DATE DUE

CRITICAL COMPANION TO

Kurt Vonnegut

CRITICAL COMPANION TO

Kurt Vonnegut

A Literary Reference to His Life and Work

SUSAN FARRELL

Facts On File
An imprint of Infobase Publishing

Critical Companion to Kurt Vonnegut

Facts On File, Inc.
An imprint of Infobase Publishing
132 West 31st Street
New York NY 10001

Library of Congress Cataloging-in-Publication Data

Farrell, Susan Elizabeth, 1963–
Critical companion to Kurt Vonnegut: a literary reference to his life and work /
Susan Farrell.
p. cm.
Includes bibliographical references and index.
ISBN 978-0-8160-6598-1 (acid-free paper) 1. Vonnegut, Kurt—Handbooks,
manuals, etc. I. Title.
PS3572.O5Z67 2008
813'.54—dc22   2007037900

Text design by Erika K. Arroyo

Printed in the United States of America

VB Hermitage 10 9 8 7 6 5 4 3 2 1

This book is printed on acid-free paper and
contains 30 percent postconsumer recycled content. ·

CONTENTS

ACKNOWLEDGMENTS

I would very much like to thank everybody who helped me with this project. My research assistant, Zach Turpin, devoted numerous hours to fact-checking and to tracking down sources, never flagging in his good cheer and enthusiasm for the work. Michael Phillips, in the interlibrary loan department at the College of Charleston, provided invaluable assistance in obtaining materials. I would also like to thank Mr. Vonnegut's literary agent and lawyer, Don Farber, of New York City, who helped with permissions. Joe Petro III was extremely generous in his support for the project and in allowing me to reproduce two of his silkscreens of Mr. Vonnegut's artwork. Thanks also to Michael Taylor and the research librarians at the Lilly Library at the University of Indiana who guided me through their Vonnegut collection and provided some of the photographs reproduced here. Susan Sutton and the librarians at the Indiana Historical Society were friendly and helpful as well. I would like to thank my editor at Facts On File, Jeff Soloway, and the staff there for their smart and insightful revision suggestions. Finally, I could not have finished this project without the generous support of my colleagues and students at the College of Charleston, who inspire me every day. I would especially like to thank Joe Kelly, who helped with every step of this project, encouraging me, reading portions of the manuscript, and providing the time and opportunity for me to conduct research and to write.

INTRODUCTION

Kurt Vonnegut was one of the most popular and admired writers of the post–World War II era in American literature. Many of his irreverent imaginings have entered the lexicon of American popular culture, ranging from the use by college students of the term *karass* to rock bands named "The Billy Pilgrims" and "Ice Nine Kills" to the ubiquitous phrase "So it goes," which appeared in Vonnegut's *New York Times* obituary. Because Vonnegut's playful, humorous, and deceptively simple style of storytelling made his work accessible to a large audience, it is easy to overlook how fully his fiction illustrates the pressing literary, philosophical, and social concerns of the late 20th century. Vonnegut's anti-realistic novels helped usher in the postmodern period in American literature. Like other examples of postmodern art, such as Andy Warhol's paintings of soup cans, Vonnegut's writing blurs the line between high and low culture. His works often include jokes, drawings, risqué limericks, cartoonish characters, flying saucers, and other elements of science fiction at the same time that they ask important questions about the nature of human beings and their purpose in the world. He frequently used the techniques of metafiction (fiction that calls attention to its own artificiality) to examine questions of narrative and the relationship between art and reality. But perhaps most important, Vonnegut's fiction offers a scathing critique of social injustice, war, and environmental degradation while managing simultaneously to express love and compassion for the weak, bewildered, and often lonely human beings he depicts.

Often labeled a science fiction writer, especially early in his career, Vonnegut studied science at Cornell University and came to believe that contemporary writers should not avoid talking about technology because technology is such an integral part of American life.

Yet, Vonnegut was a Luddite who typed his essays and stories on a typewriter rather than a computer; he always relied on the U.S. Postal Service rather than e-mail; and he warned repeatedly of the dangers of technological advancement. Repeatedly, his work depicts dystopic futures brought about by good intentions and improved technologies. Machines take over routine human labor in *Player Piano*, leaving people feeling useless and outmoded. The eradication of human disease leads to massive overpopulation in stories such as "Tomorrow and Tomorrow and Tomorrow" and "Welcome to the Monkey House." Advances in military science create weapons of destruction like *ice-nine* in *Cat's Cradle* or the neutron bomb that destroys Midland City, Ohio, in *Deadeye Dick*. Yet, science fiction itself, especially as represented in the work of iconic hack writer Kilgore Trout, is a way for Vonnegut's characters to reinvent themselves and to imagine new worlds different from the United States of the late 20th century that they find themselves in.

Vonnegut's characters tend to be hapless, often bewildered, and lonely people who are the victims of fateful circumstances beyond their control. Characters such as engineer Paul Proteus; Nazi propagandist Howard W. Campbell, Jr.; disaffected millionaire Eliot Rosewater; war survivor

Billy Pilgrim; used car salesman Dwayne Hoover; and neanderthaloid genius Wilbur Swain are all basically well-intentioned people who find themselves traumatized by life in 20th-century America and who respond by trying to imagine and create new worlds more suitable to their dreams. Yet, despite their best attempts, the new worlds created by Vonnegut's characters are often doomed. The Ghost Shirt Revolution in *Player Piano* collapses when people cannot stop from attempting to repair the very machines they had just destroyed. *Ice-nine*, designed to make travel easier for the U.S. Marine Corps, ends up destroying almost all life on the planet. Wilbur Swain's system of eradicating loneliness by assigning all Americans new, computer-generated middle names backfires when members of the artificial families begin to feud and start wars with one another, shattering the country into separate fiefdoms. While Vonnegut repeatedly depicts failed utopian schemes such as these, he nevertheless professes love for characters who try to change the world against all odds. Paul Proteus's finest moment occurs when he commits himself to the doomed Ghost Shirt Movement, telling his former boss that he is the revolutionary group's true leader. Eliot Rosewater, while perhaps unable to effect true social reform on any large scale, nevertheless brings hope and cheer into the lives of those around him by his insistence on being kind. Wilbur Swain's middle-name scheme does supply Americans with a new sense of belonging, at least for a short period. And even Kilgore Trout, the cynical and wasted science fiction writer, continues to write in the face of poverty and adversity, eventually producing a healing mantra that brings great comfort to those who hear it: "You were sick but now you're well again, and there's work to do" (*Timequake* 196).

As several critics have noted, Vonnegut preached the necessity of maintaining human kindness and common decency in the face of the social ills confronting the contemporary world. In essays, he cites as secular saints those human beings "who behaved decently in a strikingly indecent society" (*A Man Without a Country* 106). The most admirable characters in his work tend to be nurses, doctors, schoolteachers, and firefighters—ordinary people who refuse to give in to despair, who work to help others in the most trying of circumstances. Above all, Vonnegut remained throughout his career a profoundly moral writer, someone who was unafraid to thumb his nose at authority: at fundamentalist versions of organized religion, at military science that treats human beings as disposable, at a U.S. government willing to commit atrocities at home and overseas, and at literary critics who disregarded his work as "serious literature" because it was too popular and too accessible. A self-described atheist, Vonnegut nevertheless pleaded with readers to retain what he called "the most ridiculous superstition of all: that humanity is the center of the universe, the fulfiller or the frustrator of the grandest dreams of God Almighty" (*Wampeters* 165).

While much has been written about Vonnegut, the vast majority of published criticism focuses on a few of his novels—especially *Player Piano, Cat's Cradle, Slaughterhouse-Five,* and *Breakfast of Champions*. This book, for the first time, offers a look at Vonnegut's entire literary output—novels, short stories, essays, plays, and miscellaneous pieces. It examines Vonnegut's work in the context of postmodern American literature, providing information about Vonnegut's influences and his connections to other artists and writers, his family, his dominant themes, ideas, characters, and settings. This volume is intended both for the casual reader or the student who wants to learn more about Vonnegut's life and work, as well as for the more serious scholar or researcher looking for a convenient Vonnegut reference tool.

How to Use This Book

Part I of this volume offers an overview of Vonnegut's life. Part II provides detailed synopses and commentaries on Vonnegut's literary works, including his 14 novels, nearly 50 short stories, five essay collections, and three plays, as well as a libretto, a teleplay, a children's book, and more. The entries for the novels, stories, and plays contain subentries describing all the individual characters in the work, as well as a handful of related fictional places, objects, and subjects. Part III includes entries on people, places, events, and topics that are important to Vonnegut's work. These entries cover biographical background and historic, literary, and artistic influences and allusions. Throughout the text, references to entries in Part III are given in SMALL CAPITAL LETTERS, indicating a cross-reference. Part IV contains the appendixes, including a chronology of Vonnegut's life, a bibliography of Vonnegut's works, a bibliography and collection of brief entries on the works ascribed to Vonnegut's fictional alter-ego Kilgore Trout, and a bibliography of secondary sources.

A Note on Editions

All page numbers for Vonnegut works cited in this book are from the following editions:

Bagombo Snuff Box. 1999. Reprint, New York: Berkley Books, 2000.

Between Time and Timbuktu. 1972. Reprint, New York: Dell, 1973.

Bluebeard. 1987. Reprint, New York: Dell, 1998.

Breakfast of Champions. 1973. Reprint, New York: Dell, 1999.

Cat's Cradle. 1968. Reprint, New York: Dell, 1998.

Deadeye Dick. 1982. Reprint, New York: Dell, 1999.

Fates Worse Than Death. 1991. Reprint, New York: Berkley Books, 1992.

Galápagos. 1985. Reprint, New York: Dell, 1999.

God Bless You, Dr. Kevorkian. 1999. Reprint, New York: Washington Square Press, 2001.

God Bless You, Mr. Rosewater. 1965. Reprint, New York: Dell, 1998.

Happy Birthday, Wanda June. New York: Samuel French, 1971.

Hocus Pocus. 1990. Reprint, New York: Berkley Books, 1991.

Jailbird. 1979. Reprint, New York: Dell, 1999.

"L'Histoire du Soldat." *The Paris Review* 40.148 (Fall 1998): 188–204.

Like Shaking Hands with God. 1979. Reprint, New York: Washington Square Press, 2000.

A Man Without a Country. 1961. Reprint, New York: Seven Stories Press, 2005.

Mother Night. 1961. Reprint, New York: Dell, 1999.

Nothing Is Lost Save Honor. Jackson, Miss.: Nouveau Press, 1984.

Palm Sunday. 1981. Reprint, New York: Dell, 1999.

Player Piano. 1952. Reprint, New York: Dell, 1974.

The Sirens of Titan. 1959. Reprint, New York: Dell, 1998.

Slapstick. 1976. Reprint, New York: Dell., 1999.

Slaughterhouse-Five. 1969. Reprint, New York: Dell, 1999.

Sun Moon Star. New York: Harper & Row, 1980.

Timequake. 1997. Reprint, New York: Berkley Books, 1998.

Wampeters, Foma and Granfalloons. 1979. Reprint, New York: Dell, 1999.

Welcome to the Monkey House. 1968. Reprint, New York: Dell, 1998.

PART I

Biography

Kurt Vonnegut
(1922–2007)

Kurt Vonnegut's funny, irreverent, and wildly inventive fiction has resonated with Americans, especially college students and disaffected young people, for more than 50 years. Best known for a trio of novels published in the 1960s and early 1970s—*Cat's Cradle, Slaughterhouse-Five,* and *Breakfast of Champions*—Vonnegut is also the author of 11 other novels and nearly 50 short stories, as well as numerous essays, plays, and autobiographical pieces. While his style tends to be simple and accessible—he uses a conversational tone, short chapters, and almost childlike descriptions at times—his subject matter is often very serious. Underlying his jokes, humorous drawings, and descriptions of flying saucers and time travel, Vonnegut expresses social criticism about the suffering and atrocities human beings experienced in the 20th century—from the effects of war and atomic weaponry, to racism, social injustice, and environmental destruction. Vonnegut's characters, who frequently recur from one novel to the next, tend to be lonely and somewhat bewildered dreamers who try to invent new worlds when the ones they live in become unbearable. While his fiction is often set in the Midwest America of his youth, or else in upstate New York or CAPE COD, places where he spent significant time as an adult, Vonnegut's imaginative, nonrealistic style can also transport readers to prisons in Israel, to the battlefields of Germany, or to Mars, the moons of Saturn, or the planet Tralfamadore.

Kurt Vonnegut, Jr., was born in INDIANAPOLIS, Indiana, on November 11, 1922, to KURT VONNEGUT, SR., and EDITH LIEBER VONNEGUT. Both the Lieber and Vonnegut families had roots in Indianapolis stretching back to the mid-19th century. All eight of Vonnegut's great-grandparents, according to family historian JOHN RAUCH, "were part of the vast migration of Germans to the Midwest in the half century from 1820 to 1870" (*Palm Sunday* 18). Vonnegut's immigrant forbears were unusually talented and well educated. They included merchants and musicians, teachers and

1975 portrait of Kurt Vonnegut *(photo by Bernard Gotfryd/Getty Images)*

civil servants, and they tended to be religious free thinkers and atheists. In a 1973 interview in *Playboy* magazine, Vonnegut explains that, growing up, he never rebelled against organized religion: "I never had any. I learned my outrageous opinions about organized religion at my mother's knee" (*Wampeters* 240). His paternal great-grandfather, CLEMENS VONNEGUT, whom the author describes as the ancestor who "most beguiles" him (*Palm Sunday* 23), was a respected advocate of progressive public education who founded the Vonnegut Hardware Store, a business still in operation during Vonnegut's boyhood. One of his maternal great-grandfathers, PETER LIEBER, fought in the Civil War, sustained a crippling leg injury, and later bought the brewery that he renamed P. Lieber & Co., and which was run by family members until the Prohibition years.

Vonnegut's father, Kurt, Sr., was the oldest son of BERNARD VONNEGUT, SR., an Indianapolis architect who had trained in Germany and Boston, and

NANETTE SCHNULL VONNEGUT, an outgoing, sociable woman admired for her beauty and excellent singing voice. Kurt, Sr., following in the footsteps of his father, also became an Indianapolis architect, studying first at the American College in Strasbourg, Germany, for three years and later earning his bachelor of science degree from the MASSACHUSETTS INSTITUTE OF TECHNOLOGY. On November 22, 1913, Kurt, Sr., married Edith Lieber, a wealthy young Indianapolis woman who had experienced a difficult childhood. Edith's father, ALBERT LIEBER, ran the P. Lieber & Co. Brewery and lived a fashionable life in high society. Vonnegut refers to this grandfather as a "rascal," arguing that Lieber's "emotional faithlessness to his children . . . contributed substantially" to the later suicide of Vonnegut's mother (*Palm Sunday* 33). When Albert's first wife, ALICE BARUS LIEBER, died, Edith, the oldest of the couple's three children, was only six. Albert remarried an eccentric violinist named ORA D. LANE, who abused her three stepchildren. Albert eventually divorced Lane, but great damage to his children had already been done. According to John Rauch, all three of the Lieber children, under the pernicious treatment of their stepmother, "suffered a distinctive psychic trauma from which they never fully recovered" (*Palm Sunday* 35).

Despite his mother's difficulties and what he remembers as a basic sadness within both parents, Vonnegut describes his childhood growing up in Indianapolis as a relatively happy one, although he tells readers of the short work *Like Shaking Hands With God* that he understands it is "shameful" for a writer to confess to a happy childhood (51). He was very close to his older brother, BERNARD, (born in 1914) and his sister, ALICE (born in 1917). Both siblings figure prominently in Vonnegut's later fiction and essays. The family, comfortably well-to-do during Vonnegut's earliest childhood, suffered financial setbacks during the Great Depression years as clients at Kurt, Sr.'s, architectural firm became increasingly scarce. Thus, while his older siblings had attended private schools, Kurt, Jr., was educated in Indianapolis public schools, a seeming misfortune that turned out to be a blessing in disguise. The writer speaks frequently of the excellent education he received as a young man and his good

fortune to have been born in Indianapolis in the 1920s. In the 1991 essay collection, *Fates Worse Than Death*, he writes:

> That city gave me a free primary and secondary education richer and more humane than anything I would get from any of the five universities I attended. . . . It had a widespread system of free libraries whose attendants seemed to my young mind to be angels of fun with information. There were cheap movie houses and jazz joints everywhere. There was a fine symphony orchestra, and I took lessons from Ernst Michaelis, its first-chair clarinet. (97)

At SHORTRIDGE HIGH SCHOOL, Vonnegut played clarinet in the school band and served as writer and editor for the school newspaper, THE SHORTRIDGE ECHO, one of only two daily newspapers operating in U.S. high schools at the time. Vonnegut explains that his experience at the *Echo* trained

Kurt Vonnegut's high school yearbook photo, 1940
(Courtesy of Indiana Historical Society)

him to write not for a teacher, but for a large audience, who gave immediate feedback to his work. He adds that writing came easily to him and was something he loved to do, just as his brother, Bernard, was good at mathematics and physics and his sister, Alice, excelled at drawing and sculpting (*Wampeters* 260).

Growing up, Vonnegut also enjoyed sharing jokes with both his siblings. He writes, in a self-interview originally published in *The Paris Review*, that he first learned to be funny at the family dinner table. As the youngest child in the family, the only way he could get anyone to listen to him, he explains, was by telling jokes. To hone his humor, he listened intently to radio comedians popular during the 1930s, studying and copying their styles of delivery. Vonnegut adds that he and Alice used to argue about what was the funniest joke in the world, and that when the two of them worked on jokes together, they "could be almost as funny as LAUREL AND HARDY" (*Palm Sunday* 103). Vonnegut's love of slapstick comedy, as well as his close relationship with his older sister, are childhood memories he would later memorialize in his novel *Slapstick*.

After graduating from Shortridge High School in 1940, Vonnegut enrolled at CORNELL UNIVERSITY in Ithaca, New York, as a biochemistry major. Although he would have preferred to study literature or the humanities, or to become an architect like his father and grandfather before him, both Kurt, Sr., and his older brother, Bernard, pushed him toward the sciences, his father, himself a frustrated artist, arguing that it was a waste of time and money to study subjects that he characterized as "so much junk jewelry"—literature, history, and philosophy (*Palm Sunday* 57). Vonnegut, however, did not have much aptitude for the sciences and did poorly in his course work. Despite joining a fraternity, he disliked Cornell and did not feel that he fit in well until he joined the staff of the college newspaper, THE CORNELL DAILY SUN. Serving first as a staff writer and later as editor for the *Sun*, Vonnegut found a home at the newspaper. Nevertheless, when he came down with a severe case of pneumonia during his junior year, Vonnegut was not overly distressed to withdraw from the univer-

Vonnegut with high school friends, ca. 1940 *(Courtesy of Indiana Historical Society)*

sity. He had been on academic probation and in danger of flunking out in any case.

Having enlisted in the U.S. Army in November 1942, a few months before he actually left Cornell, Vonnegut was sent to basic training in 1943, where he was taught to fire a 240-millimeter howitzer, the largest mobile fieldpiece in use by the army at that time. Although his previous college experience qualified him for Officer Candidate School, the army had enough officer candidates at the time. Instead, Vonnegut was sent back to college as part of the Army Specialized Training Program (ASTP), where he studied mechanical engineering, first at Carnegie Technical Institute and later at the University of Tennessee. In *Fates Worse Than Death*, Vonnegut tells about being "yanked out of college again when what the Army needed, with the invasion of Europe in prospect, was riflemen and more riflemen" (95). He was sent to Camp Atterbury, just south of Indianapolis, where he met his longtime friend BERNARD V. O'HARE, the war buddy who figures prominently in *Slaughterhouse-Five*. Despite his lack of infantry training, Vonnegut, along with O'Hare, was made a battalion intelligence scout, whose job was to sneak across enemy lines to surreptitiously gather information. His unit would be shipped overseas in late summer of 1944, after the D-day invasion. But during his months at Camp Atterbury, Vonnegut was stationed so close to home that he "was able to sleep in [his] own bedroom and use the family car on weekends" (*Fates* 96).

On one of those weekends, May 14, 1944, Vonnegut's mother, Edith, died from an overdose of sleeping pills. In interviews, Vonnegut remembers his mother as a highly intelligent and cultivated woman who was well traveled and fluent in three languages. When the family's finances became strapped during the Great Depression years, Edith began writing short stories, hoping to make money selling them to magazines. Vonnegut writes of her obsession: "She took short story courses at night. She studied magazines the way gamblers study racing forms" (*Conversations* 177). Although Vonnegut insists that his mother was a good writer, she was never able to sell her stories. According to her son, this was because "she had no talent for the vulgarity the slick magazines required" (*Conversations* 178). Depressed by the family's reduced circumstances, her own failure as a writer, and by Kurt, Jr.'s impending overseas assignment, and doped up on prescription drugs and alcohol, Edith committed suicide the night before Vonnegut returned home on leave for Mother's Day weekend. His mother's death is an event that shapes much of Vonnegut's later fiction. He will compare Edith to fictional character Celia Hoover in *Breakfast of Champions*, a woman who kills herself by swallowing Drano. The novel *Deadeye Dick* will spiral around a terrible tragedy that occurs on Mother's Day, 1944. Vonnegut even speculates that his early career as a writer of short stories for slick magazines was an attempt to live out his mother's dreams.

As a soldier, however, Vonnegut did not have much time for grief. His unit, the 106th Infantry Division, was sent overseas three months after his mother's death. Vonnegut, along with the five other battalion scouts in his unit, and about 50 other American soldiers, was captured by the German army in December 1944 during the BATTLE OF THE BULGE, the last main German offensive of World War II. In an interview, Vonnegut describes being trapped with a group of soldiers in a deep gully in Luxembourg, in the midst of a snowstorm without any food. German soldiers, speaking through a loudspeaker, told the Americans they were surrounded and that their situation was hopeless. Initially, the group of Americans fixed their bayonets, hoping to fight off the Germans, but when 88-millimeter shells began to explode in the treetops overhead, the American soldiers threw down their weapons and emerged. Vonnegut and his fellow American prisoners were shipped to DRESDEN in railroad boxcars, an event fictionalized as one of Billy Pilgrim's war experiences in *Slaughterhouse-Five*. British mosquito bombers attacked the prisoner train at one point, hitting a boxcar containing most of the officers from Vonnegut's division and killing nearly all of them (*Palm Sunday* 77–79).

Following the cramped and terrifying journey, Vonnegut was first sent to a large prison camp south of Dresden. Later, because the articles of the Geneva Convention required privates to work for their keep, Vonnegut was sent as a laborer to Dresden, where he worked in a factory that manufactured a vitamin-fortified malt syrup for pregnant women. He and his fellow soldiers were housed in a cement-block slaughterhouse, where they were able to survive the Allied carpet bombing that took place on the night of February 13, 1945. Vonnegut and the other prisoners-of-war were put to work in the days immediately following the bombing, digging bodies out of the rubble and burned remains of the city. He describes this gruesome task in an interview that initially appeared in *The Paris Review* in 1977:

> Every day we walked into the city and dug into basements and shelters to get the corpses out, as a sanitary measure. When we went into them, a typical shelter, an ordinary basement usually, looked like a streetcar full of people who'd simultaneously had heart failure. Just people sitting there in their chairs, all dead. . . . We brought the dead out. They were loaded on

wagons and taken to parks, large open areas in the city which weren't filled with rubble. The Germans got funeral pyres going, burning the bodies to keep them from stinking and from spreading disease. (*Palm Sunday* 80–81)

What struck Vonnegut most after his Dresden experience was both the scale of the devastation he had witnessed as well as the secrecy that attended the operation. While the figure of 135,000 dead given by British historian (and later Holocaust denier) DAVID IRVING has since been discredited, Vonnegut nevertheless witnessed one of the deadliest and swiftest civilian massacres in history. Current figures estimate that between 25,000 and 35,000 people died in the Dresden bombing. It was not until the publication of *Slaughterhouse-Five* that the tragedy truly registered in the mainstream American consciousness.

Vonnegut's Dresden novel would have to wait to be written until more than 20 years after the writer's return from the war in May 1945, however. Back in Indianapolis as a 22-year-old war veteran with a Purple Heart, Vonnegut soon married his childhood sweetheart, Jane Cox (see JANE YARMO-LINSKY). The pair had initially met in kindergarten and had been high school classmates together; the marriage took place on September 1, 1945. In December, the newlyweds moved to Chicago, where Kurt enrolled in the UNIVERSITY OF CHICAGO as a graduate student in anthropology. Jane, a Swarthmore College graduate, received a full scholarship to undertake graduate studies in Russian, although she never earned her degree, dropping out of school when she became pregnant with the couple's first child, MARK. During his time at Chicago, Vonnegut was heavily influenced by the work of Anthropology Department chair DR. ROBERT REDFIELD, who studied what he termed "folk societies." According to Dr. Redfield, primitive peoples tended to live in small, close-knit groups of relatives in which individuals were valued for themselves rather than for what they could contribute to the group as a whole. Such groups were small enough that everybody knew everybody else and a modern division of labor was unnecessary. The idea that human beings are genetically constructed to

live in such circumstances and thus have difficulty tolerating the crowded anonymity and loneliness of modern American life, would become one of the dominant themes in Vonnegut's later fiction, in which characters—such as Eliot Rosewater and Dr. Wilbur Swain—frequently propose utopian schemes to help people regain a sense of community and belonging. Despite his affection for several of his professors at Chicago, Vonnegut's master's thesis, "On the Fluctuations Between Good and Evil in Simple Tales," was unanimously turned down by his thesis committee. He would, however, finally be awarded the master of arts degree from the University of Chicago in 1971, when the anthropology faculty decided that his novel *Cat's Cradle* made a significant contribution to the field of cultural anthropology.

During his time as a graduate student at the University of Chicago, Vonnegut also worked as a reporter for the Chicago City News Bureau, a job he describes in the introduction to *Slaughterhouse-Five*, where he explains that reporters "would telephone in stories to writers wearing headphones, and the writers would stencil the stories on mimeograph sheets" which were then stuffed into pneumatic tubes that ran under the streets of Chicago to all the newspapers in town (8). Although his early work on *The Shortridge Echo* and *The Cornell Daily Sun* had prompted Vonnegut to consider a career in journalism, his brief stint as a reporter in Chicago seems to have soured him on such a possibility. In the description in *Slaughterhouse-Five*, Vonnegut seems dismayed by the callous disregard for the feelings of others evinced by his fellow journalists—especially by the tough women reporters and writers who had moved into the profession when so many men went to war. He tells readers the story of one of these "beastly girls" (9) who convinces him to telephone the young wife of a war veteran who had just died in a grisly accident in order to get her reaction to the death. The point is that Vonnegut realizes he cannot simply report what he saw in Dresden and make a book out of it. He must turn to literature as a way to express his moral outrage as well as the empathy he feels for his fellow human beings, emotions that have no room in straightforward news stories.

Leaving Chicago in 1947, Vonnegut moved to Schenectady, New York, to take a job in the public relations department at GENERAL ELECTRIC, where his older brother, Bernard, had worked as an atmospheric scientist since 1945. In 1946, Bernard had made a significant discovery for the G.E. laboratories—he had invented a method of using silver iodine to seed clouds in order to produce snow and rain, a discovery still in use in the early 21st century. At General Electric Vonnegut began his career as a fiction writer, gathering material for his first short stories as well as his early novels—*Player Piano* and *Cat's Cradle* especially—from his experiences there. Partly motivated to write his way out of what he considered a "very disagreeable" job (*Conversations* 111), and wanting to earn more money to support his growing family (his son Mark was born in May 1947 and his oldest daughter, Edith, in 1949), Vonnegut wrote a short piece, "Report on the Barnhouse Effect," which he claims is the first story he ever wrote, and mailed it to *Collier's* magazine. In the *Paris Review* interview, Vonnegut explains what happened next:

> Knox Burger was fiction editor there. Knox told me what was wrong with it and how to fix it. I did what he said, and he bought the story for seven-hundred and fifty dollars, six weeks' pay at G.E. I wrote another, and he paid me nine-hundred and fifty dollars, and suggested that it was perhaps time for me to quit G.E. (*Conversations* 190)

Magazine fiction writing during the first half of the 20th century paid quite well. Americans had a large appetite for stories that appeared in weekly magazines such as *Collier's*, the *Saturday Evening Post*, and *Cosmopolitan*. As Vonnegut explains in his collection *Bagombo Snuff Box*, the lucrative field of short story magazine writing would die out in the later 1950s, with the advent of television. Families gathered around the television set in the evening rather than read stories out loud. Vonnegut, however, was fortunate to make his start in the business before the window of opportunity completely closed.

Earning a comfortable salary from sales of short fiction allowed Vonnegut to quit his job at General

March 1969 photo of Vonnegut at his home in Barnstable, Cape Cod *(photo by Israel Shenker/ Getty Images)*

Electric in 1951 and move his family to Cape Cod, Massachusetts, where he would live for the next 20 years. With more time to devote to writing, Vonnegut settled down to serious work on *Player Piano*, a novel largely inspired by his years at General Electric. As he explains in a 1973 *Playboy* interview:

> I was working for General Electric at the time, right after World War Two, and I saw a milling machine for cutting the rotors on jet engines, gas turbines. This was a very expensive thing for a machinist to do, to cut what is essentially one of those Brancusi forms. So they had a computer-operated milling machine built to cut the blades, and I was fascinated by that. This was in 1949 and the guys who were working on it were foreseeing all sorts of machines

being run by little boxes and punched cards. *Player Piano* was my response to the implications of having everything run by little boxes. (*Conversations* 93)

In another interview, Vonnegut tells literary critic Robert Scholes that the satirical scenes from *Player Piano* that take place at The Meadows, where Paul Proteus and his fellow engineers and managers are sent for a weeklong company morale-building adventure, were modeled on a yearly retreat held by General Electric at a place called Association Island, which was shut down after the book came out (*Conversations* 113).

Published by Scribner's in 1952, the novel received a positive review in the *New York Times* from influential critic and novelist Granville Hicks, who compared *Player Piano* to Aldous Huxley's *Brave New World*, but argued that Vonnegut was able to keep his future "closer to the present" than Huxley succeeded in doing, and to have more "fun" with his subject matter as well. Hicks closed his review by calling Vonnegut a "sharp-eyed satirist" (Hicks 5;16). Yet, the novel did not make much of a splash among serious writers and critics. When new editions were released, as part of the Doubleday Science Fiction Book Club in 1953 and as a Bantam paperback retitled *Utopia 14* in 1954, Vonnegut's reputation became that of a SCIENCE FICTION writer, a genre derided by the literary establishment. The inclusion of "Report on the Barnhouse Effect" in a science fiction anthology edited by Robert A. Heinlein in 1952 helped lay the groundwork for this view of Vonnegut's work, as did several of the short stories he published in *Collier's* magazine in 1950 and 1951, including the science fiction–themed "Thanasphere" (September, 1950), "EPICAC" (November, 1950), and "The Euphio Question" (May, 1951). In Vonnegut's first book of collected essays, *Wampeters, Foma, and Granfalloons*, published in 1974, he discusses being "a soreheaded occupant of a file drawer labeled 'science fiction'" (1) ever since the publication of *Player Piano*. While he argues that serious critics tend to "mistake the drawer for a urinal," Vonnegut defends the genre, seeing it as occupied simply by writers who "notice technology"

and deploring the notion that "no one can simultaneously be a respectable writer and understand how a refrigerator works" (1).

Vonnegut earned the majority of his income from short story writing during the 1950s, publishing numerous pieces, even quite early in his career, that were decidedly not science fiction. Stories such as "Mnemonics" (April, 1951), "The Foster Portfolio" (September, 1951), "More Stately Mansions" (December, 1951) and "Any Reasonable Offer" (January, 1952), all appearing in *Collier's*, explore the lives of ordinary, suburban mid-century Americans who struggle with jobs and marriage. As his own family expanded—daughter Nanette was born in 1954—Vonnegut looked to other methods of earning money as well. During the 1950s, he taught at a school for learning disabled children for a brief period and operated a Saab auto dealership on Cape Cod. But Vonnegut's family life took a traumatic turn in 1958, when his sister, Alice, died of cancer 48 hours after her husband, JAMES CARMALT ADAMS, had been killed in a commuter train crash in New York City. The Vonneguts adopted the three oldest Adams boys, 14-year-old JAMES, 11-year-old STEVEN, and nine-year-old KURT, after their parents' deaths. A much younger brother, PETER NICE, a baby at the time, was eventually adopted by his father's first cousin, who lived in Birmingham, Alabama. As Vonnegut makes clear in the novel *Slapstick,* the death of Alice affected him immensely, not only because he took in her orphaned children, but because his older sister, he explains, was the person for whom he always imagined he was writing his fiction. Jane Cox Vonnegut would later chronicle this tragic period in a memoir called ANGELS WITHOUT WINGS: *A Courageous Family's Triumph Over Tragedy*, published posthumously in 1987 and made into a television movie called *A Promise to Keep* in 1990.

Vonnegut continued to write in the midst of family turmoil, turning back to the form of the novel at the end of the decade, and soon publishing as paperback originals two wildly different novels: *The Sirens of Titan* in 1959 and *Mother Night* in 1962. *The Sirens* details a Martian invasion of Earth, masterminded by a disaffected millionaire who wants to start a new religion, but who subsequently discovers that all of his own actions, as well as all of human history, have been controlled by robotic aliens from the planet Tralfamadore. Characters in *Mother Night*, unlike those in *The Sirens of Titan*, never make excursions to other planets, but are firmly rooted in real history. The novel details the career and arrest of Nazi propagandist and American double-agent Howard W. Campbell, Jr., who is supposedly writing his confessions from an Israeli prison cell. Because both books were published as paperbacks, they were not reviewed in the ordinary literary journals, and they received scant attention from the mainstream literary establishment. In between these two novels, Vonnegut also collected what he considered his best published magazine stories from the 1950s. These were published as the volume *Canary in a Cat House* in 1961. Although the collection soon went out of print, all of the stories from *Canary* (except for "Hal Irwin's Magic Lamp," which would appear in the later collection *Bagombo Snuff Box*) were reprinted in the 1968 volume *Welcome to the Monkey House*.

Although Vonnegut was now established as a published writer, sales of his books were small and he remained largely unknown. When his paperback editor, Samuel Stewart, of the Western Printing Company, moved to Holt, Rinehart, & Winston, he arranged for Vonnegut's next novel, *Cat's Cradle*, to come out in hardback. An apocalyptic tale of destruction caused by the invention of the fantastical weapon *ice-nine*, a thinly veiled metaphor for the ATOMIC BOMB, *Cat's Cradle* was a critical success, earning accolades from such well-known writers as Graham Greene, who praised the book as one of the three best novels of the year, and American novelist Terry Southern, who wrote a complimentary review in the *New York Times,* which concluded with the following paragraph:

> *Cat's Cradle* is an irreverent and often highly entertaining fantasy concerning the playful irresponsibility of nuclear scientists. Like the best of contemporary satire, it is work of a far more engaging and meaningful order than the melodramatic tripe which most critics seem to consider "serious."

While *Cat's Cradle* hardly made Vonnegut a household name, it did increase the small but devoted fan base the author had earned from his previous novels. *Cat's Cradle* was particularly popular among college students, earning Vonnegut something of a cult following on campuses, where students often introduced the author's work to their professors.

Another turning point in Vonnegut's career came in 1965, when he accepted a two-year teaching position at the prestigious Iowa Writer's Workshop. Vonnegut was able, for the first time, to immerse himself in a community of creative writers, both students and fellow faculty members. His fifth novel, *God Bless You, Mr. Rosewater,* is the story of a tenderhearted but hapless millionaire who hopes to create a better world by being intensely sympathetic to all of his fellow human beings; it was published by Holt, Rinehart & Winston in 1965 as well. Reviewer Martin Levin, writing for the *New York Times,* described *Mr. Rosewater* as "a book that is devoid of anything as square as a plot, its text broken up into short epiphanies, like poetic cantos, with typographical squiggles for segues" (BR41). Levin describes here the start of the style that would mark Vonnegut's work for the next several decades. *Mr. Rosewater* is also the novel that introduces Vonnegut's recurring character and sometime alter ego, science fiction writer Kilgore Trout. Despite his reluctance to characterize the book as a proper novel, Levin nevertheless praises Vonnegut as "a writer with an excellent ear, a knack for arresting imagery, and a Message" (BR41).

With *Mr. Rosewater* finished, Vonnegut turned back to his short fiction as well as to the book he had been trying to write for the last 20 years—his Dresden novel. *Welcome to the Monkey House,* a collection of Vonnegut's magazine stories from the 1950s and 60s, appeared in 1968. The previous year, as the recipient of a Guggenheim Fellowship, Vonnegut was able to return to Dresden with his war buddy, Bernard V. O'Hare, to conduct research for the book that would become *Slaughterhouse-Five*. Published in March 1969, as the first of a three-book contract Vonnegut had signed with Delacorte Press and publisher SEYMOUR LAWRENCE, *Slaughterhouse-Five* was an instant success, reaching number one on the *New York Times* best-seller list and changing Vonnegut's life forever. The novel tells the tale of preposterous soldier Billy Pilgrim, a tall, ungainly chaplain's assistant from ILIUM, New York, who is captured by Germans during World War II and survives the Dresden bombing in a concrete slaughterhouse. Back in Ilium as a middle-aged optometrist, Billy is kidnapped by space aliens who take him to the planet Tralfamadore to be mated with an American porn star. Billy's war experiences, however, have left him "unstuck in time" so that he travels back and forth between his Tralfamadorian experiences, his war memories, and his time in Ilium, unable to control where he will go next. Framed by opening and closing chapters that detail Vonnegut's own attempts to compose the novel, *Slaughterhouse-Five* marks Vonnegut's turn toward more autobiographical writing, toward the melding of fact and fiction that he would rely on in most of his later novels. The *New York Times* set the tone for critical reaction to the novel in a review that concluded, "It sounds crazy. It sounds like a fantastic last-ditch effort to make sense of a lunatic universe. But there is so much more to this book. It is very tough and very funny; it is sad and delightful; and it works." *Slaughterhouse-Five* not only thrust Vonnegut into national prominence as a writer, it made him a wealthy man. Adding to the income he received from book sales, Vonnegut was able to sell the screen rights as well. The book was turned into a film in 1972, directed by George Roy Hill. The screen version of *Slaughterhouse-Five* remains, both in the estimate of critics as well as the author himself, the most successful film adaptation of any of Vonnegut's work.

Vonnegut maintained a high profile after the publication of *Slaughterhouse-Five*, speaking frequently at colleges and universities, writing articles and book reviews, dabbling again in journalism, and even trying his hand at playwriting. He traveled to Africa in 1970 to report on the collapse of the Republic of BIAFRA, which had been struggling to gain independence from Nigeria, and wrote about his experiences for *McCall's* magazine. That same year, he accepted a visiting appointment at HARVARD UNIVERSITY to teach creative writing. His play, *Happy Birthday, Wanda June*, opened in New York City in 1971. At the same time his pro-

fessional career was blossoming, Vonnegut's personal life was very much in flux. He separated from his wife, Jane Cox Vonnegut, in 1971, and moved from Cape Cod to Manhattan, where he began living with photographer JILL KREMENTZ, who would become his second wife in 1979, after he and Jane were officially divorced. The separation from Jane was clearly a traumatic event for Vonnegut, who ascribes the breakup to a number of factors, including the emptiness both felt as the six children they had raised together grew up and left home, as well as to Jane's becoming a born-again Christian, a change the freethinking Vonnegut had a difficult time accepting. The two managed to remain close friends, however. Jane married diplomat ADAM YARMOLINSKY, and Vonnegut wrote a very touching tribute to his ex-wife, who died of cancer in 1986, in his novel *Timequake*. To add to Vonnegut's family problems, his son Mark suffered a major nervous breakdown in early 1971, was hospitalized in a mental institution in Vancouver, and diagnosed as a schizophrenic. Mark eventually recovered from his illness and in 1975 published a book about his experiences, *The EDEN EXPRESS: A Memoir of Insanity*. He graduated from Harvard Medical School and became a well-respected pediatrician, ascribing his earlier mental breakdown to manic-depressive disorder rather than the schizophrenia with which he had originally been diagnosed.

Despite a tumultuous personal life, Vonnegut published three more novels in the 1970s as well as his first collection of speeches and essays. *Breakfast of Champions*, a METAFICTIONAL work in which Vonnegut appears as a character and introduces himself to his own fictive creation, Kilgore Trout, came out in 1973 to mixed critical reviews, but great popular success. While Vonnegut had first introduced a few of his line drawings as illustrations in *Slaughterhouse-Five*—a tombstone, a latrine sign, a sketch of Montana Wildhack's breasts with a locket dangling between them—he includes many more illustrations in *Breakfast of Champions*, several of these quite cartoonish and irreverent, such as a drawing of a sphincter and one of girl's underwear. Such drawings attained the status of icons—in later years, Vonnegut often signed autographs with his signature sphincter and sold reproductions of the drawing as silkscreens produced by Kentucky artist JOE PETRO, III.

The same year that *Breakfast* appeared, Vonnegut accepted a position teaching creative writing at the CITY UNIVERSITY OF NEW YORK as Distinguished Professor of English Prose, a post he resigned the following year. His first collection of speeches, observations, and essays, *Wampeters, Foma, and Granfalloons*, appeared in 1974, and his eighth novel, *Slapstick,* came out in 1976. Much to Vonnegut's disappointment, *Slapstick,* a novel about a pair of genius "Neanderthaloid" twins who become dullards when separated from each other, meant to metaphorically represent Vonnegut's relationship with his sister, Alice, was greeted with critical derision. In an interview, Vonnegut explained what he believed to be the viciousness of the novel's critics as well as the devastation he felt as a result of the negative reviews.

> *Slapstick* may be a very bad book. I am perfectly willing to believe that. Everybody else writes lousy books, so why shouldn't I? What was unusual about the reviews was that they wanted people to admit now that I had never been any good. The reviewer for the Sunday *Times* actually asked critics who had praised me in the past to now admit in public how wrong they'd been. . . . I never felt worse in my life. (*Palm Sunday* 93)

Stung by such criticism, Vonnegut, in his next novel, *Jailbird,* published in 1979, turned away from the whimsical future-based fantasy of *Slapstick.* Like the earlier *Mother Night, Jailbird* is a novel grounded in real historical events that mingles historical figures with fictional characters. It follows the career of ill-fated Walter F. Starbuck, a well-intentioned man caught up in some of the most shameful episodes of 20th-century American history, including the SACCO AND VANZETTI case of the 1920s, the McCarthy red-baiting of the 1950s, and the Watergate scandal of the 1970s.

Vonnegut remained prolific over the 1980s and 1990s, publishing a children's book, *Sun Moon Star* (1980), with illustrations by graphic artist IVAN CHERMAYEFF, two more books of collected speeches, essays, and anecdotes, which he characterized as "autobiographical collages," *Palm Sunday* (1981) and

Fates Worse Than Death (1991), as well as five more novels. *Deadeye Dick* (1982) is about a young man named Rudy Waltz who accidentally shoots a pregnant neighbor woman when he is 12 years old and who lives a cautious, fearful life forever after. This novel, while retaining the characteristic Vonnegut style of short paragraphs, humorous understatement, and a tone of resigned pessimism, is a more straightforward coming-of-age story than Vonnegut's previous works. Although it lacks space aliens and imaginative flights of fancy from science fiction writer Kilgore Trout that many readers had come to expect of Vonnegut's work, *Deadeye Dick* still communicates the sense of impending apocalypse that is one of the hallmarks of Vonnegut's fiction, this time through a neutron bomb, which by the end of the novel has killed all the people in Rudy Waltz's hometown of MIDLAND CITY, Ohio. Despite writing tales involving large-scale death and destruction, Vonnegut was optimistic enough in 1982 to take on the challenge of raising young children again, at the age of 60. In December of that year, Vonnegut and Jill Krementz, who had married on November 24, 1979, adopted an infant daughter, Lily.

Vonnegut turned back to the adventures of Kilgore Trout in his next novel, *Galápagos,* published in 1985. Narrated by the cynical science fiction writer's son, Leon Trout, a VIETNAM WAR veteran who has lived as a ghost for a million years and witnessed the de-evolution of human beings to furry, seal-like creatures with small brains—a vast improvement over 20th-century humans, Leon insists—*Galápagos* is classic Vonnegut. While critics had panned the silliness of *Slapstick,* were noncommittal in reviews of *Jailbird,* and found *Deadeye Dick* to be somewhat facile and shapeless, several reviewers, led by Herbert Mitgang of the *New York Times,* felt that Vonnegut was back in fine form in *Galápagos,* praising the humanity underlying his dark humor. Although artistically productive during this period, Vonnegut was also battling severe depression. In the mid-80s, like his mother before him, Vonnegut attempted suicide by ingesting a combination of sleeping pills and alcohol. After his recovery, he wrote and spoke frankly about the mental problems affecting his mother and son, and about his own depression, especially in the autobiographical work *Fates Worse Than Death,* in which he claims that most writers, himself included, have "proved to be depressives from families of depressives" (29).

With his next novel, *Bluebeard*, published by Delacorte in 1987, Vonnegut explored the world of abstract art, a form that would increasingly draw his energy and attention over the next two decades of his life. *Bluebeard* is narrated by Rabo Karabekian, an ABSTRACT EXPRESSIONIST painter whom readers first met in *Breakfast of Champions*. To contrast Rabo, the novel offers what is perhaps Vonnegut's strongest female character, a brassy, talkative widow and lover of sentimental art named Circe Berman. Through these characters, Vonnegut explores the ins and outs of abstract versus representational painting, offering great sympathy and insight into both forms of visual art. Although one of the best of Vonnegut's later novels, many prestigious publications, including the *New Yorker, Newsweek,* and the *Times Literary Supplement,* opted not to review it. Following *Bluebeard,* Vonnegut turned once again to a novel in the vein of the more historically oriented *Mother Night* and *Jailbird. Hocus Pocus,* published in 1990, like those two earlier novels, contains the confessions of a well-intentioned man, Eugene Debs Hartke, imprisoned for crimes not entirely of his own commission. Like Leon Trout in *Galápagos,* Hartke is a Vietnam veteran. As he writes his book from a prison cell while waiting trial after being wrongfully accused of inciting a prison break and assault on a small college town, Hartke makes lists of all the women he has made love to as well as all the people he had killed in the war. The two lists end up having exactly the same number of people. Like Howard W. Campbell, Jr. in *Mother Night,* Hartke is a hopelessly complicated man, a morally ambiguous figure who, in many ways, seems the victim of fate.

Timequake, the book that Vonnegut publicly declared to be his final novel, was published in 1997. Perhaps the most metafictional of all Vonnegut's works, a novel in which he talks frequently with his character Kilgore Trout, and which he ends with a giant clambake that freely mixes fictional characters with autobiographical figures from his own life, and even literary critics, *Timequake* offers a fitting end to Vonnegut's fiction-writing career. The novel depicts an aging writer looking back and coming to terms with a long and productive artistic life. While *Timequake* may be Vonnegut's last novel,

the writer's creative output did not end with this book. He published a second collection of short stories gathered from his magazine fiction-writing career, *Bagombo Snuff Box,* in 1999. *God Bless You, Dr. Kevorkian,* a collection of short, humorous radio addresses delivered in New York City, also appeared in 1999. In addition, he continued to give speeches and lectures, and to contribute articles and opinion pieces to journals and newspapers, particularly to the left-leaning *In Our Time.*

In early 2000, however, Vonnegut nearly died in a small fire in his Manhattan brownstone, a fire that appeared to be the result of the writer's carelessness in smoking his unfiltered Pall Mall cigarettes. Rescued by a neighbor and by his teenage daughter Lily, Vonnegut spent several days in the hospital in critical condition, suffering from smoke inhalation. He eventually made a complete recovery and went on to publish in 2005, at the age of 82, another volume of speeches, anecdotes, and opinions, *A Man Without a Country.* A deeply pessimistic book, *A Man* depicts

Vonnegut at opening of Lincoln Center Theater Presents *Awake and Sing!* April 17, 2006 *(photo by Brad Barket/ Getty Images)*

an aging and somewhat bitter Vonnegut who compares himself to MARK TWAIN in later life. While he points out that humor "is a way of holding off how awful life can be" (129), he also admits that, as writers and humorists get older, they can "get just too tired, and the news is too awful, and humor doesn't work anymore" (129). The book emphasizes Vonnegut's disappointment with the presidential administration of George W. Bush, leading the country into war with Iraq. In publicity appearances to support this book, Vonnegut recemented his earlier connection to young people, even appearing on *The Daily Show*, the immensely popular satirical news program hosted by comedian Jon Stewart.

If Vonnegut felt that humor had begun to fail him as he moved into the 21st century, he was able to turn to the visual arts for compensation. In a brief author's note at the end of *A Man Without a Country*, Vonnegut explains that the illustrations that appear in the book are the result of a relationship he had developed with a Kentucky artist named Joe Petro III, whom Vonnegut says "saved [his] life" (143). Petro produces silk screen prints of line drawings and other artwork made by Vonnegut, and these works are sold by ORIGAMI EXPRESS, a partnership formed by the two men. In 2004, Joe Petro arranged an exhibition of Vonnegut family artwork at the Indianapolis Art Center. The show contained not only work produced jointly by Vonnegut and Petro, but also paintings by Kurt Vonnegut, Sr. as well as by Vonnegut's grandfather Bernard, his daughter Edith, and son Mark. Vonnegut writes at the end of *A Man Without a Country* about how important this art show was to him, as it brought him full circle back to his hometown of Indianapolis and united four generations of his family. Vonnegut emphasizes in this book and elsewhere that, despite his often expressed pessimism, the human ability to create art as well as to connect with small groups of like-minded individuals, where one can feel a true sense of belonging, are the things that make life worth living. Kurt Vonnegut died on April 11, 2007, after sustaining brain injuries from a fall at his Manhattan home.

In April 2008, one year after Vonnegut's death, a posthumous collection, *Armageddon in Retrospect*, was published by Putnam. This collection contains

Silkscreen, *Trout in Cohoes* (© 2007 Origami Express LLC, Kurt Vonnegut, and Joe Petro III. www.vonnegut.com)

12 new and previously unpublished pieces revolving around the theme of war, including a long letter Vonnegut wrote home to his family while a prisoner of war in Dresden, several stories from early in his career, and the final speech he wrote. It includes, as well, an affectionate and humorous introduction written by Mark Vonnegut, the author's son.

BIBLIOGRAPHY

Allen, William Rodney, ed. *Conversations with Kurt Vonnegut*. Jackson: University of Mississippi Press, 1988.

———. *Understanding Kurt Vonnegut*. Columbia: University of South Carolina Press, 1991.

Klinkowitz, Jerome. *Kurt Vonnegut*. London: Methuen, 1982.

Morse, Donald E. *Kurt Vonnegut*. San Bernardino, Calif.: Borgo Press, 1992.

Schatt, Stanley. *Kurt Vonnegut, Jr.* Boston: Twayne, 1976.

Vonnegut, Kurt. *Palm Sunday: An Autobiographical Collage*. New York: Delacorte Press, 1981.

PART II

Vonnegut's Works

"Adam"

"Adam," the tale of Holocaust survivors whose newborn son represents a whole new world for them, was initially published in *Cosmopolitan* magazine in April 1954 and later reprinted in both the 1961 collection *Canary in a Cat House* and the 1968 *Welcome to the Monkey House*.

SYNOPSIS

"Adam" is the story of Heinz Knechtmann, whose wife, Avchen, has a baby in a Chicago hospital one night. A seemingly drab little man who works in a dry-cleaning plant, Mr. Knechtmann is very excited about the new baby, especially compared to another man at the hospital, Mr. Sousa, whose wife has just given birth to his seventh daughter. As the night progresses, readers discover that the Knechtmanns are survivors of a Nazi concentration camp where Heinz saw all the members of his family led away and killed. The couple's first child had been born in a displaced person's camp, but had not lived. Mr. Knechtmann will meet a series of Americans in Chicago the night his new baby is born, from hospital personnel to men drinking at a bar, to a coworker out drinking with his girlfriend. None of these Americans will recognize, as the Knechtmanns do, the miracle represented by the birth of their child.

COMMENTARY

Just as in the story "The Manned Missiles," when Mikhail Ivankov recognizes that "there must be great suffering before great joy" (*Welcome* 286), in "Adam," Heinz and Avchen Knechtmann truly recognize the miracle of their son's birth because they had suffered so greatly growing up as children in Nazi concentration camps during World War II. The Americans who surround the couple fail to recognize the fragility of life. Thus, they cannot truly recognize its joys either. Mr. Sousa, the other father at the hospital, complains about the birth of his seventh daughter. The tired doctor carelessly mixes up the identities of Mrs. Sousa and Mrs. Knechtmann. The bartender who drinks with

the two new fathers would rather toast the White Sox than his customers' newborns. Harry, Mr. Knechtmann's coworker, is embarrassed by Heinz's announcement and does not really know how to respond to him. There is even an indication that the brand-new baby, Peter Karl Knechtmann, will be an American through and through, as he refuses to look when his father taps on the glass window of the baby nursery, and will not "share the moment" (309) with Heinz any more than any other of the Americans will.

Depressed by the lack of response he encounters, Heinz goes home that night and thinks to himself, "Another Knechtmann is born, another O'Leary, another Sousa. Who cares? Why should anyone care? What difference does it make? None" (313). Yet, despite this initial depression, the story ends happily. Although Mr. Knechtmann, traveling on the downtown train to the hospital that morning is "a gray, uninteresting man, a part of the city" (313), he changes completely when he enters his wife's hospital room, where he feels only "what he had always felt in her presence—love and aching awe and gratitude for her" (314). Avchen, who has experienced the same terrible childhood suffering as her husband, Heinz, recognizes that their son's birth represents the couples' very survival. "They couldn't kill us, could they, Heinz?" she whispers to her husband (314). Their son is like Adam, a new creation that is "the most wonderful thing that ever happened" (314).

CHARACTERS

Bartender   In a bar across the street from the hospital where his new son is born, Heinz Knechtmann buys a drink for the bartender and Mr. Sousa. The bartender, a father of eight himself, is not overly impressed with the news of Knechtmann's new son and, like Mr. Sousa, is more interested in the White Sox than in new babies.

Harry   On his way home from the hospital after his son is born, Heinz Knechtmann sees a coworker from the dry-cleaning plant, Harry, who is out with a girlfriend. Bursting with his news and eager to tell someone, Knechtmann informs Harry and the girl that he is a brand-new father. While his coworker congratulates him on the birth, the conversation between the two men is awkward.

Harry's Girlfriend Heinz Knechtmann's coworker Harry has obviously been out drinking with a girlfriend when he bumps into his colleague from the dry-cleaning plant when returning home from the hospital very late at night. The girl is somewhat perplexed by Mr. Knechtmann, looks at him with "slightly derisive eyes" (312), and giggles when he departs.

Knechtmann, Avchen Avchen Knechtmann is the wife of Heinz Knechtmann. Like her husband, she was raised "behind barbed wire" (307) in a concentration camp and appreciates the miracle the birth of their son represents.

Knechtmann, Friederich Friederich Knechtmann was a playwright and a relative of Heinz Knechtmann who was killed by the Nazis during World War II.

Knechtmann, Heinz Heinz Knechtmann is a 22-year-old German concentration camp survivor who has migrated to Chicago with his wife, Avchen. When the couple gives birth to a baby boy, they recognize the miracle of life more fully than native-born Americans do, who take the birth of a new baby for granted.

Knechtmann, Helga Helga Knechtmann was Heinz Knechtmann's beautiful harp-playing mother, who was killed during World War II.

Knechtmann, Karl Karl Knechtmann was the name of Heinz and Avchen's first child. Born in a displaced person's camp in Germany, Karl did not survive.

Knechtmann, Kroll Kroll Knechtmann, a botanist, was a relative of Heinz Knechtmann; he was killed during the war.

Knechtmann, Peter Peter Knechtmann was a great-uncle of Heinz Knechtmann. He was a surgeon killed by the Nazis during the war.

Knechtmann, Peter Karl Peter Karl Knechtmann is the name Heinz Knechtmann gives to his newborn son. The child's first name comes from a great-uncle of Heinz's who had been a surgeon, and his middle name comes from Heinz's father.

Nurse At the lying-in hospital in Chicago, an unnamed nurse informs Mr. Knechtmann that his wife had a son. The nurse pronounces his name, "as almost all Americans did, a colorless Netman" (306).

Powers, Dr. Dr. Powers is the young, tired, red-headed doctor who delivers the Knechtmann's new son. He initially gets Mrs. Knechtmann mixed up with Mrs. Sousa and seems too weary to recognize the miracle that the birth represents to the Knechtmanns.

Soldier In the hospital lobby, Heinz Knechtmann sees a soldier making a call home to inform his family of the baby his wife just gave birth to. Heinz longs to make a call as well, but his own family is gone, killed by the Nazis during the war.

Sousa, Mr. Mr. Sousa is a Chicago man at the same lying-in hospital as the Knechtmanns. He is disappointed when he is told that his wife has given birth to a girl, his seventh daughter. Later, Mr. Sousa will have a drink in a bar across the street from the hospital with Mr. Knechtmann. He and the bartender will be more interested in baseball than in the new babies.

Sousa, Mrs. Mrs. Sousa gives birth to a seventh daughter the same night that the Knechtmann's son is born.

FURTHER READING

Reed, Peter. *The Short Fiction of Kurt Vonnegut.* Westport, Conn.: Greenwood Press, 1997.
Welcome to the Monkey House. New York: Dell, 1998.

"All the King's Horses"

Vonnegut's fourth published story, a cold war allegory called "All the King's Horses," first appeared in *Collier's* magazine in February 1951. The story was later reprinted in both *Canary in a Cat House* and *Welcome to the Monkey House*.

SYNOPSIS

"All the King's Horses" tells the story of Colonel Bryan Kelly, whose military transport plane crashes in China when he is on his way, with his wife and twin sons, to a post as a military attaché in India. Also on the plane is a group of enlisted men going to the Middle East as technical specialists. Although all 16 people on board survive the plane crash, the little group of Americans is immediately captured by a communist guerrilla chief named Pi Ying and marched through the jungle to a decaying palace, where they are held in an underground room. Pi Ying, accompanied by a surly military Russian army observer named Major Barzov, soon informs Colonel Kelly of the guerrilla band's plans for the Americans: They will be forced to act as life-size chess pieces in a game of wits that Pi Ying will play against Kelly. Any human chess pieces that Kelly loses in the course of the game will face immediate execution, while anyone left alive should Kelly win will be released. If the American commander refuses to play the game, all of the American prisoners will be shot immediately.

When the chess game commences, Pi Ying plays aggressively, more determined to wreak havoc on the Americans than to use a long-term winning strategy. Conversely, Colonel Kelly plays defensively, concerned to save as many lives as he can. After several moves and the loss of four American soldiers, Kelly sees clearly a strategy that will win him the game, but the price he must pay to save the lives of the remaining Americans is extremely high. He will be forced to sacrifice one of his 10-year-old sons, who is serving as a knight in the white army. Nevertheless, Kelly steels himself and orders his son to make the move that will bring about his death. Before the boy can be taken, how-

ever, a Chinese girl who had been observing the game with great distress stabs Pi Ying and then herself to death. The Russian, Major Barzov, steps into Pi Ying's place and continues the game, offering Kelly the chance to take back his last move, the one that lost him his son. Kelly grimly refuses, and Barzov concedes that 10-year-old Jerry Kelly can stay with his family until the game ends. When Colonel Kelly checkmates the major a few moves later, it initially seems that the boy will be executed, but Barzov finally declares that, since his country is not officially at war with the United States, he will offer all the prisoners safe transport out of the country.

COMMENTARY

Set during the early years of the cold war, "All the King's Horses" attempts to put a human face on decisions made during battle. Pi Ying tells Colonel Kelly that chess games, like battles, can very rarely be won without sacrifices and that, philosophically, the game he is required to play is no different "from what he had known in war" (95). When the colonel's wife, Margaret, demands to know how Pi Ying, "For the love of God," can do such a thing to children (96), he asks angrily, "Is it for the love of God that Americans make bombs and jet planes and tanks?" (96). Although certainly not a sympathetic character, Pi Ying does point out the hypocrisy of Americans, for whom death becomes real only when it affects them personally. Kelly himself wavers between the cold, steely resolve required of commanders in battle, who are able to see human beings as expendable assets, and the hopeless despair of a man who loses the "illusion of the game," and realizes that "the pieces in his power" are real human beings whose lives depend on the decisions he makes (99). The only chance for the Americans to survive is for Kelly to harden himself and see his young son in terms of "pure geometry . . . a rigid mathematical proposition" (102). Forcing himself to see this way, a "refreshing, chilling wind" seems to blow over him. The true horror of war, Vonnegut suggests, is that, in order to survive, men must become like machines, denying their humanity. Whether readers believe

Kelly makes the right decision in sacrificing his son or not, we are meant to see that this decision is the only logical solution allowed by the circumstances of war.

The chess metaphor also suggests the lack of control that ordinary people have over their own lives. The majority of characters in this story are pawns whose moves are controlled completely by outside forces. Not only do these ordinary characters lack control of their movements, they do not even understand the game that they are playing. Vonnegut makes it clear that not even the wisecracking pilot or the self-sacrificing sergeant knows the rules of chess, any more than do Kelly's family members or the scared young corporal. Even when the tall T-4 seems to break out of the game, tackling the nearest guard, the end result of his act of FREE WILL is that another chess master, Major Barzov, simply steps in to replace Pi Ying, and the T-4, along with the rest, are right back where they started. In the end, the remaining American men and the Kelly family survive only because fear of precipitating an international incident forces Major Barzov to see them to safety. As he explains, his winning the game "would have made no difference" in the fates of the Americans (109). Thus, even the supposed rules that the game is played by collapse into illusion—they really make no difference in the end. The control the chess masters initially seem to exert over their circumstances also vanishes into the whim of outside forces larger than themselves.

CHARACTERS

Barzov, Major   The man really running the show at Pi Ying's rebel guerrilla camp seems to be the Russian military observer Major Barzov rather than the Chinese guerrilla chief. When Pi Ying is stabbed to death, the major takes over the chess game, losing largely because of Pi Ying's initial short-sighted play. Yet, the major lets the Americans go at the end of the story, hinting darkly that there will be another Russian/American showdown soon.

Corporal   A scared young American corporal reluctantly plays one of the pawns in the human chess game. When he refuses to move as Colonel

Kelly orders, rebel leader Pi Ying threatens him with being tortured to death.

Kelly, Colonel Bryan   Colonel Bryan Kelly, a man of gigantic stature, both physically and morally, is on his way to India with his family to accept a post as a military attaché when his transport crash lands in the jungles of Asia. When forced to play the human chess game with guerrilla leader Pi Yeng, Kelly is willing to sacrifice one of his own sons to save the lives of as many Americans as possible.

Kelly, Jerry and Paul   Jerry and Paul Kelly are the 10-year-old twin sons of Colonel Bryan Kelly. The boys, who never seem to fully understand what is happening to them, are forced to play the role of knights in the human chess game at the story's center. Although Colonel Kelly makes the tortured decision to sacrifice Jerry's life for the greater good, the boy is spared at the end of the game.

Kelly, Margaret   Margaret Kelly is Colonel Bryan Kelly's traumatized wife, made to play the role of white queen in the human chess game that risks the lives not only of herself, her husband, and his men, but of her 10-year-old sons as well.

Oriental Guard   After Colonel Bryan Kelly's interview with rebel leader Pi Ying, a "small Oriental guard" accompanies Kelly back to the room where the American prisoners are being held.

Oriental Woman   A young Chinese woman, who seems to be a love interest for Pi Ying, though this is never made specific in the story, becomes very distraught while watching the chess game. When she realizes that young Jerry Kelly has been sacrificed, she stabs Pi Ying and then herself to death.

Pi Ying   Pi Ying is the communist guerrilla chief who captures Colonel Kelly, his family, and his men after their plane crashes on the Asiatic mainland. Pi Ying forces Kelly to play the human chess game for the Americans' lives. While clearly relishing the torment he's causing Kelly, Pi Ying is also trying to impress Major Barzov, the Russian military observer visiting him. Pi Ying, however, in his bloodthirstiness, plays a poor game and is on the verge of losing when he is stabbed to death by the young Chinese woman who is watching the game as his companion.

Pilot The pilot of Colonel Kelly's plane is a cynical lieutenant who plays a white bishop in the human chess game. The pilot's refusal to be cowed, and his baiting of Pi Ying, puts the enlisted men somewhat more at ease, so that they begin "to talk among themselves—like a baseball team warming up" (97).

Sergeant One of the enlisted men on Colonel Kelly's plane is a "gruff, tired" (90) sergeant who insists on taking the dangerous position of king's pawn in place of a scared young corporal. The sergeant is summarily shot when Pi Ying orders one of his pieces to take the king's pawn.

T-4 One of the enlisted men on Colonel Kelly's plane is a "lanky T-4" (96) who tells Kelly to put the soldiers where he wants on the chessboard and to "save the soft spots" for Kelly's wife and kids (96). After Jerry Kelly is taken by one of Pi Ying's pieces, the T-4 dives into a guard, tackling him. In the ensuing bedlam, the young Chinese woman stabs guerrilla leader Pi Ying to death.

FURTHER READING

Reed, Peter. *The Short Fiction of Kurt Vonnegut.* Westport, Conn.: Greenwood Press, 1997.
Welcome to the Monkey House. New York: Dell, 1998.

"Ambitious Sophomore"

One of four Vonnegut stories about Lincoln High School band director George M. Helmholtz, "Ambitious Sophomore" first appeared in the *Saturday Evening Post* on May 1, 1954. The story was later reprinted in the collection *Bagombo Snuff Box.*

SYNOPSIS

"Ambitious Sophomore" opens with Lincoln High School's assistant principal, Stewart Haley,

haranguing band director George M. Helmholtz about a $95 bill just received for a band uniform. The school has recently bought the band 100 new uniforms to outfit the 100 boys who play in it, and Haley demands to know why another uniform is necessary. It turns out that this particular uniform is specially designed with padded shoulders and tapered waist for the bell-shaped piccolo player Leroy Duggan. Duggan plays beautifully, but is so self-conscious in his normal band uniform that he falls to pieces. Helmholtz quiets Haley by paying for part of the new uniform out of his own pocket, and the new outfit soon works its magic on Leroy, who becomes extremely confident when wearing it.

On the day of the state marching band contest, Helmholtz plans for the Lincoln High School Ten Square Band to stop in front of the judges' stand and shoot off fireworks, then for Leroy to play a piccolo solo. But the young man's newfound confidence has emboldened him to speak to a pretty blond piccolo player in a rival band. The drum major of this band looks closely at Leroy's uniform, pushes and prods it, and, upon discovering the padding, seizes the jacket, tearing it apart. Helmholtz is forced to outfit Leroy in an ordinary spare uniform and fully expects the young man to play so poorly that Lincoln High will lose the contest. To his surprise, Leroy plays beautifully, even without his special costume. The story ends when Helmholtz discovers his car has a flat tire. Unfortunately, he had sold his spare to help pay for Leroy's uniform. Nevertheless, Helmholtz is undaunted. He happily takes a streetcar home, clutching the band's first place trophy in his lap.

COMMENTARY

"Ambitious Sophomore" is a story about George M. Helmholtz's love for the high school band he directs, its members, and the music they make. His generosity in buying Leroy Duggan the special uniform is motivated not only by Helmholtz's desire to win the marching band contest, but also because he feels it is his "duty . . . to bring the best music out of" each student he teaches (155). "If a boy's shape prevents him from making the music he's capable of making," he tells assistant principal

Stewart Haley, "then it's my duty to get him a shape that will make him play like an angel" (155). Readers have seen Helmholtz's dedication to his students in other Vonnegut stories as well, including "The Kid Nobody Could Handle," reprinted in *Welcome to the Monkey House*. In both of these stories, Hemholtz's kindness to students changes them in a significant way. Leroy Duggan, by the end of "Ambitious Sophomore," is able to talk with the pretty blond piccolo player from the rival band even after his special uniform has been destroyed. Haley points out that Leroy does not miss the padded shoulders anymore because "he's a man now, bell-shaped or not" (165). He just needed a temporary boost of confidence to come out of his shell. Leroy's newfound love interest prompts the assistant principal to ask Helmholtz whether he knows anything about love. The story ends ironically, with Helmholtz thinking about love as he walks back to his car, clutching the first-place trophy: "If love was blinding, obsessing, demanding, beyond reason, and all the other wild things people said it was, then he had never known it, Helmholtz told himself" (165). Of course, readers are to understand that these are the exact feelings Helmholtz has for his famous Ten Square Band. Of all the characters in the story, he is the one who knows the most about love.

CHARACTERS

Bearden, Miss   Miss Bearden is the secretary to Coach Jorgenson at Lincoln High School. Like the coach, she admires Leroy Duggan dressed in his new band uniform.

Blond Piccolo Player   Leroy Duggan's newfound confidence, given him by the new band uniform with the padded shoulders, allows him to talk to a pretty blond piccolo player in a rival band at the state contest.

Crane, Harold   Harold Crane, head of the English Department at Lincoln High School, buys George Helmholtz's spare tire from him for $20. Helmholtz needs the money because he has helped purchase Leroy Duggan's new band uniform out of his own pocket.

Delivery Boy   A delivery boy sent by the tailor Mr. Kornblum brings Lincoln High assistant principal Stewart Haley a bill for $95 for a specially designed band uniform to be worn by Leroy Duggan. This bill causes the story's initial confrontation between Haley and band director George M. Helmholtz.

Drum Major   At the state marching band contest, a drum major from a rival band discovers that Leroy Duggan's uniform is deeply padded. The boy tears the jacket off him, destroying the new uniform.

Duggan, Leroy   High school sophomore Leroy Duggan, described by band director George Helmholtz as "probably the finest piccoloist in this hemisphere" (154), is also bell-shaped and extremely self-conscious. A new band uniform with padded shoulders, however, gives Leroy the new confidence to talk to girls and to march without missing a step, all the while playing beautifully. When his uniform is torn apart by a rival drum major, Leroy is able to retain his new self-assurance, even without the uniform as a prop.

Haley, Stewart   Haley Stewart is assistant principal of Lincoln High School. One of his jobs is to reign in his profligate band director, George Helmholtz, who is constantly asking for more money for his marching band.

Helmholtz, George M.   Described as "a good, fat man who saw no evil, heard no evil, and spoke no evil" (151), George M. Helmholtz is the Lincoln High School band director, who lives for his music. The story depicts Helmholtz using his own money to pay for a special padded uniform for his star piccolo player, Leroy Duggan. When Leroy's uniform is destroyed shortly before the state marching band contest, Helmholtz is convinced that Lincoln High School cannot win. He is delighted when Leroy plays his heart out and the band is awarded first place, so much so that he does not mind having to take the streetcar home, hardly noticing the flat tire on his own car that he cannot afford to fix.

Jorgenson, Coach   When Leroy wears his new, padded uniform down the high school hallway past the athletic office, Coach Jorgenson admires the young man, commenting that "only in this band-happy school would they make a piccolo player out of a man built like a locomotive" (157).

Kornblum, Mr.   Mr. Kornblum is the tailor who sews the new, specially padded uniform for piccolo player Leroy Duggan.

FURTHER READING

Reed, Peter. *The Short Fiction of Kurt Vonnegut.* Westport, Conn.: Greenwood Press, 1997.
Welcome to the Monkey House. New York: Dell, 1998.

"Any Reasonable Offer"

First published in *Collier's* magazine in July 1952, "Any Reasonable Offer," a story largely about class prejudice, was later reprinted in the 1999 collection, *Bagombo Snuff Box.*

SYNOPSIS

"Any Reasonable Offer" is narrated by a real estate salesman who tells the story of Colonel and Mrs. Bradley Peckham, an extremely refined couple who come to him one day asking to see the Hurty mansion, a property the narrator is trying to sell. When the narrator takes the couple to the house, they are impressed with the grounds and the swimming pool, but insist that they must live with the house a few days to "get the newness out of it" (47). The Peckhams spend many hours at the mansion over the next several days, swimming in the pool, drinking cocktails mixed for them by Mr. Hurty, and enjoying the lush grounds. When the narrator tries to finish the sale, by getting Mr. Hurty to tell the couple that another man is about to make an offer on the house, the Peckhams walk away in disdain, saying that "they couldn't possibly be interested in anything that would appeal to a retired brewer from Toledo" (49). The next house the narrator shows the couple is a huge monstrosity he has been trying to sell for three years: the Hellbrunner place. The

Peckhams behave much the same way here as they did at the Hurty mansion, though this time they avoid closing the deal by telling Mrs. Hellbrunner that the colonel is being sent to Bangkok. Eventually, the narrator calls the National Steel Foundry in Philadelphia where the colonel claimed to have been "straightening things out" (44). He discovers that *Mr.* Peckham (not *Colonel*) is simply a draftsman at the company who cannot afford elaborate vacations. The story ends with the narrator himself going to Newport and pulling the same scheme on a real estate agent that the Peckhams had pulled on him.

COMMENTARY

"Any Reasonable Offer" is a story that plays on assumptions about social class and also on characters' greed. The Peckhams are able to get away with their scam because of the inherent class prejudices of both the narrator and his clients. For instance, Mrs. Hellbrunner, a member of a wealthy, prestigious family that has been trying to sell her enormous mansion for the past three years, cannot understand how the narrator was able to sell Dennis Delahanty's "awful little cracker-box" (42) in one day while her own home has sat on the market for three years. Like the wealthy Mr. Hurty, Mrs. Hellbrunner is taken in by the Peckhams' clothes, accents, and snobbery. If an ordinary, middle-class couple had taken advantage of their hospitality as the Peckhams do, neither Mr. Hurty nor Mrs. Hellbrunner would have stood for it.

Moreover, as with any good scam, the characters are undone by their own greed. Although the Peckhams and Mr. Hurty treat the narrator "like a Seeing Eye dog or overnight bag" (45), he accepts this treatment gladly because he expects a good commission at the end: "The Peckhams had some distance to go," he says, "before offending four thousand dollars' worth of my pride" (44). The narrator is willing to trade his dignity for a big commission. And the mansion owners are duped by their greed as well. Hoping to make a large profit on their homes, they allow the Peckhams unprecedented freedom to roam their properties. When the narrator himself is able to run the same scam as the

Peckhams at the end, Vonnegut's SATIRE of wealth and class divisions in America is driven home. The enterprising narrator, always willing to lie to make a sale, has simply taken his lies to the next level. And the greedy clients, eager to turn a profit and respectful of someone they believe to be their social equal, are so dazzled by his supposed wealth that they do not ask too many questions.

CHARACTERS

Delahanty, Dennis   Dennis Delahanty is one of the narrator's clients. When the narrator manages to sell Delahanty's home after bringing only one client to see it, Delahanty tries to close the deal behind his agent's back to avoid paying the commission he owes.

Hellbrunner, Mrs.   Mrs. Hellbrunner is the owner of an enormous 27-room mansion that has been on the market for three years. She is angry with the narrator when he is able to sell Dennis Delahanty's house in one afternoon and accuses him of not working hard enough to sell her place. Mrs. Hellbrunner will be completely taken in by the Peckhams when they come to see her home, inviting them for dinner, buying them cigars, plying them with brandy, etc. When the Peckhams walk away from the deal, Mrs. Hellbrunner still does not suspect a con; she believes the colonel is simply too polite to bargain about the price.

Hurty, Mr.   The owner of a luxurious estate that the narrator is trying to sell, Mr. Hurty is the first person taken in by the Peckhams' scam. He fires the narrator as his real estate agent when the Peckhams refuse to close the deal, saying they could not possibly be interested in a house "that would appeal to a retired brewer from Toledo" (49).

Narrator   A real estate agent used to being abused by his clients, the narrator is at first taken in by the Peckhams because he expects to receive a big commission if he is able to sell an expensive home to them. When he finally realizes that he has been scammed, he decides to run a similar scam himself and ends the story by staying at the Van Tuyl estate, an elaborate mansion in Newport.

Peckham, Colonel Bradley   Colonel Bradley Peckham is really a con artist who works as a drafts-man at the National Steel Foundry in Philadelphia. Because he and his wife are unable to afford luxurious vacations, the couple pose as potential buyers of huge mansions. The owners then allow the Peckhams to spend hours and hours enjoying themselves in their homes because they believe the couple will soon make an offer to buy them.

Peckham, Pam   Pam Peckham is the wife of Colonel Bradley Peckham. She is complicit with her husband in the scams he runs to attain luxury vacations for free.

FURTHER READING

Bagombo Snuff Box. New York: Berkley Books, 2000.
Reed, Peter. *The Short Fiction of Kurt Vonnegut*. Westport, Conn.: Greenwood Press, 1997.

Bagombo Snuff Box

Published by Putnam in 1999, the collection *Bagombo Snuff Box* includes 23 magazine short stories that, with the exception of "Hal Irwin's Magic Lamp," which appeared in the 1961 volume, *Canary in a Cat House*, had not previously been collected into book form. The book also includes a preface by Vonnegut scholar Peter Reed, author of the 1997 critical work, *The Short Fiction of Kurt Vonnegut*, as well as an introduction by the author, in which Vonnegut claims that "there is no greatness in this collection . . . nor was there meant to be" (3). Rather, he tells readers, the stories "may be interesting . . . as relics" from another time (3). The stories in *Bagombo Snuff Box* appeared in magazines such as *Collier's*, the *Saturday Evening Post*, and *Cosmopolitan*, during the years 1950 to 1963. A few of the stories, including "The Powder-Blue Dragon," "The Boy Who Hated Girls," and "Hal Irwin's Magic Lamp," include endings that have been significantly revised from their initial magazine publications, as Vonnegut informs readers in the coda appearing at the end of the volume. The contents of *Bagombo Snuff Box* are:

FURTHER READING

Bagombo Snuff Box. New York: Berkley Books, 2000.

"Bagombo Snuff Box"

A commentary on post–World War II suburban life, the story "Bagombo Snuff Box" first appeared in *Cosmopolitan* magazine in October 1954. Later, it was reprinted as the title story of the collection *Bagombo Snuff Box*.

SYNOPSIS

The story opens in a bar with Eddie Laird reminiscing about the last time he was in this particular city, 11 years previously, when he served in the Air Force during World War II. Readers soon discover that Eddie has an ex-wife in town, a woman named Amy to whom he was married for six months when he was 22 and she was 18. Laird eventually screws up his courage and phones Amy. He ends the conversation by inviting himself out to the suburban house where she lives with her new husband and two children. When Laird arrives, the small home is chaotic, with supper cooking and Amy changing a baby's diaper. He is welcomed by Harry, Amy's husband. The two men talk, with Laird telling Harry about his adventures over the past 11 years. He flew planes for a pearling outfit in Ceylon, prospected for uranium in the Klondike, hunted diamonds in the Amazon, etc. Laird also gives Harry a gift he has brought for the family, a small, jewel-encrusted snuff box from Bagombo, Ceylon. Amy soon joins the men, and Laird continues to wow the couple with stories of his world travels. Soon, Harry and Amy's nine-year-old son, Stevie, arrives home. When Laird introduces himself to the boy as a major, Stevie asks where his uniform is. The boy also asks why the snuff box has a label on the bottom that says "Made in Japan." Finally, Stevie insists that Ceylon is off the coast of Africa although Amy believes the island is off India. When the family turns to Laird to respond, he rushes out of the house and departs in his waiting taxi. The story closes with Laird back in his hotel room that night, calling his second wife, Selma, on the phone. Readers find out that Laird is, in fact, a traveling salesman who lives a staid middle-class existence in a subdivision in Levittown, New York, with his wife and several children.

COMMENTARY

Levittown, New York, where readers discover that Eddie Laird actually lives at the end of the story, was the first mass-produced American suburb, built mostly between 1947 and 1951, although officially finished in 1958. Levittown, then, is the model of the contemporary American suburb, which not only represents the American dream of affordable home ownership, but also suggests a certain type of bland conformity, of cookie-cutter sameness. In "Bagombo Snuff Box," published in 1954, Vonnegut comments on both the good and bad associated with suburban life. Clearly, the characters feel hemmed in by their ordinary, domestic lives and long for adventure and romance. Amy is reluctant to invite Eddie Laird to her home because "the house is a horror" and she's "a witch" (171). She worries that such a visit will be a "hideous letdown" for someone who has traveled "from Ceylon by way of Baghdad, Rome, and New York" (171). Harry, too, seems to become increasingly dissatisfied with his very ordinary life as he listens to Eddie's wild tales. He asks whether "there are a lot of jobs waiting for Americans in places like" Ceylon and if they are "recruiting" (173). After listening to Eddie, Harry speaks sharply to his wife, and both Harry and Amy scold their son, Stevie, in a new way, suggesting the increasing discontent beginning to stir within them.

At the same time, Vonnegut does not completely dismiss suburban life as insipidly conformist. On the phone, Amy tells Eddie that, when she gets a chance to catch her breath, she can see that her life is "sweet and good" (171). And tender moments pass between her and Harry, such as when she takes her husband's hand and squeezes it, and "peace settled over the house once more" (176). The real hero of the story is perhaps nine-year-old Stevie, who, unlike his parents, is not so foolish as to be hoodwinked by the possibility of a better life on the other side of the world. Stevie's eyes are "frank, irreverent, and unromantic" (178), and he refuses to simply accept Eddie Laird's exotic tales at face value. Because he is not disposed to long for something he does not have, and because he is too young to regret the life he does have, he is able to look at facts squarely and expose Eddie's lies.

By the end of the story, however, readers see that Eddie is not a bad man. While he play-acts at being a romantic adventurer in front of his ex-wife and her second husband, he is actually a devoted family man himself. In his telephone conversation with his wife, Selma, Eddie is concerned about his children and shows himself to be involved in the small details of their lives. He asks about Arthur's troubles in school and about Dawn's dentist visit. In addition, he tells Selma that he loves her, and his wife seems to genuinely return his affection. Although he may be only a traveling potato chip salesman rather than a Ceylonian adventurer, Eddie Laird has made a good life for himself over

the past 11 years. While Vonnegut pokes gentle fun at the sameness and drudgery of suburban life, he nevertheless seems to have an underlying affection for it.

CHARACTERS

Amy Amy is Eddie Laird's ex-wife whom he has not seen in 11 years. The two were married for a short six months while Eddie served in the Air Force. Amy is reluctant to see Eddie again because she fears that her ordinary, suburban life will pale in comparison to the adventures Eddie claims to have had over the past 11 years. Yet, despite his grandiose claims, Eddie turns out to be living much the same life as Amy herself.

Arthur Arthur is Eddie Laird's school-age son who is having trouble with reading in school. Readers only learn of the boy's existence at the very end of the story, since Eddie Laird has claimed to be a bachelor.

Bartender The story opens in a bar, with Eddie Laird telling the bartender that he has not been in this city for 11 years. The bartender tells Eddie about some of the changes that have occurred since Eddie was stationed there while serving in the air force during World War II.

Dawn At the very end of the story, readers learn that Eddie Laird actually has several children, including a daughter named Dawn, who needs new braces.

Harry Harry is the second husband of Eddie Laird's ex-wife, Amy. Harry is taken in by Eddie's tall tales about his romantic adventures and begins to seem dissatisfied with his own typical suburban life. But soon Eddie's stories begin to unravel, and Harry's confidence returns enough that he can mock Eddie by calling out a supposed phrase in the "Buhna-Simca" (176) language as Eddie flees in his taxi.

Laird, Eddie When Eddie Laird returns to the city where his first marriage took place and visits his ex-wife, Amy, whom he has not seen for 11 years, he invents a romantic, adventurous past for himself until his lies are uncovered by Amy's nine-year-old son. It turns out that Eddie's life is not much different from Amy's—both have remarried, live an ordinary middle-class life in the suburbs, and struggle financially to care for their growing families.

Selma   At the very end of the story, readers discover that Eddie Laird has a second wife named Selma. The story closes with a phone call Eddie makes to Selma, which reveals that he lives a mundane, middle-class suburban existence much as Amy and Harry do.

Stevie   Stevie is the nine-year-old son of Eddie Laird's ex-wife, Amy, and her second husband, Harry. The boy, whose eyes are described as "frank, irreverent, and unromantic" (178), sees through Eddie's lies and eventually exposes him for a fraud.

FURTHER READING

Bagombo Snuff Box. New York: Berkley Books, 2000.
Reed, Peter. *The Short Fiction of Kurt Vonnegut.* Westport, Conn.: Greenwood Press, 1997.

Between Time and Timbuktu

Between Time and Timbuktu is a National Educational Television production based on the writings of Kurt Vonnegut that first aired on March 13, 1972. Later that same year, the television script was published in book form, a handsome edition that includes numerous still photographs of the program taken by JILL KREMENTZ. In his preface to the book, Vonnegut states that the script was initially put together from unrelated incidents in several of his stories by "some friendly people at National Educational Television in New York and at WGBH in Boston" (xiii). Vonnegut himself later tinkered with it as well, like MARY SHELLEY's Victor FRANKENSTEIN creating a "new creature" (xiii) from assembled parts. He describes this new creature as "clumsy, funny-looking, and almost pathetically eager to please," but as also having "a soul" (xiii).

Despite this, Vonnegut also says in the preface that he is through with film—the medium is too realistic, too technological and too expensive for his tastes. Perhaps most important, he concludes that film limits the imagination, filling in details that are left up to readers in literature.

SYNOPSIS

The script opens with a spokesman from the Blast-off Space Food Company arriving at the INDIANAPOLIS home of Stony Stevenson to tell the young man that he has won the company's recent jingle contest. As his prize, Stony is awarded with a trip on the rocket ship *Prometheus-5,* which will blast him into a space-time warp called a chronosynclastic infundibulum. He will be the first poet in space. The action then shifts to a television news program being broadcast live from Mission Control Space Flight Center. The countdown commences, and Stony's rocket is launched with much fanfare and celebration. Eventually, however, Mission Control loses contact with the poet-astronaut, and the screen fades to black. The next six months pass with only occasional contact between Stony and the Space Center back on Earth. Around Christmastime, Stony passes through the time warp, loses consciousness, and begins to have several strange adventures.

He first finds himself waking up on the Island of San Lorenzo, where he meets a religious leader named Bokonon who, along with a group of Native followers, is on the run from the island's fascist government. Although Bokonon freely admits that the religion he has invented is made up of "harmless lies" (82), the island's president, Bokonon's former best friend, wants to execute him and his followers on "the hook" (87). Stony does not stay long on the island, however; he soon fades back into unconsciousness. This time, when he wakes, he finds himself a member of a jury that is hearing evidence against Dr. Paul Proteus, who is lying on a table strapped to electronic lie detector equipment. The doctor is accused of being part of a revolutionary group whose goal is to "wag[e] war on lawless technology" (104). After watching a cartoonish film presented by the court that praises the benefits of technology, Stony is again whirled through time and space. In his next adventure; he encounters a scientist and a general who discuss a radical new technology called *ice-nine* that will help U.S. Marines in battle by freezing mud into a hard, slick surface that they can travel over easily.

Back in the time warp again, Stony is transported to a planet where the inhabitants are forced to wear "handicaps"—heavy weights attached to their bodies, radio receivers plugged into their brains, masks and funny noses to cover their faces—which are intended to make everyone equal. He also visits a planet that suffers so severely from overpopulation that the government has invented "Ethical Suicide Parlors" to encourage inhabitants to kill themselves painlessly and make more room for others. In Stony's final escapade, he is transported to heaven, where he meets a little girl named Wanda June who was run over by an ice cream truck on her 10th birthday. In heaven, Stony also meets Nazi leader ADOLF HITLER, who makes all the people in heaven, including Wanda June, vanish by telling them that there is no afterlife, no heaven. Soon, Stony faces Hitler alone. The two men have a mental duel, in which Stony, using only his imagination, is able to make Hitler disappear. The play closes with Stony crawling out of a grave back on Earth and strolling out of the cemetery. The tombstone he leaves behind bears the epitaph "Everything was beautiful and nothing hurt."

COMMENTARY

Stony Stevenson's six space adventures in *Between Time and Timbuktu* are drawn from three Vonnegut novels—*Player Piano, The Sirens of Titan,* and *Cat's Cradle*—from two short stories—"Harrison Bergeron" and "Welcome to the Monkey House"—and from the play *Happy Birthday, Wanda June.* The teleplay itself is episodic, having much in common with picaresque novels, satirical works that usually depict a character of low social class on some kind of journey. Stony is the kind of anti-hero often found in the picaresque. Lacking the long years of training and education usually supplied to astronauts, he wins his position by virtue of writing the best jingle in a contest promoted by the manufacturers of Blast-off Space Food. He is ill-equipped and ill-prepared for his journey and, like

Don Quixote or Jonathan Swift's Gulliver, often seems befuddled by the people he meets and the places he visits. Stony, in fact, is named after an unfortunate character in Vonnegut's second novel, *The Sirens of Titan,* who is strangled to death by his own best friend, Malachi Constant (called "Unk" when he joins the Martian Army), who is under the control of a radio antenna implanted in his head. After Stony's death in that novel, Unk longs to reunite with his friend. He is able to die a happy man when the Talfamadorian space alien Salo hypnotizes Unk into believing that Stony has come for him in a rocket ship to take him to Paradise. Stony's namesake in *Between Time and Timbuktu* travels to Paradise in his rocket as well, although he first visits many strange and unexpected places before arriving there. The teleplay ascribes Stony's mysterious travels to the fact that he is shot into a chrono-synclastic infundibulum, a time warp that also plays an important role in *The Sirens of Titan,* and which transports Stony without warning from one alien scene to the next.

Stony's first adventure, on the island of San Lorenzo where he meets the holy man Bokonon, is drawn from *Cat's Cradle.* The teleplay retains the key aspects of Bokononism, including details of the religion's founding by two best friends, one who becomes the island dictator and the other who becomes the outlawed prophet. Just as in the book, the teleplay's Bokonon freely admits that his religion is made up of "harmless lies" (82), designed to comfort a population crushed by poverty and despair. Bokonon's final speech in this section reflects a theme that is prevalent in many of Vonnegut's works and which serves as the "moral" to his novel *Mother Night.* Admitting that real executions are being carried out in San Lorenzo, Bokonon says to Stony: "I suppose that it goes to show that you have to be very careful what you pretend to be . . . because one day you may wake up to find that's what you are" (89). The power of the human imagination, of pretending, is an idea that is revisited at the very end of the play, when Stony uses his imagination to challenge Adolf Hitler in heaven.

After losing consciousness in San Lorenzo, Stony is thrust into his second space adventure and into an earlier Vonnegut novel, his very first book, *Player Piano.* This scene in the teleplay derives from the trial of Dr. Paul Proteus in that novel. Proteus is charged with being the leader of a revolutionary anti-technology group, the Ghost Shirt Society (inexplicably changed to the "Gray Shirt Society" in the teleplay). This section seems to have been chosen for inclusion in *Between Time and Timbuktu* because it illustrates Vonnegut's frequent critique of technology and scientific advancement. While the silly corporate video Stony Stevenson watches with the rest of the jury members argues that technology has benefited John Averageman, readers of the teleplay see technology's more sinister applications, especially in Stony Stevenson's third adventure, which focuses on the invention of *ice-nine,* the doomsday device from *Cat's Cradle* that ends up destroying the Earth and nearly every living thing on it, except for a small band of survivors. In this adventure, Vonnegut's condemnation of new forms of military weaponry is especially apparent. The teleplay highlights the fact that *ice-nine* is created at the behest of a Marine general who wants to be able to move his soldiers more efficiently.

Stony's fourth and fifth adventures come directly from two of Vonnegut's most popular and most science-fiction oriented short stories: "Harrison Bergeron" and "Welcome to the Monkey House." Both stories depict future dystopic worlds in which human beings have attained long desired goals, but at tremendous cost. The Harrison Bergeron adventure depicts a planet so obsessed with equality that all citizens with above-average physical or mental ability are forced to wear handicaps on their bodies to weigh them down, make them more ugly, or limit their ability to think. When Harrison Bergeron tears off his handicaps, he reveals almost superhuman good looks, intelligence, and agility, but he is shot dead almost immediately by Diana Moon Glampers, the handicapper general. On the next planet Stony visits, humans have finally conquered death and disease, but the consequence is overpopulation so severe that Ethical Suicide Parlors are established where people can go to kill themselves and make more room for others. In both cases, as happens so often in Vonnegut's fiction, utopian schemes backfire, creating unforeseen problems

and instituting new societies that are worse than the old ones being replaced.

Stony's final space adventure in *Between Time and Timbuktu* takes place in heaven and draws at least partly from Vonnegut's play, *Happy Birthday, Wanda June.* Portions of that play depict 10-year-old Wanda June in heaven playing shuffleboard with Nazi SS Officer Major Siegfried Von Konigswald. In the teleplay, Von Konigswald is replaced by Adolf Hitler himself. Vonnegut's frequently expressed view that conventional religions offer "foma" or comforting lies, is driven home when readers see Adolf Hitler tell the crowds in heaven that there is no afterlife. No longer able to trust the foma that had allowed them to believe they were in heaven, all of heaven's inhabitants vanish, eventually leaving only Stony and Hitler. The two men engage in a mental duel, which Stony describes as pitting "Death against . . . imagination" (262). Stony is finally able to overcome Hitler by imagining him gone. He then makes the heavenly crowd reappear and disappear at will, illustrating how completely the human imagination is able to shape reality. In this final scene, readers may begin to suspect that Stony's journey has perhaps been simply an interior one, into the recesses of his own mind. At one point, when talking to Hitler, the astronaut touches his head and says, "It's all up here . . . you . . . them . . . this . . . Mission Control . . . the moon, the sun, the stars" (261). The play closes with Stony returned to Earth, determined not to worry, but to simply "smile . . . smile . . . smile . . ." (277). Paradise might be only a lie, but choosing to believe such a lie can make life bearable.

CHARACTERS AND RELATED ENTRIES

Abernathy, Sandy Sandy Abernathy is a television reporter who covers a protest led by the evangelist Dr. Bobby Denton at the launch of *Prometheus-5.*

Averageman, John A John Averageman appears in a brief film touting technology's wonders that is shown by the prosecution at the trial of Dr. Paul Proteus in one of Stony Stevenson's space adventures. Initially skeptical about the benefits of technology, John Averageman is eventually persuaded that technology has made him richer than Caesar and Napoleon.

Bergeron, Harrison   Harrison Bergeron appears in Stony Stevenson's fourth space adventure as a mentally and physically superior individual who refuses to wear the handicaps assigned him. He interrupts a nationally televised ballet, persuades the lead ballerina to remove her handicaps as well, then performs a wonderful, nearly super-human dance with her. Both Bergeron and the ballerina are shot dead in the midst of their performance by handicapper general Diana Moon Glampers. These events are lifted from Vonnegut's well-known short story "Harrison Bergeron," though the teleplay transforms Bergeron from a 14-year-old adolescent into a young man of 23.

Blast-off, Miss   A beauty queen, Miss Blast-off accompanies the Blast-off Space Food contest announcer when he goes to INDIANAPOLIS to award Stony Stevenson first prize in the company's jingle contest.

Bokonon   The fraudulent religious leader Bokonon from Vonnegut's novel *Cat's Cradle* appears in *Between Time and Timbuktu* in Stony Stevenson's first adventure after hurtling through the chronosynclastic infundibulum. The poet-astronaut awakens on the island of San Lorenzo, where he meets Bokonon and a group of native followers, who are on the run from government soldiers trying to capture and execute them. Bokonon, as he does in *Cat's Cradle*, asserts that his religion is based on "harmless lies" (82) that bring comfort to people crushed by poverty and despair.

Cemetary Gardener   The last person Stony Stevenson meets in his space adventures is actually a cemetery gardener back on Earth. At the end of the play, Stony is transported to the burial plot his stepfather had bought for him in Brooklyn. He emerges from a grave whose headstone reads—as does the tombstone Billy Pilgrim in *Slaughterhouse-Five* imagines for himself—"Everything was beautiful and nothing hurt" (276). The gardener, not recognizing the astronaut, informs Stony that the

grave is really a memorial since Stony's body is not actually buried there. He tells Stony that his space capsule splashed down in the Pacific. Inside was found only a half-bottle of Tang and a note containing the words that were carved on the tombstone.

Contest Announcer   The teleplay opens with an unnamed television announcer from the Blast-off Space Food Company declaring Stony Stevenson as the winner of their recent jingle contest. As his prize, Stony is awarded a rocket trip into space.

Deaf Juror   When Stony Stevenson is transported to the trial of Dr. Paul Proteus, one of his fellow jurors turns out to be almost completely deaf. Absurdly, the lawyers have asked the man whether he favors capital punishment, but not whether he can hear.

Denton, Dr. Bobby   A fundamentalist preacher from Vonnegut's novel *The Sirens of Titan* who warns against space travel, Dr. Bobby Denton appears in *Between Time and Timbuktu* to lead a protest at the rocket launch of *Prometheus-5*. He leads his followers in a countdown of the Ten Commandments, which occurs simultaneously with Mission Control's launch countdown.

Director   In Stony Stevenson's fourth space adventure, a television director begs Harrison Bergeron to stop his disruption of the televised ballet, reminding him that his actions are completely illegal.

Drunk   In Stony Stevenson's third space adventure, he initially meets a drunk on the sidewalk of an unknown planet. Stony asks the man for a dime so that he can telephone Mission Control. The drunk gives Stony all his change, sobbingly repeating that Stony's story is the saddest tale he has ever heard.

General   An unnamed Marine general appears in Stony Stevenson's third space adventure. The general persuades brilliant scientist Dr. Hoenikker to develop a material that will turn mud into a hard surface, making it easier for Marines to deploy over land. The material Dr. Hoenikker invents turns out to be *ice-nine*, an extremely dangerous compound that has the potential to freeze all the Earth's water, thus destroying all life on the planet. This scenario is lifted from Vonnegut's fourth novel, *Cat's Cradle*.

Gesundheit, Walter Walter Gesundheit is a news broadcaster modeled on the real-life Walter Cronkite. Gesundheit anchors the television broadcast of Stony Stevenson's rocket launch.

Glampers, Diana Moon A character who initially appears in Vonnegut's short story "Harrison Bergeron," Diana Moon Glampers is the "handicapper general" in Stony Stevenson's fourth space adventure. Her job is to assign handicaps to people with above-average physical or mental abilities. Any individual deemed more capable than the norm is required to wear heavy sandbags, distorting facial masks, or a radio antenna wired to the skull in an attempt to make all people absolutely equal. As in the short story, Diana Moon Glampers ends up shooting the defiant Harrison Bergeron dead.

Girl Pool Lead Caroler Echoing a scene from *Cat's Cradle*, in Stony Stevenson's third space adventure in *Between Time and Timbuktu*, a group of secretaries known as the "girl pool" visits Dr. Hoenikker's office to sing Christmas carols. The lead caroler introduces the women before they begin to sing. In both works, this scene illustrates the strange aura of innocence surrounding Dr. Hoenikker's sinister undertakings.

Hitler, Adolf Adolf Hitler, who also appears as a character in Vonnegut's third novel, *Mother Night*, shows up in Stony Stevenson's sixth and final space adventure in *Between Time and Timbuktu*. Stony meets Hitler in heaven, and the two men engage in a mental duel. While Hitler is able to make all of heaven's residents, with the exception of Stony, disappear when he tells them that there is no afterlife, Stony is finally able to make Hitler disappear by using his imagination.

Hoenikker, Dr. Dr. Hoenikker, the inventor of doomsday device *ice-nine* in Vonnegut's fourth novel, *Cat's Cradle*, appears in one of Stony Stevenson's space adventures. In *Between Time and Timbuktu*, Dr. Hoenikker runs a laboratory in which he freezes well-known people after their deaths, hoping to thaw them out and bring them back to life at some future point. Stony witnesses the brilliant scientist come up with the idea of *ice-nine* as he discusses military issues with a Marine general.

Howard, Lionel J. Lionel J. Howard appears in Stony Stevenson's fifth space adventure as a client at an Ethical Suicide Parlor—government-run facilities that encourage citizens to kill themselves and thus help alleviate the planet's terrible overpopulation problem. Mr. Howard insists that he has the right to ask one final question before he dies. Nancy, the suicide hostess, however, forces him to take the drugs that will kill him before he can ask his question. Mr. Howard gains consciousness long enough to pose the question—"What . . . what are people—for?" (243), but dies before he can receive an answer.

Martin, Miss Miss Martin appears in Stony Stevenson's third space adventure as the secretary to Dr. Hoenikker, the brilliant scientist who invents the doomsday device *ice-nine*.

Nancy Nancy is a hostess at an Ethical Suicide Parlor in Stony Stevenson's fifth space adventure, which derives from Vonnegut's short story "Welcome to the Monkey House." Her job is to make her clients, who have altruistically agreed to kill themselves in order to help the planet's gross overpopulation problem, comfortable before they die. Mistaking Stony for a fellow Suicide Parlor worker, she sends him to bring client Lionel J. Howard his final meal.

News Announcer In addition to Walter Gesundheit and Bud Williams, Jr., who appear in the opening scenes of the teleplay, a news announcer also plays a role in Stony Stevenson's fourth space adventure, lifted from "Harrison Bergeron." The announcer introduces the televised ballet production that Harrison Bergeron will interrupt.

Pirandello, Colonel Donald "Tex" Colonel Donald "Tex" Pirandello works at Mission Control. Known as the "voice of *Prometheus-5*" (26), Tex is the Space Flight Center spokesman who communicates with the press about Stony Stevenson and his rocket journey into space.

Policeman When Stony Stevenson awakes to his fourth space adventure, he finds himself being chased by an unnamed policeman who threatens him with a gun. The events that take place in this escapade derive from "Harrison Bergeron."

Promotheus-5 *Promotheus-5* is the name of the rocket ship that transports jingle contest winner Stony Stevenson into space.

Prosecutor Stony Stevenson's second space adventure draws on scenes from Vonnegut's first novel, *Player Piano*. In this section of the play, Stony finds himself a member of a jury witnessing the trial of Dr. Paul Proteus, who is lying on a table strapped to electronic lie detector equipment. An unnamed government prosecutor is making his case against Proteus, whom he accuses of leading a revolutionary anti-technology movement.

Proteus, Dr. Paul The protagonist of Vonnegut's first novel, *Player Piano*, Dr. Paul Proteus appears briefly in *Between Time and Timbuktu* on Stony Stevenson's second space adventure, when the astronaut is transported into the midst of a trial. Dr. Proteus is lying on a table, wired to a lie detector, as he listens to a government prosecutor detail charges against him. Dr. Proteus defends himself against accusations of sabotage by claiming he only wanted what was best for his country.

Short-Order Cook Stony Stevenson, on his fifth space adventure, meets a short-order cook on a planet so overpopulated that the government encourages its citizens to kill themselves in Ethical Suicide Parlors. The cook is responsible for preparing last meals for the Parlors' clients.

Soldier In Stony Stevenson's first space adventure, on the island of San Lorenzo, he witnesses soldiers searching for the religious leader Bokonon and his followers. One of the soldiers has a brief speaking role in the play. He rather bufoonishly states that he has his enemy on the run, then complains about his working conditions.

Stagehands In Stony Stevenson's fourth space adventure, two stagehands named Mike and Larry at a television studio are astonished when Stony appears without wearing handicaps of any kind. Sandbags are soon strapped onto the astronaut, and he is fitted with a clown nose and a radio antenna to weaken his physical and mental abilities.

Stevenson, Mrs. Mrs. Stevenson is the mother of poet-astronaut Stony Stevenson. After Stony is launched into space, Mrs. Stevenson is interviewed on national television by former astronaut Bud Williams, where she discusses such personal issues as her relationships with her three husbands and her family's experiences with the welfare system.

Stevenson, Stony The protagonist of the teleplay, Stony Stevenson, is a character readers first met in Vonnegut's second novel, *The Sirens of Titan*. He is the best friend in the Martian Army of Unk, (who is, in fact, the former millionaire playboy Malachi Constant). Unk, controlled by a radio antenna implanted in his head, is forced to strangle Stony Stevenson to death and spends the rest of the novel longing to reunite with his friend. In *Between Time and Timbuktu*, Stony Stevenson is an aspiring poet who enters and wins first place in the Blast-off Space Food Jingle Contest. Stony's prize is the chance to be the only passenger aboard a rocket ship shot into a time warp deep in space. The play chronicles Stony's strange adventures in space as he moves between various scenarios lifted from several previous Vonnegut works. Stony defeats Adolf Hitler in heaven at the end of the play, and returns safely to Earth.

Wanda June Wanda June, a character from Vonnegut's play, *Happy Birthday, Wanda June*, appears in Stony Stevenson's sixth and final space adventure, in which he is transported to heaven. The little girl tells the astronaut that she is in heaven because she was run over and killed by an ice cream truck on her 10th birthday. Wanda June ends up disappearing along with the rest of the heavenly host when Adolf Hitler announces that there is no afterlife.

Williams, Bud, Jr.   Bud Williams, Jr. is a former astronaut who, along with Walter Gesundheit, broadcasts the live news program covering the rocket launch of Stony Stevenson. Williams later conducts a rather awkward interview with Stony's mother.

FURTHER READING

Between Time and Timbuktu. New York: Dell, 1973.

"Big Space Fuck, The"

"The Big Space Fuck" first appeared in a 1972 book, *Again, Dangerous Visions: Forty-six Original Stories Edited by Harlan Ellison.* Widely considered the first published short story to use the expletive *fuck* in its title, the story was reprinted in Vonnegut's *Palm Sunday: An Autobiographical Collage* in 1981.

SYNOPSIS

"The Big Space Fuck," which Vonnegut calls the "dirtiest story" he ever wrote (*Palm Sunday* 207), takes place in the United States in the year 1989. Earth has become nearly uninhabitable because of environmental destruction and overpopulation. As a result, the U.S. government decides to stage the Big Space Fuck, "which was a serious effort to make sure that human life would continue to exist somewhere in the Universe" (207). A rocket ship is loaded with 800 pounds of freeze-dried "jizzum" and will be fired into the Andromeda Galaxy at midnight on the Fourth of July. That night, Dwayne and Grace Hoobler are watching the countdown to liftoff on their television when their friend the county sheriff knocks on the door, bringing the sad news that the Hoobler's daughter, Wanda June, is suing her parents for ruining her

childhood. In the ruined Earth of the future, children are encouraged to sue their parents, partly in an effort to discourage reproduction since there is no longer enough to eat. The sheriff also reports that Wanda June decided to sue because she is in jail, charged with heading a shoplifting ring. To avoid prison, she must prove that her behavior is the fault of her parents. Dwayne and Grace are heartbroken by the sheriff's news, and the sheriff himself is torn up about having to bring such bad news to his friends. He stumbles out into the night, crying, and is immediately devoured by a giant lamprey eel, who had oozed out of the polluted Great Lakes. Upon hearing the sheriff's scream, Dwayne and Grace rush outside and are instantly devoured as well. Meanwhile, the television set continues to play in the empty house, counting down toward the rocket's liftoff.

COMMENTARY

A somewhat silly story largely devoid of characterization or plot, "The Big Space Fuck" serves mostly to illustrate Vonnegut's ideas about politeness and obscenity. In the collection *Palm Sunday,* he expresses his belief that enforced politeness—the good manners taught to members of his generation by his parents and others—can in fact be quite dangerous. People who are offended by obscenity, by the specific naming of body parts and bodily functions, have often also shut their eyes to other distressing or unpleasant things in the world, such as environmental devastation, social injustice, violence, and racism. Vonnegut believes that human beings must be able to face and to name these unpleasant things, or they will never be able to bring about change. Thus, throughout his essays and fiction, he seems to admire the "bad manners" of the younger generation who are not only willing to use so-called obscene language, but who face obscene circumstances head-on. As he writes in the preface to *Breakfast of Champions,* itself considered "obscene" by certain readers, Vonnegut makes his living by "being impolite" (2), by refusing to gloss over or ignore unpleasantries. The title for "The Big Space Fuck" derives at least partly from the notion that that is exactly what the U.S. government is trying to do in the story. Playing with one of the slang definitions of the word *fuck*, which can mean to take advantage of, to betray, cheat, or victimize, Vonnegut depicts human beings who have not only screwed up Earth, polluting it beyond livability, but who now plan to send human sperm into space to do the same thing in distant galaxies.

CHARACTERS

Astronaut   As Dwayne and Grace Hoobler are watching the countdown to the Big Space Fuck on television, an aged astronaut appears on the screen. The astronaut says he wishes he could go where his freeze-dried jizzum is going, but he will stay at home instead, "with his memories and a glass of Tang" (210).

County Sheriff   The Ohio county sheriff who brings the bad news about Wanda June's lawsuit to the Hooblers is much more intelligent than his friend Dwayne. Thus, his jizzum makes up part of the 800 pounds freeze-dried and placed aboard a rocket for the Big Space Fuck. But despite his superior intelligence, the sheriff succumbs to the same fate that will strike Dwayne and Grace Hoobler. He is devoured by a giant lamprey eel that has crawled out of the heavily polluted Lake Erie.

Hoobler, Dwayne   Dwayne Hoobler is a guard at the Ohio Adult Correctional Institution who lives with his wife, Grace, in a modest home on the shore of what used to be Lake Erie, which is now nearly filled with solid sewage. Not terribly bright, Dwayne has no jizzum aboard the rocket that will perform the Big Space Fuck, since a person must have an I.Q. of over 115 to get his jizzum accepted. Dwayne is dismayed to learn, on the night of the rocket launch, that his daughter, Wanda June, is suing him and Grace for ruining her childhood. Yet, he does not have long to dwell on this bad news, since he is devoured by a man-eating lamprey that crawled out of Lake Erie at the end of the story.

Hoobler, Grace   Grace Hoobler is Dwayne Hoobler's dim-witted wife. Like her husband, she is devastated by the sheriff's news that the couple is being sued by their own daughter, Wanda June. Also like

Dwayne, Grace is eaten alive by a giant lamprey on the evening of the Big Space Fuck.

Hoobler, Wanda June   Wanda June Hoobler, the daughter of Dwayne and Grace Hoobler, is arrested in New York City for leading a shoplifting ring. In order to avoid prison, she decides to sue her parents, claiming they ruined her childhood and that they are the ones truly responsible for her bad behavior.

Interviewer   A television interviewer speaking with Senator Flem Snopes the night of the Big Space Fuck asks the senator to stand up so that the television audience can get a good view of the codpiece he is wearing, a recent fashion trend honoring the rocket launch to Andromeda.

Newcomb, John L.   John L. Newcomb is named in Wanda June Hoobler's lawsuit against her parents as a potential lover her father had lost for her by being "half in the bag whenever a suitor came to call" (212).

Scientist   A scientist on television the night of the Big Space Fuck explains that the Andromeda Galaxy has been selected as a target because of 87 time warps between Andromeda and Earth. If the rocket passes through any of these time warps, its load of freeze-dried jizzum could be multiplied a trillion times.

Snopes, Senator Flem   Senator Flem Snopes of Mississippi is the chairman of the Senate Space Committee. He is interviewed on television the night of the Big Space Fuck and proclaims his pride that his hometown of Mayhew had been chosen as the site of the biggest jizzum-freezing plant in America.

Bluebeard

Published in 1987 by Delacorte, *Bluebeard*, like many other Vonnegut works, focuses on man's inhumanity to man. Yet, the novel also shows that even in the midst of war and death and sorrow the innate human impulse is a creative one. The book explores this human desire to create as it investigates the nature of art itself: What makes great art? What is the relationship between art and reality? While Vonnegut has specifically examined literary art in earlier works such as *Breakfast of Champions,* in *Bluebeard* he is interested in visual art. The novel presents a dialogue between abstract and representational painting, pointing out both the value and shortcomings of each school. It ends by imagining a type of art in which the usual boundaries separating the real and the artificial fall away, an art that is able to capture the complexity, sorrow, and beauty of life itself.

SYNOPSIS

Bluebeard is the autobiography of ABSTRACT EXPRESSIONIST artist Rabo Karabekian, a character Vonnegut readers first met in the author's 1973 novel, *Breakfast of Champions.* Karabekian is writing his memoirs in 1987, at the age of 71, at the urging of Circe Berman, a brassy, voluptuous widow he recently met on the beach and who invited herself to live as a guest in his beachfront home in East Hampton, Long Island. Karabekian's beloved second wife, Edith Taft Karabekian, died two years previously, and since that time, Karabekian has been lonely, rattling around his mansion with only the company of his cook, Allison White, her 15-year-old daughter, Celeste, and his novelist friend, Paul Slazinger, who spends most of his time at Karabekian's home. Mrs. Berman, though opinionated, loud, and bossy, also breathes fresh life into Karabekian's lonely existence, and despite their differences, the two characters manage to form a solid friendship. As Karabekian relates his life story, the novel makes frequent jumps back and forth in time between his past experiences as a boy and young man and his current life with Circe Berman.

I. The Past

Chapters 1–5

As Karabekian relates his life story, readers discover that he was born in 1916, in San Ignacio, California, the son of Armenian immigrants to the United States. Karabekian's parents met in Persia,

where both had fled during the Turkish massacre of the Armenians. His mother, playing dead amid a group of corpses during the Turkish atrocity, had found a small fortune in jewels pouring out of the mouth of a dead woman lying next to her; the jewels enable her to make the trip to Persia. Later, she and her new husband travel to Egypt, where they are swindled out of their fortune by a fellow Armenian named Vartan Mamigonian, himself a survivor of an earlier Turkish massacre. Mamigonian convinces the Karabekians to buy, sight unseen, a beautiful house in San Ignacio, California, where he tells the naïve couple that a large community of immigrant Armenians live. These people would be very eager to have Mr. Karabekian as a teacher for their children, Mamigonian explains. When the Karabekians actually arrive in San Ignacio, there is no house and no immigrant community. In fact, they are the only Armenians in the whole city. Mr. Karabekian, bitter and cynical, goes to work as a cobbler, and Mrs. Karabekian works in a cannery.

Chapters 6–21

Rabo is his parents' only child. Because he shows great artistic talent as a young boy, his mother, eager to better the family's station in life, encourages Rabo to write letters to the well-known artist and illustrator Dan Gregory, who lives in New York City and is also of Armenian heritage. Rabo's letters are not answered by Gregory himself, but rather by Marilee Kemp, a woman claiming to be Gregory's assistant, but who actually turns out to be his mistress. This correspondence continues for several years, long after the death of Rabo's mother from a tetanus infection when the boy is 12 years old. The letters grow increasingly intense until Marilee finally invites Rabo to come to New York City to serve as Dan Gregory's apprentice. Much later, Rabo will discover that the apprenticeship was Marilee's idea, agreed to by Gregory only because he felt guilty after throwing Marilee down a flight of stairs and breaking several of her bones. When he arrives in New York, Rabo soon discovers that Gregory is a cruel and exacting master, a strict representationalist who hates all forms of modern art. Rabo and the older Marilee, though, develop a close friendship. The two especially enjoy sneaking off together to New York's Museum of Modern

Art, a place they are expressly forbidden to visit by Gregory. One afternoon, Gregory catches the pair exiting the museum. Though Rabo will be fired as Gregory's apprentice, the teenage virgin makes love to Marilee that day, enjoying three hours of ecstatic bliss.

Chapters 22–32

After his dismissal by Dan Gregory, Rabo works for a time in New York City, but eventually enlists in the Army Corps of Engineers and fights in World War II as the commander of a special unit of artists assigned to develop new camouflage techniques. Near the end of the war, Rabo is wounded and captured on the border of Germany. He is kept for a short time as a prisoner of war in DRESDEN before being marched with other captured officers to a valley on the border between Czechoslovakia and East Germany, and freed on V-E day. Upon his release, Karabekian undergoes cosmetic surgery at Fort Benjamin Harrison, having lost an eye when he was wounded in battle. He ends up marrying Dorothy, one of his nurses at the military hospital. When Rabo is recovered, the young couple moves to New York City, where they start a family and make plans for Rabo to become a businessman. Rabo, however, still longs to be an artist, and he begins to spend time with a group of abstract expressionist painters, drinking with them and helping them out financially, much to Dorothy's displeasure. He eventually rents a potato barn to use as a studio on Long Island and moves his family out to the country. Before long, fed up with Rabo's hard-drinking artist friends and his neglect of his family, Dorothy leaves him, taking their two young sons, Terry and Henri, with her.

II. The Present

Following his divorce from Dorothy, Rabo marries the widow Edith Taft Fairbanks, the owner of the potato barn he rents as a studio. Edith and Rabo live together in her Long Island mansion very happily for 20 years, until her unexpected death from a heart attack. Lonely and reclusive after the death of his "darling Edith," Rabo stays in the mansion the couple had shared, living uneventfully for two more years, until a chance meeting on the beach

one day with the widow Circe Berman changes his life again. The outspoken, take-charge Mrs. Berman moves into Rabo's house and orders him to begin writing his autobiography so that he will not simply spend all day doing nothing. Rabo soon discovers that Circe Berman is actually the best-selling young adult author Polly Madison, whose books depict very realistic situations facing contemporary teenagers. Mrs. Berman and Rabo have a prickly relationship and very different views of art. She appreciates only realistic art, while Rabo collects abstract expressionist paintings and views Mrs. Berman's artistic tastes as hopelessly kitschy and sentimental. Eventually, Mrs. Berman convinces Rabo to take a trip to New York City, which he had not visited for years and years. While he is gone, she redecorates the foyer of his mansion with garish wallpaper and chromos of children on swings, removing the abstract expressionist paintings he had been so fond of. Incensed with rage after he discovers the changes to his foyer, which had previously been featured in a prominent art magazine, Rabo has it out with Mrs. Berman, each attacking the other's taste in art.

Chapters 33–37

Despite their differences, Rabo and Circe Berman form an uneasy truce after their confrontation. By the end of the novel, it will be Mrs. Berman to whom Rabo finally reveals his biggest artistic secret. For the past several years, he had kept his potato barn padlocked, not letting anyone enter. There has been a great deal of speculation in the artistic community about what Rabo Karabekian has locked in there. Mrs. Berman, extremely nosy and pushy, has been constantly bothering Rabo for the keys to the barn. But the barn remains off-limits, like the room in Bluebeard's castle in the famous children's tale. After the two share a pleasant farewell supper on Mrs. Berman's last night in the Hamptons, Rabo finally agrees to show her what's inside the potato barn. The mystery turns out to be an enormous eight-paneled painting, eight feet high and 64 feet long. Ultra-realistic in its attention to detail, the painting depicts the scene that Karabekian witnessed in the Czechoslovakian valley on V-E day. Painted while he was grieving for his beloved wife, Edith, the painting is titled, "Now It's the Women's Turn."

COMMENTARY

Rabo Karabekian's existence begins, like the 20th century itself, in atrocity. The child of parents who meet as they are fleeing a genocide—the Turkish massacre of Armenians—Rabo's childhood is an unhappy one. He is the son of a bitter, distant father who is trapped by his memories of the friends and relatives he lost in the carnage, and who therefore has given up on life itself: "*If anybody has discovered what life is all about,*" Rabo imagines his father saying, "*it is too late. I am no longer interested*" (19). While his mother, who actually had a worse experience during the Turkish brutality, having to play dead among the corpses, remains fairly optimistic, she dies of a tetanus infection when Rabo is only 12 years old, leaving him motherless like so many of Vonnegut's characters, including Eliot Rosewater in *God Bless You, Mr. Rosewater,* the

Hoenniker children in *Cat's Cradle,* Bunny Hoover in *Breakfast of Champions,* and Leon Trout in *Galápagos.* All the missing mothers in Vonnegut's fiction may serve as a testament to the suicide of Vonnegut's own mother when he was 21 years old. The novel follows Rabo's relationships with a series of women, beginning with Marilee Kemp and ending with Circe Berman. As the first of Vonnegut's novels to explicitly incorporate gender disparity as a major theme, Rabo's relationships with the various women in his life suggest a longing for nurturing and balance. His grief over his dead wife, Edith, causes him to paint his masterpiece, "Now It's the Women's Turn," and his rebirth, through the aid of Circe Berman, causes him to reveal the painting's existence to the world at large.

Marilee Kemp is the first substitute mother figure with whom Rabo Karabekian interacts. When Rabo, at Marilee's urging, moves to New York City to become Dan Gregory's apprentice, he describes the event as a rebirth: "So I went to New York City

Armenian refugees on Black Sea beach with household possessions, 1920 *(courtesy of the Library of Congress)*

to be born again" (72). Unlike his parents, whose roots in Turkey were deep, Rabo has no "sacred piece of land" or "shoals of friends and relatives" that he leaves behind in San Ignacio (72). Like many 20th-century Americans, then, it is easy for him to start anew. Rabo writes that his mind is "as blank as an embryo's" as he crosses the continent in "womblike Pullman cars," and that, when the train plunges into a tunnel under New York City, he is "out of the womb and into the birth canal," to be "born" 10 minutes later in Grand Central Terminal (72). Later, referring to the abortion that Dan Gregory forces Marilee to undergo, Circe Berman will suggest to Rabo that he was a "replacement for the Armenian baby which had been taken from [Marilee's] womb in Switzerland" (76). So, as Rabo is reborn in New York City, Marilee does indeed serve as a surrogate mother, though she will move from mother-figure to lover as their relationship develops.

Part of Rabo's rebirth in New York involves the loss of his earlier naiveté. While in San Ignacio, he was able to believe that Dan Gregory himself admired his artistic endeavors and wanted him as an apprentice. In New York, however, he must realize that Dan Gregory cares nothing about him, and that it is really Marilee Kemp who has arranged the trip. Rabo will also witness Dan Gregory's cruelness to Marilee, though it will take him several more years, until he visits her in Florence after the war, to realize that Gregory had thrown Marilee down the stairs for sending some of his precious art supplies to the young Rabo in San Ignacio. Only the guilt over Marilee's broken bones causes Gregory to agree to accept Rabo as his apprentice. In fact, when Gregory talks about Marilee, Rabo writes, "he never mentioned her name again. She simply became 'women'" (151). And in his diatribes against women, Gregory argues that men and women have separate, distinct roles. He tells Rabo that "no woman could succeed in the arts or sciences or politics or industry, since her basic job was to have children and encourage men and take care of the housework" (152). While the young Rabo politely agrees with Dan Gregory at this point, he later criticizes Gregory's sexist thinking.

Once in New York, Rabo is also introduced to the fundamental artistic debate of the novel. Dan Gregory is an entirely realistic artist, an illustrator, whose ability to mimic the real world in his paintings is the root of his fame. In fact, Gregory views all modern art as "the work of swindlers and lunatics and degenerates" (147). He also associates modern art with dangerously democratic principles, pointing out to the young Rabo that, if Gregory's hero, Benito Mussolini, took over America, he would "burn down the Museum of Modern Art and outlaw the word *democracy*" (147). Gregory, in his abhorrence of democracy, has an overinflated view of the importance of artists in the world, seeing them as gods on earth: "Painters—and storytellers, including poets and playwrights and historians," he tells Rabo, "are the justices of the Supreme Court of Good and Evil, of which I am now a member, and to which you may belong someday" (150). The older Rabo, writing his memoirs, follows this comment with one of his own: "How was *that* for delusions of moral grandeur!" (150). Partly as a reaction to the fascist and cruel Dan Gregory, Rabo will reject realistic art completely, blaming people like Gregory for causing a great deal of "senseless bloodshed" (150).

Marilee and Rabo, against Gregory's express orders, begin to visit the Museum of Modern Art together. This is where Rabo's later appreciation of abstract expressionism develops. While he believes that Gregory's delusions of moral grandeur cause bloodshed and suffering, abstract art, Rabo explains, refuses to present a moral stance on the world. He tells readers that the abstract expressionist paintings in his collection at his home on Long Island "are about absolutely nothing but themselves" (9). Later, in Florence, we'll see that Marilee Kemp agrees with Rabo's views about the dangers of realistic art. She tells Rabo she had considered hiring women and children to paint the blank spaces on her rotunda with "murals of the death camps and the bombing of Hiroshima and the planting of land mines, and maybe the burning of witches and the feeding of Christians to wild animals in olden times" (255). Yet, she decides not to do this, arguing that "that sort of thing, on some level, just eggs men on to be even more destructive and cruel, makes them think: 'Ha! We are as powerful as gods!'" (255). This indictment of realism echoes, in many ways, Vonnegut's criticism of traditional storytelling in his earlier novel *Breakfast of Champions*, the work that introduced Rabo Karabekian. In that novel, Vonnegut explained that it was "innocent and natural" for people to behave "abominably" because they're simply doing their best "to live like people in story books" (*Breakfast* 215). Rabo's refusal to assign artists an elevated moral position also reflects Vonnegut's debunking of literary art in the opening chapter of *Slaughterhouse-Five*, where BERNARD V. O'HARE speaks of Vonnegut's writing as his "trade" (5), and where Vonnegut refers to himself not as an arbiter of morality, but simply as a "trafficker in climaxes and thrills and characterization . . ." (5). In *Bluebeard*, both Marilee's and Rabo's dedication to modern art suggests a rejection of the pretensions to morality by realistic artists like Dan Gregory.

Gregory's belief in his own godlike stature is driven home when he catches his mistress and his apprentice coming out of the museum they have been forbidden to enter: "Your loving Papa asked just one thing of you as an expression of your loyalty: 'Never go into the Museum of Modern Art,'" he seethes (175). Gregory behaves here like God castigating Adam and Eve for eating the apple in Eden. The parallel is made especially clear when Rabo describes his and Marilee's walk home later that afternoon: "[T]he supposition was that we would be leaving the Garden of Eden together, and would cleave to one another in the wilderness through thick and thin" (180). Yet, in their rebellion against the tyrannical Gregory, Rabo and Marilee create a new Eden of their own making. Rabo writes that they "were about to do the one thing other than eat and drink and sleep which our bodies said we were on Earth to do," and further, "there was no vengeance or defiance or defilement in it" (181). The two make love for three hours, Marilee initiating the not yet 20-year-old Rabo into the mysteries and pleasures of sexual ecstasy. In fact, Rabo will connect this "brainless lovemaking" with abstract expressionist painting when he says that it, too, "was about absolutely nothing but itself" (181). Later, Rabo's artist friend Terry

Kitchen describes those three hours as a "non-epiphany" (183), a moment in which human beings are "contentedly adrift in the cosmos," when "God Almighty lets go of the scruff of your neck and lets you be human for a little while" (184). While realistic art and storytelling offer moments of epiphany, in which divine beings reveal themselves or spiritual insight is achieved, abstract art eschews such moments, refusing to be "about" anything at all, and thus releasing people from the burdens of spiritual insight.

Any remaining innocence Rabo carries from his childhood disappears completely when Marilee informs him that their lovemaking does not mean that the two will move into the future together, "smiling bravely and holding hands" (192). Marilee, abused horribly by Gregory, nevertheless realizes that the great illustrator is her meal ticket and that she must return to him. The women who nurture Rabo throughout the book are decidedly practical and nonromantic. Telling Rabo that he is "still a little boy" (193), Marilee parts ways with him, a parting that will set the stage for the next key relationship in Rabo's life, his marriage to his first wife, Dorothy. Rabo's longing for nurturing is evident when he meets Dorothy while he is undergoing cosmetic surgery for the eye injury he received during World War II. Dorothy is his nurse at the army hospital at Fort Benjamin Harrison. While Marilee introduced Rabo to the artistic world of New York City, Dorothy tries very hard to remove Rabo from that world. Dorothy is a sensible woman, concerned that Rabo should provide for his growing family. Thus, the two make plans that Rabo will give up his artistic endeavors and become a businessman. If his dream with Marilee was to become a great painter, Rabo's dream with Dorothy is to be a "good father" (85). Yet, Rabo, as he is writing his memoirs, sees himself as a failure in both of these dreams. He neglects Dorothy and his young sons, preferring instead to drink in bars with a group of abstract expressionist artists he has met in New York City. When, in later life, Rabo's cook, Allison White, berates him for not treating her as a full-fledged human being, for, in fact, not even knowing her name, Rabo is reminded of his relationship with Dorothy: "This was dismayingly close to what my first wife Dorothy had said to me," Rabo writes, "that I often treated her as though I didn't even care what her name was, as though she really weren't there" (140). Rabo's failings as a husband and father cause him much anguish: "Of all the things I have to be ashamed of," he writes, "the most troublesome of this old heart of mine is my failure as a husband of the good and brave Dorothy, and the consequent alienation of my own flesh and blood, Henri and Terry, from me, their Dad" (258). Before Rabo can become the great artist he had always dreamed of being, he must first learn to love and appreciate women.

This process begins when Rabo remeets Marilee Kemp in Forence, Italy. Reborn as the Contessa Portomagiorre, Marilee has transformed herself from a victim, a woman abused by her lover, Dan Gregory, into an outspoken feminist. Offended by the crude remarks Rabo makes on the telephone, Marilee, when she sees Rabo in person, rages against men, against war, and against the effects of both on women. She tells Rabo that the real war is "always men against women, with the men only pretending to fight among themselves" (238). When Rabo replies that men can "pretend pretty hard" sometimes, Marilee argues that the men who pretend the hardest "get their pictures in the paper and medals afterward" (239). While Rabo has received medals for saving fellow soldiers and for the injuries he suffered, women like Marilee's servant Lucrezia, who lost both an eye and a leg after stepping on a mine while trying to do a kind act for a neighbor, received nothing. Marilee, in fact, has turned her palazzo into a kind of home for women injured and abused during the war. She defends her sex vigorously, berating Rabo for his assumption that women are "useless and unimaginative (239). "All they ever think of planting in the dirt," she tells Rabo "is the seed of something beautiful or edible. The only missile they can ever think of throwing at anybody is a ball or a bridal bouquet" (239). While Marilee's views on the differences between the sexes might be somewhat exaggerated—later, Rabo writes that she was "ahead of her time . . . believing that men were not only useless and idiotic, but downright dangerous" (244)—she nevertheless makes Rabo think in a new way. For the first time, he must

examine his own status as a privileged member of society as well as his own earlier attitudes about women and their roles.

After Marilee thoroughly embarrasses him, the two are able to become friends again. She appreciates what Rabo tells her about the new abstract art being produced by him and his friends in New York City, pointing out that this group is doing "the last conceivable thing a painter could do to a canvas"—writing "The End" (254). Marilee also argues that no piece of contemporary art should try to do anything different: "After all that men have done to the women and children and every other defenseless thing on this planet," she explains to Rabo," "it is time that not just every painting, but every piece of music, every statue, every play, every poem and book a man creates should say only this: 'We are much too horrible for this nice place. We give up. We quit. The end!'" (254). Yet, the theme of renewal, of rebirth, of starting over, so recurrent in the novel, is evoked again when Marilee suggests a name for Rabo's group of painter friends. Despite her view that that abstract expressionist art says "The End," Marilee proposes that Rabo and his group call themselves the "Genesis Gang," a name that suggests beginnings, since they are trying to create a new form of nonmoral art, of art that is about nothing but itself.

After this meeting with Marilee, Rabo is able to begin again in a new marriage, this time with the former Edith Taft, a kind, generous woman who does not try to change Rabo, but allows him to be what he is. Described in Rabo's autobiography as an "Earth Mother" who fills their home with "love and merriment" (7), Edith allows Rabo to redeem himself as a husband. His relationship with Edith also allows Rabo to cope with the great disaster that strikes his abstract paintings—having used a bogus "postwar miracle" (21) product called Sateen Dura-Luxe to paint his canvases, all his pictures are now cracking and peeling, and in fact, disappearing. His paintings are returning to blank canvases. This phenomenon suggests that Rabo, now happy in his life, has also started over as a blank canvas. When a curator at the Guggenheim Museum returns the remains of his famous "Windsor Blue Number Seventeen" to him, Rabo works hard to remove all traces of "faithless Sateen Dura-Luxe" from them, restretching and repriming the canvases. He explains to Edith that this "eccentric project" is "an exorcism of an unhappy past, a symbolic repairing of all the damage" Rabo had done to himself and others during his "brief career as a painter" (292).

Yet, even amid the seeming Eden Rabo is able to create with Edith, sorrow inevitably creeps in when she dies unexpectedly of a heart attack 20 years into their marriage. As Vonnegut writes in the opening pages of *Slaughterhouse-Five*: "Even if wars didn't keep coming like glaciers, there would still be plain old death" (4). Even great art cannot stop death, cannot freeze moments in time, as Vonnegut in *Slaughterhouse-Five* tells us the French author CÉLINE tried to do. Time marches inexorably forward. In fact, in *Bluebeard*, Rabo explains that the greatest works of art are able to depict the movement of time itself. What limits Dan Gregory as an artist, despite his impressive skill, is that, while his pictures were "truthful about material things . . . they lied about time" (90). Dan Gregory celebrates only moments frozen in time, lacking "the guts or the wisdom, or maybe just the talent, to indicate somehow that time was liquid, that one moment was no more important than any other, and that all moments quickly run away" (90). So, rather than a real artist, Dan Gregory is a "taxidermist" who can never capture the essence of life, the fact that life is never still, that, by definition, life is moving "from birth to death, with no stops on the way" (90). This essential fact of life, crystallized in his grief for Edith, causes Rabo to paint his final masterpiece, the huge, elaborate canvas he locks in the potato barn. He tells his friend, the novelist Paul Slazinger, that what he has hidden in the barn is "the emptiest and yet the fullest of all human messages . . . Good-bye" (211). The painting is his good-bye to Edith, but Rabo expects it to be his good-bye to the larger world as well. For two years after Edith's death, Rabo himself is like the walking dead, his Long Island mansion a mausoleum.

Unexpectedly, however, yet another rebirth is in store for Rabo Karabekian. When he meets Circe Berman on the beach, Rabo's life, as well as his artistic vision, takes another dramatic turn. Although the two clash, disagreeing about nearly everything, including the role and purpose of art, Rabo realizes that he wants "someone as vivid as [Circe] is to keep [him] alive" (146). Circe Berman shares much in common with the Greek sorceress she is named after. In *THE ODYSSEY*, the mythic Circe at first seems to be a malevolent force to Odysseus and his sailors, turning Odysseus's men into swine. Yet, she soon releases them from their animal forms, bringing them back to human shape handsomer and stronger than before, and offering them comfort and hospitality. Mrs. Berman plays a similar role, calling Rabo her "Lazarus," and arguing that she has brought him "back to life" (137). The mythic Circe was mistress of potions and herbs; we learn that the widow Berman is a pill addict. But perhaps Circe Berman's most important role in the novel is to guide Rabo to a newfound appreciation for representational art and the fact that art can, in fact, *say* something about the contemporary world.

Circe Berman's views on art provide a necessary balance and corrective to the artistic vision embraced by Rabo Karabekian. In the guise of wildly popular young adult novelist Polly Madison, Circe looks unflinchingly at the problems facing contemporary teenagers, writing smart and realistic books that mean a great deal to ordinary people. Rabo, on the other hand, tends to be elitist in his views of art. He often wallows in the past, using his conversations with Celeste, his cook's 15-year-old daughter, to bemoan the lack of knowledge he sees in contemporary teens. He belittles the artistic taste of Celeste's mother, Allison White, by selling the only painting in his collection she really liked—a magazine illustration of two black boys and two white boys painted by Dan Gregory. Allison points out that she is uneducated, and that the abstract paintings in Rabo's collection simply don't "*mean* anything" to her (142). The painting by Dan Gregory, though, Allison could appreciate because it "was really about something" (143). She explains to Rabo that she "used to look at it and try and guess what would happen next" (143). Finally, Rabo jeers at the chromos of children on swings that Circe hangs in his foyer, arguing that "anybody with half a grain of sense about art" would see these pictures as "a *negation* of art," as "black holes from which no intelligence or skill can ever escape" (136). He calls Circe's pictures "kitsch," in fact, condescendingly asking the widow if she knows the meaning of the word. We see that Rabo's artistic snobbery is also tied up with the gender superiority often felt by males when Circe replies that she wrote a book called *Kitsch,* and Celeste explains that "it's about a girl whose boyfriend tried to make her think she has bad taste, which she does—but it doesn't matter much" (138).

While Rabo Karabekian's embracing of abstract expressionism is a corrective to the dangerously fascist artistic views of Dan Gregory, Circe Berman teaches Rabo to revalue representational art. She defends her pictures of little girls on swings by arguing that their value lies in the very fact that they *are* about something: "Try thinking what the Victorians thought when they looked at them," she tells Rabo, "which was how sick or unhappy so many of these happy, innocent little girls would be in just a little while—diptheria, pneumonia, smallpox, miscarriages, violent husbands, poverty, widowhood, prostitution—death and burial in potter's field" (138). Realistic art, which makes a specific connection to the world, can attempt to change that world for the better. Rabo himself uses this same defense of the sentimental pictures when three writers from the Soviet Union come to tour his collection. Like Rabo, the men originally view Mrs. Berman's chromos as sentimental and "trashy" (166). But after Rabo connects the pictures to the horrors awaiting the little girls, the men are ashamed and leave the house unanimously "agreeing that these were the most important pictures" they had seen (166). The parting words of the writers to Rabo are "No more war, no more war," showing that even "trashy" art can affect people deeply, and perhaps constitute the first step in changing the world for the better.

But that is not to say that Vonnegut believes Rabo should completely reject abstract expressionism in favor of realistic art. Both types of art, Vonnegut seems to argue, can coexist alongside each other. As critic David Rampton points out, Rabo, at the very end of the novel, turns his mansion into "a museum that serves as a commentary on the art history that the novel explores." Visitors begin by viewing "the doomed little girls on swings in the foyer" then move on to "the earliest works of the first Abstract Expressionists," and finish their tour with "the perfectly tremendous watchamacallit in the potato barn" (299). Rabo's gigantic painting that he has locked in the barn all these years, "Now It's the Women's Turn," suggests the culmination of art. Every square inch of the painting is "encrusted with the most gorgeous jewelry" (297). The jewelry is humanity itself in all its motley and teeming glory. Although an impossible feat in the real world, Vonnegut has imagined a painting that depicts *all* of life, that is somehow equivalent to life itself. It is a painting that expresses the creative impulse, the impulse to life, as it depicts the moment "when the sun came up the day the Second World War ended in Europe" (298). The painting suggests great sorrow, the suffering caused by World War II as well as Rabo's grief over Edith's death, yet it is also a testament to the human will to survive. As Rabo said to Circe Berman earlier, when she accused him of having survivor's syndrome, "Everybody who is alive is a survivor" (35). Circe Berman finally teaches Rabo to love himself again, to look at his hands with "love and gratitude," and to say out loud, "Thank you, Meat," for the wonderful work they have accomplished (318). Circe has brought Rabo back to life, and in finally showing her his painting, Rabo has offered a new beginning both to Circe Berman and to the world at large. The painting depicts the world poised on the brink of a rebirth, turned over to women, who will now take their chances with it.

CHARACTERS AND RELATED ENTRIES

Aiken, Conrad   Real-life 20th-century poet Conrad Aiken figures in the novel when Terry Kitchen tells Rabo Karabekian that Aiken lectured at Yale when Kitchen was in law school there. According to Aiken, the sons of gifted men go into fields occupied by their fathers, but where their fathers are weak. Terry Kitchen tells Karabekian, though, that he could never do such a thing to his own father.

Aiken, Sr.   Terry Kitchen tells Rabo Karabekian that Conrad Aiken's father, a doctor and politician, also fancied himself a poet, which is why Aiken became a poet. Conrad Aiken's real-life father, William Ford Aiken, was indeed a well-respected doctor. The fictional Aiken, Sr., though, ends up killing his wife and then himself.

Arnold, General Benedict An actual American general during the Revolutionary War who deserted to the British, Benedict Arnold appears in *Bluebeard* when Rabo Karabekian tells readers that Paul Slazinger's ancestor served as a mercenary in the war and was captured during the second Battle of Freeman's Farm, in which General Arnold defeated British General John Burgoyne.

Bauerbeck, Nelson After Rabo Karabekian is fired as Dan Gregory's apprentice, he decides to take lessons in how to be a serious painter. He brings his portfolio to a teacher named Nelson Bauerbeck, a representational painter in New York City. Although Bauerbeck declares Karabekian's work technically perfect, he refuses to accept him as a student because he believes the young man has no passion.

Berman, Abe Abe Berman was Circe Berman's brain surgeon husband who died of a stroke six months before Rabo Karabekian meets Circe on the beach. Circe confides to Karabekian that her dead husband, whom she loved very deeply, is the audience she imagines as she writes her Polly Madison books.

Berman, Circe A blunt, outspoken 43-year old recent widow whom Rabo Karabekian meets on his private beach, Circe Berman soon moves in with the artist and begins rearranging his life. She bullies him into writing his autobiography, which turns out to be the novel *Bluebeard*, and she redecorates the foyer of his mansion that Karabekian is so proud of. A realistic writer herself, author of the best-selling Polly Madison young adult books, Circe also mocks Karabekian's collection of abstract paintings, arguing that they "are a *negation* of art. . . . they suck up the dignity, the self-respect, of anybody unfortunate enough to look at them" (136). Circe Berman, while often annoying to Karabekian, also brings color and excitement into his drab life. She is the

one to whom he will eventually show his masterpiece painting, "Now It's the Women's Turn," and he will dedicate his autobiography to her as well.

Beskudnikov When Dan Gregory is five years old, he is taken to live with Russian currency engraver Beskudnikov, who takes the boy on as an apprentice when he turns 10 years old. When Gregory turns 15, Beskudnikov promises to promote him to journeyman if he can draw by hand a one-ruble note so realistic that it can fool the merchants in the marketplace. The penalty for counterfeiting at that time was public hanging. The young apprentice ends up making a bill so realistic that he is able to trick the great Beskudnikov himself into spending it in the marketplace. Beskudnikov escapes hanging, though, because no one ever discovers the forgery.

Beskudnikov's Wife The wife of Russian artist and engraver Beskudnikov rescues Dan Gregory from his drunk and abusive parents when he is five years old. She takes him in just as she might a stray animal and gives him to the servants to raise.

Brooks, Jim Jim Brooks is a painter friend of Rabo Karabekian. When Karabekian makes love to Marilee Kemp, he is reminded of what Brooks once said about the way he painted: "I lay on the first stroke of color. After that, the canvas has to do at least half the work" (181). Karabekian tells readers that the "first stroke" between him and Marilee was a kiss the two shared just inside the front door of Dan Gregory's brownstone mansion.

Burgoyne, General John An actual British general during the American Revolutionary War, John Burgoyne enters into *Bluebeard* when Rabo Karabekian tells readers that Paul Slazinger's ancestor served as a mercenary in General Burgoyne's army.

Coates, Arnold Arnold Coates is a newspaper editor in San Ignacio, California, who hires the teenage Rabo Karabekian to draw editorial cartoons for his newspaper, the *Luma County Clarion*. Coates is fervently antiwar and despises what he considers the bloodthirstiness of Europeans. He urges Rabo to get out of San Ignacio, but prays that the boy will never become a soldier.

Cooley, Franklin Franklin Cooley is a man hired by Rabo Karabekian to mow his extensive lawns. All that Karabekian knows about Cooley is that he drives an "old, babyshit-brown Cadillac Coupe de Ville" (215) and is father to six children. Karabekian remarks that he does not even know if Franklin Cooley can read and write, then muses about the high number of illiterates in America.

Coulomb, Marc A Bulgarian Armenian raised in Paris, Marc Coulomb (originally named Marktich Kouyoumdjian) meets Rabo Karabekian in Central Park after the young artist has been fired as Dan Gregory's apprentice. Coulomb wants to help out a fellow Armenian, so he buys Rabo a new suit, shirt, tie, and shoes, and gets him a job at a local advertising agency. Though Rabo never sees Coulomb again after that day, he later reads the man's newspaper obituary and discovers that Coulomb had been a hero in the French Resistance during the war and, at the time of his death, had become the head of the largest travel organization in the world.

de Medici, Innocenzo Innocenzo "the Invisible" de Medici was a banker in Florence and the richest and most reclusive member of the famous de Medici family. He originally owned the palazzo that is later occupied by the Count and Contessa Portomaggiore.

Fairbanks, Charles Warren Edith Taft Karabekian's first husband, Richard Fairbanks, is descended from Charles Warren Fairbanks, U.S senator and vice president under Theodore Roosevelt.

Fairbanks, Richard, Jr. The first husband of Edith Taft Karabekian, Richard Fairbanks, Jr. is described by Rabo Karabekian as an "affable idler" (275). Fairbanks, like Edith, is descended from an important political family, one of his relatives having served as vice president to Theodore Roosevelt.

Fields, W. C. An actual early 20th-century actor and comedian, W. C. Fields appears in *Bluebeard* as a guest at Dan Gregory's dinner party the first evening the young Rabo Karabekian spends in New York.

Finkelstein, Isadore Izzy Finkelstein is a tailor who likes to drink with Rabo Karabekian and his abstract expressionist painter friends in New York City. When he measures Karabekian for a suit one day, he tells him that he was a tank gunner in Patton's Third Army during World War II. After Finkelstein's death from a stroke, Karabekian discovers that the tailor was a secret painter as well.

Finkelstein, Rachel The wife of tailor Izzy Finkelstein, Rachel Finkelstein holds a one-man show of her husband's secret paintings after his death.

Ghiberti, Lorenzo An actual 15th-century Italian artist, Lorenzo Ghiberti, according to Rabo Karabekian, sculpted a bust of Innocenzo de Medici as a child. When de Medici was 15 years old, he smashed the bust and threw the pieces into the Arno.

Gorky, Arshile A real-life Armenian-American abstract expressionist painter who escaped the Turkish genocide of Armenians, Arshile Gorky is claimed by Rabo Karabekian as one of his many painter friends who committed suicide. Gorky hanged himself in 1948.

Gregory, Dan Dan Gregory is a fictional illustrator with whom Rabo Karabekian serves an apprenticeship in New York City. Described as perhaps the most important illustrator in American history, Gregory's ability to realistically depict minute detail is astounding. Yet, the man himself is a bully and a fascist, who hits his girlfriend, abuses young Rabo, and admires Benito Mussolini. Dan Gregory dies in Egypt in 1940, shot by British soldiers while fighting for the Italians.

Gregory, Mrs. According to Dan Gregory, his father had "stolen" his mother "away from her people and all she knew when she was only sixteen, promising her that they would soon be rich and famous in Moscow" (106). Yet, Gregory's father remains only a stable boy and the family lives in poverty.

Gregory, Sr.   Dan Gregory's father was a horse trainer in Moscow who could rise no higher than stable boy because, in Gregory's words, "the horse world there was run by Polacks" (106).

Hildreth, Gerald   Gerald Hildreth is the taxi driver who takes Circe Berman to the airport when she leaves Rabo Karabekian's house. Hildreth used to be on the East Hampton rescue squad and is the person who found artist Jackson Pollack's body after the car accident that killed him. Hildreth also cleaned up the mess after Terry Kitchen's suicide.

Hovanessian, Kevork   An Armenian who owns an estate in Southampton formerly owned by J. P. Morgan, Kevork Hovanessian also owns Twentieth Century-Fox. Rabo Karabekian cites Hovanessian as an example of how well Armenians have done in the United States.

"Hungarian Rhapsody Number Six"   "Hungarian Rhapsody Number Six" is the title of one of Rabo Karabekian's paintings. After being purchased by the Guggenheim Museum, the painting, like all of Karabekian's work, begins to crumble and dissolve, because of the inferior Sateen Dura-Luxe paint Karabekian used to make it. A woman curator at the Guggenheim notices a face emerging from behind the top layer of crumbling paint. The face turns out to be a portrait of Karabekian's friend, Paul Slazinger, whom the curator herself used to date.

"I Tried and Failed and Cleaned Up Afterwards, so It's *Your* Turn Now"   "I Tried and Failed and Cleaned Up Afterwards, so It's *Your* Turn Now" is the title Rabo Karabekian gives to the eight reprimed and whited panels that previously had made up the painting "Windsor Blue Number Seventeen" before it had crumbled and peeled due to the inferior Sateen Dura-Luxe paint Karabekian had used to paint it.

Jolson, Al   A real-life actor and singer in the early 20th century, famous for singing in black face and appearing in *The Jazz Singer*, the first "talkie" film, Al Jolson figures in *Bluebeard* as a guest at Dan Gregory's dinner party the first night Rabo Karabekian arrives in New York.

Jones, Fred   Fred Jones is assistant to illustrator Dan Gregory. An aviator during World War I, Jones is tall and handsome and dignified, though he treats Rabo Karabekian scornfully. Fred Jones will stick with Gregory to the very end, dying alongside him in Egypt in 1940 when the two are shot by British soldiers because they are wearing Italian uniforms.

Karabekian, Dorothy   The first wife of Rabo Karabekian, Dorothy Karabekian was working as a nurse in a military hospital when she met the injured Rabo. The two married, moved to New York, and quickly had two sons. A practical woman concerned about having enough money to raise her young sons, Dorothy encourages Rabo to give up art and become a businessman. She eventually ends up leaving Rabo and taking her sons with her. Soon after her divorce, she remarries an insurance agent and has a much happier life than she had with Rabo.

Karabekian, Edith Taft   Edith Taft Karabekian, grandniece to U.S. President William Howard Taft, rents the potato barn adjoining her family mansion on Long Island to the Karabekian family (Rabo, Dorothy, and their two sons). Edith ends up marrying Rabo after her first husband dies and after Rabo's marriage falls apart. The two live together very happily for 20 years until Edith's unexpected death of a heart attack.

Karabekian, Henri   See Steel, Henri, below.

Karabekian, Mr.   Rabo Karabekian's parents were both Armenians who survived the Turkish massacre early in the 20th century. Mr. Karabekian, a teacher at the time, hides in the privy behind the schoolhouse to escape the violence. He meets his future wife, Rabo's mother, while both are in Persia, fleeing from the Turks. The couple migrates to California, believing they are buying a large beautiful house and joining a vibrant Armenian community. Upon their arrival in San Ignacio, however, they discover they have been swindled out of their savings. Mr. Karabekian sets up shop as a cobbler, cynically refusing to study English, to teach, or to write poetry any longer. Near the end of his life, his artistic temperament emerges in the beautiful, elaborate cowboy boots he designs. Mr. Karabekian ends up dying in San Ignacio in 1938, while watching a movie at the Bijou Theater.

Karabekian, Mrs. Rabo Karabekian's mother was an Armenian who barely escaped massacre by the Turks by lying still under a pile of corpses and pretending to be dead. When the Turks finally leave, she sees a fortune in jewels pouring from a dead woman's mouth. Scooping up the jewels that have fallen on the ground, she escapes, making it to Persia where she meets Rabo's father, an Armenian from another village. The couple wind up in Egypt, where they are swindled out of their savings and tricked into migrating to San Ignacio, California. Mrs. Karabekian ends up working in a cannery in San Ignacio, where she dies of a tetanus infection when Rabo is 12 years old.

Karabekian, Rabo The protagonist of *Bluebeard* is abstract artist Rabo Karabekian, a character Vonnegut readers first met in the 1973 *Breakfast of Champions*. Karabekian is writing his autobiography at the age of 70 at the urging of his house guest, Circe Berman. We discover that Karabekian is the child of Armenian immigrants, born in 1916 in San Ignacio, California. As a young man with artistic talent, he goes to New York City to serve as an apprentice to the great illustrator Dan Gregory. Later, during World War II, he heads up a platoon of army engineers composed completely of artists, whose mission is to invent and test new types of camouflage. Karabekian loses an eye in the war and ends up marrying a nurse from the military hospital where he is sent to recuperate. Upon returning home, he and Dorothy settle down and have two sons. Though Dorothy wants him to become a businessman as they had originally planned, Karabekian instead prefers to associate with abstract expressionist artists, often drinking with them in bars until late at night. He ends up moving out to Long Island, where he buys a potato barn, which is

intended to serve as his art studio. Eventually Dorothy leaves him, taking the couples' sons with her. Karabekian remarries Edith Taft, a widow, and the two live happily for the next 20 years. After Edith's death, Karabekian rattles around the large Long Island house that had belonged to Dorothy, lonely and at loose ends, until he has a chance meeting on the beach with another widow, the loud, bossy Circe Berman, who turns out to be a well-known writer of young adult novels. Mrs. Berman moves in with Karabekian and encourages him to start writing his autobiography. Shortly before Mrs. Berman is scheduled to leave Long Island, Karabekian brings her out to the locked potato barn, which he had forbidden anyone to enter. Inside is Karabekian's masterpiece, a wonderfully realistic, enormous painting of V-E day. The novel ends with Karabekian leading tours of his home and barn, his painting the central attraction.

Karabekian, Terry See Steel, Terry, below.

Karpinski, Big John John Karpinski is Rabo Karabekian's neighbor to the north in East Hampton, Long Island. Karpinski is a New York native and a potato farmer.

Karpinski, Big John's Father Big John Karpinski's potato barn in East Hampton originally belonged to his father, a man who was treed by a grizzly bear in Yellowstone Park at the age of 60. After this encounter, Big John's father read every book about bears he could find.

Karpinski, Dorene Dorene Karpinksi is the wife of Big John Karpinski, Rabo Karabekian's neighbor to the north in East Hampton, Long Island. At the end of the novel, the Karpinskis decide to divide up their farm to sell in six-acre, ocean-view lots and retire to Florida.

Karpinski, Little John Little John Karpinski is the son of Rabo Karabekian's neighbor, potato farmer John Karpinski. After he is caught selling dope as a high school student, Little John joins the army and is sent to Vietnam, where he is killed by a land mine.

Kasabian, F. Donald Donald F. Kasabian is an Armenian, an executive vice president at the Metropolitan Life company, and Rabo Karabekian's neighbor to the west in East Hampton. Karabekian mentions the man in order to point out how well Armenians have done for themelves in the United States.

Kemp, Marilee Dan Gregory's mistress and a former Ziegfeld Follies showgirl, Marilee Kemp answers the fan letters that the young Rabo Karabekian writes to Gregory. She keeps up the correspondence for several years, ultimately orchestrating Rabo's apprenticeship to Dan Gregory in New York, an arrangement the famous illustrator agrees to only because he feels guilty for having pushed Marilee down the stairs and broken several of her bones. After their meeting, Rabo and Marilee form an even stronger attachment to each other, often sneaking away to visit New York's Museum of Modern Art, a place despised and forbidden by Dan Gregory. The young man ends up losing his virginity to the older Marilee after the two are caught coming out of the museum by Gregory. For Karabekian, this sexual encounter is ecstatic and memorable. Later, Marilee moves to Italy with Gregory, and, after the artist's death, marries the homosexual Count Portomaggiori and serves as an American spy during the war years. Karabekian meets Marilee, now the Contessa Portomaggiore, in Italy briefly after the war and helps her decorate her palazzo with abstract expressionist art.

Kennedy, Jackie Jackie Kennedy, widow of President JOHN F. KENNEDY, appears in the novel as the guest of honor at a dinner party in Southampton attended by Circe Berman and her date, a psychiatrist she met on the beach outside Rabo Karabekian's mansion.

Kim, Bum Suk Kim Bum Suk is a South Korean political exile who writes a book called *Private Art Treasures of Tuscany*. In the book, he includes photographs of the palazzo of Innocenzo de Medici, the home owned by Marilee Kemp after she becomes the Contessa Portomaggiore. Rabo Karabekian is able to supply readers with very specific information about the palazzo after reading Kim's book.

Kitchen, Terry Terry Kitchen is a fictional abstract expressionist painter who is Rabo Karabekian's best friend during his New York City days and his early years on Long Island. A graduate of Yale Law School from a wealthy family, Kitchen transforms into a real artist when Rabo Karabekian buys him a spray rig, which Kitchen uses to paint giant canvases. In 1956, Kitchen ends up shooting his own father in the shoulder in an alcoholic haze, then putting the gun into his mouth and killing himself immediately afterward.

Kitchen, Terry, Sr. Terry Kitchen's father is a corporate lawyer, civil rights champion, and first-rate cellist who, when he is about 60 years old, visits his estranged son in a tavern where Terry is drinking with his painter friends. At the time, Rabo Karabekian does not know who the distinguished older gentleman is, but Terry tells him it is either his father or else a clever imitator. Six years later, Terry Kitchen shoots his father in the shoulder while in an alcoholic haze, then turns the gun on himself, committing suicide.

Lucrezia Lucrezia, whose last name we never learn, is a servant to Contessa Portomaggiore in Florence, Italy. Lucrezia lost a leg and an eye when she stepped on a mine trying to bring eggs to a new mother. The contessa, Marilee Kemp, uses the example of Lucrezia to bemoan the violence men do against women during wartime.

Madison, Polly Polly Madison is the pen name Circe Berman uses to write her ultra-realistic and best-selling young adult novels.

Mamigonian, Leo Leo Mamigonian is the son of swindler Vartan Mamigonian, who tricked Rabo Karabekian's parents out of their fortune. Coincidentally, Leo Mamigonian is also the suspected Eyptian arms dealer who buys Marilee Kemp's Florentine palazzo after her death.

Mamigonian Vartan Vartan Manigonian is an Armenian shoe manufacturer in Egypt who swindles Rabo Karabekian's parents out of their money and tricks them into moving to San Ignacio, California.

Named after a great Armenian national hero who fought the Persians in the fifth century, Mamigonian, like Mr. and Mrs. Karabekian, is the survivor of a Turkish massacre against the Armenians, though an earlier one than Rabo's parents endured.

Maria   Maria, whose last name we never learn in the novel, is Marilee Kemp's cook in Florence. Marilee, or the Contessa Portomaggiore, has all female servants, many of them injured or harmed during World War II. Maria, like Rabo Karabekian, lost an eye in the war.

Mayor of Florence   The mayor of Florence gives Marilee Kemp, now the Contessa Portomaggiore, a painting depicting the death of her husband, British spy Bruno Portomaggiore, by a fascist firing squad near the end of World War II.

Mencken, Barbira   Barbira Mencken is the actress ex-wife of novelist Paul Slazinger. During divorce proceedings, she changes her name from plain "Barbara" to "Bar-*beer*-ah." Later, when Rabo Karabekian visits New York as an old man, he will catch a glimpse of Barbira coming out of one of the brownstones that used to belong to Dan Gregory.

Mussolini, Benito   Italian fascist dictator Benito Mussolini is one of the actual historical figures who appears in *Bluebeard*. In the novel, illustrator Dan Gregory is obsessed with Mussolini, even moving to Italy to support Mussolini before World War II and "to make paintings of the Italian Army in action" (115).

"Now It's the Women's Turn"   "Now It's the Women's Turn" is the title Rabo Karabekian gives to his enormous, jeweled, ultra-realistic painting of a Czechoslovakian valley on V-E day, which he had painted while grieving for his beloved wife, Edith, and subsequently hid in his potato barn.

Only Way to Have a Successful Revolution in Any Field of Human Activity, The   Abstract painter Rabo Karabekian's writer friend Paul Slazinger is said to be at work on his first volume of nonfiction, which is titled *The Only Way to Have a*

Successful Revolution in Any Field of Human Activity. Slazinger argues that for real change to occur, a team of three specialists must work to promote it. Such teams must include an authentic genius, a highly intelligent and respected citizen who admires the genius, and a person who is able to explain anything, no matter how complicated, so that others can understand.

Picasso, Pablo   The great cubist painter appears as a character in *Bluebeard* when Rabo Karabekian goes to his home to make sure he is all right during the liberation of Paris in World War II. Picasso opens the door only a crack and begs not to be disturbed. Marilee Kemp later tells Rabo Karabekian about a collage of a cat Picasso had made by cutting up an advertising poster drawn by Dan Gregory.

Pollock, Jackson   An actual abstract expressionist painter, famous for his large canvases and "drip" technique, Jackson Pollock bought a large house in East Hampton, Long Island, with a barn on the property that he used as a studio. Thus, he is in many ways the inspiration for Rabo Karabekian. Pollock also figures as a character in *Bluebeard*; he is a good friend of Karabekian and the fictional Terry Kitchen. The three artists, in fact, become known as the "Three Musketeers" since they are so often together. Pollock died in an alcohol-related car crash in 1956, a death that Rabo Karabekian recounts in the novel.

Pomerantz, Floyd   On his visit to New York City, Rabo Karabekian meets a fellow East Hamptonite named Floyd Pomerantz, who gives Karabekian a lift home in his stretch limousine. On the way, Pomerantz asks if Karabekian still thinks there is time for him to become a painter. Earlier, we discover, the man had asked Paul Slazinger if there was time for him to become a writer. In response to Pomerantz, Slazinger proposes a "Money Hall of Fame" to convince people like him that they have already "extorted more than enough money from the economy" (121).

Portomaggiore, Count Bruno   Count Bruno Portomaggiore is Benito Mussolini's minister of culture in Italy during World War II. Oxford-educated and homosexual, the count marries the former Marilee Kemp in an attempt to hide his true sexual bent. Always kind and thoughtful to Marilee, unlike her previous lover, Dan Gregory, the count turns out to have been "head of the British spy apparatus in Italy all through the war" (157). He will be executed by a fascist firing squad near the end of the war.

Portomaggiore, Contessa   See Kemp, Marilee, above.

Private Art Treasures of Tuscany   *Private Art Treasures of Tuscany* is an invented book said to be written by a South Korean political exile named Kim Bum Suk. Rabo Karabekian reads the book to get an idea about what the Italian palazzo owned by the former Marilee Kemp looks like.

Roberto   When Rabo Karabekian returns to New York as an old man, he has dinner at the Century Club. He asks about the club's old maître d', a man named Roberto, and is told that he had been killed by a bicycle messenger who was riding the wrong way down a one-way street.

Rothko, Mark   Mark Rothko was a real-life painter, often classified as part of the abstract expressionist school. He appears in *Bluebeard* as one of the many artists Rabo Karabekian becomes friends with in New York City after World War II. Like many of Karabekian's artist friends, Rothko died a suicide, slashing his wrists with a knife in 1970.

Sateen Dura-Luxe   At the height of his fame, Rabo Karabekian uses a newly invented acrylic wall paint called Sateen Dura-Luxe which promises to "outlive the smile on the Mona Lisa" (21). Unfortunately for Karabekian, however, the paint ends up cracking and disintegrating, eventually returning all his abstract paintings to blank canvases.

Savonarola, Girolamo   Girolamo Savonarola is a Dominican monk who, in 1494, orders murals scraped off the walls of the palazzo in Florence later owned by the Count Portomaggiore. Savon-arola wishes to dispel all traces of paganism from Florence.

Shoup, Martin   When Rabo Karabekian is rejected as a student by painter Nelson Bauerbeck as a young man in New York City, he signs up for a course in creative writing instead, taught by famous short story writer Martin Shoup. Shoup advises Karabekian to drop the course when the young artist declares himself unable to put the appearance of things into words.

Slazinger Ancestor   The first ancestor of Paul Slazinger to come to America was a Hessian grenadier serving as a mercenary to a British general during the Revolutionary War. He is taken prisoner during the second Battle of Freeman's Farm and never returns home to Germany again.

Slazinger, Paul   Novelist and World War II veteran Paul Slazinger is a good friend of Rabo Karabekian. Slazinger, in fact, spends most of his time at Karabekian's house, eating his food and enjoying the creature comforts of Karabekian's mansion. Though he no longer writes himself, just as Karabekian no longer paints, Slazinger is initially scornful of Circe Berman's literary comments, not realizing that she is best-selling young adult novelist Polly Madison. When he discovers the truth, Slazinger helps Mrs. Berman redo Karabekian's foyer in a way that he knows will outrage his old friend. At the end of the novel, Slazinger goes crazy at least temporarily, comes to believe that Polly Madison's books are "the greatest works of literature since *Don Quixote*" (208), and begins work on a nonfiction book titled *The Only Way to Have a Successful Revolution in Any Field of Human Activity*.

Solomon, Syd   When Circe Berman asks Rabo Karabekian how to tell a good picture from a bad one, Rabo replies that the best answer he ever heard to that question was given by a painter named Syd Solomon. Speaking to a 15-year-old girl at a cocktail party, Solomon explained that, to tell a good painting from a bad one, all you had to do "is look at a million paintings, and then you can never be mistaken" (165). Syd Solomon is a real-life figure, a second generation abstract expressionist painter from Long Island.

Steel, Henri   One of Rabo Karabekian's sons, Henri Steel (named for Rabo's favorite painter, Henri Matisse) has, like his brother, Terry, taken his stepfather's last name. Henri Steel works as a civilian contract compliance officer at the Pentagon and has one daughter. He does not speak to his father any longer.

Steel, Roy   Roy Steel is Dorothy Karabekian's second husband, an affable insurance salesman. Rabo Karabekian's sons, Henri and Terry, end up taking their stepfather's surname and dropping Karabekian.

Steel, Terry   Terry Steel is one of Rabo Karabekian's sons, named for Rabo's dear friend, the artist Terry Kitchen. Like his brother, Henri, Terry goes by his stepfather's surname. At the present time of the novel, Terry Steel works as a publicity man for the Chicago Bears and has two sons of his own. He no longer speaks to his father Rabo, however.

Taft, William Howard   The 27th president of the United States, William Howard Taft is a great-uncle of Edith Taft Karabekian, Rabo Karabekian's beloved second wife.

Tarkington, Booth   An actual historic figure, Booth Tarkington was a Pulitzer Prize–winning American author writing in the early 20th century. Along with Al Jolson and W. C. Fields, he appears as a guest at Dan Gregory's dinner party the night Rabo Karabekian arrives in New York.

Trippingham, Mona Lisa   Mona Lisa Trippingham is an insurance inspector from the Matsumoto Company. She finds eight large canvases in the company basement that are the remains of the panels Rabo Karabekian had painted for the GEFFCo company, which formerly owned the Matsumoto Building. Having taken an art appreciation course at Skidmore College in which the professor showed slides of "Windsor Blue Number Seventeen," both before and after it fell apart, Ms. Trippingham rec-

ognizes what the canvases used to be. She offers to return the canvases to Karabekian, who will later use them to paint his masterpiece, "Now It's the Women's Turn."

Underground, The   *The Underground* is the name of a Polly Madison young adult novel that is about children of a parent who survived some sort of mass killing. Polly Madison is the pen name used by fiction writer Circe Berman.

Unnamed Abstract Expressionist Widows   Determined to discover whether the Polly Madison books have any real literary merit, Rabo Karabekian telephones the widows of a couple of his old abstract expressionist buddies who have teenage grandchildren. The women declare the books to be intelligent and frank, but not great literature.

Unnamed American Agent   Right before World War II, an American agent from the War Department disguised as a common workman visits Marilee Kemp in Florence, Italy. He persuades Marilee to agree to marry Count Portomaggiore and to serve as an American spy during the war.

Unnamed Armenian Woman   When Rabo Karabekian's mother is playing dead during the Turkish massacre of the Armenians, she looks into the face of an old Armenian woman's corpse, which is lying with its mouth open. Inside the woman's mouth and on the ground below it is a fortune in jewels. Mrs. Karabekian scoops up the jewels on the ground and uses these to make it to safety in Egypt, though she and her husband are swindled out of this fortune before they come to America.

Unnamed Art Collector   Circe Berman buys a series of pictures of little girls on swings from an unnamed art collector at an antique show in Bridgehampton. These are the paintings she uses to redecorate Rabo Karabekian's foyer while he is out of town in New York.

Unnamed Bank Robber   When an unnamed bank robber wearing a "babyshit brown" suit escapes on the streets of New York, Rabo Karabekian is mistakenly picked up for questioning because he is wearing a suit of the same color.

Unnamed Bookseller and Librarian Curious about the literary merits of the Polly Madison books, but unwilling to read them himself, Rabo Karabekian telephones a bookseller and a librarian in East Hampton, who proclaim the books to be "useful, frank, and intelligent, but as literature hardly more than workmanlike" (209).

Unnamed Boyfriend of Celeste White On Circe Berman's last night in East Hampton, Rabo Karabekian hires a boyfriend of his cook's daughter, Celeste, to drive him and Circe to Sag Harbor for supper and back home again afterward. Rabo plans to have a few drinks and does not want to drive himself.

Unnamed Canadian Bombadier In his elaborate painting, "Now It's the Women's Turn," Rabo Karabekian depicts a dying Canadian bombadier, shot down over Hungary, clinging to his leg and looking up to him as if he were God.

Unnamed Clerk at East Hampton Hardware Store After Edith Karabekian's death, the grieving Rabo drives to a hardware store in East Hampton, where he buys stacks of art supplies that he will use to paint "Now It's the Women's Turn." Karabekian speaks only one word to the young store clerk who asks if he is a painter: "Renaissance" (294).

Unnamed Dresden Prisoner of War Rabo Karabekian is captured when World War II is almost over. Sent to a prisoner of war camp in DRESDEN, where rations are very scarce, Karabekian and his comrades elect a fellow prisoner of war to divide the remaining food into equal shares. The man remains "sleek and contented-looking" while the other prisoners become skeletons by feasting on the crumbs that fall on his knife and the table when he divides the food.

Unnamed Father of Circe Berman Circe Berman tells Rabo Karabekian that her father owned a pants factory in Lackawanna, New York. He hanged himself when he went bankrupt.

Unnamed German Boy Izzy Finkelstein tells Rabo Karabekian the story of how, as a tank gunner in World War II, a German boy had shot a rocket launcher at his tank. Finkelstein and the other soldiers shoot the boy before they realize how young he is.

Unnamed German Dandies Two "dandified young German businessmen" (189) come to see Rabo Karabekian's abstract expressionist collection on Long Island one day, posing as art enthusiasts. Circe Berman and Karabekian piece together enough of their German conversation, however, to discover that the two men are actually real estate developers, interested in turning Karabekian's mansion into beachfront condominiums.

Unnamed German General After the war, Rabo Karabekian is summoned to Florence to testify in a lawsuit about two paintings that had been taken by American soldiers from a German general in Paris. The general had evidently stolen the paintings from a private house in Florence, and the original owners are suing to recover them.

Unnamed Guggenheim Curator One day in his potato barn in East Hampton, Rabo Karabekian sketches a quick caricature of Paul Slazinger on a canvas that he later covers with layers of Sateen Dura-Luxe to make a painting called "Hungarian Rhapsody Number Six." Bought by the Guggenheim Museum, the painting begins to disintegrate like all of Karabekian's work. A woman curator, worried that the museum has stored the painting improperly, calls Karabekian to check. She tells the artist a face is emerging from behind the layers of paint. When Rabo tells her to call the pope, she replies that she would, except for one thing: She used to date Paul Slazinger.

Unnamed Gypsy Boy When Circe Berman asks about an old gypsy woman depicted in the painting, "Now It's The Women's Turn," Rabo Karabekian makes up a background story for her, explaining that one of the gypsy queen's subjects, a 14-year-old boy, was caught stealing a ham from a Slovak mortar squad. The soldiers make the boy lead them back to the gypsy camp, where they kill everyone they find there.

Unnamed Gypsy Queen   A dead, bloated woman depicted in the painting "Now It's the Women's Turn" is an old queen of the gypsies who was starving to death and tried to steal a chicken from a farmhouse. She dies when the farmer shoots her in the abdomen.

Unnamed Handless Servant   At Marilee Kemp's palazzo in Florence, Rabo Karabekian is served tea by a servant who has two steel clamps in place of hands. He learns that her husband had plunged her hands into boiling water in order to make her tell him who her lovers had been while he was away at war. Gangrene set in, and the hands had to be amputated.

Unnamed Hermaphrodite Cook   Dan Gregory's cook in New York City, who dies two weeks after the young Rabo Karabekian's arrival, is discovered to be a hermaphrodite by an undertaker after her death. In his autobiography, Karabekian calls this piece of information "the most trivial footnote imaginable in a history of abstract expressionism" (153).

Unnamed Italian Prisoner of War and his Wife   After the war, Rabo Karabekian goes to Florence to testify in a lawsuit concerning stolen paintings that his unit had catalogued. An unnamed Italian prisoner of war in Le Havre, who was supposed to crate the paintings, had secretly shipped them to his wife in Rome.

Unnamed Italian Sculptor   Rabo Karabekian recounts a time when his first wife, Dorothy, read in a magazine something an Italian sculptor had said about the abstract expressionist painters: "These Americans are very interesting. They dive into the water before they learn to swim" (281). To prove to Dorothy that he really *can* draw, Rabo picks up a green crayon and sketches two beautiful portraits of their sons on the Sheetrock of the kitchen wall.

Unnamed Japanese Major   Although no Japanese were present at the V-E day scene Rabo Karabekian depicts in his painting, "Now It's the Women's Turn," he nevertheless paints in a Japanese major lurking near a ruined watchtower, since he believes the Japanese share responsibility for turning Americans into "a bunch of bankrupt militaristic fuckups" (304).

Unnamed Letter-to-the Editor Writer   After an art magazine publishes an article claiming that Rabo Karabekian has the world's greatest abstract expressionist painting locked in his potato barn in order to artificially inflate the prices of the other paintings in his collection, an unnamed man writes a letter to the editor stating he knew Karabekian in the war and claiming that Karabekian stole masterpieces of art that should have been returned to their rightful owners in Europe. The letter writer further claims that these masterpieces are what Karabekian has locked in his potato barn.

Unnamed Maid   Before the war in Italy, Marilee Kemp's personal maid brings a workman to see her. The man turns out to be from the U.S. War Department; he asks Marilee to work as an American spy in Italy during the war.

Unnamed Maître d'   When Rabo Karabekian has supper at the Century Club on his return visit to New York City as an old man, he is greeted by a new maître d'. The man tells Karabekian that the club's former maître d', Roberto, had been killed in an accident involving a bicycle messenger driving the wrong way down a one-way street.

Unnamed Maori Corporal   In the hodge-podge of humanity depicted in Rabo Karabekian's painting, "Now It's the Women's Turn," is the tiny figure of a Maori corporal reading a newspaper. The corporal is perched on an ammunition box, on which is inscribed the date of the events that the painting depicts: V-E day, or May 8, 1945.

Unnamed Men Fighting   After Rabo Karabekian and Marilee Kemp are caught coming out of the

Museum of Modern Art by Dan Gregory, they walk home together. On the way, they stop to watch a pair of unnamed white men fighting in front of a bar on Third Avenue. This is the same afternoon that Karabekian will lose his virginity to Marilee.

Unnamed Milanese Automobile Dealer After Marilee Kemp's death, her palazzo is inherited by her late husband's second cousin, an automobile dealer in Milan, who immediately sells it to an Egyptian arms dealer.

Unnamed New York Photographer During his New York artist days, Rabo Karabekian rents studio space for himself and Terry Kitchen in a loft owned by a New York photographer.

Unnamed Policeman in Grand Central Terminal When no one comes to pick up young Rabo Karabekian in Grand Central Terminal when he first arrives in New York to become Dan Gregory's apprentice, the boy shows Gregory's address to a policeman, who tells Rabo that the house is only eight blocks away.

Unnamed Policemen Investigating a Bank Robbery When Rabo Karabekian is still married to Dorothy and living in New York, he is nabbed on the street by two unnamed policemen who are looking for a bank robber wearing a "babyshit brown" suit. Because Karabekian is wearing a suit of the same color, the policemen mistake him for the robber. They later apologize and let him go.

Unnamed Pretty Girl Rabo Karabekian tells Circe Berman the story of a pretty 15-year-old girl who, at a cocktail part, asked Karabekian's painter friend SYD SOLOMON how to tell a good painting from a bad one. Solomon replied that all she had to do was look at a million paintings, and then she would know the difference.

Unnamed Prominent Sexologist When Rabo Karabekian has supper at the Century Club on his return visit to New York City, he meets a writer of young adult novels whose wife is a prominent sexologist. Karabekian imagines that it must be "burden-

some" to be married to a woman "so sophisticated in sexual techniques" (119).

Unnamed Psychiatrist While Circe Berman is staying at Rabo Karabekian's house, she goes to a big dinner party for Jackie Kennedy in Southampton with an unnamed psychiatrist she met on the beach.

Unnamed Relative of Edith Karabekian At the Karabekian's wedding reception, Rabo's new wife, Edith, tells a female relative that Rabo is her "tamed raccoon" (276).

Unnamed San Ignacio Morticians The San Ignacio mortician who buried Rabo Karabekian's mother goes bankrupt and leaves town to seek his fortune. So, a different mortician buries Rabo's father. Ironically, this mortician had come to San Ignacio to seek his fortune. The bottom half of Rabo's father's casket is closed, but this second mortician informs Rabo that his father is indeed wearing pants and also that he is being buried in one of the fancy pairs of cowboy boots he designed late in life. For some reason, the mortician also believes that Rabo's father is a Mohammedan and is quite excited to show how uncritically pious he can be. Rabo tells the mortician to say "Praise Allah" when he closes the coffin lid, and the mortician happily complies.

Unnamed Scottish Glider Pilot One of the figures depicted in Rabo Karabekian's large, ultra-realistic painting, "Now It's the Women's Turn," is a Scottish glider pilot who had been captured on D-day.

Unnamed Sergeant Major in the Moroccan Spahis When Rabo Karabekian shows Circe Berman his elaborate painting, "Now It's the Women's Turn," he points out a figure who is a sergeant major in the Moroccan Spahis, captured in North Africa.

Unnamed Servants to Dan Gregory When Dan Gregory throws Marilee Kemp down the stairs, two unnamed servants, who happen to be standing at the bottom of the staircase, witness the fall. Thus, Gregory cannot pretend it was an accident.

Unnamed Soldiers at Fort Benning Rabo Karabekian wins a soldier's medal by pulling two unconscious enlisted men out of a burning barracks while he's giving a course in camouflage techniques to officer candidates at Fort Benning, Georgia.

Unnamed Soviet Writers The day after Circe Berman redecorates Rabo Karabekian's foyer, installing realistic chromos of children on swings, three Soviet writers come to the house for a tour of Karabekian's abstract art collection. Puzzled by the trashiness of these pictures, the writers ask Karabekian about them. The artist replies by using Mrs. Berman's own words about the horrors awaiting these children in the future. After this explanation, the writers are embarrassed and agree that these paintings are the most important pictures in Karabekian's house.

Unnamed SS Guard One of the characters Rabo Karabekian depicts in his painting, "Now It's the Women's Turn," is a concentration camp guard who has thrown away his SS uniform, but who is still nervous about being found out in the midst of a crowd of concentration camp victims he brought to the valley and dumped.

Unnamed Stage Manager for the Zeigfield Follies When Rabo Karabekian visits Marilee Kemp in Florence, she tells him that the stage manager for the Ziegfeld Follies, where she was a young dancer, loved her so much that he told her she had to be "part of his stable of whores" (235) or he'd fire her and have somebody throw acid in her face.

Unnamed Steel/Karabekian Grandchildren Rabo Karabekian has three grandchildren—two boys (the sons of Terry Steel) and a girl (the daughter of Henri Steel). Because his sons do not speak to him, Rabo has never met his grandchildren. Yet, he tells Circe Berman that he is leaving everything he owns to his sons after his death, providing they

change their names and the names of his grandchildren back to Karabekian. Both Terry and Henri took on their stepfather's surname, Steel, after their mother's divorce and remarriage.

Unnamed Woman with W. C. Fields When Rabo Karabekian sits at the top of the stairs in Dan Gregory's mansion the first night he is in New York, he hears W. C. Fields introduce the woman he is with to Gregory, using these words: "This, my child, is Dan Gregory, the love child of Leonardo da Vinci's sister and a sawed off Arapahoe" (99).

Unnamed Writer of Young Adult Novels At the Century Club in New York, when he returns to the city as an old man, Rabo Karabekian meets a writer of young adult novels who is married to a prominent sexologist. When Karabekian delicately inquires whether making love to a woman so sexually sophisticated is burdensome, the writer replies that Karabekian "has certainly hit the nail on the head" (119).

Unnamed Young Man from the State Department The day after Circe Berman redecorates Rabo Karabekian's foyer, a young man from the U.S. State Department leads three writers from the Soviet Union on a tour of Karabekian's art collection. When asked why Karabekian has such trashy pictures in his foyer, the artist gives the men Mrs. Berman's lecture about the horrors awaiting the children on the swings in the future. The men are all terribly embarrassed and apologetic for their insensitivity.

Unnamed Yugoslavian Partisans Rabo Karabekian explains to Circe Berman that two of the figures depicted in the painting, "Now It's the Women's Turn," are Yugoslavian partisans.

Vitelli, Giovanni Giovanni Vitelli is the 15th-century Italian artist who painted the original murals on the now blank walls of the Florentine palazzo owned by Count Portomaggiore. Because the murals were later ordered scraped off by a Dominican monk, Rabo Karabekian calls Vitelli "the Rabo Karabekian of his time" (230) whose equivalent for Sateen Dura-Luxe was Christian fundamentalism.

White, Allison   Allison White, a divorced woman of about 40, works as a cook for Rabo Karabekian in his Long Island mansion after Edith Karabekian's death. Disgusted that Rabo treats her so impersonally and does not even know her name—he merely refers to her as "the cook"—she threatens to walk out, but is convinced to stay in her job by Circe Berman.

White, Celeste   Celeste White is the 15-year-old daughter of Rabo Karabekian's cook, Allison White. Celeste is given the run of Karabekian's mansion; she and her friends eat his food, lounge by his pool, and enjoy his private beach. Rabo uses Celeste and her friends as sounding boards, frequently asking them questions about history and regularly being astonished at their ignorance.

Whitehall, Major General Daniel   Major General Daniel Whitehall, commander of the combat troops of the Army Corps of Engineers during World War II, commissions Rabo Karabekian to paint his portrait. This general, after carefully dropped hints by Karabekian, orders the creation of the new camouflage unit made up of enlisted men with artistic experience, the unit Karabekian will command during the war.

"Windsor Blue Number Seventeen"   Said to be Rabo Karabekian's most famous painting, "Windsor Blue Number Seventeen" was 64 feet long and eight feet high, and hung in the lobby of the GEFFCo headquarters in New York City before it started to disintegrate because it had been painted with Sateen Dura-Luxe. Later in the novel, Karabekian uses the canvases of "Windsor Blue Number Seventeen" to paint his masterpiece: "Now It's the Women's Turn."

Wu, Sam   Sam Wu is a Chinese laundryman in New York who worked for a period as Dan Gregory's cook. After hearing on the radio about how lonesome soldiers could be overseas, Sam Wu asks for Rabo Karabekian's address so that he can write

to him during the war. Wu writes faithfully to Karabekian and even stores the paintings that Karabekian buys in Europe. After Karabekian retrieves his paintings from Wu when the war is over, he never sees the Chinese laundryman again.

FURTHER READING

Kopper, Edward A., Jr. "Abstract Expressionism in Vonnegut's *Bluebeard*." *Journal of Modern Literature* 17, no. 4 (1991): 583–584.
Morse, Donald E. "Thinking Intelligently about Science and Art: Kurt Vonnegut's *Galápagos* and *Bluebeard*." *Extrapolation* 38, no. 4 (1997): 292–303.
Rampton, David. "Into the Secret Chamber: Art and the Artist in Kurt Vonnegut's *Bluebeard*." *Critique* 35, no. 1 (1993): 16–26.

"The Boy Who Hated Girls"

"The Boy Who Hated Girls," one of several Vonnegut stories about Lincoln High School band director George M. Helmholtz, was first published in the *Saturday Evening Post* on March 31, 1956. It later appeared in the 1999 collection *Bagombo Snuff Box*.

SYNOPSIS

The story opens with Helmholtz working one-on-one with trumpet player Bert Higgens, a member of the highly selective Ten Square Band who has forgotten how to march. Because Higgens's affliction seems so unusual, Helmholtz takes him to see the school nurse, Miss Peach, who discovers that Helmholtz had given private lessons to the boy for two years and taken him out for sodas afterward. But when Bert was promoted to the Ten Square Band, the lessons stopped, and Helmholtz began working with other boys who needed extra help. Miss Peach feels that Helmholtz has been a substitute father for Bert, whose own father is not involved in his life. He has regressed because he wants to regain Helmholtz's attention. The story ends with Bert dating Charlotte, a pretty girl he had claimed to hate earlier. He tells Helmholtz some hurtful things Charlotte has said about the band director—that he is not really interested in people, but only in music. Helmholtz, realizing that Charlotte's accusations have some truth to them, goes to see Miss Peach about his own problems.

COMMENTARY

A story about the high cost of being completely devoted to art, "The Boy Who Hated Girls" differs from other Vonnegut stories involving Lincoln High School band director George M. Helmholtz. While the band director is often described as kind and good-natured, and helps numerous students, especially in the stories "The Kid Nobody Could Handle" and "Ambitious Sophomore," in this story, readers see a slightly darker side of Helmholtz. He has served as a father figure to trumpet player Bert Higgens for the past two years, not only giving him private trumpet lessons, but taking the boy out for sodas and talks afterward. Thus, when he turns his attention to a new boy who needs his help, Bert feels abandoned and begins getting drunk in an attempt to regain the band director's special attention. Helmholtz, though, has been blind to how his behavior affects the boy. Miss Peach, the school nurse, accuses him of "playing fast and loose with kids' emotions," and points out that Bert's worship of him is "a casual thing" to the band director (239). Although Helmholtz at first bristles at these accusations, claiming that psychology such as that practiced by Miss Peach tries to prevent people from "being nice to each other" (241), nevertheless "guilt rode on his back like a chimpanzee" (240).

The nurse's observations are only enforced by Helmholtz's phone call to trumpet teacher Larry Fink. Fink tells him that Bert is not really a musician at all, that he was not very talented and only worked so hard because of his love for Helmholtz. The conversation ends with Fink telling Helmholtz that, in his innocence, he has "turned a person who never should have been a musician into an actor instead" (242). Helmholtz must face the awful truth of his own emotional shortcomings when Bert tells him, at the end of the story, what Charlotte has said about him: that he is "disconnected from real life, and only pretend[s] to be interested in people" (244). Readers are meant to

see the justice in this accusation since music is playing in Helmholtz's mind even in the course of this painful conversation, and he has trouble focusing on what Bert is telling him. Helmholtz does finally realize the huge price he pays for being such a consummate musician and lover of music when he tells Miss Peach at the very end of the story that he has come to talk about himself, not Bert this time.

CHARACTERS

Charlotte Charlotte is a girl whom band director George M. Helmholtz often sees with trumpet player Bert Higgens. Charlotte tells Bert that Mr. Helmholtz is "nuts" (245), that he is disconnected from real people, and that all he cares about is music. Although Bert is originally so infatuated with Mr. Helmholtz that he claims to hate Charlotte, he will begin dating the girl at the end of the story after Helmholtz turns his attention from Bert to other band members who need his help.

Fink, Larry Larry Fink is the best trumpet teacher in town. When students of Mr. Helmholtz finally make the Ten Square Band, he turns them over to Fink for lessons. This is what has happened to Bert Higgens, but Bert is so distraught to lose Helmholtz's special attention that he begins drinking and forgets how to march at band performances.

Haley, Stewart Stewart Haley is the assistant principal of Lincoln High School, who constantly complains about the money band director George M. Helmholtz spends on his beloved band.

Helmholtz, George M. The lead character in several Vonnegut short stories, George M. Helmholtz is the band director of Lincoln High School who completely dedicates himself to his music and his students. In "The Boy Who Hated Girls," however, the kindly Helmholtz must examine his own conscience when one of the boys he has worked diligently with, Bert Higgens, begins to regress in his playing and marching. The school nurse accuses Helmholtz of getting too involved in Bert's life, then dropping him for other needy students.

Higgens, Bert   Bert Higgens is a trumpet player at Lincoln High School who has been taking private lessons from band director George M. Helmholtz for the last two years. Helmholtz serves as a substitute father to the boy, whose own father had wandered away from the family years before. When Bert makes the Ten Square Band and is turned over to another trumpet player in town for lessons, he starts drinking during band performances and rehearsals, wanting to regain the attention he once received from Helmholtz. At the end of the story, the emotionally needy boy turns his affection to a girl named Charlotte, who believes that Helmholtz is "really nutty" (245).

Peach, Miss   Miss Peach is the school nurse who tells band director George Helmholtz that he is inadvertently being cruel to his students by showing them so much attention, then dropping them for other needy students once they show improvement.

Shakely, Norton   Norton Shakely is the student whom George Helmholtz begins giving private lessons to after Bert Higgens is promoted to the Ten Square Band.

FURTHER READING

Bagombo Snuff Box. New York: Berkley Books, 2000.
Reed, Peter. *The Short Fiction of Kurt Vonnegut.* Westport, Conn.: Greenwood Press, 1997.

Breakfast of Champions

In Vonnegut's seventh novel, *Breakfast of Champions*, published by Delacorte/ SEYMOUR LAWRENCE in 1973, readers see an author approaching his 50th birthday and attempting to come to terms with the long-ago suicide of his mother and death of his father, as well as his own pessimism and suicidal impulses. In the opening chapter, Vonnegut writes, "This book is my fiftieth-birthday present to myself. I feel as though I am crossing the spine of a roof—having ascended one slope" (4). The sense of descending, of a life spiraling into decline,

Cover art from *Breakfast of Champions* (used by permission of Dell Publishing, a division of Random House, Inc.)

is everywhere evident in this novel, in both the characters of Pontiac dealer Dwayne Hoover, who is inching steadily toward madness, and in Kilgore Trout, who decides to go to MIDLAND CITY to show the community what a failed artist looks like. The life of the country as a whole is in no better shape in *Breakfast of Champions*. Vonnegut critiques racial, economic, and gender inequality in America, and he exposes the damage that Americans have done to their environment. He grapples with the notion that human beings are simply robots, programmed to act in irresponsible ways, and lacking FREE WILL. Yet, as in most of Vonnegut's work, the cynicism is mitigated at the end by a faith in the redemptive powers of art. Though traditional forms of art may have contributed to the social and psychological problems Vonnegut outlines in the novel, there is the possibility that new artistic forms will allow us to see the world in new and meaningful ways, in turn allowing us to revalue our fellow human beings.

SYNOPSIS

Chapters 1–2, 4

As Vonnegut tells readers in chapter 1, *Breakfast of Champions* is "a tale of a meeting of two lonesome, skinny, fairly old white men on a planet which was dying fast" (7). The two men who will ultimately meet at the end of the novel are Dwayne Hoover, a Pontiac dealer who is going insane, and Kilgore Trout, the SCIENCE FICTION writer who appears in numerous Vonnegut novels. The occasion for the meeting of these two characters is an Arts Festival that takes place in Midland City, Ohio, Dwayne's home town, in the autumn of 1972. Kilgore Trout has been invited to attend the festival as a visiting artist. Although he is an extremely prolific writer, Trout is very much unknown, since most of his work is published in pornography magazines. He is invited to the festival only on the recommendation of local millionaire Eliot Rosewater, another character appearing in numerous Vonnegut novels, who is a huge Kilgore Trout fan. Rosewater promises to lend the festival an extremely valuable El Greco oil painting on the condition that the organizers invite Trout as a visiting artist. The novel's chapters alternate between those set in Midland City, a typical, medium-size American city in the Midwest, and those that follow the journey of Kilgore Trout to the festival.

When readers first meet Dwayne Hoover, they are told that he is being consumed by bad chemicals in his head, which are "no longer content with making him feel and see queer things. They wanted him to *do* queer things, also, and make a lot of noise" (39). Dwayne, though "fabulously well-to-do" (13) and owner of numerous businesses around town, has had a difficult life; his wife, Celia, committed suicide by eating Drano, and he is estranged from his only son, a homosexual named Bunny, who plays piano in a cocktail lounge at the Holiday Inn. Dwayne's bad chemicals make him cruelly chastise longtime employee Harry LeSabre,

the sales manager at Dwayne's Pontiac dealership, for his boring wardrobe and drab style. Dwayne orders Harry to acquire a new look for Hawaiian Week, a sales promotion coming up at the dealership the following week. Harry, who is secretly a transvestite, is crushed by Dwayne's tirade, believing Dwayne has discovered his secret affinity for dressing in women's clothing. The weekend that follows turns out to be a bad one for both Harry and Dwayne—Harry frets about whether his secret is discovered while Dwayne's bad chemicals force him, at one point, to put a loaded revolver into his mouth and contemplate suicide, though he eventually opts to shoot up his expensive bathroom instead.

Chapter 3, 5–8

Kilgore Trout, meanwhile, has dusted off his ancient high school tuxedo and set out for Midland City, not to accept acclaim for his long-neglected writings, but to show everyone at the arts festival what an "unhappy failure" he is (37). As he tells his parakeet, Bill, "I'm going out there to show them what nobody has ever seen at an arts festival before: a representative of all the thousands of artists who devoted their entire lives to a search for truth and beauty—and didn't find doodley-squat!" (37). He first hitches a ride from his rented apartment in Cohoes, New York, to New York City to scour pornography shops for copies of his books. He ends up getting mugged and beaten on 42nd Street late at night after leaving a dirty movie theater, losing all the money he had been sent by the festival organizers for travel expenses. When Trout is questioned by the police about the crime, he cannot supply any information about his attackers, adding that, as far as he knows, they might not even have been Earthlings: "For all I know," Trout continues, "that car may have been occupied by an intelligent gas from Pluto" (77). When a newspaper reporter leads off a story the following morning with that quote from Trout, other papers pick up the story and rumors about "The Pluto Gang" spread terror through the city. Eventually, a Puerto Rican gang in the city adopts the name for themselves, painting it on the back of their leather jackets.

Chapters 9, 11, 13, 15

While Trout is wreaking havoc in New York, Dwayne is heading toward havoc in Midland City. Back at work following the long Veterans Day weekend, Dwayne's senses are becoming increasingly distorted. When he walks across the parking lot of the Holiday Inn he partially owns to his Pontiac dealership, the asphalt seems to sink and rise with each step, as if Dwayne is walking on a trampoline. He brushes brusquely past an ex-convict named Wayne Hoobler, who is polishing cars on the sales lot, desperately hoping that Dwayne will give him a job. He completely ignores Harry LeSabre, his sales manager who has donned a green leotard, pink T-shirt, and grass skirt for Hawaiian Week, again crushing Harry. Dwayne returns to normal briefly in a meeting with his twin stepbrothers, Lyle and Kyle Hoover, who have come to see Dwayne about a problem with Sacred Miracle Cave, a tourist trap Dwayne owns in partnership with them. The cave's underground stream has become polluted by some sort of industrial waste that has formed "bubbles as tough as ping-pong balls" (119). The bubbles have been moving up the cave's passageways and are threatening to engulf the main cavern room, The Cathedral of Whispers, where numerous weddings and funerals have taken place.

Later that afternoon, Dwayne asks his secretary, Francine Pefko, to drive to a motel in nearby Shepardstown with him. After the two make love, Dwayne's bad chemicals emerge again when he hurls abuse at Francine because he thinks she is hinting that she would like Dwayne to buy her a Colonel Sanders' Kentucky Fried Chicken franchise. Eventually, Dwayne calms down, apologizes, and tells Francine he has lost his way and needs someone to give him answers. Francine suggests he talk to one of the artists coming to the Midland City Arts Festival, pointing out that "they don't think like other people" (171). Cheered by her suggestion, Dwayne resolves to do just that.

Chapters 10, 12, 14, 16–19

The artist who Dwayne eventually receives new ideas from—Kilgore Trout—is steadily moving closer to Midland City all the while. He hitches rides, first with a truck driver who is worried about environmental destruction. Trout tells the driver that he, Trout, used to be a conservationist too, but isn't any more because God clearly doesn't care for the environment any more than man does. Trout rides with the truck driver all the way to West Virginia, where the two see the devastating results of strip mining. Trout next accepts a ride from a traveling salesman named Andy Lieber, who drives a Ford Galaxie. When the Galaxie is stopped because of a traffic accident not far outside of Midland City, Trout decides to get out and walk the rest of the way. As he crosses Sugar Creek, the small river running along the shoulder of the interstate, his feet become encased in a thick plastic coating, a result of the same industrial pollution ruining the Sacred Miracle Cave.

Meanwhile, as Trout rapidly approaches, Vonnegut himself arrives at the cocktail lounge of the Holiday Inn to watch the interaction he has planned between his characters Dwayne Hoover and Kilgore Trout. He wears sunglasses and sits at a dark table so as not to be recognized. Also in the cocktail lounge are several other of Vonnegut's creations: a feisty cocktail waitress named Bonnie MacMahon and two visiting festival artists, gothic novelist Beatrice Keedsler and minimal painter Rabo Karabekian. Karabekian is the creator of the first piece of art purchased by the Mildred Barry Memorial Center for the Arts, the Midland City sponsor of the arts festival. The painting consists of a field of avocado green paint with a vertical stripe made out of Day-Glo orange reflecting tape. All of Midland City is outraged by the price paid for this painting—$50,000. Vonnegut writes that he, too, is outraged. When the cynical and arrogant Karabekian loudly insults Mary Alice Miller, the Queen of the Festival of the Arts, and a champion swimmer, waitress Bonnie MacMahon can take no more. She tells Karabekian that the city doesn't think much of his painting, that she's seen better pictures done by a five-year-old. Next comes what Vonnegut calls "the spiritual climax of this book" (224), the point at which Vonnegut is transformed by his own characters. Though he himself had not liked Karabekian previously, had considered him a "vain and weak and trashy man, no artist at all" (225), Vonnegut is reborn when Karabekian stands up in the cocktail lounge and gives a noble speech, defending not only his painting, but minimal art in general, as stripping away the superfluities of human existence to show the "unwavering band of light" (226) at the core of each of us that makes us sacred.

Chapters 20–24

When Kilgore Trout finally arrives in the cocktail lounge, Dwayne, who had been quiet during the confrontation between the painter and the waitress, is spurred by his bad chemicals to accost the science fiction writer and demand that Trout give him "the message" (258). Trout, in a desperate attempt to evade Dwayne, allows the Pontiac dealer to snatch up Trout's novel *Now It Can Be Told*, which Dwayne is able to read in minutes, because of a speed-reading course he had taken previously at the Young Men's Christian Association. The novel leads Dwayne to believe that he is the only person in the universe with free will, that everyone else is a fully programmed robot put on Earth simply as part of an enormous experiment by the Creator of the Universe to test Dwayne's reactions. Believing that everyone surrounding him is a machine, Dwayne goes on a violent rampage, smashing his son Bunny's face into his piano keyboard, savagely beating Francine Pefko, and biting off the tip of Kilgore Trout's index finger. Altogether, Dwayne hurts 11 people so badly that they have to go to the hospital. Dwayne himself is bundled off to the hospital as well. Later, the people Dwayne injured sue him, making him destitute. Dwayne ends up on skid row, no longer fabulously well-to-do, but just another drifter with "doodley-squat" (288).

Epilogue

While the main action of the novel concludes after the rampage in the cocktail lounge, Vonnegut adds an epilogue in which he introduces himself to Kilgore Trout, whom he describes as "the only character I ever created who had enough imagination to suspect that he might be the creation of another human being" (246). When Trout leaves the hospital with his bandaged hand, Vonnegut is sitting in a rented car in the dark night a few blocks away, waiting to intercept him. As Trout arrives in Vonnegut's sight, however, a giant Doberman pinscher named Kazak, who was "a leading character in an earlier version of this book" (293) springs out of the night to attack Vonnegut, who had gotten out of the car to smoke a cigarette. Filled with adrenaline, Vonnegut leaps over the car, landing on his hands and knees in the middle of the street. Kilgore Trout, already uncomfortable at the nearness of his creator, backs away and begins to run. Vonnegut chases him down, finally getting Trout to stop. He explains to the nervous and disbelieving Trout that he is Trout's Creator and that Trout is, right now, a character in the middle of a book. To convince the science fiction writer of the truth of what he says, Vonnegut quickly transports him around the world, into space, and back to Earth. Vonnegut then offers Kilgore Trout an apple, and tells him that he is setting him free. As Vonnegut disappears and the book draws to a close, Trout calls out to him, "*Make me young, make me young, make me young!*" (302), a cry that ends the novel.

COMMENTARY

Vonnegut dedicates *Breakfast of Champions* to the memory of Phoebe Hurty, a wealthy INDIANAPOLIS widow whom he tells readers in the opening chapter hired him to write advertising copy during the Depression years. Phoebe Hurty would talk bawdily to Vonnegut and his friends. He remembers that she was "funny" and "liberating" and "impolite" (2) and taught the teenagers in her charge to behave the same way. Yet, behind Phoebe Hurty's irreverence was an optimism that the country would improve when prosperity arrived. Phoebe Hurty, Vonnegut tells us, "was able to believe that the impoliteness she recommended would give shape to an American paradise" (2). He laments the fact that while Phoebe's sort of impoliteness is now fashionable, no one believes anymore in a new American paradise. Like *God Bless You, Mr. Rosewater*, this novel has great sympathy for utopian projects, for characters who believe that they can make the world a better place. In many ways, *Breakfast of Champions* chronicles Vonnegut's own struggles with despair and cynicism, the pull to accept things as they are in the world, to adopt a deterministic outlook, rather than try to change them for the better.

Vonnegut confesses, in this opening chapter, his own tendency to see human beings as robots, as machines, programmed to respond to stimuli in certain ways by the chemicals coursing through their bodies. He writes, "I tend to think of human beings as huge, rubbery test tubes . . . with chemical reactions seething inside" (3). Thus, when Vonnegut depicts Dwayne Hoover and his incipient madness, he is always careful to mention the "bad chemicals" that force Dwayne to behave in the odd ways he does. Vonnegut also sees the monumental effects of chemicals in the diseases he witnessed as a boy growing up in Indianapolis: the jerky, robotic movements of syphilitics on the street, the goiters that resulted from too much iodine in a person's diet. When merely ingesting one-millionth of an ounce less of iodine each day can so drastically alter a human being's life, when people can ruin their brains by taking sleeping medication as Vonnegut's mother did, or cheer themselves up by ingesting a tiny pill, as Vonnegut says he does, it is easy to see that the human body is an extremely complex and delicately calibrated instrument.

The impulse to view humans as a conglomeration of chemical reactions quite often, in fact, seems to be a kind and charitable response to pain and suffering. The young patrolman at the end of *Mother Night,* for instance, who wants to go back to school to study chemistry because he believes bad human behavior is the result of faulty chemicals, is certainly a kinder, more humane character than those who want to punish and destroy Howard W. Campbell, Jr. for his Nazi activities. Yet, when Vonnegut writes about his own tendency to view characters this way, he describes it as a "temptation" (4). He writes, "So it is a big temptation to me, when I create a character for a novel, to say that he is what he is because of faulty wiring, or because of microscopic amounts of chemicals which he ate or failed to eat on that particular day" (4). The problem is that this view of human behavior verges dangerously close to the idea that humans are basically automatons, with no free will. This is the idea that Kilgore Trout expresses in his novel, *Now It Can be Told,* the book that provokes Dwayne Hoover

into a savage rampage at the end of the novel. Trout's novel, written in the form of a long letter from the Creator of the Universe to one of his creations, leads Dwayne to believe that he is the only person in the Universe with free will, that all the people surrounding him are merely robots put on Earth to test his responses. This is the "bad idea," according to Vonnegut, that will set Dwayne's "bad chemicals" into motion. "Bad chemicals and bad ideas," Vonnegut writes, "were the Yin and Yang of madness" (14). The bad idea Dwayne digests in the Trout novel—that all human beings except himself are robots—turns Dwayne "into a monster" (14).

Thus, *Breakfast of Champions,* like *Slaughterhouse-Five,* grapples with notions of free will versus DETERMINISM. While it may be tempting to read both novels as advocating a deterministic outlook, as suggesting a kind of nihilistic passivity in the face of human beings' inability to change their world, it is instead exactly this tendency that both novels warn against. The refusal of the Tralfamadorians in *Slaughterhouse-Five* to try to save the universe, despite their foreknowledge of how it will end, along with their willed blindness toward atrocity, are not that much different from Kilgore Trout's giving up of writing about "the way things could be and should be on the planet, as opposed to how they really were" (106), or from Dwayne's deliberate blindness to the pain and suffering he causes to so many people. Things go dreadfully wrong in the world, Vonnegut proposes in *Breakfast of Champions,* when people give up on utopian ideals, when they believe they can have no real effect on other human beings, and when they accept the deterministic view that the future cannot be changed for the better. This is the mindset that initially grips both Vonnegut himself as narrator of the book and his fictional alter ego, Kilgore Trout, but it is also the mindset that both men will overcome by novel's end.

Like any good SATIRE, though, *Breakfast of Champions* must first show what's wrong with the world in its present state before it raises the possibility of redemption or change. And there is plenty that Vonnegut believes is wrong with America in the early 1970s, when the book was written. Following as it does on the heels of the civil rights movement of the 1950s and 60s and the later black power movement of the 1960s and '70s, *Breakfast of Champions* very much takes on the issue of race in America. In chapter 1 of the novel, Vonnegut briefly and sardonically discusses several of the symbols and historical fallacies undermining the American national mythology. He complains that schoolchildren are taught lies about American history: that in 1492, their continent was discovered by human beings, that the European sea pirates who first arrived on the continent "eventually created a government which became a beacon of freedom to human beings everywhere else" (10). Instead, Vonnegut explains to readers, the sea pirates, who were white, used black human beings as "machinery" (11). "Color," he adds, "was everything" (11). Thus, whenever Vonnegut introduces a new character in the book, he mentions that character's race, whether it is the "two lonesome, skinny, fairly old white men" (7) who are the novel's protagonists—Dwayne Hoover and Kilgore Trout—or very minor characters like the "angel-faced white child" (124) Trout glimpses in West Virginia or the unnamed "black bus boy" and "black waiter" (40) who listen to Dwayne sing as he crosses the lobby of the new Holiday Inn. This device forces readers to see and consider race; it is not something we can overlook as we read the novel. In addition, Vonnegut introduces both white and black characters in the same way. While the mainstream tendency in America has been to see whiteness as the norm and blackness as a racially charged deviation, Vonnegut struggles against such a view, requiring readers to consider the racial status of each of his characters, whether the beneficiaries of racial privilege or the victims of racial oppression.

Dwayne Hoover's adoptive father provides a good example of racial prejudice and the resulting racial disparity that is part of the past of Midland City and neighboring Shepherdstown. Dwayne remembers a story his stepfather told him when he was 10 years old: "Why there were no Niggers in Shepherdstown" (244). During World War I, when black Americans migrated in large numbers from the rural South to the more urban, industrialized North, the people of Shepherdstown, Dwayne's stepfather explains, "didn't want Niggers in their

town, so they put up signs on the main roads at the city limits and in the railroad yard" (245). When a black family gets off a boxcar in Shepherdstown one night during the Great Depression, not seeing the signs, or perhaps unable to read them, a white mob attacks and murders the father. Himself a racist who changes his name from Hoobler to Hoover because there are so many blacks named Hoobler in Midland City, Dwayne's stepfather tells the Shepherdstown story "gleefully" (246). The legacy of slavery and racial prejudice is everywhere apparent in contemporary Midland City as well, since most of the black characters, such as Lottie Davis, Dwayne Hoover's maid, Eldon Robbins, a dishwasher at the Holiday Inn, or Wayne Hoobler, just released from the Adult Correctional Institution at Shepherdstown, either work in menial, low-paying jobs or have spent time in prison. When Wayne Hoobler appeals to Dwayne for a job, mentioning the striking similarity of the two men's names, Dwayne, as a white businessman, is blind to the brotherly ties between them that Wayne speaks of; he simply brushes past Wayne, ignoring his plea.

Breakfast of Champions, like previous Vonnegut novels—especially *God Bless You, Mr. Rosewater*—also critiques an unjust capitalist economic system. While pointing out that America is opposed to communism, which Vonnegut describes as "a theory that what was left of the planet should be shared more or less equally among all the people" (12), he explains that America instead has adopted an economic system in which "everybody . . . was supposed to grab whatever he could and hold on to it" (13). The result of such a system, Vonnegut adds, is that "Some Americans were very good at grabbing and holding, were fabulously well-to-do. Others couldn't get their hands on doodley-squat" (13). The people who don't have doodley-squat want their lives to improve. Unable to improve their surroundings, "they did their best to make their insides beautiful instead" (72). In their attempts to change their lives, these people often ingest chemicals, usually with disastrous results. Kilgore Trout, walking in the down-and-out neighborhood of 42nd Street in New York City, witnesses an unconscious 14-year-old white boy who has swallowed a half pint of paint remover and ingested cattle medicine; he is also propositioned by two young black prostitutes who have eaten a tube of Norwegian hemorrhoid remedy. Vonnegut presents the drug problem in America as stemming directly from economic disparity. The whole city of New York is dangerous, he tells readers, largely because of "the uneven distribution of wealth" (71).

But the tragic results of a capitalist economy are seen not only in the seedy neighborhoods of big cities. When Trout is traveling across the country in the Pyramid Company truck, he stops at a diner in West Virginia where he talks to an ex–coal miner who explains that "the mineral rights to the entire county in which they sat were owned by the Rosewater Coal and Iron Company" (129). The old miner tells a story of how he and other miners once tried to force the Rosewater Company to "treat them like human beings" (130). But, the miner explains, "Rosewater always won" (130). The Rosewater family, like the Rumfoords, stand in many Vonnegut novels as symbols of the rich robber barons of late 19th-century America who grew fabulously wealthy, often by profiting off the labor of poorer Americans.

The environmental destruction caused both by Americans' love affair with technology and by large corporations ravishing the American landscape is another target of Vonnegut's satire in the novel. In West Virginia, where Kilgore Trout talks to the old coal miner, he notices that much of the state's surface has been demolished as men and machinery have tried to make the ground yield up its coal. Vonnegut describes the environmental disaster left behind by strip mining:

> The surface of West Virginia, with its coal and trees and topsoil gone, was rearranging what was left of itself in conformity with the laws of gravity. It was collapsing into all the holes which had been dug into it. Its mountains, which had once found it easy to stand by themselves, were sliding into valleys now.
>
> The demolition of West Virginia had taken place with the approval of the executive, legislative, and judicial branches of the State Government, which drew their power from the people. (123)

Vonnegut notes the irony in the fact that the government, supposedly "of the people, by the people, for the people," to quote from ABRAHAM LINCOLN's GETTYSBURG ADDRESS, has approved the practices of a coal industry that not only strips the earth of its beauty, but that treats its workers little better than slave labor. The theme of environmental disaster continues when Lyle and Kyle Hoover report to Dwayne about the creeping toxic waste that threatens to destroy the Sacred Miracle Cave. The underground stream that passes through the cave is increasingly "polluted by some sort of industrial waste which formed bubbles as tough as ping-pong balls" (119). The bubbles are rising in the cave passageways, threatening to engulf the main tourist attractions, especially the Cathedral of Whispers, a large, natural opening that has served as the setting for numerous weddings and funerals. Of course, the Hoovers do not seem particularly concerned about the lurking environmental disaster in the cave, not so much as with the potential loss of tourist revenue. The cave's natural beauty had already been commodified and commercialized before being poisoned by industrial waste. At the end of the novel, readers will see that the toxic residue in the caves has seeped out to infect Sugar Creek, the stream running through Midland City itself. When Kilgore Trout wades through the creek on his way to the Holiday Inn, his feet become completely encased in a thin, tough plastic film, a fitting symbol for the ways human destruction of the natural environment may eventually suffocate us and may become the shroud entwining the entire human race.

Yet, Kilgore Trout, who used to be a conservationist who lamented the destruction of the natural world, tells the Pyramid truck driver that he is no longer affected the same way by the devastation he sees: "I used to weep and wail about people shooting bald eagles . . . , but I gave it up. There's a river in Cleveland which is so polluted that it catches fire about once a year. That used to make me sick, but I laugh about it now" (86). Trout tells the truck driver he realized that "God wasn't any conservationist, so for anybody else to be one was sacrilegious and a waste of time" (87). Though the truck driver (and probably the reader as well) has a hard time determining whether Trout is being serious or not, his cynicism is evidence of the despair that he has fallen into. Although he used to write stories warning about the dangers that accompany technological advancements, such as *Plague on Wheels*, about Kago who brings automobile technology to Earth, unwittingly causing all life on the planet to die, Trout now nonchalantly declares that he accepts the environmental destruction he used to bemoan. Vonnegut writes about Trout, "his head no longer sheltered ideas of how things could be and should be on the planet, as opposed to how they really were. There was only one way for the Earth to be, he thought: the way it was" (105–106). Trout has accepted a deterministic worldview.

Along with its critiques of the social ills of racism, economic disparity, and environmental destruction, *Breakfast of Champions* is the first Vonnegut novel that moves toward a critique of gender oppression in America. While many of Vonnegut's female characters in previous novels come across as selfish, mean-spirited, or rather simple-minded compared to the often kinder and more thoughtful men (Anita Proteus in *Player Piano*, Beatrice Rumfoord in *The Sirens of Titan*, Diana Moon Glampers in *God Bless You, Mr. Rosewater*, Valencia Merble in *Slaughterhouse-Five*), in *Breakfast of Champions*, Vonnegut begins to analyze gender differences in a more probing way. When he introduces Patty Keane, the 17-year-old Burger Chef waitress, for instance, he notes that she "was stupid on purpose, which was the case with most women in Midland City" (140). Although women have "big minds" because they, like men, are "big animals," Vonnegut points out that, "in the interests of survival, [women] trained themselves to be agreeing machines instead of thinking machines" (140). Here, Vonnegut recognizes that women are as mentally capable as men, but that social training and opportunity can account for inequality in gender achievement. Lacking social opportunity, women must have friends and make themselves agreeable in order to get along in the world.

In addition, Vonnegut is more sympathetic in this novel to a homosexual character than he had been in the past. While Bunny Weeks seems a pale imitation of a "real man" such as Harry Pena in *God Bless You, Mr. Rosewater*, in *Breakfast of Champions*, Bunny Hoover is presented as a complex character deserving of readers' respect and sympathy. Vonnegut condemns Dwayne's decision to send Bunny to military school when Bunny, as a 10-year-old child announces he would rather be a woman than a man, because "what men did was so often cruel and ugly" (184). Military schools, according to Vonnegut, are institutions "devoted to homicide and absolutely humorless obedience" (184). Vonnegut himself has much in common with Bunny, as both their mothers were "beautiful in exotic ways," both "boiled over with chaotic talk about love and peace and wars and evil and desperation" (186), and both committed suicide, leaving painful legacies that their sons must learn to cope with. *Breakfast of Champions*, Vonnegut hints, is largely about his attempts to come to terms with his mother's suicide. While American novelist Thomas Wolfe's editor told him to keep in mind the unifying idea of a hero's search for a father as he wrote, Vonnegut believes that it may be more important for authors to search for mothers. "It seems to me," he writes, "that really truthful American novels would have the heroes and heroines alike looking for *mothers* instead. This needn't be embarrassing. It's simply true. A mother is much more useful" (276).

The longing for a mother expressed in this novel suggests the desire for a nurturing, uncritical type of love, for strong bonds with fellow human beings. We have seen that this type of bond is something that both Kilgore Trout and Vonnegut himself seem to have lost as the novel opens. Trout believes he is a failure, that his writing has no appreciable effect on people, and he decides to travel to Midland City as "a representative of all the thousands of artists who devoted their entire lives to a search for truth and beauty—and didn't find doodley-squat!" (37). Vonnegut believes much the same thing about his own work. He feels lousy about his novel, he tells readers in his preface, saying that it was written by Philboyd Studge, a fictive persona suggesting a clumsy, lumbering, pedantic author. Even more, Vonnegut feels completely adrift in America of the early 1970s. *Breakfast of Champions,* he writes, is an attempt to clear his head of all the junk that is in there. He laments, "I have no culture, no humane harmony in my brains. I can't live without a culture anymore" (5). As the son of a suicide, he confides, his greatest fear is that he, too, will commit suicide.

Yet, despite all its depiction of social ills, its satire of an America that has lost its way, *Breakfast of Champions* is a story of redemption as well. Both fictional author Kilgore Trout and narrator-author Kurt Vonnegut come to realize at the novel's end that they do indeed have an effect on other human beings, that their art is not as meaningless or ignored as they might have thought. Ironically, Trout is awakened to the effect of his words on others by the savage rampage Dwayne Hoover embarks on after reading Trout's novel *Now It Can Be Told.* Vonnegut writes, "It shook up Trout to realize that even *he* could bring evil into the world—in the form of bad ideas" (15). But the recognition that he is capable of affecting the world enough to bring evil into it changes Trout significantly. After Dwayne is taken to a lunatic asylum, Trout "became a fanatic on the importance of ideas as causes and cures for diseases" (15). No longer content to let the world determine his fate, Trout makes use of the free will inherent in all human beings; he becomes a mental health researcher and advocate, disguising his theories as science fiction, and achieving recognition as a great artist and scientist. When Trout dies, a quote from his last novel, which could serve as an epitaph for Vonnegut's body of work as well, is carved on his tombstone: "We are healthy only to the extent that our ideas are humane" (16).

But perhaps even more important in the novel is the transformation and rebirth of Vonnegut himself, in what he calls the "spiritual climax of this book" (224). When he enters the cocktail lounge in the Holiday Inn, Vonnegut tells us, "I had come to the conclusion that there was nothing sacred about myself or about any human being, that we were all machines, doomed to collide and collide and collide" (225). Having given in to the "temptation" he describes in the book's preface, that of

viewing human beings in a mechanistic way, and thus accepting a deterministic outlook on human existence, the last thing Vonnegut expects is to be rescued by one of his own characters. He especially does not expect to be saved by artist Rabo Karabekian, who was, in Vonnegut's opinion, "a vain and weak and trashy man, no artist at all" (225). Yet, in a moving testament to the power of the human imagination, Vonnegut's own creation surprises him. In response to Bonnie MacMahon's heated comment that she does not think much of his painting, that she has seen better pictures done by a five-year-old, Karabekian slides off his barstool, standing up to face the crowd that has gathered. He explains to the crowd his stripped-down painting:

> "It is a picture of the awareness of every animal. It is the immaterial core of every animal—the 'I am' to which all messages are sent. It is all that is alive in any of us. . . . It is unwavering and pure, no matter what preposterous adventure may befall us. A sacred picture of Saint Anthony alone is one vertical, unwavering band of light. If a cockroach were near him, or a cocktail waitress, the picture would show two such bands of light. Our awareness is all that is alive and maybe sacred in any of us. Everything else about us is dead machinery." (226)

With these words, Karabekian restores Vonnegut's faith in the sacred nature of human beings, countering his earlier suggestion that people are simply rubbery test tubes filled with seething chemical reactions. Salvation in this novel, as in the work of mid-20th-century American writer Flannery O'Connor, comes from the least likely of places. Since Karabekian is Vonnegut's fictional creation, salvation for Vonnegut comes through his own art, an art he had previously disparaged and was ready to give up.

The art that offers redemption, though, a new way of seeing the world, must be a new kind of art. While Rabo Karabekian's minimal painting strips away the superfluities and distractions of everyday existence to show the sacred nature of human beings, Vonnegut's novel strips away literary convention, also in an attempt to lend dignity and value to human existence. As in *Slaughterhouse-Five*, where traditional war narratives can glamorize violence and convince children to take up arms, Vonnegut in *Breakfast of Champions* criticizes conventional storytelling. As Vonnegut approaches his 50th birthday, he realizes that it was "innocent and natural" for people "to behave so abominably, and with such abominable results" (215). They are simply "doing their best to live like people invented in story books," he explains (215). Americans shoot one another so often because shooting is a common literary device, a way to end books. Americans are treated by their governments as unimportant because "that was the way authors customarily treated bit-part players in their made-up tales" (215). The new art Vonnegut visualizes refuses to fall into the trap of old-fashioned storytellers who make people believe life has leading characters, significant details, lessons to be learned, a beginning, a middle, and an end. He decides to "shun storytelling" and instead, "write about life" (215). All people in his books will be equally important, all facts will be equally weighty, nothing will be left out. Vonnegut's theory of a new kind of storytelling explains the form of *Breakfast of Champions*, the inclusion of all the simple felt-tip pen drawings, the facts about men's penis size, the perfect willingness to follow any digression that occurs to him. His book is chaotic because he believes human beings must adapt to the requirements of chaos; we do not live in an orderly world, and orderly literature is therefore a lie. Vonnegut is a writer for whom art matters, but he recognizes that in a messy, POSTMODERN, fragmented world, art itself must be messy, postmodern, and fragmented as well.

The novel ends with Vonnegut overturning what is perhaps the most rigid boundary in conventional literary fiction—the separation of the real world of the author from the fictional world of his characters. In a burst of generosity following his transformation upon hearing Karabekian's speech, Vonnegut decides to introduce himself to his character Kilgore Trout, and like Tolstoy freeing his serfs at the age of 50, sets Trout free. Kilgore Trout, after all, Vonnegut explains, is the only character he ever created "who had

enough imagination to suspect that he might be the creation of another human being" (246). The confrontation between Trout and his Creator, Vonnegut, shows how created worlds can take on a life of their own. Vonnegut imagines his fiction, but cannot fully control it. He is like the god in the Kilgore Trout story *Now It Can Be Told*, who is constantly surprised by the actions of the man he creates. Kazak, the large black Doberman pinscher who appeared in an earlier version of the novel, refuses to be cut out of the book completely; Vonnegut has some difficulty convincing Trout he is who he says he is.

Though art can be chaotic and unruly, as we have seen, it still matters to Vonnegut. As in his earlier novels *Player Piano* and *Cat's Cradle*, *Breakfast of Champions* recognizes and asserts the beauty of symbols and symbolic action, and in doing so, the value of art itself. "Symbols can be beautiful" (206), Vonnegut tells readers earlier in the book when he includes a drawing of an apple. And it is an apple that Vonnegut offers Kilgore Trout at the novel's end. Symbols are perhaps so beautiful to Vonnegut because they are messy and indeterminate; in literature symbols carry an array of meanings, meanings so complex that they can sometimes be difficult to articulate fully. In the Christian tradition, apples are associated with the fall of man, the entrance of sin into the world. In the Garden of Eden, God forbids Adam and Eve to eat apples from the tree of knowledge of good and evil. Yet, in *Breakfast of Champions*, Vonnegut the Creator offers Kilgore Trout, his Adam, an apple as a final gift. He offers Trout knowledge rather than trying to keep it from him, and unlike the Christian god, Vonnegut accepts the inevitability of sin in the human world.

Mirrors are another example of the beauty of symbolism in the novel. It is telling that, throughout the key scene in the cocktail lounge, Vonnegut wears mirrored sunglasses. Though he claims simply that he does not want to be recognized, the symbolism associated with the mirrored glasses is rich and provocative. When Vonnegut's characters look at the Creator of the Universe, what they see reflected back is an image of themselves. Vonnegut perhaps suggests here that humans create gods in their own

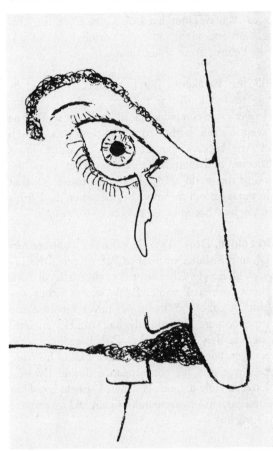

Illustration of Vonnegut with tear, from *Breakfast of Champions* (used by permission of Dell Publishing, a division of Random House, Inc.)

images; they imagine gods who reflect their own needs and desires. The mirroring image works to tie Kilgore Trout to Vonnegut as well. Often said by critics to be Vonnegut's alter ego, Trout's final plea to his Creator, "*Make me young, make me young, make me young!*" (302), reflects Vonnegut's own uneasiness as he approaches his 50th birthday, his sorrow about the passing of time, about the inevitability of death and decay in the human world. A tear leaks out of his eye as he holds a mirror up to his face. The books itself becomes a mirror—an item that Kilgore Trout actually calls a leak—as life is reflected in art, and as art reflects that life back to us.

CHARACTERS AND RELATED ENTRIES

"And so on" The phrase "And so on" is used throughout *Breakfast of Champions* as a kind of punctuation mark—it frequently ends short passages or acts as a transition phrase between passages. Reminiscent of the phrase "So it goes," used throughout his previous novel, *Slaughterhouse-Five*, the repeated refrain "And so on" seems to some critics and reviewers an almost gimmicky attempt on Vonnegut's part to replicate the success of his previous book. Yet, the phrase captures one of the key themes of *Breakfast of Champions*: Vonnegut's attempt to create a new kind of storytelling. The phrase signals to readers that what he is able to include in the novel is not all of life, with nothing left out, as he would like to do. "And so on" suggests that there is more out there, that despite Vonnegut's best attempts, a book is a finite medium that cannot include the totality of messy, chaotic human existence. But the phrase at least acknowledges the book's attempt to do so, and thus distinguishes it from the type of storytelling that Vonnegut says in the book he will "shun"—storytelling that makes people believe real life has "leading characters, minor characters, significant details . . . lessons to be learned . . . and a beginning, a middle, and an end" (215).

Arthur Vonnegut tells readers that part of cocktail waitress Bonnie MacMahon's fortune, which he never gets a chance to tell her, is that her brother, Arthur, will find eleven dollars in a taxicab in Atlanta.

Bannister, George Hickman George Hickman Bannister was a 17-year-old boy who was killed while playing high school football in Midland City in 1924. He now has the largest tombstone in Calvary Cemetery, and the high school field house is named after him.

Barry, Fred T. The chairman of the Midland City Festival of the Arts, Fred T. Barry is also the wealthiest man in Midland City and owner of the Barrytron Corporation, which had started out selling washing machines under the name Robo-Magic during the

Depression years. Fred T. Barry pays for the new Center of the Arts, a building that looks like "a translucent sphere on stilts" (32), and arranges to purchase the extremely expensive minimal painting by Rabo Karabekian. While Fred Barry is the same age as Kilgore Trout, the two men do not look anything alike; Barry, in fact, as he grows older and happier, and loses more and more of his hair, comes to look like an "ecstatic old Chinaman" (33).

Barry, Mildred   Mildred Barry is the late mother of wealthy Midland City businessman and arts patron Fred T. Barry. The new Mildred Barry Memorial Center for the Arts in Midland City is named for her, and the large arts festival is organized to celebrate the center's opening. A former music hall entertainer in England, Mildred could imitate the calls of numerous birds of the British Empire. The black servants who worked for the Barry family found this hilarious and learned to mimic the bird calls perfectly. The craze spread over the years, so that at the novel's present time almost all black people in Midland City can imitate the birds as well.

Barry, Sr.   Fred T. Barry's father, whose first name we never learn, made a fortune as a bootlegger and swindler during the 1920s. During the Depression, Mr. Barry, Sr. kept all his money in cash and thus retained his wealth. Barry also worked as an property agent for Chicago gangsters who wanted their children and grandchildren to get into legitimate businesses.

Barrytron Ltd.   Barrytron Ltd. is a weapons-manufacturing company founded by Fred T. Barry. Barry also serves as chairman of the Midland City Festival of the Arts, the group that invites Kilgore Trout to the city as a visiting artist. Barrytron Ltd., which began life as an automatic washing machine company called Robo-Magic in 1934, also figures into the novel *Hocus Pocus*. Eugene Debs Hartke's father, a chemical engineer, is employed by Barrytron as "Vice-President in Charge of Research and Development" (24).

Bearse, Alfy   Kilgore Trout, like Vonnegut himself, has difficulty remembering people's names and faces. When Trout lived on CAPE COD, the only acquaintance he could greet warmly by name was Alfy Bearse, a one-armed albino.

Bill the Parakeet   Bill is a parakeet owned by Kilgore Trout. Just as the dog Sparky is Dwayne Hoover's sole companion at night, Trout is all alone except for Bill. Both men talk to their pets, though Dwayne babbles about love while Kilgore Trout "sneered and muttered to his parakeet about the end of the world" (18). Trout also teases Bill that the parakeet will die before he does when the Earth's atmosphere becomes too poisonous to breathe.

Breedlove, Don   Don Breedlove is a gas-conversion unit installer who raped Patty Keene, the 17-year-old Burger Chef waitress, after a local high school basketball game. Patty, whose father was dying of cancer at the time, never reported the crime because she already had trouble enough. Later, readers find out that Don Breedlove is no teenager, but has a wife and three kids of his own. Breedlove gets his comeuppance during Dwayne Hoover's violent rampage when Dwayne hits Don in the ear, causing tremendous pain and permanent hearing loss.

Brown, Payton   During his rampage in and around the Holiday Inn, Dwayne Hoover tells ex-convict Wayne Hoobler about a young black man named Payton Brown whose life Dwayne tried to save unsuccessfully. At age 15-and-a-half, Payton Brown became the youngest person to die in the electric chair at the Shepherdstown Adult Correctional Institution.

Browning, Gloria   Gloria Browning is a 25-year-old cashier at Dwayne Hoover's Pontiac Village. She has recently had a hysterectomy following a botched abortion. Don Breedlove, the gas-conversion unit installer who raped Patty Keane, was the father of the fetus.

Burger, Knox   KNOX BURGER is a friend Vonnegut cites in the novel's preface, who one time said that a clunky novel ". . . read as though it had been written by Philboyd Studge" (4). Vonnegut then adds that he himself feels like Philboyd Studge when he is writing.

Cohen, Abe   A Midland City jeweler who is in the Holiday Inn cocktail lounge to witness Rabo Karabekian's defense of minimalist art, Abe Cohen comments that, "If artists would explain more, people would like art more" (241).

Davis, Benjamin   Vonnegut tells readers that, in an earlier version of *Breakfast of Champions*, he had Benjamin Davis, the husband of Dwayne Hoover's maid Lottie Davis, take care of Kazak, the big black Doberman pinscher who attacks Vonnegut at the end of the novel. A trumpet player with the Midland City Symphony Orchestra, Benjamin Davis does not get paid for his symphony work, so he moonlights as Kazak's trainer.

Davis, Lottie   Lottie Davis is Dwayne Hoover's black servant, who cleans and cooks for him. Though she and Dwayne like each other a lot, they do not talk much. In an earlier version of the book, Vonnegut tells readers, he gave Lottie a husband, Benjamin Davis, who cared for the giant Doberman pinscher, Kazak, that attacks Vonnegut in the novel's epilogue.

di Capistrano, Paulo   Vonnegut tells readers that, four days after the end of the novel, freed convict Wayne Hoobler will be picked up and questioned by policemen for suspicious behavior outside Barrytron Ltd. He will be found carrying a membership card to the Playboy Club of America, made out to Paulo di Capistrano, which he had found in the garbage can in back of the new Holiday Inn.

Don   An astronaut in a novel Kilgore Trout makes up while he is watching pornographic movies in New York, Don, whose last name readers never learn, visits a planet where all animal and plant life, except for humanoids, has been killed by pollution. The humanoids now eat food made from petroleum and coal. They take Don to see a dirty movie on their planet, which consists of close-up shots of humanoids eating ordinary food until they are glutted.

Fairchild, Will   The man that the Midland City airport is named after, Will Fairchild was a war hero and maternal uncle of gothic novelist Beatrice Keedsler. One night in 1926, Fairchild shot five of his relatives to death, along with three servants, two policemen, numerous animals, and finally himself. An autopsy showed that Will Fairchild suffered from a brain tumor that caused him to commit the murders.

Fairyland   Ex-convict Wayne Hoobler fantasizes about a better world, which he privately calls "Fairyland." Hoobler imagines the word written in lights and capital letters inside his head. Later, when Hoobler sees the runway lights from the Will Fairchild Memorial Airport all lit up at night, he believes that he is finally viewing the Fairyland that he had so long imagined.

Farrow, Dudley   Dudley Farrow is a hunter in the Kilgore Trout novel *The Smart Bunny*, about a female rabbit who is as smart as SHAKESPEARE and EINSTEIN. The rabbit decides her mind is a liability like a tumor and decides to have it removed, but before she can make it to the city, Farrow shoots and kills her.

Farrow, Grace   Grace Farrow is the wife of Dudley Farrow in the Kilgore Trout novel *The Smart Bunny*. After Dudley kills the genius rabbit, he and Grace decide not to eat her, because of her overly large head, which they fear is the result of disease.

Garr, Mary   Mary Garr is the wife of Vernon Garr, a mechanice at Dwayne Hoover's Exit Eleven Pontiac Village. Mary is a schizophrenic who believes that Vernon is "trying to turn her brains into plutonium" (42), thus keeping Vernon from noticing the strange behavior of Dwayne Hoover.

Garr, Vernon   Vernon Garr is a white mechanic who works for Dwayne Hoover at his Midland City Pontiac agency. When Harry LeSabre believes that Dwayne is acting strangely, he tells Francine Pefko, Dwayne's secretary, to ask Vernon Garr whether Dwayne is still the same.

"Good-bye Blue Monday"   The phrase "Good-bye Blue Monday" becomes a repeated refrain in *Breakfast of Champions* as well as the novel's subtitle. It was originally the motto of the Midland City Robo-Magic Corporation, which produced automatic washing machines during the Great Depression. Women traditionally did the family washing on Mondays, and the new machines promised to make their lives easier. As the company changed names and directions over the years, eventually becoming Barrytron, Limited, the motto stuck. Dwayne Hoover, who was a civilian employee of the U.S. Army Air Corps during World War II, is also said to have painted the motto on a 500-pound bomb that was to be dropped on Hamburg, Germany.

Gooz   Gooz is the main character in the Kilgore Trout novel called *The Barring-gaffner of Bagnialto* or *This Year's Masterpiece*, the book that served as toilet paper in the Georgia jail cell of the Pyramid truck driver. The novel is set on a planet where the value of artworks is based on the spin of a wheel of chance. A humble cobbler named Gooz paints a picture of a cat, which, with one spin of the wheel, becomes worth 18,055 *lambos*, the equivalent of 1 billion Earthling dollars.

Harper, Colonel Looseleaf   Colonel Looseleaf Harper is the pilot of Eliot Rosewater's chartered plane that lands at the Will Fairchild Memorial Airport in Midland City shortly after Dwayne Hoover has been arrested for injuring 11 people. The plane's landing is what causes the runways to light up and look like Fairyland to ex-convict Wayne Hoobler. Vonnegut claims that Colonel Harper was the pilot who dropped an ATOMIC BOMB on Nagasaki, Japan, but he is actually a fictional creation of Vonnegut's.

Heath, Durling   Kilgore Trout has difficulty remembering the names and faces of casual acquaintances. In Cohoes, New York, where he is living when the novel begins, the only person he calls by name is a red-headed Cockney midget named Durling Heath. Trout drops by the shoe repair shop where Heath works frequently, to chatter idly.

Heath, in his Cockney accent, eventually screams at Trout: "Stop bloody *hounding* me!" (108).

Hoobler, Josephus   The farm on which the Sacred Miracle Cave was discovered was started by an ex-slave named Josephus Hoobler, who was freed by his master. Hoobler's descendents continued to run the farm until the Depression years, when the mortgage was foreclosed. Dwayne Hoover's bigoted stepfather contemptuously referred to the land as ". . . a God damn Nigger farm" (121).

Hoobler, Wayne   Wayne Hoobler, a 26-year-old young black man just released from the Adult Correctional Institution in Shepherdstown, is first seen polishing cars in the lot at Dwayne Hoover's Pontiac dealership. While in prison, he had read Dwayne's newspaper ads, and he hopes to get a job working for Dwayne, especially since the two men's names are so similar. Yet, Dwayne's bad chemicals initially make him ignore Wayne Hoobler. At the end of the novel, when Dwayne goes on his violent rampage and attacks Wayne in the car lot, Wayne dodges every blow aimed at him, making Dwayne believe he is fighting a dodging machine. At the end of their confrontation, all the lights at the Will Fairchild Memorial Airport, across the Interstate from the Pontiac dealership, come on at once. Wayne believes the airport is the Fairyland that he's dreamed of.

Hoover, Celia   Celia Hoover is the late wife of Pontiac dealer Dwayne Hoover. She committed suicide by eating Drano, after keeping secret that she had gone "crazy as a bedbug" (185).

Hoover, Dwayne   One of the novel's protagonists, Dwayne Hoover is an aging Pontiac dealer in Midland City. Although he is "fabulously well-to-do" (13), owning portions of numerous businesses around town, Dwayne has had a difficult life. His wife, Celia, committed suicide by eating Drano, and he is estranged from his homosexual, piano-playing son, Bunny. Dwayne is also going insane as the novel begins—bad chemicals in his head are making him think and act in peculiar ways. The action of the novel works to bring Dwayne ever closer to his doom, as the science fiction writer Kilgore Trout, whose ideas will spark a savage rampage on Dwayne's part, travels to Midland City. When the two men meet in the cocktail lounge of the Midland City Holiday Inn, Dwayne snatches Trout's novel *Now It Can Be Told* from him, believing it will provide him the answers he has been seeking from life. The novel leads Dwayne to believe he is the only creature in the universe with free will, and that all other people are machines. Fully accepting this delusion, Dwayne brutally beats 11 people, including his son, Bunny, and his mistress/secretary, Francine Pefko. He bites off the tip of Kilgore Trout's index finger as well. Though we never see Dwayne after he is bundled off to the mental hospital, Vonnegut tells readers that he will be sued by all the people he injured to the extent that he loses all his money, ending up destitute on Skid Row.

Hoover, George "Bunny" The homosexual son of Dwayne Hoover, Bunny Hoover makes his living playing piano in the cocktail lounge of the Midland City Holiday Inn. When he had told his father, at age 10, that he wished he were a woman because "what men did was so often cruel and ugly" (184), he was sent to military school, where he earned high grades and many medals. Bunny currently lives on Skid Row, though, and is estranged from Dwayne. At the end of the novel, Bunny will be the first person Dwayne cruelly attacks after reading the Kilgore Trout novel that convinces him other humans are really just machines.

Hoover, Lyle and Kyle The twins Lyle and Kyle Hoover are Dwayne Hoover's younger stepbrothers, the natural children of Dwayne's adoptive parents. They own the Sacred Miracle Cave in partnership with Dwayne, and live in matching yellow ranch houses on either side of the Cave gift shop and entranceway. Readers meet Lyle and Kyle when they arrive at Dwayne's Pontiac dealership to inform him that the industrial pollution infecting the cave is creeping ever higher, threatening some of the cave's chief tourist draws.

Hoover, Mrs. Dwayne Hoover's adoptive mother, whose first name is never given, is the natural mother of the twins Lyle and Kyle Hoover. She and Mr. Hoover adopted Dwayne, believing they could never have children of their own, but the adoption seemed to trigger something in their bodies that allowed them to have children after all.

Hoover, Sr. Readers never learn the first name of Dwayne Hoover's adoptive father, referred to as his "stepfather" by Vonnegut. We do discover, though, that the man was a racist bigot, referring to Bluebird Farm, started by ex-slave Josephus Hoobler as ". . . a God damn Nigger farm" (121), and changing his name from Hoobler to Hoover when he moved from West Virginia to Midland City because there were so many black people in Midland City named Hoobler.

Hurty, Phoebe Phoebe Hurty is the woman to whom Vonnegut dedicates the novel. A 40-year-old widow when the 16-year-old Vonnegut meets her during the Great Depression, Phoebe Hurty wrote an advice-to-the-lovelorn column for the Indianapolis *Times* as well as advertisements for a local department store. She hires the young Vonnegut to write ad copy, and he soon becomes friends with her two teenage sons. Vonnegut writes that Phoebe Hurty was bawdy, funny and liberating, and taught him to be impolite in his thinking and conversation, something he now makes his living doing.

Joyce, Leroy Cocktail waitress Bonnie MacMahon tells visiting artists Beatrice Keedsler and Rabo Karabekian the story of Leroy Joyce, which she heard from her husband, a guard at the Shepherdstown Adult Correctional Institution. Sentenced to the electric chair for rape, Leroy Joyce cuts off his own penis, puts it in a cup, and gives it to a guard, believing that this will negate his death sentence.

Kago The main character in Kilgore Trout's novel *Plague on Wheels*, Kago is a tiny Zeltoldimarian who visits a planet inhabited by automobilelike creatures that are slowly going extinct. Although the Zeltoldimarian crew is too tiny to save the automobile creatures, they roam the universe, telling everyone they meet how wonderful the now extinct beings had been. They eventually arrive on Earth, and not realizing how strongly ideas affect Earthlings, Kago and his crew tell them about the automobile planet. Within a century of Kago's visit, Earthlings have destroyed their own planet by building automobiles that they come to worship. Kago is killed while attempting to explain the evils of the automobile in a bar in Detroit; mistaking Kago for a kitchen match, an automobile worker tries to strike him repeatedly on the underside of the bar.

Karabekian, Rabo Rabo Karabekian is a minimal painter invited to be a visiting artist at the Midland City Arts Festival. His painting, *The Temptation of Saint Anthony*, is the most expensive piece of art purchased for the permanent collection of the new Mildred Barry Memorial Center for the Arts. Karabekian's painting consists of a thin vertical strip of Day-Glo orange reflecting tape set against an avocado green background. When Karabekian insults local heroine Mary Alice Miller in the cocktail lounge of the Holiday Inn, waitress Bonnie MacMahon blows up, telling him the citizens of Midland City don't think much of his painting, that a five-year-old could have done better. Karabekian rises and gives an impassioned defense of minimalist art, which causes Vonnegut, as a character in his own book, to undergo a spiritual rebirth of sorts.

Kazak Kazak is the name of the Doberman pinscher that attacks Vonnegut right before his meeting with Kilgore Trout at the end of the novel. Vonnegut tells us that Kazak had been a leading character in an earlier version of *Breakfast of Champions* and points out that the materials writers work with can be quite dangerous. Kazak shares a name with the large black dog belonging to Winston Niles Rumfoord in *The Sirens of Titan*.

Keedsler, Beatrice Beatrice Keedsler is a gothic novelist who grew up in Midland City and is invited back to be honored at the Arts Festival. She has several drinks with Rabo Karabekian in the Holiday Inn cocktail lounge, witnesses his impassioned defense of minimalist art, and is socked in the jaw by Dwayne Hoover on his violent rampage.

Keene, Mr. The father of 17-year-old waitress Patty Keene dies of colon cancer, leaving his teenage daughter greatly in debt, because of all the medical bills. As Vonnegut points out, in this country, "one of the most expensive things a person could do was get sick" (139).

Keene, Patty Patty Keene is a 17-year-old waitress at the Burger Chef owned by Dwayne Hoover. Her father has recently died of cancer, leaving Patty with enormous medical bills to pay. When Dwayne comes into the restaurant to eat, Patty is thrilled, believing that Dwayne, with his great wealth, could solve all her problems. She also feels sorry for Dwayne, because of his wife's suicide, his son's homosexuality, and his dog's lack of a tail, and would like to comfort him with "her young body, with her bravery and cheerfulness" (147). Yet, when Patty gets the courage to call Dwayne on the phone later that night, he has already been on his rampage and is occupying a padded cell at the County Hospital.

Key, Eddie The ambulance driver of the emergency vehicle that transports the injured people to the hospital at the end of the novel, Eddie Key, though considered a black man, is a direct descendant of Francis Scott Key, the white author of "The Star-Spangled Banner." Eddie has memorized huge amounts of his family's history, familiarizing him with a "teeming past" (279) that makes life much more interesting to him than it is to Dwayne Hoover or to Kilgore Trout or to most white people in Midland City.

Lancer and his Owner Vonnegut tells readers that the dog excrement Kilgore Trout gets on his clothing during the attack by the Pluto Gang comes from a greyhound named Lancer owned by a girl he used to know in New York. Because Lancer and the girl lived in a tiny, one-room apartment six flights up, the dog's "entire life was devoted to unloading his excrement at the proper time and place" (203).

Lembrig, Dr. Thor Vonnegut tells readers that when Kilgore Trout is a very old man he will be asked by Dr. Thor Lembrig, the secretary-general of the United Nations, if he fears the future. Trout will respond, "Mr Secretary-General, it is the *past* which scares the bejesus out of me" (192).

LeSabre, Grace Grace LeSabre is the wife of Harry LeSabre, the sales manager at Dwayne Hoover's Exit Eleven Pontiac Village. Contemptuous of Dwayne and of Midland City in general, Grace is more interested in her sex life and average number of monthly orgasms than in staying in Midland City, "the asshole of the Universe" (168). She persuades Harry to move to Maui with her after Dwayne's bad chemicals make him treat Harry cruelly at the car dealership.

LeSabre, Harry Dwayne Hoover's sales manager at the Pontiac agency, Harry LeSabre, is a closet transvestite who is terrified that his secret has been discovered when Dwayne's bad chemicals make him chastise Harry for his drab style of dress. When Harry shows up for Hawaiian Week at the Pontiac dealership dressed in a green leotard, grass skirt, and pink T-shirt that reads "Make Love, Not War," Dwayne ignores him, further adding to Harry's fears. Harry is later convinced by his wife, Grace, with whom he has a rich sex life, to "split to a condominium on Maui and *live* for a change" (168).

LeSabre Maid Grace and Harry LeSabre employ a black maid whose name is never given but who is referred to by the couple as "the reindeer," a code word the LeSabres use to refer to all black people so that they can speak about racial matters without giving offense.

Lieber, Andy Hitchhiking to Midland City, the second ride Kilgore Trout accepts is with Andy Lieber, a traveling salesman in a Ford Galaxie. An overweight, 32-year-old white man, Lieber is happy with his life since he sets his own hours and chooses the products he sells. He tells Trout that he is "one of the few remaining free men in America" (172). Lieber lets Trout out close to Midland City, when traffic has stopped because of an accident, and Trout walks the rest of the way to the Holiday Inn.

Lingamon, Cynthia Anne Cynthia Anne is an infant who is killed for excessive crying by her own father, Ned Lingamon, the most-decorated veteran in Midland City.

Lingamon, Ned Having served in Vietnam, Ned Lingamon is the most-decorated veteran in Midland City. On the afternoon before Dwayne Hoover's rampage, Lingamon calls his friend Harold Newcomb Wilbur, the bartender at the Holiday Inn cocktail lounge, to tell him that he, Lingamon, is in jail for killing his infant daughter, Cynthia Anne.

MacMahon, Bonnie Bonnie MacMahon is the cocktail waitress at the lounge of the Midland City Holiday Inn who says "Breakfast of Champions" every time she serves a martini. She blows up at Rabo Karabekian when the artist insults local heroine Mary Alice Miller, telling him the residents of Midland City don't think much of his painting, and prompting Karabekian's inspired defense of minimalist art.

MacMahon, Ralph The husband of cocktail waitress Bonnie MacMahon, Ralph MacMahon is a guard in the Sexual Offender's Wing of the Adult Correctional Institution at Shepherdstown. Bonnie is forced to work as a waitress because Ralph lost all their money by investing in a car wash.

Maritimo, Dr. Alfred Midland City's leading orthodontist, Dr. Alfred Maritimo is also part-owner of the new Holiday Inn, along with Dwayne Hoover and Bill Miller.

Maritimo, Carlo Carlo Maritimo is a partner in the Maritimo Brothers Construction Company. He is in the cocktail lounge of the Holiday Inn to witness artist Rabo Karabekian's defense of minimalist art; afterward he marvels with other city residents about their new understanding of Karabekian's painting.

Maritimo, Gino Gino Maritimo is one of the partners in the Maritimo Brothers Construction Company, which is responsible for the pollution in Sugar Creek. Gino is the dope king of Midland City and the uncle of arts aficionado Milo Maritimo.

Maritimo, Guillermo "Little Willie"   The grandfather of Milo Maritimo, "Little Willie" Maritimo was a bodyguard of famous gangster Al Capone.

Maritimo, Milo   Milo Maritimo is a "beautiful young desk clerk" (235) at the Midland City Holiday Inn. A graduate of the Cornell Hotel School, Milo is the homosexual grandson of Guillermo "Little Willie" Maritimo, a bodyguard of Al Capone. Milo greets Kilgore Trout effusively when he arrives at the hotel, having read Eliot Rosewater's entire collection of Trout stories and novels. Milo is thrilled about the Midland City Arts Festival, believing that it will bring an artistic renaissance to the city.

Martha the Psychiatrist   Vonnegut mentions that the name of his psychiatrist is also Martha, like his character Martha Simmons, who dies of rabies after being bitten by an infected bat. Vonnegut comments that he likes Martha a lot, that she teaches her patients how to "comfort one another intelligently" (276).

Mendoza, José   José Mendoza is a member of the Puerto Rican gang in New York City that adopts the name the Pluto Gang after Kilgore Trout is quoted in a newspaper story as saying that, as far as he knew, his mugging might have been committed by an intelligent gas from Pluto. A good painter, Mendoza paints the emblem of the gang on the back of their jackets.

Miasma, Khashdrahr   Khashdrahr Miasma is one of the physicians aboard the disaster vehicle that transports the injured people to the hospital at the end of the novel. He is from Bangladesh and does not help out much during the emergency because he is so ultra-sensitive to criticism. He had been reprimanded earlier in the day for amputating a patient's foot that might have been saved. Khashdrahr Miasma is also the name of the Shah of Bratpuhr's nephew in *Player Piano*, though the

characters seem to be different men with different backgrounds.

Miller, Bill/Don   Early in the novel, Bill Miller is chairman of the Parole Board at the Adult Correctional Institution at Shepherdstown and also part-owner, along with Dwayne Hoover and Dr. Alfred Maritimo, of the new Midland City Holiday Inn (65). Later in the novel, Don Miller, Mary Alice Miller's father, is said to be the chairman of the Parole Board and to have approved Wayne Hoobler's release from prison (262). Bill and Don Miller are likely the same man, and Vonnegut has likely made a mistake with the character's name.

Miller, Mary Alice   Fifteen-year-old Mary Alice Miller, a local Midland City girl, is the Women's Two Hundred Meter Breast Stroke Champion of the World. She is the most famous person in Midland City, and is also the Queen of the Arts Festival. Minimal painter Rabo Karabekian's scorn for Mary Alice causes cocktail waitress Bonnie MacMahon to denigrate his painting, in turn causing Karabekian's moving defense of art and Vonnegut's spiritual rebirth.

Ojumba   One of ambulance driver Eddie Key's ancestors, a man named Ojumba, had been kidnapped on the West Coast of Africa by an ancestor of Nigerian physician Cyprian Ukwende. Ojumba was transported on a slave ship to Charleston, South Carolina, and auctioned off "as a self-propelled, self-repairing farm machine" (279).

Pefko, Francine   Francine Pefko is Dwayne Hoover's extremely competent secretary at the Pontiac dealership in Midland City. A widow whose husband, Robert, was killed while serving in Vietnam, Francine is also Dwayne's mistress. Dwayne's bad chemicals, though, make him treat Francine very badly during the course of the novel, first accusing her of trying to bilk him for a Colonel Sanders' Kentucky Fried Chicken franchise, then beating her savagely at the end of the novel, under the delusion that she, like all the other people surrounding him, is merely a machine and not a human being at all. Francine Pefko is also the name of a secretary in *Cat's Cradle*.

Pefko, Robert   The late husband of Francine Pefko, Robert Pefko was a West Point graduate and career army officer killed during the war in Vietnam.

Pluto Gang   When Kilgore Trout is mugged on the streets of New York City, the police ask him about the occupants of the white Oldsmobile he had seen following him. In reply to their queries, Trout says, "For all I know, they may not even have been Earthlings . . . for all I know, that car may have been occupied by an intelligent gas from Pluto" (76–77). The *New York Post* picks up the story, getting all the details wrong. The newspaper writes that 82-year-old "Kilmer Trotter" was kidnapped by "Pluto bandits" (77). Soon, the whole city begins to fear "The Pluto Gang," and, eventually, an actual gang of Puerto Rican boys adopts the name for themselves.

Robbins, Eldon   A black dishwasher at the Midland City Holiday Inn and ex-convict himself, Eldon Robbins invites freed convict Wayne Hoobler into the hotel kitchen for a meal. Robbins reveals to Wayne a peephole through which the kitchen staff can spy on the guests in the cocktail lounge, saying "When you get tarred of watchin' television . . . you can watch the animals in the zoo" (219).

Robo-Magic Corporation   The Robo-Magic Corporation, founded in Midland City by Fred T. Barry in 1934 to sell automatic washing machines, figures in both *Breakfast of Champions* and *Hocus Pocus*, with the corporation's motto, "Goodbye Blue Monday," even serving as the subtitle for *Breakfast of Champions*. The company's focus changes many times over the years, eventually becoming Barrytron Ltd.

Rockefeller, Nelson   Nelson Rockefeller, real-life governor of New York, shakes Kilgore Trout's hand in a grocery store in Cohoes one time. Trout, though, has no idea who Rockefeller is, even though the man "owned or controlled more of the planet than many nations" (109).

Rosewater, Eliot   A character readers have met in previous Vonnegut novels, Eliot Rosewater in *Breakfast of Champions* is the eccentric millionaire responsible for the Midland City Festival of the Arts' inviting Kilgore Trout as a visiting artist. When Fred T. Barry, the festival chairman, asks Rosewater to loan a valuable oil painting to the festival, he agrees on the condition that Kilgore Trout be invited.

Sacred Miracle Cave   Sacred Miracle Cave is a tourist destination outside of Shepherdstown. Operated by the younger twin stepbrothers of Dwayne Hoover—Lyle and Kyle Hoover—the cave is slowly being overtaken by pollution released into Sugar Creek by the Barrytron plant. The industrial waste has formed bubbles as hard as Ping-Pong balls that are beginning to fill passageways in the cave and that will soon engulf the cave's main attraction: the Cathedral of Whispers, where thousands of people, including Dwayne, Lyle, and Kyle, have had their wedding ceremonies performed.

Shepherdstown   Shepherdstown is a small city that neighbors Midland City. The town is home to the Adult Correctional Institution at Shepherdstown, the prison that Wayne Hoobler has just been released from as the novel begins.

Simmons, Newbolt and Martha   The emergency vehicle that transports the 11 people injured by Dwayne Hoover to the hospital is called the Marsha Simmons Memorial Mobile Disaster Unit. Martha Simmons was the wife of County Commissioner Newbolt Simmons; she died of rabies after trying to be kind to a rabid bat that ended up biting her. Newbolt and Dwayne Hoover had shared a brief friendship because each man's wife had died such a strange death within a month of each other.

Skag, Delmore   A character in one of Kilgore Trout's novels (whose title we never learn), Delmore Skag is an Earthling who learns to reproduce himself in chicken soup. Though a bachelor, Skag has several babies a day and becomes a famous family man. While Skag had hoped to force his country to pass laws outlawing excessively large families, the legislature instead passes laws prohibiting the possession of chicken soup by unmarried persons.

Sparks, Jon When Vonnegut enters the cocktail lounge of the Midland City Holiday Inn, he explains that he is wearing a bracelet bearing the name of Warrant Officer First Class Jon Sparks, who was an American taken prisoner during the Vietnam War.

Sparky Because Dwayne Hoover is a widower, his only companion at night is a Labrador retriever named Sparky. Sparky has no tail because of an automobile accident many years before, so he has no way to show friendliness to other dogs and is forced to fight all the time. Vonnegut writes that Sparky is modeled after a real dog his brother owns, who has to fight all the time because he has no tail to wag.

Stockmayer, Professor Walter H. When discussing the pollution in Midland City's Sugar Creek, Vonnegut includes a diagram of a portion of a plastic molecule. He tells readers that the man who taught him how to diagram the molecule was Professor Walter H. Stockmayer of Dartmouth University.

Studge, Philboyd Philboyd Studge is the name invented for a clunky, cumbersome type of novelist by Vonnegut's friend Knox Burger. Vonnegut says he feels like Philboyd Studge often when he is writing.

Sugar Creek Sugar Creek is the name of the stream that runs through the center of Midland City. The creek is so polluted by residue from the Barrytron plant that Kilgore Trout's feet become encased in plastic when he crosses the creek on foot after a traffic jam causes him to abandon the truck in which he had hitchhiked a ride to the city's outskirts.

Temptation of Saint Anthony, The The *Temptation of Saint Anthony* is a painting by abstract artist Rabo Karabekian. Because the painting consists only of a strip of Day-Glo orange reflecting tape against an avocado green background, the people of Midland City are outraged by the high price paid for it. Yet, it is Karabekian's impassioned defense of this painting that narrator Vonnegut tells readers induces in him a profound spiritual transformation.

Thomas, Headley When Vonnegut is drinking in the cocktail lounge in the Midland City Holiday Inn, he tells waitress Bonnie MacMahon that he can tell fortunes. Though he never gets a chance to tell Bonnie her fortune, he lets readers know that Bonnie's cat will be run over by a motorcycle rider named Headley Thomas.

Trout, Kilgore Kilgore Trout is Vonnegut's ubiquitous science fiction writer, who appears in many of his novels. Though only a secondary character in previous works such as *God Bless You, Mr. Rosewater* and *Slaughterhouse-Five*, Kilgore Trout takes center stage in *Breakfast of Champions*. At the beginning of the novel, Trout is invited to attend the Midland City Festival of the Arts, even though he is a largely unknown writer whose material is published as filler in pornographic magazines. His biggest fan, Eliot Rosewater, has wrangled the invitation from the festival organizers. Trout hitchhikes from his rented apartment in New York to Midland City, planning to attend the festival in order to show what an unhappy failure he is. When he finally arrives in Midland City, he meets local Pontiac dealer Dwayne Hoover in the cocktail lounge of the Holiday Inn. Dwayne, who is going slowly insane, snatches one of Trout's books from him, *Now It Can Be Told*. Trout's novel makes Dwayne believe he is the only creature in the universe with free will, that all other people are simply machines designed to provoke reactions in Dwayne. This delusion leads Dwayne into a savage rampage in which he injures 11 people so severely that they are taken to the hospital. He even bites off the tip of Trout's index finger in the melee. After Trout's release from the hospital, he is confronted by Vonnegut himself—his Creator—who explains that Trout is a character in one of Vonnegut's novels. To prove his assertion, Vonnegut quickly transports Trout around the Earth and into outer space, then back to Midland City. Vonnegut tells Trout that he is setting him free, just as Tolstoy freed his serfs and Jefferson his slaves. The novel ends with Trout pathetically begging Vonnegut to make him young again as the author disappears.

Trout, Leo, Jr.   Although Kilgore Trout had been married and divorced three times, he has only one child, a son named Leo, who left home forever at the age of 14 to join the Marines. Leo, Jr. sends his father a note from boot camp which reads, "I pity you. You've crawled up your own asshole and died" (114). This is the last Kilgore Trout ever hears from his son, though he is visited by two F.B.I. agents who claim that Leo has deserted from his unit in Vietnam and committed high treason by joining the Viet Cong. This son, with his name changed to "Leon," is the narrator of Vonnegut's later novel Galápagos.

Trout, Leo, Sr.   When Kilgore Trout was a child, his father, Leo Trout, Sr., worked for the Royal Ornithological Society in Bermuda, where Kilgore was born. Leo assigns his son the "melancholy task" (30) of measuring the wingspan of dead Bermuda erns, the birds that Leo studies, a likely cause of the pessimism that overwhelms Kilgore Trout in later life.

Ukwende, Cyprian   A HARVARD-educated Nigerian who is working as an intern at the County Hospital in Midland City, Cyprian Ukwende helps man the disaster vehicle nicknamed *Martha* that takes the 11 people injured by Dwayne Hoover to the hospital at the end of the novel.

Unnamed Angel-Faced Child   Driving through West Virginia in the Pyramid truck, Kilgore Trout sees a broken guardrail over a gully. In a brook in the gully is a wrecked automobile and several old kitchen appliances. An unnamed "angel-faced white child, with flaxen hair" (124) stands next to the brook, clasping a bottle of Pepsi-Cola to her chest. She waves to Trout as he passes by.

Unnamed Birth Mother and Father of Dwayne Hoover   Dwayne Hoover was adopted by a Midland City couple when he was a young child. Dwayne's birth mother, we find out, was "a spinster school teacher who wrote sentimental poetry and claimed to be descended from Richard the Lion-Hearted" (45). His birth father was a typesetter who seduced Dwayne's mother when he set her poems in type. Dwayne's mother died giving birth to him, and Dwayne's typesetter father disappeared, thus causing Dwayne to be put up for adoption.

Unnamed Bus Boy and Waiter   Dwayne Hoover, as his bad chemicals take charge of him, begins to sing songs that had been popular in his youth. One day, strolling across the lobby of the new Holiday Inn that he is part-owner of, Dwayne sings loudly. An unnamed black bus boy and a waiter hear Dwayne singing. The bus boy says, "Listen at him sing," to which the waiter replies, "If I owned what he owns, I'd sing, too" (40–41).

Unnamed Clerk at Holiday Inn   When Dwayne Hoover checks into his own Holiday Inn very early in the morning after the night he puts the gun in his mouth, then drives to sit in a vacant lot, the new night clerk does not recognize Dwayne and makes him fill out a full registration form.

Unnamed 14-Year-Old Murderer   In discussing the nature of guns, Vonnegut tells readers that, in the same week Dwayne Hoover ran amok, a 14-year-old Midland City boy shot his mother and father to death because he did not want to show them a bad report card.

Unnamed 14-Year-Old Drug User   When Kilgore Trout walks out of the pornographic movie theater in New York, he sees a 14-year-old white boy lying unconscious in a doorway on 42nd Street. The boy, a drug addict, had swallowed half a pint of paint remover and two pills intended to prevent Bang's disease in cattle.

Unnamed Hitchhiking Family   On his ride through West Virginia in the Pyramid truck, Kilgore Trout sees a white man hitchhiking with his pregnant wife and nine children. The truck driver comments that the man looks like Gary Cooper, a movie star of the 1920s and '30s, and Trout agrees.

Unnamed Idiot and Nurse   At the diner where Kilgore Trout and the truck driver who gives him a ride to West Virginia stop to eat, Trout sees an adult male idiot eating as well, with his nurse in tow. The man is happy and has a wonderful appetite. As Trout watches him shovel food into his mouth, he says to himself, "Stoking up for another day" (91).

Unnamed Kitchen Workers   Two unnamed black kitchen workers at the Midland City Holiday Inn are among the victims of Dwayne Hoover's rampage.

Unnamed Miner   In the West Virginia diner, where Kilgore Trout stops to eat with the Pyramid truck driver, he sits next to a very old man who had worked in coal mines from the age of 10 to 62. The miner tells Trout it does not seem right that some people can own what is underneath the earth, trumping the rights of the people who live above. He complains particularly about the Rosewater family, having worked for the Rosewater Coal and Iron Company his whole life.

Unnamed Movie Theater Manager   When Kilgore Trout decides to sleep all night in a pornographic movie theater in New York, the manager tells him he must leave after the last movie has ended. The two men form a temporary friendship as they walk out of the theater together, and the manager explains to Trout that his family doesn't know he runs a dirty movie theater—they think he is an engineer. The manager is mugged and beaten on 42nd Street along with Trout.

Unnamed State Policemen   Dwayne Hoover's violent rampage ends when he is subdued by two unnamed state policemen on the median divider of the interstate highway that runs through Midland City.

Unnamed Old Woman   When Kilgore Trout enters Philadelphia with the truck driver who has

given him a ride from New York, he sees an old white woman fishing through a garbage can. Trout, who no longer thinks about "how things could be and should be on the planet" (106), decides that everything must be as it is; it is necessary that the old woman should be picking through garbage at that particular time and place.

Unnamed Pimp   The two young black prostitutes who proposition Kilgore Trout in New York City work for an unnamed pimp who is "splendid" and "cruel," and who acts as a god to the women, taking their free will away, which is fine with them (74).

Unnamed Prostitutes   After Kilgore Trout leaves the pornographic movie theater in New York with the theater's manager, two young black prostitutes, high on Norwegian hemorrhoid crème, proposition the men.

Unnamed Sleeping Policeman   Late one night, after placing a revolver in his mouth and contemplating suicide, Dwayne Hoover jumps into the black Plymouth Fury he is driving, speeds down the interstate, slams into a guardrail, and jumps a curb, coming to rest in a vacant lot. No one hears or sees anything, though, because a policeman who is supposed to cruise the area once every hour is "cooping," or sleeping on the job, in an alley about two miles away.

Unnamed Tourists   Three unnamed white tourists, on their way to the Grand Canyon from Erie, Pennsylvania, are among the victims of Dwayne Hoover's rampage.

Unnamed Truck Driver   A truck driver whose name readers never learn gives Kilgore Trout a ride from New York City all the way to West Virginia. A former hunter and fisherman, the driver is worried about environmental destruction, at least until Trout tells him that God does not seem to be any kind of conservationist. The driver tells Trout he can't tell if the writer is kidding or not, and Vonnegut adds, "After Trout became famous, of course, one of the biggest mysteries about him was whether he was kidding or not" (88). The two men converse on their long trip about friendship, about family, and about aluminum siding, among other things. Eventually, the driver tells Trout about a book he read, which was being used as toilet paper in a jail in Libertyville, Georgia, where the driver had been briefly imprisoned for speeding. Trout feels woozy when he realizes the book was *The Barring-gaffner of Bagnialto* or *This Year's Masterpiece*, one of his own novels.

Unnamed Truck Driver's Brother   The truck driver who gives Kilgore Trout a ride from New York through West Virginia tells Trout about his brother who works in a factory that produces chemicals designed to kill plants and trees in Vietnam. The driver points out that, through such work, his brother is committing suicide and adds that it seems like "the only kind of job an American can get these days is committing suicide in some way" (88).

Unnamed Truck Driver's Brother-in-Law   The truck driver who gives Kilgore Trout a ride from New York explains that his brother-in-law owns the truck. In fact, the brother-in-law owns 28 trucks and is president of the Pyramid Trucking Company. When Trout asks why he named the company Pyramid, the driver responds that his brother-in-law liked the sound of the name, prompting Trout to dream up a story about a planet where the language keeps turning into pure music because the creatures who live there are so in love with sounds.

Unnamed Workman   After Dwayne Hoover eats lunch at the Burger Chef, he wanders over to the construction site of the new Midland City high school and admires a "tremendous earth-moving machine" (150). Dwayne asks an unnamed white workman how many horsepower the machine has, and the workman replies that he doesn't know how many horsepower, but that the workers call the piece of equipment "The Hundred-Nigger Machine" (150).

Valentine, Jimmy   Jimmy Valentine was a safecracker who first appeared in a story by noted short story writer O. Henry in the early 20th century. Later plays and movies have kept the Jimmy Valentine legend alive. The Valentine character is

famous for sandpapering his fingers so they will be extra-sensitive for breaking into safes. Vonnegut has Kilgore Trout write a short novel called *The Son of Jimmy Valentine*, in which Jimmy's son Ralston sandpapers his fingers so they will be extra-sensitive when making love to women.

Valentine, Ralston   Ralston Valentine is the hero of Kilgore Trout's novel *The Son of Jimmy Valentine*. Unlike his famous criminal father, who sandpapers his fingers for safe-cracking, Ralston sandpapers his fingers so that he can please women when making love. He is so good at touching women the way they want to be touched that tens of thousands of women abandon their husbands to become his willing slaves and eventually elect him president of the United States.

Vonnegut, Kurt   Vonnegut uses the METAFIC-TIONAL technique of presenting himself as a character in his own book when he enters the cocktail lounge at the Midland City Holiday Inn. Unexpectedly, the depressed and cynical author finds a new lease on life when his character Rabo Karabekian resoundingly defends minimalist art, even though Vonnegut previously did not have much respect for Karabekian as a man or an artist. Kilgore Trout, the only Vonnegut character with enough imagination to suspect he might be a fictional creation, is unsettled by Vonnegut's proximity. The novel ends with Vonnegut confronting Trout, offering him an apple, and setting him free. In the last lines of the book, the pathetic science fiction writer begs Vonnegut to make him young again.

Vonnegut, Kurt, Sr.,   Although Vonnegut's father never actually enters the novel as a character, he is referred to frequently. Vonnegut gives Kilgore Trout many of his father's characteristics as an old man, including his varicose veins, marked up shins, and long slender feet.

Vonnegut, Edith Lieber   Vonnegut's mother, like his father, is not an actual character in the novel, but is mentioned often. In many ways, the depression left by his mother's suicide seems to be the motivating factor in Vonnegut's writing the book.

Commenting on how novelist Thomas Wolfe wrote about a hero's search for a father, Vonnegut says, "It seems to me that really truthful American novels would have the heroes and heroines alike looking for *mothers* instead. . . . A mother is much more useful" (276). Vonnegut's own mother is also the inspiration for Bunny Hoover's mother, Celia, who kills herself by eating Drano. Both women were beautiful in exotic ways and yet neurotically afraid of having their pictures taken, both were "crazy as bedbugs" (185), and both left their sons a legacy of trauma after their suicides.

Washington, Elgin Elgin Washington is a 26-year-old black pimp who operates out of the Midland City Holiday Inn. When readers see him, he is a patient in the local hospital, the very man, in fact, whose foot Dr. Khashdrahr Miasma had mistakenly amputated. When Kilgore Trout passes Washington's deluxe private room on his way out of the hospital, Washington wheedles him to come in and promise to do the pimp a favor. Not really having any specific favor in mind, Elgin Washington makes Trout listen to him imitate the call of a nightingale.

Wilbur, Harold Newcomb Harold Newcomb Wilbur is the bartender at the cocktail lounge of the Midland City Holiday Inn. Wilbur, who fought in World War II, is the second-most decorated veteran in Midland City.

Young, Mary Mary Young, the oldest inhabitant of Midland City, dies in the County Hospital while Dwayne Hoover is sitting in a vacant lot very late one night in a Plymouth Fury, listening to the radio. Mary, the daughter of slaves from Kentucky, is connected to Dwayne slightly, because she used to do laundry in the Hoover household when Dwayne was a little boy. As Mary dies, all she has to say is, "Oh my, oh my" (64).

Zog Zog is the protagonist in a Kilgore Trout story, "The Dancing Fool." From Margo, a planet where creatures communicate by means of farts and tap dancing, Zog comes to Earth to tell Earthlings how wars can be prevented and how cancer be cured. As soon as his flying saucer touches down

in Connecticut, Zog sees a house on fire. He rushes in, farting and tap dancing, to warn the inhabitants about the danger they are in, but is brained with a golf club by the home's owner.

FURTHER READING

Breakfast of Champions. New York: Dell, 1999.

McGinnis, Wayne. "Vonnegut's *Breakfast of Champions*: A Reductive Success." *Notes on Contemporary Literature* 5, no. 3 (1975): 6–9.

Merrill, Robert. "Vonnegut's *Breakfast of Champions*: The Conversion of Heliogabalus." *Critique* 18, no. 3 (1977): 99–108.

Messent, Peter B. "*Breakfast of Champions*: The Direction of Kurt Vonnegut's Fiction." *Journal of American Studies* 8, no. 1 (1974): 101–114.

Morse, Donald E. "The 'Black Frost' Reception of Kurt Vonnegut's Fantastic Novel *Breakfast of Champions*." *Journal of the Fantastic in the Arts* 11, no. 2 [42] (2000): 143–153.

Simpson, Josh. "'This Promising of Great Secrets': Literature, Ideas, and the (Re)Invention of Reality in Kurt Vonnegut's *God Bless You, Mr. Rosewater, Slaughterhouse-Five*, and *Breakfast of Champions* Or 'Fantasies of an Impossibly Hospitable World': Science Fiction and Madness in Vonnegut's Troutean Trilogy." *Critique* 45, no. 3 (2004): 261–271.

Canary in a Cat House

Canary in a Cat House, published as a paperback original by Fawcett in 1961, is Vonnegut's first collection of short fiction. The book includes 12 stories previously published in magazines ranging from *Collier's* to *Galaxy Science Fiction* to *Cosmopolitan*, during the years 1950 to 1958. The 12 stories are:

1. "Report on the Barnhouse Effect"
2. "All the King's Horses"
3. "D.P."
4. "The Manned Missiles"
5. "The Euphio Question"
6. "More Stately Mansions"
7. "The Foster Portfolio"
8. "Deer in the Works"
9. "Hal Irwin's Magic Lamp"

10. "Tom Edison's Shaggy Dag"
11. "Unready to Wear"
12. "Tomorrow and Tomorrow and Tomorrow"

While *Canary in a Cat House* went out of print for several decades, 11 of the stories appearing in the collection were later republished in the 1968 volume, *Welcome to the Monkey House.* "Hal Irwin's Magic Lamp," the only story from *Canary* omitted from *Welcome to the Monkey House,* appears in Vonnegut's 1999 collection of short fiction, *Bagombo Snuff Box.* The original *Canary in a Cat House* was republished by Buccaneer Books in 1991.

Cat's Cradle

Cat's Cradle, published in hardcover by Holt, Rinehart & Winston in 1963, is the novel that began the buzz and cult following that Vonnegut continued to attract during the 1960s and early 1970s. Like *Player Piano,* Vonnegut's first novel, *Cat's Cradle* warns against the dangers of irresponsible scientific advancement undertaken without adequate concern for the human costs that technological progress may wreak. The book is the child of World War II, its apocalyptic vision inspired by the invention of atomic weaponry. But *Cat's Cradle* is also about truth and illusion, about the comforting lies humans tell themselves and one another in order to make tolerable a world that is often cruel and unfathomable. Religion, along with art and love itself, are examples of what the "spurious holy man" (272) Bokonon calls *foma,* harmless untruths that can help human beings live lives that make them, in the words of the novel's epigraph, "brave and kind and healthy and happy." Though the human race may be fated for destruction, the best we can do, Vonnegut seems to say, is take comfort where we can find it, love one another as well as we can, and live according to the illusion that man is a sacred being.

SYNOPSIS

Chapters 1–36
Written in the first person by a freelance writer named John, whose last name we never learn,

Cat's Cradle begins with the story of Dr. Felix Hoenikker, one of the chief creators of the ATOMIC BOMB. John is collecting material for a book to be called *The Day the World Ended,* which will chronicle what important Americans were doing on August 6, 1945, the day the first atomic bomb was dropped on Hiroshima. Though Dr. Hoenikker is dead, John writes to his youngest son, a midget named Newt Hoenikker, asking for anecdotes about the day. Newt, a CORNELL UNIVERSITY pre-med student who has just flunked out of school and is still living in his fraternity house, writes back, telling the narrator about his unusual family. Dr. Hoenikker had worked for the General Forge and Foundry Company of ILIUM, New York. Still a child at heart, Felix Hoenikker left all responsibility for family and home to his wife, Emily, who died giving birth to Newt. After Emily's death, Dr. Hoenikker's oldest daughter, Angela, who was 16 when her mother died, takes on the responsibility of raising baby Newt as well as Frank, the middle child. A lonely, homely girl fiercely devoted to her father, Angela's one passion in life is playing the clarinet. Readers also find out from Newt's letter to the narrator that Frank, his older brother, an eccentric and friendless child, has been out of touch with his siblings for many years. According to Newt, the last the Hoenikker family has heard of Frank is that he is wanted by the Florida police, the F.B.I., and the Treasury Department for running stolen cars to Cuba.

When the narrator happens to go to Ilium about a year later while working on another story, he decides to look up the Hoenikkers. Though no Hoenikkers are currently living in Ilium, he meets several people in a bar who knew Frank in high school. A prostitute named Sandra tells the narrator that the kids used to call Frank Secret Agent X-9, because he was a secretive boy who dedicated himself to making model airplanes. The next day, at the Ilium General Forge and Foundry Company, John meets Dr. Asa Breed, who had been Dr. Felix Hoenikker's supervisor during the years of the Manhattan Project when the atomic bomb was being developed. Rumors circulate in Ilium that Dr. Breed was in love with Emily Hoenikker, and that he, not Felix Hoenikker, is the father of Angela,

Frank, and Newt. Whether or not the rumors are true, Dr. Breed respected Dr. Hoenikker as a scientist. Dr. Breed carefully explains to the narrator that his laboratory is one of the few in the country where pure research, rather than research for commercial use, is conducted. Dr. Hoenikker was allowed to explore whatever interested him, in the name of pure science, whether it was the nucleus of atoms or the behavior of turtles. Yet, that did not stop important people from suggesting projects to Felix. Dr. Breed tells the narrator that, at the time of his death, Felix Hoenikker had been working on a scheme suggested to him by a Marine general who was tired of Marines having to crawl through mud to fight their battles. Felix had been experimenting with a substance called *ice-nine*, a chemically altered version of ordinary ice, which was extremely strong, firm, and durable, with a very high melting point. A single grain of *ice-nine* could instantaneously turn an entire body of water into a solid. Though Dr. Breed believes that Felix's work was still in the hypothetical stage when he died, readers discover that Felix had actually developed the substance. After their father's death, his three children divided the *ice-nine* among themselves.

Chapters 37–60

Several weeks after his trip to Ilium, the narrator, reading a special supplement to the Sunday *New York Times* back in his New York City apartment, discovers what has happened to the elusive Frank Hoenikker. The paid advertisement touts a banana republic in the Caribbean called the Republic of San Lorenzo. In it is a picture of "a narrow-shouldered, fox-faced, immature young man" who is identified as "Major General Franklin Hoenikker, *Minister of Science and Progress in the Republic of San Lorenzo*" (80). Coincidentally, the narrator is later assigned by a magazine to do a story in San Lorenzo, not about Frank, but about Julian Castle, an American millionaire who had moved to the island to found a free hospital in the jungle there. On the airplane on his way to the island, the narrator meets several fellow Americans traveling to San Lorenzo, including Horlick Minton, the new American ambassador to the republic, and his wife, Claire, a bicycle manufacturer named H. Lowe Crosby and his wife,

Hazel, and Angela and Newt Hoenikker, who are traveling to the island to attend an engagement party for their brother Frank and the beautiful Mona Aamons Monzano, the adopted daughter of the island's dictator, Miguel "Papa" Monzano.

On the plane, the Mintons give the narrator a book to read, *San Lorenzo: The Land, the History, the People,* written by Philip Castle, son of the man the narrator has come to write a story about. Fascinated, the narrator learns a bit about the history of the island and its outlawed religion, Bokononism, which was started by a black man named Lionel Boyd Johnson, who was born in 1891 on the island of Tobago to a wealthy Episcopal family. After several adventures at sea as a young man, Johnson was approached by an idealistic Marine deserter named Earl McCabe, who offered him $500 to sail him to Miami. The boat went down in a storm near San Lorenzo, and Johnson and McCabe barely managed to swim ashore, naked and exhausted. There they found a depressed, poverty-ridden population and an island completely lacking natural resources or a benevolent government. Determined to establish a Utopia on San Lorenzo, McCabe overhauled the economy and the laws and Johnson started a new religion. When it eventually became clear that no new government was ever going to be able to help the people as they needed, the new religion started by Johnson (who was called "Bokonon" in the local dialect) was where the population turned for hope. Bokonon asked McCabe to outlaw him and his religion, Bokononism, in order to give "the religious life of the people more zest, more tang" (173). The two also developed a fiendish punishment for those caught practicing Bokononism—the Hook—a device law-breakers are impaled on and where they are left to dangle until they die. At first only for show, the hook eventually became used for real executions as Bokonon and McCabe settled into the roles they had assigned themselves. When McCabe died, his former major-domo, Papa Manzano, became dictator of San Lorenzo. When the narrator arrives on the island, Papa Manzano is 70 years old, dying of cancer, and expects his own major-domo, Frank Hoenikker, to succeed him.

Chapters 61–93

At his hotel shortly after his arrival, the narrator receives a frenzied phone call from Major General Frank Hoenikker, who refuses to divulge any details over the phone, but demands that the narrator come out to his house right away on extremely urgent business. The narrator takes San Lorenzo's one taxicab to Frank's house, an architectural wonder straddling a waterfall. Frank's house was built by Mona Aamons Monzano's father, Nestor Aamons, a native Finn who had been invited to San Lorenzo to design Julian Castle's hospital, the House of Hope and Mercy in the Jungle. At his arrival, the narrator finds Newt and Angela Hoenikker, along with the philanthropist Julian Castle, waiting for Frank as well. After waiting for many hours, which are filled with conversations about Newt's art, the native religion Bokononism, and the history of the island, all the lights suddenly go out because of an electricity failure, apparently a common event in San Lorenzo. The narrator eventually falls asleep for a brief period, then is awakened by loud banging noises and a flood of lights as the power is restored. Frank has finally arrived with a generator and with his bride-to-be, Mona Aamons Monzano.

Leading the narrator down a flight of stairs to what he calls his den, a natural cave behind the waterfall, Frank finally divulges his pressing business. Much to the narrator's shock, Frank offers him the position of president of the Republic of San Lorenzo, confessing that he himself is no good at facing the public and that nobody else on the island wants the job. Though he adamantly refuses at first, the narrator eventually weakens, concluding, as a good Bokononist would, that God is running his life and that fate has conspired to push him toward this destiny. When Frank tells him that marrying Mona Aamons Monzano is part of the bargain, the narrator becomes enthusiastic about the position, having fallen in love with Mona instantly when he saw her picture in the advertising supplement about San Lorenzo back in New York. Frank brings Mona down into the cave to talk with the narrator, and the two practice *boko-maru*, the ritual rubbing together of the soles of the feet that is one of the major rites of Bokononism. Yet, when the narrator tells Mona that, after they are married, he'll want her to practice *boko-maru* exclusively with him rather than with anyone she wishes, Mona replies that she will not marry a *sin-vat*, "a man who wants all of somebody's love" (208). To keep from losing her, the narrator eventually relents, asking Mona if he can join her religion and become a Bokononist.

Chapters 94–116

When everything is settled between the narrator and Mona, Frank drives the narrator to the palace where Papa Monzano lies dying, in order to receive his blessing. Papa, it turns out, has been secretly practicing Bokononism throughout his rule, though the religion remains outlawed; he demands that his last rites be performed according to the Bokononist rather than the Christian ritual. Leaving Papa still clinging to life, Frank and the narrator agree that the new president of the Republic of San Lorenzo will be announced at that afternoon's air show in honor of the Hundred Martyrs to Democracy, a ceremony that Ambassador Minton has traveled to the island to attend. At a buffet on the palace battlements during the ceremony, the narrator eats a chunk of albatross meat that upsets his stomach and desperately searches for a bathroom. He finds one adjoining the suite of Papa Manzano. Upon leaving the bathroom, the narrator is stopped by Papa's doctor, an ex-Nazi named Dr. Schlichter von Koenigswald, who is wild-eyed with shock. Babbling that Papa is dead after ingesting something from a cylinder he had kept hanging around his neck, Dr. Koenigswald leads the narrator into Papa's chambers. The narrator is amazed to see Papa turned into a solid, stonelike statue, with blue frost on his lips and nostrils. After touching the dead man's lips, Dr. Koenigswald is transformed into a statue as well. It turns out that the capsule around Papa's neck had contained *ice-nine*, given to him by Frank Hoenikker.

The narrator orders the three Hoenikker children brought to Papa's room, where they confess to possessing the dangerous substance. The three, along with the narrator, work frenziedly to clean up the death site, then return to the ceremonies on the battlements. When one of the planes from the air show accidentally crashes into the palace, a rock slide is triggered, and the whole building begins to crack and shake. In the chaos, Papa Monzano's body is launched out of its death chamber and into the sea below. Immediately, there is a huge noise and the entire sea is frozen solid, the earth turns white and frosty, and the sky darkens and fills with tornadoes as the *ice-nine* is unleashed into the world.

Chapters 117–127

The narrator and Mona manage to escape into a deep oubliette in the dungeon below the palace, which had been furnished as a bomb shelter, with plenty of food and emergency supplies. After staying in their shelter for seven days, the two venture out into the barren world above to look for other survivors. Climbing a ridge, they stumble upon a broad natural bowl formation, in which lie thousands upon thousands of dead bodies, each frozen solid with a finger near the mouth, indicating a mass suicide by *ice-nine*. Near the death site, the narrator and Mona find a large boulder with a note placed on it. The note explains that all these people had captured the holy man Bokonon and begged him to tell them what to do. The "mountebank," as the note calls Bokonon, tells the people that God is surely trying to kill them, and they should have the good manners to die. The note, we find out, is signed by Bokonon himself. Leaving the bowl, Mona playfully runs ahead of the narrator, asking him if he would wish any of the dead alive again. When he does not answer quickly enough, she laughingly reaches down, touches the ground, then touches her finger to her lips and immediately dies.

Dazed with grief, the narrator is eventually found by H. Lowe Crosby, the bicycle manufacturer, his wife, Hazel, and Newt Hoenikker, who have been riding around surveying the damage in the island's one taxicab. The only other living person on the island is Frank Hoenikker. The five survivors live together for six months, managing rather well since there is plenty of food available, the weather is uniformly dry and hot, and they enjoy excellent health, all germs having been wiped out by *ice-nine*. Hazel cheerfully dubs the little group the Swiss Family Robinson. It is during this sixth-month period that the narrator writes the book we have been reading. Depressed and cynical, the narrator explains to Newt as the two are riding around in the taxicab foraging for supplies that he dreams of climbing up Mount McCabe, the island's tallest geographic feature, and planting "some magnificent symbol" at the top (284), though he has no idea what the symbol would be. Suddenly, looking out the window, the narrator spots "an old Negro man" sitting by the side of the road (286). The man turns out to be Bokonon himself. Though he initially takes no notice of the two men's arrival, Bokonon does answer the question put to him by the narrator about what he is thinking. He replies that he is thinking about the final sentence for *The Books of Bokonon* and hands the narrator a piece of paper. On it, Bokonon has written that if he were a younger man he would write a history of human stupidity, climb to the top of Mount McCabe, lie down with the book for a pillow, then reach down onto the ground for a grain of blue-white frost and make a statue of himself, "grinning horribly, and thumbing my nose at You Know Who" (287). These are the last words of the novel; we never know if the narrator takes Bokonon's advice or not.

COMMENTARY

The theme of illusion versus reality is evident from *Cat's Cradle*'s title and epigraph. Prefaced by the warning that "Nothing in this book is true," the novel asks us to consider what truth is. While readers recognize that they are reading a work of fiction, and thus an invented or "untrue" story, at the same time, we expect literature to deliver another, deeper kind of truth through the fictional stories it presents—to tell us something true about human nature or the human experience. In *Mother Night*, Vonnegut, in his role as the editor of Howard W. Campbell's confessions, writes of his belief that "lies told for the sake of artistic effect . . . can be, in a higher sense, the most beguiling forms of truth" (ix–x). In *Cat's Cradle*, though, Vonnegut suggests that literature itself might be just another kind of *foma*, harmless untruths or illusions that make life seem more meaningful than it actually is. *The Books of Bokonon*, after all, which freely admit to being *foma* invented to give people hope, begin with a caveat similar to the one Vonnegut begins his book with: "All of the true things I am about to tell you are shameless lies" writes Bokonon (5). But just because religion and art might be based on lies, that does not mean that these things should be easily dismissed or that they have no value in life. The novel's narrator early on provides another Bokononist warning: "Anybody unable to understand how a useful religion can be founded on lies will not understand this book either" (5–6). In many ways, then, the novel is about the need for illusion, to find hope in a world teetering on apocalypse.

The novel's title conveys the theme of illusion in the motif of the cat's cradle, which first appears when Newt Hoenikker responds to the narrator's request for memories of August 6, 1945, the day the atomic bomb was dropped on Hiroshima. Newt writes a long letter back, concluding with a memory of his father's only attempt to play with his young son. Dr. Felix Hoenikker, toying with the string that had been tied around a manuscript about the end of the world, sent him by prison inmate Marvin Sharpe Holderness, eventually shapes it into a cat's cradle between his hands. But when Dr. Hoenikker goes down on his knees on the carpet to show the cat's cradle to six-year-old Newt, all Newt sees is a "tangle of string" in his face, accompanied by a father with pores "as big as craters on the moon," with ears and nostrils "stuffed with hair" and a cigar whose smoke "made him smell like the mouth of Hell"—in short, "the ugliest thing" little Newt has ever seen (12). Newt is frightened and runs out of the house crying. "No wonder kids grow up crazy," Newt speculates at his brother Frank's house in San Lorenzo later in the novel, "A cat's cradle is nothing but a bunch of X's between somebody's hands and little kids look and look and look at all those X's . . ." and what do they see? *No damn cat, and no damn cradle* (166). Because of this incident, the term *cat's cradle* becomes shorthand Newt uses to refer to illusions, to comforting lies that people conjure in their imaginations out of the chaos and ugliness of life, just as the cat's cradle is conjured out of the tangle of string. For instance, when the narrator, after learning about the cruel way Harrison C. Connors treats Newt's sister, Angela, protests that he thought the marriage was a happy one, Newt replies, "See the cat? See the cradle?" (179),

the same comment he makes scoffingly about religion a few pages later.

Newt's childhood memory of the cat's cradle suggests the illusion that Dr. Hoenikker is interested in his own child, in other humans in general, when, in fact, this incident is the only time Felix ever tries to make any contact with his son. Dr. Hoenikker represents something Vonnegut warns against repeatedly in his work: a form of science that is completely cut off from human considerations. We see evidence of this when, in his letter to the narrator, Newt relates what happens after he runs crying from the cat's cradle incident. Angela slaps Newt for saying he hates their father, and Frank punches Angela in the stomach. When Angela yells for her father, Frank scornfully tells her that Father won't come. Newt explains that Frank was right:

> Father stuck his head out a window, and he looked at Angela and me rolling on the ground, bawling, and Frank standing over us, laughing. The old man pulled his head indoors again, and never even asked later what all the fuss had been about. People weren't his specialty. (17)

Dr. Hoenikker behaves like the turtles that he becomes so fascinated by, pulling his head back into his shell to avoid human interaction. Like the notorious Dr. FRANKENSTEIN in MARY SHELLEY's novel, who leaves behind his cherished Elizabeth and Clerval in Geneva for his mad pursuit of science in Ingolstadt, Dr. Hoenikker's sin lies in sacrificing ties of family and friendship in order to devote himself single-mindedly to scientific investigation. The morality of his pursuits is never a concern to Dr. Hoenikker at all; when a fellow scientist tells him that "Science has now known sin" after the test of the atomic bomb at Alamogordo, Felix replies simply, "What is sin?" (17).

Other characters in the novel share Newt's views of Felix Hoenikker as a cold man of science, cut off from human concerns. Dr. Breed's secretary, Naomi Faust, explains that Dr. Hoenikker was unknowable, pointing out that the things that matter to most people—"intimate things, family things, love things" (54)—were not very important to Felix. While the legendary Dr. Faust sold his soul to the devil in exchange for knowledge, the ironically named Naomi Faust says she does not understand how truth, all by itself, can be enough for a person, a comment the narrator recognizes as being Bokononist in sentiment. And Marvin Breed, the tombstone salesman, speculates that Felix Hoenikker was "born dead" because he "never met a man who was less interested in the living" (68). Breed goes on to conjecture that, perhaps the problem with the world is that there are "too many people in high places who are stone-cold dead" (68). It is fitting then, that the "stone-cold" Felix Hoenikker develops the doomsday device that will eventually reduce the whole world to ice and the human beings who ingest it to stone.

Is such destruction inevitable in the novel? Is it the fate of humankind to destroy itself? As in many of his works, in *Cat's Cradle*, Vonnegut raises questions about fate and DETERMINISM versus FREE WILL. Are human actions preordained and determined according to some inescapable plan, or do people have the ability to shape the future through the choices they make? The novel's narrator, John, certainly presents his own journey toward San Lorenzo and Bokononism as if he is fated toward this particular end. He tells us about experiencing a *vin-dit* in the tombstone salesroom when he sees his own last name carved on the pedestal of the stone angel. A *vin-dit,* according to Bokononist thought, is "a sudden, very personal shove in the direction of Bokononism" (69). And moreover, Bokononism teaches the narrator that "God Almighty" knows all about him and has elaborate plans for him (69). The narrator, looking back on his life as a good Bokononist, interprets all events that happen to him as nudges toward his final fate. Thus, when he lends his apartment to the poet Sherman Krebbs over the Christmas holidays, the narrator believes that Krebbs has served as a *wrang-wrang,* in Bokononist thought, a member of a person's *karass* who acts as a type of negative warning, steering an individual away from a wrong path. Krebbs, the narrator believes, came into his life to show him that the path of nihilism, or a belief in the utter meaninglessness of existence, is not for him.

The narrator, in fact, presents himself from the very beginning of the novel as a Biblical JONAH figure. The first line in the book is "Call me Jonah," a sentence hearkening back to the famous opening of Herman Melville's MOBY-DICK, "Call me Ishmael" as well as to the story of Jonah in the Bible. Like the narrator of *Cat's Cradle,* Ishmael in Melville's novel is an outsider, a wanderer who witnesses great destruction and survives to tell the tale. Although it would be an oversimplification to read *Cat's Cradle* as a biblical allegory, both Ishmael in *Moby-Dick* and John in *Cat's Cradle* share traits with the biblical Jonah who is ordered to go to the city of Nineveh to preach against wickedness there, but who initially resists his fate, ending up in the belly of a whale as punishment. Like Jonah, John is at first reluctant to accept his fate, working on his book about the end of the world only leisurely and haphazardly. But also like Jonah, John eventually comes to accept that his destiny is mapped out by God and thus that he cannot resist it. While Jonah preaches to the Ninevites about the great destruction God has planned for their wickedness, John, too, is a prophet of mass destruction, who writes his history as a warning, against the sin of a science divorced from moral considerations.

While the people of Nineveh in the Bible story are spared by God because they repent, Jonah is unhappy about this, believing that the Ninevites deserved the destruction with which they were threatened. There is a similar sense of pessimism in Vonnegut's novel, a sense that humans deserve to be destroyed, that they have brought their terrible end upon themselves. The Books of Bokonon often express futility and fatalism in regard to human existence. The narrator remembers, for instance, reading *The Fourteenth Book of Bokonon,* which is entitled "What Can a Thoughtful Man Hope for Mankind on Earth, Given the Experience of the Past Million Years?" The entire book, the narrator explains, consists of only one word: "Nothing" (245). We see a similar sense of futility in Bokonon's understanding of what it means to be fully grown up; Bokonon defines maturity, the narrator explains, as "a bitter disappointment for which no remedy exists, unless laughter can be said to remedy anything" (198). As in most of Vonnegut's novels, BLACK HUMOR may be the only response to the absurd and frightening world we find ourselves in.

Indeed, the whole idea of human beings having a meaningful purpose in life is presented in Bokononist thought as an invention of man, not of God. Bokonon, in *The First Book,* tells a variation of the creation story in Genesis. In Bokonon's version, God in "His cosmic loneliness" creates man out of mud. When man sits up, he asks politely, "What is the *purpose* of all this?" (265). The following conversation then takes place:

> "Everything must have a purpose?" asked God.
> "Certainly," said man.
> "Then I leave it to you to think of one for all this," said God. And he went away.

Although it might be a foolish pursuit to try to discover purpose in human life—Bokonon writes in his Books that "anyone who thinks he sees what God is Doing" (5) is a fool—nevertheless, as humans, Vonnegut seems to believe, we are compelled to try to find meaning. As a Tralfamadorian tells Billy Pilgrim in *Slaughterhouse-Five,* of all the creatures in the universe, Earthlings are the "great explainers" (85). Or, as Bokonon writes in one of his calypsos:

> Tiger got to hunt,
> Bird got to fly;
> Man got to sit and wonder, "Why, why, why?"
> Tiger got to sleep,
> Bird got to land;
> Man got to tell himself he understand. (182)

As humans, we crave answers to the large questions of existence, even though those answers might never be forthcoming.

If discovering true meaning in life is a fool's errand, an impossibility, we are left with the logical question of what to do about this. If life has no discernable purpose, does that mean that life is meaningless? Should we simply give up on the attempt to create meaning? Some critics have called Vonnegut a "quietist," someone who advocates a resigned passivity to life. But it is entirely possible that Vonnegut offers a very different solution to the problem of finding meaning in human life than simply giving up. In *Cat's Cradle,* at least, Vonnegut suggests the possibility that we can turn human life into a work of art in order to create our own meaning out

of meaninglessness. McCabe and Bokonon do just this in their attempt to create a Utopian society in San Lorenzo. By creating the "living legend of the cruel tyrant in the city and the gentle holy man in the jungle" (174), the happiness of the islanders increases. The San Lorenzo natives become like actors "employed full time . . . in a play they understood" (174–175). When Julian Castle explains this transformation to the narrator, John marvels: "So life became a work of art" (175). Simply giving up and leaving the islanders to the hell they are living in is no more an option for McCabe and Bokonon than abandoning the Ninevites is for Jonah. In the Bible story, Jonah is admonished by God for his desire to leave Ninevah to its destruction; God teaches Jonah to love the sinful Ninevites. In *Cat's Cradle,* McCabe and Bokonon, despite their ultimate failure to create a Utopian paradise, love the San Lorenzans and try to give them hope, sacrificing themselves in the process.

Throughout the novel, Vonnegut emphasizes the importance of art in helping people find meaning in life. When Philip Castle tells the narrator jokingly that he is thinking of calling a general strike of all writers "until mankind finally comes to its senses" (231), John responds that his conscience would not let him support such a strike. The narrator and Philip Castle speculate that, without art, people would begin dying, whether like flies or mad dogs. Julian Castle, when asked how men die when they are deprived of the consolations of literature, responds: "In one of two ways . . . putrescence of the heart or atrophy of the nervous system" (232), and he begs John and Philip to keep writing. While this conversation is not meant to be taken entirely seriously, it does acknowledge the necessity of art in our lives. We see a similar, if less jocular, example of the importance of art when the narrator listens to Angela Hoenikker play her clarinet for the first time. Intensely moved by the music, the narrator's hair stands on end and he shrieks at Julian Castle, "My God—life! Who can understand even one little minute of it?" (182). Angela's art moves the narrator to ask big questions about life. Julian's reply to John's agitated plea is: "Don't try . . . Just pretend you understand" (182).

Pretending is what Bokonon advocates all along in his invented religion and what the novel advocates in its epigraph as well—that we should live as if the *foma* that helps us find meaning is true. If such *foma* as religion and art help us be more brave and kind, better human beings, surely these are useful lies. Bokononism, despite Bokonon's own acknowledgment that the religion is "trash" (265), does teach people to love one another, especially through the invented ritual of *boko-maru*. As the narrator writes, "We Bokononists believe that it is impossible to be sole-to-sole with another person without loving the person, provided the feet of both persons are clean and nicely tended" (158). Going sole-to-sole during *boko-maru* helps human beings connect soul-to-soul. Of course, Vonnegut being Vonnegut, he cannot resist throwing in the humorous and somewhat deflating qualifier that the practioners' feet must be clean and well-tended.

Further, if we live according to *foma*, there is the possibility that we can make what we believe come true. Bokonon makes up a legend about the lifeboat, later painted gold and made the bed of the island's president, that he and McCabe row to San Lorenzo. The golden boat, writes Bokonon, "will sail again when the end of the world is near" (109). Although an invention of Bokonon's, the legend becomes reality when the golden lifeboat carrying Papa Monzano's body crashes into the sea below, setting off the *ice-nine* disaster. Similarly, both Bokonon himself and Earl McCabe eventually grow into what they initially only pretended to be, Bokonon knowing the "agony of the saint" and McCabe "the agony of the tyrant" (175). Readers may be reminded of *Mother Night* here, with its clearly stated moral: "We are what we pretend to be, so we must be careful about what we pretend to be" (v). The line between truth and fiction in *Cat's Cradle* is thin and permeable, as is often the case with POSTMODERN literature. What is pretense and what is truth when what we pretend to be is what we really are? Where does art stop and reality begin? With truth and fiction so easily interchangeable, again it makes sense to live one's life according to the *foma*, the harmless untruths that help make us better people.

However, Vonnegut is not an author to offer easy answers to big questions about the meaning of life. While the book may advocate living by the *foma* "that make you brave and kind and healthy and happy" (epigraph), there is a cruel paradox in the Bokononist worldview. The narrator describes this paradox as "the heartbreaking necessity of lying about reality, and the heartbreaking impossibility of lying about it" (284). So, at the same time that Bokonon invents *boko-maru* and comforts people with the belief that God has plans for them, that all humans are organized into teams called *karasses* in order to do God's will, at the same time that he declares man is the only thing sacred to Bokononists, he also shamelessly advocates mass suicide at the end of the book. Perhaps we are to read this as Bokonon's final acceptance of the "heartbreaking impossibility" of *foma* to provide comfort any longer after the apocalyptic *ice-nine* disaster has occurred. While the narrator gasps "What a cynic!" (273) after reading Bokonon's note explaining the mass suicide, Mona Aamons Monzano certainly takes the note in stride, seeing suicide as the only logical response to the catastrophe that has just taken place. The narrator, after all, never answers when Mona asks if he would wish any of the dead back alive again, hesitating so long that Mona reaches down to scoop up some of the *ice-nine* and press it to her own lips.

Later, in a conversation with Newt Hoenikker, the narrator proclaims Bokononism "Such a *depressing* religion!" (284) and calls Bokonon himself a "jigaboo bastard" (285). Still trying to cling to a sentimental belief that man is sacred, the narrator speaks of "meaningful, individual heroic acts" (285) including the deaths of Julian Castle and his son, who, in their final hours, return to their jungle hospital to provide comfort to their patients, and of Angela Hoenikker, who dies playing her clarinet. "Soft pipes, play on," the narrator murmurs "huskily" (285), thinking of Angela. Immediately, Newt responds that maybe the narrator "can find some neat way to die, too" (285), a comment not only deflating to the narrator's lofty sentiments, but very Bokononist in spirit. Perhaps the way Bokonon handles the cruel paradox of the religion he invents—the necessity of lying about reality, yet the impossibility of doing so—is by telling lies, but then not hiding the fact that he does so. Thus, he admits throughout the *Books of Bokonon* that nothing he says is true, that his stories are "trash," and so forth. Bokonon does not necessarily expect his followers to believe the lies he tells, but only to *act* as if these lies are true.

As in *Player Piano*, when Paul Proteus realizes that the ex-minister Lasher "had created the revolution as a symbol, and was now welcoming the opportunity to die as one" (320), in *Cat's Cradle*, symbolic action matters. That is why the narrator, at the end of the novel, blurts out to Newt his "dream of climbing Mount McCabe with some magnificent symbol and planting it there" (285). But the narrator has a hard time figuring out what his magnificent symbol should be. Not until he meets Bokonon and reads the final sentence that Bokonon has planned for his *Books* does the narrator identify an appropriate symbol to plant on the mountain. The paper with the final sentence written on it, which Bokonon hands the narrator, reads:

> If I were a younger man, I would write a history of human stupidity; and I would climb to the top of Mount McCabe and lie down on my back with my history for a pillow; and I would take from the ground some of the blue-white poison that makes statues of men; and I would make a statue of myself, lying on my back, grinning horribly, and thumbing my nose at You Know Who. (287)

The history that the narrator is writing, the novel *Cat's Cradle* itself, and *The Books of Bokonon* all become inextricably entwined in this final page. Each begins with a warning that the pages contained within are nothing but lies, and each can be read as a history of human stupidity.

Bokonon, in fact, comments on histories. The narrator explains, "'Write it all down,' Bokonon tells us. He is really telling us how futile it is to write or read histories. 'Without accurate records of the past, how can men and women be expected to avoid making serious mistakes in the future?' he asks ironically" (237). Bokonon never expects men and women to learn from history and avoid

making mistakes in the future. Just as in *Slaughterhouse-Five* Vonnegut talks about turning into a pillar of salt for looking back at the past, we see the futility of history-writing; recording history, Vonnegut suggests, probably will not change the future as we might hope. Yet, again as in *Slaughterhouse-Five*, when Vonnegut says that he loves LOT'S WIFE for looking back at the destruction of Sodom and Gomorrah "because it was so human" (22), in *Cat's Cradle* we also get the sense that looking back, that attempting to explain and understand the past, are very human, empathetic things to do, despite their potential futility. Histories might not change things, might not provide warnings to the future, but humans must *try* nonetheless. This, then, is being fully human and is a way of "thumbing [one's] nose" at God, at fate, at destiny, at determinism itself. *Cat's Cradle*, as Vonnegut's "history of human stupidity," becomes the symbol he wants to plant—though it might not save us from death and destruction in the end, at least the black humor will cause us to go out "grinning horribly."

CHARACTERS AND RELATED ENTRIES

Aamons, Celia A native San Lorenzan, Celia Aamons marries the Finnish architect Nestor Aamons and is the mother of Mona Aamons Monzano.

Aamons, Nestor A native Finnish architect captured by the Russians and liberated by the Germans during World War II, Nestor Aamons is forced by the Germans to fight in Yugoslavia. In Yugoslavia, he is captured first by Chetniks, then by Communist partisans who attack the Chetniks. He is liberated by the Italians, who put him to work designing fortifications in Sicily. He eventually steals a fishing boat and escapes to Portugal, where he meets Julian Castle, an American draft dodger and sugar millionaire. Castle persuades him to come to San Lorenzo to design a charity hospital, the House of Hope and Mercy in the Jungle. Aamons dies in San Lorenzo shortly after the birth of his beautiful daughter, Mona.

boko-maru *Boko-maru* is a Bokononist ritual designed to kindle love and affection between religious practitioners. The ritual involves two people rubbing the soles of their feet together.

Bokonon   Lionel Boyd Johnson, whose last name is pronounced "Bokonon" in the native San Lorenzo dialect, is a black British subject born in 1891 on the island of Tobago. The youngest child of a wealthy Episcopalian, Johnson sailed alone to London as a 21-year-old to enroll in the London School of Economics and Political Science. His education, however, is interrupted by the outbreak of World War I. After enlisting, serving in the field for two years, then being hospitalized for two more years after suffering a gas attack at the Battle of Ypres, he encounters several adventures while sailing home to Tobago. Winding up in Haiti, he is approached by an idealistic Marine deserter named Earl McCabe, who pays Johnson to sail him to Miami. A storm, though, sinks the boat, and McCabe and Johnson end up on the island of San Lorenzo, where they determine to establish a Utopian country. McCabe reforms the economy and laws while Johnson "cynically and playfully" (172) invents a new religion, Bokononism. Eventually, the two men agree between themselves that no governmental reform will make the people of San Lorenzo less miserable, so they decide that McCabe will outlaw Bokononism to make the religion more appealing. Bokononism is a religion filled with paradox, and it becomes difficult for readers to determine whether Bokonon is a charlatan or a saint. Though he supplies the masses of San Lorenzans with hope for many years, after the *ice-nine* disaster, he induces thousands of people to commit suicide. The only time we actually see Bokonon in the novel, rather than simply hearing about him secondhand, is at the very end, when the novel's narrator stumbles upon him sitting by the side of the road. In this scene, Bokonon apparently tries to persuade the narrator to commit suicide as well.

Bokononism   Bokononism is the popular, though outlawed, religion of many native San Lorenzo islanders. The religion was founded by a black man named Lionel Boyd Johnson, born to a wealthy Episcopalian family on the island of Tobago in 1891. When Johnson and a U.S. Marine deserter

named Earl McCabe become shipwrecked on the tiny island of San Lorenzo, they try to help the poverty-stricken inhabitants by inventing a new government and a new religion. To make the religion more appealing, its founder, Johnson, redubbed "Bokonon" in the native dialect, asks McCabe, the island's new political leader, to outlaw it. Thus, Bokononism is born. The religion is strangely paradoxical, freely admitting that the beliefs it teaches are lies, but also encouraging people to live by these lies, or *foma*, in order to lead happier, more fulfilling lives.

Books of Bokonon, The   *The Books of Bokonon* are the primary religious texts of the followers of Bokononism. The paradoxical nature of this invented religion becomes evident when the novel's narrator, John, reveals to readers the first sentence in *The Books of Bokonon*: "All of the true things I am about to tell you are shameless lies" (5).

Breed, Dr. Asa   Vice president of the Research Laboratory at the General Forge and Foundry Company, Dr. Asa Breed supervised Dr. Felix Hoenikker during the production of the atomic bomb. Early in the novel, Dr. Breed gives the novel's narrator, John, a tour of the laboratory, explaining that Dr. Hoenikker was allowed to research anything that interested him, since the laboratory's mission was pure research rather than commercial applications. Though he respected Dr. Hoenikker as a scientist, Dr. Breed is rumored by people in Ilium to have had a long-standing affair with Dr. Hoenikker's wife, Emily. Many people, in fact, believe that Dr. Breed is the true father of Angela, Franklin, and Newton Hoenikker.

Breed, Jr.   The novel's narrator, John, discovers, while gossiping with two bartenders and a prostitute in an Ilium bar, that Dr. Asa Breed had a son who quit his job at the General Forge and Foundry Company on the day the atomic bomb was dropped on Hiroshima. Breed, Jr., whose first name is never given, explains to the older bartender that all scientific inventions are eventually turned into weapons and that he no longer wants to help politicians fight wars, which is why he is quitting.

Breed, Marvin A tombstone salesman in Ilium, Marvin Breed is the younger brother of Dr. Asa Breed. He meets John, the novel's narrator, when the cab driver who had driven John to the older Hoenikker graves wants to buy a more suitable tombstone for his own mother. Marvin Breed supplies the narrator with some background information about Emily Hoenikker. He used to date her in high school before losing her to his older brother, Asa, who subsequently lost her to Felix Hoenikker. A great admirer of Emily's, Marvin has no use for Felix Hoenikker, whom he speculates was "born dead" (68) since he has so little interest in living human beings.

"busy, busy, busy" "Busy, busy, busy," is a repeated refrain appearing throughout *Cat's Cradle*. It is what Bokononists are taught to whisper whenever they think about "how complicated and unpredictable the machinery of life really is" (66).

calypso Calypso is the name the religious teacher Bokonon gives to the short poems appearing throughout *The Books of Bokonon*.

Castle, Julian The narrator originally travels to the island of San Lorenzo to write a story about Julian Castle, who, in Albert Schweitzer fashion, founded the House of Hope and Mercy in the Jungle, a hospital for the poor. A former American sugar millionaire who had lived a decadent and wasteful existence, Julian Castle is 60 years old when he meets the narrator and "had been absolutely unselfish for twenty years" (84). Though he tends to be cynical, Julian Castle is also a devout Bokononist who offers the Bokononist rites to the patients he treats at the hospital. Both Julian and his son, Philip, die in the *ice-nine* disaster.

Castle, Philip The son of hospital founder Julian Castle, Philip Castle is both an artist and writer whose work, *San Lorenzo: The Land, the History, the People*, the narrator reads on the plane on the way to San Lorenzo. Claire Minton, the American ambassador's wife, who used to work as an indexer, deduces from the index of Castle's book that, although Philip grew up with the beautiful Mona Aamons Monzano and is deeply in love with her, he will never marry her because he is a homosexual. Readers first see Philip Castle when he is making a mosaic of Mona Aamons Monzano in the lobby of the Casa Mona, the hotel where the narrator, H. Lowe Crosby, the American bicycle manufacturer, and his wife, Hazel, are staying. After arguing with Castle and discovering that he is actually the owner of the hotel, the Crosbys leave "The Pissant Hilton" in a huff. Like most characters, Philip dies at the end of the novel in the *ice-nine* disaster.

Connors, Harrison C. Harrison C. Connors is the "strikingly handsome" (116) playboy husband of Angela Hoenikker. A former laboratory assistant to Dr. Felix Hoenikker, Connors is currently president of the Fabri-Tek Company, a firm that does top-secret government work. Cruel and unfaithful to his wife, Angela, Connors, we discover, married her in exchange for a portion of the *ice-nine* that she acquired at her father's death.

Castle Sugar, Inc. The Castle Sugar Company colonized the island of San Lorenzo in 1916, during the sugar boom of World War I. The company ran the island like a feudal fiefdom for several years, but never made a profit, and withdrew from its San Lorenzo holdings in 1922 when Lionel Boyd Johnson and Corporal Earl McCabe arrived.

Connors, Mrs. Harrison C. See Hoenikker, Angela, below.

Crosby, H. Lowe An American bicycle manufacturer whom the narrator meets on the plane on the way to San Lorenzo, H. Lowe Crosby is tired of his employees' ingratitude at his Chicago plant, so he plans to start a bicycle company in San Lorenzo. Scornful of communists and "pissants," Crosby believes that dictatorships are often very good things. Though the narrator says Crosby "wasn't a terrible person and he wasn't a fool," he nevertheless confronts the world "with a certain barn-yard clownishness" (92). Crosby, along with his wife, Hazel, is one of the few survivors of the *ice-nine* disaster.

Crosby, Hazel   The wife of the American bicycle manufacturer H. Lowe Crosby, Hazel Crosby is delighted when, on the plane to San Lorenzo, she discovers that the novel's narrator is from Indiana and thus a fellow Hoosier. Obsessed with Hoosiers, Hazel tells the narrator to call her "Mom," something she tells all young people from Indiana she meets. Hazel, along with her husband, the narrator, and Newt and Frank Hoenikker, survives the *ice-nine* disaster at the end of the novel. We last see her stitching together an American flag for the little group of survivors, whom she has cheerfully dubbed the Swiss Family Robinson.

Day the World Ended, The   *The Day the World Ended* is a book started but never finished by John, the narrator of *Cat's Cradle*. It is an account of what important Americans were doing on August 6, 1945, the day the first atomic bomb was dropped on Hiroshima, Japan. John becomes entangled in the affairs of the Hoenikker family in the course of conducting research for the book since Dr. Felix Hoenikker, father of Angela, Frank, and Newt, was one of the key scientists working on the Manhattan Project to develop the bomb.

duffle   *Duffle* is a term used by the religious teacher Bokonon to refer to "the destiny of thousands upon thousands of persons when placed in the hands of a *stuppa*" or a "fogbound child" (199).

duprass   In *Cat's Cradle*, a *duprass* is a *karass* composed of only two people. The novel's narrator, John, believes that Horlick and Claire Minton, whom he meets on the plane on the way to the island of San Lorenzo, are a "flawless example" (86) of a *duprass*. Bokonon also teaches that members of a *duprass* die within a week of each other. The Mintons, later in the novel, die "within the same second" (88).

Dynamic Tension   The prophet Bokonon teaches that good societies can be built "only by pitting good against evil, and by keeping the tension between the two high at all times" (102). Bokonon calls this equilibrium "Dynamic Tension," a term borrowed from Charles Atlas, a mail-order muscle-builder.

Faust, Naomi   Described as a "merry desiccated old lady" (37), Naomi Faust is Dr. Asa Breed's secretary at the General Forge and Foundry Company in Ilium, whom we first see decorating the office for Christmas. Naomi later explains to the narrator her view of Dr. Felix Hoenikker, describing him as unknowable because the usual things that matter to a person—family, love, intimacy—were not important to Dr. Hoenikker. Though she is told by Dr. Breed that Dr. Hoenikker's main interest was in truth, Naomi explains to the narrator, in a very Bokononist fashion, that she has "trouble understanding how truth, all by itself, could be enough for a person" (54).

foma   According to the teachings of Bokononism, *foma* are harmless untruths that can help people lead happier lives. The novel's epigraph includes a quote from *The Books of Bokonon* 1:5, which urges adherents of this religion to "Live by the *foma* that make you brave and kind and healthy and happy." In Vonnegut's view, organized religion and art both provide sustaining illusions to human beings, and thus are examples of *foma*.

General Forge and Foundry Company   Dr. Felix Hoenikker spends his professional life working in the research laboratory of the General Forge and Foundry Company in Ilium, New York. During his tenure at the company, he contributes significantly to the development of the atomic bomb and also invents the doomsday device *ice-nine*.

granfalloon   The prophet Bokonon teaches that a *granfalloon* is a false *karass*. A *granfalloon* is a group of people that seem to be connected in some way, but whose connections have nothing to do with God's plan for them. Political parties, sports teams, and companies are all examples of *granfalloons*.

Hoenikker, Angela   Angela Hoenikker is pulled out of school at the age of 16 to care for her father, Dr. Felix Hoenikker, after her mother's death. A homely girl who is fiercely devoted to Dr. Hoenikker, Angela's one passion in life is playing the clarinet, which she does beautifully. The narrator first meets Angela on the plane to San Lorenzo, where she and her youngest brother, Newt, are traveling to attend the engagement party of the family's middle child, Franklin Hoenikker. Like her brothers, Angela possesses a small amount of *ice-nine*, which the siblings had divided among themselves at their father's death. Frank Hoenikker hints, after Papa Monzano's death, that Angela had used the *ice-nine* to entice her handsome and unfaithful husband, Harrison C. Connors, into marrying her. Angela dies in the *ice-nine* disaster at the end of the novel.

Hoenikker, Celia The novel's narrator discovers, from talking with Angela and Newt Hoenikker, that their father has a sister named Celia. Celia Hoenikker raises giant schnauzers on Shelter Island in New York. Although the children do not really know her, she sends a Christmas card every year.

Hoenikker, Emily Emily Hoenikker is the wife of Dr. Felix Hoenikker and mother of Angela, Franklin, and Newton. Described as prettier than an angel in high school, Emily first dated Marvin Breed, who later becomes an Ilium tombstone maker, then his older brother, Asa Breed, who later runs the research laboratory at the General Forge and Foundry Company, before marrying Felix Hoenikker. Because she is a long-suffering wife largely ignored by her husband during their marriage, many in Ilium believe she had a long-term affair with Dr. Asa Breed, and that Dr. Breed is the true father of all three Hoenikker children. Readers, however, never find out if these rumors are true. Giving birth to little Newt, Emily dies as a result of a pelvis injury obtained in an earlier car wreck, when she had gone to retrieve a car abandoned in traffic by her absentminded husband.

Hoenikker, Dr. Felix One of the main creators of the atomic bomb, Felix Hoenikker is also the father of Angela, Franklin, and Newton Hoenikker. The novel's narrator, John, never actually meets Dr. Hoenikker, but learns about him from his children and from his coworkers. A scientist who disassociates himself completely from his own family and from human relationships in general, Dr. Hoenikker develops the insidious compound *ice-nine* just before his death, and thus is respon-

sible for bringing about the actual end of the world, an end hinted at in his work on the bomb and in the title of the book the narrator is working on: *The Day the World Ended*. In an interview in *The Paris Review*, Vonnegut said that Dr. Felix Hoenikker is a "caricature" (*Palm Sunday* 91) of real-life Nobel Prize–winning chemist and physicist and star of the GENERAL ELECTRIC research laboratory, DR. IRVING LANGMUIR.

Hoenikker, Franklin Franklin Hoenikker is the middle child of Dr. Felix Hoenikker and his wife, Emily. A silent and friendless boy dubbed "Secret Agent X-9" by his fellow high school students, Frank spends most of his teenage years working at Jack's Hobby Shop, where he builds elaborate models and secretly conducts a love affair with Jack's wife. As a grown man, Frank moves to the island of San Lorenzo, where he becomes the republic's Minister of Science and Progress and major-domo to the island's dictator, Miguel "Papa" Monzano. Pegged to be the new president of San Lorenzo after Papa's death, and to marry his beautiful adopted daughter, Mona Aamons Monzano, Frank convinces the novel's narrator, John, to take over both duties. When Papa dies, readers discover that Frank had attained his lofty position in San Lorenzo by giving his share of *ice-nine* to Papa Monzano. Frank is one of the few survivors of the *ice-nine* catastrophe; the last we see of him, he is constructing ant farms and marveling at the survival instincts of the tiny creatures.

Hoenikker, Newton The youngest son of Dr. Felix Hoenikker, Newton Hoenikker is a 21-year-old midget who has just flunked out of Cornell University when the novel's narrator requests memories of his father. The most forthcoming of the Hoenikker children, Newt supplies the narrator with many anecdotes about his strange family. Like his siblings, Newt possesses a small amount of *ice-nine*. At the end of the novel, we discover that part of Newt's *ice-nine* is in the possession of the Union of Soviet Socialist Republics because Newt had given some of the substance to Zinka, the midget Russian ballerina with whom he had a brief love affair. Newt is also an artist who paints a picture consisting of "scratches made in a black, gummy impasto," which he tells the narrator is a cat's cradle. One of the survivors of the *ice-nine* apocalypse, Newt is driving in San Lorenzo's single taxicab with the narrator when the two encounter the holy man Bokonon.

Hoenikker, Rudolph Rudolph Hoenikker is the identical twin brother of Dr. Felix Hoenikker. Although readers never meet him in the novel, Angela and Newt tell the narrator about Rudolph, explaining that their father hardly ever mentioned his twin. The last the children heard, Rudolph Hoenikker was a manufacturer of music boxes in Zurich, Switzerland.

Holderness, Marvin Sharpe Marvin Sharpe Holderness, imprisoned for killing his own brother, writes a manuscript about the end of the world, *2000 A.D.*, which he sends to Dr. Felix Hoenikker. Because the book includes a sex orgy right before the world blows up, the teenage Frank Hoenikker steals the book, and he and Newt Hoenikker read it over and over. When their sister, Angela, finds the book, she burns it as "dirty rotten filth" (10). Dr. Felix Hoenikker, who was not interested in literature, never read the book, but played with the string that had tied the manuscript together, making a cat's cradle out of it and scaring his little son Newt with it the only time he ever tried to play with the child.

Horvath, Dr. Nilsak Dr. Nilsak Horvath is a scientist who works at the General Forge and Foundry Company in Ilium. Though we never actually meet him in the novel, we meet his secretary, Miss Francine Pefko. Dr. Horvath, apparently, is a "famous surface chemist . . . who's doing . . . wonderful things with films" (32). Miss Pefko tells Dr. Breed and John, the novel's narrator, that she does not understand a thing she writes down when she takes dictation from Dr. Horvath.

House of Hope and Mercy in the Jungle, The The House of Hope and Mercy in the Jungle is the hospital started by Julian Castle on the island of San Lorenzo.

Humana, Dr. Vox A native San Lorenzan who is also a Christian minister, Dr. Vox Humana, named after an organ stop, arrives at Papa Monzano's deathbed to administer the last rites. Because Catholicism and Protestantism have been outlawed on the island along with Bokononism, Dr. Humana has to invent his own ritual, which involves a chicken and a butcher knife. When Dr. Humana is actually let in the room, Papa orders him to leave, declaring that he is a member of the Bokononist faith and will not accept the Christian last rites. Dr. Humana is also a talented artist who draws caricatures of world leaders on the targets the air show planes fire at.

ice-nine *Ice-nine* is a doomsday device invented by Dr. Felix Hoenikker at the request of a Marine general who wants a method of freezing muddy ground so that military troops can travel more easily. After the doctor's death, his children, Angela, Frank, and Newt Hoenikker, divide the *ice-nine* among themselves. Each Hoenikker child trades the technology for either love or position. When Frank's portion of the *ice-nine*, which he had traded to Papa Monzano on the island of San Lorenzo in exchange for a political appointment, is accidentally released into the ocean surrounding the island, all water on Earth freezes, causing an apocalyptic natural disease. Only a small group of San Lorenzans survive the catastrophe and become the last remaining people on Earth at the novel's end.

Jack The owner of Jack's Hobby Shop, where Frank Hoenikker worked during most of his teenage years, Jack shows the narrator an extremely elaborate model town built by Frank. Gushing that Frank was a misunderstood genius, the hobby store owner has no idea that Frank was sleeping with his wife during the years he worked there.

John John, whose last name is never divulged, is the freelance journalist who is the narrator of the novel. At the beginning of *Cat's Cradle*, John is working on a book to be called *The Day the World Ended* about the events of August 6, 1945, the day the first atomic bomb was dropped on Hiroshima. Because Dr. Felix Hoenikker was so intricately involved in developing the bomb, John writes to the Hoenikker children, soliciting memories of the day. He learns more about the family when Newt, Dr. Hoenikker's youngest son, writes him back. John later discovers that Dr. Hoenikker's elusive older son, Franklin, is employed as a minister of science on the small Caribbean island of San Lorenzo, a place John himself is coincidentally sent a bit later to write a magazine story. In San Lorenzo, John is astonished when Frank Hoenikker recruits him to be the new president of the republic. He eventually agrees to accept the job and is delighted to discover that marrying the beautiful Mona Aamons Monzano is part of the bargain. When the island is destroyed by the *ice-nine* possessed by the Hoenikker children, John is one of a very few survivors. *Cat's Cradle* is presented as having been written during the six months following the cataclysmic release of the chemical compound. Though readers never learn John's fate definitively, the end of the novel hints that he will commit suicide, as thousands and thousands of native San Lorenzans did earlier.

Johnson, Lionel Boyd   See Bokonon, above.

kan-kan   In Bokononist belief, a *kan-kan* is the instrument that brings a person into his or her *karass*, or group of people that God assembles to do his will. The novel's narrator, John, tells readers that his own *kan-kan* is the book he never finished, *The Day the World Ended*, which brings him into contact with the Hoenikker family.

karass   Bokononists believe that "humanity is organized into teams . . . that do God's Will without every discovering what they are doing" (2). Such a team, which "ignores national, institutional, occupational, familial, and class boundaries," (2–3) is called a *karass*. If a person is tangled up with another person over and over again in life, that person is most likely a member of his or her *karass*.

Knowles, Lyman Enders   A "small and ancient Negro" (58) who operates the elevators at the General Forge and Foundry Company in Ilium, Lyman Enders Knowles is, in the narrator's opinion,

insane. The old man grabs his own behind and cries "Yes, yes!" whenever he makes a point. Among other things, Knowles tells the narrator that Dr. Felix Hoenikker is not really dead but has merely entered a new dimension, and he calls the Hoenikker children "Babies full of rabies" (60).

Krebbs, Sherman   Sherman Krebbs is the poor poet the novel's narrator lets stay in his New York City apartment for two weeks over Christmas while he is away on his trip to Ilium. Described as a "platinum blond Jesus with spaniel eyes," Krebbs, in a "nihilistic debauch" (77), wrecks the narrator's apartment while he is gone, even killing his cat. The narrator later speculates that Krebbs was a member of his *karass*, the group of people Bokononism teaches will reappear again and again in our lives, serving it as a *wrang-wrang*, a person who steers someone away from a wrong path. Through Krebbs's example, the narrator realizes that nihilism is not for him.

McCabe, Earl   Described as a "brilliant, self-educated, idealistic Marine deserter" (107), Earl McCabe steals his company's recreation fund in Haiti in 1922 and offers the young Lionel Boyd Johnson (Bokonon) $500 to sail him to Miami. When the boat is wrecked in a storm, Johnson and McCabe make it onto the island of San Lorenzo, where they decide to set up a Utopia. McCabe reforms the government and legal system, while Johnson invents a new religion, which comes to be called Bokononism. Eventually, the two men decide together that McCabe should outlaw Bokononism in order to make the religion more appealing to the people. Both Johnson/Bokonon and McCabe grow into the roles they have devised for themselves, Johnson becoming more saintlike and McCabe more tyrannical and cruel. When McCabe dies, he anoints his major-domo, Miguel "Papa" Monzano, as his successor.

Minton, Claire   The wife of the American ambassador to the republic of San Lorenzo, Claire Minton meets the novel's narrator on the plane on the way to San Lorenzo. The Mintons, the narrator realizes, are members of a *duprass*, which is a *karass,* or group of people linked by fate, consisting of only two. Claire explains that her husband, Horlick, lost his job with the U.S. State Department because of a letter she wrote to the *New York Times,* about how Americans are always looking for love in forms and places where they cannot possibly find it. Claire also used to work as an indexer, and she is able to tell the narrator a great deal about Philip Castle based on the index to his book, *San Lorenzo: The Land, the History, the People.* The Mintons die together at the end of the novel, after the plane at the air show crashes into the palace. The couple hold back from being saved and plunge into the ocean holding hands; the narrator writes that "their good manners killed them" (259).

Minton, Horlick   The American ambassador to the republic of San Lorenzo, Horlick Minton, along with his wife, Claire, meets the novel's narrator on the plane on the way to San Lorenzo. Minton, we discover, became ambassador after having been fired from the U.S. State Department. According to H. Lowe Crosby, the American bicycle manufacturer, Minton was fired for being soft on communism. However, Horlick believes he was fired for being too pessimistic. The Mintons are traveling to the island to help commemorate the Hundred Martyrs to Democracy, a group of San Lorenzoans killed on their way to fight in World War II. At the ceremony at the end of the novel, Minton delivers a moving speech in which he says that all men killed in war are really murdered children. It turns out that the Minton's own son had been killed in World War II. Horlick and Claire Minton die at the end of the novel, when one of the air show planes crashes into the palace, too polite to try to save themselves.

Moakely, George Minor   George Minor Moakely was a man hanged in Ilium in 1782 for murdering 26 people. On the scaffold, he sang a song proclaiming that he was not sorry for his crimes. John, the novel's narrator, hears this story from Dr. Asa Breed during his tour of the General Forge and Foundry Company.

Monzano, Miguel "Papa"   Papa Monzano is a self-educated native of San Lorenzo who had been

major-domo to Corporal McCabe, the founder, along with Bokonon himself, of the republic. Upon McCabe's death, Monzano became the island's dictator. When the narrator reaches San Lorenzo, Papa is dying of cancer. Though he has named Franklin Hoenikker, his own major-domo, as his successor, Frank is reluctant to take the position and instead persuades the narrator to become San Lorenzo's new president. Papa, wracked with pain caused by the cancer, kills himself by ingesting *ice-nine,* which had been given to him by Frank Hoenikker. Papa's body, tainted by *ice-nine,* is what causes the apocalyptic disaster that ends the novel. During a ceremonial air show, a plane crashes into the palace, crumbling the walls and sending Papa's body plummeting into the ocean below. Instantly, the entire world is frozen by *ice-nine.*

Monzano, Mona Aamons   The heartbreakingly beautiful daughter of Finnish architect Nestor Aamons, who had come to San Lorenzo to design Julian Castle's House of Hope and Mercy in the Jungle, Mona Aamons Monzano is adopted by Miguel "Papa" Monzano after her father's death and becomes an icon of hope for the people of the island. Although she is initially engaged to marry Franklin Hoenikker, who is Papa's chosen successor, Mona good-naturedly agrees to marry the novel's narrator instead when he consents to become the new president of the republic of San Lorenzo. She refuses, however, to promise the narrator that she will practice the Bokononist ritual of *book-maru,* the rubbing together of the soles of the feet, with him exclusively. Reluctantly, the narrator agrees that she may practice the ritual with whomever she wishes. Mona survives the *ice-nine* disaster by fleeing with the narrator into a deep oubliette under the palace dungeon, where they live for seven days. When the two emerge into the frozen world above and discover thousands of dead bodies in a natural bowl formation in the mountains, Mona reaches playfully toward the ground and kills herself with the *ice-nine.*

Pefko, Francine   Described as "twenty, vacantly pretty, and healthy—a dull normal" (32), Francine Pefko is the secretary of Dr. Nilsak Horvath at the General Forge and Foundry Company in Ilium. Embarrassed to be singled out of a crowd and introduced to the novel's narrator, John, by Dr. Asa Breed, Francine Pefko asserts her lack of understanding of anything she types and offers the observation that "You scientists *think* too much." Later, Dr. Breed admonishes Francine for referring to the laboratory's education exhibits as "magic," arguing that the lab is involved in science, in explaining mystery, not in reinforcing superstition. Francine Pefko is also the name of Dwayne Hoover's secretary in *Breakfast of Champions*, although it is unclear whether these characters are meant to be the same person.

pool-pah In *The Books of Bokonon*, the term *pool-pah* is translated variously as "shit storm" or "wrath of God" (244). A great *pool-pah* is created in the book after Frank Hoenikker gives his portion of the doomsday device *ice-nine* to Papa Manzano, dictator of the island of San Lorenzo.

Rumfoord, Remington, IV Remington Rumfoord, IV is the "young rakehell of the Rumfoord family" (106). The young Lionel Boyd Johnson (Bokonon) works on Rumfoord's estate in Newport, Rhode Island, as a gardener and carpenter for a time. After the end of World War I, Rumfoord proposes to sail his steam yacht around the world and invites Johnson to serve as first mate. When the yacht is rammed in a fog in Bombay harbor, only Johnson survives. The Rumfoord family appears in several other Vonnegut novels as well, most notably in *The Sirens of Titan* and *Slaughterhouse-Five*.

Sandra A prostitute whom the narrator, John, meets in a bar in Ilium, Sandra knew Frank Hoenikker in high school. She tells John how the kids used to call Frank "Secret Agent X-9." She also relates the story of Dr. Felix Hoenikker not showing up to give the high school commencement speech he was scheduled to deliver, and Dr. Asa Breed substituting at the last minute.

San Lorenzo San Lorenzo is the name of the poverty-stricken Caribbean island where Lionel Boyd Johnson, later known as the prophet Bokonon, and Earl McCabe attempt to fashion a Utopia by inventing a new religion and a new government.

saroon Bokononists use the verb *saroon* to describe what happens when a person acquiesces to a *vin-dit*, or cosmic shove into Bokononist belief. When the novel's narrator, John, agrees to become president of San Lorenzo, he *saroons*, finally accepting the Bokononist view that God is running his life and has work for him to do.

sinookas Practitioners of the Bokononist religion believe that *sinookas*, or the tendrils of one's life, become tangled with the *sinookas* of other people who are members of one's *karass*, a small group of individuals unknowingly assembled by God to do His bidding.

sin-wat *Sin-wat* is the Bokononist term for "a man who wants all of somebody's love" (208). Mona Aamons Monzano accuses the novel's narrator, John, of being a *sin-wat* when he demands that she practice the ritual of *boko-maru* exclusively with him after their marriage.

Stanley Stanley is the servant at the home of Frank Hoenikker on the island of San Lorenzo. He is the first plump native the narrator has seen.

stuppa Bokononists define a *stuppa* as a leader who controls the destinies of thousands upon thousands of people, but whose leadership skills are no better than those of a "fogbound child" (201).

Tum-bumwa In 1786, African blacks took over a British slave ship and ran it ashore on San Lorenzo. There they proclaimed the island an independent nation with Tum-bumwa as its emperor. Described as a "maniac" (126), Tum-bumwa orders the construction of not only the San Lorenzo Cathedral but of the massive fortifications and presidential castle on the north side of the island. Local legend says that 1,400 people died while building the fortifications, half of them executed in public for "substandard zeal" (126).

2000 A.D. *2000 A.D.* is a novel about the end of the world written by Marvin Sharpe Holderness, a minor character in *Cat's Cradle*. Holderness sends his manuscript to atomic bomb scientist Dr. Felix Hoenikker, along with a cover letter explaining that the author is currently in prison for killing his own brother. Although Dr. Hoenikker never reads the manuscript, his children do, mostly because it includes a scene depicting a wild sex orgy that takes place right before the world ends. Dr. Hoenikker is interested only in the string that ties the manuscript together, which he later uses to play a game of cat's cradle.

Unnamed bartender (younger) The novel's narrator, John, meets a bartender while he is killing time in an Ilium bar one evening before he can meet Dr. Asa Breed the next day. The bartender, along with a prostitute named Sandra, had both gone to high school with Frank Hoenikker. They supply John with some background information about the Hoenikker family. The last we see of Sandra and the bartender, they are both remembering that they read in the paper a few days before that the secret of life had been discovered. Ironically, though, neither one can remember what the secret is, though the bartender suggests it has something to do with proteins.

Unnamed bartender (older) While John, the novel's narrator, is conversing in an Ilium bar about the Hoenikker family with a bartender and a prostitute named Sandra, an older bartender comes in, who tells John about his memories of August 6, 1945, the day the atomic bomb was dropped on Hiroshima. On that day, he had served a drink to a man who was quitting his job at the General and Forge and Foundry Company because he did not want to help create weapons. The man turned out to be the son of Dr. Asa Breed.

Unnamed cab driver When the narrator hires a cab in order to visit the grave of Dr. Felix Hoenikker, his driver is so moved by the monument the Hoenikker children have erected to their mother that he decides to buy a new stone to mark his own mother's grave. So he and John drive to Avram Breed and Sons tombstone store, where they meet Dr. Asa Breed's younger brother, Marvin. In the tombstone salesroom, the narrator has his first *vin-dit*, or nudge toward Bokononism, when he discovers that the name carved on the pedestal of the stone angel the cab driver wants to buy is the same as his own last name.

Unnamed fat woman On his tour of the General Forge and Foundry Company in Ilium, John, the novel's narrator, sees a "winded, defeated-looking fat woman in filthy coveralls" (33) who trudges behind him at one point, looking resentfully at Dr. Asa Breed. John speculates that the woman hates people who think too much—Francine Pefko has just accused scientists in the lab of thinking too much—and John feels that, because of this, she is "an appropriate representative for almost all mankind" (33).

vin-dit A *vin-dit* is described as "a sudden, very personal shove in the direction of Bokononism" (69). The narrator John experiences his first *vin-dit* in the salesroom of a tombstone shop when he sees his own last name carved on the pedestal of a stone angel.

von Koenigswald, Dr. Schlichter Dr. Schlichter von Koenigswald is the personal physician to San Lorenzo's dictator, Papa Monzano. A member of the German S.S. for 14 years and a camp physician at Auschwitz, Dr. von Koenigswald came to San Lorenzo to work at Julian Castle's House of Hope and Mercy in the Jungle in order to do penance for his years as a Nazi. Castle tells the narrator that von Koenigswald is making great strides, "saving lives right and left" (186). If he continues at his present rate, Castle adds, "the number of people he's saved will equal the number of people he let die—in the year 3010" (186–187). Von Koenigswald perishes at the end of the novel, after tending to the body of Papa Monzano. When he goes to wash his hands, the water in the basin turns to ice. Von Koenigswald touches his tongue to the frozen substance and is instantly frozen solid himself.

wampeter Adherents of Bokononism believe that a *wampeter* is a pivot that holds together a *karass,* or small group of individuals assembled by God to do His bidding. Bokonon also teaches that, "at any given time, a *karass* actually has two *wampeters*—one waxing in importance, one waning" (52). The novel's narrator, John, tells readers that the *wampeter* of his *karass* just "coming into bloom" (52) at the beginning of the novel is the crystalline substance *ice-nine.*

wrang-wrang A *wrang-wrang* is a specific person in a *karass* (a small group of individuals who keep meeting again and again in life and make up a team assembled by God to do his will) whose purpose is to steer people away from a certain path in life. The novel's narrator, John, believes that the demented poet Sherman Krebbs, whom he lets stay in his apartment over Christmas, serves as a *wrang-wrang* in his *karass.* Krebbs steers John away from the path of nihilism after destroying John's apartment in a nihilistic debauch.

Zah-mah-ki-bo Bokononists believe that individuals have specific fates or inevitable destinies that they cannot resist. *Zah-mah-ki-bo* is the term they use to refer to this destiny.

Zinka Zinka is a Ukranian midget, a ballerina for the Borzoi Dance Company. Newt Hoenikker, also a midget, sees the company perform in Ilium and then again at Cornell University, where he waits for her outside the stage door with a dozen roses. Zinka defects from the U.S.S.R., asks for political asylum in the United States, and disappears with Newt for a week before appearing back at the Russian embassy, claiming that Americans are too materialistic and that she wants to go home. We find out later that Zinka had been a Russian agent who seduced Newt Hoenikker in order to get some of the *ice-nine* for her government.

FURTHER READING

Cat's Cradle. New York: Dell, 1998.
Leverence, W. John. "*Cat's Cradle* and Traditional American Humor." *Journal of Popular Culture* 5, no. 4 (1972): 955–963.
Mangum, Bryant. "*Cat's Cradle's* Jonah-John and the Garden of Ice-Nine." *Notes on Contemporary Literature* 9, no. 3 (1979): 9–11.
McGinnis, Wayne. "The Source and Implications of *Ice-Nine* in Vonnegut's *Cat's Cradle.*" *American Notes and Queries* 13, no. 3 (1974): 40–41.
Scholes, Robert. "Fabulation and Satire—Black Humor: *Cat's Cradle* and *Mother Night.*" In *The Fabulators.* New York: Oxford University Press, 1967. 35–55.
———. "Vonnegut's *Cat's Cradle* and *Mother Night.*" In *Fabulation and Metafiction.* Urbana, Ill.: University of Illinois Press, 1979. 156–162.
Zins, Daniel L. "Rescuing Science from Technocracy: *Cat's Cradle* and the Play of Apocalypse." *Science-Fiction Studies* 13 (1986): 170–81.

"The Chemistry Professor"

The musical-drama "The Chemistry Professor" appears as a chapter in Vonnegut's 1981 collection, *Palm Sunday: An Autobiographical Collage.* In the introduction, Vonnegut tells readers that his friend, Broadway producer Lee Guber, asked him, during the summer of 1978, to write a modern version of the Robert Louis Stevenson classic THE STRANGE CASE OF DR. JEKYLL AND MR. HYDE for the musical stage. Vonnegut complies, setting his version of the classic story on a contemporary college campus in the late 1970s.

SYNOPSIS

"The Chemistry Professor" opens at Sweetbread College, a small liberal arts institution outside Philadelphia. A group of students has just read in the campus newspaper that the college will be closing its doors forever because it has gone bankrupt. To try to save the college, the students decide to write and perform a Broadway musical, eventually agreeing that their play will be an updated version of the Robert Louis Stevenson novella *The Strange Case of Dr. Jekyll and Mr. Hyde.* Meanwhile, chemistry professor Dr. Henry Jekyll retreats to his lab to try to make a discovery that will win him the Nobel Prize and thus restore the college to its former glory. As the students begin to rehearse their play, a real-life Jekyll and Hyde story unfolds at the college as well. Dr. Jekyll creates a potion out of LSD and chicken tonic, supplied to him by roast chicken entrepreneur Fred Leghorn, the stepfather of student body president Jerry Rivers. When he drinks the potion, Dr. Jekyll turns into a raving, maniacal giant chicken. Soon the Hyde-like chicken comes crashing onto the theatrical stage, interrupting the fictional Jekyll and Hyde story. Fred Leghorn chases the giant chicken, eventually shooting him three times. The story ends with Dr. Jekyll, still in the guise of the Mr. Hyde chicken, dying tragically. The students abandon their play idea and decide instead, at the prompting of Leghorn, to roast the giant chicken and bury it in an unmarked grave.

COMMENTARY

Although in *Palm Sunday* Vonnegut explains that, unlike Robert Louis Stevenson, he was never paid for his work on the Jekyll and Hyde story, he also claims (perhaps ironically) that he considers his play "excellent, if a little slapdash and short" (239). Contemporary readers may be disinclined to agree with this assessment. The play that Vonnegut ended up writing is a bizarre blend of the classic Stevenson monster story and a 1940s Busby Berkeley musical extravaganza. Borrowing the plot from numerous Mickey Rooney–Judy Garland vehicles such as *Babes in Arms* and *Girl Crazy*, in which a group of talented young people decide to stage a musical in order to raise money for some cause, "The Chemistry Professor" very self-consciously spoofs the genre, designating certain students as Rooney and Garland look-alikes.

The humor of Vonnegut's play comes from the wholesome innocence of those early 1940s movies clashing with the very different cultural ideas about politically active, drug-experimenting college students in the 1970s. The students Vonnegut depicts in "The Chemistry Professor" are meant to be seen as impossibly anachronistic and unrealistic. Less successful, perhaps, is the humor that Vonnegut tries to mine out of chicken parts entrepreneur Fred Leghorn and the crazed giant chicken that serves as

the Mr. Hyde character. The end of the play is particularly unsatisfying since Vonnegut drops the plot-line about the students trying to raise money. While readers might have expected the giant chicken to be roasted and sold for its parts, thus solving Sweetbread College's financial difficulties, the students at the end agree to bury the chicken parts in an unmarked grave, and the school's impending bankruptcy seems to have been forgotten.

CHARACTERS AND RELATED ENTRIES

Cathcart, Sally   Sally Cathcart, described as a "Judy Garland look-alike," is a cheerleader at Sweetbread College who is in love with student body president Jerry Rivers. In the student production of *Dr. Jekyll and Mr. Hyde,* Sally plays the role of a prostitute with a heart of gold.

Jekyll, Dr. Henry   A chemistry professor at Sweetbread College, and the only faculty member with a "statewide reputation" (243), Dr. Henry Jekyll attempts to save the college by inventing a new chemical potion that will win him the Nobel Prize. Instead, his concoction, made of chicken tonic and LSD, turns him into a giant, crazed chicken. Dr. Jekyll dies at the end of the play, shot by chicken magnate Fred Leghorn.

Jekyll, Hortense   Hortense Jekyll is the beautiful and neglected wife of Sweetbread College chemistry professor Dr. Henry Jekyll. Although her husband has difficulty even remembering her first name, Hortense is loyal to Henry to the end, throwing herself sobbing upon the body of the dead, giant chicken—all that remains of her husband—as the final curtain drops.

Kimberly   Kimberly is a student at Sweetbread College, described in the stage directions as a "particularly pretty and scatterbrained coed" (240). In the students' revised version of *Dr. Jekyll and Mr. Hyde,* she plays a nursery maid, whose infant charge is blown up when Mr. Hyde distracts her and places a bomb in the perambulator she is pushing.

Leghorn, Fred   Fred Leghorn, the "shrewd hayseed king of the mechanized chicken industry"

(241), is also the fifth husband of the mother of Sweetbread College student body president Jerry Rivers. When he comes to visit Jerry, he brings a flask of chicken tonic used by one of his competitors and offers chemistry professor Dr. Henry Jekyll a generous sum of money to analyze its contents. Dr. Jekyll, however, uses the tonic to create a strange potion that turns him into a giant chicken. Leghorn will eventually save the students by shooting the Jekyll/chicken with a gun taken from the campus police officer.

Pops   Pops is a "doddering campus cop" (242) at Sweetbread College who plays a police officer in the student production of *Dr. Jekyll and Mr. Hyde*. Pops is the first character to see and be terrorized by the giant chicken that will end up disrupting the student play.

Rivers, Jerry   Jerry Rivers is student body president at Sweetbread College. Jerry's mother has been married five times, and his current stepfather is chicken magnate Fred Leghorn, who has come to Sweetbread to visit Jerry when the news of the college's bankruptcy is announced. In the student theatrical, Jerry plays the leading role of Dr. Jekyll.

Sam   Sam is the studious boyfriend of Kimberly. He, too, is an undergraduate at Sweetbread College. In the student play, he takes the part of Dr. Jekyll's best friend, a lawyer named Utterson who is choked to death by Mr. Hyde.

Sweetbread College   Sweetbread College is the setting for "The Chemistry Professor," an updated version of the Robert Louis Stevenson novella, *The Strange Case of Dr. Jekyll and Mr. Hyde*.

Whitefeet, Elbert   Elbert Whitefeet is the ineffectual, philosophy-reading college president who has run Sweetbread College into bankruptcy by investing in cocoa futures.

FURTHER READING

Palm Sunday: An Autobiographical Collage. New York: Dell, 1999.

"The Cruise of *The Jolly Roger*"

"The Cruise of *The Jolly Roger*," about a World War II veteran attempting to find a meaningful civilian life, was first published in the magazine *Cape Cod Compass* in April 1953. It was later reprinted in the 1999 collection *Bagombo Snuff Box*.

SYNOPSIS

A story about a previously homeless man who joins the army, becomes a major, is injured in an explosion, and returns to civilian life, "The Cruise of *The Jolly Roger*" focuses on the difficulties veteran Nathan Durant has fitting back into ordinary America when his war days have ended. Upon his release from a veteran's hospital, he buys a cabin cruiser, christens it *The Jolly Roger*, and motors around the Massachusetts coast. Depressed by the tranquility at Martha's Vineyard, he goes to CAPE COD, where he meets a group of young artists who invite him to lunch. But Durant ends up boring them with war stories. He moves on to New London, Connecticut, the hometown of a buddy killed in World War II. Although nobody in the town at first remembers Durant's friend, George Pefko, a legal secretary named Annie eventually figures out that he was a member of a large, transient family that lived out on the dunes. A small square in the town has even been named for him. As Annie takes Durant to see the square, a Memorial Day parade of schoolchildren passes by. When a young boy lays a bunch of lilacs on the plaque commemorating Pefko and makes a simple statement that the veteran had died so that the townspeople could be "safe and free" (132), Durant is genuinely moved.

COMMENTARY

In this story, the main character, Nathan Durant, has trouble with his own sense of identity. Because he grew up homeless during the Great Depression, he has no real hometown, and readers never find out much about his family background. In fact, he does not seem to belong much of anywhere until he "found a home in the United States Army" (121). Because the only home he knows is the army,

Durant has trouble imagining what life will be like when he is released at the age of 36. Vonnegut writes, "For want of exciting peacetime dreams of his own, for want of a home or family or civilian friends, Durant borrowed his neighbor's dream" (122). It is only because the man in the bed next to him at the veteran's hospital had talked ceaselessly about buying a boat that Durant purchases *The Jolly Roger*. And even the name he gives the boat is not of his own invention. Lifted from numerous pirate vessels, the name is suggested by a group of children at the boatyard. Later, the young artists Durant meets will laugh at the boat's name, considering it highly unoriginal.

Durant's lifelong lack of belonging is only compounded when he visits the various small New England towns along the Atlantic shoreline. Like the story "Miss Temptation" from Vonnegut's *Welcome to the Monkey House*, "The Cruise of *The Jolly Roger*" is about the difficulties returning veterans have fitting back into the civilian world. During his 17 years in the army, the world has moved on without Durant. He no longer retains the glamour lent him by his army uniform, and beautiful women no longer show any interest in him. While the young artists try to be polite, clearly their interests are quite different from Durant's, and he only bores them when he flounders through a long, overly detailed story about the injuries he sustained in Korea. In New London, Durant learns from the postmistress about the scorn the world at large has for transients like himself and his friend. When Annie suggests that George Pefko's father brought his family to New London to pick cranberries, the postmistress sniffs that she "wouldn't exactly call this their hometown" (128).

Later, the policeman in the Memorial Day parade, who is "fat with leisure, authority, leather, bullets, pistol, handcuffs, club, and a badge" (131), suggests that most people care only about exterior trappings. The policeman's badge and pistol seem designed for show rather than for the kind of dangerous service a man like Nathan Durant has performed for his country. The overinflated words that the teacher urges young Tom to pronounce when Durant asks why he laid flowers on Pefko's plaque—"Tell them you're paying homage to one of the fallen valiant who selflessly gave his life" (132)—are similarly false. They, like the policeman's accessories, are simply for display. There is nothing genuine or heartfelt about them. The teacher's lofty statement is contrasted to the simple words of the young schoolboy Tom, who quietly tells Durant that Pefko "died fighting so we could be safe and free. And we're thanking him with flowers, because it was a nice thing to do" (132). Tom's innocent, yet genuine sentiments affect Durant in a way that the showy parade and lofty words of the teacher do not. In what is perhaps a somewhat superficial, sentimental ending, the boy's words spark new life into Durant. The wounded veteran is finally able to imagine a future for himself, and he invites the secretary Annie for a ride on his boat.

CHARACTERS

Annie Annie is a legal secretary who comes into the post office when Nathan Durant is asking the postmistress about his dead war buddy, George Pefko. While the postmistress does not remember any Pefkos living in the town, Annie remembers a large, transient family that arrived to pick cranberries many years before. She is also able to tell Durant that a small square in the village is named for his dead friend. At the end of the story, Durant invites Annie to lunch, then for a ride on *The Jolly Roger*.

Durant, Nathan Nathan Durant is homeless during the Great Depression, but eventually settles in as an officer in the U.S. Army, where he remains for 17 years until he is severely injured in a bomb explosion in Korea. Upon his release, he buys a cabin cruiser, *The Jolly Roger,* and motors around the New England coast, missing the companionship and adventure he knew during his army days. After putting in at several towns, he ends up in New London, Connecticut, the hometown of a dead war buddy. There Durant's interest in life is revived by a young boy who retains the simple, true values Durant himself has lost.

Ed, Teddy, Lou, and Marion Ed, Teddy, Lou, and Marion are four artists in their late 20s whom Major Nathan Durant meets in Provincetown,

Cape Cod. Marion asks to sketch him and then invites him to lunch. At the lunch, Durant feels awkward and left out until Ed asks him about his war injuries. The major clearly bores the young people, though, when he launches into a long, convoluted tale about his experiences.

Pefko, George   George Pefko was a friend of Nathan Durant's who was killed in World War II. Like Durant himself, Pefko was transient as a boy, moving from town to town. But, because he had enlisted in the army from New London, Connecticut, he considered the village his hometown. In his wanderings after the war, Durant goes to New London to look up anyone who might have known Pefko.

Tom   Tom is a schoolboy who marches in New London's Memorial Day parade. He lays a bunch of lilacs on the plaque dedicated to George Pefko, Nathan Durant's friend who was killed in World War II. When Durant asks what the boy's gesture means, he is extremely moved by Tom's simple, genuine answer, that Pefko "died fighting so we could be safe and free" (132).

Unnamed Beautiful Woman   When Nathan Durant arrives at Chatham, Cape Cod in *The Jolly Roger,* he finds himself "beside a beautiful woman at the foot of a lighthouse there" (122). While he had been quite successful with women during his army days, now "the spark was gone" (122), and the woman looks away from him, without interest.

Unnamed Injured Veteran   While in the army hospital recovering from his injuries, Nathan Durant lies in a bed next to an unnamed veteran who talks constantly about his dream of owning a boat. Because of this man, Durant buys *The Jolly Roger.* Vonnegut writes that, "for want of exciting peacetime dreams of his own . . . Durant borrowed his neighbor's dream" (122).

Unnamed Policeman   A town policeman, described as "fat with leisure, authority, leather, bullets, pistol, handcuffs, club, and a badge" (131), rides in the New London, Connecticut, Memorial

Day parade. This character serves as a contrast to the much more humble-appearing Nathan Durant, who lacks the fancy trappings of the policeman, but whose own experience with guns was not just for show.

Unnamed Postmistress   In New London, Connecticut, Nathan Durant asks the town postmistress about his dead war buddy George Pefko. The woman does not remember any Pefkos living in the town.

Unnamed Teacher   When Nathan Durant asks why the young boy Tom has laid flowers on the plaque commemorating George Pefko, a teacher prompts him to answer that he's "paying homage to one of the fallen valiant who selflessly gave his life" (132). Tom's much more simple, straightforward answer, however, ends up moving Nathan Durant so profoundly that he feels "the old spark" of his life come back (132).

Unnamed Young Man and Woman   A "gaudily dressed young man with a camera in his hands and a girl on his arm" (123) clicks Nathan Durant's photograph in Provincetown on Cape Cod. When Durant tells the girl that he is not a painter, however, the couple loses interest in him.

FURTHER READING

Bagombo Snuff Box. New York: Berkley Books, 2000.
Reed, Peter. *The Short Fiction of Kurt Vonnegut.* Westport, Conn.: Greenwood Press, 1997.

"Custom-Made Bride"

A story that comments on the role of women in the 1950s, "Custom-Made Bride" first appeared in the *Saturday Evening Post* on March 27, 1954, and was later reprinted in the 1999 collection *Bagombo Snuff Box.*

SYNOPSIS

"Custom-Made Bride" is narrated by an adviser from an investment counseling firm who is sent to the home of famous designer and artist Otto Krummbein to straighten out his finances since Krummbein has neglected to pay income tax on any of his lavish earnings. The narrator arrives to find that Krummbein's home is extremely modern; it looks like a glass matchbox resting on a brick spool. Krummbein's wife, Falloleen, dressed in a leopard-print leotard, with silver hair and one huge hoop earring, is beautiful, sleek, and ultra-modern as well. The narrator, who sets to work immediately on the finances, soon tells the artist that he must begin to live on an allowance. The couple decides to begin saving money by spending a quiet evening at home, the very first time they have done this in their month-long marriage. Alone together, the artist and his wife discover they have nothing much to say to each other. They both wind up downstairs in Krummbein's studio at the end of the evening, where the narrator is working, looking for entertainment. In the course of their conversation with the narrator, readers discover that Falloleen herself is one of Otto's designs. He has transformed the plain, mousy Kitty Cahoun, the girl he originally married, into the glamorous Falloleen. But both the artist and his wife miss Kitty. The story ends with the couple striking a compromise—Falloleen will remain on the exterior, but "the soul of Kitty Cahoun" (148) will shine through.

COMMENTARY

"Custom-Made Bride" is a short, comic story that mines its humor at least partly from the contrast between the stodgy, sensible narrator and the ultra-stylish Krummbeins. The narrator has a solid profession as "a customer's man for an investment counseling firm" (133). His clothes are drab and conservative. He wears a "uniform" consisting of a "gray suit, Homburg hat, and navy blue overcoat" and he is saving money to buy "a half-dozen more white shirts" (133). The Krummbeins, on the other hand, are anything but sensible. Otto lives completely for aesthetics and has the financial sense "of a chickadee" (134). Out-of-date and unstylish surroundings cause him to become mentally depressed, so he constantly redesigns things to be as modern and stylish as possible. His wife, Falloleen, is in

many ways Otto's most stunning creation. The narrator describes Falloleen as "sheathed in a zebra-striped leotard," with hair that is "bleached silver and touched with blue," and wearing a "barbaric gold hoop" in one ear (136). When the narrator enters the Krummbeins' home, two opposite worlds collide. Yet, each man has something to offer the other. The narrator actually likes the way the lemon yellow pocket handkerchief that Otto gives him looks. And Otto is willing to submit to the narrator's financial supervision in order to avoid going to prison for not paying his taxes. One of the surprising things about the story is how well Otto and the narrator seem to get along.

The story is also interesting in that it makes a comment on the ornamental role many wives were expected to play in the 1950s. Nearly 10 years before the publication of Betty Friedan's 1963 bestseller, *The Feminine Mystique*, which examined the stultifying lives of American housewives, "Custom-Made Bride" exposes the emptiness of a woman whose only function is to serve as a beautiful object, as an enhancement and extension of her husband and his career rather than as an individual in her own right. Kitty recognizes that a life dedicated solely to style creates a woman that is "dull and shallow, scared and lost, unhappy and unloved" (147). But even more, Vonnegut shows that reducing women to such ornamental roles will not produce happiness in the husband either. He has Otto admit that he "lived in terror of being left alone" with Falloleen, who "was a crashing bore when she wasn't striking a pose or making a dramatic entrance or exit" (148). Otto insists that he never meant to remake Kitty's soul, which is one of "only four things on earth that don't scream for redesigning" (148). Yet, Otto, and perhaps Vonnegut himself, is not willing to give up the notion that women should still be beautiful to look at, even while being individuals on the inside. The other three things that Otto says need no improvement are the egg, the Model-T Ford, and "the exterior of Falloleen" (148). The story closes with the couple agreeing that Falloleen will remain, though she will be only the exterior Mrs. Krummbein, while Kitty Cahoun lives as the woman inside the glamorous body.

CHARACTERS

Cahoun, Kitty See Krummbein, Falloleen, below.

Krummbein, Otto Otto Krummbein is a designer and an artist who longs to make everything around him as modern and stylish as possible. Thus, he constantly redesigns whatever he comes in contact with, whether furniture, cars, or even people. He has transformed his wife, the plain Kitty Cahoun, into the sleek and glamorous Falloleen. Otto even tries to redesign the narrator, asking him to remove his maroon tie and giving him a lemon yellow pocket handkerchief for dramatic effect. By the end of the story, however, Otto admits that Falloleen is a "crashing bore" and he urges his wife to rediscover Kitty inside herself.

Krummbein, Falloleen Mrs. Krummbein, the new wife of Otto Krummbein, loves her husband so much that she willingly allows him to transform her into the sleek, beautiful, and ultra-modern Falloleen. However, Faloleen eventually breaks down and tells her husband that she wants to be plain Kitty Cahoun again. The two compromise at the end of the story, agreeing that Mrs. Krummbein will retain the exterior of Falloleen, but the soul of Kitty.

Murphy, Hal Hal Murphy is artist Otto Krummbein's lawyer and also a friend of the narrator. Murphy is the one who asks the narrator to straighten out Krummbein's finances.

Narrator The story's narrator is a financial adviser for an investment firm. His friend, lawyer Hal Murphy, asks him to take on artist and designer Otto Krummbein as a client, a man in danger of going to prison for income tax evasion. When he goes to Krummbein's home, the narrator is amazed by its extremely modern appearance. He is even more astonished by Krummbein's wife, the chic, modern Falloleen. Yet, by the end of the evening, the narrator is able to see through the Krummbeins' high-living façade. The couple confess to him their boredom with each other and their dissatisfaction with Otto's most stunning creation, Falloleen.

He witnesses their final pledge to let the plain, mousy Kitty Cahoun reemerge.

FURTHER READING

Bagombo Snuff Box. New York: Berkley Books, 2000.
Reed, Peter. *The Short Fiction of Kurt Vonnegut.* Westport, Conn.: Greenwood Press, 1997.

Deadeye Dick

Like many of Vonnegut's previous novels, *Deadeye Dick*, published in 1982 by Delacorte/ SEYMOUR LAWRENCE, has an apocalyptic feel to it. While *Cat's Cradle* introduced the environmental disaster of *ice-nine*, *Slaughterhouse-Five* explored the devastating firebombing of DRESDEN, and *Slapstick* depicted a world ravaged by fatal diseases, *Deadeye Dick* has its own doomsday device: a neutron bomb that wipes out the entire population of MIDLAND CITY, Ohio. In his preface, Vonnegut tells readers that the neutron bomb represents the disappearance of so many of the people he cared about in INDIANAPOLIS when he was young. "Indianapolis," he writes, "is there, but the people are gone" (xiii). In many ways, an aging Vonnegut echoes here the lament expressed in *Slapstick*, his longing for the days before World War I when an extended clan of parents, grandparents, aunts, uncles, siblings, and cousins resided in Indianapolis. The neutron bomb suggests the lack of belonging felt by many contemporary Americans, including both Vonnegut himself and his protagonist Rudy Waltz. Later in the novel, Rudy uses the word *egregious* to define himself, explaining that the word does not mean "terrible or unheard of or unforgivable" as most people think, but that, instead it means "outside the herd" (150). *Deadeye Dick*, then, expresses the sorrow and loneliness of a man who does not belong anywhere, who is afraid of life itself.

SYNOPSIS

Chapters 1–8
Deadeye Dick is the story of Rudy Waltz, born in 1932 in Midland City, Ohio, the same setting Vonnegut used in his earlier novel, *Breakfast of*

Champions. At the present time, Rudy is 50 years old, the year is 1982, and Midland City has been destroyed by a neutron bomb. Rudy and his older brother, Felix, escaped death because they were in Haiti at the time, having become the new owners of the GRAND HOTEL OLOFFSON there. As Rudy looks back on his life, he tells his story in the first person, beginning by chronicling the life of his colorful and eccentric father, Otto Waltz. Born in 1892, Otto is heir to a family fortune made through the sale of a quack medicine called Saint Elmo's Remedy. He is the only child of a doting mother who firmly believes her son could be the next Leonardo da Vinci; thus she provides him with a painting studio and private tutor. The tutor, August Gunther, however, turns out to be a rapscallion more interested in corrupting Otto than in teaching him about painting. While the two travel the Midwest, supposedly on tours of galleries and art studios, they actually visit bars and whorehouses. By the time Gunther is discovered and fired, Otto Waltz is already 18 years old, has contracted gonorrhea, and is, in Rudy's words, a "fully committed . . . good-time Charley" (3).

The 18-year-old Otto is then sent by his family to live with relatives in Vienna, Austria, and to enroll in the famous academy of Fine Arts. Although his portfolio is scorned by a professor at the academy, Otto meets another rejected art student there, a young ADOLF HITLER, and the two become, for a short while, close friends. Otto even buys one of Hitler's paintings, "The Minorite Church of Vienna," which he will later hang over his bed back in Midland City. As an American millionaire "disguised as a ragged genius" (7), Otto lives it up in Vienna for four years, eventually asking influential friends to help get him a commission in the Hungarian Life Guard because he so admires their panther skin uniforms. At this point, Otto is summoned to a meeting with the American ambassador to the Austro-Hungarian Empire, Henry Clowes, and told that he will lose his American citizenship if he joins a foreign army. Clowes also informs Otto that his parents have threatened to cut off his allowance unless he returns home immediately, and Otto complies, returning to the United States at the age of 22.

Back home, Otto eventually converts his family's conical-shaped former carriage house into a home/studio, marries a wealthy and much younger neighbor girl, Emma Wetzel, and has two sons, Felix and Rudy. Although continuing to fancy himself an artist, Otto never actually produces any paintings, but he does reflect fondly on his former life in Austria and his friendship with Adolf Hitler. Emma and Otto even travel to Germany for six months in 1934 as the guests of Hitler, who is now chancellor of the country. Otto returns with an enormous Nazi flag, which he flies proudly in his studio. Otto is so enamored of Hitler and the Nazis, in fact, that he greets Felix's friends by saying "Heil Hitler" to them. As World War II approaches, Otto is increasingly ostracized and scorned for his devotion to Germany, so that he eventually takes down his Nazi flag and stops talking about Hitler. But he continues his eccentricities in other ways, becoming so obsessed with the reputed beauty of Felix's prom date, Celia Hildreth, that he embarrasses the girl thoroughly when Felix brings her by to meet his family, causing her to run home in tears before the dance begins.

Chapters 9–18

While young Rudy escapes the brunt of Otto's Nazi phase, his childhood comes to an abrupt end through a tragic incident that occurs on Mother's Day, 1944, when he is 12 years old. Otto had purchased an enormous gun collection on his European honeymoon and keeps it locked in the attic of his studio home. On this day, Otto gives Rudy the key to the gun room, believing the boy to be older than he actually is. That afternoon, Rudy goes to the attic and plays with the guns, eventually loading a Springfield rifle with ammunition and shooting it out the window. In a tragic accident, the bullet happens to enter the second story of a nearby home and kill a pregnant housewife who is vacuuming her floors. When the sheriff comes to the Waltz home to inquire about the death, Otto immediately figures out what happened and blames himself. Both Rudy and Otto are taken to jail, where they are mistreated and abused by the policemen and guards, largely because of Otto's great wealth and his Nazi-sympathizing past. After a few days,

Otto is charged with criminal negligence and Rudy is released from jail. The policeman who drives the boy home, however, pins the nickname on him that will stick for the rest of his life: Deadeye Dick.

As a result of this experience, Rudy Waltz largely withdraws from life. Otto ends up serving two years in prison, and the Waltz family loses its fortune when they are sued by the Metzgers, the family of the dead woman. Having to let all their servants go, Otto and Emma begin to rely more and more on Rudy, who does all the cooking and cleaning for his spoiled and formerly wealthy parents. The only bright spot in Rudy's high school years is when he writes an essay about his hero, John Fortune, a local Midland City man and former friend of Otto Waltz who had left the Midwest to travel to Katmandu to search for Shangri-La. Praised highly by his English teacher, Rudy decides he wants to become a writer. When he tells Otto his dream, though, Rudy's father orders him to become a pharmacist instead, which he does. Rudy enrolls as a pharmacy major at Ohio State University but continues to care for his parents, commuting home three or four times a week. While he is in college, Rudy also takes a course in playwriting. He converts his John Fortune essay into a play called *Katmandu,* which he continues to work on even after graduating from college and taking a job as the all-night pharmacist at Schramm's Drugstore back in Midland City. The play eventually wins a national contest, allowing it to be produced in New York City.

Chapters 19–27
When Rudy is 27 years old, he moves to New York briefly to attend the six weeks of rehearsals for *Katmandu.* In New York, he sleeps on the couch of his very successful NBC executive brother, Felix, and Felix's third wife, Genevieve. On opening night of the play, Rudy overhears a ferocious argument between his brother and wife, prompted by Genevieve's suggestion that Felix encourage his younger brother to take a bath. While Rudy has largely shut down his feelings and thus is not hurt by Genevieve's comment, the fight and the subsequent revelation that Rudy is a murderer breaks up his brother's marriage. It turns out that *Katmandu,* too, is a flop, closing after one night to great

critical derision. Rudy returns to Midland City with Felix, only to discover that a terrible blizzard has blanketed the city. The Waltz brothers find their parents at the hospital, their father dying of double pneumonia. After Otto's death, Rudy moves with his mother into a small, two-bedroom tract house in a nearby subdivision called Avondale. He continues to cook and clean for Emma for many years until she dies of brain tumors brought on by a radioactive mantelpiece in the home's living room. Felix and Rudy sue the construction company, which allows them to buy a hotel in Haiti, where they are presently living.

Epilogue
The novel closes with the Waltz brothers returning to Midland City, along with their lawyer, Bernard Ketchum, and Hippolyte Paul De Mille, the headwaiter at the Grand Hotel Oloffson in Haiti, for a brief visit after the neutron bomb has killed the entire population of the county. As they tour the ghost town, tightly controlled now by the military, the small group winds up in Calvary Cemetery, contemplating the vast number of dead. Hippolyte Paul, a voodoo practitioner, upsets Felix by offering to raise the ghost of his former prom date, Celia Hildreth. Eventually, Rudy allows the old man, determined to perform a miracle, to raise the ghost of barnstormer and World War I ace Will Fairchild instead.

COMMENTARY
Deadeye Dick is a novel that explores how small accidents of fate can shape entire human lives and even the lives of those in the future. If Otto Waltz's mother had not hired August Gunther as her son's painting instructor initially, Otto would not have gotten into trouble and been sent away to Vienna, he would not have had a chance encounter with the young Hitler, he might not have returned to Germany and bought a gun collection on his honeymoon, and Rudy Waltz would not have shot the Springfield rifle out the widow that fateful Mother's Day. Without this one small, initial mistake, the lives of the members of the Waltz family would have been entirely different. Because of his own involvement in the fatal shooting accident, the

story's narrator, Rudy Waltz, is keenly aware of the power seemingly small mistakes have over human lives. He tells readers that his "principal objection to life" is that "it is too easy, when alive, to make perfectly horrible mistakes" (6). Rudy's solution to this problem is to become less than alive, to withdraw from any meaningful human interaction at all. "Watch out for life" (1), Rudy's warning to all the as yet unborn people in the world, becomes his motto. The novel explores the tragedy of Rudy's largely unlived life, a life that turns out to be mostly epilogue with very little story, as Rudy himself admits at the end of the novel.

Immediately following his return home after the shooting accident, Rudy's one desire is to get into bed and pull the covers over his head. He tells readers, "That was my plan. That is still pretty much my plan" (105). His guilt over the shooting, along with the treatment he receives at the hands of the abusive policemen, convince Rudy that human life is too painful to be borne, and that the best course of action is to withdraw completely from human interaction: "During my time in the cage," he writes, "I concluded that the best thing for me and for those around me was to want nothing, to be enthusiastic about nothing, to be as unmotivated as possible, in fact, so that I would never again hurt anyone" (126–127). In his attempt to avoid hurting anyone ever again, Rudy retires to the one place he found comfort as a child: the domestic realm. As a young boy, Rudy's favorite place in his father's cavernous house was the small, warm galley kitchen, where the black servants did actual work while talking and laughing easily. The cook, Mary Hoobler, acted as a substitute mother to Rudy, offering him more warmth and practical knowledge than his own mother ever did. Thus, Rudy transforms himself into a servant to his spoiled parents. The recipes that he scatters frequently throughout the novel also attest to the comfort Rudy felt in the kitchen as a young boy. Often, Rudy will follow some devastating confession with a recipe. For instance, when he tells readers about the "profound spiritual change" (29) that Otto undergoes in Germany, and his subsequent conviction to "become a spokesman in America for the new social order which was being born in Ger-

many" (30), the next paragraph, without transition or explanation, simply offers the recipe for Mary Hoobler's barbecue sauce. Rudy's withdrawal from the larger world is also what leads to his sexlessness in later life, his status as a "neuter." He tells readers that, as a 12-year-old boy, he had resolved not to "touch anything on this planet, man, woman, child, artifact, animal, vegetable, or mineral—since it was very likely to be connected to a push-pull detonator and an explosive charge" (127). The irony of this statement is that, despite Rudy's resolve, an explosive charge—the neutron bomb accidentally unleashed by the U.S. government—does indeed destroy everyone in Midland City.

Toward the end of the novel, at Celia Hildreth's funeral, we discover that Rudy's status as one of the living dead is not confined to him alone, but that it works as a metaphor for the citizens of Midland City in general. Rudy writes that there was "no reason to expect that anything truly exciting or consoling would be said" at the funeral, since "not even the minister . . . believed in heaven or hell. Not even the minister thought that every life had a meaning, and that every death could startle us into learning something important, and so on" (222–223). In fact, not only is the corpse "a mediocrity that had broken down after a while" (223), so are the mourners, so is Midland City, whose "center was already dead," and so is the planet itself, which "was going to blow itself up sooner or later anyway, if it didn't poison itself first" (223). The neutron bomb, then, becomes a metaphor for what is happening already in Midland City. It pushes a place that is already filled with the walking dead one step further, merely hastening the breakdown that is already taking place.

The neutron bomb that destroys Midland City also points up Vonnegut's recurring suspicions of technological achievement. Vonnegut equates advanced technology with a culture of weaponry throughout the novel, showing, as he did in *Cat's Cradle*, that scientific achievement does not necessarily signify human progress or enlightenment. Hitler's Nazi scientists, for instance, work feverishly to invent new ways of carrying out mass murder more efficiently. But Rudy Waltz grows up in a gun culture that predates the extremes of World War

II. The decapitation of August Gunther in a shooting accident before Rudy is even born brings this point home. Gunther's tragic death, however, does not stop the shooter, Sheriff Francis X. Morissey, or one of the witnesses, Otto Waltz, from bringing their sons to the rifle range to play with guns many years later. Weaponry in the novel is depicted as having particularly far-reaching and lasting effects; the weapons of technology spread their tentacles into the future, continuing to cause destruction long after their initial use. The radioactive mantelpiece that will eventually kill Emma Waltz, for instance, is made with cement left over from the Manhattan Project, the World War II venture in which scientists developed the ATOMIC BOMB. Similarly, the gun collection that Otto buys from the family of his dead German friend will provide the means for Rudy's accidental shooting of Eloise Metzger. Vonnegut shows how the technology of weaponry sacrifices human life in the name of scientific achievement. The irony of movie crews coming to Midland City to document "without the least bit of fakery, the fundamental harmlessness of a neutron bomb" (259) that has killed the city's entire population is readily apparent. Harm done is measured not in terms of human lives lost, but of property saved. When Rudy visits the military-controlled and depopulated city at the end of the novel, he says, "It was almost as though Midland City were at last being run the way it should have been run all along" (260–261). Without messy human citizens around to muck things up, the city functions smoothly indeed.

Vonnegut's views on weapons in the novel are perhaps best expressed by Eloise's husband, *Bugle-Observer* editor George Metzger. Though Metzger has every right to be angry at Rudy for the carelessness that caused his wife's death, and though the Midland City detectives and police certainly expect him to seek revenge, Metzger instead publishes a short statement in his newspaper:

"My wife has been killed by a machine which should never have come into the hands of any human being. It is called a firearm. It makes the blackest of all human wishes come true at once, at a distance: that something die.

"There is evil for you.

"We cannot get rid of mankind's fleetingly wicked wishes. We can get rid of the machines that make them come true. "I give you a holy word: DISARM." (98)

For Vonnegut, humans are not inherently moral creatures. The best we can do, as he has argued repeatedly in his work, is to behave as if we were, to pretend a goodness that we do not really possess. Guns and weaponry in general, however, cater to the worst qualities of humanity, making it easy for us to live as our worst selves.

The antidote to guns and weaponry for Vonnegut is often art. In a 1970 speech to the graduating class at Bennington College (published in his 1974 essay collection, *Wampeters, Foma, and Granfalloons*), Vonnegut has this to say about art versus military science:

Which brings us to the arts, whose purpose, in common with astrology, is to use frauds in order to make human beings seem more wonderful than they really are. . . .

The arts put man at the center of the universe, whether he belongs there or not. Military science, on the other hand, treats man as garbage—and his children, and his cities, too. Military science is probably right about the contemptibility of man in the vastness of the universe. Still—I deny that contemptibility, and I beg you to deny it, through the creation of [and] appreciation of art. (166–167)

Art is one way that Rudy Waltz can cope with the tragedy he has experienced in his life. He relates his most troubling and embarrassing recollections in the form of stage plays, telling readers: "I have this trick for dealing with all my worst memories. I insist that they are plays. The characters are actors. Their speeches and movements are stylized, arch. I am in the presence of art" (94). Rudy indeed uses fraud to make human beings seem more wonderful than they really are. His own play, *Katmandu*, while scorned by the New York theater critics, nevertheless allows Rudy to retain the illusion of a world in which human beings may act heroically, a world where it is not simply foolish to search for a deeper meaning in life rather than to walk the earth as members of the living dead. John Fortune, a "hero in the trenches in the First World War" (21), though perhaps sad and deluded in his actual search for *Shangri-La,* is a meaningful icon for Midland City residents Fred and Mildred Barry, who see the play in New York, and for the provincial audience who attend the play's performance in Midland City three years later. Even though the 50-year old Rudy Waltz believes, like his father Otto before him, that Shangri-La is "bunk" (129), Reverend Harrell, officiating at Celia Hildreth's funeral, can claim that the play "enriched lives all over town" (224).

At the same time, it is important to remember that art *does* contain the element of fraud. Rudy's play certainly seems silly to readers, especially when the New York actor Sheldon Woodcock, who plays the role of John Fortune, points out the droning repetition and logical inconsistencies in the script. Vonnegut is self-consciously aware of the fraud he himself commits in his own writing. When he announces in his preface that he will now "explain the main symbols in this book" (xii), and makes such statements as, "Haiti is New York City," and "The neutered pharmacist who tells the tale is my declining sexuality" (xiii), his METAFICTIONAL musings seem all too facile. While partly serious here, Vonnegut is also poking fun at a type of literary criticism that asserts easy, one-on-one correlations between symbols and meaning. And while the correlation between art and life is an important theme in this work, it is not an easy correlation to untangle. Art, as we have seen in Vonnegut novels, works in deep and complex ways. Thus, Otto Waltz's selfish spectacle, in which he severely embarrasses both his own son, Felix, and Felix's prom date, Celia Hildreth, by posing, in Rudy's words, as the "King of the Early Evening," is nevertheless an "artistic masterpiece" (52), the only real work of art Otto will ever produce in his life.

While art can ennoble our lives, Rudy also recognizes the dangers inherent in trying to live one's life as art. "It may be a bad thing that so many people try to make good stories out of their lives," he writes near the end of the novel, "A story, after all, is as artificial as a mechanical bucking bronco in a drinking establishment" (237). When people fail to live up to the stories they invent for themselves, they are often disappointed and their lives seem like failures. Stories also demand action and drama in ways that can cause trouble in real life. Recognizing that America's story involves World War II and the building of the atomic bomb, Rudy points out that "it may be even worse for nations to try to be characters in stories. Perhaps these words should be carved over doorways of the United Nations and all sorts of parliaments, big and small," he cautions: "LEAVE YOUR STORY OUTSIDE" (237). Readers may be reminded here of Vonnegut's cautions against conventional storytelling in his earlier novel *Breakfast of Champions,* also set in Midland City. In that book, Vonnegut pointed out that it was "innocent and natural" for people to behave "abominably," because they are simply "doing their best to live like people invented in story books" (215). Thus, he shuns traditional storytelling, resolving instead to "write about life" (215) itself, without leaving anything out.

Despite attempts to ennoble ourselves through art, and the ability of art to make human life seem more meaningful than it really is, *Deadeye Dick* closes by asking the question of where our reliance on art has really brought us. The novel's final scene takes place in Midland City's Calvary Cemetery, where so many of those killed by the neutron bomb are buried. The Haitian headwaiter, Hippolyte Paul De Mille, who accompanies the Waltz brothers and lawyer Bernard Ketchum to the cemetery, is a voodoo practioner who assumes the role of artist at the end. Not content to leave the dead at peace, Hippolyte Paul insists upon actually raising one of the spirits from its grave. Like a novelist who brings symbols and metaphors to life, Hippolyte Paul's voodoo makes vivid and concrete what has been an important metaphor in the novel—that Midland City citizens are broken down "mediocrities"—the walking dead. While Celia Hildreth, who had anesthetized herself at the end of her life by overdosing on amphetamine pills, is a likely candidate since she was clearly one of the living dead, the spectacle of a raised Celia is too dreadful for her former prom date, Felix, to contemplate, so Rudy allows Hippolyte Paul to raise a substitute instead, World War I flying ace Will Fairchild. Rudy, to make this final work of art complete, acts as "the William

Shakespeare of Midland City" and invents a story to accompany the ghost of Fairchild—that the daredevil pilot is looking for his parachute. Rudy then concludes his tale by writing, "You want to know something? We are still in the Dark Ages. The Dark Ages—they haven't ended yet" (271). Despite human technology and scientific progress, Vonnegut seems to be saying that human beings are still superstitiously casting spells in the dark, trying desperately to understand life and make life bearable by inventing stories that make them seem more wonderful than they really are.

CHARACTERS AND RELATED ENTRIES

Adams, Steve When Sally Freeman and Felix Waltz split up during their senior year of high school, Sally turns to Steve Adams, the captain of the basketball team, for consolation, in turn causing Felix to invite Celia Hildreth to the senior prom.

Adams, Tiger Tiger Adams is the pilot of the private plane that belongs to the Barrytron Corporation. He flies Fred and Mildred Barry to the New York premier of Rudy Waltz's play, *Katmandu.*

Bannister, George Hickman George Hickman Bannister was a 17-year-old killed in a high school football game in 1924. Bannister now has a 62-foot gray marble obelisk with a stone football on top dedicated to his memory in Calvary Cemetery in Midland City.

Barry, Fred T. Fred T. Barry is the founder and owner of the Barrytron Corporation in Midland City. He flies to New York to see the production of Rudy Waltz's play, *Katmandu,* and raves about it afterward. Later in life, he will feud with Emma Waltz over the value of modern art. He eventually surrenders to Mrs. Waltz, sells his company to the RAMJAC Corporation, and moves away from Midland City. Barry is also a character in *Breakfast of Champions.*

Barry, Mildred Mildred Barry is the mother of Fred T. Barry. She accompanies her son to the New York production of *Katmandu,* whistling and clapping enthusiastically when the performance ends.

The Midland City Arts Center is named after Mildred Barry, both in this novel and in *Breakfast of Champions.*

Brokenshire, David David Brokenshire is a British doctor who has been a prisoner of the Japanese for many years during World War II. He is studying folk medicine in Katmandu when John Fortune is brought to him on a stretcher with double pneumonia. Although Fortune dies, he scribbles a last message for Brokenshire to bring back to Midland City. Six years later, the doctor keeps his promise. Fortune's last words are these: "To all my friends and enemies in the buckeye state. Come on over. There's room for everybody in Shangri-La" (135).

Butler, Nicholas Murray The president of Columbia University, Nicholas Murray Butler, visits the Waltz house when Rudy Waltz is a boy. Most famous visitors to Midland City are brought to Otto Waltz's studio because there is not much else to see of interest in the town. An actual historical figure, Butler was president of Columbia from 1902 to 1945 and the winner of a Nobel Peace Prize.

Clowes, Henry Henry Clowes is the fictional American ambassador to the Austro-Hungarian Empire at the beginning of World War I. When Otto Waltz goes to Vienna and asks friends if they can get him a commission in the Hungarian Life Guard, Clowes summons the young millionaire to a meeting, then warns him he will lose his American citizenship if he joins a foreign army. Further, Clowes has written a letter to Otto's parents, telling them that their son is not really a painter and that he has been "spending money like a drunken sailor" (8). When Otto learns that his parents will discontinue his allowance if he stays in Vienna, he agrees to return home.

Davis, Lottie The Hoovers' black maid, Lottie Davis, is the only person Rudy Waltz hears crying at the funeral for Celia Hoover.

De Mille, Hippolyte Paul Hippolyte Paul De Mille is the headwaiter at the Grand Hotel Oloffson in Port au Prince, Haiti. A practitioner of voodoo, Hippolyte Paul offers to raise the ghost of Felix Waltz's long-ago prom date Celia Hildreth Hoover when he visits the Midland City cemetery with Felix and Rudy Waltz and Bernard Ketchum after the neutron bomb has depopulated the city. When Felix refuses, Rudy agrees to let Hippolyte Paul raise the ghost of an old barnstormer, Will Fairchild, to cheer him up.

Duveneck, Frank Frank Duveneck, Vonnegut tells readers in his preface, is one of the four real artists who appear in the novel. An American realist painter who lived from 1848 to 1919, Duveneck is an actual historical figure. He appears in the novel when art historian Cliff McCarthy calls Rudy Waltz to let him know that Rudy's father, Otto, appeared in a diary kept by the famous painter. Though Duveneck admired Otto's studio, he also wrote in the diary that Otto should be shot for "seeming to prove the last thing that needs to be proved in this part of the world: that an artist is a person of no consequence" (240).

Fairchild, Will A former World War I flying ace, Will Fairchild died while stunt flying at the Midland County Fair in 1922. The Midland City airport is named after him. At the end of the novel, Hippolyte Paul De Mille raises the ghost of Will Fairchild at Calvary Cemetery in Midland City.

Finkelstein, Izzy When Felix Waltz was in junior high school, his father Otto embarrassed him by flying a Nazi flag in the house and greeting his friends with the phrase, "Heil Hitler." Even the Jewish boy Izzy Finkelstein was greeted this way by Otto Waltz.

Fortune, John John Fortune is a Midland City native who is a friend of Otto Waltz. At a drunken party one night, Fortune drops a timber on Otto's foot, crushing it. Fortune will go on to become a decorated veteran in World War I and the best man at Otto Waltz's wedding. Later, as World War II approaches, Fortune ceases speaking to Otto because of his Nazi sympathies. John Fortune eventually dies in Katmandu, inspired to seek Shangri-La by James Hilton's book, *Lost Horizon*. Rudy

Waltz will one day write a prize-winning play about Fortune, called *Katmandu*, which is produced in New York, but which closes after a single night.

Fortune, Mrs. John Fortune's wife, whose first name is never given, dies of cancer in 1938, prompting Fortune's trip to the Himalayas to seek "far higher happiness and wisdom than was available, evidently, in Midland City" (33).

Freeman, Sally Sally Freeman had been Felix Waltz's girlfriend for most of his senior year in high school. But their breakup precipitates Felix's invitation to Celia Hildreth to the senior prom instead.

Gatch Brothers When Rudy Waltz is at the hospital with his parents after the terrible Midland City blizzard, a man whom he suspects is one of the Gatch brothers tells a nurse at the counter that he has a leg full of shrapnel from World War I. Rudy, who overhears the comment, doubts that Gatch ever fought in any war. The Gatch brothers used to work for the Maritimo Brothers Construction Company until they were fired for theft. Later, another Gatch brother (or possibly the same one that Rudy saw in the hospital), who works as a floor waxer at the Will Fairchild Memorial Airport, finds Celia Hoover collapsed in a heap on the runway and takes her home.

Gatch, Mary or Martha or Marie At the hospital after the blizzard, when Rudy sees one of the Gatch brothers, he is reminded of the man's daughter, a girl named Mary or Martha or Marie, who was two years ahead of Rudy in school. The girl was a shoplifter and continually tried to make friends by offering people presents of items she stole.

Gunther, August A German cabinetmaker hired to tutor Otto Waltz in painting and drawing, August Gunther corrupts the boy, taking him to whorehouses and bars when the two go on overnight trips supposedly to visit galleries and painters' studios. When Otto is 18, the two are found out, and Gunther is "denounced and fired and blacklisted" (3). The rascally cabinetmaker dies under mysterious circumstances in the autumn of 1916, when he goes goose hunting with Otto Waltz, John Fortune, and other young men. His headless body is discovered at the mouth of Sugar Creek, just west of Cincinnati. Later in the novel, readers discover that Police Chief Francis X. Morissey had accidentally shot Gunther in the head with a 10-gauge shotgun during the hunting expedition. The other young men, realizing the shooting was an accidental, kept the secret for years.

Gunther, Grace   Grace Gunther is the only child of painting tutor and cabinetmaker August Gunther.

Harrell, Reverend Charles   The Reverend Charles Harrell is the minister at Celia Hoover's funeral, who, according to Rudy Waltz, does not believe in heaven or hell or that every life has a meaning any more than anyone else at the funeral believes these things.

Hildreth, Celia's Brother   None of Celia Hildreth Hoovers' family members are at her funeral. Rudy Waltz tells readers that one of her brothers was killed in the Korean War.

Hildreth, Shirley   According to Rudy Waltz, someone he knows in Midland City swears that he saw Celia Hildreth Hoovers' sister Shirley as an extra in a remake of the movie *King Kong*.

Hitler, Adolf   The real-life Nazi leader Adolf Hitler appears in the novel when Otto Waltz briefly befriends him in Vienna, Austria, after both are rejected from the Academy of Fine Arts. Angry at the professor who scorns both his and Hitler's portfolios, Otto immediately produces more cash than the professor makes in a month in order to buy a picture from Hitler called "The Minorite Church of Vienna." Later, back in Midland City, Otto exaggerates his relationship with Hitler and flies Nazi flags in his studio, until this gets him in trouble at the beginning of World War II.

Hoobler, Cynthia   When Rudy Waltz goes to New York for the production of his play, *Katmandu*, he hires Cynthia Hoobler, Mary Hoobler's

daughter-in-law, to care for his parents while he is gone.

Hoobler, Mary   Mary Hoobler is the African-American cook to the Waltz family during Rudy's youth. She teaches the boy everything she knows about cooking and baking and serves as a mother figure to him, especially since Emma Waltz is so distant.

Hoover, Bunny   In the hospital after the Midland City blizzard, Rudy Waltz sees the 11-year-old Bunny Hoover, son of Celia and Dwayne Hoover, holding the hand of his exhausted mother as she sleeps on a couch in a hospital lounge. Bunny, as detailed both in *Deadeye Dick* and in *Breakfast of Champions*, will grow up to be a "notorious homosexual" (194). Disowned by his father, he makes a living playing piano at the Midland City Holiday Inn.

Hoover, Celia Hildreth   Celia Hildreth, though from a poor and illiterate family, is the prettiest girl in town when Felix Waltz is in high school. Felix invites Celia to their senior prom, but is humiliated by his father when they stop by the Waltz house on the way there. Otto, obsessed by Celia's reputed beauty, has lit the house with hundreds of candles and donned his Hungarian Life Guard uniform. When the young couple pull up, Otto calls out: "Let Helen of Troy come forward—to claim this apple, if she dare!" Embarrassed and confused, Celia runs home, refusing to continue the date. Later in life, Celia will marry Dwayne Hoover, a wealthy Midland City car dealer. She will end up committing suicide by ingesting Drano, the popular drain unclogger, an event previously detailed in Vonnegut's novel *Breakfast of Champions*.

Hoover, Dwayne   Dwayne Hoover is a rich Pontiac dealer in Midland City who marries Celia Hildreth. Though he appears only briefly in *Deadeye Dick*, Dwayne is one of the main characters in Vonnegut's earlier novel *Breakfast of Champions*.

Horton   A man named Horton, who lives in Cincinnati, is the owner of Schramm's Drugstore, where Rudy Waltz works as an all-night pharmacist.

Hyatt, Malcolm   Malcolm Hyatt, who went to high school with Otto Waltz, is Rudy Waltz's predecessor as all-night pharmacist at Schramm's Drugstore. Hyatt is killed by a robber while at work.

Karabekian, Rabo   A painting by minimalist artist Rabo Karabekian, which is purchased by Fred T. Barry for the Midland City Arts Center, is one of the works that sparks Emma Waltz's outrage about modern art. Karabekian and his painting, *The Temptation of Saint Anthony*, also play a prominent role in *Breakfast of Champions.*

Ketchum, Bernard   Bernard Ketchum serves as George Metzger's attorney in the suit brought over the accidental shooting death of Metzger's wife, Eloise. Years later, Rudy and Felix Waltz hire Ketchum to sue the Maritimo Brothers Construction Company, among others, over the radioactive mantelpiece that kills their mother. Ketchum eventually becomes a partner with the Waltz brothers in the purchase of the Grand Hotel Olaffson in Haiti.

Ketchum Children   Bernard Ketchum has two grown sons who no longer speak to him. One had deserted to Sweden during the VIETNAM WAR, and the other becomes a welder in Alaska after flunking out of HARVARD Law School.

Ketchum, Mrs.   Bernard Ketchum's wife, whose first name is never given, is present at the swimming pool of the Grand Hotel Olaffson when Rudy Waltz asks Ketchum to tell him about the Metzgers.

Krementz, Jill   A photographer and author, JILL KREMENTZ is Kurt Vonnegut's real-life second wife. She is mentioned in the novel's preface when Vonnegut tells readers about the Grand Hotel Olaffson in Port au Prince, Haiti, where he and Jill liked to stay. In the novel, Rudy Waltz and his brother, Felix, have purchased the hotel and lived in it for several months.

Maritimo, Dr. Alan   Dr. Alan Maritimo was a veterinarian who had decided against going into the construction business owned by his family. His whole household is killed in the neutron bomb

explosion. When Rudy and Felix Waltz visit the Midland City cemetery, they are able to bring Hippolyte Paul De Mille along by claiming that he is the brother of a Haitian cook who had worked for Dr. Maritimo.

Maritimo, Gino and Marco   Gino and Marco Maritimo, poor immigrants from Italy, robbed by hoboes on a train when they first arrive in the country, are generously fed and given work by Otto Waltz when they appear at the Waltz carriage house. From that time forward, the Maritimo brothers are fiercely loyal to Otto, even when they become the powerful and wealthy owners of a construction company and Otto is a despised Nazi. The Maritimo brothers also appear in Vonnegut's earlier novel *Breakfast of Champions.*

Maritimo, Julio   The son of Marco Maritimo, Julio Maritimo is drafted to serve in World War II at the same time as Felix Waltz. Julio, unlike Felix, is killed in the war.

Maritimo, Mrs. Gino   Rudy Waltz gives readers the recipe for Mrs. Gino Maritimo's *spuma di cioccolata*. Mrs. Maritimo is married to Italian immigrant and construction company co-owner Gino Maritimo.

McCarthy, Cliff   In his preface to the novel, Vonnegut tells readers that there are four real painters in *Deadeye Dick*. The living one, he explains, is his friend in Athens, Ohio—Cliff McCarthy. An actual historic figure who taught at Ohio University, McCarthy appears in the novel when he visits the Waltzes to try to learn more about Otto Waltz. McCarthy is writing a book about Ohio painters, but he has never heard of Otto. McCarthy is the one who discovers that the Waltz's mantelpiece is radioactive when film he accidentally left on it turns black.

Meeker, Jimmy   The Meekers lived next door to Rudy and Emma Waltz in Avondale. After the neutron bomb explosion, when Rudy visits his old house, he is moved to see young Jimmy Meeker's tricycle outside the neighboring home. Rudy is severely reprimanded by a police captain, however, when he touches the child's tricycle and rolls it back and forth a few inches.

Metzger, Eloise Eloise Metzger is the pregnant housewife accidentally shot to death by Rudy Waltz on Mother's Day, 1944. She had been vacuuming on the second floor of her house about eight blocks away from the Waltz studio.

Metzger, Eugene and Jane Eugene and Jane Metzger are the children of Eloise Metzger, the woman Rudy Waltz accidentally shoots to death. Both children are named after activist reformers—Eugene after labor organizer EUGENE DEBS, and Jane after Nobel Prize–winning social reformer Jane Addams. When the Metzgers' lawsuit against the Waltzes is settled, the family moves to Florida. In later life, Eugene Metzger moves to Athens, Greece, and operates several oil tankers, while Jane Metzger lives with a refugee Czech playwright in Hawaii.

Metzger, George The husband of accidental shooting victim Eloise Metzger, George Metzger is the city editor of local newspaper, the *Bugle-Observer*. Metzger refuses to beat Rudy Waltz when given the opportunity by the policemen who have put the young boy on display in a cage. He later publishes a brief notice of his wife's death in the paper, blaming guns for the accident and begging people to disarm.

Mitchell, Jerry Jerry Mitchell was Felix Waltz's worst enemy in high school. He used to torture cats and dogs and pretend to be performing scientific experiments. As an adult, Mitchell becomes a doctor. Many of his patients, including Celia Hoover and Mitchell's own wife, become addicted to amphetamines he prescribes them.

Morrissey, Bucky Bucky Morrissey is the son of Midland City police chief Francis X. Morrisey. Bucky and his father are one of the father and son teams shooting rifles at the firing range, alongside Otto, Felix, and Rudy Waltz, on the morning of the day that Rudy accidentally shoots Eloise Metzger to death.

Morrissey, Francis X. Francis X. Morrissey is the police chief of Midland City who in his youth accidentally shot August Gunther in the head, killing him instantly. Morrissey is the officer who first arrives at the Waltz house after the accidental shooting death of Eloise Metzger many years later. Though Chief Morrissey tries hard to give the family an out, Otto Waltz immediately takes responsibility for the crime.

Pefko, Captain Julian Julian Pefko is the police captain in charge of Rudy Waltz and his small group as they visit the neutron bomb site in Midland City. He chastises Rudy at one point for touching a child's tricycle, reminding him of the "Hands in your pockets" rule (259).

Pendleton, Dr. Miles When Emma Waltz is at the hospital after the Midland City blizzard, she receives an experimental frostbite treatment invented right there that very morning by Dr. Miles Pendleton.

Penfield, Frederic Courtland In the book's preface, Vonnegut tells readers that *Deadeye Dick* is a work of fiction and that he has taken some liberties with history. For instance, he explains, the real United States ambassador to Austria-Hungary at the beginning of World War I was Frederic Courtland Penfield, though the book includes a fictional ambassador named Henry Clowes.

Piatigorsky, Gregor Gregor Piatigorsky is said by Rudy Waltz to be one of the famous people brought to visit his father's studio. An actual historic figure, Piatigorsky was a famous Russian cellist.

Rettig, John John Rettig, Vonnegut tells readers in his preface, is one of the four real painters in the novel. Rettig is an actual historical figure, a painter, set designer, and potter from Cincinnati, Ohio, who lived from 1855 to 1932, spending much of his adult life in Holland. In the novel, Otto Waltz once owned a painting by Rettig called "Crucifixion in Rome," which Waltz considers one of the 10 greatest paintings in the world. When the Waltzes are forced to sell their art collection,

"Crucifixion in Rome" is the only valuable painting in the lot. It is purchased by the Cincinnati Art Museum because it was painted by a locally born artist.

Roosevelt, Eleanor On the same Mother's Day that Felix Waltz leaves to fight in World War II and that Rudy Waltz accidentally shoots Eloise Metzger, Eleanor Roosevelt comes to lunch at the Waltz house while she's on a morale-boosting tour of war plants.

St. Elmo's Remedy The Waltz family made its fortune primarily by selling a quack medicine called "St. Elmo's Remedy" that is actually grain alcohol "dyed purple, flavored with cloves and sarsaparilla root, and laced with opium and cocaine" (2).

Schramm's Drugstore Schramm's Drugstore is where Rudy Waltz takes a job as an all-night pharmacist upon his return to Midland City after graduating from college.

Seitz, Al and Sue In the novel's preface, Vonnegut tells us that Al and Sue Seitz are the actual owners of the Grand Hotel Olaffson in Port au Prince, Haiti.

Shoup, Naomi Naomi Shoup is Rudy Waltz's high school English teacher. She is the one who first encourages him to write about John Fortune, the subject of his prize-winning play, *Katmandu.*

Skinner, Cornelia Otis One of the famous visitors to Midland City who is brought to see Otto Waltz's studio, Cornelia Otis Skinner was an actual historic figure, a well-known author and actress in the first part of the 20th century.

Sparky Sparky is the name of Dwayne Hoover's Labrador retriever, who greets Celia Hoover when one of the Gatch brothers drives her home after finding her in a collapsed heap on an airport runway.

Squires, Anthony Anthony Squires is the ordinary patrolman who drives Rudy Waltz home after

his humiliating prison experience. Squires heaps abuse on Rudy during the drive and ultimately gives him the nickname "Deadeye Dick." Readers are told that Anthony Squires in later life will become chief of detectives, then suffer a nervous breakdown. He eventually dies in the neutron bomb explosion.

Squires, Barbara Barbara Squires is married to Dr. Jerry Mitchell, Felix Waltz's worst enemy in high school. She is also the daughter of police officer Anthony Squires, who gave Rudy Waltz the nickname "Deadeye Dick."

Stacks, Herb Herb Stacks is Rudy Waltz's dentist, who has been to Katmandu three times. In fact, the Stacks family escapes the neutron bomb because they are in Nepal at the time.

Ulm, Lowell Lowell Ulm is the director of civil defense in Midland City. He brings his Geiger counter to the small two-bedroom home Rudy Waltz shares with his mother in the Avondale subdivision and confirms that the mantelpiece is radioactive.

Unnamed Black Woman in Jail When Rudy Waltz is taken to jail for the accidental shooting death of Eloise Metzger, only one other prisoner is there at the time, an unnamed "black woman from out of town, who had been taken off a Greyhound bus after beating up the white driver" (81). This is the woman who introduces Rudy to the concept of peepholes opening at birth and closing at death.

Unnamed Czech Playwright When Jane Metzger, the daughter of shooting victim Eloise Metzger, grows up, she moves to Hawaii and lives with a refugee Czech playwright.

Unnamed Drunk at the Drugstore One night around 2:00 A.M., a drunken man wanders into Schramm's Drugstore and demands a chocolate malted milkshake. Seeing the name Rudolph Waltz above the pharmacy counter, he asks Rudy whether he's the one who shot the woman or the one who put the woman through the windshield, a reference to Rudy's older brother, Felix, who was responsible for a car accident that severely injured his first wife.

Unnamed Farmers Two farmers in bib overalls are passing out leaflets in the coffee shop of the Quality Motor Court where Rudy Waltz and his party are staying during their visit to the neutron bomb site. The farmers turn out to be members of an organization called Farmers of Southwestern Ohio for Nuclear Sanity. This group believes that Midland City was bombed purposefully by the U.S. government in order to bring slavery back to the country. Midland City, according to the farmers, is going to be used to house the slaves who will be imported from Haiti and Jamaica and "places like that" (264).

Unnamed Girl in Tollbooth On an intoxicated drive back to Midland City after losing his job as president of NBC in New York, Felix Waltz remembers proposing marriage to a girl he picked up at a tollbooth on the Ohio Turnpike.

Unnamed Haitian Painter When Felix goes to get more champagne on the evening that he and his brother, Rudy, and the Ketchums sit around talking late at night around the swimming pool of the Grand Hotel Olaffson, he carefully steps over an unnamed Haitian painter who has fallen asleep on the stairs. Felix must be careful because Haiti, the only nation ever born out of a successful slave revolt, has strict laws guarding against white or lightly colored people who menace Haitians in a manner that suggests a master-and-slave relationship.

Unnamed Hoboes Four unnamed American hoboes rob Italian immigrants Gino and Marco Maritimo of their suitcases, coats, hats, and shoes, as they are riding a boxcar across the United States. The Maritimos are ultimately helped by Otto Waltz.

Unnamed Japanese Lunatic A Japanese man, whom Rudy Waltz describes as a "lunatic" since the word is related to craziness and the moon, comes into Schramm's Drugstore one night and convinces Rudy to come outside to see something wonderful in the moonlight. The object the Japanese man is so excited about is the conical slate roof of the Waltz carriage house, which in the moonlight looks to the man like the sacred Japanese volcano Fujiyama.

Unnamed Policemen After Rudy Waltz is arrested for accidentally shooting Eloise Metzger to death, two unnamed policemen shove his face into some black, gummy ink used for fingerprinting, remarking that he is a "proper-looking nigger now" (84). These same policemen are the ones who put Rudy into a large cage in the basement of the courthouse. Later, a police detective will encourage George Metzger, the dead woman's husband, to beat Rudy with a piece of cable while six other policemen egg him on.

Unnamed Professor at the Academy of Fine Arts When Otto Waltz presents his portfolio for review at the Academy of Fine Arts in Vienna, it is returned to him with scorn by an unnamed professor who tells him that his work is "ludicrous" (5). Another young painter, who turns out to be Adolf Hitler, has his portfolio rejected at the same time. To get revenge on the professor, Otto Waltz pulls a pile of cash from his wallet and buys one of Hitler's works, "The Minorite Chruch of Vienna," on the spot.

Unnamed Robber A robber from out of town kills Malcolm Hyatt, the all-night pharmacist prior to Rudy Waltz at Schramm's Drugstore. The robber is later sentenced to die in the electric chair.

Unnamed Secret Service Agent An unnamed Secret Service agent who accompanies Eleanor Roosevelt to the Waltz household makes a comment about Otto's gun collection, showing that the Secret Service had checked the family out in advance.

von Furstenberg, Rudolf An old friend of Otto Waltz from his Vienna days, Rudolf von Furstenberg is killed in World War I, but Otto and Emma visit what remains of his family on their honeymoon. Otto Waltz buys an enormous gun collection from the von Furstenberg family and names his second son, Rudy, after his old friend.

Vonnegut, Kurt   Though he is not named in the novel, Vonnegut seems to appear briefly as a character at Celia Hoover's funeral. Rudy Waltz sees a man wearing large mirrored sunglasses looking at him from one end of a pew. This is how the Vonnegut character is described in *Breakfast of Champions*, the novel that shares its Midland City setting with *Deadeye Dick.*

Waltz, Barbara   Barbara Waltz is Felix Waltz's fifth wife, and the first one to truly love him. She is a 23-year old X-ray technician who is pregnant with Felix's first legitimate child.

Waltz, Charlotte   Felix Waltz breaks up with his fourth wife, Charlotte, during the period that he is president of the National Broadcasting Company and living in a penthouse overlooking Central Park. Rudy and Emma Waltz read in a gossip column that Felix and Charlotte have divided the penthouse with a line of chairs, and that neither one is supposed to enter the other's territory. Charlotte gets so mad at Felix at one point that she cuts all the buttons off his clothes and throws them down the incinerator.

Waltz, Donna   Donna Waltz is Felix Waltz's first wife. Even though he knows her only slightly—in fact, he is unable to tell her apart from her identical twin sister, Dina—Felix marries Donna after accidentally putting her through the windshield in a car wreck. Later, Felix refers to this marriage as a "shotgun wedding" (140).

Waltz, Emma Wetzel   Born in Midland City in 1901, Emma Wetzel is the only child of Richard Wetzel, an extremely wealthy banker. She marries the 30-year-old Otto Waltz in 1922, when she is 21 years old and a new graduate of Oberlin College. Emma will remain devoted to Otto their whole married life. After her husband's death, she moves with her younger son, Rudy, a pharmacist, into a little two-bedroom home in a subdivision called Avondale. Emma will eventually die of tumors in her brain, the result of a radioactive mantelpiece in the tiny tract house. Before she does, though, the tumors affect her personality, causing her to crusade zealously against modern art at the very end of her life.

Waltz, Felix   Rudy Waltz's older brother, Felix, has such a deep, beautiful voice that he is nicknamed "The Velvet Fog" in school. When he invites the most beautiful girl in town, Celia Hildreth, to the high school senior prom, Otto Waltz embarrasses both teenagers so deeply that Celia runs away from Felix, crying that she hates rich people. Later in life, Felix will fight in World War II and return home to eventually become president of NBC, with a penthouse and a limousine. He burns out early, though, eventually losing his network job and going through four marriages and divorces before attaining his fifth wife. In the novel's present time, Felix has become the proprietor, along with his brother Rudy, of the Grand Hotel Olaffson in Port au Prince, Haiti.

Waltz, Genevieve   Genevieve Waltz was Felix Waltz's third wife. Felix now refers to her as "Anyface" because she has almost no eyebrows and very thin lips, thus paints these features on. The marriage dissolves when Rudy stays with the couple in New York while his play is in rehearsals. When Genevieve whispers to Felix that Rudy needs to take a bath before the big opening, Felix blows up at her, embarrassing her at work. The two nearly make up, but Genevieve moves out when she finds out that Rudy is a murderer.

Waltz, Grandfather and Grandmother   Otto Waltz's parents are wealthy and influential citizens of Midland City, Ohio, whose family fortune came mostly from a quack remedy made out of grain alcohol, opium, and cocaine. Otto's mother, mistakenly believing her only child to be artistically gifted, builds him a studio and hires a painting tutor who soon corrupts the boy. The Waltzes die before the beginning of World War I, when carbon monoxide leaks into their farmhouse from a faulty heating system.

Waltz, Great-Grandfather and Great-Grandmother   The carriage house that Otto Waltz converts into a home and studio, described as a "stone-by-stone replica of a structure in an illustration in her favorite book of German fairy tales" (8), was a present from Great-Grandfather Waltz to his homesick wife from Hamburg, Germany.

Waltz, Otto Rudy Waltz's eccentric father, Otto, was born in 1892, the only child of a family that made its fortune by peddling a quack medicine called St. Elmo's Remedy. As a young man, Otto leads a wild life, visiting brothels and drinking heavily with his painting teacher, August Gunther. Otto eventually goes to Vienna, Austria, hoping to be accepted into the famous Academy of Fine Arts. Though rejected because of the poor quality of his work, Otto meets another young aspirant to the Academy, Adolf Hitler, and the two enjoy a brief friendship. When Otto's parents summon him back to the United States, he eventually marries the wealthy and much younger Emma Wetzel and converts an enormous old carriage house into a studio where he lives with his wife and two sons, Felix and Rudy. His admiration of Adolf Hitler eventually gets him into trouble with his neighbors and local officials, especially after both he and his youngest son, Rudy, are arrested after Rudy's accidental shooting of a neighbor woman. Otto Waltz eventually dies at the age of 68, after a devastating blizzard strikes Midland City.

Waltz, Rudy The novel's protagonist, Rudy Waltz is born into a rather odd family in Midland City, Ohio, in 1932. His father, Otto, is an eccentric would-be painter who revels in a brief friendship he had with Adolf Hitler in Vienna before World War I. Rudy's passive, yet wealthy mother, Emma, worships her husband, but largely leaves her sons to be raised by servants. As a 12-year-old boy, on Mother's Day, 1944, Rudy, playing with his father's gun collection in the attic of the Waltz's studio/house, accidentally shoots a woman in a neighboring house, killing her instantly. This earns him the nickname "Deadeye Dick," which will stick with him the rest of his life. The accident haunts Rudy, who becomes a pharmacist and lives alone with his mother much of his adult life. As the novel opens, Midland City has been com-

pletely depopulated by a neutron people. Rudy, now 50, and his older brother, Felix, are living in Haiti, the proprietors of the Grand Hotel Olaffson in Port au Prince.

Wetzel, Richard Richard Wetzel is the "founder and principal stockholder of the Midland County National Bank" (13). He is also the father of Emma Wetzel Waltz, Rudy Waltz's mother.

Woodcock, Sheldon Sheldon Woodcock is the New York actor who plays John Fortune in the production of Rudy Waltz's play, *Katmandu*. He has a frustrating conversation with Rudy about the character's motivation, pointing out logical inconsistencies in the role.

Woollcott, Alexander One of the famous visitors to Midland City brought to visit Otto Waltz's studio, Alexander Woollcott is described by Rudy Waltz as a "wit and writer and broadcaster" (62). Woollcott is an actual historic figure, a critic and commentator for *The New Yorker* magazine in the early 20th century and a member of the Algonquin Round Table literary group.

FURTHER READING

Broer, Lawrence L. "Kurt Vonnegut vs. Deadeye Dick: The Resolution of Vonnegut's Creative Schizophrenia." In *Spectrum of the Fantastic,* edited by Donald Palumbo, 95–102. Westport, Conn.: Greenwood, 1988.

Deadeye Dick. New York: Dell, 1999.

Morse, Donald E. "Kurt Vonnegut's *Jailbird* and *Deadeye Dick*: Two Studies of Defeat." *Hungarian Studies in English* 22 (1991): 109–119.

"Deer in the Works"

"Deer in the Works," a commentary on what it means to work for a large, soulless corporation, was initially published in *Esquire* magazine in April 1955. It was later reprinted in the 1961 collection, *Canary in a Cat House,* as well as the 1968 volume, *Welcome to the Monkey House.*

SYNOPSIS

The story opens with David Potter, a 29-year-old married man with a set of twin boys and brand-new twin girls, applying for a job in sales and advertising at the ILIUM Works, the second-largest industrial plant in the United States. Potter has owned and run a small-town weekly newspaper for the past eight years, but with the arrival of his new babies he feels the need for a more secure position, even though his wife urges him to stay with the newspaper work that he loves. After an intense interview, Potter is hired. When he and his new boss, Lou Flammer, receive news that a deer has gotten caught in the Works, David is told to start immediately. Believing that this story could be picked up by the national press and garner the company much attention, Flammer sends David to the other end of the Works to meet a photographer and to get the story of the deer. David, though, ends up losing his way in the massive, tangled Works. At one point, he wanders into an auditorium, is mistaken for a scientist at the conference that is going on there, and drinks three martinis before stumbling out again. When he eventually gets to the section of the plant where the deer was spotted, the animal has broken antlers and is trapped by a dozen company policemen with drawn pistols. David ends up unwiring a gate and letting the deer escape, then follows the animal right out of the plant, never looking back.

COMMENTARY

Like Vonnegut's first novel, *Player Piano*, published in 1952, three years before "Deer in the Works," this story is a send-up of large, bureaucratic corporations that treat workers as cogs in a machine rather than as individual human beings. Not only is the Federal Apparatus Corporation (the company that runs the Ilium Works) enormous, but like the National Industrial, Commercial, Communications, Foodstuffs, and Resources Organization in *Player Piano*, it has ties to the government and military. The reason that the corporation is increasing its staff by one-third is "in order to meet armament contracts" (222). Here, Vonnegut anticipates President Dwight D. Eisenhower's 1961 farewell address to the nation that warned of the dangers wrought

by the "total influence" of the U.S. "military-industrial complex." The Federal Apparatus Corporation seems to be representative of just such a power monopoly. The highly bureaucratic nature of the Ilium Works is driven home when David calls his wife, Nan, on the phone and reports the benefits the company offers workers: "a five per cent bonus in company stock—twelve years from now" (227), three weeks of vacation after putting in 15 years of work, and so on. When he becomes a member of this enormous organization, David's life will be controlled by such considerations. The prototypical company man is the "old and bright-eyed" (228) worker David meets on a busy street in the Works who has dedicated his life to the company and has a small lapel pin declaring his 50 years of service to prove it.

In the story, Vonnegut emphasizes the unnaturalness of such a life. The Ilium Works are described as a man-made, mechanistic world within a world. When David steps out onto a street in the Works, he walks on hot asphalt, trucks honk at him, and a cinder blows in his eyes. A world of machinery has replaced the natural world. And even more, workers soon grow so accustomed to the mechanized world that surrounds them that it begins to seem their natural environment. The old man David meets on the street is so acclimated to the artificial world of the Works that he prefers this man-made environment, "the clangor and smells and nervous activity" (228) to nature itself—April in Paris. The deer that gets caught inside the company's fences represents the incongruity between the artificial, machine-laden world of the Works and the natural world. An ambassador from nature, the deer cannot survive long inside. When David finally catches up with the animal, its antlers are broken, and it is soon to be shot and turned into venison for a company picnic. David's freeing of the deer is a freeing of himself as well. The story suggests that, had he stayed with the company, he too would be destroyed. He would no longer be able to write what he believes in, as he did for his weekly paper, but would have to write unnatural stories puffing the company and its activities. He would be trapped inside the bureaucracy of the company, selling his soul and his humanity for job security.

CHARACTERS

Company Policemen A group of company policemen, suggesting both the enormous size and authoritative structure of the Ilium Works, appears at both the beginning and end of the story. Company policemen are initially seen ushering job applicants into the company in groups of three. At the end, a dozen of these men, with drawn pistols, have cornered a terrified deer that has gotten lost in the giant Works.

Dilling, Mr. Mr. Dilling is the first company official David Potter speaks to when he applies for a job at the Ilium Works. Impressed by David's newspaper work, Mr. Dilling, who is about the same age as David and a family man as well, sends him to see Lou Flammer about a position.

Dunkel, Stan Stan Dunkel is described as "a grinning, bald, big-toothed man" (234), who works in sales at the Ilium Works. When David Potter gets lost in the Works on his way to get the story of the trapped deer, Dunkel mistakes him for a scientist and asks him what features he wants in an "X-ray spectrogoniometer" (235). The quick-thinking David replies that such a machine should be "sturdy" (235).

Flammer, Lou Lou Flammer is the publicity supervisor at the Ilium Works. A man who, like David Potter, also used to work on a weekly newspaper, Flammer has now become a complete company man. He hires David and sends him to report on the deer that has gotten caught in the Works.

Jason, Ed Ed Jason is a recent college graduate who works as David Potter's assistant at the small, weekly newspaper Potter owns. Jason's father wants to buy the newspaper for his son, which is one of the reasons that David feels it is a good time to leave newspaper work behind and obtain a more secure job at the Ilium Works.

McGarvey McGarvey is the name of the photographer who is sent to take pictures of the deer caught in the Ilium Works. David is to meet McGarvey at the site where the deer had been flushed out. Like David, though, the photographer gets lost on his way. He pulls up in a company limousine with Lou Flammer at the end of the story and is able to snap a picture before David lets the deer out a nearby gate.

Old Man When David Potter is sent to speak with Ilium Works publicity supervisor Lou Flammer, he is directed to the correct office by an "old and bright-eyed" (228) man who has worked 50 years for the company. The man's many years of service are represented by a small button on his lapel. This old man perhaps serves as a warning to David of his own future if he takes a job with the enormous company.

Plumber The deer is first spotted in the Ilium Works when a plumber is sent to repair a drinking fountain at a softball field near Building 217. The plumber discovers the deer hiding under the bleachers and flushes him out.

Potter, David David Potter is a young married man whose wife has just given birth to twin baby girls, adding to the twin boys already in the family. Although he loves working on the small-town newspaper that he owns and operates, he believes that his new, larger family requires him to obtain a more secure position. The Ilium Works, though, is a huge bureaucracy that threatens to stifle David, even on his first day. He escapes the company's clutches, along with the poor, terrified deer at the end of the story.

Potter, Nan David Potter's wife, Nan, has just given birth to twin girls when the story begins. Nevertheless, when her husband calls her in her hospital room to tell her about his new job at the Ilium Works, she encourages him to stick with the newspaper work that he loves rather than sacrifice himself for the sake of the family.

Receptionist A young woman receptionist who is sending job applicants to meet various company officials is too "sober" (223) and beaurocratic to laugh at the little joke David Potter makes when he comes before her.

FURTHER READING

Reed, Peter. *The Short Fiction of Kurt Vonnegut.* Westport, Conn.: Greenwood Press, 1997.
Welcome to the Monkey House. New York: Dell, 1998.

"Der Arme Dolmetscher"

One of only a few Vonnegut stories set in the army during World War II, "Der Arme Dolmetscher" first appeared in *The Atlantic Monthly* in July 1955. It was later reprinted in the 1999 collection, *Bagombo Snuff Box.*

SYNOPSIS

"Der Arme Dolmetscher," which translates as "The Army Interpreter," is narrated by an American soldier fighting in Belgium during World War II who is named battalion interpreter after his commanding officer hears him reciting the only German he knows: the first stanza of a poem by Heinrich Heine, "Die Lorelei," which he learned from a college roommate. Neither the battalion commander nor the battalion executive officer listen to the narrator's protests that he does not really know German, and he is assigned to be stationed in the local burgomaster's house to keep the man under surveillance. On his way there, the narrator meets three Pennsylvania Dutchmen who had been turned down for interpreters' jobs. The men warm up to the narrator and give him a pamphlet with several missing pages that translates English phrases into German. The narrator studies the pamphlet carefully, but the only phrases he learns are meant to be used in the heat of battle and for interrogation purposes. The narrator ends up sneaking away from the burgomaster's house in the middle of the night, realizing that he will be useless as an interpreter. He returns to his battalion headquarters, where he pretends that the burgomaster speaks a different dialect than he is used to. Soon after his arrival, four German Tiger tanks arrive at headquarters, and soldiers with submachine guns round up the Allied officers and troops. The only phrase the narrator can find in his pamphlet to say to them is the German for "Don't shoot." Ironically, the story ends with a German tank officer pulling out a translation pamphlet of his own and beginning to interrogate his prisoners using the same phrases that appear in the narrator's own pamphlet.

COMMENTARY

Partly a SATIRE on army incompetence, "Der Arme Dolmetscher" shows an ordinary soldier being promoted into a position as translator that he cannot possibly fulfill. His commanding officers seem strangely unbothered when the narrator insists that he cannot really speak German. Readers find out that the colonel, who in civilian life is a hotel detective from Mobile, Alabama, has a history of making imprudent decisions. The narrator says, "The Colonel felt his role carried with it the obligation to make quick, headstrong decisions. He made some dandies before the Wehrmacht was whipped, but the one he made that day was my favorite" (226). The ridiculousness of the narrator's elevation to battalion translator is truly brought home when he imagines the only drama that his smattering of German words would allow him to master. He dreams up a scenario in which he is required to console the burgomaster's beautiful daughter but ends up discovering that she and her father are really Nazi agents whom he then heroically captures and interrogates. Though the stuff of romantic war movies perhaps, this imagined scenario in no way resembles the narrator's real-life army experiences in which absurdity and incompetence rule the day. When the narrator returns to battalion headquarters, the southern colonel lackadaisically drawls that the camp is surrounded by German tanks, though he still seems to believe that the Americans will "whomp 'em" like they "whomped" the Germans when on maneuvers back in "Nawth Ca'lina and Tennessee" (230). The story ends ironically, with the German army not much better off than the American one, since the German tank officer carries a phrase book of his own.

CHARACTERS

Burgomaster The narrator, when he is named battalion interpreter, is stationed at the home of a local Belgian burgomaster, a government official roughly equivalent to an American mayor. The narrator, though, realizing he will be useless as an interpreter since he does not know German, leaves the burgomaster's home the very first night he is there to return to battalion headquarters.

Burgomaster's Daughter   While trying to sleep at the home of the Belgian burgomaster, the narrator imagines a drama that would make use of the only German he knows—the words from the first stanza of the poem "Die Lorelei" and the interrogation phrases from the translation pamphlet given him by the Pennsylvania Dutchmen. The scenario he dreams up involves a romantic liaison with the burgomaster's daughter, followed by the discovery that both she and her father are really Nazi agents.

Colonel   The narrator's battalion commander is a colonel who, in civilian life, is a hotel detective from Mobile, Alabama. When the colonel overhears the narrator recite a stanza of poetry in German, he names him battalion interpreter even though the narrator insists he does not really speak German.

Executive Officer   The executive officer of the narrator's army battalion is a dry-goods salesman from Knoxville, Tennessee, in civilian life. He and the battalion's commanding officer, a colonel, both agree that the narrator knows more German than anyone else in the battalion and should therefore be taken off latrine duty and serve instead as the unit's interpreter.

German Tank Officer   At the end of the story, four German tanks surround battalion headquarters, and two dozen German infantryman with submachine guns round up the Americans inside. A German tank officer soon "swaggers" (23) in and begins questioning the men using a German/English translation pamphlet that contains the same phrases as the pamphlet the narrator himself had studied earlier.

Narrator   The story's narrator is an ordinary American soldier fighting in Belgium in World War II who is mistakenly given the position of battalion interpreter even though he does not speak German.

He is captured, along with the entire staff at battalion headquarters, at the end of the story. A German tank officer interrogates the Americans, using a German/English phrase book very similar to the one the narrator himself had been given to study.

Pennsylvania Dutchmen   On his way to the Belgian burgomaster's house, where he is newly stationed, the narrator rides in the back of a truck with "three disgruntled Pennsylvania Dutchmen who had applied for interpreters' jobs months earlier" (226). Eventually the men warm up to the narrator and give him a tattered English/German phrase book with several missing pages.

FURTHER READING

Bagombo Snuff Box. New York: Berkley Books, 2000.
Reed, Peter. *The Short Fiction of Kurt Vonnegut*. Westport, Conn.: Greenwood Press, 1997.

"D.P."

The story "D.P.," one of the few Vonnegut stories that uses American World War II soldiers as characters, was initially published in the *Ladies' Home Journal* in August 1953. It later appeared in both *Canary in a Cat House*, Vonnegut's 1961 collection of short fiction, and his 1968 collection, *Welcome to the Monkey House*.

SYNOPSIS

"D.P." is set in Germany, shortly after World War II has ended. It is about a six-year-old black boy with blue eyes who lives in an orphanage run by Catholic nuns. Though the boy's official name is Karl Heinz, he is called "Joe" because the townspeople believe he resembles the African-American boxer, JOE LOUIS. The oldest boy at the orphanage, Peter, tells Joe that his father is an American soldier and his mother is a German woman. The nun who cares for the boys, though, denies this story, telling the six-year-old that no one knows who his father and mother are. But Joe takes Peter's words to heart and, one day, while he is on a walk with the group, he sees an enormous African-American soldier near the woods. Believing this is his father, Joe runs away from the orphanage that night to the place where he saw the soldier. It turns out that a whole unit of African-American soldiers is in the woods, on maneuvers, though they plan to move out in the morning. Joe spies the large soldier he had seen earlier, who is a sergeant in the unit, and runs to him. The soldiers are amazed to find a little black German boy in the woods. They give him chocolate and other gifts, and someone eventually fetches the lieutenant who can speak German. This is how they discover that Joe has run away from the orphanage. The lieutenant, along with the sergeant, whom Joe clings to and calls "Papa," drive the little boy back to the orphanage in their jeep. Once back, Joe is a star, sharing his gifts and telling the other children about his father who has promised to return for him and take him back home across the ocean.

COMMENTARY

The "D.P." of the story's title stands for "Displaced Person," a term that came into use during World War II to describe the vast number of people who had been removed from their native countries. While Germany is not the country of origin for many of the orphans living in this small town—the village carpenter and mechanic even amuse themselves trying to guess the nationalities of the various children—six-year-old Joe's dark skin color sets him apart as not belonging in a very visible way. In this story, Vonnegut explores a theme that will become paramount in his later fiction—the need for extended families to create a sense of belonging. Even at the young age of six, Joe realizes that he is set apart from the others, and when he sees the African-American sergeant coming out of the woods, he says to the nun: "He's one of my people" (165). Despite the kindness of the nun who looks after him, Joe longs to fit in, to be around people who look like him.

Another significant feature of the story is the nickname given the young orphan boy. He is dubbed "Joe" by the German village carpenter after legendary American boxer Joe Louis, also known as the Brown Bomber. Already a hero to many African Americans in the 1930s, Joe Louis's defeat of Ger-

man boxer Max Schmeling for the World Heavyweight Championship in 1938 was perceived as an American defeat of Nazi Germany, elevating Louis to heroic stature among American whites as well as blacks. Thus, for the African American soldiers who come upon Joe hiding in the woods, the boy's declaration that he is Joe Louis causes the woods to echo "with glee" (168). For the soldiers, Joe Louis is not only a symbol of an African American overcoming racism in America, but for America besting the Germans. The soldiers shower the little underdog with gifts, turning him into a hero back at the orphanage just as Joe Louis is a hero to them. Whether the soldiers will actually return for the boy as they promise might be doubtful, but Joe's statement that the sergeant cried when the two parted shows how deeply moved he was to meet the little boy. Having finally met some of "his people," and being convinced that there is a place he belongs in the world, the six-year-old can more happily return to his dreamy ways at the orphanage.

CHARACTERS

Carpenter An old village carpenter in the German town where the orphanage is located nicknames a six-year-old black orphan "Joe" after the American boxer, Joe Louis. When African-American soldiers come to the town on maneuvers one day, the carpenter tells Joe to look sharply in the woods up the slope past the school and he will see his father.

Corporal Jackson When the sergeant and the lieutenant leave to drive the child Joe back to the orphanage, a soldier named Corporal Jackson is put in charge of the men who remain behind. Jackson asks the lieutenant to tell the nuns back at the orphanage that "Joe was a *good* boy" (168).

Heinz, Karl See Joe, below.

Joe Joe, whose real name is Karl Heinz, is a six-year-old black boy with blue eyes who has been raised in a German orphanage run by Catholic nuns in the 1940s. Too young to remember his real parents, but likely the product of a relationship between an American soldier and a German woman, Joe runs away one night after spotting an African-American soldier whom he believes is his father. A unit of African-Americans soldiers treats him kindly, then drives him back to the orphanage, leaving Joe to believe that the soldier he mistakes for his father will come back for him soon.

Lieutenant When the orphan boy Joe runs away to the soldiers' camp, the enlisted men eventually send for their lieutenant, who can speak German. The lieutenant drives Joe back to the orphanage, along with the sergeant, whom Joe believes is his father.

Little Girl When Joe wakes up the next morning after his adventures with the African-American soldiers, a little girl, one of his fellow orphans, "wonderingly" asks Joe questions about his father (171).

Mechanic Every day when the orphans walk through the town, an old carpenter and a young mechanic try to guess the nationalities of the children. Both agree that the six-year-old black boy they call "Joe" is an American.

Nun The Catholic nun who oversees the orphans on their walks through town is kind to Joe and tries to distract him from 14-year-old Peter's hurtful comments.

Peter Peter, age 14, is the oldest child in the German orphanage where the story is set. Because Peter can remember his parents and his siblings and his home, he seems "superhuman" (163) to Joe and the other children. Peter is the one who initially tells Joe that his father is an American soldier. At the end of the story, Joe usurps Peter's role as the star of the orphanage, the child other children listen to with fascination.

Sergeant A large black sergeant is the first African-American soldier that the six-year-old orphan Joe spots on his walk. Joe thus firmly believes that the man is his father, and when he runs away to find the soldiers later that night, Joe clings to the sergeant and refuses to let go.

FURTHER READING

Reed, Peter. *The Short Fiction of Kurt Vonnegut.* Westport, Conn.: Greenwood Press, 1997.
Welcome to the Monkey House. New York: Dell, 1998.

"EPICAC"

A SCIENCE FICTION story depicting a machine that develops human emotions, "EPICAC" first appeared in *Collier's* magazine in November 1950. It was later reprinted in the 1968 collection, *Welcome to the Monkey House.*

SYNOPSIS

EPICAC is a giant supercomputer built by Dr. Ormand von Kleigstadt to help figure out the complicated mathematics of modern war. EPICAC's story is narrated by an unnamed mathematician who operates the computer on the night shift. Also working on the night shift is another "crackerjack mathematician" (299), Pat Kilgallen, whom the narrator falls completely in love with. However, he is unable to convince Pat to marry him because he is so unromantic. One night, "for the plain hell of it" (300), the narrator punches the question "What can I do?" into EPICAC's circuitry, using a simple code. To his great surprise, the computer spits out another question: "What's the trouble?" (300). The narrator then punches his problems into the supercomputer, including dictionary definitions of "love" and "girl" and other words that EPICAC does not understand. When the narrator explains the word *poetry* to the machine, EPICAC begins "clicking away like a stenographer smoking hashish" (300) and spits out a beautiful 208-line poem titled "To Pat" (300). The next night, the machine produces a sonnet. The narrator uses EPICAC's poems to woo Pat, but soon discovers that the machine itself is in love with the beautiful mathematician. When the narrator explains that women cannot love machines, EPICAC goes haywire and blows up. Yet, the machine turns out to have been a gracious loser. Before he short-circuits himself because he cannot have Pat, he leaves the narrator a "modest wedding present" (304), which turns out to be more than 500 love poems. The narrator plans to give Pat one of the poems on each wedding anniversary.

COMMENTARY

"EPICAC" is a lighthearted retelling of the famous *Cyrano de Bergerac* story, with a computer playing the role of the big-nosed, sword-fighting poet. While Cyrano de Bergerac was an actual 17th-century French playwright, he is better known as a character in several works that fictionalize his life. French poet Edmond Rostand published a play about Cyrano in 1897, in which the title character is in love with a beautiful woman named Roxanne, but is persuaded to woo her for another man, the more handsome Christian, who lacks Cyrano's way with words. The story has also been turned into several well-known film versions, including a 1987 Steve Martin comedy called *Roxanne*. Vonnegut's story retains the tongue-tied, unromantic figure in the character of the narrator, who loves his fellow mathematician Pat Kilgallen, but who lacks the poetic sensibility to win her over. Ironically, it is a computer, usually considered a soulless machine, that supplies the romantic poetry to win Pat. Clearly, this is a case in which a machine is more human than the humans who build and program it. Designed as an instrument to wage war more efficiently, EPICAC is more interested in love than war. The narrator certainly views EPICAC as a person. He talks about the computer as a "he" rather than an "it" and often supplies substitute words in parentheses to describe EPICAC's functioning, as in the following passage: "I won't go into details about how EPICAC worked (reasoned)" (298).

Finally, what destroys EPICAC is his acceptance of his machinelike nature. When the narrator is unable to counter the computer's claims that he is smarter and writes better poetry and lasts longer than his rival, the narrator tells him that women cannot love machines because of "fate," which he defines as "predetermined and inevitable destiny" (303). While human beings in many Vonnegut works are presented as the victims of fate themselves, the idea that he is a prisoner of a predetermined destiny and thus will never win the woman

of his dreams, causes EPICAC to short-circuit himself. Even a machine cannot bear to live a predetermined, machinelike existence. EPICAC's sacrifice for the narrator's happiness at the end, his gift of 500 poems, shows that this truly was a machine who acted with the greatest humanity possible.

CHARACTERS AND RELATED ENTRIES

EPICAC   The supercomputer EPICAC becomes a character in the story as the narrator presents the machine as more human than many human beings. EPICAC, while able to do the complex computations required of him, is nonetheless sluggish in this pursuit. A whole army of technicians cannot figure out what is wrong, but the narrator soon discovers that the machine in more interested in poetry and romance than in the science of war. Although the computer short-circuits himself in the end because he cannot marry Pat Kilgallen, the narrator says that he "shall always remember him as a sportsman and a gentleman" (304) since EPICAC writes 500 poems for the narrator to give Pat before he expires.

Kilgallen, Pat   Pat Kilgallen is not only "beautiful," "warm," and "soft," but she is a "crackerjack mathematician" (299) as well who loves poetry and romance. She initially refuses to marry the story's narrator because she believes he is not warm and romantic enough. When the narrator presents her with the poems written by EPICAC, however, Pat relents and promises to marry him if he will write her a poem each anniversary. The narrator agrees, mostly because a year is so far away. EPICAC helps the narrator out in the end by leaving him with 500 love poems for Pat before short-circuiting himself in despair.

Narrator   The story's narrator is a rather prosaic mathematician in love with a beautiful colleague named Pat Kilgallen. When he accidentally discovers that the computer EPICAC's true vocation is poetry, the narrator uses the poems the machine produces to woo Pat. Much to his dismay, however, he soon finds out that EPICAC himself is in love with Pat. At first, when EPICAC rightly points out that he writes better poetry than the narrator and is smarter than him, the narrator does not know how to respond. He silences EPICAC, however, when he explains that women cannot love machines because of "predetermined and inevitable destiny" (303).

von Kleigstadt, Dr. Ormand Dr. Ormand von Kleigstadt designed the supercomputer EPICAC to help calculate the complex mathematical equations associated with modern warfare. When the poetry-loving computer ends up short-circuiting himself, a tearful and choked-up Dr. von Kleigstadt calls the narrator with the tragic news.

Wyandotte College Wyandotte College is a fictional institution of higher learning appearing in several Vonnegut short stories reprinted in the collection *Welcome to the Monkey House,* including "Report on the Barnhouse Effect," "The Euphio Question," "EPICAC," and "Tomorrow and Tomorrow and Tomorrow." In "EPICAC," Wyandotte College houses the giant, poetry-writing supercomputer.

FURTHER READING

Reed, Peter. *The Short Fiction of Kurt Vonnegut.* Westport, Conn.: Greenwood Press, 1997.
Welcome to the Monkey House. New York: Dell, 1998.

"The Euphio Question"

"The Euphio Question," a SCIENCE FICTION story that satirizes the rise of television, was first printed in *Collier's* magazine in May 1951. The story was later reprinted in both *Canary in a Cat House* and *Welcome to the Monkey House.*

SYNOPSIS

The narrator of "The Euphio Question," a sociology professor at Wyandotte College, tells the story of his friend and colleague Dr. Fred Bockman, a physicist who is interviewed on the radio one day about his discovery of noise being transmitted by radio waves from what appear to be blank spots in space. The radio show host, Lew Harrison, has his engineer play the noise, which is not much more

than a "wavering hiss" (191), for his listeners. For the five minutes that the hiss sounds, Harrison, Bockman, and the narrator, who has been watching the interview, experience complete and total happiness. Later, they discover that everyone in the town, whether actually listening to the broadcast or not, had a similar experience. Soon, Lew concocts a plan to produce and market table-top devices that will receive the outer-space transmissions and broadcast them into peoples' homes, producing instant and complete happiness.

A few days later, Dr. Bockman has constructed a model of the device, which the men decide to call the "euphoriaphone" or "euphio" for short. The three men assemble in Bockman's home, along with Bockman's wife, Marion, the narrator's wife, Susan, and his 10-year-old son Eddie, to test the new euphio. After the device is flipped on, everyone in the little group immediately experiences total happiness and contentment. They cease to pay much attention to the outside world and barely notice when first a milkman comes to the door, then a state trooper to complain about the milkman's truck blocking the road. These two visitors are completely sucked into the happiness the device is emitting and join the group. Eventually, more people show up, including a troop of Boy Scouts, numerous parents who come looking for their missing sons, and a Western Union boy. Nobody minds when the winds whip up, and the "tail end of [an] Atlantic hurricane" (199) begins knocking down trees and blowing freezing cold air through a broken window.

Eventually, however, a tree crashes into a power line, shutting off the euphio. As the crowd comes out of its dazed condition, they realize they are cold and starving and that several people have sustained serious injuries. They also discover, to their amazement, that 36 hours have passed since the experiment began. The Boy Scouts set to work, finding blankets, making food, and generally restoring order. Soon, the power comes back on, and the narrator and Bockman notice the euphio beginning to start up again. The two men completely destroy the machine. Nevertheless, readers find out at the end of the story that Lew Harrison has not let the matter die, as Bockman and the narrator wished. He has petitioned the Federal Communications Commission for permission to start selling the devices. The narrator has been telling the story as part of his FCC testimony opposing Lew's plans. Yet, the story closes with the narrator experiencing the same euphoria and complacency he had earlier and praising the project—Lew has obviously set up a euphio nearby to influence the commission's decision.

COMMENTARY

"The Euphio Question" was written in 1951, just as television sets were beginning to work their way into middle-class American homes. By the mid-1950's, televisions would become quite commonplace. This story, then, can be viewed as a prescient SATIRE of television culture. The narrator describes the euphio, or euphoriaphone, as a gadget that fulfills "what a lot of people vaguely foresaw as the crowning achievement of civilization: an electronic something-or-other, cheap, easily mass-produced, that can, at the flick of a switch, provide tranquility" (189). But the happiness provided by the euphio is so complete that it sedates people, making them forget to eat, to sleep, and to care for themselves and each other. Just as the drug soma in Aldous Huxley's *Brave New World* (1932) controls the masses not through harsh laws or totalitarian regimes, the euphio turns human beings into pleasure-seeking zombies, unable to act or think for themselves. The story anticipates Ray Bradbury's immensely popular 1953 novel, *Farenheit 451*, which also satirizes the rise of American television culture, depicting characters who are hypnotized by wall-size television sets and who have retreated from intellectual or physical activity in favor of the narcoticlike effects provided by their televisions.

Vonnegut also ridicules the consumerist bent of American culture in the early 1950s. The euphios are not only dangerous as a new technology—scientific inventions in Vonnegut's works often cause more harm than good—but they also represent the ludicrous notion that people can buy happiness. Happiness, in Lew Harrison's view, is simply another consumer good that can be manufactured and sold to middle-class Americans eager to own all the modern conveniences. In his testimony before the Federal Communications Commission, the story's narrator admits that the euphio does indeed deliver everything that Lew Harrison promises. "The question is," he continues, "whether or not America is to enter a new and distressing phase of history where men no longer pursue happiness but buy it" (205). Echoing the "unalienable rights" guaranteed in the U.S. Declaration of Independence—"Life, Liberty, and the Pursuit Happiness"—the narrator creates the specter of an American changed drastically from Thomas Jefferson's vision. Ultimately, though, his impassioned speech does no good as the euphio clicks on and the narrator's mind becomes imprisoned by the happiness the device brings him.

CHARACTERS AND RELATED ENTRIES

Bockman, Dr. Fred   Dr. Fred Bockman is a physicist at Wyandotte College who is invited onto Lew Harrison's weekly radio program to discuss his discovery of noises being transmitted via radio signals from voids in space. Bockman initially opposes the idea of marketing euphoriaphones, but is persuaded by Lew to test out a model device. After the disastrous test, Bockman helps the narrator destroy the euphio.

Bockman, Marion   Marion Bockman is the wife of Dr. Fred Bockman and a participant in the test of the euphio. Like her husband, she is horrified by the events that occur in her home.

Bockman's Euphoria   Bockman's Euphoria is the name given to the phenomenon of hissing noises that are transmitted by radio waves from what appear to be blank spots in space. Discovered by physicist Dr. Fred Bockman, these noises induce euphoric feelings in human listeners.

Boy Scouts and their Parents   A troop of Boy Scouts who come to the Bockman's door, collecting old newspapers, is drawn in by the euphio. Later, several of the boys' parents, who arrive in search of their sons, are drawn in as well. When the power goes out and the device shuts down, the Boy Scouts, "with the incredible stamina of the young"

(202), heroically pull themselves together enough to fetch blankets and food and tend to the injured.

Eddie Eddie is the narrator's baseball-loving 10-year-old son. During the test of the model euphio, the wild and somewhat obnoxious Eddie immediately becomes docile and complacent, laying his head in his mother's lap.

Engineer An engineer at Lew Harrison's radio studio first flips the switch to transmit the outer space signals from Dr. Fred Bockman's radio antenna. The noise sedates everyone with a contentment so complete that they cannot act. The only reason that the hiss gets turned off after five minutes is because the engineer's cuff catches on the switch accidentally.

euphio "Euphio" is a shortened version of euphoriaphone, a table-top device that receives outer-space transmissions and broadcasts them into peoples' homes, producing instant and complete happiness. These devices, however, have the unanticipated side effect of entrancing people so completely that they forget to eat and sleep and become like drug-addicted zombies.

Harrison, Lew Lew Harrison is the loudmouthed radio announcer who invents the scheme to produce and market euphoriaphones after interviewing Dr. Fred Bockman on his weekly radio program. Even after the disastrous test of the device at Bockman's home, the greedy Lew does not drop his plan, but instead petitions the Federal Communications Commission for permission to develop and sell the happiness-producing machines. When one of Lew's euphios turns on automatically at the very end of the story, the narrator's objections to his scheme evaporate and Lew seems to have won out.

Milkman A milkman who comes to the Bockman's door during the test of the euphio gets pulled into the wave of happiness, leaving his milk truck blocking traffic in the street outside.

Narrator The story's narrator is a sociology professor at Wyandotte College who is testifying before the Federal Communications Commission regarding Lew Harrison's request to begin marketing the euphoriaphone. The narrator tells a cautionary tale about the terrible experiences he and a small group had when testing one of the devices. Nevertheless, Lew outsmarts him in the end, when a nearby euphio on a timing device clicks on, causing the narrator's objections to vanish in the wave of numbing happiness that overcomes him.

Repairman As Lew Harrison is arguing with the others about the euphio while the power is out, a repairman briefly sticks his head in the house to announce that the electricity will be back on in about two minutes.

State Trooper When a state trooper knocks at the Bockman's door to complain about the milk truck blocking traffic, he too is pulled into the wave of happiness in the house.

Susan The narrator's wife, Susan, like everyone else at the test of the model euphio device, is overcome with happiness. At one point, she kisses the loathsome Lew Harrison for about five minutes, to her husband's approving chuckle.

Western Union Boy A Western Union boy who had wandered unnoticed into the Bockman's home during the euphio test tells the assembled crowd, after the power goes out and they are released from their spell of happiness, that he arrived on a Sunday night. Therefore, it must be Monday morning.

Wyandotte College Wyandotte College is a fictional institution of higher learning appearing in several Vonnegut short stories reprinted in the collection *Welcome to the Monkey House,* including "Report on the Barnhouse Effect," "The Euphio Question," "EPICAC," and "Tomorrow and Tomorrow and Tomorrow." Both the narrator of "The Euphio Question" and Fred Bockman are professors at Wyandotte.

FURTHER READING

Reed, Peter. *The Short Fiction of Kurt Vonnegut.* Westport, Conn.: Greenwood Press, 1997.
Welcome to the Monkey House. New York: Dell, 1998.

Fates Worse Than Death: An Autobiographical Collage

Published by Putnam in 1991, *Fates Worse Than Death: An Autobiographical Collage* is called by Vonnegut a "sequel" (19) to *Palm Sunday*, the collection of essays, speeches, reviews, and autobiographical tidbits he had published 10 years earlier. *Fates Worse Than Death* takes a look back at the decade of the 1980s, assembling the short commentaries, opinion pieces, and autobiographical sketches that Vonnegut wrote during that decade. As with his previous collection, he stitches these pieces together with current observations and transitional remarks. He also includes several photographs in the book, as well as an appendix that presents a variety of items, some written by other authors, such as a brief essay about literature by the Czech writer Karel Capek and the afterword to a new edition of THE EDEN EXPRESS, a book written by his son MARK VONNEGUT that chronicles the young man's mental breakdown. Vonnegut's focus in this collection begins on his own family; he includes brief pieces on his father and mother and son Mark as well as meditations on his ex-wife, JANE COX VONNEGUT YARMOLINSKY, and his current wife, photographer JILL KREMENTZ. Because his family has been affected by mental illness and addiction, these are also topics he addresses in this autobiographical collage. As in all his work, in *Fates Worse Than Death*, Vonnegut considers American and worldwide social ills, including war, weaponry, environmental destruction, and racism. He examines the damage he believes is caused by traditional CHRISTIANITY and offers alternative religious practices. Finally, he examines the role of art in the contemporary world, discussing both literary and visual art as potential spiritual expressions that may serve as a substitute for organized religion.

Family/Mental Illness

Perhaps the dominant theme in all of Vonnegut's work, both his fiction and nonfiction, is the need that individuals have for large, supportive family structures. In *Fates Worse Than Death*, as in his two previous essay collections, he discusses the theory of folk societies advocated by his former

UNIVERSITY OF CHICAGO professor DR. ROBERT REDFIELD. Dr. Redfield argues that every society in world history has passed through a stage of isolation and group cohesion, in which members are united through kinship bonds. In such folk societies, Vonnegut explains, "there was such general agreement as to what life was all about and how people should behave in every conceivable situation that very little was debatable" (122–123). Although he does, perhaps for the first time in an essay about Dr. Redfield's ideas, warn of sentimentalizing such communities—according to the professor himself, "they were hell for anyone with a lively imagination or an insatiable curiosity or a need to experiment and invent" (123)—nevertheless Vonnegut tells readers of his own longing to belong to a folk society, even describing this desire as his "Holy Grail" (124). While folk societies were cohesive and rooted to a single place, Vonnegut argues that the "Great American Experiment" has quite opposite values. America, he explains, "is an experiment not only with liberty but with rootlessness, mobility, and impossibly tough-minded loneliness" (35). Thus, as an American, Vonnegut feels he never had a true sense of belonging to a specific, like-minded group. Even more, he goes on to argue that his lack of cultural identification is exasperated by his German-American background. Largely because of anti-German sentiment generated by both world wars, German-Americans are "the least tribal and most acculturated segment" of the American population (199).

Although Vonnegut feels he lacks the large, communal support of a folk society, he does view the INDIANAPOLIS of his boyhood, before his parents died and his friends and relatives scattered to different places, as conferring some of the sense of belonging a person might gain from a folk society. "It was a tradition in the Indianapolis branch of our once large and cohesive family," he writes, "that we should go east to college but then come back to Indianapolis" (22). Nevertheless, as he meditates on his parents and his relationship to them, Vonnegut laments the fact that the cohesiveness of the Vonnegut clan in Indianapolis seemed to come to an end with his generation. The book is dedicated to his father, KURT VONNEGUT, SR., a second-generation Indianapolis architect. In *Palm Sunday*, Vonnegut tells readers of his longing to follow in the footsteps of his father and grandfather and become an architect, like them working in his hometown of Indianapolis, and of his father's discouraging of this ambition. While also mentioning these facts in *Fates Worse Than Death*, Vonnegut's memories of his father in this collection are kinder and more flattering than readers have seen before. He describes Kurt, Sr. as a "unicorn," a frustrated artist out of place in the American Midwest of the early 20th century. Vonnegut writes, "While other fathers were speaking gloomily of coal and iron and grain and lumber and cement and so on, and yes, of HITLER and Mussolini, too, my father was urging friends and startled strangers alike to pay attention to some object close at hand, whether natural or manmade, and to celebrate it as a masterpiece" (24–25). Above all, Kurt Sr. in this collection comes off as a "gentle and innocent man" (36) whom his son loves and admires.

Vonnegut also presents his father as the long-suffering husband of a wife who is going insane. Elsewhere in his work, Vonnegut speaks of his mother's troubled childhood and the abuse she received at the hands of her stepmother. In this collection, he tells how his mother's insanity manifested itself in the "pure" and "untainted" "hatred and contempt" (36) that she spewed at her husband in the late hours of the night, between midnight and dawn. Witnessing such vitriol in his parents' relationship, Vonnegut, while admitting that his two marriages were far from perfect, nevertheless has almost entirely kind words to say about his first wife, Jane Vonnegut Yarmolinsky, who "adored her kids" and whose kids "adored her" in return (155) and his current "dear, gifted wife" (88), Jill Krementz. Even for his mother, whose mental problems, augmented by alcohol and the Phenobarbitals prescribed by her family doctor, caused her to commit suicide in May 1944, Vonnegut feels compassion, arguing that her crazed diatribes were compulsions she could not control: "For her it was like throwing up. She had to do it. Poor soul! Pour soul" (36). At a meeting of the American Psychiatric Association in 1988, Vonnegut discusses his family's desire at the time to keep his mother's illness and eventual suicide

a secret. Yet, in this speech, as in several other autobiographical pieces, Vonnegut is quite candid about his mother's illness as well as the mental breakdown of his son Mark, who was diagnosed in the early 1970s as a schizophrenic, though later, after his full recovery, this diagnosis was updated to manic-depression. He also speaks of his Uncle Alex's alcoholism, and, later in the collection, of his own battles with depression and, briefly, of his 1984 suicide attempt. In *Fates Worse Than Death*, as in his novels, Vonnegut argues that people are at least partly bundles of chemical reactions. When a person's chemicals misfire, that person should be treated with sympathy and support, just as any physical illness would be treated. He greatly admires groups such as ALCOHOLICS ANONYMOUS that provide such support.

Social Ills: War, Weaponry, Environmental Destruction, Racism

While speaking openly about his family's experiences with mental illness and about human beings who experience misfiring chemicals in their brains, Vonnegut also acknowledges that often the cause of depression and other psychiatric disorders may be a society that has gone insane. He tells readers about a failed novel he began writing 20 years previously, called *SS Psychiatrist*, about an MD at Auschwitz whose "job was to treat the depression of those members of the staff who did not like what they were doing there" (32). His point, he explains, was that "workers in the field of mental health at various times in different parts of the world must find themselves asked to make healthy people happier in cultures and societies which have gone insane" (32). Vonnegut very specifically points out what he believes are the insanities of America in the second half of the 20th century. Chief among these is Americans' love of weaponry and propensity toward war.

Reminding readers of his own father's gun collection and membership in the National Rifle Association, Vonnegut nonetheless explains how he feels when he hears people such as the actor Charlton Heston applauding that Americans are allowed to keep military weapons in their homes: "I feel exactly as though he were praising the germs of some loathsome disease, since guns in civilian hands, whether accidentally or on purpose, kill so many of us day after day" (81). Further, he argues that Western civilization has been blighted by the numerous people "who are tragically hooked on preparations for war" (134). And unfortunately, these "compulsive war-preparers" (135) are the ones who hold positions of power. Vonnegut writes, "Western Civilization cannot be represented by a single person, of course, but a single explanation for the catastrophic course it has followed during this bloody century is possible. We the people, because of our ignorance of the disease, have again and again entrusted power to people we did not know were sickies" (135). Vonnegut sees war-mongering as a disease, much like alcoholism or obsessive gambling. If we treat war-preparers sympathetically as sick individuals and remove them "from the levers of power," Vonnegut believes that Western civilization will then be able to begin "a long, hard trip back to sobriety" (135).

Specific war-related atrocities that Vonnegut discusses include the fire-bombing of DRESDEN, which he witnessed firsthand as a prisoner of war, an experience that makes up the basis of his classic novel *Slaughterhouse-Five,* and the atomic bombing of Japan at the end of World War II, among others. He insists here, and throughout his writings, that the German city of Dresden had no military significance during World War II, and thus that the Allied bombing of the city was wrong. Vonnegut is more ambiguous about the bombing of Hiroshima, calling it a "racist atrocity of atrocities" (100), yet recognizing that the city's destruction "had military significance" (100), since it prevented an Allied invasion of Japan, which would inevitably have cost even more lives. The bombing of Nagasaki, however, Vonnegut unambiguously opposes. In fact, responding to readers who find his speeches and novels "hopelessly ambiguous," Vonnegut includes in *Fates Worse Than Death* a list of bombings and attacks conducted by the United States from World War II forward, quite unambiguously assessing those that were justified. While he finds the bombing of Hamburg, Germany during World War II to have been necessary, and while he remains uncertain about Hiroshima, he very spe-

cifically condemns the bombings of Dresden, Nagasaki, Hanoi, Cambodia, Libya, and Panama City.

But Vonnegut also explains that even without the human-promulgated wars and weaponry that have scarred the 20th century, humans must face the fact that nature itself can be an enemy. Vonnegut argues that people in the 20th century have been the first in world history "to get reliable information about the human situation: how many of us there were, how much food we could raise or gather, how fast we were reproducing, what made us sick, what made us die" and so on (110). And the news has not been good. Nature sets fires to forests, sends glaciers down from the North Pole, turns farms into deserts, pushes up tidal waves, and showers down "white-hot boulders from outer space" (111). Nature, Vonnegut tells readers in a letter written to Earthlings of the year 2088 at the behest of the Volkswagen Company, is "ruthless when it comes to matching the quantity of life in any given place at any given time to the quantity of nourishment available" (111). And he adds that 20th-century Earthlings have only exasperated environmental problems, gobbling up everything in sight, making love, then doubling in size again and again. Vonnegut suggests that humans cannot win an ultimate victory over nature and that what we must do instead is concede to her "stern but reasonable surrender terms" (112). These terms include reducing and stabilizing the human population; ceasing to pollute the air, water, and soil; stopping preparations for war; teaching children how to inhabit a small planet without killing it; ceasing to believe that SCIENCE AND TECHNOLOGY will solve all human problems; and abandoning the notion that we can be destructive and wasteful because later generations will be able to explore and inhabit new planets. If we do not make these concessions, Vonnegut argues, human beings might as well carve these words in great big letters on a wall in the Grand Canyon:

WE PROBABLY COULD HAVE SAVED OURSELVES,
BUT WERE TOO DAMNED LAZY TO TRY VERY HARD.

AND TOO DAMN CHEAP.

While Vonnegut fully seems to expect the world destruction he foresees—in a sermon preached at the Cathedral of St. John the Divine in New York City, he said, "My guess is that we will not disarm, even though we should, and that we really will blow up everything by and by" (145)—he nevertheless admits in the collection that the world *is* getting better in many ways. Recognizing that "old poops" forecasting doom, a type he calls a "Royal Astronomer," have been around for centuries, Vonnegut challenges the clichés often expressed by the older generation: "Things aren't as good as they used to be. The young people don't know anything and don't want to know anything. We have entered a steep decline" (113). He tells readers that when he was a boy, lynchings of black people were common, that an apartheid stricter than that practiced in South Africa was enforced in Indianapolis, and that Jews were not welcome in universities and other places. In fact, in a graduation speech delivered at the University of Rhode Island in Kingston in 1990, Vonnegut reports telling the students that "the most extraordinary change in this country" since he was a boy is "the decline in racism" (83). That is not to say that racism no longer exists in America. He criticizes the 1980s neo conservative political movement in America as accepting the worn-out notion of the "White Man's Burden" (127), and he condemns George H. W. Bush for fanning racist fears in his 1988 presidential campaign against Michael Dukakis. While praising the great strides the United States had made in racial relations, Vonnegut recognizes that a legacy of slavery and racism still affects many Americans.

Slavery itself is one of the many social ills Vonnegut explores in this collection. He links slavery to war mongering in his sermon at the Cathedral of St. John the Divine when he speculates that human beings make hydrogen bombs and prepare for war not because we fear death at the hands of our enemies—death will come in any case—but because we fear "fates *worse* than death" (140), a phrase that becomes the title of this collection. Yet, the only fate that Vonnegut acknowledges to be worse than death is being crucified. And he severely doubts that any invading army is going to come to America to crucify its citizens the way that

Romans crucified people in biblical times. Even the fear of being enslaved, he argues, a fate most Americans probably consider to be worse than death, finally provides insufficient justification for preparing and utilizing what today would be called weapons of mass destruction. The last time that Americans were slaves and the last time that Russians were slaves, he adds, "they displayed astonishing spiritual strengths and resourcefulness" (143), committing suicide less often than their masters. Because slaves so clearly want to go on living, Vonnegut argues that perhaps slavery "*isn't* a fate worse than death" (143)—people are tough and able to endure terribly trying circumstances. Vonnegut also believes that fears of being enslaved by a conquering army are grossly unrealistic. But his point here, and throughout the collection, is that no fate we can imagine justifies the destruction of human life threatened by the current buildup of weapons and the constant preparation for war.

Religion

Another frequent target for Vonnegut, and one that he does not spare in *Fates Worse Than Death*, is traditional Christianity. If human beings are cruel in their production of war weaponry and in their treatment of the environment, these cruelties are only encouraged by conventional Christianity, he argues. He tells readers that the stories he has written have gotten him into trouble "with the sincerely Christian far right" (80), beginning with a story in which time-travelers go back to biblical times and discover that Jesus was only five feet, two inches tall. Vonnegut asserts that he likes Jesus better than the story's critics do, since he "didn't care how tall or short He was" (80). More liberal brands of Christianity are not always better, either. Vonnegut tells the story of looking for an Episcopal Church in which to celebrate his marriage to Jill Krementz, herself an Episcopalian. When he tries a New York City church long associated with the theater community and affectionately called "The Little Church Around the Corner," he tells readers that he never in his life "caught more hell for having been divorced" (87). The powerful church woman he speaks to treats Vonnegut's divorce from his first wife "as the most unforgivable thing she had ever heard" (87). Needless to say, the couple found a different church to get married in.

But Vonnegut's most extensive discussion of traditional Christianity comes in a piece newly written for the collection, in which he describes attending the 1985 world premiere of Andrew Lloyd Webber's new musical setting for a Requiem Mass whose text was composed in the 16th century. Vonnegut is dismayed by the lyrics to the Mass, which he argues promised a "Paradise indistinguishable from the Spanish Inquisition" (71). Because of the Mass's emphasis on stern heavenly judgment and the fear such judgment should instill in sinful human beings, Vonnegut calls it both "sadistic and masochistic" (71). After the premiere, Vonnegut tells readers he went home and stayed up half the night composing a new Requiem Mass. He includes copies of the 1570 original and his own revision in the index to the collection. In Vonnegut's Mass, he asks that sinful human beings receive peace and forgiveness. He asserts that his prayers will be unheard and that the "sublime indifference" of any supernatural being will ensure that humans never "burn . . . in some everlasting fire" (228). After having a New York University instructor translate his lyrics into Latin and finding a Juilliard graduate to set his words to music, Vonnegut's Requiem was actually premiered in a Unitarian Universalist Church in Buffalo, New York, in March 1988.

Vonnegut extends the analogy between war and religion when he asserts, at a lecture delivered to a Unitarian gathering in Rochester, New York, in 1986, that the two commandments he is able to distill from the religious revival going on in the country at the time are "Stop thinking" and "Obey," orders he compares to what he was taught as an infantry private undergoing basic training. In this same lecture, he mentions all the Christian crosses he saw proudly displayed on Nazi uniforms and flags when he was fighting in World War II and wonders "what makes Christians so bloodthirsty?" (158). Vonnegut's answer to his own question is that traditional Christianity requires its adherents to love their neighbors, a task Vonnegut claims is simply too difficult for most ordinary human beings to accomplish. Love, for Vonnegut, as he discusses in earlier novels and essay collections, is always a

dangerous concept. Here Vonnegut explains that love implies its opposite: hate. If people fail at loving their neighbors, they come to the "seemingly inevitable conclusion that they must hate instead" (160). As a solution, Vonnegut proposes doing away with the Christian requirement to "love" one's neighbors and substituting "respect" instead. Just as in the prologue to his novel *Slapstick*, he argues for "a little less love and a little more common decency" (3), in this lecture he claims that respecting and behaving decently toward one's fellow human beings is not only more valuable than loving them, but more realistic as well.

In this collection, as he does throughout his writings, Vonnegut advocates a spirituality more centered on human values than focused on a supernatural being or the promise of heavenly rewards and punishments. The "saints" (191) that he praises in the book are human beings, such as his wife, Jill, who did her best to help the Vietnamese people while working as a photographer in that country during the war years, his friend DR. ROBERT MASLANSKY, who treats addicts committed to Bellevue Hospital, southern lawyer MORRIS DEES, who risks his own life to challenge racist groups in court, and the various CARE workers he met while surveying the human tragedy in Mozambique. Vonnegut's HUMANISM is particularly evident in the verse with which he concludes the collection: "Man alone is able to do/What's seemingly impossible . . . He alone may/Reward the good,/Punish the wicked,/Heal and save" (202). In Vonnegut's view, human beings do indeed have spiritual yearnings that must be fulfilled in order to make life seem meaningful, but he does not believe that humans should simply accept religious dogma handed to them. In his fiction and essays, he constantly reworks traditional Christian notions, unafraid to try to improve on what he sees as failings in received wisdom.

Reading/Writing/Art

As he does in his two previous essay collections, *Wampeters, Foma, and Granfalloons* and *Palm Sunday*, in *Fates Worse Than Death* Vonnegut substitutes the experience of reading itself for more conventional religion. In an essay written for the *New York Times* but unpublished until the release of this collection, Vonnegut discusses dabbling in Transcendental Meditation during the 1960s. While his meditative experiences provided fairly pleasant "little naps" (187), Vonnegut explains that he soon realized that he already had access to what was, for him, a much deeper, more spiritually fulfilling form of meditation: reading. Since he was "eight or so," he explains to readers, he "had been internalizing the written words of persons who had seen and felt things" that were new to him (188). He returned from these "Western-style meditation" (188) experiences a wiser human being, having absorbed the wisdom of others. While books may have started as "practical schemes for transmitting or storing information," he argues that an unforeseen consequence of reading is that it allows people to "create a spiritual condition of priceless depth and meaning" that may ultimately be "the greatest treasure at the core of our civilization" (188).

In *Fates Worse Than Death*, Vonnegut also discusses the making of art as a meditative, deeply subconscious experience. In an essay about the artist JACKSON POLLOCK written for *Esquire* magazine, Vonnegut compares ABSTACT EXPRESSIONIST painting to jazz music, arguing that these are the only two art forms Americans took leadership roles in developing. Pointing out that Pollock was capable of producing realistic images in "photographic detail," having been trained by the American master of representational art, Thomas Hart Benton, he goes on to explain that Pollock rejected realism in his art, preferring instead to "surrender his will to his unconscious as he went about his job" (42). And Vonnegut delights in the idea of a school of art that rejects "tired old stories" (43) in favor of the organic unfolding of the human unconscious: "Had any psychological experiment yielded a more delightful suggestion than this one," he asks, "that there is a part of the mind without ambition or information, which nonetheless is expert on what is beautiful?" (44). Moreover, Vonnegut considers abstract expressionism, despite its lack of realistic subject matter, as a deeply moral artistic movement. Anti-realism, he argues, is an "appropriate reaction . . . to World War II, to the death camps and Hiroshima" (44). The real world has shown itself to be diseased and ugly, so that all human and natural objects are tainted. Thus, painters retreat to the inner works of the mind and the imagination for inspiration.

In several of his novels, including *Slaughterhouse-Five*, *Breakfast of Champions*, and *Bluebeard*, Vonnegut justifies his own nonrealistic literary endeavors, pointing out the social ills he believes literary realism has engendered. In this collection, he also touches on his experiments with anti-realistic art, explaining the secret connection he always felt to the American experimental author Donald Barthelme since both writers were the sons of architects. As such, he argues, they both "tried hard to make every architect's dream come true, which is a dwelling such as no one has ever seen before, but which proves to be eminently inhabitable" (55). Thus, Vonnegut describes himself and Barthelme as "aggressively unconventional storytellers" (55) in their quest to build truly original edifices. Vonnegut asserts that one of the chief ways his own writing is unconventional is that in many of his books, "individual human beings are not the main characters" (129). Neither, he says, are the villains in his work individual human beings; they are, instead, "culture, society and history" (31). Yet, as the above quote about sons of architects suggests, Vonnegut also wants his novels to be "eminently inhabitable," to be inviting to readers rather than obscure, overly difficult, or off-putting despite their unconventionality. He describes, in a lecture given in Idaho to a group of HEMINGWAY scholars, his love for the simple, straightforward language of Hemingway's work despite his frequent distaste for Hemingway's subject matter. This simple prose is a style that Vonnegut has emulated in his own work, while at the same time overturning such traditional conventions as the realistic characters and plots that Hemingway employed.

While he believes that reading can be a sacred activity and that the production of art can be an avenue to the beauty of the human unconscious, Vonnegut at the same time expresses a somewhat paradoxical self-deprecation for his role as a writer. As he has done throughout his career, in *Fates Worse Than Death* he presents writing as a trade, a craft he has developed in order to earn a living, similar to what is done by an ironworker or a baker or a cobbler, a point also made in the essay "On Literature" by the Czech writer Karel Capek, which Vonnegut admired enough to include in his appendix to the collection. The work of translating fiction, in fact, he believes is as difficult and worthy of praise as the original work of creating it. In an essay about translations of his own novels, Vonnegut expresses his belief that "translators should be paid the same royalties as authors" (178). Further, Vonnegut is not afraid to face the pitfalls of his chosen profession. He acknowledges that American humorists such as himself, "those who choose to laugh rather than weep about demoralizing information," become "intolerably unfunny pessimists if they live past a certain age" (183). For men, Vonnegut sets that age at 63. Of course, he was 68 years old when this collection was published. Thus, he explains that his latest novel, *Hocus Pocus*, set for publication in September 1991, is "a sardonic fable in a bed of gloom" (184). Nevertheless, Vonnegut goes on writing, as he believes MARK TWAIN went on writing, because American humorists also have "a clear image in their heads of what American citizens ought to be" (186). Vonnegut's utopian dream of creating ideal citizens, while perhaps impossible to fulfill, all the same serves as the inspiration and driving force behind *Fates Worse Than Death*.

FURTHER READING

Fates Worse Than Death. New York: Berkley Books, 1992.

"Find Me a Dream"

"Find Me a Dream," initially published in *Cosmopolitan* magazine in February 1961, is one of Vonnegut's short, sweet love stories, along the lines of "Long Walk to Forever." The story was reprinted in the 1999 collection, *Bagombo Snuff Box*.

SYNOPSIS

"Find Me a Dream" is set in Creon, Pennsylvania, a town known for its ability to produce quality sewer pipes. The story opens on a Friday night, with Andy Middleton, clarinetist and leader of a dance band called The Creon Pipe-Dreamers, leaving a country club dance to get some fresh air on the adjoining golf course. On the first tee, he comes upon a pretty young woman crying. The two have a brief conversation, during which the woman shows her musical knowledge as she recognizes how poorly Middleton's band is playing. She asks Andy for a drink, and he obliges her, going into the crowded country club bar while she remains outside on the golf course. In the bar, the bartender tells Andy that Arvin Borders, manager of the Creon Works of the General Forge and Foundry Company, is searching everywhere for his new fiancée, a young New York actress with two little daughters and the widow of a famous jazz musician. Back on the golf course, Andy finds out that the young woman is indeed Hildy Matthews, the actress whom Arvin Borders plans to marry. Hildy explains that she falls in love easily and loves lavishly and truly afterward. She has agreed to marry Borders, despite his obsession with sewer pipes, because she needs to support her daughters and he is a wealthy businessman. However, the story ends with Hildy proposing to Andy, explaining that she thinks she could love him very much.

COMMENTARY

"Find Me a Dream," set as it is in Creon, Pennsylvania, also known as "Pipe City" for the town's main industry and obsession, plays on the notion of "pipe dreams." Pipe dreams are usually defined as fantastic or unrealistic fantasies; the phrase derives from the pleasant dreams experienced by opium smokers. Meeting Hildy Matthews on the golf course is like a pipe dream come true for bandleader Andy Middleton. Not only is Hildy young and pretty, but she is the widow of the most famous jazz musician in the world. She has a deep appreciation for and understanding of music, unlike almost everyone else in the very prosaic town of Creon, where "pipe dreams" are more likely to refer to dreams of what people can buy with the money they earn from selling sewer pipes than anything else. Andy tells Hildy at the end that his own big dreams have all but vanished— dreams of being "half the musician" (291) her husband was, and dreams of love.

But Andy Middleton also fulfills Hildy's own pipe dreams. He combines the best elements of both her former husband and her new fiancée, Arvin Borders. A lover of music unlike the stodgy Arvin Borders, Andy is also an upright and responsible man, contrasting the famous jazz musician Hildy was previously married to, a man who, in the words of Borders, was "a dope fiend, an alcoholic, a wife-beater, and a woman-chaser" (288). Yet, the story also shows that the practical Hildy makes her own dreams come true. She tells Andy that one of the things she does best is to love, adding, "I don't mean pretending to love. I mean really loving" (290). When she makes up her mind to love Arvin Borders, she really loves him, despite the deep differences between the two. Thus, at the end of the story, when Hildy tells Andy that she will both encourage him as a musician and also give him "the big and beautiful love" (293) he wants, readers believe her. Hildy is an actress, perhaps, trained to play roles, but marrying Andy Middleton is the one role she seems born to play.

CHARACTERS

Bartender An unnamed bartender at the Pipe City Golf and Country Club informs bandleader Andy Middleton that factory manager Arvin Borders is searching for his date, young New York actress Hildy Matthews.

Borders, Arvin Arvin Borders is a 46-year-old bachelor who is the manager of the Creon Works of the General Forge and Foundry Company. Obsessed with sewer pipe, as are most people in the town, Borders uncharacteristically brings a young New York widow and actress named Hildy Matthews to a Friday night dance at the Creon country club one night. Borders cares so little about music that he does not even recognize the name of Hildy's former husband, the most famous jazz musician in the world. Hildy ends up leaving Borders for bandleader Andy Middleton by evening's end, justifying herself by speculating that Borders would ruin his career by marrying a woman like her.

Matthews, Hildy Hildy Matthews is a small-time New York actress and the widow of the most famous jazz musician in the world. She comes to the small manufacturing town of Creon, Pennsylvania, as the date of factory manager Arvin Borders. She has agreed to marry Borders mostly because he is a wealthy businessman who can support her and her two young daughters, left destitute after her husband's death. When Hildy meets bandleader Andy Middleton on the golf course, however, she changes her dreams, realizing that Middleton would be a much better match for her.

Middleton, Andy Andy Middleton is a clarinet player and leader of a dance band who seems somewhat out of place in Creon, Pennsylvania, since he is not obsessed with sewer pipes as most of the other town residents are. He is intrigued when he comes upon pretty, young New York actress Hildy Matthews crying on the country club golf course one evening. When Hildy proposes to him at the end of the story, Middleton accepts, even though she is already the fiancée of factory manager Arvin Borders.

FURTHER READING

Bagombo Snuff Box. New York: Berkley Books, 2000.
Reed, Peter. *The Short Fiction of Kurt Vonnegut.* Westport, Conn.: Greenwood Press, 1997.

"Fortitude"

"Fortitude," Vonnegut explains in the preface to his essay collection *Wampeters, Foma, and Granfalloons*, where it was first published, is a "screenplay for an unproduced short science-fiction film" (xvii). While he writes that he is content to leave several of his short stories uncollected, he thinks highly enough of this brief screenplay to include it as the only piece of fiction that appears in *Wampeters*. The play is a contemporary updating of MARY SHELLEY's classic horror tale, FRANKENSTEIN, first published in 1818.

SYNOPSIS

The story involves a genius doctor named Norbert Frankenstein who has dedicated his life to keeping alive the rich widow Mrs. Sylvia Lovejoy. The 100-year-old Mrs. Lovejoy's physical body consists of a head on a tripod, connected to wires and pipes that run to an underground room, where numerous mechanical organs work to keep her functioning. The play opens when a young Vermont family doctor, Elbert Little, comes to visit Dr. Frankenstein in his laboratory. The older doctor proudly shows Dr. Little around, introducing him to Mrs. Lovejoy and explaining that even the rich widow's emotions are controlled by machines, so that she is kept happy and contented. However, Mrs. Lovejoy's hairdresser, Gloria, tells Dr. Little a different story. Gloria claims that the "little spark" that is left of the original Sylvia Lovejoy wants only to die, ending the hell that has become her life. To help Mrs. Lovejoy, Gloria smuggles a loaded pistol into her room. Dr. Frankenstein and his assistant, Dr. Tom Swift, however, have configured Mrs. Lovejoy's mechanical arms in such a way that she cannot point a gun at herself. When she realizes this, she instead unloads the pistol into Dr. Frankenstein's body. The story ends with Dr. Frankenstein as a head on a tripod as well, hooked up to the same bodily organs as his beloved Sylvia, the two prepared to face a long future together.

COMMENTARY

Clearly indebted to Mary Shelley's classic novel, "Fortitude" also depicts a protagonist named Dr. Frankenstein who creates a monster when he is unable to accept the limits of the human life span. Both Shelley's Victor Frankenstein and Vonnegut's Norbert Frankenstein have beloved mothers who die young. Both men are scientific geniuses who study intensely to gain the knowledge that will allow them to create life artificially. Both unwittingly end up creating monsters. While Shelley's story responded to scientific advances of her time, particularly experiments with electricity, Vonnegut's screenplay comments on medical advances of the decade in which he began his writing career. Great leaps in medicine were made in the middle part of the 20th century. The miracle drug penicillin had recently been discovered, and Jonas Salk created a vaccine for polio. More important for Vonnegut's purposes, the first kidney transplant

was successfully performed in 1954. In the preface to *Wampeters, Foma, and Granfalloons*, the collection in which the screenplay was first published, Vonnegut speaks of his era as a "miracle age of organ transplants and other forms of therapeutic vivisection" (xv). Yet, suspicious of technology as always, Vonnegut takes a look at these medical wonders and speculates about the dark side of such scientific advancements.

Dr. Elbert Little in the drama represents old-fashioned medicine. Though not as technologically informed as Dr. Frankenstein, Dr. Little is a more humane doctor. He is a family practitioner from Vermont who cares for numerous patients in a poor township. Part of the problem Vonnegut foresees with the burgeoning medical technology of the 1950s is its cost. Much is made of the expense of the various mechanical organs that keep Mrs. Lovejoy alive. Vonnegut fears a future in which the wealthy can afford life-extending medical care that is completely unavailable to those of more modest means. In addition, Vonnegut suggests that the new medical technology ceases to treat people as human beings, seeing the human body instead as a machine that must be kept functioning at all costs. Dr. Frankenstein is tone-deaf when it comes to human interaction. He completely misunderstands Dr. Little's comment that Mrs. Lovejoy has exhibited a great deal of courage and fortitude in her treatment, explaining condescendingly to the younger doctor that, "We knock her out, you know. We don't operate without anesthetics" (45). Even more important, he misreads his patient. Dr. Frankenstein is blind to what the hairdresser Gloria sees in Sylvia—the "tiny little spark of what she used to be" (61). He believes that human emotions can be completely controlled by mechanical devices, even saying to Dr. Little, "What the hell do we have to watch her face for? We can look at the meters down here and find out more about her than she can know about herself" (56). Dr. Frankenstein operates according to a mechanistic view of human beings, a notion that Vonnegut works hard to dispel in so much of his fiction.

The ending of the story is chilling. Sylvia Lovejoy's unhappiness is made manifest when she repeatedly shoots Dr. Frankenstein with the pistol smuggled in by Gloria. Through this action she gains for herself the exact opposite of what she wants: an eternity as a half-machine, with the doting doctor hooked up to wires and apparatus at her side. Although Dr. Frankenstein has carefully planned for a future in which he would be kept alive artificially alongside Sylvia, readers cannot help but speculate that this future will not be as bright as he expects. Even the insensitive doctor, Vonnegut suggests, will tire of the eternal half-human existence to which he has damned himself.

CHARACTERS

Derby, Howard A hospital mail clerk described as a "merry old fool," Howard Derby delivers the thousands of letters that Sylvia Lovejoy receives every year. The rich widow, unable to move or leave her room, entertains herself by keeping up a voluminous correspondence with people from the outside world.

Frankenstein, Dr. Norbert A character in the tradition of Mary Shelley's famous Dr. Victor Frankenstein, who created a human being out of dead body parts and who has become a SCIENCE FICTION icon, Dr. Norbert Frankenstein is similarly ignorant about what true humanity consists of. Like Victor Frankenstein in Shelley's novel, Norbert loses his beloved mother and desires to cheat death as a result. He uses a combination of science, engineering, and medical know-how to keep rich widow Sylvia Lovejoy artificially alive years and years after her physical body has fallen apart. Norbert, though, never understands the hell he has created for his beloved Sylvia. When he is shot by his patient at the end of the play and finds himself next to her, also a head on a tripod wired to machines, he is content, since this is the ending that he had long foreseen for himself.

Gloria Gloria is a beautician who is hired to take care of rich widow Sylvia Lovejoy's face and hair. Though uneducated according to Dr. Frankenstein's standards, Gloria understands the suffering that Mrs. Lovejoy is experiencing. Caring for her

client a great deal and believing that Mrs. Lovejoy only wishes to end her suffering, Gloria smuggles a loaded pistol into the old woman's room.

Little, Dr. Elbert Dr. Elbert Little is a young general practitioner from Vermont who has recently been chosen by *Reader's Digest* magazine as the American family doctor of the year. When Sylvia Lovejoy reads about Dr. Little, she begs him to come visit and bring cyanide, since she can no longer bear her existence, kept alive on machines as she is. Dr. Little, who cannot hide his horror at what Dr. Frankenstein has created, observes the events unfold as Sylvia first tries to kill herself and eventually ends up shooting Frankenstein. Dr. Little's role is to serve as a humane foil to Dr. Frankenstein, a representative of old-fashioned medical care in the face of Frankenstein's love of technology.

Lovejoy, Mrs. Sylvia The 100-year-old widow of a multimillionaire, Mrs. Sylvia Lovejoy's physical self is a head on a tripod, wired to an entire room filled with pumps and mechanical body parts that work around the clock to keep her alive. Although her moods are also controlled by the machines she is wired to, the spark of her real self shows through occasionally. At these times, she is able to recognize the hell that her existence has become. When she is unable to commit suicide with the loaded pistol her hairdresser smuggles into her room, she turns the gun on Dr. Frankenstein instead.

Swift, Dr. Tom Dr. Tom Swift, who is named after the mechanical whiz hero of a series of early 20th-century children's book, is Dr. Norbert Frankenstein's first assistant. Dr. Swift helped to design the machines in the underground room that keep Sylvia Lovejoy alive. He also runs the machines' complicated controls, although Dr. Frankenstein makes the actual decisions about Mrs. Lovejoy's care.

FURTHER READING

Wampeters, Foma and Granfalloons. New York: Dell, 1999.

"Foster Portfolio, The"

A story about a man who is forced to hide his artistic bent in a grim, materialistic world, "The Foster Portfolio" was first published in *Collier's* magazine in September 1951. It was later reprinted in both *Canary in a Cat House* and *Welcome to the Monkey House.*

SYNOPSIS

"The Foster Portfolio" is narrated by an unnamed salesman for an investment counseling firm. Used to handling large accounts of other peoples' money, the salesman is somewhat annoyed when one evening he is called to the home of Herbert Foster, clearly a man of modest means with little to invest. At the Foster home, the narrator meets Herbert's "shrewish" (60) wife, Alma, and the couple's toddler son, Herbert, Jr., before being taken into a bedroom where Herbert gives him a list of his securities to look over. Much to the narrator's astonishment, Herbert turns out to be an extremely wealthy man, with holdings of more than $850,000. As the weeks pass, the narrator's firm invests the money wisely and it continues to grow. Meanwhile, Herbert steadfastly refuses to touch his inheritance. The narrator learns from Alma that Herbert's father, a jazz pianist, had abandoned Herbert and his mother when Herbert was very young. His mother, however, according to Alma, was "a saint," who taught her son to be "decent and respectable and God-fearing" (67). The narrator also learns that Herbert has a second job to make ends meet, working Friday, Saturday, and Sunday nights at a restaurant. Increasingly curious, the narrator discovers the name of the restaurant where Herbert works and goes to see him one night. The place turns out to be a dive—"tough, brassy, dark, and noisy" (71)—and no one working there has ever heard of Herbert Foster. Yet, the narrator discovers Herbert's secret. He has been playing jazz piano under the name Firehouse Harris, living out the life of his much-reviled father three nights of every week.

COMMENTARY

"The Foster Portfolio" is as much about the narrator of the story as it is about Herbert Foster. The story is told by an unreliable narrator who is clearly

a product of his money-loving society. Vonnegut carefully details the expensive suits, shirts, and ties the narrator dons as he strives to create the appearance that he is like a "minister or physician" (59), there to take loving care of his old lady clients, although his real concern is with the money he can make from them. Despite the narrator's claims to "have nothing against people in moderate circumstances," he fully participates in the "unsavory habit" of his profession—"sizing up a man's house, car, and suit, and estimating his annual income" (60). When the narrator determines that Herbert Foster is worth only six thousand a year, he immediately loses interest in the man, and repeatedly suggests that it is time for him to call a cab and leave the house. After Herbert shows the narrator his hidden portfolio, however, the narrator's attitude changes; he perks up and begins calling Herbert "Sir" (63). The narrator's real love of money is most evident in his description of what his firm is able to do with Herbert Foster's portfolio. "A sound portfolio is a thing of beauty," he says, adding that, "Putting one together is a creative act" (71). Herbert's portfolio, moreover, is the firm's "masterpiece" (71). For this narrator, moneymaking is an art form.

Herbert Foster, on the other hand, is a man to whom money itself does not matter that much. He is a torn, conflicted character who seems to have had a shrewish, overbearing mother as well as wife. When the narrator mistakes the portrait of Herbert's mother for a picture of Alma herself, Alma Foster, replies that "everybody" makes the same mistake (66). Alma's admiration of Herbert's mother makes readers suspect that she was a rather grim woman who dominated Herbert mercilessly as she taught him to be "decent and respectable and God-fearing" (67). In fact, readers may even begin to suspect that Herbert's "saint" of a mother is the reason that his father abandoned the family to play jazz piano. While Herbert truly wants to do the right thing by his family and make his mother proud, he is still his father's son, a lover of music and an artist at heart. Yet, he rejects the shallow, crass materialism of the narrator, for whom Herbert's inheritance represents "winters in Florida, *filet mignon* and twelve-year-old bourbon, Jaguars, silk underwear and handmade shoes" (66). The narrator, who is devoted solely to the art of making money, believes that Herbert belongs in the "bughouse" (69). Herbert, though, unlike the narrator, is a real artist who hides his wealth in order to buy himself the freedom to play the music he loves. As an artist, he delicately balances his life between the duty to others inculcated by his mother and the joyous indulgence that is his father's legacy.

CHARACTERS

Foster, Herbert's Father Alma Foster informs the narrator that Herbert's father was a jazz pianist who abandoned his family when Herbert was a boy. As a result, Herbert's mother raised him to despise his father and everything he stood for.

Foster, Alma The wife of Herbert Foster, Alma Foster has no idea that her husband has a massive inheritance squirreled away or that he lives a secret life as a jazz pianist. Described as a "skinny, shrewish-looking woman" (60), Alma seems to be a fairly unpleasant person whom Herbert wishes to escape from when he can, while not abandoning her completely as his father had abandoned Herbert and Herbert's mother.

Foster, Herbert A hard-working man who prides himself on earning his own way and sacrificing for his family, Herbert Foster lives out the values instilled in him by his saintly mother who had been abandoned by her jazz-playing husband when Herbert was a child. Nonetheless, as the narrator of the story learns at the end, Herbert lives a secret life three nights a week when he escapes his shrewish wife and demanding toddler by playing jazz piano at a dark and noisy restaurant. Herbert must keep his large inheritance a secret from his family because the illusion of not earning enough money allows him to maintain his respectable reputation while giving him an excuse to slip out of the house on weekends for a second job.

Foster, Herbert, Jr. Herbert Foster, Jr. is the two-year-old son of Alma and Herbert Foster. Readers see him repeatedly banging on a piano the first time the narrator visits the Foster home, perhaps suggesting that the child will grow up with his father's and grandfather's love of music.

Foster, Mrs. Herbert Foster's mother, whose first name is never given, was abandoned by her husband, a jazz pianist, when Herbert was a young child. As a result, she raised Herbert to be "decent and respectable and God-fearing" (67) and to revile his jazz-playing, smoke-breathing, gin-drinking father. When the narrator remarks on how similar Mrs. Foster and Herbert's wife, Alma, look, readers suspect that Mrs. Foster must have been a rather grim woman, despite Alma's calling her a "saint" (67).

Foster, Herbert's Grandfather Herbert Foster's paternal grandfather supported Herbert and his mother after Herbert's father abandoned the family for a life of jazz music. Herbert adored his grandfather, who left Herbert the enormous legacy that Herbert keeps secret from his wife, Alma.

Harris, Firehouse Firehouse Harris is the name that Herbert Foster performs under when he plays jazz piano on weekends at a noisy, crowded restaurant.

Narrator The narrator of "The Foster Portfolio" is a salesman for an investment counseling firm. Although he claims to "have nothing against people in moderate circumstances" (60), and is not a wealthy man himself, the narrator nevertheless respects the power of money and clearly treats Herbert Foster differently after Foster reveals his vast securities holdings.

Unnamed Bartender and Crone When the narrator goes to the restaurant where Herbert Foster works on weekends, both an unnamed bartender and an old crone making hamburgers claim never to have heard of a man named Herbert Foster.

FURTHER READING
Reed, Peter. *The Short Fiction of Kurt Vonnegut.* Westport, Conn.: Greenwood Press, 1997.
Welcome to the Monkey House. New York: Dell, 1998.

Galápagos

Galápagos, published in 1985 by Delacorte/ SEY-
MOUR LAWRENCE, is a novel that imagines human
beings evolving all over again, in a very different
direction than current evolution has taken us. Set
quite deliberately in the GALÁPAGOS ISLANDS, so
important to CHARLES DARWIN's formulation of
the theory of natural selection, the novel questions
popular conceptions of Darwin's theories, especially concerning progress, species adaptation, and
survival of the fittest. Like most of Vonnegut's novels, *Galápagos* raises basic questions about human
beings and what happens to them. Are people basically good or bad? Do we have control over our
own destinies, or are our fates largely the result of
chance and accident? Why, with all their potential,
are human beings so often cruel and self-destructive? Is the human race as we know it doomed to
annihilation? And if so, is this a fate that is well
deserved?

SYNOPSIS

Book One, Chapters 1–16
Galápagos is narrated by Leon Trout, son of SCI-
ENCE FICTION writer Kilgore Trout. Leon is writing
the book far in the future—1 million years after the
events he describes have taken place. At this point
in the distant future, human beings have evolved
smaller brains, furry skins, and flipperlike hands,
as well as the ability to remain underwater for long
periods of time. They have become more like seals,
in fact, than like humans of the year 1986, when
most of the events in the novel occur. Leon has
witnessed these evolutionary changes over the past
millennia as a ghost. He actually died while working as a welder in a Swedish shipyard back in the
1980s. Rather than enter the afterlife, however,
Leon chooses to live as a ghost in order to study
human beings and their motivations.

In his account, Leon takes readers back to the
year 1986, when a much-publicized and celebrity-
studded trip to the Galápagos Islands off the coast
of Ecuador is being planned. Billed as "The Nature
Cruise of the Century," the trip is to be taken
aboard a luxury ship called the *Bahia de Darwin*,
the very ship that Leon Trout had been helping

build when he was decapitated by a falling sheet
of steel in a shipyard accident. The passenger list
for the cruise includes Jacquelyn Kennedy Onassis, Mick Jagger, Henry Kissinger, Walter Cronkite,
and numerous other rich and famous people. As
the departure date approaches, however, a nearly
global economic catastrophe, which strikes especially hard in Ecuador and other South American
countries, makes it highly unlikely that the much-
anticipated cruise will take place. The well-known
passengers all bow out, preferring to stay in the
United States, where the economy is still sound.
Yet, six passengers who have signed up for the
cruise still show up in Guayaquil, Ecuador, on the
eve of departure, having various reasons to hope
that the *Bahia de Darwin* will depart as planned.

These six passengers include James Wait, a con
man who signs up for the cruise to escape his 17th
wife, a rich widow he married for her money. Wait
preys on lonely and wealthy women whom he pretends to love, marrying them, cleaning out their
bank accounts, then departing. Also in Guayaquil
is Mary Hepburn, a former high school biology
teacher from ILIUM, New York. Mary's much-loved
husband, Roy, had signed the couple up for the
cruise shortly after discovering he had an inoperable
brain tumor. One of his dying wishes is that Mary
will take the cruise anyway, even though he's no
longer there to accompany her. Wealthy American
entrepreneur Andrew MacIntosh and his 19-year-
old blind daughter, Selena, are two more passengers
who arrive in Guayaquil. MacIntosh hopes to sign
a lucrative business deal aboard the ship with Zenji
Hiroguchi, a Japanese computer genius who has
invented a hand-held language translation device.
Zenji and his pregnant wife, Hisako, traveling as
guests of the MacIntoshes, round out the list of
remaining passengers.

Book One, Chapters 17–30
All of these guests are put up at the Hotel El
Dorado in Guayaquil the day before the *Bahia de
Darwin* is scheduled to depart. As the economic
situation in Ecuador worsens, and as mobs of starving people begin congregating in the street, the
hotel has been barricaded by barbed wire in an
attempt to keep the visitors safe. Zenji Hiroguchi

and Andrew MacIntosh, however, are both shot to death on the street outside the Hotel El Dorado by an insane ex-soldier who believes that Zenji's hand-held translation device, called Mandarax, is a radio that can scramble his brains. The soldier runs off after the shooting, but he leaves a shop door open behind him that allows six little native Indian girls, members of the nearly extinct Kanka-bono tribe, to make their way to the Hotel El Dorado, where James Wait, in a rare act of kindness, feeds the starving children peanuts, oranges, and cocktail onions from the bar. Mary Hepburn enters the bar at this point, sees James Wait acting kindly, and strikes up a conversation with him. Wait, viewing the widow as a potential target for his marriage scam, talks to Mary very nicely, feigning sympathy for her loss of her husband, Roy.

Book One, Chapters 31–38

All the while these events are taking place, the situation in the streets is worsening. Hotel manager Siegfried von Kleist decides to try to bus the remaining four guests out to the wharf where the *Bahia de Darwin* is docked. He drives James Wait, Mary Hepburn, Selena MacIntosh, and Hisako Hiroguchi, along with the six Kanka-bono girls through the streets of Guayaquil as rioters and starving mobs bang on the bus's sides and windows. During the trip, James Wait's heart begins to fibrillate. He has suffered a heart attack that will prove fatal in the next few days. It turns out that mobs are also at the wharf, stripping all the food and luxury trappings off the *Bahia de Darwin*. Ecuador's situation at this point is made even more dire because neighboring Peru declares war on the country and begins a bombing campaign. While the bus makes it to the wharf at last, and the four passengers and the Kanka-bono girls are able to scramble aboard the ship, Siegfried von Kleist is killed when a tidal wave, caused by an exploding bomb, washes the bus off the wharf and out to sea. The *Bahia de Darwin's* captain, Siegfried von Kleist's older brother, Adolf, is already on the ship, having gotten extremely drunk since he believed the cruise was to be cancelled. But he is able to launch the ship, and the passengers finally make it out to sea and away from the turmoil of Ecuador.

Book Two, Chapters 1–7

The next five days are spent aboard the *Bahia de Darwin*. Adolf von Kleist has gotten the ship hopelessly lost since he was drunk while he was navigating that first night. In addition, all the stores of food and bedding have been plundered by starving mobs, so the passengers are extremely hungry and uncomfortable. The Kanka-bono girls, in fact, steal Selena MacIntosh's seeing-eye dog and kill and eat her. In the midst of all this, James Wait dies of the heart attack he had experienced on the bus ride. Before he expires, though, he convinces Mary Hepburn to marry him; Captain von Kleist performs the ceremony. Mary never learns Wait's true nature or even his real name since he had been traveling under an alias. She lives out the rest of her long life firmly believing that Wait was a good and compassionate man.

Book Two, Chapters 8–14

The ship eventually runs aground on the Galápagos island of Santa Rosalia, where the castaways begin a new life for themselves. Selena MacIntosh and Hisako Hiroguchi pair off, together raising Hisako's daughter, Akiko, who is born on the island with a strange genetic abnormality—fur-covered skin. Mary Hepburn and Captain Adolf von Kleist live together as a couple, although their relationship is fraught with bickering and distrust. The Kanka-bono girls start their own community away from the other passengers. Though the little group initially expects to be rescued, it appears that the outside world has forgotten them. Narrator Leon Trout tells readers that all human beings in the outside world die before long, anyway. Millions starve during the economic collapse, but even worse, a new bacterium enters the human population, preventing reproduction.

The survivors of the *Bahia de Darwin* on the island of Santa Rosalia become the forebears of a whole new race of human beings when Mary Hepburn, trained as a biologist, begins experimenting with genetic engineering. She uses the Captain's sperm to impregnate each of the Kanka-bono girls. The first child born is nicknamed Kamikaze, and he will later mate with the furry Akiko Hiroguchi to produce seven children. As evolution proceeds over the next million years, all humans will inherit Akiko's warm, protective fur. They will lose the big brains that marked earlier humans, and as a result, live more peacefully, if with less conscious awareness and ambition than earlier humans had. Narrator Leon Trout judges this to be a change for the better.

COMMENTARY

Most popular conceptions of Darwin's theories, as critic Daniel Cordle points out, posit evolution as a progression from a more primitive to a more sophisticated state of being, as a bettering of species over time, with human beings at the pinnacle of this progression. Think, for example, of the frequently occurring picture in school textbooks of the evolution of man—a small primate depicted on the left-hand side of the illustration slowly grows erect and develops into modern man on the right-hand side. Further, popular views of Darwin also hold that species which advance and adapt deserve to do so, that such species are the "fittest" to survive. As *Galápagos* narrator Leon Trout writes, Darwin's book, *On the Origin of Species*, "did more to stabilize people's volatile opinions of how to identify success or failure than any other tome" (14). Even though Darwin does not discuss morality in relation to species adaptation, Trout suggests in this comment that Darwin's theories have been popularized in such a way that moral stigma is attached to species survival. Human beings, then, congratulate themselves for reaching the top of the evolutionary chain, for being a species that "made it," that succeeded more fully than any other species in history.

Leon Trout, and by extension Vonnegut himself, questions these assumptions about natural selection and the survival of the fittest. While chance certainly plays a part in Darwin's theories, the chance adaptations that get passed on are those that help a species survive. Yet, in *Galápagos*, rather than show a process of carefully controlled adaptation, in which change occurs slowly over time and only the fit survive, Vonnegut often depicts survival and eventual evolutionary change as occurring by complete accident rather than adaptation or natural selection. For instance, the fact that the Kanka-bono bloodline is carried to all future

human beings is the product of pure chance. While the Kanka-bono tribe is so nearly extinct that the Ecuadorian ambassador to the United Nations can write a poem titled "The Last Kanka-bono," Trout tells us that the seeming inevitability of the tribe's extinction is premature. Because deranged soldier Geraldo Delgado leaves a shop door open, the last remaining Kanka-bonos are saved. The ambassador instead should have wept for "The Last Mainland South American" (or North American or European or African or Asian), Trout tells readers. Survival in this case occurs simply by chance; although other races and peoples thrived over the globe and the Kanka-bonos were reduced to six remaining members, it is the Kanka-bono genes that survive and get passed on to future humans. Similarly, the novel depicts the effects of chance in the instance of several diseases carried through the genes, such as the von Kleist family's Huntington's chorea and Selena MacIntosh's retinitis pigmentosa. Each von Kleist brother has a fifty-fifty chance of developing Huntington's chorea; that Siegfried manifests the disease while Adolf never does seems the result of mere luck rather than natural selection. Accordingly, narrator Leon Trout often refers to the von Kleists not by name, but as either the "lucky" or the "unlucky" brother. James Wait's heart attack aboard the bus bound for the *Bahia de Darwin* is another example of a chance happening that drastically affects future evolution. Wait's heart attack necessitates a detour to a hospital, which, Trout tells readers, "surely saved the lives of all on board" (217) and made possible the later evolution of the human species.

In addition, Vonnegut questions the popular view of Darwin's theories as presenting a gradual progression in human development over time. Leon Trout sees human beings' big brains as merely an evolutionary change without being an improvement. Our big brains, in fact, cause quite a bit of mischief. The economic crisis that brings about widespread famine in the year 1986, for instance, is depicted as "purely a product of oversize brains" (24). Trout writes that "there was still plenty of food and fuel and so on for all the human beings on the planet, as numerous as they had become, but millions upon millions of them were starting to starve to death now" (24). The reason for this, Trout explains, is "all in people's heads"—a crisis in paper wealth, something arbitrarily assigned value by human beings, is causing as much disruption as if the planet had "been knocked out of orbit by a meteor the size of Luxembourg" (24). The novel depicts other social ills caused by humans' big brains as well, many of which should be familiar objects of SATIRE to readers of Vonnegut's other novels. Machines are putting human beings out of work, as when Roy Hepburn gets furloughed so that the GEFFCo plant can modernize and automate operations. Even literature and poetry become the province of machines as Zenji Hiroguchi's hand-held Mandarax device spits out verse on cue, having the ability to quote, but not to interpret the quotes it emits. In addition, human big brains are depicted as being quite often self-destructive. When readers first meet Mary Hepburn, her brain is telling her to put a plastic garment bag over her face and deprive her cells of oxygen, despite the fact that, as a high school biology teacher, she had taught her students "that the human brain was the most admirable survival device yet produced by evolution" (26). And Trout states that his own big brain instructed him to "join the United States Marines and go fight in Vietnam" (29), advice that "can be charitably described as questionable" (29).

Despite all the invective that Trout spouts about human beings' big brains, *Galápagos*, like most Vonnegut novels, also expresses a certain amount of affection for contemporary humans, despite all the flaws. Readers might ask how they are expected to react to Leon Trout's insistence that the de-evolution of human beings to small-brained seal-like creatures is a good thing, an improvement in human character. Does Trout really mean what he says? Are readers supposed to take his words at face value? The answer is complex: Vonnegut, always the pessimist, certainly shows the damage human beings have done to their planet and one another. At the same time, the novel offers moments that suggest the loss of big brains over the million years that Trout observes humanity might be a tragedy rather than the triumph Trout claims it is. One of the novel's most touching moments occurs when

Roy Hepburn is on his deathbed. A few seconds after Roy seems to have expired, his lips move again, and he whispers his final words to Mary:

> "I'll tell you what the human soul is, Mary," he whispered, his eyes closed. "Animals don't have one. It's the part of you that knows when your brain isn't working right. I always knew, Mary. There wasn't anything I could do about it, but I always knew." (45)

Roy asserts here that human beings' self-consciousness is what sets them apart from the animals, what gives them a soul. Thus, the very act of being able to criticize ourselves for own flaws might be what makes us human. Later in the novel, Trout points out that the new humans have lost self-awareness. "Do people still know that they are going to die sooner or later?" he asks. "No," writes Trout, answering his own question, "Fortunately, in my humble opinion, they have forgotten that" (320). While the new humans might be happier, are they really even humans? Or, along with the loss of self-consciousness, have they lost their souls, their human uniqueness, and become a new kind of animal?

In addition, part of the irony of what happens on the island of Santa Rosalia is that Mary Hepburn's big brain, her tinkering with artificial reproduction, allows the human race to survive. Trout writes, "In the face of utter hopelessness on Santa Rosalia, she still wanted human babies to be born there. Nothing could keep her from doing all she could to keep life going on and on and on" (100). So, despite the enormous destructive capabilities of human beings, there is still a human impulse toward creation, to doing everything possible to continue life. Without the aid of Mary's big brain, the same brain that had earlier given her instructions to kill herself, the human race would not have survived. And there are moments in the novel when Trout lovingly points out instances of human kindness that seem to move him profoundly. When Selena MacIntosh and Hisako Hiroguchi pair off to raise Hisako's daughter, Akiko, Trout's professed cynicism vanishes, at least temporarily: "How tenderly Hisako and Selena would care for each other during the coming years!" "What a beautiful and sweet-natured child they would rear! How I admired them!" (194). And later, as subsequent generations that follow the original colonists begin to develop a common language and religion, common jokes and songs and dances, Trout writes, "It went very fast—that formation from such random genetic materials of a perfectly cohesive human family. That was nice to see. It almost made me love people just as they were back then, big brains and all" (299). Nevertheless, Vonnegut being Vonnegut, Selena and Hisako will eventually kill themselves in a suicide pact, and the cohesive human family will lose language and religion and art as they devolve over time. Yet, these fleeting moments are beautiful despite their transitory nature.

The complexities of Leon Trout's perceptions of the human race arise at least partly from his own upbringing, the guilt he feels about helping his father, science fiction writer Kilgore Trout, drive away Leon's mother, who walked out on the family when Leon was 11 years old, unable to stand Kilgore's cynical nature any longer. While Leon's mother loved to dance, wanted to have friends and go out upon occasion, all Kilgore Trout did was sit at home and wallow in his pessimism, "doing nothing . . . but writing and smoking all the time—and I mean all the time" (280). When Kilgore Trout appears to his son aboard the *Bahia de Darwin*, he urges Leon to step into the blue tunnel leading to the afterlife, arguing that the more Leon learns about people, "the more disgusted" he will become (277). Leon, though, while often donning the same cynical guise as his father, is torn. When he ran away from home at age 16 to find his mother, he was also seeking to find the goodness in humanity that she had continued to believe in. Kilgore Trout reminds his son that his mother's favorite quote was from ANNE FRANK, who wrote in her diary, "In spite of everything, I still believe people are really good at heart." This quote becomes painfully, tragically ironic for readers who, of course, know that Anne Frank was doomed to die in the Nazi death camps. But at the same time, Anne Frank's simple statement can also be read as a courageously optimistic refusal to be brought low by human brutality. It is telling that Kilgore insists Leon is just like his mother and that Leon, despite all his professed

pessimism, chooses his mother's favorite quote as the epigraph to the book he is writing.

Most critics who discuss *Galápagos* wrestle with this question of Leon Trout's pessimism, some arguing that we are to accept his view that humans are better off without big brains at face value, others that these assertions are actually undermined in the novel. One critical view that merits special mention, though, is an argument put forth by Oliver Ferguson. Ferguson, comparing Leon Trout to Billy Pilgrim in *Slaughterhouse-Five*, argues that readers are not even supposed to take at face value Leon's assertions that he is a ghostwriting the book 1 million years after the voyage of the *Bahia de Darwin*. When the Swedish doctor at the end of the novel praises Kilgore Trout, Leon experiences an intense emotional release, and, in his own words, "actually went crazy for a little while" (256). Ferguson argues that Leon does not just go crazy for a little while, but that, in his frenzied state, he retreats into his imagination and invents the story of de-evolution he tells in *Galápagos*. Just as Billy Pilgrim creates Tralfamadore as a coping device to both overcome his fear of death and justify his own passivity in the face of brutality, Leon's tale provides an imagined solution to all the problems he sees inherent in 20th-century society: "domestic discord, economic free-booting, environmental despolation, and war." Thus, according to Ferguson, the "true" parts of the book include Leon's family upbringing, as well as his experiences in Vietnam and Sweden. The other events are a "lunatic construct," Leon's working out of the guilt and conflicted emotions he feels about his parents and his killing of an old woman in Vietnam. To resolve his guilt, he invents a world in which human brains are not big enough either to cause destruction or to feel guilty about the destruction they wreak.

Through an intriguing interpretation of the novel that does a nice job of making connections with Vonnegut's other work, in the end *Galápagos* does not offer much evidence for such a reading of Leon Trout. In *Slaughterhouse-Five*, Vonnegut lets readers know that Billy's Tralfamadorian scenario is lifted from a Kilgore Trout book belonging to Eliot Rosewater which he had read in the mental hospital. Readers also discover that he learns about Montana Wildhack in a pornographic bookstore in New York. In addition, Billy has a head injury, possibly resulting in brain damage, which he received in the plane crash on Sugarbush Mountain. The case for viewing Tralfamadore as Billy's fantasy invention is simply much stronger than the evidence for reading Leon Trout's tale in such a way. Nevertheless, the two books do have in common a desire on the part of their protagonists to go back to the beginning of human history and start all over again. Both novels imagine a new sort of Eden, with new Adams and Eves who repopulate the world. In fact, Leon Trout tells readers early on in *Galápagos*, "If there really was a Noah's ark, and there may have been—I might entitle my story 'A Second Noah's Ark'" (5). In a similar vein, Trout refers to Captain Adolf von Kleist, whose genetic material infuses all human beings born on Santa Rosalia in the future as Adam, and the six Kanka-bono girls who will bear his children as Eves. In both *Slaughterhouse-Five* and *Galápagos*, though, it is extremely questionable how much of a paradise these new Edens really are, despite the protagonists' longings for such worlds.

In *Galápagos*, as in most Vonnegut novels, it is through the artistic process that human beings are most self-conscious, and thus, as Roy Hepburn points out on his deathbed, most in possession of their own souls. Leon Trout, in his ghostly form, becomes a figure for the writer who studies human beings and attempts to learn the truth about human motivations, no matter how difficult this task may finally be. When Kilgore Trout urges Leon to step into the blue tunnel, Leon hesitates, protesting that he has not yet completed his research: "I had chosen to be a ghost," he explains, "because the job carried with it, as a fringe benefit, license to read minds, to learn the truth of people's pasts, to see through walls, to be many places all at once, to learn in depth how this or that situation had come to be structured as it was, and to have access to all human knowledge" (276). A writer who invents human characters and situations has similar powers to the ones Leon Trout describes. A fiction writer through his or her imagination can read minds and gain access to all human knowledge.

Despite their differences, both Leon and his father (as well as Vonnegut himself) are writers and thus students of human nature. And Kilgore Trout, in the title of one of his own novels, provides the description of contemporary human beings that perhaps best sums up Vonnegut's own position: *The Era of Hopeful Monsters*. Even with all the terrible destruction human beings have brought about, they are still capable of great beauty; the repeated references to Beethoven's Ninth Symphony attest to this. As Leon points out at the end of the novel, the hammerhead shark that eats Captain von Kleist is perfectly designed according to the Law of Natural Selection:

> It was a flawless part in the clockwork of the universe. There was no defect in it which might yet be modified. One thing it surely did not need was a bigger brain.
>
> What was it going to do with a bigger brain? Compose Beethoven's Ninth Symphony?
>
> Or perhaps write these lines:
>
> All the world's a stage,
> And all the men and women merely players.
> They have their exits and their entrances;
> And one man in his time plays many parts . . . ?
>
> —William Shakespeare (1564–1616)

Clearly, despite his professed disdain for big brains, Leon Trout admires the artistic genius of human beings and the beauty they are capable of producing.

Even in the face of the guilt and trauma Leon experienced as a soldier in the Vietnam War, he still finds compassion. The novel ends with Leon telling readers of his visit to a Swedish doctor working in Thailand after he had contracted syphilis from a Saigon prostitute during the war. When the doctor asks if Leon is related to "the wonderful science-fiction writer Kilgore Trout" (323), Leon is moved to tears for the first time in his life. The doctor is the first person he meets outside of his hometown who has ever heard of Kilgore Trout, much less who appreciates his writing. Sensitive to Leon's suffering, the doctor prescribes what he calls a very "strong medicine" (324) for Leon—political asylum in Sweden. When Leon protests that he cannot speak Swedish, the doctor replies, "You'll learn . . . You'll learn, you'll learn" (324), words that end the novel. These final words suggest that big brains can, in fact, serve humans well, if only they will learn to behave compassionately to one another; these same big brains supply humans with such a capacity in the first place.

CHARACTERS AND RELATED ENTRIES

Bahia de Darwin The *Bahia de Darwin* is an Ecuadorian luxury passenger ship built to take tourists on nature cruises to the Galápagos Islands. This is also the ship that the novel's narrator, Leon Trout, had been helping to build in a Swedish shipyard when he was accidentally decapitated and turned into a ghost. The *Bahia de Darwin*, stripped of its luxury trappings by starving mobs, eventually takes a small group of tourists and native Indian girls to the island of Santa Rosalia, where they become the ancestors to an entirely new form of human beings.

Boström, Hjalmar Arvid When Leon Trout is working as a ship welder in Sweden, he attends the funeral of the shipyard's foreman with a fellow welder named Hjalmar Arvid Boström. As the two men are leaving the church, Boström says, "Oh, well—he wasn't going to write Beethoven's Ninth Symphony anyway" (266), a comment that Trout will repeat several times after a death occurs in the book.

Boström's Grandfather Swedish welder Hjalmar Arvid Boström tells Leon Trout that he first heard the phrase about a dead person who wasn't going to write Beethoven's Ninth Symphony anyway from his German grandfather, who had been an officer in charge of burying the dead during World War I. Trout explains that this is one of the cynical things a soldier might say to a thoughtful new recruit who is bothered by witnessing death.

Braxton, Carter When he is a little boy, Leon Trout's mother tells him that he is related, through her side of the family to Carter Braxton, one of the signers of the Declaration of Independence.

Carson, Johnny Well-known talk show host Johnny Carson appears in the book briefly when Captain Adolf von Kleist appears on *The Tonight Show* to talk about "The Nature Cruise of the Century."

Claggett, Noble Noble Claggett is one of Mary Hepburn's high school biology students, who is eventually killed in the Vietnam War. He writes a poem about the courtship dance of the blue-footed booby bird that goes like this:

> Of course I love you,
> So let's have a kid
> Who will say exactly
> What its parents did;
> "Of course I love you,"
> So let's have a kid
> Who will say exactly
> What its parents did;

Mary will remember this poem for the rest of her life.

Cortez, Ricardo Ricardo Cortez is the Peruvian pilot who drops a second bomb in Ecuador, onto the Colombian freighter the *San Mateo*, mistakenly believing it to be the *Bahia de Darwin*. He had previously had a conversation with a fellow airman, Guillermo Reyes, about whether anything felt better than sexual intercourse. Reyes, the pilot to drop the first Peruvian bomb on Ecuador, reported back to Cortez at the time that dropping the bomb was more fun than sex.

Cruz, Hernando Hernando Cruz is the first mate of the *Bahia de Darwin*. While the captain is mostly a charming figurehead, Cruz is the one who actually knows how to run the ship. As the economic collapse in Ecuador escalates, however, Cruz decides to walk away from the ship and return home to his pregnant wife and 11 children who need him.

de la Madrid, Dr. José Sepulveda Dr. José Sepulveda de la Madrid is the president of Ecuador. He writes a letter to all the passengers signed up for "The Nature Cruise of the Century," inviting them to a state breakfast at the Hotel El Dorado. Mary Hepburn never receives the letter, though, since her and Roy's names were left off the passenger list by Bobby King, "so as not to raise the embarrassing question of who they were" (117).

Delgado, Geraldo Private Geraldo Delgado is an 18-year-old Ecuadorian army deserter and paranoid schizophrenic who believes that he is the greatest dancer in the world and the son of Frank Sinatra. The starving Delgado happens to break into the back of a defunct souvenir shop across the street from the Hotel El Dorado at exactly the same moment that Zenji Hiroguchi and Andrew MacIntosh are walking in front of it. Believing that Zenji's Mandarax interpreting machine is a radio that will scramble his brains, Delgado shoots both Hiroguchi and MacIntosh in the head, then runs off. Because he leaves the back door to the souvenir shop open, the six starving Kanka-bono girls are able to make their way to the hotel and later onto the *Bahia de Darwin*. Delgado will rape a woman the next day and become father to one of the last 10 million or so children to be born on the South American mainland.

Donald Donald is Roy and Mary Hepburn's four-year-old golden retriever. When Roy's brain tumor begins to affect his mind, he believes that he was a U.S. sailor during ATOMIC BOMB testing on the Bikini Atoll and that he was forced to tie Donald, along with numerous other animals, to stakes in the ground to endure the explosions. Later, after Roy's death, when a man Mary works with named Robert Wojciehowitz attempts to court her, Donald, barking in an attempt to be friendly, scares Wojciehowitz so much that the man climbs a tree and refuses to come down for an hour.

Donoso, Dr. Teodoro Dr. Teodoro Donoso is a poet and physician from Quito, as well as Ecuador's ambassador to the United Nations. He becomes good friends with promoter Bobby King while the two work together to plan "The Nature Cruise of the Century." Ambassador Donoso tells King at one point that he does not believe there are any real Kanka-bonos left in existence; one of his poems, in fact, is called "The Last Kanka-bono," and is about the tribe's extinction. What Dr. Donoso does not

know is that, soon enough, every human being in the world will be predominantly Kanka-bono in genetic makeup.

El Dorado Hotel The El Dorado Hotel is the place in Guayaquil, Ecuador, where the passengers who signed up for "The Nature Cruise of the Century" aboard the *Bahia de Darwin* gather to wait for the ship's departure.

Fitzgerald, Father Bernard Father Bernard Fitzgerald is an 80-year-old Roman Catholic priest from Ireland who has lived with the Kanka-bono tribe in Ecuador for 50 years. When the Kanka-bono village is sprayed with insecticide, killing all the residents, six young girls are saved because they are at choir practice with Father Fitzgerald. The priest tramples an SOS message into the mud of a riverbank, which catches the attention of bush pilot Eduardo Ximinez, who flies in and rescues the girls.

Flemming, Willard Willard Flemming is the alias used by James Wait in Ecuador. Mary Hepburn, whom Wait marries on the ship, the *Bahia de Darwin*, never learns his real name. She calls him "Mr. Flemming" throughout their acquaintance and continues to think of him this way long after his death.

GEFFCo Mary Hepburn's husband, Roy, is furloughed from his job as a millwright at the enormous GEFFCo plant in Ilium, New York, so that the company can modernize and automate operations. The enormous corporation also makes a brief appearance in the novel *Bluebeard,* when Rabo Karabekian's famous painting "Windsor Blue Number Seventeen" is hung in the lobby of the GEFFCo headquarters on Park Avenue in New York.

Gokubi Gokubi is the name given by computer genius Zenji Hiroguchi to the first generation of hand-held language translation computers he invents.

Hepburn, Mary The book's protagonist, Mary Hepburn, is a high school biology teacher from

Ilium, New York. Her husband, Roy, signs the couple up for "The Nature Cruise of the Century," but dies of cancer before the ship is scheduled to leave. Mary goes to Ecuador alone, determined to carry out Roy's final wish that she take the cruise without him. At the Hotel El Dorado in Guayaquil, Mary witnesses James Wait (who is calling himself "Willard Flemming") being kind to a group of starving Indian girls. Later, after Wait has a heart attack, Mary succumbs to his repeated entreaties and marries him aboard the ship, the *Bahia de Darwin*. Wait dies a few minutes after the ceremony; thus, Mary never discovers that he was a conniving con man. When the ship runs aground on the island of Santa Rosalia, Mary lives with Captain Adolf von Kleist for many years. She turns out to be responsible for the continuation of the human race when she uses von Kleist's sperm to impregnate each of the Kanka-bono girls. Mary lives to the ripe old age of 80, when she is eaten by a great white shark.

Hepburn, Roy   The husband of novel's protagonist, Mary Hepburn, Roy Hepburn works as a millwright for a large company called GEFFCo in Ilium, New York. A sober, steady man who has never missed a day of work in his 29 years at the company, Roy develops a malignant brain tumor and signs both himself and Mary up for "The Nature Cruise of the Century" to the Galápagos Islands. Later, he loses his job when GEFFCo furloughs all its workers to modernize the Ilium plant. Roy dies of the brain tumor three months before the cruise begins, but he makes Mary promise him two things before he expires: that she will continue the cruise without him, and that she will remarry as soon as she can. Mary fulfills both promises by traveling to Guayaquil and marrying the con man James Wait aboard the *Bahia de Darwin*.

Hiroguchi, Akiko   The daughter of Hisako and Zenji Hiroguchi, Akiko is born on the island of Santa Rosalia after her father's death. Akiko has an unusual genetic trait: Her skin is covered by a coat of soft, downy fur, which protects her from sunburn and cold water when she swims. This is a trait she will pass on to her own seven children and eventually, through natural selection, to all future

humans. Akiko's children are fathered by Kamikaze, the first son born to a Kanko-bono woman whom Mary Hepburn impregnated with the sperm of Captain Adolf von Kleist. Akiko is a gentle, nurturing woman who takes care of the captain when he develops Alzheimer's disease and who remains good friends with Mary Hepburn until the old lady's death at the age of 80.

Hiroguchi, Hisako   The wife of Japanese computer genius Zenji Hiroguchi, the pregnant Hisako Hiroguchi escapes, along with a few others, from the economically devastated and war-torn Ecuador aboard the *Bahia de Darwin*. Her husband, Zenji, however, never makes it onto the ship, having been shot dead the day before. When the ship runs aground on the island of Santa Rosalia, Hisako pairs off with the blind Selena MacIntosh. Together, the two women raise Hisako's infant daughter, Akiko, who is born with a downy covering of fur all over her body. After Akiko grows up and leaves home, Hisako, who has suffered from depression her whole life, and her partner Selena drown themselves in the ocean.

Hiroguchi, Zenji   A Japanese computer genius who invents hand-held language translation devices, Zenji Hiroguchi signs up for "The Nature Cruise of the Century" as the guest of wealthy American entrepreneur Andrew MacIntosh, who wants to become business partners with him. Zenji never actually makes it onto the *Bahia de Darwin*, however. He is shot in the head by an Ecuadorian thief after he runs out into the street to try to escape the overbearing presence of MacIntosh the day before the ship is to depart.

Hoover, Bunny   Though never explicitly named in the novel, Bunny Hoover is the son that is the product of Celia Hoover's seduction of 16-year-old James Wait. In previous Vonnegut novels, readers believed that Bunny was actually Dwayne Hoover's son. But Bunny's musical talent and good looks come from Wait, his actual father.

Hoover, Celia   Celia Hoover, wife of Pontiac dealer Dwayne Hoover, and a character appearing in previous Vonnegut novels, has sex with James Wait when he is 16 years old. Wait had been hired to mow the Hoover's lawn when the drug-addled and reclusive Celia seduces the teenager. Wait ends up fathering a son with Celia, though Dwayne always believes that the boy is his.

Hoover, Dwayne The main character in Vonnegut's earlier novel *Breakfast of Champions* and also appearing in *Dead-Eye Dick*, car dealer Dwayne Hoover turns up in *Galápagos* when he hires the teen-age James Wait to mow his lawn several times in Midland City, Ohio.

Kanka-bono girls When Geraldo Delgado leaves open the back door to a decrepit souvenir shop across the street from the Hotel El Dorado, six starving little girls from the Kanka-bono tribe enter and eventually make their way to the hotel, where James Wait feeds them peanuts, oranges, and maraschino cherries from the bar. The girls are orphans from the Ecuadorian rain forest to the east. Their parents and other relatives were all killed by insecticides sprayed from the air. The girls survived because they were at choir practice with a Roman Catholic priest. They were later flown to Guayaquil by bush pilot Eduardo Ximénez, who deposits them at an orphanage. They stay there until they are taken away by a dirty old man named Domingo Quezeda, the only Kanka-bono speaker in Guayaquil, who teaches them thievery and prostitution. The girls finally run away from Quezeda and end up at the Hotel El Dorado and eventually on the *Bahia de Darwin*. On the island of Santa Rosalia, the girls form their own community; they are eventually impregnated by Mary Hepburn, using the sperm of Captain Adolf von Kleist. In this way, the six girls, Sinka, Lor, Lira, Dirno, Nanno, and Keel, become the mothers of the entire human race.

Kanka-bonos The Kanka-bonos are a nearly extinct tribe of native Indians living in Ecuador. The last remaining members of the tribe are six young girls who end up departing the war-ravaged and starving country on the ship *Bahia de Darwin*, with a few foreign tourists. Many years after the ship is stranded on the island of Santa Rosalia,

former high school biology teacher Mary Hepburn uses sperm obtained from the ship's captain to impregnate the Kanka-bono girls. Their progeny will eventually repopulate the Earth with a new species of furry, seal-like human beings.

Kaplan, Mrs. Mrs. Kaplan is the name stitched over the pocket of the war-surplus combat fatigues worn by Mary Hepburn. James Wait calls Mary "Mrs. Kaplan" and extols the virtues of the Jewish people the entire time they are acquainted, even though she had told him her true name when they first met.

Kazakh Kazakh is Selena MacIntosh's seeing-eye dog. She will meet her end aboard the *Bahia de Darwin* when the six starving Kanka-bono girls steal her and eat her while Selena is sleeping.

Kenzaburos, The Zenji and Hisako Hiroguchi travel under the name Kenzaburo so that Zenji's company will not recognize his name on the passenger list of the *Bahia de Darwin* and discover that he is negotiating a business deal with Andrew MacIntosh.

King, Bobby Bobby King is a middle-aged American advertising man who runs the publicity campaign for "The Nature Cruise of the Century." He is successful in signing up a long list of celebrities, including Jackie Kennedy Onassis, Mick Jagger, and Walter Cronkite. The economic collapse in Ecuador prevents any of these celebrities from actually taking the much-touted trip.

MacIntosh, Andrew Described by the narrator as "an American financier and adventurer of great inherited wealth" (19), Andrew MacIntosh, a widower, signs up for "The Nature Cruise of the Century," along with his 19-year-old blind daughter Selena, so that he can make what he hopes will be a lucrative business deal with his guest, Zenji Hiroguchi. The hearty and callous MacIntosh, "who had come into this world incapable of caring much about anything" (107), nevertheless pretends to be an ardent conservationist. Both MacIntosh and Hiroguchi end up being shot dead by an Ecuadorian thief before either man steps foot on the *Bahia de Darwin*.

MacIntosh, Mrs. Andrew MacIntosh's wife, whose name is never given, dies giving birth to her daughter, Selena.

MacIntosh, Selena The 19-year-old blind daughter of Andrew MacIntosh, Selena MacIntosh is one of the passengers on the completely stripped down *Bahia de Darwin* the night it leaves war-torn Ecuador. Although her seeing-eye dog Kazakh is killed for food on board the ship, Selena makes it safely to the island of Santa Rosalia, where she pairs off with Hisako Hiroguchi and helps raise Hisako's furry daughter, Akiko. Selena ends up dying in a suicide pact with Hisako when she is 48 years old.

Mandarax Mandarax is the name inventor Zenji Hiroguchi gives to his second generation of hand-held language translation devices. The small computer is capable of producing famous quotes on command, but incapable of interpreting what these quotes mean. Nevertheless, former high school biology teacher Mary Hepburn becomes so attached to the device that when Captain Adolf von Kleist throws the Mandarax into the water off the island of Santa Rosalia she dives in after it, even though she is 80 years old. A great white shark immediately swallows both Mary and the Mandarax.

Matsumoto Company Matsumoto is the name of the Japanese company that is hired to automate the GEFFCo plant in Ilium, New York where Roy Hepburn worked. Zenji Hiroguchi, the young computer genius who invents the hand-held language translation device called Mandarax, also works for the Matsumoto Company.

Nureyev, Rudolf Famed ballet dancer Rudolf Nureyev is having supper at Elaine's restaurant in New York with Jacqueline Kennedy Onassis and the MacIntoshes when publicity man Bobby King spots them. King will later persuade Nureyev and Mrs. Onassis to sign up for "The Nature Cruise of the Century."

Onassis, Jacqueline Kennedy Cruise promoter Bobby King meets Jacqueline Kennedy Onassis, former wife of President JOHN F. KENNEDY, Jr., at a restaurant one evening, where she is having a late supper with Andrew and Selena MacIntosh and the ballet dancer Rudolf Nureyev. King suggests that she watch an educational film called *Sky-Pointing* about the mating dance of the blue-footed booby bird. Mrs. Onassis is so moved by the film that she reserves staterooms on the ship *Bahia de Darwin* for "The Nature Cruise of the Century."

Orlon Orlon is one of the sons of Akiko Hiroguchi and Kamikaze von Kleist. Like all of Akiko's children, he is born on the island of Santa Rosalia. He enters the novel briefly as a four-year-old who has just broken his arm, an event that calls Akiko away from the reunion of Captain Adolf von Kleist and Mary Hepburn, who had not seen each other for 10 years. Because Akiko is not there to watch the captain, he grabs the Mandarax translation device out of Mary's hands and throws it into the sea. When Mary goes in after it, a great white shark eats her. The captain, confused by the blood in the water, jumps in as well and is eaten by a hammerhead shark.

Ortiz, Jesus Jesus Ortiz, "a twenty-year-old descendant of proud Inca noblemen" (7) is the bartender at the Hotel El Dorado in Guayaquil, Ecuador. Described by the narrator as "one of the nicest people in this story" (7), Ortiz originally assumes that the rich hotel patrons he serves deserve the good things they experience in life. He is devastated, therefore, when millionaire entrepreneur Andrew MacIntosh forces him to serve two filet mignons to his daughter's seeing-eye dog. The entire country of Ecuador is starving at this point, and Ortiz is horrified to see MacIntosh's callous disregard of this fact. As a result, Ortiz turns into a "ravening terrorist" (93) by disconnecting all the telephone lines at the hotel, thus cutting off communication with the outside world.

Pépin, Robert Robert Pépin is the chef hired to run the galley aboard the *Bahia de Darwin*. Bobby King makes Pépin into a celebrity by calling him "the greatest chef in France" (119) in all the publicity releases about the cruise.

Prince Richard of Croatia-Slavonia Described as a "bloated plutocrat" (176) descended from European royalty, Prince Richard runs an antique store on upper Madison Avenue. One day in a bar he picks up homosexual prostitute James Wait. Though not homosexual himself, Prince Richard pays Wait to perform a strange sexual act upon him; he requests that Wait strangle him to the point that he loses consciousness, count slowly to 20, and then release his neck. Wait, on an impulse, murders the prince when he decides to count to 300 rather than 20.

Princess Charlotte After James Wait murders Prince Richard of Croatia-Slavonia, his widow becomes a successful designer of neckties, referring to herself as "Princess Charlotte" even though she's really from Staten Island.

Quezeda, Domingo When the orphanage that takes in the six Kanka-bono refugees puts out a call for an interpreter, they discover that the only person in Guayaquil who speaks Kanka-bono is "an old drunk and petty thief" (169) named Domingo Quezeda. The son of a philosophy professor at the Central University in Quito, Quezeda turns out to be the grandfather of one of the girls, having lived with the Kanka-bono tribe for three years as a young man. Quezedo, however, is a dirty old man who teaches the girls thievery and who sexually molests them in preparation for turning them into prostitutes. The young girls eventually escape from Quezeda and make their way to the Hotel El Dorado, onto the *Bahia de Darwin*, and finally to the island of Santa Rosalia.

Reyes, Guillermo Guillermo Reyes is a young Peruvian pilot who drops a bomb into a radar dish on top of the control tower at the Guayaquil International Airport. Later, he reports back to a fellow airman that dropping the bomb had been "more fun than sexual intercourse" (205).

Rosenquist, Per Olaf Per Olaf Rosenquist is described by Leon Trout as "an obtuse and unpopular shipyard foreman" (266) whom he met while working in Sweden as a ship welder. Rosenquist dies young, of heart problems, and Trout first hears the phrase, "Oh well—he wasn't going to write Beethoven's Ninth Symphony anyway" (266) at Rosenquist's funeral.

Santa Rosalia Santa Rosalia is the name of the northernmost Galápagos Island where a small group of tourists and native Indian girls become stranded and eventually repopulate the world.

Tharp, Naomi Naomi Tharp is the neighbor woman who helps raise Leon Trout after his biological mother walks out on the family. When Leon's father, Kilgore Trout, appears to him aboard the *Bahia de Darwin*, Naomi Tharp is standing in the blue tunnel leading to the afterlife as well. She encourages Leon to step into the tunnel, almost persuading him to do so, but Leon is called back to Earth by Mary Hepburn's cries of "Land ho!"

Tibbets, Paul W. Paul W. Tibbets is the pilot who dropped an atomic bomb on Hiroshima, Japan during World War II, exposing Hisako Hiroguchi's mother to radiation, and thus possibly contributing to Hisako's daughter, Akiko, being born furry and to the eventual furriness of the entire human race.

Trout, Mrs. The wife of Kilgore Trout walks out on her husband and son when Leon is 10 years old. Mrs. Trout, who loved dancing and wanted the couple to have a normal life, including making friends and taking trips, apparently became fed up with Kilgore Trout's hatred of the human race. Though he at first sides with his father, jeering at his mother alongside Kilgore Trout, by the age of 16 Leon has become so disgusted with his father that he runs away from home to look for his mother.

Trout, Kilgore A prolific science fiction writer who appears in many Vonnegut novels, most notably *God Bless You, Mr. Rosewater*, *Slaughterhouse-five*, *Breakfast of Champions*, and *Timequake*, Kilgore Trout's main role in *Galápagos* is as the father of the novel's narrator, Leon Trout. Leon's mother walked out on the family when Leon was

10, unable to stand any longer the cynicism and reclusiveness of her husband. Though a bad father in life, the dead Kilgore Trout nevertheless appears to his son, Leon, aboard the ship *Bahia de Darwin*, standing at the end of the blue tunnel leading into the afterlife and urging his son to step into it. Trout tells Leon that, if he doesn't enter the tunnel now, he won't see his father again for a million years. The two are interrupted by Mary Hepburn shouting, and Leon's curiosity overwhelms him so that he steps out of the tunnel and toward Mary, causing Kilgore Trout and the tunnel to vanish. Thus, Leon remains a ghost observing the human race for the next million years.

Trout, Leon The novel's narrator, Leon Trout is the son of science fiction writer Kilgore Trout, who appears in numerous Vonnegut novels. Leon is telling the story of the doomed *Bahia de Darwin* 1 million years in the future, after humans have evolved into seal-like creatures without the large brains that once burdened them. Readers discover that Leon's mother had left Kilgore Trout when Leon was 10 years old. Subsequently, Leon runs away from home as a teenager, joins the United States Marine Corps, and fights in the Vietnam War. After shooting an old Vietnamese grandmother in the war, he deserts the Marines and is given political asylum in Sweden, where he works as a welder in a shipyard in Malmo, helping to build the *Bahia de Darwin*. Trout is accidentally decapitated by a falling sheet of steel while working in the shipyard. Unlike most dead people, however, he refuses to "set foot in the blue tunnel leading into the Afterlife" (239), preferring to live as a ghost researching the lives of human beings.

Trout's Best Friend Leon Trout's best friend in Vietnam is killed by an old Vietnamese woman with a hand grenade. Readers never learn the name of this friend, although Trout kills the old woman in revenge.

Trout's Worst Enemy The grenade, thrown by an old Vietnamese grandmother, that kills Leon Trout's best friend in his platoon in Vietnam kills Trout's worst enemy in the platoon at the same time.

Unnamed Argentinian Millionaires Bush pilot Eduardo Ximinez drops off the Kanka-bono girls in Guayaquil because he is headed there to pick up two Argentinian millionaire sportsmen and take them to the Galápagos island of Baltra for deep sea fishing.

Unnamed French Anthropologist Bush pilot Eduardo Ximénez had just dropped off a French anthropologist on the Ecuador-Peru border when he sees from the air an SOS sign trampled in the mud of a riverbank by the Roman Catholic priest who was holding choir practice with six little Kanka-bono girls when their village was sprayed by insecticide.

Unnamed High School Girl When explaining whether or not he reproduced back when he was alive, Leon Trout tells readers that he impregnated a high school girl in Santa Fe, New Mexico, when he was a teenager. The girl had an abortion, though.

Unnamed High School Girl's Father The father of the Santa Fe girl impregnated by Leon Trout was the principal of their high school. He is the one who pays for his daughter's abortion.

Unnamed Manhattan Pimp When James Wait moves to Manhattan as a teenager, a pimp there befriends him and teaches him how to be successful as a homosexual prostitute.

Unnamed Rape Victim After he shoots Andrew MacIntosh and Zenji Hiroguchi in the head, Geraldo Delgado rapes a woman who later gives birth to one of the last 10 million or so children to be born in South America.

Unnamed Saigon Prostitute After Leon Trout shoots an old woman in Vietnam, he is hospitalized for "nervous exhaustion" (321). While on a pass from the hospital, he contracts syphilis from an unnamed Saigon prostitute.

Unnamed *San Mateo* crewmen The Colombian crewmen of the *San Mateo* hoist a cow aboard the ship. The cow is crippled in the incident, but will take about a week to die so that her meat will remain fresh. Later, the crew members will all die in an explosion when Peru begins bombing Ecuador. About this episode, the narrator writes, "the Colombianos had treated the cow abominably, but . . . retribution had been swift and terrible" (233).

Unnamed Swedish Doctor After Leon Trout contracts syphilis from a prostitute in Vietnam, he seeks treatment from a Swedish doctor practicing medicine in Bangkok, where Trout has been sent for R & R. This doctor will ask Leon if he is the son of "the wonderful science-fiction writer Kilgore Trout" (323), a question that makes Leon cry, since the doctor, as far as Leon knows, is the only person outside of Cohoes, New York, who has ever heard of Kilgore Trout.

Unnamed Vietnamese Grandmother When Leon Trout is a Marine serving in Vietnam, he shoots a toothless and stooped Vietnamese grandmother who had just killed Trout's best friend and worst enemy in his platoon with a hand grenade.

von Kleist, Adolf The charming and urbane captain of the *Bahia de Darwin* who appears on American talk shows to help promote "The Nature Cruise of the Century," Adolf von Kleist is a figurehead who does not actually know much about ships. On the night that the war breaks out, Adolf gets drunk on board, never expecting actual passengers to show up. When his younger brother, Siegfried, brings the hotel guests on the bus, Adolf is bumbling and incompetent, humiliated by his drunken state. Later, he tries to make amends by appearing to be a competent navigator, but ends up grounding the ship on the island of Santa Rosalia rather than bringing it to the naval base on the Galápagos island of Baltra as he had planned. Yet, his incompetence ironically saves the passengers in the end since civilization itself is doomed, and the survivors of the *Bahia de Darwin* will have to repopulate the Earth. After the passengers become marooned, Captain von Kleist lives with Mary Hepburn for 10 years. Unbeknownst to him, however, she uses his sperm to impregnate each of the six Kanka-bono girls. In this way, von Kleist becomes the ancestor of the entire human population that will develop on Santa Rosalia.

von Kleist, Gottfried and Wilhelm A pair of old German brothers in Quito, Ecuador, and the paternal uncles of Siegfried and Adolf von Kleist, Gottfried and Wilhelm von Kleist are the owners of the *Bahia de Darwin*, the luxury ship designed to take tourists on visits to the Galápagos Islands. They design the ship so that its passengers "would never be out of touch with the rest of the world for an instant" (22). Ironically, the ship runs aground on the island of Santa Rosalia, and the survivors and their descendants remain out of touch with the rest of the world for a million years.

von Kleist, Kamikaze The child of Captain Adolf von Kleist and a Kanka-bono woman, Sinka, Kamikaze is the first child produced by Mary Hepburn's genetic engineering. When Kamikaze is only 13 years old, he fathers a child by the furry Akiko Hiroguchi. Later, he will father six more children with Akiko, but also take pleasure in copulating with any woman on the island he can lay his hands on.

von Kleist, Mrs. The mother of Adolf and Siegfried von Kleist is killed by her husband, Sebastian, when he is suffering from the effects of Huntington's chorea.

von Kleist, Sebastian An Ecuadorian sculptor and architect who is the father of Adolf and Siegfried, Sebastian von Kleist has the disease Huntington's chorea, which manifests itself when he is 54 years old, causing him to go mad and murder his own wife.

von Kleist, Siegfried Siegfried von Kleist, the younger brother of ship's captain Adolf von Kleist, works as manager of the Hotel El Dorado in Guayaquil, Ecuador. A middle-aged man from a very wealthy family, Siegfried has never married because there is a fifty-fifty chance that he carries a gene for Huntington's chorea, which killed his father. On the afternoon of November 27, 1986, the disease begins to manifest itself, and Siegfried goes temporarily mad, but veers back into sanity. That evening he heroically tries to save the hotel guests, all of whom are signed up for "The Nature Cruise of the Century," by driving them on a bus, along with the six Kanka-bono girls, to the *Bahia de Darwin*. The trip is extremely difficult, though, since Peru has declared war on Ecuador and begun bombing. One of the explosives ends up creating a tidal wave that washes the bus off the wharf, drowning Siegfried von Kleist, although his passengers all make it safely onto the ship.

Wait, James James Wait is a con man who signs up for "The Nature Cruise of the Century," but who dies of a heart attack on board the ship, the *Bahia de Darwin*. The product of an incestuous relationship between a father and daughter, Wait grew up in a series of abusive foster families. As a young man, he worked for a time as a homosexual prostitute in Manhattan, eventually murdering a "bloated plutocrat" (176), Prince Richard of Croatia-Slavonia, during a perverse sexual experience. Wait makes his living by courting and marrying wealthy, lonely women, then stealing all their money and deserting them. At the opening of the novel, he has practiced this con on 17 such women and become a millionaire. When Wait hears about the widow Mary Hepburn, he decides that she will be a perfect mark. Mary, though, happens to witness Wait acting kindly to several young Indian girls and is convinced that he is a good man. The two are married aboard the *Bahia de Darwin* by the ship's captain just before Wait's death. During his suffering, Wait has actually fallen in love with Mary, and Mary lives the rest of her life thinking he was a good man.

Wait's Parents The parents of James Wait, whose names are never given, are a father and daughter who have an incestuous relationship, then run away from town together shortly after Wait's birth. Although Wait has no way of knowing it, the narrator, Leon Trout, tells readers that both of Wait's parents died of heart attacks in their early 40s.

Wait's 17th Wife Though never given a name, we find out that James Wait's 17th wife is a 70-year-old widow in Skokie, Illinois. Wait ends up in Guayaquil, Ecuador, because it sounds to him like the last place in the world she would ever think of looking for him.

Wojciehowitz, Doris Doris Wojciehowitz was the wife of teacher Robert Wojciehowitz, until she died and left him a widower. She makes Robert a gift of an expensive Jaguar car right before her death to show him what a good husband he had been. This is the car that Robert will drive to Mary Hepburn's house to propose marriage to her.

Wojciehowitz, Joseph The son of Doris and Robert Wojciehowitz, Joseph Wojciehowitz is a "lout" (262) who, in a drunk driving accident, wrecks the Jaguar his mother had bought for his father shortly before her death.

Wojciehowitz, Robert Robert Wojciehowitz is head of the English Department at Ilium High School, who begins asking Mary Hepburn for dates only two weeks after her husband, Roy's, death. When he drives to Mary's house to propose to her one day, he is chased into a tree by the Hepburn's golden retriever, Donald. Wojciehowitz is so embarrassed by the incident that he leaves Mary Hepburn alone after that.

Wojciehowitz, Mrs. Robert Wojciehowitz is frightened of dogs because he and his mother—Mrs. Wojciehowitz—were attacked by a Doberman pinscher when he was five years old.

Ximénez, Eduardo Eduardo Ximénez is a bush pilot who saves the six little Kanka-bono girls when their village in the rain forest is sprayed by insecticide. He ends up taking them to an orphanage in Guayaquil, where kindly nuns take responsibility for them.

FURTHER READING

Ferguson, Oliver W. "History and Story: Leon Trout's Double Narrative in *Galápagos*." *Critique* 40, no. 3 (1999): 230–238.

Galápagos. New York: Dell, 1999.

Morse, Donald E. "Thinking Intelligently about Science and Art: Kurt Vonnegut's *Galápagos* and *Bluebeard*." *Extrapolation* 38, no. 4 (1997): 292–303.

"Go Back to Your Precious Wife and Son"

One of Vonnegut's stories that explores the nature of marriage, "Go Back to Your Precious Wife and Son" first appeared in *Ladies' Home Journal* in July 1962. The story was reprinted in the 1968 collection, *Welcome to the Monkey House*.

SYNOPSIS

The narrator is a storm window salesman who is hired to install a bathtub enclosure in the home of movie star Gloria Hilton and her fifth husband, writer George Murra. While working in the upstairs bathroom, the narrator overhears a vicious argument between the actress and writer. The narrator leaves the house, but when he returns later in the day to install storm windows, Murra invites him to have a drink. As the two men get drunk together, the narrator discovers that Murra had left his first wife, whom he married at the age of 18, and his teenage son, John, for Gloria Hilton. It turns out that the narrator was also married at age 18 and has a son. As he becomes increasingly drunk, the narrator begins to emphathize with Murra's situation and treats his wife rudely when he returns home that evening.

The next day, when the narrator arrives at Murra's home to finish the work, the writer's son, John, is there, having been called away from school for what he believes is an emergency. Murra, however, just wants to speak with the boy. John, believing that his father's behavior has been "contemptible" (213), refuses to forgive his father. The narrator suggests that Murra give the boy a kick in the pants, which he does, and John is startled into actually listening to his father's explanations. That night, when the narrator returns to his own home, his wife is gone and does not return for several hours. Yet, the story ends happily. The narrator's wife has forgiven his previous drunken and disrespectful behavior and, much to the narrator's relief, finds their new bathtub door, which the narrator had etched with a depiction of Gloria Hilton's face, amusing.

COMMENTARY

"Go Back to Your Precious Wife and Son" is another story, like "Long Walk to Forever," that shows suitability and companionship are more important to a successful marriage than either glamour or romance. Both writer George Murra and the story's narrator married when they were only 18 years old to girls that they knew well. Murra at one point describes his wife as a woman he'd "known so long she was practically like a sister" (215). Both marriages are beset by money worries and bickering over small things, as most marriages are. Yet, things begin to go wrong for each man when he is seduced by the lure of romance, especially the kind of sentimental love promised by popular culture and film. When Murra sells one of his books to the movies and is hired to write a screenplay, movie star Gloria Hilton sweet talks him with lines about how the two were "*made* for each other" and admonitions that he should "dare to be happy" (215).

Yet, as the narrator himself discovers, these romantic promises are mere illusions. When he sees Gloria Hilton through the bathroom register, with her hair in curlers, without any makeup or fancy clothes, she looks like any ordinary middle-aged wife: "I swear, that woman wasn't any prettier than a used studio couch," he thinks to himself (208). Although, when drunk, the narrator temporarily succumbs to the same dreams of romantic love that had felled Murra, ultimately, his practical, Yankee nature saves him from such illusions. Unlike the fast-living Murra, who is from Los Angeles, the narrator is decidedly practical and nonromantic even in his dream of "making it." Rather than imagine himself working in the movies as Murra does, the narrator imagines himself selling storm windows to the biggest hotel in town. His advice that the writer kick his son "in the pants" (218) rather than continue to torture himself with recriminations turns out to be solid, practical advice as well, forcing the boy to listen to his father for a change. The story ends by showing that the narrator's wife has a similar practical attitude toward marriage. She does not tear herself up over her husband's rudeness to her when drunk. Instead, she spends the day alone—shopping, eating in a restaurant, and seeing a movie—and she has a "swell time" (220). She is able to laugh at the bathtub door finally, recognizing that her husband loves her and will not make the same mistake that George Murra did.

CHARACTERS

Crocker, Harry   Harry Crocker is a local plumber who has coffee with the narrator during the time he is working on Gloria Hilton's bathtub. The movie star has ordered that a portrait of herself be etched on the bathtub door, at exactly the height her head will reach when she stands up in the tub. Crocker jokingly asks if the narrator insisted on measuring the movie star himself.

Hilton, Gloria   A movie star currently on her fifth husband, Gloria Hilton has moved to New Hampshire with George Murra because people who "are really people" live there, and the couple is tired of all the "phonies" in Los Angeles (212). However, Gloria ultimately leaves George, uttering the line, "Go on back to your precious wife and your precious son" (209). George had divorced his first wife and abandoned his teenage son to marry Gloria.

Murra, George   George Murra is a writer who has left his first wife and his son, John, in order to marry famous movie star Gloria Hilton. He explains to the narrator that, when he sold a book to the movies and was hired to write the screenplay, he was seduced by the romantic image of Gloria Hilton. He had married young, and he and his first wife spent many years broke and bickering over minor things as married couples will do. Murra, though, regrets his actions and is pleased when his son finally forgives him and his first wife agrees to take him back.

Murra, John   John Murra is the 15-year-old son of writer George Murra, who has left the boy and his mother to marry famous movie star Gloria Hilton. Resentful and angry at his father, John agrees to listen to him only after Murra gives him a kick in the pants at the narrator's recommendation.

Murra, Mrs.   George Murra married his first wife when the two were still teenagers. The pair, like most young married couples, had their fair share of bickering and trying to make ends meet, but George realizes he made a terrible mistake in divorcing her to marry movie star Gloria Hilton. The first Mrs. Murra, however, agrees to take George back near the end of the story.

Narrator   The story's narrator is a Yankee storm window salesman and installer. After his experience installing a bathtub enclosure in the home of movie star Gloria Hilton and writer George Murra, he develops a newfound appreciation for his own wife and son.

Narrator's Wife   The story's narrator married his wife when he was only 18 years old, the same age writer George Murra was when he married his first wife, whom he subsequently divorced in order to marry movie star Gloria Hilton. Although the narrator's wife is annoyed by her husband's rude and drunken remarks after spending the afternoon with Murra, she is able to forgive him after enjoying some time by herself. She clearly has a good sense of humor since she laughs about the couple's new bathtub door rather than get angry at her husband.

Narrator's Son   When the narrator returns home after witnessing George Murra's reconciliation with his son, John, his own son tearfully tells him that his mother has gone out and might never return again. The boy, though, drops his "high and mighty tone" (220) when his father threatens to give him "a swift kick in the pants" (220).

FURTHER READING

Reed, Peter. *The Short Fiction of Kurt Vonnegut.* Westport, Conn.: Greenwood Press, 1997.
Welcome to the Monkey House. New York: Dell, 1998.

God Bless You, Dr. Kevorkian

God Bless You, Dr. Kevorkian is an odd little collection of very short vignettes in which Vonnegut imagines chatting with assorted people in the afterlife. Published in 1999 by Seven Stories Press, the book transcribes a series of 90-second radio spots Vonnegut delivered on air for the National Public Radio Station WNYC in downtown Manhattan as part of a station fundraiser. In each vignette, Vonnegut has supposedly been strapped to a gurney in the famous death chamber at the Huntsville State Prison in Texas. His close friend DR. JACK KEVORKIAN has supplied him with enough drugs to instigate a near-death experience. During these sessions, Vonnegut claims to travel down the "blue tunnel" of the afterlife to the "Pearly Gates" of heaven (7). There, he interviews dead people, both ordinary and famous, both heroes and villains, about their experiences on the other side.

In the book's introduction, Vonnegut does not shy away from the irony that he himself is a humanist who does not believe in an afterlife. He explains that, as a humanist, he has "tried to behave decently without any expectation of rewards or punishments" after he is dead (9). Humanists, he says, dedicate themselves to serving their communities as best they can rather than some abstract, supernatural entity. HUMANISM is an "Earthbound" and "unmajestic" belief system, he adds, that is really just a synonym for "good citizenship and common decency" (12). Among the human values that Vonnegut celebrates in this introduction is the need to appreciate what we have in the here and now rather than looking toward future rewards. He tells the story of his uncle ALEX VONNEGUT, a HARVARD-educated life insurance agent in INDIANAPOLIS, who always made a point of acknowledging sweet, enjoyable moments in life, no matter how fleeting. Alex would interrupt conversations during these moments with the words, "If this isn't nice, what is?" (14). In addition, Vonnegut advocates that humans should value and appreciate their Earthly communities, particularly family groups. As in all of his work, he emphasizes the importance of large, extended families in supplying human beings with the companionship and support every individual needs in order to survive.

Each of the 21 vignettes focuses on a different, departed member of the family of human beings. Some of the people Vonnegut purports to interview are famous writers and thinkers, whom he treats with a gently humorous tone. These include such luminaries as WILLIAM SHAKESPEARE, who refuses to clearly answer Vonnegut's questions about the true author of the plays or about his romantic predilections; SIR ISAAC NEWTON, who faults himself for not coming up with the ideas of evolution, relativity, or germ theory; and MARY SHELLEY, who prefers to speak about her famous parents and husband rather than discuss the ATOMIC BOMB. Vonnegut also imagines visits to longtime heroes of his, people who dedicated themselves to fighting against social injustice. These interviews tend to be somewhat more bitter and even angry in tone. The great defense attorney CLARENCE DARROW, for instance, claims that the current practice of allowing televisions into courtrooms merely confirms that the American justice system is more concerned with entertaining spectators than with achieving true justice. Vonnegut also claims to interview early 20th-century labor organizer and perennial Socialist Party (*see* SOCIALISM) candidate EUGENE DEBS in one of the vignettes. Vonnegut includes the Debs quote that he cites often in his writing and speeches and which serves as the epigraph to his novel *Hocus Pocus*: "As long as there is a lower class, I am in it. As long as there is a criminal element, I am of it. As long as there is a soul in prison, I am not free" (38). But readers detect Vonnegut's bitterness when he tells Debs that today in America these words are ridiculed and that the fastest-growing industry in our country is the building of prisons.

Vonnegut does not restrict his interviews in the afterlife to heroes of the past. He also visits several notorious criminals and villains. Chief among these is ADOLF HITLER himself, who purportedly feels remorse on the other side. Vonnegut imagines Hitler desiring that a modest monument be built to him at the United Nations headquarters in New York. The monument would bear the grossly inadequate two-word German sentence: "Entshuldigen Sie," which means, "I Beg Your Pardon," or "Excuse Me" (46). He also imagines the killer of MARTIN LUTHER KING, JR., JAMES EARL RAY, regretting his Earthly behavior in the afterlife. Ray, who is "no moron" (57), is, however, still an unrepentant bigot after death. He is only sorry for his crime because he realizes that King's death by an assassin's bullet cemented the civil rights leader's saintlike reputation worldwide.

In one of the book's final sketches, Vonnegut depicts himself following condemned murderer KARLA FAYE TUCKER down the blue tunnel shortly after her execution in Texas. The whole book, set as it is in the death chamber of the Huntsville State Prison, expresses an anti–death penalty sentiment. Nowhere is this so clear as in the piece about Tucker. Karla Faye does not deny being a murderer, but she says that the governor of Texas should accompany her to death, since he too is a murderer. The piece ends with Vonnegut returning to the world, but having to immediately vacate the facility so that another execution can be carried out.

Perhaps the most touching of the short pieces are the ones that depict less well known people, often ordinary human beings with some extraordinary quality about them. Among these are SALVATORE BIAGINI, a 70-year-old retired construction worker who died in Queens, New York, of a heart attack after saving his beloved pet schnauzer from attack by a pit bull. Several extremely devoted husbands and wives are interviewed as well, including ROBERTA GORSUCH BURKE, married for 72 years to Admiral Arly A. Burke, who chose as her simple epitaph: "A Sailor's Wife," and HAROLD EPSTEIN, a certified public accountant who died at the age of 94 after remaining "love birds" with his "sweet wife Esta" throughout his long life (39). Epstein, Vonnegut reports, was also passionate about gardening, practicing what he and Esta called "garden insanity" (40), a hobby that brought the couple great joy. Other passionate hobbyists are included as well, such as PETER PELLEGRINO, a hot-air balloonist who found heaven on Earth when crossing the Alps in a balloon, and DR. PHILIP STRAX, a poet and radiologist who loved women. Dr. Strax not only penned "feminist" verses, he was instrumental in developing mammogram technology that would save thousands of women's lives.

Finally, the message of Vonnegut's series of radio spots might be that heaven and hell are *not* to be found in the afterlife, but that human beings create their own heaven and hell here on Earth. The emphasis in these short vignettes is never on what the dead people are doing in the afterlife—in fact, no one seems to do much at all once they pass through the Pearly Gates—but on what they

did in their Earthly lives. Whether writing literary masterpieces, making beneficial scientific discoveries, crusading for the poor and oppressed, or simply creating nice moments with loved family members, human beings have the ability to make Earth a better place. Similarly, human beings create hell as well, through war, violence, and intolerance. Like all of Vonnegut's writing, this quirky little book pleads for humans to build a world based on compassion, kindness, and human decency.

FURTHER READING

God Bless You, Dr. Kevorkian. New York: Washington Square Press, 2001.

God Bless You, Mr. Rosewater

Published in 1965 by Holt, Rinehart & Winston, *God Bless You, Mr. Rosewater,* while highly critical of a class-based America that privileges its wealthy citizens over its poorer, might nonetheless be Kurt Vonnegut's most optimistic novel. Like many of Vonnegut's books, *Mr. Rosewater* toys with Utopian ideals, asking what it would take to make the world a better place. Unlike some of his other novels, though, especially *Player Piano, The Sirens of Titan, Cat's Cradle,* and *Slapstick,* books in which characters attempt to install large-scale Utopias, whether through armed revolution or through inventing new religions or political systems, Eliot Rosewater's revolution is much smaller in scope. He practices Utopian ideals one person at a time, helping out the lonely, the useless, and the throw-away members of American society by providing compassion and advice. One of the very few Vonnegut novels to offer what might be called a happy ending, *God Bless You, Mr. Rosewater* posits that by simply being kind to one another human beings might be able to at least partially bring about the better world they crave.

SYNOPSIS

Chapters 1–3

The novel opens with young lawyer Norman Mushari contemplating how to get his hands on part of the fortune of the Rosewater family, his law firm's most lucrative clients. Because the charter of the Rosewater Foundation calls for the expulsion of any officer proved insane, and because office gossip has it that Eliot Rosewater, the foundation's president, is a lunatic, Mushari hopes to become rich by representing the Rosewater next in line for the presidency—a distant cousin named Fred living in Rhode Island. Thus, Mushari begins to collect evidence intended to confirm Eliot Rosewater's incompetence. The first item in his collection is a long letter Eliot writes, which is intended to be given to the foundation's next president after Eliot's death. Mushari also collects 53 letters written by Eliot to his wife, Sylvia, who is in the process of divorcing him. From these letters, Mushari learns some of Eliot's background.

Born in 1918, the son of a prominent U.S. senator, Eliot is raised on the East Coast and in Europe, despite his ostensible family home being located in Indiana. He leaves HARVARD Law School in 1941 to volunteer for the army, where he serves with great distinction. Near the end of the war, he is diagnosed with combat fatigue and hospitalized in Paris, where he meets his wife-to-be, Sylvia DuVrais Zetterling. After his release, he marries Sylvia, returns to finish his law degree at Harvard, goes on to earn a doctorate in international law, and takes on the presidency of the Rosewater foundation. For the next several years, Eliot does considerable charitable work with the Foundation, all the while drinking heavily. In 1953, Eliot disappears for a week, during which time he drunkenly crashes a SCIENCE FICTION writers' convention, although he is disappointed to find that his favorite writer, Kilgore Trout, is not in attendance. This begins for Eliot a period of several months of drunken traveling around the country, mixing with volunteer FIRE-MEN and bums. Although he returns home, enters psychoanalysis, and stays sober for a year, Eliot's drunken wanderings soon begin again. He eventually winds up in Rosewater, Indiana, his ancestral hometown, where he will stay through most of the novel.

Chapters 4–7
Having convinced Sylvia to move with him to Rosewater, Eliot and his wife snub the wealthy and prestigious citizens of the town, but pour considerable amounts of money and sympathy into the poorer sections. Continuing his obsession with volunteer firemen, the "only social life" the Rosewaters have that is "untainted by pity" is through their involvement with the Rosewater Volunteer Fire Department (50). Five years after moving to Rosewater, however, Sylvia suffers a nervous collapse and burns the firehouse down. Placed in a private mental hospital in INDIANAPOLIS, Sylvia is treated there by a young psychiatrist named Dr. Ed Brown, who makes his reputation by describing her illness in an academic paper. Calling her disease *samaritrophia*, or "hysterical indifference to the troubles of those less fortunate than oneself" (51), the doctor notes that the cure—quelling Sylvia's troublesome conscience, thus turning her into a completely shallow person—may have been worse than the disease. Nevertheless, supposedly "cured," Sylvia flies off to Paris, where she becomes a member of the international jet set before falling to pieces again in July 1964. Treatment this time leaves Sylvia "silent and sad, almost unbearably deep again" (57). Though she wishes to return to Rosewater out of a sense of duty, Sylvia's doctor warns her that a return might be fatal, telling her instead that she must divorce Eliot and lead a very quiet life. Back in Rosewater, Eliot moves out of the Rosewater family home and into an office on Main Street, housed above a liquor store and a cheap diner. He paints on his windows and doors the following words:

ROSEWATER FOUNDATION
HOW CAN WE HELP
YOU?

Eliot proceeds to offer advice, money, and aspirin to any lonely or needy residents of the town of Rosewater who call or come by, eventually becoming venerated by the townspeople as something of a saint.

Meanwhile, Eliot's father, the famous Senator Lister Ames Rosewater, is scheming to get Eliot to give up the life he has chosen, to instead return to Washington and play the role of senator's son. He tells his lawyers that he blames himself for the way Eliot has turned out—that as a child, he was made much of as a fire department mascot, which ruined him for ordinary life. The senator's lawyer adds some important background on Eliot, arguing that some of his problems stem from his experience in World War II, where he inadvertently killed three volunteer firemen, not realizing they were not enemy soldiers. The senator eventually calls Eliot on the phone to try to persuade him to leave Indiana. He puts Sylvia on the line to speak with Eliot, and the estranged husband and wife agree to meet for one final farewell at the Bluebird Room of the Marriott Hotel in Indianapolis.

Chapters 8–11

Norman Mushari, who had been listening in on the phone call, is terrified that Eliot and Sylvia will reconcile and have a child. This would ruin his plan for the Rosewater fortune to revert to the Rosewater next in line for the presidency of the foundation, Fred Rosewater, who lives in Pisquontuit, Rhode Island. Norman decides to visit the Rhode Island Rosewaters immediately. The action of the novel at this point shifts to Rhode Island, where Fred is an insurance salesman completely ignorant of his ties to the famous Rosewaters of Indiana. A portly man who pushes insurance coverage at two cafes most of the day, and whose wife spends all her time with a rich lesbian in town, Fred longs to answer sexually suggestive ads in a racy newspaper, but is too afraid to do so. On the day of Norman Mushari's arrival in Pisquontuit, Fred, after spending the afternoon sleeping in his sailboat as he often does, returns home to his sleeping, drunken wife, who had spent the afternoon lunching with her rich friend Amanita Buntline. The son of a suicide, Fred himself thinks about swallowing a large number of sleeping pills at this point, but remembers his son, little Franklin Rosewater. Going to his son's room for comfort, Fred finds a pornographic picture stuck under the pillow. Sickened and confused, he retreats to the basement of the house, where he finds a history of the Rosewater family written by his father, but which Fred had never bothered to read before. Wearily he opens the book, but soon becomes elated when he discovers in the book's first two pages that his ancestors had been quite illustrious.

Excited, Fred insists that his wife, Caroline, come to the cellar to look at the book herself.

Awed by her husband's newfound authority, Caroline complies, but stomps upstairs in disgust when she and Fred discover that the insides of the book had been completely eaten away by termites—the only parts remaining are the first two pages and the back cover. Completely overcome with despair, Fred decides to hang himself, and is in fact putting the noose around his neck when Franklin calls down the stairs that a man is there to see him. Barely escaping the indignity of being caught in the act of trying to kill himself, Fred jumps off the stool he had climbed on and quickly hides the noose. The visitor turns out to be none other than Norman Mushari, who informs Fred that his Indiana relatives are swindling him out of millions and millions of dollars. Mushari concludes by saying, "I am here to tell you about a relatively cheap and simple court action that will make those millions yours" (207). Fred immediately faints.

Chapters 12–14

Meanwhile, back in Rosewater, Indiana, it is time for Eliot to get on a bus for Indianapolis for his farewell meeting with Sylvia. Before he leaves the office, he receives a visit from his father, the senator, who is pleased to see that Eliot has bought new clothes. While Eliot bathes himself in his small bathroom, the senator, looking around Eliot's cramped quarters, discovers a love poem Eliot had written Sylvia two years before. Shocked by the poem's mention of pubic hair, which the senator has a strong aversion to, Eliot's father is made even more uncomfortable when Eliot emerges from the bathroom stark naked. As the two converse, Eliot begins absentmindedly playing with his own pubic hair, finding one that is a foot long and extending it to its full length. The senator explodes, asking why Eliot hates him, spewing out that Eliot has ruined his life, and storming out of the office. Eliot remains calm for a few minutes after the senator's departure, but then freezes, stiff as a corpse.

Although he is able to start moving again in a few minutes and walk to the bus stop, Eliot does not recognize anyone who speaks to him on the street. He manages to get himself on the bus, but as it approaches Indianapolis, Eliot imagines that the city is engulfed in a giant fire-storm, like the ones that destroyed DRESDEN during the war. Everything goes black for Eliot. When he awakes, he finds himself dressed in tennis whites and sitting in a garden by a fountain. It turns out that he is in the same private mental hospital in Indianapolis where Sylvia had been placed earlier, and that Eliot has lost a year of his life. Facing him on a bench are four men in business suits, who turn out to be Eliot's father, Dr. Brown the psychiatrist, the family lawyer, and a fourth man Eliot does not recognize until his father addresses him as "Mr. Trout." The man is Kilgore Trout, the science fiction writer Eliot so admires but has never met. The men have been devising a strategy to prove Eliot's sanity. During his missing year, Eliot had told his father to find Kilgore Trout, who could explain all the reasons why Eliot behaved as he did in Rosewater. Trout explains that Eliot had been involved in one of the greatest social experiments of all time: how to love people who have no use.

The novel ends at the mental hospital, with Eliot figuring out a solution to everyone's problems. After the senator laments Eliot's lack of a child and heir, Eliot has an idea "for settling everything instantly, beautifully, and fairly" (272). He writes a generous check to Fred Rosewater, but also tells his father that he does indeed have children. It turns out that Norman Mushari had gone around Rosewater, bribing people to say bad things about Eliot. Beginning with a woman named Mary Moody, who claimed that Eliot was the father of her twins, now 57 babies in Rosewater County are said to have been fathered by Eliot. The senator explains that blood tests have proved the women's claims are not true, but Eliot instructs his lawyer to draw up legal papers acknowledging that each of these children is his, regardless of blood type. The children of Rosewater County, then, will have full rights of inheritance to the Rosewater fortune. Eliot's final words in the novel are directed to his lawyer. "And tell them," he says, referring to all his adopted children, "to be fruitful and multiply" (275).

COMMENTARY

God Bless You, Mr. Rosewater begins by asserting that a sum of money "is a leading character in this tale about people" (1), which is appropriate since the novel is very much about money—about social class, about the disparity between the haves and the have-nots, and even about the capitalistic free enterprise system in general. Eliot Rosewater's letter to his unknown heirs, supposed to be opened only upon his death but commandeered by Norman Mushari, uncovers a hidden history of how the great American fortunes were made. The America Eliot evokes in the letter is one of robber barons and ill-begotten riches. The actual names of historic American millionaire families such as Rothschild, DuPont, and Rockefeller pepper Eliot's ancestry, alongside fictional names of wealthy families such as Rumfoord, well-known to Vonnegut's readers.

The sordid Rosewater family history, which stands in for the larger, hidden history of wealthy America, is that the great Rosewater fortune was started when Eliot's great-grandfather paid a village idiot named Fletcher Moon to fight in his stead during the Civil War, then took advantage of the wartime economy to increase the profits made by his factories and farms. Vonnegut comments on the American class system when he has Eliot write about "the folly of the Founding Fathers" (8). Their mistake, according to Eliot, was that, while America was intended to be a Utopia, the Founding Fathers "had not made it the law of the Utopia that the wealth of each citizen should be limited" (8). Eliot continues, "Thus did a handful of rapacious citizens come to control all that was worth controlling in America. Thus was the savage and stupid and entirely inappropriate and unnecessary and humorless American class system created" (9). Further, Eliot explains, because of the greed of citizens like Noah Rosewater, "the American dream turned belly up" (9). While Americans cherish an image of themselves as inhabiting a classless society, a world in which merit is rewarded and any deserving citizen can pull him or herself up to the highest economic level, Eliot acknowledges that American resources are, in fact, finite, and that a new American motto, to replace *E pluribus unum*, might be "*Grab much too much, or you'll get nothing at all*" (10). One of the terrible ironies of *God Bless You, Mr. Rosewater* is that Eliot Rosewater, one of the only people in the novel to recognize the reality of what has happened to the American dream, to the country's original Utopian ideals, is labeled insane by the same system that celebrates rampant greed and sees the poor as inherently inferior to the wealthy.

The novel raises questions about sanity and insanity. What does it mean to be sane in a society that itself seems insane in many ways, that seems to have inverted its original ideals of equality and justice? The novel opens by quoting extensively not only from Eliot's letter to his heirs, but from a famous speech given by Eliot's father, Senator Lister Ames Rosewater, a man considered completely sane not only in the eyes of the huge corporations that control the country, but also to the American public at large, which keeps returning him to office. The senator's speech is about the Golden Age of Rome, and in it he praises Emperor CAESAR AUGUSTUS as a "great humanitarian" (27) who "wrote morals into law, and . . . enforced those unenforceable laws with a police force that was cruel and unsmiling" (29–30). The senator goes on to extol the cruel punishments devised by the Romans for lawbreakers, including being strung up by the thumbs, thrown down wells, and fed to lions. Rather than institute such punishments in present-day America, though, even though he would like to, the senator suggests instead a return to what he calls a "true Free Enterprise System, which has the sink-or-swim justice of Caesar Augustus built into it" (31). By putting these two extensive texts side by side, Vonnegut helps readers to see that Eliot's writings are the more compassionate and sane. By comparison, the senator's make him seem like a bloodthirsty madman. Yet, society labels the senator sane and Eliot insane.

Similar issues are also explored when Vonnegut describes the nervous breakdown and psychiatric treatment of Eliot's wife, Sylvia DuVrais Zetterling Rosewater. Incorporating yet another lengthy text written by a character into his own text, Vonnegut has Dr. Ed Brown make his reputation by the article he publishes on Sylvia's treatment. Dr. Brown calls Sylvia's disease "Samaritrophia," which he defines as "hysterical indifference to the troubles of those less fortunate than oneself" (51). In order to make Sylvia "sane" again, according to society's standards of sanity and insanity, the doctor does

not free her repressed social conscience, but makes sure that it stays buried deep within. In other words, he turns Sylvia into a shallow woman, a move the doctor himself is uncomfortable with, but one he must make for Sylvia to conform to her society's definition of normal. "The therapist," Dr. Brown writes about himself in the academic paper, "after a deeply upsetting investigation of normality at this time and place, was bound to conclude that a normal person, functioning well on the upper levels of a prosperous, industrialized society, can hardly hear his conscience at all" (54). Samaritrophia, then, he concludes, is less a disease than the common condition of healthy Americans at a certain economic level. Again, Vonnegut asks readers to question definitions of sanity and insanity—what does it mean to be insane when the generalized insanity of lacking compassion for one's fellow human beings is classified as normal, healthy behavior?

These three texts—Eliot's letter, the senator's speech, and Dr. Brown's academic paper—set up differing views about wealth and poverty in present-day America. Vonnegut's technique of including long excerpts from other texts serves as an example of what is often called "bricolage"—a characteristic frequently associated with postmodern literature. According to critics who write about POSTMODERN-ISM, postmodern literature often makes meaning by including fragments or pieces of other texts, which often tell competing stories, arranged together to make something new. The term is closely related to the term *collage* from the world of art. In a collage, an artist combines scraps of various materials, and it is in the combination that the artistry lies. Vonnegut's inclusion in *God Bless You, Mr. Rosewater* of Eliot's long letter, of the senator's famous speech, of the academic paper written by Dr. Ed Brown, as well as his insertion of numerous excerpts from books by Kilgore Trout and a long passage from a novel Eliot himself is writing, come together to form a collage of competing stories about Eliot Rosewater and the world he lives in. As in much postmodern literature, the task of determining meaning is left largely to the reader. Just as post–World War II society is viewed as multifaceted, heterogenous, fragmented, the literature that describes this period is often fragmented as well. In a world that is suspicious of any kind of monolithic or singular "Truth" with a capital T, individuals are left to wend their way among the fragments; finding meaning then becomes a subjective process of sorting through complex and competing "truths."

Another characteristic often associated with postmodern literature is the melding together of what are traditionally considered high culture forms, such as literature and oil painting, and forms associated more with popular culture. Mingling low and high is something Vonnegut does throughout his work, especially through his inclusion of science fiction scenarios and stories, like the Mars invasion in *The Sirens of Titan* or Billy Pilgrim's trip to Tralfamadore in *Slaughterhouse-Five*. For Vonnegut, both in *God Bless You, Mr. Rosewater* and in other novels as well, science fiction is one way of getting at meaning. Though long scorned by critics as not "real" literature or "high" literature, science fiction, Vonnegut believes, can sometimes ask the large questions about meaning and purpose in human life better than more conventionally literary works can. Eliot Rosewater admires science fiction writers even though he admits that they "couldn't write for sour apples" (19). That does not matter, according to Eliot, because, as he explains to the science fiction writers at the convention he crashes in Milford, Pennsylvania:

> "You're all I read any more. You're the only ones who'll talk about the *really* terrific changes going on . . . the only ones with guts enough to *really* care about the future, who *really* notice what machines do to us, what wars do to us, what cities do to us, what big, simple ideas do to us, what tremendous misunderstandings, mistakes, accidents and catastrophes do to us." (18)

Perhaps at least partly a dig at some of his own critics who dismissed Vonnegut early in his career as "merely" a writer of science fiction, nevertheless Eliot's sentiments here are heartfelt. In many postmodern works, meaning, which again is fragmented and subjective, can be attained through forms of popular culture as well as through traditional "high" art—think, for instance, of pop artist Andy Warhol's soup cans, pictures that depict an ordinary consumer product but that elevate it to the status of high art when the pictures are hung in galleries and exhibited at art shows. Popular forms, which reflect our culture back to us, perhaps tell us more about ourselves than traditional high art can.

At the same time it shows how science fiction can answer big social questions, *God Bless You, Mr. Rosewater* is also the novel that introduces readers to Kilgore Trout, Vonnegut's science fiction hack writer and cultural prophet, who will appear again and again in Vonnegut's later work. While in *Mr. Rosewater* Kilgore Trout does seem to be a legitimate visionary—he explains Eliot's "social experiment" in Rosewater, Indiana, for instance, in a way that makes sense not only to readers, but to Senator Rosewater as well—in later novels, Trout's prophetic gifts become more dubious. He becomes an increasingly seedy character as we see him propositioning women and exploiting young newspaper carriers in *Slaughterhouse-Five* and pathetically begging to be made young again at the end of *Breakfast of Champions*. Nevertheless, many critics read Kilgore Trout as a stand-in or double for Vonnegut himself, an underappreciated writer who, with great imagination, invents ludicrous and humorous scenarios to warn people about the folly of their current ways.

In *Mr. Rosewater,* as in Vonnegut's other novels, Kilgore Trout's writings are always found published in pornographic magazines or sold in pornographic bookstores. When Norman Mushari looks for a copy of *2BRO2B*, the Trout novel that Eliot praises so highly at the science fiction convention, it turns out that "no reputable bookseller had ever heard of Trout" (20). Mushari finds the book only at "a smut-dealer's hole in the wall . . . amidst the rawest pornography" (20). Surely Vonnegut is commenting on what we, as a society, find obscene. Obscenity becomes a recurring subtext in the novel; Senator Rosewater has, in fact, written a definition of obscenity into law, and this piece of legislation—the Rosewater Law—is the senator's most enduring legislative legacy. Obscenity, according to the Rosewater Law, "is any picture or phonograph record or any written matter calling attention to reproductive organs, bodily discharges, or bodily hair" (95). Readers also find out that the senator has a neurotic aversion to bodily hair, an aversion

Vonnegut plays up to great effect in what is perhaps the novel's funniest scene, when Eliot horrifies the senator by playing with one of his pubic hairs, pulling the hair out to its full length, and looking shyly at his father, "incredulously proud of owning such a thing" (227) and provoking an outraged tirade on the part of the senator.

The question Vonnegut wants us to ask is: What does it say about our society that we abolish sex and the human body, making the distribution and publication of "obscene" material punishable by large fines and prison terms, but we close our eyes to the obscene extremes of wealth and poverty that exist in this country? What Mushari does not understand when he finally finds *2BRO2B* in the porn shop is that the novel is not a "dirty book" (21). "He didn't understand that what Trout had in common with pornography wasn't sex but fantasies of an impossibly hospitable world" (21). So, both Trout's works and sexually pornographic material are Utopian, in a way—both imagine worlds different from the world that actually exists today, worlds more hospitable to human beings. It should be no surprise that pornography, then, is deemed obscene in a society that has come to reject the Utopian ideals it was originally built upon. After all, Eliot's grandfather, Samuel Rosewater, Eliot tells us, teaches this simple lesson: "*Anybody who thought that the United States of America was supposed to be a Utopia was a piggy, lazy, God-damned fool*" (10). Thus, science fiction writers are marginalized, along with writers of sexually explicit material, marked as dangerous and obscene Utopian thinkers.

Eliot Rosewater himself is a Utopian thinker; in fact, Eliot's psychiatrist tells the senator at one point that Eliot is "bringing his sexual energies" to Utopia (99). Eliot dares to ask the question that underlies much of Trout's as well as Vonnegut's own writing: "What in hell are people *for?*" (22), a quote from a character in *2BRO2B* as he is strapped into a chair in a suicide parlor and contemplates the question he will finally get to ask God. When Eliot tells Sylvia that he is moving to Rosewater, Indiana, he explains that he is doing so "to *care* about" (43) the people there. "I look at these people, these Americans," Eliot explains, "and I realize that they can't even care about themselves any more—

because they have no *use*" (43). We hear echoes of Vonnegut's first novel, *Player Piano*, in this passage when Eliot continues, "The factory, the farms, the mines across the river—they're almost completely automatic now" (43–44). So the problem of what do with a population deprived of useful work and thus of their dignity in an age of rapid technological advancement becomes a pressing concern in *God Bless You, Mr. Rosewater*, as it was in the earlier *Player Piano*. Kilgore Trout, at the end of the novel, explains the problem that Eliot's great social experiment was attempting to solve when he tells the senator and the other men that Eliot, in Rosewater, "dealt on a very small scale with a problem whose queasy horrors will eventually be made worldwide by the sophistication of machines" (264). The problem, Trout points out, is this: "How to love people who have no use?" (264).

Finding an answer to this problem becomes Eliot's life mission. He even sees himself as akin to SHAKESPEARE's HAMLET, not only because he is in Elsinore at one point—the name of Hamlet's kingdom in Denmark—working with the Elsinore Volunteer Fire Department, but because of the sense that he, like Hamlet, has "an important mission" to accomplish and that both become "temporarily mixed up about how it should be done" (36). Eliot and Hamlet do share quite a bit—a troubled and complex relationship with a father that sets the plot into motion, a love interest who goes insane, a desire to do right followed by periods of paralysis that prevent them from acting. Shakespeare's play is evoked as well in Kilgore Trout's novel *2BRO2B*, as the title echoes the question Hamlet asks to begin his famous soliloquy—"To be or not to be?" Trout's novel reflects some of the problems Vonnegut himself is concerned with since it depicts an America in which almost all of the work is done by machines and people have little use. Because there is also a serious overpopulation problem, the government has set up suicide parlors on every major intersection, hoping to tempt people to end their own lives. To be or not to be, then, becomes a vital question for Trout's characters as it does for Eliot's clients in Rosewater, Indiana.

As Eliot sets about to help the people who come to see him at the Rosewater Foundation in

Indiana, he tells Sylvia that he is going to be an artist: "I'm going to love these discarded Americans, even though they're useless and unattractive," he explains, "*That* is going to be my work of art" (44). As in *Cat's Cradle,* when Bokonon invents a new religion so that life itself can become a work of art, for Eliot art occupies a larger canvas than the narrow definition usually given it. Traditional art, in fact, has failed Eliot. When Eliot first meets Sylvia in Paris after the war, Sylvia's father, a world-famous cellist, introduces him as "the only American who has so far noticed the Second World War" (85). He goes on to explain that Eliot despises art, but in a way that the cellist cannot help but respect: "What he's saying, I think," Sylvia's father continues, "is that art has failed him, which I must admit, is a very fair thing for a man who has bayoneted a fourteen-year-old boy in the line of duty to say" (85). For a man who has both witnessed and committed horrible atrocities during the war, traditional forms of art simply lose their meaning, do not work anymore. Vonnegut will continue this theme in his next novel, *Slaughterhouse-Five,* when he invents a new form for telling war stories because traditional forms are no longer adequate. Yet, it is also his wartime experiences that make Eliot so compassionate. Part of his great love for his fellow humans is an attempt to make up for the volunteer FIREMEN he unwittingly killed in Germany. Again, Vonnegut makes a similar point in *Slaughterhouse-Five* when he says that "The nicest veterans" he knew when he lived in Schenectady, "the kindest and funniest ones, the ones who hated war the most, were the ones who'd really fought" (11). Ironically, it is a knowledge of the full extent of human barbarity that can lead to the greatest human kindness.

The thing that Eliot never forgets about the lonely and destitute people who seek him out in Rosewater is that they, like him, are human beings. When the senator asks Sylvia to tell him "one good thing" (68) about the people Eliot helps, she says their goodness is a "secret thing" (68). Pressed by the senator, Sylvia breaks down and tells him, "The secret is that they're human" (68). When she sees no flicker of recognition in the faces of the senator or the lawyers, she goes into the bathroom and

weeps. That is not to say, though, that Vonnegut romanticizes or sentimentalizes the poor and downtrodden. On the contrary, he writes that Eliot's clients, the people who leaned on him regularly, "were a lot weaker . . . and dumber" than Eliot imagines (72). Diana Moon Glampers, for instance, is said to be "ugly, stupid, and boring," which is the reason that nobody had ever loved her. And later, the narrator describes Mary Moody as a "slut," as "a suspected arsonist, a convicted shoplifter, and a five-dollar whore" (213). Yet, despite this, Eliot treats these people with compassion, understanding their basic humanity. When Sylvia asks Eliot what he will say at the baptism of Mary Moody's twins, he responds that he will tell the babies that there is only one rule he knows of: "God damn it, you've got to be kind" (129).

The problem of people who have no meaningful purpose in life, who have little use to society, exists in Pisquontuit, Rhode Island, as well, in the less well known side of the Rosewater family. Fred Rosewater's father committed suicide, and Fred himself, a lonely man with a distant, superior-feeling wife, and an "unattractive, fat little" son (137) who buys pornographic pictures, contemplates suicide often and even attempts to hang himself before being interrupted by Norman Mushari. And the moneyed class is not much better off. Stewart Buntline, in many ways, is simply a wealthier, thus more decadent version of Fred—his wife, Amanita, is a proclaimed lesbian who takes a liking to Caroline Rosewater, and his daughter deals in the pornography that Franklin Rosewater buys. Bunny Weeks, the restaurant owner, collects objects from the past, particularly harpoons, but these once useful objects, associated with masculine adventure and high drama—some of the harpoons are said to have come from the hide of MOBY-DICK himself—have been reduced to decorations as they are turned into objects of display in the shop attached to Bunny's restaurant. Even Bunny's homosexuality can be read as a kind of artificiality, especially considering the prevalent homophobic attitudes of the time the book was written. Bunny is not a "real man," but a weakling, as his name implies, especially when contrasted to the fisherman Harry Pena and his blatantly heterosexual sons.

Harry is one character in Pisquontuit who has a definite use and purpose in life, largely because he has reverted to working with his hands in an old-fashioned kind of way. While Bunny's restaurant *The Weir* and his shop *The Jolly Whaler* nod to a past when men earned their living fishing, Harry is a genuine fisherman. Bunny's patrons, in fact, are given opera glasses at each table so that they may watch Harry and his sons at work. And the work they do is described in nearly reverent terms by the narrator. "It was a magic time," he writes, describing Harry and his sons using nets to haul in fish, "Even the gulls fell silent as the three, purified of all thought, hauled net from the sea" (182). And when they have finished their work, hooking the fish violently and slamming their heads to finish them off, Harry and his boys laugh, curse, and are said to be "as satisfied with life as men can ever be" (184). Vonnegut's idealization of vigorous, masculine pursuits such as the fishing trips of Harry Pena and his sons is also seen in his obsession with volunteer firemen, not only in *God Bless You, Mr. Rosewater*, but in many of his other novels. Like the Penas, the work of firemen is highly physical, demanding and dangerous, done in company with other men, and less morally ambiguous than the work of say, lawyers, public relations representatives, or insurance salesmen—careers that are often skewered in Vonnegut's writings. At the same time that he romanticizes these masculine pursuits, Vonnegut also ironically undercuts Harry Pena. Bunny Weeks explains to Amanita and Caroline that Harry, unbeknownst to him, is bankrupt and will soon lose his business: "'That's all over, men working with their hands and backs. They are not needed,'" he explains (186). The narrator writes that Bunny, "to his credit, was not happy about this" (186). Bunny, though presented as a kind of synthetic man himself, laments that society has no use any longer for genuine men of Harry's type.

Eliot Rosewater offers a different model for behavior in a world that destroys the Harry Penas. Neither hypermasculine like Harry nor artificial like Bunny, Eliot is a bundle of contradictions. Critic Jerome Klinkowitz describes Eliot as "a well-meaning but rather oafish, ill-smelling, overweight person" (*Kurt Vonnegut* 58). Klinkowitz adds that

Vonnegut does not idealize Eliot since he is "alternately kind and rude" to the people of Rosewater, since he "leaves them at the drop of a hat," and since his charitable acts have only a very small effect in the world (60). Despite these considerations, Eliot certainly remains one of Vonnegut's most admirable characters. At the end of the novel, when Eliot is brought to Dr. Brown's private mental hospital in Indianapolis after his final breakdown, these words are seen cut into the rim of a fountain there: "Pretend to be good always, and even God will be fooled" (255). Eliot, in trying to be good as best he knows how, has at least brought comfort to a few destitute souls who depended on him.

Eliot Rosewater is, in many ways, the opposite of Howard W. Campbell, Jr. in *Mother Night*. While Campbell pretends to be bad, hiding his goodness deep inside, Eliot pretends to be good, suppressing the unkind parts of himself. And as Vonnegut points out again and again, we are what we pretend to be. Eliot's attempt at goodness, then, his great social experiment in human kindness, is characterized by Kilgore Trout as successful: "If one man can do it, perhaps others can do it, too," Trout explains. "It means that our hatred of useless human beings and the cruelties we inflict upon them for their own good need not be parts of human nature. Thanks to the example of Eliot Rosewater, millions upon millions of people may learn to love and help whomever they see" (269). Eliot's final act of adopting all 57 children he is said to have fathered in Rosewater County not only neatly solves the problem of Norman Mushari's lawsuit, but also is an astounding act of generosity, in which he pretends to be something he is not—a father. But Eliot's pretense, his intense desire to be good, to do the right thing, is what gives the novel its happy ending.

CHARACTERS AND RELATED ENTRIES

Avondale Avondale is the name of the upper-middle-class suburb of brick ranch houses built in a cornfield in Rosewater County. When Eliot and Sylvia Rosewater first return to Rosewater County to live, they are looked up to as royalty by the people of Avondale. Later, after the Rosewaters become champions of the poor, they become contemptible figures to the social climbers of Avondale.

Bella   The propietor of Bella's Beauty Nook in Rosewater, Indiana, Bella is a 314-pound woman who suffers a mild heart attack when Eliot Rosewater pushes the button setting off the fire horn he has bought the city, which is described as "the loudest fire alarm in the Western Hemisphere" (217).

Barry, Roland   Roland Barry is a young man who works at the Sunoco station in Rosewater, Indiana. Roland had suffered a nervous breakdown 10 minutes after being sworn into the army, and now receives a 100 percent disability pension and cannot speak above a whisper. Though Roland has visited Eliot Rosewater nearly every day for a year, Eliot cannot remember the young man's name on his way to the bus station for his farewell meeting with Sylvia, because Eliot had suffered a nervous breakdown himself after the visit from his father. Nevertheless, Roland thanks Eliot for saving his life and gives him a poem he has written in his honor.

Boyle, Sergeant Raymond   The hero of *Pan-Galactic Three-Day Pass*, a Kilgore Trout novel Eliot Rosewater reads in the bus station on his way to Indianapolis to see Sylvia, Sergeant Raymond Boyle is the only Earthling on an outer-space exploratory expedition. While on the trip, Boyle is given an emergency three-day pass back home and informed that the entire Milky Way has died in his absence.

Brown, Dr. Ed   The psychiatrist who treats Sylvia Rosewater after her nervous collapse, Dr. Ed Brown makes his professional reputation by a paper he writes describing her illness which he calls *samaritrophia*, or "hysterical indifference to the troubles of those less fortunate than oneself" (51). In the paper, Dr. Brown suggests that the cure, repressing Sylvia's social conscience and turning her into a shallow, pleasure-seeking person, might be worse than the illness itself. Dr. Brown appears again at the end of the novel when Eliot Rosewater becomes a patient at the same hospital where Sylvia had been treated previously.

Buntline, Amanita   Amanita Buntline is the wealthy lesbian in Pisquontuit, Rhode Island, who

showers Caroline Rosewater with gifts and attention. The two women spend many hours lunching at The Weir, the expensive restaurant owned by Bunny Weeks.

Buntline, Castor   Castor Buntline is the owner of a broom factory in Providence, Rhode Island, which is staffed completely by blind Union veterans of the Civil War. He hires George Rosewater to work in his factory and names a whiskbroom after him—the "General Rosewater" model. Having established the great Buntline fortune through his factory, Castor and his son Elihu move south to become carpetbagging tobacco growers.

Buntline, Elihu   Elihu Buntline is the son of Castor Buntline, broom factory owner and founder of the Buntline fortune. Using broom profits, father and son eventually move south and become tobacco farmers.

Buntline, Lila   The daughter of rich lesbian Amanda Buntline, Lila Buntline is a tall, "horse-faced" (13) 13-year-old who is the best sailor in the Pisquontuit Yacht Club. Lila is also the town's leading purveyor of pornography, buying all the steamy titles from the news store before anyone else sees them, and reselling them to her friends and classmates for a tidy profit. The pornographic picture Fred Rosewater finds under his son's pillow had been purchased from Lila Buntline.

Buntline, Stewart   Stewart Buntline is the rich heir of the Buntline fortune who is married to Amanita and is the father of Lila. Considered the best-looking man in Pisquontuit, Stewart has retreated into drink and dissolution after having been discouraged by his lawyer, Reed McAllister, from giving of all of his money away 20 years previously.

Calvin, Ned   Diana Moon Glampers praises Eliot Rosewater's healing skills in their phone conversation, reminding him that he has cured a twitch that Ned Calvin had in his eye since he was a little boy.

Campbell, Archibald   The leader of the Lowland Presbyterian Army, Archibald Campbell is also the eighth earl of Argyll, whose forces are defeated by Rosewater forbear James Graham in mid-17th-century Scotland. Archibald Campbell is a real historical figure whom Vonnegut incorporates into his novel.

Chaplain from *Pan-Galactic Three-Day Pass* The expedition chaplain in Kilgore Trout's novel *Pan-Galactic Three-Day Pass*, which Eliot Rosewater reads in the bus station on his way to Indianapolis to say farewell to Sylvia, informs Sergeant Raymond Boyle that the entire Milky Way has died. The chaplain is from the planet Glinko-X-3 and is described as "an enormous sort of Portuguese man-o'-war, in a tank of sulfuric acid on wheels" (250).

Commanding Officer from *Pan-Galactic Three-Day Pass* In the Kilgore Trout novel *Pan-Galactic Three-Day Pass*, which Eliot Rosewater reads in the bus station on his way to Indianapolis to say farewell to Sylvia, Sergeant Raymond Boyle's commanding officer is from the planet Tralfamadore, is about as tall as an Earthling beer can, and looks like a toilet plunger.

Deal, Selena Selena Deal works as the upstairs maid in the home of the Buntlines in Pisquontuit, Rhode Island. An 18-year-old orphan raised in an orphanage founded by the Buntlines in 1878, Selena is "a pretty girl who played the piano beautifully and wanted to be a nurse" (189). After working for the Buntlines for a month, Selena writes a letter to the head of the orphanage, explaining that it is difficult for her to stay with the Buntlines because of their condescending attitude and ignorance. The letter, however, does not have a complaining tone, but is sweet and self-reproaching. Selena closes by saying maybe she is too wicked to realize how wonderful Pisquontuit really is and that "maybe this is a case of pearls before swine" (194), evoking the novel's subtitle.

Ewald, Lincoln An "ardent Nazi sympathizer during the Second World War" (240), Lincoln Ewald operates a small stand in Rosewater, Indiana, that sells shoelaces, razor blades, soft drinks,

and newspapers. Though Eliot does not recognize Lincoln when he passes him on his way to the bus station to visit Sylvia, he good-naturedly returns Lincoln's greeting of "Heil Hitler."

Finnerty, Noyes A former high school basketball star in Rosewater, Indiana, Noyes Finnerty had strangled his 16-year-old wife for infidelity in 1934 and was sent to prison for life. Paroled at the age of 51 with the help of Eliot Rosewater, Noyes works as a janitor in Charley Warmergran's insurance office. When Eliot comes into the office on his way to the bus station to visit Sylvia, Noyes realizes that something momentous has happened to Eliot. Noyes explains that he believes Eliot has heard "the big click," a phenomenon Noyes learned about in prison, when he would see men suddenly calm down after years of criminal behavior.

Fleming, Pearl A resident of Rosewater, Indiana, Pearl Fleming supposedly threw her crutch away after a meeting with Eliot Rosewater. Diana Moon Glampers uses this incident as evidence that Eliot is better than any doctor in the town.

Get With Child a Mandrake Root *Get With Child a Mandrake Root* is a novel written by Arthur Garvey Ulm, an impoverished poet Eliot Rosewater meets at a cocktail party in New York. Eliot writes Ulm an enormous check after Ulm tells Eliot he wants to be free to tell the truth no matter what his economic situation. After receiving the check, Ulm tries hard to discover what Eliot wants him to write about, but Eliot merely insists on the truth and ends up humiliating the obsequious poet. Fourteen years later, Eliot receives in the mail the manuscript for *Get With Child a Mandrake Root*, which turns out to be 800 pages of violent pornography.

Glampers, Diana Moon A 68-year-old virgin who is one of Eliot Rosewater's best clients at the Rosewater Foundation in Indiana, Diana Moon Glampers is described as "ugly, stupid and boring" (73). A lonely woman whom nobody has ever loved, Diana is afraid of electricity since both her parents were killed by lightning, and she has chronic kidney trouble. She utters the book's title,

"God bless you, Mr. Rosewater," after being comforted by him on the phone one evening. Diana Moon Glampers, interestingly, also appears as the Handicapper General in Vonnegut's short story, "Harrison Bergeron."

Graham, James   The father of John Graham who adopts the family name of Rosewater as a pseudonym during the Puritan Revolution, James Graham was an ardent royalist whose title is the fifth earl and first marquis of Montrose. Also a poet who led an army into the Scottish highlands, James was hanged in 1650.

Graham, John   See Rosewater, John, 1, below.

Herald, Randy   Randy Herald is the showgirl depicted on the cover of the tabloid newspaper *The American Investigator* that is read by the men in the news store in Pisquontuit, Rhode Island. The headline over Miss Herald's picture declares: "I want a man who can give me a genius baby!" (136). When the men at the news store begin to joke about helping Randy Herald with her request, Fred Rosewater uses the opportunity to praise their "brides," and to mention that loving husbands protect their brides with hefty insurance coverage.

Herrick, Cleota   Cleota Herrick is the wife of Noah Rosewater, one of Eliot Rosewater's Civil War–era ancestors. Noah marries Cleota because, although she is the "ugliest woman in Indiana" (7), she has $400,000, which Noah uses to expand his munitions factory and buy more farms.

Leech, Leonard   Leonard Leech was Norman Mushari's favorite professor at CORNELL UNIVERSITY Law School. Leech told Norman that, in order to get ahead in law, a lawyer should look for situations where large amounts of money are about to change hands. A good lawyer can get a portion of such sums for himself. Leech thus inspires Norman's meddling in the Rosewater affairs.

Leonard, Dawn   In her phone conversation with Eliot Rosewater, Diana Moon Glampers tells him he is better than a doctor because he has cured

Dawn Leonard's boils, as well as other ailments suffered by poor townspeople.

Little, Sherman Wesley   A suicidal tool-and-die maker in Rosewater, Indiana, Sherman Wesley Little calls Eliot for help after seeing his name and phone number on a sticker in a phone booth. Little is a World War II veteran just laid off from his job; his second child suffers from cerebral palsy. Eliot awards him a Rosewater Fellowship of $300.

McAllister, Reed   A partner in the law firm of Mcallister, Robjent, Reed and McGee, Reed McAllister is the lawyer for Stewart Buntline of Pisquontuit, Rhode Island. McAllister had convinced the young, idealistic Stewart 20 years before the action of the book takes place not to give away all his money to help the poor. He still sends Stewart pamphlets touting the value of the free enterprise system from time to time.

McAllister, Thurmond   One of the partners in the law firm of McAllister, Robjent, Reed and McGee, Thurmond McAllister is described as "a sweet old poop who was seventy-six" years old (4). He is the main lawyer for Senator Lister Ames Rosewater and is present at the mental hospital at the end of the novel when Eliot Rosewater regains his senses. McAllister is the lawyer Eliot directs to draw up legal papers adopting 57 children of Rosewater County, Indiana.

Moody, Foxcraft and Melody   Foxcraft and Melody are the names Mary Moody gives her twins, whom she asks Eliot to baptize. At the end of the novel, Mary claims that Eliot is the true father of the twins.

Moody, Mary   A resident of Rosewater, Indiana, Mary Moody is one of the people helped by Eliot Rosewater's foundation. When Mary has twins, she asks Eliot to baptize them. Eliot plans to tell the babies at the baptism that there's only one rule he knows: "God damn it, you've got to be kind" (129). Later, after Eliot's mental collapse, Mary claims that he is the father of her twins, setting up a kind of hysteria among other women in

Rosewater County. By the end of the novel, more than 50 women claim that Eliot fathered their children as well.

Moon, Fletcher   Fletcher Moon is the local village idiot whom Noah Rosewater pays to fight in his place during the Civil War. Moon is killed by Stonewall Jackson's artillery at the second battle of Bull Run.

Mushari, Norman   A young lawyer of Lebanese extraction just out of Cornell University Law School, Norman Mushari is "the youngest, the shortest, and by all odds the least Anglo-Saxon male employee" (3) in the law firm of McAllister, Robjent, Reed and McGee. Because of these reasons, he is ignored and made fun of by the other employees in the firm. What his fellow lawyers do not know, though, is that Norman is scheming to get a chunk of the fortune of the Rosewater family, his firm's biggest client. To do this, he will need to prove that Rosewater Foundation president Eliot Rosewater is insane so that he will be expelled and the presidency passed on to distant cousins in Rhode Island, whom Norman hopes to represent. Toward the end of the novel, Norman travels to Rhode Island, where he meets Fred Rosewater and tells him that he is being swindled out of millions of dollars by his well-known relatives. Though Norman does represent Fred Rosewater in a lawsuit, he never makes the fortune he hopes for since Eliot Rosewater ends up adopting 57 children in Rosewater County to be his legal heirs.

Ned the Carpenter   Ned, whose last name is never given, is a carpenter in Pisquontuit, Rhode Island, to whom Fred Rosewater has sold insurance coverage. He is among the men who discuss the picture of Randy Herald in the tabloid newspaper in the Pisquontuit news store.

New Ambrosia   New Ambrosia is a former Utopian community described as having been situated in the southwest corner of Rosewater County. New Ambrosia's members "practiced group marriage, absolute truthfulness, absolute cleanliness, and absolute love" (46). Although the community has

disappeared by the time Eliot Rosewater returns to the area, the brewery they started, the home of Rosewater Golden Lager Ambrosia Beer, remains. Vonnegut's description of the brewery might be a nod to the fact that his own maternal ancestors had started a brewery in Indianapolis in the 19th century.

Oglethorpe, James E.   An actual historical figure, James E. Oglethorpe was the founder of the original U.S. colony of Georgia. In the novel, Oglethorpe convinces John Rosewater, an ancestor of the Rhode Island Rosewaters, to accompany him on his expedition to Georgia.

Parrot, Wilfred   Wilfred Parrot is the head of the orphanage in Pisquontuit, Rhode Island, where Selena Deal is raised. Parrot runs a happy orphanage; all of the children call him "Daddy," and he sees to it that each child learns to cook and dance and paint and play a musical instrument. Selena addresses the letter she writes from the Buntlines to "Daddy Parrot."

Peach, Delbert   A town drunk in Rosewater, Indiana, Delbert Peach goes to visit Eliot Rosewater right before Eliot is scheduled to leave on the bus for Indianapolis for his final farewell with Sylvia. Delbert insists that Eliot will never return to the town, though Eliot reassures him he will. As his parting gift to Eliot, Delbert swears off liquor forever.

Pena, Harry   A professional fisherman in Pisquontuit, Rhode Island, and also chief of the local volunteer fire department, Harry Pena was formerly an insurance salesman in Pittsfield, Massachusetts, who almost killed himself cleaning his living room rug with carbon tetrachloride. Harry becomes a fisherman when his doctor tells him he must work out of doors from then on or else die. A real man's man, Harry delights in working with his hands with the help of his sons. The wealthy patrons of The Weir, Bunny Week's restaurant, often watch Harry and his sons work as they eat. Bunny discloses to Amanita Buntline and Caroline Rosewater, though, that Harry is bankrupt and will soon lose his business. Bunny seems to admire Harry as the last of a dying breed—men who work honestly with "their hands and backs" (186).

Pena, Manny and Kenny Manny and Kenny Pena are the two big sons of Harry Pena, who work alongside their father on his fishing boat.

Pisquontuit Pisquontuit was an Indian chief who drank himself to death in 1638. The town of Pisquontuit, Rhode Island, where Fred Rosewater lives, is named after him.

Rosewater, Abraham Abraham Rosewater is the son of Faith Merrihue and George Rosewater, the blind Civil War veteran. Abraham becomes a Congregationalist minister who travels to the Congo as a missionary where he marries Lavinia Waters and has a son named Merrihue.

Rosewater, Caroline The wife of Fred Rosewater, Caroline Rosewater was a philosophy major in college who pities herself for being married to a man as "poor and dull" as Fred (155). As a result, she spends all her time drinking and shopping with a rich lesbian named Amanita Buntline even though she's snubbed by some of Amanita's friends, like restaurant owner Bunny Weeks.

Rosewater, Cynthia Niles Rumfoord The mother of Fred Rosewater, Cynthia Niles Rumfoord was a minor heiress when she married Merrihue Rosewater in Pisquontuit, Rhode Island. Her husband commits suicide after losing all his own as well as Cynthia's money in the stock market crash of 1929.

Rosewater, Eliot The novel's protagonist, Eliot Rosewater was born in 1918 to a life of ease and wealth. His father is a well-known U.S. senator, and his forbears are equally illustrious. Eliot attends Harvard Law School, serves in World War II with great distinction and earns a doctorate in international law. He marries Sylvia DuVrais Zetterling, an artistic Parisienne beauty, and settles in as president of the Rosewater Foundation. Soon, though, Eliot begins drinking heavily and wandering the

country, spending time with volunteer firemen and various down-and-out people he meets. Eventually he moves with Sylvia from Washington D.C. to Rosewater, Indiana, where he lives for five years, generously helping the poor and needy in the community. When Sylvia has a nervous collapse and leaves the town, Eliot moves into a seedy office and provides money, advice, and sympathy for the town's poor, lonely, and desperate citizens, achieving a status of near-sainthood among the people he helps. Eliot himself has a mental breakdown after a visit from his father. He loses a whole year of his life, returning to his senses in a mental hospital in Indiana, where he learns of the lawsuit being fought over his sanity. At the end of the novel, desiring to settle everything "instantly, beautifully, and fairly" (272), Eliot has legal papers drawn up, declaring 57 children in Rosewater County his legal heirs with full inheritance rights.

Rosewater, Eunice Eliot Morgan The former Eunice Eliot Morgan married Senator Lister Ames Rosewater and was Eliot Rosewater's mother. Women's chess champion of the United States in 1927 and 1933, Eunice also is the author of a historical novel about a female gladiator, *Ramba of Macedon.* Eunice died in a sailing accident in Cotuit, Massachusetts, in 1937, a catastrophe Eliot feels responsible for.

Rosewater, Faith Merrihue Faith Merrihue is a 14-year-old orphan who works as George Rosewater's "eyes and . . . messenger" (143) in Castor Buntline's broom factory after the Civil War. When Faith turns 16, George marries her, and the couple becomes the forebears of Fred Rosewater's line.

Rosewater, Franklin Described as an "unattractive, fat little boy" (137), Franklin Rosewater is the son of Fred and Caroline Rosewater of Pisquontuit, Rhode Island. When Fred finds a pornographic picture hidden under Franklin's pillow, he becomes so depressed that he contemplates suicide.

Rosewater, Fred Fred Rosewater is an insurance salesman in Pisquontuit, Rhode Island. Unaware of his family connection to the famous Rosewaters of Indiana until the arrival of Norman Mushari, Fred is a sad man who puts up a hearty front, but who often contemplates suicide. His wife, Caroline, does not respect him, preferring to spend all her time with a rich lesbian friend, and his son, Franklin, hides pornographic pictures in his room. In fact, it is only Mushari's arrival at his home that saves Fred from hanging himself. Mushari convinces Fred that the Indiana Rosewaters are trying to swindle him out of millions of dollars. With Mushari as his lawyer, Fred brings a lawsuit claiming that Eliot Rosewater is insane and that Fred should inherit control of the Rosewater Foundation. Though unsuccessful because Eliot adopts numerous children in the county, thus establishing a large group of legal heirs, Fred nevertheless receives a $100,000 check from the generous Eliot at the end of the novel.

Rosewater, Frederick, I   Frederick Rosewater, a distant ancestor to the novel's Fred Rosewater, was the third son of John Graham, also known as John Rosewater. Frederick is the direct ancestor of the Rhode Islander Rosewaters.

Rosewater, George   The younger brother of Eliot's great-grandfather, Noah Rosewater, George Rosewater is cheated out of his share of the family farm and saw factory by Noah while he, George, is off fighting in the Civil War. Injured in the war and promoted to general, George returns home blind but cheerful. He visits the families of each Rosewater County boy under his command during the war, "praising them all, mourning with all his heart for the boys who were wounded or dead" (141). George Rosewater eventually obtains a job in a broom factory, where the whisk broom called the "General Rosewater," a brand name that enters ordinary speech for a time, is named after him. George is the ancestor of Fred Rosewater's side of the family.

Rosewater, George, I   A distant ancestor of General George Rosewater, the blind Civil War hero, the first George Rosewater left the Scilly Islands in England in 1700 to go to London to become a florist.

Rosewater, Geraldine Ames Rockefeller   The former Geraldine Ames Rockefeller is the mother of Senator Lister Ames Rosewater and wife of Samuel Rosewater, Eliot's grandfather.

Rosewater, John, I   The Rosewater family was founded by John Rosewater when he arrived on St. Mary Island in Cornwall in 1645, accompanying the 15-year-old Prince Charles, who was later to become Charles II. Originally named John Graham, John chose the name Rosewater as a pseudonym, needed because he and the prince are fleeing the Puritan Revolution. Fred Rosewater reads this information in the family history written by his father, which had been collecting dust in the basement for many years.

Rosewater, John, II   The second John Rosewater is the younger son of George Rosewater, the ancestor who had gone to London in 1700 to become a florist. John was imprisoned for debt in 1731, but freed in 1732 by James E. Oglethorpe, who paid his debts on the condition that John accompany him to Georgia as chief horticulturalist. John Rosewater becomes the principle architect of the city of Savannah.

Rosewater, Lavinia Waters   The daughter of a Baptist missionary serving in the Congo, Lavinia Waters marries Abraham Rosewater. Lavinia dies giving birth to a son, Merrihue Rosewater.

Rosewater, Senator Lister Ames   Eliot Rosewater's famous father, Senator Lister Ames Rosewater, spends most of his adult life as a conservative politician serving in the U.S. Congress. His one regret in life is that his son, Eliot, throws over his wealth and connections to live among the poor and needy in Rosewater, Indiana, and consequently, the senator constantly schemes to pull Eliot away from this life. Visiting Eliot in his Rosewater office, the senator flies into a rage when, just out of a bath, the naked Eliot begins absentmindedly playing with his own pubic hair. The senator had earlier written a definition of obscenity called the Rosewater Law, which he considers his legislative masterpiece. One of the definitions of obscenity in the senator's law is any material that calls attention to bodily hair. His father's anger in this scene is at least partly what causes Eliot's final mental breakdown.

Rosewater, Merrihue Merrihue Rosewater is the son of missionary Abraham Rosewater and the former Lavinia Waters. When his mother dies giving birth to him, Merrihue is nursed by a Bantu woman. When Merrihue is still young, he returns to Rhode Island with his father, to the village of Pisquontuit. Merrihue becomes a realtor when he grows up and divides his father's land into lots. He marries Cynthia Niles Rumfoord, and the two become the parents of Fred Rosewater. Merrihue Rosewater shoots himself to death after losing all his money in the stock market crash of 1929.

Rosewater, Noah Eliot Rosewater's great-grandfather, Noah Rosewater is described as "a humorless, constipated Christian farm boy turned speculator and briber during and after the Civil War" (6–7). It is Noah who establishes the family fortune. After paying a village idiot to fight in his place during the war, he converts the family farm to the raising of hogs, and the family saw factory to the manufacturing of swords and bayonets, in the process cheating his younger brother, George, out of his share of the family inheritance. When he marries a homely but extremely wealthy woman, Noah is able to build his holdings into an empire.

Rosewater, Samuel The son of Noah Rosewater and the grandfather of Eliot Rosewater, Samuel Rosewater worked tirelessly for the Republican Party during his lifetime. He bought newspapers and preachers and taught that anyone who thought the United States was supposed to be a Utopia was a lazy fool.

Rosewater, Sylvia DuVrais Zetterling An artistic Parisienne from a good family, Sylvia DuVrais Zetterling marries Eliot Rosewater in Paris while he is recuperating from combat fatigue following his distinguished service in World War II. Initially sympathetic to Eliot's eccentricities and his love of the poor and downtrodden, Sylvia lives with Eliot first in Washington, D.C., then in Rosewater, Indi-

ana, for five years before she has a mental breakdown. Treated at a private mental hospital by Dr. Ed Brown, Sylvia is cured by having her social conscience repressed. She temporarily becomes a shallow, pleasure-seeker, flying to Paris and joining the international jet set for a period before she has a second nervous collapse. Following treatment this time, she becomes "silent and sad, almost unbearably deep again" (57). Though she wants to return to Rosewater out of a sense of duty, her doctor tells her such a move could be fatal. He advises her to instead divorce Eliot and build a life of her own. Sylvia takes the doctor's advice.

Rumfoord, Lance When Norman Mushari first arrives in Rhode Island on a visit to Fred Rosewater, he kills the afternoon by driving to Newport and touring the famous Rumfoord Mansion—a family and estate that appears in several Vonnegut novels, notably in *The Sirens of Titan*. On the tour, Mushari is offended by the way the six-foot, eight-inch-tall Lance Rumfoord "sneered whinnyingly at him" (195). As Mushari leaves the estate, Lance comes loping after him to tell Mushari that his mother guessed that Norman had once served as a sniper in the United States Infantry. Norman, though, denies having such a past.

samaritrophia *Samaritrophia*, or "hysterical indifference to the troubles of those less fortunate than oneself" (*God Bless You, Mr. Rosewater* 51), is the disease that Dr. Ed Brown diagnoses Eliot's Rosewater's wife, Sylvia DuVrais Zetterling, as having. Dr. Brown makes his reputation when he publishes an academic paper describing this disease.

Trout, Kilgore Kilgore Trout is the prolific science fiction writer who appears in several later Vonnegut novels, most notably in *Slaughterhouse-Five*, *Breakfast of Champions*, and *Timequake*. A personal hero of Eliot Rosewater, who is a huge science fiction fan, Kilgore Trout actually appears in person at the end of the novel. While Eliot was out of his senses for a year, he had told his father to contact Trout, who could explain why Eliot lived the life he did in Rosewater, Indiana. Though Senator Rosewater thinks Trout is simply a good public relations man, Trout explains quite truthfully that Eliot had been living out a social experiment while in Rosewater—trying to figure out how to love people who have no use.

Ulm, Arthur Garvey   Arthur Garvey Ulm is a poet to whom Eliot Rosewater gives $10,000 after Arthur tells him he wants to be free to tell the truth. Upon receiving the check, Ulm freezes and begs Eliot to tell him what to write about. Eliot then speaks sharply to Ulm, causing the poet to flee in tears. Years later, Ulm sends Eliot a copy of his about-to-be-published novel, *Get With Child a Mandrake Root.* Although Eliot does not remember him at all, Ulm's cover letter profusely thanks Eliot for forcing him to tell the truth about society. When Eliot turns to the novel itself to discover the truths Ulm burns to tell, he encounters trite, mildly violent pornography.

Unnamed Fisherman   On his way to the bus station to visit Sylvia, Eliot Rosewater meets an unnamed fisherman, a black man about his father's age, riddled with cancer, whom the Rosewater Foundation had given a grant to buy morphine. Eliot cannot remember the man's name or his troubles when he meets him.

Unnamed Lunch Counter Girl   When Ned the carpenter leaves behind a copy of *The American Investigator* in the news store in Pisquontuit, Fred asks an unnamed girl working behind the lunch counter who reads such trash. Although the girl "might have responded truthfully that Fred himself read it from cover to cover every week" (147), she is an idiot who notices nothing. Her only response is "Search me," something the narrator describes as "an unappetizing invitation" (148).

Unnamed New Egypt Fireman   On one of his drunken excursions across the country, Eliot Rosewater carouses with volunteer firemen in New Egypt, New Jersey. An unnamed fireman tells Eliot he must be crazy for wearing a suit he traded a bum for. Eliot replies that he doesn't want to look like himself but like the fireman, whom he calls "the salt of the earth" (26).

Unnamed Psychiatrist   Eliot, after one of his drunken excursions across the country, sobers up and enters psychoanalysis where he is treated by an unnamed psychiatrist. The psychiatrist resigns the case after a year, however, telling Sylvia that Eliot is untreatable because all he talks about in their sessions is history. Later in the novel, Senator Rosewater speaks to the same psychiatrist about his son, but will gain no insight into Eliot because the psychiatrist is, instead, interested in talking about the senator's own neuroses, especially in relation to his abhorrence of pubic hair.

Wainwright, Tawny   A 14-year-old girl made pregnant by her own stepfather, Tawny Wainwright is having her medical bills paid by the Rosewater Foundation. Eliot sees Tawny in the bus stop candy store, reading *The American Investigator,* when he is on his way to Indianapolis for his final farewell with Sylvia. Later, readers discover that Tawny is one of the Rosewater women who claim that Eliot Rosewater is the father of their babies.

Wakeby, Stella   Stella Wakeby is a resident of Rosewater, Indiana, who calls Eliot Rosewater for help one night, even though she had previously considered herself and her family to be more *Senator* Rosewater people than *Eliot* Rosewater people.

Warmergran, Charley   The fire chief of Rosewater, Indiana, Charley Warmergran is a close friend of Eliot Rosewater's. At the end of the novel, when Eliot has a mental breakdown after his father's visit to his seedy office, Charley realizes something is wrong because Eliot comes into his insurance office and begins to congratulate him for an award he received three years previously.

Weeks, Bunny   The owner of Pisquontuit's fanciest restaurant, The Weir, Bunny Weeks is a "tall homosexual from New Bedford" (173). His restaurant looks out on the fish traps of Harry Pena and his sons, and Bunny provides his patrons with opera glasses on the tables so that they may watch Harry at work. A close friend of Amanita Buntline, Bunny continually forgets who Caroline Rosewater is, though he's met her numerous times. Bunny

Weeks is the one who delivers the news to Amanita and Caroline that Harry Pena is bankrupt.

Weeks, Captain Hannibal The great-grandfather of Bunny Weeks, the owner of The Weir restaurant in Pisquontuit, Rhode Island, Captain Hannibal Weeks is famous as the man who finally killed Moby-Dick. Seven of the harpoons in Bunny's collection are said to have come from the hide of the great white whale.

Winters, Dr. Dr. Winters is the physician Diana Moon Glampers goes to see in Rosewater, Indiana. She complains to Eliot Rosewater that he treats her like a cow, that he's a drunk veterinarian, and that he tells her that her kidney trouble is all in her head.

FURTHER READING

God Bless You, Mr. Rosewater. New York: Dell, 1998.

Godshalk, William L. "Vonnegut and Shakespeare: Rosewater in Elsinore." *Critique* 15, no. 2 (1973): 37–48.

Leff, Leonard. "Utopia Reconstructed: Alienation in Vonnegut's *God Bless You, Mr. Rosewater.*" *Critique* 12, no. 3 (1971): 29–37.

Simpson, Josh. "'This Promising of Great Secrets': Literature, Ideas, and the (Re)Invention of Reality in Kurt Vonnegut's *God Bless You, Mr. Rosewater, Slaughterhouse-Five,* and *Breakfast of Champions* Or 'Fantasies of an Impossibly Hospitable World': Science Fiction and Madness in Vonnegut's Troutean Trilogy." *Critique* 45, no. 3 (2004): 261–271.

"Hal Irwin's Magic Lamp"

An odd little story, "Hal Irwin's Magic Lamp" is one of three stories that Vonnegut, in the "Coda" to *Bagombo Snuff Box,* says he rewrote substantially from their earlier magazine versions, because their original denouements were "so asinine" (349). The story was first published in *Cosmopolitan* magazine in June 1957. It was reprinted in *Canary in a Cat House* in 1961, but was the only story in that early collection not to reappear in 1968's *Welcome to the Monkey House.* The story, in revised form, did, however, make it into the 1999 collection, *Bagombo Snuff Box.*

SYNOPSIS

Hal Irwin builds his magic lamp, an old teapot rigged up with a doorbell buzzer, in his basement in INDIANAPOLIS in 1929. He plans to use it for an elaborate ruse he will play on his wife, Mary, the young woman he has been married to for two years. Hal works in a brokerage firm and has secretly made a fortune in stocks and bonds, but he has kept this information from Mary, who believes the couple is actually quite poor. Hal hires a local black woman named Ella Rice to come to his house and pretend to be a genie. He will have Mary rub the lamp while Hal wishes for big expensive items such as a new car and fancy house—things he has already bought and kept hidden from Mary. After each wish Hal makes, Ella says, "you got it," and one of the expensive new possessions is revealed to Mary. Needless to say, Hal's plan does not come off exactly as he had anticipated. Mary feels sorry for Ella, who is pregnant and in pain, and becomes angry at Hal for using her in the way he does. She is also a sensible, practical, and religious woman who does not mind being poor and enjoys doing her own housework and cooking. When she and Hal go to live in the new mansion, Ella comes with them. Mary lavishes more attention on Ella's newborn son, Irwin, than on her husband. When the stock market crashes later that year, Hal is wiped out and, realizing that Mary does not really love him anyway, jumps out of a seventh-story window. Destitute, Mary returns home to her father's farm, and Ella goes to the church where Irwin was baptized, where she is given food and a place to sleep.

COMMENTARY

This story, like "The Package," satirizes the notion that wealth can buy happiness. Just as Earl Fenton in "The Package" is a poor judge of character, completely misreading the motives of his old college friend Charley Freeman, Hal Irwin does not understand his wife, Mary, at all. Although his idea to build the magic lamp and surprise Mary could be viewed as sweet, Hal Irwin clearly missteps by keeping Mary in the dark about the couples' finances for the past two years. Ten years older than his wife, which allows him to "buffalo her about a lot of things" (340), Hal treats Mary in a patronizing way, giving her only a "piddling allowance" to run the house. He does not understand Mary's religious nature, her compassion for others, or her complete lack of interest in becoming rich. In fact, Hal's surprise for Mary completely backfires. In hiring Ella Rice, Hal betrays to Mary his callousness for the suffering of others as well as his racial insensitivity—he did not consider hiring a black man to play the role of genie because he is "scared of black men" (343). While Mary had never loved Hal, she had previously at least "managed to like him" (345). But she hates the new house and "gigantic car" so much "that she couldn't even like Hal anymore" (345) and their relationship falls apart. Thus, when the stock market crashes and Hal is ruined financially, he chooses to commit suicide, knowing that "he wasn't loved at home even in good times" (346). Back at her father's farm at the end of the story, Mary still worries about the homeless people she had seen in the black church where she left Ella Rice. Her father tells her that "the poor take care of the poor" (347), a line that brings the story to a close. The suggestion is that the rich, like Hal Irwin himself, do not do their duty by the poor, who are forced to fend for themselves.

CHARACTERS

Irwin, Hal   Hal Irwin works as "a customer's man in a brokerage house" (340), where he manages to amass a fortune that he initially keeps secret from his much younger wife, Mary. Hal's scheme to impress Mary with a new car and mansion and servants, however, backfires because he does not know his wife very well. When he loses everything in the stock market crash of 1929, Hal commits suicide by jumping out of a seventh-story window.

Irwin, Mary   Mary Irwin, who is 10 years younger than her husband, Hal, is a hard-working and empathetic young woman who has no desire to be rich. Unlike Hal, she cares about the plight of those poorer than herself and soon becomes more attached to Ella Rice and her baby, Irwin, than

she is to her husband, whom she grows to dislike. When Hal is ruined in the stock market crash and kills himself, Mary returns home to her father's farm to live.

Rice, Ella   Ella Rice is the black servant of a friend of Hal Irwin's. Hal initially hires Ella to dress up like a genie who will appear to answer the wishes he makes when he rubs his magic lamp. Yet, the pregnant and tired woman is quickly befriended by Hal's wife, Mary, who invites her to come live in the Irwin's brand-new mansion. When Hal kills himself after the stock market crash, both Ella and Mary are left destitute. Ella goes to the black church where her newborn baby, Irwin, had been baptized and where she is taken care of, along with numerous other needy people.

Rice, Irwin   Irwin Rice is the newborn son of Ella Rice, the black woman hired by Hal Irwin to play the role of genie. Hal's wife, Mary, soon grows to love the baby "ten times more" (345) than she loves her own husband.

FURTHER READING

Bagombo Snuff Box. New York: Berkley Books, 2000.
Reed, Peter. *The Short Fiction of Kurt Vonnegut.* Westport, Conn.: Greenwood Press, 1997.

Happy Birthday, Wanda June

Happy Birthday, Wanda June premiered off-Broadway in New York at the Theater de Lys (now the Lucille Lortel) on October 7, 1970. The production, starring Marsha Mason as Penelope Ryan, William Hickey as Colonel Looseleaf Harper, and Kevin McCarthy as Harold Ryan, ran through March 1971, closing after 143 performances only when an actor's strike shut down numerous off-Broadway theaters that year. Since then, the play has experienced significant revivals, including a New York staging in 1983 and Los Angeles productions in 2001 and 2004, all of which received generally favorable reviews. A movie version of the play, produced in 1971 fared less well. It was panned by

Full cast photo from 2001 Los Angeles production of *Happy Birthday, Wanda June,* directed by Robert Weide *(photo by Ed Krieger)*

critics as well as by Vonnegut himself, who wrote in his essay collection *Palm Sunday* that he tried, unsuccessfully, to remove his name from the credits. Partly a rewriting of Homer's epic THE ODYSSEY and partly a response to the VIETNAM WAR, still raging at the time, *Happy Birthday, Wanda June* questions traditional western notions of masculinity and heroism, finally offering a scathing critique of HEMINGWAY-like machismo.

SYNOPSIS

Happy Birthday, Wanda June is the story of Penelope Ryan, the beautiful, 30-year-old wife of macho big-game hunter Harold Ryan. As the play opens, Harold has been missing for eight years, his plane having crashed in the Amazon rain forest, and is presumed dead. Penelope is being pursued by two suitors: gentle, peace-loving doctor Norbert Woodly and vacuum cleaner salesman Herb

Shuttle, who worships the memory of Harold Ryan. Penelope also has a 12-year-old son, Paul, who resents his mother's suitors and longs for the return of the father he does not quite remember. Shuttle, to appease Paul on the anniversary of his father's birth, buys a left-over bakery cake with the inscription, "Happy Birthday, Wanda June" written on it. He plans to scrape the words *Wanda June* off the cake and present it to Paul. Audience members soon discover that Wanda June is a ghost in heaven; she is a 10-year-old girl run over and killed by an ice cream truck on her birthday. The action of the play occasionally reverts to Wanda June and other ghosts, who make comments from heaven.

Harold Ryan and his sidekick, Colonel Looseleaf Harper, return to Penelope's apartment very late the same night as the play's action begins. Ryan turns out to be an angry, sexist, and violent oaf who smashes Dr. Woodly's 200-year-old violin, chases Penelope out of the apartment, and tries to turn his son, Paul, into a man by buying him a gun and teaching him to curse. His cruelty eventually turns even his friend Looseleaf Harper and the adoring Herb Shuttle against him a few days after his return. The play ends with a confrontation between Penelope, who has returned to the apartment to gather her clothes, Dr. Woodly, who has come back to the Ryan apartment to face his rival, and Harold Ryan himself. Penelope snatches up the gun that Ryan has bought for Paul and orders both men to leave the apartment, but Ryan takes the gun from her and shoves Penelope and young Paul out the front door. In the struggle that ensues between Ryan and Woodly, the doctor unnerves the older, more violent man by calling him "comic." Deflated, Ryan attempts to shoot himself with the gun that had been trained on Woodly. Yet, he fails even in this attempt, missing his shot at the end.

COMMENTARY

Happy Birthday, Wanda June is, at its heart, a retelling of Homer's classic poem *The Odyssey*. Like Odysseus in the Homerian epic, Harold Ryan has been wandering far from home for many years while his wife, Penelope, waits for him. Both women are courted by suitors during their husband's absence, and both have a son who is eager for his father's return. In a letter to Robert Weide, the producer and director of the 2001 Hollywood staging of *Wanda June*, Vonnegut comments on the Homerian backdrop of his play:

> I once led a Great Books Study Group on Cape Cod, and we read and discussed Homer's *Odyssey*. I found the behavior of Odysseus after arriving home unexpectedly from the Trojan War hilariously pig-headed and somehow Hemingway-esque. And then I remembered the blowhard father of a girl I dated in high school, who had heard of huge rubies to be found in the Amazon Rain Forest, and wanted to quit his job and go look for them. The rest is history.

In *Wanda June*, Vonnegut sends up the classic western model of a male hero, from Odysseus to Hemingway: macho fighters and killers who love

and leave many women. Harold Ryan, who brags about the men he has killed in war, the animals he has killed on safari, and the women he has slept with (among them three ex-wives) fits this mold well. Yet, in the play, he clearly proves himself a violent boor whom nobody can stand to be around for long. To contemporary readers and viewers, the character comes off as almost a cartoonish stereotype of a male chauvinist when he commands Penelope to prepare him breakfast after the cook quits her job: "You're a woman, aren't you," he demands, "Then we *have* a cook" (50). The world has changed in the eight years that Harold has been gone—presumably from 1962 to 1970, since the play seems to be set contemporaneously with the time it is written. Traditional gender roles, in particular, have begun to be transformed with the rise of the women's liberation movement, and Penelope has grown accustomed to exerting her independence in the interval.

Set in 1970, the play is also read by most critics as a critique of the violence taking place during the Vietnam War era. In Penelope's opening lines, she introduces *Happy Birthday, Wanda June* as "a simple-minded play about men who enjoy killing—and those who don't" (5). Contrasted with Harold Ryan and his admirer, Herb Shuttle, is Penelope's suitor and possible fiancée, Dr. Norbert Woodly, a gentle peacenik replete with love beads and hippie attire in many productions, who finds it "disgusting and frightening that a killer should still be a respected member of society," and who argues that "gentleness must replace violence everywhere, or we are doomed" (5). Woodly represents a new type of hero. Penelope recognizes this when she tells her husband that "the old heroes are going to have to get used to this . . . the new heroes who refuse to fight. They're trying to save the planet. There's no time for battle, no point to battle anymore" (69). Yet, Vonnegut also shows that the roots of the old machismo run deep. Even the forward-looking, globally aware, and environmentally concerned Woodly returns to the Ryan apartment at the end of the play to face his rival. Penelope, who has grown to abhor macho heroics, condemns *both* Harold Ryan and Dr. Woodly when she calls the two men "disgusting" (72).

She tells Woodly that she loved him when he stayed away, but that she hates him for returning "like a federal marshal in a western film . . . high noon in the Superbowl" (72). Finally, despite the loaded gun that appears onstage, Woodly wins his battle with Ryan through words, not through violence. He deflates the aging hunter when he tells Harold how "comical" he appears to men like Woodly. The play ends with an impotent, seemingly shrunken Harold unable to even use violence against himself. He tries to shoot himself, but somehow misses as the shuffleboard-playing ghosts in heaven—10-year-old Wanda June, Nazi officer Siegfried Von Konigswald, and Harold's ex-wife, Mildred, who serve as a sort of Greek chorus commenting on action both human and divine—look on.

CHARACTERS

Harper, Colonel Looseleaf Colonel Looseleaf Harper is the idiotic sidekick of big-game hunter and adventurer Harold Ryan. Harper, also a very minor character in Vonnegut's 1973 novel, *Breakfast of Champions*, is said to be the pilot who dropped the ATOMIC BOMB on Nagasaki, Japan. He, along with his friend Ryan, has been held captive by Indians in a jungle for the past eight years. Although mentally deficient, Harper proves himself to be a kinder man than Ryan and ultimately rejects the violent hunter's cruel behavior.

Mildred Mildred is Harold Ryan's third ex-wife. Like Major Von Konigswald and Wanda June, she appears in the play as a ghost in heaven. A tough, voluptuous alcoholic, Mildred tells Von Konigswald that Harold drove each of his first three wives to drink because he suffered from premature ejaculation.

Ryan, Harold Harold Ryan is a 55-year-old big-game hunter. A hard-drinking, violent, and womanizing man who has been married four times, Harold has been missing for the past eight years after his plane went down in the Amazon rain forest on an expedition to hunt for diamonds with his sidekick, Colonel Looseleaf Harper. When he finally returns home, he discovers that his wife,

Penelope, is being courted by various suitors and is possibly engaged to one of them. Despite his bluster and violence, Harold Ryan is broken at the end of the play by the gentle Dr. Norbert Woodly, who calls him "comic."

Ryan, Paul Paul Ryan is the 12-year-old son of Penelope and Harold Ryan. Paul does not know his father, since the man has been missing and presumed dead since Paul was four years old. Resentful of his mother's suitors, Paul romanticizes his missing father and longs for his return. Yet, when Harold actually does return, he is cruel to Paul, alternately ignoring the boy and baiting him about being a "man." Confused and somewhat dazed at the end of the play, Paul refuses to shoot his father, even though Harold eggs him on.

Ryan, Penelope Penelope Ryan is the beautiful, 30-year-old fourth wife of big-game hunter Harold Ryan. Having married Harold when she was very young and working as a car-hop at a hamburger restaurant, Penelope has not seen her husband for eight years. When he returns, Penelope, much changed in the interval, is horrified by the man she married so long ago. Yet, her affection for Dr. Norbert Woodly also evaporates when he returns to the Ryan apartment at the end of the play. She abhors the violence that she expects will result from the encounter between the two men. Viewers last see Penelope when she is pushed out of the apartment with her son, Paul. It appears that none of the rivals vying for her affection will play a role in her future.

Shuttle, Herb Herb Shuttle is a vacuum cleaner salesman who courts Penelope Ryan. He is also an ardent admirer of her missing husband, big-game hunter Harold Ryan. At first enchanted by Harold when he returns, Herb Shuttle eventually discovers the extent of Harold's cruelty. Disillusioned, Herb exits the plays, warning Harold that he will not have any remaining friends if he continues to treat people so callously.

Von Konigswald, Major Siegfried Major Siegfried Von Konigswald, seen as a ghost in the play, was a notorious Nazi officer known as the Beast of Yugoslavia. He reminisces for audience members about having been killed by Harold Ryan, who strangled the major with his bare hands. Despite his horrendous crimes in life, he nevertheless goes to heaven, where he plays shuffleboard with little Wanda June.

Wanda June Wanda June is a 10-year-old girl, killed by an ice-cream truck on her birthday. The only real connection she has with the characters in the play is that Herb Shuttle ends up buying the cake her parents ordered for her, but never picked up. Audience members see Wanda June after she is in heaven. As a ghost, she explains what heaven is like, and observes the action at the very end of the play when Harold Ryan attempts to shoot himself.

Woodly, Dr. Norbert Dr. Norbert Woodly is a gentle, nonviolent obstetrician who lives in an apartment across the hall from Penelope Ryan and has been courting her since her husband is missing and presumed dead. When Harold Ryan returns, Woodly initially leaves. He comes back at the end of the play, however, to confront Ryan. Penelope, surprisingly, does not admire him for this, but wishes he had stayed away from the violent confrontation that is sure to ensue. In their final struggle, Woodly ends up besting Harold Ryan by forcing the boisterous hunter to recognize himself for the comic stereotype he has become.

FURTHER READING

Happy Birthday, Wanda June. New York: Samuel French, 1971.

"Harrison Bergeron"

Easily Vonnegut's best-known and most anthologized story, "Harrison Bergeron" was first published in the *Magazine of Fantasy and Science Fiction* in 1961, reprinted in *National Review* in 1965, and then published as the second story in *Welcome to the Monkey House* in 1968.

SYNOPSIS

"Harrison Bergeron" is set in the United States in the year 2081, when absolute equality among citizens has been mandated by the 211th, 212th, and 213th Amendments to the Constitution. In order to achieve such equality, the office of the United States Handicapper General supplies handicaps to those Americans who are smarter, more talented, or better-looking than average. Highly intelligent people are forced to wear mental handicap radios in their ears, which transmit terrible noises whenever they start to think deeply about anything. Beautiful people are made to wear disfiguring masks or to mar their faces. Those deemed above average in other ways wear heavy metal weights attached to their bodies. The laws detailing these handicaps are strictly enforced, with hefty fines and prison times for anyone caught breaking them.

The story opens in the living room of George and Hazel Bergeron. George, whose intelligence is far above normal, wears a handicap radio and numerous weights. Hazel, who "had a perfectly average intelligence, which meant she couldn't think about anything except in short bursts" (7) is not required to wear handicaps. The Bergerons have a 14-year-old son, Harrison, who had been taken away by the Handicapper-General men in April. As George and Hazel are watching perfectly average ballerinas on television one day, a news flash comes on announcing that Harrison Bergeron has escaped from jail. Readers discover that Harrison is seven feet tall, extremely good-looking, and a genius; in other words, he is abnormal in every way.

Just as a police photograph of Harrison Bergeron is being displayed on the television, there is a terrible shriek and thundering noise like an earthquake and the real, live Harrison appears in the TV studio, loudly proclaiming, "I am the Emperor! . . . Everybody must do what I say at once!" (12). Harrison quickly tears away the heavy metal weights restricting his movement, rips off the tremendous pair of earphones and heavy spectacles designed to limit his ability to think, and removes the red rubber clown nose he is made to wear as well. Revealing a man beneath the handicaps who "would have awed Thor, the god of thunder" (12), Harrison then proclaims that he will choose his Empress. The most graceful of the ballerinas rises to her feet and pulls away her mask to reveal a woman of blinding beauty underneath. Harrison orders the musicians to play, then he and the ballerina begin to dance, breaking not only the laws of the land, "but the laws of gravity and the laws of motion as well" (13) as the two rise 30 feet into the air on each leap. As the couple kisses, suspended high in the air, the U.S. Handicapper General, Diana Moon Glampers, enters the studio with a double-barreled shotgun and shoots the Emperor and Empress to death.

The story closes back in the living room of George and Hazel Bergeron. After the shooting, their television tube burns out. Hazel turns to comment to George, but George has gone to the kitchen for a can of beer. When he returns, he notices that Hazel has been crying. Asked what she is crying about, Hazel responds that she is not quite sure: something sad on television. George, ever dutiful, tells her to forget sad things. "I always do," replies Hazel, and the couple resumes their life as if nothing unusual has happened.

COMMENTARY

Picking up on themes Vonnegut first explored in his 1959 novel, *The Sirens of Titan*, "Harrison Bergeron" depicts a state of equality in the America of 2081 that looks very much like the type of equality demanded by the Church of God the Utterly Indifferent in *Sirens*. In both cases, those who are above average in any way are made to wear physical handicaps on their bodies so as not to have an unfair advantage over those citizens less gifted than themselves. In addition, both works show characters who are kept from thinking by radio receivers—implanted in the skulls of the members of the Martian Army in *Sirens*, and worn over the ear by people with above-average intelligence in "Harrison Bergeron." Both works depict the American ideal that "all men are created equal" gone amok. As in many of Vonnegut's works, "Harrison Bergeron" creates a Utopia that misfires, leading to more social problems than are cured.

Clearly the equality that has been achieved in 2081 in "Harrison Bergeron" is a perfectly uniform mediocrity. Vonnegut especially decries the squashing of artistic and intellectual talent and

ability demanded by his futuristic America, as the show being televised in the Bergeron's living room depicts a ballet performed by handicapped artists in a broadcast controlled by the government. Readers sympathize with sensitive and intelligent George Bergeron, who cringes in pain when horrifying sounds play over the radio receiver he is forced to wear over his ear. Vacuous Hazel Bergeron makes readers shudder at the specter of the "average" American, a creature Vonnegut describes as unable to think "about anything except in short bursts" (7). Diana Moon Glampers, the U.S. Handicapper General, seems vicious and vengeful in her shooting of Harrison and the ballerina. The very ludicrousness of the attempts to average out society, as in *Sirens of Titan*, clearly satirizes what Vonnegut sees as a human tendency to despise those more gifted than themselves—the hypocrisy of an America that purports to celebrate individuality, yet rewards mediocrity.

For all these reasons, it may be tempting to read "Harrison Bergeron," as many critics do, in the context of U.S.–Soviet relations during the cold war, and thus as presenting a warning against the erasure of individuality associated with communistic forms of government. Nevertheless, as Darryl Hattenhauer points out, this reading oversimplifies the story and ignores political opinions asserted by Vonnegut elsewhere in his work. Certainly in novels such as *Breakfast of Champions*, where Vonnegut describes communism as "a theory that what was left of the planet should be shared more or less equally among all the people" (12), he seems more sympathetic to SOCIALISM than he does to capitalism, which he describes as a system in which "everybody . . . was supposed to grab whatever he could and hold on to it" (13). It is also important to remember that Vonnegut's Utopias always fail, despite the good intentions of those who try to create them. One of the reasons it is so tempting to read "Harrison Bergeron" as an anticommunist manifesto is because we never see the world before 2081—we are thrust into the action when the 211th, 212th, and 213th Amendments to the Constitution have already been passed, and the Handicapper General has already been at work for quite a while. Unlike other Vonnegut works, in

"Harrison Bergeron" we see the bad results without the good intentions.

Though the future depicted in "Harrison Bergeron" is chilling, the story is also quite funny in its wild exaggerations. Fourteen-year-old Harrison is not only a smart, handsome boy; he is seven feet tall, devastatingly good-looking, and a genius. Harrison does not simply dance with the "blindingly beautiful" (12) ballerina; the two leap into the air so joyfully and gracefully that they reach the ceiling and pause suspended 30 feet above the ground, breaking not only the laws of the land, but the laws of gravity as well. Readers might begin to suspect that Vonnegut, whose son Mark was 14 years old just like Harrison when the story was published, might be poking a bit of fun at the grandiose self-importance of adolescent males who often feel like misunderstood geniuses by the authority figures surrounding them. While Vonnegut clearly satirizes a society that strives so hard to be equal that it ends up worshipping mediocrity, Harrison's behavior when he bursts into the television studio shows that a society completely accepting of unequal abilities might not be that much better. When Harrison frees himself from the handicaps that hold him back, he does not announce that he will release others from their fetters or that he will work to make America better for everyone; he proclaims himself Emperor, adding, "Everybody must do what I say at once!" He intends to set up a kingdom with himself as absolute ruler, even choosing an Empress and promising to make barons and dukes and earls of the musicians who play well. In a darkly funny way, Harrison epitomizes the teen rebel popularized in such 1950s films as *Rebel Without a Cause* and *The Wild One*.

Diana Moon Glampers, however, the gun-toting authority figure, shoots Harrison and his Empress dead, causing their adolescent dream of rebellion to come crashing down alongside their physical bodies. When readers return to George and Hazel Bergeron's living room, the dramatic events on television have somehow caused the tube of the Bergerons' TV set to blow out. Many critics read Hazel's inability to recall exactly what the "real sad" (14) thing she saw on the television was, even though she herself is handicap-free, as indicative

of the medium's mind-numbing effects. Americans, Vonnegut suggests, watch television like zombies, fascinated and even hypnotized by what they see onscreen, but also shutting down their thinking while under the television's spell. The most frightening part of this story may well be the ease and lack of emotion with which the tie between parents and child, a bond supposedly strong and instinctual, is broken. The story ends with Hazel cheered up, comforted by George's advice to forget anything sad she might have seen, which in this case is the murder of her own son. Things have returned to the status quo as Hazel turns her attention again to the transmitted noises George is receiving over his radio-earphone, stupidly repeating her comment that "that one was a doozy" (14).

CHARACTERS

Ballerina   When the news flash comes in that Harrison Bergeron has escaped from jail, a ballet is being broadcast on television. One of the ballerinas, clearly stronger and more beautiful than the others because of her hideous mask and heavy handicaps, reads the actual announcement when the newsman stutters over his words. When Harrison Bergeron himself comes crashing into the studio, proclaiming himself Emperor, this same ballerina rises up to cast off her handicaps and become his Empress. The two leap gracefully and joyfully into the air, embracing and kissing 30 feet above the ground before being shot to death by Handicapper General Diana Moon Glampers.

Bergeron, George   George Bergeron is the father of genius teenage outlaw Harrison Bergeron. A man of high intelligence, George is burdened by pounds of lead weight attached to his body and is forced to wear a mental handicap radio in his ear, which transports unbearable noises when he tries to think deeply about any subject. Thus, he has trained himself not to think much at all. He misses the drama of his son proclaiming himself Emperor and getting shot on TV because he is in the kitchen getting a can of beer. Although his wife, Hazel, is crying when he returns, she is unsure why. George tells her to forget anything sad she might have seen on television.

Bergeron, Harrison The story's title character, Harrison Bergeron is a 14-year-old genius who is so good-looking, smart, and talented that he's forced to wear more handicaps than anyone else in the country. Readers learn early in the story that he's recently been taken from his home by the Handi-capper General. Readers first see Harrison Bergeron as he crashes into the television studio where his jail escape has just been announced. On live TV, he tears away his handicaps, proclaiming himself Emperor. When a ballerina consents to be his Empress, the two dance, leaping into the air "in an explosion of joy and grace" (13). As Harrison and the ballerina kiss while suspended in air, 30 feet above the ground, the Handicapper General rushes into the studio and shoots the young couple dead.

Bergeron, Hazel Harrison Bergeron's mother, Hazel Bergeron is a woman of ordinary intelligence who, in fact, seems to be average in every way. Thus, unlike her more gifted husband and son, she is not required to wear limiting handicaps. A kindly but dim woman, Hazel witnesses the death of her son on television and is saddened by it. However, she is unable to sustain any thought for very long and cannot explain to her husband, George, why she is crying when he returns from the kitchen. Vaguely realizing that she saw something sad on television, she immediately concedes to her husband's admon-ishment to forget about it and happily returns to her ordinary life.

Glampers, Diana Moon Diana Moon Glampers holds the position of Handicapper-General in the year 2081, when the story is set. She is in charge of determining the handicaps that individuals with above average intelligence, looks, or talent must wear. When Harrison Bergeron escapes from jail, bursts into a television studio, rips away his handicaps, and dances joyfully with his Empress, the ballerina, Diana Moon Glampers shoots the couple to death with a double-barreled shotgun. Diana Moon Glampers is also the name of a very different character in Von-negut's novel *God Bless You, Mr. Rosewater.*

Handicapper General The Handicapper Gen-eral is a government officer whose job is to supply handicaps to American citizens who are smarter, better-looking, or more physically capable than average. People with above-average intelligence are forced to wear radio antennas that make it difficult to think; beautiful people wear disfiguring masks; and strong people wear heavy weights attached to their bodies. The idea behind this policy is to make everyone perfectly equal so that no Americans feel bad about themselves.

Television Announcer As George and Hazel Bergeron are watching television in their living room, an announcer breaks into the ballet being broadcast with an important news bulletin. How-ever, like all television announcers in the year 2081, he has a serious speech impediment. The announcer, after excitedly trying to get out the words "Ladies and gentleman" for a half minute, turns the bulletin over to one of the ballerinas, who reads out loud to the audience the news of Har-rison Bergeron's escape from jail.

FURTHER READING

Hattenhauer, Darryl. "The Politics of Kurt Vonnegut's 'Harrison Bergeron'." *Studies in Short Fiction* 35, no. 4 (1998): 387–392.
Reed, Peter. *The Short Fiction of Kurt Vonnegut.* West-port, Conn.: Greenwood Press, 1997.
Welcome to the Monkey House. New York: Dell, 1998.

Hocus Pocus

Published in 1990 by Putnam, *Hocus Pocus*, like Vonnegut's earlier novels *Mother Night* (1962) and *Jailbird* (1979), depicts a basically decent, but flawed main character who becomes corrupted by historical events. While Vonnegut explores the SACCO AND VANZETTI case, World War II, the McCarthy Era, and the NIXON presidency in those two previous novels, the defining moment of his-tory in *Hocus Pocus* is the VIETNAM WAR. Eugene Debs Hartke ends up a career officer in the U.S. Army fighting in Vietnam nearly by accident, after a chance encounter with a recruitment officer at a state science fair when he is a high school senior changes his life plans. Like many Vonnegut characters, Hartke seems to be a prisoner of fate, locked in a downward spiral, a pawn of history rather than a shaper of it. *Hocus Pocus* continues Vonnegut's career-long critique of social injustice, war, violence, and bureaucratic ineptitude, as it asks important questions about the ability of individuals to determine their fate in the world.

SYNOPSIS

Chapters 1–6
Hocus Pocus is the story of Eugene Debs Hartke, who is writing the book as he sits in prison in Scipio, New York, awaiting trial for masterminding a prison break and assault on the town for which he is actually not responsible. Hartke is the son of a chemical engineer and homemaker who was raised in MIDLAND CITY, Ohio, the setting for many Vonnegut novels. Though he had wanted to attend the University of Michigan and study music, Eugene's father, knowing his son's commission will impress their friends and neighbors, convinces him to go to the United States Military Academy at West Point instead. After graduation, Eugene marries his best friend's sister, Margaret Patton, has two children, and embarks on a military career, serving several years in Vietnam, where he rises to the rank of lieutenant colonel and helps in the 1975 evacuation of Saigon. After this event Eugene resigns his commission in the army.

Chapters 7–18
Eugene returns to the United States when he is 35 years old. Sam Wakefield, a former commanding officer of his in Vietnam, who has become president of Tarkington College, a small school for learning disabled students in New York State, offers him a job teaching physics. Eugene gladly accepts the position, moving his wife and children and his mother-in-law, Mildred Patton, who is going slightly crazy by this time, to the Mohiga Valley. The Hartke family spends the next 25 years there. For the first 15 of these years, Eugene teaches at Tarkington College. Meanwhile, his wife Margaret, due to a family history of insanity, which neither she nor Eugene knew about when they married, has begun to go crazy as well. Eugene keeps both

Margaret and her mother, Mildred, at home, caring for the women, but embarrassing and alienating his children in the process. As grown-ups, neither one of the Hartke children speak to their father.

Having grown comfortable in his teaching position and continuing to take care of the two crazy women while having numerous affairs with women at the college, Eugene is surprised and devastated when, on graduation day of 1991, he is fired from his job by the Tarkington board of trustees. A student, Kimberly Wilder, daughter of conservative talk show host and newspaper columnist Jason Wilder, had been secretly tape-recording comments Eugene made to friends and students all over campus. Though often quite innocent, the comments are construed by Wilder and the board of trustees as wildly anti-American. But the evidence that makes Eugene's firing truly inevitable is a dossier of affidavits gathered by a private detective, which attests to Hartke's "having been a shameless adulterer" from the moment he and his family arrived in Scipio (149). It does not help matters that one of Eugene's most frequent tryst partners was Zuzu Johnson, the wife of college president, Henry "Tex" Johnson.

Chapters 19–34
On the same day that he is fired from his position at the college, however, Eugene discovers that the New York State Maximum Security Adult Correctional Institution at Athena, across the lake from Tarkington, is hiring teachers. He travels to the prison in a pick-up trip with John Donner, a man who is seeking a job teaching shop at the prison. Although Donner does not get the job, prison warden Hiroshi Matsumoto, a survivor of the atomic bombing of Hiroshima who feels a connection to Eugene because of his service in Vietnam, hires Hartke on the spot. Eugene works diligently at the high-security, Japanese-run prison for the next eight years, befriending many of the all-black inmates. He moves from Scipio into a house on the lake separating the prison and college, next door to Warden Matsumoto, whom he eventually comes to know and respect. However, on a cold night in the winter of 1999, a group of Jamaican drug dealers sets off bombs at the prison in an attempt to free

Jeffrey Turner, the head of their drug cartel, who is serving 25 consecutive life sentences. While the Jamaicans and Turner get away, the break ends up freeing all the inmates at Athena, since the Japanese guards, who regard their work as a business rather than a mission, do not put up a fight.

Chapters 35–38

After the Jamaicans' assault on the prison, a charismatic ex-drug dealer and murderer named Alton Darwin persuades a group of prisoners to follow him in an attack on the town of Scipio. Though most of the prison inmates simply return to the prison where they have food and shelter, Darwin's contingent makes it to Scipio, where they assault the town mercilessly. Numerous prisoners, townies, and college personnel are killed in the ensuing battle, which lasts two days. The victorious Darwin then sets himself up as president of a new country. Because he has taken the Tarkington College board of trustees hostage, Darwin believes government officials will negotiate with him and give him what he wants. Yet, Darwin ends up getting fatally shot by college president Tex Johnson while ice skating on the college ice rink. The entire rebellion is eventually suppressed when the 82nd Airborne Division of the U.S. Army, along with National Guard troops, are called in. During this time, Eugene Hartke has been unharmed by the prisoners, since they know and trust him from his years teaching at the prison. After the assault is quelled, his wife and mother-in-law are taken to an insane asylum in Batavia, New York, and an army lieutenant colonel named Harley Wheelock III names Hartke as the new mayor of the town of Scipio. In order that he will be respected, Harke is also given the rank of brigadier general in the National Guard.

Chapters 39–40

A few weeks later, the former Tarkington College is turned into a prison, and Hartke is chosen as the new warden. During his brief career as prison warden, Hartke meets his illegitimate son, Rob Roy Fenstermaker, the product of a brief affair he had with a war correspondent in the Philippines. Until the boy comes to visit Hartke in Scipio, he had no idea of his son's existence. Rob Roy has recently discovered that Hartke is his true father.

He has come to say good-bye before leaving the country, since he has just been acquitted of wrongful charges of child molestation stemming from his work in a free child care center he had set up and run in Dubuque, Iowa. Though he meets Rob Roy only once, Eugene feels closer to this son than he does to his legitimate children.

The novel ends with Eugene Hartke being dealt a double blow. First, he moves from prison warden to inmate when government officials begin to suspect that he had masterminded the entire prison break since he seemed to be on such good terms with the prisoners during the assault on Scipio. As he is writing his memoirs, Hartke is suffering from tuberculosis and awaiting trial. But perhaps even more devastating to him is the news of Hiroshi Matsumoto's suicide in Hiroshima, Japan. Hartke speculates that the suicide is a result of Matsumoto's having lived through the ATOMIC BOMB attack on Hiroshima so many years before. In the end, Hartke in prison is compiling two lists: the number of women he has slept with during his life, and the number of people he has killed during his years in the army. The final numbers on the lists are exactly the same. Hartke says that this is the number he wants carved on his tombstone when he dies.

COMMENTARY

The story of Eugene Debs Hartke is one of a much sinned-against and also much-sinning man who is coming to terms with past events while imprisoned, perhaps for the rest of his life. In this sense, the novel has much in common with *Mother Night*, in which we also read the memoirs of an imprisoned man with a violent, war-filled past awaiting trial. While Howard W. Campbell, Jr., served as a Nazi propagandist during World War II, however, Eugene Hartke's war was in Vietnam. But the guilt or innocence of both men is similarly debatable. Campbell certainly contributed to the Nazi war effort, developing terribly anti-Semitic propaganda although he was working as a secret American agent the whole time. Hartke, although wrongfully accused of masterminding the Athena prison break, nevertheless killed numerous civilians in Vietnam while complying with orders from his superiors. Thus, both men, who start out innocently enough as lovers of the arts, become corrupted by the machinery of war and must live with their own complicity with evil as best they can.

Like Howard W. Campbell, Jr., who starts out as an idealistic young playwright, Eugene Debs Hartke has a similar interest in the arts as a young man. A member of an all-white soul band during his high school years, Hartke's dearest wish is someday to be a jazz pianist. Although that ambition is never fulfilled, Hartke is at least given the opportunity to play the impressive Tarkington College Lutz Carillon, a huge set of bells controlled by a keyboard, an endeavor that provided him "the happiest moments in [his] life, without question" (7). But Hartke's life starts with idealistic promise in another way as well. Named for noted socialist, labor leader, and pacifist Eugene Debs (see SOCIALISM) at the behest of his maternal grandfather, Benjamin Wills, Hartke would seem to be destined to live a life dedicated to helping those less unfortunate than himself. Hartke's grandfather, a humble groundskeeper at Butler University and a socialist himself, makes Eugene memorize, before he is eight years old, the best-known words of his famous namesake: "While there is a lower class I am in it. While there is a criminal element I am of it. While there is a soul in prison I am not free" (2). So, like Howard W. Campbell, Jr. of *Mother Night*, Eugene Hartke's early life shows promise of great things to come.

Nevertheless, both men are soon corrupted by war. Campbell, who at first refuses to be politically involved, writing plays about idealized romance and ignoring the ever-increasing brutality surrounding him, is recruited as an American spy and does such a good job of pretending to be a Nazi that it becomes impossible to tell which side he helps more: the Allies or the Third Reich. Hartke's Vietnam experiences are similarly damaging. To his surprise, even though he never wanted to be a professional soldier, he turns out to be a good one. Hartke writes that during the years he was a commissioned officer in the U.S. Army, he "would have killed Jesus Christ Himself or Herself or Itself or Whatever, if ordered to do so by a superior officer" (2). In fact, he adds that there was a "microscopic

possibility" that he had actually "called in a white-phosphorus barrage or a napalm air strike on a returning Jesus Christ" (2). Although he is wrongly accused of masterminding the Athena prison break, he writes that, in Vietnam, he "really was the mastermind" (153). He explains, "During my last year there, when my ammunition was language instead of bullets, I invented justifications for all the killing and dying we were doing which impressed even me! I was a genius of lethal hocus pocus!" (154). The novel's title suggests illusions created when lies are told to make things seem better than they actually are. Hartke himself learns to become quite an accomplished liar, both in his personal and his professional life. He not only tells outrageous lies to Harriet Gummer, the war correspondent who will become the mother of his illegitimate son, Rob Roy Fenstermaker, but like Howard W. Campbell, Jr., he becomes an expert at propaganda. "And during my final year in Vietnam, when I was in Public Information," Hartke writes, "I found it as natural as breathing to tell the press and replacements fresh off the boats or planes that we were clearly winning, and that the folks back home should be proud and happy about all the good things we were doing there" (27). Hartke participates fully in the public relations deceptions practiced by his government in Vietnam.

Perhaps the most disturbing hocus pocus involving the Vietnam War, given the class-consciousness instilled in Hartke by his socialist grandfather, is the government's ability to make vanish the high cost of war paid by the lower classes. Hartke speaks of the dead American soldiers, "teenagers mostly, all packaged and labeled and addressed on loading docks in Vietnam" (31). He speculates that very few Americans "knew or cared how these curious artifacts were actually manufactured" (31). Asserting that he is really fired from Tarkington College because of his "ugly, personal knowledge of the disgrace that was the Vietnam War" (99), Hartke also points out that none of the Tarkington trustees and none of their sons and daughters had been sent to Vietnam. In the prison, however, and in the town of Scipio, "there were plenty of somebody's sons who had been sent over there" (99). The sons of the poor come home in those neat packages Hartke described earlier. And, even more, in his position as an officer, who eventually had thousands and thousands of inferiors to whom he gave orders, Hartke himself, named for champion of the poor and pacifict Eugene Debs, acted in the interests of the exploiter class. "You know who was the Ruling Class that time?" (253), Hartke asks after relating a story about pitching a hand grenade into a tunnel and killing a woman, her mother, and her baby, "Eugene Debs Hartke was the Ruling Class" (253).

Hartke's tragic Vietnam experiences, in fact, cause him to begin to romanticize World War II as a "good war" in a way that often occurs in Vietnam War literature. Hartke longs to have fought in the earlier war. Speaking about Ernest Hubble Hiscock, the former Tarkington student killed in World War II while serving as a Navy nose-gunner, Hartke says: "I would have given anything to die in a war that meaningful" (57). Hartke's idealization of World War II is related to the class issues that so disturb him in relation to Vietnam. While he views American involvement in Vietnam as relying disproportionately on the sons of the poor, he discovers, in reading about World War II, that "civilians and soldiers alike, and even little children, were proud to have played a part in it" (167). He continues, "It was impossible, seemingly, for any sort of person not to feel a part of that war, if he or she was alive while it was going on. Yes, and the suffering or death of soldiers and sailors and Marines was felt at least a little bit by everyone" (167). While there is perhaps a germ of truth to these speculations, it is nevertheless important to note that Hartke only *reads* about World War II, while having actually experienced combat in Vietnam. Vonnegut's point is that it is easy to long wistfully for a war one only knows about through books. Certainly, elsewhere in his body of work, Vonnegut shows enough horrible atrocities occurring during World War II—schoolgirls being boiled alive in *Slaughterhouse-Five*, Jews being gassed and slaughtered in *Mother Night*—that a sanitizing idealization of that war becomes impossible. Perhaps the real problem for Hartke is that the Vietnam War seems anticlimactic as it follows the war he learns to think of as "the Finale Rack of so-called Human Progress" (204). This line comes from the SCIENCE FICTION story "The Protocols of

the Elders of Tralfamadore," which Hartke reads in his old copy of the pornographic magazine, *Black Garterbelt*. A Finale Rack is a fireworks term, referring to the piece of lumber that holds the profusion of explosives that are lit up to perform the grand finale in fireworks shows. If World War II truly was the Finale Rack of human progress, the Vietnam War is reduced to an afterthought.

As Hartke's life seems to spiral downward into war and violence, the dominant image in the novel becomes the perpetual motion machines commissioned by college founder Elias Tarkington. The beautiful, carefully crafted machines are designed with the utmost optimism; Elias "foolishly expected [the machines] to go on running, after he had given them an initial spin or whack, until Judgment Day" (13). Yet, the longest Hartke and his students can get any of the machines to run is a mere 51 seconds. To Hartke, "the restored devices demonstrated . . . how quickly anything on Earth runs down without steady infusions of energy" (14). The machines represent the novel's theme of antiprogress, of entropy even, the eventual winding down of things to an inert state of uniformity. *Entropy*, a term that originally comes from the field of physics, is a measure of the dispersal of energy in a system, sometimes referred to as disorder. The second law of thermodynamics states that in a closed system, entropy, or dispersal of energy, always increases. As particles exchange heat, the heat will become increasingly distributed over a number of particles until no heat is exchanged any longer; a uniform level of dispersal has been achieved. If a hot cup of coffee is left on the kitchen counter, eventually the coffee will become lukewarm, closer to the temperature of the surrounding air. A cup of coffee never spontaneously heats up. Writers of POSTMODERNISM, beginning in the late 1950s with Vonnegut's generation, borrowed the notion of entropy from scientific thought and used it to describe a world that seems increasingly chaotic and random, a world moving to a uniform sameness whether that be globalized mass culture, a general winding down of intellectual ideas, or the end of meaningful communication entirely. The notion of entropy has always been present in Vonnegut's work, from his depiction of the steady march through time toward death in

Slaughterhouse-Five, to the increasing disorder and eventual decay of the government in *Slapstick*, to the de-evolution of the human species in *Galápagos*. In *Hocus Pocus*, the perpetual motion machines suggest a futility, a downward spiral, which Eugene Hartke claims "can surely be applied to this whole ruined planet nowadays" (14). The single drawing in the book, repeated a number of times, is, in fact, a tombstone with different words printed on it. Vonnegut never lets readers forget that this is the direction all humans, and even the planet itself, are moving toward.

Because human beings in the novel are presented much like the perpetual motion machines, doomed to wind down, to reach an inevitable end, there is a great emphasis, as in all Vonnegut novels, on fate, on DETERMINISM, and on the lack of control human beings have over their own lives. In describing the founding and early history of Tarkington College, Hartke states that "accident after accident" made Tarkington "what it is today. . . . The 2 prime movers in the Universe are Time and Luck" (21). In addition, Hartke's own life direction is largely the result of accident. A chance encounter with Sam Wakefield, the army recruiter, at the Ohio State Science Fair changes Hartke's life forever. Hartke points out that if he had simply chosen another exit as that 18-year-old boy, his life could have led to the University of Michigan, to journalism and music-making, to a wife who did not go insane, and to children who loved and respected him. But because he chose the particular exit he did, his life led to war and prison. Perhaps the book's most significant indicator of the deterministic forces shaping human beings is the computer game GRIOT™. In the game, a person's age, race, education, present situation, drug use, and so on, are entered into the computer. GRIOT™ then spits out a story about what is likely to happen to that person, based on what has happened to real people with the same general attributes. Although amazingly prescient in most cases, the more poverty-ridden and oppressed a person's background, the more likely GRIOT™ is to predict their futures accurately. The Athena prisoners end up smashing the GRIOT™ game in the Pahlavi Pavilion because, after they punch in their statistics, the machine shows all of them

going to prison to serve long sentences. In *Hocus Pocus*, people are often presented as being prisoners of forces beyond their control. Accidents of their environment shape peoples' destinies, and FREE WILL does not play much of a part in how human lives turn out.

Yet, at the same time, there are characters who can live outside of the grim statistics of the GRIOT™ program. Helen Dole, a 26-year-old black physics Ph.D. who is interviewed for Eugene Hartke's old job at Tarkington College at the end of the novel is just such a character. Born in South Korea and raised in Berlin, Dr. Dole, though "as badly treated by many people over there as she would have been over here" (281), nevertheless escapes the worst of what it means to be black in America. "She didn't have to think every day about some nearby black ghetto where life expectancy was worse than that in what was said to be the poorest country on the planet, which was Bangladesh" (281–282). Although her overseas birth is certainly an accident of fate, not under her own control, Dr. Dole still asserts free will in her refusal to be the kind of placid teacher expected by the Tarkington board of trustees. When the board asks her to promise that she will never discuss politics or history or economics or sociology with her students, she blows up at them, pointing out that their inherited wealth is the product of class and race exploitation. Because Helen Dole refuses to fit stereotypical expectations, the members of the board of trustees, Jason Wilder included, do not have any idea how to respond to her. Hartke writes, "He may never have had to debate with a person whose destiny GRIOT™ would have described as unpredictable" (285). Helen Dole's insistence on looking reality in the face and telling the truth about it makes her a real teacher, not just a mouthpiece of the ruling class.

In his role as teacher, Eugene Hartke perhaps tries to atone for the sins he commits during the Vietnam War. At Athena Prison, he tried to give the most honest answer he could to any question put to him (90). "I simply described the truth of the inquirer's situation in the context of the world outside as best I could. What he did next was up to him" (90). Further, that is what Hartke calls being a real teacher. Denying that he was the "mastermind of a treasonous enterprise," Hartke explains that all he "ever wanted to overthrow was ignorance and self-serving fantasies" (90). In his honesty as a teacher, Hartke is overcoming the "hocus pocus" he delivered in Vietnam. However, Jason Wilder's definition of a teacher is very different from Hartke's. When Hartke is summoned before the board of trustees, Wilder calls him an "unteacher" (127) for being overly negative and pessimistic. Wilder objects particularly to the sign posted in the library above the exhibit of the perpetual motion machines: "THE COMPLICATED FUTILITY OF IGNORANCE." Focusing on the word *futility* especially, Wilder argues that such a slogan destroys students' self-esteem. Although Hartke points out that *ignorance* is the truly negative word in the sign, Wilder seems to want a teacher concerned more with puffing up the sons and daughters of the ruling class than a teacher concerned with overcoming ignorance. He advocates just the same kind of hocus pocus practiced in Vietnam—indulging in comforting lies to hide an ugly or unbearable truth.

As with most Vonnegut protagonists, Eugene Debs Hartke remains a puzzlingly ambiguous character. A man who starts out with promise and idealism, he is corrupted by war. Yet, his unflinching honesty, both as a teacher and in his account of his own life, goes at least partly toward mending the sins he committed as a professional soldier and undoing the hocus pocus of illusions with which Americans comfort themselves. Nowhere is the ambiguity of Hartke's character so well symbolized as in the two lists he keeps in prison: one of all the women he has made love to and the other of all the people he has killed. While lovemaking in Vonnegut's work is often depicted as a creative act, Hartke has committed an equivalent amount of destruction in the world. The two lists are exactly the same. How to interpret this fact? Do the killings and lovemakings balance each other out so that Hartke's ultimate effect on the world finally amounts to zero? Or is Vonnegut parodying the very notion that a human life can be reduced to a number? After all, Hartke does not simply *tell* readers the number he wants carved on his tombstone.

Afraid that readers, when they hear the number exists, will simply flip to the end of the novel "to learn the number in order to decide that it is too small or too big or just about right or whatever without reading the book," Hartke has devised "a lock to thwart them" (323). Rather than tell the number, he provides a complicated word problem that only those who have read the whole book will be able to solve. Perhaps Vonnegut is stating that a human life must be taken in its entirety, must be judged for what it is, not simply reduced to a number. Readers have to know his entire story in order to understand Eugene Hartke's character. Human character is a puzzle that cannot be solved easily or quickly by flipping to the end of a life and passing judgment.

CHARACTERS AND RELATED ENTRIES

Akbahr, Abdullah Abdullah Akbahr is imprisoned at Athena for murders committed during drug wars. When Eugene Hartke first meets him, he is reading a copy of the anti-Semitic work *The Protocols of the Elders of Zion*. Later, Akbahr becomes a short story writer; his most memorable work is the autobiography of a talking deer that lives in the National Forest.

Astor, Madelaine Peabody A former student of Eugene Hartke's, Madelaine Peabody Astor serves on the board of trustees that fires him from his teaching job at Tarkington College. Later, Madelaine writes Eugene a letter explaining that Jason Wilder had threatened to denounce the college if Hartke were not fired.

Barber, Kensington Kensington Barber was the provost of Tarkington College in 1922, when Letitia Smiley disappeared. Eugene Hartke speculates that Barber killed the beautiful young student, then went insane.

Bergeron, Bruce Bruce Bergeron is the homosexual son of Tarkington board of trustees member and environmentalist Ed Bergeron. A former student at Tarkington College and an excellent dancer, Bruce Bergeron joins the Ice Capades as a chorus boy after he graduates, but is soon found murdered, strangled by his own belt, and having close to 100 stab wounds on his body.

Bergeron, Ed   A wealthy, environmentally-minded member of the board of trustees of Tarkington College, Ed Bergeron is the one friend Eugene Hartke has on the board. But Bergeron is unable to attend the board meeting the day Hartke is fired and thus cannot defend him. Later, an old tape of Bergeron debating Jason Wilder on environmental issues is played at Athena prison and generates "considerable interest" among the inmates who ask Hartke: "Who right, Professor—beard or mustache?" (143).

Blankenship, Dr. Martin Peale   Dr. Martin Peale Blankenship, a close friend of conservative columnist Jason Wilder and a fellow Rhodes scholar of Wilder's as well, delivers the graduation address at Tarkington College the day Eugene Hartke is fired from his job. Dr. Blankenship is a UNIVERSITY OF CHICAGO economist who would later become a quadriplegic after a skiing accident in Switzerland.

Carpathia   *Carpathia* is a novel said to be written by Felicia Tarkington, daughter of Mohiga Wagon Company founder Aaron Tarkington. *Carpathia* is the story of "a headstrong, high-born young woman in the Mohiga Valley who fell in love with a half-Indian lock-tender" working on the Onondaga Canal (10).

Casey, Dwight and his Wife   Muriel Peck becomes a professor of English at Tarkington College when another English professor named Dwight Casey asks for Eugene Hartke's old job, thus creating a vacancy for Muriel. When Casey's wife, whose family was big in the Mafia, inherits a great deal of money, he quits his job and moves to the south of France.

Chung, Lowell   Lowell Chung is the most successful student athlete ever to attend Tarkington College. He is an equestrian who won a bronze medal in the Olympics in 1988 and who dares Eugene Hartke to ride a horse for the first time. As a student, Chung is typical of the strangely limited yet gifted Tarkington students; he "couldn't read

or write or do math worth a darn" (66), but he's a whiz at physics.

Chung, Lowell's Mother   The mother of student Lowell Chung, who is said to own half of Honolulu, serves as a member of the Tarkington College board of trustees even though she does not speak English and has to have everything said at meetings translated into Chinese. Mrs. Chung dies of tetanus before the Athena prison escape and thus will not be taken hostage with the rest of the board members.

Clarke, Arthur   Arthur Clarke is a "fun-loving billionaire" (174) who leads the motorcade of motorcycles and limousines through the Tarkington campus on the day that Eugene Hartke is fired. He is there to receive an honorary degree.

Clewes, Dr. Alan   Dr. Alan Clewes is an Episcopalian priest and HARVARD graduate who taught Latin, Greek, Hebrew, and the Bible at the Mohiga Valley Free Institute.

Darwin, Alton   Alton Darwin is a murderous drug dealer imprisoned at Athena. A highly intelligent man who is verbally gifted and who can do complicated arithmetic in his head, Darwin is the charismatic leader who persuades a group of prisoners to attack the neighboring town of Scipio. Darwin is fatally shot by Tarkington College president Tex Johnson while ice skating at the college's Cohen Rink. His last words echo a statement made by his South Carolina great-grandfather, who pretended to be a stunt pilot shortly after World War I: "See the Nigger fly the airplane" (75), a comment suggesting the racist expectations of blacks in America.

Darwin's Great-Grandfather   The great-grandfather of prison escapee Alton Darwin worked with stunt pilots in South Carolina after World War I. Darwin, a black man, would sit in the plane's front cockpit while a barnstormer crouched down in the rear cockpit and worked the controls. People would come from miles around "to see the Nigger fly the airplane" (68).

de Wet, Marthinus Mr. and Mrs. Marthinus de Wet is the owner of a gold mine in Krugersdorp, South Africa, whose wife is a Tarkington alumna. Mrs. de Wet writes a letter to *The Musketeer* about the modernization of the Lutz Carillon. Although she's not upset that the bells can now be played by a keyboard, she protests that the famous sour bells will be relathed until they are properly in tune.

Dole, Helen Helen Dole is a 26-year-old black woman with a Ph.D. in physics who had come to Tarkington College the day before the prison break to be interviewed for Eugene Hartke's old job. Born in South Korea and raised in Berlin, Dr. Dole is internationally sophisticated and well aware of racism. She blows up at the Tarkington board of trustees when they ask her to promise never to discuss politics, history, economics, or sociology with her students.

Dole, Mr. Helen Dole's father had been a master sergeant in the U.S. Army, serving first in Korea, where Helen was born, and later in Berlin.

Donner, John and his Son Described as an "ugly mountain of a man," John Donner is the father of the boy whose bicycle Eugene Hartke finds and borrows on the day he is fired from Tarkington College. Later that afternoon, Donner and Hartke end up going to Athena Prison together for teaching interviews—Donner wants to teach shop there, but does not get the job. Hartke speculates that John Donner might be a pathological liar and that the owner of the bicycle might not be his son at all.

Dresser, Paul Paul Dresser composed the melody of the ballad "Mary, Mary, Where Have You Gone?" written by Henry Moellenkamp. The song is said to have been one of the most popular ballads at the turn of the last century and to later have become the alma mater of Tarkington College. Dresser was an actual historic figure—a popular late 19th-century American composer and brother of novelist Theodore Dreiser.

Eastman, George Real-life photography pioneer George Eastman enters the novel when Eugene Hartke tells readers that Sam Wakefield's suicide note says the same thing as Eastman's: "My work is done" (54).

Elders of Tralfamadore At the top of his old Vietnam foot locker, delivered to Eugene Hartke 16 years after the end of the war, is a copy of a pornographic magazine called *Black Garterbelt*. Hartke reads a science fiction story from the magazine called "The Protocols of the Elders of Tralfamadore" in which intelligent threads of energy (the Elders of the title) feed crazy ideas to Earthlings—such as the notion that the world was made by a large, male animal who looked just like them—in order to make them hate strangers and try to exterminate one another. The Elders use humans to test the survival skills of germs they want to send all through the universe.

Everett, Norman and his Son Norman Everett is the old campus gardener at Tarkington College. Everett's son was paralyzed from the waist down by a mine in Vietnam and now lives permanently in a V.A. hospital in Schenectady.

Fedders, John W., Jr. John W. Fedders, Jr. is a member of the Tarkington College board of trustees who was raised in Hong Kong and thus can serve as interpreter for the Chinese-speaking board member, Mrs. Chung.

Fenstermaker, Lowell Meat packer Lowell Fenstermaker marries Eugene Hartke's former lover Harriet Gummer and raises Hartke's son, Rob Roy, as his own.

Fenstermaker, Rob Roy Rob Roy Fenstermaker is Eugene Hartke's illegitimate son, conceived in 1975 during Eugene's brief dalliance with Harriet Gummer, a war correspondent working in the Philippines. Eugene discovers his son's existence only near the end of the novel, after the Athena prison escape, when Rob Roy comes to see him in Scipio. The young man had been tried for child molestation in Dubuque, Iowa, where he had been running at his own expense a free child care center. Rob Roy had inherited a fortune from his stepfather, a meatpacker named Lowell Fenstermaker. After being acquitted of the wrongful child molestation charges, Rob Roy has decided to leave the country for Italy; he wants to meet his real father, though, before he goes. At this meeting, Eugene confirms to his son that he had told numerous lies about himself and his life to Rob Roy's mother when he knew her in the Philippines years before.

Florio, Lucas Lucas Florio is commander of the "Rainbow Division" of the New York National Guard, a unit that started out as an experiment in desegregation during World War II, but that had since resegregated, since army leaders, like prison operators, believed people were more comfortable with those of their own race. Florio loans some of his troops to Eugene Hartke after Hartke is made a brigadier general in the National Guard.

French, Mary Alice Mary Alice French is a high school student from Cincinnati who wins the Ohio State Science Fair the year Eugene Harke also enters. Eugene speculates that she wins because "of the moral contrast" (39) between her exhibit and Eugene's, which are both on crystallography. Mary Alice clearly made her project herself, unlike Eugene, whose father made his.

Governor of New York Harley Wheelock III, the leader of the counterassault on the prisoners holding Scipio, contacts the governor of New York, who officially grants Eugene Hartke the rank of brigadier general in the National Guard and installs him as new mayor of Scipio.

Guido Guido works at the crematorium behind the cinema complex at the Rochester city limits. Guido is the source of the only remaining gas in the area after the Athena prison break and assault on Scipio.

Gummer, Harriet Harriet Gummer was a young war correspondent working for *The Des Moines Register* in the Philippines at the end of the Vietnam War. Eugene Debs Hartke meets her during a stopover in Manila after he resigns his army commission in 1975. Unbeknownst to him at the time,

he fathers a son with Harriet, who appears later in the novel as Rob Roy Fenstermaker. The boy is named after the cocktails that Harriet and Eugene drank together during their brief love affair. Eugene includes Harriet on the very short list of all the women he actually loved.

Hall, Pamela Ford Pamela Ford Hall is artist in residence at Tarkington College the year that Eugene Hartke is fired. She and Eugene become lovers one night after drinking blackberry brandy. Later, a drunken Eugene stumbles to the Pahlavi Pavilion and regales the students with horror stories from his days in Vietnam, an incident that Kimberly Wilder will secretly tape-record, something that will be pivotal in his losing his job. Pamela's year as an artist takes a definite downturn when she is humiliated at a one-woman show in Buffalo, New York, after her sculptures blow off their pedestals and melt against hot pipes concealed in the museum's baseboards. Pamela later moves to Key West, Florida, and marries novelist Paul Slazinger.

Hall, Pamela Ford's ex-Husband The ex-husband of Pamela Ford Hall, Tarkington's artist in residence, used to slap and kick her and mock her efforts to become a serious artist. In the divorce settlement from this man, Pamela receives a 12-year-old Buick sedan that mechanic Whitey VanArsdale tries to convince her needs a new transmission.

Handy, Fred Fred Handy is the old college roommate of Eugene Hartke's father. When Mr. Hartke is dismissed by Barrytron, Fred tries to cheer him up by taking him on a yacht cruise down the Inland Waterway from New York to Florida. But the trip depresses Mr. Hartke even more because of all the plastic bottles polluting the water, bottles he had helped develop as a chemical engineer.

Hanson, Miss Miss Hanson is an elderly woman in a wheelchair who donates the Hanson Centre for the Arts to the city of Buffalo, New York. At the centre's grand opening, three doors are thrown open to accommodate Miss Hanson's wheelchair, causing the bag lady sculptures of Pamela Ford

Hall to blow off their pedestals and begin to melt on the floor.

Hartke, Eugene Debs   The protagonist of the novel, Eugene Debs Hartke, is named after labor organizer and socialist politician Eugene Debs at the request of his maternal grandfather. Born in 1940 in Wilmington, Delaware, and raised in Midland City, Ohio, Hartke is the son of a chemical engineer and a housewife. As a young man, Hartke attends the U.S. Military Academy at West Point and becomes a commissioned officer in the U.S. Army, serving for nearly 15 years. He sees extended combat duty in Vietnam, attaining the rank of lieutenant colonel by the end of American involvement there. After the war, Hartke marries, has two children, and accepts a position teaching physics and music at Tarkington College in New York, where he stays for another 15 years. When Hartke is abruptly fired from Tarkington, he obtains a job teaching at the prison in Athena, New York, just across the lake from the college. He teaches there for several years, until a violent prison escape takes place in 1999. When the prisoners are finally recaptured, Tarkington is converted from a college into a prison, and Hartke serves as warden for a brief period. As he is writing *Hocus Pocus*, Hartke himself has become a prisoner at Athena, arrested for supposedly masterminding the escape. At the novel's present time, he is awaiting trial.

Hartke, Eugene Debs, Jr.   The son of Eugene and Margaret Hartke, Eugene, Jr. is described as a beautiful boy who started a rock-and-roll band in high school. At the novel's present time, however, Eugene Sr. has no idea where his son is, since Eugene, Jr. hates his father and no longer communicates with him.

Hartke, Margaret Patton   Margaret Patton Hartke is the wife of Eugene Debs Hartke. Margaret's brother, Jack, had been Eugene's roommate at West Point; the couple met when Jack's family came out from Wyoming to see him graduate. At first a "pretty and personable" (5) young woman, after a few years of marriage, Margaret goes insane like her mother, Mildred, before her. Eugene takes

care of the two crazy women for years and years, but after the Athena prison escape, both Margaret and her mother are sent to an insane asylum in Batavia, New York. Eugene does include Margaret on the short list of women he loved, explaining that the first four years of their marriage, before Eugene came home "with the clap" (101) were good ones.

Hartke, Melanie   Melanie is the daughter of Eugene Hartke and Margaret Patton Hartke. After studying mathematics at Cambridge University, Melanie moves to Paris, where she lives with another woman and teaches English and math in an American high school. Grossly overweight like her paternal grandmother, Melanie is estranged from her father and barely communicates with him.

Hartke, Mrs.   Eugene Debs Hartke's mother is a terribly overweight homemaker who is killed, along with her husband, when the roof of a gift shop at Niagara Falls caves in on her 20 years before the book's present time. We do not find out much about Mrs. Hartke in the novel, except that Eugene, as a high school student ends up doing most of the housework and cooking for the family because it is difficult for his enormous mother to get around. One of the few things Eugene tells readers about his mother is that she agreed with every decision her husband ever made, which, according to Eugene, made her a "blithering nincompoop" (4).

Hartke, Sr.   Eugene Debs Hartke's father is a chemical engineer who works at the Robo-Magic Corporation (later Barrytron Ltd.) in Midland City, Ohio. When Eugene is a high school senior, his father, publicly humiliated after being beaten up by the husband of a woman he is having an affair with, decides to save face by having his son win the local science fair competition. Eugene's father makes the project entirely by himself, thus winning his son a trip to the state finals, where the father and son team are disqualified for cheating. Mr. Hartke dies in a "freak accident" (4) at Niagara Falls when a gift shop roof caves in on him.

Hiscock, Ernest Hubble   The Lutz Carillon at Tarkington College is modernized to become a memorial to Ernest Hubble Hiscock, an alumnus who was killed at the age of 21 while serving as a nose-gunner on a Navy bomber during the Battle of Midway in World War II. Eugene Hartke writes that he himself "would have given anything to die in a war that meaningful" (57).

Hiscock, Mr. and Mrs. The parents of Ernest Hubble Hiscock, divorced but still friends, chip in to have the Lutz Carillon modernized as a memorial to their war hero son. The bells are mechanized so that one person can play them by means of a keyboard.

Hiscock's Roommate An unnamed roommate of Ernest Hubble Hiscock—himself a war hero as well—writes a letter to *The Musketeer* arguing that the memorial Hiscock would have wanted most was a promise by the board of trustees to keep student enrollment the same size it had been when he was a student at Tarkington College.

Hooper, Charlton The extremely tall son of Scipio fire chief Lyle Hooper, Charlton Hooper is an all-star basketball center in high school. Though he is invited to try out for the New York Knicks, he instead accepts a scholarship to MIT and becomes a top scientist working on the Supercollider atom smasher outside Waxahachie, Texas.

Hooper, Lyle Lyle Hooper is fire chief of Scipio and owner of the Black Cat Café. Eugene Harke calls Hooper "the best-liked man in this valley" (215). The townspeople do not seem to mind at all that much of Hooper's business comes from men visiting the prostitutes working in vans in the café's parking lot. Lyle is executed by the escaped prisoners after shooting several of them in an ambush. His last words appear printed on a drawing of a tombstone: "OK, I admit it. It really was a whorehouse" (219).

Hooper, Mrs. Lyle Hooper's wife discovers in mid-life that she is a lesbian and runs off to Bermuda with the girls' high school gym teacher.

Humanoids of Tralfamadore In the story "The Protocols of the Elders of Tralfamadore," which

Eugene Hartke reads in his Vietnam-era pornographic magazine *Black Garterbelt*, the Elders have given up trying to influence the humanoids of Tralfamadore and turn their attention to Earthlings instead. This is because the Tralfamadorians have senses of humor and refuse to take themselves too seriously, while Earthlings are quite willing to believe that they are the "glory of the Universe" (202).

Johnson, Henry "Tex" Henry "Tex" Johnson is the president of Tarkington College during the Athena prison escape. Acting as a sniper in the college bell tower, he kills 11 inmates and wounds 15 others before being shot himself. When the enraged prisoners find his body in the tower, they crucify it. Eugene Hartke had been having an affair with the president's wife, Zuzu.

Johnson, Sr. Although Tex Johnson claims to be descended from a defender of the Alamo, Eugene Hartke discovers, from Tex's wife, Zuzu, that Tex's father was actually an illegal immigrant from Lithuania who settled in Corpus Christi after jumping ship when the Russian freighter he had been working on put in for repairs.

Johnson, Zuzu Zuzu Johnson is the wife of Tarkington College president Henry "Tex" Johnson. Eugene Hartke has been having a long-standing affair with her, unbeknownst to Tex, and even counts her on the short list of women he actually loved. Like her husband, Zuzu is shot and dies when the prisoners attack Scipio.

Kern, Shirley Shirley Kern is the first name on Eugene Harke's list of all the woman he has made love to, excluding his teen years, which he finds impossible to remember clearly.

Kissinger, Henry Real-life former U.S. secretary of state Henry Kissinger appears briefly in the novel as part of the motorcade led onto the Tarkington campus by billionaire Arthur Clarke.

LeGrand, Pierre A student of Eugene Hartke's at Tarkington College, Pierre LeGrand is extremely wealthy but unpopular. When he is unable to win friends by giving them expensive gifts, he tries to hang himself from the water tower on top of Musket Mountain. Hartke cuts him down and saves his life. Two years later, Pierre successfully commits suicide when he jumps off the Golden Gate Bridge.

LeGrand, Mrs. The mother of Tarkington College student Pierre LeGrand is so grateful when Eugene Hartke saves her son's life that she gives him a brand-new Mercedes, which costs more than Hartke's annual salary.

LeGrand's Grandfather Tarkington College student Pierre LeGrand's maternal grandfather had been dictator of Haiti and had robbed the country's treasury when he was overthrown. This accounts for the great wealth of the LeGrand family.

Lutz, André André Lutz, from Liege, Belgium, was the chief engineer at the Mohiga Wagon Company who later became a professor of chemistry at the Mohiga Valley Free Institute. Lutz is the one who donates the bell carillon to the school, after having cast them at his own expense from abandoned weaponry gathered up after the Battle of Gettysburg.

Lutz, Mrs. André Lutz's wife, a French woman, teaches French and watercolor painting at the newly formed Mohiga Valley Free Institute.

"Mary, Mary, Where Have You Gone?" Henry Moellencamp, a learning disabled descendant of the founder of Tarkington College who goes on to become an outstanding orator and U.S. senator, is said to have composed the lyrics to "one of the most popular turn-of-the-century ballads" (20), a song called "Mary, Mary, Where Have You Gone?" The song soon becomes the alma mater of Tarkington College.

Matsumoto, Hiroshi The warden at Athena Prison, Hiroshi Matsumoto, is a survivor of the atom bombing of Hiroshima, which took place when he was eight years old. As an adult, Matsumoto works for the Sony Corporation, first running a hospital in Louisville and then the prison at

Athena. He hires Eugene Hartke to teach at the prison in an attempt to be humane to the prisoners and allows Hartke to live in a house next door to him on the lake for many years. After the prison escape, Matsumoto runs into the National Forest, where he gets lost in the woods; he is wearing only sandals with no socks on his feet. Gangrene sets in, and he ends up losing both his feet. Matsumoto eventually moves back to Hiroshima and kills himself by committing hara-kiri.

Mellon, Hortense Hortense Mellon is a student at Tarkington College and the niece of graduation speaker Dr. Martin Peale Blankenship. All that Eugene Hartke remembers about her is that she could play the harp and that she had false upper teeth, since her own teeth had been knocked out by a mugger as she was leaving a friend's debutante party at the Waldorf-Astoria.

Mellon, Mr. Hortense Mellon's father, like many Tarkington College parents, lost a huge amount of money after buying stock in a company called Microsecond Arbitrage, perpetrators of what Eugene Hartke calls "the biggest swindle in the history of Wall Street" (92).

Moellenkamp, Henry Henry Moellenkamp is the first member of his illustrious family to attend Tarkington College. He is also the student who inspires the college's dedication to disabled and incapacitated students. Despite his inability to write and a severe stammer, Henry goes on to attend Oxford University, to become a brilliant public speaker, and to serve as a U.S. congressman for 36 years. His family becomes major donors to the college.

Moellenkamp, Henry's Grandfather Henry Moellenkamp's grandfather had married one of the daughters of Aaron Tarkington and served on the board of trustees at Tarkington College. The grandfather originally suggests changing the name of the Mohiga Valley Free Institute to Tarkington College when Henry is a student there since the original name "sounded too much like a poorhouse or a hospital" to him (18).

Moellenkamp, Robert W. Robert W. Moellenkamp is the chairman of the board of trustees of Tarkington College when Eugene Hartke is fired from his teaching job. Though Moellenkamp is illiterate, he is legendary for his "phenomenal memory" (150), and he quotes from SHAKESPEARE's *Romeo and Juliet* when he fires Hartke. Later, Moellenkamp loses a fortune from his investments in the Microsecond Armitrage Company, which has perpetrated a huge Wall Street swindle.

Mohiga Wagon Company The Mohiga Wagon Company of Scipio, New York, which manufactures Conestoga covered wagons that pioneers use to make the trip west, is said to have been founded in the early 19th century by the dyslexic genius Aaron Tarkington. Tarkington's son Elias founds the Mohiga Valley Free Institute, later to become Tarkington College.

Nakayama, Senator Randolph and his Family Eugene Hartke's lawyer is friends with the U.S. ambassador to Japan, former senator Randolph Nakayama. The lawyer tells Hartke that both sets of the Senator's grandparents were put into a concentration camp by the U.S. government during World War II. The senator's father, however, served in an infantry division of Japanese-Americans that became the most decorated unit taking part in the Italian campaign of World War II. Hartke asks his lawyer to find out from the ambassador whether Hiroshi Matsumoto left a note after his suicide.

Patton, Jack Eugene Hartke's roommate at West Point, fellow soldier in Vietnam, and brother-in-law, Jack Patton is a young man who refuses to take anything seriously. His comment on everything that happens is: "I had to laugh like hell" (46). Patton is killed by a sniper in Hue, Vietnam, while serving as a lieutenant colonel in the Combat Engineers.

Patton, Mildred Eugene Hartke's mother-in-law, Mildred Patton, goes insane after she comes to live with her daughter and son-in-law. Soon, Margaret Patton Hartke will go insane as well. Eugene takes care of the two crazy women for years and years

during the time he's a professor at Tarkington College and also while he's teaching at Athena prison. After the prison escape, however, Mildred and her daughter are sent to an insane asylum in Batavia, New York.

Patton, Sr. All that readers find out about the father of Jack and Margaret Patton is that he was a student at the School of Veterinary Science at the University of Wyoming in Laramie when he met his wife, Mildred.

Peck, Jerry The husband of Muriel Peck, Jerry Peck dies after inhaling too much paint remover when he and Muriel are trying to restore an old-time ice cream parlor in Scipio. Jerry Peck is a direct descendant of John Peck, the first president of Tarkington College.

Peck, John John Peck, a cousin of the Tarkington family, becomes the first president of the Mohiga Valley Free Institute when he is only 26 years old.

Peck, Muriel Muriel Peck is a bartender at the Black Cat Café in Scipio when Eugene Harke is fired from his job at Tarkington College. A literature major at Swarthmore College as a young woman, Muriel later becomes an English professor at Tarkington. She and Eugene become lovers after he begins teaching at Athena Prison, and she will appear on the very short list of women he truly loved. Muriel eventually dies during the attack on Scipio after the prison escape.

Polk, Dalton Dalton Polk was Elias Tarkington's physician. Later, he will teach biology and Shakespeare at the Mohiga Valley Free Institute.

Pratt, Mary Mary Pratt was Eugene Hartke's high school English teacher who made him memorize the first lines of HAMLET's famous "To Be or Not To Be" soliloquy, which Hartke quotes to the board of trustees after he is fired from his job.

"Protocols of the Elders of Tralfamadore, The" "The Protocols of the Elders of Tralfamadore" is a science fiction story appearing in the pornographic magazine *Black Garterbelt*. The magazine is a gift to Eugene Debs Hartke from his brother-in-law, Jack Patton. The story is about super-intelligent threads of energy from the planet Tralfamadore who trick human beings into fighting among themselves so that the energy threads can test out the survival skills of germs that they plan to send all over the universe. Clearly, the title of the story plays on the well-known anti-Semitic work, *The Protocols of the Elders of Zion*, which Athena Prison inmate Abdullah Akbahr is reading when Eugene Hartke first meets him.

Roosevelt, Claudia   A Tarkington College student and the girlfriend of Lowell Chung, Claudia Roosevelt "was a whiz at arithmetic, but otherwise a nitwit" (66). Claudia loans Eugene Hartke a gentle old mare to ride his first time on horseback.

Shaw, Marilyn   Marilyn Shaw is the head of the Department of Life Sciences at Tarkington College. Like Eugene Hartke, she served in Vietnam, having been a nurse during the war. Sam Wakefield finds Marilyn after the war and offers her a job at Tarkington College just as he does for Eugene Hartke.

Shaw, Marilyn's Husband   Marilyn Shaw's husband had divorced her and married someone else while she was serving in Vietnam. Apparently, though, Marilyn did not care; Eugene Hartke suspects that she and Sam Wakefield might have been lovers during the war.

Shultz, Hermann   Originally the brewmaster at the Tarkington brewery in Scipio, New York, Hermann Shultz goes on to teach botany and German and flute at the Mohiga Valley Free Institute. Shultz and his wife die within one day of each other during a diptheria epidemic in 1893 and are buried near the college stable at the novel's present time, their bodies having recently been moved to make room for the school's new Pahlavi Pavilion.

Shultz, Sophia   Sophia Shultz is the wife of 19th-century botany, German, and flute professor Her-

mann Shultz, who teaches at the Mohiga Valley Free Institute.

Slazinger, Paul   Paul Slazinger, a key character from Vonnegut's previous novel, *Bluebeard*, appears briefly in *Hocus Pocus* as Tarkington College's writer in residence the year Eugene Hartke is fired from his job.

Smiley, Letitia   Letitia Smiley was a beautiful, dyslexic Tarkington senior who disappeared from campus in 1922. Eugene Hartke speculates that it is Letitia's skull that is dug up by the forensic medicine specialist who comes to campus to examine bodies after the prison break.

Steel, Terrence W.   Terrence W. Steel is the private detective hired by conservative columnist Jason Wilder to investigate Eugene Hartke's sex life. Steel's report puts the nail in the coffin of Hartke's career as a college physics professor.

Stern, Damon   Head of the History Department at Tarkington College, the unicycle-riding Damon Stern is a close friend of Eugene Hartke. Although he, too, speaks unfavorably about his country, he escapes the wrath of the board of trustees because, in Hartke's words, Stern is a comedian who wants his students to leave his classes feeling good, so he only talks about U.S. "atrocities and stupidities" from the distant past (116). Stern is killed while trying to save the Tarkington College horses during the prison break.

Stern, Wanda June   Wanda June Stern is the wife of history professor Damon Stern. She and her children escape Scipio before the prisoners' assault because her husband wakes her up in the middle of the night and tells her to drive the family Volkswagen to Rochester with the headlights off.

Stone, Fred   Fred Stone is a Tarkington College student whom Eugene Hartke catches brazenly stealing a beer mug from the college bookstore. Hartke writes a letter to the boy's father about the incident.

Stone, Sydney   The extremely wealthy father of Tarkington student Fred Stone, Sydney Stone also serves on the Tarkington board of trustees. He is glad to fire Eugene Hartke because Hartke had earlier caught Stone's son, Fred, stealing from the college bookstore.

Tarkington, Aaron   Aaron Tarkington was the founder of the Mohiga Wagon Company in the early 19th century. Though unable to read and write himself, he was an inventor and an educated man who had his wife read out loud to him for two hours every evening. Aaron is also the father of Elias Tarkington, founder of the Mohiga Valley Free Institute, later to become Tarkington College.

Tarkington, Elias   The son of businessman Aaron Tarkington, Elias Tarkington was a mechanic who, after being wounded during the Civil War when a Confederate soldier mistakes him for ABRAHAM LINCOLN, comes home to Scipio and obsessively tries to build perpetual-motion machines. Elias never marries and has no heirs, so in his last will and testament he bequeaths his estate to Scipio, to become the Mohiga Valley Free Institute. Later, the school becomes Tarkington College.

Tarkington, Felicia   The youngest daughter of Aaron Tarkington, Felicia Tarkington is the author of a novel called *Carpathia*, "about a headstrong, high-born young woman in the Mohiga Valley who fell in love with a half-Indian lock-tender" on the Onondaga Canal (10).

Tarkington, Mrs. Aaron   Aaron Tarkington's wife reads to him for two hours every night because her husband is dyslexic and never learned to read or write himself.

Tarkington College   Tarkington College is the university in Scipio, New York, where Eugene Debs Hartke teaches physics for 15 years.

Turner, Jeffrey   The prison escape at Athena occurs when the members of a Jamaican drug cartel blow up the prison's main gate in an attempt to free Jeffrey Turner, their imprisoned chief. Both Turner and the attackers vanish after the assault, never to be seen again.

Unnamed Astronaut   An retired astronaut who tells Muriel Peck he has diarrhea is among the celebrities in Arthur Clarke's motorcade that stop to use the toilets in the Black Cat Café.

Unnamed Aunt of Student   The report of the private detective hired by Jason Wilder to investigate Eugene Hartke's sex life contains a misunderstanding of what happened between Hartke and the aunt of a student who went up into the college bell tower together. While the detective assumed the two made love up there, the woman was actually an architect who wanted to see the tower's post-and-beam joinery.

Unnamed Baseball Players   Two highly paid black baseball players are among the revelers who accompany Arthur Clarke to the Tarkington campus to receive his honorary degree.

Unnamed Book Reviewer   A book reviewer for the *New York Times* is one of the members of Arthur Clarke's motorcade when he comes to Tarkington College. The reviewer had just written a rave review of Clarke's autobiography, *Don't Be Ashamed of Money*.

Unnamed Confederate Soldier   When Elias Tarkington goes to Gettysburg as a civilian observer during the Civil War, an unnamed confederate soldier shoots him through the chest, mistaking him for Abraham Lincoln because Tarkington is "a tall and skinny man with chin whiskers and a stovepipe hat" (12).

Unnamed Coroner   An unnamed New York State coroner, a black man who looks white, comes to Scipio to assist with exhuming the bodies of those killed during the prison escape. When Eugene Hartke asks him if the state could take possession of the bodies, the coroner tells Hartke not to get his hopes up since the county is broke, the state is broke, and the country is broke. The coroner himself is broke as well, having lost money in Microsecond Arbitrage.

Unnamed Forensic Medicine Specialist An unnamed specialist in forensic medicine comes to Tarkington College after the prison escape to examine bodies. He is particularly interested in the body of Tex Johnson, who had been crucified. He tells Eugene Hartke of the word *crurifragium*, which refers to breaking the legs of a crucified person in order to shorten the period of suffering.

Unnamed Girl with a Hand Grenade and her Father Eugene Hartke tells readers that the Athena prison break was big news for only about 10 days before being replaced by a story about a girl in rural Northern California who blew up her high school prom committee with a Chinese hand grenade. She had taken the grenade from the collection of her father, a gun nut.

Unnamed Guards and Prisoners in Truck One day, when Eugene Hartke takes his wife, Margaret, and mother-in-law, Mildred, fishing, a prison truck stops nearby. Three shackled prisoners and two guards briefly emerge. While Mildred remains obsessed with her fishing, Margaret and Eugene gawk at the prisoners. Eugene compares this event to viewing pornography, since the prisoners were "common things nice people shouldn't see," but Margaret compares seeing the shackled prisoners to "seeing animals on their way to a slaughterhouse" (79).

Unnamed Honduran General When Eugene Hartke tells readers about the heavy test line he puts on his mother-in-law's fishing reel, he mentions briefly that he had done the same thing once for a three-star general in Honduras, whose aide he was.

Unnamed Horror Story Author A famous author of horror stories is among the celebrities in billionaire Arthur Clarke's motorcade that comes to Tarkington College on the day Eugene Hartke is fired.

Unnamed Jewelry Saleswoman The private detective hired by Jason Wilder to investigate

Eugene Hartke's sex life reports two trysts Hartke had with an unnamed woman who came to Tarkington College to sell class rings.

Unnamed Lawyer In prison, Eugene Hartke has been assigned a defense lawyer whose name is never given. The lawyer is happy to see Hartke's two lists, though—of all the women he has made love to and of all the people he has killed—because he thinks they show that Hartke is in a deeply disturbed mental state, which might help him get acquitted of masterminding the Athena prison escape.

Unnamed Lemon Car Owner The only diesel automobile in Scipio belongs to a Tarkington parent who had painted large yellow lemons all over it because the car worked so poorly. Eugene Hartke mentions this anecdote in telling readers that the backhoe, which he uses to rebury the exhumed bodies, has a tank full of diesel fuel.

Unnamed Letter Writer One of the Tarkington alumni who writes a letter to *The Musketeer* protesting the modernization of the Lutz Carillon is an alcoholic and compulsive gambler imprisoned for fraud. One of the things the inmate had been looking forward to upon his release was returning to Tarkington to ring the bells with ropes again.

Unnamed Little Japanese Girl After former prison warden Hiroshi Matsumoto commits suicide by disemboweling himself in Hiroshima, the first person to find the body is an unnamed little girl.

Unnamed Lottery Winner An old black woman who had just won $57 million in the New York State lottery is one of the revelers who accompany billionaire Arthur Clarke to campus to receive his honorary degree.

Unnamed Lover When an unnamed woman Eugene Hartke was making love to several years before asks if Hartke's parents are still alive, he makes up an elaborate lie about them being killed on safari in Tanganyika.

Unnamed Male Companion When Henry Moellenkamp attends Oxford University in the late 19th century, he brings with him an unnamed male companion who reads aloud to him and writes down the thoughts Henry can express only orally.

Unnamed Man Who Works for Architect A man who works for the architect who is designing Tarkington College's new student recreation center appears one day at Muriel and Jerry Peck's ice-cream parlor in Scipio to tape measure and record everything about the store. Later, an identical ice-cream parlor is built for students on the Pahlavi Pavilion, putting the Pecks out of business.

Unnamed Married Woman and her Husband When Eugene Hartke is a senior in high school, his father has an affair with an unnamed married woman whose husband catches them in the act and beats up Mr. Harke, giving him a black eye.

Unnamed Nephew of the Mayor Although Eugene Hartke expected many black people to be shot after the prison break just for being black, this only happens to one man: the nephew of the mayor of Troy, New York. The mayor's nephew is only winged, however.

Unnamed Old Friend of Mildred Patton An old friend of Eugene Hartke's mother-in-law, Mildred Patton, sits next to the Hartke family in a restaurant one night. From this friend Eugene learns about the craziness affecting his wife's family.

Unnamed Painting Owner One of the odd people collected by billionaire Arthur Clarke and traveling in his motorcade with him is a man who had inherited from his father a Mark Rothko painting worth $37 million.

Unnamed Parent When Eugene Hartke sulks by the Tarkington College stables after being fired from his job, an unnamed parent of a graduating student tells him to cheer up because 1 billion Chinese were "about to throw off the yoke of Communism" (183) and become customers for American automobiles, tires, and gasoline.

Unnamed Relatives of Mildred Patton An old friend of Mildred Patton, Eugene Hartke's mother-in-law, informs Hartke that Mildred's mother and grandmother were both patients at the State Hospital for the Insane in Indianapolis, Indiana. In addition, he tells Hartke that a maternal uncle of Mildred had also gone insane, as a senior in high school, and set fires all over town. This is the first time either Eugene or Margaret hear about mental illness in the Patton family.

Unnamed Science Fair Exhibitor When Eugene Hartke goes to the science fair in Cleveland, Ohio, one of the exhibit tables is empty because an unnamed exhibitor was rear-ended by a drunk driver while pulling out of his driveway in Lima, Ohio. The accident would not have been as serious if the student's science project, which included several bottles of different acids, had not been in the trunk and broken, touching off a fire that consumed both vehicles.

Unnamed Servants of the Warden Athena Prison warden Hiroshi Matsumoto employs three house servants, all convicts over 70 years old who are "coked to the gills on Thorazine" (259). After the prison escape, Eugene Hartke wakes up the three old men and takes them to his house by the lake to help care for Mildred and Margaret.

Unnamed Student from Cincinnati Eugene Hartke reminisces about a student he once had at Tarkington College from Cincinnati. Although he is 21 years old and extremely rich, the student barely looks 12; he's short and speaks in a high, squeaky voice and completely lacks social graces. When Eugene asks if he knew Mary Alice French in Cincinnati, the student begs Eugene never to talk to him again, and to tell everyone else not to talk to him as well.

Unnamed Tape Donor and his Adopted Son When the adopted son of a member of the board of directors of the Museum of Broadcasting is sent to Athena prison for strangling his girlfriend, his father donates hundreds of tapes of old TV shows to the prison.

Unnamed United Parcel Service Man   A young man from the United Parcel Service delivers Eugene Hartke's Vietnam foot locker to him 16 years after Hartke left the war. The UPS man is so young and naïve that he waits around to see what is in the box he has just delivered. He is especially impressed by the pornographic magazine *Black Garterbelt*, the top item in the foot locker.

Unnamed Vietnam Soldiers   During Eugene Hartke's three years in Vietnam, he heard "plenty of last words by dying American footsoldiers" (12). He specifically remembers one unnamed boy of 18 whose last words were "Dirty joke, dirty joke" (12). Another time, he tells the story about a young soldier who stepped on an antipersonnel mine. When his best friend asks what he can do to help, the young soldier replies: "Turn me off like a light bulb, Sam" (26).

Unnamed West Point Cheater   When Jack Patton and Eugene Hartke fail to report a cadet who cheated on a final examination in electrical engineering at West Point, they are punished by having to walk a three-hour tour in the Quadrangle. The cheater, who told Jack and Eugene about the incident many months after the fact, while drunk at a football game, is thrown out of the academy.

Unnamed West Point Snitch   Another cadet who is present when a drunk cadet confesses to Jack Patton and Eugene Hartke that he cheated on an exam several months previously, turns in all three for violating the academy's honor code. The snitch will later be fragged during the Vietnam War—purposefully killed by his own men.

Unnamed Wife of the Tennis Coach   Eugene Hartke is in the bushes on top of Musket Mountain with the wife of the college's tennis coach when he saves student Pierre LeGrand from hanging himself.

Unnamed Wounded Soldiers   Eugene Hartke reminisces about watching *2001: A Space Odyssey* in Vietnam twice. During one of the film's showings, a young black soldier in a wheelchair in the front row says to a buddy, also in a wheelchair, "You tell *me*: What was that all about?" (175). His friend, a white soldier replies, "I dunno, I dunno. I'll be happy if I can just get back to Cairo, Illinois" (175).

Updike, Norman   Norman Updike is the mortician who takes charge of moving the bodies of Hermann Shultz and his wife, Sophia, to make room for the college's new Pahlavi Pavilion. Updike points out to Hartke that it takes bodies much longer to rot than most people realize.

Van Arsdale, Herbert   Herbert Van Arsdale (who is not related to mechanic Whitey VanArsdale) was president of Tarkington College in the 1920s, when Letitia Smiley disappeared from campus. When Provost Kensington Barber goes insane that summer, Van Arsdale publicly ascribes his breakdown to "exhaustion brought on by his tireless efforts to solve the mystery of the disappearance of the golden-haired Lilac Queen" (193).

VanArsdale, Whitey   Whitey VanArsdale is a mechanic in Scipio who tells all his customers that they have broken transmissions. Eugene Hartke warns Pamela Ford Hall about Whitey's tricks.

Wakefield, Andrea   Sam Wakefield's wife, Andrea, who would become dean of women at Tarkington College, is estranged from her husband and sleeping in a separate room at the time of his suicide. She dies herself two years before the prison break at Athena.

Wakefield, Sam   Eugene Hartke first meets Sam Wakefield at the state science fair in Cleveland, Ohio, when he is a high school senior. Wakefield is an army recruiter who convinces Eugene's father that the boy should attend West Point Military Academy. Later, Sam is Eugene's commanding officer in Vietnam, where he awards Eugene a Silver Star "for extraordinary valor and gallantry" (42). After Wakefield quits the army in order to speak out against the war, he becomes president of Tarkington College and hires Eugene as a physics professor. Three years later, Sam Wakefield commits suicide by shooting himself in the head.

Wheelock, Harley, II Harley Wheelock II was three years ahead of Eugene Hartke at West Point. He drowned trying to save a suicidal Swedish woman in Germany. Wheelock's son leads the attack on the prisoners at Scipio.

Wheelock, Harley, III Harley Wheelock III is the lieutenant colonel who leads the counterassault on the prisoners occupying Scipio. Wheelock assigns Eugene Hartke the rank of brigadier general in the National Guard and makes him the acting governor of Scipio.

White, Gloria Gloria White is a 60-year-old movie star who rides on the back of Arthur Clark's motorcycle in the "motorcade of highly successful Americans" (174) that tears through the Tarkington campus on graduation day.

Wilder, Jason A "celebrated Conservative newspaper columnist, lecturer, and television talk-show host" (89), Jason Wilder is the man who gets Eugene Hartke fired from Tarkington College. Wilder becomes outraged at liberal comments made by Hartke, and has his daughter, Kimberly, secretly tape-record the professor all around campus. Jason Wilder later becomes a member of the Tarkington board of trustees and is held hostage during the prison escape at Athena.

Wilder, Kimberly Kimberly Wilder is conservative pundit Jason Wilder's learning-disabled daughter. She follows Eugene Hartke all over campus, trying to get him to say outrageous things and secretly tape-recording his comments. Kimberly's tapes are played back to Hartke when he is fired by the board of trustees.

Wills, Benjamin Benjamin Wills is Eugene Debs Hartke's maternal grandfather. A socialist and atheist who works as a groundskeeper at Butler University in Indianapolis, Indiana, Wills is the one who chooses to name his grandson after a famous labor organizer and socialist politician. Before Wills's death in 1948, when young Eugene is eight years old, he makes sure his grandson memorizes the most famous words uttered by the original

Eugene Debs: "While there is a lower class I am in it. While there is a criminal element I am of it. While there is a soul in prison I am not free."

FURTHER READING

Hocus Pocus. New York: Berkley Books, 1991.

"The Hyannis Port Story"

"The Hyannis Port Story," set in the Kennedys' summer hometown on CAPE COD, Massachusetts, was sold to the *Saturday Evening Post* in 1963. However, due to the assassination of President JOHN F. KENNEDY, who appears as an actual character in the story, it remained unpublished until it appeared in the 1968 collection, *Welcome to the Monkey House.*

SYNOPSIS

Set in the early 1960s, "The Hyannis Port Story" is narrated by a storm window salesman who is hired by a wealthy Republican, Commodore William Rumford, to install storm windows on his home in HYANNIS PORT, Massachusetts. Commodore Rumfoord, an ardent Barry Goldwater supporter, mistakenly believes the narrator is a staunch Republican as well, after meeting him at a Lion's Club dinner in New Hampshire. When the narrator arrives in Hyannis Port, the place is overrun with tourists trying to get glimpses of the famous Kennedy family, whose compound is located in Hyannis Port, right across the street from Rumford's four-story "cottage." Rumford himself is extremely annoyed by all the Kennedy hoopla. He invites the narrator to stay for dinner and to spend the night, and he spends the early part of the evening complaining bitterly about how the Kennedy family, whom he views as recent interlopers, have ruined Hyannis Port. Eventually, though, he receives a phone call from Raymond Boyle, a Secret Service agent, who informs Rumford that his son, Robert Taft Rumfoord, has been caught sneaking onto Joseph Kennedy's boat with a girlfriend. The girl turns out to be Sheila Kennedy, a fourth cousin of the famous family, recently arrived from Ireland. The young couple comes to dinner at the Rumfoord home, and

Sheila turns out to be "so intelligent, so warm, and so beautiful" that she bewitches the Rumfoords. That night, the commodore neglects to turn the floodlights on to light up the huge portrait of Barry Goldwater he keeps on the second-story verandah, facing the Kennedy compound. The story ends with President Kennedy himself, accompanied by a son-in-law of Soviet leader Nikita Khrushchev, asking Rumfoord to light the portrait, so that he can find his way home.

COMMENTARY

"The Hyannis Port Story" is a *Romeo and Juliet* style tale not only about two competing families but also about two diametrically opposed political camps in the United States during the early 1960s: Goldwater Republicans and Kennedy Democrats. Barry Goldwater, the political figure supported by Commodore Rumfoord, was a longtime Arizona senator, a founder of American conservatism, and the Republican candidate who ran for U.S. president against Democrat Lyndon B. Johnson in 1964. Rumfoord, of course, is himself quite politically conservative, and further, he seems to coerce his son, Robert, into the kind of conservative politics that will benefit wealthy old families like his own. Robert's speech to the Lions Club concerns getting the country back to "First Principles," but as the narrator wryly notes, one of the First Principles "was getting rid of the income tax" (147), a suggestion that draws great applause from club members. The narrator also speculates that Robert does not "care much more about politics" than he himself does, noting that the young man "looked as though he'd just as soon be somewhere else" (147).

Nevertheless, the young man represents his father's views that the Kennedys and their associates are socially inferior to the Rumfoords and other old families. In his speech, he points out that BOBBY KENNEDY "actually couldn't golf for sour apples" and that Pierre Salinger, White House press secretary, "was one of the worst golfers in the world, and didn't care for sailing or tennis at all" (148). Ironically, high social standing is defined by the Rumfoords as an ability to excel in leisure activities, not in terms of how well these men run the country. The commodore's ethnocentrism becomes

readily apparent when he refers to the Kennedys as the "Irish mafia" (153) and when he mocks their Catholicism by speculating that a helicopter that lands at the compound carries "Pope John the Sixth" (152). In addition, while the commodore brags about his own family arriving in Hyannis Port in 1884, he tells the narrator that the Kennedys "only got here the day before yesterday" (154), though readers soon discover the family actually arrived in 1921, a date 40 years previous, which Rumfoord fully expects the narrator to view as very recent.

Commodore Rumfoord, however, is forced to reassess his views about his neighbors when his son, Robert, is caught sneaking aboard Joseph Kennedy's yacht with a beautiful female Kennedy cousin in tow. Rumfoord is at first brash with Raymond Boyle, the Secret Service agent who calls him to tell him the news. Readers discover that Rumfoord has been a thorn in the Kennedy side for quite a while when the narrator says that Boyle "was known around the Kennedy household as the *Rumfoord Specialist* or the *Ambassador to Rumfoordiana*" (154). But just as in SHAKESPEARE's *Romeo and Juliet*, two young lovers place their affection for each other above their loyalty to their own, feuding families. Sheila Kennedy, with her warmth and charm, completely wins over Commodore Rumfoord, whose decision not to turn on the lights of his giant Goldwater portrait that night shows he is reconsidering his radical anti-Kennedy agenda. When the president himself shows up in Rumfoord's driveway that evening, the commodore speaks to him respectfully. Kennedy views the old man with affection and humor; his request that the commodore turn on his Goldwater sign suggests that the president believes Rumfoord is entitled to whatever political opinions he chooses.

CHARACTERS

Boyden, Hay   Hay Boyden, a building mover in North Crawford, New Hampshire, and a loyal Kennedy Democrat, attends the Lions Club meeting where Robert Taft Rumfoord speaks. He stands up at the end of the talk and says "some terrible things to the boy" (148). When the narrator speaks heatedly to Boyden after the meeting about a dispute over a bathtub enclosure the narrator had sold him, Commodore William Rumfoord believes the narrator is defending Robert's talk. This is why the commodore invites the narrator to install storm windows at his home in Hyannis Port.

Boyle, Raymond Raymond Boyle is the Secret Service agent who is assigned by the Kennedys to be the "*Rumfoord Specialist*" (154). A polite but firm man who has protected both Republican and Democratic presidents, Boyle informs Commodore Rumfoord that his son, Robert, has been apprehended on Joseph Kennedy's yacht with a young woman.

Defense Minister of Pakistan When the narrator finally gets through the crush of tourists, he drives behind the defense minister of Pakistan down a deserted portion of Irving Avenue toward the Rumfoord home.

John the Butler The Rumfoord family's butler, a man named John, answers the phone when the narrator calls and promises to tell the Secret Service to allow the narrator through the crush of tourists. Later, John brings a big bowl of Goldwater campaign buttons to the commodore on the verandah.

Kennedy, John F. U.S. president John F. Kennedy appears in the story at the end when he parks in front of the Rumfoord cottage, gets out of the car, and asks why the commodore has not turned on the lights of his giant Barry Goldwater portrait. The president tells Rumfoord that Nikita Khrushchev's son-in-law is with him and would very much like to see it. Finally, the president asks Rumfoord to keep the portrait lit so that he can find his way home.

Kennedy, Sheila A fourth cousin of the powerful American Kennedy family just arrived from Ireland, Sheila Kennedy is "so intelligent, so warm, and so beautiful" (158) that she wins over even staunch Goldwater supporter Commodore William Rumfoord when she becomes engaged to his son.

Khrushchev's Son-in-Law At the end of the story, President John F. Kennedy tells Commodore

Rumfoord that he has with him "Mr. Khrushchev's son-in-law" (160) who would very much like to see the gaudily lit-up Goldwater portrait that Rumfoord keeps on his second-story verandah. Nikita Khrushchev was the real-life head of the Soviet Union during the time the story takes place.

Narrator The narrator of the story is a storm window salesman and installer who lives in North Crawford, New Hampshire. A man with no strong political affiliation, the narrator is rather bemused when Commodore Rumfoord mistakes him for a Goldwater Republican. Above all, the narrator, unsure of his own social standing, is an outsider to the rich and privileged lifestyle he witnesses in Hyannis Port, and thus is able to provide an objective, ordinary citizen's view of the wealthy and powerful people he meets there.

Program Chairman The unnamed program chairman of the North Crawford Lions Club is a Goldwater man who invites Robert Taft Rumfoord to speak to the club "about the Democratic mess in Washington and Hyannis Port" (147).

Reuther, Walter An actual union organizer and powerful Democratic Party operative in the 1950s and '60s, Walter Reuther appears in the story as a character when he is said to be aboard the *Marlin*, Joseph Kennedy's yacht, when Robert Taft Rumfoord is apprehended trying to sneak aboard.

Rumfoord, Clarice Clarice Rumfoord is the long-suffering wife of Commodore William Rumfoord, who is mostly seen sighing quietly at her husband's excesses. At the end of the story, she encourages the commodore in his conviction to find some kind of work, telling him that "it's awfully hard for a woman to *admire* a man who actually doesn't do anything" (159).

Rumfoord, Commodore William Commodore William Rumfoord, an ardent Goldwater supporter, invites the story's narrator to install storm windows on his extremely large "cottage" in Hyannis Port, Massachusetts. Scornful of the Kennedy family and Democrats in general, the commodore is from a very old, very wealthy Hyannis Port family. The only thing he has actually been commodore of is the Hyannis Port Yacht Club in 1946. By the end of the story, however, when his own son becomes engaged to a warm, beautiful, intelligent Kennedy cousin, he must reassess his social and political views, at least a little bit.

Rumfoord, Robert Taft Robert Taft Rumfoord, a college student who is president of a Republican student organization, speaks at a North Crawford Lions Club meeting attended by the story's narrator. Later, when the narrator is invited to the Rumfoord home to install storm windows, Robert is caught sneaking onto Joseph Kennedy's yacht with Sheila Kennedy. The young couple, clearly in love, cause both the Rumfoords and the Kennedys to soften toward one another.

Stevenson, Adlai A real-life Democratic politician, best known for his two failed campaigns for U.S. president against Dwight Eisenhower in the 1950s, Adlai Stevenson was named U.S. ambassador to the United Nations by President John F. Kennedy. Stevenson appears as a character in the story when he, like the narrator, gets stuck in the line of traffic on Irving Avenue outside the Kennedy family compound. Later, he is on Joseph Kennedy's yacht when Robert Taft Rumfoord is caught sneaking aboard.

FURTHER READING

Reed, Peter. *The Short Fiction of Kurt Vonnegut.* Westport, Conn.: Greenwood Press, 1997.
Welcome to the Monkey House. New York: Dell, 1998.

Jailbird

Much like Vonnegut's earlier novel *Mother Night,* *Jailbird*, published in 1979 by Delacorte/ SEYMOUR LAWRENCE, mingles actual historical figures with fictional characters in order to explore a turbulent period of American history. While *Mother Night*'s fictional characters interact with Nazis such as ADOLF HITLER, Heinrich Himmler, and Adolf Eich-

mann, *Jailbird*'s protagonist, Walter F. Starbuck, mixes with historical figures from what Vonnegut considers three of the most shameful periods in 20th-century America: the early 1920s with its Red Scare and SACCO AND VANZETTI executions; the early 1950s with the Communist denunciations led by Senator Joseph McCarthy; and the Watergate scandal of the early 1970s. As in *Mother Night,* actual historical figures such as lawyer Roy M. Cohn, Watergate co-conspirators H. R. Haldemann, John D. Ehrlichman, Charles Colson, John Mitchell, and even President RICHARD M. NIXON make appearances in the book. But *Jailbird* is also the story of an ordinary man, Walter F. Starbuck, and how he is a pawn of history. Despite his desire to fight injustice done to working people, Starbuck eventually ends up as part of the corrupt system he originally abhors.

SYNOPSIS

Prologue
The novel opens, as many Vonnegut novels do, with a prologue in which the author introduces some of his characters and themes and relates these to his own life. Vonnegut begins by discussing a lunch he and his father and his Uncle Alex (see ALEX VONNEGUT) had with prominent labor organizer POWERS HAPGOOD, whom Vonnegut tells us is the role model for Kenneth Whistler, a character in the novel. The prologue to *Jailbird* is concerned mostly, though, with explaining the events of the fictional Cuyahoga Massacre in Cleveland, Ohio, in which several striking workers and their supporters were gunned down by armed sharpshooters hired by the factory owner. This information sets the stage for the story of Walter F. Starbuck that will follow, a story that involves the history of organized labor and political radicalism in 20th-century America.

Chapters 1–7
Told in the first person by Starbuck, the novel begins on the day that he is released from the Federal Minimum Security Adult Correctional Facility on the edge of Finletter Air Force Base. Starbuck's memoirs detail not only what happens in the two days following his release from prison, but also wind

back in time as he relates stories from his past. Starbuck is the child of servants who worked in the wealthy McCone household; the McCones are owners of the Cuyahoga Bridge and Iron Company and perpetrators of the Cuyahoga Massacre. As a boy, Starbuck receives special attention from Alexander Hamilton McCone, who teaches the boy to play chess and ends up paying for his education at HARVARD UNIVERSITY. We also find out that Starbuck goes to work for the U.S. government after studying in Oxford on a Rhodes scholarship. He travels to Germany at the end of World War II as a civilian member of the Defense Department to oversee logistics during the Nuremberg Trials. This is where he meets his wife, Ruth, who is a Jewish concentration camp survivor who works as Starbuck's interpreter.

After their return from Germany, the couple buys a house in Chevy Chase, Maryland, where they live happily until Starbuck, being interviewed for a promotion within the Defense Department, rather innocently testifies under oath about the communist leanings of friends. This testimony ruins the career of Leland Clewes, an up-and-coming young man in the State Department and gets Starbuck fired from his job. Ruth has to support the couple and their young son for the next several years through her work as an interior decorator while Walter is unemployed. In 1970, Starbuck is offered a minor position in the Nixon administration, as adviser to the president on youth affairs. Though he has very little to do with the president himself, only meeting him face-to-face one time, Starbuck participates in the Watergate conspiracy; this is why he has been sent to prison. His beloved wife dies from massive heart failure two weeks prior to the start of his prison term.

Chapters 8–11

Upon his release from Finletter two years later, Starbuck is given a ride to the airport in Atlanta by limousine chauffeur Cleveland Lawes, who had just dropped Virgil Greathouse, former U.S. secretary of health, education, and welfare, off at Finletter to begin serving his own prison sentence as a Watergate co-conspirator. At the airport, Starbuck catches a plane to New York, where he plans to

become a bartender, having received his doctorate of mixology degree by correspondence while in prison. In New York, he checks into the Hotel Arapahoe, now a decrepit flophouse, though formerly a splendid dining and dancing establishment. Starbuck had taken a college date, Sarah Wyatt, there to dinner years before, an evening he reminisces fondly about in his memoirs. Sarah Wyatt later marries Leland Clewes, the friend Starbuck had unwittingly denounced as a communist. That evening, when Starbuck puts his things away in the Hotel Arapahoe, he discovers a drawerful of various clarinet parts; unbeknownst to him, the parts had been stolen from a truck hijacked on the Ohio Turnpike, a robbery in which the driver was killed. He does not think too much about the parts, though, falling into bed exhausted.

Chapters 12–19

The next morning, Starbuck rises at six A.M. After having breakfast at the Royalton Coffee Shop, where the waitress and owner are kind to him, and after spending several hours sitting listlessly on a park bench, he walks out into the city and bumps into the man whose life he's ruined, Leland Clewes. As Starbuck is talking with Clewes, an old, rumpled bag lady interrupts, and it soon becomes apparent that she knows Starbuck as well. Clewes is not angry about Starbuck's testimony, but thanks him, saying that the prison term he ended up serving for perjury about his communist affiliations was the best thing that ever happened to him. The bag lady turns out to be one of Starbuck's old college girlfriends, Mary Kathleen O'Looney, who is in actuality the extremely wealthy and reclusive Mrs. Jack Graham, main stockholder of the RAMJAC Corporation. Deathly afraid that she will be killed for her wealth, Mary Kathleen lives life disguised.

Starbuck is then led by Mary Kathleen to two secret places in the city. They first go to the basement deep under Grand Central Terminal where she lives; they next ride an elevator to the roof of the Chrysler Building, where the open-air, bird-filled showroom of the American Harp Company is located. On the roof, Mary Kathleen explains to Starbuck that after the death of her husband, Jack Graham, she was so unhappy that she turned to alcohol. She was sent to a private sanitarium in Louisville, Kentucky, where she was given shock treatments. As a result she lost 20 years of her memory, including the years that Starbuck was in the news for ruining Leland Clewes's career. Readers also find out more about Mary Kathleen's and Starbuck's political activism during their student days, when both were under the influence of radical labor organizer Kenneth Whistler, who had helped arrange protests before the Sacco and Vanzetti executions. The reunion of Starbuck and Mary Kathleen O'Looney is soon interrupted, however, when the police come and rearrest Starbuck because he had made an off-hand remark about clarinet parts to the harp company's ancient salesman upon arrival, not realizing the parts in his hotel room were stolen, involved a murder, and that numerous police circulars about the crime had been distributed.

Chapters 20–Epilogue

Starbuck is taken to a New York City police station, put into a padded cell in the basement, and forgotten for many hours until famous lawyer Roy M. Cohn, hired by Mary Kathleen, procures his release. Starbuck is then put into a limousine and taken to the penthouse apartment of RAMJAC Corporation president Arpad Leen. Also in the limousine are Cleveland Lawes, the Georgia chauffeur, as well as Israel Edel, the night clerk at the Hotel Arapahoe, and Frank Ubriaco, the owner of the Royalton Coffee Shop. At his penthouse, Leen tells each of the men that he will be a new vice president of the RAMJAC Corporation. Though bewildered about this change in their fortunes, what the men do not know is that Mary Kathleen is rewarding everyone who showed special kindness to Walter Starbuck after his prison release. Finally figuring out that Mary Kathleen is actually Mrs. Jack Graham, Starbuck leaves to search for her. He finds her in a toilet stall of the Grand Central Terminal basement, having been hit by a RAMJAC taxicab. Much to Starbuck's sorrow, Mary Kathleen ends up dying that night, although before she expires, she tells Starbuck about her will, hidden in her left shoe, in which she leaves the RAMJAC Corporation to the American people. Starbuck decides to conceal the will, believing this is a gift the American people

are not ready for. He enjoys his RAMJAC vice presidency for the next two years, though his concealment of the will is eventually discovered. The novel ends with a large farewell party that Leland and Sarah Clewes throw for Starbuck before he is returned to prison.

COMMENTARY

The heart and soul of *Jailbird* is the 1920 Sacco and Vanzetti case, a historical event in which two Italian immigrants and political anarchists were executed by a U.S. government seemingly more concerned about punishing radical activism than with determining the true guilt or innocence of the convicted men. The novel's epigraph quotes from a letter Nicola Sacco wrote to his 13-year-old son Dante just before his execution. In it, Sacco pleads for Dante to "help the weak ones . . . the prosecuted and the victim, because they are your better friends." The novel's prologue concerns itself with another American miscarriage of justice against working people: the Cuyahoga Massacre in which 14 factory workers and onlookers are gunned down after being fired from their jobs for refusing to accept a drastic pay cut. Although the massacre is fictional, Vonnegut tells readers that it is culled from actual events; he describes it as a "mosaic composed of bits taken from tales of many such riots in not such olden times" (15). The prologue also lets readers know that the book is at least partly inspired by the real-life figure Powers Hapgood, a Harvard-educated labor organizer who gave up a life of ease and prosperity to fight for workers' rights. Kenneth Whistler is based on Hapgood. *Jailbird* is largely about organized labor and political radicalism; its dominant theme is the unjust treatment of working-class people, along with corporate and government corruption, in 20th-century America.

In many ways, Walter F. Starbuck is an American everyman; his story at first seems to follow the ideal rags-to-riches trajectory associated with the American dream. Born to working-class immigrant parents, Starbuck begins life as Walter Stankiewicz—his family anglicizes the name to Starbuck in the hopes that their son will assimilate more easily into the dominant American culture. Catching the

Bartolomeo Vanzetti (left) and Nicola Sacco, manacled together, enter the courthouse at Dedham, Massachusetts, where they will receive the death penalty for murder, 1927 *(courtesy of the Library of Congress)*

eye of the wealthy Alexander Hamilton McCone, Starbuck attends Harvard University, the epitome of American educational achievement. He wins a Rhodes scholarship and later accepts a government job, idealistically hoping to make the world a better place. Initially, his communist sympathies do not seem as if they will count against him. As Starbuck writes when remembering his youth, it was once entirely acceptable for a young man in this country to be a communist:

> What could be so repulsive after all, during the Great Depression, especially, and with yet another war for natural wealth and markets coming, in a young man's belief that each person could work as well as he or she was able,

and should be rewarded, sick or well, young or old, brave or frightened, talented or imbecilic, according to his or her simple needs? (54)

Despite his rise from poverty, his sterling education, and his idealistic dreams of helping those in need, Starbuck winds up on the wrong side of history again and again. He ruins a close friend, Leland Clewes, and sends him to prison through his testimony during the McCarthy period; he conspires with corrupt politicians during the Watergate affair; and he participates in the mega-corporate takeover of America as a vice president in the RAMJAC Corporation. So is Walter Starbuck a good man or a bad man? What are readers to think of him and his escapades in American history?

A former government official turned private lawyer named Timothy Beame, whom Starbuck visits when he is seeking work after losing his position with the Department of Defense, certainly believes that Starbuck's actions caused irreparable harm to the government. Beame accuses Starbuck and Clewes of destroying "the good reputation of the most unselfish and intelligent generation of public servants this country has ever known" (122). When Starbuck protests that he merely told the truth about his and Clewes's early communist leanings, Beame responds that Starbuck told a "fragmentary truth" (122) that led Americans to believe that "educated and compassionate public servants are almost certainly Russian spies" (123). Despite his bluster, Beame acknowledges that Starbuck's crimes were partly the result of being in "the wrong place at the wrong time," though he still calls Starbuck a "nincompoop" who "set humanitarianism back a full century" (123). Starbuck himself sees his life as a series of accidents, but these accidents, he confides to readers, are partly the result of weakness in character: "The most embarrassing thing to me about this autobiography, surely, is its unbroken chain of proofs that I was never a serious man" (227), he confesses, adding, "Never have I risked my life, or even my comfort, in the service of mankind. Shame on me" (227–228).

Like many Vonnegut characters, Starbuck seems to be the victim of large forces beyond his control. The character is perhaps named after the first mate in Melville's MOBY-DICK, a thoughtful Quaker who opposes Captain Ahab's mad pursuit of the white whale, but who is finally unable or perhaps too weak to prevail against the obsessed captain. Like Melville's Starbuck, Vonnegut's character is a well-intentioned man whose heart is in the right place, yet who is finally the plaything of fate, not always able to act according to his better nature. Vonnegut's Starbuck cannot help asking, late in life, whether anything he did, any of his lofty commitments, made any difference at all. Amazed at how nature makes his little dog believe that a rubber ice-cream cone toy is a puppy, Starbuck ponders about his own "equally ridiculous commitments to bits of trash," concluding that it finally does not matter much since "We are here for no purpose,

unless we can invent one" (301). Walter Starbuck, then, is a character through whom Vonnegut can explore his favorite recurring theme of fate versus FREE WILL.

Do humans have the ability to act freely and change the world, or are they simply, as Vonnegut writes about Billy Pilgrim in *Slaughterhouse-Five*, "the listless playthings of enormous forces" (164)? As in many Vonnegut novels, perhaps the best solution to this conundrum is to behave *as if* one has free will, even in the face of overwhelming evidence to the contrary. Starbuck says that as he is writing these memoirs at the "rueful age of sixty-six" (54), despite all his misadventures in history, his "knees still turn to water" with admiration and respect when he encounters anyone "who still considers it a possibility that there will one day be one big happy peaceful family on Earth—the Family of Man" (54–55). Like Eliot Rosewater in *God Bless You, Mr. Rosewater*, Walter Starbuck admires the utopian impulse, no matter how impossible it may be to create utopias in the real world. Vonnegut himself seems to share this admiration. Mary Kathleen O'Looney perhaps sums up Starbuck's character best with her dying words, when she forgives him for pretending to love her as a young man. "You couldn't help it that you were born without a heart," she tells him, "At least you tried to believe what the people with hearts believed—so you were a good man just the same" (283). Readers might be reminded of Vonnegut's novel *Cat's Cradle*, in which the religious prophet Bokonon advises adherents of his philosophy to live by the *foma*, or harmless untruths, that "make you brave and kind and healthy and happy" (epigraph). Perhaps the only way to bring genuine goodness into the world is to pretend it exists, no matter the real circumstances. We see a similar idea in the prologue when Vonnegut mentions John Figler, the high school student who has read all of Vonnegut's work and sums up "the single idea" that lies at the heart of his writing: "Love may fail, but courtesy will prevail" (2). In the absence of real love, humans can still treat each other with the respect due loved ones, with courtesy and kindness. To Vonnegut, this "seven-word telegram" (2) seems a true and complete summation of his life's work.

In many ways, *Jailbird* is also a love story—Walter Starbuck's reminiscences about the four women he loved during his life: his mother, his wife, Ruth, his college girlfriend, Sarah Wyatt, and his radical lover, Mary Kathleen O'Looney. While Starbuck may have failed all of these women to a certain extent, and while genuine love may be impossible in a contemporary world in which the elegant and romantic dining room of the Hotel Arapahoe has been turned into a sleazy theater showing hard-core pornographic films, nevertheless, Starbuck's relationships with the women in his life have helped him through difficult times. Starbuck, in fact, tells readers that he still believes what used to be a commonly held notion among men: "that women were more spiritual, more sacred than men" (50). The four women he has loved have all been martyrs to a certain extent. His mother, a Russian Lithuanian immigrant, spent her life working as a servant in the wealthy McCone household. His wife, Ruth, is a concentration camp survivor who retains her brilliance and multiple accomplishments, despite the cynicism resulting from her wartime experiences. The formerly wealthy Sarah Wyatt becomes a trained nurse, coping with death and disease through humor. Mary Kathleen O'Looney, whose own mother was killed by industrial carelessness, crusades to help the poor and oppressed, losing her own sanity in the process. The women that Starbuck has loved are "sacred"—living examples of those Christ calls "blessed" in the Sermon on the Mount: those who mourn, those who are meek, those who hunger and thirst for righteousness, those who are merciful, and so on.

Indeed, New Testament CHRISTIANITY plays a large role in this novel. Starbuck writes that, as a young man, he had "expected the story of Sacco and Vanzetti to be retold as often and as movingly, to be as irresistible, as the story of Jesus Christ some day" (228). He even imagines the execution of the two men as a Christian passion play, with the role of the three wise men played by the committee appointed by Governor Fuller to investigate the Sacco and Vanzetti verdicts. In this version, though, Starbuck decries the so-called wisdom of the wise men—the committee votes that justice would be done if the execution is carried through.

While Starbuck abhors the cruelties done in the name of religion and the vengeful Christianity of a man like Emil Larkin, the born-again Watergate conspirator jailed alongside him at Finletter Prison, he nevertheless admires Christ's message of love and redemption. Starbuck imagines himself, when he is working as President Nixon's special adviser on youth affairs, sending a telegram each week to the administration that reads: "Young people still refuse to see the obvious impossibility of world disarmament and economic equality. Could be fault of New Testament (quod vide)" (56). As critic Peter Scholl argues, Vonnegut "cannot stand the theology of Christianity, but would have its ethics. His books propose that absurdity lies at the heart of the cosmos, and thus making any sort of moral statement is at least a little foolish. Still, paradoxically, he insists that man must be treated with kindness and respect, as though he were the center of the universe and possessed of an eternal soul" (11).

Perhaps the way the novel most clearly retains Christian ethics is through its recognition and praise of those who display common decency and kindness in a cruel world. When Starbuck tells Mary Kathleen O'Looney about the people who had treated him humanely after his release from Finletter Prison, she exclaims, "They're saints! . . . So there are still saints around!" Vonnegut himself has written about the possibility of saints in the modern world in a 2003 article that appeared in the alternate news magazine *In These Times*:

> And hey, listen: A sappy woman sent me a letter a few years back. She knew I was sappy, too, which is to say a lifelong northern Democrat in the Franklin Delano Roosevelt mode, a friend of the working stiffs. She was about to have a baby, not mine, and wished to know if it was a bad thing to bring such a sweet and innocent creature into a world as bad as this one is. I replied that what made being alive almost worthwhile for me, besides music, was all the saints I met, who could be anywhere. By saints I meant people who behaved decently in a strikingly indecent society. Perhaps some of you are or will become saints for her child to meet.

Several of the "saints" depicted in *Jailbird*, the people who behave decently in an indecent society, refer specifically to Christ's Sermon on the Mount. In the novel's prologue, Vonnegut tells a story about a judge who asks labor organizer Powers Hapgood why a man "from such a distinguished family and with such a fine education" chose to live the life he did. Hapgood responds simply, "Because of the Sermon on the Mount, sir" (12). Later, Starbuck relates that the fictional character Kenneth Whistler, modeled after the real-life Hapgood, also said those words to a judge. Finally, at the end of the novel, at his farewell party before being returned to prison, a record from many years before is played in which Starbuck is asked by Congressman Nixon why someone like him, the son of immigrants who had benefited from American capitalism, has been so ungrateful to the economic system that aided him. Though he acknowledges that his answer to Nixon is not original, and that, in fact, nothing about him "has ever been original" (306), Starbuck nevertheless repeats the words uttered by his one-time hero, Kenneth Whistler: "Why? Because of the Sermon on the Mount, sir" (306). Despite his lack of originality, at least Starbuck pretends to be like those he admires, and in Vonnegut's world, that might be the best one can do.

CHARACTERS AND RELATED ENTRIES

Agnew, Spiro T. An actual historical figure, Spiro T. Agnew was vice president during the Nixon administration, forced to resign his office after pleading *nolo contendere* to charges of tax evasion and accepting bribes. He appears in *Jailbird* at the meeting about the Kent State shootings, when Nixon makes a joke about Walter Starbuck's smoking habits.

Barlow, Frank X. Frank X. Barlow is one of the pen names used by Finletter prisoner Dr. Robert Fender, a science fiction writer of some note. In the novel, Starbuck sums up a story about a former judge from the planet Vicuna, published in *Playboy* magazine under the Barlow pseudonym.

Beame, Timothy When Walter Starbuck is fired from his government job after his involvement

in sending Leland Clewes to prison, he goes to numerous old friends looking for work. Most are very polite though unhelpful. The exception is "an arrogant old man" (119) named Timothy Beame who served as an assistant secretary of agriculture during the Roosevelt administration. Beame invites Starbuck to his office, then cruelly berates him for destroying "the good reputation of the most unselfish and intelligent generation of public servants this country has ever known" (122).

"Bonnie Failey" "Bonnie Failey" is a fictional poem, said to be written by Henry Niles Whistler about an infant who was shot and killed at the Cuyahoga Massacre. Supposedly, the poem is later set to music, and according to Vonnegut, is "still sung today" (26).

Borders, Lance and Leora Leora Borders is Walter Starbuck's secretary during the time he is a vice president at the RAMJAC Corporation. She appears at Starbuck's farewell party with her husband, Lance, who has just undergone a radical mastectomy. Lance tells Starbuck that one in 200 mastectomies are actually performed on men.

Capone, Al The famous Chicago gangster Al Capone appears in *Jailbird* briefly when Walter Starbuck tells readers that Capone believed Sacco and Vanzetti should have been executed because "Bolshevism is knocking at our gates . . ." (236).

Carter, Clyde A third cousin and look-alike to President Jimmy Carter, Clyde Carter is a guard at the Federal Minimum Security Adult Correctional Facility on Finletter Air Force Base who befriends prisoner Walter Starbuck. Both Carter and Starbuck are doctors of mixology, having taken a correspondence course in bartending. At the end of the novel, Clyde becomes a vice president of the Chrysler Air Temp Division of the RAMJAC Corporation and attends the farewell party for Starbuck at the home of Leland and Sarah Clewes.

Carter, Claudia Claudia Carter is the wife of Finletter prison guard Clyde Carter. She appears briefly at the end of the novel, at the farewell party for Walter Starbuck.

Chessman, Caryl An actual historical figure who was put to death in a California gas chamber in 1960 for supposedly robbing and sexually assaulting two women, Caryl Chessman was also an eloquent writer with a sharp legal mind who published four books while in prison. Chessman became a cause celebré in the 1950s, with prominent actors, politicians, and other well-known figures campaigning for his release, arguing that his death sentence was a gross miscarriage of justice. Chessman appears in the novel when prison guard Clyde Carter mentions that the executed man's last words were "It's all right" (92).

Claycomb, Judge Judge Claycomb (whose first name is never given) appears in the novel's prologue. He is the judge who listens in court to Powers Hapgood's tales of strikes, arrests, and other labor intrigues. When Judge Claycomb asks Hapgood why a man from such a distinguished family would choose to live such a life, Hapgood replies, "Because of the Sermon on the Mount, Sir" (12).

Claycomb, Moon Moon Claycomb, a high school classmate of Vonnegut's, is the son of Judge Claycomb. Because of his acquaintance with Moon, Vonnegut is able to remember the judge's name when he relates the story about Powers Hapgood's reference to Christ's Sermon on the Mount in court.

Cleveland Chief of Police When the striking workers gather on Christmas morning, 1894, at the Cuyahoga Bridge and Iron Company, the Cleveland chief of police climbs a scaffold and reads the riot act, ordering the crowd to disperse. When nothing happens, the chief calmly climbs down again; he did not expect the workers to comply with his order, and he wisely keeps his officers safe inside a fence for their own protection.

Clewes, Leland Leland Clewes is the up-and-coming young diplomat in the State Department who has presidential aspirations and whose career is ruined when Walter F. Starbuck testifies that he had previously been a communist. Clewes eventually serves time in prison for perjury. Starbuck and Clewes meet again after many years when Clewes surprisingly thanks Starbuck, saying prison was the best thing that ever happened to him. At the end of the novel, Clewes and his wife, the former Sarah Wyatt, who used to be Starbuck's girlfriend, throw a farewell party for him before he returns to prison.

Clewes, Sarah Wyatt One of the four women Walter F. Starbuck claims to have loved during his life, Sarah Wyatt is a student at Pine Manor College in Wellesley, Massachusetts, when he is a student at Harvard University. Walter invites Sarah to the Hotel Arapahoe for a fancy dinner and dancing, and the two end up dating off and on for the next seven years. Sarah's family owns the Wyatt Clock Company, notorious for an industrial tragedy in which 50 women workers experienced radium poisoning after being hired to paint ships' clocks. A beautiful but cynical girl, Sarah eventually marries Leland Clewes, Starbuck's former friend whom he inadvertently outed as a communist. The Clewes rekindle their friendship with Starbuck by the end of the novel and throw him a farewell party before his return to prison.

Cohn, Roy M. Roy M. Cohn is a minor character in the novel's prologue. He is modeled after real-life anticommunist lawyer Roy M. Cohn, who had been chief counsel of the Senate Investigating Committee during the anticommunist hearings headed by Senator Joseph McCarthy in the 1950s. The fictionalized Cohn, retained by the RAMJAC Corporation, gets Walter Starbuck out of jail after he is arrested on suspicion of killing a truck driver and stealing a load of clarinet parts.

Colson, Charles W. Charles W. Colson, an actual historical figure known as the "evil genius" of the NIXON administration, served seven months in prison for his role in the Watergate scandal. The fictionalized Colson appears at the emergency meeting Nixon calls to discuss the Kent State shootings. Colson became a born-again Christian in prison, and thus is the possible role model for the Emil Larkin character in the novel.

Cuyahoga Bridge and Iron Company The Cuyahoga Bridge and Iron Company, founded by the wealthy Daniel McCone, is said to be the largest single employer in Cleveland, Ohio, in 1894, when the Cuyahoga Massacre takes place.

Cuyahoga Massacre The Cuyahoga Massacre is a fictional event described in the prologue of *Jailbird* in which several striking workers at the Cuyahoga Bridge and Iron Company are killed by anti-riot sharpshooters hired by their employers. Although Vonnegut terms the Cuyahoga Massacre an "invention," he nevertheless claims it is drawn from accounts of real riots and acts of violence committed against striking workers, which occurred "in not such olden times" (15).

Denny, Kyle Kyle Denny is a Harvard classmate of Walter Starbuck's, a football player from Philadelphia who took Sarah Wyatt out twice. When asked what he thought of Sarah, Kyle replied, "nobody home!" (148).

di Sanza, Dr. Carlo Dr. Carlo di Sanza is a fellow prisoner of Walter Starbuck's at Finletter. A naturalized American citizen who holds a doctorate in law from the University of Naples, di Sanza is serving his second term in prison for promoting a Ponzi scheme through the U.S. mail. Di Sanza is also a vociferous patriot who tells Starbuck upon his release to remember that the United States is "still the greatest country in the world" (94).

Edel, Israel The night clerk at the decrepit Hotel Arapahoe when Walter Starbuck stays there after being released from prison, Israel Edel holds a doctorate in history from Long Island University, but the night clerk position is the best job he can find. Edel is later rewarded with a vice presidency in the RAMJAC Corporation for his kindness to the old jailbird Walter Starbuck; Edel gives Starbuck the hotel's bridal suite to stay in, and he patiently and ruefully explains to him the nature of the pornography films being shown in the room that once housed the hotel's fancy restaurant.

Edel, Norma Norma Edel is the wife of Hotel Arapahoe night clerk Israel Edel. She has always hated Walter Starbuck for some unknown reason. Nevertheless, she appears at his farewell party at the end of the novel.

Ehrlichman, John D. John D. Ehrlichman is an actual historic figure who served as assistant to the president for domestic affairs during the Nixon administration. He served 18 months in prison for his role in the Watergate scandal. Like other key administration officials, Ehrlichman is present at the meeting in which Nixon jokes about Walter F. Starbuck's smoking habits.

Einstein, Albert The great 20th-century physicist makes an appearance in the novel as a ghost and the hero of the Robert Fender science fiction story "Asleep at the Switch."

Fender, Dr. Robert Bob Fender is a fellow inmate of Walter F. Starbuck's at Finletter prison. A veterinarian who had been convicted of treason during the Korean War after falling in love with a beautiful North Korean agent, Fender is also a science fiction writer of some note who publishes under the names "Frank X. Barlow" and "Kilgore Trout." Several of his stories, including one about the planet Vicuna and another called "Asleep at the Switch," are summarized in the novel. A lifer who cannot get out of prison to attend the farewell party for Walter Starbuck, Fender nevertheless sends a telegram, which bears only the words "Ting-a-ling," a reference to his Vicuna story.

Figler, John In the novel's prologue, Vonnegut mentions that he received a letter from John Figler, a high school student from Crown Point, Indiana, on November 16, 1978. In the letter, John Figler says that after reading almost everything by Vonnegut he is prepared to state the single idea that lies at the core of Vonnegut's work: "Love may fail, but courtesy will prevail" (2). Vonnegut explains that Figler's axiom seems true and complete to him and that he is "now in the abashed condition" of realizing he need not have written several books when "a seven-word telegram would have done the job" (2).

Finletter Federal Minimum Security Adult Correctional Facility The Finletter Federal Minimum Security Adult Correctional Facility is the prison where Walter F. Starbuck, the protagonist and narrator of *Jailbird*, serves his sentence for his role in the Watergate conspiracy. Starbuck is being released from Finletter as the novel begins.

Gibney, Peter On the morning after his release from prison, Walter F. Starbuck walks the streets of New York City. When he passes the Century Association on West 43rd Street, he remembers how he had once been a luncheon guest there of the composer Peter Gibney. Gibney, a Harvard classmate of Starbuck's, abruptly ends their relationship after the Leland Clewes affair.

Graham, Jack Jack Graham was a reclusive engineer who founded the RAMJAC Corporation. He dies before the novel opens, leaving his widow, Mrs. Jack Graham (the former Mary Kathleen O'Looney), to run the giant conglomerate. Graham had met Mary Kathleen one night in a Kentucky coal mining town when she had fled the alcohol-induced violence of Kenneth Whistler.

Graham, Mrs. Jack Mrs. Jack Graham, the majority stockholder in the RAMJAC Corporation, is even more reclusive than her late husband. She has not been seen in public for five years; her orders for running the company come in the mail and are accompanied by her signature and a complete set of fingerprints. The reclusive multimillionaire, however, turns out to be the bag lady Walter Starbuck meets on the street after being released from prison—the former Mary Kathleen O'Looney. See below.

Grant, Robert Referred to by Walter Starbuck as one of the "three wise men" (237) who comments on the Sacco and Vanzetti case, Robert Grant was an actual former probate judge put on a committee by Governor Fuller of Massachusetts to investigate the trial. The committee upheld the death sentences of Sacco and Vanzetti.

Greathouse, Virgil Virgil Greathouse, a completely fictional character unlike Haldeman, Colson, Ehrlichman, and others, is the former secretary of health, education, and welfare in the Nixon administration. Convicted in the Watergate Scandal, Greathouse begins serving his prison sentence on the same day that Walter Starbuck finishes serving his. Starbuck witnesses Greathouse, along with two of his lawyers, arrive at Finletter Air Force Base in a limousine. The limousine driver, Cleveland Lawes, ends up giving Starbuck a ride into Atlanta.

Haldeman, H. R. The actual White House chief of staff to President Richard Nixon, H. R. Haldeman was convicted of conspiracy and obstruction of justice for his role in the Watergate scandal and sentenced to an 18-month prison term. Like other historical figures, Haldeman is said to be present at the emergency meeting Nixon calls to discuss the Kent State shootings.

Hapgood, Mary Donovan Mary Hapgood, a real life socialist activist and political candidate, was married to union organizer Powers Hapgood. Vonnegut mentions her in the prologue to *Jailbird* when he explains that his first vote in a national election was for the presidential ticket of Norman Thomas and Mary Hapgood.

Hapgood, Norman and Hutchins Norman and Hutchins Hapgood, brothers of William Hapgood and uncles of Powers Hapgood, were both "socialistically inclined journalists and editors and book writers in and around New York" (10), whom Vonnegut mentions briefly in the novel's prologue.

Hapgood, Powers Powers Hapgood, an actual historical figure, is described by Vonnegut in the novel's Prologue as an INDIANAPOLIS man of his father's generation, who is "sometimes mentioned in histories of American labor for his deeds of derring-do in strikes and at the protests about the executions of Sacco and Vanzetti" (2). A Harvard-educated man who became a coal miner and labor organizer, Powers Hapgood is the model for the fictional Kenneth Whistler. In the prologue, Vonnegut tells of a lunch he had with his father, his Uncle Alex, and Powers Hapgood. Hapgood tells the others he had been in court all morning to testify about violence on a picket line. The judge had allowed Hapgood to tell story after story about his involvement with organized labor, but finally asks him why a well-educated man from a distinguished family would live as he did. Hapgood replies, "Because of the Sermon on the Mount, sir" (12).

Hapgood, William William Hapgood, an actual historical figure, was the father of Powers Hapgood. In the novel's prologue, Vonnegut tells how William Hapgood founded a cannery in Indianapolis in 1903 called the Columbia Conserve Company. Set up as an experiment in industrial democracy, in which workers controlled the company and received fair wages and generous benefits, the company was a success until the Great Depression years destroyed it.

Helms, Richard M. An actual historical figure who headed the C.I.A. from 1966 to 1973, Richard M. Helms is said to be present at the emergency meeting called by President Nixon to discuss the Kent State shootings. This meeting is the only time Walter F. Starbuck meets Nixon in person.

Hotel Arapahoe The Hotel Arapahoe is the former luxury hotel become a decrepit flophouse. Walter Starbuck, after his release from prison early in the novel, checks into the New York hotel, mostly out of nostalgia for the time he had brought a date there for an evening of dinner and dancing when he was a young man. Ironically, the former elegant dining room of the Arapahoe has now been turned into an adult theater showing hardcore pornographic films, and thus mocking romance altogether. The Hotel Arapahoe is where Starbuck finds the drawer filled with stolen clarinet pieces that will get him in trouble with the law once again.

Izumi Izumi is a beautiful North Korean agent and nightclub singer whom science fiction writer Bob Fender meets and falls in love with while he is stationed overseas during the Korean War. Though Izumi realizes Fender really is only a meat inspector when he smuggles her onto his military base, she nevertheless falls in love with him as well after the two spend the night together. When Izumi's spy ring is discovered, Fender hides her in his apartment for 11 days. On the 12th day, the two are arrested and never see each other again. Fender can only assume that Izumi has been summarily executed by the South Koreans.

Jarvis, Colin Described as "an ordinary foundryman with a gift for oratory" (15), Colin Jarvis leads the striking factory workers at the Cuyahoga Bridge and Iron Company. When he is jailed on trumped-up murder charges in late November, his wife, Ma Jarvis, takes over his leadership role.

Jarvis, Ma The wife of jailed strike leader Colin Jarvis, Ma Jarvis leads a delegation of striking workers' wives to the Cuyahoga Bridge and Iron Company on December 15, 1894, to deliver the message that the workers will return on any terms. Rebuffed, Ma tells a reporter that the striking workers will return on Christmas morning. The Cuyahoga Massacre, in which many of the workers are killed and injured, takes place that day.

Johannsen Nils Nils Johannsen is the president of Johannsen Grinder, the company that fired all its workers who joined a union while Walter Starbuck was a Harvard University student. Kenneth Whistler, in a rally for the fired workers, tells the story of Johannsen being caught using loaded dice in a crap game at a tea dance years before.

Kincaid, Edwin Edwin Kincaid is the fictional governor of Ohio who mobilizes a company of National Guard infantrymen to protect the Cuyahoga Bridge and Iron Company from striking workers who have promised to return on Christmas morning, 1894.

Kissinger, Henry The real-life secretary of state in both the Nixon and Ford administrations, Henry

Kissinger appears in the novel at Nixon's emergency meeting to discuss the Kent State shootings. Vonnegut states that Kissinger "had yet to recommend the carpet-bombing of Hanoi on Christmas Day" (75), linking Kissinger in readers' minds with the villainous factory owner Daniel McCone, who instigated the Christmas Day Cuyahoga Massacre in Cleveland, Ohio.

Kramm, Doris   The ancient secretary of ancient harp salesman Delmar Peale, Doris Kramm weeps when she meets Walter Starbuck on the roof of the Chrysler Building in New York the morning after his release from the Finletter prison. She has just received two pieces of bad news: She will be forced to retire immediately now that the RAMJAC Corporation has taken over the American Harp Company, and her great-grandniece was killed in an auto crash.

Larkin, Emil   A fictional creation who appears amid the actual historical figures involved in the Watergate scandal, Emil Larkin is described as "the President's most vindictive advisor and dreaded hatchet man" (74). Sent to his prison for his role as a Watergate co-conspirator, Emil Larkin becomes a born-again Christian who tries to bully Walter F. Starbuck into praying with him. Larkin is possibly modeled on the real-life figure Charles W. Colson, who was considered the "evil genius" of the Nixon administration and became a born-again Christian while serving a prison term for his involvement in the Watergate scandal.

Lawes, Cleveland   Cleveland Lawes is the limousine driver who gives Walter Starbuck a lift to Atlanta after dropping Virgil Greathouse off at the Finletter prison. Although Lawes has only a grammar school education, he reads five books a week waiting for people in the limousine. When Lawes was in the army, he became a prisoner of the Chinese Communists in North Korea. When the war was over, Lawes went to China and worked for two years as a deck hand on the Yellow Sea; when he decided to go home, Chinese and American diplomats at the highest level debated terms under which he would be allowed to return to America.

Cleveland Lawes is eventually made a vice president in the RAMJAC Corporation for his kindness to Walter Starbuck.

Lawes, Unnamed Cousin   When African-American Cleveland Lawes was a boy, his family experienced many racist incidents including an unnamed cousin of his being burned alive by a mob.

Lawes, Eucharist   The wife of chauffeur Cleveland Lawes, Eucharist Lawes, or Ukey, appears at the farewell party for Walter Starbuck at the end of the novel. She is a southerner homesick for the South, where she believes people are friendlier and more relaxed.

Lawes, Sr.   When Cleveland Lawes was a boy, his father, whose first name is not given, was dragged out of his house and horsewhipped by the Ku Klux Klan one night.

Leen, Arpad   Arpad Leen, who grew up in Fiji, is the president and chairman of the board of directors of the RAMJAC Corporation. Described as an "able and informed and brilliant and responsive executive" (136), Leen dutifully follows the orders of his boss, Mrs. Jack Graham, and hires Walter Starbuck, along with several people who were kind to Starbuck upon his release from prison, as vice presidents of the RAMJAC Corporation. Never having met Mrs. Graham personally, Leen begins to suspect that Walter Starbuck is the reclusive multimillionaire disguised as a man. At the end of the novel, Leen goes to work for a mysterious company called BIBEC, which some people believe is a Russian front organization.

Leen, Dexter   Dexter Leen is the 10-year-old son of Arpad Leen, who lets Walter Starbuck borrow his dancing shoes, "black patent leather evening slippers with little bows at the insteps" (276). Dexter has given his parents an ultimatum: He will commit suicide if they make him continue to go to dancing school.

Leen's Butler   When the men to be rewarded by Mrs. Jack Graham are assembled at Arpad Leen's penthouse, Walter Starbuck asks the butler to bring him a *pousse-café*, a rainbow-colored drink he learned about from his correspondence bartendering course.

Leen's Daughter   Arpad Leen's daughter is having her debut at the Waldorf-Astoria Hotel the night he rewards all the men noticed by Mrs. Jack Graham for being "honest and kind" (256). Leen's duties cause him to miss this big event.

Leen's Mother and Father   Arpad Leen's father is a Hungarian Jew and his mother is a Greek Cypriot. The couple met when they were working on a Swedish cruise ship in the late 1920s. They jumped ship in Fiji, where they run a general store.

Lowell, A. Lawrence   One of the "three wise men" who comments on the Sacco and Vanzetti case, Abbot Lawrence Lowell was the president of Harvard University who chaired the committee appointed to look into the trial by Massachusetts Governor Fuller. The committee upheld the convictions and death sentences.

Madeiros, Celestino   An actual historic figure, Celestino Madeiros confessed to being present during the Braintree murders supposedly committed by Sacco and Vanzetti before the executions took place. Though Madeiros claimed Sacco and Vanzetti were not present, his testimony was questionable and did not exonerate the men. He ended up being executed for unrelated crimes on the same day as Sacco and Vanzetti.

McCone, Alexander Hamilton   The younger son of Cuyahoga Bridge and Iron Company owner Daniel McCone, Alexander Hamilton McCone at the age of 22 witnesses the Cuyahoga Massacre, after which his previously slight stammer becomes so pronounced that he can barely speak at all. In later life, McCone becomes Cleveland's leading art collector and philanthropist. He takes great interest in the young son of his cook and chauffeur, teaching the boy, Walter Starbuck, to play chess and eventually paying for his education at Harvard University. When McCone discovers that Starbuck

has become a communist at Harvard, he becomes furious and descends on Starbuck in his borrowed apartment in Cambridge, where the college boy has just made love for the first time to Mary Kathleen O'Looney. When McCone slams out of the apartment, declaring himself through with Starbuck forever, Starbuck says that the door also slammed on his childhood and he became a man.

McCone, Alice Rockefeller   The wife of Alexander Hamilton McCone, Alice Rockefeller McCone is embarrassed by her husband's speech impediment and thus spends most of her time in Europe with her daughter, Clara.

McCone, Clara   Clara McCone is the daughter of Alexander and Alice McCone. Alexander rarely sees his daughter because she lives with her mother in Europe most of the time.

McCone, Daniel   Daniel McCone is the founder and owner of the Cuyahoga Bridge and Iron Company, a fictional business that Vonnegut presents as the largest employer in Cleveland, Ohio, at the end of the 19th century. When McCone tells his factory workers that they must accept a 10 percent pay cut, half walk out, leading eventually to the Cuyahoga Massacre, in which 14 people, most of them striking workers and their family members, are shot to death on Christmas Day.

McCone, John   The older son of Daniel McCone, John McCone had flunked out of the MASSACHUSETTS INSTITUTE OF TECHNOLOGY his freshman year and gone to work at his father's iron company, soon becoming the senior McCone's "most trusted aide" (16). John McCone is 25 when the Cuyahoga Massacre occurs. The workers hate both John and his father, although they acknowledge that the men "knew more about shaping iron and steel than anybody else in the world" (16).

Mitchell, John N.   United States attorney general during the Nixon administration, John Mitchell served prison time for his involvement in the Watergate scandal. Mitchell is one of the actual historical figures who appears at the emergency meeting Nixon calls to discuss the Kent State shootings.

Nixon, Richard M. The novel includes several characters who are actual historical figures, the best known of whom is U.S. President Richard M. Nixon. Walter F. Starbuck is given a position in the Nixon administration as his special adviser on youth affairs. The only time Starbuck ever meets Nixon in person is when he is called to an emergency meeting about the war protesters shot to death at Kent State University. Though Starbuck prepared an elaborate plan for the president to follow, he is never asked to speak. The only time the president notices him is to make a joke about the three cigarettes Starbuck nervously has going all at once.

O'Looney, Francis X. Francis X. O'Looney is a deputy sheriff in Morris County who arrests an engraver for drunken driving one night. The man tells O'Looney that the only time he's seen his unusual name before was on the crypt of Mary Kathleen O'Looney, whose doors he engraved. Francis X. O'Looney then becomes curious about whether he's related to Mary Kathleen; he ends up bringing the RAMJAC Corporation tumbling down when he researches her fingerprints and it is discovered that Walter Starbuck had concealed Mary Kathleen's will for two years.

O'Looney, Mrs. Francis X. Francis X. O'Looney's wife divorces him after he falls in love with his fantasy version of Mary Kathleen O'Looney, a woman he never actually met.

O'Looney, Mary Kathleen Mary Kathleen O'Looney is one of the four women Walter Starbuck claims to have loved during his life. The daughter of a woman who contracts radium poisoning while working for the Wyatt Clock Company, Mary Kathleen is a radical activist whom Walter Starbuck meets and sleeps with during his senior year at Harvard. The two attend an inspiring talk by labor organizer Kenneth Whistler, and Mary Kathleen later follows Whistler to Kentucky, where he is working in a coal mine. Fleeing Whistler's drunken abuse one night, she runs into the arms

of a young mining engineer named Jack Graham, whom she ends up marrying. In later life, Mary Kathleen becomes the reclusive and eccentric head of the RAMJAC Corporation, known only as Mrs. Jack Graham (see above), and lives out her life disguised as a bag lady. Mary Kathleen ends up dying in a toilet stall under Grand Central Terminal, having been hit by one of her own company's taxicabs.

O'Looney, Mary Kathleen's Mother Mary Kathleen O'Looney's mother was one of the 50 women who died from radium poisoning after painting clocks for the Wyatt Clock Company; this fact might have helped radicalize Mary Kathleen.

Padwee, Dr. Howard Dr. Howard Padwee is Walter Starbuck's veterinarian, who tells Starbuck that his dog is experiencing a false pregnancy; she believes a toy rubber ice-cream cone is her puppy.

Peale, Delmar Delmar Peale is an ancient salesman at the American Harp Company showroom on the roof of the Chrysler Building in New York City. When Mary Kathleen O'Looney brings Walter Starbuck to the showroom, Starbuck jokes about the clarinet parts he had found in his room at the Hotel Arapahoe. Delmar Peale, knowing the parts are stolen, calls the police, who eventually arrest Starbuck and return him to jail.

President of the I.B.A.A.W. and His Daughter The start of Walter Starbuck's prison term at Finletter overlaps with the end of a term being served by the lifetime president of the International Brotherhood of Abrasives and Adhesives Workers. The man's 23-year-old daughter runs the union from her villa in the Bahamas while her father is away.

RAMJAC Corporation The RAMJAC Corporation is the huge, multinational conglomerate in *Jailbird* that has consumed numerous other businesses and thus controls the vast majority of the American economy. Founded by reclusive engineer Jack Graham, the enormous company is taken over by his widow, the former Mary Kathleen O'Looney, after her husband's death. When Mary Kathleen herself dies, she leaves behind a will instructing that the enormous corporation be given to the American people. But Walter Starbuck, believing American citizens are not ready for such a gift, conceals it, and, as a result, is sent back to prison at the end of the novel.

Redfield, Colonel George Colonel George Redfield is the son-in-law of the governor of Ohio; he is commissioned to lead the militia called up to protect the Cuyahoga Bridge and Iron Company from striking workers. The owner of a lumber mill, Colonel Redfield has no military experience but wears the costume of a cavalryman. Consumed with rage when the crowd of striking workers refuses to disperse, Redfield orders his militiamen to advance with bayonets at the ready, crushing the crowd backward. After the massacre has ended, Redfield, who disappeared in the crowd, is found on a side street, "naked and out of his head, but otherwise unharmed" (33).

Rivera, Jerry Cha-Cha Jerry Cha-Cha Rivera is a nightclub comedian of Puerto Rican extraction who is the former husband of Walter F. Starbuck's daughter-in-law and the biological father of his adopted grandchildren, Juan and Geraldo Stankiewicz.

Sacco, Mrs., Dante and Inez Sacco When Nicola Sacco of the infamous Sacco and Vanzetti case moves to Milford, Massachusetts, to work in a shoe factory, Vonnegut tells readers that he married, got a house with a garden, and had two children, Dante and Inez, all historically accurate facts.

Sacco, Nicola Nicola Sacco, an actual historical figure, was an Italian immigrant and anarchist who was executed, along with Bartolomeo Vanzetti, in 1927 for robbery and murder in a politically charged case most historians feel was a gross miscarriage of justice. The Sacco and Vanzetti case, with its shameful treatment of political activists and workers, is, in many ways, the inspiration for *Jailbird*.

Salsedo, Andrea A few weeks prior to the arrests of Sacco and Vanzetti, a printer named Andrea

Salsedo, a friend of Bartolomeo Vanzetti's and an anarchist as well, was arrested by federal agents. After being held for several weeks incommunicado, Salsedo died after plunging from the 14th-story window in an office in the Department of Justice. Walter Starbuck reports this historic fact in *Jailbird* when he discusses the Sacco and Vanzetti case.

Shapiro, Dr. Ben A Harvard classmate of Walter F. Starbuck, Dr. Ben Shapiro cares for the ill, malnourished Ruth Starbuck after Walter first meets her. Ben Shapiro is also the best man at the Starbucks' wedding and delivers their son, Walter, Jr. Dr. Shapiro eventually dies in Israel in the Six-Day War and has an elementary school named in his honor in Tel Aviv.

Sills, Morty Morty Sills is a tailor to whom Arpad Leen sends Walter Starbuck before he actually takes up his new position as a vice president of the Down Home Records division of the RAMJAC Corporation.

Sri Lankan Finance Minister When Walter Starbuck is taken to prison for a second time on suspicion of the clarinet parts robbery, the precinct is in an uproar because the finance minister from Sri Lanka had been thrown into the East River by rioters. The Sri Lankan is later rescued, "clinging to a bell buoy off Governor's Island" (241).

Stankiewicz, Juan and Geraldo The sons of Walter Starbuck's daughter-in-law from a previous marriage, Juan and Geraldo Stankiewicz receive reparations from West Germany because Ruth Starbuck's family bookstore was confiscated by the Nazis during World War II.

Stankiewicz, Walter F. The son and only child of Walter and Ruth Starbuck, Walter F. Stankiewicz readopts the original family name to repudiate his father. Described by Starbuck as "a very unpleasant person," Walter Stankiewicz works as a book reviewer for the *New York Times*. He is married to an African-American woman and adopts her two sons from a previous marriage to a Puerto Rican comedian. After not seeing his father for many years, Stankiewicz comes to the farewell party for Walter Starbuck at the Clewes' home. He turns out to be homely and unhealthy: a short, fat, bald chain smoker who is nervous and wretched about meeting his father again.

Stankiewicz, Mrs.   Mrs. Stankiewicz, an African-American nightclub singer, is the wife of Walter F. Stankiewicz, son of the novel's protagonist, Walter F. Starbuck. She is also the mother of Juan and Geraldo Stankiewicz, children from her marriage to Puerto Rican comedian Jerry Cha-Cha Rivera. Mrs. Stankiewicz comes to the farewell party for her father-in-law and treats Walter Starbuck with the "honors due a grandfather" (305).

Starbuck, Anna Kairys   The mother of the novel's protagonist, Walter F. Starbuck, Anna Kairys Starbuck was born in Russian Lithuania, but winds up as a cook to the wealthy McCone family when she migrates to the United States.

Starbuck, Ruth   The wife of Walter Starbuck, Ruth Starbuck is fluent in many languages as well as being a skilled artist and pianist. She was originally an Austrian Jew, born in Vienna, where her family owned a rare-book store until it was confiscated by the Nazis. Initially hidden by a Christian family during the war years, Ruth is eventually discovered, arrested, and sent to a concentration camp outside Munich. She meets Walter Starbuck in Germany, where he is overseeing logistics related to the Nuremberg trials. The two eventually marry, have a son, return to the United States, and buy a cottage in Chevy Chase, Maryland. When Walter loses his government job, Ruth supports the family by working as an interior decorator. She eventually dies of congestive heart failure in 1974, two weeks before her husband is arrested for his involvement in the Watergate scandal.

Starbuck, Stanislaus Stankiewicz   An immigrant from Russian Poland, Stanislaus Stankiewicz, Walter F. Starbuck's father, works as a chauffeur and bodyguard for Alexander Hamilton McCone. Stankiewicz is convinced to change his family name to Starbuck by McCone, who argues that Walter

will have a better chance of succeeding at Harvard University with an Anglo-Saxon name.

Starbuck, Walter F.   The novel's narrator and protagonist, Walter F. Starbuck is the son of Anna Kairys Stankiewicz, a cook in the wealthy McCone household and Stanislaus Stankiewicz, Alexander Hamilton McCone's bodyguard and chauffeur. As a boy, Walter becomes the protégé of McCone, and the two play chess together for hours. When Walter is 10 years old, McCone convinces the Stankiewiczes to change their family name to Starbuck; McCone has promised to pay for Walter's education at Harvard University, and he believes the boy will have an easier time there if he has an Anglo-Saxon name. After graduating from Harvard, Starbuck wins a Rhodes scholarship to Oxford, then lands a job in Franklin Roosevelt's Department of Agriculture. At the age of 32, he goes to Germany to oversee logistics associated with the Nuremberg trials. While in Germany, Starbuck meets his future wife, Ruth, who is a 26-year-old Jewish concentration camp survivor. In 1949, Starbuck's life takes a turn for the worse when, under oath, he names a group of men who had been communists, but who had later proved their patriotism. One of these men is a rising star in the State Department, Leland Clewes, whose career is ruined by Starbuck's revelation. After this, Starbuck's government friends begin to turn against him, and he cannot find work for many years until he is offered a minor appointment in the administration of Richard M. Nixon. Starbuck ends up getting rounded up in the Watergate investigations and sentenced to prison. He serves two years at the Federal Minimum Security Adult Correctional Facility on Finletter Air Force Base and is just being released as the novel opens. Most of the book's events take place in the two days following Starbuck's release from prison. He ends up meeting an old girlfriend named Mary Kathleen O'Looney, who is now a wealthy widow and head of the RAMJAC Corporation, though she lives disguised as a bag lady. After several adventures, including winding up back in jail briefly because of a mix-up over stolen clarinet parts, Starbuck is made a vice president in the RAMJAC Corporation, where he works for two years. As the novel ends, he is being sent back to prison for concealing Mary Kathleen's will for two years after her death.

Stratton, Samuel W. One of the "three wise men" who comment on the Sacco and Vanzetti case, Samuel W. Stratton was the president of the Massachusetts Institute of Technology. An actual historic figure, Stratton was appointed by Governor Fuller of Massachusetts to serve on the committee that ultimately upheld the Sacco and Vanzetti verdicts.

Sutton, Mr. Mr. Sutton was Sarah Wyatt's grandfather, who committed suicide by jumping out of his office window on Wall Street when the stock market crashed in 1929.

Sutton, Mrs. The grandmother of Walter F. Starbuck's college girlfriend Sarah Wyatt, Mrs. Sutton lives in a tiny two-bedroom apartment filled with furniture and objects from her former, more lavish lifestyle. Walter meets Mrs. Sutton when he picks Sarah up for their dinner at the Hotel Arapahoe; the old woman becomes very fond of him.

Sutton's Chauffeur Although Sarah Wyatt's grandmother Mrs. Sutton lives in a tiny, cramped apartment, she still retains several servants, including an ancient chauffeur who comes into the room during Walter Starbuck's first visit to ask if Mrs. Sutton will be going anywhere in "the electric"—her electric car—that night (143).

Thayer, Webster An actual historic figure, Webster Thayer was the presiding judge during the Sacco and Vanzetti case. Vonnegut depicts Thayer as extremely biased against the two accused men, and the judge has often been criticized by scholars and commentators for the way he conducted the trial.

Thomas, Norman A real-life figure who was the Socialist Party candidate for president several times in the 1920s, '30s and '40s, Norman Thomas appears in the prologue to *Jailbird* when Vonnegut states that his first vote in a national election was for the presidential ticket of Norman Thomas and Mary Hapgood.

Tillie Tillie is the aged maid of Sarah Wyatt's grandmother, Mrs. Sutton. She is the last of Mrs. Sutton's servants to die; the old woman's own death follows Tillie's by two weeks.

Trout, Kilgore The prologue to *Jailbird* begins with the words, "Yes—Kilgore Trout is back again. He could not make it on the outside. That is no disgrace. A lot of good people can't make it on the outside" (1). Yet, Kilgore Trout does not appear as an actual character in the novel, as he does in so many other Vonnegut works including *God Bless You, Mr. Rosewater, Slaughterhouse-Five,* and *Breakfast of Champions.* Instead, the name is used as a pseudonym by Dr. Robert Fender, a "science fiction writer of some note" (82), as well as a veterinarian who is serving a life term for treason at the prison on Finletter Air Force Base. "Asleep at the Switch" is a story published by Fender under the name Kilgore Trout, and Fender is said to be currently at work on a science fiction novel about economics, which will also be published under the Kilgore Trout pseudonym.

Ubriaco, Frank Frank Ubriaco is the owner of the Royalton Coffee Shop in New York City, where Walter Starbuck goes for breakfast the morning after his release from prison. Ubriaco has a withered hand after french-frying it while trying to retrieve a watch that had fallen into a vat of boiling oil. Like Israel Edel and others, Ubriaco is kind to Starbuck and will later by rewarded by Mrs. Jack Graham with a vice-presidency in the RAMJAC Corporation.

Ubriaco, Marilyn Marilyn Ubriaco is the 17-year-old wife of Royalton Coffee Shop owner Frank Ubriaco. She appears briefly at the end of the novel at the farewell party for Walter Starbuck.

Unnamed Baby-faced Policeman On the morning after his release from prison, Walter Starbuck walks out from the Hotel Arapahoe into the city, where he encounters a baby-faced policeman who seems as uncertain of his role in the city as Starbuck himself is.

Unnamed Female Drug Addict and Baby When he is in Bryant Park the morning after his release from prison, Walter Starbuck hears a disturbing news story on the portable radio held by a young Hispanic man; an "imbecilic young female drug addict" (179) from Ohio forgot to feed her German shepherd dog, and the dog attacked and partially ate the woman's baby.

Unnamed Flatiron Custodian Leland Clewes tells the men assembled in Arpad Leen's penthouse about a custodian in the Flatiron Building who tells war stories about World War II. He speculates that the custodian could have been the mysterious Mrs. Jack Graham disguised as a man.

Unnamed Frenchman While waiting in the Atlanta airport for a plane to New York City following his release from prison, Walter F. Starbuck's reading is interrupted by an unnamed Frenchman who is disturbed because Starbuck is wearing a red ribbon in his label, identifying him as a *chevalier* in the French Légion d'honneur. After a brief exchange of words, the Frenchman icily plucks the ribbon from Starbuck's collar and continues on his way.

Unnamed Guard in Osaka An unnamed guard in Osaka, where Bob Fender is stationed during the Korean War, carelessly waves Fender onto the base one night, not realizing that he has the North Korean agent Izumi hidden in his car. The guard is later acquitted at a court-martial.

Unnamed Gypsy Violist During their date at the Hotel Arapahoe, an unnamed gypsy violist plays for Sarah Wyatt and Walter Starbuck. When Walter accidentally tips him a ludicrously lavish $20, the man runs out into the night, never to be seen again. Sarah Wyatt is deeply offended because she believes the tip is an effort to impress her, and she calls Starbuck an "inconceivable twerp" and an "unbelievable jerk" after the incident, though she forgives him later.

Unnamed Hispanic Man After he leaves the coffee shop on the morning after his release from prison, Walter Starbuck goes to Bryant Park, where he sits on a bench for three hours, as if in a trance. He is aroused by a young Hispanic man listening to the news on a portable radio.

Unnamed Joggers In Bryant Park, on the day after Walter Starbuck's release from prison, a man and woman in matching orange-and-gold sweatsuits jog by. Starbuck explains that he already knows about the jogging craze from prison and that he finds joggers to be "smug" (178).

Unnamed Lawyers When chauffeur Cleveland Lawes drops Virgil Greathouse off at the Finletter prison, he is accompanied by two sleek lawyers. One of the lawyers later turns out to be Arpad Leen's lawyer as well, who picks up in a limousine all the men to be rewarded by Mrs. Jack Graham with executive positions in the RAMJAC Corporation.

Unnamed Man with Sandwich Board Walter Starbuck finds himself positioned between an unnamed man with a sandwich board and a bag lady when he sees Leland Clewes on the streets of New York City, making the meeting between the two men seem like a musical comedy.

Unnamed Messenger Boy at RAMJAC and his Father After Walter Starbuck becomes a vice president of the RAMJAC Corporation, he asks a messenger boy who is about his age if he remembers the execution of Sacco and Vanzetti when he was a boy. The man replies that he remembers his father, a bank president in Montpelier, Vermont, saying he was sick and tired of people talking about Sacco and Vanzetti all the time and he was glad when the case ended.

Unnamed Middle-Aged American Woman Mary Kathleen O'Looney, also known as Mrs. Jack Graham, decides to release herself from her reclusivity for one day while she's in Managua, Nicaragua. She befriends a middle-aged American woman who is weeping in a park because her husband died that morning. Trying to help, Mary Kathleen brings the widow back to the RAMJAC luxury hotel with her, where the poor woman ends up being murdered and having her hands cut off after being mistaken for Mary Kathleen.

Unnamed Militia Captain A group of militiamen, consisting mostly of farm boys from southern Ohio, is called up to protect the Cuyahoga Bridge and Iron Company against striking workers, The captain of this group is the postmaster of Greenfield, Ohio.

Unnamed Militia Lieutenants The two lieutenants of the militia called up to protect the Cuyahoga Bridge and Iron Company are the twin sons of the president of the Greenfield, Ohio, Bank and Trust Company. The banker had done a favor for the governor of the state, and his sons' commissions were his reward.

Unnamed Neighbor Woman When the Starbucks live in their bungalow in Chevy Chase, Maryland, their son, Walter Jr., is so embarrassed by them that he tells playmates in the neighborhood he is adopted. An unnamed neighbor woman invites Ruth and Walter over for coffee one afternoon to try to discover who Walter Jr.'s real parents are.

Unnamed News Dealer The morning after his release from prison, Walter Starbuck leaves the Hotel Arapahoe and buys a copy of the *New York Times* from an unnamed news dealer; Starbuck seems surprised when the dealer accepts the two thin dimes he offers for the paper.

Unnamed Newspaper Reporter After Ma Jarvis and her delegation of women is rebuffed on their December 15, 1894, visit to the Cuyahoga Bridge and Iron Company, an unnamed newspaper reporter for *The Cleveland Plain Dealer* asks her what she plans to do next. Not really knowing what to do next, Ma Jarvis gives a "brave answer" anyway, telling the reporter: "We will be back" (20). This promise leads to the Christmas Day Cuyahoga Massacre.

Unnamed Night Clerk When Walter Starbuck returns to the Hotel Arapahoe after the death of Mary Kathleen O'Looney, there is a new night clerk to replace Israel Edel. This clerk, who normally works at the Carlyle Hotel, is "exquisitely dressed and groomed" (285) and mortified to be working at the Arapahoe.

Unnamed Owner of the Hotel Arapahoe When Walter Starbuck takes Sarah Wyatt on a date to the Hotel Arapahoe, they are received by the owner himself, who speaks French with Sarah and ushers the young couple to a table.

Unnamed Pakistani Ambulance Attendants When Mary Kathleen O'Looney dies in the basement of Grand Central Terminal, the two ambulance attendants who come to pick up the body are Pakistani and speak Urdu as their first language.

Unnamed Patient of Sarah Wyatt Clewes When Walter Starbuck talks to the former Sarah Wyatt on the phone again after many years, Sarah, now a registered nurse, continues their old routine of telling corny jokes. Starbuck finds out later that Sarah needed some kind of escape that night because a patient of hers, whom Sarah liked very much, had just died of a congenital heart defect.

Unnamed Patient's Children and Husband Walter Starbuck, reading the newspaper the morning after Mary Kathleen O'Looney's death, finds no mention of it, though he does read an obituary for the patient of Sarah Wyatt Clewes who had died of a congenital heart defect. The patient left behind three children; her husband had died in an automobile accident a month before. This incident is reminiscent of the deaths of Vonnegut's sister, Alice, and her husband, JAMES CARMALT ADAMS, which he describes in his previous novel, *Slapstick*.

Unnamed Police Captain When Ma Jarvis leads a delegation of striking workers' wives to the Cuyahoga Bridge and Iron Company on December 15, 1894, an unnamed police captain tells the women they are violating the law by assembling in such great numbers. He orders them to disperse, and the women comply.

Unnamed Puffy Old Woman   Only about a dozen other patrons are eating dinner at the Hotel Arapahoe when Walter Starbuck takes Sarah Wyatt there on a date. One of the diners is a puffy old woman who wears a diamond necklace and eats alone, except for a Pekingese dog in her lap, who also wears a diamond necklace.

Unnamed Religious Fanatics   When Walter Starbuck first sees Leland Clewes on the street of New York City on the day after his release from prison, Clewes appears to be "a leading man in a musical comedy" (181) because of the group of religious fanatics in saffron robes chanting and dancing behind him.

Unnamed Sailor and Captain in Osaka   After Bob Fender has hidden the North Korean agent Izumi in his apartment for 11 days, he innocently asks a sailor from New Zealand if, for a thousand dollars, he would take a young woman on board and away from Japan. The sailor reports this conversation to his captain, who reports it to American authorities, leading to the arrest of both Fender and Izumi.

Unnamed Shady Colonel   Walter F. Starbuck is able to get a suitable wardrobe for his future wife, Ruth, from a shady colonel in Germany who is an old Harvard acquaintance of his. With the new clothes from the black market, Ruth is able to work as Walter's interpreter during the period of the Nuremberg War Crime Trials.

Unnamed Sharpshooters   Four unnamed sharpshooters, supplied by the Pinkerton Agency, set up in the bell tower of the Cuyahoga Bridge and Iron Company on Christmas morning, 1894. These sharpshooters, along with company guards, actually fire into the crowds of striking workers and onlookers, causing the Cuyahoga Massacre.

Unnamed Story about Vicuna by Frank X. Barlow   In *Jailbird*, Walter F. Starbuck sums up for readers a story about the planet Vicuna, which supposedly appeared in *Playboy* magazine as Starbuck was writing his memoirs. The story is about a Vicunian judge who is forced to leave his own planet after scientists discover a way to extract time from the topsoil. Soon the Vicunians have so wasted the valuable resource that they have no future left. While the judge's body remains behind on Vicuna, his soul flies to Earth and inhabits the body of a little old man at a minimum security prison for white-collar criminals. The story's author is said to be Frank X. Barlow, a pen name used by Finletter prison inmate Dr. Robert Fender.

Unnamed Waiter at the Hotel Arapahoe   An unnamed waiter at the Hotel Arapahoe, where Walter Starbuck and Sarah Wyatt go on their first date, delivers a plate of Cotuit oysters to the table, a dish specifically ordered by Starbuck's patron, Alexander Hamilton McCone.

Unnamed Waitress at the Royalton Coffee Shop   The morning after his release from prison, Walter Starbuck has coffee at the Royalton Coffee Shop in New York City; he is amazed by the kindness of the unnamed waitress there who calls him "honeybunch" and "darling" (174).

Unnamed Withered Old Man   One of the few other patrons of the Hotel Arapahoe, when Walter Starbuck takes Sarah Wyatt there on a date, is a withered old man who hunches over his food, hiding it with his arms. The couple later learns that the old man had been eating caviar.

Unnamed World War II Englishman   When Walter Starbuck is about to be released from prison, he changes into his civilian clothes. His tie is especially old; Starbuck explains that he had worn it during World War II. During that period, an unnamed Englishman, working with him on medical supplies for the D-day landing, told Starbuck the tie identified him as an officer in the Royal Welsh Fusiliers, a most unlucky regiment.

Vanzetti, Bartolomeo   An actual historical figure, Bartolomeo Vanzetti was an Italian immigrant and anarchist executed, along with Nicola Sacco, on trumped-up charges of robbery and murder in 1927. The Sacco and Vanzetti case became an international cause during the 1920s, tarnishing America's social and political reputation. The case very much serves as the inspiration for Vonnegut's examination of the organized labor movement and political radicalism in *Jailbird*.

von Strelitz, Arthur   Arthur von Strelitz is an associate professor of anthropology at Harvard University who loans his apartment to Walter Starbuck and Mary Kathleen O'Looney on the afternoon they first make love.

von Strelitz, Sr.   The father of anthropology professor Arthur von Strelitz would become commander of an S.S. Corps during World War II in Germany and die of pneumonia during the siege of Leningrad.

Vonnegut, Alex   Alex Vonnegut is KURT VONNEGUT, SR.'s, younger brother; he appears in the novel's prologue when Vonnegut describes a lunch he has with his father, his Uncle Alex, and labor organizer Powers Hapgood. Though Alex is quite conservative, he is friends with the radical Powers Hapgood from his Harvard days.

Vonnegut, Edith Lieber   Vonnegut refers to his mother in the novel's prologue when he describes the lunch he has with his father, his uncle ALEX VONNEGUT, and Powers Hapgood. At that time, Vonnegut is a 22-year-old soldier just returned from World War II. His mother "had declined to go on living, since she could no longer be what she had been at the time of her marriage—one of the richest women in town" (3).

Vonnegut, Kurt, Sr.,   Vonnegut mentions his father, Kurt Vonnegut, Sr., in the novel's prologue when he mentions the lunch he and his father and his uncle Alex Vonnegut have with labor organizer Powers Hapgood. Vonnegut describes his father as "a good man in full retreat from life" (5); after lunch with Powers Hapgood, Vonnegut Sr. tells his son he had had no idea there was any question

about the guilt of the unjustly executed Sacco and Vanzetti.

Walker, Shelton   Shelton Walker is the assistant secretary of the army in the Eisenhower administration who fires Walter Starbuck from his government position following his involvement in the Leland Clewes scandal.

Whistler, Henry Niles   On Christmas morning, 1894, when the crowd of striking workers gather at the Cuyahoga Bridge and Iron Company, they read a beautiful letter written by the poet Henry Niles Whistler, a Harvard man who comes to Cleveland to bolster the spirits of the workers.

Whistler, Kenneth   Inspired by real-life union organizer Powers Hapgood, Kenneth Whistler is a Harvard-educated labor organizer and coal miner who is the idol of Walter F. Starbuck as a young man. Starbuck and Mary Kathleen O'Looney see Whistler speak at a rally for the International Brotherhood of Abrasives and Adhesives Workers in Cambridge, where he mesmerizes the crowd with talk of a saner, more equitable society. Kenneth Whistler had also led the pickets outside the prison where Sacco and Vanzetti were executed. Mary Kathleen O'Looney will later hitchhike to Kentucky to live with Whistler briefly, though she will meet her husband, Jack Graham, one night after she flees Whistler's shanty because he has become violently drunk.

Winkler, Kermit   The morning after he is released from prison, Walter Starbuck walks out from the Hotel Arapahoe into the city and buys a newspaper. After this simple transaction, Starbuck has the "whimsical" idea of calling up Kermit Winkler, the secretary of the Treasury and a Harvard man, to tell him how well his dimes worked in Times Square (172).

Wyatt, Mr.   The father of Sarah Wyatt, Mr. Wyatt is a Harvard man who had once been the largest yacht dealer in Massachusetts, a business that went belly-up during the Great Depression. He is later supported by his wife, who runs a catering business out of their home.

Wyatt, Mrs. Sarah Wyatt's mother supports the family by running a catering business after her husband's yacht dealership goes broke during the Great Depression years. The Wyatts eventually die penniless.

Wyatt, Radford Alden Radford Alden Wyatt is the brother of Sarah Wyatt and the Harvard roommate of Walter Starbuck. Wyatt eventually drops out of Harvard, takes a job as an orderly in a tuberculosis sanitarium, and contracts tuberculosis himself. In later life, Wyatt runs a small welding shop in the village of Sandwich on CAPE COD.

FOR FURTHER READING

Jailbird. New York: Dell, 1999.

Morse, Donald E. "Kurt Vonnegut's *Jailbird* and *Deadeye Dick*: Two Studies of Defeat." *Hungarian Studies in English* 22 (1991): 109–119.

"The Kid Nobody Could Handle"

One of Vonnegut's four published stories about high school band director George M. Helmholtz, "The Kid Nobody Could Handle" initially appeared in the *Saturday Evening Post* in September 1955 before being reprinted in the 1968 collection, *Welcome to the Monkey House.*

SYNOPSIS

"The Kid Nobody Could Handle" is the story of high school band director George M. Helmholtz, a fat, kind man who loves his job. One morning, when George's wife is out of town, he is eating breakfast in a diner with Bert Quinn, the restaurant's owner and a shrewd, cynical businessman, who bested Helmholtz in a land deal several years before. George asks about a 15-year-old boy mopping the floor whose name he does not know. The boy, Jim Donnini, is the son of Quinn's brother-in-law. When Jim's mother died, his father married Quinn's sister, then subsequently walked out on her, leaving Jim behind. The teen had spent time in foster homes before finally being sent away

from Chicago, where he had grown up, to live with Quinn in the small town where the story takes place. Helmholtz, taking an interest in the boy, offers him a ride to school, but Jim is rude and uncommunicative in the car. After his first class, Helmholtz is summoned to a special faculty meeting where he discovers the school had been vandalized the night before.

That night, Helmholtz dreams that his band rehearsal room was vandalized and that his big bass drum was destroyed. He dresses and rushes to the school only to discover that his drum is fine. But he hears noises in a nearby chemistry lab and discovers Jim Donnini flinging bottles of acid around the room. Rather than call the police, though, Helmholtz takes Jim to the band room, speaks with him, and gives him his most valuable possession—a beautiful trumpet that had belonged to John Philip Sousa. The next morning at the diner, Bert Quinn has discovered what happened the night before and says that he is going to send Jim back to Chicago. Helmholtz, realizing that another rejection will completely destroy the boy, becomes so angry and depressed that he smashes up the trumpet that Quinn had returned to him and collapses in tears. Watching him, Jim Donnini is filled with pity. Something in his eyes turns human again. The story ends with Jim taking the lowest seat in the lowest band at the high school, with the repaired John Philip Sousa trumpet at the ready.

COMMENTARY

"The Kid Nobody Could Handle," published in 1955, picks up on the American interest in teenage delinquency, popularized in the 1950s by movies such as 1953's *The Wild One*, about two rival motorcycle gangs, and 1955's *Rebel Without a Cause*, about a troubled teen coming to a new town. Jim Donnini is the product of a broken home, a kid nobody wants. His rough background rather than any specific character failing seems to have made him into a hopeless, angry boy as the story begins. As in many of his novels and short stories, Vonnegut emphasizes the need for individuals to feel that they belong. In his later work, such as the novel *Slapstick*, this longing to belong is represented by Vonnegut's insistence on the importance of extended families, even artificially constructed ones. Family is exactly what Jim Donnini is lacking. His mother's death and his father's abandonment leave the boy alone in the world. He is sent to live with Bert Quinn only by court order, and clearly, the self-centered old wheeler-and-dealer does not know how to handle him.

George Helmholtz seems in many ways to be a prototype for Vonnegut's later recurring character Eliot Rosewater. Though not from a wealthy, powerful family like Rosewater, Helmholtz, with his good-natured optimism and simple kindness to other human beings, prefigures Rosewater, who treats people with compassion and humanity, and who makes the memorable statement that some critics believe sums up Vonnegut's own philosophy: "God damn it, you've got to be kind" (*God Bless You*, 129). While Quinn believes that the way to change Jim Donnini's behavior is to "ride his tail" (273), Helmholtz talks patiently to the troubled teen and seems to truly care about him. Although Helmholtz does not have a specific plan for changing Jim—he acts instinctually and in a rather confused way—he nevertheless treats the boy like a valuable human being, even giving Jim his most valued possession. In the end, this compassion pays off. When Helmholtz collapses in despair, Jim is finally able to feel the sort of compassion for another human being that the band director had shown him earlier. Moreover, compassion in this story is contagious. Vonnegut even suggests that the new spark of humanity and life in Jim's eyes affects hardened old Bert Quinn: "Quinn looked at Jim, and something like hope flickered for the first time in his bitterly lonely old face" (282). As in *Slapstick*, Vonnegut suggests that loneliness is the cause of much of the world's misery and that simple kindness to one another may be the best weapon against it.

CHARACTERS

Donnini, Jim   Jim Donnini is a tough 15-year-old from Chicago who has been sent by the courts to live with his stepmother's brother, Bert Quinn, in a small town. Jim has had an extremely hard life; his mother has died and his father has abandoned him. He has been in and out of foster homes as well. The

only thing that matters to him in the beginning of the story is his pair of black boots that he polishes obsessively. Although a lost cause to most people, Jim shows by the end of the story that he is still an emotional human being who can sympathize with others who are suffering.

Helmholtz, George M.   Described as "a very kind fat man with a headful of music" (270), George Helmholtz is the local high school band director, who is extremely dedicated to his students. The toughest kid he ever meets, though, is Jim Donnini. Although Helmholtz's kindness to the boy initially seems futile, it eventually pays off. He genuinely cares what happens to Jim, and the tough teenager senses this and is finally able to change by the end of the story.

Quinn, Bert   Bert Quinn is a "small, dark humorless man" who has "only two moods: one suspicious and self-pitying, the other arrogant and boastful" (271). A thoroughly unlikable man, Quinn believes the best way to handle tough teenager Jim Donnini is to "ride his tail till he straightens up and flies right" (273–274). In the end, however, George Helmholtz's kindness turns out to be a better approach. When Jim shows pity for the band director, Quinn himself is affected by the change in the boy and experiences a flicker of hope for the first time in his lonely life.

FURTHER READING

Reed, Peter. *The Short Fiction of Kurt Vonnegut.* Westport, Conn.: Greenwood Press, 1997.
Welcome to the Monkey House. New York: Dell, 1998.

L'histoire du Soldat

L'histoire du Soldat was originally a modernist theatrical work, premiering in September 1918, with music by Igor Stravinsky and a French libretto written by C. F. Ramuz. The story was based on a Russian folk tale and involved a soldier who trades his violin to the devil. In the early 1990s, Robert Johnson, artistic director of the New York Philomusica

Chamber Ensemble, decided to update the piece and asked Vonnegut to write a completely new libretto, which the author decided to base on the life of PRIVATE EDDIE SLOVIK, the only U.S. soldier executed for desertion since the Civil War. The updated version of *L'histoire du Soldat* premiered at Alice Tully Hall in New York City on May 6, 1993. A text version of Vonnegut's libretto was subsequently published in *The Paris Review* in fall of 1998.

SYNOPSIS

The piece opens with the actor who plays a major general of an American infantry unit taking on the role of narrator and explaining to the audience that the original Ramuz story, "intentionally silly" and "whimsical" as it was, did not match Stravinsky's brilliant and ironic music or the tragic zeitgeist of the World War I years. He then transforms into a weary American general who is commanding an invasion of Germany near the end of World War II. A dazed, bedraggled soldier soon enters the scene and confesses that he has run away from the fighting at the front. The general calls in a military policeman who arrests the soldier and quarters him in a ruined farmhouse in the countryside. The M.P. reads the soldier Article Number Fifty-eight from the Articles of War, which provides for the execution of deserters, but he also assures the soldier that the U.S. Army has not carried out this penalty for 80 years, and that he will most likely end up with a short prison term. A Red Cross volunteer then arrives at the farmhouse and announces that Supreme Headquarters has decided to make an example of the deserting soldier and actually execute him by firing squad, a decision that she says "sickens" the division commander. The commander is so reluctant to carry out the sentence that he comes to the farmhouse and offers the soldier a deal: If he will return to the front and fight, all will be forgiven. The soldier refuses, explaining that, if he returned, he would simply run away again. The general then urges the soldier to act crazy in order to save himself, but the soldier refuses this reprieve as well, explaining that he is not a "nut," just a disgrace to the human race. The next scenes show the soldier and the M.P.

talking. The soldier has accepted his fate, arguing that he feels like he is doing something worthwhile for the first time in his life. The execution is carried out while various characters read aloud from an 1863 army manual that details the organization and duties of a firing squad. The soldier's last words are "Remember me." The play ends with the characters removing their costumes and addressing the audience directly, explaining that the libretto is based on the case of Private Eddie Slovik.

COMMENTARY

In the play's prologue, the major general, serving as narrator, explains that Charles-Ferdinand Ramuz's original libretto depicts a soldier that is "unlike any real soldier in all of history." While the narrator concedes that demanding realism in a work of fiction can be a "perfectly inane" requirement, nevertheless he argues that Igor Stravinsky's music, which seems to respond to the suffering and deaths of millions of real soldiers, does not match the innocence of Ramuz's story. Thus, the tale has been updated and turned into a "real down-and-dirty soldier's story," in which the ironies of the deserting soldier's position match the "wry melodic ironies" of Stravinsky's music. Viewers begin to see these ironies immediately when the unnamed soldier appears on stage. He tells the general that he has run away from the front because he desires exactly what the army itself is supposedly fighting for—freedom from fear. Yet, this desire, exalted as a motive of the Allied forces, ends up getting the soldier executed at the end of the piece. Other ironies enter in as well when the soldier, who is to be executed for cowardice, is the only character brave enough to face his crime unflinchingly. Despite the general's urging that he save himself by returning to the front or by feigning insanity, the soldier refuses, unafraid to admit the truth of his situation. In addition, when the soldier refuses to cooperate with the general's scheme to stop the execution, he seems to exchange roles with the commander, telling the Red Cross girl that he is the one "giving the orders now." The Red Cross girl replies that the soldier has "turned the general,/Who's one in a million, into a chickenhearted civilian." Thus, the play questions traditional notions of bravery and cowardice—these labels become meaningless as the characters are complex and shifting in their behavior.

Vonnegut's libretto not only shares the ironic stance taken in most of his work, it also uses the characteristic Vonnegut technique of METAFICTION. While the interior story told in the play is loosely based on the execution of Private Eddie Slovik, the players also drop their characters to address the audience directly and comment on the action that they have just portrayed. Following the soldier's final words, the actors become sickened with the scene they have just presented and strip off their costumes. The general speaks directly to the audience when he says, "No more acting." It is important to Vonnegut that viewers not simply dismiss this theatrical piece as a work of imaginative fiction, so he has the actors explain to the audience actual historical details surrounding the death of Eddie Slovik. The actor playing the general also suggests how the audience might begin to interpret what they have just seen when he says to his fellow actor in the role of the executed soldier, "Not coming down from the cross?" The suggestion is that viewers may understand the soldier as a Christ figure—someone who dies for sins committed by others, in this case, the violence and horror of a war which the soldier was drafted into. Eddie Slovik, the actors tell the audience at the end, had no actual last words. Vonnegut puts the phrase "remember me" into his mouth to remind viewers of the real horror of war, that war destroys individuals—in the words he uses in his classic novel *Slaughterhouse-Five*, turning them into the "listless playthings of enormous forces" (164).

CHARACTERS

Major General   The major general is an American commander of an infantry unit that invades Germany near the end of World War II. When he comes across a deserting soldier, he finds the man reprehensible and orders him arrested by a military policeman. Yet, the general is sickened by the decision made at Supreme Headquarters to actually execute the man. He offers the soldier a reprieve of his sentence if he will return to the front, but the soldier refuses. The general is then forced to carry out the soldier's execution by firing squad. The major general breaks character at both the beginning and the end of the play to directly address the audience.

Military Policeman   A thoughtful military policeman arrests the soldier who has deserted from the fighting at the front. He talks with the soldier in several scenes, initially comforting him that his sentence will not be carried out. The military policeman often comments ironically on the action of the play.

Red Cross Girl   A Red Cross volunteer, who is having a sexual affair with the major general, first brings the news to the soldier and the military policeman that Supreme Headquarters actually plans to execute the soldier for desertion. The Red Cross girl has her own problems—the general she is sleeping with does not even know her name, mixing her up with her predecessor in the position, who was killed by stepping on a bomb.

Soldier   The soldier in the play is modeled after the real-life Private Eddie Slovik, shot by a firing squad in 1945—the only man executed by the U.S. Army for desertion since the Civil War. In Vonnegut's libretto, the soldier is honest about his fear and refuses to return to the front or pretend that he is insane to avoid his sentence. He even comes to accept his fate at the end of the play, believing that he is giving his life for his country since other soldiers will fight better because of what happened to him.

FURTHER READING

"L'Histoire du Soldat." *The Paris Review* 40, no. 148 (Fall 1998): 188–204.

"The Lie"

A story about class privilege and the arrogance of those born into wealth, "The Lie" was first published in the *Saturday Evening Post* in February 1962. The story was later reprinted in the 1968 collection, *Welcome to the Monkey House*.

SYNOPSIS

"The Lie" tells the story of the extremely wealthy Dr. Remenzel and his wife, Sylvia, who are taking their 13-year-old son, Eli, to Whitehill, an exclusive boy's preparatory school that male members of the Remenzel family have attended for generations. The Remenzels are also huge donors to the school, and the doctor, as his chauffeur-driven Rolls-Royce speeds along, is looking over plans for a new dormitory the family is having built there. Sylvia, whose own family of origin had no money at all, is particularly fascinated by the Whitehill School and the Remenzel legacy. Her husband, however, warns her that Eli should receive no special treatment just because he is a Remenzel. Readers soon discover that Eli is keeping a secret from his parents, however. He has failed the school's entrance examination and torn up a letter denying him admission. When the family stops to have lunch with one of Dr. Remenzel's old school friends, Eli runs away from the table, and Whitehill's headmaster, also at the restaurant with several members of the school's board of overseers, awkwardly informs the couple of their son's failure. While Sylvia immediately wants to find and comfort Eli, the doctor, forgetting his own insistence that his son not receive special treatment, talks to several members of the board, insisting that his son be admitted. To his dismay, each of them refuses. Rejoining his shamed wife and son outside the restaurant and recognizing his bad behavior, Dr. Remenzel apologizes to them at the end.

COMMENTARY

"The Lie" is a story about class relations. Although wealthy Dr. Remenzel is scrupulous in his behavior, always doing the correct thing, such as insisting that scholarship boys like his old friend Tom Kilyer belong at Whitehill School, and that the African boys have met the school's standards, readers nevertheless see that he is still something of a snob. He is constantly worried that his lower-class wife will embarrass him publicly by asking for special favors for their son, Eli, and he gives her strict orders not to do so. Sylvia is the partner in the marriage who initially seems more interested in the Remenzels' fortune and long family history and who, in fact,

seems a bit star-struck by her husband's wealth and power. Possibly even racist in her first reaction to the possibility of an African student rooming with Eli, nevertheless, she gives up the Whitehill dream much more easily than her husband in the end. Ironically, Dr. Remenzel, when he learns that his son has been denied admission, does exactly what he spoke so strongly against previously. He requests special favors for his son. Underneath his high-minded rhetoric, the doctor clearly expects to be treated like a Remenzel. Sylvia, however, wants what is truly best for Eli. Unlike her husband, she realizes what her son must be going through and rushes to comfort him. She sees that it would be a "cruel thing" (251) to send her son to the school if he is not capable of doing the work. "The Lie" of the story's title, then, has a double meaning by the end. Although readers initially take the title to refer to Eli's lie of omission to his parents, perhaps the bigger lie in the story involves Dr. Remenzel's lies to himself.

CHARACTERS AND RELATED ENTRIES

Barkely, Ben Ben Barkely is the black chauffeur who drives the Remenzels to the Whitehill School in their Rolls-Royce.

Kilyer, Tom Tom Kilyer was a classmate of Dr. Remenzel's when the two were boys at the Whitehill School. He was a scholarship student, however, unlike the wealthy Remenzels, whose family not only could afford to pay his way, but also could make large donations to the school. As his family is being driven to the school in his Rolls-Royce, Dr. Remenzel spies Kilyer driving behind them in a beat-up old car and realizes that Kilyer, too, is driving his son to the school. The men arrange to have lunch together at a restaurant near Whitehill.

Kilyer's Son The 13-year-old son of Tom Kilyer makes the highest score ever recorded on the Whitehill entrance examination, unlike Eli Remenzel, who failed the exam but was too ashamed to tell his parents.

Remenzel, Eli Thirteen-year-old Eli Remenzel has been told his whole life about the wonderful

Whitehill Preparatory School for Boys and the Remenzel legacy there. Thus, when he fails the school's entrance exam, he is humiliated and afraid, and he tears up the notification letter and the test scores without telling his parents. The truth comes out when the school's headmaster bumps into the Remenzels at lunch during the school's admission events. Eli is particularly horrified when his father refuses to admit defeat and approaches members of the school's board of overseers to ask for special treatment for his son.

Remenzel, Dr. The story opens with Dr. Remenzel taking his son, Eli, to the preparatory school he himself as well as numerous Remenzel forbears attended. When the doctor discovers that Eli failed the entrance exams, he is horrified and breaks his own strict rules about Remenzels not asking for special treatment. At the end, however, he is abashed and apologizes for his behavior to his wife and son.

Remenzel, Sylvia Dr. Remenzel's wife, Sylvia, does not come from the same kind of moneyed background that her husband does. Thus, the doctor is always worried that she will say something to embarrass him. At the end of the story, though, when the couple discovers that Eli has failed the entrance examination, Sylvia behaves better than her husband, comforting her son and quickly giving up her dream of a Whitehill School education for him.

Warren, Dr. Donald Dr. Donald Warren is the headmaster of the Whitehill School, who is forced to tell the Remenzels over lunch that their son, Eli, failed the school's entrance examination and has been denied admittance.

Whitehill School for Boys Whitehill School is an exclusive boy's preparatory school. Thirteen-year-old Eli Remenzel is being driven to the school by his wealthy parents as the story opens. Although it is his father's fondest wish that his son attend Whitehill, where generations of Remenzels have gone, readers soon discover that Eli failed the school's entrance exam, but kept that fact secret from his father, afraid to disappoint him.

FURTHER READING

Reed, Peter. *The Short Fiction of Kurt Vonnegut.* Westport, Conn.: Greenwood Press, 1997.
Welcome to the Monkey House. New York: Dell, 1998.

Like Shaking Hands With God: A Conversation About Writing

This short volume, published by Seven Stories Press in 1999, transcribes a public discussion about writing held between Kurt Vonnegut and LEE STRINGER at a Union Square bookstore in Manhattan on the evening of October 1, 1998. Stringer is the author of *Grand Central Winter* and *Sleepaway School*, books detailing his three-year stint at a juvenile detention center as a young teenager and the decade he spent homeless and crack-addicted on the streets of New York City. An ardent admirer of Stringer's work, Vonnegut compares the writer to Jack London in a blurb for *Grand Central Winter*. In front of an audience of several hundred, the two men, in between readings from their work, discuss their love of writing, the care that goes into their craft, and their level of political engagement. The book closes with a second, private conversation that took place among Vonnegut and Stringer as well as original conversation moderator Ross Klaven and Daniel Simon of Seven Stories Press over lunch in January 1999.

Vonnegut begins his portion of the public discussion by talking about his experiences teaching creative writing at the UNIVERSITY OF IOWA Writers' Workshop, at the CITY COLLEGE OF NEW YORK, and at HARVARD UNIVERSITY. He tells the audience that the best students in these programs were not necessarily those who wanted to become writers, but rather the ones who were passionate, who cared deeply about a particular subject matter. Vonnegut believes that having something important to *say* is the basis of successful writing and that matters of style—"the language . . . the right words . . . the paragraphing" (16)—will follow. One of the reasons he says he admires Lee Stringer so much is because Lee "had a hell of lot on [his] mind" (16); he had an interesting subject matter to write about. But one of the things that makes writing so challenging, according to Vonnegut, is that "literature is the only art that requires [an] audience to be performers" (17). Readers work in partnership with authors to experience a work of literature, and, as he points out in his novel *Timequake*, reading is a very difficult activity that requires a great amount of skill to do well. Readers are not only required to decode "idiosyncratic arrangements in horizontal lines of only twenty-six phonetic symbols, ten Arabic numbers, and about eight punctuation marks" (18), they also must detect irony, points at which an author says one thing but means something else. Writers, then, must necessarily write for a small audience because they need readers who are so highly skilled. He ends this portion of his discussion, to laughter, by thanking his audience members "for learning how to do this virtually impossible thing" (18).

The two writers also discuss the idea that literary writing has no specific practical use. Vonnegut mentions that his students at City College were disappointed to find out "there was no job at the end of the course" (19). Both he and Stringer acknowledge, however, that books may have political consequences, although both men, Stringer in particular, are somewhat uncomfortable seeing themselves as editorialists or social reformers. Stringer talks about the difficulty of rescuing himself through his writing, pointing out that it would be presumptuous, if not impossible, to try to rescue others as well. Vonnegut, in response to a question about the right relationship for a writer to have with social issues, replies that he "was always interested in good citizenship" (70), in living by the values he learned in junior civics class at SHORTRIDGE HIGH SCHOOL in INDIANAPOLIS. Nevertheless, like Stringer, he actually speaks more about what his writing has done for him as an individual than how it has changed society or attempted to redress social injustice. Vonnegut discusses in particular the relationship between writing and psychoanalysis, telling his audience about a letter he wrote to *Harper's* magazine in

response to talk about "the death of the novel." In his letter, Vonnegut argued that "people will continue to write novels, or maybe short stories, because they discover that they are treating their neuroses" (32). Practicing art is not a way to make money or become famous, he continues, "it's a way to make your soul grow" (32). Lee Stringer makes a similar statement, though he uses a different metaphor. He talks about the joy of working through problems in writing, and finally figuring something out, moments he describes as "like shaking hands with God" (52). Both writers, then, see their craft as a vehicle for self-discovery and personal growth as well as a way to communicate with a small group of like-minded others.

The volume closes on an interesting philosophical note; the two writers, at the private lunchtime conversation, discuss their views of heaven and the afterlife. Stringer argues that human beings paint a picture of heaven that is "filled with things that are nice" (74), but finally, with things that humans are just not very interested in. He concludes that people are actually more concerned with staying out of hell than in going to heaven. In response to these comments, Vonnegut asks the small group of men whether, given the option, they would prefer to sleep for eternity after death or return to Earth. Stringer replies that making the assumption that "heaven's just this blank, eternal sleep" (75) is one way people keep themselves in hell. He says that, if eternal blankness were the option, he would prefer to come back to Earth. Vonnegut, however, claims that eternal sleep would be "absolutely okay" with him (76). The answer that Vonnegut most admires, though, is that given by Dan Simon, who says he would opt for eternal sleep as long as he was given the opportunity to dream. Vonnegut tells the group that, in his answer, he "really was counting on dreaming" (76). For Vonnegut here, as elsewhere in his work, the life of the unconscious imagination can be the place that true art springs from, and an eternal retreat into that world would not be an unwelcome move.

FURTHER READING

Like Shaking Hands with God. New York: Washington Square Press, 2000.

"Long Walk to Forever"

In his Preface to *Welcome to the Monkey House*, Vonnegut calls "Long Walk to Forever" a "sickeningly slick love story" that he initially titled "Hell to Get Along With" (xv). When the story was first printed in the *Ladies' Home Journal* in August 1960, the editors retitled it "Long Walk to Forever." Despite Vonnegut's disparaging comments about this piece, he nevertheless thought enough of it to include it in his 1968 collection, a book that omits many previously published Vonnegut stories.

SYNOPSIS

"Long Walk to Forever" tells the story of 20-year-olds Newt and Catharine, who have grown up as next-door neighbors. Newt has joined the army, and Catharine is about to be married to a man named Henry Stewart Chasens. The story opens with Newt knocking on Catharine's door and inviting her to go on a walk with him. Though at first reluctant, Catharine eventually agrees. Newt has gone AWOL (absent without leave) from the army to rush home to see Catharine after his mother wrote to him about the impending marriage. On their walk, Newt confesses his love for his next-door neighbor. Catharine is at first upset and insists that she loves her fiancé, Chasens. Eventually, the two wander into an apple orchard, where Newt falls asleep. Catharine stays awake and watches him nap for an hour before she wakes him. The young couple agree they must part, and Newt begins to walk toward town, planning to hitch a ride and turn himself in. But just as he is leaving, he turns around and calls Catharine's name, and she runs to him and puts her arms around him, leaving readers to believe that she will choose to marry Newt instead of the man she is engaged to.

COMMENTARY

A short, sweet love story, "Long Walk to Forever" is a reverse Garden of Eden myth, one that ends happily in an apple orchard, with the couple's newfound knowledge creating a Paradise rather than expelling them from it. As in several of his novels, Vonnegut seems suspicious of conventional romantic love, suggesting that friendship and the "common decency" he speaks of in *Slapstick* might be a better basis for marriage than traditional romance. Catharine and Newt had always shared a "playful, comfortable warmth between them" (51), even though there had never been any talk of love. Catharine, at the opening of the story, however, as she is reading her "fat, glossy" (51) bridal magazine, seems to have fallen prey to traditional romance. Although she protests that she loves Henry Stewart Chasens, whose name suggests the kind of wealthy "good catch" such a magazine might advise young women to make, Catharine also has difficulty explaining to Newt exactly what is good about the man. Newt himself is not the traditional romantic hero; his shyness causes him to speak absently, "even in matters that concerned him deeply" (51). Yet, Newt is also a sympathetic character. He never pushes Catharine into doing something against her will; he simply states, honestly and simply, how he feels about her, and he readily agrees to leave her forever if that is what Catharine wants. As the young couple stroll past a school for the blind, readers realize that the pair have been blind as well; they belong together. The small steps of their lives as next-door neighbors have added up to this walk, where they finally confess their love for each other.

CHARACTERS

Catharine Twenty-year-old Catharine is about to be married to Henry Stewart Chasens when the story opens. When her next-door neighbor, Newt, invites her on a long walk and confesses his love for her, she initially tells him that he is too late and that she is determined to go through with the wedding. Eventually, though, she will give in to her true desires; the story ends when she runs to Newt and puts her arms around him.

Chasens, Henry Stewart Although readers never actually meet Henry Stewart Chasens, Catharine's fiancé when the story opens, they may suspect that Catharine's love for him is more a product of social pressure on young women to marry than a genuine attachment. Not only does Chasens sound rich and stuffy, judging from his name, but Catharine is hard pressed to explain Chasen's good qualities to Newt.

Newt   Newt is a young soldier who goes AWOL from the army when his mother writes to him that his longtime next-door neighbor Catharine is about to be married. A shy, unheroic, but appealing young man, Newt acts courageously in confessing his love to Catharine. Readers cannot help but be satisfied that Catharine chooses Newt over the stuffy-sounding Henry Stewart Chasens at the end of the story.

Newt's Mother   Newt's mother, obviously able to see the love and warmth between her son and Catharine, even though the young people themselves are blind to it, writes to Newt at his army camp to inform him of Catharine's impending marriage.

FURTHER READING

Reed, Peter. *The Short Fiction of Kurt Vonnegut.* Westport, Conn.: Greenwood Press, 1997.
Welcome to the Monkey House. New York: Dell, 1998.

"Lovers Anonymous"

One of the first Vonnegut stories to address the issue of women's role in society, "Lovers Anonymous" appeared in the women's magazine *Redbook* in October 1963. It was later reprinted in *Bagombo Snuff Box.*

SYNOPSIS

Set in North Crawford, New Hampshire, and narrated by a storm window salesman, "Lovers Anonymous" tells the story of Sheila Hinckley White, a very pretty and intelligent local girl whom all the young men in the town wanted to marry when they were in their early 20s. Much to their surprise, however, Sheila dropped out of the University of Vermont in her junior year to marry bookkeeper Herb White. On the evening of Sheila's wedding day, a group of drunken young men formed the club Lovers Anonymous to commemorate their feelings for Sheila. The group has been somewhat jokingly in existence for the past decade. When the story opens, rumors are going around that trouble is brewing between Sheila and Herb. Herb has moved into the ell of his home, where he has set up a mattress and kerosene stove and is keeping house for himself. Soon Sheila is seen turning a big red book in to the library, called *Woman, the Wasted Sex,* or *The Swindle of Housewifery.* The narrator checks out the book and begins reading it himself, learning how women have been mistreated through the years, their brains wasted in trivial domestic matters. When he is hired by Herb to install storm windows in the ell, the narrator runs into Sheila, who tells him she is going back to the university and that she and Herb are happier than they have ever been before. At the end of the story, the narrator gives the book to his own wife to read.

COMMENTARY

"Lovers Anonymous" is a story that responds to a large, cultural conversation about the role of women taking place in America in the early 1960s. Prompted largely by the 1963 publication of Betty Friedan's *The Feminine Mystique,* which argued that American housewives often felt worthless and unfulfilled because they were expected to find their identity through their husbands and children, this conversation erupted a few years later into the women's liberation movement of the late 1960s and early 1970s. Vonnegut's story, published in October 1963 in the women's magazine *Redbook* seems to react very specifically to Friedan's influential book. The book that Sheila Hinckley White checks out of the library, *Woman, the Wasted Sex,* or *The Swindle of Housewifery,* can be read as a mock *Feminine Mystique.* Vonnegut's attitude toward the new expectations of women can be difficult to discern, but it is clear that he is not simply satirizing or undercutting the idea of women's liberation.

Sheila White is treated by the narrator with respect. Although she begins as a love object for the men in town, nevertheless they have high expectations for her. When she writes in her high school yearbook that she would discover a new planet or serve on the Supreme Court or become president of a company, the narrator adds that "she was kidding, of course, but everybody—including Sheila . . . had the idea that she could be anything she set her heart on being" (330). The local boys, in fact, are terribly surprised when she drops out of the University of Vermont in the middle of her junior year to marry Herb. Yet, when she speaks with the narrator about her previous ambitions to run a company at her wedding, Sheila seems to have swallowed the dominant 1950s view about the role of women hook, line, and sinker. She tells him, "I'm taking on a job a thousand times as important—keeping a good man healthy and happy, and raising his young" (330). When he asks her about her future seat on the Supreme Court, she replies, "The happiest seat for me, and for any woman worthy of the name of woman . . . is a seat in a cozy kitchen, with children at my feet" (331). Asked about discovering planets, Sheila says, "Planets are stones, stone-dead stones. . . . What I want to discover are my husband, my children, and through them, myself" (331). The pat platitudes that Vonnegut has Sheila respond with in this scene suggest that he is spoofing ideas about women's destiny being completely tied up with their domestic roles rather than satirizing the notion that women can and should strive to be more.

In addition, both Herb White and the narrator as well as Sheila herself are greatly affected by reading *Woman, the Wasted Sex, or The Swindle of Housewifery*. The narrator seems persuaded by the author's argument that women have been mistreated over the years, and Herb begins to feel terribly guilty that Sheila has not used her intelligence in a more productive manner. Yet, perhaps the most interesting part of the story occurs when the narrator speaks with Sheila when he comes to the house to install the storm windows on Herb's ell. To the narrator's surprise, who considers "Herb's moving into the ell . . . a great tragedy of recent times," Sheila tells him to report back to the group Lovers Anonymous that she and Herb "have never been this happy before" (336). But it is not her own liberation from housewifery that Sheila is so pleased about so much as it is Herb's newfound freedom. When she sees Herb sleeping happily on his mattress in the ell the first morning he moves there, she tells the narrator that she realizes "he'd been a slave all his life, doing things he hated in order to support his mother, and then me, and then me and the girls. His first night out

here was probably the first night in his life that he went to sleep wondering who he might be, what he might have become, what he still might be" (336). Vonnegut suggests here that a reexamination of stereotypical male and female gender roles can be a liberating exercise for *both* sexes. The story even ends with the narrator giving his own wife the book to read. Yet, as is often the case in his work, Vonnegut mitigates the social critique with a joke at the end. When the other men in Lovers Anonymous warn that, after reading the book, the narrator's wife will "walk out on" the narrator and their kids to "become a rear admiral" (337), the narrator claims to have prevented that possibility with the "magic bookmark" (338) he inserted into the volume—his wife's old high school report card.

CHARACTERS

Battola, Will Will Battola is a local plumber who is a member of the group Lovers Anonymous, formed by heartbroken young men in North Crawford when Sheila Hinckley married Herb White.

Boyden, Hay Hay Boyden works as a house mover and wrecker in North Crawford. He is one of the founding members of the partly tongue-in-cheek group Lovers Anonymous.

Deal, Selma Selma Deal is a woman who works at the lunch counter of the local drugstore. She makes wisecracks when members of Lovers Anonymous eat lunch together one day.

Narrator As in several Vonnegut stories, the narrator of "Lovers Anonymous" is a storm door and window salesman in North Crawford, New Hampshire. He tells the story of Sheila Hinckley White, a well-educated local woman who became a housewife, breaking the hearts of many young men in the town. When Sheila reads a book condemning housewifery as a waste of women's brains, the narrator is intrigued and reads the books himself.

Narrator's Wife The story's narrator gives his own wife the big red book about the drudgery of housewives to read at the end of the story. But to ensure that she will not become overly ambitious, he puts an old report card of hers in the book to use as a bookmark.

Owley, Reva Reva Owley sells cosmetics at the North Crawford drugstore and also runs the small library that is housed there. She tells the narrator that *Woman, the Wasted Sex,* or *The Swindle of Housewivery,* is a very popular book.

Parker, Theodore Theodore Parker is a real-life figure who is written about in *Woman, the Wasted Sex,* or *The Swindle of Housewivery,* the book that Sheila White checks out of the local library. A Unitarian minister in Boston around the time of the Civil War who was friends with Ralph Waldo Emerson, Parker argued that women wasted their brains when they devoted themselves to housework.

Pelk, Kennard Kennard Pelk is the local police chief and also a member of the group Lovers Anonymous. He reports to the group that Herb White has started to live in the ell of his home rather than in the main house with his wife, Sheila.

Tedler, Al Al Tedler works as a carpenter in North Crawford and is a member of Lovers Anonymous. Tedler reports to his fellow club members that Herb White is building a double-studded wall between the ell and the rest of his house.

White, Herb Herb White is a bookkeeper and war veteran who never went to college. He surprises the whole town of North Crawford when he marries pretty Sheila Hinckley, a local girl who attends the University of Vermont. When Sheila becomes liberated from housewifery at the end of the story, Herb is happier as well, no longer having to feel responsible for taking care of her.

White, Sheila Hinckley Sheila Hinckley White is a very smart and pretty local girl with big dreams who drops out of college to marry bookkeeper Herb White. The local men of the town form the group Lovers Anonymous when Sheila marries, since they had all been half in love with her themselves. After a decade of marriage, Sheila reads a book decry-

ing housewifery, and her relationship with her husband changes dramatically. When Herb moves into another part of the house, both he and Sheila feel freer and happier than they had previously.

FURTHER READING

Bagombo Snuff Box. New York: Berkley Books, 2000.
Reed, Peter. *The Short Fiction of Kurt Vonnegut.* Westport, Conn.: Greenwood Press, 1997.

"The Manned Missiles"

"The Manned Missiles" is the only Vonnegut story written in epistolary form (a literary mode in which a story is told through letters). Commenting on the U.S./Soviet space race of the late 1950s, the story was first published in *Cosmopolitan* magazine in July 1958 before being reprinted in 1961 in *Canary in a Cat House* and again in 1968 in *Welcome to the Monkey House.*

SYNOPSIS

"The Manned Missiles" is a story that consists of two letters. The first is written from a Russian stone mason, Mikhail Ivankov, to an American gas station operator named Charles Ashland. The letter concerns Ivankov's son Stepan, a Russian scientist who becomes the first man in space. Readers soon discover that Stepan did not survive his space mission and that his death was somehow caused by or related to the death of Ashland's son, Bryant, an air force pilot who was the first American man in space. Mikhail's letter attempts to explain to Charles Ashland his love for his son, his bewilderment about space travel, and his desire for world peace. The letter, though, rather than being delivered to Ashland, falls into the hands of Russian ambassador Mr. Koshevoi, who reads it out loud in the United Nations. After this, the letter appears in all the American newspapers, and numerous experts give Ashland advice about how to answer it. Eschewing the experts, Ashland answers the letter in his own simple way. The second half of the story contains the text of Ashland's response letter, in which he, like Mikhail Ivankov, explains his simple but overwhelming love for his son, his ignorance of politics and his son's mission, and his understanding of what Ivankov himself is going through. In Ashland's letter, readers discover that Bryant Ashland had been sent into space to spy on Stepan Ivankov and that both men had died in a terrible accident when Ashland's rocket flew too close to Ivankov's ship.

COMMENTARY

"The Manned Missiles," published in 1958, is Vonnegut's comment on the U.S.-Soviet space race of the same era. Much to the surprise of Americans, the Soviets had launched *Sputnik,* the first artificial satellite in space, on October 4, 1957. They followed this launch with *Sputnik 2* in November 1957, which carried aboard a dog named Laika, the first living passenger in space. The anxieties set off by these early Soviet successes prompted the United States, which had believed itself ahead of the Soviets in missile technology, to hurry along its own space program. NASA was established in 1958 and the Project Mercury space program by 1959. Perhaps the main question asked in this story is whether the suffering and sacrifices associated with space travel will be worthwhile. As always, Vonnegut is suspicious of new technological advancements and wonders whether these scientific achievements will do human beings more harm than good.

These same questions are also asked by the story's two narrators: the Russian Mikhail Ivankov and the American Charles Ashland. In his letter, Ivankov writes that he "knew great suffering in the war," and further, that he understands "there must be great suffering before great joy" (286). The problem for the simple stone mason, though, is that he "could not see the joy to be earned by" space travel (286). To him, it is a terrible thing to send a man out into space, lonely and unweighed down by Earth's gravity. Ashland is similarly skeptical about technology, writing that he moved his family from Pittsburgh to Florida so that they would "be far away from any bomb targets, in case there was another war" (293). Much to his chagrin, however, scientists start building rockets in Florida, so close to the Ashlands that they have a framed view of

launches out of their living room picture window. These men are both presented as decent, ordinary, salt-of-the-earth people. Though of an older generation than their sons, they are not stupid, and they are not selfish men. They both remind readers of the costs often associated with new technological advances.

The story, though, is not simply an indictment of science, as Vonnegut stories sometimes are. Both dead sons, the Russian Stepan Ivankov and the American Bud Ashland, fully support the space program that ends up costing them their lives. And like their fathers, these men are presented as decent, kind, and thoughtful human beings. Mikhail, in his letter, emphasizes that his son was not "a great warrior" (287). He was a lover of peace and of knowledge who firmly believed that space offers numerous "poetic and scientific joys" (288) for the betterment of human beings. Similarly, Bud Ashland was not the "mad dog" or "gangster" that the Russian ambassador, Mr. Koshevoi, first makes him out to be. Charles Ashland, in his letter, explains that Bud was, above all else, "dignified" (294). He was "straight and serious and polite" (294) and courageously dedicated himself to flying despite a strong premonition that he would die young. Thus, there is no easy answer to the question of whether the joys of space travel will compensate for the sufferings such scientific knowledge will create. Perhaps the most striking thing for readers is a sense of the similarities that bind the Russian family to the American one. Despite political differences, despite the animosity of the cold war, the story ends with Charles Ashland writing that he "grasp[s] the hand" of Mikhail Ivankov, the man who, in so many ways, should be Ashland's enemy.

CHARACTERS

Ashland, Bryant Captain Bryant Ashland, known to his family as Bud, grew up with a single-minded desire to be in the air force and to fly. He is described by his father as a "dignified" young man: "straight and serious and polite and pretty much alone" (294). Although not a violent man, Bud accepts the secret mission he is given by the air force in his quiet, dignified way. By the time

Charles Ashland writes his letter, the crash that takes both Bud's life and the life of Soviet scientist Stepan Ivankov is considered to have been an accident by world experts.

Ashland, Charlene   Charlene Ashland, who works for the telephone company in Jacksonville, Florida, is the twin sister of Bud Ashton. She urges her father, in the letter he writes to the father of dead Soviet scientist Stepan Ivankov, to tell a story about Bud as a child. Taking Charlene's advice, Charles writes about the pair of goldfish the twins used to own. The fish looked so much alike they were impossible to tell apart, yet when eight-year-old Bud found one floating upside down in the tank, he reported to Charlene that *her* goldfish had died. Charlene hopes that this story, "cute and silly" (291) as it is, will make the Russian father laugh and like the Ashland family better.

Ashland, Charles   Charles Ashland is the father of dead American air force pilot and space explorer Captain Bryant Ashland. When the father of a dead Soviet space explorer, killed in a crash with Bryant Ashland's rocket, writes him a letter that appears in U.S. newspapers, Ashland answers it. The second half of the story consists of the text of Ashland's letter.

Ashland, Hazel   Hazel Ashland is the wife of Charles Ashland and mother of dead space explorer Captain Bryant Ashland.

Ivankov, Aksinia   Aksinia Ivankov is the widow of Russian space explorer Stepan Ivankov. She is a pediatrician who works hard at her job in an attempt to forget her grief for Stepan.

Ivankov, Alexei   Alexei Ivankov is Mikhail Ivankov's 17-year-old son. Originally enthusiastic about weapons in space, he learns from his older brother, Stepan, that such "childish violence" (288) is not the goal of space exploration. Alexei speaks fluent English and writes the letter in English to Charles Ashland that Mikhail dictates in Russian.

Ivankov, Mikhail   Mikhail Ivankov, a Russian stone mason, is the father of Soviet scientist and first man in space, Major Stepan Ivankov. When his son dies in a space crash between his rocket ship and that of American air force pilot Captain Bryant Ashland, Mikhail writes a letter to Ashland's father, Charles. The text of this letter makes up the first half of the story.

Ivankov, Olga   Olga Ivankov is the wife of Mikhail Ivankov and the mother of dead Russian spaceman Major Stepan Ivankov. Before her son's death, Olga had laughed at her husband's fear of space travel.

Ivankov, Stepan   Major Stepan Ivankov is a Soviet scientist and the first man in space. He dies when his rocket ship crashes with a ship piloted by American pilot and astronaut Bryant Ashland. Stepan's father, Mikhail, subsequently writes a letter to Bryant's father, Charles Ashland. In his letter, Mikhail describes Stepan as a "man of peace," as a brilliant scientist, and as a "thoughtful" and "serious" person who uncomplainingly accepted the suffering he knew would come with space exploration (287).

Ivanoff, Prokhor   Prokhor Ivanoff is a Russian dairy manager arrested for theft. When the Soviets send a rocket to space with a dog inside, a joke goes around that Ivanoff rather than the dog has been launched into space. This joke makes Mikhail Ivankov consider "what a terrible punishment it would be to send a human being up there" (285).

Koshevoi, Mr.   Mr. Koshevoi is the Soviet ambassador who intercepts the letter Mikhail Ivankov writes to American Charles Ashland and reads it out loud at the United Nations. Although Koshevoi initially believes Captain Bryant Ashland deliberately crashed into the rocket ship of Major Stepan Ivankov, he eventually comes to accept, as do all the scientific experts, that the crash was an accident.

Waterman, Earl   Earl Waterman is a U.S. congressman who comes to talk to the Ashlands about their son's death. Though Bud's mission must remain secret, Waterman assures the Ashlands that Bud had done "one of the most heroic things in United States history" (295).

FURTHER READING

Reed, Peter. *The Short Fiction of Kurt Vonnegut.* Westport, Conn.: Greenwood Press, 1997.
Welcome to the Monkey House. New York: Dell, 1998.

Man Without a Country, A

A Man Without a Country, edited by Daniel Simon and published by Seven Stories Press in 2005, collects a series of anecdotes, opinions, and observations made by Vonnegut at the age of 82. Somewhat in the style of the earlier collections *Palm Sunday* and *Fates Worse Than Death,* though shorter and less autobiographical than either of those books, *A Man Without a Country* touches on familiar Vonnegut themes: his love of humor and joking, his admiration for champions of social justice, the importance of art and music as forces that make people more human, the necessity of extended families, a suspicion of technology and weaponry, and fears of environmental destruction. What is new in this collection is the insertion throughout of photographs of silk-screened "samplers" (141) of Vonnegut quotes, made in partnership with the Kentucky artist JOE PETRO III, as well as an even more intense sense of despair and pessimism than readers have seen in his previous essay collections as the aging author contemplates what he considers the grotesque absurdities of the George W. Bush administration and the U.S. war in Iraq.

Vonnegut opens the collection by explaining to readers that his ability to tell jokes grew out of being the youngest member of his family. In order to get family members to pay attention to him at the dinner table, he had to learn to be funny. He listened religiously to the top-notch comedians of the Depression era on the radio, learning techniques from them—"what jokes were and how they worked" (2). Arguing that humor is often a reaction to pain and frustration and is often motivated by

fear, Vonnegut reiterates his especial love for LAUREL AND HARDY, which he had discussed previously in the prologue to his 1976 novel, *Slapstick.* What he loves about the pair is the "terrible tragedy" that they somehow encapsulate in their comedy. "These men are too sweet to survive in this world," Vonnegut explains, "and are in terrible danger all the time. They could be so easily killed" (4). Yet, this book is also a meditation on aging, and the 82-year-old Vonnegut, thinking particularly about the example of MARK TWAIN, understands that while humor "is a way of holding off how awful life can be" (129), he also realizes that, eventually, "you get just too tired, and the news is too awful, and humor doesn't work anymore" (129). So, while he reasserts humor as a defense mechanism, Vonnegut also questions whether he has lost the skill to be funny as a way of protecting himself from the pain of life.

The pain of being human turns out to be one of the main topics of this collection. Vonnegut not only asserts his view that "all great literature—*Moby Dick, Huckleberry Finn, A Farewell to Arms, The Scarlet Letter, The Red Badge of Courage, The Iliad* and *The Odyssey, Crime and Punishment, The Bible,* and 'The Charge of the Light Brigade'—are all about what a bummer it is to be a human being" (8–9), he also points out what he considers to be the especially distressing aspects of the world in the early years of the 21st century. Topping out this list is the American and increasingly worldwide dependency on fossil fuels. Prompted by a war in Iraq that many critics believe to be at least partly related to U.S. energy needs, Vonnegut calls fossil fuels "the most abused, addictive, and destructive drug of all time" (42). Further, he believes that "our leaders are now committing violent crimes to get what little is left of what we're hooked on" (42). Vonnegut's pessimism about the future of human beings is clearly displayed when he argues that human beings "have now all but destroyed this once salubrious planet as a life-support system in fewer than two hundred years" (43). He foresees a bleak future for Earth, suggesting that if humans continue to behave "as though there were no tomorrow" (45), it is very likely there is not going to be a tomorrow at all.

Vonnegut's despair in this little book revolves not only around environmental devastation, it also encompasses the current U.S. political administration, which Vonnegut believes is only hastening human destruction. The book's title—*A Man Without a Country*—arises from Vonnegut's hatred of the direction his country is taking. He writes,

> In case you haven't noticed, as the result of a shamelessly rigged election in Florida, in which thousands of African Americans were arbitrarily disenfranchised, we now present ourselves to the rest of the world as proud, grinning, jut-jawed, pitiless war-lovers with appallingly powerful weaponry—who stand unopposed.
>
> In case you haven't noticed, we are now as feared and hated all over the world as the Nazis once were.
>
> And with good reason.

The reason the U.S. is so hated, Vonnegut explains, is because Americans, in conducting a preemptive war, have dehumanized millions of human beings around the world because of their religion and race. President George W. Bush, he argues, has gathered around him a group of people with psychopathic personalities, "smart, personable people who have no consciences" (99). These include not only warmongers, but also business executives, such as those at Enron and WorldCom, who have enriched themselves while ruining others and who "still feel as pure as the driven snow" (100), government officials who are attempting to destroy the public school system in America, communications experts who tap phones and institute programs for domestic spying, and "craven," "unvigilant" media personnel (103) who refuse to inform the public about what is really going on in the government. While Vonnegut has spoken harshly about past administrations, especially the Nixon presidency during the late years of the VIETNAM WAR, the degree of bitterness and pessimism he expresses in *A Man Without a Country* is more extreme than readers have seen in his previous work.

Despite the despair and anger that often infiltrate this book, Vonnegut is still able to believe that certain things make human life worth living. Chief among these are the secular saints that he describes here and elsewhere in his work, particularly in his 1997 novel, *Timequake*. For Vonnegut, saints are "people who behaved decently in a strikingly indecent society" (106). In *A Man Without a Country*, as he does throughout his body of work, Vonnegut praises great champions of social justice. Labor organizer and five-time Socialist Party candidate for U.S. president, EUGENE DEBS, is cited as one of Vonnegut's personal heroes, as is HARVARD graduate, coal miner, and union sympathizer POWERS HAPGOOD of INDIANAPOLIS. He praises as well Mary O'Hare, the wife of his war buddy BERNARD V. O'HARE, a registered nurse who convinced Vonnegut to tell the unheroic truth about war in his breakthrough novel, *Slaughterhouse-Five*. He reiterates his love for the profoundly human side of Jesus Christ, especially for Christ's words in the Sermon on the Mount, in which He promises that the meek shall inherit the Earth, the merciful shall obtain mercy, and the peacemakers shall be called the Children of God. The saint that Vonnegut discusses most fully in this collection, though, is a largely unknown obstetrician from Budapest named IGNAZ SEMMELWEIS, who was born in 1818. Semmelweis, convinced that Louis Pasteur's germ theory was accurate, begged the well-respected and haughty doctors in a poverty-stricken maternity hospital in Vienna, Austria, to wash their hands before examining expectant mothers. Although his exhortations greatly reduced the maternal death rate, Semmelweis was ostracized by his social superiors and eventually committed suicide. Vonnegut calls Semmelweis his "hero" (89) and uses him as an example for young people, to contrast the psychopathic personalities that he believes fill out the Bush administration.

The arts are also what make life worth living for Vonnegut. In this collection, he argues that the arts "are not a way to make a living" (24). Instead, they are a "very human way of making life more bearable" and even more, "practicing an art, no matter how well or badly, is a way to make your soul grow" (24). So, his best advice to young people is to create something, to practice an art, whether it is just singing in the shower, dancing to the radio, telling stories, or writing a poem to a friend. Vonnegut reiterates in the book his love of music, quoting friend and jazz historian Albert Murray, who informs him that, during the slave era in the United States, "the suicide rate per capita among slave owners was much higher than the suicide rate among slaves" (68). Murray speculates that this is at least partly due to the African-American invention of blues music, which may not be able to eliminate depression completely, but can drive depression "into the corners of any room where it's being played" (68). Vonnegut is so fond of music, in fact, that he requests—"should [he] ever die, God forbid"—as his epitaph the following: "THE ONLY PROOF HE NEEDED FOR THE EXISTENCE OF GOD WAS MUSIC" (66). In this collection and throughout his work, Vonnegut substitutes the arts, whether music, literature, or painting, for traditional religious sentiment. The book ends with a brief statement about the artwork that is reproduced in its pages—photographs of original silk screens designed by Vonnegut and produced by Kentucky artist Joe Petro III. Beginning in the early 1990s, Vonnegut became much more involved in the visual arts, mostly through his partnership with Petro. He even goes so far as to tell readers that, in retrospect, it seems quite possible that Joe Petro III saved his life. Although he does not elaborate on this comment, readers understand that it is his involvement in the arts that makes life meaningful for Vonnegut. Just as the Vonnegut character is redeemed by his own creation, the abstract artist Rabo Karabekian, in his 1973 novel, *Breakfast of Champions*, the arts restore to Vonnegut a belief in the sacred nature of human beings.

FURTHER READING

A Man Without a Country. New York: Seven Stories Press, 2005.

"Miss Temptation"

A story about a young veteran's distrust of women and sexuality, "Miss Temptation" first appeared in the *Saturday Evening Post* in April 1956. It was later reprinted in the collection *Welcome to the Monkey House*.

SYNOPSIS

Set in the early 1950s, "Miss Temptation" is about the return of Corporal Norman Fuller to his small, New England hometown after serving 18 months in Korea. When Fuller arrives home, it is summer, and a 19-year-old "bit-part actress" (75) named Susanna, who is working in summer theater and renting a room over the village fire station, has been bewitching the town with her black eyes and hair, her creamy skin, her hoop earrings, and her belled ankle bracelets. Susanna wakes up at noon each day to begin "her stately, undulating, titillating, tinkling walk" (75) to the local drugstore, where she buys the New York papers. The day after Fuller's return from Korea, he is sitting on one of the soda fountain stools when Susanna enters the drugstore. Upon seeing her, the puritanical young soldier turns on his stool, which gives out a loud screech heard by the entire town, and proceeds to humiliate the young woman publicly, shaming her for the way she walks and dresses. The next morning, Susanna has packed her trunk and is preparing to leave the town. Bearse Hinkley, the knowing old drugstore pharmacist, sends Corporal Fuller up to her room with the young woman's New York papers. The two confront each other, and Fuller is forced to recognize Susanna's humanity. The story ends with Susanna having her trunk brought back to her room, and the two young people begin a stroll together through the town, arm in arm.

COMMENTARY

"Miss Temptation" is reminiscent of ERNEST HEMINGWAY's well-known 1925 short story, "Soldier's Home," about Harold Krebs, a returning World War I soldier who no longer fits into the small-town life he left to go to war, and who has a particular problem with the changes the town girls have gone through while he has been gone. Like Krebs, Corporal Norman Fuller has a cheerful mother who tries to interest him in his old activities. But also like Krebs, Fuller feels he no longer belongs in the town, and he seems to particularly resent women upon his return. Yet, Vonnegut's story, unlike the earlier Hemingway story, is more interested in condemning the zealous bigotry of its main character than in showing the malaise of the damaged and alienated soldier. Fuller's public humiliation of Susanna, for the sexualized way she walks and dresses, is presented as a throwback to the New England witch hunts when Vonnegut writes that "the wraith of a Puritan ancestor, stiff-necked, dressed in black, took possession of Fuller's tongue" and that the young man speaks with "the voice of a witch hanger . . . redolent with frustration, self-righteousness, and doom" (81). Fuller even refers to his condemnation of the actress as a "religious experience" (80) and suggests to his mother that he plans to attend divinity school.

Fuller's anger stems largely from his high school experiences with beautiful girls, whom he believes would not look at a boy without "a car and an allowance of twenty bucks a week to spend on 'em" (82). His lack of success with girls in high school is only compounded by his army experiences, when he is confronted by numerous "professional temptresses . . . who had beckoned from makeshift bed-sheet movie screens, from curling pinups on damp tent walls, from ragged magazines in sandbagged pits" (80). In fact, when Fuller actually speaks to Susanna, he finds himself wishing that "she were in black and white, a thousandth of an inch thick on a magazine page" (86). It would be easier for Fuller to deal with the flat stereotypes of women he has internalized than the real-life human being he meets when he actually speaks with the young actress. But Susanna insists to Fuller that she indeed has "a soul" (86) and that high school boys like him were quick to condemn her without even speaking to her. When Susanna suggests the two take a walk together so that Fuller can undo his earlier humiliation of her and "welcome [her] back to the human race" (88), readers understand that Susanna is really the one welcoming Corporal Norman Fuller back to the human race.

CHARACTERS

Fuller, Corporal Norman An angry young soldier just returned from serving 18 months in Korea, Corporal Norman Fuller begins the story with a self-righteous zeal that seems the legacy of his witch-hanging Puritan forebears. Later, readers discover that Fuller's resentment of the beautiful young actress Susanna stems largely from his lack of success with girls in high school and during his army days. Thus, he views women as wicked temptresses who mock him with what he cannot have. After actually speaking with Susanna and being forced to recognize how he hurt her in the drugstore, his views begin to change, and he comes to see women as fellow human beings rather than merely sexual objects.

Fuller, Mrs. Norman Fuller's cheerful widowed mother encourages him to see old friends and date girls after his return from Korea. Norman, however, responds in a surly way, stating that he has no friends anymore and that all the girls he knows are already married.

Hinkley, Bearse Bearse Hinkley is the 72-year-old town pharmacist who sells the New York newspapers to Susanna every day. After Corporal Norman Fuller publicly humiliates the young actress, Hinkley shames Fuller into recognizing his own egotism. Hinkley, by sending Fuller to Susanna's room with her newspapers the next day, initiates the reconciliation between the two young people.

Susanna Described as having "feathery hair and saucer eyes . . . as black as midnight," "skin the color of cream," "hips . . . like a lyre," and a "bosom [that] made men dream of peace and plenty for ever and ever" (75), Susanna is a 19-year-old bit-part actress who is working in summer theater in the small New England village where the story takes place. She captivates the entire town each day with her titillating walk from her rented room to the drugstore to buy newspapers. When she is publicly humiliated by a young soldier just returned from Korea, however, she packs her trunk to leave town, deciding to stay only after she frankly explains to Corporal Fuller how he has hurt her.

FURTHER READING

Reed, Peter. *The Short Fiction of Kurt Vonnegut.* Westport, Conn.: Greenwood Press, 1997.
Welcome to the Monkey House. New York: Dell, 1998.

"Mnemonics"

One of Vonnegut's earliest published stories, "Mnemonics" first appeared in *Collier's* magazine in April 1951. The story, which concerns the transformation of a diffident, timid office worker into an unlikely lady's man, was later reprinted in the 1999 collection, *Bagombo Snuff Box*.

SYNOPSIS

In "Mnemonics," Alfred Moorhead has recently attended a memory clinic held by his company. The clinic's instructor taught him to create imaginative scenarios in his mind to remember lists of items. Back at his office, Moorhead has done so well with the technique that he has become much more efficient in his work and recently been promoted. He is very happy, except for one thing. For two years, he has "silently adored" (35) his secretary, Ellen, but been afraid to tell her. One day, Moorhead's boss calls with a long list of items that Moorhead needs to remember and insists that Moorhead write the items down. However, Moorhead cannot find a pencil, so he forces himself to remember the list. To do so, he imagines scenarios involving famous, beautiful actresses. When the phone call ends, Moorhead has 43 items to remember and, sweating profusely, hurries to find a pencil before his imagined scenarios fade away. He manages to write all the items down, except for the very last one. The final scenario to confront him involves a beautiful woman standing in front of him with a sheaf of papers, but he can remember nothing about the details of the scenario. So he reaches out, grabs the woman, and murmurs, "Now, baby . . . what's on *your* mind?" (39). It turns out that this last woman is his real-life secretary Ellen, who is delighted to finally be noticed by her boss.

COMMENTARY

Like many stories by O. Henry, a 19th-century short fiction writer much admired by Vonnegut as a young man, "Mnemonics" is a sweet, humorous little piece with a surprise ending. Alfred Moorhead seems like the ultimate milquetoast character in many ways. He is too timid to tell his secretary, Ellen, that he has secretly adored her for two years,

the "richest moments in his life" occur when he is daydreaming (38), and he is initially too feeble-minded to remember a list of five items told him by the instructor at the memory clinic. Nevertheless, Moorhead turns out to be an unlikely hero. Although his imagined scenarios involving beautiful actresses might at first seem pathetic, they get Moorhead what he wants in the end. He is able to work more efficiently, spend less time looking for things in his files, and he even receives a promotion at work. But most important, his imagination, which he confuses with real life at the end of the story, wins him his secretary, Ellen. It is only in his daydreams that he is able to act bravely with women, and because he believes Ellen is simply another one of his 43 created scenarios, he speaks to her as he would to one of his fantasy women. The surprise at the end is that Ellen has secretly returned his love these past years and has only been waiting for Moorhead to notice her.

CHARACTERS

Clinic Instructor   An instructor at a memory clinic attended by Alfred Moorhead teaches his clients to improve their memories by creating imagined scenarios in their minds. The scenarios, he tells his pupils, must be of their own invention since each person's personality is clearly different. This frees Moorhead to create images involving beautiful actresses, and the technique does indeed dramatically improve his memory.

Ellen   Ellen works as a secretary to Alfred Moorhead. She clearly has secretly been in love with her boss, just as he has been with her, since she is so pleased by his accidental sexual advance at the end of the story.

Moorhead, Alfred   Timid, dreamy Alfred Moorhead works in an office and moons over his secretary, Ellen. His life changes, however, after he attends a memory clinic held by his company, where he learns to imagine pictures in his mind to remember lists of items. At the end of the story, Moorhead's mind-pictures, which always involve beautiful actresses, become confused with real life, causing him to proposition his secretary. The story ends happily for Moorhead, though, since Ellen is delighted by finally receiving sexual attention from her boss.

Thriller, Ralph L. Ralph L. Thriller is Alfred Moorhead's boss. Toward the end of the story, Thriller calls Moorhead with a list of important items he needs to remember. Although Thriller insists that Moorhead write the list down, Moorhead tries instead to remember the items, using the techniques taught him at the company's memory clinic.

FURTHER READING

Bagombo Snuff Box. New York: Berkley Books, 2000.
Reed, Peter. *The Short Fiction of Kurt Vonnegut.* Westport, Conn.: Greenwood Press, 1997.

"More Stately Mansions"

"More Stately Mansions," a domestic drama about a housewife with artistic ambitions, was first published in *Collier's* magazine in December 1951 before being reprinted in both *Canary in a Cat House* in 1961 and *Welcome to the Monkey House* in 1968.

SYNOPSIS

"More Stately Mansions" is narrated by a man who moves with his wife into a new house in a small village. The first neighbors to welcome them are the McClellans. Grace McClellan is completely obsessed with home redecorating. She subscribes to numerous home magazines, which she seems to have nearly memorized. When she visits the narrator and his wife, Anne, she immediately walks from room to room, making elaborate suggestions for improvements. Eventually, after the couples have been acquainted for a while, the narrator and Anne are finally invited to the McClellan's house for drinks. Expecting the McClellans' home to be a spectacular showcase, the narrator is astonished when he discovers the house is actually dirty, decrepit, and bare. Grace, though, is undaunted, and explains in loving detail what she hopes to do

with the house one day. Meanwhile, her husband, George, is patient and sympathetic to his wife's excesses.

Two years after the couples meet, Grace McClellan comes down with a viral infection that requires hospitalization. While she is in the hospital, George inherits a small legacy from a relative he had never met. He decides to use the money to completely redo their house while Grace is away, and he asks the help of the narrator and Anne, who throw themselves into the project. By the time Grace is released from the hospital, the house is perfect, done up exactly according to the plans she had outlined in such specific detail. The friends anticipate Grace's reaction with great glee, but when she actually arrives home, she seems to take the changes completely in stride. Grace believes the house has always been decorated this way, and that George has simply kept things clean and well-ordered while she has been gone.

COMMENTARY

Grace McClellan, despite her annoying behavior, fits the definition of an artist Vonnegut will develop in later works such as *Bluebeard*. She completely loses herself in home redecorating, forgetting the outside world as she obsessively discusses furniture and color patterns. Like Circe Berman in *Bluebeard*, Grace McClellan's artistic bent is more pedestrian and lowbrow than that of other characters, especially the male narrator. While it would be easy for Vonnegut to simply mock such a character, the story presents Grace more complexly, especially in light of her relationship with her husband, George. He himself is not condescending toward his wife. Instead, the narrator sees him give Grace a glance that is "affectionate and possessive" (137). When George is among friends whom he knows will not bait his wife, he "did nothing to discourage or disparage her dreaming" (143). In fact, George appreciates Grace's upbeat tendency to live in the future; she never reproaches him for the very little money he earns in his leather goods shop, which prevents her from buying the kind of home furnishings she would like. Despite the seeming strangeness of this couple, each provides the other uncritical support. At the story's end, it becomes clear that Grace has retreated completely into her imagination. She believes the curtains that Anne was not able to match exactly to her desired shade of yellow have simply faded while she has been away, suggesting her conviction that the house has *always* been as beautifully decorated as it is now. Yet, Grace makes this observation while George is out of the room, mixing drinks. It is unclear whether he, too, realizes his wife's delusions. In any case, the narrator and his wife allow the couple to retain their illusions, accepting their drinks "wordlessly" (146) at the end as their neighbors continue to occupy a world of their own making.

CHARACTERS

Anne   Anne is the wife of the narrator of the story. The couple meet the McClellans when they move into a new house in a small village. Anne learns to bear Grace McClellan's idiosyncrasies with patience and forbearance, coming to like the woman despite her single-minded obsession with home decorating.

Jenkinses   Although readers never actually meet the Jenkinses, they are a neighboring family. Grace McClellan disapproves of them because they bought two new Hitchcock chairs at one point, but then stopped their redecorating efforts.

McClellan, George   George McClellan, Grace's husband, is initially silent and hesitant with the narrator and Anne. When he discovers, however, that the new couple is not going to "bait his wife about interior decorating" (143), he grows more friendly and talkative. George adores his wife and is patient with her obsession. He seems to appreciate the fact that she never blames him for not earning more money at his little leather goods store, but instead cheerfully makes plans for the future.

McClellan, Grace   Grace McClellan, though difficult for the narrator and Anne to be around because of her obsession with home decorating, which is all she ever talks about, is not a bad person. She never complains about her own lack of wealth, and she excitedly lends her expertise to her neighbors (whether they want it or not). When her husband,

George, completely makes over their home while she is in the hospital, readers realize that Grace's obsession has turned into madness; she can no longer distinguish fact from fantasy.

Narrator   The narrator of the story is bemused by Grace McClellan's obsession. He admits, though, that his wife, Anne, bears the brunt of Grace's one-track conversations, since he often spends time with George McClellan while the women talk. The narrator comes to like George quite a bit and to admire the patience and love he shows his difficult wife.

FURTHER READING

Reed, Peter. *The Short Fiction of Kurt Vonnegut*. Westport, Conn.: Greenwood Press, 1997.
Welcome to the Monkey House. New York: Dell, 1998.

Mother Night

Vonnegut's third novel, *Mother Night*, published as a Fawcett paperback in 1962, explores the fine, ambiguous line between good and evil in the world. It examines one of the darkest chapters of human history—the Nazi holocaust of the Jews—and asks pressing questions about the human capacity to both commit appalling atrocities and perform

Nick Nolte and Sheryl Lee in 1996 film version of *Mother Night* ("Mother Night" © MCMXCVI, New Line Productions, Inc. All rights reserved. Photo by Atilla Dory. Photo appears courtesy of New Line Productions, Inc.)

astonishing acts of heroism. By focusing on How- ard W. Campbell, Jr., a Nazi propagandist secretly working as an American agent, the novel asks whether an individual can be forgiven for loath- some acts if his ultimate intentions are good. In other words, do the ends justify the means? In what many critics consider to be Vonnegut's grimmest novel, his answer to this question seems to be a resounding "no." He tells us in his 1966 introduc- tion added to the novel that *Mother Night* is the only story he has written whose moral he knows. And that moral, he explains, is this: "We are what we pretend to be, so we must be careful about what we pretend to be" (v). Howard W. Campbell, Jr.'s, great crime is to have "served evil too openly and good too secretly," something Vonnegut, as editor, tells readers is also "the crime of his times" (xiii).

SYNOPSIS

Chapters 1–10

Mother Night is presented as the "confessions" of Howard W. Campbell, Jr., notorious Nazi propa- gandist, written while he is in Israel waiting to be put on trial for war crimes. The book begins with an "Editor's Note," signed by Kurt Vonnegut him- self, in which he claims that his involvement with the project is simply "to pass on, in the most satis- factory style," the American edition of Campbell's confessions (x). While he has had to make some textual decisions, such as changing a few names to protect people still living, reconstructing Camp- bell's German poems, and making certain cuts in the text on the advice of his lawyers, Vonnegut claims that, in all other ways, the text is Campbell's own. Howard W. Campbell, Jr., begins his story by explaining that he is writing this book in the year 1961, and that it is addressed to Mr. Tuvia Friedmann, director of the Haifa Institute for the Documentation of War Criminals. Mr. Friedmann is so eager to have Campbell's writings to add to his archives that he has provided a typewriter, a stenographic service, and research assistants to aid Campbell in the project.

Campbell, born in 1912 in Schenectady, New York, is the son of an engineer who worked for the GENERAL ELECTRIC Company, but who was sel- dom home because of his work. Campbell's mother was a musician and alcoholic who doted on him as a young boy, but who ceases paying any atten- tion to him out of fear she will harm him. When Howard is 11 years old, his father is assigned to the General Electric office in Berlin, Germany, where he spends the next two decades of his life. Married to the beautiful actress Helga Noth when he is 26, the grown-up Campbell becomes a suc- cessful playwright in Germany, popular with the rising Nazi party, whose high-ranking officials he mingles with socially. In 1938, three years before America's entry into World War II, Campbell is recruited as an American spy by a man he knows as Major Frank Wirtanen. Campbell's assignment is to work himself as high up with the Nazis as pos- sible. Eventually becoming the leading expert on American problems in the Nazi Ministry of Popular Enlightenment and Propaganda, Campbell works as a writer and broadcaster of Nazi propaganda to the English-speaking world, gaining a notorious reputation for his anti-Semitic hate speech. Yet, all the while he is spreading Nazi propaganda, Camp- bell is also secretly broadcasting coded messages to American agents.

Chapters 11–22

In the last weeks of the war, Campbell, by now high on the list of Nazi war criminals, is captured by Lieutenant Bernard B. O'Hare of the U.S. Army. Though the American intelligence service refuses to either confirm or refute Campbell's insistence that he was acting secretly as their agent during the war, they deny the existence of Major Frank Wirtanen. The Americans, however, do manage to save Campbell from hanging. He is given money and told to disappear into New York City since he is still a highly sought-after war criminal. Camp- bell's wife, Helga, had been captured while enter- taining troops in the Crimea and is presumed dead, so Campbell goes to New York by himself, where he rents an apartment and lives a very quiet and lonely life for 13 years. One day in 1958, though, he buys a war-surplus wood-carving kit that he uses to whittle a set of chessman. Excited about his accomplishment, Campbell bangs on the door of his neighbor, whom he does not know at all, to show him the set. The neighbor turns out to be a "foxy old man" (48) named George Kraft, a painter with whom Campbell begins an intense friendship. Campbell soon tells Kraft his whole story.

About a year after he meets Kraft, Campbell receives in the mail two important items. One is a racist newspaper called *The White Christian Minuteman,* which contains a small article lamenting the fact that Howard W. Campbell now lives in poverty in New York City, and publishing his actual address. The other is from Bernard B. O'Hare, who has discovered where Campbell lives and promises to turn him in as a war criminal. A week later, Campbell is paid a visit by the Reverend Doctor Lionel J. D. Jones, D.D.S., D.D., publisher of *The White Christian Minuteman.* Jones, who arrives with several associates in tow, is a huge fan of Campbell and announces that he has brought Campbell a gift: the return of his wife, Helga. Overcome with emotion at seeing each other again, Helga and Campbell embrace, and Helga tells the wretched story of her hard life since the war. Meanwhile, August Krapptauer, Jones's 63-year-old bodyguard, has gone down several flights of stairs to fetch Helga's luggage. When he arrives back at the apartment, he drops dead from a heart attack.

Chapters 23–30
After spending a wonderful night with his returned Helga, Howard Campbell is astonished the next morning when she confesses that she is not actually Helga at all, but Helga's much younger sister, Resi Noth. At first bewildered, Campbell eventually accepts Resi as his Helga, and the two spend the day happily shopping and drinking. When they return to Campbell's apartment, they are met by a "bald, bristly fat man" (144), an unnamed World War II veteran who beats Campbell severely in honor of his fallen comrades in the war. Campbell loses consciousness, and when he come to, he finds himself in the cellar of the home of Dr. Lionel J. D. Jones, which has been furnished for meetings of the Iron Guard of the White Sons of the American Constitution, a youth group organized by August Krapptauer before his death. Resi had called Jones after the beating since he was the only person she knew they could trust. Also waiting in the basement is Campbell's old friend George Kraft. While

Campbell had been unconscious, Resi Noth and Kraft had developed a plan for the three of them to escape the country to Mexico City since the newspapers have gotten ahold of Campbell's story, neighbors and curiosity seekers have staked out his apartment, and the Republic of Israel is demanding he be sent there for trial. Before they are able to escape, though, Jones asks Campbell to deliver the eulogy at a memorial service for Krapptauer, and Campbell agrees.

Chapters 31–39
At the service Campbell meets up again with Frank Wirtanen, the agent who originally recruited him as a spy. Someone in the darkened room puts a note into Campbell's pocket, urgently requesting that he slip away from the ceremony and meet Wirtanen in a vacant store across the street. Once there, the agent tells Campbell that George Kraft and Resi Noth are both communist spies, and that as soon as the plane they're escaping on lands in Mexico City, they plan to put him on another plane for Moscow. The Russians want to exhibit Campbell to the world "as a prime example of the sort of Fascist war criminal this country shelters" (198). Even though Campbell now knows Kraft and Noth for what they truly are, he nevertheless returns to Jones's basement since the two are still the only people in the whole world for whom he cares. When Campbell confronts them with his newly gained knowledge, Resi Noth breaks down, declaring that she has really fallen in love with him, and that she was not going to go through with the plan to send him to Moscow. When Campbell informs her that American agents are surrounding the place and that he won't fight to protect her, Resi declares that there's nothing to live for, if not love, and kills herself by ingesting a cyanide capsule she had carried with her. George Kraft is arrested by the American agents and taken to prison along with Dr. Jones and the rest of the *White Christian Minuteman* crew.

Chapters 40–45
Having nowhere to go and nothing to do, Howard W. Campbell decides to return to his old apartment. Once there, he encounters Bernard B. O'Hare, the army lieutenant who had originally

arrested him in Berlin. Aging, pale, and unhealthy, O'Hare recounts to Campbell the numerous disappointments in his life since the war, as well as declaring that he believes it is his destiny is to "take apart" Campbell, whom he considers a "yellow-belly," evil Nazi (249). Instead, Campbell hits O'Hare with a pair of fire tongs, breaking his arm. In great pain, O'Hare eventually leaves the apartment. Campbell then goes downstairs and finds himself knocking on the door of his neighbor, Dr. Abraham Epstein, who had spent his childhood in Auschwitz. Campbell tells Epstein he wishes to go to Israel to stand trial for his crimes against humanity. Although Epstein claims to have forgotten his Auschwitz memories and wants nothing to do with politics, his mother, also an Auschwitz survivor, understands that Campbell *has* to turn himself in. The two Epsteins call Zionist friends of theirs, who take Campbell into custody and surrender him to Israeli officials.

At the end of the novel, Campbell, waiting for his trial in the Israeli prison, receives a letter from the man he knew as Frank Wirtanen, who offers to come forward, identify himself, and vouch that Campbell was a secret American agent during the war. Previously, Campbell's lawyers had told him that verifying the existence of Wirtanen was the only chance Campbell had to be acquitted. Yet, at this point, Campbell finds the prospect of becoming a free man again "nauseating" (267). He determines, instead, that this night will be the night he "will hang Howard W. Campbell, Jr., for crimes against himself" (268). The German phrase *auf wiedersehen*, or good-bye, closes the novel.

COMMENTARY

The opening chapters of *Mother Night*—the author's introduction and the editor's note—set the stage for the type of personal and literary commentary on his own work that Vonnegut frequently uses in his later novels, especially *Slaughterhouse-Five*, *Breakfast of Champions*, and *Slapstick*. Though here billed as the more traditional introduction and editor's note, these self-reflective devices allow Vonnegut to comment not only on the story he is presenting, but also on the very nature of fiction. Such commentary develops in his later work into a more full-blown use of METAFICTION, which is a type of self-conscious fiction, often associated with POSTMODERN literature, that is about storytelling itself, about how stories affect one's perception of the world, and about how language shapes reality. For instance, the 1969 *Slaughterhouse-Five* is, in many ways, about Vonnegut's struggle to write the story of his DRESDEN experiences, and the novel asks questions about how one should write about atrocity. *Breakfast of Champions*, published in 1973, goes even further, introducing Vonnegut as a character in his own story, and drawing attention to the fictional status of other characters such as Kilgore Trout, who actually meets his creator—Vonnegut—at the end of the book. In *Mother Night*, the beginnings of metafiction are evident when Vonnegut states the moral of his novel in the introduction and when he has his own character, Howard W. Campbell, Jr., comment on the book's title and dedication in the editor's note.

Vonnegut also comments about the nature of art in his editor's note when he tells us that Howard W. Campbell, Jr.'s, vocation as a playwright makes his writings "concerned with more than mere informing or deceiving" (ix). Campbell is an artist, and art *requires* the telling of lies, according to Vonnegut. Further, writing for the theater may be the most unreal form of art there is. "No one is a better liar," the editor writes, "than a man who has warped lives and passions onto something as grotesquely artificial as a stage" (ix). Yet, with that said, the editor goes on to venture the opinion that "lies told for the sake of artistic effect—in the theater, for instance, and in Campbell's confessions, perhaps—can be, in a higher sense, the most beguiling forms of truth" (ix–x). So, while acknowledging that fiction making consists of telling lies, the editor also believes, paradoxically, that literary art is an avenue to get at truth, truth in a "higher sense" than otherwise accessible.

The editor's comment is also interesting because it affects the reading of Campbell's confessions that follows. Vonnegut slyly raises the possibility that Campbell might be lying in his confessions, that the story he tells, which is presented as truth—the very word *confession* suggests getting at a hidden truth— might actually consist of "lies told for the sake of artistic effect." This editor's note teaches readers to be skeptical about Campbell's story—was there really a Major Frank Wirtanen? Was Campbell really working for the Americans during the war? We have only his word for these "facts," since no one else ever saw his "Blue Fairy Godmother" as he calls Wirtanen. And Campbell, after all, is a fiction maker, someone who makes his living inventing lies. Perhaps the point is that, finally, it does not much matter whether Campbell is telling the absolute truth in his confessions or not; what he is able to convey is the artistic truth of what it feels like to commit reprehensible acts, all the while believing in one's own basic goodness buried deep inside.

Mother Night also anticipates Vonnegut's later works in the style he adopts. Critic Stanley Schatt points out that, "When Vonnegut wrote his first two novels, *Player Piano* and *The Sirens of Titan*, he used a conventional narrative style and a third-person point of view" (52). Schatt argues that Vonnegut's first two novels can be considered social SATIRES, while *Mother Night* tends more toward BLACK HUMOR, which most critics agree is more ethically ambiguous, with less of a desire to reform society and more of a tendency to laugh at human foibles, than satire (53). *Mother Night* presents the beginnings of Vonnegut's clearly identifiable sentence-level style as well—the almost child-like understatement and lack of moral judgment in describing horrific happenings that becomes a hallmark of his later fiction. A couple of examples from the introduction include his description of the victims of the Dresden firestorm as "seeming pieces of charred firewood two or three feet long—ridiculously small human beings, or jumbo fried grasshoppers, if you will" (vii) as well as his flat statement about the victims' relatives who came to watch the prisoners of war dig bodies out of the shelters: "They were interesting, too" (vii). Vonnegut's reduction of these events to their simplest terms and his refusal to attach moral outrage to them amplifies the horror for readers and becomes a technique he relies on heavily in his later fiction.

Campbell's actual story begins when he is in a Jerusalem prison, awaiting trial for war crimes. He starts by introducing readers to four different prison guards who watch over Campbell in rotating shifts.

These guards are very different from one another and represent four different reactions to atrocity, each of which will be explored in more detail in Campbell's confessions. The first guard is the 18-year-old Arnold Marx, who "knows nothing about" World War II and who is "not interested" in it (3). Arnold represents the desire to deny or repress knowledge of the Holocaust as a way of coping with the tragedy. Like young Dr. Epstein later in the novel, for Arnold Nazi atrocities become part of the distant past, mingling with the whole sordid history of human behavior, and best not dwelt upon. In fact, Arnold, through the archaeological work he does with his father, is more interested in ancient history than in the recent past. He tells Campbell about Hazor, an ancient Canaanite city he is working to help excavate: "About fourteen hundred years before Christ . . . an Israelite army captured Hazor, killed all forty thousand inhabitants, and burned it down" (4). Later, Solomon rebuilt the city, but then, about 700 B.C. TIGLATH-PILESER THE THIRD, an Assyrian, burnt it down again. Vonnegut includes this detail to show what becomes an important theme in much of his fiction—the futility of trying to change the world. War crimes have been committed throughout history. Today's victims, the Jews, were yesterday's tyrants. So, one way of dealing with Nazi atrocity is simply to chalk it up to natural human behavior, to relegate it to the string of horrors that make up past history and thus render it invisible.

The guard who relieves Arnold Marx is Andor Gutman, an Estonian Jew who spent two years of his life in Auschwitz. Unlike Arnold, Andor does remember the war. His reaction to the Nazi atrocities he witnessed and experienced is one of despair; in the concentration camp, Andor gives in to the suicidal impulse that many people suffer in the face of great horror. Andor explains to Campbell that he had just volunteered for the Sonderkommando, a special detail whose duties included shepherding condemned persons to the gas chambers, then hauling their bodies out afterward, when Himmler ordered the Auschwitz ovens closed down. In this way, Andor's life is saved, since members of the Sonderkommando are themselves killed after performing their gruesome task. Angry at himself afterward and unable to understand why he volunteered for the position of corpse carrier, Andor expresses his shame to Campbell. Campbell, though, says that he is able to understand the temptation to volunteer.

The impulse to commit suicide is something that motivates Campbell himself, as he is unable to live with the contributions he made to the Nazi cause during the war. The crooning, nearly hypnotic call for the corpse carriers at Auschwitz becomes a recurring motif in the book as Campbell symbolically commits suicide by turning himself in to the Epsteins, Mrs. Epstein gently murmurs the call to Campbell before he is taken away:

> "*Leichentrager zu Wache*," she crooned.
> A beautiful language, isn't it?
> Translation?
> "Corpse-carriers to the guardhouse."
> That's what that old woman crooned to me.
> (260)

The impulse to suicide is evident at the end of the novel as well, when Campbell, though he has received the letter from Wirtanen and thus has the means to free himself, states that he is nauseated by the idea of freedom and decides to hang himself instead.

The third man who guards Campbell in the Israeli prison is Arpad Kovacs, a Hungarian Jew who joined the hated and feared Schutzstaffe, or S.S., in order to save his life. Kovacs represents yet another reaction to wartime atrocity. He has become hard and cruel himself, doing anything necessary to get by and to survive the brutality that he is subject to. Expressing only contempt for the "complacent bastards" he calls "briquets" because they did nothing to save themselves when the Nazis took over (11), Kovacs chides Campbell that his notorious anti-Semitic broadcasts were not ferocious enough, that they lacked zest: "If any member of my S.S. platoon had spoken in such a friendly way about the Jews," he tells Campbell after reading the transcript of one of Campbell's radio broadcasts, "I would have had him shot for treason!" (13). Kovacs's viciousness is strangely effective in that, on his recommendation, 14 S.S. men are shot as suspects for leaking information to the Jews when it is Kovacs himself

who is doing the leaking. Yet, the problem with Kovacs's reaction to the horror of Nazi Germany is that in his methods and in his cruelty he comes to resemble so closely the Nazis that he abhors.

Like the willful forgetting of Arnold Marx and the suicidal despair of Andor Gutman, the hardening of Arpad Kovacs is a trait that becomes a theme in the rest of the confessions. Howard W. Campbell, Jr., like Dr. Faust in *FAUST*, the play from which the book's title is derived, has sold his soul to the devil in that he out-Nazis the Nazis with his virulent propaganda. Campbell's father-in-law, Werner Noth, recognizes this when he tells Campbell that he would not turn him in even if Campbell were a spy because Campbell could never have served the Americans as well as he served the Nazis (99). Major Wirtanen also acknowledges Campbell's service to the enemy in the following exchange:

> "three people in all the world knew me for what I was—" I said. "And all the rest—" I shrugged.
> "They knew you for what you were, too," he said abruptly.
> "That wasn't me," I said, startled by his sharpness.
> "Whoever it was—" said Wirtanen, "he was one of the most vicious sons of bitches who ever lived." (188)

Howard W. Campbell, Jr. is caught up in a cruel catch-22 in the novel. In order to survive and to serve his country, he has to be a good Nazi. Yet, in being a good Nazi, he betrays his country and does not deserve to survive. Vonnegut, like JOSEPH HELLER, whose novel *Catch-22* was published the same year as *Mother Night*, sees the terrible irony and absurdity of such situations. Also like Heller, Vonnegut offers no remedies for society's flaws; perhaps the best we can do is laugh darkly at the cosmic jokes played upon us.

The final prison guard we meet in Jerusalem represents a fourth reaction to atrocity, one that Howard W. Campbell, Jr., will also admit to in his confessions: an overwhelming numbness and lack of emotion. Bernard Mengel is a Polish Jew who once saved his own life "by playing so dead that a German soldier pulled out three of his teeth without suspecting that Mengel was not a corpse" (15). After undergoing such unspeakable brutality, Mengel tells Campbell that during the war and immediately afterward he got so he couldn't feel anything. When he helps hang Rudolf Hoess, the commandant at Auschwitz, by buckling a strap around his ankles, Mengel feels no satisfaction in the act. He explains that after hanging Hoess he packed up his clothes to go home. The catch on his suitcase broke, so he buckled it shut with a leather strap. "Twice within an hour I did the very same job," Mengel says, "—once to Hoess and once to my suitcase. Both jobs felt about the same" (16).

Campbell feels a similar numbness during his 13-year solitary life in New York City, and the numbness returns after the betrayal of George Kraft and Resi Noth, his only friends in the world. Right before she takes the cyanide capsule, Resi declares that she has nothing left to live for. All she has is her love for Campbell, but she recognizes that Campbell does not love her in return. "He is so used up," Resi explains, "that he can't love any more. There is nothing left of him but curiosity and a pair of eyes" (230). And even curiosity fails Campbell in the end. After the death of Resi and the arrest of Kraft, Campbell is led into the street by an American agent, and he completely freezes. He explains that his inability to move comes not from guilt or a sense of loss or a fear of death or even rage against injustice. "What froze me," Campbell writes, "was the fact that I had absolutely no reason to move in any direction. What had made me move through so many dead and pointless years was curiosity. Now even that had flickered out" (232). Campbell has become completely numb and emotionless at this point and is prepared to commit a symbolic suicide by turning himself in to the Israeli officials.

One of the darkest aspects of this novel is that there is no forgiveness or escape available to Campbell, no matter how much he desires it. During the years he lives in the tiny attic apartment in New York City, Campbell overlooks a small private park, walled off from the street by houses. Watching this "little Eden" (23) where children play hide-and-seek, Campbell is especially moved by the "sweetly mournful cry that meant a game . . . was over, that those still hiding were to come out of hiding, that

it was time to go home" (24). The cry, he writes, "was this: 'Olly-olly-ox-in-free'" (24). Though he longs for someone to call him home and stop his own endless game of hide-and-seek, that call never comes for Campbell. Major Wirtanen had told him initially that to do his job as an American spy well he would have to commit high treason and that he could never be forgiven (44). The longing for escape and redemption, then, permeates the novel as the refrain "Olly-olly-ox-in-free" competes with the crooned "Corpse carriers to the guardhouse" throughout the book, the first suggesting the possibility of forgiveness and absolution, the second that no escape from atrocity exists.

Much of Campbell's life, in fact, has been spent looking for a way to escape a traumatic and brutal world. The plays he writes as a young man are medieval romances, "about as political as chocolate *éclairs*" (33). The play that he is beginning to write when he is recruited by Major Frank Wirtanen is another romance, titled "Nation of Two," which "was going to show how a pair of lovers in a world gone mad could survive by being loyal only to a nation composed of themselves—a nation of two" (34). This play is inspired by his love affair with Helga Noth. The two remain friendly with Nazi officials, closing their eyes to the faults of their fascist patrons, and instead, attempting to live only for each other, for the "nation of two" that they create between themselves. As a young man, Campbell seems naïve in his insistence that the world of politics has nothing to do with him. He also seems naïve in his faith in romance. Major Wirtanen is able to use Campbell's overly simplistic worldview against him when he sells Campbell on the idea of becoming a spy by telling him he has seen his plays and that through these works he has learned something about Campbell himself: that he admires "pure hearts and heroes," that he loves good and hates evil, and that he believes in romance (39). Only *before* his wartime experiences, though, does Campbell entertain such firm, black-and-white convictions about heroes and villains, about good and evil, and about the ability of love to conquer all.

The novel shows that Campbell and Helga's attempt to isolate themselves from the larger world is doomed to failure. When he first meets Wirtanen, Campbell insists that he's "not a soldier, not a political man" but an artist (38). If war comes, he continues, "I won't do anything to help it along . . . it'll find me still working at my peaceful trade" (38). But, as Wirtanen points out, "this war isn't going to let anybody stay in a peaceful trade" (38). He adds that the worse "this Nazi thing gets" (38), the less easily Campbell will be able to sleep at night. Vonnegut suggests here that true artists cannot remain unengaged in politics. The very act of refusing to take sides can be a silent affirmation of evil. Campbell's previous simplistic notions of heroes and pure hearts are muddied forever when he accepts Wirtanen's proposition. He begins "to strut like Hitler's right-hand man" (39), playing his part so perfectly that nobody sees the "honest" self he hides "so deep inside" (39). The waters are muddied for readers as well, who have difficulty distinguishing a clear-cut motive for Campbell's decision to become a spy. Is he a true hero, willing to sacrifice himself—his love, his reputation—for a cause that is noble? Does Wirtanen convince him that a real artist must be politically engaged? Or is he so caught up in the romance of his own plays that he can not resist playing the role of tragic, doomed hero? Or, equally plausible, perhaps he is a towering egomaniac, willing to throw over his beloved Helga for the satisfaction of performing "some pretty grand acting" (39). It is curious, after all, that Campbell never tells Helga about his life as a spy, even though he freely admits to readers that he would have lost nothing by telling her the truth. Moral ambiguity is the hallmark of this novel.

Schizophrenia is a word used repeatedly by Vonnegut in the novel to describe the moral ambiguity of 20th-century life and the complexity of human motives. George Kraft, for instance, can simultaneously admire the organization ALCOHOLICS ANONYMOUS as "the greatest contribution America had made to the world" (53) while using the institution for his spy drops. He can be a true friend of Campbell's at the same time that he is secretly a communist agent planning to use Campbell cruelly to advance the Russian cause. As Wirtanen tells Campbell, Kraft's secret life of espionage does not mean that the friendship between the two men was false: "He's like you," Wirtanen tells Campbell, "He can be many things at once—all sincerely" (197). This schizophrenia is similarly evident in the behavior of the Nazis themselves who are able to appreciate and admire fine art while inflicting horrible suffering on their fellow human beings. Campbell's father-in-law, Werner Noth, for instance, cherishes his "luminously beautiful blue vase" carried by the Polish slave woman though he has absolutely no regard for the woman herself. Similarly, Rudolf Hoess plays beautiful classical music at Auschwitz that the prisoners hear as they are being herded to the gas chambers.

Howard W. Campbell himself is the character in the novel whose "several selves" (184) are most widely divergent. Thus, at the same time that Campbell's initial reluctance to become politically engaged is morally objectionable, readers can also find much to admire in his rejection of traditional patriotism and overzealous nationalism. When he and Resi are walking in New York City on Veterans Day, Campbell explains that he neither hates nor loves America: "I can't think in terms of boundaries," he tells her. "Those imaginary lines are as unreal to me as elves and pixies. I can't believe that they mark the end or the beginning of anything of real concern to a human soul. Virtues and vices, pleasures and pains cross boundaries at will" (133). Readers are surely intended to respect the sentiments Campbell expresses, especially when the insistence on ethnic boundaries and the playing up of nostalgic nationalism contributed heavily to the success of the Third Reich in Germany.

But readers also learn that hate masquerading as national loyalty is not the sole province of the Nazis. When Campbell's presence in America is exposed in the press, he states that it was the anger of his neighbors "that really stank of sudden death" (161). The "more barbaric" newspapers print letters that demand Campbell be displayed across the country in an iron cage, that volunteer their author's services on firing squads, and that express confidence that "other, stronger, younger people" would know what to do (161). Campbell calls these last letter writers "patriots" and muses that there has probably never been a society "without strong and young people eager to experiment with homicide, provided no very awful penalties are attached to it" (161). And later, in his final confrontation with Bernard B. O'Hare, Campbell decries the tendency to see the world in stark terms of black and white, no matter which side a person may be fighting for. He denounces O'Hare roundly for imagining his battle with Campbell as a war with pure evil. "There are plenty of good reasons for fighting," Campbell chides O'Hare, "but no good reason ever to hate without reservation, to imagine that God Almighty Himself hates with you, too. Where's evil? It's that large part of every man that wants to hate without limit, that wants to hate with God on its side" (251). America, these examples show, has its own share of fanatics not so unlike the Germans during the Third Reich: We have our own fascists, white supremacists, and self-deluded hate-mongers who call themselves patriots.

If hatred and the conviction that one is fighting absolute evil are human ills in the novel, readers see these traits contrasted with the kindness and essential human decency of the patrolman who guards Campbell's apartment. Despite recognizing Campbell as the source of all the trouble that has been occurring—the threats, vandalism, and destruction directed against Campbell's apartment—the young patrolman does not scold or condemn him. Instead, he explains that America is "a free country" and that "everybody gets protected exactly alike" (235). Even though his own father was killed in Iwo Jima, the patrolman recognizes that there were probably "good people killed on both sides" of the war (235). Finally, rather than blame people for bad things that happen, or condemn certain humans as evil, the patrolman speculates that chemicals cause much of the misery in the world—the different chemicals that people ingest in different countries, the chemicals that naturally exist in the blood. The patrolman even dreams of going back to school and learning more about chemicals so that he can help make the world a better place. While the patrolman might seem naïve, his refusal to hate or to blame makes him a fundamentally decent and kind-hearted character, unlike so many of the rabid fascists and nationalists Campbell meets.

Howard W. Campbell, Jr., for all of his moral schizophrenia, is perhaps best viewed as an artist, someone who acknowledges truth when he finds it and helps others to see that truth. Although his early plays perhaps worked to create illusion rather than truth, Campbell's confessions are his greatest work of art in that he shows the moral uncertainty and the complexities of human behavior that exist in the real world. Whether or not Campbell actually served as an American spy, he recognizes within himself the capacity for both good and evil. While he leaves open the possibility that he acted as a real hero, Campbell never excuses or glosses over the crimes that he committed along the way, even arguing that he is more deserving of punishment than Adolf Eichmann because he, Campbell, understood the difference between right and wrong and had enough of an imagination to anticipate the cruel consequences of the lies he told. As an artist, Campbell tells Major Wirtanen that he admires form: "I admire things with a beginning, a middle, an end," he explains, "and, whenever possible, a moral, too" (185). If Campbell had been a romantic hero like the ones in his plays, he would have killed himself when he lost Helga, he explains to Wirtanen, but he missed his cue. Still, Campbell's probable suicide at the close of the novel makes sense for an artist who appreciates form and who likes stories to have ends. Though too late to be the pure romantic hero of his earlier, simpler work, Campbell knows when it is time to exit; his suicide, coming right after the promise of exoneration is a logical playing-out of his new, darkly ironic and morally ambiguous art.

CHARACTERS AND RELATED ENTRIES

Bodovskov, Stepan   An interpreter for the Russians when the first Russian troops enter Berlin, Stepan Bodovskov finds the trunk containing the manuscripts of Howard W. Campbell, Jr. in a theater loft. Bodovskov, who is fluent in German, begins translating some of Campbell's works into Russian, eventually passing off almost all of Campbell's manuscripts, including the play *The Goblet* and the pornographic novel *Memoirs of a Monogamous Casanova*, as his own. Bodovskov is eventually arrested and shot, not for plagiarizing the work of Campbell, but for the crime of originality. He had begun to write his own fiction, including a 2,000-page satire on the Red Army. Howard W. Campbell, Jr., is told Bodovskov's story by Major Frank Wirtanen, in the scene in which Wirtanen warns him that George Kraft and Resi Noth are really communist agents.

Brewer, Ansel   Ansel Brewer is one of the dead war buddies memorialized by the bald, bristly, fat man who attacks Howard W. Campbell, Jr., outside his New York City apartment. Brewer was run over by a Tiger tank at Aachen.

Buchanon, Private Irving   When the unnamed bald, bristly fat man brutally beats Howard W. Campbell, Jr., he announces that the first punch is in memory of Private Irving Buchanon, a buddy of his who was killed in Omaha Beach where "the Germans cut his nuts off and hung him from a tele-phone pole" (146).

Campbell, Howard W., Jr.   *Mother Night* is pre-sented as the confessions of Howard W. Campbell, Jr., written in his own hand and simply edited by Vonnegut. Campbell is an American who moves to Berlin with his family as a child, and is raised speak-ing German and moving comfortably in German culture. A budding author and playwright, Camp-bell marries the beautiful actress Helga Noth when he is 26 years old. The happy couple is popular with the Nazis, moving in social circles frequented by high-ranking party officials. In 1938, Campbell is recruited as an American spy by Major Frank Wirtanen, a U.S. intelligence agent. Campbell's assignment is to continue working his way up the ranks of the party and ingratiating himself with the Nazis. He succeeds so well in his job that he becomes one of the most notorious Nazi propagan-dists, delivering virulently anti-Semitic radio broad-casts to the West. All the while, Campbell is also secretly delivering coded messages to the Allies. Captured after the war by army lieutenant Bernard B. O'Hare, Campbell narrowly escapes hanging. Though unacknowledged by the Americans as a spy, he is given money and sent to New York City, where he lives anonymously for the next 13 years.

Campbell's whereabouts are eventually discovered by the Reverend Doctor Lionel J. D. Jones, a rabid white supremacist, and also by a bevy of World War II veterans who would like to see Campbell executed for his war crimes. Betrayed by his friend George Kraft and by his late wife's sister, Resi Noth, who are secret Russian communist agents, Campbell decides to turn himself in to the Israeli secret service. He writes his confessions awaiting trial for war crimes in a Jerusalem prison. Although he receives a letter from Wirtanen at the end of the novel giving him the means to prove his inno-cence, Campbell is so cynical and filled with self-loathing by this time that he determines instead to hang himself in prison. Howard W. Campbell, Jr., appears again, as an American Nazi agent trying to convert American prisoners of war to a unit called the Free American Corps, in *Slaughterhouse-Five*, Vonnegut's 1968 novel about the Allied bombing of Dresden.

Campbell, Howard W., Sr.   Raised in Ten-nessee, the son of a Baptist minister, Howard W. Campbell, Sr., is the father of the Nazi propagan-dist and novel's protagonist, Howard W. Campbell, Jr. Campbell, Sr., worked as an engineer for the General Electric Company when his son was young, and was seldom home since he lived for his work. "The man was the job and the job was the man," Campbell, Jr. writes (25). In 1923, when Harold, Jr. is 11 years old, the older Campbell is assigned to the General Electric office in Berlin, Germany, where he moves with his family. Both Campbell, Sr., and his wife die before the end of World War II, possibly of broken hearts at the behavior of their son, but nevertheless leaving Howard, Jr. a sizable inheritance.

Campbell, Virginia Crocker   Virginia Crocker Campbell is the wife of Howard W. Campbell, Sr., and mother of Howard, Jr. A housewife and ama-teur cellist who played with the Schenectady Sym-phony Orchestra, Virginia is talented and beautiful, but also an alcoholic. Howard, Jr., recounts a mem-ory of his mother, drunk, filling a saucer with rub-bing alcohol and table salt, placing the mixture on the kitchen table between herself and her son, and lighting it with a kitchen match. When the sodium flame makes both their faces look an eerie yellow, Virginia tells her son that that's what they'll look like when they're dead. After this incident, Howard, Jr., states that he was no longer his mother's favored companion as he had been when younger. Having scared herself with this demonstration, and afraid that she might hurt Howard, Virginia cuts herself off from her son, hardly even speaking to him from that moment on. Virginia, along with her husband, Howard, Sr., dies before the end of World War II, never knowing that her traitorous Nazi son was really an American agent.

Dobrowitz, Alvin Alan Dobrowitz, though raised in America, is Howard W. Campbell, Jr.'s, defense lawyer in Israel. Dobrowitz, eager to prove Campbell's innocence, emphasizes the importance of producing the "barest proof" (263) that a man named Major Frank Wirtanen existed and recruited Campbell as an American spy.

Eichmann, Adolf Known as the chief executioner of the Third Reich, Adolf Eichmann is an actual historical figure largely responsible for organizing the Nazi's attempted genocide of Jews and other "undesirable" persons. In *Mother Night,* Howard W. Campbell, Jr., meets Adolf Eichmann briefly at an Israeli prison in Tel Aviv. Eichmann, like Campbell, is also writing the story of his life. When Campbell asks Eichmann if he feels guilty for murdering 6 million Jews, Eichmann replies "Absolutely not" (165). His trite defense for his actions is that he was just following orders. Later, Eichmann offers to lend Campbell some of the 6 million for his own book, joking that he does not really need them all. Campbell's final contact with Eichmann comes when Eichmann smuggles him a note from his prison in Tel Aviv to Campbell's prison in Jerusalem. The note, astonishing in its amorality, reads, "Do you think a literary agent is absolutely necessary?" (168). Campbell replies with the deadpan comment, "For book club and movie sales in the United Sates of America, absolutely" (168).

Epstein, Dr. Abraham A downstairs neighbor in the New York apartment that Howard W. Camp-

bell, Jr., lives in for 13 years after World War II, Dr. Abraham Epstein spent part of his childhood in the Auschwitz concentration camp. Dr. Epstein, however, wants to forget Auschwitz and everything associated with it. Nevertheless, memories of that period keep intruding as Dr. Epstein is asked to treat August Krapptauer after his heart attack and as Campbell chooses to surrender to Epstein and his mother at the end of the novel.

Epstein, Mrs. Mrs. Epstein and her son, Dr. Abraham Epstein, live downstairs from Howard W. Campbell, Jr., in his New York apartment building. Campbell meets the Epsteins soon after they move into the building because he needs a doctor to see to his infected thumb. An Auschwitz survivor, Mrs. Epstein is immediately suspicious of Campbell, remembering that there was a radio broadcaster in Berlin by that name. Campbell, though, denies he is *that* Howard W. Campbell. At the end of the novel, when Campbell decides to surrender to Israeli agents, he goes to the Epsteins to turn himself in. Despite her son's reluctance to get involved, Mrs. Epstein complies with Campbell's wishes, explaining that Campbell's nearly catatonic state reminds her of thousands of people she'd seen at Auschwitz who longed for someone to tell them what to do next.

Friedmann, Tuvia Tuvia Friedmann is director of the Haifa Institute for the Documentation of War Criminals. Howard W. Campbell, Jr., addresses his confessions to Mr. Friedmann who is so eager to add Campbell's work to his archives that he has provided Campbell with a typewriter, a free stenographic service, and the use of research assistants so that his account will be as complete and accurate as possible.

Gingiva-Tru White supremacist Lionel Jason David Jones, who is originally trained as a dentist, invents a product called Gingiva-Tru, which is said to be "a wonderfully lifelike, gum-stimulating substance for false teeth" (65). Convicted of spreading German propaganda during World War II, Jones serves eight years in prison. Upon his release, he is a wealthy man, partly because Gingiva-Tru had sold so well during his incarceration.

Goblet, The   Playwright and later Nazi propagandist Howard W. Campbell, Jr., as a young man, writes a romantic play called *The Goblet* about a pure young maiden who guards the Holy Grail and an upright young knight who wins it. When the two fall in love, they begin to have impure thoughts about each other, eventually falling into a night of tender lovemaking although they believe they will be damned to hell for losing their purity. The next day, the Holy Grail appears to them, signifying that Heaven approves their love, and the couple lives happily ever after. This play illustrates the disjunction between Campbell's romantic ideals and the reality of the rising Nazi atrocities surrounding him, which he ignores for so long. But Campbell never receives credit for the play. A Russian soldier named Stepan Bodovskov finds Campbell's manuscripts in a trunk as the war is ending, translates several of the works into Russian, and passes them off as his own. *The Goblet* becomes a huge hit in war-ravaged Russia.

Goebbels, Dr. Paul Joseph   Like other Nazi figures in the novel, Dr. Paul Joseph Goebbels was a real, historical person. He served as Hitler's propaganda minister during the war. When the war ended, Goebbels's wife, Magda, murdered all six of their children in their sleep the night before she and Goebbels took their own lives. In the novel, Goebbels is the boss in the German Ministry of Popular Enlightenment and Propaganda. When Campbell uses a phrase from the Gettysburg Address in one of his propaganda pieces, Goebbels decides to steal other phrases to use at dedications of German cemeteries. He first demands to know, though, if Lincoln was Jewish, since he has the suspicious first name Abraham.

Gutman, Andor   Andor Gutman is a guard in the Israeli prison where Howard W. Campbell, Jr., is being held for war crimes. Forty-eight years old, and described as a "sleepy, not very bright Estonian Jew," Andor spent two years incarcerated at Auschwitz. In the concentration camp, Andor volunteered for the Sonderkommando, the special detail that leads condemned prisoners into the gas chambers, then brings their bodies out. After performing this duty, members of the Sonderkommando are themselves gassed, and the first job of their successors is to dispose of their remains. Just before Andor can take up his new assignment, Himmler orders the ovens closed down, and Andor escapes certain death. He explains to Campbell in the prison that he does not understand why anyone would volunteer to be a corpse carrier in the camps and is ashamed of himself for having done so. Campbell, though, says he understands and does not see volunteering as a shameful act.

Himmler, Heinrich   An actual historical figure, Heinrich Himmler was the commander of the German Schutzstaffel, or S.S., the paramilitary organization that enforced Nazi policies during World War II. Himmler is mentioned in *Mother Night* when Howard W. Campbell, Jr., states that he received a letter of thanks from Himmler himself for the grotesquely anti-Semitic shooting practice targets he had designed in 1941.

Hitler, Adolf   Although the Nazi Fuehrer is mentioned often in *Mother Night*, as are other historical figures such as Rudolf Hoess and Dr. Paul Joseph Goebbels, Hitler never actually appears in the novel. He does, however, communicate with Howard W. Campbell, Jr., when he sends Campbell a note stapled to the top of the Gettysburg Address, in which he says that Lincoln's speech almost made him weep, adding that "all northern peoples are one in their deep feelings for soldiers" (21).

Hoess, Rudolf Franz   A historical figure, Rudolf Hoess was the commandant of Auschwitz, who worked to make the mass killings at the concentration camp more efficient. Sometimes called the greatest mass murderer in history, Hoess oversaw the death of 2.5 million Jews at the camp. He enters into *Mother Night* in the memories of Israeli prison guard Bernard Mengel, a fictional character who helped hang Hoess in 1947.

Horthy, Dr. Lomar   Dr. Lomar Horthy is the chemist who teams with the Reverend Doctor Lionel J. D. Jones to develop Viverine, an embalming fluid, and Gingiva-Tru, a gum-stimulating substance for false teeth.

Jones, the Reverend Doctor Lionel J. D. A great admirer of Howard W. Campbell, Jr., the Reverend Doctor Lionel J. D. Jones, D.D.S. is the publisher of *The White Christian Minuteman*, a "scabrous, illiterate, anti-Semitic, anti-Negro, anti-Catholic hate sheet" (59). Born in Haverhill, Massachusetts, in 1889, Dr. Jones was raised as a Methodist in a family of dentists. Though he attends dental school at the University of Pittsburgh, Jones is expelled in 1910, supposedly for scholastic failure, though really because of his widely broadcast beliefs that "the teeth of Jews and Negros proved beyond question that both groups were degenerate" (64). Jones finds works in a funeral home and marries the much older widowed owner, whom he lives with happily for many years. Only after his wife's death does Jones revert to his old ideas and begin publishing the racist newspaper, which eventually gets financed as a propaganda tool of the German Third Reich. Arrested as a war criminal in 1942, Jones serves eight years in prison and is released as a wealthy man due to the success of an embalming fluid and gum-stimulating substance for false teeth he had invented years earlier. Dr. Jones, along with several racist associates, pays a visit to his hero Campbell after hearing from George Kraft that the notorious Nazi propagandist is still living. Later, Jones hides Campbell in his basement to protect him from Israeli agents seeking to bring him to trial. Arrested when American agents raid the house, Jones stays loyal to Campbell to the end. Imagining himself a true American patriot, Jones repeats to the F.B.I. agents who take him into custody Nathan Hale's famous line spoken to the British just before his execution: "My only regret is that I have but one life to give to my country" (227).

Keeley, Father Patrick Father Patrick Keeley is a 73-year-old unfrocked Catholic priest who serves as secretary to the Reverend Doctor Lionel J. D. Jones. An alcoholic gun enthusiast, Father Keeley had been chaplain to a Detroit gun club that had been organized by Nazi agents to shoot Jews. Unfrocked by the pope for the virulently anti-Semitic sentiments Keeley expressed in his prayers, the ex-priest drifts into Skid Row for many years before meeting Jones. Father Keeley is arrested along with Jones's other supporters when the American agents raid their basement hideout. Since no specific charges are pressed against him, the American agent Frank Wirtanen speculates that he will return to Skid Row.

Klopfer, Arndt Arndt Klopfer is the photographer who makes portraits of Howard W. Campbell, Jr., and other well-known Nazis, including Adolf Eichmann. Klopfer appears again in the novel when the Reverend Doctor Lionel J. D. Jones tells Campbell that Klopfer is the man who will meet him in Mexico City after he, Resi Noth, and George Kraft make their escape.

Kovacs, Arpad Described as "a Roman candle of a man, loud and gay" (11), Arpad Kovacs is the Israeli prison guard who relieves Andor Gutman at six each night. A Jew in Nazi Hungary, Kovacs saved himself during the war by joining the Hungarian S.S., and is thus entirely sympathetic to the plight of Howard W. Campbell, Jr., even telling Campbell that his hateful, anti-Semitic radio broadcasts were weak and lacked the proper fervor. Ironically, Kovacs played such a "pure and terrifying Aryan" (13) that his superiors put him in a special detachment whose mission was to discover who in the S.S. was leaking information to the Jews when Kovacs himself was responsible for the leaks.

Kraft, George George Kraft is the elderly neighbor whose door Howard W. Campbell, Jr., knocks on when he feels compelled to show someone the chess set he has carved. Kraft is an extremely talented painter and chess player who becomes an intimate friend of Campbell's. Really a Russian agent named Colonel Iona Potapov, George Kraft, like Campbell himself, is able to compartmentalize his different identities so that he both genuinely likes Campbell as a friend and yet plans to hand him over to the Russian authorities as a Nazi war criminal. Kraft is the one who writes a letter to the Reverend Doctor Lionel J. D. Jones, publisher of the racist newspaper *The White Christian Minuteman*, informing him that Campbell is alive and well and living in New York. He also asks Jones to send a complimentary copy of the paper to

Bernard B. O'Hare, thus orchestrating Campbell's discovery. Along with fellow communist agent Resi Noth, Kraft pretends that he will escape on a plane to Mexico City with Campbell, though the two spies really plan to send Campbell immediately on another plane to Moscow. Their plan is foiled when Campbell is warned of it by Major Frank Wirtanen. Kraft is eventually arrested by American agents when Dr. Jones's basement, where Campbell had been hiding, is raided.

Krapptauer, August   The former Vice-Bundesfuehrer of the German-American Bund (an actual organization of ethnic Germans living in the United States who openly supported Hitler), August Krapptauer serves as bodyguard to the Reverend Doctor Lionel J. D. Jones. Krapptauer's greatest lifetime achievement was arranging a joint meeting of the Bund and the Ku Klux Klan in New Jersey in 1940, where he declared that the pope was a Jew. Krapptauer dies of a heart attack after he carries the luggage of Resi Noth up the numerous flights of stairs to Howard W. Campbell, Jr.'s New York City apartment. Krapptauer had organized a group of fascist youth called the Iron Guard of the White Sons of the American Constitution, who hold their meetings in Dr. Jones's basement.

Marx, Arnold   One of Howard W. Campbell, Jr.'s, guards in the Israeli prison, Arnold Marx is 18 years old, knows nothing about what happened during the war, and is not interested in finding out. Arnold was three when Hitler died, was born in Israel, and is studying to be a lawyer. Arnold is also interested in archaeology and spends most of his spare time with his father excavating the ruins of the Canaanite city of Hazor. He knows more about the history of Hazor than he does about the history of Hitler and the Jews during World War II.

McCarty, Eddie   A dead war buddy of the bald, bristly, fat man who attacks Howard W. Campbell, Jr., outside his New York City apartment, Eddie McCarty, who had dreams of becoming a doctor, was instead "cut in two by a burp gun in the Ardennes" (146). The fat man dedicates to McCarty a sharp kick delivered to Campbell's ribs.

Memoirs of a Monogamous Casanova   Howard W. Campbell, Jr., is the author of *Memoirs of a Monogamous Casanova*, a pornographic book recounting the erotic life he shared with his beloved wife, Helga, during the first two years of their marriage. The manuscript of the memoir is found locked in a trunk with Campbell's other papers at war's end by a Russian soldier named Stepan Bodovskov, who passes many of Campbell's works off as his own. *Memoirs of a Monogamous Casanova* is one of these and becomes a huge best seller in Russia and Eastern Europe. It is such an "attractive, strangely moral piece of pornography" (203) that the communist governments of these countries wink at its publication.

Mengel, Bernard   Bernard Mengel is a Polish Jew who guards Howard W. Campbell, Jr., in the Israeli prison from midnight until six in the morning. Mengel once saved his own life in World War II by "playing so dead that a German soldier pulled out three of his teeth without suspecting that Mengel was not a corpse" (15). Mengel is surprised that Campbell has such a bad conscience about what he did during the war, since everyone else he has met argues, no matter which side he was on, that he acted in the only way a good man could act. In 1947, before migrating to Israel, Mengel had helped to hang Rudolf Franz Hoess, the commandant at Auschwitz, but felt no satisfaction in the job since, like other survivors of the war, he had become emotionally numb.

Noth, Eva   The mother of Helga and Resi Noth and wife of Werner Noth, Berlin chief of police, Eva Noth is a sausagelike woman seen only once in the novel when she stands at a second-story window of the Noth family home in Berlin to witness the shooting of Resi's dog by Howard W. Campbell, Jr.

Noth, Helga   The elder daughter of Werner Noth, the Berlin chief of police, Helga Noth becomes the actress wife of Howard W. Campbell, Jr., during the time that he is a popular Nazi playwright and propagandist. Politically apathetic, Helga and Campbell form what they call a "nation of two" (34), shutting out the horror of Nazi atrocities they themselves participate in by loving each other uncritically and passionately. Helga disappears and is presumed dead when the Russians attack German troops she is entertaining in the Crimea during the war. Although Campbell hires private detectives and offers an enormous reward for information about Helga following the war, he is never given definitive proof as to whether she is alive or dead.

Noth, Resi The younger sister of Howard W. Campbell, Jr.'s, wife, Helga Noth, Resi Noth first falls in love with her sister's husband when she is a 10-year-old girl in Berlin. Resi's father, Werner Noth, the Berlin chief of police, asks Campbell to shoot Resi's dog because the family is evacuating the city and can not take the dog with them. Resi, rather than being opposed to this plan, listlessly tells Campbell to take the dog; she believes it will be better off dead anyway. Campbell meets up with Resi again in 1959 in New York City, when the Reverend Doctor Lionel J. D. Jones brings Resi to Campbell's apartment, thinking that she is Helga, Campbell's long-lost wife. Though she initially poses as Helga, fooling Campbell completely, soon Resi admits her true identity. Campbell, at first bewildered and disappointed, shortly decides to accept Resi as his Helga. Their brief day of love is interrupted when an angry World War II veteran beats up Campbell on the street, believing him to be a Nazi war criminal. Campbell is rescued and taken to Dr. Jones's basement, where Resi and George Kraft, Campbell's chess-playing friend, plan for the three to escape to Mexico City together. Campbell, though, discovers from the American agent Frank Wirtanen that both Resi and George Kraft are really communist agents planning to send him to Moscow to answer for his war crimes. When confronted, Resi tearfully tells Campbell that she has fallen in love with him and was not going to go through with the plan. When Campbell refuses to protect her from the American agents, Resi kills herself with a cyanide capsule, claiming that if she can no longer live for love there is nothing left to live for.

Noth, Werner The Berlin chief of police, Werner Noth is the father of Helga Noth, the well-known

actress who marries Howard W. Campbell, Jr., and of the much younger Resi Noth, who assumes Helga's identity many years after her disappearance. When Campbell goes to say good-bye to his father-in-law as the war draws to a close, he witnesses Werner Noth berating a Polish slave woman for almost dropping an expensive blue vase while the Noth house is being evacuated. Like the Nazis who played beautiful music at the concentration camps, Noth's cruelty to other human beings is starkly contrasted to his love of precious art. During this encounter, Noth tells Campbell that it does not matter if he was an American spy because Campbell never could have served the Americans as well as he served the Germans through his propaganda. Noth is later hanged from one of his own apple trees by slave laborers, though the insightful writer of a magazine article about the event ultimately concludes that Noth was no better and no worse than any other big city chief of police.

O'Hare, Bernard B. The American army lieutenant who first captures Howard W. Campbell, Jr., at the end of World War II, Bernard B. O'Hare discovers Campbell's whereabouts many years later in New York City and pledges to have him hanged or deported to Germany. At the end of the novel, after the arrest of George Kraft and death of Resi Noth, Campbell wanders back to his old apartment, where he finds O'Hare waiting for him. O'Hare, who believes that Campbell is his nemesis, and that his life's work is to capture him, is drunk and seething with resentment over his own disappointing life: his failed businesses and more children than he can support. Vowing to "take [Campbell] apart," O'Hare is stunned when, instead, Campbell breaks O'Hare's arm with a pair of fire tongs. After lecturing O'Hare on the true nature of evil—arguing that real evil is hating without reservation and imagining that God hates with you—Campbell sends O'Hare away, and he's not seen again in the novel. Interestingly, a very different character named BERNARD V. O'HARE will turn up later in Vonnegut's novel *Slaughterhouse-Five*, though the later O'Hare has V rather than B for a middle initial.

"Olly-olly-ox-in-free" Howard W. Campbell, Jr., a Nazi propagandist and secret American double agent during World War II, holes up in a tiny apartment in Greenwich Village for 13 years following the end of the war. The apartment overlooks a little private park where children play and which Campbell refers to as a "little Eden" (23). After games of hide-and-seek in this little Eden, Campbell hears the children give a "sweetly mournful cry that meant . . . those still hiding were to come out of hiding, that it was time to come home. The cry was this: 'Olly-olly-ox-in-free'" (24). Campbell himself, forced to hide from his past and from the many people who want to hurt or kill him, longs to hear such a cry himself, but never does. The phrase becomes a repeated refrain throughout the novel, used to express Campbell's desire to be forgiven for his war crimes and welcomed home.

Potapov, Colonel Iona See Kraft, George, above.

Potapov, Ilya Ilya Potapov is the oldest son of Colonel Iona Potapov, the Russian agent better known to Howard W. Campbell, Jr., as George Kraft, his chess-playing friend in New York City. Potapov's son, Ilya, is a famous rocket expert.

Potapov, Tanya The wife of Colonel Iona Potapov, known to Howard W. Campbell, Jr., as George Kraft, his chess-playing friend and neighbor in New York, Tanya Potapov lives in Borisoglebsk, Russia, and has not seen her husband in 25 years.

Rowley, Mrs. Theodore In the editor's note that precedes the book, Vonnegut claims that the poems written in German in Howard W. Campbell, Jr.'s, manuscript were extremely difficult to decipher because he worked them over so many times, crossing out and rewriting. Mrs. Theodore Rowley, of Cotuit, Massachusetts, whom Vonnegut describes as "a fine linguist, and a respectable poetess in her own right" (xi), is supposedly the person Vonnegut commissioned to handle the delicate job of reconstructing Campbell's German poems.

Scharff, Hattie Hattie Scharff is the widowed owner of Sharff Brothers Funeral Home in Pitts-

burgh. She marries the Reverend Doctor Lionel J. D. Jones when he is 24 years old and she is 58. The marriage, though, is a happy one, and it keeps Jones distracted from his racist theories until Hattie's death in 1928.

Schildknecht, Heinz One of Howard W. Campbell, Jr.'s, colleagues in the Nazi Propaganda Ministry, whose expertise lies in propagandizing Australians and New Zealanders, Heinz Schildknecht is Campbell's closest friend in Germany and his doubles partner in Ping-Pong. When Campbell goes to visit his in-laws, the Noths, to say good-bye at the end of the war, he borrows "for all eternity" Schildknecht's beloved motorcycle, a machine Schildknecht loves more than he loves his wife. At the end of the novel, readers discover that Schildknecht is really a Jew, "a member of the anti-Nazi underground during the war, an Israeli agent after the war and up to the present time" (262), who is eager to testify against Campbell at his war crimes trial.

Shoup, Mary Alice Mary Alice Shoup is the widow of the president and former owner of an embalming school in Little Rock, Arkansas. When she advertises for a new president, the Reverend Doctor Lionel J. D. Jones applies and wins the job. Mary Alice later marries Jones, when he is 40 and she is 68. Like Jones's earlier marriage to Hattie Scharff, his second marriage makes him temporarily a "happy, whole, and quiet man" (66). Upon Mary Alice's death, however, Jones reverts to publishing his racist propaganda.

Sparrow, Harold J. See Wirtanen, Major Frank, below.

Szombathy, Lazlo Lazlo Szombathy is the garbage man who finds the noose the bald, bristly fat man brings for Howard W. Campbell, Jr., and that Resi Noth throws away in an ash can. Szombathy had been a Freedom Fighter against the Russians in Hungary, shooting and killing his own brother who was the Hungarian minister of education. Szombathy hangs himself with the noose intended for Campbell, leaving a suicide note pinned to his pants, which explains that he is bitter over not being allowed to practice veterinary medicine in America though he was a well-respected animal doctor in Hungary. He closes his note "in a final fandango of paranoia and masochism" (150), claiming he knows how to cure cancer, but that American doctors only laughed at him when he tried to share his knowledge.

Unnamed bald, bristly fat man   A man who is never named, but is described as being "bald, bristly [and] fat" (144) brutally beats Howard W. Campbell, Jr., when he and Resi Noth are returning to Campbell's New York apartment. As he hits and kicks Campbell, the man dedicates his blows to war buddies who were killed by the Germans in World War II.

Unnamed teacher and his wife in German bunker   Howard W. Campbell, Jr., remembers a time when he and Helga took shelter in a deep underground bunker during an air raid in Berlin. Also occupying the shelter were a German teacher, his wife, and their three children. The woman hysterically cries to God, asking what he wants of them; unable to quiet her, the husband knocks her out. He then apologizes for his wife's behavior to a vice admiral also in the bunker, who absolves the man, saying his wife's behavior was understandable. The teacher backs away from the vice admiral, murmuring "Heil Hitler" and returns to his wife to try to revive her.

Unnamed young patrolman   When Howard W. Campbell, Jr., returns to his apartment in New York at the end of the novel, after the arrest of George Kraft and Resi Noth, he encounters a young patrolman guarding the building. The patrolman does not forbid Campbell from entering the building, since "it's a free country and everybody gets protected exactly alike" (235). Although his father was killed in Iwo Jima, the young patrolman bears no hatred toward Campbell, instead recognizing that good people were killed on both sides. When both Campbell and the patrolman confess that they believe more wars will come, the patrolman offers his theory that people are bad because of internal chemical reactions beyond their control. He con-

fides in Campbell that he would like to go back to school to learn more about chemistry.

Viverine   White supremacist Reverend Doctor Lionel Jason David Jones, who was originally trained as a dentist and later worked as a funeral home director, invents a new type of embalming fluid called Viverine, which comes to dominate the market, making Jones a wealthy man.

Von Braun, Werner   Wernher Von Braun, an actual historical figure, was a German rocket scientist who helped develop ballistic missiles for the Nazis before surrendering to the Americans near the end of the war. Von Braun came to the United States after the war, where he worked on missile programs for the U.S. Army and later was integral in designing the Saturn rockets used by NASA in the 1960s. In *Mother Night*, George Kraft shows Howard W. Campbell, Jr., a copy of *Life* magazine that features Von Braun on the cover. Campbell tells Kraft that he knew Von Braun in Germany, where the baron danced with Campbell's wife, Helga, at a birthday party. Campbell also relates that he ran into Von Braun very recently on 52nd Street in New York. Shocked by Campbell's reduced circumstances, Von Braun had offered to get him a job in public relations.

Westlake, Ian   Ian Westlake is the journalist who writes the magazine story "Hangwomen for the Hangman of Berlin" about Howard W. Campbell, Jr.'s, father-in-law, Werner Noth. Westlake is an Englishman and a liberated prisoner of war who had witnessed the hanging shortly after being released from his captivity by the Russians.

White Christian Minuteman, The   The *White Christian Minuteman* is the title of the racist and anti-Semitic newspaper published by the Reverend Doctor Lionel J. D. Jones, D.D.S., D.D.

Wilson, Robert Sterling   Robert Sterling Wilson, 73, chauffer to the Reverend Doctor Lionel J. D. Jones, is known as "The Black Fuehrer of Harlem" (75). Sent to prison as a Japanese spy in 1942, Wilson tells Howard W. Campbell, Jr. that he supported the Japanese because he wished to be on the side of the "colored folk" during the war (89). All the while he performs servile duties for Jones, Wilson admonishes both his employer and Campbell for their views of "colored people" (90). Wilson argues that the Japanese and other colored people are soon going to develop a hydrogen bomb of their own. Ironically, Wilson also believes that the Japanese are going to drop their bomb on China, stubbornly refusing to admit that the Chinese are colored people, too. Last seen in the novel, Wilson is being arrested, along with Jones and the rest of his crew, when their basement hideout is raided by American agents.

Wirtanen, Major Frank   Major Frank Wirtanen is the American agent who recruits Howard W. Campbell, Jr., as a spy. Campbell meets Wirtanen only three times in the novel: once in 1938 when he is recruited, again immediately after the war in Wiesbaden, Germany, and finally, in New York City in 1959 in a vacant store across the street from the house of white supremacist Dr. Lionel J. D. Jones. Campbell often refers to Wirtanen in the narrative as his "Blue Fairy Godmother," since nobody believes in the American intelligence agent but him. American officials deny that a man named Frank Wirtanen ever served the government in any branch. Wirtanen becomes crucial to Campbell's defense when he is put on trial for war crimes in Israel. Campbell's lawyers tell him that the only way he can prove his innocence is to somehow show that Wirtanen existed and that he recruited Campbell to be an American agent. In prison at the end of the novel, Campbell receives a letter from Wirtanen, who supplies his real name—Harold J. Sparrow—rank, and serial number to Campbell, even offering to affirm under oath the truthfulness of Campbell's claim that he was working for the Americans. By this point, however, Campbell finds the prospect of freedom "nauseating" (267), and he determines to hang himself in prison.

Yadin, Yigael   Yigael Yadin, who was chief of staff of the Israeli Army during the war with the Arab States, directs the excavation of the ancient Canaanite city of Hazor, the project to which the

18-year-old prison guard Arnold Marx and his father dedicate almost all of their spare time.

FURTHER READING

Han, Eungoo. "Kurt Vonnegut's *Mother Night*: Fiction and Life." *Journal of English Language and Literature* 41, no. 3 (1995): 741–760.

Jamosky, Edward and Jerome Klinkowitz. "Kurt Vonnegut's Three *Mother Nights*." *Modern Fiction Studies* 34, no. 2 (1988): 216–219.

Marvin, Tom. "'Who Am I This Time?': Kurt Vonnegut and the Film *Mother Night*." *Literature Film Quarterly* 31, no. 3 (2003): 231–236.

Mother Night. New York: Dell, 1999.

Scholes, Robert. "Fabulation and Satire—Black Humor: *Cat's Cradle* and *Mother Night*." *The Fabulators*. New York: Oxford University Press, 1967. 35–55.

———. "Vonnegut's *Cat's Cradle* and *Mother Night*." *Fabulation and Metafiction*. Urbana, Ill.: University of Illinois Press, 1979. 156–162.

"New Dictionary"

More a short reflective essay than a story as such, "New Dictionary" is included here because it was reprinted in the 1968 short story collection, *Welcome to the Monkey House*. The piece was originally published under the title "The Random House Dictionary," and first appeared in the *New York Times* in October of 1966.

SYNOPSIS

"New Dictionary" provides readers with Vonnegut's meditations upon buying and using a copy of the newly printed Random House Dictionary of the English Language. His new dictionary mixes biographical and place names among the ordinary words and even includes a color atlas of the world and concise dictionaries of French, Spanish, German, and Italian, additions Vonnegut has mixed feelings about. The essay compares three editions of the Merriam-Webster dictionary to his new Random House and includes comments from various scholars and reviewers regarding the works.

COMMENTARY

In this short piece, Vonnegut clearly shows that he admires dictionaries as treasure troves of information. His new Random House dictionary, he says, "is heavy and pregnant, and makes you think" (118). Yet, he also realizes that dictionary publishing is a capitalist competition. New dictionaries vie to be the most up-to-date as they include recently coined words and winnow their predecessors for bloopers. Vonnegut speculates, in fact, that the giant corporations General Motors or Ford may be the next "to crash the unabridged dictionary game" (122). There is money to be made in the business of controlling the English language. As he meditates upon his new Random House dictionary, Vonnegut debunks some of the lofty connotations of dictionaries, recognizing that many young people come to dictionaries, as he did when a child, to look for dirty words hidden between the covers, "where only grownups were supposed to find them" (119). Moreover, dictionaries have distinct personalities, with reviewer Mario Pei complaining of the "residual prudishness" (119) of the third revised edition of the Merriam-Webster and Vonnegut noting the relative, though still limited, frankness of the Random House.

Vonnegut also points out that a dictionary's tendency to be prescriptive or descriptive also adds to its personality. "Prescriptive" and "descriptive" are linguistic terms that relate to grammar use. Prescriptive grammars or dictionaries lay down rules for language use, while descriptive grammars or dictionaries look at the way language is actually used and try to generate rules from real speech and usage patterns. Generally, prescriptive grammar advocates take a conservative position, believing that the English language will decline if proper rules are not followed, while descriptive grammarians believe language rules are artificial to begin with and emphasize that language is constantly changing over time. Vonnegut, rather than explaining the differences in these terms, imagines a prescriptive dictionary as being like an "honest cop" and a descriptive one as "a boozed-up war buddy from Mobile, Ala." (120). Vonnegut's attitude toward this debate is difficult to determine. While he clearly respects literary scholar Robert

Scholes's admonition that Richard Yates should buy a prescriptive dictionary, Vonnegut nevertheless derides America as a nation "populated by parvenus with the heebie-jeebies" (120) about language, people so unsure of themselves that they will not use colloquial expressions for fear of seeming illiterate. Further, he concedes that the typical American "is going to go on speaking and writing the way he always has, no matter what dictionary he owns" (123). The final sentence of Vonnegut's essay—"Moral: Everybody associated with a new dictionary ain't necessarily a new Samuel Johnson" (123)—nicely sums up his mixed feelings about prescriptive and descriptive language. While he condemns the "anything goes" attitude of Random House publisher Bennett Cerf, who is no new Samuel Johnson (the highly esteemed 18th-century dictionary writer), Vonnegut nevertheless uses the "colloquial" (120) and "illiterate" (120) word "ain't" to do it.

CHARACTERS

Narrator   The essay's narrator is a version of Vonnegut himself, who describes his delight and frustration with his new Random House dictionary.

Scholes, Professor Robert   A real-life scholar of modern literature who has published extensively on Vonnegut's work, Professor Robert Scholes retired from Brown University in 1999. He appears in "New Dictionary" having dinner with Vonnegut and novelist Richard Yates one evening. When Yates asks Scholes which unabridged dictionary he should buy, Scholes replies that Yates "should get the second edition of the 'Merriam-Webster,' which was *prescriptive* rather than *descriptive*" (120).

Yates, Richard   Richard Yates is a real-life essayist, short story writer, and novelist who makes an appearance at a dinner with Vonnegut and literary scholar Robert Scholes in "New Dictionary." Yates has just received a "gorgeous grant for creative writing" (119) and wants to buy a new dictionary with some of the money. Professor Scholes recommends that Yates buy the second edition of the Merriam-Webster, though Scholes and Vonnegut agree that Yates is already a master of the English language—"the sort of man lexicographers read in order to discover what pretty new things the language is up to" (120).

FURTHER READING

Reed, Peter. *The Short Fiction of Kurt Vonnegut.* Westport, Conn.: Greenwood Press, 1997.
Welcome to the Monkey House. New York: Dell, 1998.

"Next Door"

"Next Door," a piece about a little boy dragged too soon into the adult world, was first published in *Cosmopolitan* magazine in April 1955. The story was later reprinted in the 1968 collection, *Welcome to the Monkey House.*

SYNOPSIS

In "Next Door," the Leonards and the Hargers share a duplex with only a thin wall separating the two families. One evening, the Leonards, who have just moved in, decide to go to the movies. After arguing for a bit about whether their eight-year-old son, Paul, is old enough to stay alone, they make up their minds to leave him by himself for the evening. When his parents leave, Paul settles down to look through his microscope, but soon begins to hear a terrible racket from next door, where a man and woman are shouting at each other over the music on a radio. Paul turns up his own radio to drown out the sound of the "awful, unbelievable" (126) fight, and lands on the same program playing next door, in which a deejay named All-Night Sam is accepting song dedications. As the fight escalates, Paul calls the radio and asks All-Night Same to dedicate the next song "From Mr. Lemuel K. Harger to Mrs. Harger" (128). The message Paul dictates is: "I love you. . . . Let's make up and start all over again" (128). Sam, believing Paul is trying to get his own parents to stop fighting, is moved, and makes the dedication.

At first, there's immediate silence next door, but then the voices start up again. The woman at the Hargers, Paul discovers, is named Charlotte

and is Mr. Harger's girlfriend, not his wife. Paul hears talk of a gun, then hears three shots ring out. When he runs outside to see what happens, the woman is racing from the apartment. She grabs Paul and gives him a wad of cash to keep him quiet before rushing out into the night. Soon, a policeman arrives at the house and, much to Paul's surprise, Mr. Harger appears, rumpled but uninjured, to speak with him. Immediately, a cab pulls up and Mrs. Harger tearfully emerges, embraces her husband, and the two retreat into their side of the house. The story closes with the Leonards returning home from the movies and babying Paul as they remove his clothes and tuck him into bed. However, the ball of cash falls out of Paul's pocket, and Mrs. Leonard notices that it smells of Tabu perfume.

COMMENTARY

"Next Door" is a story about an eight-year-old who is forced to grow up too soon. While it begins with a heated discussion between the Leonards about whether Paul is old enough to be left alone, even Mr. Leonard, who insists his son is no longer a little boy, would be shocked by what actually happens while he and his wife are absent. Paul, who really still is a young boy, is naïve about many things. Unused to the passions and jealousies of adulthood, he believes that, if he does not intervene, "the man and woman" next door "would kill each other" (127). Though he is certainly enterprising in taking matters into his own hands and calling up the radio program, he also has a misplaced confidence in the ability of adults to solve problems. He is so impressed "with the wisdom and authority" of the deejay All-Night Sam that he believes Sam is "speaking like the right-hand man of God" (129). Paul trusts Sam completely, not realizing that Sam himself is misreading the situation, since he believes Paul is trying to make his *own* parents stop fighting. Sweet and naïve Paul even gets a lump in his throat as he thinks "about the beautiful thing he and Sam were bringing to pass" (129).

But Paul's interference in the Harger's lives, his decision to intervene in adult lives, moves him into the harsh realities of the adult world. As Paul waits to see the results of his actions, "childhood dropped away, and he hung, dizzy, on the brink of life, rich, violent, rewarding" (130). Paul is horrified when the knowledge of Mr. Harger's infidelity becomes clear to him. Paul's childhood truly ends, though, when he lies to the policeman, claiming not to have heard any shots, as the "ball of money in [his] pocket seemed to swell to the size of a watermelon" (132). Paul is now implicated in the adult intrigue he had not even imagined at the evening's start. The end of the story, when Mrs. Leonard returns home to sing nursery rhymes to Paul and tell him about the "cunning little" bear cubs (133) in the short subject before the film, seems terribly ironic in light of what readers have just witnessed. While his mother rattles on about little boys' pockets containing "childhood's mysteries" such as "an enchanted frog" or "a magic pocketknife from a fairy princess" (133), the wadded ball of "ones, fives, tens, twenties," which exudes "the pungent musk of perfume," falls out of his pocket, belying the innocence that Mrs. Leonard so desperately wants to believe in for her little boy.

CHARACTERS

All-Night Sam   All-Night Sam is the radio deejay who broadcasts the dedication from Mr. Harger to his wife that eight-year-old Paul Leonard calls in, believing that Paul is trying to make his own parents stop fighting.

Charlotte   Charlotte is the girlfriend of Lemuel K. Harger. When Paul Leonard hears the two viciously fighting, he believes Harger is fighting with his wife and calls in the radio dedication to try to make them stop. Charlotte, though, is infuriated when she hears the radio announce that Mr. Harger still loves his wife and wants to get back together with her. Charlotte shoots at Harger three times, apparently missing, but too distraught to notice. As she runs out of her apartment, she gives Paul Leonard a wad of cash to keep quiet about what he has seen and heard.

Harger, Lemuel K.   The next-door neighbor of the Leonards, Lemuel K. Harger is having an affair

with a woman named Charlotte, who attempts to shoot him after she hears the radio dedication, supposedly from Mr. Harger to his wife.

Harger, Rose   The wife of Lemuel K. Harger, Rose Harger rushes home to her husband after hearing the radio dedication. Apparently, she had left him because he was having an affair with another woman.

Leonard, Mr.   Mr. Leonard is the father of eight-year-old Paul. He and his wife leave Paul alone in the house the night of the story, while they go to the movies.

Leonard, Mrs.   While Mrs. Leonard is at first hesitant to leave her eight-year-old son, Paul, alone while she and her husband go to the movies, she finally agrees to do so. At the end of the story, when the wad of cash and lipstick-stained Kleenex, all carrying the "musk of perfume" (133) falls out of Paul's pocket, she must reassess her view that Paul is still just a little boy.

Leonard, Paul   The protagonist of "Next Door" is eight-year-old Paul Leonard, an enterprising young boy left to his own devices one evening. He tries his best to stop the terrible fighting he hears next door, but his attempt backfires when he discovers that Mr. Harger is arguing with his girlfriend, not his wife. Paul Leonard is a little boy forced to grow up too soon.

Policeman   After the shots heard from the Hargers' apartment, a policeman arrives to investigate. After Mr. Harger claims not to have heard anything, the policeman turns to Paul and asks if he heard shots. While the arrival of Mrs. Harger initially impedes Paul's ability to answer, the policeman asks again, and Paul, thinking about the ball of money in his pocket, replies that he heard nothing either.

FURTHER READING

Reed, Peter. *The Short Fiction of Kurt Vonnegut.* Westport, Conn.: Greenwood Press, 1997.
Welcome to the Monkey House. New York: Dell, 1998.

"A Night for Love"

One of Vonnegut's stories about both the difficulties and charms of marriage, "A Night for Love" first appeared in the *Saturday Evening Post* in November 1957. The story was later reprinted in the 1999 collection *Bagombo Snuff Box*.

SYNOPSIS

"A Night for Love" offers alternating glimpses into the lives of two very different families on one moonlit evening—the working-class Whitmans and the wealthy Reinbecks. The Whitmans' daughter, Nancy, is out on a date with young Charlie Reinbeck, and the couple are several hours late returning home. Turley Whitman, a company policeman at Reinbeck Abrasives Company, is extremely worried and wakes up his wife, Milly. Readers soon discover that Milly, as a pretty young woman herself, had gone on two dates with company owner Louis C. Reinbeck, and Turley is still jealous of this long-ago relationship. Meanwhile, Natalie Reinbeck, at her large and expensive home, is also jealous of her husband's past relationship with Milly, and imagines that he has never gotten over their brief affair. The story ends with both pairs of husband and wives reconciling as they acknowledge the romantic properties of the moonlight. Nancy and Charlie, meanwhile, have eloped and started their own life together.

COMMENTARY

Like other Vonnegut stories about marriage, "A Night for Love" dismantles conventional, sentimental ideas about romance, showing that a couple's degree of companionship and a long history together are what make a solid marriage. The conflict in this story develops at least partly because the romantic, moonlit night pervades the common sense of both the Whitmans and the Reinbecks, and makes each couple dwell on what might have been rather than on what is. The solid, usually kindly company policeman Turley Whitman begins to doubt his wife's affection for him as the moonlight, combined with his daughter's absence, makes him remember Millie's brief past relationship with wealthy Louis C. Reinbeck. His suspicions of his wife turn Turley into a petulant child who wakes his wife out of sleep, insults her by claiming she was "sawing wood" (267), and tries to reassert his manhood by "dominat[ing] his wife, his rooms, and his house" (270). While Turley feels unequal to Reinbeck because of the class differences separating the two men, it is ironic that a very similar scenario to the one being played out in the Whitman house is taking place at the Reinbeck mansion. Natalie Reinbeck is also jealous of her husband's past relationship with Milly, telling him, "Face it, you would have been a thousand times happier if you'd married your Milly O'Shea" (278).

The troubles between the two couples end only when Louis realizes that his past relationship with Milly was shaped by moonlight—by romantic visions that really have no place in the real world. He tells Natalie that he had "been thinking it really had been something big" between Milly and himself so long ago, but that now he realizes "all it was was pure, beautiful, moonlit hokum" (281). Milly, similarly tells Turley that, because of the moonlight all those years ago, she "just had to fall in love," even though she and Louis did not even "like each other very well" (281). Unlike their parents, however, Nancy Whitman and Charlie Reinbeck give in to the romantic impulse of the moonlight: "They'd decided that Cinderella and Prince Charming had as good a chance as anybody for really living happily ever after. So they'd married" (282). Yet, the end of the story implies that this marriage, if it is to endure, will have to be made of more than just moonlight and romance. Vonnegut writes, "So now there was a new household. Whether everything was all right remained to be seen. The moon went down" (282). Romantic moments are fleeting and temporary; marriage, according to Vonnegut, is something that takes place in the harsh light of day.

CHARACTERS

Reinbeck, Charlie   Charlie Reinbeck is the son of wealthy company owner Louis C. Reinbeck. He ends up eloping with Nancy Whitman, the daughter of his father's old girlfriend, the former Milly O'Shea.

Reinbeck, Louis C. Louis C. Reinbeck is the wealthy owner of the Reinbeck Abrasives Company, which he inherited from his father and grandfather. One night, his son, Charlie, goes out on a date with Nancy Whitman, the daughter of the former Milly O'Shea, a woman Reinbeck himself had dated as a young man. Reinbeck begins to become nostalgic for his relationship with Milly as the evening progresses. Yet, by the end of the story, he realizes that his wife, Natalie, is the woman he truly loves.

Reinbeck, Natalie Natalie Reinbeck, originally from Boston, is the wife of wealthy Louis C. Reinbeck. On the night that her son stays out late on a date with Nancy Whitman, the daughter of Louis's old girlfriend, Milly, Natalie becomes extremely jealous. But when Louis realizes that his relationship with Milly was based only on the moonlight, not on real feelings of love, he is able to reassure Natalie that she is the only woman for him.

Whitman, Milly Milly Whitman is the wife of Reinbeck Abrasives Company policeman Turley Whitman. As a young woman, she used to be the prettiest girl in town and even went on two dates with wealthy Louis C. Reinbeck himself. Milly is mortified when her husband mentions her past relationship with Reinbeck when he calls the company owner on the phone to discuss the fact that their children are very late coming home from a date. She is able, however, to reassure Turley of her love for him by the end of the story.

Whitman, Nancy Nancy Whitman is the daughter of Turley and Milly Whitman. When she stays out very late on a date with Charlie Reinbeck, son of her father's boss, Turley becomes very worried about her. At the end of the story Nancy and Charlie elope.

Whitman, Turley Described as "a huge, kind, handsome man" (265), Turley Whitman works as a company policeman in charge of parking lot security at the Reinbeck Abrasives Company. Worried when his daughter stays out very late on a date with the son of company owner Louis C. Reinbeck,

Whitman eventually calls Reinbeck on the phone to express his concerns. It turns out that Whitman's anxiety on this night stems as much from jealousy over his wife's former relationship with Louis Reinbeck as from worry about his daughter's whereabouts.

FURTHER READING

Bagombo Snuff Box. New York: Berkley Books, 2000.
Reed, Peter. *The Short Fiction of Kurt Vonnegut.* Westport, Conn.: Greenwood Press, 1997.

"The No-Talent Kid"

The first of Vonnegut's four published stories dealing with Lincoln High School band director George M. Helmholtz, "The No-Talent Kid" was initially published in the *Saturday Evening Post* in October 1952 before being reprinted in the collection *Bagombo Snuff Box.*

SYNOPSIS

"The No-Talent Kid" is the story of high school band director George M. Helmholtz, who is plagued by a student clarinet player named Walter Plummer. Plummer is the worst player in the whole high school, but is so tone deaf that he has no idea of his own deficiency. In fact, Plummer believes that he is a good player, and he longs to get into the school's top band, the A Band, so that he can earn a letter sweater. He wastes Mr. Helmholtz's time every two weeks, on challenge day, when he attempts to outplay the school's best musicians. Because he always loses these contests, Plummer believes that Mr. Helmholtz is treating him unfairly.

Besides his problems with Plummer, Mr. Helmholtz's other big concern is obtaining a seven-foot bass drum for the band. While his high school had won the state marching band contest for 10 years in a row, the prize was awarded to another high school the previous year because they had just such an impressive instrument. Mr. Helmholtz's dreams seem within his grasp when he reads in the paper that a local men's club is selling all its assets. One of the items to be sold is an enormous bass drum.

Although he repeatedly calls the telephone number listed in the paper, Helmholtz receives only a busy signal. He later discovers that Walter Plummer has purchased the drum ahead of him. Although Helmholtz offers to buy the drum for more than the boy paid for it, Plummer insists that he be allowed to play the drum in the school's A Band. At the end of the story, the two reach a compromise. Plummer will earn his letter sweater by being allowed to pull the drum along and seeing that it does not capsize.

COMMENTARY

This story involves ordinary, everyday people acting out small-town American life of the early 1950s. Although the characters' concerns might seem insignificant in the larger scheme of world events, or in light of some of the earth-shattering inventions and discoveries of other Vonnegut stories, nevertheless, the issues the story's characters deal with are pressing and urgent to them. To a small town band director such as George M. Helmholtz, it is a matter of vital importance that his high school band acquire the seven-foot bass drum it needs to win state contests. His conflicted relationship with the "no-talent kid" Walter Plummer is the cross he must bear. And Mr. Helmholtz accepts this burden as gracefully as any self-sacrificing hero. He is consistently kind to the annoying boy, patiently devoting numerous hours to judging Plummer's ill-conceived challenges of better players than himself. Similarly, to Plummer, the issue of whether or not he makes it into the high school's A Band, which he sees as part of his ongoing struggle with Mr. Helmholtz, is as serious as the epic battle between Hector and Achilles. Although completely untalented as a musician, Plummer proves himself to be a smart entrepreneur, buying the bass drum before Helmholtz can, and then using the prize as a bargaining tool.

It may be difficult for readers to determine how to interpret the end of the story. On the one hand, it might be tempting to read the bass drum as Mr. Helmholtz's Achilles' heel—his one weak spot. In such a reading, Mr. Helmholtz might be seen as making a bargain with the devil—compromising his principles by allowing Plummer into the A Band in order to obtain the drum that he has coveted

for so long. On the other hand, it is also possible to interpret the story in a less pessimistic fashion. While Mr. Helmholtz does allow Plummer into the A Band, he works out a compromise in which the boy will not destroy the band's musical excellence. Rather than allowing Plummer to play the drum, which he initially insists upon, Mr. Helmholtz defuses the situation by allowing Plummer to be the drum's puller. Thus, everyone is happy, and Mr. Helmholtz's A Band will still be the same musically superior group it was before the addition of Plummer.

CHARACTERS

Delaney, Ed   When Walter Plummer announces that he wants to challenge Flammer, a musical genius, to a playing contest, band director George Helmholtz suggests that he begin, instead, by challenging Ed Delaney, the last chair clarinetist in the high school's B Band.

Flammer   A boy named Flammer is the most talented musician at Lincoln High School. He is the first-chair clarinetist in the A Band. Tone-deaf Walter Plummer, believing he is as good as Flammer, challenges him in a playing contest, and believes he is treated unfairly when he loses.

Helmholtz, George M.   A fat, sweet-tempered band director who appears in a number of Vonnegut short stories, George M. Helmholtz lives for music and truly cares about his students. Although he is flummoxed by Walter Plummer, the "no-talent kid" of the title, he still treats the boy as kindly as he can. When Helmholtz agrees to allow Plummer to join the A Band as the bass drum's puller, it is difficult to determine whether he has made a deal with the devil or reached a mutually beneficial compromise solution.

Plummer, Walter   Walter Plummer is a high school clarinet player who is long on confidence but short on talent. Refusing to believe that he has no chance of making the school's A Band, Plummer insists on challenging the school's best musicians every two weeks. Although a failure as a musician, Plummer is nevertheless an enterprising young man who runs his own paper route and who makes hard bargains to obtain what he wants. He finally works his way into the A Band by buying an enormous bass drum before band director George Helmholtz has a chance to purchase it himself, and then refusing to sell the drum to Helmholtz.

Plummer, Mrs. When band director George Helmholtz calls Walter Plummer's house to tell him he left his newspapers under Helmholtz's hedge, he talks to Plummer's mother, who says that her son just ran out of the house to sell his clarinet.

Sublime Chamberlain of the Inner Shrine of the Knights of Kandahar When the treasurer of the men's club the Knights of Kandahar runs off with the club's money, the Sublime Chamberlain promises to make good on the group's debts by selling off all their assets. Included in the items for sale is an enormous bass drum that George Helmholtz covets for the Lincoln High School marching band.

Treasurer of the Knights of Kandahar George Helmholtz reads in the newspaper that the treasurer of the Knights of Kandahar, a respected citizen, has run off with the organization's funds. This is what precipitates the Knights' selling of their seven-foot bass drum.

FURTHER READING

Bagombo Snuff Box. New York: Berkley Books, 2000.
Reed, Peter. *The Short Fiction of Kurt Vonnegut.* Westport, Conn.: Greenwood Press, 1997.

Nothing Is Lost Save Honor: Two Essays

This limited edition of two essays, "Nothing Is Lost Save Honor" and "The Worst Addiction of Them All," was published by Nouveau Press in 1984 as part of a fund-raising effort by the Mississippi Civil Liberties Union, a group whose work, Vonnegut writes in a postscript to the collection, he "ardently supports." Vonnegut donated the essays, which had

previously been copyrighted in his name, to be sold by the MCLU for profit: the volume "is like a cake at a cake sale," he states in the postscript. Only 300 copies were produced, each one signed by the author. The essay "Nothing Is Lost Save Honor" was initially delivered as a lecture at the Cathedral of St. John the Divine in New York City on May 23, 1982, and was copyrighted the same year under the title "Fates Worse Than Death." "The Worst Addiction of Them All" was originally published in *The Nation* magazine and was copyrighted in 1983. Both of the essays are also collected in the 1991 volume, *Fates Worse Than Death: An Autobiographical Collage.* For a fuller discussion of the issues discussed in these essays, see the entry in this book for *Fates Worse Than Death.*

FURTHER READING

Nothing Is Lost Save Honor. Jackson, Miss.: Nouveau Press, 1984.

"The Package"

"The Package," a story about a man who confuses material wealth with success and happiness, was first published in *Collier's* magazine in July 1952. The story was later reprinted in the 1999 collection, *Bagombo Snuff Box.*

SYNOPSIS

The story of Earl and Maude Fenton, who have just returned from a cruise around the world, "The Package" begins with the couple walking into their brand-new home, which has been completely decorated and furnished with all the modern conveniences while they have been traveling. Immediately, the Fentons receive two phone calls. One is from an old college fraternity brother of Earl's, Charley Freeman, whom Earl has not heard from in years. The other is from a home magazine, wanting to write an article about the Fentons' new house. Earl invites both Freeman and the home magazine staff over. As Earl and Maude show off their new house to the magazine writers and pose in different costumes for the staff photographer, they become increasingly resentful of Charley Freeman. Earl, extremely sensitive to his lack of wealth as a college boy, feels uncomfortable around Charley and begins to relive the animosity he held toward the wealthier students at that period in his life. He points out repeatedly to the magazine staff that he is a self-made man and that he deserves the good things that have happened to him. Noticing that Charley is wearing old, frayed clothing, the couple begins to suspect that he has looked them up to scam them in some way. Eventually, the Fentons concoct a story about Maude's sister coming to dinner unexpectedly and staying the night so that they can get out of the invitation to stay over which they had originally extended to Charley. Earl's old fraternity brother takes the hint quickly and departs. Later, when the Fentons' contractor, who had brought the magazine people to the house that afternoon, returns to retrieve the hat he left behind, the Fentons learn that Charlie had lived in China for the past 30 years, where he had run a hospital until getting jailed and eventually ejected from the country by the communists. At this news, the Fentons feel miserable. The story ends with Earl looking among all his new, fancy buttons and gadgets, wishing for a button he could push to start the day all over again.

COMMENTARY

"The Package" is a SATIRE on a particular type of American—the "self-made man." Although Earl Fenton prides himself on "being a plain, ordinary, friendly fellow for all of his success" (57), readers see through his outward heartiness to the insecurity that lies beneath. A man deeply conscious of class differences, Earl's distaste for his old friend Charley Freeman arises from his inability to see and judge Charley as an individual apart from his social class, the very flaw that Earl faults his old college fraternity brothers for in regard to himself. Clearly, however, Earl's resentments about his college life come from his own insecurities, not from any unkindnesses actually done to him. When Maude asks Earl to explain some of the things that Charley did to him in college, Earl "waved the subject away with his hand. There weren't any specific incidents that he could tell Maude about"

(58). Yet, Earl's own embarrassment at having been a waiter in college so poisons his mind that he feels bitter toward Charley and is predisposed to be suspicious of him even before the man arrives at his home. Not even knowing much about his old friend, Earl continually insists on his moral superiority to Charley because Earl started out poor and worked hard for what he has achieved. Yet, Maude and Earl prove that they are the true class snobs when they notice Charley's threadbare suit and immediately suspect him of trying to "bamboozle" (69) them out of money.

Part of Earl's short-sightedness is that he equates success solely with material prosperity, the ability to buy the things that he was not able to afford in his younger years. In the Fentons' view, the "package" makes the man. So they have purchased the best, most impressive package they can find. Vonnegut thinks that this is a view shared by many Americans. The home magazine writer, sent to do a story on the Fentons' new house, says that the angle of the story will be that the Fentons have returned from a world cruise "to a complete package for living—everything anybody could possibly want for a full life" (62). Contractor Lou Converse adds that the Fentons' "package" is complete, "right down to a fully stocked wine cellar and a pantry filled with gourmet specialties. Brand-new cars, brand-new everything but wine" (62). Material possessions are what make a full life according to the cultural mythology advanced in such magazines. Any kind of spirituality or deeper meaning in life has been eclipsed. This point becomes clear when the Fentons' enormous new outdoor grill is described as a "stone edifice" and the Fentons kiss beside it as they had done "beside the Great Pyramid, the Colosseum, and the Taj Mahal" (60). The Fentons' great work of beauty, their cultural monument, is a barbecue grill, a totem of consumption. Similarly, Earl tells Charley the house itself is "more'n a house. It's the story of my life . . . my own personal pyramid, sort of" (70).

"The Package" also critiques the shallow, overly optimistic jingoism of popular philosophers such as Norman Vincent Peale, whose hugely best-selling *The Power of Positive Thinking* was published in 1952, the same year "The Package" appeared in *Collier's*. Earl congratulates himself not only for his material prosperity and his success in bettering his social position, but for the empathy he believes he has for other downtrodden people. He reminds Maude that many people on the cruise "didn't want to look at all that terrible poverty in Asia, like their consciences bothered them" (60). "But us," he continues, "well, seeing as how we'd come up the hard way, I don't guess we had much on our consciences, and we could look out at those poor people and kind of understand" (60). The problem is that Earl and Maude *look at* the poverty, but *do* nothing about it. This speech of Earl's is followed immediately by his declaration that he is going to grill himself and his wife a sirloin steak "as thick as a Manhattan phone book" (60). In his later conversation with Charley Freeman, Earl is equally reductive about the problems of poverty in Asia. Expecting the Chinese to pull "themselves up by their bootstraps" as he and Maude have done, he repeats Peale-like clichés such as: "There's nothing wrong with Asia that a little spunk and common sense and know-how won't cure" (67). These comments are met with skepticism by Charley Freeman, who has actually spent the last 30 years of his life building hospitals in China before being thrown in jail by the communists and forced to leave the country.

Despite all the flaws of the Fentons, Vonnegut does not depict them as evil people, but simply as self-deluded. They are meant to represent a type of shallow, blind, and self-congratulatory American, unaware of true suffering in the world. At least the Fentons have the grace to be ashamed of themselves at the end of the story, when Lou Converse reveals Charley Freeman's past to them. As Earl Fenton searches for a button to push or switch to flick, he realizes that his complex gadgetry cannot fulfill all his wishes. He cannot take back the shameful way he and Maude treated Charley Freeman.

CHARACTERS

Angela and Arthur Angela is the name of Maude Fenton's sister, and Arthur is her husband. In order to get rid of Charley Freeman, Maude and Earl pretend that Angela is coming to visit unexpectedly with her husband and children.

Converse, Lou Lou Converse is the contractor who has designed the Fentons' luxurious new home, with all of its push-button gadgets and latest technology. Lou is the one who brings the home magazine people over to the house to write a story about it. He also informs the Fentons about Charley Freeman's past at the end of the story.

Fenton, Earl Earl Fenton is a self-made millionaire who has recently sold the plant he operates, whose children are grown, and who has just returned from a world cruise with his wife, Maude. While the Fentons were gone, they ordered a brand-new home to be built and decorated and outfitted with all the modern conveniences. Upon their return, the couple is eager to show off their new house in a magazine spread as well as to Earl's old college fraternity brother, Charley Freeman. Earl, however, is ashamed of himself and his treatment of Charley by the end of the story. His own accomplishments fall flat after he hears the news of Charley's self-sacrificing heroics in China.

Fenton, Earl Jr. and Ted One of Earl Fenton's sons, Earl Jr., has become a doctor while the other, Ted, has become a lawyer. His sons' occupations indicate that Fenton has risen in the world from his college days, when he worked as a waiter.

Fenton, Maude Maude Fenton is the wife of self-made millionaire Earl Fenton. She encourages Earl in his resentment about his poverty during his college days and wants to hear more about the slights he received. Maude also fans the flames of Earl's suspicions in regard to Charley Freeman; she helps Earl concoct the story of her sister's visit in order to get rid of Charley.

Freeman, Charley Charley Freeman is the old college fraternity brother of Earl Fenton who calls him up unexpectedly soon after the Fentons arrive home from a world cruise. Although Charley is gracious and unassuming, Earl feels resentment toward the man because Charley is from a wealthy family while Earl had to work his way through college. At the end of the story, readers, along with Earl, discover that Charley had spent the last 30 years in China, running a hospital for the poor.

Maid   The Fentons' maid, who answers the phone and fetches Earl the steak he will grill, is a symbol of the couples' wealthy status and their rise from working-class roots.

Slotkin   Slotkin is the name of the foreign photographer who works for the home magazine that is writing a story about the Fentons' new house. He takes numerous photographs of Earl and Maude in different costumes in different rooms of their mansion.

Writer   The home magazine doing a spread on the Fentons' new house sends out a young, pretty woman writer to get the story.

FURTHER READING

Bagombo Snuff Box. New York: Berkley Books, 2000.
Reed, Peter. *The Short Fiction of Kurt Vonnegut.* Westport, Conn.: Greenwood Press, 1997.

Palm Sunday: An Autobiographical Collage

Palm Sunday: An Autobiographical Collage, published in 1981 by Delacorte/ SEYMOUR LAWRENCE, is a follow-up to Vonnegut's previous essay collection, the 1974 *Wampeters, Foma, and Granfalloons.* Like the earlier collection, *Palm Sunday* is a miscellaneous collection of essays, reviews, and speeches from the previous decade or so of Vonnegut's career. Also like *Wampeters, Palm Sunday* includes a formerly unpublished short play. This collection differs from the previous one, however, in the more personal, autobiographical direction it takes. In *Palm Sunday,* Vonnegut includes large chunks of a family biography researched and written by his uncle, JOHN RAUCH, an INDIANAPOLIS lawyer and the husband of KURT VONNEGUT, SR.'s, first cousin, GERTRUDE SCHNULL RAUCH. In addition, he includes personal vignettes focusing on his military experience, his divorce from his first wife, JANE COX VONNEGUT

YARMOLINSKY, and detailing the lives of several of his six children.

Billed in the subtitle as a "collage," in his introduction to the book Vonnegut claims to have invented a "marvelous new literary form" (xi). With tongue firmly in cheek, he opens his introduction with the line: "This is a very great book by an American *genius*" (xi), a statement he subsequently undermines when he settles on the term blivit to describe his "masterpiece" (xii). A *blivit,* Vonnegut explains, is a word he learned during his adolescence, meaning "two pounds of shit in a one-pound bag" (xii). Simultaneously boostering and undercutting the collection, he nevertheless recognizes, as he did in *Wampeters,* the inadequacy of conventional literary genres in describing his work—his fiction as well as his essay collections. He proposes that the *New York Times Book Review* should "establish a third category for best sellers," for any book "combining fact and fiction" (xii). That way, "authors of blivits could stop stepping in the faces of mere novelists and historians and so on" (xii). But perhaps the image most appropriate for describing *Palm Sunday* is that of FRANKENSTEIN'S monster. Vonnegut himself uses such a metaphor when he tells about putting the pieces together and discovering that he "would have to write much new connective tissue" (xiii) between them. A metaphor deriving from the physical body seems appropriate to a work like *Palm Sunday,* which is intensely personal in many ways. The various body parts that Vonnegut stitches together with new connective tissue to create *Palm Sunday* include meditations on reading, censorship, and obscenity, discussions of literary style, assessments of other writers as well as of his own work, essays on the Vonnegut ancestry and on his personal life history, reflections on religion, spirituality and human dignity, and finally, an examination of humor and joking as responses to the painful elements of life.

Reading/Censorship/Obscenity
Throughout the collection, Vonnegut meditates on the value and significance of reading and writing. He includes a speech given at the dedication of a new library at Connecticut College in 1976, which he closes by asserting that "language" and

"literature" as well as the "freedom to say or write whatever we please in this country" are all "holy" to him (150). Here, and elsewhere, he describes reading and writing as profound and nourishing forms of meditation. In his 1978 graduation speech at Fredonia College in New York, Vonnegut argues that reading and writing are "sacred" activities, far surpassing "any dream experienced by a Hindu on a mountaintop," because, by reading well, any human being "can think the thoughts of the wisest and most interesting human minds throughout history" (163). The adjectives Vonnegut uses to describe reading and writing—"sacred" and "holy"—show that, for him, these secular activities replace religious conventions. He perceives that reading and writing fulfill spiritual needs in human beings.

Because he values reading so highly, Vonnegut speaks out against censorship in this volume. The first chapter in the collection is titled "The First Amendment," and in it Vonnegut declares that he is a member of "the last recognizable generation of full-time, life-long American novelists" (1). This is partly because television killed the lucrative short story trade of the 1930s, '40s and early '50s, a phenomenon he describes in more detail in his introduction and coda to the short story collection *Bagombo Snuff Box*, and partly because "accountants and business school graduates" now dominate the book publishing industry (2), and these types are afraid to take chances on first books by young authors. But even more, Vonnegut suggests that what might really set his literary generation apart is that they "were allowed to say absolutely anything without fear of punishment" (3). He fears that the First Amendment may be repealed soon on the grounds of decency—protecting children from a supposedly noxious atmosphere. He goes on to detail a particularly egregious incident of censorship in which his novel *Slaughterhouse-Five* was actually burned in Drake, North Dakota. Vonnegut includes a passionate letter he wrote in 1973 to the chairman of the Drake School Board. In it, he defends the First Amendment on the grounds that children should be exposed to as much information and as many diverse opinions as possible, that it is ignorant, un-American, and uncivilized to try to protect children by sheltering them from

coarse language when it is "evil deeds and lying" that really harm children.

Finally frustrated when he receives no response from the school board chair, Vonnegut concludes that:

> Whenever ideas are squashed in this country, literate lovers of the American experiment write careful and intricate explanations of why all ideas must be allowed to live. It is time for them to realize that they are attempting to explain America at its bravest and most optimistic to orangutans. (8)

Although he says he has given up on defending the Constitution to "dimwitted Savonarolas" (8), Vonnegut still speculates about why so many ordinary Americans have contempt for the First Amendment. He believes it is because of the hierarchy of laws set down by Thomas Aquinas and believed in by most people "down to the marrow of" their bones (9). The highest law, according to this hierarchy is divine law, followed by the laws of nature. Human law comes in a "lousy" (9) third in such a scheme. Therefore, far too many American citizens believe that "our courts and policemen and prisons [should] be guided by divine or natural law" (10). Of course, the problem is that divine law and natural law are unknowable. Our government, then, must work according to human law. American freedom, Vonnegut believes, will vanish "by the surrender of our destinies to the highest laws" (10).

As Vonnegut points out in this essay, one of the reasons *Slaughterhouse-Five* is most often censored is because of coarse language. In a later essay titled "Obscenity," he tells readers about his first mother-in-law, a "gallant and pretty little woman" (201) named RIAH FAGAN COX, who imagined that Vonnegut "used certain impolite words" in his books "in order to cause a sensation, in order to make the books more popular" (202). Cox tells Vonnegut that her friends can no longer bear to read his work. Similarly, Vonnegut reports that an article in *Indianapolis Magazine* said much the same thing. While praising his earlier work, the article chastises the "obscene" language and line drawings that appear in his 1973 novel, *Breakfast of Champions*. Vonnegut responds to these criticisms by pointing out that Mrs. Cox and others consider it bad manners to use so-called dirty words. Yet, as he explains in *Wampeters, Foma, and Granfalloons* as well as in the preface to *Breakfast of Champions*, Vonnegut is skeptical about enforced politeness. He worries that conventional good manners are merely excuses for not talking about things that are painful or ugly: "But even when I was in grammar school," he writes, "I suspected that warnings about words that nice people never used were in fact lessons in how to keep our mouths shut not just about our bodies, but about many, many things—perhaps too many things" (203). He goes on to tell a story about his father slapping him for asking a couple visiting the family during the Great Depression how much a sapphire ring worn by the woman cost. Vonnegut's parents had such good manners, taught to them in childhood, that they could not even suspect that the couple were crooks, trying to con them out of their remaining life savings.

In a similar vein, Vonnegut speculates about 19th-century British Queen Victoria and her revulsion toward obscenity. He suggests that the real reason the queen feared obscenity was because she refused to pay attention to the cruder, crueler aspects of life—if she could hide the supposed ugliness of bodily functions, she could also close her eyes to other impolite topics: "the suffering of the Irish, or the cruelties of the factory system, or the privileges of the nobility, or the approach of a world war, and on and on" (206). If the queen would "not even acknowledge that human beings sometimes farted," Vonnegut writes, "how could she be expected to hear without swooning of these other things?" (206). In a direct challenge to just such enforced rules of politeness, Vonnegut recounts the "dirtiest story" he ever wrote. Called "The Big Space Fuck," the story was printed by Harlan Ellison in a 1972 anthology called *Again, Dangerous Visions*. The story, set in the near future in America, depicts an environmentally ravaged Earth. In an effort to make sure that human life will continue in the Universe, since it cannot endure much longer on Earth, the U.S. government devises a plan to send a rocket ship filled with "eight hundred pounds of freeze-dried jizzum" (208) into the Andromeda Galaxy. Vonnegut presents the story

unapologetically, proudly proclaiming that it is "the first story in the history of literature to have 'fuck' in the title" (207). He believes that the world needs less politeness about natural bodily functions as well as about pressing social and environmental concerns. If people remain afraid to discuss dirty, ugly, or unpleasant topics, they will continue to pretend such things do not exist, and real change can never occur.

Literary Style/Writers

In this volume, Vonnegut not only explains his own willingness to use crude language in his works, he also explores other aspects of literary style, both his own and that of other writers. In the chapter titled "When I Lost My Innocence," he explains how he believes people come to be writers: "You feel somehow marginal, somehow slightly off-balance all the time," he notes (59), adding that this is exactly how he felt as a chemistry major at Cornell University. When asked by the International Paper Company in May 1980 to write an essay about literary style, Vonnegut jokes that he has been elected to write about such a topic after nearly flunking chemistry and never having taken a course in literature or composition at college. Nevertheless, he shares with readers the ideas about literary style he has developed over the course of his career. Pointing out that newspaper reporters and technical writers "are trained to reveal almost nothing about themselves in their writings" (68), he argues that other writers *do* reveal things about themselves. It is these self-revelations—both accidental and intentional—that Vonnegut believes make up literary style. They tell readers what sort of person they are spending time with when they read a writer's work.

As far as advice about literary style for fledgling writers, Vonnegut recommends that a writer must begin with interesting ideas. Caring about one's subject matter, rather than playing fancy language games, will make for a compelling style, he argues. He also urges writers to keep their language simple, pointing out that "two great masters of our language, WILLIAM SHAKESPEARE and James Joyce, wrote sentences that were almost childlike when their subjects were most profound" (69). He praises the opening line of the Bible—"In the beginning God created the heavens and the earth"—for its simplicity as well, noting that this is "a sentence well within the writing skills of a lively fourteen-year-old" (69). Another recommendation Vonnegut makes to young writers is to "never include a sentence which does not either remark on character or advance the action" (70). He advises writers to cross out all sentences that do not illuminate their topic in a new and useful way. In addition, writers should adopt a style that echoes the speech they heard as children. His own style, he argues, reflects his Midwest background. Common speech in Indiana, he says, "sounds like a band saw cutting galvanized tin, and employs a vocabulary as unornamental as a monkey wrench" (70). Finally, Vonnegut recommends that writers employ clarity in their style. Although Vonnegut himself dreamed "of doing with words what Pablo Picasso did with paint or what any number of jazz idols did with music" (71), he realizes that he would not be understood by readers if he did so. Readers, he believes, have a difficult enough task decoding "thousands of little marks on paper" (71) and interpreting these marks as it is, without writers making their job even more difficult. Vonnegut, then, insists on clarity even though he points out, in the book's final chapter, that, to literary critics and academics in this country, "clarity looks a lot like laziness and ignorance and childishness and cheapness. . . . Any idea which can be grasped immediately is for them, by definition, something they knew all the time" (291). Clearly, Vonnegut is frustrated by certain negative reviews of his own work. Earlier in the collection, Vonnegut writes that "he never felt worse in [his] life" (93) than after the critical thrashing he received for his novel *Slapstick.*

Perhaps Vonnegut's most arresting point about writing, though, is his demystification of the literary arts. In this volume, especially in the self-interview that appeared in *The Paris Review* in 1977, he insists that writing is a trade more than an art. Similar to the way he writes about himself as a "trafficker in climaxes and thrills and characterization [etc.]" in chapter 1 of *Slaughterhouse-Five*, in the self-interview Vonnegut compares a writer working on a novel to a carpenter building a house or a

mechanic repairing an automobile. If a writer is too lazy or unable to stage confrontations in his work, that writer "should withdraw from the trade" (100). He also insists that, while studies have shown that writers tend to be more depressed than the general population, the IQs of writers are perfectly average. The "power" good writers have is not immense talent but "patience" (116). "We have discovered," Vonnegut says, "that writing allows even a stupid person to seem halfway intelligent, if only that person will write the same thought over and over again, improving it just a little bit each time. . . . Anybody can do it. All it takes is time" (116). Vonnegut eschews the romantic notion of the writer as tortured genius, preferring instead to ascribe writing ability to hard work and plenty of revision.

Many of the essays collected in this volume contain assessments of other writers' works. Having suffered from negative reviews himself, Vonnegut seems careful in these pieces to focus on works and on writers that he truly admires and respects. The first sustained review that appears in the book is of JOSEPH HELLER'S 1974 novel, *Something Happened*, a giant novel set in the large corporations and suburbs of the conformist mid-20th century. While somewhat skeptical about how the novel will be received, Vonnegut nevertheless argues that it "could become the dominant myth about the middle-class veterans who came home from [World War II] to become heads of nuclear families" just as Heller's earlier *Catch-22* "is now the dominant myth about Americans in the war against fascism" (121). Vonnegut also includes in the volume a speech he gave in honor of the writer IRWIN SHAW at the Players Club in 1979. Proclaiming Shaw's novel *The Young Lions* to be "the best American novel about World War Two" (125), Vonnegut pinpoints what he admires so much in Shaw's work: He knows how real Americans "talk and feel," a skill "highly unusual in our literary history" (126). Also, in 1979, Vonnegut spoke at the funeral of novelist JAMES T. FARRELL, whom he extolled for emphasizing "rationality and compassion and honor at the expense of piety" in his work (130). Other writers Vonnegut praises in the collection include MARK TWAIN, whom he sees as the creator of numerous American myths, and whom he tells readers he named his firstborn son after; the humorist H. L. MENCKEN, who found religious people to be comical; the great 18th-century satirist JONATHAN SWIFT, author of *Gulliver's Travels,* a masterpiece that contains "rage and joy and irrationality" (238); and even the French Nazi-sympathizer LOUIS-FERDINAND CÉLINE, whom Vonnegut argues "gave us in his novels the finest history we have of the total collapse of Western civilization in two world wars, as witnessed by hideously vulnerable common women and men" (267).

But Vonnegut, while appreciating the writers mentioned above, is not elitist in his taste. Confessing the "barbarous opinion" that he finds *The Spoon River Anthology* by Edgar Lee Masters to be "a very great book," Vonnegut admits, further, that he sees "much to celebrate in the shrewd innocence of many of the poems now being set to country music" (138). In two different places in the collection, he quotes verses from country songs written by members of the singing group the Statler

Mark Twain, 1907 *(courtesy of the Library of Congress)*

Brothers. The song "The Class of '57," whose lyrics contrast the big dreams of the members of a high school graduating class with what the students are actually doing many years later, seems to Vonnegut to be "an anthem for [his] generation" (142). And he describes the song "Flowers on the Wall" as a "great contemporary poem" that tells of "a man's cold sober flight into unpopulated nothingness" (278). Vonnegut believes this song does a good job explaining the emotions and circumstances he himself experienced after his divorce. It should be no surprise to readers that Vonnegut, whose own work is such a mixture of high and low forms, should be attracted both to more "literary" writers as well as to more popular expressions. Nor does his own work escape assessment in *Palm Sunday.* Toward the end of the collection, he gives himself a report card in which he frankly rates his works against one another. *Cat's Cradle* and *Slaughterhouse-Five* come out on top, rating grades of "A+" in relation to his other works, while the play *Happy Birthday, Wanda June* and the novel *Slapstick* do less well, both earning marks of "D."

Ancestry/Autobiography

While Vonnegut looks back on his own writing career toward the end of the collection, *Palm Sunday* as a whole devotes many pages to his personal and family life as well. Along with the 1997 novel, *Timequake,* this is the most autobiographical of Vonnegut's works. The second chapter in the collection, "Roots," consists mostly of large chunks of a family history written by Vonnegut's uncle, John Rauch. These excerpts detail the lives of Vonnegut's eight great-grandparents, all of whom "were part of the vast migration of Germans to the Midwest in the half century from 1820 to 1870" (21). In addition, readers learn about Vonnegut's paternal grandfather, the architect BERNARD VONNEGUT, SR., his maternal grandfather, the flamboyant and wealthy ALBERT LIEBER, as well as the upbringing and courting of Vonnegut's own parents: Kurt Vonnegut, Sr., and EDITH LIEBER VONNEGUT. The motive for Vonnegut's including such detailed description of his lineage seems to be partly a reclaiming for himself of a sense of culture. As Vonnegut discusses elsewhere, particularly in the prologue to his novel *Slapstick*, the anti-German feelings generated by World War I largely destroyed his sense of having a specific culture to call his own. In this essay, he writes about his parents' shame for their German ancestry:

> ... the anti-Germanism in this country during the First World War so shamed and dismayed my parents that they resolved to raise me without acquainting me with the language or the literature or the music or the oral family histories which my ancestors had loved. They volunteered to make me ignorant and rootless as proof of their patriotism. (19–20)

Vonnegut longs to regain a sense of family pride in a shared past. He even wishes that he could have become a third-generation Indianapolis architect, following in the footsteps of his father and grandfather. However, Kurt, Sr. discouraged this ambition, directing his son to study chemistry in college rather than architecture or the humanities.

One of Vonnegut's dominant themes, in both his essays and his fiction, is his admiration for large family groups. Because, growing up, he felt somewhat alienated from his parents and ignorant of his German cultural heritage, he writes that he spent his later years searching for artificial families to fit into. In a speech given at CORNELL UNIVERSITY on the 100th anniversary of the founding of *THE COR-NELL DAILY SUN*, Vonnegut explains that he found just such a family working on the staff of the college newspaper. "I found a family here at the *Sun*," Vonnegut tells the students, "or I no doubt would have invited pneumonia into my thorax during my freshman year" (59). Vonnegut's appreciation for extended families is also evident in a graduation speech delivered at Hobart and William Smith Colleges in 1974, in which he tells about visiting the struggling African country BIAFRA as it was being defeated by Nigeria in the early 1970s, a trip he explores in more detail in his previous essay collection, *Wampeters, Foma, and Granfalloons*. He explains to the students that the Biafran people survived because of their large family groups who took care of their members. He contrasts the Biafran system to nuclear families in America, arguing that the divorce rate in America is so rampant because "the

nuclear family doesn't provide nearly enough companionship" (188). Contemporary Americans also tend to disperse from the places where they were born, a trend Vonnegut laments, as he quotes 19th-century American Transcendentalist writer HENRY DAVID THOREAU, who famously said, "I have traveled extensively in Concord" (53). To Vonnegut, this quote suggests "what every child seemingly *must* feel about the place where he or she was born"—that there is "more than enough to marvel at for a lifetime" (53), in every child's own hometown.

Vonnegut, of course, did not stay in his hometown of Indianapolis his whole life. After spending several years as a poor student at Cornell, he enlisted in the U.S. Army in 1943 and was sent overseas as an infantry battalion scout. In the self-interview from *The Paris Review*, Vonnegut discusses his military experience in some detail. Here, as elsewhere in his work, he speaks of his hatred of officers, as well as his capture by the Germans during the BATTLE OF THE BULGE. When asked to describe the firebombing of DRESDEN—the pivotal event that shapes his most critically acclaimed novel, *Slaughterhouse-Five*—Vonnegut tells of a beautiful, urbane city transformed into rubble. As a prisoner of war, Vonnegut was made to dig out corpses from the underground shelters. He describes entering these shelters, usually ordinary basements, and finding what "looked like a streetcar full of people who'd simultaneously had heart failure. Just people sitting there in their chairs, all dead" (80). Vonnegut also explains that he had no idea of the scope and importance of the firebombing until years after his return home from the war. Only when he began to read about the tragedy and speak to other veterans about it did he decide his experiences in Dresden were worth writing about.

Yet, despite his decision to write about Dresden, Vonnegut is not blind to the tricky morality involved in such an undertaking. *Slaughterhouse-Five* not only cemented Vonnegut's reputation, it also made him a wealthy man. He explains, in his introduction to a new, deluxe edition of the novel, that "only one person on the entire planet benefited from the raid" on Dresden (84). And that person was Vonnegut himself. "I got three dollars for each person killed. Imagine that" (84).

Although Vonnegut frequently acknowledges, both in this collection and elsewhere in his work, that World War II was a "just war" (162), he nevertheless bemoans the fact that young men in our society are so eager to go to war, speculating that war service stands in for the puberty ceremonies that more traditional societies offer young men to mark their passage into adulthood. Because the United States withholds such ceremonies, young men want to go to war to show that they are really men, no longer boys. In *Palm Sunday*, as in all his work, Vonnegut criticizes society's war machinery and laments the effects of this machinery. Despite his experiences in Dresden, he says it was not until "the atomic bomb was dropped on Hiroshima" (62) that he truly lost his innocence. The "flash at Hiroshima" (63), he argues, revealed the sickness of the human soul—a soul "so sick that it did not want to live anymore" (63). Vonnegut's experiences in World War II and Dresden, along with the dropping of the ATOMIC BOMB, form the imaginative launching point for many of his finest novels—not only *Slaughterhouse-Five* but also the apocalyptic *Cat's Cradle* and the underrated morality tale *Mother Night*.

Perhaps the most intensely personal portion of *Palm Sunday*, however, involves Vonnegut's recounting of his life experiences following his return from Dresden. In the chapter titled "Playmates," he speaks about marriage and raising children. Noticing that most literature deemed "great" ignores domestic experience, Vonnegut writes of the importance of such experience in his own life: ". . . the most meaningful and often harrowing adventures which I and many like me have experienced have had to do with the rearing of children" (143). Later in the collection, he speaks frankly about personal crises, including his son MARK VONNEGUT's descent into madness and subsequent recovery as well as his divorce from his first wife, Jane Cox Vonnegut. Just as in the prologue to *Slapstick*, Vonnegut asks for "a little less love, and a little more common decency" (3). In a 1980 speech at a Unitarian Church in Cambridge, Massachusetts, Vonnegut derides the notion of romantic love: "As every married person here knows," he says, "love is a rotten substitute for respect" (197). Thus, in the self-interview that appears in

the collection, Vonnegut can write that "no real women" and "no love" appear in his fiction (94). He worries that if an author writes about love the topic will begin to take over the work: "Once that particular subject comes up, it is almost impossible to talk about anything else. Readers don't want to hear about anything else. They go gaga about love" (95). Vonnegut points out that he has other things he wants to talk about.

Nevertheless, he does explore the topic of love and marriage in the essays collected here. He speaks of the embarrassment ensuing from his divorce, the wrong-headed notion that his breakup with Jane was a story "of booze and wicked women" (278), and the feelings of uselessness that arose from his children growing up and leaving the house and no longer depending on him. He speaks of the limits of the nuclear family and praises the extended families found in folk societies, a topic he elaborates more fully in his previous collection, *Wampeters, Foma, and Granfalloons*. Finally, Vonnegut claims that his divorce was more a matter of him and Jane growing apart and going in different directions than anything else. Interestingly, he adds that religious differences constituted the couples' major disagreements toward the end of their marriage. Jane Cox Vonnegut, as well as Vonnegut's daughters, EDITH and NANETTE, all became born-again Christians at one point, a choice that Vonnegut describes as "painful" to him. This experience explains why Vonnegut chose as the epigraph to *Palm Sunday* a quote from his freethinking great-grandfather CLEMENS VONNEGUT: "Whoever entertains liberal views and chooses a consort that is captured by superstition risks his happiness." Although elsewhere in the collection, Vonnegut says that it is "all right" with him that his first wife and both his daughters now work "white magic through rituals and prayers" (217), he himself is a religious skeptic, and the differences between his views and Jane's finally became too overwhelming for the marriage to endure.

Religion/Spirituality/Human Dignity

Vonnegut attributes his religious skepticism to a long history of free thinking and agnosticism in his forbears. "I am of course a skeptic about the divinity of Christ and a scorner of the notion that there is a God who cares how we are or what we do," he tells the audience in a speech honoring Mark Twain in 1979. "I was raised this way—in the midst of what provincial easterners imagine to be a Bible Belt" (152). Yet, despite his skepticism toward conventional religious belief and practice, in his 1974 graduation speech at Hobart and William Smith Colleges in New York, he declares the need for a new religion. While traditional religion "allows people to imagine from moment to moment what is going on and how they should behave" (181), Vonnegut points out that life seems chaotic to many contemporary Americans. People are forced to do without religion because "the old-time religions they know of are too superstitious, too full of magic, too ignorant about biology and physics to harmonize with the present day" (181). Life without a coherent moral structure, though, is dissatisfying, he argues. In imagining his new religion—a word, by the way, he tells his audience he is willing to drop in favor of "heartfelt moral code"—Vonnegut tries to make things as simple as possible. The new moral code that he eventually settles on is this: "Anything which wounds the planet is evil, and anything which preserves it or heals it is good" (185). Anyone who breaks this moral code, Vonnegut adds, would be viewed as "an evil and therefore disgusting human being" (185). He believes that what human beings really fear is not hell, but the contempt of their fellow men.

Just as it is human beings who ultimately punish one another, Vonnegut believes it is humans who confer dignity on one another. In his speech praising 19th-century Unitarian minister WILLIAM ELLERY CHANNING, delivered in Cambridge, Massachusetts, in 1980, Vonnegut extols Channing for preaching that not only members of one's own like-minded community were deserving of human dignity, but that strangers, even black ones, were as well. Adding to Channing's ideas, Vonnegut insists that human dignity is not something people are inherently born with or that God bestows on them. "Human dignity," he writes, "must be given by people to people. If you stand before me, and I do not credit you with dignity, then you have none" (194). Even more, when humans endow their fel-

low creatures with dignity, something else very important happens. Vonnegut warns the members of his audience: "If you allow yourself to see dignity in someone, you have doomed yourself to wanting to understand and help whoever it is" (195). He ends the speech by reimagining the Christian gospels, in a way quite similar to how he has Kilgore Trout rewrite the Christ story in *Slaughterhouse-Five*, when Trout presents Christ as a bum adopted by God only after he is crucified.

In Vonnegut's revision of the Gospel story, Jesus is not the son of God either, but a common human being. The Roman soldiers strip him of his dignity by humiliating him, whipping him, forcing him to wear a crown of thorns, and nailing him to a cross. But a group of ordinary people gather beneath him on the cross, talk to him, sing to him, and explain how sorry they are in an attempt to relieve his suffering. When a rich tourist comes upon this scene, he comments on the way the people seem to be worshipping this man: "My goodness," he says, "you would think he was the Son of your God!" (198). Vonnegut then imagines Mary Magdalene responding to the man: "Oh no, sir. If he were the Son of our God, he would not need us. It is because he is a common human being exactly like us that we are here—doing, as common people must, what little we can" (199). Vonnegut often refers to himself as a HUMANIST, even though this particular designation is not discussed in *Palm Sunday*. Nevertheless, in this collection, as elsewhere, Vonnegut advocates a moral code that is centered on this world, that revolves around human beings' treatment of one another rather than focusing on a supernatural being or the promise of a better life after death.

Humor/Joking

The title of this collection itself addresses the religious theme that Vonnegut treats in the book. It derives from a Palm Sunday sermon Vonnegut was invited to preach at St. Clement's Episcopal Church in New York in 1980. The church, which is also a theater, and whose congregation is made up of many actors, has a tradition of having a stranger preach once a year. When he was the person invited, Vonnegut chose to speak about Christ's Sermon on the Mount, a part of the Bible he admits to being "enchanted by" since it is extols the virtue of being merciful. Yet, Vonnegut says that Christians have long had difficulty reconciling the lovely Sermon on the Mount with the Christ presented in the first eight verses of the 12th book of John, in which Jesus is being anointed by Mary and Judas questions why the money spent on the ointment was not instead given to the poor. In the King James version of the Bible, Jesus replies, "For the poor always ye have with you; but you do not always have me" (297). Vonnegut points out that, on first glance, this passage has "two quite depressing implications: that Jesus could be a touch self-pitying, and that he was, with his mission to earth about to end, at least momentarily sick and tired of hearing about the poor" (297). Such implications disturb Vonnegut, who calls himself a "Christ-worshipping agnostic" (298), and who understands that "much un-Christian impatience with the poor" (298) has been generated by the quotation. Thus, Vonnegut reinterprets Jesus' words in John 12, explaining to the St. Clements parishioners that Christ was only joking with Judas, and not really thinking about the poor much at all at this moment. According to Vonnegut, Christ's words amounted to the following: "Judas, don't worry about it. There will still be plenty of poor people left long after I'm gone" (300). Vonnegut reads Jesus' words to Judas here as a "divine black joke," a joke that comments on Judas's hypocrisy rather than on the situation of the poor. And as readers repeatedly discover in Vonnegut's work, he is a writer who loves jokes, perhaps above all else.

Vonnegut tells readers that he himself learned how to tell jokes as the youngest member of a large family. In order to have people pay attention to him at the dinner table, he had to learn to be funny. The chapter in *Palm Sunday* that most fully examines humor and joking is titled "Funnier on Paper Than Most People." In it, Vonnegut explains how jokes work. "The beginning of each good one," he says, "challenges you to think" (160). But then, the second part of any joke "announces that nobody wants you to think. . . . You are so relieved to at last meet somebody who doesn't demand that you be intelligent. You laugh for joy" (160). Throughout his life, he adds, comedians, along with jazz musicians,

have meant more to him, have provided more comfort and enlightenment, than preachers, politicians, poets, or novelists. In an introduction he wrote for a comedy book published by the team of Bob Elliott and Ray Goulding, Vonnegut explains just what he loves about humor and joking. The comedy of BOB AND RAY, Vonnegut argues, works so well because "there is a refreshing and beautiful innocence" to it: "Man is not evil, they seem to say. He is simply too hilariously stupid to survive" (129). And further, Vonnegut says this statement is something he fully believes as well.

In his *Palm Sunday* sermon about Jesus' joking with Judas, as elsewhere in his work, Vonnegut explains that "jokes can be noble" (298). Laughs, he argues, "are exactly as honorable as tears" (298). Both forms of expression are "responses to frustration and exhaustion, to the futility of thinking and striving anymore" (298). In his fiction, often described by critics as consisting largely of BLACK HUMOR, Vonnegut similarly responds to the frustrations of the social ills and hypocrisy he sees in the world around him. He explains that he prefers to laugh rather than cry "since there is less cleaning up to do afterward—and since I can start thinking and striving again that much sooner" (298). It is fitting that Vonnegut closes his "blivit," his Frankenstein-like autobiographical collage, with the Palm Sunday sermon, which combines humor with a deep morality, both hallmarks of Vonnegut's writing.

FURTHER READING

Palm Sunday: An Autobiographical Collage. New York: Dell, 1999.

Player Piano

Published in 1952 by Scribner's, *Player Piano* is Vonnegut's first novel and, in many ways, his most formally conventional one. Though missing the short sentences and childlike understatement, the nonlinear chronologies, the space aliens, and the one-liners of much of his later fiction, *Player Piano* nevertheless introduces many of the important themes that became hallmarks of Vonnegut's work. This is the novel in which Vonnegut first questions traditional notions of scientific progress, pointing out the devastating effects that an American love of machines and technology can have on human beings. *Player Piano*, like much of Vonnegut's later work, presents ambiguous characters with utopian dreams that ultimately fail, leaving readers in a strange, post-apocalyptic world at novel's end. Nevertheless, in *Player Piano*, as elsewhere in Vonnegut's work, readers are meant to admire the creative impulse associated with these utopian schemes and to accept the human frailty that finally makes a perfect world impossible.

SYNOPSIS

Chapters 1–8

Player Piano is set in the not too far distant future in Ilium, New York, 10 years after America has won a major war, the victory mostly a result of technology and engineering expertise. "Democracy," Vonnegut writes, "owed its life to know-how" (9). The technological advances that helped win the war have been refined even further in the years after the war so that machines now do most of the ordinary work in the country. Peoples' IQ scores, recorded on punch cards and stored on computing machines, strictly delineate class lines and determine their occupations. As a result of these changes, Ilium is now divided into three parts: Managers and engineers and bureaucrats live in the northwest portion of the city and enjoy elite status. Machines dominate the northeast. The vast majority of people, though, live in the south, in an area called Homestead. Only members of the professional class in the northwest are allowed to go to college, and this class is the only one that has meaningful work to do. The bulk of Ilium's citizens, who live in Homestead, are employed by the government, assigned to work in either the Reconstruction and Reclamation Corps or the army. Both the "Reeks and Wrecks" as members of the Corps are known, and army enlistees have dead-end jobs and not much hope for the future, as their children have every likelihood of being assigned to similar positions. The elite class and the common class rarely if ever mingle. Vonnegut writes that if someone were to dynamite the

bridge crossing the Iroquois River separating the classes, "few daily routines would be disturbed. Not many people on either side have reasons other than curiosity for crossing" (9).

Doctor Paul Proteus, "the most important, brilliant person in Ilium" is the manager of the Ilium Works, one arm of the giant National Industrial, Commercial, Communications, Foodstuffs, and Resources Organization, which controls all industry and manufacturing in the United States, and where the elite group of engineers and managers is employed. The son of the late Doctor George Proteus, who had been director of the entire organization during the war years, Paul is 35, a gifted engineer, has a beautiful wife, and seems destined to rise almost as high in the company as his father. Yet, as the novel opens, Paul is vaguely dissatisfied with his work and his marriage. His discontent is given shape when his old friend Dr. Edward Finnerty, who along with Paul and Dr. Lawson Shepherd had helped shape the Ilium Works 13 years previously, arrives back in town on the evening Paul is to make an important speech at a party for the Ilium managers and engineers. A brilliant engineer himself, Finnerty had been assigned to a prestigious position in Washington, but informs Paul that he has quit his job in disgust. During his visit, Finnerty antagonizes Paul's wife, Anita, a shrewd and ambitious woman who has been pushing Paul toward trying to win a promotion, as well as Paul's immediate bosses in the organization, Kroner and Baer.

Chapters 9–12

When Finnerty persuades Paul to go drinking across the river in Homestead the next night, the two meet the radical Reverend James J. Lasher, a social scientist and Protestant minister who lectures them about the evils of the new machine-run economy and the toll it is wreaking on the mass of Homesteaders who feel useless and unfulfilled without meaningful work. Lasher prophesies the rise of a new Messiah whom the Homesteaders will eagerly follow if he promises to restore their dignity. That evening, in the saloon in Homestead, Paul is charmed by Alfy Tucci, who makes a living guessing the names of songs performed by musical groups on televison even though he watches with the volume control turned all the way down. Finnerty and Paul end the evening drinking scotch with two homely Homestead women. After imbibing heavily, Paul is inspired to drunkenly rise and deliver a pronouncement that he believes will make him the new Messiah and Ilium the new Eden. Lurching to stand on top of a table, Paul cries, "We must meet in the middle of the bridge!" The table, however, crashes from underneath Paul, and he collapses in a heap. When he comes to, Finnerty is leaving with Lasher, whom he has decided to stay with rather than with Paul, and Paul somehow makes his way home to the northwest part of Ilium.

Late to his office the next day, Paul finds Dr. Lawson Shepherd sitting at his desk and going through his drawers. The number two man at the Ilium Works, Shepherd is jealous of Paul and is trying desperately to outmaneuver him for the promotion Anita has been relentlessly pursuing on Paul's behalf. After kicking Shepherd out and returning home, he discovers that Shepherd has been to visit Anita and told her about Paul and Finnerty's wild night in Homestead. While at first Anita seems jealous about the women Paul was seen drinking with, she's actually worried more about appearances than about Paul's faithfulness to her. (Later in the novel, Anita herself carries on an affair with Shepherd.) The next night, Paul and Anita are invited to dinner at the home of his boss, Kroner. While Anita continues to push for the promotion, Paul pours out his concerns to the fatherly Kroner. Kroner urges Paul to stay on his own side of the river. Much to Paul's surprise, Kroner knows all about Lasher and Finnerty. The evening ends with Kroner pushing Paul to betray the two radicals by testifying that they are saboteurs, the most loathed type of criminals in machine-dominated Ilium. In bed that night, Paul decides to quit his job, though he keeps his resolution to himself.

Meanwhile, as Paul struggles with his job and his marriage, Vonnegut, in alternating chapters, develops a subplot about the shah of Bratpuhr, the spiritual leader of the Kolhouri sect, who is visiting America as a foreign dignitary. The shah is traveling around the country with his interpreter and nephew, Khashdrahr Miasma, and with Dr. Ewing

J. Halyard, of the U.S. Department of State, who has been assigned the task of introducing the shah to the wonders of American technology. The shah repeatedly insists on calling the ordinary people of New York he sees *Takaru*, a word that means "slave" in his language, despite Halyard's repeated attempts to persuade him that these are free citizens, not slaves. On his tour, Halyard takes the shah to visit not only Ilium, but also an army barracks, a completely average home in Chicago, and Carlsbad Caverns, where the huge computer EPICAC, the nerve center of the mechanized world, is kept. The shah mistakes the computer for a god and asks it an ancient riddle, which the Kolhouri believe will be answered one day by a wise god who will then end all suffering on Earth. When he receives no answer to his question, the shah dismissively accuses the Americans of worshiping *Baku* or false idols.

Chapters 13–26

Back in Ilium, Paul decides to surprise Anita by buying a small old decrepit farm with no modern amenities, not even running water or indoor plumbing. He dreams of escaping the machinated world by moving there with Anita and living a life of subsistence farming. While Anita, who adores antiques, is initially delighted by the farmhouse, her plan is to pillage it for objects that could be displayed in her own modern home in Ilium; she is horrified when Paul confesses he wants to live there permanently. After quarreling bitterly, the two make up and begin preparations for their trip to the Meadows, an annual retreat held each summer by the Organization to reward and reinspire their most deserving but not yet fully developed managers and engineers. Paul is to be captain of the Blue Team and will be expected to lead his group in 14 days of singing, drinking, horseplay, and competitive sports against members of the three other teams.

At the Meadows, forced to take part in heavily staged antics designed to encourage team rivalry and to watch a hokey play pitting an earnest young engineer against a dirty radical to win the hearts of ordinary men, Paul's distaste for the entire Organization comes rushing back. Kroner's earlier plan for Paul to betray Finnerty and Lasher is revisited when Paul is called to a secret meeting with Kroner and the director of the Organization. The top brass have hatched a plot for Paul to infiltrate the Ghost Shirt Society, a radical group led by Lasher whose mission is to destroy machines and topple the Organization's control of the economy; they will pretend to fire Paul and send him home from the Meadows in disgrace. Ironically, at the end of this meeting, Paul announces that he is quitting his job. Kroner and the director, who believe Paul is simply playing the role they've assigned him, laugh and encourage him.

Chapters 27–35

One evening, after being home in Ilium for a week by himself, Paul returns to the saloon in Homestead, where he is given a drugged drink. When he awakes, he finds himself tied up and being questioned by Lasher and Finnerty. Under the influence of sodium pentathol, a truth serum, Paul tells of his dissatisfaction with the Organization. Lasher and Finnerty have kidnapped Paul in order to turn him into the new Messiah Lasher spoke of earlier. They expect that Paul's famous name will lend support to their cause. When a meeting of the Ghost Shirt Society is raided by police, Paul and his cohorts are taken to prison. Kroner, still believing that Paul has infiltrated the society to betray its leaders, visits Paul in prison. Questioned about the leadership of the radical group, Paul finally declares himself to be the true leader, committing himself fully to the cause at last. At his widely televised trial, Paul makes astute political speeches in an attempt to garner support for the radical Ghost Shirts. As the trial reaches its end, however, it is disrupted by a brick thrown through a window. The Ghost Shirt revolution has begun.

Wild groups of rioters from Homestead and in cities across the nation, dressed in outlandish costumes, begin smashing machines, burning cars, and generally rampaging. The shah of Bratpuhr and his entourage get caught up in the chaos; in the last view of the shah and his nephew, their exotic attire gets them mistaken for members of the Ghost Shirt Society by one of the riot organizers. They are accused of shirking their duties and sent to the front line of the fighting in a truck. As Paul and the other Ghost Shirt leaders helplessly watch,

though, the rioters begin to spiral out of control, smashing not only their carefully planned targets, but also machines that will be needed to create a new society after the revolution. The leaders can no longer control the fury they have unleashed. Eventually, police surround the city and quell the rioters. While the society has had limited success in a few cities across the nation, the revolution has been suppressed. Disappointed and disillusioned at their loss, Paul and Finnerty are surprised by Lasher's admission that he expected to lose all along, but that they at least had to try to change things, "for the record." The novel ends with the leaders of the Ghost Shirt Society driving to the roadblock set up outside Ilium by the police. They drink a toast "to the record" before putting their hands up and marching forward to turn themselves in.

COMMENTARY

Player Piano is, above all, a novel about the dangers of a naïve belief in human progress, particularly in scientific and technological advancement. While expecting to create a postwar utopia in which merit is rewarded, people are assigned to the work they are best suited for, and machines take care of the mundane, everyday tasks previously required of human beings. American managers and engineers in the 10 years since the war have instead created a rigidly hierarchical society in which the great mass of people are bored, unfulfilled, and lack the dignity all humans crave. The novel depicts a society that, in effect, has tried to stamp out everything that makes human beings particularly human—imperfection, frailty, inefficiency, and brilliance followed by stupidity to quote the qualities praised as human virtues in the letter written by the Ghost Shirt Society at the novel's end. Although the revolution envisioned by the Ghost Shirt Society might ultimately be doomed to fail, the chaos and messiness of trying to change things shows humanity at both its best and its worst; the Ghost Shirters at least succeed in reasserting a cause to believe in in the midst of a society that has made the great mass of humanity feel useless and unimportant.

In *Player Piano* Vonnegut explores and plays with long-held stereotypes about the typical American character. Americans like to see themselves as unlike older, European, class-based societies in which social privilege is often based on inherited wealth or family stature. The idealized vision of America is one of a classless society, where any enterprising young person with brains, ambition, and a willingness to work hard can rise to the top, a society where merit rather than family background is rewarded. Yet, as the Reverend James J. Lasher points out to Paul Proteus and Ed Finnerty in the Homestead saloon, the American reality before the war did not live up to the ideal: "Used to be that the richer you were, the better you were" (94). It's just this problem that the managers, engineers, and bureaucrats of *Player Piano* have attempted to remedy after the war, when they institute a new system of job classifications based strictly on IQ scores. The idea is to create a society in which the most meritorious members do indeed move to the top. The irony of this attempt, though, is that they actually create a society even more rigid and class-bound than the old prewar America. The new assumption, as Lasher points out is that "the smarter you are the better you are" (94). He continues, arguing that "'The criterion of brains is better than money, but' he held his thumb and forefinger about a sixteenth of an inch apart—'about *that* much better'" (94). Either system, he points out, "is pretty tough for the have-nots to take" (94). The effect of the new machine-based job classifications is actually to create a new elite class and to make the superiority of this class seem natural. Vonnegut writes, "But now this elite business, this assurance of superiority, this sense of rightness about the hierarchy topped by managers and engineers—this was instilled in all college graduates, and there were no bones about it" (14). As in many Vonnegut novels, attempts to engineer a better society backfire and have the reverse effect of what is intended.

The other significant quality of the American character that Vonnegut satirizes in *Player Piano* is the American love of machinery, gadgetry and technical "know-how." The inventor THOMAS ALVA EDISON becomes a symbol of this typical American obsession, when Paul Proteus remembers that Building 58 of the Ilium Works is the site of the original machine shop set up by Edison in 1886. In his visit to Building 58 at the begin-

ning of the novel, Paul even imagines that he *is* Edison, surveying the impressive machinery "bobbing, spinning, leaping, thrusting, waving" at its work (16). While this love of mechanization is not presented in the novel as a bad thing in and of itself—in fact, Vonnegut seems to have great affection for mechanical whizzes, like Edison and like Ilium employee Bud Calhoun—nevertheless, carried to an extreme, it can become a dangerous obsession. Bud gets so carried away with his love of gadgetry that he invents himself right out of a job. He creates a machine that can do his work more efficiently than he himself can, and puts not only himself but 71 other employees out of work. This theme is repeated throughout the novel as the barber Homer Bigley tells the story of a fellow barber who invents a hair-cutting machine that is expected to replace human barbers, a skill once thought unreplicatable by machine. Even Paul himself has contributed to this trend, when he, Ed Finnerty, and Lawson Shepherd, as young engineers recorded the motions of expert machinist Rudy Hertz, eventually putting thousands of human machinists out of work.

While Western culture has long cherished, from the Enlightenment forward, ideals of human progress through increased reason and scientific advancement, the novel distrusts the very notion of progress. Paul's secretary, Dr. Katharine Finch, after typing up the speech he will deliver at the party for the Ilium managers and engineers, asks Paul about the possibility of a third Industrial Revolution. In his speech, Paul had argued that "the First Industrial Revolution devalued muscle work, then the second one devalued routine mental work" (21). In speculating about a third revolution, Paul shows what so-called progress might really lead to. He tells Katharine that, in a way, the third revolution has already been going on for quite a while, and that it involves "machines that devaluate human thinking" itself (22). Vonnegut satirizes the notion of progress when he has Katharine respond, "First the muscle work, then the routine work, then, maybe, the real brainwork" (22). If humans no longer have cause to use their brains, to think, because machines do it for them, of what use are they? Katharine recognizes the inherent horror of this situation when she adds, "I hope I'm not around long enough to see that final step" (23).

In a world that values machinery so highly, people themselves have become increasingly machine-like. The marriage between Paul and Anita seems particularly mechanistic as they carry out the conventions of marriage with none of the love and warmth we would expect to see. In fact, "Anita had the mechanics of marriage down pat, even to the subtlest conventions. If her approach was disturbingly rational, systematic, she was thorough enough to turn out a creditable counterfeit of warmth" (25). Anita's "I love you, Paul" invariably evokes the rote response from Paul, "I love *you*, Anita." The structured postwar society is so carefully engineered that "there was no place for erratic behavior" (25), whether from machines or from human beings. The remaining idiosyncratic individuals like Lasher and Finnerty are forced underground into the socially revolutionary Ghost Shirt Society. Vonnegut, though, questions the values of social conformity and an enforced, uniform happiness throughout the novel. A vibrant society needs its critics, its malcontents, its gadflies, like Socrates in ancient Greece. As the unnamed, pretty, dark-skinned woman propositioned by the shah of Bratpuhr says about her novelist husband's philosophy, "somebody's just *got* to be maladjusted; . . . somebody's got to be uncomfortable enough to wonder where people are, where they're going, and why they're going there" (233). The novel depicts far too many people who have ceded to the machines their ability to think and to question.

One way that the characters lose individuality is through the pervasiveness of enormous institutions like the National Industrial, Commercial, Communications, Foodstuffs, and Resources Organization, the army, and the Reconstruction and Reclamation Corps. As in much POSTMODERN literature, characters are often presented as simply cogs in the machinery of these giant organizations. In this respect, *Player Piano* shares much in common with other popular novels of the 1950s and early 1960s that show individuals trapped by large institutions. Sloan Wilson, for instance, in his 1955 *The Man in the Gray Flannel Suit*, condemns Madison Avenue as a huge, uncaring institution while JOSEPH HELLER

skewers the U.S. Army in his 1961 novel, *Catch-22*. The loss of individuality in the face of large, corporate entities is a theme that Vonnegut will return to throughout his work, perhaps nowhere as notably as in his 1968 novel, *Slaughterhouse-Five*, in which he writes that there are almost no characters in his story because people have become so much the "listless playthings of enormous forces" (164). All these works share a sense of the absurdity evident in the corporations and institutions that govern individuals. The Meadows shows this absurdity most clearly in *Player Piano*. Corporate unity is encouraged through activities more appropriate to athletic teams or fraternal organizations than to adult employees; men are encouraged to remain eternal adolescents rather than develop into thoughtful, mature human beings.

Because the managers, engineers, and bureaucrats of *Player Piano* worship technological progress, they view the present moment of the novel, the mechanist world they have created, as the height of human civilization. In such a view, the past becomes "humble and shoddy" (14) compared to the glorious present. Rather than have any kind of meaningful sense of history, the majority of characters in *Player Piano* view the past in a shallow, superficial way. As in much postmodern literature, with its emphasis on the "now," the present moment, history is reduced to simply another commodity or else to a cause for nostalgia—characters repeatedly romanticize the past and often create a false picture of a past that never really existed. We see these two views of history—as commodity and as nostalgia—most clearly in the examples of Anita's kitchen and at the Meadows.

Lasher, in his lecture at the Homestead saloon, describes how buying and selling have replaced religion in the new world of the novel. He describes how the process of "designing and manufacturing and distributing" has become like a "holy war" for the "crusading" managers and engineers of the present day (93). All of the folklore "cooked up by public relations and advertising men . . . to make big business popular in the old days" is now taken to heart by the very managers and engineers who hired the advertisers. "Yesterday's snow job," Lasher points out, "becomes today's sermon" (93).

In a society that worships buying and selling, it is no surprise that history itself becomes commodified. Anita's kitchen makes this process very clear. Containing dozens of antiques from the American colonial period, including "rough-hewn rafters, taken from an antique barn," "a long muzzle-loading rifle, powder horn, and bullet pouch," "candle molds" on the mantel, and "an iron cauldron, big enough to boil a missionary in" swinging in the fireplace (110), Anita's kitchen, filled with items pillaged from the past, becomes an expression of herself, of her very soul. "The kitchen was, in a manner of speaking, what Anita had given of herself to the world" (110).

Readers see, though, that Anita is interested not in real history, but only in the commodities that can be raided from it, when Paul takes her to the Gottwald farm he has purchased. At first Anita is delighted with the farm, moving about the room, touching objects "lovingly" (173) and asking Paul if it is really theirs. But she's not interested in living at the farm or even retaining its integrity as a piece of history. She wishes to scavenge what she can for use in her own home in Ilium, retaining only the antique façade of items like the grandfather clock, but replacing the interior workings with modern components. Like the managers and engineers of Ilium, Anita sees the actual past as shoddy; she wants to retain only a romanticized notion of the past through saving the superficial outsides of the objects she covets. Later in the novel, Paul's purchase of the farm shows his own tendency to romanticize the past. Though he initially believes he can return to a more simple way of life at the farm, that it is a place "where he could work with his hands, getting life from nature" (149), Paul eventually recognizes that farming is really hard, dirty work. The "hand of Nature" which Paul dreams of "guiding" turns out to be "coarse and sluggish, hot and wet and smelly" (246). Paul never returns to the farm again.

The same type of nostalgic recreation of a past that never really existed can be seen in the evoking of Native American culture at the Meadows. The organizers hire "a professional actor, painted bronze, wearing an eagle-feather war bonnet and a beaded G-string" to perform after the presentation of the Sky Manager play. Replete with the worst stereotypes of Indian speech from B westerns—"How!" and "Many moons ago"—the actor recites a history of his "brave," "proud," and "honest" people who no longer live on the island, but who have passed their spirit on to "other young men," the managers and engineers being indoctrinated at the Meadows (213). This history completely omits any mention of why the Indians no longer inhabit the island, leaving out the true history of land theft, removal to western reservations, and genocide practiced against the Indians. The falseness of the history presented is symbolized in the artificiality of the actor himself; Paul notices that he is aging, that his large belly "cast a shadow over his G-string," that he's developed varicose veins, and that his "war paint failed to hide the gray bags under his eyes" (213). For a society that believes "Civilization has reached the dizziest heights of all time!" (209), as the young engineer depicted in the Sky Manager play proclaims, then supports that view by reciting the number of television sets, electrostatic dust precipitators, and refrigerators owned by Americans, meaningful history is easily gilded over and forgotten.

The novel, though, repeatedly debunks such superficial views of history and of human progress. The chapters that depict the shah of Bratpuhr are meant to show that, despite all the so-called progress instituted by the postwar engineers, modern, sophisticated Americans are not really all that much different from humans in more primitive societies. People, according to Vonnegut, are pretty much people, both across time and across cultures. Readers cannot help but feel the rightness of the shah's insistence on calling the ordinary citizens of Ilium and elsewhere *Takaru* or slaves, despite the repeated attempts of Dr. Ewing J. Halyard to correct him. Like slaves, the vast majority of citizens of Ilium have their livelihoods controlled by a ruling elite. Like slaves, the citizens can expect their children to wind up in the same circumstances they themselves experience. And like slaves, the citizens have no hope of change except through armed resistance.

We also see the wisdom of the shah when he recognizes how vast institutions like the army are similar no matter where they appear. When visiting the camp of Pfc. Elmo C. Hacketts, Jr., the shah comments that "it would be easier to move the Himalayas than to change the Army" (71). The shah shows himself as remarkably like other distinguished visitors Dr. Halyard has guided around the country when he begins to proposition pretty American women. While Halyard "had hopefully told himself that the Shah really was different from his other guests in this respect, different from the French and Bolivians and Czechs and Japanese and Panamanians and Yaps and . . ." (229), he is forced to come to the conclusion that this is not the case: "But no. The Shah, too, was now getting curious about American-type women" (229). Finally, we see that the shah is also not that much different from the Americans when Khashdrahr Miasma, his nephew and interpreter, tells President Jonathan Lynn about the Kolhouri belief that one day a wise god will come among them and end all suffering on earth. What have the Americans done with EPICAC XIV and the other machines except build a God to worship whom they hope and believe will end all suffering on Earth?

While *Player Piano* condemns the overly simplistic views of history and progress represented by the managers and engineers of Ilium, Lasher and the leaders of the Ghost Shirt Society are depicted as having a somewhat deeper understanding of the past. The very name the group has chosen for itself—the Ghost Shirt Society—evokes Native American culture, as the Organization does at the Meadows, but in a way that does not omit the history of atrocity practiced against Indians by the U.S. government. The group's name is meant specifically to suggest the painfulness of the past. Lasher explains the 19th-century Indian Ghost Dance ritual to Paul by pointing out that "The white man had broken promise after promise to the Indians, killed off most of the game, taken most of the Indians' land, and handed the Indians bad beatings every time they'd offered any resistance" (272). The Ghost Dance, Lasher continues, "was the last, desperate defense of the old values" in what had become "a white man's world" (273). While the actor at the Meadows pretends that the Organization has retained Indian values, Lasher

and the other social revolutionaries recognize the significant changes that history brought to the Indians.

That is not to say, however, that Vonnegut presents the Ghost Shirt leaders as perfect or as invincible. Finnerty, for instance, after spending only a short period of time in Homestead, adopts the "rough, swashbuckling mannerisms" of the Homesteaders and seems to Paul "glaringly synthetic" (139), as mechanical and robotic in his actions as Anita, who plays the role of the perfect wife. And in his adulation of Lasher, Finnerty is depicted as a disciple willing to turn his own thinking over to that of his chosen leader, as he struggles "to remain intellectually as one with the dynamic Lasher" (314). Even Paul, for all his thoughtfulness and intelligence, is an imperfect character. Although he largely blames Anita for the emptiness of their marriage, Vonnegut shows that there is plenty of blame to go around. Readers sense the validity of Anita's emotional outburst when Paul confronts her at the Meadows, and she sobs that she "wasn't any damn use" to Paul at all and that she is "sick of being treated like a machine" (237). In addition, Paul is often passive, allowing himself to be swayed by whoever he is speaking to at the time, whether it is the falsely paternal Kroner selling Organization values to him, Anita encouraging his ambition, or Lasher or Finnerty condemning social injustice. While Paul is in jail after the police raid on the Ghost Shirt Society, Vonnegut writes, "Through all his adventures, he had been a derelict, tossed this way, then that. He had yet to lay a firm hand on the tiller" (288).

Paul begins to change significantly during his experiences in jail, however. When he discovers that his old rival for the Pittsburgh promotion, Fred Garth, is being held in the adjoining cell, "an exotic emotion welled up within him" (289). For the first time in his life, Paul "was sharing profound misfortune with another human being" (289). This shared misfortune allows Paul to feel a warmth for Garth that he had never felt for anyone in his life before, not even Anita or Kroner. Only after experiencing this deep fellow-feeling is Paul able to act decisively. Later, when Kroner comes to visit Paul in jail, his previous moral murkiness has cleared up. He has reached a "fork in the road" that "every child older than six" not only knew about, but also "knew what the good guys did here, and what the bad guys did here . . . Bad guys turned informer. Good guys didn't—no matter when, no matter what" (293). Paul decides to be a "good guy" when, in answer to Kroner's question about who the leader of the Ghost Shirt really is, he replies, "I am" (293). Often described as an existentialist writer, Vonnegut shows here a basic tenet of EXISTENTIAL-ISM: the idea that humans must continue to act in an absurd world filled with awful choices, even with no assurance that their actions will have the intended results. When Paul asserts to Kroner that he is the radical group's leader, that "I am" is also a testament to his individuality, his insistence that he is a person, not simply a machine, a cog designed to help run the Organization more effectively.

But Vonnegut also understands that when humans act decisively, when they become individuals as Paul has done in the jail scene with Kroner, they are still fallible and subject to human frailties. Nowhere in his work does Vonnegut present a true hero or even a true villain. All of Vonnegut's characters are motivated by complex mixtures of sordid and altruistic impulses. Paul Proteus is no exception. During the trial scene at the end of the novel, when Paul gets to make his speech about how the machines "have robbed the American people of liberty and the pursuit of happiness" (296), the prosecutor argues that Paul's loyalty to the Ghost Shirt Society is motivated as much by his unresolved hatred of his father as it is by his impulse to do good for the oppressed Homesteaders. When accused by the prosecutor of harboring an OEDI-PUS COMPLEX—the subconscious desire to kill one's own father—Paul cannot deny the charge. Yet, he argues that he should not be condemned for such a motive: "I suspect," he points out, "that all people are motivated by something pretty sordid" (299). In fact, Paul continues, "Sordid things, for the most part, are what make human beings, my father included, move. That's what it is to be human, I'm afraid" (299). Rather than condemn the sordidness of human motivations, Vonnegut seems to embrace human frailty. The Ghost Shirt letter points out that humans, to be happy, must feel useful, that

they must be engaged in meaningful enterprises, despite their imperfections. Imperfection, in fact, is one of the qualities celebrated as a virtue in the Ghost Shirt letter, along with frailty, inefficiency, and "brilliance followed by stupidity" because these are the qualities that describe human beings, and "Man is a creation of God" (286).

Thus, it should be no surprise that the Ghost Shirt revolution turns out as messy and imperfect as it does. When the rioters begin destroying the machines, they cannot be stopped; the "good die with the bad—the flush toilets with the automatic lathe controls" (311). In fact, according to Professor von Neumann, the destruction "has all the characteristics of a lynching" though it is on "such a big scale" that the professor supposes "genocide is closer" as an analogy (311). The true illogic of human activity is asserted, though, when we see Bud Calhoun begin to repair an Orange-O machine in the last few pages of the novel. Despite their previous rampage against machines, a crowd gathers around Bud, cheering him on as he manages to get the drink dispenser back in working order, even though "no one in the whole country . . . could stomach the stuff" (317). Finnerty and Paul, as young engineers helping create the nightmare that the crowd seems to be rebuilding in the Orange-O scene, are not so different from anyone else. When Finnerty tells Paul that those years were the happiest he had ever experienced, Paul replies, "Most fascinating game there is, keeping things from staying the way they are" (313).

The failure of the revolution is certainly no surprise to Lasher, who understands from the beginning much of what Paul comes to learn. "It doesn't matter if we win or lose, Doctor," Lasher explains to Paul at the end, "The important thing is that we tried. For the record, we tried!" (315). Again, in an existentialist sense, the men have exercised their freedom, choosing to act, despite their knowledge (at least Lasher's knowledge) that they will be doomed to fail. Lasher further describes this behavior as true morality when the desk he is behind seems to transform into a pulpit. "Revolutions aren't my main line of business," he tells Paul, "I'm a minister, Doctor, remember? First and last, an enemy of the Devil, a man of God!" (315). On the novel's final page, then, when all four leaders of the failed revolution make a toast "to the record," Paul studies Lasher carefully, realizing that the ex-minister is "a lifelong trafficker in symbols," and that "he had created the revolution as a symbol, and was now welcoming the opportunity to die as one" (320). When Vonnegut has Paul realize the importance of symbolism here, he is making a comment on the nature of art itself, as he does much more overtly in some of his later novels, especially *Slaughterhouse-Five* and *Breakfast of Champions*.

For Vonnegut, art, which makes meaning through symbols, is something that makes humans particularly human. The "player piano" of the novel's title suggests an attempt to mechanize art, but such mechanization drains the music of its meaning and beauty. As Rudy Hertz notes, the player piano "Makes you feel kind of creepy" as it delivers "exactly five cents worth of joy" (38). The machine stands in contrast to Ed Finnerty who, with his astounding intuition, is a "top-flight pianist" (41). At the Meadows, the soullessness of a society that utilizes art strictly for propaganda purposes is evident. There's no doubt that art affects people intensely. When Paul had first seen a play at the Meadows as a teenager, "he had been struck full force by its sublime clarity and simplicity" (211), and his faith in the Organization is restored. Yet, as an adult viewing the Sky Manager play, Paul realizes that true art should be complex and layered rather than presenting an overly "simple picture" like the "silly playlet" he has just witnessed (212). This point is driven home when the pretty dark-skinned woman talks about her writer husband later in the novel. In the brave new world of the managers and engineers of Ilium, novels are kept purposefully short and dumbed-down, and are not allowed to have themes that challenge the status quo. Vonnegut could be describing *Player Piano* itself when the woman explains that her husband's novel "had an anti-machine theme" (233). While art may not solve the world's problems any more than the Ghost Shirt Society's failed revolution does, Vonnegut closes his novel with a plea to recognize the importance of symbols in human life, and thus provides a justification for his own project of creating complex and richly layered literary art.

CHARACTERS AND RELATED ENTRIES

Alfy (see Tucci, Alfy)

Baer Along with Anthony Kroner, Baer administers the eastern division of the National Industrial, Commercial, Communications, Foodstuffs, and Resources Organization. Small, nervous, and "unconvincingly extroverted" (47), Baer is an excellent engineer who remains unengaged in moral questions. He seems to agree enthusiastically with whatever is said to him and with whoever is speaking at the time. Surprisingly, we discover that, at the end of the novel, after reading the Ghost Shirt Society letter signed by Paul Proteus, Baer walks out of his job at the Organization in sympathy with the radical group.

Barbara and Martha Barbara and Martha are the two women known only by their first names whom Ed Finnerty and Paul Proteus flirt with in the saloon in Homestead. When the two find out that Paul and Finnerty are engineers, they become decidedly chilly and ask whether the men have come across the river to have "a good laugh at the dumb bunnies" (104). Paul passes out briefly from drinking too much, and when he wakes up, Barbara and Martha have gone.

Berringer, Dr. Dave Though readers never actually meet Dr. Dave Berringer, he is the father of Fred Berringer, and he turns out to be the real inventor of Checker Charley, the checker-playing machine beaten by Paul Proteus. Apparently a talented engineer, unlike his son who is barely competent, Dave Berringer had worked on the machine as a hobby for many years.

Berringer, Dr. Fred A new, young engineer at the Ilium Works, Dr. Fred Berringer is "a short, heavy, slit-eyed blond . . . a wealthy, extroverted, dull boy from a good family of engineers and managers in Minneapolis" (50). Though a poor engineer who barely squeaked through college, Berringer is hired at Ilium Works largely on the reputation of his father, Dr. Dave Berringer. At the party where Paul Proteus gives his speech early in the novel, Fred challenges Paul, the reigning checker champion at

Ilium for many years, to a match. When the checker game is to take place later that evening, Fred comes into the room, surrounded by a snickering group of young engineers leading a machine they introduce as Checker Charley. Though Paul wants to concede the contest, Finnerty urges him forward. Paul beats Checker Charley easily when the robot starts to short out and fall apart. Fred Berringer will hold a grudge against Paul for the rest of the novel, throwing in his lot with Dr. Lawson Shepherd and conspiring against Paul at the Meadows.

Bigley, Homer   Homer Bigley is the proprietor of the barber shop where the shah of Bratpuhr and his nephew, Khashdrahr Miasma, are taken for their first American haircuts. Bigley talks nonstop in a running monologue that lasts for more than five pages while he is cutting the shah's hair. His comments deal mostly with machines putting people out of business, how barbering is a skill best done by humans, and how he hopes to retire before the new barbering machines are brought on line.

Bromley, Milford S.   Milford S. Bromley is general of the armies, commanding officer when the shah of Bratpuhr tours the army camp where Private First Class Elmo C. Hacketts is stationed. When the shah is told that the soldiers are not slaves, he wonders how the officers get the men to do what they want them to. General Bromley replies, "Patriotism, damn it" (69). Undaunted, the shah comments upon leaving that "Americans have changed almost everything on earth . . . but it would be easier to move the Himalayas than to change the Army" (71).

Calhoun, Dr. Bud   Bud Calhoun is manager of the petroleum terminal at the Ilium Works, but at least at the beginning of the novel, he seems to spend most of his time lounging around Paul's office sweet-talking his girlfriend, Paul's secretary, Dr. Katharine Finch. A very American type, Bud Calhoun is an imaginative gadget maker who likes nothing better than inventing labor-saving devices. Ironically, Bud puts himself out of a job when he invents a machine to do his own work more efficiently. While Paul believes that Bud should really

be an engineering designer since that is what he does best, the machines report that Bud has no aptitude for design, so he is reassigned to lead a Reeks and Wreck crew. Bud, along with Katharine Finch, joins the Ghost Shirt Society when both show up at one of the radical group's meetings after Paul has been kidnapped. Bud repairs an Orange-O drink machine at the end of the novel, after the rioters have smashed and destroyed everything in their path. Despite their just expressed hatred of the machines, a group of Homesteaders gathers around Bud to cheer him on. When Paul and Finnerty witness the crowd's enthusiasm for rebuilding the machines, they perhaps recognize the futility of their attempt to change the world.

Dodge, Dr. Ned   Dr. Ned Dodge is manager of Proteus Park, the prefabricated housing development in Chicago, where the shah of Bratpuhr is taken to meet an average American family. Dr. Dodge leads the shah on his tour of the Hagstrohm home, speaking sharply to Edgar Hagstrohm when he behaves disrespectfully.

EPICAC   EPICAC is a giant super computer stored in Carlsbad Caverns that serves as the nerve center of the mechanized world. When the shah of Bratpuhr is taken to see the computer, he asks it a riddle, which the Kolhouri people believe will be answered one day by a wise god who will then end all suffering on earth. When the shah's question goes unanswered, he accuses the Americans of worshipping false gods. A computer named EPICAC also appears in the short story titled "Epicac," a contemporary retelling of the Cyrano de Bergerac myth, in which a computer writes poetry that a love-struck mathematician uses to woo a beautiful colleague. But EPICAC ends up falling in love with the same woman and blows all its circuits when the mathematician tells it that women cannot love machines.

Finch, Dr. Katharine   Paul's secretary at the Ilium Works, Dr. Katharine Finch is also the only woman to work there, which perhaps explains why she works in such a subservient position despite holding a doctorate degree. Katharine is the girlfriend of the ingenious gadget-maker Bud Calhoun, manager of the Ilium petroleum terminal. Distraught when Bud invents a machine to do his own job and is subsequently reassigned to the Reeks and Wrecks, Katharine shows up as a member of the Ghost Shirt Society, along with Bud, at the end of the novel.

Finnerty, Dr. Edward Ed Finnerty came to Ilium as a young engineer with Paul Proteus and Lawson Shepherd. Five years before the novel's start, though, Finnerty was promoted to a position on the National Industrial Planning Board in Washington, D.C., where he has lived since then. A social rebel known as much for his unkempt appearance as his brilliance, Finnerty, unlike Paul and most of the other engineers and managers, comes from a dubious social background. According to Kroner, one of the bosses of the Organization, Finnerty "was a mutant, born of poor and stupid parents" (40). Paul speculates that Finnerty's womanizing, his overdrinking, and his refusal to keep up appearances may be a deliberate attempt to insult the engineers and managers of Ilium, along with their "immaculate wives" (40). Finnerty's return to Ilium on the night of Paul's speech sets the novel's plot into motion. Finnerty tells Paul he has quit his prestigious Washington job in disgust, fanning the flames of Paul's own dissatisfaction. Finnerty takes Paul to Homestead the night they meet the Reverend James J. Lasher. Fascinated by Lasher and his arguments condemning the machine economy, Finnerty leaves the saloon with him, telling Paul he has chosen to stay with Lasher rather than with Paul and Anita. Later Finnerty emerges as one of the key leaders of the Ghost Shirt Society. As the four leaders prepare to turn themselves in at the end of the novel, Paul speculates that Finnerty has gotten what he wanted from the revolution: "a chance to give a savage blow to a close little society that made no comfortable place for him" (320).

Frascati, Lou Lou Franscati, now deceased, had been the husband of Marion and the best friend of Edgar R. B. Hagstrohm, the average man chosen for the shah of Bratpuhr to meet. After Lou's death, Marion and Edgar begin having an affair, despite Edgar's marriage to Wanda Hagstrohm.

Frascati, Marion The widow of Lou Frascati, Marion is carrying on an affair with Edgar R. B. Hagstrohm, the statistically average man who had been her husband's best friend. When Edgar loses control later in the novel, blowtorches his suburban home, and goes to her house stark naked, Marion refuses to run away to the woods with him.

Garth, Fred Paul Proteus's chief competitor for the Pittsburgh promotion, Fred Garth is manager of the Buffalo Works and a much older man than Paul. Garth is a steady and reliable but unimaginative worker who has achieved his current position mostly by being the fallback safe choice for promotion throughout his career. Awkwardly, the two men are assigned to be roommates at the Meadows, where Garth tells Paul about his oldest son who has not done well on his General Classification Exams, but is being given another chance to take the test. Later, when Paul is arrested after the police raid on the Ghost Shirt Society meeting, he discovers, much to his surprise, that Fred Garth occupies the adjoining cell. Garth has been arrested for damaging the symbolic oak tree at the Meadows after learning that his son had again failed the Classification Exams. At this news, Paul begins to feel very warmly toward Fred Garth. As Vonnegut explains, "For the first time in the whole of his orderly life he was sharing profound misfortune with another human being" (289). In prison, Garth is unconcerned about potential punishment since the crime he is charged with, "attempted treeslaughter," is so patently ludicrous.

Gelhorne, Dr. Francis Eldgrin Doctor Francis Eldgrin Gelhorne is the successor of Paul Proteus's father as National Industrial, Commercial, Communications, Foodstuffs, and Resources director. Paul Proteus considers Gelhorne to be "the last of a race" (218) because he is a self-made man with no college background whom the machines would never allow to rise so far in the Organization in the novel's current time. Gelhorne comes to the Meadows to tell Paul about the plan in which he will appear to be fired from the Organization so that he can secretly infiltrate the Ghost Shirt Society.

Ghost Shirt Society   The Ghost Shirt Society is the secret revolutionary group started by the Reverend James J. Lasher. The group, whose name derives from the 19th-century Native American ghost dance ritual, plans to start a revolution by destroying the machinery that has put so many human beings out of work and wresting control of the economy from the ubiquitous Organization that currently oversees all manufacturing and production of goods. Dr. Paul Proteus is recruited by Lasher and his old friend Ed Finnerty to be a new Messiah who will draw attention to the society's cause. Although the Ghost Shirt Revolution fails at the novel's end, the society's leaders hope that it will continue to have symbolic significance.

Hacketts, Elmo C., Jr.   Elmo C. Hacketts, Jr. is a private in the army, participating in drill practice with his unit when the shah of Bratpuhr comes to visit the camp where he is stationed. Having chosen the army over the Reeks and Wrecks when his IQ scores disqualified him from all other work, Hacketts plays a bitter tape over and over in his head, reminding himself he has only 23 more years to serve, that he won't do anything not absolutely required of him, and dreaming of the day he'll be able to whip out his discharge notice and tell "some sonofabitching colonol or lieutenant or general" to "Kiss my ass, sonny" (68).

Hagstrohm, Edgar R. B.   Edgar R. B. Hagstrohm, named after his father's favorite author, EDGAR RICE BURROUGHS—the creator of Tarzan—is the "typical *Takaru*" or average man chosen by personnel machines for the shah of Bratpuhr to visit. Hagstrohm is married to Wanda, has two children, and lives in a suburban home in Chicago. In fact, he is "statistically average in every respect save for the number of his initials" (156). Hagstrohm is even typical in that he is a married man on his second extramarital affair, which is causing discord in his marriage. Later, Paul Proteus sees a photo of Edgar Hagstrohm at the police station. The brief biography accompanying the photo explains that, after

having cut up his suburban home with a blowtorch, Hagstrohm went naked to the home of his mistress, Marion Frascati, and demanded that she come to the woods with him. When she refused, he ran into a bird sanctuary and eluded police by dropping onto a passing freight train.

Hagstrohm, Edgar, Jr.   The son of Edgar R. B. and Wanda Hagstrohm, Edgar, Jr. understands that something is wrong with his parents' marriage. When Edgar, Sr. leaves the house to see his mistress after the shah's visit, Edgar, Jr. makes a special effort to comfort his mother, choosing to stay home and watch television with her rather than go to the ball game as he had planned.

Hagstrohm, Wanda   Wanda Hagstrohm is the wife of Edgar R. B. Hagstrohm, chosen as a perfect example of an average man for the shah of Bratpuhr's visit. Overweight and bored because machines do all her housework for her, Wanda lives for her children and husband. Though she knows about his affair with the widow Marion Frascati, who had been married to Edgar's best friend, Wanda is still understanding and loving to Edgar, blaming herself for no longer interesting her husband.

Halyard, Dr. Ewing J.   Employed by the U.S. Department of State, Dr. Ewing J. Halyard, "a heavy, florid, urbane gentleman of forty" (26), is the guide who leads the shah of Bratpuhr on his tour of America. Halyard is somewhat exasperated by the shah's tendency to overlook his explanations of how the country functions. While Halyard patiently explains that the government does not own the machines of the Ilium Works and elsewhere, but simply taxes them and redistributes the income, the shah confidently and astutely proclaims the system to be communism. After taking the shah to numerous spots around the country, including a visit to Carlsbad Cavern to see the famous EPICAC XIV computer, Dr. Halyard receives a letter from his undergraduate alma mater, CORNELL UNIVERSITY, informing him that he never passed his physical education exam, and thus his degree is invalid. To retain his job,

Halyard must return to Cornell to take the test he skipped 17 years previously. Halyard is dismayed when Cornell football coach Dr. Harold Roseberry pulls out a letter written by a disgruntled alumni to the president of Cornell in Roseberry's first year at the university. The letter complains bitterly about the shortcomings of the new football coach. Halyard's doom is sealed when it is disclosed that the letter had been written by Halyard himself, and that Roseberry had saved it for all the intervening years. Roseberry lets Halyard know that he, not one of his assistants, will be personally administering the makeup exam. When Halyard fails, he is stripped not only of his undergraduate degree, but his subsequent degrees and his job with the State Department as well. To add insult to injury, the machines who detected the error, ever-vigilant, start fraud proceedings against him.

Harold Paul Proteus's cellmate when he is taken to prison late in the novel, Harold is described as a "small elegant young Negro . . . who was in jail for petty sabotage" (288). Harold's crime was smashing a traffic safety education box that had been attached to a lamp post outside his bedroom window. Driven crazy by the box's repeated tape-recorded safety warnings, blared at all hours of the day, Harold is unapologetic about his crime. Though he is told he can leave jail if he says he is sorry, Harold refuses because he insists he *isn't* sorry.

Harrison, Dr. Edmund The young engineer Paul Proteus meets at lunch at the Meadows, Doctor Edmund Harrison sees through the phony theatrics and shenanigans of the Organization much as Paul himself does. Dr. Harrison brings Paul a drink after he gets kicked out of the bar at the Meadows, and later appears at The Dutch, the bar near Cornell University, where he encourages Buck Young, the promising young football player, to give up his dreams of becoming a manager or engineer and instead choose a life devoted to the gridiron.

Haycox Mr. Haycox is the member of the Reeks and Wrecks assigned as caretaker on the Gottwald farm that Paul Proteus buys. When Paul comes to

look at the farm, the cynical Haycox ridicules the fact that both he and real estate agent Dr. Pond use the title of "Doctor." At the end of the visit, Paul discovers that Mr. Haycox's father used to own the farm, but sold it to Gottwald, with the understanding that his son could stay on as caretaker for the rest of his life. Paul reassures Haycox that he will keep things as they are and retain the old caretaker's services. At the end of the novel, Haycox shows up again as a member of the Ghost Shirt Society.

Hertz, Rudy Rudy Hertz, though near retirement, was the best machinist at the Ilium Works when the young engineers Paul Proteus, Ed Finnerty, and Lawson Shepherd arrived fresh out of college 13 years before the novel begins. Their first project was to record the movements Rudy made in his work, so that they could be duplicated by the machine the three engineers constructed to replace workers like Rudy. Proud to be chosen out of the thousand machinists working in Ilium at the time, Rudy never expresses resentment or even seems to fully understand that his cooperation in the project has helped put all human machinists out of work. Paul meets Rudy again when he drives to the saloon in Homestead to buy Irish whiskey for Ed Finnerty. Excited at seeing Paul, Rudy announces his identity to the large crowd in the saloon, many of whom, unlike Rudy, do understand that engineers like Paul have put them out of work. Rudy, in fact, introduces Paul to the man with thick glasses who will later turn out to be the Reverend Lasher.

Holdermann, Bill Bill Holdermann, a "shaggy, worn-out nobody from the INDIANAPOLIS Works" (210) is acknowledged at the Meadows as the author of the propaganda play performed on the night of Paul Proteus's meeting with Kroner, Gelhorne, and MacCleary.

Homestead Homestead is the ghetto where the vast majority of people in Ilium, New York, live. The city itself is divided into three parts: managers and engineers and bureaucrats live in the northwest portion, machines dominate the northeast, and Homestead is in the south. The people of Homestead, who do not have high enough IQs to be given a coveted job overseeing the machines that do most of the work in America, have no meaningful occupation. Most of them are assigned by the government to perform tedious, fairly useless service in either the Reconstruction and Reclamation Corps or the army. These are dead-end jobs that offer a bleak future to the Homesteaders and their children. But it is also in Homestead that the Ghost Shirt Society, a radical group bent on destroying machines and reforming the social order, is founded.

Ilium Works   The Ilium Works is the name of the company in *Player Piano* where Dr. Paul Proteus is employed.

Kolhouri Sect   The shah of Bratpuhr is said to be the spiritual leader of 6 million members of the Kolhouri sect, a fictional ethnic and religious group from an unidentified part of Asia.

Kroner, Anthony   One of the administrators, along with Baer, of the entire eastern division of the National Industrial, Commercial, Communications, Foodstuffs, and Resources Organization, Anthony Kroner was also the closest friend of Paul Proteus's father. A large and kindly man, though stern when necessary, Kroner considers himself a father to all the engineers under him. In Kroner's presence, Paul feels like a child again, and is easily induced to share his concerns about the Organization when Kroner invites him to dinner one evening. Betraying the ruthlessness carefully hidden under his kindly exterior, Kroner expects Paul to betray Ed Finnerty and Reverend Lasher. When Paul refuses to do so, proclaiming that *he* is the leader of the Ghost Shirts, he not only breaks with Kroner and the Organization, but finally understands "what his father had known—what it was to belong and believe" (293).

Kroner, Janice ("Mom")   The wife of Dr. Anthony Kroner, Paul Proteus's boss in the organization, Janice Kroner encourages all the young engineers and their wives to call her "Mom." Described as "a fat repository or truisms, adages, and hom-

ilies" (123), Mom appears at social functions to dispense advice to the wives while Kroner confers with their husbands. While Mom dislikes Finnerty, who refuses to confide in her as she wishes, she does like Paul who *had* occasionally confided in her as a young man, though he seems somewhat repulsed by her now.

Lasher, Reverend James J.   The enigmatic and dynamic leader of the Ghost Shirt Society, James J. Lasher is first seen in the saloon at Homestead the night Paul Proteus goes there to buy Irish whiskey. He is the man with the thick glasses introduced to Paul by Rudy Hertz, who talks about his son being unable to find a job. Not until a few nights later when Paul returns to Homestead with Ed Finnerty does he discover the man is the Reverend James J. Lasher, an ex-Protestant minister and anthropologist with a master's degree who lectures Paul and Ed about the bad uses that scientific knowledge has been put to since the war. Finnerty is especially inspired by Lasher and leaves the saloon to stay with him rather than with Paul. Later in the novel, when the Ghost Shirt revolution fails, Lasher is the only one of the four leaders unsurprised by their lack of success. When Paul asks what was the sense of trying to change things if Lasher knew they did not stand a chance, he replies, "It doesn't matter if we win or lose, Doctor. The important thing is that we tried. For the record, we tried!" (315). He then reminds Paul that he is a minister, a man of God, who must fight evil when he sees it. The leaders drink a toast "to the record" before marching forward to turn themselves in at the end of the book.

Lubbock, Luke   Paul Proteus first sees Luke Lubbock marching in a parade in Homestead. Described as a "florid, serious old man" (88), Luke is dressed in a turban and pantaloons and carefully cradles an elephant tusk inscribed with mysterious symbols. A member of various Elks and Moose lodges, Luke finds meaning in life by joining organizations and dressing up in elaborate uniforms. He keeps reappearing throughout the novel, showing up as a busboy working at the Meadows, and finally, at the end of the novel, as a secret member of the Ghost Shirt Society, dressed as an Indian.

Lynn, Jonathan Jonathan Lynn, whose real name is Alfred Planck, is president of the United States. Described as "boyish, tall, beautiful, and disarming," Lynn was elected president not for his brains—he didn't even finish high school—but for his looks and his ability to serve as a figurehead on ceremonial occasions. The dedication ceremony of EPICAC XIV is the only scene in the novel in which Lynn appears.

MacCleary, Dr. Lou The executive manager of National Industrial Security, Dr. Lou MacCleary is present at the meeting at the Meadows when Kroner and Dr. Francis Eldgrin Gelhorne tell Paul Proteus about their plan for him to secretly infiltrate the Ghost Shirt Society.

Martha See Barbara and Martha, above.

Matheson Although Matheson never enters the story in person, we find out that he is Ilium's manager in charge of testing and placement. When Paul Proteus first meets the Reverend James J. Lasher in the Homestead saloon, he promises to call Matheson about obtaining a job for Lasher's son. Described as a "powerful bureaucrat who went about his job with the air of a high priest" (36), Matheson is disliked by Paul.

McCloud See Purdy and McCloud, below.

Meadows, the The Meadows is the name given to an outdoor retreat center where employees of the National Industrial, Commercial, Communications, Foodstuffs, and Resources Organization are taken each year to build company spirit. At the Meadows, employees are organized into four teams and encouraged to compete with one another in silly games. At night they watch hokey plays which spout company propaganda.

Miasma, Khashdrahr Nephew to the shah of Bratpuhr, Khashdrahr Miasma is also serving as the shah's translator on his tour of America. A polite and easily embarrassed young man who has never before been outside of the shah's palace, Khashdrahr at times mistranslates the shah's com-

ments to avoid awkwardness for everyone involved. For instance, when the shah, drunk on Sumklish, begins to proposition American women on the street, Khasdrahr explains unhappily that "Shah says it is a nice day" (228). At the end of the novel, after having been mistaken for Ghost Shirt Society members and driven to the Griffin Boulevard roadblock, Khashdrahr Miasma and the shah are last seen sleeping in a ditch by the side of the road just before the revolution organizers march forward to turn themselves in.

Orange-O Orange-O is a drink, dispensed by vending machines, which almost no one can stomach. Yet, after the machine-destroying riots induced by the Ghost Shirt Society leave masses of wreckage at the end of the novel, a group gathers around Bud Calhoun as he works to repair an Orange-O dispenser. Perversely, the crowd cheers when the machine starts working again. Although they despise Orange-O itself, they appreciate Bud's ingenuity in repairing the machine.

Pond, Dr. Dr. Pond is the real estate agent Paul Proteus deals with when he decides to buy the Gottwald farm. Initially excited about selling the piece of property, which has been on the market for years, Dr. Pond soon has second thoughts and refuses to sell the farm to Paul, telling him it is a matter of integrity. While Paul is at first amused, he realizes that to Dr. Pond the refusal to sell the farm *really* is a matter of integrity: "This pipsqueak of a man in a pipsqueak job had pipsqueak standards he was willing to lay his pipsqueak life down for" (148). When Paul assures him that he intends to farm only as a hobby, Dr. Pond, with great relief, relents and agrees to sell the property.

Proteus, Anita Paul's ambitious wife, Anita, had been his secretary at the Ilium Works during the war years. Paul married Anita after she told him she was pregnant as the result of an intimate war victory celebration between the two in an abandoned office. Ironically, though, Anita turns out to be barren. Unable to have children, she turns her energies toward advancing Paul's career in the organization and decorating her home with carefully constructed replicas of American colonial furnishings. Beautiful, sophisticated, yet insecure, Anita begins an affair with Dr. Lawson Shepherd as Paul's attention wanders from both her and his job. As the only engineer's wife in Ilium without any college background at all, Anita's ambitions are at least partly prompted by her fear of Homestead and the people who live there. With a lower IQ than Paul and the other elites, Anita realizes that if she had not married Paul, she herself could have easily ended up as a Homesteader.

Proteus, Dr. George Dr. George Proteus, Paul's father, was the first director of the National Industrial, Commercial, Communications, Foodstuffs, and Resources Organization, a position Vonnegut tells us, "approached in importance only by the presidency of the United States" (10). Having played a key role in winning the recent war, Dr. Proteus, who died before the novel begins, is revered by the Organization's hierarchy. Paul, though, has an ambivalent attitude toward his father. Although he is expected by his bosses in the organization to achieve a similar stature to the great man, and though he has been working toward that goal all his life, Paul seems to secretly hate his father and what he stands for. At his trial for sabotage late in the novel, Paul is accused of suffering from an Oedipus Complex—of having a subconscious rivalry with and desire to kill his father. Reluctantly, hooked up to lie detector machines, Paul acknowledges at least the partial justice of this accusation, arguing that sordid motivations compel most human activity.

Proteus, Dr. Paul The novel's protagonist, Dr. Paul Proteus is the manager of the Ilium Works. Son of former National Industrial, Commercial, Communications, Foodstuffs, and Resources director, Dr. George Proteus, Paul is being groomed for big things in the Organization. Despite his early success, Paul is vaguely dissatisfied with his life at the beginning of the novel. His marriage to his wife, Anita, whom he proposed to after she told him she was pregnant (with a child who never actually materialized), is unfulfilling. He is also having moral questions about his job: Has his success come only at the expense of the vast majority of common

people, regulated to dreary existences in Homestead? Goaded by his old friend Ed Finnerty and by the Reverend James J. Lasher, a social radical, Paul decides to quit his job with the Organization. Ironically, before he can announce his resignation, his bosses at the company put into motion a plan to pretend to fire Paul so that he can infiltrate Lasher's group, the Ghost Shirt Society, and betray the group's leaders. Kidnapped by the Ghost Shirts, Paul half-willingly, half-reluctantly allows himself to be molded into the new Messiah the group desires. Though he gets to make many astute political and philosophical statements during his trial for intended sabotage, the revolution incited by Paul, Lasher, and Finnerty eventually fails, and the novel ends with Paul, along with the other leaders, turning himself into the police.

Purdy and McCloud Purdy and McCloud are two football linemen who play for Cornell University. They are drinking at The Dutch, the university bar, when Dr. Harold Roseberry, the head Cornell football coach, tries to recruit Buck Young. At the time of the novel, college football players are payed huge sums of money, play well past the usual age for college students, and make no pretense of an interest in academics. Purdy at age 37 and McCloud at 36 are no exceptions. Unbeknownst to the two aging linemen, Dr. Roseberry plans to sell them to HARVARD UNIVERSITY, whose football team has a reputation of buying any player that comes cheap.

Reeks and Wrecks Reeks and Wrecks is the nickname given to members of the Reconstruction and Reclamation Corps. Because most meaningful work is now done by machines in the novel, the vast masses of ordinary people, those without high enough IQs to qualify them to join the elite group of managers and engineers who oversee the machines, have no meaningful way to spend their time. Therefore, the government has assigned them dead-end jobs, either as Reeks and Wrecks or in the army.

Roseberry, Dr. Harold Dr. Harold Roseberry is the head football coach at Cornell University, who we see in the university bar trying to recruit Buck Young to the team. Cornell also turns out to be the alma mater of Dr. Ewing J. Halyard, who wrote an angry letter about Roseberry's shortcomings as a coach when he was first hired several years previously. When Halyard finds out that his degree will be revoked unless he makes up a physical education test he never took as an undergraduate, Dr. Roseberry decides to administer the test personally and gain his revenge on Dr. Halyard.

Second Industrial Revolution *Player Piano* is set in a period that follows a second Industrial Revolution in America. During this second revolution, machines have taken on many of the routine mental tasks previously done by human workers, just as they had taken over much manual labor in factories during the actual Industrial Revolution (called the "First Industrial Revolution" in the novel). *Player Piano* explores the aftereffects of this second revolution, when masses of people are put out of work and crowded into ghettoes where they feel useless and bored.

Shah of Bratpuhr The ancient and wizened spiritual leader of the Kolhouri sect, the shah of Bratpuhr is visiting America as the guest of the U.S. Department of State. He is in the country to "see what he could learn in the most powerful nation on earth for the good of his people" (26). While Dr. Ewing J. Halyard, the shah's guide, is frustrated by the shah's tendency to interpret what he sees in terms of his own culture, readers nevertheless see the truth of some of the shah's pronouncements. For instance, he refuses to call the workers he sees "citizens," naming them instead *Takaru*, a word that means "slave" in the shah's language. Yet the shah turns out to be not all that different from Halyard's other guests when, with seven swigs of Sumklish, the sacred Kolhouri drink, under his belt, he begins to proposition pretty American women. The last view of the shah in the novel occurs when he and his nephew, having been mistaken for recalcitrant Ghost Shirt Society members because of their colorful dress and driven by Luke Lubbock to the front lines of the rioting, are sleeping tangled together in a trench in the midst of concertina wire, sandbags, and abandoned police cars at the Griffin Boulevard roadblock.

Shepherd, Dr. Lawson Although Dr. Lawson Shepherd came to the Ilium Works as a young engineer with Paul Proteus and Ed Finnerty 13 years previously, he now considers himself a rival and enemy of Paul's. Second-in-command to Paul at the Works, Shepherd longs to beat Paul out for a promotion to manager of the Pittsburgh Works. A competitive and jealous man, Shepherd believes that Paul is constantly scheming against him, as he is against Paul. He believes his fortunes are looking up, though, when he is named as one of the team captains at the Meadows. Unlike Paul, Shepherd takes his position as captain very seriously, training diligently in the days leading up to the retreat. At the Meadows, readers discover that Shepherd has been carrying on an affair with Paul's wife, Anita. When Anita leaves Paul after his disgrace at the Meadows, she announces that she is going to marry Dr. Shepherd as soon as she can get a divorce.

Sumklish Sumklish is the sacred drink of the Kolhouri sect, which Khashdrahr Miasma carries in a hip flask for the shah of Bratpuhr.

Third Industrial Revolution Dr. Paul Proteus speculates that America, having already experienced a first and second industrial revolution, in which machines took over the muscle work and routine mental tasks from human beings, is in the midst of yet another major industrial upheaval. In this third Industrial Revolution, Paul conjectures, machines such as EPICAC will replace the need for human thinking completely.

Tucci, Alfy Alfy Tucci is a man Paul Proteus meets in the saloon in Homestead; he makes a living by guessing the names of songs performed by musical groups on television with the volume turned all the way down. Paul is impressed by Alfy's skill as well his enterprising spirit. Later in the novel, Alfy appears as a cook at the Meadows. Unlike Luke Lubbock and other Homesteaders, though, Alfy never joins the Ghost Shirt Society. Finnerty explains that this is because he never joined anything and never will. According to Lasher, Alfy sees himself as "the great American individual . . . the embodiment of liberal thought throughout the ages" (281–282).

Tucci, Joe   The teenage brother of Alfy Tucci, Joe Tucci is depicted trying to learn how to play a matchstick counting game in the Homestead saloon late in the novel so that he will have a way to support himself other than the army or the Reeks and Wrecks. Joe, however, is not as skillful as his older brother, Alfy, who has a knack for determining songs played on the television with the volume turned all the way down. When Joe wants to give up, Alfy admonishes him to keep practicing since "anybody by the name of Tucci stands on his own two feet" (255).

Unnamed Dark-skinned Woman   A very pretty, dark-skinned woman who is never named in the novel is propositioned by the shah of Bratpuhr after he has drunk too much Sumklish. Although she does not seem like a prostitute to Dr. Ewing J. Halyard, she gets in the car with the shah, seeming to understand that he wants more than simply to give her a ride. She is desperately trying to earn money to support herself and her husband, a writer who has just completed a novel the machines disapprove of, and who has subsequently been assigned a job in public relations. The woman tells the men in the car that her husband prefers her to go out on the street rather than accept a job in public relations, because "he's one of the few men on earth with a little self-respect left" (234). After hearing her story, the shah gives the woman a ruby ring and sends her on her way.

Unnamed Judge   An unnamed judge oversees proceedings at Paul Proteus's trial for sabotage. Although the judge sternly insists on order in his court, the trial is interrupted when a brickbat shatters a courtroom window, signaling the onset of the Ghost Shirt Revolution.

Unnamed Prosecutor   At Paul Proteus's trial near the end of the novel, an unnamed prosecutor accuses him of harboring an Oedipus complex,

arguing that Paul's involvement in the Ghost Shirt Society is motivated by hatred of his father rather than by the desire to change society or help the Homesteaders. Paul does not deny the charges, conceding that all human behavior grows out of fairly sordid motivations.

van Curler, Dr. Ormand   When Paul Proteus decides to purchase the Gottwald farm, he speculates about how much farming has changed in the past years. In the present day, Dr. Ormand van Curler manages the farming of the entire country, relying on only 100 men, but millions of dollars worth of machinery. Much to his relief, Paul remembers that the Gottwald farm is *not* part of van Curler's system.

von Neumann, Professor Ludwig   A character from very late in the novel, Professor Ludwig von Neumann is one of the leaders of the Ghost Shirt Society. When Paul Proteus is brought to his first meeting of the society, he immediately recognizes Professor von Neumann, a small, elderly man who used to teach political science at Union College in Schenectady. Paul had known von Neumann slightly in Ilium, since both had been members of the Ilium Historical Society before its building had been torn down to build an atomic reactor. When the Ghost Shirt revolution fails, Paul realizes that the whole enterprise had been an interesting social experiment to the professor. Paul speculates that von Neumann "had been less interested in achieving a premeditated end than in seeing what would happen with given beginnings" (320).

Wheeler, Sergeant Elm   Elm Wheeler was the army sergeant in charge of barber Homer Bigley's unit in the war. Readers hear about Wheeler during Bigley's running monologue while cutting the hair of the shah of Bratpuhr. Sergeant Elm Wheeler was killed in the war after he received a letter from his wife saying she had had a baby though he had not seen her for two years. After reading the letter, Sergeant Wheeler went wild, destroying two enemy machine gun nests and a mortar emplacement in his rage. As a result, he is posthumously awarded the Congressional Medal for bravery.

Young, Buck A star in intrafraternity football at Cornell University, Buck Young is more interested in studying to become an engineer or manager than in playing for the official Cornell team, even though college players at this time are payed fabulously well. He reluctantly meets head coach Dr. Harold Roseberry at The Dutch, the university bar, but agrees to play for the team only after a drunk Dr. Edmund Harrison, an engineer who had been at the Meadows, tells him how ridiculous and unfulfilling the lives led by managers and engineers really are.

FURTHER READING

Magome, Kiyoko. "The Player Piano and Musico-Cybernetic Science Fiction between the 1950s and the 1980s: Kurt Vonnegut and Philip K. Dick." *Extrapolation* 45, no. 4 (2004): 370–387.

Morse, Donald E. "Sensational Implications: Kurt Vonnegut's *Player Piano* (1952)." *AnaChronist* 6 (2000): 303–314.

Mustazza, Leonard. "The Machine Within: Mechanization, Human Discontent, and the Genre of Vonnegut's *Player Piano*." *Papers on Language and Literature* 25, no. 1 (1989): 99–113.

Player Piano. New York: Dell, 1974

Reid, Susan. "Kurt Vonnegut and American Culture: Mechanization and Loneliness in *Player Piano*." *Journal of the American Studies Association of Texas* 15 (1984): 46–51.

"Poor Little Rich Town"

A story that questions the value of progress when it comes to a small, traditional, close-knit community, "Poor Little Rich Town" was first published in *Collier's* magazine in October 1952. It was later reprinted in the collection *Bagombo Snuff Box.*

SYNOPSIS

When the Federal Apparatus Corporation decides to build its new company headquarters in ILIUM, New York, people in the neighboring village of Spruce Falls are excited, hoping the new construction will perk up the real estate market in their small depressed town. This seems to be the case when Newell Cady, efficiency expert and new vice president in the company, rents with the option to buy an old mansion in the village. In order to endear themselves to Cady, the townspeople elect him to be a full member of the fire department and also to be head judge of their annual Hobby Show. Yet, Cady brings with him new ideas about how to run things more efficiently in Spruce Falls. He vetoes purchasing a new fire truck, which members of the fire department had their hearts set on; he reorganizes the way the postmistress distributes mail; and he judges the town's hobby contest in a newfangled way, refusing to award prizes to everyone who enters. Eventually, knowing that Cady is next door in the post office, separated from the fire station by only a thin partition, the volunteer FIRE-MEN loudly discuss their decision that Cady's election to the fire department violates their by-laws, since the man has not lived in Spruce Falls the requisite three years. The story ends with things in the town returning to their previous status quo.

COMMENTARY

"Poor Little Rich Town" is a story that, like much of Vonnegut's work, questions whether unbridled progress is such a good thing. Possibly a response to popular literature of the day, especially the 1948 classic *Cheaper by the Dozen,* a memoir by Frank Gilbreth and Ernestine Gilbreth Carey based on their efficiency expert father, which celebrated American ingenuity and know-how, "Poor Little Rich Town" questions the results of just such ingenuity. Like Frank Gilbreth Sr. whose story was made into a hit movie in 1950, two years before Vonnegut published "Poor Little Rich Town," Newell Cady is an efficiency expert interested in reducing waste and increasing productivity. The villagers in Spruce Falls at first welcome Cady with open arms, hoping that his moving to the town will spur other Federal Apparatus Company executives to do the same, and they will be able to sell their decaying mansions. Upton Beaton, in fact, is the only Spruce Falls resident to warn of the dangers of giving away their traditions too easily. Unimpressed by the money that stands to be made (possibly because he has family wealth of his own), Beaton asks, "What is a village profited if it shall gain a real estate boom and lose its own soul?" (94).

The villagers soon learn that Beaton was right. In his efficiency mania, Newell Cady overlooks the human dimension of the villagers' relationships to one another. He is blind to the disappointment of Stanley Atkins and Ed Newcomb when he vetoes the village's purchase of a new fire truck, and his suggestion that Spruce Falls establish rural mail delivery completely overlooks the kindness that the villagers wish to do for Mrs. Dickie in supplying her with a job, as well as the gratitude they owe her for her Mr. Dickie sacrificing his life in a fire to save others. While Cady believes the villagers are "blinded by custom" (105), Beaton believes that Cady is himself blind because "he doesn't watch people's faces and doesn't give the blind credit for the senses they do have" (105). And these senses involve caring for their friends and neighbors. The story ends with the village reverting back to its status quo, but being sure to curb Newell Cady in a way that will not hurt his feelings. The firemen pretend they are forced to ask Cady to resign only because of their by-laws, and Ed Newcomb is careful to say, in the conversation that the men plan to have Cady overhear, that the villagers all like him and are proud he wants to live in Spruce Falls. In fact, the story ends with Upton Beaton declaring to the Ilium real estate agent that Newell Cady has "a good heart" and that the villagers are "all rooting for him" (107).

CHARACTERS AND RELATED ENTRIES

Atkins, Stanley Stanley Atkins is the Spruce Falls fire chief, who at first is enthusiastic about luring Newell Cady to buy a house in the tiny village. After witnessing some of the changes Cady implements in village life, however, especially his vetoing of the purchase of a new fire engine as an unnecessary expense, Atkins changes his mind about the man and works with Upton Beaton in a scheme to curb Cady's power.

Batsford, Ted Ted Batsford is an old-time resident of Spruce Falls who has been collecting string since the second Cleveland administration. When

Newell Cady judges the town's Hobby Show, however, Batsford is not awarded his usual blue ribbon in the category of string saving.

Beaton, Upton The "last of what had been the first family of Spruce Falls" (93), the aristocratic 65-year-old Upton Beaton warns against extending so many village privileges to newcomer Newell Cady. Yet, when Cady actually begins implementing changes in the town, Beaton encourages him, possibly to hasten the demise of his power in the village. At the end of the story, Beaton works with his former rival, Fire Chief Stanley Atkins, to take the village back from Newell Cady's control.

Brayton, Hal Hal Brayton is the grocer in the tiny village of Spruce Falls. After Newell Cady begins noticing inefficiencies in the town, Brayton stops "adding bills on paper sacks" (98) and buys an adding machine. He also moves his store counters around to improve traffic flow.

Cady, Newell Described as having "the polish, the wealth, the influence, and the middle-aged good looks of an idealized Julius Caesar" (91), Newell Cady is a vice president in the Federal Apparatus Corporation who rents a mansion in the tiny village of Spruce Falls, New York. Cady, who serves as an efficiency expert at the giant company, soon begins to apply his progressive principles to village life as well. In the end, the villagers manage to stop the changes implemented by Cady without hurting the man's feelings.

Dickie, Mrs. The old postmistress of Spruce Falls, Mrs. Dickie is used to sorting the mail inefficiently and has a hard time changing her ways when directed to do so by efficiency expert Newell Cady. Toward the end of the story, readers discover that Mrs. Dickie's old-fashioned method of mail delivery is tolerated because her husband had died in a fire while saving the lives of some villagers.

Federal Apparatus Corporation The Federal Apparatus Corporation decides to build its new company headquarters in Ilium, New York. The company's new vice president moves into the nearby small town of Spruce Falls and immediately begins to change the way the townspeople conduct business. The people, however, eventually find a way to retain the status quo without hurting the feeling of the giant corporation vice president.

Hobby Show Prizewinner   When Newell Cady judges the Spruce Falls Hobby Show, he upsets the custom of awarding first-prize ribbons to everyone who enters. Instead, he awards only one ribbon, to a woman who made "a petit-point copy of the cover of a woman's magazine" (101). The prizewinner is so embarrassed to be the only person awarded that she furtively takes her entry home late in the evening, leaving her blue ribbon behind.

Mansfield, Dave   When Ed Newcomb mentions that the old mansion owned by Stanley Atkins has termites and rot, Atkins is furious, fearing that someone might have overheard and he will be unable to sell the place. Upton Beaton, though, reassures the men that the only person outside is old Dave Mansfield, who "hasn't heard anything since his boiler blew up" (103).

Newcomb, Ed   Ed Newcomb is a villager in Spruce Falls who has served 20 years as secretary of the fire department. Newcomb is eager to keep Newell Cady in town and hopes to lure other executives from the Federal Apparatus Corporation as well, since he owns one of the village's decaying mansions and is eager to sell. But, like the other villagers, he changes his mind about Cady by the story's end.

Real Estate Man   An unnamed real estate man from the city of Ilium is disappointed at the end of the story when the Spruce Falls villagers seem to have lost interest in selling the town's decaying mansions to executives of the Federal Apparatus Corporation.

Spruce Falls   Spruce Falls is a tiny village that neighbors the much larger Ilium, New York. When a big-shot corporate executive and efficiency expert moves into the small town and starts trying

to change things, the villagers manage to outwit him and retain the status quo.

FURTHER READING

Bagombo Snuff Box. New York: Berkley Books, 2000
Reed, Peter. *The Short Fiction of Kurt Vonnegut.* Westport, Conn.: Greenwood Press, 1997.

"The Powder-Blue Dragon"

Initially published in *Cosmopolitan* magazine in November 1954, "The Powder Blue Dragon" was reprinted in the 1999 collection, *Bagombo Snuff Box.* In his coda to that collection, Vonnegut tells readers that rereading the original version of "The Powder-Blue Dragon" so upset him that he "virtually rewrote the denouement" (349) before he could help himself. Thus, along with two other stories in *Bagombo Snuff Box,* "The Powder-Blue Dragon," according to Vonnegut, is a faked fossil "on the order of Piltdown Man, half human being, half the orangutan" he used to be (349).

SYNOPSIS

Kiah Higgins is a hard-working young man in a New England seaside village whose parents were both killed in a head-on collision when he was 16 years old. Since that time, he has lived in a boardinghouse, supported himself, and saved quite a nest egg by working full-time at a car dealership and waiting tables and pumping gas at night and on the weekends. When he has finally saved enough money, he tells his boss at the car dealership, Mr. Daggett, that he is going to buy a brandnew Marittima-Frascati sports car. Mr. Daggett calls Kiah's bank in disbelief, since the car is one of the rarest and most expensive in the world. Sure enough, Kiah has the money, and Daggett orders the car for him, but he cautions Kiah that the precision machine must be broken in carefully. Kiah must not drive over 60 miles an hour the first thousand miles and must not take the car to maximum speed until he has accrued 5,000 miles on it. The first time Kiah takes his new car out, he sees a cute girl driving a Cadillac convertible and follows her into a hotel cocktail lounge. Inside, he strikes up a conversation with the girl about his car, but they are interrupted by the arrival of her boyfriend, Paul, who claims that his own British Hampton is the better car. Insulted that the couple does not even bother to learn his name, Kiah mumbles that the car is not broken in yet when Paul challenges him to a race. The couple leave, and Kiah soon follows after. Despite Mr. Daggett's warning, he opens the car up, driving as fast as he can until he overtakes the Hampton. Paul drops behind, refusing to race, and Kiah drives his car full out until it dies by the side of the road. When Mr. Daggett asks him to explain, Kiah says he does not know why he killed the car, but that he is glad it is dead.

COMMENTARY

Kiah Higgins's obsession with cars probably stems from the fact that his parents were killed in a head-on collision that the police said was their own fault. His parents did not have any money, and they were driving a secondhand Plymouth Fury that was totaled in the wreck. Perhaps the young man subconsciously feels that he can escape such a fate if he buys the most expensive car he can, a precision machine that handles beautifully. Although Kiah has managed well on his own since he was 16 years old, working three jobs and saving his money diligently, he nevertheless carries with him a great deal of barely suppressed rage. He resents the summer people who come to play in the seaside village where he has had to work so hard. The story opens with two of these summer people, a couple about his own age, coming out of the drugstore that he is entering. Kiah "gave them a sullen glance, as though their health and wealth and lazy aplomb were meant to mock him" (184).

Kiah's boasting to the wealthy Paul and Marion at the end of the story similarly betrays his own insecurities. He expects the Marittima-Frascati sports car to be his ticket into the moneyed world of leisure, not realizing at first the real exclusivity of the class he so desperately wants to enter. The truth dawns on him, though, when he sees that Paul and Marion and even the bartender Ralph all know one another, but no one has even bothered to ask him his name. "So Kiah now knew

the names of all three, but they didn't know what his name was. Nobody had asked. Nobody cared. What could matter less than what his name was?" (195). Readers can see how much this incident bothers Kiah when he insists that Mr. Daggett call him by his name at the end of the story. When Kiah purposely kills his brand-new car and then says he is "glad it's dead" (196), the young man's actions seem partly a retribution for his parents' death and partly a result of the realization that the car will not change his life in the way he had hoped it would.

CHARACTERS

Customer A customer, described as "an urbane and tweedy gentleman" (186), comes into Mr. Daggett's car dealership to look at an MG sports car, which he is considering buying for his son. When he cannot remember the name of the extremely expensive sports car that his son raves about, Kiah supplies the information that the car is called a Marittima-Frascati.

Daggett Daggett is the owner of the car dealership where Kiah Higgins works. A rather angry and unkind man, he is astonished that Kiah has enough money to buy the Marittima-Frascati sports car, but after he calls Kiah's bank, he orders the car for him, warning the boy to break it in carefully. Mr. Daggett cannot understand why Kiah destroys the car at the end of the story.

Druggist The story opens with Kiah Higgins entering a drugstore in the seaside village where he lives in order to cash a personal check, just to make sure that his new checking account really works. A kindly druggist who has known Kiah for a long time cashes the check and also tries to convince the young man to be satisfied with what he has rather than always longing for more.

Higgins, Kiah Kiah Higgins is a single-minded young man who works hard during his teenage years to save enough money to buy a fancy Marittima-Frascati sports car. When he discovers that, despite the car, a great distance still separates him from the wealthy crowd who summer in the seaside village where he lives, he purposefully drives his new car so hard that he kills the engine and ruins the car.

Higgins, Mr. and Mrs. Kiah Higgins's father had been a landscape contractor, and his mother worked as a chambermaid at Howard Johnson's. Both Kiah's parents were killed in a head-on collision when Kiah was 16 years old.

Marion When Kiah takes his brand-new sports car out for a spin the first time, he sees a pretty girl driving a Cadillac convertible. He follows her to an expensive hotel cocktail lounge, where he speaks to her briefly. Later, he learns that the girl's name is Marion. She is engaged to a young man named Paul, who believes his own sports car is superior to Kiah's.

Paul Paul is the fiancé of Marion, the girl that Kiah sees driving a Cadillac convertible and follows into a hotel cocktail lounge. Contemptuous of Kiah, Paul does not believe the young man's boasts about his brand-new sports car. Kiah is insulted when Paul and Marion leave the cocktail lounge without even bothering to learn his name. He follows them in his Marittima-Frascati and makes an obscene gesture as he passes by.

Ralph Ralph is the name of the bartender at the fancy cocktail lounge where Kiah talks to Marion, the pretty girl he saw driving a Cadillac convertible. Ralph is suspicious of Kiah and believes the young man is a mechanic who is just pretending the Marittima-Frascati sports car belongs to him.

FURTHER READING

Bagombo Snuff Box. New York: Berkley Books, 2000

Reed, Peter. *The Short Fiction of Kurt Vonnegut.* Westport, Conn.: Greenwood Press, 1997.

"A Present for Big Saint Nick"

A comic send-up of gangsters, this story was first published as "A Present for Big Nick" in *Argosy* magazine in December 1954. It was retitled "A Present for Big Saint Nick" when it was printed in the 1999 collection, *Bagombo Snuff Box.*

SYNOPSIS

"A Present for Big Saint Nick" opens in a jewelry store, where ex-boxer Bernie O'Hare is buying a glow-in-the-dark watch as a Christmas present for his boss, mafia head Big Nick. Bernie's four-year-old son, Willy, sees a small plastic Santa Claus figure in the store and begins screaming in fear. It turns out that he is deathly frightened of Santa Claus. Soon another couple, the Pullmans, enter the store with their small son, who is scared of Santa as well. They, too, buy a gaudy Christmas present for Big Nick since Mr. Pullman serves as the gangster's lawyer. The next scene takes place at the annual Christmas party Big Nick holds for his employees. The O'Hares, the Pullmans, and six other couples with children are present. Big Nick, dressed as Santa, enters the room and begins bullying each child in turn, asking what the child's parents really think about him before grudgingly giving each a toy. When Willy O'Hare receives a boat from the cigar-smoking, gruff and rude Santa Claus, he asks for a rag to wipe off the dirt and blood, explaining that his mother said the toys are covered with blood and that Mrs. Pullman said Nick is dirty. Soon, the other children chime in as well, betraying unkind things their own parents have said about Big Nick. As Nick threatens to hit four-year-old Willy, Bernie O'Hare instead punches him squarely in the face, and all the families cheer. Nick goes down, threatening to kill everyone present. Before the families can leave, however, Nick tries to show off by opening Christmas gifts he has received from famous movie stars and important people. The second present he opens turns out be an explosive that blows him up. Little Willy retrieves the card from the package and keeps it as a souvenir.

COMMENTARY

A comic story that deconstructs the sentimentality usually associated with children and Christmas, "A Present for Big Saint Nick" achieves its humor by turning conventions on their head. Children are terrified of Santa Claus rather than longing for his arrival. Employees buy expensive gifts for their boss rather than the other way around. And an ex-boxer uses his former skills not to save Christmas, but to punch Santa Claus in the nose. The children, upon leaving Big Nick's party, are so happy that "they danced out of the house without their coats," although rather than glowing inside with the warmth of the Christmas spirit, they are saying things like "Jingle bells, you old poop," and "Eat tinsel, Santy" (208). And, as in most Christmas stories, the parents are delighted by their children's happiness, though again, with a twist. When Big Nick tells the parents that they "are all gonna get rubbed out" (208), the parents seem resigned rather than properly frightened:

> "I'm a dead man," said O'Hare to his wife. "I'm a dead woman, she said, "but it was almost worth it. Look how happy the children are." (208)

But the most jarring element of the story is its ending, with the gruesome explosion that blows off Big Nick's chin and nose. As the Mafia boss's "corpse" is "carted off to the morgue," Mrs. O'Hare gushes that she does not think "this is a Christmas the children are going to forget very soon" (209). Four-year-old Willy O'Hare even retains a souvenir from the memorable party, the card attached to the bomb that reads, "Merry Christmas to the greatest guy in the world," and is signed simply "The Family" (209). This is, indeed, a "family" Christmas story, though not in the traditional sense.

CHARACTERS

Big Nick A cruel and heartless gangster, Big Nick terrifies the children of his employees each year by playing Santa Claus at an annual Christmas party. Big Nick dies at the end of the story when he unwraps an explosive device disguised as a Christmas gift.

Clerk The story opens in a jewelry store, where a clerk is showing gaudy items to Bernie O'Hare and Mr. Pullman, two employees of a gangster named Big Nick who are trying to buy an appropriate Christmas present for their boss.

O'Hare, Bernie A former middleweight boxer known as the Shenandoah Blaster, Bernie O'Hare is given a job as a body guard by Mafia head Big Nick after losing his sight in one eye. O'Hare becomes a hero to Big Nick's employees and their children when he punches the gangster in the face at Nick's annual Christmas party, which he uses as an occasion to bully children and pry into their parents' real opinions about him. When Big Nick is blown up by an explosive at the end of the story, O'Hare and the other employees escape the retaliation that certainly would have come to them otherwise.

O'Hare, Wanda Wanda O'Hare is the wife of ex-boxer Bernie O'Hare and mother of four-year-old Willy.

O'Hare, Willy Willy O'Hare is a four-year-old child terrified of Santa Claus because his father's employer, a gangster named Big Nick, dresses up as Santa each year and bullies the children of his staff members. Willy gets all the employees in trouble when he repeats unkind things his parents and other employees have said about Big Nick. But Nick's death, by an explosive device disguised as a Christmas present, prevents him from retaliating against the children and their parents.

Pullman, Mr. and Mrs. Mr. Pullman is the lawyer for notorious gangster Big Nick. He and his wife, like the O'Hares, are required to attend the Christmas party Nick throws for his staff members with young children each year.

Pullman, Richard Richard Pullman is the young son of a man who works as a lawyer for Mafia head Big Nick. Like four-year-old Willy O'Hare, Richard Pullman is terrified of Santa Claus because of the annual Christmas parties at which Big Nick dresses up in a Santa suit and bullies his employees' children.

Zerbe, Gwen Gwen Zerbe is one of the children who is made to attend gangster Big Nick's annual Christmas party. After responding satisfactorily to Nick's questions about her parents' opinions of him, she is given a doll by the gangster.

Zerbe, Mr.   Mr. Zerbe works as Big Nick's chief accountant. Like the other employees at Big Nick's Christmas party, Mr. Zerbe is terrified that his daughter will say the wrong thing to the gangster and get him in trouble.

FURTHER READING

Bagombo Snuff Box. New York: Berkley Books, 2000
Reed, Peter. *The Short Fiction of Kurt Vonnegut.* Westport, Conn.: Greenwood Press, 1997.

"Report on the Barnhouse Effect"

"Report on the Barnhouse Effect" was Kurt Vonnegut's first published story. It appeared in *Collier's* magazine on February 11, 1950. The story was reprinted in the 1961 collection, *Canary in a Cat House,* and later, in the 1968 *Welcome to the Monkey House.*

SYNOPSIS

"Report on the Barnhouse Effect," set during the cold war, tells the story of Arthur Barnhouse, a psychology professor who discovers, while playing dice one night in his army barracks, that he has the ability to focus his mental powers so as to control what happens in the world. He dubs this phenomenon "dynamopsychism" and studies it for 10 years. The author of the report is a graduate student in social studies, to whom the professor eventually reveals his secret. The professor also tells the student that he has concluded he should no longer keep his research to himself: "Now I realize that I haven't any more right to it than a man has a right to own an atomic bomb" (180), he tells the narrator. Thus, he has written a short note to the U.S. secretary of state hinting at his powers. Immediately, the professor, along with the student/narrator are whisked to an old mansion near Charlottesville, Virginia, and kept under the supervision of General Honus Barker and William K. Cuthrell of the State Department for further study in a top secret experiment labeled "Project Wishing Well."

The professor, as the experiment progresses, becomes increasingly reluctant to participate as he realizes that the project is intended to wage war more efficiently rather than to benefit mankind. After the success of "Operation Brainstorm," in which the professor is able to destoy an enormous array of bombers, rockets, and military ships, Barnhouse disappears. While in hiding he begins to use his mental powers to destroy the world's stockpile of weaponry. Although the world's leaders frantically search for him, Barnhouse's whereabouts remain a mystery. Toward the end of the story, readers discover that the graduate student narrator is writing this report 18 months after Barnhouse's disappearance. The student speculates about how much longer his former professor will be able to live, since both his mother and father died at young ages and since he has so many enemies searching for him. The report concludes with the narrator receiving a note from Barnhouse in his mailbox on Christmas Eve. Once deciphered, the narrator realizes he has received instructions in dynamopsychism. The story concludes with the narrator making preparations to vanish in order to carry out the professor's work.

COMMENTARY

"The Barnhouse Effect," published in 1950, is a commentary on the very early beginnings of the nuclear arms race between the Soviet Union and the United States. Following the dropping of the ATOMIC BOMBS on Nagasaki and Hiroshima by the United States in 1945, the Soviets detonated their first atomic bomb in August 1949. During this period, both countries were also working to produce hydrogen bombs, the first of which would be tested in 1952. The story, then, like Vonnegut's 1963 novel *Cat's Cradle,* warns against the excesses of a science bent on discovering ever more powerful weaponry. As Professor Barnhouse asks the narrator at one point, "Think we should have dropped the atomic bomb on Hiroshima? . . . Think every new piece of scientific information is a good thing for humanity?" (179).

The professor shares much in common with other Vonnegut characters who develop utopian schemes in order to make the world a better place.

Although he stumbles onto the phenomenon of dynamopsychism accidentally, Barnhouse nevertheless devotes the next 10 years of his life to studying his discovery and improving his ability to utilize his own dynamopsychic powers. During these years, he comes to believe that the phenomenon will improve the human situation, telling the narrator: "I think maybe I can save the world. I think maybe I can make every nation a *have* nation, and do away with war for good. I think maybe I can clear roads through jungles, irrigate deserts, build dams overnight" (179). It is this belief that causes the professor to write to the U.S. secretary of state, revealing his secret. But, of course, as in many of Vonnegut's works, utopian schemes backfire. While the U.S. State Department is indeed interested in Barnhouse's discovery, they launch a project to develop dynamopsychism as a powerful new weapon rather than as a way of bringing prosperity to the world. While Mr. Cuthrell of the State Department winces at General Honus's crude remark to the professor that "Eternal vigilance is the price of freedom" (182), he, too, sees Professor Barnhouse as naïve, explaining that the general is right in his own way: "I wish to heaven the world were ready for ideals like yours," he tells the professor, "but it simply isn't. We aren't surrounded by brothers, but by enemies. It isn't a lack of food or resources that has us on the brink of war—it's a struggle for power. Who's going to be in charge of the world, our kind of people or theirs?" (182). It is just this mindset, Vonnegut suggests, that keeps the world at war.

The professor, while appearing to accede to such considerations, really seems to have been making preparations for his own disappearance. Immediately after the success of Operation Brainstorm, he departs. Like Billy the Poet in "Welcome to the Monkey House," Professor Barnhouse is forced to live as an outlaw. Vonnegut shows in both these stories that living as outsiders is the only option for characters who refuse to succumb to totalitarian societies. The frightening thing about "The Barnhouse Effect" is that the society in question does not have the futuristic SCIENCE FICTION setting of "Monkey House," but rather resembles the United States of 1950. But the very phenomenon of dynamopsychism suggests an ability to think outside of authoritative control, to think in a new, higher, more focused way about the world. Unlike the government and military officials in the story, the professor is able to imagine a peaceful world, and therefore, his outlaw activities do succeed, at least to a certain extent. He is able to reduce the latest "costly armaments race" that develops as countries rush to find new dynamopsychically gifted individuals into what the narrator dubs the "War of the Tattletales" (185) in which spies help the professor achieve his goals by locating military equipment and notifying the press, after which it is promptly destroyed by the professor. The story's ending, in which the narrator rolls 50 consecutive sevens on a pair of dice, suggests that the Barnhouse Effect will continue long into the future.

CHARACTERS AND RELATED ENTRIES

Admiral An unnamed admiral, watching the outcome of Operation Brainstorm on television, at first shouts that the ships in the fleet Professor Barnhouse is supposed to destroy have not been touched. Immediately after this, Mr. Cuthrell of the State Department observes that the ships' guns have all drooped downward, "their muzzles resting on the steel decks" (184).

Barker, General Honus General Honus Barker is the U.S. military commander who plans Operation Brainstorm using Professor Arthur Barnhouse's discovery of dynamopsychism. In this experiment, Barnhouse is able to destroy a fleet of 120 military ships as well as a contingent of V-2 rockets and 50 radio-controlled jet bombers.

Barnhouse, Professor Arthur Professor Arthur Barnhouse discovers the phenomenon of dynamopsychism, which allows him to focus his thoughts so specifically that he can cause things to happen in the world at large. The U.S. military and State Department use Barnhouse to run top-secret weapons experiments, but the professor, who believes his discovery should be used to equalize the world's resources, disappears. He lives underground for 18 months, periodically destroying the world's weapons stashes. At the end of the story, Barnhouse leaves the narrator a note teaching him the secrets of *dynamopsychism* so that his student can take over his work.

Cuthrell, William K.   William K. Cuthrell works for the U.S. State Department and helps General Honus Barker oversee the top secret "Project Wishing Well," which is studying Professor Barnhouse and dynamopsychism. Cuthrell explains to the professor that he wishes "the world were ready for ideals" like the ones the professor advocates, but that "a struggle for power" rather than lack of resources has led the world to the brink of war (182).

Dean of Social Studies   When the narrator arrives at the Wyandotte Graduate School, the dean of social studies apologetically assigns Professor Barnhouse as his thesis adviser. The professor, obsessed and isolated while studying dynamopsychism, has become something of a ridiculous figure on campus.

Doctor   When the narrator decides to disappear in order to help Professor Barnhouse with his plan to destroy the world's weapons, he goes to see his doctor who gives him a clean bill of health.

dynamopsychism   Dynamopsychism is the ability to focus one's mental powers so intently that one can actually control future events. The phenomenon is discovered by psychology professor Arthur Barnhouse. When the U.S. military finds out about dynamopsychism, they experiment with using Barnhouse as a weapon. The professor eventually escapes the military's clutches, and lives as a rebel, using his mental powers to destroy all weapon caches around the globe.

Foust, Senator Warren   After Professor Barnhouse disappears, Senator Warren Foust demands funds in order to screen the population "for men potentially as powerful dynamospsychically as the professor" (175). But the narrator points out that this effort will be fruitless without access to the professor's technique for channeling the force.

Guard   An unnamed and "harassed" (185) guard throws open the front door to the Charlottesville mansion and announces that Professor Barnhouse has escaped following the success of Operation Barnstorm.

Kropotnik, Commissar   Commissar Kropotnik, presumably of the Soviet Union, believes, as does U.S. Senator Warren Foust, that controlling the Barnhouse Effect will lead to control of the world. Thus, after Professor Barnhouse's disappearance, the two superpowers enter into a new arms race, this time to see who can duplicate the professor's discovery of dynamopsychism.

Narrator The story's narrator is an unnamed graduate student in social studies who had been assigned to work with Professor Barnhouse at the Wyandotte Graduate School. He is supposedly writing this report about the Barnhouse Effect 18 months after the professor's disappearance. At the story's end, after receiving a mysterious note from his former professor, the student/narrator will make preparations to disappear as well so that he can carry on the professor's work.

Operation Brainstorm   Operation Brainstorm is the code name given by the military to one of the secret experiments they conduct with Professor Arthur Barnhouse. During Operation Brainstorm, Barnhouse is able to destroy an enormous array of bombers, rockets, and military ships, using only his mental powers.

Slezak, Premier   Premier Slezak, leader of some unnamed country, builds a shelter with 12-foot-thick lead armor to try to protect himself from the Barnhouse Effect after the professor disappears and begins destroying the world's weaponry. However, the shelter does no good. The narrator writes that "the premier has been floored twice while in it" (175).

Soldier   An unnamed soldier in the bunk next to Barnhouse's when the professor first rolls the dice and gets the number seven ten times in a row, says to him, "You're hotter'n a two-dollar pistol, Pop" (176).

Wyandotte College Wyandotte College is a fictional institution of higher learning appearing in several Vonnegut short stories reprinted in the collection *Welcome to the Monkey House,* including "Report on the Barnhouse Effect," "The Euphio Question," "Epicac," and "Tomorrow and Tomorrow and Tomorrow." Professor Arthur Barnhouse teaches social studies at Wyandotte College in "Report on The Barnhouse Effect."

FURTHER READING

Reed, Peter. *The Short Fiction of Kurt Vonnegut.* Westport, Conn.: Greenwood Press, 1997.
Welcome to the Monkey House. New York: Dell, 1998

"Runaways"

A decidedly unromantic take on a Romeo and Juliet tale of young lovers, "Runaways" first appeared in the *Saturday Evening Post* in April 1961. The story was later reprinted in the 1999 collection, *Bagombo Snuff Box.*

SYNOPSIS

"Runaways" is about the 16-year-old daughter of the governor of Indiana, Annie Southard, who runs away from home with Rice Brentner, the teenage ex-reform school son of a supply clerk. Police find the pair and bring them home, but they soon run away together again, their teen romance fueled by popular songs they hear on the radio. This time, the Southards and the Brentners get together to discuss what to do about their disobedient children. Although they initially blame each other, the two couples eventually decide to give their children exactly what they want. When the teenage runaways are apprehended this time, Annie is given a message from her father that instructs the pair to come home whenever they feel like it. When they get home, their parents want the couple to get married and "start being happy as soon as possible" (310). Deflated by this message since they had been expecting a stern admonition, Annie and Rice drive home silently. When Rice drops Annie off at the governor's mansion, they

both agree that they are too young to get married any time soon.

COMMENTARY

Although readers' sympathies might initially lie with the teenage runaways, especially since Annie Southard is shown, early in the story, being forced by her father, Governor Jesse K. Southard, to read a statement to the press that expresses lies about her relationship with Rice Brentner, by the end Vonnegut shows the young couple to be self-involved and overly dramatic, like many teenagers. "Runaways" debunks the kind of young love so celebrated and romanticized in works like *Romeo and Juliet.* While neither pair of parents is particularly sympathetic—the Brentners' response to their son's mustache seems overblown, and Governor Southard and his wife seem overly class conscious and controlling—nevertheless, the real objects of SATIRE in the story are the young lovers themselves. At least the governor realizes that, for a marriage to be successful, two people must have something in common. But at only 16 years old, Annie and Rice believe they know more than their parents. After they are caught the first time, the pair "lecture[s] reporters and police on love, hypocrisy, persecution of teenagers, the insensitivity of parents, and even rockets, Russia, and the hydrogen bomb" (296).

But Annie and Rice's true narcissism comes out nowhere so well as in the conversation they have in the car the second time they run away. The pair talks at cross purposes, neither one listening to the other at all, but both self-pityingly complaining about how no one understands them. Vonnegut writes that "both would have been bored stiff if they had listened" to each other, but "they spared themselves that" (304). Instead, Annie and Rice listen to the popular music that glorifies teenage rebellion and romance, with many such lyrics actually appearing in the text. Clearly, the shallowness of their relationship is revealed at the end of the story when Governor Southard gives Annie permission to marry Rice. When the teenagers drive past a young couple with a screaming baby arguing in another car, a bit of reality begins to sink in. But no longer persecuted and unable to present themselves as victims, Annie and Rice lose interest in each other, conceding that they are, after all, "not too young to be in love," but "too young for about everything else there is that goes with love" (312).

CHARACTERS

Brentner, Mr. Mr. Brentner is the father of teenager Rice Brentner, the boy who runs away with the governor's daughter. Mr. Brentner is humiliated when the newspapers report that he is "an eighty-nine-dollar-and sixty-two-cent-a-week supply clerk in the main office of the public school system" (300). The mention of the 62¢ seems an especial insult to him.

Brentner, Mrs. Mrs. Brentner is the mother of Rice Brentner, the teenager who runs away with Annie Southard, the governor's daughter. When the Brentners are summoned to the governor's mansion, the Brentners are first intimidated by the governor's wealth and power. Mrs. Brentner, however, responding to the governor's charges of slack parenting on the Brenters' part, eventually finds the courage to challenge the governor about the way he has raised his own daughter. Governor Southard acknowledges the justice in her remarks.

Bretner, Rice A 16-year-old boy who had spent time in reform school for stealing automobiles, Rice Bretner runs away from home with Annie Southard, the teenage daughter of the governor of Indiana. Both Rice and Annie seem more intent on proving how they are misunderstood by their parents than they are in listening to each other.

Counsel, Bob Bob Counsel is the name of the wealthy young boy whom Mrs. Southard wishes her daughter would date instead of Rice Brentner. Rice pretends to be Bob Counsel when he calls Annie on the phone and persuades her to run away with him a second time.

Policemen Several policemen appear in the story. State troopers initially find the teenage runaways Annie and Rice and bring them home to their parents. Later, the second time the young people run

away together, a trooper gives Annie a message from her father, granting the young woman permission to marry Rice. Finally, a policeman greets Annie and Rice upon their return to the governor's mansion at the end of the story.

Siebolt, Dr. The second time that Annie Southard and Rice Brentner run away, Annie talks at great length about Dr. Siebolt, the Southards' family physician, whom Annie believes is the only person who truly listens to her. Ironically, neither Annie nor Rice listen to the other at all during this conversation about being misunderstood.

Southard, Annie Annie Southard is the 16-year-old daughter of the governor of Indiana. When she runs away with a working-class ex–reform school boy, her father sends state policemen to find her and bring her home. Both Annie and Rice claim to be misunderstood by their parents, but finally seem more motivated by maudlin pop songs and self-pity than by any great attachment to each other. When her parents give her permission to marry Rice, Annie loses interest in the boy.

Southard, Jesse K. The governor of Indiana, Jesse K. Southard is at first furious when his 16-year-old daughter, Annie, runs away with the shady Rice Brentner. When the pair runs off together a second time, Southard, in a meeting with the Brentners, reconsiders how to handle the young couple. He sends a message to Annie, giving his daughter permission to marry Rice. As he had hoped, the message deflates the romance from the relationship, and both teenagers decide they are too young to marry at the end.

Southard, Mary Mary Southard is the mother of teenage Annie, who runs away with Rice Brentner. Mary wishes Annie would date someone from her own upper-class background rather than Rice, whom the Southards consider a delinquent.

FURTHER READING

Bagombo Snuff Box. New York: Berkley Books, 2000
Reed, Peter. *The Short Fiction of Kurt Vonnegut*. Westport, Conn.: Greenwood Press, 1997.

The Sirens of Titan

The Sirens of Titans, first published as a Dell paperback in 1959 and reissued in hard cover in 1961, is perhaps the Vonnegut novel that reads most like SCIENCE FICTION—characters travel to different planets in space ships; humans interact with robots; Martians invade Earth; there exists a warp in space/time that scatters people throughout the universe. Despite these conventions, *The Sirens of Titan* is still a very human novel. It is a novel that is about luck, about friendship, and finally, about the purpose of human life on Earth. Like many Vonnegut books, *The Sirens of Titan* explores the question of DETERMINISM vs. FREE WILL. It asks whether human actions are predetermined and their fates inescapable, or if, instead, people act freely, influencing and shaping their own destinies.

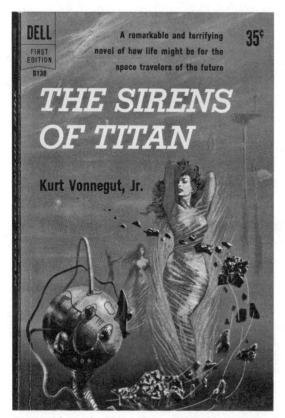

Cover art from *The Sirens of Titan* (used by permission of Dell Publishing, a division of Random House, Inc.)

SYNOPSIS

Chapters 1–3

In the beginning of *The Sirens of Titan*, Vonnegut writes that the book contains a "true story from the Nightmare Ages, falling roughly, give or take a few years, between the Second World War and the Third Great Depression" (2). So, like *Player Piano*, the novel is set in an indeterminate but not too distant future, although the narrator purports to be telling the story from a more distant future, in which humans now know how to find the meaning of life within themselves and have thus entered into an age of "goodness and wisdom" (2). The "Nightmare Ages" refers to the history of mankind before this enlightened age, when humans looked outward for meaning and found only "a nightmare of meaninglessness without end" (1–2). The story from the Nightmare Ages that the narrator tells begins in Newport, Rhode Island, at the vast estate of the wealthy Winston Niles Rumfoord. A crowd has formed outside the walls of the estate, eager to witness the materialization of Rumfoord and his dog, Kazak. Rumfoord and Kazak exist as "wave phenomena" (7), materializing on Earth only once every 59 days. This odd state of affairs was caused when Rumfoord ran "his private space ship right into the heart of an uncharted chrono-synclastic infundibulum two days out of Mars" (7). A chrono-synclastic infundibulum is a kind of funnel in outer space, in which ordinary space and time is disrupted. In these strange space funnels, what seem on Earth to be opposing truths all fit nicely together. It is very dangerous, though, for humans to go to such places, and, as a result of Rumfoord's running into one, he and Kazak, the only passenger in the space ship, are now "scattered far and wide, not just through space, but through time, too" (9).

Unfortunately for the crowd of onlookers, no one has ever been allowed inside the Rumfoord estate to witness a materialization. Rumfoord's wife, Beatrice, has always turned down requests, even by famous scientists, to attend these mysterious events. On this particular day, though, Malachi Constant from Hollywood, California, the richest man in America, a notorious playboy, and possibly the luckiest man who ever lived, has been invited specifically by Rumford to attend the materialization. Upon the two men's meeting, Rumford tells Malachi Constant that he can read his mind, and that he can predict the future, since one thing he discovered in the chrono-synclastic infundibulum is that "everything that ever has been always will be, and everything that ever will be always has been" (20). Rumford then prophesies that Constant and Rumford's wife will both go to Mars and be "bred" by the Martians "like farm animals" (21). Rumford adds that Mars will not be Constant's final destination, but that after Mars he will visit Mercury, Earth again, then Titan, one of the moons of Saturn. When Constant declares that he's not going, Rumford slips him a photograph of three beautiful women, one white, one gold, one brown—the sirens of Titan. Constant seems much less resistant to the Mars voyage after this. Rumford closes the meeting by telling Constant he will also father a son, Chrono, with Beatrice, who will pick up a little strip of metal that he will call his good-luck piece; Rumford tells Constant to keep his eye on this strip of metal because it will turn out to be "unbelievably important" (35).

Soon after the materialization, Malachi Constant returns to Hollywood and throws a wild party that lasts for 56 days. Upon waking up in a narcotic-induced stupor as the party peters out, Constant discovers that he has lost all his money. His company, Magnum Opus, willed to him by his father, who had made a fortune playing the stock market based on a random system of reading Bible verses, has gone belly up and Constant is left with nothing. After he reads a letter written by his father, whom he had met only once in his life, urging him to take on new adventures, Constant is easy pickings for two recruiters for the Martian Army who come to Earth disguised as retired schoolteachers. Meanwhile, the stock market crash that caused part of Constant's troubles has also ruined Beatrice Rumford as well, who is left with absolutely nothing except "her clothes, her good name, and her finishing school education" (45). Although assiduously trying to avoid the future Winston Niles Rumford has predicted for her, Beatrice is kidnapped by the same Martian recruiters and put on the same space ship for Mars that Malachi Constant is on.

Chapters 4–9

After this opening, which constitutes about a third of the novel, Vonnegut switches scenes radically and dramatically. Chapter 4 opens on Mars, with an infantry division of 10,000 soldiers—controlled not by shouted commands, but by radio antennas inserted in their heads—marching to a barren parade grounds where they see a man chained to a stake. One of the soldiers, a private named Unk who has been on Mars for eight years, but had been broken from lieutenant-colonel three years before, is ordered forward and made to strangle the chained man to death while the army watches. Right before he dies, the man at the stake is able to choke out his last words: *Blue stone, Unk . . . Barrack twelve. . . . letter*" (103). Because the radio antenna in his head causes horrible pains whenever Unk begins to think deeply about anything, and because he is under the watchful eye of Boaz, a supposed private, but in actuality one of the carefully planted real commanders able to control the radio antennas, it takes Unk a while to search Barrack twelve as the dying man had requested. When he does search the barrack, however, Unk discovers a letter detailing facts that the letter writer has discovered—among other things, that Unk is on Mars in the army, that his memory has been erased and a radio antenna inserted, that an invasion of Earth is planned, that Unk has a family elsewhere on Mars, with a wife named Bee and a son named Chrono, and that Unk's best friend is named Stony Stevenson. Before Unk turns to the signature page, he admiringly imagines the writer as a fearless man, willing to "expose himself to any amount of pain in order to add to his store of truth," as someone "far superior to Unk and Stony" (131–132). He is shocked to find his own signature scrawled six inches high at the bottom of the letter. Unk, who had been Malachi Constant in his previous life, "was the hero who had written the letter" (132).

When the Martian forces are finally ready to invade Earth, Boaz, the private who is really a secret commander, arranges it so that he and Unk, whom he considers his good buddy, get assigned to the mother ship, which carries all the supplies for the army. Before they can take off, though, Unk deserts from the army in Phoebe, the only city on

Mars, and tries to rescue his wife and son. Unsuccessful in his attempt, Unk is brought back to the space ship, where he is greeted by Winston Niles Rumfoord, whom we find out is the commander in chief controlling the entire Martian army. Rumfoord informs Unk that, as Malachi Constant, he had forced himself upon Beatrice Rumfoord on the space ship taking them to Mars initially and made her pregnant, then, like all ordinary members of the Martian army, had his memory erased. Unk is then launched on the mother ship with Boaz, which unbeknownst to them is programmed to take them to Mercury, not Earth. The two men miss the entire Martian invasion of Earth, which turns into a complete rout of the Martians in only 67 days.

On Mercury, the ship burrows deep into the ground, coming to rest in a series of caves far below the surface. The walls of the cave system are covered by small, kite-shaped creatures called harmoniums, who feed off sound. While the complex sensors on the base of the ship allowed it to guide itself carefully downward, the ship has no such sensors on the top, so when Boaz and Unk turn on the automatic controls to try to exit the caves, the ship simply crashes into the ceilings and walls of the cavern. After repeatedly trying and failing to get the ship out of the underground caves, Unk looks through the porthole of the ship and is amazed to discover that the harmoniums have spelled out a message: "IT'S AN INTELLIGENCE TEST!" Trapped in the caves of Mercury for two and a half years, Boaz befriends the harmoniums, coming to love the creatures who view him as a God. Unk, though, hates the creatures and spends his days tramping through the caves, searching for a way out. One day, the harmoniums, who have been occasionally forming messages to the space travelers, spell out the answer to the puzzle for Unk in five simple words: "UNK, TURN SHIP UPSIDE DOWN" (214). Unk takes the harmoniums' advice and leaves the planet for Earth, though Boaz refuses to accompany him, having made for himself a life among the creatures where he can do good.

Chapters 10–11

Back on Earth, Bee and Chrono have been sent as part of the last wave in the attack of the Martian

army. Their spaceship had crashed in the Amazon rain forest in Brazil; Bee and Chrono are the only survivors. Readers soon discover that Winston Niles Rumfoord has masterminded the entire Martian suicide in order to change the world for the better. He plans to install a new religion on Earth, primed by the shame that begins to set in for the Earthlings' mass slaughter of Martian invaders, many of whom were unarmed women and children. The name of Rumfoord's new religion is The Church of God the Utterly Indifferent (183). The two chief teachings of the new religion, according to Rumfoord are these: "Puny man can do nothing at all to help or please God Almighty, and Luck is not the hand of God" (183). Rumfoord, with his ability to see the future, is able to make many prophesies that come true. His most important prophesy involves the arrival of a Space Wanderer, "a lone straggler from the Army of Mars" (221), who would be greeted with joy and who would deliver an important message. The Space Wanderer turns out to be Unk, who, when asked by the ecstatic crowds what happened to him, replies, as predicted by Rumfoord: "I was a victim of a series of accidents, as are we all" (232).

Unk, the Space Wanderer, is then taken to the Rumfoord estate for the next materialization of Winston Niles Rumfoord himself. Huge crowds have gathered to watch the ceremony and to meet the Space Wanderer. When Rumfoord materializes, he has Bee and Chrono brought forth, who have been hawking souvenirs outside the walls of the estate with the few other Martian army survivors. The little family united, Unk is happy at last, until Rumfoord begins to question him on a raised platform in front of the crowds about his life before Mars. When Unk says he cannot remember his previous name, Rumfoord reveals to the crowd's astonishment that Unk is Malachi Constant. Rumfoord has built a hatred of Malachi Constant into the new religion since he is the symbol of a man who believes his good luck came because "somebody up there" must like him. Church members, in fact, hang effigies of Constant, small dolls called "Malachis," as part of their devotions. Rumfoord further questions Unk, asking him to name one good thing he has done in his life. When Unk replies that he had had a friend on Mars, Stony Stevenson, which is certainly a good thing, Rumfoord reveals, to Unk's horror, that the man chained to the post he had strangled back on Mars had in fact been Unk's good friend, Stony Stevenson. With a "thorough understanding now of his own worthlessness" (265), Unk sadly climbs into the rocket Rumfoord has waiting to take him to Titan. Bee and her son, Chrono, are banished along with Unk.

Chapter 12 and Epilogue

On Titan, readers meet Salo, a creature from a planet far away called Tralfamadore. Good friends with Rumfoord, who lives out most of his life on Titan when he's not materializing elsewhere, Salo is a machine like all Tralfamadorians and had been on a mission to deliver a sealed message to a far galaxy when his space ship broke down on Titan. He has been waiting for more than 200,000 Earthling years for a spare part to be sent from his home planet. It eventually turns out that the part he's been waiting for all these years is the thin strip of metal Chrono calls his good-luck piece. All of human history, in fact, has been manipulated by the Tralfamadorians to lead up to Unk, Bee, and Chrono's arrival on Titan. When Rumfoord figures out that he, too, has been used by the Tralfamadorians, he becomes enraged at Salo, who, though a machine, is very hurt by his friend's anger. Rumfoord demands that Salo open the sealed message from Tralfamadore he has been carrying all these years, although he has been programmed not to, but he dies before Salo can comply. Distraught, Salo, fighting against his very nature as a machine, opens the message and translates it for Unk, Bee, and Chrono. The urgent message, whose delivery had shaped all of human history is simply: "*Greetings*" (306). After revealing the secret message, Salo kills himself, taking himself apart and throwing the pieces in all directions.

Bee and Unk and Chrono live out the rest of their lives on Titan in peace. Bee lives in the grand palace of Rumfoord and dedicates herself to writing an enormous, nonending book called *The True Purpose of Life in the Solar System*. Chrono leaves home to live with the giant Titan bluebirds, an awe-inspiring species of native bird. Unk becomes self-sufficient, growing his own food, building his own shelter, and occasionally visiting his wife, Bee. Unk and Bee actually fall in love with each other as a very old man and woman the last year of their lives on Titan. When Bee dies, Salo, who had been put back together by Unk as one of his hobbies, sends Unk back to Earth on the spaceship. Before he does, though, he hypnotizes Unk and tells him that he will die soon, but before he does, a wonderful thing will happen to him. When Unk returns to Earth, it is the middle of winter and Salo lets him off the ship at a bus stop. The novel ends with the old man freezing to death in the snow, but imagining, as he does, that a spaceship has come for him, and that his old friend, Stony Stevenson, beckons him on board for a trip to Paradise.

COMMENTARY

As in much of Vonnegut's fiction, the characters in *The Sirens of Titan* live in an absurd world in which most of what happens to them is beyond their control. Like most humans, however, the characters in this novel like to ascribe some kind of purpose and order to the universe; they wish to supply reasons for the fates that befall them. One of the book's major themes, then, is the relationship between luck and design. Do things simply happen to characters through chance, or are their fates guided by some kind of purpose or controlling force in the universe? The story begins with this quote from Malachi Constant: "I guess somebody up there likes me" (1), implying that Malachi believes his luck proceeds from the auspices of some guiding force in the universe who wants him to succeed. Ironically, the novel will end with a very similar statement, this time spoken by Stony Stevenson in Malachi Constant's dying fantasy: "'Don't ask me why old sport,' said Stony, 'but somebody up there likes you'" (326). Winston Niles Rumfoord, though, hates the whole notion that God is responsible for luck so much that he stages an elaborate Martian invasion in order to install a new religion on Earth that views luck as just that: simple luck. After all, one of the main tenants of the The Church of God the Utterly Indifferent is that "Luck is not the hand of God" (183).

One of the most puzzling aspects of this complex and ambiguous novel is trying to figure out how Vonnegut wants readers to feel about Rumfoord. Is he a good man or a bad one? In many ways, Rumfoord is certainly an appealing character. He is authoritative, charming, and courageous; he comes from a class that has supplied "a tenth of America's presidents, a quarter of its explorers, a third of its Eastern Seaboard governors . . . [etc.]" (21). After his experience with the chrono-synclastic infundibulum, Rumfoord seems more experienced, more worldly, and has a larger vision than any other character in the book. Although he is careful never to proclaim himself a god, he takes on godlike stature as he is able to read minds and to predict the future. Finally, Rumfoord is well-intentioned. He sincerely wants to make the Earth a better place, and he is not afraid to act to bring his vision of the brotherhood of mankind about. In comparing Winston Niles Rumfoord and Malachi Constant at the beginning of the novel, the narrator states that "everything Rumfoord did he did *with* style, making all mankind look good" while "everything Constant did he did *in* style—aggressively, loudly, childishly, wastefully—making himself and mankind look bad" (24). At least in the very beginning of the book, Rumfoord certainly seems a more admirable figure than Malachi Constant.

Yet, at the same time, Rumfoord is a monster who horribly abuses the tens of thousands of Martian army recruits he kidnaps and cons into their suicide mission. And while he is from a class whose history has involved courageous leadership, it is also a class that is quite comfortable treating human beings as animals, as the means to an end rather than as ends in and of themselves. The narrator states, "If Rumfoord accused the Martians of breeding people as though people were no better than farm animals, he was accusing the Martians of doing no more than his own class had done" (22). While the American aristocracy had been happy to sacrifice individuals' happiness for the healthiness of the stock, arranging marriages "cynically on the sorts of children likely to be produced" (22), Rumfoord is perfectly willing to sacrifice the lives of thousands and thousands of innocent people in order to produce what he considers a better future on Earth.

In addition, despite having lofty intentions in creating The Church of God the Utterly Indifferent—Rumfoord intends to make humans depend on themselves rather than looking to God for guidance and approval, something he believes has accounted for much of the atrocity in human history—the practices of the church are ludicrous. In their attempts to make everyone equal, to cancel out the effects of luck in the universe, church members, who number 3 billion by the time of the Space Wanderer's arrival, wear "handicaps"—pounds and pounds of weights—on their bodies. Every member of the church, the narrator states us, "accepted handicaps gladly, wore them proudly everywhere" so that "at last, the race of life was fair" (224). But at what cost has this fairness come? When Reverend Redwine tells Unk he should carry about 50 pounds in handicaps, a "beautifully threatening tone" creeps into his voice (230) and he recalls how, in the church's early days, he and other proselytizers "had threatened unbelievers with the righteous displeasure of crowds" (230–231). Ironically, just as much coercion seems to exist in Rumfoord's new religion as in the religions he displaces.

Perhaps the best clue as to how readers are supposed to view Rumfoord comes in the depiction of "Skip's Museum," the strangely tall, yet closet-like room at the Rumfoord estate where he initially meets Malachi Constant. Rumfoord tells Constant that this little room was one of the few things he ever really wanted when he was a boy. Described as "a museum of mortal remains," the room contains "endoskeletons and exoskeletons," and other "specimens," most that a child could easily find on the beaches and in the woods of Newport, but some, such as a "complete skeleton of an adult human male" expensive gifts from family members (19). Skip's Museum indicates that Rumfoord has long been a disinterested collector of specimens, including human specimens, possibly suggesting that he is a largely amoral experimental scientist who toys with humans for his own amusement and education. Rumfoord's wife, Beatrice, certainly seems to feel this way when, furious that her husband does not seem more concerned about the dire future he's predicted for her, she destroys the museum, attacking the skeleton, swiping the shelves of their specimens and trampling them underfoot. Despite his ability to predict the future, Rumfoord is "flabbergasted" at Beatrice's actions and receives only "static" when he tries to read her mind afterward (48). For all his courage and possibly noble intentions, Rumfoord's attempts to manipulate the future and control human beings are morally bankrupt. Even though he never declares himself a god, he acts like one, and brings about just as much horror and atrocity as have the older religions he tries to eliminate.

Morality and true heroism in this novel are to be found only in the unlikeliest of places. While Malachi Constant is in many ways a despicable character in the book's opening third—selfish, lustful, taking his good fortune for granted, and even going so far as to rape the pathetic Beatrice on the Martian spaceship—he is nevertheless transformed as Unk. In the sad love story that Rumfoord tells Unk after his failed attempt to run away with Bee and Chrono, readers discover that after the rape on the spaceship Malachi Constant had a change of heart. Rumfoord explains that the lieutenant-colonel in his story (Constant himself) "realized for the first time what most people never realize about themselves—that he was not only a victim of outrageous fortune, but one of outrageous fortune's cruelest agents as well" (163). Rumfoord quotes here from HAMLET's famous "To be or not to be" soliloquy in act III of SHAKESPEARE's play:

To be, or not to be: that is the question:
Whether 'tis nobler in the mind to suffer
The slings and arrows of outrageous fortune,
Or to take arms against a sea of troubles,
And by opposing end them?

Hamlet is asking a question that is key to Vonnegut's novel as well: Is it better to simply suffer the fortune that befalls one or to act to oppose that fortune? While the answer to this question may remain ambiguous, readers should certainly note Rumfoord's point that "outrageous fortune" does not just happen to a person, but that people are also the authors of their own fates—the "agents" of human fortune. Vonnegut makes an assertion of the existence of free will in a seemingly predetermined universe. Yet, readers should also note the

irony that Rumfoord, in the midst of telling this story, never seems to come to the same kind of realization of his own culpability that Constant does. Unlike Constant, Rumfoord never openly acknowledges that he is "one of outrageous fortune's cruelest agents." Rumfoord, with his Martian suicide scheme, continues to cause pain to others, while Constant is "spoiled forever as a soldier," becoming "hopelessly engrossed in the intricate tactics of causing less rather than more pain" (163).

This transformation is what makes Unk able to act heroically in the terribly adverse conditions of the Martian army. Although he has had his memory erased seven times and is made to suffer unbelievable pain when he thinks hard about things, Unk finds strength to write himself the letter explaining what he has discovered about himself and his situation. In a quote at the beginning of chapter 5, Dr. Morris N. Castle, the director of mental health on Mars, writes:

> "We can make the center of a man's memory virtually as sterile as a scalpel fresh from the autoclave. But grains of new experience begin to accumulate on it at once. These grains in turn form themselves into patterns not necessarily favorable to military thinking. Unfortunately, this problem of recontamination seems insoluble" (105)

Rumfoord's Martian army experiment, in its attempt to turn men into machines, must fail because it goes so against the nature of human beings to become machines. As in *Player Piano*, humans are imperfect and unpredictable, and these flaws are what make people fully human.

Before he realizes that he is the author of the letter, Unk "tried to imagine the character and appearance of the writer. The writer was fearless. The writer was such a lover of truth that he would expose himself to any amount of pain in order to add to his store of truth" (131). Unlike Rumfoord, Unk causes pain only to himself, and only in the pursuit of truth. When readers discover that Unk is the letter's author, they see that he has become the "faithful messenger" he desired to be as Malachi Constant; the message he delivers is the letter to himself. And further, this letter, this message Unk writes to himself, is described as being "literature in its finest sense" (132). Commenting on the power and necessity of art as he often does in his work, Vonnegut elevates the letter to the status of literature because it "made Unk courageous, watchful, and secretly free. It made him his own hero in very trying times" (132). Art, for Vonnegut, is a search for truth that elevates human beings.

The other very unlikely place in the novel where true human goodness is evident is in the transformation of Boaz. Initially a rather unsavory character, as is Malachi Constant, Boaz originally delights in a lazy, bored way in the control he wields over other characters; his manner with the army recruits is like nothing so much as that of "a cunning bully's chucking a sissy under the chin, talking baby-talk to him" (111). Even though Boaz genuinely likes Unk, he still cannot "forbear torturing [him] from time to time" (119). Confused about exactly how he got so much power as well as about what to do with it, Boaz's aspirations amount no higher than going to Earth and having a good time in Hollywood night clubs. Yet, after the arrival of Unk and Boaz on Mercury, Boaz changes drastically. In the deep underground caves of Mercury, Boaz "had never felt better . . . He had gained weight . . . and serenity, too" (203).

Both Unk's transformation on Mars and Boaz's transformation on Mercury are due at least partly to having a renewed purpose in life, a dedication to others. While Unk has resolved to win Bee's forgiveness for the way he wronged her, Boaz devotes himself to the simple harmoniums on Mercury, who come to worship him as a god. After accidentally killing a number of harmoniums after leaving the music he was playing for them unattended, Boaz is described as "a wise, decent, weeping, brown Hercules" (215). When he makes the decision to stay on Mercury, a place where he "can do good without doing any harm" (217), Boaz's transformation is complete. Both Unk and Boaz have dedicated their lives to causing less rather than more pain in the world. Unk is amazed at Boaz's dignity at their parting; when Boaz holds up his hand for silence, it is described as "a gesture made by a thoroughly great human being" (216). Ironically, though, Boaz's greatness is driven by a

refusal to face the truth while Unk's is driven by a dedication to it. "Don't truth me, Unk, and I won't truth you" (216) becomes Boaz's refrain as he tries to avoid the knowledge that the harmoniums are really mindless creatures incapable of love and that the messages they spell out are really carefully arranged by Winston Niles Rumfoord. In return, Boaz keeps to himself the knowledge that the man Unk strangled on Mars was really his best friend, Stony Stevenson. Perhaps Vonnegut's point here is that the resolve to do no harm to others is the highest morality humans can achieve in an ambiguous and ironic world in which good intentions so often backfire. Both men find the courage to act morally because of their friendship for others—Unk's with Stony and Boaz's with the harmoniums. While these friendships may prove illusory in the end, they nevertheless allow for the possibility of true human goodness.

The third character who changes significantly through the course of the novel is Beatrice Rumfoord. While Winston Niles Rumfoord condemns Malachi Constant for "wallowing in filth" (267) before sentencing him to be sent to Titan, he charges Beatrice with an opposite crime. Her excesses, according to Rumfoord, were those of reluctance. "As a younger woman," he continues, "she felt so exquisitely bred as to do nothing and to allow nothing to be done to her, for fear of contamination. Life, for Beatrice as a younger woman, was too full of germs and vulgarity to be anything but intolerable" (266). The most significant symbol associated with Beatrice is the oil painting of her as a young girl dressed all in white "holding the reins of a pure white pony" (18). Frozen by her fear of becoming dirty, the little girl in the painting grows up to be the icy and haughty Beatrice Rumfoord. Winston Niles Rumfoord even confesses to Unk on Mars that, despite being married for several years before being kidnapped by the Martian army recruiters, Beatrice was still a virgin when the "hot-shot lieutenant-colonel got to her there in the space ship bound for Mars" (166). Beatrice's transformation into the "one-eyed, gold-toothed" hawker of cheap souvenirs, with her foul-mouthed juvenile delinquent son, Chrono, by her side, suggests an astonishing reversal of fortune.

Despite her lack of appeal in both incarnations, Beatrice, like Malachi Constant and like Boaz, has the capacity for moral goodness, a goodness largely attained through art and through the recognition of the value of human relationships. Just as Malachi/Unk is an artist who writes literature in his letter to himself and Boaz is an artist in the musical concerts he stages for the harmoniums, Bee, too, is an artist. She is a poet who, as a young woman, had published "a slim volume of poems called *Between Timid and Timbuktu*" (6). And even though, like Unk, Beatrice has had her memory erased several times on Mars, she is still drawn to art. She is, in fact, sent to the Martian hospital for further treatment after showing her supervisor a sonnet she had written about Schliemann breathing, the technique for taking in air in alien environments that Bee teaches to new recruits. In a parody of 17th-century British poet John Donne's Meditation XVII, in which he writes that "No man is an island," Bee's sonnet ends with these lines: "Every man's an island as in lifeless space we roam/Yes, every man's an island: island fortress, island home" (153).

Bee, however, will revise this view at the end of her life on Titan. Largely through the friendship of Unk, with whom she finally falls in love in their final year of life, and whom she depends on to comfort her after her disturbing birthday confrontation with her son, Chrono, who has run away to live with the Titanian blue birds, Beatrice reverses her earlier standoffishness. In the enormous tome she works on for years, *The True Purpose of Life in the Solar System*, she writes that "The worst thing that could possibly happen to anybody . . . would be to not be used for anything by anybody" (317). Bee's final words, in fact, are spoken to her mate, Unk, when she says "Thank you for using me . . . even though I didn't want to be used by anybody" (317). Bee, though a "springy, one-eyed, gold-toothed, brown old lady—as lean and tough as a chair slat" at the end of her life is also "to anyone with a sense of poetry, mortality, and wonder . . . as handsome as a human being could be" (314). Like Unk and Boaz, Bee is ennobled and made fully human by friendship.

Bee's grand book is written purposefully as a refutation of Winston Niles Rumfoord's deterministic view that the purpose of human life "was to get a grounded messenger from Tralfamadore on his way again" (314). Ironically, Rumfoord, the great manipulator, is enraged at the Tralfamadorian Salo at the end of the book when he finally acknowledges that all of human history, including his own planning and execution of the Martian invasion, has been orchestrated by the Tralfamadorians. With his ability to see into the future, Rumfoord should know all along how he is being used. This certainly seems to be the case, when, early in the novel, he speaks with Beatrice about roller coasters as a symbol of determinism. When Beatrice asks Rumfoord to help her avoid the future he has predicted, he replies that she'll still have to take the roller-coaster ride of the future, no matter what he does: "I didn't design the roller coaster, I don't own it, and I don't say who rides and who doesn't," he exlains, "I just know what it's shaped like" (54). When Beatrice expresses her distaste for roller coasters, Rumfoord tells her to stop and think about the roller coaster that Rumfoord himself is on: "Some day on Titan," he points out, "it will be revealed to you just how ruthlessly I've been used, and by whom, and to what disgustingly paltry ends" (61). Rumfoord clearly realizes that the Tralfamadorian manipulations are taking place all along, but acts as he is expected to anyway; he cannot avoid riding the roller coaster predestined for him.

While perhaps no one can avoid his or her fate, Rumfoord's big mistake is to never recognize the true value of human connection and friendship, the absolute dictum of causing no pain to others. At the very end of his life, Rumfoord cruelly breaks his decades-long relationship with Salo, crushing the little robot's spirit. In fact, it is friendship itself that allows Salo to overcome his nature as a machine. Despite being strictly programmed not to unseal his message until he reaches his destination, Salo, at Rumfoord's request, and after a great inner struggle, disobeys his orders and tears open the message, only to discover that he is too late; Rumfoord has disappeared into the solar system, never to be seen again. Anguished, Salo explains that, as a machine, he was built to be "dependable, efficient, predictable, and durable," the very opposite of human qualities. Yet, he's proved to be none of these.

Salo finally lays the message in Rumfoord's empty chair, calling the absent Rumfoord "friend" and lamenting that, in order to give the message to Rumfoord, his "old friend Salo had to make war against the core of his being, against the very nature of being a machine" (305). His love of Rumfoord has effectively transformed Salo from a machine into a human. Friendship and love in the novel might be what ultimately allow human beings to overcome determinism. After all, Constant tells Salo after spending years piecing him back together, what it had taken him and Bee nearly a lifetime to recognize, that "a purpose of human life, no matter who is controlling it, is to love whoever is around to be loved" (320). The "faithful messenger" Malachi Constant has delivered his final and most important message. Salo understands and is able at the end of the novel to give Constant back the gift of friendship, the illusion that Stony Stevenson has come to take him to Paradise.

CHARACTERS AND RELATED ENTRIES

Are Adults Harmoniums?   *Are Adults Harmoniums?* is an invented book said to be written by Dr. Frank Minot. The book argues that harmoniums on the planet Mercury are like adult Earthlings: "obscenely unmotivated, insensitive, and dull" (200).

American Philosopher Kings, The   *The American Philosopher Kings* is a fictional study of the American aristocracy by invented author Waltham Kittredge. *The Sirens of Titan's* narrator tells readers that Kittredge's book is "the most competent, if humorless" (22) analysis available of Winston Niles Rumfoord's social class.

Beatrice Rumfoord Galactic Cookbook, The   *The Beatrice Rumfoord Galactic Cookbook*, said to be a "delightful forgery" (199), is described by *Siren's* narrator as the second most popular book on Earth following the Martian War. One of the recipes in the book is for a "delicious tea snack" made of "young harmoniums rolled into tubes and filled with Venusian cottage cheese" (199).

Boaz   Boaz, although disguised as a private in the Martian army, is actually one of the secretly placed real army commanders who control the radio antennas in the skulls of ordinary soldiers. A "young colored soldier" (108) who was an orphan back on Earth, recruited to the Martian army when he was only 14, Boaz styles himself as Unk's good buddy, mostly because he knows how lucky Unk was back on Earth, and he wants Unk to show him how to have a good time in Hollywood night clubs after the Martian invasion. Boaz arranges things so that he and Unk are assigned to the mother ship during the invasion. Unbeknownst to him, however, the ship is programmed to head not for Earth, but for Mercury, where, upon arrival, it bores deep down into a series of underground caves. The caves are inhabited by thin, kitelike creatures named harmoniums; they cling to the cavern walls and feed off sound vibrations. During the three years he and Unk are stranded together on Mercury, Boaz comes to love the harmoniums, acting as a god to them and playing them music from the space ship's vast libraries. When Unk eventually figures out how to leave Mercury, Boaz decides to stay on the planet, where he can do good among the harmoniums. Boaz has changed from the Martian army commander who could not resist torturing fellow soldiers with the radio controls to a "wise, decent, weeping, brown Hercules" (215), a "thoroughly great human being" (216).

Brackman, Sergeant Henry   Unk's platoon seargeant in the Martian army, Henry Brackman, like all Martian soldiers, is controlled by a radio antenna surgically inserted in his skull. Brackman is the officer who orders Unk to strangle Stony Stevenson. Grievously injured in the Martian invasion of Earth, Brackman later turns up as one of the veterans hawking souvenirs outside the Rumfoord estate during the materializations of Winston Niles Rumfoord. The International Committee for the Identification and Rehabilitation of Martians later identifies Brackman as Private Francis J. Thompson, a soldier who disappeared in the middle of night while on guard duty in Fort Bragg, North Carolina.

Bud and Sylvia Though readers never meet Bud and Sylvia in the novel, their names are written in lipstick on the white wall by the door of the space ship that takes Unk, Bee, and Chrono to Titan. The two apparently had broken into the space ship, had a wild, sexy party together, and not bothered to clean up after themselves.

Burch, Captain Arnold The company commander of Unk's unit in the Martian army, Captain Burch comes into the barracks one day for a surprise inspection. Boaz, though, who controls the radio antenna in Captain Burch's skull, makes him abruptly leave without ever carrying out the inspection or punishing Boaz for his disrespectful attitude.

Canby, Sarah Horne Sarah Horne Canby is the fictional author of the famous children's book, *Unk and Boaz in the Caves of Mercury*, the fourth best-selling book in the period following the Martian invasion.

Castle, Dr. Morris N. Though readers never actually meet Dr. Morris N. Castle in the novel, he is the director of mental health on Mars. Dr. Castle is quoted speaking about the impossibility of completely erasing human memory at the beginning of chapter 5.

Chrono The son of Malachi Constant and Beatrice Rumfoord, Chrono spends his early childhood on Mars. First seen as a sullen eight-year-old, he is obsessed with the game of German batball, into which he pours all of his energy. To help him in the game, Chrono carries a good luck piece that will later turn out to be the spare part for the Tralfamadorian messenger Salo's spacecraft, the part he has been waiting for hundreds of thousands of years to receive. Chrono first meets his father, Unk/Malachi Constant, when Unk deserts from the Martian army in an attempt to rescue Beatrice and Chrono. Unimpressed by the news that Unk is his father, Chrono is appalled and runs away from him when Unk begins weeping uncontrollably. Later, Chrono takes part in the Martian invasion of Earth. He and his mother, Bee, arrive in the last wave of ships

sent from Mars. Their ship, however, crashes in the Amazon rain forest; Bee and Chrono are the only survivors. After living for a year in the jungle, Bee and the tough and surly 11-year-old Chrono are given jobs hawking souvenirs outside the Rumfoord estate during the regular materializations of Winston Niles Rumfoord, which draw huge crowds. Chrono is eventually sent to Titan with Bee and Unk, where he runs away to live out his life among the enormous Titanian bluebirds.

chrono-synclastic infundibula Chrono-synclastic infundibula—described as funnel-shaped time warps in which "all the different kinds of truths fit together . . . nicely" (9)—play an important role in *The Sirens of Titan*. Winston Niles Rumfoord accidentally runs his private space ship right into the heart of a chrono-synclastic infundibulum two days out from the planet Mars. As a result, he and his passenger—his dog, Kazak—are scattered throughout space and time and live as wave phenomena, materializing on Earth only at set intervals of 59 days. These strange time/space warps also appear in the teleplay *Between Time and Timbuktu*, based on Vonnegut material. Stony Stevenson is able to travel so quickly to so many different planets because his spaceship also travels through a chrono-synclastic infundibulum.

Church of God the Utterly Indifferent, The The Church of God the Utterly Indifferent is founded by Winston Niles Rumfoord after the failed Martian invasion of Earth. On the last day of the Martian War, Rumfoord materializes at his estate in Newport, Rhode Island, and tells the crowds of tourists gathered there that he brings word of a new religion that will annihilate national borders, stop war, and put an end to envy, fear, and hate. The religion's motto is: *"Take Care of the People, and God Almighty Will Take Care of Himself"* (183). It has two chief teachings: "Puny man can do nothing at all to help or please God Almighty," and "Luck is not the hand of God" (183). Rumfoord hopes the church will create a utopia on Earth by stopping religious wars, teaching people to depend on themselves rather than God, and erasing the notion that certain people are more favored by a Creator than others. The church reviles Malachi Constant, who famously explained his luck with the statement, "I guess somebody up there likes me." Like all utopias dreamed up by Vonnegut characters, however, Rumfoord's idealistic dreams result in unfortunate and even ludicrous consequences. Much like the futurisitic society of Vonnegut's short story "Harrison Bergeron," The Church of God the Utterly Indifferent ends up making its adherents wear handicaps—weights and sandbags attached to their physical bodies—in order to make all people equal. In addition, as the church grows in size, "righteously displeased crowds" (231) begin enforcing a strict conformity on the 3 billion people who are members.

Constant, Benjamin   Benjamin Constant, a tribune under Napoleon from 1799 to 1801 and lover of the wife to the Swedish ambassador to France, was an ancestor of Sylvanus, Noel, and Malachi Constant.

Constant, Malachi   Malachi Constant begins the novel as the wealthiest man in America, a young, lucky, good-looking playboy whose father, Noel Constant, left him a fortune. Constant's life changes permanently, though, after he is summoned to attend the materialization of Winston Niles Rumfoord, who exists on Earth for only one hour every 59 days. Informed by Rumfoord that he, Constant, is destined to marry Rumfoord's wife, Beatrice, on Mars, then travel to Mercury, back to Earth again, and finally to Titan, one of the moons of Saturn, Constant returns to Hollywood, throws a wild party that lasts for 56 days, and discovers, as the party peters out, that he has lost his enormous fortune. The old Malachi Constant is last seen in the company of two recruiters from the Martian army. Constant is then reborn as a character named Unk three years later. Unk is a private in the Martian army who has been busted down from lieutenant-colonel. Like all Martian army recruits, Unk is controlled by a radio antenna installed in his head. After Unk is ordered by the radio controls to strangle to death his best friend, Stony Stevenson, he is sent to Mercury with a man named Boaz, completing missing the Martian invasion of Earth. Trapped on Mer-

cury for three years, Unk is eventually allowed to leave. When he returns to Earth, he is greeted as the prophesied Space Wanderer by members of the new religion installed by Winston Niles Rumfoord, The Church of God the Utterly Indifferent. Though adored at first, Unk/the Space Wanderer is soon revealed to have formerly been Malachi Constant, a figure reviled in the new religion. Unk is then sent by Rumfoord to Titan, where he lives for many years in relative peace until he is an old man. He returns to Earth right before his death. After being hypnotized by Salo, a Tralfamadorian machine he meets on Titan, Unk dies believing that his former best friend, Stony Stevenson, has come for him in a space ship to take him to Paradise.

Constant, Noel   Malachi Constant's father, Noel Constant, is the founder of the giant corporation Magnum Opus that manages the Constant's financial affairs. Noel initially makes his fortune after holing up in room at the Wilburhampton Hotel and speculating on the stock market. His fail-proof system involves opening up a Gideon Bible and writing out the first sentence in Genesis in all capital letters. He then divides the letters into pairs and invests in companies that have the same initials. He sells his stock the instant it doubles, then invests in a new company whose initials correspond to the next paired letters from the Bible. Noel's only visitor is a chambermaid named Florence Whitehill, "who spent one night out of ten with him for a small, flat fee" (72). When Florence discovers she is pregnant, Noel marries her, gives her a mansion and a huge checking account, and tells her to continue to visit him, but not to bring the baby, Malachi. The first and only time Noel meets his son is on Malachi's 21st birthday; at this meeting, Noel divulges his speculation method. The only further contact he has with Malachi is to write him a letter, which he gives to Ransom K. Fern with the strict instructions that it be given to Malachi only if his luck "ever really turned sour" (83). Fern gives Malachi the letter after the bankruptcy of Magnum Opus. In it, Noel urges that if "somebody comes along with a crazy proposition" (89), Malachi should take them up on it, thus motivating his son to agree to join the army of Mars.

Constant, Sylvanus The father of Noel Constant and grandfather of Malachi, Sylvanus Constant was an anarchist loom fixer in New Beford, Massachusetts.

Darlington, Edward Seward Edward Seward Darlington was the half-wit stable boy at the Rumfoord estate who played German batball with Winston Niles Rumfoord and other servants when Rumfoord was a young boy.

Denton, the Reverend Bobby The Reverend Bobby Denton is a fundamentalist preacher who sermonizes about the chrono-synclastic infundibulum at his Love Crusade in Wheeling, West Virginia. Denton interprets Rumfoord's space ship as a modern-day Tower of Babel, a device by which humans aspire to the heavens. He preaches that the infundibulum is God's warning that people are not intended to use science to fly in space, but should focus instead on the planet Earth, the space ship God has already given them. "Where would you rather be tomorrow—on Mars or in the Kingdom of Heaven" (29), he asks his congregation, then leads them in "God's countdown," a recitation of the Ten Commandments.

Dun Roamin Dun Roamin is the wry name Winston Niles Rumfoord gives the replica Taj Mahal that he lives in on the planet Titan.

Fenstermaker, Isabel Described as "a frail old lady" (141), Isabel Fenstermaker is Chrono's teacher on Mars. She had been a Jehovah's Witness trying to sell a copy of *The Watchtower* to a Martian recruit when nabbed to join the Martian army. An incompetent teacher, Miss Fenstermaker's office is crammed full of ungraded papers. When Unk comes to see his son on Mars, she is easily fooled and allows him to visit Chrono in her office.

Fern, Ransom K. The president of Malachi Constant's company, Magnum Opus, Ransom K. Fern quits his job after giving Constant the news that he is broke. Fern had talked Malachi's father, Noel Constant, into hiring him as a skinny 22-year-old fresh out of the HARVARD Business School by arguing that, with his oversight, Noel could have made even more money in investments than he already has. Over the intervening years, Ransom K. Fern made good on his word, protecting the Constant family fortune from the Internal Revenue Service.

Galactic Spacecraft Galactic Spacecraft is a corporation controlled by Malachi Constant in the beginning of *The Sirens of Titan.* The last giant spaceship manufactured by Galactic Spacecraft is named *The Whale* (and later renamed *The Rumfoord*). This is the ship that will be shot toward Mars to inaugurate America's New Age of Space.

Garu, Krishna A member of the Martian army who single-handedly attacked all of India with a double-barreled shotgun, not surrendering until his gun blows up, Krishna Garu later turns up as one of the Martian veterans selling souvenirs outside the Rumfoord estate. In his former life he had been a typesetter in Calcutta, India, wanted on charges of bigamy, pandering, and nonsupport.

goofballs "Combat Respiratory Rations," more commonly called "goofballs," are pills rich in oxygen that allow human beings to breathe in the toxic atmosphere of Mars.

Gomburg, Crowther Crowther Gomburg is the fictional author of *Primordial Scales*, a history of the Constant family and their enormous corporation, Magnum Opus.

Hall, Dr. Cyril The fictitious author of *A Child's Cyclopedia of Wonders and Things to Do*, Dr. Cyril Hall's definition of a chrono-synclastic infundibulum is cited at the very beginning of the novel.

harmoniums Harmoniums are said to be the only known life form on the planet Mercury. They are translucent, kite-shaped creatures who cling to the walls of deep, underground caves, feeding on sound vibrations given off by the planet. Incapable of speech, the animals send weak telegraphic messages to one another, which translate as the phrases *"Here I am, here I am, here I am"* and *"So glad you are, so glad you are, so glad you are"* (189). After the spaceship piloted by Unk and Boaz lands on Mercury, Boaz comes to love the harmoniums, serving as a God to the creatures and playing them music from the spaceship's library. When Unk finally figures out how to leave the planet, Boaz decides to stay and live out his life among the harmoniums.

Heller, Charlene   One of the Martian veterans selling souvenirs outside the Rumfoord estate, in her former life Charlene Heller had been assistant dietician of the cafeteria of Stivers High School in Dayton, Ohio.

Helmholtz, George M.   George M. Helmholtz is one of two Martian recruiters posing as retired schoolteachers who convince Malachi Constant to join the Martian army. He and the other recruiter, Roberta Wiley, later trick Beatrice Rumfoord onto the space ship carrying Malachi. Helmholtz is also a character in four Vonnegut short stories from the 1950s, where he is a kindly, fat smalltown band director.

Kazak   Kazak is the giant black dog belonging to Winston Niles Rumfoord. As the only other passenger in the space ship when Rumfoord ran into the chrono-synclastic infundibulum, Kazak materializes along with Rumfoord every 59 days on Earth. Kazak eventually dies on Titan right before Rumfoord himself, sadly leaving Rumfoord without his faithful companion in the last minutes of his life.

Kittredge, Waltham   Fictional author of the book *The American Philosopher Kings*, Waltham Kittredge analyzes the American aristocratic class to which families such as the Rumfoords belong. Kittredge, despite his difficulty articulating his points, coins the term *un-neurotic courage* to define the quality that best describes people like the Rumfoords.

Koradubian, Martin   Martin Koradubian is an imposter who identifies himself as the "bearded stranger who had been invited into the Rumfoord estate to see a materialization" (46). Malachi Constant, wearing a false beard, is the actual person invited to witness the materialization. Koradubian,

actually a repairer of solar watches in Boston, sells his story to the magazines for $3,000. He claims that Rumfoord has told him that, in the year Ten Million A.D., all records "related to the period between the death of Christ and the year One Million A.D. would be hauled to dumps and burned" (46) in order to make more room for subsequent history. According to Koradubian, the million-year period erased from history would be referred to in later books simply as "a period of readjustment that lasted for approximately one million years" (46).

Lapp, Martin T.   Martin T. Lapp is the showman who leases the Rumfoord esate in order to sell tickets to the materializations of Winston Niles Rumfoord for a dollar apiece.

MacKenzie, Miss Joyce   Miss Joyce MacKenzie was Winston Niles Rumfoord's governess who taught him to play German batball when he was a child.

McSwann, Ross L.   The mayor of Boca Raton, Florida, during the Martian invasion, Ross L. McSwann famously said "Send us more Martians" after the citizens of Boca Raton crushed the small contingent of invaders sent to their city. McSwann is later elected a United States senator.

Minot, Dr. Frank   The fictional author of the book *Are Adults Harmoniums?* Dr. Frank Minot argues that children are fascinated by the tale of Unk and Boaz in the caves of Mercury because harmoniums are like their parents. Just like Unk and Boaz, children have to "deal solemnly and respectfully with creatures that are in fact obscenely unmotivated, insensitive, and dull" (200).

Magnum Opus, Inc.   Magnum Opus, Inc. is a Los Angeles-based corporation founded by Malachi Constant's father. The sole purpose of this company is to manage the affairs of the Constant family.

Mars   Winston Niles Rumfoord secretly begins recruiting and training an army of kidnapped Earthlings on the planet Mars. To make the soldiers obedient, their memories are erased and radio receivers are installed in their heads. This Martian army eventually invades Earth, but is completely routed in only a couple of months. Readers soon discover that the Martian suicide had been planned all along by Rumfoord, who, playing on peoples' guilt over the slaughtered Martians, many of whom were unarmed women and children, hoped to install a new religion on Earth, to be called The Church of God the Utterly Indifferent.

Mercury Unk (also known as Malachi Constant) and Boaz leave Mars in a spaceship that, unbeknownst to them, is programmed to crash land on the planet Mercury. The two men are stranded on Mercury for several years until Unk finally figures out with the help of messages left for him by Winston Niles Rumfoord how to get his spaceship out of the deep underground cave where it is trapped. Boaz, however, who has become something of a god to the planet's gentle inhabitants, called harmoniums, elects to stay on Mercury.

Moncrief, Earl The elderly butler to the Rumfoords, Earl Moncrief later turns out to have managed the entire Martian suicide, on the orders of Winston Niles Rumfoord. At the end of his life, Moncrief steps up to become Rumfoord's "ruthless, effective, and even brilliant Prime Minister of Earthling Affairs" though his outward façade as servile butler never changes (174).

Pan-Galactic Humbug *Pan-Galactic Humbug* (subtitled *Three Billion Dupes*) is a fictional book, said to be written by Dr. Maurice Rosenau, that harshly critiques Winston Niles Rumfoord's new religion, The Church of God the Utterly Indifferent.

Peterson, Mrs. Lyman R. An American living in Boca Raton, Florida, Mrs. Lyman R. Peterson shoots four members of the invading Martian army in her backyard and is posthumously awarded the Congressional Medal of Honor.

Phoebe The major city on the colonized planet Mars is named Phoebe. After her kidnapping by Martian Army recruiters, Beatrice Rumfoord works in Phoebe as an instructor at the Schliemann

Breathing School. Chrono, Beatrice's son by Malachi Constant (who is known as "Unk" on Mars), lives at the grade school in Phoebe.

Pocket History of Mars The best history of the war between Earth and Mars is said to be a slim volume called *Pocket History of Mars* written by Winston Niles Rumfoord. The novel's narrator tells readers that any later historian who tries to describe the war can do so only "in the barest, flattest, most telegraphic terms" and immediately "recommend that the reader go at once to Rumfoord's masterpiece" (167).

President of the United States Though never given a name in the novel, the president of the United States, who mispronounces words freely, gives a speech announcing a New Age of Space and praising the country's "prog-erse" (56).

Primordial Scales A supposed historical account of the Magnus Opus Corporation. *Primordial Scales* is described as being "first-rate on business details," but as suffering from the central thesis of its author Crowther Gomberg—"that Magnum Opus was a product of a complex of inabilities to love" (78).

Pulsifer, M. The "nominal commander" (116) of the entire Martian army, Pulsifer actually has a radio antenna lodged in his skull and is controlled at all times by his orderly, Corporal Bert Wright.

Redwine, the Reverend Homer C. The pastor of the BARNSTABLE First Church of God the Utterly Indifferent in CAPE COD, Massachusetts, the Reverend Homer C. Redwine is the first to notice the naked, bearded Space Wanderer (Unk), whose visit to Earth had been prophesied by Winston Niles Rumfoord. When he sees the Space Wanderer, Redwine rings the bell of his church madly, notifying the volunteer fire department, whose members transport the Space Wanderer to the Rumfoord estate in Newport, Rhode Island.

Rosenau, Dr. Maurice Dr. Marice Rosenau is the fictional author of the book *Pan-Galactic Humbug or Three Billion Dupes*, which takes a very critical view of Winston Niles Rumfoord, yet does admit that Rumfoord never claimed to be a god.

Rumfoord, Beatrice The wife of wealthy aristocrat Winston Niles Rumfoord, Beatrice Rumfoord has been estranged from her husband ever since he developed the ability to predict the future after running his space ship into a chrono-synclastic infundibulum, a strange sort of space disturbance, which has scattered him through space and time, causing him to materialize on Earth for only an hour every 59 days. Rumfoord has told Beatrice that her future involves being bred on Mars to Hollywood playboy Malachi Constant and bearing him a son. Though she tries desperately to avoid this fate, Beatrice is kidnapped by two Martian recruiters, raped by Malachi Constant on the space ship to Mars, and bears a son named Chrono. Bee and Chrono return to Earth in the last wave of ships that make up the Martian invasion. Their ship, however, crashes in the Amazon rain forest, and Bee and Chrono are the only survivors. Forced to endure in the hostile jungle and among unfriendly native tribes, the two become very tough and very close. When they make their way back to civilization, they are given jobs hawking souvenirs, along with other Martian War veterans, to the huge crowds that gather outside the Rumfoord estate for the materializations every 59 days. Bee is eventually sent by Rumfoord to Titan, a moon of Saturn, with Chrono and Malachi Constant, where she lives out her life in luxury, in the replica of the Taj Mahal built there by Rumfoord. Bee ends her days on Titan, obsessively writing a massive tome called *The True Purpose of Life in the Solar System*.

Rumfoord, Winston Niles Wealthy, aristocratic Winston Niles Rumfoord exists differently from other human beings ever since he ran his private space ship into an odd, funnel-shaped disruption in space called a chrono-synclastic infundibulum. The infundibulum scattered Rumfoord and his dog, Kazak, through time and space. Now, rather than existing punctually, as a point in time, like most Earthlings, Rumfoord materializes on Earth every 59 days and on Mars every 111 days; he spends most of the intervening time on Titan, one

of the moons of the planet Saturn. Because of the infundibulum, Rumfoord is also able to predict the future (since all time exists at once for him) and to read peoples' minds. He uses these skills to organize a giant Martian army, made up of Earthling recruits who have had their memories erased and radio antennas installed in their skulls. Rumfoord uses this army to invade Earth, even though he knows that such an invasion is a suicide mission, because he plans to represent the doomed Martians as saints who sacrificed themselves to bring about a new brotherhood of mankind on Earth, which is represented in a new religion he establishes, The Church of God the Utterly Indifferent. Rumfoord eventually dies on Titan, disillusioned by the discovery that all of his actions have been orchestrated by machines on the planet Tralfamadore, who, in fact, have manipulated all of human history in order to get a spare part to a stranded Tralfamadorian space traveler.

Salo An 11-million-year-old machine from the planet Tralfamadore with skin the color of a tangerine, Salo had left his home planet in the Earthling year 483,441 B.C. as a messenger on a mission to carry a sealed message from "One Rim of the Universe to the Other" (274). Mechanical difficulties with his space ship force Salo to land on the moon Titan, where he has been stranded for the past several hundred thousand years, waiting for a replacement part. On Titan, he meets Winston Niles Rumfoord and generously donates half his supply of UWTB (the Universal Will to Become), the "most powerful conceivable source of engery" (175) in the universe, to Rumfoord's grand scheme of the Martian suicide. Sincerely attached to Rumfoord, whom he considers a close friend, Salo is heartbroken when Rumfoord breaks off their friendship at the end of the novel after discovering that all of human history, including his own organizing of the Martian invasion, has actually been orchestrated by the Tralfamadorians' attempts to get the space ship spare part to Salo. When he begs "Skip"— Rumfoord's childhood nickname—to tell him how to repair the friendship, Rumfoord demands that Salo open his sealed message from Tralfamadore. At first unable to, because he is a machine programmed to follow orders, Salo eventually overcomes his mechanical nature and tears open the message, but too late; Rumford has died in the interval. Translated into English, the message says simply: *greetings.* After reading the message, Salo commits suicide by dismantling himself and scattering the pieces. Unk, as a hobby, works for years to put Salo back together, finally succeeding at the end of his life. Salo decides to make Unk's last days happy ones, so sends him back to Earth in a space ship and hypnotizes him to believe that his long-lost friend, Private Stony Stevenson, comes to take him away to Paradise in a space ship.

Sams, Howard W. The fictional author of *Winston Niles Rumford, Benjamin Franklin, and Leonardo da Vinci,* Howard W. Sams claims in his book that German batball was the only team sport Rumford was familiar with as a child.

Schneider, Kurt In his former life an alcoholic manager of a failing travel agency in Bremen, Germany, Kurt Schneider is one of the Martian veterans who sells souvenirs outside the Rumford estate.

Simpkins, Darlene Darlene Simpkins was a "plain and friendless girl" (246) who had disappeared from Brownsville, Texas, after accepting a ride from a swarthy stranger. When trying to discover the true identity of Bee before her life on Mars, the Committee for the Identification and Rehabilitation of Martians suspects she might actually be Darlene Simpkins.

The Space Wanderer See Constant, Malachi, above.

Stevenson, Private Stony Unk's best friend, whom he strangles to death under the control of the radio antenna inside his head, Private Stony Stevenson had been one of the secret real commanders in the Martian army. Stevenson becomes so fascinated by Unk's attempts to understand what is happening that he begins, unconsciously, to help Unk think. He is punished for this by having a radio antenna inserted in his own head and being publicly executed by Unk. Not realizing he

has strangled his friend until Rumford announces it just before sending him off to Titan, Unk continues to fantasize, throughout the novel, about a reunion between himself and Stony Stevenson. At the end of the novel, the Tralfamadorian machine Salo makes Unk's dreams come true when he hypnotizes Unk to believe, as he is dying, that Stony Stevenson has come to Earth for him in a space ship to bring him to Paradise.

Sylvia See Bud and Sylvia, above.

Thompson, Private Francis J. See Brackman, Sergeant Henry, above.

Titan Titan is the name of a moon of the planet Saturn. In *The Sirens of Titan,* it is the place where Bee (Beatrice Rumford), Unk (also known as Malachi Constant or the Space Wanderer), and their son, Chrono, live out the remainder of their lives after the Martian army invades Earth. Titan is also the place where Winston Niles Rumford lives in between his appearances on Earth, and it the place where the spaceship belonging to Salo, the Tralfamadorian robot, breaks down, and where Salo has been waiting for the past 200,000 years for a spare part.

Too Wild a Dream *Too Wild a Dream* is the title of an invented history book about the Magnum Opus Corporation. Supposedly written by an author named Lavina Waters, the book is said to be more romantic than other published histories of the company.

Tralfamadore Tralfamadore is a planet that appears in several of Vonnegut's works. In *The Sirens of Titan,* the robot Salo is a messenger from the planet Tralfamadore who has landed on the moon Titan to wait for a replacement part for his damaged spaceship. At the end of the novel, Winston Niles Rumford discovers that all of human history has been orchestrated by Tralfamadorians in order to get Salo the spare part he needs. The planet Tralfamadore also plays a key role in *Slaughterhouse-Five.* Billy Pilgrim claims to have been kidnapped by plunger-shaped Tralfamadorians and taken to a zoo on their planet, where he is mated with an Earthling ex-porn star named Montana Wildhack. Many critics believe that the Tralfamadorian episodes in the novel are fantasies that allow Billy to cope with the psychological damage he suffered during World War II. Billy's Tralfamadore stories sound very similar to a scenario he reads about in a Kilgore Trout book loaned to him by Eliot Rosewater when both men are briefly patients in a mental hospital.

Universal Will to Become Tralfamadorian space ships are powered by a phenomenon known as UWTB, or the Universal Will to Become. It is UWTB that allows the robot Salo to travel to Titan. In addition, Salo makes the Martian war effort possible when he donates half his supply of UWTB to Winston Niles Rumfoord. The novel's narrator describes UWTB as "what makes universes out of nothingness—what makes nothingness insist on becoming somethingness" (138). Earth, according to the narrator, does not have UWTB, but Earthlings have invented a piece of doggerel about the dangerous substance:

Willy found some Universal Will to Become
Mixed it with his bubble gum.
Cosmic piddling seldom pays:
Poor Willy's six new Milky Ways. (139)

Unk See Constant, Malachi, above.

Unk and Boaz in the Caves of Mercury *Unk and Boaz in the Caves of Mercury* is a fictional children's book said to be written by Sarah Horne Canby. The book tells the story of the Space Wanderer Unk and his companion Boaz whose spaceship crashes on the planet Mercury, which is inhabited only by strange creatures called harmoniums.

Unnamed Blond, Brassy Woman When Malachi Constant comes back to consciousness after the ravages of his 56-day Hollywood party, he is greeted by a "ravishing, brassy, blond woman" who brings him the telephone, through which Malachi will receive the news that he is broke. The blond woman tells Malachi that the two of them are mar-

ried, having flown to Mexico for a quickie wedding, and that her gangster boyfriend will kill Malachi if he isn't providing for her correctly. This woman might be one of the reasons Malachi is eager to join the Martian army when the recruiters catch up to him.

Wataru, Beverly June The daughter of the Rumfoord's Japanese gardener, Watanabe Wataru, Beverly June Wataru played German batball with her father, with Winston Niles Rumfoord, and with other servants when Rumfoord was a young boy.

Wataru, Watanabe The Rumfoord's Japanese gardener when Winston Niles Rumfoord was a child, Watanabe Wataru participated in German batball games with the young boy and other servants.

Waters, Lavina Lavina Waters is the fictional author of *Too Wild a Dream*, a romantic history of the Constant family and their giant corporation, Magnum Opus.

Watson, Myron S. A Martian veteran running one of the souvenir booths outside the Rumfoord estate, Myron S. Watson was an alcoholic who had been taken by the Martians from his job as a wash room attendant at the Newark airport.

The Whale/The Rumfoord *The Whale* is the last big rocket built by the Galactic Spaceship Company and is fitted with living quarters for five passengers. When the president of the United States announces a New Age of Space, *The Whale*, rechristened *The Rumfoord* in honor of Winston Niles Rumfoord, is launched into space in the direction of the planet Mars. Rumfoord tells his wife, Beatrice, and playboy millionaire Malachi Constant that they will be aboard the spaceship when it is launched. However, Beatrice and Malachi are actually transported to Mars via a flying saucer piloted by officers in the Martian army.

White, Florence When the International Committee for the Identification and Rehabilitation of Martians tries to identify who Bee had been in her former life, they believe she may have been Florence White, a "plain and friendless girl who had disappeared from a steam laundry in Cohoes, New York" (246).

Whitehill, Florence   A chambermaid at the Wilburhampton Hotel who is paid a small fee to spend one night out of every 10 with Noel Constant, Florence Whitehill will later become the mother of Malachi Constant. When she discovers that she is pregnant, Noel marries her, sets her up in a fancy mansion and gives her a checking account with a million dollars in it, though he himself continues to live at the Wilburhampton.

Wilburhampton Hotel   Malachi Constant's father, Noel Constant, lives for many years holed up in Room 223 of the Wilburhampton Hotel in Los Angeles. From this room, he begins investing in the stock market and establishes the Magnum Opus Corporation. Malachi's mother, Florence Whitehill, was a chambermaid at the Wilburhampton, whom Noel paid a small fee to spend one night out of every 10 in his room with him.

Wiley, Roberta   Along with George M. Helmholtz, Roberta Wiley is a Martian army recruiter. Posing as retired schoolteachers, the two persuade Malachi Constant to enlist in the army. They then disguise themselves as representatives of mortgage holders on the Rumfoord estate, eager to open the mansion to the tourist market in order to kidnap Beatrice Rumfoord, whom they put on the same space ship bound for Mars that Constant is traveling on.

Winslow, Bernard K.   The Martian veteran who sells mechanical birds outside the Rumfoord estates during materializations is identified by the International Committee for the Identification and Rehabilitation of Martians as Bernard K. Winslow, "an itinerant chicken sexer, who had disappeared from the alcoholic ward of a London hospital" (245).

Winston Niles Rumfoord Authorized Revised Bible, The   *Sirens'* narrator tells readers that "the best-selling book in recent times" has been *The*

Winston Niles Rumfoord Authorized Revised Bible (199). This bible is the work in which Rumfoord lays out the tenets of his newly invented religion, The Church of God the Utterly Indifferent.

Wright, Corporal Bert   Posing as an orderly to the supposed commander of the entire Martian army, General M. Pulsifer, Corporal Bert Wright is actually one of the 800 real army commanders strategically placed in low-level positions. He controls Pulsifer at all times by means of the radio antenna surgically implanted in the general's skull.

FURTHER READING

Cowan, S. A. "Track of the Hound: Ancestors of Kazak in *The Sirens of Titan*." *Extrapolation* 24, no. 3 (1983): 280–287.

Fiene, Donald M. "Vonnegut's *Sirens of Titan*." *Explicator* 34, no. 4 (1975): Item 27.

Rose, Ellen Cronan. "It's All a Joke: Science Fiction in Kurt Vonnegut's *The Sirens of Titan*." *Literature and Psychology* 29, no. 4 (1979): 160–168.

Sigman, Joseph. "Science and Parody in Kurt Vonnegut's *The Sirens of Titan*." *Mosaic* 19, no. 1 (1986): 15–32.

Sirens of Titan, The. New York: Dell, 1998

Wolfe, G. K. "Vonnegut and the Metaphor of Science Fiction: *The Sirens of Titan*." *Journal of Popular Culture* 5, no. 4 (1972): 964–999.

Slapstick

Published in 1976 by Delacorte/ SEYMOUR LAWRENCE, *Slapstick* was disappointing to many Vonnegut readers and critics, coming as it did after the great critical success of *Slaughterhouse-Five* in 1969 and the commercial success of *Breakfast of Champions* in 1973. Nevertheless, the novel continues to explore many recurring Vonnegut themes in interesting and moving ways. If *Breakfast of Champions* was Vonnegut's attempt to come to terms with the deaths of his parents, *Slapstick* is a novel that mourns the loss of his sister, ALICE VONNEGUT, from cancer in 1958, a death that, to Vonnegut, is an example of the "grotesque situational poetry" that makes up human existence. Alice's husband, JAMES CARMALT ADAMS, had died 48 hours before her in a commuter train accident, leaving their sons to be raised by Vonnegut and his wife, Jane Cox Vonnegut. (See JANE COX VONNEGUT YARMOLINSKY.) In *Slapstick*, Vonnegut reimagines Alice and himself as the grotesque Swain twins, expelled from their childhood Paradise and forced to go their separate ways. Wilbur Swain's life is subsequently devoted to an attempt to forge new family relationships, not just for himself, but for all lonely people nationwide. Although Wilbur's utopian schemes ultimately backfire, as such schemes always do in Vonnegut's works, the novel still values his desire to reestablish the extended family groups that used to provide Americans with a sense of community and belonging that they are so often lacking in the modern world.

SYNOPSIS

Prologue

Like many of Vonnegut's novels, *Slapstick* begins with a chapter in which the author introduces events from his own life. In fact, Vonnegut declares in the opening sentence that "This is the closest I will ever come to writing an autobiography" (1). He explains that *Slapstick* is a book about "what life *feels* like" to him (1). Telling readers that it is natural for him to talk about life without ever mentioning love, he argues that "common decency" (2) finally matters more than love. Vonnegut's longest experience with common decency in his own life, he explains, has been with his brother Bernard, an atmospheric scientist at the State University of New York at Albany. He details an airplane trip that he and BERNARD VONNEGUT took back home to INDIANAPOLIS for the funeral of their uncle, ALEX VONNEGUT. Between the two brothers on the airplane is an empty seat, which Vonnegut says seemed reserved for his sister, Alice, who had died many years ago of cancer, two days after her husband was killed in a commuter train wreck. Vonnegut and his wife had subsequently adopted Alice's three oldest boys. Remembering the importance of his sister in his life, Vonnegut tells readers that she is the person he has always written for. He ends the prologue by explaining that the book itself

is a story he daydreamed up on the airplane ride to the funeral. The book, he says, depicts him and his "beautiful sister" as "monsters" (20).

Chapters 1–7

The story proper begins with a very old man named Dr. Wilbur Daffodil-11 Swain sitting in a clearing in the jungle that has overtaken 34th Street in New York City, watching smoke from a cooking fire in the destroyed lobby of the Empire State Building waft into the street, and writing his autobiography. Swain was once president of the United States, but he now lives in the post-apocalyptic landscape of the city with his granddaughter and her lover. The trio's nearest neighbor is a woman named Vera Chipmunk-5 Zappa, a 60-year-old farmer who raises animals and grows food on the banks of the East River with the help of a large group of slaves. Readers also discover that Manhattan is now called "The Island of Death" (25) and that even the laws of nature are no longer constant—the force of gravity changes from day to day; on light gravity days, the Island of Death inhabitants are buoyant; on heavy gravity days, they are forced to crawl on all fours.

Yet Swain tells us that life was not always this way. He explains that he was born in New York City, christened Wilbur Rockefeller Swain, and that he had a twin sister named Eliza Mellon Swain. At birth, the twins were monstrous—each had six fingers, six toes and two extra nipples as well as the "massive brow-ridges, sloping foreheads, and steamshovel jaws" of prehistoric human beings. Explaining that he and his sister were "neanderthaloids," Swain writes that his fabulously wealthy, pretty, and young parents were "shattered by having given birth to monsters" (31). Yet, rather than institutionalize their monstrous offspring, who were not expected to have any intelligence or to live past the age of 14, Caleb and Letitia Swain instead ensconce them in an old family mansion in Galen, Vermont, with a full staff of servants under the charge of a pediatrician who looks in on them every day. Although Eliza and Wilbur are actually geniuses, at least when together, they feign idiocy to the servants and their parents, since that is what seems to be expected of them. In this way, the twins experience a near perfect childhood, exploring the mansion's secret passages, devouring the books in the well-stocked library, and propounding theories on the nature of gravity, on evolution, and on problems contained within the U.S. Constitution.

Chapters 8–19

The twins' happy childhood lasts until they are 15 years old. That year, when their parents come to make their annual birthday visit to Eliza and Wilbur, the two overhear their mother expressing a wish that her children would exhibit even "the faintest sign of intelligence" (75). Liking to solve problems and to please the grown-ups who care for them, the next morning Eliza and Wilbur reveal themselves to their parents as the geniuses they really are. What the twins do not realize, though, is that "intelligence and sensitivity in monstrous bodies . . . merely made [them] more repulsive" (81). Eventually recognizing that their intelligence makes them more tragic than ever, Eliza and Wilbur revert back to the incomprehensible sounds and childish behavior they had always practiced around adults. Yet, having betrayed themselves, the twins are not allowed to return to their paradise of idiocy. Their parents fire Dr. Mott, the pediatrician who had cared for them previously, and bring in all kinds of new specialists to run tests on the children. Separated for the testing, the twins' monumental intelligence fades, only to return when they are close together again. One of the doctors, a psychologist named Cordelia Swain Cordiner, convinces Letitia and Caleb Swain that the twins must be separated permanently.

Chapters 20–28

Wilbur, considered the more promising of the two because he can read and write, is sent to a school for severely disturbed children on CAPE COD, while Eliza remains behind, eventually being shipped off to an expensive institution designed to house people who are little more than human vegetables. As a defense mechanism to combat the grief of being separated from his sister, Wilbur slowly begins to forget the close relationship the two enjoyed for so many years. He attends HARVARD Medical School and later becomes a pediatrician. Meanwhile, the now grown-up Eliza hires a lawyer named Norman Mushari to help her sue her family for locking her up against her will. At one point, she comes to visit Wilbur in the Beacon Hill house he shares with their mother—Caleb having died in an automobile accident during Wilbur's first year in medical school. Bitter and insulting, Eliza at length begs Wilbur to touch her. When he finally complies, the two turn into a single genius again, going "berserk" (145) as well and entering into an orgy for five days—presumably both a sexual orgy as well as a frenzy of reading and intellectual activity. Following this experience, "mutual terror" (151) keeps the twins apart. Eliza moves to Machu Picchu in Peru, and Wilbur converts the old mansion in Vermont into a clinic and children's hospital.

Chapters 29–32

During all this time, as the twins grow up, reconcile briefly, and part forever, strange things have been going on in the larger world. The Chinese have been experimenting with a method of shrinking themselves so that they will take up far less space and fewer resources in the world. One evening, a tiny Chinese ambassador named Fu Manchu visits Wilbur at his hospital. He had been sent by Eliza, who told him of some of the scientific discoveries she and Wilbur made as children. After reading the twins' childhood papers, Fu Manchu seems pleased. He tells Wilbur that, as a reward, Eliza will be sent to Mars, where the Chinese have established a colony. A few weeks later, Wilbur learns that Eliza has died in an avalanche on Mars. As he's reading the telegram from Fu Manchu informing him of his sister's death, Wilbur experiences a very strange sensation of heaviness, is knocked off his feet, and sees buildings begin to collapse around him. The world has undergone its first jolt of extremely heavy gravity, a phenomenon Wilbur never knows the cause of—whether nature or an experiment by the Chinese. Disoriented, Wilbur swallows two pills of tri-benzo-Deportamil, a treatment for Tourette's disease, which he had received as free samples in the mail. Immediately, his "whole being [is] flooded with contentment and confidence" (176). Thus begins a life-long addiction to the medication.

Chapters 33–Epilogue

Under the influence of the powerful medication, Wilbur's new confidence allows him to run for the

U.S. Senate and eventually to become president of the United States. Having campaigned on the slogan "Lonesome No More!," Wilbur proposes a plan to end loneliness by creating artificial extended families for every American, a scheme he and Eliza had originally concocted together as children. Each citizen will be given a new, computer-generated middle name and number, which will ally them with a large group of others who are similarly named. Under this system, Wilbur's own middle name becomes Daffodil-11. At first wildly successful, Americans are happier than they ever were before, even though the economy is falling apart, and millions begin to die from the Albanian Flu and the Green Death, diseases caused by inhaling either Martians or microscopic Chinese. Yet, the naming eventually backfires, balkanizing the country into separate fiefdoms controlled by specific family groups. Wilbur is forced to sign a document selling the property contained in the historic Louisiana Purchase to the king of Michigan for one dollar. As the country crumbles around him, Wilbur returns to New York City to live out his life, which is where readers see him as he begins to pen his autobiography at the start of the book. The old man dies soon after the 101st birthday party thrown for him by his granddaughter, Melody Oriole-2 von Peterswald, and her lover, Isadore Raspberry-19 Cohen.

COMMENTARY

The novel's title, referring to the broad, exaggerated physical comedy of vaudeville, silent film, and early talkies, is explained in Vonnegut's prologue when he writes that he calls the book "Slapstick" because he thinks of it as a kind of "grotesque, situational poetry," much like the old film comedies of LAUREL AND HARDY. This novel, Vonnegut explains, is the closest he "will ever come to writing an autobiography" since it's about what life *"feels* like" to him (1). Like Laurel and Hardy, Vonnegut feels he is being tested constantly on his "limited agility and intelligence" (1). What he admires most about the classic comic duo is that "they did their best with every test . . . They never failed to bargain in good faith with their destinies, and were screamingly adorable and funny on that account" (1). While Vonnegut, in *Slaughterhouse-Five* says he loves LOT'S WIFE in

the Bible for looking back at the destruction of Sodom and Gomorrah because it is so human, his appreciation for Laurel and Hardy stems from their looking forward; their will to continue bargaining in good faith with their destinies shows their refusal to learn from the past, or at least to be cowed by it. For Vonnegut, there is something very human about the comedians' shtick; despite all the pratfalls, tricks, and setbacks, they always come back expecting their luck will change next time.

Vonnegut goes on to point out that Laurel and Hardy's films were never about love even though they often contained the "situational poetry of marriage" (1). Love, Vonnegut argues, should take a back seat to what he calls "common decency" (2), to treating people well and being treated well in return. It is in family relationships that Vonnegut tells us he has most often experienced this sort of common decency. The novel, then, offers an extended meditation on families and what family relationships can mean. Vonnegut points out in the prologue that he and his brother, Bernard, can "claim relatives all over the world" since Bernard is "a brother to scientists everywhere" and Vonnegut is a brother to writers, a fact they both find "amusing and comforting" (5). Readers see where the inspiration for Wilbur Swain's scheme for creating large artificial families comes from.

But this scheme also expresses Vonnegut's longing for the days when the extended Vonnegut clan of parents, grandparents, aunts, uncles, siblings, and cousins resided in Indianapolis, before World War I taught them to be ashamed of their German heritage, and family members began to wander away. When this happens, the family loses its unique identity. "We didn't belong anywhere in particular any more," Vonnegut writes, "We were interchangeable parts in the American machine" (8). The loss of family goes hand in hand with the mechanization and homogenization that mark contemporary American culture, a theme Vonnegut expresses in many of his novels. While Indianapolis "once had a way of speaking English all its own, and jokes and legends and poets and villains and heroes all its own," the city itself, he laments, has "become an interchangeable part in the American machine" as well (8). As relatives such as his uncle

Alex Vonnegut die off, the comfort of home and family become increasingly lost for Vonnegut, who describes himself as a turtle, forced to carry his home on his back.

The family member whose loss he mourns most in the book, though, is his sister, Alice. *Slapstick* is a novel inspired by Alice and about his relationship with Alice. Shortly before she dies, Vonnegut remembers Alice referring to the grotesque situational poetry of her impending death from cancer, and the fact that she will leave behind four sons, as "slapstick" (12). The cruel tricks played by destiny on the Vonnegut family only multiply when Alice's husband, James Carmalt Adams, is killed in a commuter train accident two days before Alice dies, causing Vonnegut and his wife to adopt the three oldest Adams boys. Just as *Breakfast of Champions* presented Vonnegut's efforts to understand and accept his mother's suicide, *Slapstick* is an attempt to come to terms with Alice's tragic death. Vonnegut tells readers that his sister was the person he had always secretly written for and that, after her death, he had been able to feel her presence for a number of years so that he could go on writing with Alice in mind as his audience of one. Yet, by the time of his Uncle Alex's death, Alice has begun to fade away. The novel, which he daydreams on the plane on the way to Uncle Alex's funeral, depicts Vonnegut and his "beautiful sister as monsters" (20), he tells readers. The book is an attempt to hold onto his fading memories of Alice, to capture and freeze in time his love for his long-dead sister.

As Vonnegut imaginatively recreates his relationship with his dead sister in the novel, he gives neanderthaloid twins Wilbur and Eliza Swain an idyllic childhood. The grounds of the Vermont mansion where they are brought up are "covered with apple trees" (38), evoking a biblical Eden before the fall. In their paradise of two, the twins live in innocence, believing that idiots are "lovely things to be" (44) and underestimating "the importance of good looks" (61) in the larger world outside their cozy Eden. Like Adam and Eve in the biblical story, Wilbur and Eliza spend each of their days "exactly like the one before" (47), in congruence with their fellow creatures, yet clearly the center of their own universe. However, Wilbur and Eliza's

paradise, like Adam and Eve's, is doomed to fall when the twins gain forbidden knowledge. Overhearing a private conversation between their parents, Caleb and Letitia Swain, on the eve of their 15th birthday, Wilbur and Eliza discover a "perfect Lulu of a secret" (64): that their parents wish they would die. Though not particularly disturbed at this revelation, the twins' world is shattered when they decide to make a wish of their mother's come true. The last words Letitia speaks to Caleb that fateful night express her desire that the children would show "the faintest sign of intelligence, the merest flicker of humanness in the eyes" (75). The next morning, when the twins reveal their true intelligence, the fall from Paradise is complete. Though they briefly try to regain their former happiness by returning to idiocy, their lost innocence cannot be recovered any more than Adam and Eve can return to their pure and sinless state in the garden. The twins are separated for all kinds of tests and eventually expelled from their Eden, Wilbur to a school on Cape Cod and Eliza to a mental institution; loneliness becomes their new condition.

Separated, the twins become the bland "Betty and Bobby Brown," identities they despise. The genius that they had exhibited previously appears only when the two are close together, working as a unit. Vonnegut here meditates on the incompleteness, the loneliness of the human individual. Human beings are social animals who need one another, who inevitably form family groups as support mechanisms. Later in the novel, when Wilbur will campaign for president, he argues that "all the damaging excesses of Americans in the past were motivated by loneliness rather than a fondness for sin" (183). Thus, he looks back to something he and Eliza discovered as children—the necessity of family—and he dusts off the scheme of creating artificial, extended families the twins had cooked up so many years before. Wilbur's campaign promise, "Lonesome No More!," becomes a way for him to heal the emptiness he experienced when parted from Eliza, and a way for Vonnegut the narrator to express the sorrow of his own sister's death. Both men recognize that human beings are better and stronger when they are in community with others. When Wilbur's second wife, Sophie Rothschild Swain, becomes a newly minted Peanut, but despises her computer-generated name, Wilbur points to all the new Peanuts and Daffodils who gather outside the White House. He tells Sophie to watch what will happen to this rag-tag band of "centipedes and slugs and earwigs and worms" (202), these throw-away human beings who have never felt they belonged anywhere. "The simple experience of companionship," Wilbur explains to his wife, "is going to allow them to climb the evolutionary ladder in a matter of hours or days, or weeks at most" (202). These people will become fully human only in communion with their fellow human beings.

Readers also see the benefits of community in the mind-linking experiments of the Chinese in the novel. Just as Wilbur and Eliza become geniuses when their minds combine, the Chinese have been able to make great scientific progress by teaching small groups or pairs of "congenial, telepathically compatible specialists to think as single minds" (105). The "patchwork minds" created by such teachings become the equals of great thinkers such as SIR ISAAC NEWTON and WILLIAM SHAKESPEARE. Eventually, the Chinese "combine those synthetic minds into intellects so flabbergasting that the Universe itself" seems to await their instruction (105). Yet, like most Edens, there is a serpent lurking in the shadows of the Chinese scheme. Wilbur tells readers that he was amused to learn that the Chinese scientists got the idea for linking minds from the "American and European scientists who put their heads together during the Second World War, with the single-minded intention of creating an atomic bomb" (106). Just because humans may have great intellectual gifts doesn't mean these gifts will be used for moral purposes. As we see repeatedly in Vonnegut's novels, utopian schemes, no matter how well intentioned, backfire, often garnering terrible and unexpected results. Thus, the Chinese, for all their great intellectual prowess, also bring about the Green Death, which kills millions and millions of citizens by the end of the novel. Though the Chinese "were peace-loving and meant no one any harm," in their microscopically reduced form, they were "invariably fatal to normal-sized human beings when inhaled or ingested" (265).

We see the downside to Eliza and Wilbur's linked minds as well when Eliza comes to visit her twin brother in his Beacon Hill home one day, after lawyer Norman Mushari has sprung her from the mental hospital where she spent so many years. When the two touch, they become a single genius again, but they also go "berserk," entering into a five-day-long orgy, a period of intense, frenzied activity that seems to be both intellectual and sexual in nature. The twins' love is narcissistic and excessive as well as incestuous; completely absorbed in each other, they tie all the household servants as well as Mushari and even their mother to dining room chairs for the duration, barely feeding them enough to keep them alive and letting them sit in their own bodily waste. The twins, Eliza especially, are "shattered" by this experience and stay apart afterward out of "mutual terror" (151). In fact, the only time that Wilbur will hear Eliza's voice again, at least while she's living, is during his medical school graduation party when Eliza hires a helicopter and cites part of a Shakespeare sonnet to Wilbur over a bullhorn. The portion of the poem she broadcasts is from sonnet 39, which, in its entirety, reads as follows:

O, how thy worth with manners may I sing,
When thou art all the better part of me?
What can mine own praise to mine own self
    bring?
And what is 't but mine own when I praise
    thee?
Even for this let us divided live,
And our dear love lose name of single one,
That by this separation I may give
That due to thee which thou deservest alone.
O absence, what a torment wouldst thou prove,
Were it not thy sour leisure gave sweet leave
To entertain the time with thoughts of love,
Which time and thoughts so sweetly doth
    deceive,
And that thou teachest how to make one twain,
By praising him here who doth hence remain!

The poem is about lovers so entangled in each other that they become like one; their love is so narcissistic that the speaker cannot praise his beloved without praising himself as well. Thus, the two part so that they can be separate beings again, and the poet can give his beloved due praise. In citing this poem, Vonnegut depicts the tragedy not only of Wilbur and Eiza's relationship, but of the human condition as well. We need each desperately, but we also risk losing our individual selves when we completely identify with the other.

Eliza and Wilbur's overly close family relationship has the added negative side effect of shutting out everyone who does not belong to their small, select group. Similar problems arise when Wilbur finally institutes the artificial family scheme he and Eliza had dreamed up as children. Stricken by grief over Eliza's death, which is metaphorically represented by the jolt of extremely heavy gravity he experiences immediately after reading the news of the Martian avalanche, Wilbur's campaign promise to end loneliness is at least partially motivated by the sorrow he feels over losing Eliza. Initially, the extended family scheme works well—family newspapers and clubs spring up, citizens feel a new sense of belonging, families begin policing themselves. In addition, a new kind of diversity is valued; the new Daffodil Club, for instance, housed in a building which used to be an exclusive "haven for men of power and wealth . . . well-advanced into middle age" (207) now teems with mothers and children, old people and young adults, all getting along together. Yet, when the nation itself fails, due to the Green Death and the Albanian Flu, which kill millions upon millions of citizens, all of the old problems experienced by nations begin to arise. Family groups become more exclusive and narcissistic. Vera Chipmunk-5 Zappa, for instance, recalls that Indianapolis was a Daffodil Town: "You weren't anything if you weren't a Daffodil," she tells Wilbur (239). Even worse, families develop into mini-fiefdoms and begin waging war with one another over turf. Wilbur's utopian scheme, much like Bokonon's in *Cat's Cradle*, ends up hastening a sort of apocalyptic cataclysm. Both novels end with a small group of survivors making do as best they can in a post-apocalyptic landscape.

Into the void created by the collapse of the nation comes another system of belief that, like Wilbur's extended family plan, promises to fill an emptiness within people. The Church of Jesus Christ the Kidnapped begins as a "tiny cult in Chicago," but, as Wilbur says, is "destined to become the most popular American religion of all time" (210). Just as Wilbur's new middle names are an attempt to recapture the Paradise he lost when he and Eliza were parted, The Church of Jesus Christ the Kidnapped is an attempt to reestablish an earthly Paradise as well. The church proposes that God has already sent Jesus to live again among mankind, but that the Savior has been captured by the "Forces of Evil" (211). Believers must be constantly vigilant and spend "every waking hour in trying to find Him" (212). Adherents of the new doctrine clearly feel spiritually empty and are enticed by the notion that their vigilance can usher in a new age of peace and happiness, when swords will be beat into ploughshares, and humans will be redeemed from their fallen state. Like many Vonnegut religions, such as The Church of God the Utterly Indifferent in *The Sirens of Titan*, the earnestness of the believers in the kidnapped Jesus is exceeded only by the ludicrousness of their actual practices. Vonnegut's characters constantly seek a better world, though their attempts to attain one are often horribly misguided.

Vonnegut, in fact, seems quite doubtful in most of his books about the capacity of human beings to learn from the past. He writes *Slaughterhouse-Five*, for instance, knowing full well that wars are like glaciers—they will keep coming despite people's best efforts to stop them. In *Slapstick*, the king of Michigan, Stewart Oriole-2 Mott, reads only history, and quotes to Wilbur Swain the famous line from Spanish philosopher and historian George Santayana: "Those who fail to learn from history are condemned to repeat it" (255). Wilbur mocks this view when he replies to the king:

> "Yes. . . . If our descendants don't study our times closely, they will find that they have again exhausted the planet's fossil fuels, that they have again died by the millions of influenza and the Green Death, that the sky has again been turned yellow by the propellants for underarm deodorants, that they have again elected a senile President two meters tall, and that they are again the intellectual and spiritual inferiors of teeny-weeny Chinese" (255)

The series of events leading to the destruction of the Earth is so ludicrous and so specific that it is absurd to think they would ever be repeated. Wilbur offers, as an alternative to the king, *his* view of history: "History is merely a list of surprises . . . It can only prepare us to be surprised yet again" (255). Again, Vonnegut proposes in this novel that life is "grotesque situational poetry"; no one could have predicted that his sister's death would be preceded so cruelly by her husband's fatal accident. The important thing is to continue to "bargain in good faith" with destiny; Vonnegut's characters do this over and over as they attempt to regain a lost Paradise.

One of the ironies in the novel is that Paradise itself is not really Paradise at all. When Wilbur is finally able to communicate with his long-dead sister, Eliza, over Dr. von Peterswald's device, she complains about being bored stiff, as do other residents of what the late physicist came to call "The Turkey Farm." In a very funny scene, every curse word and obscenity that young David von Peterswald involuntarily utters over the device, due to his Tourette's disease, is doubled by those who have died. The denizens of Paradise are even more bitter and unhappy than Earth-bound humans. Eliza, it turns out, wanted to talk to her brother so desperately in order to convince him to blow his brains out quickly so that he could join her in Paradise and the two could devise ways of making Eternity more tolerable. The suggestion seems to be that Paradises must be of human making, that even though humans might finally be doomed to failure in the long run, they are responsible for making the world they live in a better place rather than waiting around for redemption in the next one. And, as in the beginning of the novel, practicing "common human decency" and friendship might be the best way of doing this. One of the loveliest moments in the book, in fact, is a moment of quiet friendship, when Vera Chipmunk-5 Zappa brings Wilbur a thousand candles for his birthday party. When the two fit them into Wilbur's collection of candlesticks and light them, Wilbur writes, "I felt as though I were God, up to my knees in the Milky Way" (258).

Although Wilbur's extended family scheme has failed in many ways, he dies proud of his reforms, leaving the following poem behind:

And how did we then face the odds,
Of man's rude slapstick, yes, and God's?
Quite at home and unafraid,
Thank you,
In a game our dreams remade.

He and Eliza's childhood dream remade the game of reality for millions of Americans. His utopian scheme of large, extended families offered comfort to vast numbers, at least for a brief while. And Wilbur is able to leave behind at his death an odd new sort of family, forged out of the wreckage that has shattered America. His granddaughter, 16-year-old Melody Oriole-2 von Peterswald is pregnant with the child of her lover, Isadore Raspberry-19 Cohen. The two work together to build a tomb—a pyramid constructed out of junk—to honor the stillborn infant Melody bore four years previously. The ragtag family, made up of the dead infant, the unborn child, and the young lovers, shows that the human struggle will continue after Wilbur is gone. Though "illiterate" and "rickety," Melody has survived an arduous journey to New York to find her grandfather. Melody, as Vonnegut explains in his prologue, represents all that is left of his "optimistic imagination," of his "creativeness" (21). As Wilbur explains to Vera, when Melody arrived, it was as if he "had somehow sprung a huge leak. And out of that sudden, painless opening . . . there crawled a famished child, pregnant and clasping a Dresden candlestick" (272). Vonnegut's own imagination, damaged and rickety as it is by Alice's death, gives birth to the novel, his creativity the "famished child" that finally emerges from his grief.

CHARACTERS AND RELATED ENTRIES

Adams Boys Vonnegut tells readers in his prologue how he and his wife, Jane Cox Vonnegut, adopted the three oldest sons of Vonnegut's sister, Alice, and James Carmalt Adams after the couple died within two days of each other—a real event that occurred in 1958. The Adams boys were between the ages of eight and 14 at the time. Vonnegut explains that one of his adopted sons, on his 21st birthday and preparing to leave for the Peace Corps in the Amazon Rain Forest, says to Vonnegut, "You know—you've never hugged me" (3). Vonnegut then hugs the young man, explaining that it was "very nice . . . like rolling around on a rug with a Great Dane" (3).

Adams, James Carmalt   The editor of a trade journal for purchasing agents, James Carmalt Adams was the husband of Vonnegut's sister, Alice. Tragically, he died in a commuter train accident two days before Alice herself succumbed to cancer. The couple left behind four boys. The three oldest were adopted by Vonnegut and his wife, while the infant was adopted by a first cousin of their father.

Adams, James Carmalt, Jr.   Vonnegut tells readers that one of his adopted sons, James Carmalt Adams, Jr., is a goat farmer on a mountaintop in Jamaica when the novel is published. James, Jr., Vonnegut explains, is living out a dream of Alice Vonnegut's: "To live far from the madness of cities, with animals for friends" (16).

Adams, Kurt   Kurt Adams is one of the sons of Alice Vonnegut and James Carmalt Adams, whom Kurt and Jane Vonnegut adopted after their parents' death. In his prologue, Vonnegut tells readers of an incident in which the eight-year-old Kurt Adams, riding with Vonnegut from New Jersey to Cape Cod immediately after his parents' death, asks, "Are the kids up there nice?" (15). Vonnegut replies, "Yes, they are" (15), then tells readers that the grown-up Kurt is now an airline pilot. He adds that all the children are "something other than children now" (15), showing that the three survived their horrible ordeal.

Albanian Flu   Americans begin dying by the millions of a disease called the Albanian Flu not too long after President Wilbur Swain institutes his scheme of supplying new, computer-generated middle names to all Americans. The flu germs turn out to be tiny Martian invaders who have infiltrated human bodies. Eventually, anti-bodies in the systems of survivors repel the invasion.

Beryllium   Though he is identified in the novel only by his artificial family name, Beryllium, this man is a friend of the widow Wilma Pachysandra-17 von Peterswald. Because he is on his way to join a large settlement of his relatives in Maryland, near the White House, the widow asks him to deliver the letter she has written to the president. The Beryllium messenger, however, is shot by Byron Hatfield en route. Hatfield had mistaken him for his sworn enemy, Newton McCoy

Brown, Betty and Bobby   Betty and Bobby Brown are the names Eliza and Wilbur make up to call themselves when they are separated from each other. The names represent the "listless" and "stupid" children they become when not together. In Eliza's will, which Wilbur reads after his sister's death in a Martian avalanche, she asks that her tombstone be engraved with the words: "Here lies Betty Brown" (97).

Church of Jesus Christ the Kidnapped, The   The Church of Jesus Christ the Kidnapped begins as a tiny cult in Chicago, but eventually becomes "the most popular American religion of all time" (210). The church's adherents believe that Jesus has been kidnapped by the Forces of Evil and that their duty is to spend every waking hour trying to find Him. Thus, believers continually jerk their heads around, in the middle of whatever they are doing, as they continually search for their Savior.

Cohen, Isadore Raspberry-19   Isadore Raspberry-19 Cohen is the lover of 16-year-old Melody Oriole-2 von Peterswald. Described as "robust and rosy," Isadore, like almost all the Raspberries, still has "nearly all his teeth, and remains upright even when the gravity is most severe" (90). Isadore's cheerfulness counters the sadness of Melody's grandfather, Dr. Wilbur Daffodil-11 Swain. Isadore helps Melody build a pyramid-shaped monument out of rubbish and debris to honor the stillborn child she gave birth to when she was only twelve years old. He is the father of the child Melody is currently carrying.

Cooper, Oveta   Oveta Cooper is one of the practical nurses hired to care for the Swain twins at the old Vermont mansion. Oveta is the first person Eliza and Wilbur reveal their true intelligence to. As Eliza speaks to her in an authoritative and cultured voice, Oveta, described as "a bleak, Yankee dumpling" is "hypnotized—like a rabbit who has met a rattlesnake" (78). Yet, she meekly obeys Eliza's orders to inform the other servants of the "miracle," curtseying and replying "As you wish, Mistress Eliza" (79).

Cordiner, Dr. Cordelia Swain After Eliza and Wilbur Swain reveal their hidden genius to their parents, their usual pediatrician, Dr. Stewart Rawlings Mott, is fired, and their parents bring in a team of specialists who apply a whole battery of tests to the 15-year-old twins. One of the psychologists, a "malicious lunatic" named Dr. Cordelia Swain Cordiner, decides that Eliza and Wilbur should be parted forever, condemning the twins to live out their lives as their bland alter egos, Betty and Bobby Brown. Dr. Cordiner, who is no relation to the twins despite her middle name, is "so enraged by how much money and power" the Swain family has, and "so sick" that she perceives Eliza and Wilbur as simply "two more rotten-spoiled little rich kids" (100) who deserve whatever ill-fortune they receive.

Cry of the Nocturnal Goatsucker, The During their frenzied five-day orgy, Eliza and Wilbur Swain manage to write a manuscript for a child-rearing manual, which they call *The Cry of the Nocturnal Goatsucker*. They ascribe authorship of the manuscript to their invented alter egos, Betty and Bobby Brown. Later, Wilbur will actually publish the book under the pseudonym Dr. Eli W. Rockmell, M.D. The publisher will retitle the manual *So You Went and Had a Baby*.

Donna Donna is a slave of Vera Chipmunk-5 Zappa who plans to give Wilbur Swain the gift of a beautiful microscope, unearthed in the ruins of a hospital in New York, for his 101st birthday. Wilbur ruins the surprise when he unexpectedly comes upon Vera fiddling with the microscope herself.

Ford, Rose Aldrich Wilbur Swain only briefly mentions his first wife, the former Rose Aldrich Ford, in his memoirs. A wealthy woman who was a third cousin of Wilbur's, Rose was unhappy during the marriage because Wilbur did not love her. The brief marriage did produce a child, Carter Paley Swain, who was normal and thus uninteresting to Wilbur. After the couple divorce, Rose moves to Machu Picchu, Peru, to live in the same condominium complex as Wilbur's twin sister, Eliza. Wilbur never hears from her or from his son again.

Fu Manchu A tiny, thumb-sized ambassador from the People's Republic of China, Fu Manchu visits Wilbur Swain in his bedroom one evening at the hospital and clinic in the old Vermont mansion. Chosen as an emissary because he is so much larger than other Chinese, Fu Manchu tells Wilbur he had met his twin sister, Eliza, in Machu Picchu, Peru, where the Chinese had sent an expedition to recover Incan secrets. Eliza tells Fu Manchu that she and Wilbur have secrets even better, in the childhood papers they'd hidden in the mausoleum of Professor Elihu Roosevelt Swain. When Wilbur carries Fu Manchu out to the mausoleum, the tiny Chinese ambassador walks across the papers, reading them carefully, and seems to be especially interested in the theory of gravity the twins had proposed. Satisfied at last, Fu Manchu leaves, telling Wilbur that as a reward Eliza will be allowed to visit the Chinese colony on Mars. Three weeks later, Wilbur receives a telegram from Fu Manchu, informing him that Eliza died in a Martian earthquake. Immediately after this, gravity on Earth begins to act up for the very first time, suggesting that the Chinese, since reading the twins' theory, had been tinkering with the force.

Fu Manchu's Son The Chinese emissary who leads a delegation to Urbana, Illinois, to investigate Dr. Felix Bauxite-13 von Peterswald's apparatus that allows the living to speak to the dead turns out to be the son of Ambassador Fu Manchu, who had earlier visited Wilbur Swain at his children's hospital in Vermont. Fu Manchu's son, though, finds the apparatus uninteresting after he discovers how it works, explaining to Dr. von Peterswald's widow that the discovery could be "interesting only to participants in what is left of Western Civilization" (220).

Galen, Vermont   The spooky old Swain mansion, where neanderthaloid twins Eliza and Wilbur are raised, is located on 200 acres just outside the tiny hamlet of Galen, Vermont.

Garland, Dorothy Daffodil-7   When former U.S. president Wilbur Daffodil-11 Swain flies to INDIANAPOLIS to meet other Daffodils, he is given a warm welcome and is invited to attend a weekly family meeting of Daffodils. The meeting's chairperson, chosen by lot from all assembled, turns out to be Dorothy Daffodil-7 Garland, an 11-year-old black girl who runs the meeting with such authority that she impresses Wilbur greatly. He writes that "the little girl behind the lectern kept things moving so briskly and purposefully that she might have been some sort of goddess up there, equipped with an armload of thunderbolts" (245). As a result of watching the meeting, Wilbur is so filled with respect for parliamentary procedure that he calls ROBERT'S RULES OF ORDER "one of the four greatest inventions by Americans" (246). The others are the Bill of Rights, the principles of ALCOHOLICS ANONYMOUS, and the artificial extended families imagined by Wilbur and his twin sister, Eliza.

Grace Daffodil-13   Though readers never learn her last name, a "beautiful but disorderly" young woman named Grace Daffodil-13 stands up at the Daffodil family meeting in Indianapolis and, "crazed by altruism" (247), volunteers to take twenty refugees from the fighting in the north into her home. When she is admonished by the group as being an incompetent housekeeper, absentminded, and accident prone, Grace accepts the rebukes gracefully, staying for the rest of the meeting, and looking "sympathetic and alert" (247).

Grasso, Elmer Glenville   When he is campaigning for the office of president, Wilbur Swain is questioned by an old man named Elmer Glenville Grasso. Grasso tells Wilbur that he used to buy things he didn't need because he was lonely and the salesmen were friendly. Yet, he still is skeptical about Wilbur's new middle name scheme, asking if 10,000 brothers and sisters and 190,000 cousins

aren't an awful *lot* of relatives. Grasso also asks what happens if he gets a new artificial relative he can't stand. Wilbur tells him what to say to any such person: "Brother or Sister or Cousin . . . why don't you take a flying fuck at a rolling doughnut? Why don't you take a flying fuck at the moooooooon?" (186).

Green Death, the   The Green Death is a disease that kills off millions of Manhattanites while the Albanian Flu is ravaging the rest of the country. The Green Death turns out to be caused by microscopic Chinese who mean no harm, but who are fatal to any normal-size human that accidentally inhales or ingests them.

Hatfield, Byron   One day, after millions of citizens have already died of the Albanian Flu and the Green Death, and after gravity has begun to play havoc with the world, President Wilbur Swain, alone on the White House staircase, sees a man watching him from below. The figure, who is "dressed in buckskins and moccasins and a coonskin hat" (217), turns out to be Byron Hatfield, a descendent of the famous Hatfield family, who feuded with the McCoys. Byron had accidentally shot a man he believed to be Newton McCoy, an enemy of his. The man mistaken for a McCoy, though, had actually been a friend of Wilma Pachysandra-17 von Peterswald, and he was carrying to the president the letter the widow had written informing Swain of his twin sister Eliza's request to speak with him from beyond the grave. Byron Hatfield, a good Christian, promises to deliver the letter in the man's place.

"Hi-ho"   "Hi-ho" is a tagline repeated frequently in *Slapstick*. Like the refrain "So it goes" in *Slaughterhouse-Five* or "And so on" in *Breakfast of Champions*, "Hi-ho" is often used to punctuate short vignettes. It frequently ends troubling or strange passages that the novel's narrator, Wilbur Swain, does not know how else to comment on. The phrase can almost be read as meaning, "Oh well, life is strange, but there is not much we can do about it, except get on with it." Wilbur himself describes the phrase as a "kind of senile hiccup" (25), and tells readers that he has lived too long.

Hooligan, The   The Hooligan is a device that allows living people to talk to those who have died. It is named after a janitor, Francis Iron-7 Hooligan, who absentmindedly placed his lunch pail and a brown clay pipe on top of an abandoned particle-accelerator built by Dr. Felix Bauxite-13 von Peterswald, and subsequently heard voices coming from the pipe. Dr. von Peterswald, an open-minded scientist, believed Hooligan and instructed him to reposition his lunch pail and pipe exactly as it had been before. The doctor soon discovered that the voices were coming from the afterlife.

Hooligan, Francis Iron-7   A janitor who worked in the lab of Dr. Felix Bauxite-13 von Peterswald, Francis Iron-7 Hooligan one day absentmindedly places a piece of brown clay pipe and his lunch pail on top of a steel cabinet that contains an old particle-accelerator and immediately begins to hear voices. Dr. Von Peterswald demonstrates that he is a great scientist by believing the janitor and making him tell his story again and again and then recreating the exact conditions; von Peterswald discovers that the voices are those of dead people talking in the afterlife. The device is afterward referred to as "The Hooligan" by the few people who know about it.

Island of Death, The   The Island of Death is the name given to Manhattan after the Green Death has ravaged the island's inhabitants.

Kirk, Mary Selwyn   Mary Selwyn Kirk is one of two practical nurses hired to take care of the Swain twins at the Vermont mansion.

Kleindienst, Edward Strawberry-4   Edward Stawberry-4 Kleindienst was the valet of President Wilbur Swain. Unfortunately, he dies of Albanian Flu as do many White House staff members.

"Lonesome No More!"   "Lonesome No More!" is the campaign slogan of Wilbur Swain when he runs for president of the United States. The phrase also serves as the novel's subtitle. Wilbur runs on the platform of erasing loneliness in America. To this end, he invents an elaborate scheme of giving every U.S. citizen a new, computer-generated middle name and number that will create an instant, artificial extended family for every American. Wilbur's plan does not work out entirely as hoped. Although initially successful, the new middle names eventually splinter the country into family groups who begin to wage war on one another.

McBundy, Hortense Muskellunge-13   The private secretary to Wilbur Swain when he is president of the United States, Hortense Muskellunge-13 McBundy will later die of flu at the White House, along with many other staff members.

McCoy, Newton   When Byron Hatfield shoots the man delivering Wilma Pachysandra-17 von Peterwald's letter to the president, it is because he mistakes the messenger for Newton McCoy. Hatfield and McCoy are descendants of the famous feuding families in West Virginia.

Mott, Stewart Oriole-2   Stewart Oriole-2 Mott is the grandson of Dr. Stewart Rawlings Mott, the pediatrician hired to take care of the Swain twins. During Wilbur Swain's second term as president of the United States, when the country becomes factionalized due to the new middle names all citizens are assigned, Stewart Oriole-2 Mott becomes king of Michigan. Wilbur meets him when he is still "a skinny and supple and ascetic young soldier-saint" (51). During this meeting, the king requires Wilbur to sign a document selling all land contained in the original Louisiana Purchase to the king of Michigan for one dollar. In later life, Mott becomes "an obscene voluptuary, a fat old man in robes encrusted with precious stones" (51) who keeps a harem of children who share his middle name. Wilbur's granddaughter, Melody, is captured by Mott when she is six years old and kept in the harem until she escapes at the age of 12.

Mott, Dr. Stewart Rawlings   Described as a Texan and "a melancholy and private young man" (34), Dr. Stewart Rawlings Mott is the pediatrician hired by Caleb and Letitia Swain to look in on the neanderthaloid twins every day at the old Vermont mansion. When the twins reveal their intelligence, Dr. Mott's reaction is decidedly casual and unsurprised, unlike the rest of the servants or the twins' parents. Wilbur Swain, the book's narrator, tells readers that he is still unsure about Dr. Mott's motives: "I teeter even now between thinking that Dr. Mott loved Eliza and me, and knew how smart we were, and wished to protect us from the cruelties of the outside world, and thinking that he was comatose" (48). Whether he knew the twins' secret all along or not, Dr. Mott is nevertheless fired once they reveal it. Wilbur meets Dr. Mott again briefly during the lavish graduation party his mother throws for him after he finishes medical school. Too full of champagne to realize that Dr. Mott was his childhood pediatrician, Wilbur treats him dismissively. Dr. Mott, though, leaves a note for his former charge, which reads: "'If you can do no good, at least do no harm.' Hippocrates" (162), a dictum Wilbur has carved in stone over the front door of his medical clinic, until patients complain.

Mushari, Norman Jr. Norman Mushari, Jr. is a "fat and shifty-eyed attorney" hired by Eliza Swain to sue her family for locking her away for many years against her will. Tied to a dining room chair during the five-day orgy conducted by Eliza and Wilbur when they touch again after spending so long apart, Norman Mushari becomes severely disoriented and rips a thermostat from the wall, believing it to be a switch that controls the twins' behavior. Mushari is changed by his experience of being held captive and admits to Wilbur that he was a "bounty-hunter" when he freed Eliza from the institution where she had been confined. He explains that he made a practice of finding rich people in mental hospitals who didn't belong there, while he "left the poor to rot in their dungeons" (152). Mushari comes to Wilbur's attention only once more, when he reads in the *New York Times* that the former attorney has patented an invention—removeable taps for tap-dancing shoes. Norman Mushari, Jr. should be familiar to readers from Vonnegut's earlier novel, *God Bless You, Mr. Rosewater*—he is the attorney who persuades Fred Rosewater to sue Eliot Rosewater's branch of the family.

neanderthaloids The twins Wilbur and Eliza Swain are described as "neanderthaloids." They suffer from a new type of genetic disorder that gives them "the features of adult, fossil human beings even in infancy—massive brow-ridges, sloping foreheads, and steamshovel jaws" (30).

O'Hare, Captain Bernard Captain Bernard O'Hare, a name familiar to readers of Vonnegut's earlier novels *Mother Night* and *Slaughterhouse-Five*, appears at the White House one day after the nation has fallen apart—after millions of Americans have begun dying of the Albanian Flu and the Green Death and artificial families have begun battling over turf. Although President Wilbur Swain at first thinks O'Hare is a lunatic, he soon discovers that the man is perfectly sane. O'Hare had been stationed for the past 11-years in a secret underground silo, where a presidential helicopter with thousands of gallons of gasoline sits at the ready. He emerged from his silo to find out "what on Earth was going on" (225). Swain gets O'Hare to fly him first to Indianapolis, where they drop off Carlos Daffodil-11 Villavicencio, then on to a meeting with the king of Michigan, and finally to Urbana, Illinois, for an "electronic reunion" between Wilbur and his long-dead sister, Eliza, conducted over Dr. Felix Bauxite-13 von Peterswald's device for speaking to the dead.

Piatigorsky, Dr. Albert Aquamarine-1 Science adviser to President Wilbur Swain, Dr. Albert Aquamarine-1 Piatigorsky dies of the Albanian Flu, actually expiring in the arms of the president on the floor of the Oval Office.

Raspberry Family Kidnappers Wilbur Swain, after talking to his sister, Eliza, on "The Hooligan" device, has his helicopter pilot, Captain Bernard O'Hare, drop him off in Manhattan, where he hopes to die by inhaling microscopically tiny Chinese communists. At the end of his first day there, Wilbur is captured by six armed members of the Raspberry family who are in desperate need of a doctor. They give him the antidote to the Green Death, then take him to minister to Hiroshi Raspberry-20 Yamashiro, the head of the family who is deathly ill with pneumonia. When the fever breaks, the Raspberries bring Dr. Swain their most precious possessions. To be polite, he selects a single brass candlestick, thereby establishing his legend as the King of Candlesticks.

Rivera, Wanda Chipmunk-5   At the 101st birthday party for Wilbur Swain, the candlestick brought to him by his granddaughter, Melody Oriole-2 Mott, is kicked over and broken by an intoxicated slave named Wanda Chipmunk-5 Rivera.

Rockmell, Dr. Eli W.   During their five-day orgy in Boston, Eliza and Wilbur Swain write a child-rearing manual, which they call *The Cry of the Nocturnal Goatsucker,* by Betty and Bobby Brown. When Wilbur becomes a practicing pediatrician, he publishes the book under a pseudonym, which is an amalgam of the twins' names: Dr. Eli W. Rock-mell, M.D. The book is retitled *So You Went and Had a Baby.*

Swain, Caleb Mellon   The father of the nean-derthalaoid twins Eliza and Wilbur Swain, Caleb Swain is of normal intelligence although he is fabulously wealthy and from an aristocratic family background; he is very good at backgammon, so-so at color photography, and a kind man who adores his wife, Letitia. Caleb and Letitia refuse to send the twins to an institution at birth, instead ensconcing them in an old family mansion in Vermont where Eliza and Wilbur enjoy a happy childhood until they turn 15 and reveal their true intelligence. Caleb dies in an automobile accident during Wilbur's first year in medical school.

Swain, Carter Paley   Carter Paley Swain is the son of the novel's narrator, Dr. Wilbur Daffodil-11 Swain, from his first marriage, to Rose Aldrich Ford. Described as being "like a summer squash on the vine—featureless and watery, and merely growing larger all the time" (163), the boy is normal and thus completely uninteresting to his father, who never learns to love him. When Wilbur and Rose divorce, Carter moves with his mother to Machu Picchu, Peru.

Swain, Professor Elihu Roosevelt [Witherspoon]   The largest monument in the Swain cemetery under the apple trees at the old Vermont mansion belongs to the founder of the family's fortune and builder of the mansion, Professor Elihu Roosevelt Swain. Wilbur Swain tells readers that the professor was the most intelligent of all his ancestors. He took a degree from the MASSACHUSETTS INSTITUTE OF TECHNOLOGY when he was 18, and was an engineering professor at CORNELL UNIVERSITY by the age of 22. Tired of teaching, Elihu Swain goes on to found the Swain Bridge Company, and to become the personal friend of many heads of state. Eliza and Wilbur find out two of the professor's secrets, though: first, that "there was a mansion concealed within the mansion" (41), accessible through trap doors and sliding panels, and second that the professor's real middle name was not Roosevelt but was actually Witherspoon. He renamed himself when he entered M.I.T. so that he would seem more aristocratic. This act of renaming is what inspires the twins to concoct their scheme of giving everyone in the country new middle names. The twins also use the professor's mausoleum as a hiding place for their secret papers.

Swain, Eliza Mellon   The equally monstrous twin sister of Wilbur Swain, Eliza Swain never learns to read or write, though she is the one who directs the reading the twins do in their isolated mansion in Vermont. She also is the one who makes the great intuitive leaps that lead to many of the scientific discoveries she and Wilbur make. Yet, when the twins betray their genius and are separated for testing, she is labeled the less intelligent of the two and is sent to live in an expensive private hospital for patients who are near-vegetables. Bitterly resentful of this treatment in later life, Eliza hires attorney Norman Mushari, Jr. to sue her family. Eliza reunites briefly with Wilbur at his home in Beacon Hill after he finishes medical school. But the five-day orgiastic frenzy that results in the two touching each other again after so many years terrifies both twins. As a result, Eliza moves to Machu Pichu in Peru, where she lives until convincing a miniaturized Chinese ambassador to send her to their colony on Mars, where she dies in an avalanche shortly after arrival.

Swain, Letitia Vanderbilt Like her husband, Caleb, Letitia Swain is young, pretty, rich, and of average intelligence. Though she cares enough for her monstrous twins Eliza and Wilbur not to have them institutionalized at birth, she nevertheless, like Caleb, secretly wishes the embarrassing children would die as they grown into teenagers. Letitia, in fact, on the eve of the twin's 15th birthday expresses out loud her repressed hatred for her children, although she is sorry and ashamed afterward. Her outburst, which is overheard by Eliza and Wilbur, causes the twins to reveal their true intelligence to their parents the next day, eventually causing them to be separated for the rest of their lives, despite an incident in which Letitia vociferously defends her offspring against a dismissive psychologist. Letitia shares a house with Wilbur after he is grown up, getting to know her son quite well although she never develops a real relationship with Eliza, who had been sent as a teenager to live in an expensive hospital for the mentally infirm. Letitia Swain dies two weeks after the first attack of extremely heavy gravity strikes Earth.

Swain, Sophie Rothschild As he is vigorously campaigning for political office, buoyed up by tri-benzo-Deportamil pills, Wilbur Swain "picked up a pretty new wife, Sophie Rothschild Swain, who was only twenty-three" (184). Eventually, Sophie takes to wearing a button that reads, "Lonesome, Thank God," a slogan designed by opponents of Wilbur's artifical middle-name scheme and his campaign slogan, "Lonesome No More!" When new middle names are assigned, Sophie becomes a Peanut-3. Furious about this, Sophie eventually divorces Wilbur and moves to a condominium in Machu Pichu, Peru.

Swain, Dr. Wilbur Daffodil-11 The narrator of the story, Dr. Wilbur Daffodil-11 Swain is about to turn 101 years old and is writing his autobiography as the novel begins. We find out that he was born in New York City and that, along with his twin sister, Eliza, he was considered a neanderthaloid at birth, a sort of monstrous idiot with the physical characteristics of prehistoric people. The twins' parents, not wanting to institutionalize the

pair for the rest of their lives, instead sets them up with a platoon of servants in an old family mansion in Vermont. There, Wilbur and Eliza have an extremely happy childhood, pretending to be drooling idiots in public, but secretly devouring the vast collection of books in the mansion's library and propounding scientific theories. Not until they turn 15 and reveal to their parents their true intelligence do the twins get cast out of their childhood paradise. On the advice of a psychologist, Wilbur is separated from Eliza forever. Parted, the twins lose the genius they enjoyed when together, becoming dull "Bobby and Betty Brown." Nevertheless, Wilbur goes on to medical school to become a pediatrician and later enters politics, eventually becoming president of the United States, his confidence boosted by an addiction to a drug intended to treat the side effects of Tourette's syndrome. As president, Wilbur institutes a scheme to end loneliness in the United States by creating enormous, artificial extended families for all citizens by granting them new, computer-generated middle names. At first wildly successful, the scheme eventually leads to warring factions and balkanizes the nation. At the same time, millions and millions of people are dying from new diseases introduced by Chinese experiments. Wilbur lives out his twilight years in a post-apocalyptic setting on a decimated and destroyed Manhattan Island, accompanied by his granddaughter and her lover. He dies shortly after his 101st birthday party, his memoirs concluded by an unnamed third-person narrator.

Swain, Unnamed Son of Wilbur When Wilbur Swain visits the Urbana widow, Wilma Pachysandra-17 von Peterswald, and speaks to his dead sister, Eliza, on the device called "The Hooligan," he gives his remaining supply of tri-benzo-Deportamil to Wilma's son, who has Tourette's syndrome. Wilbur's withdrawal from the medication is so "spectacular" (267) that he must be tied to a bed for six nights and days, during which time he makes love to the widow and conceives an illegitimate son who is never named, but who in turn fathers Melody Oriole-2 von Peterswald when he is 14 years old. Wilbur's son is killed in the Battle of Iowa City when Melody is six years old.

Theodorides, Mildred Helium-20 The vice president to Wilbur Swain, Mildred Helium-20 Theodorides dies of Albanian Flu like many other White House staff members and politicians.

tri-benzo-Deportamil On the same day that the first enormous jolt of heavy gravity strikes Earth, Wilbur Swain receives in the mail an envelope from a pharmaceutical company filled with samples of a pill called tri-benzo-Deportamil, a treatment for Tourette's syndrome. Wilbur swallows two of the pills and is immediately "flooded with contentment and confidence" (176). This begins an addiction that will last for the next 30 years.

Unnamed Blacksmith At the weekly family meeting of the Daffodils in Indianapolis that Wilbur Swain attends, a strapping young blacksmith volunteers to serve as a replacement for the fallen Daffodils in the army of the king of Michigan, who is currently battling both Great Lakes pirates and the duke of Oklahoma. "Send me," the young man pleads, "There's nothing I'd rather do than kill me some 'Sooners,' long as they ain't Daffodils" (243). The young blacksmith is scolded by the assembled Daffodils for his "military ardor" (243) and reminded that war is not fun but tragic. Wilbur is impressed by the family's reaction, noting that while nations cannot acknowledge their own wars as tragedies, family groups *must* do so.

Unnamed Doorkeeper and Scribes When Wilbur Swain is summoned to an audience with the king of Michigan at his summer palace, a doorkeeper announces his arrival in pompous fashion. Three male scribes write down everything that is said, for the sake of history. The king tells Wilbur that history is all he reads, and then repeats the cliché that "Those who fail to learn from history are condemned to repeat it" (255). In response, Wilbur instructs the scribes to write that "History is merely a list of surprises. . . . It can only prepare us to be surprised yet again" (255).

Unnamed General Electric Safety Officer In the prologue to *Slapstick,* Vonnegut tells how his brother's laboratory in Schenectady, New York,

when he worked for the GENERAL ELECTRIC Company, was a "sensational mess" (4). In fact, an unnamed G.E. safety officer "nearly swooned" when he visited the office one time and "bawled out" Bernard for the mess (5). Bernard replied by tapping his forehead and saying, "If you think this laboratory is bad, you should see what it's like in *here*" (5).

Unnamed Guard at the Thirteen Club On a visit to Manhattan, Wilbur Swain sees his first Thirteen Club, "raffish establishments" started by people whose new middle names contain the number 13. Even though he is president, Wilbur is not allowed inside the club. An unnamed guard, instead of letting Wilbur in, tells him to "take a flying fuck at a rolling doughnut . . . take a flying fuck at the moooooooon" (210), the same advice Wilbur had earlier instructed Elmer Glenville Grasso to give any new artificial relatives he does not like.

Unnamed Head Nurse After gravity becomes extremely heavy on Earth for the very first time, Wilbur Swain goes out to the mausoleum behind the children's hospital to read the scientific papers he and Eliza had hidden there as children. His reading is interrupted by his head nurse, who tells Wilbur that all the frightened young patients have gotten to sleep at last. Wilbur then asks her to order 2,000 doses of tri-benzo-Deportamil, the drug intended to treat symptoms of Tourette's syndrome that Wilbur has just ingested.

Unnamed Hospital Patient When Alice Vonnegut's husband dies in a commuter train wreck, Kurt and Bernard Vonnegut do not inform her of the tragedy, since Alice herself is in the hospital, dying of cancer, and her husband is supposed to take full charge of their four boys after her death. Yet, Alice finds out about her husband's death when an "ambulatory female patient" (14) at the hospital gives her a copy of the New York *Daily News* to read, which includes a cover story about the wreck as well as a list of those killed.

Unnamed Inca Servant During Wilbur Swain's lavish graduation party at the Ritz Hotel in Boston, an Inca servant of Eliza Swain's, disguised as a bellhop, lures Wilbur deep into the woods. When the servant fires a flare, Eliza appears overhead, in a helicopter. Using a bullhorn, Eliza bellows half of a Shakespearean sonnet to Wilbur.

Unnamed Laundress The mother of Melody Oriole-2 von Peterswald is an unnamed 40-year-old laundress who is attached to the army of the duke of Oklahoma. She meets the illegitimate son of Dr. Swain when he survives the "Urbana Massacre" (272) and is pressed into service as a 14-year-old drummer boy in the duke's army. Melody's mother and father are both slain in the Battle of Iowa City when Melody is six years old.

Unnamed Radiant Youth During the same visit to Manhattan in which he is not allowed inside a Thirteen Club, President Wilbur Swain learns of the existence of The Church of Jesus Christ the Kidnapped, a tiny cult at the time, but "destined to become the most popular American religion of all time" (210). An unnamed but "clean and radiant youth" hands Wilbur a leaflet about the religion as he crosses the lobby of his hotel. The leaflet explains that the new religion believes Jesus Christ is on Earth but has been kidnapped by the Forces of Evil. Thus, practitioners of the religion must drop whatever they are doing and spend every waking hour trying to find Him. This explains why the radiant youth constantly darts his head from side to side, "firing ardent glances this way and that" (210).

Unnamed Slave Two days before Wilbur Swain turns 101 years old, an unnamed slave of Vera Chipmunk-5 Zappa brings Wilbur, Melody, and Isadore a chicken, two loaves of bread, and two liters of beer. The slave pantomimes how nourishing he is being to the three. He holds the bottles to his nipples, pretending that he has breasts that give creamy beer, causing Wilbur, Melody, and Isadore to laugh and clap their hands.

Unnamed Television Reporter After Eliza Swain's release from the mental hospital, she grants numerous television interviews, although she will not allow herself to be photographed. The inter-

views are done with Eliza sitting inside a confessional booth she had purchased from a church. In one of these interviews, an unnamed television reporter asks how Eliza spent her time in the hospital. Eliza replies that she sang the same song over and over again—"Some Day My Prince Will Come" (130). The prince she had in mind, she tells the reporter, was her twin brother, Wilbur, adding, "But he's a swine, of course. He never came" (130).

Villavicencio, Carlos Daffodil-11 Originally a White House dishwasher, Carlos Daffodil-11 Villavicencio is befriended by the president, Wilbur Swain, when the two men are given the same new middle name. As White Staff begin dying off from the Albanian Flu or else wandering away, Carlos is the one employee who stays. Later, when Captain Bernard O'Hare flies President Swain to Indianapolis, which has become densely populated with Daffodils, they decide to leave Carlos there before flying on to Wilbur's childhood home in Vermont. "I was glad to be getting rid of him," Wilbur tells readers about the dishwasher, "He bored me to tears" (228).

von Peterswald, David Daffodil-11 The son of the widow in Urbana whose late husband had discovered a way of talking to the dead through an apparatus involving a pipe and a lunch pail, David Daffodil-11 von Peterswald suffers from Tourette's syndrome. As a result, when Wilbur Swain talks to his sister, Eliza, over the apparatus, David begins shouting a string of obscenities. Dead people in the background "sensed that poor David was a kindred spirit, as outraged by the human condition in the Universe as they were" (263). So they egg the boy on, shouting obscenities of their own and doubling David's obscenities.

von Peterswald, Dr. Felix Bauxite-13 Dr. Felix Bauxite-13 von Peterswald, deceased at the time of the story, had accidentally discovered a way of speaking to the dead. Much to his dismay, however, Dr. von Peterswald also discovered that Paradise is "tedious in the extreme" (219). Thus, he refers to the other side not as "Heaven" or "Our Just Reward," but as "The Turkey Farm."

von Peterswald, Wilma Pachysandra-17   A piano teacher in Urbana, Illinois, Wilma Pachysandra-17 von Peterswald is the widow of Dr. Felix Bauxite-13 von Peterswald, a physicist who, just before his death, stumbled upon a way of talking to the dead. The son of Chinese ambassador Fu Manchu has been to visit her, to study her late husband's journals, but once the Chinese figure out the discovery, they lose interest in it. Wilma writes a letter to Wilbur Swain, explaining these events, and also informing him that she and her son have spoken to Wilbur's dead twin sister, Eliza, many times on her husband's apparatus. Eliza had begged the von Peterswalds to bring Wilbur himself to speak with her. When Wilbur visits Urbana, he discovers that "so-called 'Paradise'" (264) is utterly boring. Eliza pleads with Wilbur to blow his brains out quick so he can join her there and the two can think up ways to improve eternity. After this communication with his sister, Wilbur gives his few remaining tri-benzo-Deportamil pills to the widow's son. His withdrawal from the medication is so "spectaular" (267) that Wilbur must be tied to a bed in the widow's house for six nights and days. "Somewhere in there," Vonnegut writes, "he made love to the widow, conceiving a son who would become the father of Melody Oriole-2 von Peterswald" (267).

Vonnegut, Alex   Alex Vonnegut was the younger brother of Kurt Vonnegut's father. In the novel's prologue, Vonnegut describes a plane trip he and his older brother, Bernard, take back to Indianapolis to attend Uncle Alex's funeral. Described as "almost the last of [their] old-style relatives" (8), Alex Vonnegut represents the illustrious past of the Vonnegut family—"native American patriots who did not fear God, and who had souls that were European" (8). Although he was the cofounder of the Indianapolis Chapter of Alcoholics Anonymous, Alex Vonnegut's newspaper obituary claimed that he himself was not an alcoholic, a statement Kurt Vonnegut describes as "denial" (9).

Vonnegut, Alice   Alice Vonnegut was Kurt Vonnegut's older sister, who died in 1958 of cancer. Coincidentally, Alice's husband, James Carmalt Adams, had been killed in a commuter train wreck two days

previously. Kurt Vonnegut and his first wife, Jane, adopted Alice's three oldest sons after her death. In many ways, *Slapstick* is Vonnegut's attempt to come to terms with his sister's death. He explains to readers in his prologue that Alice was the person he had always secretly written for, "She was the secret of whatever artistic unity I had ever achieved," he adds, "She was the secret of my technique" (16–17). A few pages later, Vonnegut tells readers that he daydreamed the plot of *Slapstick* on the plane back to Indianapolis to attend his Uncle Alex Vonnegut's funeral. He says that the book depicts him and his "beautiful sister" as monsters (20).

Vonnegut, Bernard   Kurt Vonnegut's older brother, Bernard, was an atmospheric scientist at the State University of New York at Albany when *Slapstick* was published. In the novel's prologue, Vonnegut tells readers that his longest experience with human decency has been with Bernard. He describes an airplane trip the two men take together to their Uncle Alex's funeral in Indianapolis, explaining that the empty seat between them on the plane could have been reserved for their deceased sister, Alice.

Vonnegut, Jane Cox   Jane Cox Vonnegut was Kurt Vonnegut's first wife. In the prologue, Vonnegut tells readers how he and Jane adopted his sister's three oldest boys after their parents died within 48 hours of each other. Jane and Kurt Vonnegut raise the boys along with their own three children on Cape Cod.

von Peterswald, Melody Oriole-2   Melody Oriole-2 von Peterswald is the granddaughter of Dr. Wilbur Daffodil-11 Swain, her father the product of a brief union between Wilbur and Wilma Pachysandra-17 von Peterswald, a widow in Urbana, Illinois, whose late husband had invented a way to communicate with the dead. Melody was given the middle name Oriole-2 in hopes that she would be treated with mercy should she be captured by Stewart Oriole-2 Mott, the king of Michigan, who was battling the duke of Oklahoma during the period of Melody's birth. Melody, at age six, is indeed captured by the king of Michigan. But rather than being treated mercifully, she is put into a seraglio of captured children with the same middle name as the king. She eventually escapes and heads East to look for her mythic grandfather—Wilbur Swain— known now as the "King of New York." Pregnant when she arrives at the age of 12, Melody has a still-born infant son. Later, she will acquire a lover, Isadore Raspberry-19 Cohen, and the two will labor to build a pyramid out of debris in honor of the dead infant. At the close of the book, when Wilbur Swain dies, Melody is pregnant again, this time with Isadore's child.

Wainwright, The Right Reverend William Uranium-8 Reverend Wainwright is the founder of The Church of Jesus Christ the Kidnapped, which believes that Jesus is on Earth but has been kidnapped by the Forces of Evil. Thus, practitioners must devote every waking hour of their lives to constantly searching for Him. If they don't do so, the church teaches, God will destroy all Mankind.

Wilkinson, Max In his prologue to *Slapstick,* Vonnegut tells his brother Bernard that he is "sick of" writing (17). He recounts an anecdote about the writer Renata Adler, who defined a writer as "a person who hated writing" (18). When Vonnegut complains to his agent, Max Wilkinson, "about what a disagreeable profession" he has, Wilkinson writes back: "Dear Kurt—I never knew a blacksmith who was in love with his anvil" (18). Vonnegut and Bernard laugh about this joke, but Vonnegut suspects that Bernard, who loves his work, has actually experienced "an unending honeymoon with his anvil" (18).

Witherspoon, Withers Withers Witherspoon was a combination guard, chauffeur and handyman who attended Wilbur and Eliza Swain when they were children growing up in the mansion in Vermont. After the twins' true intelligence is discovered, Withers Witherspoon's job is to keep watch over one twin in the ballroom at the top of the tower at the north end of the mansion while the other twin is being tested in the dining room so as to prevent any mental telepathy between the two.

Yamashiro, Hiroshi Raspberry-20 The head of the Raspberry family in Manhattan, Hiroshi Raspberry-20 Yamashiro is deathly ill with pneumonia when he is treated by Dr. Wilbur Swain. When the fever breaks, Wilbur accepts the gift of a candlestick from the family, thus starting the tradition of everyone bringing him candlesticks as gifts and earning himself the moniker the King of Candlesticks.

Zappa, Lee Razorclam-13 The alcoholic former husband of Vera Chipmunk-5 Zappa, Lee Razorclam-13 Zappa beats Vera up during the Battle of Lake Maxinkuckee, when the two are working as cooks in the army of the king of Michigan. Following the beating, Lee steps outside of the pair's tent, where he is immediately "skewered by the lance of an enemy cavalryman" (238). When Vera tells this story to Wilbur Swain, Wilbur asks her about the moral. "Wilbur," Vera replies, "don't ever get married" (238).

Zappa, Vera Chipmunk-5 Vera Chipmunk-5 Zappa, a 60-year-old hard-working and capable woman, is the nearest neighbor to Wilbur Swain and his granddaughter, who live in the ruins of the Empire State Building in Manhattan, now called the Island of Death. A farmer who raises crops and animals along the banks of the East River in New York, Vera is also mistress to a large group of slaves who work the farm alongside her. Being a Chipmunk-5 slave is considered a very desirable position among the remaining few inhabitants of Manhattan; Melody Oriole-2 von Peterswald and Isadore Raspberry-19 Cohen both have ambitions to someday become slaves themselves. On Wilbur Daffodil-11 Swain's 101st birthday, Vera brings gifts of wine and beer and a thousand candles she has made with her slaves. Wilbur, who collects candlesticks, stands among all the lights and feels as if he is "up to [his] knees in the Milky Way" (258).

FURTHER READING

Blackford, Russell. "The Definition of Love: Kurt Vonnegut's *Slapstick*." *Science Fiction* 2, no. 3 (1980): 208–228.

Slapstick. New York: Dell, 1999.

Slaughterhouse-Five

Slaughterhouse-Five, published in 1969 by Delacorte under the guidance of SEYMOUR LAWRENCE, is the novel that catapulted Vonnegut to widespread fame. Reaching number one on the *New York Times* best-seller list, Vonnegut's DRESDEN novel is also considered a masterpiece by critics. The novel recounts the life of passive, antiheroic Billy Pilgrim, who, having come "unstuck in time" (23), stumbles back and forth between his childhood, his wartime experiences, his marriage and career as an optometrist, and his eventual kidnapping by space aliens and mating to ex-porn star Montana Wildhack. In telling Billy's story, Vonnegut deglamorizes war by dismantling traditional narrative form. While conventional war stories may provide roles for heroes that would be played by Frank Sinatra and John Wayne in the movies, *Slaughterhouse-Five* presents a war fought by children and incompetents, a war in which the Allies as well as the Nazis commit appalling atrocities. Recognizing that it might be futile to write an antiwar novel, that wars may be as hard to prevent as "glaciers" (3) or as "plain old death" (4), nevertheless Vonnegut in *Slaughterhouse-Five* looks back open-eyed at his Dresden experiences, and writes a funny, eloquent, and heartbreaking plea for human beings to remember their basic humanity.

SYNOPSIS

Chapter 1
The opening chapter of *Slaughterhouse-Five* details the trouble Vonnegut had writing "this lousy little book" (2). Having witnessed the Allied bombing of Dresden during World War II as a prisoner of war, Vonnegut tells readers that he thought the book would be easy to write; he'd simply report what he had seen and, if he did not have a masterpiece, at least he would make a lot of money. Yet, telling the story of his Dresden experiences is not as easy as Vonnegut anticipated. Stymied by a lack of memories as well as admonitions about the futility of writing an antiwar novel, Vonnegut visits an old war buddy, BERNARD V. O'HARE, in an attempt to jog his memories of the war. Vonnegut's visit to O'Hare does not turn out as he had expected either. O'Hare's wife, Mary, slams around the house, obvi-

ously angry at Vonnegut. The two men soon discover that Mary's anger stems from her fear that Vonnegut will write a book that glorifies war, that he will pretend he and O'Hare were men rather than babies and cause other babies, like the children upstairs at the O'Hare house, to want to fight in wars. Abashed, Vonnegut promises Mary that he will subtitle his Dresden book THE CHILDREN'S CRUSADE. Yet, Vonnegut declares at the end of this opening chapter that the book is a failure, that it is "so short and jumbled and jangled . . . because there is nothing intelligent to say about a massacre" (19). He compares himself to LOT'S WIFE in the Bible, who turns into a pillar of salt after being warned not to look back at Sodom and Gomorrah. Like Lot's wife, Vonnegut looks back at great destruction, something he tells readers he won't do again.

Chapters 2–4
The story proper begins in the second chapter and details the life of awkward, ungainly Billy Pilgrim, a "funny-looking child who became a funny-looking youth—tall and weak, and shaped like a bottle of Coca Cola" (23). Billy is born and raised in ILIUM, New York. Drafted by the military, he becomes a chaplain's assistant during World War II, when, like Vonnegut, he is captured behind German lines during the BATTLE OF THE BULGE and subsequently witnesses the Allied bombing of Dresden. After returning home, Billy attends optometry school and becomes engaged to the enormously obese Valencia Merble, daughter of the school's owner and founder. Soon after that, he has "a mild nervous collapse" and is treated briefly in a veteran's hospital, where he is given electric shock treatments and where he meets Eliot Rosewater, who introduces him to the SCIENCE FICTION writings of Kilgore Trout. Following his release, Billy marries Valencia, has two children, and becomes quite wealthy and successful. In 1968, on his way to an optometrist's convention, Billy severely injures his head in a plane crash that kills everyone on board but him. His wife, Valencia, accidentally dies from carbon monoxide poisoning while Billy is recovering in the hospital.

While Vonnegut provides readers with a similar synopsis of Billy's life soon after introducing the character, the book does not tell Billy's story in a linear fashion. Chapter 2 opens with the lines, "Listen: Billy Pilgrim has come unstuck in time" (23). Billy does not experience his own life in chronological order; rather, he travels back and forth in time, reliving experiences from his childhood, from the war, and from his life after the war in a seemingly random way. The bulk of the narrative, though, focuses on Billy's wartime experiences, to which he keeps returning throughout the story. An object of contempt and ridicule to his fellow soldiers, Billy finds himself a "dazed wanderer" behind enemy lines during the Battle of the Bulge in December 1944 (32). Billy is accompanied by two graceful and clever scouts as well as by Roland Weary, a violent, angry anti-tank gunner who regales Billy with stories of his father's collection of torture implements and who imagines himself as a bosom buddy of the scouts, thinking of the trio as "the three musketeers." In reality, the scouts are waiting for an opportunity to ditch both Weary and Billy, who are slowing them down. Billy himself is in bad shape, described as a "filthy flamingo," and begging to be left behind. Weary kicks and punches Billy, though, forcing him to keep moving. Eventually captured by a ragtag group of German soldiers after being abandoned by the scouts, who are later shot, Billy and Roland Weary are marched to join other American prisoners, where they are herded onto crowded boxcars and slowly driven to a prisoner-of-war camp in Dresden. Roland Weary dies of gangrene from infected footsores while on the train, but not before a rabid, pockmarked car thief named Paul Lazarro promises to avenge Weary against Billy, whom Weary believes caused his death.

Chapters 5–8

When the exhausted and bedraggled American men arrive at the camp in Dresden, they find it

Old Market in Dresden, circa 1900 *(courtesy of the Library of Congress)*

populated by cheery, jaunty British officers who were captured at the beginning of the war and have spent the last four years hoarding food, decorating their quarters, playing games, and practicing calisthenics. Having made elaborate preparations to welcome the American prisoners, including a musical production of *Cinderella*, the Brits are dismayed by their American guests, particularly by Billy, who cuts a ridiculous figure with the tiny crimson-lined coat he has been given, which fits him like a stole. The American most respected by the British officers is Edgar Derby, a physically fit and compassionate high school teacher from INDIANAPOLIS, old enough to have a grown-up son who is a Marine fighting in the Pacific theater of the war. When Nazi propagandist Howard W. Campbell, Jr. (the main character from Vonnegut's third novel, *Mother Night*) tries to recruit prisoners for a German military unit called "The Free America Corps," Derby bravely stands up to him, praising the American form of government. Ironically, Edgar Derby is shot at the end of the war in Dresden for taking a teapot that isn't his, an incident, Vonnegut explains to O'Hare in the opening chapter, that will be the climax of his Dresden novel.

Tralfamadorian Chapters

Mixed in with these traumatic war experiences and with moments from his everyday life both before and after the war are Billy's bizarre experiences on the planet Tralfamadore, where he is taken in a flying saucer after being kidnapped from Earth following his daughter's wedding. The Tralfamadorians keep Billy in a zoo on their planet, where he is mated with ex-porn star Montana Wildhack. Back on Earth, Billy writes letters to the newspapers about his Tralfamadorian experiences, describing the creatures as green, two feet tall, and shaped like toilet plungers, infuriating his daughter, Barbara, who believes that Billy is delusional. According to Billy, the Tralfamadorians do not experience time as Earthlings do—they see all of time at once, like a mountain range. In fact, they can see how the universe will end; a Tralfamadorian pilot, experimenting with new fuels for their flying saucers, will accidentally blow it up. When Billy asks if there

is some way, knowing this end, that it can be prevented, a Tralfamadorian tells Billy it has always happened and always will happen: "The moment is *structured* that way" (117). When Billy asks about FREE WILL, he is told that of the 31 inhabited planets the Tralfamadorians have studied, only on Earth is there talk of free will. The Tralfamadorians teach Billy to see time as they do. He believes he, too, can see all of time at once, claiming even to have experienced his own death many times. Billy says he always has and always will die on February 13th, 1976, at the hand of Paul Lazarro, who assassinates him in revenge for Roland Weary's death. But because all of time exists simultaneously, this foreknowledge of his own death does not disturb Billy. He passively waits for nicer moments in his life to occur—particularly his mating with Montana Wildhack in the zoo on Tralfamadore.

Chapter 10

The novel closes with Vonnegut speaking about himself again. He takes readers back to the present time he is writing the book—1968—stating that ROBERT KENNEDY was shot two nights ago and that MARTIN LUTHER KING, JR. was assassinated a month previously. He briefly details a trip that he and Bernard V. O'Hare took back to Dresden, informing readers that Billy Pilgrim is also traveling back to Dresden, though not in the present, but in 1945, two days after the Allied bombing. The scene then shifts to Billy and his fellow prisoners of war walking out of the slaughterhouse and into the moonscape that Dresden has become. The horror and scale of the atrocity are driven home when Vonnegut writes about the corpse mines that Billy and his fellow soldiers are ordered to excavate. Yet, on the very last page, Vonnegut perhaps offers some hope for the future, writing that "somewhere in there was springtime" (215). The novel's final word is spoken to Billy by a bird: "Poo-tee-weet?," the nonsense syllables that Vonnegut had earlier claimed were the only thing to be said about a massacre.

COMMENTARY

While *Slaughterhouse-Five* is certainly a novel about war, it is also a novel about narrative itself, a novel that shows how the stories people tell about the

Two men with tipcart on top of rubble in Dresden, Germany, after firebombing during World War II *(courtesy of the Library of Congress)*

world they live in help shape that world. In this sense, the book is an example of METAFICTION: fiction that takes as its subject fiction itself. Vonnegut begins the novel by outlining the difficulties he has writing his planned Dresden book. The first obstacle he faces is the seeming inability of literary art to make any real difference in the world. When he tells Harrison Starr, the famous moviemaker, about his Dresden novel, Starr asks if it's an anti-war book. When Vonnegut replies that he guesses it is, Starr says, "Why don't you write an anti-*glacier* book instead?" (3). Vonnegut explains, "What he meant, of course, was that there would always be wars, that they were as easy to stop as glaciers." He adds, "I believe that, too" (3). Because Vonnegut suggests that war is inevitable, and he seems to believe his antiwar novel might do no good, the opening chapter is packed with images of futility and impotence. The young man from Stamboul in the limerick Vonnegut remembers "soliloquize[s]" to "his tool" about its uselessness; the Yon Yonson song mindlessly repeats forever; when Vonnegut tells people about the atrocities he witnessed in

Dresden, they respond by reciting Nazi atrocities; the history book by MARY ENDELL he reads relates the 1760 Prussian destruction of Dresden. These references all suggest continued cycles of death, decay, and destruction that may be inescapable.

Another difficulty Vonnegut has in writing the book is with the inadequacy of straightforward journalism. He thought it would be easy to write about the destruction of Dresden since he was an eyewitness and could simply report what he had seen. Yet, Vonnegut also relates in this initial chapter an experience he had after the war working as a police reporter for the "famous Chicago City News Bureau" (8). The first story Vonnegut covered was about a veteran who was crushed to death when his wedding ring got caught in the ornamental iron lace of an old-fashioned office elevator. When Vonnegut phoned the story in, a "beastly girl" whose job it was to write up the story coldly told Vonnegut to call up the veteran's wife to get her reaction. Later, this same writer, while eating a Three Musketeers Candy Bar, asked Vonnegut, "just for her own information, what the squashed guy had looked like when he was squashed" (9). The point of this incident is to show how jaded and cynical constant reports of atrocity can make one. Simple reporting, divorced from the moral dimension that is more properly the realm of literature, can desensitize one to violence. Thus, Vonnegut cannot merely report what he saw in Dresden as he first thought.

Perhaps the opposite problem in writing about war is that it can so easily be glamorized. During Billy Pilgrim's honeymoon with Valencia Merble later in the novel, Valencia asks about Billy's war experiences right after they make love. "It was a simple-minded thing for a female Earthling to do," Vonnegut writes, "to associate sex and glamor with war" (121). Mary O'Hare's fear, expressed in the opening chapter, is certainly that Vonnegut intends to write a novel that will romanticize war. When Vonnegut visits his old war buddy, Bernard V. O'Hare, Mary lets her anger show. She expects that Vonnegut's book will be like other war books she has read: "You'll pretend you were men instead of babies, and you'll be played in the movies by Frank Sinatra and John Wayne or some of those other glamorous, war-loving, dirty old men. And war will look just wonderful, so we'll have a lot more of them" (14). Vonnegut solemnly pledges to Mary that he will not write that kind of book. As part of Vonnegut's promise to Mary O'Hare, then, *Slaughterhouse-Five* is a novel that radically reforms and revises traditional ways of writing about war, deflating the romance and glamour often associated with war narratives.

In fact, the book overturns traditional narrative conventions right from the start, beginning with the title page that refuses to stop. Not only does Vonnegut give the novel two subtitles, but the author's name is followed by a lengthy introduction to the book itself:

BY
Kurt Vonnegut
A FOURTH-GENERATION
GERMAN-AMERICAN
NOW LIVING IN EASY CIRCUMSTANCES
ON CAPE COD
[AND SMOKING TOO MUCH],
WHO, AS AN AMERICAN INFANTRY
SCOUT
HORS DE COMBAT,
AS A PRISONER OF WAR,
WITNESSED THE FIRE-BOMBING
OF DRESDEN, GERMANY,
"THE FLORENCE OF THE ELBE,"
A LONG TIME AGO,
AND SURVIVED TO TELL THE TALE.
THIS IS A NOVEL
SOMEWHAT IN THE TELEGRAPHIC
SCHIZOPHRENIC
MANNER OF TALES
OF THE PLANET TRALFAMADORE,
WHERE THE FLYING SAUCERS
COME FROM.
PEACE.

Fact and fiction are mixed together on this title page, as they are in the body of the text. Unlike traditional realistic novels, Vonnegut himself is present in the narrative, in both his opening and closing chapters as well as periodically in Billy Pilgrim's story, occasionally including statements such as "That was I. That was me. That was the

author of this book" (125). This method of inserting biography into fiction perhaps prevents readers from easily dismissing the events Vonnegut describes as simply part of a made-up or fictional world. Vonnegut's real-life experiences and the fact that he was an eyewitness to the bombing lend authenticity to Billy Pilgrim's story. At the same time, however, Vonnegut's presence in the text destroys the illusion of reality associated with the realistic novel; the authorial intrusions constantly remind readers that they are, in fact, reading a novel. Thus, readers cannot lose themselves in the romance of war or get caught up in the fiction, in suspense or glamour, and forget they are hearing a story.

By erasing the hard and fast line traditionally separating history and novel, (fact and fiction, the real and the invented), Vonnegut actually elevates the project of fiction writing. In this metafictive opening chapter, Vonnegut shares much in common with other POSTMODERN writers who insist that experiences of reality are constructed and shared through language, that history is not monolithic "truth," but dependent on perspective, on storytelling, and on language. For instance, the history of the Dresden bombing ascribed to by Bertram Copeland Rumfoord, a HARVARD history professor with whom Billy shares a hospital room after the plane crash, is very different from Billy's own version of the bombing. And DAVID IRVING'S *The Destruction of Dresden*, a book Rumfoord reads in the hospital, contains opposite interpretations of the bombing in the forewords by Lieutenant General IRA C. EAKER and British air marshal SIR ROBERT SAUNDBY, long portions of which are included in Vonnegut's text. History and fiction merge even more fully in the recent real-life controversy surrounding Irving's Dresden book, with many historians criticizing Irving's estimates of the numbers killed in the bombing. The point here is that history, which we like to think of as "real," as "true," is a matter of imaginative reconstruction and interpretation much like fiction writing itself.

In *Slaughterhouse-Five*, though, Vonnegut uses a number of techniques to deflate the suspense and glamour often associated with war narratives. In his opening chapter, for instance, he gives away the beginning, the climax, and the end of his story. In the third sentence of the book, he states that "a guy [he] knew really *was* shot in Dresden for taking a teapot that wasn't his," an incident that he later tells Bernard O'Hare will be the climax of his novel. The first chapter ends with these words:

> This [book] is a failure, and had to be, since it was written by a pillar of salt. It begins like this:
> *Listen:*
> *Billy Pilgrim has come unstuck in time.*
> It ends like this:
> *Poo-tee-weet?* (22)

Not content with simply disclosing the opening and closing lines of his story in advance, Vonnegut briefly sketches out the entire plot of Billy's life and death at the beginning of chapter 2. In this synopsis Billy is *not* presented us the type of hero that is usually glorified in war. Though gentle and kind, he is weak and passive and an object of ridicule, not in control of his own destiny. Vonnegut not only deflates traditional plot-driven narrative, but he undermines traditional notions of character as well. While readers might expect characters in a realistic novel to be "well-rounded" or "fleshed out," they are flat in Vonnegut's novel. He writes, "There are almost no characters in this story, and almost no dramatic confrontations, because most of the people in it are so sick and so much the listless playthings of enormous forces. One of the main effects of war, after all, is that people are discouraged from being characters" (164). The novel has no heroic characters or glorious action; nor can it be read for purposes of suspense or plot, to simply to find out what happens. Instead, Vonnegut invites readers to refocus attention on *how* the story is told, on form.

Proper storytelling is indeed one of Vonnegut's pressing concerns. In the mental hospital after Billy's nervous breakdown, Eliot Rosewater tells him about a novel by Kilgore Trout, *The Gospel from Outer Space.* A visitor from outer space (shaped much like a Tralfamadorian, incidentally) comes to Earth to study Christianity and to learn why Christians can be so cruel. "He concluded," Rosewater tells Billy, "that at least part of the trouble was slipshod storytelling in the New Testament":

He supposed that the intent of the Gospels was to teach people, among other things, to be merciful, even to the lowest of the low.

But the Gospels actually taught this:
Before you kill somebody, make absolutely sure he isn't well connected. So it goes. (108–109)

Part of the reason that Vonnegut focuses so intently on form in this novel is because of the dangers of slipshod storytelling; a story poorly told could lead to exactly what Mary O'Hare warns against: making war look wonderful so that there would be more of them.

The novel's nonchronological structure is further evidence of Vonnegut's dismantling of traditional narrative conventions. In talking with Harrison Starr about the futility of writing an antiwar novel, Vonnegut adds that, "even if wars didn't keep coming like glaciers, there would still be plain old death" (4). Life marches chronologically toward death just as conventional narrative marches chronologically toward a close. While death is inevitable, the novel suggests that literature might be a way to try to stave it off, a way to stop time, at least temporarily. At the end of the opening chapter, Vonnegut speaks of CÉLINE, a French soldier in World War I who later became a writer. Céline, Vonnegut writes, includes an "amazing scene" in one of his novels in which "he tries to stop the bustling of a street crowd. He screams on paper: *Make them stop . . . don't let them move anymore at all . . . There, make them freeze . . . once and for all! . . . So that they won't disappear anymore!*" (21). While literature has long been seen as a potential way of achieving immortality (many of SHAKESPEARE's sonnets, for instance, argue that, as long as the poem survives, the lover described in its lines will not be forgotten), Vonnegut's nonlinear narrative becomes an attempt to disrupt the steady march of time.

One of the reasons Vonnegut disrupts linear time in the novel is because, in his experience, time moves toward destruction; human history, after all, has led up to the horror he witnessed in Dresden. Just before Billy Pilgrim is captured by the Tralfamadorians, he comes "unstuck in time" and watches an old war movie both backwards and forwards. The story is about American bombers in World War II. In the backward version of the film, German fighter planes suck bullets and shells out of American airplanes and crew members. The American bombers then fly over a German city and use a "miraculous magnetism" to shrink fires, gather them into steel containers, and draw them into the bellies of the planes. When the planes return to the United States, factories work day and night to dismantle the bombs, separating the content into minerals, and replanting them in the Earth. The movie makes more sense to Billy in reverse than in forward motion. Because events in chronological or historical time lead to death and destruction, Vonnegut seems to be saying that creating a new form of literature can also create a saner, kinder world.

The scene in which Billy watches the war movie ends with him extrapolating to imagine all of time and history moving backward to create two perfect people: Adam and Eve. Christian imagery, such as this allusion to Adam and Eve, appears frequently in the novel. Many critics see Billy Pilgrim as a type of Christ figure, an innocent who is dirtied by the sins of humankind, but who delivers a message of salvation. Billy's speech, right before his assassination by Paul Lazzaro certainly seems Christ-like in a number of ways. Like Christ at the Last Supper, Billy predicts his own death to his followers. But he also promises that, if his audience only believes him, they will be able to live again after death: "If you protest," he tells the crowd after announcing his imminent assassination, "if you think that death is a terrible thing, then you have not understood a word I've said" (142). Billy serenely adds that it is time for him to be dead for a little while, "and then live again" (143). The Tralfamadorian philosophy, which Billy preaches to the crowd, offers a version of eternal life, even if it is not exactly the Christian promise of heaven and salvation. Critics who read Billy as a Christ figure also point to his name, suggesting that Billy is indeed a pilgrim, a searcher or seeker after something holy. Billy is even said to be "self-crucified" at one point, when he is riding in the boxcar containing prisoners of war (80). And finally, Vonnegut compares Billy's infrequent but silent weeping later in life to the crying of the Christ child from the book's epigraph.

But perhaps it is more convincing to see Billy as a new Adam rather than a Christ. The image of Adam and Eve recurs several times in the novel, first when Billy and Roland Weary are captured by the five German irregular soldiers behind enemy lines after the Battle of the Bulge. The commander of the motley group is a middle-aged corporal who has acquired a pair of golden cavalry boots from a dead Hungarian colonel on the Russian front. When Billy, lying on his back, stares into these boots, he sees "Adam and Even in the golden depths" (53). "They were naked. They were so innocent, so vulnerable, so eager to behave decently. Billy Pilgrim loved them" (53). Adam and Eve, then, come to represent the innocence lost during wartime. Although, as Mary O'Hare points out, wars are fought by children, these children, as they participate in wartime atrocities, rapidly lose the purity of childhood. Perhaps Billy's Tralfamadorian experiences are fantasies he concocts in order to regain his lost innocence. He and Montana Wildhack in the Tralfamadorian zoo become like Adam and Eve, starting the human race over again. Like Adam in the Garden of Eden, Billy is naked in full view of his gods, the Tralfamadorians. Also like Adam, at least before the fall, Billy is not ashamed of his nakedness. The Tralfamadorians have "no way of knowing Billy's body and face were not beautiful. They supposed that he was a splendid specimen" (113). Billy, like Adam, is given his Eve when the Tralfamadorians kidnap Montana Wildhack as a mate for him. Montana Wildhack perfectly fits into Billy's middle-aged fantasy. She is a young, beautiful, very sexually experienced woman—an ex-porn star, even—who is, nevertheless, shy and demure with Billy. Of course Billy and Montana live in a postmodern Eden rather than the biblical garden—their paradise is furnished with items stolen from a Sears Roebuck warehouse in Iowa City and comes complete with wall-to-wall carpeting, a televison, and stereophonic phonograph.

While some critics argue that Billy Pilgrim's Tralfamadorian adventures are to be read as real, as something that actually happens to Billy in his life, Vonnegut supplies much evidence to suggest that Billy's extraterrestrial kidnapping is an escape fantasy he devises, whether consciously or unconsciously, to cope with a traumatic life. Billy loves the innocence of Adam and Eve, and it seems plausible he would want to regain the innocence he lost during the war, especially with a young, sexy woman who grows to adore him. In addition, as Billy's daughter, Barbara, points out, Billy begins speaking about his Tralfamadorian experiences only after the plane crash on Sugarbush Mountain in Vermont, where he receives a serious head injury. When asked why he did not mention Tralfamadore before the accident, Billy replies, "I didn't think the time was *ripe*" (30). Readers might wonder what has suddenly made it the appropriate time for Billy to talk about his alien friends.

But the most persuasive evidence that Billy's Tralfamadorian journey takes place only in his troubled mind is the fact that he reads the whole scenario of the kidnapping he claims to have undergone in a Kilgore Trout novel supplied by Eliot Rosewater immediately after the war. When Billy goes into the pornographic book store in New York before appearing on the radio talk show, he thumbs through several Kilgore Trout novels. One, *The Big Board*, Billy realizes he has read years before, in the veteran's hospital. The book "was about an Earthling man and woman who were kidnapped by extra-terrestrials. They were put on display in a zoo on a planet called Zircon-212" (201). While *The Big Board* takes place on a different planet, Billy takes the basic outlines of the plot for his fantasy. The Tralfamadorians themselves come from another Kilgore Trout novel, *The Gospel from Outer Space*, in which the alien protagonist is shaped very much like a Tralfamadorian.

While it seems likely that Billy himself believes his Tralfamadorian fantasies, readers should understand that these fantasies not only help Billy cope with war trauma, but also justify the exceedingly passive life he lives. According to the Tralfamadorian philosophy, events in the universe are all predetermined, and there is no way to change what is meant to happen. When the Tralfamadorian guide tells Billy that the universe will end when a Tralfamadorian test pilot blows it up experimenting with new flying saucer fuels, Billy is at first horrified and asks why, with this foreknowledge, the

Tralfamadorians do not try to keep the pilot from pressing the button that will end the universe. The guide replies, simply, "He has *always* pressed it, and he always *will*. We *always* let him and we always *will* let him. The moment is *structured* that way" (117). The Tralfamadorians do not believe the future can be changed, that wars can be prevented. In fact, one of his alien kidnappers tells Billy that Earthlings "are the great explainers," constantly striving to understand why events occur, how other events may be achieved or avoided. He adds that, of the thirty-one planets he's visited, "Only on Earth is there any talk of free will" (86).

When Billy accepts the Tralfamadorian philosophy, the passivity that he has displayed his entire life—from wanting to drift quietly at the bottom of the YMCA pool after his father throws him in, to begging Roland Weary to leave him behind—is justified. If the future cannot be changed anyway, why even try? Thus, in later life, when Billy sees a black man approach his car in the Ilium ghettoes, or the crippled magazine salesmen ring his doorbell, he simply turns away. Billy's Tralfamadorian fantasies are a narcotic that helps him cope with trauma, much like the morphine he was given after losing control in the German prisoner-of-war camp. When the head Englishman comes to check on Billy in the camp hospital unit, Edgar Derby says that Billy is "dead to the world" (105), though he is not actually dead. The Englishman replies, "How nice—to feel nothing, and still get full credit for being alive" (105). Billy's Tralfamadorian experiences allow him to come to terms with all the death he has witnessed, because death has no real meaning in the Tralfamadorian philosophy; yet they also make Billy dead to the real world that he must live in and cope with on a day-to-day basis.

While in some ways the Tralfamadorian philosophy might seem larger, wiser, and more sane than the limited Earthling views of time and the universe, nevertheless Vonnegut does not recommend a simple resigned acceptance of things as they are as the proper outlook on life. The Tralfamadorians, after all, are shaped like toilet plungers, suggesting perhaps that they spend much time dealing in muck and waste? In addition, the Tralfamadorians sound suspiciously like Nazi prison guards. Just as a German guard who brutally beats an American prisoner says, "Vy you? Vy anybody?" (91) as he shoves the man back into ranks, the Tralfamadorian kidnappers reply, "Why *you*? Why *us* for that matter? Why *anything*?" (76–77) when Billy asks why they have chosen him to abduct. Rather than acting to try to change the future, the Tralfamadorians tell Billy they simply do not look at horror. They ignore wars and other unpleasantness, focusing instead on good times. "That's one thing Earthlings might learn to do, if they tried hard enough," the Tralfamadorians tell Billy, "Ignore the awful times, and concentrate on the good ones" (117). Yet, Vonnegut makes it clear that Billy, as a human being, simply cannot take the Tralfamadorians' advice. He constantly travels back to his wartime experiences; they have affected him profoundly, and he is incapable of ignoring them.

Nor does Vonnegut himself take the Tralfamadorians' advice to simply ignore the awful times. In his opening chapter, he discusses Lot's wife, who looks back on the destruction of Sodom and Gomorrah and is turned into a pillar of salt as a result. Yet, Vonnegut also says that he loves Lot's wife for looking back, "because it was so human" (22). In looking back at the great destruction of Dresden, Vonnegut is like Lot's wife. He even says that his book is a failure because it "was written by a pillar of salt" (22). While looking back may finally be futile, it is nevertheless human and empathetic to do so, to try to understand and explain atrocity, to provide warnings for the future. The repeated refrain of the novel, "so it goes," can be read as drawing attention to every death that occurs, no matter how small or how seemingly meaningless; the phrase prevents overlooking death, ignoring it, or closing one's eyes to it as the Tralfamadorians recommend to Billy Pilgrim. To simply accept death as natural, as a temporary condition as the Tralfamadorians do, would obviate the point of trying to stop it, of trying to prevent wars and other brutalities from taking place. What would be Vonnegut's point in writing his antiwar novel in the first place, or of warning his sons not to take part in massacres, not to allow news of massacres of enemies to fill them

with glee, and not to work for companies that make massacre machinery?

While the Tralfamadorians are right to recognize that life is filled with both pleasant and horrifying moments, they do not realize that for Earthlings these moments cannot be neatly separated from one another, and that humans cannot simply focus on the good times and ignore the bad. *Slaughterhouse-Five* ends with the horrifying image of the corpse mines in Dresden and the Maori prisoner who dies from repeated vomiting. Yet, Vonnegut writes, "somewhere in there was springtime" (215). Traditionally a season of hope and new beginnings, spring arrives even amid the horror of the corpse mines. When Billy and the rest of the prisoners wander out into the shady street, they see only one vehicle, a wagon drawn by two horses that is both "green and coffin-shaped" (215). Again, images of life and death are inextricably mixed together in this description and cannot be neatly separated. Finally, the novel ends with the nonsense phrase spoken to Billy by a bird: "*Poo-tee-weet?*" (215). An ambiguous ending, it is difficult to know how to read this final phrase. It seems hopeful that it is springtime and that birds are talking. Life continues, despite the devastation caused by the bombing. Yet, is the bird's call a cry of despair at making sense of what has happened in Dresden? In his opening chapter, Vonnegut tells his editor, Seymour Lawrence, that there "is nothing intelligent to say about a massacre" (19). Has Vonnegut's attempt, then, been a failure, as he claims in the opening chapter? Readers should also notice that the bird's call is followed by a question mark. Perhaps Vonnegut wants to retain ambiguity at the end. Will the warning his novel provides be heeded by future generations?

CHARACTERS AND RELATED ENTRIES

Campbell, Howard W., Jr., Howard W. Campbell, Jr., is an American-born playwright who becomes a notorious Nazi propagandist. He visits the American prisoners in the German prisoner-of-war camp to recruit them for a unit of his own invention, the Free American Corps, which is supposed to fight only on the Russian front. Costumed in an outlandish uniform, Campbell promises the Americans steak dinners and other ample repayment if they will only defect to the Nazi side. He is challenged after his speech by the American high school teacher Edgar Derby. Readers of *Slaughter-house-Five* never discover that, in *Mother Night*, Vonnegut's earlier novel, Howard W. Campbell, Jr., is actually a double agent, sending coded messages to the Allies in his propaganda broadcasts.

Corwin, Lance Lance Corwin is a time traveler in a novel by Kilgore Trout. Corwin wants to find out if Jesus really died on the cross or whether he had been taken down while still alive. Using a stethoscope to listen to Jesus' heart, Lance Corwin discovers that he really is dead.

Derby, Edgar Edgar Derby is the ex-high school teacher from Indianapolis who is captured by the Germans in World War II and sent, along with Billy Pilgrim and many others, to work in Dresden. Fit, patriotic, and kind, Derby is a leader and father-figure to the other men; he even stands up to the Nazi recruiter Howard W. Campbell, Jr., becoming an actual character in the book rather than simply the "listless plaything of enormous forces" (164), like so many others in the story. Ironically, Derby dies an ignomious death, executed by a firing squad in Dresden for stealing a teapot as the war is winding down. Derby's death, Vonnegut says at the beginning of the novel, will be the climax of the story. However, the scene is described very anticlimactically, in three sentences, which are treated almost as an aside, a few paragraphs before the novel ends.

Derby, Jr. Although his first name is not given, Edgar Derby has a son who is a Marine fighting in the Pacific theater of World War II while Derby fights the Germans. Derby's son survives the war, though Derby does not.

Derby, Margaret Edgar Derby imagines writing a letter home to his wife, Margaret, in which he tells her, ironically, not to worry because Dresden is an open city and will never be bombed.

Dog in Lazarro's Story Paul Lazarro tells Billy Pilgrim and Edgar Derby a story about a dog who

bit him once. To get revenge, Lazarro put tiny sharpened pieces of a spring into the dog's food. When the dog ate it, the springs tore up his insides, driving the dog wild with pain.

Febs The Febs, an acronym standing for "Four-eyed Bastards," are a barbershop quartet made up of optometrists, colleagues of Billy Pilgrim. The group sings at the anniversary party of Billy and Valencia, causing Billy to react grotesquely, as if he has seen a ghost. He later realizes that the four men with open mouths had reminded him of German prison guards gaping in horror after the bombing of Dresden. The Febs die in the plane crash on Sugarbush Mountain, bound for an optometry conference.

German Irregulars A group of five German irregular soldiers, consisting of two boys in their early teens, two old men, and a middle-aged corporal, capture Billy Pilgrim and Roland Weary behind enemy lines in Germany. The corporal is wearing golden cavalry boots taken from a dead Hungarian colonel. Billy, staring into the boots, believes he can see Adam and Eve in the boots' shine. The Germans bring Billy and Weary to a stone cottage where other Allied prisoners are being held before being transported to prisoner-of-war camps on crowded boxcars.

Gluck, Werner Werner Gluck is a 16-year-old German who guards Billy Pilgrim and Edgar Derby in Dresden as the two American prisoners make their way to the communal kitchens for supper. Tall and weak, Gluck resembles Billy, and in fact, unbeknown to either, the two are distant cousins. On their way to the kitchen, Gluck unwittingly opens the door to a communal shower, where about 30 teenage girls who are German refugees are taking showers. While Gluck and Billy have never seen a naked woman before, it is nothing new to Edgar Derby. These girls will later be killed in the fire-bombing.

Golliwogs After the plane crash of Sugarbush Mountain, Billy Pilgrim is rescued by Austrian ski instructors, who, in their black ski masks, look like golliwogs, or "white people pretending to be black for the laughs they could get" (156).

Lawrence, Seymour Seymour Lawrence, known as Sam, was Vonnegut's actual publisher at the time he wrote *Slaughterhouse-Five*. In the novel's opening chapter, Vonnegut imagines explaining the unusual form of his book to Lawrence: "It is so short and jumbled and jangled, Sam, because there is nothing intelligent to say about a massacre" (19).

Lazarro, Paul A diminutive, angry, boil-covered car thief from Cicero, Illinois, Paul Lazarro is an American soldier captured in Germany and sent to work in Dresden. On the box cars on the way to the prisoner-of-war camp, Lazarro makes friends with Roland Weary, who, as he dies of gangrene, makes Lazarro promise to seek revenge against Billy Pilgrim. According to Pilgrim, who believes he can see all of time at once after his visit to the planet Tralfamadore, Lazarro, who frequently brags about the people he will have killed some day, does actually end Billy's life. Lazarro assassinates Pilgrim on February 13, 1976, after Billy gives a speech to a huge crowd in Chicago about flying saucers and the nature of time.

Lot's Wife At the end of the opening chapter, Vonnegut compares himself to Lot's wife from the Bible who was warned not to look back at the destruction God visited on the sinful cities of Sodom and Gomorrah. Yet, Vonnegut loves Lot's wife for disobeying "because it was so human" (22). Both he and Lot's wife, Vonnegut says, have been turned to pillars of salt for looking back at great destruction.

Merble, Lionel Lionel Merble is the father of Billy Pilgrim's wife, Valencia Merble Pilgrim, and owner of the Ilium School of Optometry. He sets Billy up in business after Billy marries Valencia. Lionel Merble, who, incidentally, is declared by the narrator to be a machine, dies in the plane crash on Sugarbush Mountain on the way to an optometrist's convention.

Mitchell, Allison Allison Mitchell is a friend of Vonnegut's daughter Nanny. Vonnegut brings the two little girls with him when he goes to visit his old war buddy, Bernard V. O'Hare.

Müller, Gerhard A cab driver whom Vonnegut and Bernard V. O'Hare meet when they return to Dresden, Gerhard Müller had been a prisoner of the Americans during the war. Although his mother was killed in the fire-bombing of Dresden, things have improved since then for the Müller family; Gerhard lives in a pleasant apartment, and his daughter is getting an excellent education. Müller sends O'Hare a postcard at Christmastime that reads in part: "I hope that we'll meet again in a world of peace and freedom in the taxi cab if the accident will" (2). Taken by that final phrase in the postcard, Vonnegut dedicates his novel to Gerhard Müller, along with Mary O'Hare.

Nancy the Newspaper Writer In the novel's opening chapter, Vonnegut relates an incident that occurred when he worked for the Chicago City News Bureau. The first story he covered involved a veteran who was crushed to death in an elevator when his wedding ring got caught in some ornamental iron lace. When he phones the story in to Nancy, one of the "beastly girls" (9) who writes for the paper, she tells Vonnegut to call the veteran's wife and pretend to be the police captain in order to get her reaction to her husband's death. Later, "just for her own information" (9), Nancy asks what the squashed man looked like, all the while casually eating a Three Musketeers candy bar.

O'Hare Bernard V. Bernard V. O'Hare is Vonnegut's real-life old war buddy, currently working as a district attorney in Pennsylvania, whom he goes to visit in the opening chapter, in the hopes that O'Hare can stimulate Vonnegut's war memories. He and Vonnegut fly back to revisit Dresden together on a Guggenheim grant. O'Hare also appears in the novel's final chapter when he discusses with Vonnegut the number of people dying and being born in the world every day and the fact that they will all want dignity. Although sharing a very similar name with the character who captures Howard W. Campbell, Jr. in Vonnegut's novel *Mother Night*—Bernard B. O'Hare—Bernard V. O'Hare is a much more likeable figure than the angry, resentful character in *Mother Night*.

O'Hare, Mary The wife of Vonnegut's old war buddy Bernard V. O'Hare, Mary O'Hare is a pivotal character in the novel, who inspires Vonnegut to subtitle his Dresden book, *THE CHILDREN'S CRUSADE*. When Vonnegut first arrives at the O'Hare house, Mary, a trained nurse, is angry with him. Vonnegut eventually discovers her anger stems from her belief that he will write a book that glamorizes war. He solemnly promises Mary that this is not his intent and that he will make sure readers understand that wars are fought by children. Vonnegut dedicates the novel to both Gerhard Müller, the Dresden taxi driver, and Mary O'Hare.

Pilgrim, Barbara Billy Pilgrim's daughter, Barbara, marries young. After her mother's death, Barbara looks after Billy's business interests and takes care of him. "All of this responsibility at such an early age," Vonnegut writes, "made her a bitchy flibbertigibbet" (29). Barbara does not believe Billy's Tralfamadorian stories, asking him why he never mentioned the aliens before his head was injured in the plane crash.

Pilgrim, Billy The novel's protagonist, the tall, awkward, and ungainly Billy Pilgrim, was born in 1922 in Ilium, New York. He is drafted to serve in World War II after attending night sessions at the Ilium School of Optometry for one semester. A chaplain's assistant during the war, Billy is captured behind enemy lines during the Battle of the Bulge. As prisoner of war, he is sent to work in Dresden where he survives the Allied fire-bombing of the city. After his return home, Billy is briefly treated for a mild nervous collapse in a veteran's hospital, earns his degree from the optometry school, and marries the owner's daughter, Valencia Merble. Billy's father-in-law sets Billy up in the optometry business, and Billy becomes quite wealthy. After a plane crash on his way to an optometry conference, in which he receives a severe head injury, Billy begins talking about his adventures on the planet Tralfamadore. Billy claims to have been kidnapped by the Tralfamadorians, taken to a zoo on their planet, and mated with ex-porn star Montana Wildhack. Because of his Tralfamadorian experiences, Billy Pilgrim has

"come unstuck in time" (23). He now sees all of time at once, as the Tralfamadorians do, and is able to travel back and forth through his life rather than living it in strict chronological order. A passive character deeply affected by his war experiences, Billy ends the novel in the safe retreat of the Tralfamadorian zoo.

Pilgrim, Mrs. Billy Pilgrim's mother, whose first name is never given in the novel, works as a substitute organist for various churches around town when Billy is a child growing up in Ilium. She shops around for a religion she likes, but never actually finds one. Billy, though, receives a gory crucifix to hang in his room. Mrs. Pilgrim is still alive when Billy begins talking publicly about his Tralfamadorian experiences; she is a patient in Pine Knoll, a nursing home in Ilium.

Pilgrim, Robert Billy Pilgrim's son, Robert Pilgrim, is a troublemaker in high school, but joins the Green Berets afterward and fights in the VIETNAM WAR.

Pilgrim, Sr. Billy Pilgrim's father is a barber in Ilium, New York, before being killed in a hunting accident by a friend. One of Billy's strongest memories of his father is when Billy is a child learning to swim at the Y.M.C.A. pool. Billy's father throws him in the deep end, telling Billy he's going to learn by the "sink-or-swim" method (43).

Pilgrim, Valencia Merble The daughter of Lionel Merble, who owns the Ilium School of Optometry, Valencia Merble marries Billy Pilgrim, and the couple has two children, Barbara and Robert. Valencia is enormously overweight, but loves Billy. Through his ability to time-travel, Billy sees that his marriage to Valencia will be tolerable the whole way through. Valencia dies after inhaling carbon monoxide after she wrecks her car in her haste to visit Billy in the hospital following the plane crash on Sugarbush Mountain.

"Poo-tee-weet" In the opening chapter of *Slaughterhouse-Five,* in which Vonnegut discusses his difficulties in writing the novel, he includes a paragraph addressed to his editor, Seymour Lawrence. The book, Vonnegut explains to Lawrence, is "so short and jumbled and jangled . . . because there is nothing intelligent to say about a massacre" (19). Everything is quiet after a massacre, he continues, except for the birds, and the birds say all that there is to say about such carnage: "*Poo-tee-weet?*" (19). The nonsense syllables "*Poo-tee-weet?*" also serve as the final word in the novel. Critics disagree about how to interpret this ending. On the one hand, birds singing and the arrival of spring amid the horrific corpse mines in Dresden seem to suggest a promise of better things to come. At the same time, the birds' song is a nonsense word, incomprehensible to human beings, suggesting that perhaps there will never be full understanding of human atrocity and that any attempt must ultimately fail. It is also important to note that the phrase ends with a question mark, drawing attention to the ambiguity of the novel's ending.

Princess   Princess is a dog—a female German shepherd—who accompanies the five irregular German soldiers who capture Billy and Roland Weary behind enemy lines after the Battle of the Bulge.

Quintuplet Sales Clerks   When Billy Pilgrim travels to New York City, hoping to appear on television to talk about the planet Tralfamadore, he visits a pornographic bookstore in Times Square, where he had seen old dusty copies of Kilgore Trout novels in the window. The bookstore is run by "seeming quintuplets . . . five short, bald men chewing unlit cigars . . ." (202). One of the men tells Billy that the Kilgore Trout novel he's looking at is just window dressing and what he wants is in back. The clerk then produces a "really hot" item they "kept under the counter for connoisseurs" (205). The item turns out to be a pornographic picture of a woman and a Shetland pony, the same photograph that Roland Weary had shown Billy back in the war.

Rosewater, Eliot   Eliot Rosewater, the protagonist of Vonnegut's previous novel, *God Bless You, Mr. Rosewater*, appears in the mental hospital where Billy Pilgrim goes to recover from the ner-

vous breakdown he suffers shortly after returning from the war. Rosewater, a huge Kilgore Trout fan as he is in the earlier novel, has a musty carton of Trout's books under his bed, several of which he loans to Billy. Rosewater also meets Billy's mother and practices being "ardently sympathetic" to her (102).

Rumfoord, Professor Bertram Copeland   After the plane crash on Sugarbush Mountain, Billy Pilgrim shares a hospital room with Professor Bertram Copeland Rumfoord, a Harvard history professor who has broken his leg in a skiing accident. A retired brigadier general in the Air Force Reserve, Professor Rumfoord is writing a one-volume history of the Army Air Force in World War II; he is currently deciding how much to include about the bombing of Dresden in his book, a raid Rumfoord considers a great Allied triumph. When Billy tells Rumfoord that he was at Dresden, Rumfoord does not believe him, insisting that Billy simply has ECHOLALIA, a medical condition in which the patient immediately repeats what is said by people around him. Billy eventually convinces Rumfoord he really was in Dresden during the bombing, and when Rumfoord grudgingly admits it must have been difficult on the ground, Billy replies that it was all right: "*Everything* is all right, and everybody has to do exactly what he does" (198).

Rumfoord, Lance and Cynthia Landry   When Billy Pilgrim and Valencia Merble honeymoon in CAPE COD, a large yacht named the *Scheherezade* glides past their window. On it are another honeymooning couple, Lance Rumfoord and Cynthia Landry Rumfoord. The wealthy Rumfoord family has appeared in several previous Vonnegut novels, including *The Sirens of Titan* and *God Bless You, Mr. Rosewater.*

Rumfoord, Lily   The wife of Professor Bertram Copeland Rumfoord, Lily Rumfoord is a high school dropout with an I.Q. of 103 who had been a go-go girl before her marriage. Although she has difficulty reading, Professor Rumfoord demands that she read a Xerox copy of President Truman's announcement that an ATOMIC BOMB had been dropped on Hiroshima.

Sandy Sandy is Vonnegut's dog, whom he describes talking to late at night in the opening chapter of the novel. Sandy does not mind the smell of mustard gas and roses and keeps Vonnegut company while his wife sleeps.

Scouts After the Battle of the Bulge, Billy Pilgrim travels behind enemy lines in the company of two infantry scouts and Roland Weary, an anti-tank gunner. Described as "clever, graceful, and quiet," the scouts are the other two members of the trio that Weary fantasizes he belongs to: "The Three Musketeers." The scouts eventually ditch Billy and Weary to go their own way. Ironically, despite their far superior skills, the two scouts are quickly shot while Billy and Weary survive to be captured.

"So it goes" "So it goes" is probably Vonnegut's most famous tagline. In *Slaughterhouse-Five*, one critic counted 108 uses of the phrase. "So it goes" is uttered when anyone or anything in the novel dies—whether it is schoolgirls boiled alive during the bombing of Dresden, or bubbles dying in a glass of champagne. Critics take varying views of this phrase, some arguing that it adds to a resigned, fatalistic outlook in the novel, evening out all deaths and making them all seem relatively unimportant. This view is supported by Billy Pilgrim's claim that "So it goes" is a phrase he learned from the Tralfamadorians, who view death as inconsequential because it is simply one moment in the great continuum of time. Other critics argue that the phrase draws attention to each instance of death in the novel, forcing readers to notice each one. According to this view, the phrase signals a rejection of the placid, resigned acceptance of death offered by the Tralfamadorians.

Spot Spot is a dog that Billy Pilgrim owned at one point, though Spot has died by the time of Barbara Pilgrim's marriage and the beginning of Billy's Tralfamadorian adventures. Yet, while the dog was alive, "Billy had liked Spot a lot, and Spot had liked him" (62).

Starr, Harrison Harrison Starr is a well-known moviemaker to whom Vonnegut talks about the Dresden book he is writing. When Starr finds out that it will be an antiwar book, he tells Vonnegut he might as well write an "anti-*glacier* book instead" (3), suggesting that wars are as easy to stop as glaciers.

Tralfamadorian Guide When Billy Pilgrim is in the zoo on the planet Tralfamadore, a Tralfamadorian guide explains to zoo visitors how Earthlings see time. While Tralfamadorians see all of time at once, and are able to move freely back and forth between the past and the present, it is as if Earthlings have their heads encased in steel helmets, with only one eyehole that has six feet of pipe attached. Further, they are strapped to a railroad car that moves in only one direction. The guide also explains to Billy how the universe ends—that a Tralfamadorian test pilot blows it up while experimenting with flying saucer fuels. When Billy asks why the aliens don't try to prevent this fate, the guide replies that they have always let the pilot blow up the universe and they always will: "The moment is *structured* that way," he explains (117).

Tralfamadorian Kidnappers The Tralfamadorians who kidnap Billy Pilgrim and take him to their planet are small beings shaped like toilet plungers with a hand sticking out at the top. Communicating telepathically with Billy who asks "Why me" (76), a question asked of a German prison guard by an Allied prisoner a few pages later, the Tralfamadorians explain that "there is no *why*" (77), that he is simply like a bug trapped in amber. Billy's captors also explain to him that free will is a concept valid only on Earth. Finally, his captors give Billy Tralfamadorian books to read. These books consist of clumps of symbols, which, when seen all at once, "produce an image of life that is beautiful and surprising and deep" although these books have "no beginning, no middle, no end, no suspense, no moral, no causes, no effects" (88) much like the novel *Slaughterhouse-Five* itself.

Trout, Kilgore Billy Pilgrim is introduced to the work of Vonnegut's ubiquitous science fiction writer Kilgore Trout when he meets Eliot Rosewater in a mental hospital shortly after the war. Billy borrows many Trout novels from Rosewater's huge library, and Kilgore Trout soon becomes Billy's favorite writer. One of the novels Billy reads, *The Big Board*, is about an Earthling man and woman who are kidnapped by aliens and put on a display in a zoo on faraway planet, a scenario sounding suspiciously similar to what Billy says happens to him on Tralfamadore. Billy actually meets Trout later in the novel; he coincidentally happens to live in Ilium, New York, where he has been working as a circulation man for the *Ilium Gazette*, bullying the newspaper boys in his charge. Billy invites Trout to his and Valencia's anniversary party, where the writer flirts with a vacuous young woman named Maggie White. In *Slaughterhouse-Five*, Trout appears as a much seedier figure than he did in the earlier *God Bless You, Mr. Rosewater*.

Unnamed American Prisoner of War and German Prison Guard   As the American prisoners are marched into a camp in Germany, one unnamed American mutters something that an English-speaking German guard does not like. The guard knocks down the American, causing him to lose two teeth. The prisoner is astonished, and asks the guard, "Why me?" to which the guard replies, "Vy you? Vy anybody?" (91). This response links the German prison guard to Billy's Tralfamadorian captors who also say, "Why *you*? . . . Why *anything*?" (76).

Unnamed Army Umpire   When Billy Pilgrim is on maneuvers in South Carolina after being drafted into the army, there are "umpires everywhere, men who said who was winning or losing the theoretical battle, who was alive and who was dead" (31). One Sunday morning, when Billy is playing hymns at an outdoor church service, an umpire brings them the news that the whole congregation is now theoretically dead after having been spotted from the air by a theoretical enemy. Later, Billy remembers this as a very Tralfamadorian experience, since the men are both dead and eating breakfast at the same time.

Unnamed Black Man in Ilium   On his way to a Lions Club luncheon meeting in Ilium, New York, in 1967, Billy Pilgrim drives his Cadillac through the Ilium ghetto, which is described as looking "like Dresden after it was fire-bombed" (59). While Billy is stopped at a traffic light, a black man approaches his car and taps on the window, wanting to talk about something. Billy, though, simply drives on, ignoring the man.

Unnamed Blind Innkeeper and his Family   After the bombing of Dresden, Billy Pilgrim and his fellow survivors march out of the city, astonished at the moonscape that Dresden has become. Eventually, they come to a suburb untouched by the fire and explosions. A blind innkeeper, along with his sighted wife and two young daughters, feeds the American prisoners soup and beer and puts them up for the night in the inn's stable.

Unnamed Boy Optometry Patient and his Widowed Mother   While Billy Pilgrim is examining the eyes of a 12-year-old in his optometry office in Ilium, he matter-of-factly tells the boy about his experiences on Tralfamadore. Billy wants to comfort the child because his father had been killed in Vietnam, so he tells the boy not to worry, that his father is still very much alive in certain moments. This causes the boy's widowed mother to tell the receptionist that Billy has evidently gone crazy. Billy's daughter, Barbara, takes him home after the incident.

Unnamed Civilian Cameramen   When the Allied prisoners of war are marched to the railroad yard for transportation after the Battle of the Bulge, two civilian cameramen have set up a motion-picture camera on the Luxembourg-Germany border. Though they have long since run out of film, one of the cameramen focuses on Billy Pilgrim's face for a moment, then focuses "at infinity again" (65).

Unnamed Crippled Salesmen   As Billy Pilgrim is napping one afternoon in 1967 in Ilium, New York, a crippled man rings the doorbell. Looking out the window, Billy sees another crippled man ringing a doorbell across the street. Billy knows what the men are up to; he had been warned at a Lions Club meeting about a scam in which crippled salesmen sell subscriptions to magazines that never arrive. Though he has been told to call the police if he sees these men, Billy instead weeps, closes his eyes, and travels in time back to Luxembourg at the end of the war.

Unnamed Dresden Drunk When Bernard V. O'Hare and Vonnegut first discuss their Dresden memories, one of the few incidents they recall involves a guy who "got into a lot of wine in Dresden" (13) and had to be taken home in a wheelbarrow.

Unnamed English Blue Fairy Godmother The Englishman at the prisoner-of-war camp who plays Cinderella's Blue Fairy Godmother in the play the officers put on for their American guests breaks Paul Lazarro's arm later that night when Lazarro tries to steal cigarettes from under the Englishman's pillow. When the Englishman goes to visit Lazarro in the hospital unit, Lazarro threatens to have him killed. Nonplussed, the Blue Fairy Godmother replies that he might just kill Lazarro instead.

Unnamed English Infantry Colonel An unnamed English infantry colonel is the head English officer at the camp where Billy Pilgrim and his fellow American prisoners are taken after their capture. The English colonel visits Billy in the hospital shed after Billy loses control following the production of *Cinderella*. Because Billy is on morphine, he is dead to the world. "How nice," the colonel says, "to feel nothing, and still get full credit for being alive" (105), a state in which Billy often seems to operate. The same Englishman later gives the Americans a lecture on maintaining personal hygiene while in the prisoner camp.

Unnamed English Prisoner of War When Billy Pilgrim first arrives at the prisoner-of-war camp occupied by British officers, one of them chides Billy for the outlandish costume he is wearing—the tiny coat, the strange footwear. The officer says to Billy, "Ohhhh—Yank, Yank, Yank—that coat was an *insult*" (98). Then he tells Billy not to let Jerry do things like that to him, although Billy doesn't know who "Jerry" is—that this is a slang term referring to the Germans.

Unnamed Female Optometry Patient After Billy Pilgrim is captured at the end of World War II and brought to the stone cottage where Allied prisoners of war are being held, he travels forward in time to his optometry office in Ilium, New York, where he is examining the eyes of an unnamed female patient. The woman remarks that Billy had become very quiet and distant for a period of time and fears that he has found some terrible disease in her eyes.

Unnamed German Cook After Billy Pilgrim, Edgar Derby, and 16-year-old German guard Werner Gluck accidentally stumble upon the naked teenage girls in the shower in Dresden, they arrive at the communal kitchen where an unnamed cook is waiting to serve them soup. She asks Gluck if he isn't awfully young to be in the army and Edgar Derby if he isn't awfully old. She asks Billy Pilgrim what he is supposed to be, then sighs that "All the real soldiers are dead" (159).

Unnamed German Major In the prisoner of war camp in Dresden, an unnamed German major who is close friends with the English officers interred at the camp apologizes to them for having to temporarily put up with the American enlisted men. He then reads long passages about the deficiencies of American fighting men from a monograph written by Howard W. Campbell, Jr.

Unnamed German Photographer After the Battle of the Bulge, the Allied prisoners are marched to boxcars by German soldiers. Along the way, an unnamed German war correspondent with a Leica camera takes pictures of the bedraggled prisoners. Because the photographer wants a photo of an actual capture, two German guards stage one by throwing Billy Pilgrim into the shrubbery. When Billy emerges, "his face wreathed in goofy goodwill" (58), the guards pretend to be capturing him for the photographer.

Unnamed German Soldier in Black When the Allied prisoners of war are marched to the boxcars after their capture, they pass a convoy of military vehicles hurrying German reserves to the front. One unnamed soldier in black, "having a drunk hero's picnic all by himself on top of a tank" (64) spits on Roland Weary as he and Billy Pilgrim pass by.

Unnamed German Surgeon When the bedraggled American prisoners of war are marched into Dresden to take up their work assignments, they are spotted by an unnamed surgeon who has spent the entire day operating. Highly offended when he sees Billy Pilgrim dressed in his "blue toga and silver shoes, with his hands in a muff" (149), he asks Billy if he thinks war is funny, if he's trying to mock the Germans, and if he's proud to represent America in such a state. Billy's only response is to take out the diamond and partial denture he found in the lining of his coat and hold it out to show the surgeon, smiling inexplicably.

Unnamed German Train Guards A group of four unnamed German soldiers guard the Allied prisoners of war being transported through Germany via boxcar. The guard's car, with bunks that have quilts and a table with wine and sausage, looks like heaven to Billy Pilgrim when he gets a glimpse inside.

Unnamed Hanged Pole Billy Pilgrim, three days after his arrival in Dresden, accidentally witnesses a Polish farm laborer hanged in public for having had sexual intercourse with a German woman.

Unnamed Hobo On the boxcars that transport the Allied prisoners of war to a camp in Germany, Billy Pilgrim meets an unnamed 40-year-old former hobo who repeatedly insists that he has been in worse places and worse situations than their current one. The former hobo, however, dies on the journey.

Unnamed Hungarian Airlines Pilot and Steward When Vonnegut and Bernard V. O'Hare return to Dresden in 1967, they take a Hungarian Airlines plane from East Berlin. The pilot looks like Adolphe Menjou, with a large handlebar mustache. A young steward serves the men rye bread and salami and butter and cheese and white wine.

Unnamed Idiotic Englishman In the opening chapter, Vonnegut remembers the massive prisoner exchange he took part in at the end of World War II in a beet field along the Elbe River. He eventually climbs into an American truck with numerous other Allied prisoners, most of whom have some sort of souvenir from the war. An "idiotic Englishman" (6) bounces a canvas bag containing his souvenir on Vonnegut's instep, all the while rolling his eyes and swiveling his "scrawny neck" (6), expecting someone to try to steal his prize. The souvenir turns out to be a trite tourist trinket—a plaster model of the Eiffel Tower with a clock inside.

Unnamed Literary Critics In New York City, Billy Pilgrim does not get on television as he wants, but he does get on a radio talk show that involves a group of literary critics discussing whether or not the novel is dead. In this scene, Vonnegut spoofs well-known writers and issues in literary criticism of the late 1960s. Participants in the radio show allude to Norman Mailer, William Styron, and Tom Wolfe, among others—respected authors of the period. When it is Billy's turn to talk, he discusses Tralfamadore and is gently expelled from the studio.

Unnamed Little League Coach Billy Pilgrim, at one point, travels in time to 1958, where he attends a banquet in honor of his son's little league team. The coach becomes choked up praising the team, saying he would consider it "an honor just to be *water* boy for these kids" (46).

Unnamed Maori Prisoner of War After the destruction of Dresden, when the prisoners of war are made to dig for bodies, Billy Pilgrim is paired with a Maori prisoner who dies of the dry heaves. He tears himself to pieces, throwing up again and again.

Unnamed Marine Major When Billy Pilgrim attends a Lions Club luncheon meeting in 1967 in Ilium, New York, the speaker is an unnamed Marine major who advocates increased bombing of North Vietnam to teach the communists a lesson.

When Billy is introduced to the major, he tells him about his son, Robert, who is a Green Beret serving in Vietnam.

Unnamed Mongolian Idiot and his Mother While Billy Pilgrim is in the hospital after the plane crash on Sugarbush Mountain, he travels briefly back in time to 1958, when he is in his Ilium optometry office examining the eyes of a young male Mongolian idiot while the boy's mother acts as interpreter.

Unnamed Newspaper Boy When Billy Pilgrim meets Kilgore Trout for the first time, the science fiction writer is working as a circulation man for the local newspaper, the *Ilium Gazette*. Billy sees Trout bullying a group of newspaper boys, one of whom quits because the work is so hard, the hours are so long, and the pay is so meager. When Trout tells the boy about all the millionaires who had carried newspapers as boys, the cynical news boy responds: "Yeah—but I bet they quit after a week, it's *such* a royal screwing" (168). Billy Pilgrim then helps Trout deliver the boy's abandoned newspapers.

Unnamed Newspaper Girl As circulation man for the *Ilium Gazette*, Kilgore Trout tells a group of newspaper delivery boys that whoever sells the most subscriptions will win a trip for himself and his parents to Martha's Vineyard. It turns out that one of the newspaper boys is actually a newspaper girl, who is "electrified" at the possibility of winning the free trip. When she asks if she can bring her sister along if she wins, Trout replies, "Hell no . . . You think money grows on *trees*?" (167).

Unnamed Obstetricians Near the end of the novel, Billy Pilgrim travels in time to Dresden two days after World War II officially ends. He is sleeping in a coffin-shaped wagon when he hears crooning noises made by a middle-aged couple, two German obstetricians, who are horrified by the condition of the horses drawing the wagon. Although Billy and his fellow prisoners had not noticed, the horses' mouths are bleeding, their hooves are broken, and they are extremely thirsty. When the couple make Billy get out of the wagon to see the condition of the animals, he bursts into tears even though he had not cried about anything else in the war.

Unnamed Old Man with Baby Buggy During his hospital stay in Vermont after the plane crash on Sugarbush Mountain, Billy Pilgrim travels in time back to Dresden in May 1945, two days after the end of World War II. Traveling in a coffin-shaped wagon back to the slaughterhouse with five other Americans for souvenirs of the war, Billy sees only one other person—an old man pushing a baby buggy that contains pots and cups and an umbrella frame and other items he had found in the destruction.

Unnamed Old, Old Man When Billy Pilgrim is in the hospital in Vermont with Professor Bertram Copeland Rumfoord, he briefly travels back in time until he is 16 years old, waiting to see a doctor about his infected thumb. Waiting in the office is one other patient—an old, old man who is suffering terribly from gas. He says to Billy, "I knew it was going to be bad getting old . . . I didn't know it was going to be *this* bad" (189).

Unnamed Rabbi In the stone cottage where Billy Pilgrim and Roland Weary are brought after being captured behind enemy lines, Billy sleeps with his head resting on the shoulder of an unprotesting army captain, a chaplain who is a rabbi.

Unnamed Ranger at Grand Canyon Billy Pilgrim travels in time back to his childhood, when his family visited the Grand Canyon on a trip out west. Billy hates the canyon, sure he is going to fall in. At one point his mother touches him, and he wets his pants. An unnamed ranger is at the canyon to answer tourists' questions. When a Frenchman asks if many people commit suicide by jumping in, the ranger replies, "Yes sir . . . About three folks a year" (89).

Unnamed Ranger at Carlsbad Caverns On their family trip out west, the Pilgrims also visit Carlsbad Caverns. Terrified, just as he was at the

Grand Canyon, Billy fears that the ceiling will cave in. A ranger, who leads tourists through the caverns, turns out all the lights at one point, telling people they have probably never been in total darkness before. In the darkness, Billy is not sure if he is alive or dead until his father takes out his watch, which has a radium dial. This small detail connects Billy's childhood memories to a scene at the prisoner-of-war camp in Germany, where he sees a Russian soldier with a face like a radium dial.

Unnamed Russian Prisoner of War When Billy Pilgrim gets off the train at the prisoner-of-war camp, he sees his first Russian. The man is described as having "a round, flat face that glowed like a radium dial" (82). When Billy passes within a yard of the soldier, the Russian looks "directly into Billy's soul with sweet hopefulness" (82) as though Billy might have good news for him.

Unnamed Russian Prisoner of War 2 After leaving the hospital unit in the prisoner-of-war camp, pumped full of morphine, Billy gets caught in a barbed wire fence that he does not see in the dark night. An unnamed Russian prisoner notices Billy, who seems to dance with the fence like a "curious scarecrow" (124) as he tries to unsnag himself. The Russian speaks gently to Billy and patiently undoes the snags for him so that Billy can dance off into the night.

Unnamed Russian Soldiers When Vonnegut and Bernard V. O'Hare first try to conjure up war memories in the book's opening chapter, one of the only things that comes to mind is an incident involving two Russian soldiers who had looted a clock factory. Vonnegut remembers the two driving a horse-drawn wagon full of clocks, happy and drunk and smoking cigarettes they had rolled in newspaper.

Unnamed Telephone Operator In the opening chapter, Vonnegut describes trying to call up old girlfriends on the phone late at night while his wife sleeps. When he asks for the number of a "Mrs. So-and-So" (7), an unnamed telephone operator tells him there is no such listing.

Unnamed Train Porter In 1944, Billy Pilgrim takes a train from South Carolina, where he is on army maneuvers, to Ilium, New York, for his father's funeral. After falling asleep on the train, Billy is awoken by a porter who tells him that he "sure had a hard-on" while he slept (127).

Unnamed University of Chicago Professor At a cocktail party, Vonnegut tells a UNIVERSITY OF CHICAGO professor about the Dresden raid he had witnessed. The professor, a member of the Committee on Social Thought, replies by telling Vonnegut about Nazi atrocities in the concentration camps. All that Vonnegut can say in response is, "I know, I know. I *know*" (10). Vonnegut relates this incident in the book's opening chapter.

Unnamed Veteran Killed in the Elevator In the opening chapter of the novel, Vonnegut tells about the first story he covered as a reporter for the Chicago City News Bureau, about a veteran who was crushed to death when his wedding ring got caught in the ornamental iron lace of an old-fashioned elevator.

Unnamed Veteran's Wife After Vonnegut phones in the story to the Chicago City News Bureau about the veteran crushed in the elevator, he is told to call the veteran's wife and inform her of her husband's death so that he can get her reaction for the story. The wife "said about what you would expect her to say. There was a baby. And so on" (9).

Unnamed Woman at Party At a New Year's Eve party in 1961, a drunken Billy is unfaithful to his wife, Valencia, for the first and only time. He has sex with an unnamed woman who sits on top of a running gas dryer.

Vonnegut, Kurt Kurt Vonnegut himself is a character in *Slaughterhouse-Five*, appearing as narrator in the opening chapter, the closing chapter, and occasionally throughout the book, in lines such as: "That was I. That was me. That was the author of this book" (125). While it is tempting to read this figure as the real-life Kurt Vonnegut, readers should remember that the Vonnegut telling the story is a fictional creation, despite having characteristics in common with the biographical Vonnegut. It is a fairly typical technique of metafiction for an author to include him or herself as a character in the work. Such a device allows the author to explore the relationship between fact and fiction, categories not necessarily considered as distinct and separate in postmodern literature as they are in more traditional writing.

Vonnegut, Nanny When Vonnegut goes to visit his old war buddy, Bernard V. O'Hare, he brings with him his daughter Nanny and her friend Allison Mitchell. On their way home, Vonnegut brings the two little girls to visit the New York World's Fair, where they "saw what the past had been like, according to the Ford Motor Company and Walt Disney, saw what the future would be like, according to General Motors" (18).

Vonnegut's Boss at General Electric Vonnegut tells readers in the opening chapter that, after the war, he became a public relations man for GENERAL ELECTRIC in Schenectady, New York. He describes his boss there as "one of the toughest guys I ever hope to meet" (10). A former lieutenant colonel in public relations in Baltimore, the boss sometimes asked Vonnegut sneeringly why he hadn't been an officer in the war.

Vonnegut's Father In the opening chapter, Vonnegut remembers that his father, shortly before he died, pointed out that Vonnegut never wrote a story with a villain in it. Vonnegut explains that was one of the things he learned in college after the war, when they were teaching that "nobody was ridiculous or bad or disgusting" (8). In the novel's final chapter, Vonnegut writes that his father, a sweet man, left Vonnegut his gun collection which now collects rust.

Vonnegut's Wife Vonnegut, as narrator of the opening chapter, mentions how he telephones old girlfriends late at night, after his wife has gone to bed. When Vonnegut joins her, she always asks what time it is. He also mentions his wife when he

talks about the period in his life when he worked for General Electric in Schenectady, New York.

Weary, Mr. Roland Weary's father, whose first name is never given, is a plumber in Pittsburgh who collects torture devices. Mr. Weary, in fact, belongs to a club composed of people who collect similar items.

Weary, Mrs. All readers find out about Roland Weary's mother is that she is given horrific gifts by her husband—a Spanish thumbscrew in working condition, and a model of the "Iron Maiden of Nuremberg," a notorious torture device.

Weary, Roland Roland Weary is an anti-tank gunner who wanders behind enemy lines with Billy Pilgrim and two infantry scouts. Described as "stupid and fat and mean" (35), Weary grew up in Pittsburgh, the son of a plumber whose hobby was collecting torture devices. Weary fantasizes that he and the scouts make up a loyal trio of friends called "The Three Musketeers," who are kept back by the pathetic college-boy, Billy Pilgrim, whom Weary pushes and prods into moving when Billy wants to give up. The two scouts soon ditch Weary and Billy, but are shot almost immediately afterward. The two misfit survivors are captured by a scraggly group of German irregulars and sent on a boxcar to a prisoner-of-war camp. On the train, Weary dies of gangrene, but not before making Paul Lazarro vow to get revenge against Billy Pilgrim, whom Roland Weary believes is responsible for his death.

White, Maggie Originally a dental assistant, Maggie White is a pretty but vacant young woman who has given up her career to become a homemaker for an optometrist. She is a guest at Billy and Valencia's anniversary party, where she is in awe at the famous writer Kilgore Trout. Trout flirts with Maggie and teases her, telling her that it is illegal to write untrue stories, and that she better watch what she says or she will burn in hell.

Wild Bob Wild Bob is a full colonel suffering from double pneumonia whom Billy Pilgrim meets as the Allied prisoners of war are being loaded onto boxcars. Wild Bob had lost an entire regiment, about 4,500 men, in the war. He asks Billy what outfit he was with, but Billy cannot remember. When Wild Bob asks if Billy is from the Four-fifty-first, Billy replies, "Four-fifty-first what?" (66). A bit later, delirious with a high fever, the colonel calls out "If you're ever in Cody, Wyoming, just ask for Wild Bob" (67). Wild Bob dies on the boxcar on the way to the German prisoner camp, but the "just ask for Wild Bob" refrain is repeated often throughout the novel.

Wildhack, Montana   Montana Wildhack is the 20-year-old ex-porn star whom Billy Pilgrim says he is mated to on the planet Tralfamadore. At first horrified to be on display in the Tralfamadorian zoo, Montana comes to love and trust Billy. At the end of the book, the two have a child together, and the last readers see of Billy and Montana, she is nursing their baby in the zoo on Tralfamadore. The two have become like Adam and Eve, starting all humanity over again. Montana has a locket hanging between her breasts, with the SERENITY PRAYER carved on the outside, which is one of the novel's three illustrations.

FURTHER READING

Bergenholtz, Rita. "Food for Thought in *Slaughter-house-Five.*" *Thalia* 18, nos. 1–2 (1998): 84–93.

Cacicedo, Alberto. "'You Must Remember This': Trauma and Memory in *Catch-22* and *Slaughter-house-Five.*" *Critique* 46, no. 4 (2005): 357–368.

Chabot, C. Barry. "*Slaughterhouse-Five* and the Comforts of Indifference." *Essays in Literature* 8, no. 1 (1981): 45–51.

Edelstein, Arnold. "*Slaughterhouse-Five*: Time Out of Joint." *College Literature* 1 (1974): 128–139.

Greiner, Donald J. "Vonnegut's *Slaughterhouse-Five* and the Fiction of Atrocity." *Critique* 14, no. 3 (1973): 38–51.

Harris, Charles B. "Time, Uncertainty, and Kurt Vonnegut, Jr.: A Reading of *Slaughterhouse-Five.*" *Centennial Review* 20, no. 3 (1976): 228–243.

Hartshorne, Thomas L. "From *Catch-22* to *Slaughterhouse V*: The Decline of the Political Mode." *South Atlantic Quarterly* 78, no. 1 (1979): 17–33.

Isaacs, Neil D. "Unstuck in Time: *Clockwork Orange* and *Slaughterhouse-Five.*" *Literature/Film Quarterly* 1, no. 2 (1973): 122–131.

Jarvis, Christina. "The Vietnamization of World War II in *Slaughterhouse-Five* and *Gravity's Rainbow.*" *War, Literature, and the Arts* 15, nos. 1–2 (2003): 95–117.

Matheson, T. J. "This Lousy Little Book: The Genesis and Development of *Slaughterhouse-Five* as Revealed in Chapter One." *Studies in the Novel* 16, no. 2 (1984): 228–240.

McGinnis, Wayne. "The Arbitrary Cycle of *Slaughterhouse-Five*: A Relation of Form to Theme." *Critique* 17, no. 1 (1975): 55–68.

Merrill, Robert, and Peter A. Scholl. "Vonnegut's *Slaughterhouse-Five*: The Requirements of Chaos." *Studies in American Fiction* 6, no. 1 (1978): 65–76.

Nelson, Joyce. "*Slaughterhouse-Five*: Novel and Film." *Literature/Film Quarterly* 1, no. 2 (1973): 149–153.

Simpson, Josh. "'This Promising of Great Secrets': Literature, Ideas, and the (Re)Invention of Reality in Kurt Vonnegut's *God Bless You, Mr. Rosewater, Slaughterhouse-Five*, and *Breakfast of Champions* Or 'Fantasies of an Impossibly Hospitable World': Science Fiction and Madness in Vonnegut's Troutean Trilogy." *Critique* 45, no. 3 (2004): 261–271.

Slaughterhouse-Five. New York: Dell, 1999.

Vees-Gulani, Susanne. "Diagnosing Billy Pilgrim: A Psychiatric Approach to Kurt Vonnegut's *Slaughterhouse-Five.*" *Critique* 44, no. 2 (2003): 175–184.

"Souvenir"

First printed in *Argosy* magazine in December 1952, "Souvenir" touches on Vonnegut's experiences as a prisoner of war during World War II. The story was later reprinted in *Bagombo Snuff Box* in 1999.

SYNOPSIS

"Souvenir" opens with a shy young farmer entering a city pawnshop and trying to sell a bejeweled pocketwatch with a German inscription for $500. Joe Bane, the pawnshop owner, immediately recognizes that the watch is worth a great deal more, but he offers the young man only $100 for it.

The farmer, whose name is Eddie, begins to tell the story of how he acquired the watch. He explains to Bane that he and his buddy Buzzer were prisoners during World War II. When the war ended, the two found themselves released in Germany in the midst of countless fleeing refugees. After drinking a bottle of brandy with some newly freed Canadian prisoners, the two Americans stumbled upon a pair of Germans, a young blond man and a well-dressed older man, who wished to make it through the Russian lines. The Germans first tried to surrender to the Americans, then tried to persuade the two young men to sell their uniforms to them. The older German's expensive, jewel-laden pocketwatch was offered in exchange.

When Soviet tanks arrived on the scene, the younger German took advantage of the confusion to suddenly shoot Buzzer in the head. He also shot at Eddie, but missed. The older German, who could not speak English and had no hope of passing himself off as an American to the Russian troops, put his own pistol in his mouth and killed himself. Meanwhile, the younger German stripped off Buzzer's uniform and fled. Although Eddie was forced to leave his friend's body where it was lying on the ground, he picked up the watch, which was also left behind.

At the conclusion of this tale, Eddie puts the watch back into his pocket, so moved by his own story that he can no longer bring himself to sell it, even though Joe Bane offers him $500 as the young farmer leaves his shop. The story ends with a shoeshine boy bringing Bane a translation of the watch's German inscription, which he had been sent to get from a German restaurant owner down the street. The watch, it turns out, had been a gift from Adolf Hitler.

COMMENTARY

"Souvenir" is a story that builds on Vonnegut's own experiences during World War II. Like the two young American soldiers Eddie and Buzzer, Vonnegut was a prisoner of the Germans, released to wander free when the war ended. He returns to this scene in his later novels *Slaughterhouse-Five* and *Bluebeard* as well, imaginatively recreating this pivotal moment in his life in varying ways in each

work. "Souvenir" also forecasts the mixing of actual historical figures and created characters that are a hallmark of Vonnegut's later fiction, especially the novels *Mother Night* and *Jailbird*. In "Souvenir," he depicts real-life Nazi general and military strategist Heinz Guderian interacting with the fictional characters of the drunken American soldiers. "Souvenir," then, is an important story in Vonnegut's development, since it lays out themes and techniques that he will return to often.

The story is also chilling in its irony. Though narrated in a fairly lighthearted way by the young veteran Eddie, readers are meant to note the terrible injustice of Buzzer's death. Much like Erich Maria Remarque's World War I classic *All Quiet on the Western Front*, in which the protagonist, Paul Bäumer, is killed on a very quiet day near the end of the war after the most brutal and horrific of the fighting has died down, Buzzer survives the war itself, only to be shot while in a drunken daze after the war has ended. Even more, he had become drunk while toasting victory with fellow Allied prisoners, never dreaming that the victory would bring his death.

Vonnegut also shows how little Eddie's and Buzzer's sacrifice means to those back home in America. Joe Bane, the greedy pawnshop owner, tries to cheat the young veteran out of his hard-won souvenir, dismissing Eddie's tragedy by suggesting the young man merely "cop[ped]" the watch "off some German prisoner" or found it "lying around in the ruins" (112). Nevertheless, by allowing Eddie to tell his story, Joe Bane seals his own loss on the deal. As Eddie leaves the shop, he thanks Bane for letting him know what the watch "is worth" (120), even though he never learns that the watch was a gift from Adolf Hitler, which increases its value enormously. For Eddie, the watch's value is not monetary as it is for Joe Bane. The watch reminds Eddie of the terrible sacrifice of his buddy's life.

CHARACTERS

Bane, Joe   Described as a "fat, lazy, bald man" who is "lonely" and "untalented" (109), Joe Bane is a pawnshop owner whose only pleasure in life is acquiring objects cheaply and selling them at a profit. When Eddie, the shy young farmer, comes into his shop to sell an expensive pocketwatch, Bane tries to con him into selling the watch for a tiny fraction of its real value. But Bane is unable to make the bargain, a defeat especially crushing in light of the news at the end of the story that the watch had been a gift to a German general from Adolf Hitler himself.

Buzzer   Buzzer is Eddie's war buddy, a fellow prisoner of the Germans who ends up getting shot in the head after the war has ended.

Canadian Prisoners   When the war ends and Eddie and Buzzer are freed, they meet a pair of Canadian prisoners of war who share a bottle of brandy with them. The young Americans' encounter with the fleeing Germans then takes place in an alcohol-induced haze.

Eddie   Eddie is a shy young farmer fallen on hard times who enters a city pawnshop to sell a German pocketwatch he obtained during World War II. After he tells the pawnshop owner the violent and tragic story of how he acquired the watch, though, Eddie realizes that he cannot sell it.

Guderian, Heinz   The older, well-dressed German refugee who kills himself turns out to have been real-life Nazi general Heinz Guderian. The pocketwatch he offers Eddie and Buzzer in exchange for their uniforms was a gift from Adolf Hitler.

Shoeshine Boy   When Joe Bane sees that Eddie's pocketwatch has a German inscription on it, he does a rubbing of the foreign words, then gives a shoeshine boy a dime to obtain a translation from a German restaurant owner down the street. The boy returns after Eddie has already left the shop, having decided not to sell the watch after all. He brings the news that the watch had been a gift to Nazi general Heinz Guderian from Adolf Hitler.

Young, Blond German   The young, blond English-speaking German refugee whom Eddie and Buzzer meet in their drunken stupor is desperate to make it through the Russian lines. When the young Americans refuse to trade their uniforms for the bejeweled pocketwatch, the young German shoots Buzzer in the head and steals his uniform so that he can pass himself off as an American prisoner.

FURTHER READING

Bagombo Snuff Box. New York: Berkley Books, 2000.
Reed, Peter. *The Short Fiction of Kurt Vonnegut.* Westport, Conn.: Greenwood Press, 1997.

Sun Moon Star

Sun Moon Star is a children's picture book, published by Harper & Row in 1980, with text by Kurt Vonnegut and abstract illustrations by award-winning graphic and industrial designer IVAN CHERMAYEFF. The story is based on a well-known Bible verse—Mathew 1:23—which predicts the birth of Jesus Christ:

> Behold,
> a virgin shall be with child,
> and shall bring forth a son,
> and they shall call his name Emanuel,
> which being interpreted is,
> God with us.

Using this verse as an epigraph to the book, Vonnegut imagines the Creator of the Universe born as a human child into the world. Accustomed to an all-knowing and perfect darkness, the Creator must learn to see through human eyes when he takes on the form of a male infant born in a stable.

The book contrasts celestial and human vision when it shows the infant Christ mistaking many ordinary things he sees for heavenly objects. For instance, he first looks upon a crude lamp fashioned from a rag soaked in oil and believes that he sees a supernova—the exploding Christmas star. He mistakes the crystal necklace worn by a Roman matron for a sky full of stars, believes his mother, Mary, is the Sun itself, that the midwife who delivers him is the Moon, and that his father Joseph is a star as well. The child closes his eyes only to discover that human beings imagine they see things even when their eyes are closed. As in many

Vonnegut works, it is the imagination that makes people fully human. In this story, the infant Christ must experience the human imagination to transform from a celestial being into a human creature. Thus, he dreams colors when he sleeps—green, orange, purple. By the end of the story, the child's transition to human form is complete. He sees the actual Sun and recognizes it for what it is. A new day begins, with an ox and an ass led out of the stable to begin the day's work. The story closes with the line, "And life went on." The charm of this little book is that Vonnegut is not particularly concerned with the life that follows—Christ's life as detailed in the Gospels. Instead, he imagines, with childlike simplicity, the crucial moments when a God becomes a man.

FURTHER READING

Sun Moon Star. New York: Harper & Row, 1980.

"Thanasphere"

Vonnegut's second published short story, "Thanasphere," first appeared in *Collier's* magazine in September 1950. The tale of a scientist forced to confront mystical circumstances that cannot be explained by hard data or scientific fact, "Thanasphere" later appeared as the lead story in the 1999 collection, *Bagombo Snuff Box.*

SYNOPSIS

"Thanasphere" tells the story of a manned rocket secretly launched into space by the United States Air Force. When the pilot, Major Allen Rice, makes contact with project leaders back on Earth, however, he mentions that he hears strange voices inside his ship. At first rocket scientist Dr. Bernard Groszinger and project leader Lieutenant General Franklin Dane believe that either Rice has gone crazy or that he is perpetrating a hoax. But with each contact, the voices become stronger, and Rice begins to give the men back on Earth more specifics about the voices: names and dates that he tells them to check out. Eventually, the scientists must accept that what Rice is hearing are voices of the

dead, spirits floating in outer space. When amateur radio operators begin overhearing some of the communications between Rice and the ground crew, Dane and Groszinger jam the frequency, fearful of how the knowledge that dead spirits are floating in outer space will affect the inhabitants of Earth. They also abort the mission, deciding to bring Rice down. In the final communication they receive from the pilot, he talks about seeing shining lights, one of which takes the form of his dead wife, Margaret. The story ends with Rice's capsule splashing down in the ocean. Readers are never told exactly what happens to the pilot, but no wreckage is found by a British liner that witnesses the crash, and Air Force scientists continue to publicly deny testing any rockets.

COMMENTARY

"Thanasphere" pits the world of science against that of spirituality. Dr. Bernard Groszinger begins the story as a young man who trusts fully in science. He believes that nothing can go wrong with the secret rocket launch called Project Cyclops because "machines, not men, were guiding the flight" (17). He and General Dane have even chosen a man to pilot the rocket whom they believe is "as much like a machine as possible" (17). Yet, Dr. Groszinger, for all his scientific acumen, does not necessarily know as much as he thinks he does. When Groszinger lies to reporters about the state of rocket technology, Vonneguts writes, "He knew a great deal more than he was saying, but somewhat less than he himself thought" (16). Groszinger, with his love of machinery and equations, discounts the notion that there might be inexplicable, mysterious, or spiritual forces in the world that cannot be explained by the hard data of his science. He initially insists that Major Rice's claims to hear voices in space can be credited to one of two causes: Either Rice has gone insane or he is perpetrating a hoax. While the general seems somewhat willing to believe Rice, Groszinger speaks sharply over the microphone to the astronaut: "This is *Groszinger* you're talking to, and you're dumber than I think you are if you think you can kid me" (21). At this point, Groszinger is still cocky about his scientific beliefs.

When he is finally forced to accept that the voices Major Rice hears in space belong to spirits of the dead, Dr. Groszinger's world turns upside-down. He and General Dane trade roles, with Dane becoming the more sure and confident of the two men, insisting that the new information be kept secret. Dr. Groszinger, though, experiences a new uncertainty. He seems bewildered as he goes to his university office the morning after the discovery: "He had hoped that getting away for a couple of hours would clear his head—but the feeling of confusion and helplessness was still with him. Did the world have a right to know, or didn't it?" (27). For the first time, Dr. Groszinger has to use his imagination rather than rely on scientific data as he tries to envision "the world of the future—a world in constant touch with the spirits, the living inseparable from the dead . . . Would it make life heaven or hell?" (30). This new uncertainty also clouds the fate of Major Allen Rice. The radio operator, upon hearing that Rice has heard the voice of his dead wife in space, insists that the rocket pilot "don't want to live" (30) anymore. Readers also learn that Rice will have to guide the ship himself to a safe landing, since the rocket's preprogrammed automatic landing will be interrupted. When no wreckage is found, and Rice does not appear at the end of the story, readers may presume that the man crashed the ship on purpose, to rejoin the spirit of his dead wife.

Perhaps the greatest irony in the story is that despite the earth-shaking new knowledge gained by General Dane and Dr. Groszinger, the status quo is maintained at the end. Dr. Groszinger speculates that, if his secretary heard the news of the dead spirits in outer space, her reaction might be simply a shrug: "Maybe that was the spirit of this era of the atom bomb, H-bomb, God-knows-what-next bomb—to be amazed at nothing" (29). Even an answer to humankind's most pressing existential question—what happens to human beings after they die—might not be enough to cause wonder in a world so numbed by scientific achievement. The story ends the way it began, with Dr. Groszinger lying to a reporter about rocket technology. Although everything has changed for the scientist, nothing has changed in the external world.

CHARACTERS

Carl Carl, whose last name readers do not learn, is the nephew of dead Hollywood actor Grantland Whitman. Major Rice, in space, hears the voice of Whitman claiming that Carl has tampered with his will.

Dane, Lieutenant General Franklin Lieutenant General Franklin Dane is the leader of Project Cyclops, the secret rocket launch conducted by the U.S. Air Force. General Dane is interested only in military applications of the secret test and does not care about scientific discoveries. He says to Dr. Groszinger: "For all I know, the moon is made of green cheese. So what. All I want is a man out there to tell me that I'm hitting what I'm shooting at. I don't give a damn what's going on in outer space" (25). Dane considers the mission a failure, since his military questions remain unanswered.

Groszinger, Dr. Bernard A young rocket scientist working for the Air Force, Dr. Bernard Groszinger feels that nothing can go wrong with the secret mission called Project Cyclops because the entire rocket trip is controlled by computer. The pilot is really just an observer aboard the ship. The scientifically-minded Groszinger at first has difficulty accepting Major Allen Rice's reports of voices in outer space, but must reconsider his entire worldview when he finally realizes that Rice is hearing the voices of the dead.

Guard After learning about the dead spirits in outer space, Dr. Groszinger returns to his office, where he is greeted by a cheerful Irish guard coming out of the building. Dr. Groszinger speculates about how the guard would react if he knew about the ghosts in space.

Newsmen At the beginning of the story, when amateur astronomers report seeing a fleck crossing the face of the Moon, a newsman asks Dr. Bernard Groszinger if it is possible that the fleck was a spaceship. Dr. Groszinger laughs at the man's question and lies in his response, telling the reporter that it will be at least 20 years before a rocket ship leaves the Earth. At the end of the story, another reporter asks the doctor what exists beyond the stratosphere. Groszinger replies that it is only "dead space" (32) out there, and suggests that it be called the "thanasphere" (33). The story ends with Groszinger lying to this reporter as well, repeating the claim that it will be at least 20 years before rocket technology is advanced enough to launch a ship into outer space.

Radio Operator   An Air Force sergeant serves as the radio operator who makes contact with Major Allen Rice in outer space. Although the radio operator at first argues that people on Earth have a "right to know" (25) about the spirit world discovered by Rice, he is convinced by General Dane to keep his mouth shut about what he has heard.

Rice, Major Allen   Major Allen Rice is the pilot aboard the experimental rocket ship the Air Force launches into space. He is chosen for the job because he is an experienced World War II veteran and a "childless widower" (18) who devotes himself to work. He is the last man the project leaders would expect to begin hearing voices in space. At the end of the story, readers are led to suspect that Rice has purposefully crashed his ship so that he can join his dead wife, Margaret, whose spirit he had seen in outer space.

Rice, Margaret   Margaret Rice is the dead wife of rocket pilot Major Allen Rice. In his last communication, Rice tells the ground personnel that he sees the spirit shape of Margaret, "smiling, misty, heavenly, beautiful" in outer space (31).

Ritter, Harvey   Harvey Ritter is a widower with two children in Scotia, New York. One of the voices Major Allen Rice hears in space is that of Ritter's dead wife, Pamela.

Ritter, Pamela   Major Rice claims that one of the voices he hears in space belongs to Pamela Ritter of Scotia, New York, who urges her husband to remarry for the children's sake. Dr. Groszinger later receives a telegram confirming the death of a Mrs. Ritter and the existence of a widower with children in Scotia.

Secretary   When Dr. Groszinger returns to his office the morning after he learns of the dead spirits in outer space, his secretary is routinely dusting his desk. Groszinger wonders how she would react if he told her of his discovery.

Tobin, Andrew   One of the voices that Major Rice hears in space is that of Andrew Tobin, who claims that his brother murdered him in Indiana in 1927. The ground personnel check out the names and dates Rice supplies and discover that they are accurate.

Tobin, Paul   Paul Tobin is a leading businessman in Evansville, Indiana. While in outer space, Major Allen Rice hears the voice of Tobin's dead brother Andrew, who claims that Paul murdered him.

Whitman, Grantland   Another voice Major Rice hears in space is that of dead Hollywood actor Grantland Whitman, who insists that "his will was tampered with by his nephew Carl" (27).

FURTHER READING

Bagombo Snuff Box. New York: Berkley Books, 2000
Reed, Peter. *The Short Fiction of Kurt Vonnegut.* Westport, Conn.: Greenwood Press, 1997.

"This Son of Mine"

A meditation on father/son relationships, "This Son of Mine" first appeared in the *Saturday Evening Post* in August 1956 before being reprinted in *Bagombo Snuff Box* in 1999.

SYNOPSIS

"This Son of Mine" is the story of factory owner Merle Waggoner and his son, Franklin, a student at CORNELL UNIVERSITY, whom Merle expects to take over his life's work someday. Franklin, though, has no love for the centrifugal pump factory and is not sure what he wants to do with his life. As the story opens, he has just gravely disappointed Merle by telling his father he wants to be an actor, although later he will take back this announcement and agree to take over the factory when Merle dies. The story also revolves around another father and son, lathe operator Rudy Linberg, who was Merle's very first employee, and his son, Karl, also a lathe operator. The Linbergs appear to be like two peas in a pod, with exactly the same interests in life and both exhibiting exemplary crafting skills. The main action in the story occurs when the two father-and-son pairs decide to go shooting together. After a long day outdoors, as the Sun begins to set, Karl confesses to Franklin that all of the chummy togetherness exhibited by him and his father is Rudy's way of making Merle jealous. Rudy had the opportunity to buy into the factory when Merle first started it, but decided not to. As the years have passed, he has remained a wage worker while Merle has grown rich. As a result, Rudy is resentful and tries to get back at Merle by grooming Karl into the exact type of son Merle himself would most want. Yet, Karl's unexpected confession to Franklin changes nothing. The story ends with the young men keeping up the façade that they wish to be just like their fathers.

COMMENTARY

This story is about the troubled relationships between fathers and sons. Both Merle Waggoner and Rudy Linberg see their sons as extensions of themselves, and both want their sons to follow in their footsteps. Although Merle tries to be supportive of his son's stated desire to be an actor, saying he is glad Franklin has "big dreams" of his own and giving him the advice to "Give 'em hell boy—and be yourself" (255), he cannot help but be bitter that Franklin has no desire to run the factory into which Merle has poured his whole life. And Rudy is so resentful of Merle's success that he manipulates his relationship with his own son to make Merle jealous. Although Merle believes that Karl has crafted the metal sheet and snug-fitting cube he is given for his birthday, just like the one his father made years before, readers find out at the end of the story that it is Rudy who has skillfully lathed both puzzles. The cube and metal sheet, in fact, become symbols for how the fathers would like their relationships with their sons to work—the cube, representing the son, fits smoothly and perfectly into the opening cut out for it.

But family relationships do not run as smoothly as a cube fitting a hole. Generational conflict between fathers and sons is sure to occur. Merle Waggoner sees his differences with Franklin in these terms, lamenting that new people are taking over the town's businesses "instead of the sons" (258). Merle cannot understand the younger generation, and asks Franklin, "What is it about the sons? . . . What is it? All the wars? Drinking?" (258). Franklin is unsure how to answer his father's question, but he does feel great guilt and thinks of his generation as "the killers of their fathers' dreams" (259). Karl Linberg, similarly, feels a great burden of responsibility to his father, perhaps even more than Franklin does. "Your father doesn't just have you," he explains to the wealthy factory owner's son, "He's got his big success. . . . All my old man's got is me" (262). While the story ends with a return to the status quo—Rudy and Karl play musical duets together and the music seems to be saying "that fathers and sons [are] one" (264)—there is nevertheless an ominous feel to the end. Readers suspect that these relationships are bound to explode soon, that the status quo cannot hold for long. Vonnegut writes that the music is also saying "that a time for a parting in spirit was near—no matter how close anyone held anyone, no matter what anyone tried" (264). In the end, sons must be themselves; they cannot simply be carbon copies of their fathers.

CHARACTERS

Aunt Margaret Franklin Waggoner's Aunt Margaret is his father's sister. Since Franklin's mother is dead, Margaret serves as a maternal substitute for the young man.

Ferguson, Guy Guy Ferguson works for the General Forge and Foundry Company in ILIUM, New York, which has offered to buy Merle Waggoner's pump factory for $2 million.

Jackson, George Miramar George Miramar Jackson is a security guard at Merle Waggoner's pump factory. Franklin Waggoner cannot remember the man's name when George pulls up his sports car for him, suggesting that Franklin's heart is really not in the factory or its employees.

Linberg, Karl Karl Linberg is the 20-year-old son of Rudy Linberg. Like his father, he is a lathe operator, a musician, and an excellent shot. In fact, he initially seems to want nothing more than to live a life exactly like Rudy's. At the end of the story, however, Karl confesses to Franklin Waggoner that the relationship between him and his father is not so ideal as it seems. Rudy has crafted the gift Karl gives to Merle Waggoner himself—an expertly made puzzle—and passed it off as his son's work. Karl tells Franklin, in fact, that Rudy has dedicated his life to making Merle "eat his heart out" for a son like Karl (263).

Linberg, Rudy Rudy Linberg is an expert craftsman who has worked at Merle Waggoner's pump factory for years and years. Rudy, in fact, was Merle's first employee. Yet, readers discover at the end of the story that Rudy secretly resents Merle. When Rudy had a chance to become part owner of the factory when it was first started, he refused to do so, and thus has remained an employee his whole life while Merle has become an extremely wealthy man. In retaliation, Rudy has groomed his son, Karl, to be exactly the sort of boy Merle would want for his own.

Waggoner, Franklin Franklin Waggoner is the 20-year-old son of wealthy factory owner Merle Waggoner, who has made his fortune through hard work and big dreams. Franklin, a student at Cornell University, is not sure what he wants to do with his life, but he does know that running his father's factory has absolutely no appeal for him; he is not nearly so ambitious as his father. Yet, wanting to please Merle, Franklin eventually agrees to take over the factory one day.

Waggoner, Merle Merle Waggoner, a 51 year-old widower, is the owner of a very successful centrifugal pump factory, which he founded many years before. His fondest wish, as he grows older, is that his only son, Franklin, will take over the factory when he dies. He is dismayed when Franklin announces that he wishes to be an actor. Although he tries to support his son, he cannot help but let his bitterness show, eventually making Franklin feel so guilty that he changes his mind and agrees to run the factory after Merle's death.

FURTHER READING

Bagombo Snuff Box. New York: Berkley Books, 2000.
Reed, Peter. *The Short Fiction of Kurt Vonnegut.* Westport, Conn.: Greenwood Press, 1997.

Timequake

Timequake, published by Putnam in 1997, is a culmination of the metafictive project Vonnegut began in his earlier novels *Slaughterhouse-Five* (1969) and *Breakfast of Champions* (1973). METAFICTION, a characteristic often associated with POSTMODERN literature, is fiction that is about the writing of fiction,

Cover art from *Timequake* (used by permission of G.P. Putnam's Sons, a division of Penguin Group USA, Inc.)

about how storytelling shapes the human world. Thus, *Timequake's* main theme is that of a writer looking back at and coming to terms with his long career. Even more than in the two earlier books, in *Timequake* fictional characters mingle with biographical figures from Vonnegut's own life as both he and his fictional alter ego, Kilgore, Trout mourn the fact that life is often "a crock of shit" (3, 106), but also celebrate the ability of art to "make people appreciate being alive at least a little bit" (1).

SYNOPSIS

Prologue

In the prologue to *Timequake,* Vonnegut tells readers that in the winter of 1996 he found himself "the creator of a novel which did not work" (xiii). He asks readers to think of that book, which he had spent a decade writing, as *Timequake One.* He refers to the current book as *Timequake Two* and describes it as a "stew" made from the best parts of his discarded novel mixed with his "thoughts and experiences during the past seven months or so" (xiv). The main event of the earlier novel, which Vonnegut tells readers about in the current one, is a timequake that "zaps everybody and everything in an instant from February 13th, 2001, back to February 17th, 1991" (xv). Thus, everyone has to relive 10 years of their lives exactly as they had done previously, unable to change a single thing that happens. FREE WILL kicks in again on the second of February 13, 2001, and people are released from the prisons of their past. The fictional elements of the current *Timequake* mostly follow the story of the recurring Vonnegut character Kilgore Trout during the period just before the onset of the timequake and just after it ends. As Vonnegut tells readers in his prologue, "Most of what I have chosen to preserve from *Timequake One* has to do with [Trout's] adventures and opinions" (xv). Trout, however, is not thrilled when the 10-year rerun ends. "Oh Lordy," he says, "I am much too old and experienced to start playing Russian roulette with free will again" (xvi). Trout, whom Vonnegut describes as his fictional "alter ego" (xv), seems to express Vonnegut's own views here as he is released from the timequake experience of rewriting a novel that did not work the first time around.

Fact and fiction mix more thoroughly in this book than anywhere else in Vonnegut's work as the two aging writers exchange ideas, relate stories from their lives, and celebrate their long collaboration at the clambake that ends the novel.

Chapters 1–19

Kilgore Trout begins *Timequake* as a homeless person who has been caught by police in a sweep of the New York Public Library and moved, with about 30 others, to a shelter at the former Museum of the American Indian on West 155th Street. Vonnegut tells readers that Trout had been a hobo since 1975, following the news of the death of his son, Leon, in a shipyard accident in Sweden. Since that time, Trout has been throwing away the numerous stories he writes rather than sending them out for publication. One of the stories he throws away is called "The Sisters B-36," about three beautiful sisters, two of whom are artists while the third is a scientist. The scientist sister, jealous of her two popular and creative sisters, invents television and all kinds of other machines that limit the imagination. An African-American security guard named Dudley Prince working next door to the shelter, at the AMERICAN ACADEMY OF ARTS AND LETTERS, sees Kilgore Trout (whom he mistakes for a bag lady) throwing away his story. Prince retrieves it, reads it, and takes the story to be a message for the academy "from God himself" (64). He shows it to Monica Pepper, executive secretary of the academy, and her husband, the paralyzed composer Zoltan Pepper. Although Monica regards the story as "ridiculous" (68), Zoltan is "electrified" (68) by it, not because of the story's content, but because of the author's name. Zoltan Pepper, as a high school student in Florida, had plagiarized a Kilgore Trout story and been made to wear a placard with the letter *P* around his neck for a week by his English teacher. In any case, Trout continues to write a new story about every 10 days and to throw them away in the outdoor trash can where Dudley Prince retrieves and ponders them, "hoping to discover some important message from a higher power encoded therein" (75).

Chapters 20–29

When the timequake actually occurs, on February 13, 2001, Dudley Prince is zapped back to prison, where he had been serving a life sentence after having been unjustly convicted of raping and murdering a little girl before being exonerated by DNA evidence seven years later. The Peppers are sent back 10 years as well, to the time before Zoltan was paralyzed as a result of his wife diving on top of him in a swimming pool accident. Vonnegut says that he himself had dumped a very hot cup of chicken noodle soup in his lap when the timequake struck. Thus, when the timequake ends and free will kicks in again, he goes back to sweeping the scalding noodles off his trousers. Kilgore Trout, in the former Museum of the American Indian, is one of the first people to realize when the timequake ends. For the past 10 years, he, like everyone else, has lived without free will, forced to repeat everything just as they had done it the first time. But Trout recognizes that something is different on the second of February 13, 2001. He confirms the existence of free will by saying a string of nonsense words out loud, something he had not been able to do during the 10-year rerun.

Chapters 30–53

A phenomenon called Post-Timequake Apathy, or PTA, has kicked in, along with the return of free will. People are so stunned by having to act on their own again that they become frozen. As a result, car crashes and accidents of all kinds are rampant. Zoltan Pepper, in fact, is killed by a runaway hook and ladder truck while ringing the doorbell of the academy, where he has come to pick up his wife, Monica. Dudley Prince barely escapes death from a falling chandelier when the academy's smoke alarm goes off, causing him to freeze in indecision as he is about to answer the door. Kilgore Trout brings Dudley Prince back to life again. Instead of "trying to sell the concept of free will, which he himself didn't believe in" (179), Trout says to Prince, "You've been very sick! Now you're well again" (179). This mantra, with the added dictum that "there's work to do," becomes known as "Kilgore's Creed," and will be broadcast on television and radio nationwide. Meanwhile, Trout, with the help of Monica Pepper and Dudley Prince, turns the former Museum of the American Indian into a makeshift hospital and the American Academy of Arts and Letters into a makeshift morgue.

Chapters 54–63

When martial law goes into effect in New York, relieving the group of their responsibilities, Kilgore Trout, Monica Pepper, Dudley Prince, and Jerry Rivers (Zoltan Pepper's chauffeur, who had just dropped him off at the academy when free will returned) drive off in Pepper's limousine for Xanadu, a writer's retreat in Rhode Island. Because the whole world is so grateful to Trout for his healing mantra, "You were sick, but now you're well again, and there's work to do," he is given the job of creating sound effects backstage at the Xanadu production of a play, ABE LINCOLN IN ILLINOIS. After the play, a clambake honoring Trout is held on the beach. A mixture of fictional characters and real people from Vonnegut's own life, including relatives, friends, literary critics, and business associates, attend the party, which brings to an end what Vonnegut writes in his prologue will be his "last book" (xvii). Fittingly, the novel closes with an affirmation and celebration of the life of Vonnegut's greatest character and his alter ego, Kilgore Trout.

COMMENTARY

Having experienced long-term writer's block and having worked for 10 years on a novel that he considers a failure—*Timequake One*—Vonnegut himself is undergoing what feels like a timequake as he rewrites his earlier book. As he revisits his immediate past in the novel, Vonnegut questions, as he does elsewhere in his work, whether human beings can actually learn anything from history. The fact that those who experience the timequake have to repeat their lives exactly as they played out the first time suggests that the past, rather than teaching how to approach the future, is a prison people cannot escape. In his earlier novel *Slapstick*, Vonnegut had a character assert that people do not learn from history because history is "merely a list of surprises" (255). In this novel, Vonnegut remembers that his first wife, JANE COX VONNEGUT YARNOLINSKY, won her Phi Beta Kappa key at Swarthmore College by writing that "all that could be learned from history was that history itself was absolutely nonsensical, so study something else, like music" (222). Further, Vonnegut tells readers that he "agreed with her, and so would have Kilgore Trout" (222). Nevertheless, he takes on the project in *Timequake* of looking back at his personal history and memorializing the family and friends, both factual and fictional, who made a difference in his life. This book both mourns the loss of the past, the passing of people and places that cannot be held onto, and celebrates the ability of the artist to reclaim, at least temporarily, a bit of that past back again.

Art and life mingle freely in *Timequake*. SCIENCE FICTION writer Kilgore Trout, Vonnegut's alter ego throughout his writing career, frequently serves as a mouthpiece for Vonnegut's own ideas. Both agree that life is "undeniably preposterous," but as Trout points out at the clambake, "our brains are big enough to let us adapt to the inevitable pratfalls and buffoonery . . . by means of manmade epiphanies" (22). Vonnegut tells readers that some of the most important manmade epiphanies for him have been "stage plays," which are like timequakes since actors know everything they are going to say and do and how everything is going to turn out in the end when the curtain first rises, "yet they have no choice but to behave as though the future were a mystery" (23). Thus, Vonnegut's real-life timequake (the rewriting of the novel) is turned by him into a fictional timequake (the brief contraction of the universe that sends everybody in the book back to February 17, 1991). This fictional timequake serves as a metaphor for the way art (particularly stage plays) work. Finally, art helps Vonnegut adapt to the preposterous nature of real life. Speeches and situations from plays he has seen become for him as a young man the "emotional and ethical landmarks" that he lives by (25). Vonnegut turns life into art, then art helps him adapt to life. As in much postmodern fiction, the line separating fact and fiction has become blurred and permeable.

Because art and life are so inextricably intertwined in Vonnegut's view, he spends much of *Timequake* contemplating the role of art and artists in contemporary life. He laments what he sees as the diminishment of art by technology in the late 20th century, when computer programs can compose "acceptable, if derivative" (36) string quartets and design parking garages in the style of Thomas Jefferson in under half an hour. Kilgore Trout's most prominent story in the novel addresses this

same issue. In "The Sisters B-36," the scientific youngest B-36 sister, Nim-nim, jealous of her popular, artistic sisters, invents televisions and automobiles and computers and machine guns in order to stunt children's imaginations and turn them away from art. The children who grow up without imaginations, unable to read stories together, become "among the most merciless creatures in the local family of galaxies" (21). In Vonnegut's view, artistic pursuit teaches human beings compassion for one another. Art not only mitigates human cruelty, but also has the power to make life interesting and enjoyable. Vonnegut tells readers early on that he believes "a plausible mission of artists is to make people appreciate being alive at least a little bit" (1). He also remembers a conversation he had with his thesis adviser when he was a graduate student studying anthropology at the UNIVERSITY OF CHICAGO. Vonnegut's adviser explains that artists "are people who say, 'I can't fix my country or my state or my city, or even my marriage. But by golly, I can make this square of canvas, or this eight-and-a-half-by-eleven piece of paper, or this lump of clay, or these twelve bars of music, exactly what they *ought* to be!'" (162).

One way that Vonnegut rearranges life in his writing, makes it more what it "*ought* to be," is by reimagining the friends and family that he has lost throughout his life and bringing them back together in the book itself. Here, as elsewhere in his work, especially the novel *Slapstick,* which mourns the loss of his sister, Alice, Vonnegut emphasizes the importance of large, extended families in giving human beings the support and companionship they need in order to cope with life. While lamenting the INDIANAPOLIS "diaspora" (152) that scatters his boyhood friends and family members far and wide, Vonnegut, in writing about these long-lost friends and relations, can bring them back to life and gather them back together. Vonnegut bothers to write because "Many people need desperately to receive this message: 'I feel and think much as you do, care about many of the things you care about, although most people don't care about them. You are not alone'" (221). As he writes to his older brother, Bernard, Vonnegut believes that "any work of art is half of a conversation between two human beings" (168). Literature itself can serve as the extended family that so many contemporary Americans miss in their real lives.

At the same time, Vonnegut does not overly romanticize art. Always the skeptic, always the cynic, he recognizes that perhaps the only artists able to actually "make people appreciate being alive" are the Beatles (1). Even his Chicago thesis adviser killed himself by swallowing potassium cyanide. Vonnegut deglamorizes fiction writing, referring to it as an addiction as deadly as alcohol or gambling, arguing that, rather than these vices, writers are "hooked on making idiosyncratic arrangements in horizontal lines, with ink on bleached and flattened wood pulp, of twenty six phonetic symbols, ten numbers, and about eight punctuations marks" (32). Rather than a lofty image of the literary artist heroically supplying inspiration to a desperate populace, the writer is reduced to just another needy human being feeding his addiction as best he can. Readers might remember here the opening chapter of *Slaughterhouse-Five* in which Vonnegut deglamorizes fiction writing along with war, calling himself a "trafficker in climaxes and thrills and characterization and wonderful dialogue and suspense and confrontations" (5). In addition, Vonnegut points out in *Timequake* that his addiction to writing, like any addiction, can have very unpleasant effects on those close to him. Both he and Kilgore Trout can be like black holes to anyone who imagines themselves a friend of theirs (32). The dangers of romanticizing the artist are evident when Vonnegut explains that his sister would have been glad to see the words Monica Pepper spray paints across the front door of the American Academy of Arts and Letters, hoping to ward off would-be intruders: "FUCK ART!" (98). Alice felt patronized by her father's glowing praise of her own attempts to make art as a girl, recognizing that she was being "lavishly praised for very little because she was a pretty girl," and sensing her father's underlying belief that "only men could become great artists" (98).

In *Timequake*, Vonnegut also continues his critique against a strict representational type of art, a critique begun in *Slaughterhouse-Five*, articulated more fully in *Breakfast of Champions*, and applied to the visual arts in *Bluebeard*. In this novel, Kilgore

Trout insists that he does not write "literature"—literature is for the "la-di-da monkeys next door" at the Academy of Arts and Letters. Trout explains to a bum on a cot next to his at the homeless shelter that "those artsy-fartsy twerps next door create living, breathing, three-dimensional characters with ink on paper . . . as though the planet weren't already dying because it has three billion too many living, breathing, three-dimensional characters!" (71). He continues, arguing that if he had wasted his time creating characters, he "would never have gotten around to calling attention to things that really matter: irresistible forces in nature, and cruel inventions, and cockamamie ideals and governments and economies that make heroes and heroines alike feel like something the cat drug in" (72). Vonnegut, in fact, tells readers that both he and Trout create "*caricatures* rather than characters" (72). Thinking back through Vonnegut's novels, this assessment seems a fair one, and it can be understood in several ways. First, as Vonnegut will point out later in *Timequake*, human beings are unpredictable and messy, so the idea of *real* humans having a coherent character is a false one to begin with. When Vonnegut's early literary agent shoots himself to death, a friend says the man couldn't possibly have committed suicide because "it was so *out of character*" (162). Recognizing the wishful thinking evident in this line of argument, Vonnegut replies, "Even with military training, there is no way a man can accidentally blow his head off with a shotgun" (162). In addition, as Vonnegut explains in *Slaughterhouse-Five*, most of the people he writes about are "so sick and so much the listless playthings of enormous forces" (164) that they are prevented from being what we like to think of as well-rounded characters, fully functioning human beings acting on their own free will in the world.

Flat characters, moreover, are often said to be one of the defining characteristics of postmodern literature. While the great modern writers (Faulkner, Woolf, Joyce, and so forth), working in the years between the world wars, were also skeptical of universal truth, as are the writers of Vonnegut's generation, they tended to believe that truth could still be found in the individual consciousness, that truth was a matter of individual perspective. That is why those writers were so concerned with point of view in their works, sometimes juxtaposing different versions of the same story, as in Faulkner's *The Sound and the Fury*, or else relying on stream-of-consciousness techniques to try to detail the workings of the individual mind, as in James Joyce's *Ulysses*. Postmodern writers, by contrast, tend to be skeptical about the notion of coherent individual identity. They question the view that human beings are fully realized, autonomous individuals, often positing instead that they are constructs of social environments or even suggesting that what people think of as free will, individual autonomy, might actually be a matter of neurobiology: chemical impulses firing in brains. Vonnegut himself suggests this notion often, sometimes referring to humans as machines or as chemical stews and depicting characters who are prisoners of the bad chemicals in their systems that force them to act in certain ways.

Vonnegut's tendency to write "caricatures rather than characters," however, should not be taken to mean that he considers storytelling itself frivolous or unimportant. On the contrary, for Vonnegut and other postmodern writers who tend to see the world as linguistically constructed—who believe that people at least partly create reality through language, through the stories they tell—storytelling becomes an activity of the utmost importance. In *Slaughterhouse-Five*, Kilgore Trout retells the Gospel story of Christ's crucifixion since "slipshod storytelling in the New Testament" (108) is at least partly responsible for human beings' cruelty to one another. In *Timequake*, Trout rewrites another Bible story that seems responsible for some of the ignorance and suffering Vonnegut encounters in the contemporary world—the story of humankind's fall in the Garden of Eden. In Trout's version of the Garden of Eden story, God's creation of man is viewed as a cruel, indulgent experiment: "'The Garden of Eden,' said Trout, 'might be considered the prototype for the Colosseum and the Roman Games'" (29). Satan, who is a woman in Trout's story, is not evil. She has compassion for the newly created Adam and Eve and desires to make their existence less painful since she sees what God can't, that to be alive "was to be either bored or scared stiff" (29). Satan offers Eve an apple filled "with all sorts of ideas that might at least relieve the boredom" of human existence (29–30). In this version of the story, knowledge is not sinful; it is what makes life bearable. The new version encourages human beings to be curious, to learn, to create music, to sing, to dance, and, most important, to make love. Although Satan's gift has disastrous consequences for a small minority of human beings, Vonnegut writes that "her record for promoting nostrums with occasionally dreadful side effects is no worse than that of the most reputable pharmaceutical houses of the present day" (30). Readers might be reminded here that at the end of *Breakfast of Champions* Kilgore Trout's creator—Vonnegut himself—offers his creature an apple as a gift as well, signifying again, knowledge, curiosity, and even free will, the opportunity to, perhaps, become his own god.

While Vonnegut rewrites Bible stories, which in their traditional form present bad or dangerous morality, he nevertheless wants to retain what he considers the basic decency of the Christian tradition, at least as outlined in the New Testament. Appreciating the power of storytelling to change lives and alter one's view of reality, he points out that "the two most subversive tales of all remain untouched, wholly unsuspected" (40) by authority figures who want to censor books in public schools: the story of Robin Hood and "the life of Jesus Christ as described in the New Testament" (41). In addition, Vonnegut claims as one of his three favorite quotations the question uttered by Christ of his disciples: "Who is it they say I am?" (78). Vonnegut also appreciates the beauty and poetry of the King James Bible, calling LANCELOT ANDREWES, "the chief translator and paraphraser" who worked on it, "the greatest writer in the English language so far," greater than SHAKESPEARE himself (131). As readers of his earlier novel *Jailbird* recognize, Vonnegut particularly values Christ's Sermon on the Mount, seeing it as the basis for the EUGENE DEBS statement he tells us he still quotes in every public speech he delivers: "While there is a lower class I am in it, while there is a criminal element I am of it; while there is a soul in prison, I am not free" (142). Faith, Vonnegut recognizes, can teach compassion for others in ways similar to art. When a convicted felon writes him a letter, asking what he should do now that he is about to be released into a world where he has no friends or relatives, Vonnegut replies "Join a church," pointing out that "what such a grown-up waif needs more than anything is something like a family" (84).

Yet, finally, Vonnegut transforms the ethics of CHRISTIANITY and the sense of belonging promised by religious faith into his own brand of secularism. He mentions his experience as honorary president of the AMERICAN HUMANIST ASSOCIATION, pointing out that humanists are people who "try to behave decently and honorably without any expectation of rewards or punishments in an afterlife" (82). Rather than serve an unknowable Creator of the Universe, humanists try to serve their communities. Saints in Vonnegut's secular religion are people who do just that. As Vonnegut explains in a letter to a woman who asks whether it is morally right to bring a new baby into the world, saints are people who behave unselfishly and capably, often in the most unexpected places. Further, these saints make "being alive almost worthwhile" for Vonnegut (239). In *Timequake* and throughout Vonnegut's body of work, readers meet many examples of these secular saints, who are often doctors and nurses; his physician friend who works at Bellevue Hospital is one, as is the obstetrics nurse whose influence keeps her son from dropping the third ATOMIC BOMB in the Kilgore Trout story "No Laughing Matter." Mary O'Hare in *Slaughterhouse-Five,* also a trained nurse, is a saint, as are the obstetricians who take pity on Billy Pilgrim's horse at the end of the novel. Volunteer FIREMEN are certainly part of Vonnegut's pantheon of secular saints (which explains his near-obsession with these figures over the course of his 14 novels). Teachers, like Helen Dole in *Hocus Pocus* or the head of the University of Chicago Russian Department in *Timequake,* who tells the Vonneguts that "pregnancy is the *beginning,* not the end, of life" (126), often make the list as well.

Perhaps Vonnegut's most unexpected saint is crotchety, cynical, old science fiction writer Kilgore Trout. The words he speaks to African-American security guard Dudley Prince after free will returns following the 10-year timequake—"You were sick but now you're well again, and there's work to

do" (196)—become a healing mantra known as Kilgore's Creed. Schoolteachers recite the words to their students at the beginning of each day; ministers use them in wedding ceremonies; even hotel clerks repeat them in guests' wake-up calls. Trout's words are so appreciated, in fact, that he's given the job of blowing the antique steam whistle during the production of *Abe Lincoln in Illinois* at the Rhode Island writers' retreat Xanadu. The members of the Pembroke Mask and Wig Club, who stage the performance, want Trout to feel "that he was home at last, and a vital member of an extended family" (228). Through his fictional alter ego, Kilgore Trout, Vonnegut also imaginatively recreates his own large, extended family. The clambake/cast party honoring Trout that ends the novel collects together both boyhood friends and relatives of Vonnegut who had been scattered in the Indianapolis diaspora as well as figures from his later life. Dead loved ones are brought back to life as they are represented by fictional doubles. Monica Pepper, for instance, is a stand-in for Vonnegut's sister, Alice, while the party bakemaster is a double for his literary agent, SEYMOUR LAWRENCE, and a "pert young" biochemistry teacher represents Vonnegut's first wife, Jane Cox. Vonnegut's unlikely saint Kilgore Trout ends the novel with a speech celebrating the power of the human imagination, which he argues travels "a million times" faster than the speed of light (242). This most emblematic and ubiquitous Vonnegut character—cynical, pessimistic, and skeptical about the very concept of free will—is redeemed by his new sense of belonging, and at the end of what Vonnegut says will be his last novel, he proclaims the beauty of the human *soul.*

CHARACTERS AND RELATED ENTRIES

Note: Because this novel is such a mixture of autobiography, personal reflection, and fiction, it is difficult to identify "characters" as such. In this list, I have included all fictional characters, as well as all Vonnegut relatives and all writers, artists, or celebrities with whom the narrator actually interacts. Vonnegut mentions and/or reflects on many other writers, artists, and celebrities in the novel. The most important of these appear in the "A to Z" encyclopedia section of this book.

Adams, Jim Jim Adams was the husband of Vonnegut's sister, ALICE VONNEGUT. He was killed in a commuter train accident two days before Alice died of cancer, leaving their three oldest boys to be raised by Vonnegut and his first wife, Jane Cox. Before his death, Jim had plunged the family into debt by manufacturing a toy called Putty Puss, which never became popular.

Adams, Jim Jr. Jim Adams, Jr., is one of the sons of Vonnegut's sister, Alice, whom he adopts after her death. Vonnegut describes Jim, Jr., as an "ex-Peace Corps guy" who is now a psychiatric nurse" (221).

Adams, Kurt Kurt Adams is the youngest of the three brothers that Vonnegut adopts when his sister, Alice, dies. Vonnegut tells readers that Kurt is now a pilot with Continental Airlines; all he'd ever wanted to do since childhood was fly, and his dream has come true.

Adams, Steve Steve Adams is one of the sons of JAMES CARMALT ADAMS and Alice Vonnegut, whom Kurt Vonnegut and his wife adopted after the death of their parents. In *Timequake*, Vonnegut remembers Steve coming home for Christmas vacation after his freshman year at Dartmouth, close to tears after having read *A Farewell to Arms*. Vonnegut himself, moved by Steve's reaction, rereads the novel and interprets it as an attack on the institution of marriage. He tells Steve that the tears he wanted to shed are "tears of *relief*! It looked like the guy was going to have to get married and settle down. but then he didn't have to. Whew! What a close shave!" (93).

Adler, Ted Vonnegut reminisces about the house he and his first wife, Jane lived in on CAPE COD. Because the ell where Vonnegut did his writing was falling down, he hired a friend named Ted Adler to build him a new one. When Adler has finished, he surveys his handiwork and says, "How the hell did I *do* that?" (78).

Asimov, Dr. Isaac When Vonnegut speaks at a American Humanist Association memorial service

for Dr. Isaac Asimov, past honorary president of that organization, he says to the audience, "Isaac is up in Heaven now" (83), a comment that leaves the association members rolling in the aisles with laughter.

B-36 Mother The mother of the three sisters in Kilgore Trout's story "The Sisters B-36" is very rich and thus able to finance her unpopular scientist daughter Nim-nim's diabolical inventions.

B-36 Sisters Kilgore Trout's story "The Sisters B-36" is about three sisters whose last name is B-36. All three sisters are beautiful, but only two of the three are popular. These two are both artistic, while the unpopular sister, Nim-nim, is a scientist. Envious of her sisters, Nim-nim invents televisions and automobiles and other machines that destroy the imaginations of children on the family's home planet of Booboo. As a result, "Booboolings became among the most merciless creatures in the local family of galaxies" (21).

Barus, Carl Vonnegut's maternal great-uncle Carl Barus was a founder and president of the American Physical Society. Barus had argued that ionization was unimportant in condensation, a theory later proved wrong by Scottish physicist CHARLES THOMSON REES WILSON.

Böll, Heinrich Vonnegut tells readers he asked the "late great German novelist Heinrich Böll what the basic flaw was in the German character" (48). Böll replies that it is obedience.

Booboo Booboo is the matriarchal home planet of three sisters whose last name is B-36 in the Kilgore Trout story "The Sisters B-36."

Booth, John Wilkes Vonnegut tells readers that the deranged actor who assassinated President ABRAHAM LINCOLN was a character in *Timequake One*, the novel he had been working on for the previous decade. In that book, he had the fictitious Julia Pembroke, wife of the assistant secretary of the Navy, give birth to Booth's child after he drugs her one night following a performance.

Booth, Junius and Edwin Junius and Edwin Booth, brothers of Lincoln assassin John Wilkes Booth, appear in *Timequake One* when they meet Julia Pembroke one night after a performance of Shakespeare's *Julius Caesar*. John Wilkes had played the role of Marc Antony, Junius had played Brutus, and Edwin had played Cassius. The Booth brothers, along with their British father, Junius Brutus Booth, Vonnegut writes, "constituted what remains to this day the greatest family of tragedians in the history of the English-speaking stage" (224).

Bowen, Julius King Julius King Bowen is said to be the endower of the Xanadu writer's retreat in Rhode Island. Vonnegut describes him as a "never-married white man who made a fortune during the 1920s and early 1930s with stories and lectures about the hilarious, but touching, too, efforts by American black people to imitate successful American white people, so they could be successful, too" (88).

Braun, Eva ADOLF HITLER'S longtime mistress, Eva Braun, is a character in the Kilgore Trout story "Bunker Bingo Party." The story briefly shows Hitler marrying Braun in his bunker beneath Berlin in April 1945, just before the end of World War II.

Burger, Knox Knox Burger was a Cornell classmate of Vonnegut's and later publisher of his work; he appears at the giant clambake at the end of *Timequake*. Knox Burger also appears briefly in Vonnegut's earlier novel *Breakfast of Champions*.

Craig, David Vonnegut tells about "a redheaded boyhood friend" (91) named David Craig, now a builder in New Orleans, who won a Bronze Star in World War II for shooting a German tank with a bazooka.

Cosby, Janet Vonnegut's lecture agent, Janet Cosby, is one of the guests at the giant clambake that ends *Timequake*.

Cox, Harvey and Riah Harvey and Riah Cox are the parents of Vonnegut's first wife, the former Jane Cox. In *Timequake*, Vonnegut states

that the Coxes sent their daughter to a boarding school and bought her expensive clothes so that she could "marry a man whose family had money and power" (99).

Deal, Borden Borden Deal was a southern novelist and friend of Vonnegut's who defined the gothic novel in the following way: "A young woman goes into an old house and gets her pants scared off" (236).

Delicto, Flagrante Flagrante Delicto, whose name is a well-known Latin phrase meaning "in the act of committing a crime (or in the act of having sex)," is a groom described as a "heartless womanizer" (177) in Kilgore Trout's play *The Wrinkled Old Family Retainer*.

Dictu, Mirabile Mirabile Dictu, whose name is a well-known Latin phrase that means "wonderful to relate," is a bride in the Kilgore Trout play *The Wrinkled Old Family Retainer*.

Downs, Roger A classmate of Vonnegut's from high school, Roger Downs is a superb Ping-Pong player who beats another classmate, Skip Failey, so severely that he is said to have "cut" Skip "a new asshole" (149).

Emmy The daughter of Vonnegut's Uncle Dan, Emmy is not only Vonnegut's cousin, but was also his lab partner in high school physics. At the time the novel was written, 1996, Emmy lived about 30 miles from Vonnegut's boyhood friend David Craig in Louisiana.

Failey, William H. C. "Skip" Skip Failey is a boyhood friend of Vonnegut's who thought he was unbeatable at Ping-Pong until he plays a classmate named Roger Downs who, Skip reports, "cut [him] a new asshole" (149).

Farber, Don and Anne Don Farber, a lawyer and literary agent, who appears at the clambake at the end of *Timequake* along with his wife, Anne, is described as Vonnegut's "closest business associate."

Francis, Dick Vonnegut meets the author Dick Francis at the Kentucky Derby and is surprised he is not a bigger man since he used to be a champion steeplechase rider.

Goebbels, Joseph and Family Adolf Hitler's minister of propaganda, Joseph Goebbels, and his wife and children appear in the Kilgore Trout story "Bunker Bingo Party." Nazi officers in Hiter's Berlin bunker just before the end of World War II amuse themselves playing a game of bingo that the Goebbel children had brought into the bunker with them.

Grass, Günter Vonnegut remembers that the German novelist and artist Günter Grass, upon hearing that Vonnegut was born in 1922, said to him: "There are no males in Europe your age for you to talk to" (13).

Hardy, Albert Albert Hardy, the protagonist of a Kilgore Trout story of the same name, is a working-class Londoner born in 1896, "with his head between his legs, and his genitalia sprouting out of the top of his neck" (86). When free will kicks in again after the timequake, Trout is able to finish the story—he has Hardy blown to pieces during World War I. Hardy is buried in France, in the Tomb of the Unknown Soldier, his body parts reassembled as though he had been just like everyone else.

Hickenlooper, John, Jr. and Sr. The owner of the Wynkoop Brewing Company, which bottled a special beer for the Denver art show of Vonnegut and JOE PETRO III, is John Hickenlooper, Jr., the son of an old fraternity buddy of Vonnegut's from Cornell University. Because Hickenlooper Sr. had died when his son was only seven years old, Hickenlooper Jr. does not remember him well. Vonnegut is able to tell Hickenlooper Jr. funny stories about his father.

Hitler, Adolf Adolf Hitler appears in *Timequake* as a character in the Kilgore Trout story "Bunker Bingo Party," set in Hitler's bunker underneath Berlin at the end of World War II. Bored, the Nazi officials eventually become absorbed in playing bingo, a game the children of propaganda minister Joseph Goebbels have brought with them.

Hitz, Benjamin Benjamin Hitz was the best man at the wedding of Kurt Vonnegut and Jane Cox Vonnegut in Indianapolis. Now, Vonnegut tells readers, Hitz is a widower in Santa Barbara, California. A character named Dr. Benjamin Hitz also appears in Vonnegut's short story "2BRO2B."

Hotchner, A. E. HEMINGWAY biographer A. E. Hotchner is a friend of Vonnegut's. Vonnegut asked Hotchner whether Hemingway "had ever shot a human being, not counting himself" and Hotchner replied "No" (48).

Hurty, Phoebe Phoebe Hurty, the woman to whom Vonnegut dedicates his earlier novel *Breakfast of Champions*, hired him in high school to write advertising copy for a clothing store. Like many important figures from Vonnegut's life, Phoebe Hurty has a doppelgänger at the clambake at the end of the novel.

"If this isn't nice, what is?" In numerous speeches, as well as in *Timequake*, Vonnegut reminisces about ALEX VONNEGUT's ability to appreciate the good moments in life. Uncle Alex would often interrupt conversations to draw attention to small moments of happiness with the phrase, "If this isn't nice what is?" Vonnegut points out that people could learn something from his Uncle Alex, that the world be a better place if all people took time to notice when they are happy.

Johnson, Fred Bates When Vonnegut tells his father he wants to work for a newspaper, Kurt, Sr. sends him to see his old friend Fred Bates Johnson, a lawyer who had worked as a reporter for a now-defunct Indianapolis newspaper as a young man. Vonnegut explains to Johnson his careful plan to first work on a tiny paper, then slowly, over the course of several years, work his way up to reporting for *The Indianapolis Times*. Immediately afterward, Johnson makes one phone call and gets Vonnegut a job with the Indianapolis paper he had aspired to.

Joy's Pride *Joy's Pride* is the name of the American bomber ordered to drop a third atomic bomb on Japan during World War II in the Kilgore Trout story "No Laughing Matter" that appears in *Timequake*. The pilot, however, whose ship is named after his mother, Joy Peterson, an obstetrics nurse in Corpus Christi, Texas, refuses to do so.

Kilgore's Creed When Kilgore Trout gently urges security guard Dudley Prince out of his Post-Timequake Apathy, he says, "You were sick, but now you're well again, and there's work to do" (196). This assertion, which comes to be called "Kilgore's Creed," soon catches on with teachers who use it to encourage students to face the day's work, with ministers performing wedding ceremonies, and even with hotel desk clerks delivering wake-up calls. In fact, Vonnegut tells readers that in the two weeks following the return of free will, "Kilgore's Creed did as much to save life on Earth as Einstein's *E equals mc squared* had done to end it two generations earlier" (197).

Klinkowitz, Jerome Jerome Klinkowitz is a literary critic who has written extensively on Vonnegut's work and thus appears as a character at the clambake that ends *Timequake*.

Krementz, Jill The photographer Jill Krementz is Vonnegut's second wife. In *Timequake*, Vonnegut discusses Jill's up-to-date office in comparison to his old-fashioned one.

Lawrence, Seymour Seymour Lawrence was Vonnegut's publisher for *Slaughterhouse-Five*. He was also instrumental in getting Vonnegut's earlier books back into print. The bakemaster at the clambake at the end of *Timequake* is a look-alike for Seymour Lawrence.

Leeds, Marc Marc Leeds "wrote and published a witty encyclopedia" (235) of Vonnegut's life and work, and thus is present at the clambake at the end of *Timequake*.

Leonard, John Well-known book reviewer and literary critic John Leonard appears at the clambake party at the end of *Timequake*.

Lieber, Albert and wife Albert Lieber is the son of Vonnegut's maternal great-grandfather PETER LIEBER. Albert inherited the family brewery from his father and ran it until Prohibition put him out of business in 1920. When Albert's first wife died, he married a crazy violinist who hated the three children from his first marriage (including Vonnegut's mother) and abused them both physically and mentally.

Lieber, Albert II Vonnegut has a cousin named Albert Lieber, who is named after Vonnegut's maternal grandfather. Albert, a nuclear scientist in Del Mar California, is the son of Vonnegut's Uncle Pete.

Lieber, Alice Barus Alice Barus Lieber was the first wife of Vonnegut's maternal grandfather Albert Lieber, and the mother of Vonnegut's mother, Edith. In *Timequake*, Vonnegut says that Alice Lieber died while giving birth to her third child, Vonnegut's Uncle Rudy. In *Palm Sunday*, though, Vonnegut tells readers his grandmother died of pneumonia.

Lieber, Pete Pete Lieber, named after Vonnegut ancestor PETER LIEBER who fought in the Civil War, is one of Vonnegut's maternal uncles. Lieber not only flunked out of the MASSACHUSETTS INSTITUTE OF TECHNOLOGY, but he, his brother, Rudy, and Vonnegut's mother, Edith, were all abused by their stepmother as children.

Lieber, Peter Peter Lieber is one of Vonnegut's great-grandfathers, on his mother's side. A German immigrant and freethinker wounded in the leg in the Civil War, Lieber became a brewer in Indianapolis. The secret ingredient in his beer, allowing him to win a gold medal at the Paris Exposition of 1889, was coffee.

Lieber, Rudy Rudy Lieber is Vonnegut's uncle, his mother's youngest brother. According to what Vonnegut tells readers in *Timequake*, his grandmother, Alice Barus Lieber, died giving birth to Rudy. Earlier, however, in the essay collection *Palm Sunday*, Vonnegut had asserted that Alice Barus Lieber died of pneumonia.

Littauer, Colonel Kenneth Colonel Kenneth Littauer, described as "the first pilot to strafe a trench during World War One," was Vonnegut's first literary agent; he sold a dozen of his early stories, enabling Vonnegut to quit his job with GENERAL ELECTRIC.

Locke, John   John Locke was a fraternity brother of Vonnegut's from Cornell. He sold candy and soft drinks and cigarettes with John Hickenlooper, Sr. out of a big closet on the second floor of the fraternity house.

Max   Max is Vonnegut's grandson, the son of his daughter Nanny. In *Timequake*, Vonnegut tells readers about Max writing a "really swell report" (121) for school on SIR ISAAC NEWTON.

McCarthy, Cliff   Photographer and Vonnegut friend Cliff McCarthy, who also appears in *Deadeye Dick*, is present at the clambake that ends *Timequake*.

McCarthy, Kevin   Kevin McCarthy is a professional actor who is a guest at the clambake at the end of *Timequake*.

Mihalich, Jeff   A young University of Illinois physics major named Jeff Mihalich writes Vonnegut a letter saying he is having great trouble with college physics even though he had done well in the subject in high school. Vonnegut replies that Jeff should read *The Adventures of Augie March* by Saul Bellow, which will teach him that "we shouldn't be seeking harrowing challenges, but rather tasks we find natural and interesting, tasks we were apparently born to perform" (148).

Muir, Edward   A poet and advertising man Vonnegut describes as a member of his *karass*, Ed Muir was at the University of Chicago the same time as Vonnegut, as well as in Schenectady, New York, Cape Cod, and Boston when Vonnegut lived in those places. When Vonnegut writes Muir a letter, explaining his case of writer's block, his friend sends Vonnegut's words back to him, formatted as a poem. Vonnegut mentions that Muir is always getting mixed up with Scottish poet Edwin Muir.

New York State Maximum Security Adult Correctional Institution at Athena   The New York State Maximum Security Adult Correctional Institution at Athena is the prison in *Hocus Pocus* where Eugene Debs Hartke teaches for eight years before a massive jail break that Hartke is later wrongly accused of masterminding. The same prison is also said to be the place in which Dudley Prince, a security guard in *Timequake*, is unjustly incarcerated after being accused of a rape and murder he did not commit.

Nolte, Nick   Professional actor Nick Nolte is listed as one of the guests at the clambake that ends *Timequake*.

Offit, Sidney   Sidney Offit, whom Vonnegut describes as his "closest social pal" (235) appears at the clambake/cast party that ends *Timequake*.

O'Hare, Bernard V.   Vonnegut's war buddy from his earlier novel *Slaughterhouse-Five* makes a brief appearance in *Timequake* when Vonnegut tells readers that O'Hare lost his faith as a Roman Catholic during World War II. Vonnegut also mentions that O'Hare was with him when he was released from being a prisoner of war along the Czech border in May, 1945, a scene that Rabo Karabekian paints in *Bluebeard*.

Palladio   Palladio is the name of a computer program in *Timequake* that helps nonarchitects design buildings. Frank Pepper, the older brother of paralyzed composer Zoltan Pepper in the novel, hears about the program from a drugstore clerk, buys it, and tries it out. When the computer is able to successfully design a three-story parking garage in the architectural style of Thomas Jefferson, Frank goes home and blows his brains out, convinced the program will render his skill and training useless.

Pembroke, Abraham Lincoln I, III, and IV   The first Abraham Lincoln Pembroke is the illegitimate son of Julia Pembroke from her tryst with John Wilkes Booth. In 1889, he founded what would become the largest textile mill in New England. In 1947, his grandson, Abraham Lincoln Pembroke

III, locked out his striking workers and moved the company to North Carolina. Abraham Lincoln Pembroke IV later sold the mill to an international conglomerate.

Pembroke, Elias   Elias Pembroke, a "fictitious Rhode Island naval architect who was Abraham Lincoln's Assistant Secretary of the Navy during our Civil War" (223) was a character in *Timequake One*, the book Vonnegut supposedly spent a decade on before giving up. Because he is neglectful of his wife, Julia, she ends up falling in love with Lincoln assassin John Wilkes Booth.

Pembroke, Julia   A character from *Timequake One*, Julia Pembroke is the wife of Elias Pembroke, the fictitious assistant secretary of the Navy during the Civil War. Julia falls in love with actor John Wilkes Booth and arranges to meet him after a performance of *Julius Caesar* in New York City, where the actor drugs her and makes her pregnant. After this event, Julia returns home to Rhode Island and passes her son off as belonging to Pembroke.

Pepper, Frank   The older brother of composer Zoltan Pepper, Frank Pepper is an architect who kills himself after being told by a pharmacist that his 16-year-old daughter is designing buildings with the help of a computer program.

Pepper, Monica   Monica Pepper is a character from *Timequake One*, the novel Vonnegut supposedly wrote and discarded. The executive secretary of the Academy of Arts and Letters, Monica bears a striking resemblance to Vonnegut's sister, Alice. Monica is married to composer Zoltan Pepper, who became paralyzed after she accidentally landed on top of him in a swimming pool after performing a swan dive. Zoltan dies after the timequake ends in 2001. Late in the novel, Vonnegut claims that it is 2010 and that Monica Pepper Vonnegut is now his wife, as fact mingles with fiction.

Pepper, Zoltan   Composer Zoltan Pepper, like his wife, Monica, is a fictional character from *Timequake One*. Zoltan has been paralyzed from the waist down after a swimming pool accident

and is further demoralized when the "tone-deaf kid next door" is able to compose a string quartet in the style of Beethoven, using a computer program. Zoltan Pepper, as a high school student, had plagiarized a Kilgore Trout story and been forced to wear a placard with the letter *P* around his neck for a week in class. Zoltan is killed when the timequake ends, struck by a firetruck whose driver did not realize free will had kicked in.

Peterson   In Kilgore Trout's story "No Laughing Matter," a man named Peterson is the pilot of the bomber *Joy's Pride*. When he's ordered to drop a third atomic bomb, this time on Yokohama, Japan, Peterson and his crew refuse to do so and are court-martialed.

Peterson, Joy   Because of Joy Peterson, his "sweet widowed mother" (10), the pilot of *Joy's Pride* in the Kilgore Trout story "No Laughing Matter" is unable to drop a bomb on Yokohama, Japan. Joy is an obstetrics nurse in Corpus Christi, Texas, and her son realizes that she would never condone a bombing, much less one carried out by a plane named for her.

Petro, Joe III   Joe Petro III is an artist in Lexington, Kentucky, who prints Vonnegut's paintings using a silk screen process.

Pieratt, Asa   Asa Pieratt is a literary critic of Vonnegut's work who appears at the clambake at the end of *Timequake*.

Pinsky, Robert   Vonnegut tells readers he recently heard the poet Robert Pinsky [author of a translation of Dante's *Inferno*] give a reading, "in which he apologized didactically for having had a much nicer life than normal" (13). Vonnegut muses that he should do the same thing.

Post-Timequake Apathy or PTA   Following the hiccup in time that forces everyone to relive the past 10 years of their lives exactly as they had lived them the first time, most people do not realize or care that free will has kicked in again. They are suffering from a condition that comes to be called

"Post-Timequake Apathy" or "PTA," a disorder brought on by living so long without free will.

Prince, Dudley   Dudley Prince is an African-American armed guard working at the American Academy of Arts and Letters next door to the homeless shelter where Kilgore Trout is staying. When he sees Kilgore Trout, whom he believes is a bag lady, throw one of his stories into the trash can on the street outside the academy, Prince retrieves it out of boredom. He believes that the story, "The Sisters B-36," might be a message from God. Prince had found God in prison while serving time for the rape and murder of a little girl, a crime of which he is entirely innocent. When the timequake ends and free will kicks in again, Prince is saved from the runaway fire truck that kills Zoltan Pepper because a smoke alarm goes off right before he answers the door, making Prince freeze in indecision. Kilgore Trout is able to make Prince move again by saying the words that become Kilgore's Creed: "You've been very sick! Now you're well again" (179). Later, when Trout tells Prince that he has free will, Prince tells Trout what he can do with free will: "You can stuff it up your ass," he says (194).

Rackstraw, Loree   A literary critic and academician, Loree Rackstraw appears at the clambake at the end of *Timequake*.

Rauch, John   John Rauch is an uncle of Vonnegut's who provided him with a history of his family in America. Rauch is one of the many figures from Vonnegut's life who has a double at the clambake at the end of *Timequake*.

Reed, Peter   Peter Reed is a Vonnegut critic and academician who appears at the clambake at the end of *Timequake*.

Rivers, Jerry   Jerry Rivers is the limousine driver who drops Zoltan Pepper off at the American Academy of Arts and Letters, right before the timequake ends and free will kicks in again. Rivers is instrumental in spreading Kilgore's Creed—"you were sick, but now you're well again, and there's work to do"—around the city since he gets the mes-

sage broadcast on both radio and TV from coast to coast.

Schadenfreude, Dr.   The protagonist of a Kilgore Trout story of the same name, Dr. Schadenfreude (whose name means taking joy in the sufferings of others) is a psychiatrist who allows his patients to talk only about "dumb or crazy things that had happened to total strangers in supermarket tabloids or on TV talk shows" (70). If the patients mention themselves, the doctor becomes livid and barks that nobody cares about *them*, that they are "boring, insignificant piece[s] of poop" (70) and similar insults.

Scrotum   Scrotum is the wrinkled old family retainer in the Kilgore Trout play of the same name. He appears at a wedding, "crying his rheumy eyes out behind a potted plant" (178).

Seren, Leo   Vonnegut discusses a gathering that took place at the University of Chicago on August 6, 1995 to commemorate the 50th anniversary of the detonation of the first atomic bomb. One of the speakers at the event is real-life atomic physicist Leo Seren, who became a pacifist after helping to produce the bomb. Vonnegut remembers that Seren apologized to the gathering for his role in the making of the bomb, not realizing that "being a physicist, on a planet where the smartest animals hate being alive so much, means never having to say you're sorry" (5).

Smith, Frank   The son of African-American maid Rosemary Smith and Abraham Lincoln Pembroke III, a descendant of Lincoln assassin John Wilkes Booth, Frank Smith is a half black/half white amateur actor who gives a stunning performance as Abraham Lincoln in the Pembroke Mask and Wig Club's production of *Abe Lincoln in Illinois*. Kilgore Trout does the play's sounds effects and is honored afterward at a cast party, the clam bake held at the writer's retreat Xanadu.

Smith, Rosemary   A character from *Timequake One*, Rosemary Smith is an African-American housemaid who is impregnated by Abraham Lincoln Pembroke III, the grandson of the illegitimate son of John Wilkes Booth. Rosemary gives birth to Frank Smith, who turns out to be one of the greatest actors in the history of amateur theatricals.

Squibb, John John Squibb is the builder husband of Vonnegut's daughter Edith.

Squibb, Will and Buck Will and Buck Squibb are the sons of Vonnegut's daughter Edith and her husband, John Squibb. The Squibb family lives in the big old house on Cape Cod, where Vonnegut and his first wife, Jane, had raised their children.

Stewart, Ella Vonnegut Ella Vonnegut Stewart is a first cousin of Kurt Vonnegut, Sr. She is married to Kerfuit Stewart and owns a bookstore in Kentucky. The Stewarts do not stock Vonnegut's book at their store because they find his writing obscene.

Stewart, Kerfuit Kerfuit Stewart is the son-in-law of Vonnegut's great aunt, Emma Vonnegut, and the former owner of Stewart's Book Store in Louisville, Kentucky. When Emma used to say that she hated the Chinese, Kerfuit "admonished her that it was *wicked* to hate that many people all at once" (10).

Styron, William The well-known author William Styron was a friend of Vonnegut's who appears in *Timequake* when Vonnegut asks him how many people on the planet have lives worth living. Styron and Vonnegut, working together, come up with 17 percent as a likely figure. Later, Vonnegut tells readers that Styron believed the dropping of the atomic bomb on Hiroshima saved his life, since he was a Marine during World War II, training to invade Japan. While Vonnegut respects Styron's opinion, he also points out that he knows a single word that proves the obscene, murderous capabilities of the U.S. government: "Nagasaki" (196).

Sunoco, Fleon Fleon Sunoco is the mad-scientist protagonist of the Kilgore Trout story "Dog's Breakfast." Sunoco believes really smart people have little radio receivers in their heads, which give them all their bright ideas. Thus, at night, he dissects high-IQ brains, refusing to believe that "an unassisted human brain, which is nothing more than a dog's breakfast, three and a half pounds of blood-soaked sponge, could have written 'Stardust,' let alone Beethoven's Ninth Symphony" (107).

Timequake One *Timequake One* is the name Vonnegut gives to the terrible novel he claims to have worked on for nearly a decade in the prologue to his novel *Timequake*. He tells readers to think of the current *Timequake* as "a stew" made from the best parts of that previous novel "mixed with thoughts and experiences during the past seven months or so" (xiv).

Trout, Kilgore *Timequake* is perennial Vonnegut character Kilgore Trout's swan song as much as it is Vonnegut's. The science fiction writer, whom Vonnegut describes in the prologue as his "alter ego" (xv), first appears in the novel in a homeless shelter next door to the Academy of Arts and Letters in Manhattan. He has been caught up in a police sweep of about 30 homeless men, whom Trout calls "sacred cattle" (53), that had been living at the New York Public Library. Although he is perhaps the most prolific short story writer in history, Trout spends the majority of his life as a hobo. In this book, readers learn somewhat different details about Trout's childhood than are presented in earlier Vonnegut works. For instance, although Trout's father studies erns in Bermuda in both *Breakfast of Champions* and *Timequake*, in the earlier book his name is Leo Trout while this novel calls Trout's father Raymond. Readers also discover for the first time that Trout's father killed his mother when Kilgore was 12 years old. Like everyone else on Earth, Trout is caught up in the timequake, the blip in the universe that causes everyone to have to relive the past 10 years of their lives exactly as they occurred the first time. But when the timequake ends and free will kicks in again, Trout, who claims that he does not even believe in free will, is able to shake people out of their Post-Timequake Apathy (or PTA) by saying the words, "You were sick, but now you're well again, and there's work to do" (196), a mantra that becomes known as Kilgore's

Creed. At the end of the novel, Trout is honored for these words by being included as a member of the large, extended family that gathers in the summer of 2001 at a clambake on the beach at Xanadu, a writer's retreat in Rhode Island. In this novel, Vonnegut tells readers that Trout dies on Labor Day, 2001, when he is 84 years old.

Trout, Leon   Leon Trout, son of Kilgore Trout, is mentioned only briefly in *Timequake*, though he is a major character in Vonnegut's earlier novel *Galápagos*. The details readers find out about Leon in this book match those of the earlier novel: Leon is a deserter from the United States Marine Corps who is accidentally decapitated in a shipyard accident in Sweden, where he had been working as a welder.

Trout, Mrs.   Kilgore Trout, in his memory of the timequake called *My Ten Years on Automatic Pilot*, writes that his mother was a poet and a housewife who was murdered by her husband, college professor Raymond Trout, when Kilgore was 12 years old.

Trout, Raymond   Kilgore Trout's father, called Raymond in this novel, but Leo in *Breakfast of Champions*, is a SMITH COLLEGE ornithology professor, who murders Trout's mother when Kilgore is only 12 years old, then hides the body in the basement.

Ulm, Arthur Garvey   Arthur Garvey Ulm, a poet and resident secretary of the Xanadu writer's retreat, serves as a double for Vonnegut's war buddy Bernard V. O'Hare at the clambake/cast party that ends the novel.

Uncle Dan   Vonnegut tells the story of returning home from World War II, and his Uncle Dan clapping him on the back and bellowing, "You're a *man* now!" (79). This is an anecdote that Vonnegut told often, in graduation speeches and interviews. In *Timequake*, he follows the story of Uncle Dan with the line, "I damn near killed my first German" (79).

Unnamed Bakemaster   The bakemaster at the Xanadu cast party at the end of *Timequake* is a

local man paid to stage such parties. Vonnegut tells readers that the bakemaster looked like his late publisher, Seymour Lawrence.

Unnamed Bag Lady   After Kilgore Trout throws his story "The Sisters B-36" into the trash can outside the American Academy of Arts and Letters, a bag lady approaches him and asks if he is okay. Trout replies, "Ting-a-ling! Ting-a-ling!," the punch line of the dirty joke his insane father told him on the night he murdered his mother.

Unnamed Biochemistry Professor   A "pert young woman who teaches biochemistry at Rhode Island University" (233) serves as the double for Jane Cox Yarmolinsky, Vonnegut's first wife, at the clambake at the end of the novel.

Unnamed Bums   When a bum on a neighboring cot at the homeless shelter wishes Kilgore Trout a Merry Christmas, Trout replies, "Ting-a-ling! Ting-a-ling!," the punch line of a dirty joke his father had told him shortly after murdering his mother. Later, another bum on a cot (or perhaps the same one) tells Trout he might be able to get some money by selling his stories to the people next door, at the American Academy of Arts and Letters. Trout responds with a scornful speech about "artsy-fartsy" literature (71).

Unnamed Chaperone   Julia Pembroke, a character in *Timequake One*, drugs her chaperone when she goes to New York City to have a tryst with famous actor John Wilkes Booth.

Unnamed Clerk at the Homeless Shelter   When Kilgore Trout checks into the homeless shelter at the former Museum of the American Indian, he tells the clerk that his name is VINCENT VAN GOGH and that he has no living relatives.

Unnamed Convict Letter Writer   When a man who has been a prison convict for many years is about to be released back into society, he writes to Vonnegut asking for advice. Vonnegut, reminding readers that he is honorary president of the American Humanist Association, writes back: "Join a church" (84), arguing that what the man needs right now more than anything else is "something like a family" (84).

Unnamed District Attorney A zealous district attorney prosecutes Dudley Prince for a brutal murder he did not commit in hopes of being nominated governor of New York. Six years later, this district attorney is "found wearing cement overshoes on the bottom of Lake Cayuga" (66).

Unnamed Father and Baby Vonnegut reads about a teenage father who shakes his baby to death because the child would not stop crying. He uses this story to emphasize the need for extended families.

Unnamed Florist The Kilgore Trout story "Golden Wedding" is about a florist who tries to boost his business by convincing couples who work together that they are entitled to celebrate several wedding anniversaries a year.

Unnamed Head of the Russian Department at Chicago When Jane Cox Vonnegut became pregnant as a graduate student studying Russian at the University of Chicago, she and Vonnegut seek out the head of the department to tell him that Jane "had to quit because she had become infected with progeny" (126). The department head replies, "My dear Mrs. Vonnegut, pregnancy is the *beginning*, not the end, of life" (126), a response Vonnegut says he will always remember.

Unnamed Judge The court-martial judge in Kilgore Trout's story "No Laughing Matter" must bang his gavel at one point and declare that what *Joy's Pride* pilot Peterson and his crew had done in refusing to drop an atomic bomb was "no laughing matter" (12). What made the people in the courtroom laugh were stories of what had happened when Peterson returned to the base with the bomb still attached to the plane: "People jumped out of windows. They peed in their pants" (12).

Unnamed Literary Agent As a young man, Vonnegut asks advice of his then literary agent

about how to end stories without killing all the characters. The agent replies, "Nothing could be simpler, dear boy: The hero mounts his horse and rides off into the sunset" (161–162). Vonnegut then informs readers that this agent later killed himself with a 12-gauge shotgun.

Unnamed Nazi Captain When Vonnegut and Bernard V. O'Hare are released after being prisoners of war in Dresden, they enter a barn and finding a dying captain of the Nazi SS, whose last words are: "I have just wasted the past ten years of my life" (140).

Unnamed Patient When Vonnegut is walking down the street talking to an old physician friend, they pass an ex-patient of the doctor's who is clearly homeless and carrying a bag of aluminum cans he had collected. Vonnegut describes the man as one of Kilgore Trout's "'sacred cattle,' somehow wonderful despite his economic uselessness" (164).

Unnamed Physician Friend Vonnegut tells readers about walking with an unnamed physician friend of his who works with mentally disturbed patients at Bellevue Hospital. When Vonnegut asks his friend why half his patients did not commit suicide, the doctor replies that the same question had occurred to him. But when he asks patients about it, they are horrified, protesting that "an idea *that sick* had never entered their heads!" (163).

Unnamed Plumber An unnamed plumber, who is a member of the Pembroke Mask and Wig Club, puts a "gaily mournful whistle" on top of a tank of compressed air for Kilgore Trout to blow at the end of the play *Abe Lincoln in Illinois*. The plumber resembles Vonnegut's older brother, Bernard.

Unnamed Thesis Adviser Vonnegut tells the story of his thesis adviser at the University of Chicago, when he was a graduate student in anthropology, telling him that artists are people who cannot fix their country or state or even their marriage. They can, however, "make this square of canvas, or this eight-and-a-half-by-eleven piece of paper, or this lump of clay, or these twelve bars of music, exactly what they *ought* to be!" (162). Later, this adviser kills himself by swallowing potassium cyanide.

Unnamed Vonnegut Cousin Vonnegut tells the story of a cousin of his who brought home an awful report card when he was in high school. When his father asked him about it, the cousin replied, "Don't you *know*, Father? I'm dumb, I'm *dumb*" (212).

Unnamed Wedding Guest An unnamed male wedding guest in Kilgore Trout's play *The Wrinkled Old Family Retainer* says, as the groom is kissing the bride, "All women are psychotic. All men are jerks" (178).

Unnamed Woman at the Postal Center Vonnegut describes a woman who works at a local Manhattan postal center with whom he says he is secretly in love. The woman's face, which she constantly alters with new hairstyles and makeup, is "like a Thanksgiving dinner" (218).

Voce, Sotto Sotto Voce, whose name is a well-known Italian phrase meaning to speak softly or in an undertone, is a male guest at the wedding in Kilgore Trout's play *The Wrinkled Old Family Retainer*.

Vonnegut, Alex Vonnegut's paternal uncle, Alex Vonnegut, also an important figure in the earlier novels *Slapstick* and *Jailbird*, is a Harvard-educated insurance salesman. In *Timequake*, Vonnegut tells readers that Uncle Alex taught him to notice when things were going well for him, urging him to say out loud at such times: "If this isn't nice, what is?" Alex also introduces his teenage nephew to the great socialist writers such as GEORGE BERNARD SHAW, Eugene Debs, and John Dos Passos, even though Alex himself becomes extremely politically conservative in later life.

Vonnegut, Alice Vonnegut's sister, Alice, or Allie, who died of cancer when she was 41 years old, leaving her three older sons for Kurt and Jane Vonnegut to raise, seems to be as much of an inspiration for this novel as she is for Vonnegut's earlier

book *Slapstick*. In *Timequake*, Vonnegut reminisces about Allie's pessimism, her love of watching people fall down, her hatred of hunting, and her skepticism about art and religion.

Vonnegut, Bernard Vonnegut's older brother, Bernard, who also appears as a character in *Slapstick*, was a scientist who spent his life studying thunderstorms and the seeding of clouds. Although Bernard claimed not to like paintings because "they didn't *do* anything, just hung there year after year" (165), Vonnegut tells readers that his brother became an artist toward the end of his life, creating interesting and beautiful shapes from "squoozles" of paint pressed between pains of glass. When Bernard asks his younger brother whether these shapes are art or not, Vonnegut is inspired to write him a letter in which he argues that "any work of art is half of a conversation between two human beings" (168). In his epilogue to *Timequake*, Vonnegut describes Bernard's death from cancer on April 25, 1997, at the age of 82.

Vonnegut, Bernard, Sr. Vonnegut's paternal grandfather was an Indianapolis architect named Bernard Vonnegut, whom Kurt's older brother, Bernard, is named for. Vonnegut tells readers that his grandfather Bernard sent his uncle Alex Vonnegut to Harvard University "in order that he might become *civilized*" (182).

Vonnegut, Edith Vonnegut's daughter Edith, born in 1949, is affectionately called "Edie Bucket" (28) by her family. Vonnegut also tells readers that Edith is now a professional artist.

Vonnegut, Edith Lieber In *Timequake*, Vonnegut describes his mother, Edith Vonnegut, who committed suicide when the writer was 21 years old, as "addicted to being rich, to servants and unlimited charge accounts, to giving lavish dinner parties, to taking frequent first-class trips to Europe" (32). During the Great Depression, she experienced "withdrawal symptoms" (32), perhaps accounting for her suicide.

Vonnegut, Emma Vonnegut remembers that his "late great-aunt" (10) Emma Vonnegut always said that she hated the Chinese, despite her son-in-law's scolding her that it was wrong to hate so many people at once.

Vonnegut, Irma Irma Vonnegut is Vonnegut's paternal aunt, who said to him one time that "*All Vonnegut men are scared to death of women*" (182).

Vonnegut, Kurt, Jr. The novel is narrated by a fictional version of Kurt Vonnegut, Jr., who is 74 years old and looking back over the most recent events in his life. Vonnegut tells the story of writing a previous novel, which he calls *Timequake One*, a novel he spent nearly a decade on, but which did not work, which "stunk" so much that he abandons it. He thinks of his current book as *Timequake Two*, and he describes it as "a stew" made from the best parts of his previous book "mixed with thoughts and experiences during the past seven months or so" (xiv). In this version of *Timequake*, Vonnegut relates autobiographical details from his own life, mixing actual relatives and friends together with fictional characters. At the end of the novel, which Vonnegut says is his "last book" (xvii), he imagines himself at a clambake attended by relatives, friends, and critics as well as by Kilgore Trout and other fictional characters. This party seems to be his farewell to a long fiction-writing career.

Vonnegut, Kurt, Sr. One of the family members Vonnegut reminisces about in *Timequake* is his father, Kurt, Sr. An Indianapolis architect, Kurt Vonnegut, Sr., became a "gun nut and hunter in order to prove that he wasn't effeminate, even though he was in the arts" (42). He later gives up both hunting and fishing, though, at the request of his children. Kurt, Sr., is also remembered as praising his daughter Alice's attempts at art so extravagantly that he actually seemed to be "rubb[ing] her nose in how limited her gifts were" (98). Allie felt patronized because she was a pretty girl; in Indianapolis during the Great Depression, it was believed that "only men could become great artists" (98).

Vonnegut, Lily Lily Vonnegut, born in December 1982, is the adopted daughter of Vonnegut

and his second wife, photographer Jill Krementz. In *Timequake*, Vonnegut remembers her appearing in a production of Thornton Wilder's OUR TOWN when she was 13 years old.

Vonnegut, Mark Vonnegut's son Mark is a Harvard-educated pediatrician and author of THE EDEN EXPRESS: A MEMOIR OF INSANITY. In *Timequake*, Vonnegut recalls a comment Mark made when asked by a reporter what it was like growing up with a famous father. Mark replied, "When I was growing up, my father was a car salesman who couldn't get a job teaching at Cape Cod Junior College" (16). Vonnegut describes another comment made by his son as one of his three favorite quotations: "We are here to help each other get through this thing, whatever it is" (78).

Vonnegut, Nanette One of the daughters of Kurt and Jane Vonnegut, Nanette Vonnegut is described in *Timequake* as a "middle-aged professional artist" like her sister Edith (98).

Vonnegut, Raye Vonnegut's Aunt Raye is married to his uncle Alex Vonnegut, whom she considers a fool.

Wilkerson, Mrs. Florence Mrs. Florence Wilkerson was the high school teacher in Florida who made Zoltan Pepper wear a placard bearing the letter P around his neck for plagiarizing one of Kilgore Trout's short stories.

Wang, Kimberly Kimberly Wang is a 10-year-old girl of Chinese-American and Italian-American heritage whom Dudley Price is unjustly convicted of raping and murdering in a crack house.

Weide, Robert Robert Weide, who made a film version of Vonnegut's previous novel, *Mother Night*, appears at the clambake at the end of *Timequake*. He is named as one of five men half Vonnegut's age who kept him going because of their interest in his work.

Xanadu Writer's Retreat Xanadu is the name of the writer's retreat in *Timequake* where a giant clambake is held on the beach to honor Kilgore Trout.

Yarmolinksy, Adam Adam Yarmolinsky is the second husband of Jane Cox Yarmolinsky, who was Vonnegut's first wife.

Yarmolinsky, Jane Cox Vonnegut married his first wife, Jane Cox, (whom he had met in kindergarten) in September 1945. In *Timequake*, he reminisces frequently about Jane, noting that she was a Phi Beta Kappa graduate of Swarthmore College, and that she was "life-loving and optimistic" (133). After their divorce, Jane married ADAM YARMOLINSKY, but remained good friends with her former husband. Vonnegut recounts a phone call between himself and his ex-wife soon before she was to die of cancer in 1986. Jane asked Vonngut what would "determine the exact moment of her death" (135), and Vonnegut, in reply, invented a story about a boy throwing a stone over the harbor in BARNSTABLE, Cape Cod. When the stone hits the water, he tells her, she will die.

Young, Ida Ida Young was an African-American woman who worked for the Vonnegut family when Kurt Vonnegut was young. At the clambake at the end of *Timequake*, readers are told that Rosemary Smith, mother of star actor Frank Smith, resembles Ida Young.

Zine, Clara Clara Zine is a strikingly beautiful member of the office staff of the American Academy of Arts and Letters. Monica Pepper is convinced that Clara Zine was smoking the cigar that set off the academy's smoke alarm right as the timequake ended, but Clara denies ever having smoked a cigar in her life.

FURTHER READING

Hickenlooper, John. "*Timequake*, Princess Di and the Great Apocalypse." *Bloomsbury Review* 18, no. 1 (1998): 3.

Morse, Donald E. "Abjuring Rough Magic: Kurt Vonnegut's *Timequake*." *New York Review of Science Fiction* 10, no. 10 [118] (1998): 1, 8–11.

Timequake. New York: Berkley Books, 1998.

"Tom Edison's Shaggy Dog"

One of Vonnegut's more humorous and whimsical short pieces, "Tom Edison's Shaggy Dog" was first published in *Collier's* magazine in March 1953. It was later reprinted in the 1961 collection, *Canary in a Cat House*, as well as in the 1968 *Welcome to the Monkey House*.

SYNOPSIS

"Tom Edison's Shaggy Dog" begins with two old men sitting on a park bench in Tampa, Florida, one morning. One of the men, Harold K. Bullard, has been regaling the other man, who is trying to read a book, with his life story for over an hour, repeating the same information many times. The unnamed listener eventually grows so annoyed by Bullard and by Bullard's Labrador retriever, who is continually sniffing his ankles and who seems especially interested in the plastic buttons on his garters, that he moves to another bench. Bullard, however, follows him. This is when the previously quiet man begins to tell Bullard about an event from his own life. He claims to have lived next to THOMAS EDISON in Menlo Park, New Jersey, in 1879, while Edison was working on his most famous invention—the electric light bulb. Stumbling accidentally into Edison's laboratory one day, the speaker, a nine-year-old boy at the time, sees Edison attached by the ears to a small black box. The contraption turns out to be an intelligence analyzer—an instrument that measures the intelligence of whoever is hooked up to it. Edison tries out his invention on the narrator, and the needle indicator barely moves. But the narrator then makes what he calls his "one and only contribution to the world" (116). He suggests Edison try out the device on his own dog, Sparky. With Sparky strapped to the analyzer, the needle swings wildly to the right, indicating an intelligence even superior to Edison's own. A scientist unafraid to face the truth, Edison reasons that dogs have been fooling human beings for thousands of year, pretending to be dumb creatures while living an easy life. Sparky eventually speaks to Edison and the narrator, confirming Edison's suspicions, but begging the two to keep his secret.

In exchange, he tells Edison to try a carbonized cotton thread as the filament for his light bulb, and he gives the narrator a stock market tip that makes him independently wealthy for the rest of his life. Sparky, however, when he leaves Edison's laboratory, is immediately torn to pieces by a pack of dogs that had been listening outside the door. Having reached the end of his tale, the old man stands up, takes off his garters, and gives them to Bullard's Labrador retriever as "a small token of esteem" for an "ancestor of [his] who talked himself to death" (117).

COMMENTARY

A shaggy dog story is a long, detailed, often rambling, but humorous tale, frequently more amusing to its teller than to its listener. Vonnegut's "Tom Edison's Shaggy Dog" is a shaggy dog story both in its style and its subject matter, since the story is basically an extended joke about dogs—Harold K. Bullard's Labrador retriever and Thomas Edison's dog, Sparky. Reminiscent of MARK TWAIN stories such as "The Celebrated Jumping Frog of Calaveras County," in which an unnamed eastern narrator is held prisoner by the extended stories of a garrulous old westerner named Simon Wheeler, Vonnegut's story, like Twain's, gets it humor from the contrast between the main characters and from the reactions of the listener to the story being told. While in Twain's story, the local man, Wheeler, puts an outsider in his place, readers see the opposite occur in "Tom Edison's Shaggy Dog." The outsider, the stranger who seems to be a newcomer to Florida, still buttoned up in his serge wool coat, bests the garrulous old bore Harold K. Bullard at his own game.

CHARACTERS AND RELATED ENTRIES

Bullard, Harold K.   Harold K. Bullard is a non-stop talker who bores his victims by regaling them with self-important, repetitious stories of his own life. He is bested, however, by the stranger he meets in the park.

Bullard's Dog   Harold K. Bullard's dog is a Labrador retriever who repeatedly sniffs around the stranger's ankles, annoying him by aggressively putting his wet nose to his shins and trying to bite the plastic buttons on the man's garters.

Edison, Thomas   The famed 19th-century inventor is a character in the story the unnamed old man tells Harold K. Bullard. In the stranger's story, Edison's dog, Sparky, is the true genius behind the invention of the electric light bulb.

intelligence analyzer   Prolific 19th-century inventor Thomas Edison creates a machine called an intelligence analyzer, which is able to determine the brain capacity of anyone hooked up to it. Using the contraption, Edison soon discovers that his dog, Sparky, is super-intelligent. Sparky, wanting to keep his large brain a secret, tells Edison the key to making the electric light bulb work in return for his owner's silence.

Sparky   Thomas Edison's dog, Sparky, is the main figure in the ludicrous story the unnamed stranger in the park tells Harold K. Bullard. Sparky, like all dogs, has super intelligence. The animals have been hiding this fact for thousands of years, though, so that they can live the easy life while human beings take care of all their needs. Found out by Edison's intelligence analyzer, Sparky trades valuable information to Edison and the narrator so that they will keep his secret. Sparky, however, is torn to pieces by a pack of angry dogs who overhear his conversation in Edison's laboratory.

Unnamed Old Man   The unnamed old man forced to listen to Harold K. Bullard on the park bench in Tampa, Florida, seems a more imaginative and resourceful sort than the other old man, Harold K. Bullard. Peacefully trying to read a book when he is accosted by Bullard and his annoying dog, the stranger puts the old bore in his place with his wild tale of Thomas Edison's dog, Sparky.

FURTHER READING

Reed, Peter. *The Short Fiction of Kurt Vonnegut.* Westport, Conn.: Greenwood Press, 1997.
Welcome to the Monkey House. New York: Dell, 1998.

"Tomorrow and Tomorrow and Tomorrow"

Originally titled "The Big Trip Up Yonder" when it first appeared in the *Galaxy Science Fiction* magazine in January 1954, this story was retitled "Tomorrow and Tomorrow and Tomorrow" when it was reprinted in the 1961 collection, *Canary in a Cat House*, and in the 1968 *Welcome to the Monkey House*.

SYNOPSIS

"Tomorrow and Tomorrow and Tomorrow" is set in America in the year 2158. The elimination of disease and the invention of an anti-aging agent called anti-gerasone have contributed to a huge overpopulation problem in the country. The story opens with 112-year-old Lou and 93-year-old Emerald Schwartz arguing on the balcony of the three-room apartment they share with 10 other couples, all related to them, and the patriarch of the family, an old man named Harold D. Schwartz, who occupies the only private bedroom in the small apartment. Frustrated, Em is complaining bitterly to her husband about Gramps Schwartz, who controls his family by constantly updating and revising his will, according to which of his relatives is currently in his favor. In addition, the old man commands the television set and coerces his numerous relatives to bring him breakfast in bed. He eats bacon and eggs while the other family members subsist on food manufactured from processed seaweed and sawdust. His younger relatives tolerate this behavior only because each couple hopes someday to inherit Gramps's private room.

One night, Lou catches his great-grandnephew Morty diluting Gramps' anti-gerasone potion in the bathroom. Aghast at his relative's actions, but afraid to alert Gramps, Lou attempts to empty the giant bottle of diluted anti-gerasone and refill it from numerous smaller bottles. But when he drops the giant bottle on the bathroom floor, the crash gives him away. Gramps, oddly, remains calm about the affair, simply telling Lou to clean up the mess. But Lou and Em nevertheless spend the night petrified about what Gramps will do to them. When

the household wakes up the next morning, they discover that Gramps is missing from his bed. He has left behind a farewell note and a codicil to his will, stating that his possessions are to be divided absolutely evenly among his relatives. Because each couple so desires the private bedroom, a free-for-all breaks out among them. Eventually, the police arrive and haul the 11 couples off to jail. The next scene shows Lou and Em stretching out luxuriously on cots in four-by-eight-foot private cells, each with its own washbasin and toilet, extremely satisfied to have achieved such privacy. Back at the apartment, readers discover that Gramps has returned and hired the best lawyer he can find to get his relatives a conviction. The story ends with the old man sending away for a bottle of new, super anti-gerasone, which will not only keep him young, but also take away his wrinkles and aged appearance as well.

COMMENTARY

Another story that warns of the unintended side effects of a new technology that at first seems to promise the betterment of the human condition, "Tomorrow and Tomorrow and Tomorrow," like the story "Welcome to the Monkey House," depicts a grimly overpopulated and resource-depleted future. Anti-gerasone acts as the mythical and often sought-after fountain of youth, granting its users near immortality, but it also makes life unbearable for the majority of people on the planet. In this story, Vonnegut explores the dark, selfish side of human nature as well. While the younger Schwartzes hope for Gramps to choose to die soon and leave one of the 11 couples sharing the small apartment his private bedroom, Gramps is too wily for them. He not only recognizes his relatives' base desires, but he also manipulates them for his own benefit, constantly dangling the promise of his impending death so that his family members will treat him as a king.

Television is also a target of SATIRE in this story, as it is in much of Vonnegut's 1950s short fiction. The Schwartz family, rather than living their own lives fully, are mesmerized by a long-running soap opera about a family named the McGarveys. In fact, when Lou drops the bottle of anti-gerasone in the bathroom, the rest of his family hears the crash because the 29,121st episode of the television show has just ended. In addition, the Schwartzes mark their lives by huge, televised sporting events. Gramps hints that he will give up his anti-gerasone after the Five-Hundred-Mile Speedway Race, and all his family members surreptitiously check the race dates. When Gramps actually disappears, the only reason his family members can think of to be sad is because the old man will not be able to see how the Speedway Race turned out, "Or the World Series . . . Or whether Mrs. McGarvey got her eyesight back" (327). The Schwartz's own family life is so miserable that they retreat into the television world.

Finally, this story, like "The Euphio Question," also critiques America's increasing consumer culture. As in that story, in "Tomorrow and Tomorrow and Tomorrow" happiness is just another consumer product—something that can be bought and sold and that can turn a profit. At the end of the story, Gramps watches a television commercial advertising "super-anti-gerasone," which promises not only to extend the life span but also to return to its users "all the sparkle and attractiveness of youth" (330). In this future world, people are imprisoned in hellish lives by the lure of advertising and by their own selfish desire to live forever. The ironic ending of the story shows that the only place the Schwartz relatives can find a decent amount of freedom and privacy is in jail. Vonnegut presents readers with a twist on HENRY DAVID THOREAU's famous statement: "Under a government which imprisons any unjustly, the true place for a just man is also a prison." When society itself becomes an overcrowded prison, prison may be the only place that offers a modicum of privacy and individuality.

CHARACTERS AND RELATED ENTRIES

Anti-gerasone Anti-gerasone is an anti-aging liquid that keeps human beings alive indefinitely. Although the drug at first seems like a great boon to humankind, its use eventually causes serious overpopulation problems on the planet.

Bullard, Dr. Brainard Keyes The Schwartz's television set informs the family that Dr. Brain-

ard Keyes Bullard, president of Wyandotte College, gave a speech in which he said that "most of the world's ills can be traced to the fact that Man's knowledge of himself has not kept pace with his knowledge of the physical world" (321). Gramps Schwartz snorts derisively at this pronouncement, pointing out that people were saying the exact same thing 100 years before.

Haggedorn, Elbert The Schwartz family hears on their television set about a possible tragedy taking place in Iowa. Two hundred rescue workers are trying to save a 183-year-old man named Elbert Haggedorn, who has somehow become trapped. This incident shows the ludicrous lengths to which these people of the future will go to extend human life, even with rampant overcrowding and resource depletion.

Hitz, Lowell W. Highlighting the overpopulation problem in the story, the Schwartz's television set informs them of the birth of Lowell W. Hitz, the 25-millionth child to be born at the Chicago Lying-in Hospital.

Schwartz, Eddie Eddie Schwartz is the 73-year-old son of Lou and Em Schwartz. Em treats Eddie like a child still, at one point telling him not to get sarcastic with his father and not to speak with his mouth full.

Schwartz, Emerald Emerald Schwartz is the 93-year-old wife of Lou Schwartz, who is grandson to family patriarch Harold D. Schwartz, or "Gramps." The story opens with Em so mad at the old man that she proposes the idea to her husband of diluting Gramps's anti-gerasone. Yet, Em soon comes to her senses and apologizes for her awful idea. At the story's end, Em is very happy in her jail cell; she at last has the privacy she had craved.

Schwartz, Harold D. Harold D. Schwartz, known as "Gramps," is the 172-year-old patriarch of a large family that all lives together in a small, three-room apartment in an enormous New York housing development. The crafty old man controls his numerous relatives by choosing various favorites and by constantly updating his will to disinherit those relatives who are out of favor. After the revelation that a relative has diluted Gramps's anti-gerasone fluid, the old man disappears, having concocted a scheme to get all of his relatives out of the apartment. When his family is hauled off to jail, Gramps returns to the apartment, which he now has all to himself. He ends the story quite self-satisfied and happy.

Schwartz, Lou Lou Schwartz is the 112-year-old grandson of family patriarch Harold D. Schwartz. Although frustrated by his grandfather's controlling behavior, as all his relatives are, Lou actually tries to do Gramps a favor by replacing his diluted anti-gerasone. Unfortunately, his good deed backfires when he drops the bottle and his relatives believe that he is the one diluting the potion. Yet, Lou is happy at the end of the story when he stretches out on his cot in the jail cell. He and his wife, Em, have finally achieved privacy.

Schwartz, Melissa Melissa Schwartz is one of the 23 relatives who lives in the crowded Schwartz apartment in New York. She is mentioned briefly by Em Schwartz, who tells her husband that Melissa has gone 30 years without having a baby.

Schwartz, Morty Mortimer Schwartz is the great-grandnephew of Lou Schwartz. The recently married Morty has been forced to honeymoon with his new wife in the crowded hallway of the small apartment. Lou catches Morty diluting Gramps's anti-gerasone fluid one evening and tries to repair the damage, but drops the bottle and is himself suspected of trying to do away with the controlling old man.

Schwartz, Verna One of the numerous Schwartz relatives living in the small, cramped New York apartment in which the story takes place, Verna Schwartz is dying to have a baby, but the overcrowded conditions she lives in make this impossible.

Schwartz, Willy Willy Schwartz is Lou Schwartz's father. Willy becomes Gramps's favorite after the old man hears Lou make a sarcastic remark under his breath.

Winkler, Gramma Daring to hope that Gramps Schwartz will soon choose to end his life, Em Schwartz reminds her husband, Lou, that an old woman named Gramma Winkler, from their building, died not long ago. Lou, though, insists Gramma's death was an accident, not a choice. She was killed by a subway while carrying a six-pack of anti-gerasone.

Wyandotte College Wyandotte College is a fictional institution of higher learning appearing in several Vonnegut short stories reprinted in the collection *Welcome to the Monkey House*, including "Report on the Barnhouse Effect," "The Euphio Question," "Epicac," and "Tomorrow and Tomorrow and Tomorrow." Dr. Brainard Keyes Bullard, president of Wyandotte College, gives a televised speech bemoaning human beings' lack of self-knowledge in "Tomorrow and Tomorrow and Tomorrow."

FURTHER READING

Reed, Peter. *The Short Fiction of Kurt Vonnegut.* Westport, Conn.: Greenwood Press, 1997.
Welcome to the Monkey House. New York: Dell, 1998.

"2BRO2B"

First published in the journal *Worlds of If* in January 1962, "2BRO2B" was later reprinted in the collection *Bagombo Snuff Box*. Like several other Vonnegut stories, "2BRO2B" depicts a grim future, in which Earth is choked by overcrowding, and human beings are considered expendable.

SYNOPSIS

"2BRO2B" is set many hundreds of years in the future, after a cure for aging has been discovered. The population of Earth had subsequently grown to 40 billion people, but is now carefully controlled. To prevent overcrowding, Dr. Benjamin Hitz has invented the concept of Ethical Suicide Studios, where volunteers willingly choose to die to make room for others. The story's title is the gimmicky phone number given to such places (the "zero" in the number is pronounced "naught"). "2BRO2B" opens with Edward K. Wehling, Jr. waiting in the lobby of the Chicago lying-in hospital for his wife to give birth to triplets. Meanwhile, a "sardonic old man" (314) is busy painting a mural on the hospital wall. The mural depicts a carefully tended and beautiful garden, meant to represent the careful pruning done by the Suicide Studios. Wehling, however, is in despair, since he must find three volunteers willing to die in order for all his newborn babies to be allowed to live. So, far, Wehling's maternal grandfather is the only volunteer he has found. Soon two people enter the lobby: Leora Duncan, a suicide hostess whose portrait is to be painted into the mural, and the famous, handsome Dr. Hitz himself. Wehling ends up pulling out a revolver and shooting Leora Duncan and Dr. Hitz to death before turning the gun on himself, thus creating three spots for his babies. The story ends with the old painter coming down off his ladder, thinking about using the gun to shoot himself, but calling the phone number of the Suicide Studio instead.

COMMENTARY

Like two other Vonnegut short stories—"Welcome to the Monkey House" and "Tomorrow and Tomorrow and Tomorrow"—"2BRO2B" imagines a grossly overcrowded future for the planet Earth after aging, disease, and death have been conquered. Thus, as in those two stories, peoples' fondest wishes, their desire to better human conditions, have created terribly dystopic societies. While in "Tomorrow and Tomorrow and Tomorrow" characters live as best they can with the overcrowding and depletion of resources, in "Monkey House" and "2BRO2B," people are encouraged to voluntarily end their own lives. The society depicted in "2BRO2B," however, is not as obviously totalitarian as that of "Monkey House," where sex is considered sinful and people are forced to ingest pills that completely numb the lower half of their bodies. In "2BRO2B," a pleasant guise covers up the strict population control that is practiced. The

mural on the wall of the Chicago lying-in hospital depicts a beautiful, extremely well tended garden. An Edenic picture, the mural is intended to represent the new society ushered in by Dr. Benjamin Hitz, where people are carefully pruned and there is enough room for everyone, just as each plant in the painting has "all the loam, light, water, air, and nourishment it could use" (314). Dr. Hitz himself, a "blindingly handsome man" (315) is like a god presiding over this new Eden, worshipped by suicide hostesses such as Leora Duncan.

However, the dark underside of this seemingly beautiful world is recognized by the mural's painter, a "sardonic old man" (314) who is never given a name in the story. Anticipating themes of later Vonnegut novels such as *Breakfast of Champions* and *Bluebeard*, which explore the nature of art and realism, the old man decries his own painting. While the orderly sees the mural as realistic, commenting that it "must be nice to be able to make pictures that look like something" (345), the painter scoffs at him and points to a "foul dropcloth" on the hospital floor, saying, "Frame that, and you'll have a picture a damn sight more honest than this one" (315). The painter's cynical view of Hitz's new society is underscored by the dilemma facing Edward K. Wehling, Jr. The new father of triplets, Wehling has been able to find only one volunteer willing to die, so he must choose only one of his babies to save. The new father is also torn up by the fact that his own maternal grandfather is the volunteer who will sacrifice his life for one of the newborns. After Wehling shoots Leora and Dr. Hitz and then himself to death, the old painter contemplates what he considers to be the awful contradiction of human existence: "the mournful puzzle of life demanding to be born and, once born, demanding to be fruitful . . . to multiply and to live as long as possible—to do all that on a very small planet that would have to last forever" (322). As in many of his works, Vonnegut shows that the very nature of what it means to be human creates conditions unacceptable for human life.

CHARACTERS

Duncan, Leora Described as a "coarse, formidable woman," Leora Duncan is a gas chamber hostess who comes to the Chicago lying-in hospital to have her portrait added to the mural that is being painted on the wall. A true believer in the Ethical Suicide Studios, Leora acts like a shy teenager when her hero, Dr. Benjamin Hitz, also enters the hospital lobby. However, Leora is shot dead at the end of the story by the distraught father of brand-new triplets, Edward K. Wehling, Jr.

Hitz, Dr. Benjamin   Dr. Benjamin Hitz, a "blindingly handsome man" (315), is chief obstetrician at the Chicago lying-in hospital. He is also the inventor of Ethical Suicide Studios, which keep the Earth's population under control. Like Leora Duncan, he is shot dead at by Edward K. Wehling, Jr., a distraught father of triplets. In the novel *Timequake*, Vonnegut states that the real-life Benjamin Hitz was best man at his first wedding.

Orderly   While the old painter is hard at work at the Chicago lying-in hospital, an unnamed orderly comes down the hall, whistling a popular song that celebrates the Ethical Suicide Studios. The orderly stops to admire the cheerful mural being painted on the wall, but the old man painting it scorns him, claiming that the mural does not at all represent what life is really like.

Painter   The main character in the story is a "sardonic old man" (214) who is painting a mural on the wall of the Chicago lying-in hospital. Unlike most of the other characters, the painter is cynical about the brave new world created by population control. After he witnesses the double homicide and suicide at the end of the story, he calls the suicide number and sets up an appointment for himself.

Wehling, Edward K., Jr.   Edward K. Wehling, Jr. is a new father of triplets. Yet, rather than being excited about the births of his children, Wehling is in despair. The triplets will only be allowed to live if he can find three volunteers willing to die and give up their places in the world to the new babies. Thus far, the only volunteer Wehling has is his maternal grandfather, which means that he will have to choose one out of his three babies to

save. Completely distraught, Wehling pulls out a revolver at the end of the story and shoots to death suicide hostess Leora Duncan as well as obstetrician Dr. Benjamin Hitz. He then turns the gun on himself.

FURTHER READING

Bagombo Snuff Box. New York: Berkley Books, 2000.
Reed, Peter. *The Short Fiction of Kurt Vonnegut.* Westport, Conn.: Greenwood Press, 1997.

"Unpaid Consultant"

First published in *Cosmopolitan* magazine in April 1955, "Unpaid Consultant" is a story that explores the lengths people will go to in order to make a marriage work. The story was reprinted in the 1999 collection, *Bagombo Snuff Box.*

SYNOPSIS

"Unpaid Consultant" is narrated by a man who works for an investment counseling firm. One day, an old high school sweetheart, who has become a famous singer and television star named Celeste Divine, invites the narrator over to dinner to give her advice about her investment portfolio. The narrator, however, barely has a chance to speak with Celeste since her husband, Harry, dominates the conversation with talk about his work as a consultant to the ketchup industry. Harry is obsessed with ketchup and seems very knowledgeable about the entire industry. Several weeks later, a prospective client, Mr. Arthur J. Bunting, who has just sold his family's ketchup factory, comes to see the narrator. The two go to a restaurant for lunch, where they bump into Harry and Celeste, whom the narrator invites to join them. But Harry inadvertently insults Mr. Bunting by complaining about the way the ketchup industry is run and suggesting that all kinds of changes need to be made. Mr. Bunting leaves in a huff. Later, the narrator discovers that Harry had called Mr. Bunting to apologize. Bunting accepted the apology and promised to keep a secret for Harry—that he never actually worked for the ketchup industry, but only pretended to so that he would not feel inferior to his wealthy and famous wife. Harry has actually been working as an auto mechanic all along and will continue to do so, although he implies to the narrator at the end of the story that he plans to pass himself off as a birdseed expert next.

COMMENTARY

The story's narrator is a bachelor who is cynical about women. He begins the story by writing that most married women want nothing to do with old boyfriends. But, he adds, "if they happened to need something an old beau sells . . . they'll come bouncing back into his life, all pink and smiling, to get it for wholesale or less" (211). Thus, he is not surprised when the wealthy, beautiful, and famous Celeste Divine calls him for investment advice. Before having dinner with Celeste, the narrator is curious about how her husband, Harry, is able to handle his wife's fame, fully expecting Harry to be "either a cadaver or a slob" (213), for the man to be destroyed by the adulation heaped upon his beautiful wife. To the narrator's surprise, though, he sees that "the years had left [Harry] untouched" (214). And Celeste, rather than the selfish, grasping woman the narrator expects, is kind and considerate to both Harry and the narrator. In fact, underneath the narrator's outward cynicism, readers suspect he may still carry a torch for Celeste. He comments several times on her attractiveness and tries his best to start conversations about her records and her television show. By the end of the story, the narrator learns something about the lengths people are willing to go to make a marriage work. Harry fakes his entire ketchup industry connection to buy himself the self-respect that would be lacking if he were merely Mr. Celeste Divine. And Celeste is simply happy that Harry has blossomed and is willing to put up with his obsession because it makes him happy. When, in the final lines of the story, Harry punches the narrator playfully in the arm after explaining what "thixotropy" means and says, "There—you learned something new today" (224), readers sense that he is speaking about more than ketchup.

CHARACTERS

Bunting, Arthur J. Arthur J. Bunting is a prospective client of the narrator's whose family has run a ketchup factory for three generations. Bunting has just sold his factory, though, and seems to regret the decision. When he meets Celeste Divine's husband, Harry, at a restaurant, he takes great offense at Harry's suggestion that the ketchup industry has been mismanaged for years. Later, Harry telephones Bunting to apologize and also to betray his secret that he is not really an important ketchup industry consultant as he had claimed.

Divine, Celeste A former high school sweetheart whom the narrator has not seen for 17 years until she invites him to dinner one night to ask for financial advice, Celeste Divine is a famous singer and television star. She is still married to Harry, the high school boy she dated after the narrator.

Harry Celeste Divine's husband, Harry, is an automobile mechanic whom she married right out of high school. When Celeste becomes famous, Harry is at first at loose ends and feels inferior to his much-beloved wife. But after studying the ketchup industry and passing himself off as a consultant, he finds a new lease on life. He abandons ketchup at the end of the story when Arthur J. Bunting discovers his secret. Harry tells the narrator that he plans to take up birdseed instead.

Narrator The story's narrator is an investment counselor who is invited to the home of his old high school sweetheart, Celeste Divine, to give her financial advice. The narrator becomes fascinated with Celeste's husband, Harry, who claims to be a consultant for the ketchup industry. At the end of the story, the narrator discovers that Harry is still working as an auto mechanic and had only passed himself as a ketchup expert to maintain his self esteem.

FURTHER READING

Bagombo Snuff Box. New York: Berkley Books, 2000.
Reed, Peter. *The Short Fiction of Kurt Vonnegut.* Westport, Conn.: Greenwood Press, 1997.

"Unready to Wear"

"Unready to Wear," a SCIENCE FICTION story set in a utopian future, was first published in the *Galaxy Science Fiction* magazine in April 1953. The story was later reprinted in the 1961 collection, *Canary in a Cat House*, as well as in 1968's *Welcome to the Monkey House*.

SYNOPSIS

"Unready to Wear" is a science fiction story set at some time in the near future. Absentminded and disheveled mathematician Dr. Ellis Konigswasser has discovered how to separate human psyches from their bodies. Millions of people no longer need to eat, sleep, or experience illness, and their lives have improved tremendously as a result. People still slip into bodies occasionally for old time's sake; the best of the abandoned bodies are maintained at storage centers for this purpose. But for the most part, bodies are an inconvenience no longer necessary. However, there is still a group of people who refuse to become "amphibious," the term given to those who have parted from their bodies. They believe themselves to be at war with the amphibious people, though humans who have abandoned their bodies are quite content and invulnerable to attack since they have no bodies to harm.

One day, the story's narrator and his wife, Madge, a pioneering amphibious couple, fly over to peek at "the enemy"—those who insist on remaining in their bodies. Spying a storage center stocked with "the most striking woman's body" (263) the narrator has ever seen, as well as an equally handsome male body, the couple speculate that perhaps the enemy is attempting to become amphibious as well. Marge, wanting to try on the spectacular female body, enters it and is immediately surrounded by the enemy. The bodies had been a trap. The narrator, hoping to help Marge, enters the male body and is trapped as well. The two are jailed and put on trial the next day. Charged with "desertion" of the human race, they are found guilty, but when they threaten that the amphibious people will enter enemy bodies and march them off cliffs, Marge and the narrator are freed and return to their previous happy existence.

COMMENTARY

The possibility that human beings' behavior is the result of chemical exchanges in the physical body is one that Vonnegut will develop in many later works. In *Breakfast of Champions*, for instance, written 20 years after the story "Unready to Wear," Vonnegut writes that he tends "to think of human beings as huge, rubbery test tubes . . . with chemical reactions seething inside" (3), and he repeatedly ascribes Dwayne Hoover's increasingly erratic behavior to "bad chemicals" working in his brain. This view echoes Dr. Ellis Konigwasser's belief that the body is "a bag of skin, blood, hair, meat, bones, and tubes" (257). Because the physical body causes so many irritations and inconveniences for human beings, Vonnegut's story imagines a utopia where the physical body is simply left behind. Utopian schemes in Vonnegut's works, however, such as the Martian invasion of Earth in *Sirens of Titan* or the settlement of San Lorenzo in *Cat's Cradle*, almost always backfire, often bringing about more problems than they solve.

The surprising thing about "Unready to Wear" is that the utopia created when Dr. Konigswasser discovers how to sever the human psyche from the physical body is not undercut or satirized by Vonnegut. When the story's narrator says, "Nobody but a saint could be really sympathetic or intelligent for more than a few minutes at a time in a body—or happy, either, except in short spurts" (261), readers are meant to believe him. This point becomes clear in the trial scene at the end of the story. While Vonnegut uses Madge, who is unable to resist trying on a truly stunning female body, to gently poke fun at women, her weakness is generally presented as harmless. The people in the story who are the real objects of Vonnegut's SATIRE are the "enemy," those unwilling to leave their physical bodies behind. The prosecutor at the trial speaks for his group when he argues that human life is "a battle" which the amphibious people have "deserted" (265). The choice of metaphor illustrates that this is a violent, war-mongering group who use fear to suppress nonconformity. The prosecutor does not care about actual human happiness, but values "progress" and "ambition" as good things in and of themselves, equating them with "greatness" (266–267). The main charge against the narrator and Madge at the trial is that the amphibious ones have dared to change human life for the better. The enemy stubbornly try to hold onto the status quo, no matter how uncomfortable, unfair, or even cruel that status quo might be. The escape of the narrator and Madge at the end of the story is ludicrously easy—all they have to do is talk back to the prosecutor and the balance of power begins to shift. In this story, Vonnegut suggests that, with imagination and daring and lack of fear, human beings *can* make the world a better place. Paradoxically, however, humans might have to achieve the impossible feat of evolving into something not really human anymore to do it.

CHARACTERS

Konigswasser, Dr. Ellis   Dr. Ellis Konigswasser is an absentminded but brilliant old scientist with a decaying body who often forgets to eat and sleep. Because his own physical body means so little to him, he simply and unknowingly separates from it one day. Later, he writes best-selling books explaining his technique for dividing the psyche from the body, which he calls becoming "amphibious." Soon, millions of people because amphibious and live quite happily without physical bodies.

Madge   Madge is the narrator's beloved wife. The couple first learns to become amphibious when they discover that Madge does not have long to live. A stereotypical 1950s woman in many ways, Madge enjoys fashion, makeup, and hairstyles, and causes great trouble for herself and her husband when she cannot resist entering the beautiful, statuesque female body the "enemy" uses as bait. When she and her husband are released by the enemy at the end of the story, the irrepressible Marge demands that the female body she had tried on be mailed to her, "in payment for all the trouble" (268) the enemy has caused them.

Major   When Madge and the narrator enter into the beautiful bodies used as bait by the enemy, they are captured by a group of soldiers led by a "cocky young major," who is so pleased by his vic-

tory that he does "a jig along the shoulder of the road" (264).

Narrator   The story's narrator is a genial, late middle-aged man, happy to leave his short, paunchy, aging body behind. He defends the amphibious lifestyle at his trial quite eloquently at the end of the story, when readers also discover his previous line of work for the first time—he had been in the "pay toilet business" for 30 years before becoming amphibious. At this point, it becomes clear exactly why the narrator has no regrets about leaving physical bodies behind.

Prosecutor   At the trial the "enemy" hold for the amphibious narrator and his wife, Marge, a prosecutor accuses them of deserting the human race in "the battle of life" (265). The prosecutor believes that becoming amphibious represents the end of "progress" (266) and the end of "ambition" (267), necessary components of human existence in his view.

FURTHER READING

Reed, Peter. *The Short Fiction of Kurt Vonnegut.* Westport, Conn.: Greenwood Press, 1997.
Welcome to the Monkey House. New York: Dell, 1998.

Wampeters, Foma & Granfalloons

Wampeters, Foma & Granfalloons is a collection of Kurt Vonnegut's speeches, essays, and reviews published in 1974 by Delacorte/ SEYMOUR LAWRENCE. As Vonnegut explains in his preface, the title comes from three words used in his novel *Cat's Cradle*. A *wampeter* is an object that unites a group of people who are otherwise unrelated. Their lives revolve around this object, and the object holds the group together. *Foma* are comforting lies people tell themselves in order to make life more bearable than it would otherwise be. A *granfalloon* is an association of people, such as fans of a sports team or members of a political party, who pride themselves on being part of a group, although this group ultimately has no larger meaning in the way the universe works. Vonnegut explains his choice of title when he writes that, "Taken together, the words form as good an umbrella as any for this collection" (xiii). The book expresses Vonnegut's views about American culture and politics of the 1950s, '60s, and early '70s: The objects that unite us (*wampeters*), the lies we tell ourselves (*foma*), and the groups we associate with (*granfalloons*). His major themes are those addressed by his novels: art and writing, SCIENCE AND TECHNOLOGY, social injustice, the human search for enlightenment, and the necessity of family and community.

Writing and Art

Sprinkled throughout the collection are essays in which Vonnegut discusses his own background and development as a writer. In the *Playboy* interview that closes the book, he is asked how he happened to begin writing. Vonnegut explains his experience as a reporter for one of the very few daily newspapers on the high school level, THE SHORTRIDGE ECHO. Perhaps the most valuable part of this experience for Vonnegut was writing for a large audience rather than simply for a teacher. "And if I did a lousy job," he recalls, "I caught a lot of shit in twenty-four hours" (260). His high school newspaper experience trained Vonnegut to write often and to have people actually read his work. In other places, however, he reminisces about his father's pushing him into studying science rather than creative writing at college. In his "Address to the National Institute of Arts and Letters, 1971," Vonnegut recounts telling his son that the happiest day of his life was when he was admitted to the UNIVERSITY OF CHICAGO as a graduate student in the Department of Anthropology: "At last! I was going to study man!" (177). Yet, he becomes discouraged when he decides to specialize in physical anthropology and is set to measuring human brain cavities. Archaeology, where he discovers that "man had been a maker and smasher of crockery since the dawn of time" (178), is no better. Eventually, he tells about confessing to his faculty adviser that he longs to study poetry rather than science, but is worried that his wife and father will object. His faculty adviser offers Vonnegut the perfect solution to his dilemma: "How would you like to study poetry

which *pretends* to be scientific?" (178) he asks the young Vonnegut and welcomes him to the field of cultural anthropology. Although the thesis he writes at Chicago will be rejected, Vonnegut points out in the *Playboy* interview that what he learns about cultural relativity while in graduate school is essential knowledge that should be taught to all first graders. The youngest students should learn that "culture isn't a rational invention: that there are thousands of other cultures and they all work pretty well: that all cultures function on faith rather than truth; that there are lots of alternatives to our own society" (279). Finally able to combine his interests in science and poetry in graduate school, Vonnegut will continue to juggle these seemingly disparate fields when he begins publishing fiction.

Vonnegut also discusses his experiences as a writing teacher. Although he himself longed to study poetry in graduate school and in fact taught creative writing at several places, including the Iowa Writer's Workshop, in a short essay called "Teaching the Unteachable," which originally appeared in the *New York Times Book Review*, Vonnegut comments that "You can't teach people to write well" (25). Writing well, he believes, "is something God lets you do or declines to let you do" (25). But he explains that what places like the Iowa Workshop are able to do is to provide a community of writers for aspiring students. This community makes "writing fiction seem a dignified and useful enterprise" (29). Such programs are much more successful than writing conferences that purport to teach people to write in a few days; students at the Iowa Writer's Workshop toil together as apprentice writers for years rather than days. Ironically, though, Vonnegut explains that he ended up quitting the Iowa Workshop not because the students lacked the talent to write, but rather because they were so talented and productive that Vonnegut found no time to do his own writing.

Vonnegut muses not only on his own writing experiences, but also on the value and purpose of the literary arts in general. Just as his novels are often metafictive in form, commenting on the art of writing and narrative, the opinion pieces in this collection speak to similar issues. In his preface, Vonnegut admits that he has rewritten certain pieces, especially the *Playboy* interview that closes the collection: It is what I *should* have said, not what I *really* said," he explains (xx). But he uses this example to point out what he finds "most encouraging about the writing trades: They allow mediocre people who are patient and industrious to revise their stupidity, to edit themselves into something like intelligence. They also allow lunatics to seem saner than sane" (xx). Thus, writing may tell lies, but Vonnegut has no problem with this. He believes that works of the imagination may have the power to make these lies into reality, what he calls the "power to create" (xxv). "If a person with a demonstrably ordinary mind, like mine," he explains, "will devote himself to giving birth to a work of the imagination, that work will in turn tempt and tease that ordinary mind into cleverness" (xxv). The line between fact and fiction is always a tenuous one for Vonnegut. Readers may be reminded here of the moral attached to his third novel, *Mother Night*: "We are what we pretend to be, so we must be careful about what we pretend to be" (v). In *Wampeters, Foma & Granfalloons*, this dictum is put in more positive terms: By pretending to be clever, and taking on the adventure of writing fiction or producing art, one may eventually grow into the intelligence that was initially only a fiction.

Vonnegut most fully lays out his view of art and writing in his "Address to Graduating Class at Bennington College, 1970." He urges the students he is addressing to cling to superstition and untruth if they want to make the world a better place: "If you want to become a friend of civilization," he says, "then become an enemy of truth and a fanatic for harmless balderdash" (165). While it may seem surprising that a graduation speaker would recommend that students become enemies of truth, Vonnegut's point is that he wants the students to maintain their idealism in spite of the disheartening things going on in the world around them. The superstition he especially begs students to retain is the belief that "humanity is at the center of the universe, the fulfiller or the frustrator of the grandest dreams of God Almighty" (165). And the arts may be the best way to spread this superstition. The purpose of art, he adds, "is to use frauds in order to make human beings seem more wonderful than they really are" (166). By putting man at the center of the universe, "whether he belongs there or not" (167), the arts imagine a saner, kinder, more just world than the real one. Vonnegut believes that by imagining such a world, by pretending that such a world exists, humans may be able to actually create it. He closes his preface by arguing that the only way Americans "can rise above their ordinariness, can mature sufficiently to rescue themselves and to help rescue their planet, is through enthusiastic intimacy with works of their own imagination" (xxv). While art itself may be *foma*, harmless untruths we tell to comfort ourselves, nevertheless Vonnegut believes in the power of these untruths to change the world. In his "Address to P.E.N. Conference in Stockholm, 1973," Vonnegut writes that he is persuaded writers are tremendously influential despite the fact that many political leaders, Americans especially, believe that fiction is "harmless," just "so much hot air" (228), and thus they allow writers unprecedented freedom to write what they want. Writers have power because they give people, especially young people, myths to live by. Eventually, these myths take on the status of truth.

But because writers *do* have such great influence, Vonnegut also believes that they must be very careful in what they write. Novelists have the power to do much harm as well as good. In his "Address at Rededication of Wheaton College Library, 1973," he tells his audience that he wishes to apologize for all fiction writers. "We have ended so many of our stories with gunfights, with showdowns and death," he explains, that "millions and millions of simpletons have mistaken our stories for models of modern living" (216). He attributes fiction writers' reliance on violent resolutions to their stories to laziness; it is difficult to end stories, and shootouts provide convenient endings. Echoing much of what he says about the craft of writing in *Breakfast of Champions*, Vonnegut also blames conventional storytelling for instilling the belief in readers that some people are more important than others—writers focus on the lives of their main characters, while other characters are "as disposable as a box of Kleenex tissues" (217). Because conventional storytelling has done so much damage in the world, Vonnegut's own work attempts to defy conventions. He acknowledges the difficulties critics have had in categorizing his unconventional work. He examines, in particular, two "file drawers" (1) that his work sometimes gets put into: NEW JOURNALISM and SCIENCE FICTION.

Vonnegut expresses his admiration for the group of writers known as the New Journalists in several places in the collection, most notably in his preface and in "A Political Disease," his review of HUNTER S. THOMPSON's *Fear and Loathing on the Campaign Trail '72*. The New Journalism was a style of writing that arose in the early 1960s, mostly among New York magazine and newspaper writers such as Tom Wolfe, Gay Talese, Jimmy Breslin, and several others. Wolfe, the genre's chief theorist, defines New Journalism as factual reporting that uses techniques borrowed from fiction—including dialogue, scene-by-scene construction of action, a varied narrative voice, and symbolic details—in order to make journalistic writing more lively, vivid, and in-depth for readers. In his preface, Vonnegut argues that New Journalists are truth tellers who are unafraid to be charming and entertaining. They, like the ancient Greek historian Thucydides, are good teachers who try not to put their students "to sleep with the truth" (xvii). He adds that he is crazy about the writing of Dr. Hunter S. Thompson, whose work he sees as "the literary equivalent of Cubism" (234), since it breaks all the conventional rules, and in the process, shows "luminous new aspects of beloved old truths" (234). Although Vonnegut "guesses" that he, too, is something of a New Journalist, pointing out that the pieces on BIAFRA and the Republican Convention of 1972 that appear in this collection are "loose and personal" (xvii), and thus fit the definition, he also says that he does not believe he will write many more articles in that vein. Fiction itself, he concludes, is an even "more truthful way of telling the truth than New Journalism is" (xviii), since fiction writers can *show* their readers more than New Journalists can. A fiction writer, he says, "can take the reader anywhere, including the planet Jupiter, in case there's something worth seeing there" (xviii). Vonnegut finally opts for the greater freedom of fiction, though he believes

the goals of both fiction and New Journalism—to entertain and to teach—are quite similar.

The other way that Vonnegut's work, especially his earlier writing, is often characterized is as science fiction. He tells of writing his first novel, *Player Piano*, and of being "a soreheaded occupant of a file drawer labeled 'science fiction' ever since" (1). While he argues that serious critics tend to "mistake the drawer for a urinal" (1), Vonnegut defends the genre, seeing it as occupied simply by writers who "notice technology" (1). In his essay "Science Fiction," published initially in the *New York Times Book Review*, he deplores the notion that "no one can simultaneously be a respectable writer and understand how a refrigerator works" (1). He closes the essay by arguing that, sooner or later, he expects writers "in the mainstream" to begin to include technology in their works, so that the genre of science fiction will eventually become obsolete. Until then, he tells readers, aspiring writers could do worse than "throw in [to their stories] a little chemistry or physics, or even witchcraft, and mail them off to the science fiction magazines" (5). Yet, Vonnegut also admits that plenty of bad science fiction writing exists. Editors and anthologists and publishers of science fiction distribute "the worst writing in America, outside of education journals," alongside "some of the best" (5). In his essay "Excelsior! We're Going to the Moon! Excelsior!," a short piece first published in the *New York Times Magazine*, Vonnegut more fully distinguishes between low-level and quality science fiction. He quotes the great science fiction writer ISAAC ASIMOV, who defines three stages in the development of American science fiction: 1) adventure dominant, 2) technology dominant, and 3) sociology dominant. Vonnegut agrees with Asimov that a focus on sociology is to be desired, not just in science fiction, but in life itself. Interpreting sociology broadly, "as a respectful objective concern for the cradle natures of Earthlings on Earth" (87), Vonnegut writes that he hopes Asimov's stages are "a prophetic outline of Earthling history, too" (87). In Vonnegut's view, then, good science fiction writers, like all good writers, focus on the nature of human beings while also paying attention to the changing world that surrounds those human beings. Because significant world changes come largely from science and technology, these areas constitute one of his concerns in the collection, as in most of his fiction.

Science and Technology

In *Wampeters, Foma, and Granfalloons*, as elsewhere in his work, Vonnegut shows himself to be highly suspicious of new technologies. The play "Fortitude," which depicts an ancient woman kept alive only with the aid of complicated machines, warns readers to be careful what they wish for. As in his short stories "Tomorrow and Tomorrow and Tomorrow" and "2BRO2B," the human desire for long life and the eradication of disease is realized at a very high price. Sylvia Lovejoy, the aged patient of Dr. Norbert Frankenstein in "Fortitude," seems barely human as machines stand in for failed body parts. Even her emotions are controlled by Dr. Frankenstein's machines so that Sylvia is kept artificially happy. When the "tiny spark" of her real self, the self she used to be, shines through, Sylvia's sole desire is to end a life that has become unbearable. Similarly, in "Excelsior! We're Going to the Moon! Excelsior!," Vonnegut argues that "most of the true tales of masterfulness in new environments with new technologies have been cruel or greedy" (81). New technologies, for the most part, have left "tremendous messes to be cleaned up, ravaged landscapes dotted by shattered Earthlings and their machines" (81). He speaks specifically of the two world wars, of the discovery of the New World, of the African slave trade, and of the chemical DDT as examples of destructive uses of new technologies.

In several places in the collection, Vonnegut discusses his opposition to the U.S. space program—perhaps the most ambitious technological pursuit in human history. "We have spent something like $33 billion on space so far," he points out, adding that "We should have spent it on cleaning up our filthy colonies here on earth" (81–82). Vonnegut sees no rush to explore the Moon, partly because it is so expensive to do so and the money could better be used on Earth, and partly because he believes there is nothing on the Moon that humans really want: "There's no atmosphere . . . there's nothing to eat or drink, nobody to talk to" (270).

But more important, as he explains in the *Playboy* interview, the space program seems like "a vaudeville stunt . . . publicity and show business, not science" (270). While a human footprint on the Moon could be a "sacred" object signifying that "Earthlings have done an unbelievably difficult and beautiful thing which the Creator, for Its own reasons, wanted Earthlings to do" (88), Vonnegut also realizes that such a footprint would be immediately profaned by profit-making corporations as a "merchandising scheme" (89). Human nature, as far as Vonnegut can tell, dictates that those who most push new technologies and deeper explorations of the world, those who "have felt that the Creator clearly wanted this or that," have "almost always been pigheaded and cruel" (89). Perhaps the real motive behind the expensive space program, Vonnegut cynically suggests in the *Playboy* interview, is the tremendous thrill received by those who actually witness rocket launches.

Despite his skepticism about scientific advancements, Vonnegut makes it clear that he does see positive changes in the scientific community. In his "Address to the American Physical Society," delivered in 1969, he speaks of a letter he received from a physics professor named George Norwood, who calls himself a "humanistic physicist" (97). Vonnegut praises Norwood, pointing out that, in his view, a "virtuous physicist is a humanistic physicist" (97). Such a physicist, he argues, pays attention to people, listens to them, and does not knowingly cause harm to human beings or to the planet. A humanistic physicist does not help politicians or soldiers and understands the potential danger of new scientific discoveries. While Vonnegut believes that "old-fashioned" scientists tended to be "morally innocent" (99), like Dr. Felix Hoenikker in *Cat's Cradle*, one of the fathers of the ATOMIC BOMB and the inventor of the doomsday device *ice-nine*, he argues that "younger scientists are extremely sensitive to the moral implications of all they do" (99). Scientists like the fictional Dr. Hoenikker, Vonnegut argues, are the product of World War II, a war "against pure evil" in which there was no need to moralize: "Nothing was too horrible to do to any enemy that vile" (101). Thus, scientists had a "can do" attitude and never questioned the morality of their inventions. Younger scientists, though, have lost the moral innocence of their forbears. And Vonnegut considers this loss to be largely a good thing: "Any young scientist . . . when asked by the military to create a terror weapon on the order of napalm, is bound to suspect that he may be committing modern sin. God bless him for that" (104). Vonnegut's admiration for the young people of the 1960s and '70s extends beyond scientists, however. Throughout the collection, Vonnegut examines the youth culture of his day and expresses his admiration for young peoples' fight against social injustice in the world.

Social Injustice

Vonnegut recognizes his immense popularity with the younger generation. Early in his preface, he tells readers about a question asked of him after a speech by a middle-aged man who seemed to be a recent refugee from Europe: "You are a leader of American young people," the man said. "What right do you have to teach them to be so cynical and pessimistic?" (xiv). The question stumps Vonnegut, who claims to be simply a writer, not a leader of young people. And although he says the question cut short his speaking career, that he could no longer be "the glib Philosopher of the Prairies it had once been so easy" for him to be (xiii), Vonnegut does seem to have a special relation to the youth culture of the 1960s and '70s. In a short essay called "Good Missiles, Good Manners, Good Night," he tells of going to high school with "a nice girl named Barbara Masters," who married the U.S. secretary of defense for President NIXON, Melvin Laird. When a friend tells him that Mrs. Laird has read and liked his books, Vonnegut is somewhat puzzled, since he is a pacifist. The next time he is in Washington, he leaves a message for her. Although Mrs. Laird never answers, Vonnegut says that if he had been invited into the Laird home, he "would have smiled and smiled" (107). His generation had learned to respect one another's opinions and to be polite at all costs. Vonnegut ends the essay ironically, telling readers that, if he had been invited into Mrs. Laird's home, he "would have thanked God . . . that no members of the younger generation were along. Kids don't learn nice manners in high

school anymore" (107). Vonnegut's distaste for the polite manners that smooth over political atrocities becomes evident in the final lines of the essay. He writes about members of the younger generation: "If they met a person who was in favor of building a device which would cripple and finally kill all children everywhere, they wouldn't smile. They would bristle with hatred, which is rude" (107). Clearly, Vonnegut admires these young people who refuse to politely ignore cruelty and morally reprehensible actions. These "kids" have learned to be impolite, a necessary lesson that Vonnegut, in *Breakfast of Champions*, says he himself learned from his first employer Phoebe Hurty as a teenager in INDIANAPOLIS.

In "Why They Read Hesse," a short essay first published in *Horizon* magazine, Vonnegut again explores the attitudes and politics of the younger generation. He concludes that HERNAN HESSE offers young people "hope and romance" (111), qualities hard to find in late 20th-century America. Moreover, Hesse's novel *Steppenwolf*, described by Vonnegut as a "wholly Germanic, hopelessly dated jumble" (111), appeals to the younger generation, he speculates, because "the politics espoused by the hero of *Steppenwolf* coincide with those of the American young . . . He is against war. He hates armament manufacturers and superpatriots" (113). But the quality in *Steppenwolf* Vonnegut believes young people respond to most intensely is "the homesickness of the author" (115). Like Herman Hesse, who "cleared the hell out of Germany just before the holocaust began" (116), Vonnegut believes that many young Americans at that time were considering clearing out. Dissatisfied with the world political situation, with environmental destruction, and with racism and social injustice, these young people, Vonnegut believes, long to return to their safe and happy childhoods. Yet, as Vonnegut points out at the end of the essay, "the next holocaust will leave this planet uninhabitable," so that simply moving to another country is not an option for members of the younger generation as it was for Hesse.

Nevertheless, Vonnegut also believes that too much of a burden has been placed on young people of the '60s and early '70s. In his address to the

Bennington College graduating class of 1970, he says, "Another great swindle is that people your age are supposed to save the world" (169). Vonnegut reminds his audience that they are still young, and that they need to "do a certain amount of skylarking" (169) before settling down and trying to bring about serious political change. But when they are a bit older and have acquired more power and knowledge of the world, Vonnegut urges the Bennington students to "work for a socialist form of government" (170). He sees SOCIALISM as the political option kindest to "the old and the sick and the shy and the poor and the stupid, and . . . people nobody likes" (170). Free enterprise, he tells the students, has already had its chance. Moreover, he argues that it is not simply empty idealism to speak about a future in which wealth is distributed more fairly, and there is a "modest plenty for all" (170); in Sweden such a system already exists, and there is no reason Americans cannot have such a government as well.

Vonnegut's own political stance is much more sympathetic to the views of the younger generation he often addresses than to the government officials and establishment figures that the children of the 1960s despise. In several of the essays in the collection, he comments on what he perceives to be the dominant social injustices of the late 1960s. He visits the short-lived country of BIAFRA in Africa, which declared its independence from Nigeria in May 1967 only to be defeated by the oppressive Nigerian regime less than three years later. While sympathetic to the Biafran cause, Vonnegut is also suspicious of charismatic leaders in general and wonders if he "had been a fool to be charmed by" Biafran General Ojukwu (157). "Was he yet another great leader," Vonnegut wonders, "who would never surrender, who became holier and more radiant as his people died for him?" (157). Vonnegut admits to feeling despair while in Biafra and speculates that his constant joking is a "response to misery" he cannot do anything to change (148). In an essay titled "In a Manner That Must Shame God Himself," Vonnegut shows that he is disgusted by the political scene in America as well. He is astonished while covering the 1972 Republican National Convention when

a minister tells him that the U.S. president has a deeper responsibility to God than to the U.S. people. The sermon that opens the convention, Vonnegut claims, argues for the *"Divine Right of Presidents"* (194). Vonnegut goes on to explain that, in his view, the two real political parties in the United States are "Winners" and "Losers." The Republicans and Democrats are only imaginary parties. While both imaginary parties are run by Winners, the Democrats are less openly contemptuous of Losers than the Republicans are. And the Republican scheme for lasting world peace, Vonnegut explains, is simple: *"Ignore agony"* (206).

Perhaps the most pressing example of agony that Vonnegut confronts in the book results from U.S. involvement in Vietnam. In his essay "Torture and Blubber," he very clearly deplores U.S. government policies in Vietnam: "Simply: We are torturers, and we once hoped to win in Indochina and anywhere because we had the most expensive torture instruments yet devised" (171). In his "Address at Rededication of Wheaton College Library, 1973," Vonnegut explores the mindset that he believes led the U.S. into war in Vietnam. Members of his generation, he argues, "had the illusion of being very, very good during the Second World War" because it was so clearly a just war (214). Yet, this illusion proved dangerous. Because American enemies during World War II "were so awful, so evil," Americans began to believe that, by contrast, they "must be remarkably pure" (215). Atrocities such as the My Lai massacre, which Vonnegut mentions specifically in this speech, occur because Americans have the illusion of purity and believe that they are always and naturally on the side of good. This leads to a lack of restraint in the use of weapons. But, in reality, Vonnegut argues, Americans are not pure. "All human beings," he insists, "are to some extent greedy and cruel—and angry without cause" (215). And alongside the suffering in Vietnam caused by the war, Vonnegut sees another devastating consequence: the war, he says, "has broken our hearts" (273). The U.S. war in Vietnam, he argues, has alienated ordinary Americans from their government and taken away the illusion that citizens have control over their political affairs.

It is interesting that Vonnegut, in his preface, denies that an imaginative writer can "have any political effectiveness in his creative prime" (xiv) and argues that a writer who "tries to put his politics into a work of the imagination . . . will foul up his work beyond all recognition" (xiv). This is a view that he contradicts in the *Playboy* interview that closes the collection. In this final piece, Vonnegut claims that his purpose as a writer is to change the social injustices that he describes in the book. He tells the magazine that his "motives are political" (237). He believes that "the writer should serve his society," and that writers should be "agents of change" (237). While Vonnegut is able to be more outspoken and plain in the political commentary collected in this book than in his fiction, nevertheless his political views seep into his novels and stories as well, informing everything he writes. By the end of the collection, Vonnegut acknowledges and accepts that his imaginative writing, as well as his public speaking, are attempts to remedy the social injustices he so deplores in the world around him.

Portrait of Madame Helena Petrovna Blavatsky *(courtesy of the Library of Congress)*

Enlightenment

The sticking point, of course, is how to make a better world. Another main concern of *Wampeters, Foma, and Granfalloons* is the attempt of human beings to better themselves, to attain personal enlightenment, and in the process, to hopefully create a more humane society. In two essays, "The Mysterious Madame Blavatsky" and "Yes, We Have No Nirvanas," Vonnegut examines mystical movements that purport to grant their followers self-knowledge and enlightenment. MADAME HELENA PETROVNA BLAVATSKY was a 19th-century world traveler and Russian immigrant to America who cofounded the THEOSOPHICAL SOCIETY, a group dedicated to "worldwide brotherhood," to the belief "that there is much to be learned from all religions," and to the notion "that there are many odd and important adventures in life which science cannot explain" (129). While Vonnegut satirizes Madame Blavatsky by quoting some of her pseudo-mystical and baffling writings—"To reach the knowledge of that SELF thou hast to give up Self to Non-Self, Being to Non-Being, and then thou canst repose between the wings of the GREAT BIRD" (128)—

he also admires Madame Blavatsky for her charm and her refusal to live by ordinary conventions. "This would be a drab and empty world indeed if it weren't for zany men and women," Vonnegut writes (130). Madame Blavatsky was not only extremely brave, traveling over several continents as a lone woman, she was also brilliant, mastering a dozen or more languages, and generous in her longing "for a far more glamorous and complicated spiritual life for all mankind" (130). Vonnegut concludes his essay on Madame Blavatsky by saying that he is "charmed and amused that she was an American citizen for a little while" (139). Although she was "bizarre," she was also "something quite lovely: She thought all human beings were her brothers and sisters—she was a citizen of the world" (139). As in his novels, Vonnegut has great affection for kindly and well-meaning utopian visionaries, no matter how misguided such characters may eventually turn out to be.

Vonnegut, however, is somewhat more critical of another well-intentioned mystic he examines in "Yes, We Have No Nirvanas": MAHARISHI MAHESH YOGI, the founder of Transcendental Meditation.

Although he begins the essay by telling a Unitarian minister friend that the Yogi is not "a fake" (31)— "It made me happy just to see him. His vibrations are lovely and profound" (31)—nevertheless, Vonnegut is suspicious of the Yogi's claim that changing one's self and thus the world at large, is "easy as pie" (31). The Yogi's lectures, Vonnegut explains, are "cheerful and encouraging"; audience members "are told lovingly that this thing is easy, never fails to make a person more blissful and virtuous and effective, if it is done correctly" (32). The technique of Transcendental Meditation, Vonnegut adds, claims to "offer tremendous pleasure" while opposing "no existing institutions or attitudes" and demanding "no sacrifices or outward demonstrations of virtue" (34). Vonnegut actually sees some of the effects of TM in his own wife and daughter, who are devotees of the practice. "Nothing pisses them off anymore," he explains, "They glow like bass drums with lights inside" (31).

But Vonnegut's criticism of the technique arises from the fact that practitioners of Transcendental Meditation expect to change not only themselves but the larger world as well. "Every time you dive into your own mind," TM devotees believe "you are actually dealing effectively with the issues of the day" (35). While he understands the attraction of a pseudo-religion that purports to change the world so easily, Vonnegut nevertheless argues that the Yogi's ideas have much in common with the free enterprise marketplace values he frequently heard praised while working as a public relations man at GENERAL ELECTRIC in Schenectady, New York. The Yogi's message, Vonnegut believes, boils down to the idea that any "oppressed person could rise" by practicing Transcendental Meditation: "He would automatically do his job better, and the economy would pay him more, and then he could buy anything he wanted. He wouldn't be oppressed anymore. In other words, he should quit bitching, begin to meditate, grasp his garters, and float into a commanding position in the marketplace, where transactions are always fair" (38). To Vonnegut, this doctrine sounds suspiciously similar to the idea that the oppressed should simply pull themselves up by their own bootstraps. He tells his wife that Maharishi "talks economics like a traveling secre-

tary of the National Association of Manufacturers" (41). He also points out that the crowds who go to see Maharishi Mahesh Yogi are overwhelmingly white and middle-class, noting as well that many more politically-oriented students walked out when the Yogi spoke at HARVARD UNIVERSITY. While Vonnegut is attracted to the Yogi on a personal level—he is a "darling man" (37)—nevertheless, he believes that social injustices can cripple individual human beings' ability to better their lot. Changing the world, Vonnegut suggests throughout the collection, depends largely on changing the social and political institutions that oppress people rather than being simply a matter of individual human beings changing themselves.

Family and Community

Vonnegut's own remedy for bettering some of the social ills in the world reflects a recurring theme in his fiction: the necessity of large, extended family groups that would provide support and encouragement to individuals. In his preface, he writes that his own long-range utopian schemes "have to do with providing all Americans with artificial extended families of a thousand members or more. Only when we have overcome loneliness can we begin to share wealth and work more fairly. I honestly believe that we will have those families by-and-by, and I hope they will become international" (xxii). In *Slapstick*, published in 1976, Vonnegut explores just such a scheme. U.S. president Wilbur Swain gives new, computer-generated middle names to all American citizens, who then form family groups according to these new middle names. While the project does not quite generate the utopian society Wilbur had envisioned—utopian schemes in Vonnegut's fiction are almost always doomed to failure—it does at least work toward abolishing loneliness in the country, at least for a time. In his essay on the Biafran War, Vonnegut actually witnessed the real-life effects of the kind of extended family groups he envisions in America. While the Biafrans are tragically defeated by the Nigerians, Vonnegut notes that he "never met a bitter Biafran" (149). He speculates that this lack of bitterness, along with the Biafrans' ability to endure so much hardship, arises from the large and powerful family groups that make up the culture. The Biafrans, Vonnegut writes, "all had the emotional and spiritual strength that an enormous family can give" (149). When Vonnegut questions General Ojukwu about his family, the general replies "that it was three thousand members strong. He knew every member of it by face, by name, and by reputation" (150). Further, these families take care of their members. Vonnegut points out that there are no orphanages, no old people's homes, and no public charities in Biafra. Families in Biafra provide the services that Americans often expect from their government.

In his "Address to the National Institute of Arts and Letters, 1971," Vonnegut explains that his ideas about family and community were largely formed while he was a graduate student in anthropology at the University of Chicago. The head of the Department of Anthropology at that time was DR. ROBERT REDFIELD, whose ideas about what he called "folk societies" influenced Vonnegut greatly. Dr. Redfield, while acknowledging the great variety among primitive societies, also argued that those societies had certain characteristics in common: "They were all so small that everybody knew everybody well, and associations lasted for life. The members communicated intimately with one another, and very little with anybody else" (179). Further, there was not much division of labor in primitive societies, and people were valued for themselves, not for their utility to the group. Vonnegut uses Dr. Redfield's theories to argue that all human beings, even modern humans, are "chemically engineered to live in folk societies" (180). Lacking such folk societies, humans tend to "feel lousy all the time" (180). Thus, Vonnegut speculates, modern humans spend much of their time trying to recapture feelings of belonging by creating artificial folk societies, an "affectionate clan or village or tribe" (181) where they are surrounded by like-minded individuals who treat them as brothers. Lions Clubs, fraternal lodges, and professional organizations are examples of such attempts.

Vonnegut expands his theories about human beings' longing to live in folk societies in the *Playboy* interview at the end of the collection. He dis-

cusses the transience of modern Americans who no longer live in permanent communities and the loneliness that results. "I would like people to be able to stay in one community for a lifetime," Vonnegut tells the magazine interviewer, "to travel away from it to see the world, but always to come home again. This is comforting" (242). When asked about the popularity of communes among young people, Vonnegut replies that he certainly understands the impulse of these young people to live communally, to recreate "the ways human beings have lived for 1,000,000 years" (243). The problem with communes, however, is that members are not really relatives, and thus do not have enough in common so that "hellish differences" arise (243). The children of commune founders, he believes, will have an easier time living together than the founders themselves since they will have shared attitudes and experiences and thus resemble a real family more closely.

Finally, the *Playboy* interviewer asks Vonnegut if he has done any research on his theory about family and community. Vonnegut openly admits that he has not. "I'm afraid to," he adds, "I might find out it wasn't true. It's a sunny little dream I have of a happier mankind. I couldn't survive my own pessimism if I didn't have some kind of sunny little dream" (243). Vonnegut's theories about extended families, according to his own admission, may be simply *foma*, comforting lies people tell themselves in order to make life more pleasant. Yet, as in his fiction—*Cat's Cradle* especially—*foma* is not to be discounted. Such harmless untruths, he tells readers in the epigraph to that novel, can help people lead "brave and kind and healthy and happy" lives. And finally, the illusion may become the reality. Despite his much ballyhooed pessimism and cynicism, Vonnegut tells the *Playboy* interviewer that "People are too good for this world" (244). In *Wampeters, Foma, and Granfalloons*, Vonnegut critiques a number of social and cultural ills, but he never gives in to the despair that is always lurking in the background of his work.

FURTHER READING

Wampeters, Foma and Granfalloons. New York: Dell, 1999.

Welcome to the Monkey House

Welcome to the Monkey House is Vonnegut's second collected volume of short fiction, published by SEYMOUR LAWRENCE /Delacorte Press in 1968. The collection contains 25 stories, most of which had previously appeared in magazines such as *Collier's,* the *Saturday Evening Post,* and *Cosmopolitan,* as well as an author's preface, written specifically for the collection. Eleven of the stories in "Welcome to the Monkey House" had also appeared in the 1961 collection, *Canary in a Cat House,* which had gone out of print by the time *Monkey House* was published. The collection contains one story, "The Hyannis Port Story," which had been sold to the *Saturday Evening Post* in 1963, but never printed because of the assassination of President JOHN F. KENNEDY, who appears as a character in the story. The contents to *Welcome to the Monkey House* read as follows:

FURTHER READING

Reed, Peter. *The Short Fiction of Kurt Vonnegut.* Westport, Conn.: Greenwood Press, 1997.
Welcome to the Monkey House. New York: Dell, 1998.

"Welcome to the Monkey House"

One of Vonnegut's best-known short stories, "Welcome to the Monkey House" is a SCIENCE FICTION tale set in a dystopic future in which Earth is grossly overpopulated and human beings are expendable. The story first appeared in *Playboy* magazine in January 1968 and was later reprinted as the title story to the collection *Welcome to the Monkey House.*

SYNOPSIS

"Welcome to the Monkey House" is set in the near future, when the population on Earth has reached 17 billion—an unsustainable number. The government has instituted laws that require each person to ingest, three times a day, "ethical birth control" pills. But because moralists feared that "society would collapse if people used sex for nothing but pleasure" (38), the pills make whoever takes them completely numb from the waist down, thus removing all sexual desire. These pills were actually invented by J. Edgar Nation, a druggist from Grand Rapids, who, on an Easter Sunday outing with his family was horrified by the sexual behavior of monkeys in the zoo. He immediately began development of a pill that "would make monkeys in the springtime fit things for a Christian family to see" (36). Alongside the birth control pills, the government has also instituted Ethical Suicide Parlors and actively encourages people, via frequently broadcast television commercials, to end their lives.

The story opens with the news that an outlaw named Billy the Poet, a "nothinghead" who refuses to take his ethical birth control pills and who travels the country deflowering Suicide Hostesses, is headed toward the Suicide Parlor in Hyannis, Massachusetts, on CAPE COD. The parlor receives a call claiming to be from Billy, which the police trace to the next door Howard Johnson's restaurant, where they immediately race to catch the famous criminal. Meanwhile, one of the Suicide Hostesses, Nancy McLuhan, remains behind to cajole a senile old grandpa at the parlor to ask for the needle that will end his life. Alone with Nancy, the old man rips off his mask, revealing himself to be Billy the Poet. Billy takes Nancy through underground sewers to the old Kennedy compound in Hyannis, which has been turned into a museum. When her own body-numbing birth control pills have worn off, she is deflowered by Billy with the help of his gang of outlaws. Afterward, Billy tells the distraught Nancy that she just experienced what was a typical wedding night for a young virgin 100 years ago. He also reassures her that she will come to enjoy sex eventually, just as the young 19th-century wives did. Finally, the outlaw tells Nancy that he might not see her again for many years, but that he loved her. To convince her of this, he leaves her with a copy of the famous love sonnet "How Do I Love Thee?" by Elizabeth Barrett Browning, as well as a bottle of birth control pills that prevent pregnancy without eradicating sexual desire. The bottle is labeled, "Welcome to the Monkey House."

COMMENTARY

With its futuristic, dystopic setting, "Welcome to the Monkey House" reads like a science fiction story. The Hyannis, Massachusetts, of the future is part of a world that is enormously overpopulated and that, as a result, treats human beings as expendable—objects to be gotten rid of as efficiently as possible. Though staffed by kindly Suicide Hostesses and furnished with comfortable Barcaloungers, the Suicide Parlors are really nothing more than death camps, their most horrifying aspect that the clients are willing participants in their own extermination. In addition, nearly everything in this future society is automated. Because very few people have jobs, most spend their time watching government-run television, brainwashed by messages broadcast every 15 minutes urging them to conform to government policies. Echoes of George Orwell's *1984* sound here, as do concerns of other Vonnegut science fiction stories, such as the well-known "Harrison Bergeron."

But the biggest contributor to the dystopia depicted in "Welcome to the Monkey House" is the new society's puritanical crusade against sexual pleasure. Although the overpopulation problem could be addressed by simply blocking people's reproductive capabilities, pleasure itself is seen as morally offensive. Thus, the pills that J. Edgar Nation develops prohibit all sexual desire. Moreover, sexual pleasure in the story is tied to artistic pleasure as the outlaw figure is imagined specifically as a poet whose mission is to reintroduce love into the world. Vonnegut satirizes American western mythology of outlaws and sheriffs as well as 20th-century cops-and-robbers stories in the names of his characters. Billy the Poet is the romantic outlaw figure, evoking 19th-century bank robber Billy the Kid while J. Edgar Nation pokes fun at F.B.I. founder and longtime director, J. Edgar Hoover, a conservative moral crusader thought by some historians to be a closet homosexual and cross-dresser, and thus considered a hypocrite by many.

The story, as it reworks these highly masculine and even macho traditions, might be offensive to women readers in its depiction of women who are kidnapped and raped, seemingly for their own good. Yet, it is important to notice that the rape of Nancy McLuhan, as depicted in the story, is not violent or even particularly sexualized; it is described, instead, as "clinical," and rather than feeling "cocky or proud" afterward, Billy is left terribly depressed (47). Furthermore, Vonnegut ties the fictional rape experience to the very real sexual oppression experienced by women in the 19th-century. Billy tells Nancy that what she just experienced "is a typical wedding night for a strait-laced girl of a hundred years ago" (48). Here, Vonnegut critiques sexual mores that keep women inexperienced and ignorant of sexual matters, demanding such strict chastity of them that they are revolted by sex when they first experience it. The story instead views women as naturally sexual beings who, when freed of social constraints, can experience sexual pleasure as fully as men. Above all, the story advocates the sexual revolution that was taking place across the country at the time of its publication in 1968.

CHARACTERS AND RELATED ENTRIES

Billy the Poet   Outlaw Billy the Poet, whose name is clearly a play on the often romanticized 19th-century bank robber Billy the Kid, refuses to take his ethical birth control three times a day as the law demands, and is thus categorized as a "nothinghead." But his larger crime consists of traveling around the country and deflowering the virgin hostesses who staff the country's Federal Ethical Suicide Parlors. The story depicts Billy's kidnap and rape of Nancy McLuhan, a Suicide Parlor Hostess from Hyannis, Massachusetts. Although Billy first contacts the women he will abduct by sending them slightly obscene poems, the poem he leaves Nancy at the end of the story is a love poem—Elizabeth Barrett Browning's famous "How Do I Love Thee?"

Billy's Gang   When Nancy McLuhan is kidnapped by Billy the Poet, she is surprised to find that he has a whole gang, consisting of at least four men and four women, working with him.

Crocker, Pete   Pete Crocker is the sheriff of Barnstable County who arrives at the Federal Ethical Suicide Parlor in Hyannis on Cape Cod to tell the hostesses that Billy the Poet is headed their way. Crocker later is lured to the next door Howard Johnson's restaurant by Billy and his gang, leaving hostess Nancy McLuhan alone in the Suicide Parlor to be kidnapped by Billy.

Federal Ethical Suicide Parlors   "Welcome to the Monkey House" depicts a future in which the eradication of disease and increased human longevity have so overpopulated the world that the government has instituted Federal Ethical Suicide Parlors, where altruistic citizens are encouraged to end their lives in order to make more room for other people.

Kennedy, Ma   Ma Kennedy, a descendant of the famous Kennedy clan, which, by the time of the story, has produced 14 U.S. or world presidents, is the current president of the world. She is an ex-Suicide Hostess who hangs clichéd, homey sayings in her office at the Taj Mahal.

Kraft, Mary   Mary Kraft is one of the hostesses at the Federal Ethical Suicide Parlor in Hyannis, Massachusetts. A beautiful, six-foot-tall woman who, like all hostesses, wears white lipstick, heavy eye makeup, a purple body stocking, and black leather boots, Mary escapes kidnapping and rape at the hands of Billy the Poet by accompanying the police to the Howard Johnson's restaurant where they believe the outlaw is hiding.

Mailman   An unnamed mailman delivers a letter to Suicide Hostess Nancy McLuhan that contains, written in smeared pencil, a bawdy song sent by Billy the Poet.

McLuhan, Nancy   A six-foot-tall hostess at the Federal Ethical Suicide Parlor in Hyannis, Massachusetts, Nancy McLuhan's job is both to comfort and to cajole along the parlor's patients as they end their lives. Nancy, like all Suicide Hostesses, is smart, tough, trained in the martial arts, and a true believer in the government's program of enforced birth control and voluntary suicide. When she is kidnapped and deflowered by Billy the Poet, however, Nancy's initial disgust begins to waver as the outlaw explains that his mission is simply "to restore a certain amount of innocent pleasure to the world" (49).

Nation, J. Edgar   Outlaw Billy the Poet, disguised as a "Foxy Grandpa" (34), tells Nancy McLuhan the well-known story of J. Edgar Nation, a druggist from Grand Rapids who is considered the father of ethical birth control. Nation, who takes his wife and 11 children on an outing to the zoo one Easter Sunday, is horrified when his whole family sees "a monkey playing with his private parts" (36). He immediately rushes home and develops a pill that controls pregnancy by taking away all sexual desire. At the time that the story is set, with rampant overpopulation a pressing concern, all people on Earth are required to ingest Nation's pills three times a day.

FURTHER READING

Reed, Peter. *The Short Fiction of Kurt Vonnegut.* Westport, Conn.: Greenwood Press, 1997.
Welcome to the Monkey House. New York: Dell, 1998.

"Where I Live"

Originally published in *Venture* magazine under the title "You've Never Been to Barnstable?" in October 1964, and republished in 1968 as the first story in *Welcome to the Monkey House,* "Where I Live" explores changes that have come to CAPE COD due to tourism and the ability of a small town named BARNSTABLE VILLAGE to withstand these changes. Although some critics, such as Donald Morse, consider this piece to be nonfiction, its use of third-person point of view and its focus on a fictional encyclopedia salesman belie this view.

SYNOPSIS

"Where I Live" is quite simply structured, without much of a plot. An encyclopedia salesman comes to tiny Barnstable Village on Cape Cod, to the Sturgis Library, America's oldest library building. Pointing out to the "easily alarmed librarian" (1) that the most recent reference book in the library's collection is a 1938 *Britannica,* the salesman makes the case that a lot has happened since 1938. The librarian sends the salesman away to visit some of the library's directors, giving him a list that includes names such as Cabot and Lowell. Told he might catch several directors at once if he visits the Barnstable Yacht Club, the salesman sets off down a narrow, bumpy road in that direction. When he gets there, he is dismayed to discover that the yacht club is simply a narrow shack, with no bar, telephone, or electricity. Discouraged, the salesman goes to lunch in a dumpy news store, then to the local museum, still hoping to run into a library director. Bored by the museums' exhibits, the salesman takes the "customary cure" (2) for visitors to Barnstable Village, and flees to nearby Hyannis, the "commercial heart of Cape Cod" where he finds "cocktail lounges, motor courts, bowling alleys, gift shoppes, and pizzerias" (2), and he works out his frustrations by playing miniature golf. The story at this point abandons the encyclopedia salesman. The rest of the story supplies musings by the narrator about the character of Barnstable Village and its residents.

COMMENTARY

The shabby yacht club, lacking a bar, telephone, and electricity; the "aggressively un-cute, un-colonial" (2) Barnstable News Store; and the lack of entertainment in the town ensure that tourists will not make the trek to Barnstable Village, or that they will be disappointed if they do. Casual visitors to the village escape as soon as they can to the much more bustling, tourist-friendly Hyannis, the "commercial heart of the Cape" (3). Yet, the narrator does not bemoan this shabbiness; instead he loves it, pointing out that while "few Cape villages have much chance of coming through the present greedy, tasteless boom with their souls intact" (4), there is a good possibility that the soul of Barnstable Village will survive. Part of the reason for this is that, unlike the artificiality of the more touristy villages on Cape Cod, Barnstable Village is a real place. According to the narrator, it "is not a hollow village, with everything for rent, with half of the houses empty in the winter" (4). Instead, people live there year round, working at different occupations. In Barnstable Village, carpenters and masons are valued along with architects, teachers, and writers: "It is a classless society," the narrator explains, "a sometimes affectionate and sentimental one" (4).

In many ways, this story is a classic example of local color fiction, a genre popular in late 19th-century America. Local color stories are not plot-centered; what happens is not so important as the delineation of a particular place and a particular type of character associated with that place. Often, these stories portray an outsider who comes in and tries to change things but who is flummoxed by the local residents. Because of their allegiance to the status quo, these stories are often profoundly conservative in nature; local residents reject change and win out over intrusive outsiders in the end. While "Where I Live" certainly follows this model in many ways, one of the ironies in the story is that the stubborn locals, who refuse to change, are all themselves outsiders. The narrator writes that "all of the anachronistic, mildly xenophobic, charming queerness of Barnstable Village might entitle it to the epithet, 'Last Stronghold of the True Cape Codders,' if it weren't for on thing: Hardly anyone in the village was born on Cape Cod" (5). Instead, the villagers come from Evanston and Louisville and Boston and Pittsburgh, and "God-only-knows-where" and are "slowly replacing authentic rural Yankees" (5). Thus, the story plays with notions of authentic and false; it shows that true value is not necessarily a matter of who you are or where you were born, but of the choices you make. The narrator speculates that the "real Cape Codders," if they "could rise from their churchyard graves" (6) would approve of the current Barnstable villagers.

CHARACTERS

Encyclopedia Salesman   The encyclopedia salesman who comes to Barnstable Village is an outsider who expects that the recent Cape Cod tourist boom will have made the village amenable to visitors. When he does not find the luxurious yacht club, the fine restaurants, or the attractions he expects, he flees to bustling Hyannis to play miniature golf. The Sturgis Library does eventually purchase new encyclopedias, although "the school marks of the children and the conversation of the adults have not conspicuously improved" as a result (6).

Librarian   The librarian, who is described as being "easily alarmed" (1), sends the encyclopedia salesman to search for the library's directors, who could authorize a purchase of updated reference materials. The salesman's visit, although he never finds the directors, obviously makes an impression on the librarian since, at the end of the story, new encyclopedias have been purchased.

Nicholson, Father Robert   The story's narrator describes St. Mary's Church on Main Street in Barnstable Village as having "the most enchanting church garden in America" (6). The garden is the work of Father Robert Nicholson, an Episcopalian minister, and "a good man who died young" (6). Father Nicholson, talking to a Roman Catholic and a Jew at a cocktail party one evening, describes the villagers as "Druids" (6).

Treasurer of Barnstable Comedy Club (old)   The Barnstable Comedy Club had the same treasurer for 30 years, a man who refused to say what

the club's balance was for fear that members would spend it foolishly. This treasurer resigned the year before the story is set.

Treasurer of Barnstable Comedy Club (new)   The new treasurer of the Barnstable Comedy Club announces that the club has a balance of $400 in its coffers. The members immediately blow all the money "on a new curtain the color of spoiled salmon" (3), justifying the position of the former treasurer, who refused to admit the club's balance, in fear that members would spend it foolishly.

FURTHER READING

Reed, Peter. *The Short Fiction of Kurt Vonnegut.* Westport, Conn.: Greenwood Press, 1997.
Welcome to the Monkey House. New York: Dell, 1998.

"Who Am I This Time?"

A sweet love story that reflects Vonnegut's love of the theater and theatrical productions, "Who Am I This Time" first appeared under the title "My Name Is Everyone" in the *Saturday Evening Post* in December 1961. The story was reprinted as "Who Am I This Time" in the 1968 collection, *Welcome to the Monkey House.*

SYNOPSIS

The story's first-person narrator is a storm window and door salesman who belongs to an amateur theatrical society in a small town called North Crawford. The narrator is asked to direct the society's production of TENNESSEE WILLIAMS's play *A STREETCAR NAMED DESIRE,* because the group's usual director, 74-year-old Doris Sawyer, is busy with her sick mother. Not really wanting to direct, the narrator accepts the position on the condition that Harry Nash, the club's only real actor, take the part of Stanley Kowalski, made famous by Marlon Brando. Harry Nash is an extremely shy man who is able to overcome his complete awkwardness around people only when acting out the identity of a character in a play. When asked to take any role, Harry always replies, "Who am I this time?," a statement that becomes the story's title.

Because Harry never attends meetings, the narrator must go to the hardware store where Harry works to offer him the role of Stanley. On the way there, he stops at the telephone company office to complain about a mistake in his bill, where he meets a beautiful but numb, almost machine-like young woman. Because the theater company lacks younger women, the narrator invites the girl, Helene Shaw, to try out for the role of Stella. Helene's tryout, however, goes very disappointingly; she is wooden onstage, unable to express any emotion. The narrator tries hard to cast another Stella, but all the other women who audition are more appropriate for the role of Blanche. Eventually, he hits on the idea of having Helene try out again, this time opposite Harry Nash acting as Stanley. During the audition, Harry practically *becomes* Marlon Brando playing Stanley Kowalski; he lights a fire under Helene as well, who is now able to play the part of Stella beautifully.

As rehearsals progress, the whole company is inspired by the acting of Harry and Helene, and the narrator is quite pleased and proud of himself. When the play opens one Thursday night, it is a huge success. Helene is somewhat distressed after the curtain falls, however, to discover that Harry is nowhere to be found. The narrator explains that Harry disappears after his performances, returning to his ordinary existence as an extremely shy and awkward man unable to interact socially. The next night, Helene's performance is not nearly so good as on opening night; she seems distracted. On the third and closing night of the production, however, Helene shines again. Even Harry has to work hard to keep up with her. When the final curtain comes down, Helene holds Harry's hand, despite his discomfort, refusing to release it unless he promises to stay around long enough for her to go downstairs and get a present she wants to give him. Harry reluctantly agrees, and Helene dashes off to return with a copy of SHAKESPEARE's *Romeo and Juliet*, bookmarked to some lines, which she begs Harry to read. Though initially reluctant, Harry soon turns into the very essence of Romeo, speaking Romeo's love lines passionately and beautifully as Helene

reads the part of Juliet. The pair leave together and are married one week later.

COMMENTARY

"Who Am I This Time" expresses many of Vonnegut's familiar themes. People in an increasingly mechanized contemporary America are themselves often machinelike, numb. The narrator meets Helene Shaw because the telephone company has installed an automatic billing machine, which "didn't have all the bugs out if yet" (16). When the narrator tries to joke with Helene Shaw about machines eventually delivering themselves, she does not seem very interested, leading the narrator to wonder "if she was interested in anything" (16). He adds that, "She seemed kind of numb, almost a machine herself, an automatic phone-company politeness machine" (16). Similarly, Harry Nash seems less than human without a script to prompt him; he avoids all social events because, on his own, "he never could think of anything to say or do" (16). Readers may be reminded here of the wooden, nearly robotic relationship between Paul and Anita Proteus in *Player Piano* and of the way Vonnegut calls himself a writing machine in *Breakfast of Champions*. In many of Vonnegut's works, characters are unable to think intelligently, and human relationships become rote and mechanical.

Yet, as in other Vonnegut works, art can be redeeming and transformative. Harry, when he is playing a character in a play, becomes larger than life. Helene, speaking with the narrator and Doris Sawyer at her audition, lights up when she begins to talk about the movie stars she admires. Although she has moved around her whole life and been unable to make lasting attachments to real people, Helene confesses that she used to pretend she was married to various male movie stars. "They were the only people who came with us," she explains, "No matter where we moved, movie stars were there" (20). For both Harry and Helene, the artificial world of the stage and screen is more real and immediate than the world they actually live in. While a synopsis of the story might make these characters sound pathetic, the narrator does not present them that way. At the end of the story, the clever Helene proclaims herself "the luckiest girl in town" (28). Because the pair read plays together each night, Helene's life with Harry is rich, varied, and exciting: "I've been married to Othello, been loved by Faust and been kidnapped by Paris," she explains to the narrator (28). Literature has transformed the lives of these characters, providing them a new world of the imagination more richly textured and satisfying than the drab real world could ever be.

CHARACTERS

Miller, Lydia   Lydia Miller plays Blanche Dubois in the local community theater production of *A Streetcar Named Desire*. During rehearsals, she realizes that Helene Shaw, the play's Stella, is falling in love with Harry Nash, who portrays Stanley. Lydia takes Helene aside and warns her that the real-life Harry is nothing at all like Stanley and will disappoint her. When Helene becomes angry, Lydia slinks away "feeling about as frowzy and unloved as she was supposed to feel in the play" (25).

Miller, Verne   Verne Miller is the husband of Lydia Miller, the actress who plays Blanche Dubois in the North Crawford production of *A Streetcar Named Desire*. Verne is also Harry Nash's boss at Miller's Hardware Store.

Narrator   Though never given a name, the narrator of the story is a salesman who peddles storm windows and doors in the town of North Crawford. He is initially reluctant to direct the community theater production of *A Streetcar Named Desire*, but agrees to do so on the condition that Harry Nash play the role of Stanley Kowalski. Highly pleased with himself when Helene Shaw, a young woman he had met at the telephone company, is transformed by acting opposite Harry, the narrator is more concerned about his play than about the possibility that Helene will wind up being hurt by Harry when Harry melts back into his ordinary life. But things turn out well in the end when Helene tricks Harry into continuing to act. When the narrator meets Helene again after she and Harry are married, she confides that she is the luckiest girl in town. The narrator explains that he has been

asked to direct another play and begs Helene and Harry to star.

Nash, Harry   Harry Nash is a clerk at Miller's Hardware Store in North Crawford. A lonely man who is not married, does not go out with women or even with men friends, and who stays away from all social gatherings, Harry "never could think of anything to say or do without a script" (16). When he is acting, however, Harry is completely transformed, actually seeming to become the character he is portraying. He is the best actor in the town, and the story's narrator casts him as Stanley Kowalski in *A Streetcar Named Desire*. During rehearsals, the young woman playing Stella, Helene Shaw, falls deeply in love with Harry. Though Harry tries to return to his drab ordinary life after the last curtain falls, Helene gives him a gift of Shakespeare's *Romeo and Juliet* and begs Harry to read Romeo's lines. Thus, she hooks him; the two marry and live a rich and fulfilling life reading plays together.

Sawyer, Doris   Doris Sawyer is a 74-year-old woman who usually directs the plays put on by the North Crawford Mask and Wig Club. However, because her mother is ill, she insists that the story's narrator direct the production of Tennessee Williams's *A Streetcar Named Desire*. Doris helps the narrator cast the play, and like the narrator, she initially despairs at Helene Shaw's audition, but is delighted when Helene is transformed by the acting ability of Harry Nash.

Shaw, Helene   Helene Shaw has lived in North Crawford only a short time when the story opens. She travels from town to town in her job with the telephone company, teaching local girls how to use the company's new billing machine. When the narrator invites her to try out for the role of Stella in *A Streetcar Named Desire*, Helene is touched and surprised, telling him that no one has ever invited her to become involved in community activities. When she goes to the audition, though, she is terribly wooden in her acting. She explains to the narrator and Doris Sawyer that she wants to feel love, but has trouble relating to people since she has always moved around so much her whole life, even when she was a child. When she reads Stella's lines again, however, opposite Harry Nash playing Stanley this time, Helene is transformed. During rehearsals, she falls deeply in love with Harry, though she is warned by another actress that when the play is over Harry will revert to his drab self. Helene cleverly circumvents this by continually bringing plays to Harry for him to read with her. She and Harry soon marry and continue to act out parts, both very happy in the relationship.

FURTHER READING

Reed, Peter. *The Short Fiction of Kurt Vonnegut.* Westport, Conn.: Greenwood Press, 1997.
Welcome to the Monkey House. New York: Dell, 1998.

PART III

Related People, Places, and Topics

Abe Lincoln in Illinois *Abe Lincoln in Illinois,* a play written by Robert E. Sherwood that won the Pulitzer Prize for drama in 1938, is the production put on by the Pembroke Mask and Wig Club just before the clambake that ends the novel *Timequake.* Kilgore Trout is given the honor of doing the sound effects for the play.

abstract expressionist painting   Abstract expressionism is a post–World War II artistic movement originating in New York City. Considered to be the first truly original school of painting to have begun in America, abstract expressionism involved a diverse group of painters including JACKSON POLLOCK, Willem de Kooning, and Mark Rothko. Although the movement encompassed a multiplicity of styles, ranging from Pollock's drip paintings to the more figurative works of de Kooning, most of the paintings produced shared certain characteristics such as the use of large canvases, the "overall approach" to a canvas (filling the whole canvas, treating all parts of a canvas as equally important), an emphasis on spontaneity and improvisation that was intended to unleash the creativity of the subconscious mind, and an aversion to the social realism of 1930s painting. Vonnegut himself is an admirer of abstract expressionism, and this school of painting figures into several of his novels. In *Breakfast of Champions,* abstract artist Rabo Karabekian paints a Mark Rothko–like picture called "The Temptation of Saint Anthony," which consists of a vertical strip of Day-Glo orange reflect-

ing tape set against an avocado green background. Although the residents of MIDLAND CITY originally scorn this picture, Vonnegut, as a character in his own novel, finds redemption when Karabekian defends the simplicity and stripped-down essence of the painting. The novel *Bluebeard,* which is said to be the autobiography of Rabo Karabekian, returns to the question of the value of abstract expressionist art, pitting the abstract painter Karabekian against the lover of sentimental and realistic painting, the widow and young adult novelist Circe Berman. In *Bluebeard,* Vonnegut values both schools, recognizing merits and shortcomings in each. The novel ends with Vonnegut imagining a new kind of painting that seems to blend realism and abstract expressionism, somehow managing to break down the barriers that separate art from life itself.

Achebe, Chinua   Vonnegut first met Ibo writer Chinua Achebe when he went to Africa in 1970 as a sympathizer to the tiny Biafran nation, which had declared its independence from Nigeria in 1967, but which was then being defeated in a crushing war with the much larger country. Vonnegut's essay about BIAFRA was later reprinted in the collection *Wampeters, Foma, and Granfalloons.* In it, the young novelist, author of *Things Fall Apart,* tells Vonnegut that he no longer listens to the news, because it is always so bad. In the novel *Timequake,* Vonnegut explains that Achebe eventually left Africa to teach at Bard College in New York. When Vonnegut asks how the ethnic Ibo group is

Chinua Achebe and Langston Hughes in Lagos, Nigeria, July 1962.

doing now that a military junta is ruling Nigeria, Achebe replies that Ibos play no role in the government, nor do they wish to.

Adams, India   India Adams is the daughter of Vonnegut's oldest adopted son, James Adams, and his wife BARBARA D'ARTHANAY. In the collection *Palm Sunday*, Vonnegut writes that his granddaughter's name "resonates with the innocent imperialism of earlier white colonists" in the New England wilderness (225).

Adams, James, Jr.   James Adams is the oldest son of Vonnegut's sister Alice and her husband, JAMES CARMALT ADAMS. Fourteen years old when both his parents died, James, along with his two younger brothers, was adopted by Vonnegut and his wife, JANE COX VONNEGUT YARMOLINSKY. In the collection *Palm Sunday*, Vonnegut tells readers that, as an adult, James Adams became a Peace Corps volunteer in Peru, then a goat farmer in Jamaica, and later a cabinetmaker in Leverett, Massachusetts (225).

Adams, James Carmalt   James Carmalt Adams was the husband of Vonnegut's older sister, ALICE VONNEGUT. An editor for a trade journal aimed at purchasing agents, Adams died in 1958 in a commuter train crash in New York two mornings before Alice Vonnegut succumbed to cancer. Vonnegut and his wife, Jane, subsequently adopted the three oldest Adams boys.

Adams, Kurt   The youngest of the three Adams brothers adopted by Vonnegut and his wife, Jane, in 1958, Kurt Adams was nine years old at the time. In *Palm Sunday*, Vonnegut tells readers that Kurt later went on to become an airline pilot and "a builder on speculation of beautiful post-and-beam houses which are entirely heated by wood stoves" (228), and that he married an artist named LINDSAY PALERMO.

Adams, Steven   Steven Adams is the middle child of the three Adams boys whom Vonnegut and his wife, Jane, adopted after the deaths of ALICE VONNEGUT and her husband JAMES CARMALT ADAMS. Eleven years old when he joined Vonnegut's household, Steve went on to graduate from Dartmouth University before moving to Los Angeles to become a television comedy writer. In *Palm Sunday*, Vonnegut says that he knows Steve "least well" of all his children, "since, to his credit, he has had the least need" of Vonnegut's help in his life (227).

Ainsworth, Dr. Mary   Dr. Mary Ainsworth is one of the lesser-known individuals whom Vonnegut imagines interviewing in the afterlife in his short book *God Bless You, Dr. Kevorkian*. Dr. Ainsworth was a developmental psychologist who studied the mother-infant bond, a connection Vonnegut is interested in as a possible explanation for his own psychology.

Alcoholics Anonymous   Alcoholics Anonymous, a self-help group for recovering alcoholics, is an organization for which Vonnegut has a great fondness, and which he discusses in many of his essays and fiction pieces. Vonnegut views Alcoholics Anonymous as providing its members with a feeling of belonging—the type of supportive extended family that used to exist in more primitive societies, but which is largely lacking in modern-day America. In the prologue to his novel *Slapstick*, Vonnegut notes that his uncle, ALEX VONNEGUT, cofounded the INDIANAPOLIS chapter of Alcoholics Anonymous. Although Alex's obituary mentioned his involvement in the group, it stated that Alex was not himself an alcoholic, a denial that Vonnegut views as a "nice-Nellyism from the past" (9).

Algren, Nelson   In the collection *Fates Worse Than Death*, Vonnegut tells readers about attempting to arrange a meeting between the British-Indian novelist SALMAN RUSHDIE and American author Nelson Algren, who chronicled the lives of the down-and-out in seedy South Chicago. Rushdie wished to meet Algren because he believed the author had written the most intelligent review published of his novel *Midnight's Children*. When Vonnegut called Algren's house, however, he discovered that the author had died of a heart attack that very morning.

American Academy of Arts and Letters   The American Academy of Arts and Letters is an organization made up of 250 writers, composers, painters, sculptors and artists, whose mission is to promote the fine arts. Kurt Vonnegut was elected to a lifetime membership in the organization in 1973. The academy figures prominently in Vonnegut's novel *Timequake*. Not only do characters Monica Pepper and Dudley Prince work there, but the academy's office is located next door to the homeless shelter in Manhattan where Kilgore Trout has been living. Vonnegut also discusses the academy in his collection *Fates Worse Than Death*, in which he says it is a "random matter" who gets voted in and who does not, since "it is the loonies who do the nominating and then the voting, which is to say the artists and writers and musicians who already belong" (67).

American Humanist Association   Kurt Vonnegut served as honorary president of the American Humanist Association, an organization founded in 1941 to promote human rights, civil liberties, and equality. In several of his works, he discusses the AHA, often pointing out that he succeeded the late SCIENCE FICTION writer ISAAC ASIMOV in his "functionless capacity" as president (*Timequake* 82).

Andrewes, Lancelot   Lancelot Andrewes was an English clergyman and scholar during the Renaissance who oversaw the translation of the King James Version of the Christian Bible. In his novel *Timequake*, Vonnegut says that Lancelot Andrewes was "the greatest writer in the English language so far" (131).

Angels Without Wings   *Angels Without Wings: A Courageous Family's Triumph over Tragedy* is a memoir written by JANE COX VONNEGUT YARMOLINSKY, Vonnegut's first wife, about the family's adopting of the three Adams boys after the deaths of ALICE VONNEGUT and JAMES CARMALT ADAMS. Yarmolinsky had left the work unfinished when she died of cancer, but the book was completed by her publisher and published posthumously in 1987. *Angels Without Wings* was made into a 1990 television movie called *A Promise to Keep*.

Armenian genocide   During the years 1915–17, hundreds of thousands (some estimates say more than a million) ethnic Armenians were killed during mass evacuations and executions in the Ottoman Empire. Although Turkey long denied that a genocide took place, attributing the Armenian deaths to disease, famine, and interethnic fighting, most scholars today use the term *genocide* in discussing the killings, and view them as a systemic attempt by the Ottoman Empire to exterminate Armenians. The Armenian genocide plays an important role in Vonnegut's novel *Bluebeard*. Both of Rabo Karabekian's parents are Armenian survivors of Turkish massacres.

Armistice Day   Armistice Day is the older name for the U.S. holiday currently called Veterans Day, which falls on November 11. It was originally instituted to celebrate the signing of the armistice that brought an end to World War I. Vonnegut's birthday is November 11, and he writes in some of his works about his love for the original holiday. In *Breakfast of Champions*, for instance, he explains to readers that "Armistice Day was sacred. Veterans' Day is not" (6).

Asimov, Isaac   The late, Russian-born SCIENCE FICTION writer Isaac Asimov, whom Vonnegut

Dr. Isaac Asimov, 1965 *(courtesy of the Library of Congress)*

succeeded as honorary president of the AMERICAN HUMANIST ASSOCIATION after Asimov's death in 1992, figures into several Vonnegut works. In the novel *Timequake*, Vonnegut tells readers about speaking at a Humanist Association memorial service for Dr. Asimov. He told the crowd, "Isaac is up in Heaven now," a joke Vonnegut claims left the audience rolling in the aisles with laughter. Isaac Asimov also appears in a short vignette in *God Bless You, Dr. Kevorkian*, as one of the people Vonnegut imagines interviewing in the afterlife. Vonnegut asks Asimov how he accounts for his incredible productivity, and Asimov replies "Escape," then ends the book by quoting French philosopher Jean-Paul Sartre: "Hell is other people" (78).

atomic bomb   The dropping of the atomic bombs on Hiroshima and Nagasaki at the end of World War II concerns Vonnegut deeply and is something that he writes about often. The apocalyptic doomsday device *ice-nine* in the novel *Cat's Cradle* can be read as a metaphor for the bomb and for the amoral science that allowed its invention. One of Vonnegut's repeated themes is a critique of scientific and technological advancements achieved at the expense of human beings. Elsewhere in his work, however, Vonnegut acknowledges that the Hiroshima bombing might have been justified. In the novel *Timequake*, for instance, he defers to the opinion of his friend, the writer William Styron, who claims that the Hiroshima bomb saved his life. Yet, after relating this anecdote, Vonnegut adds that he knows of a single word that proves the American government "was capable of committing obscene, gleefully rabid and racist, yahooistic murders of unarmed men, women, and children, murders wholly devoid of military common sense" (196). That word is *Nagasaki*.

B

Barnstable Village After quitting his job with the GENERAL ELECTRIC Company in 1951, Vonnegut moved with his family to Barnstable Village, on CAPE COD, Massachusetts, where he owned and operated the first Saab dealership in America. Although the car dealership went bankrupt, Vonnegut stayed on Cape Cod, except for brief stints as a visiting writer in various locales, for the next 20 years. Many of the stories in *Welcome to the Monkey House* are either set specifically in Barnstable or else in similar small New England villages modeled after Barnstable. The story "Where I Live" focuses particularly on Barnstable; it is a story about the changes that increased tourism has brought to Cape Cod, and the fight of Barnstable villagers to ward off these changes.

Barus, Alice Möllman Alice Möllman Barus was one of Vonnegut's maternal great-grandmothers, the wife of musician KARL BARUS.

Barus, Karl Professor Karl Barus, who taught voice, violin, and piano in INDIANAPOLIS in the mid-19th-century, was one of Vonnegut's maternal great-grandfathers. An intellectual and art lover who also conducted orchestras, Barus is said by JOHN RAUCH, in his account of the Vonnegut ancestry reprinted in *Palm Sunday*, to have had an "incalculable" influence on the musical taste and sophistication of the entire city (32).

Battle of the Bulge The Battle of the Bulge is the popular name given to a German World War II offensive conducted in December 1944 and known officially as the Ardennes Offensive. A surprise attack that caught the Allies off guard, the battle was deadly to American troops—more than 75,000 Americans were killed, wounded, or captured in the fighting. Among those captured was the 22-year-old infantry scout Kurt Vonnegut, who was taken to DRESDEN as a prisoner of war, where he survived the Allied firebombing that took place in February of 1945. Vonnegut writes a fictional account of these experiences in his best-known and most critically acclaimed novel, *Slaughterhouse-Five*.

Beagle, the The *Beagle* is the name of the ship on which CHARLES DARWIN, beginning in 1835, took a five-year scientific voyage to South America and the GALÁPAGOS ISLANDS. In the novel *Galápagos*, narrator Leon Trout compares the *Bahia de Darwin*—a luxury liner built to take tourists to the islands made famous by Charles Darwin so many years before—to the original *Beagle*, pointing out how much smaller and simpler the earlier ship had been.

Bernstein, Leonard In the novel *Timequake*, the chair used by Monica Pepper at the AMERICAN ACADEMY OF ARTS AND LETTERS is said to have once belonged to the American composer and conductor Leonard Bernstein.

Biafra The Republic of Biafra was a tiny country that seceded from Nigeria in 1967, but which was forced to give up its independence in 1970 through military conquest by the larger country. Vonnegut visited Biafra just before its fall and writes about this experience in an article that is reprinted in the collection *Wampeters, Foma, and Granfalloons*. Sympathetic to the Biafran cause and appalled by the suffering he witnesses in the country, Vonnegut writes of his admiration for the spirit of the Biafran people.

Biagini, Salvatore   Salvatore Biagini was a retired construction worker who suffered a fatal heart attack while protecting his beloved dog from an attack by a pit bull in Queens, New York. He is one of the people whom Vonnegut imagines interviewing in the afterlife in *God Bless You, Dr. Kevorkian*. Vonnegut seems drawn to Biagini because he was a "heroic pet lover," who tells the writer that dying for his pet schnauzer "sure as heck beat dying for absolutely nothing in the Viet Nam War" (26).

Bierce, Ambrose   Ambrose Bierce was a late 19th-century American fiction writer, journalist, and critic who was famous for his bitter and acerbic wit as well as for his mysterious disappearance in Mexico in 1913. In Vonnegut's collection *A Man Without a Country*, he writes that he considers "anybody a twerp who hasn't read the greatest American short story, which is 'Occurrence at Owl Creek Bridge,' by Ambrose Bierce" (7–8).

Birnum, Birnum   Birnum Birnum, an Australian aborigine who organized demonstrations that won citizenship for his people, is one of the departed souls whom Vonnegut imagines interviewing in the afterlife in *God Bless You, Dr. Kevorkian*. When Vonnegut asks him for his opinion on the neighboring native Tasmanians, Birnum Birnum replies that "they were victims of the only completely successful genocide of which we know" (28).

black humor   Black humor is a mode of artistic expression in literature, drama, and film in which usually serious or tragic subjects—war, death, atrocity—are treated in a darkly comic fashion in order to express the cruelty or absurdity of the contemporary world. In literature, black humor is

most often associated with the work of Vonnegut, JOSEPH HELLER, Thomas Pynchon, Philip Roth, and other writers who came to prominence in the 1950s and '60s.

Blake, William   Eliot Rosewater, in *God Bless You, Mr. Rosewater*, runs his foundation out of a former dentist's office. The optimistic Eliot has painted the words of a poem by William Blake over the signs the dentist had nailed to the risers of the stairs. The poem reads, "The Angel that presided o'er my birth/Said, "Little creature, form'd of Joy and Mirth,/Go love without the help of any Thing on Earth." In response, Eliot's father, the negative and moralistic Senator Rosewater writes another William Blake poem in pencil on the wall at the foot of the stairs. The lines the senator writes make up the concluding stanza of Blake's poem "The Clod and The Pebble":

> Love seeketh only Self to please,
> To bind another to Its delight,
> Joys in another's loss of ease,
> And builds a Hell in Heaven's despite.

Blavatsky, Helena Petrovna   Ukranian-born Helena Blavatsky, better known as Madame Blavatsky, was a 19th-century mystic and founder of the THEOSOPHICAL SOCIETY, an organization dedicated to the practice of mediumship, or attempts to contact the spirits of the dead, as well as to the study of Eastern religions and spiritual practices, and to a belief in worldwide brotherhood and the underlying unity of all religions. In his collection *Wampeters, Foma, and Granfalloons*, Vonnegut includes an essay titled "The Mysterious Madame Blavatsky" in which he gently mocks some of the more convoluted and pseudo-mystical of Blavatsky's pronouncements, all the while appreciating the charm and audacity of a woman who dared to travel the globe and to believe that "all human beings were her brothers and sisters" (139).

Bob and Ray   The American comedy team of Bob Elliott and Ray Goulding, better known as Bob and Ray, were popular performers on radio and television primarily during the 1940s, '50s and '60s.

Vonnegut counts himself as a devoted fan of their comedy and wrote the introduction to their 1975 book, *Write If You Get Work: The Best of Bob & Ray*, in which he describes the comedians' jokes as "remarkably literary," as "fun to read as well as to hear" (*Palm Sunday* 127).

Bolívar, Símon   In Vonnegut's novel *Cat's Cradle*, the only city on the island of San Lorenzo is named Bolivar, in honor of "the great Latin-American idealist and hero" (133), Símon Bolívar. The historical Bolívar was a Venezuelan who, in the early 19th-century, led the fight for independence of several South American countries.

Böll, Heinrich   Winner of the 1972 Nobel Prize for literature, Heinrich Böll was a German World War II veteran who started writing fiction after his return from the war. Vonnegut discusses Böll, whom he met at an international congress of the writers' organization P.E.N. in Sweden in 1973, in the preface to his collection *Fates Worse Than Death*. The German writer, according to Vonnegut, represented "one of the last shreds of native German sorrow and shame about his country's part in World War II and its prelude" (14). Vonnegut reports that Böll told him "he was despised by his neighbors for remembering when it was time to forget" (14).

Bonner, Elena   Elena Bonner was the pediatrician wife of Soviet physicist and nuclear scientist ANDREI SAKHAROV. In his novel *Timequake*, Vonnegut suggests that Bonner, who accepted the Nobel Peace Prize on behalf of her husband in 1975, whom the Soviet Union would not allow to leave the country, was more deserving of the prize herself for her work healing children than Sakharov was for demanding a halt to the testing of weapons that he had helped create.

Brown, John   John Brown, the 19th-century radical abolitionist hanged for leading an assault on the Federal Armory at Harpers Ferry, Virginia, is one of the dead people that Vonnegut imagines interviewing in *God Bless You, Dr. Kevorkian*. In this piece, Vonnegut writes that he congratulated

Brown "on what he'd said on his way to be hanged before a gleeful, jeering throng of white folks . . . 'This is a beautiful country.' In only five words, he had somehow encapsulated the full horror of the most hideous legal atrocities committed by a civilized nation until the Holocaust" (30).

Buckley, William F., Jr.   In *Palm Sunday*, Vonnegut reprints an essay on conservative thinker and writer William F. Buckley, Jr. that first appeared in the journal *Politics Today* in 1979. In this essay, Vonnegut ostensibly praises Buckley's good looks and impressive accomplishments, as well as his geniality, but at the same time subtlety points out Buckley's fortunate circumstances in being born into a wealthy, aristocratic family and critiques his views as representing an uncharitable form of social Darwinism.

Burger, Knox   Knox Burger was a fiction editor at *Collier's* magazine, where Vonnegut published his first story, "Report on the Barnhouse Effect," in 1950. In a *Paris Review* interview reprinted in the collection *Palm Sunday*, Vonnegut claims that Knox Burger "discovered and encouraged more good young writers than any other editor of his time" (102). Burger later served as literary agent for Vonnegut's son Mark. Vonnegut also refers to Knox Burger in the Preface to *Breakfast of Champions*, where he cites Burger as saying that a clunky novel ". . . read as though it had been written by Philboyd Studge" (4).

Burke, Roberta Gorsuch   Roberta Gorsuch Burke is one of the departed souls whom Vonnegut imagines interviewing in *God Bless You, Dr. Kevorkian*. The widow of navy admiral Arly A. Burke, Roberta Burke seems to have caught Vonnegut's eye for having been so devoted to her husband for more than 70 years of marriage. The epitaph Roberta chooses for her tombstone says simply, "A Sailor's Wife."

Burroughs, Edgar Rice   In *Player Piano*, Edgar R. B. Hagstrohm, an ordinary worker and family man who lives in suburban Chicago, is named after his father's favorite writer, Edgar Rice Burroughs, author of the 1912 best seller *Tarzan of*

the Apes as well as a host of other books in the Tarzan series. Precisely because he is deemed to be so completely average, Hagstrohm is chosen to be the recipient of a visit by the shah of Bratpuhr, who desires to observe an ordinary American family in action. Ironically, Hagstrohm breaks out of his stultifying, machinelike normalcy when he cuts up his home with a blowtorch and—perhaps desiring to emulate his namesake's most famous creation—runs naked to the home of his mistress and demands that she come live in the woods with him.

Caesar Augustus In *God Bless You, Mr. Rose-water*, Senator Rosewater (Eliot's father) delivers a famous speech in the Senate chamber on the Golden Age of Rome in which he extols Roman ruler Caesar Augustus for ruthlessly enforcing morality that he had written into law.

Cape Cod Vonnegut lived in BARNSTABLE VILLAGE, on the Massachusetts peninsula of Cape Cod, from 1951 to 1971. He writes about this region frequently, especially in his short fiction of the 1950s.

Céline, Louis-Ferdinand Louis-Ferdinand Céline was the pen name of early 20th-century French writer and physician Louis-Ferdinand Destouches. Wounded during service in the French cavalry in World War I, Céline went on to publish his most famous work, *Journey to the End of the Night*, in 1932. He was later criticized and imprisoned as an outspoken anti-Semite and suspected Nazi sympathizer during the World War II years. Céline is mentioned in the opening chapter of *Slaughterhouse-Five*, in which Vonnegut describes an "amazing scene" (21) from the novel *Death on the Installment Plan*. In the autobiographical collage *Palm Sunday*, Vonnegut tells of writing introductions for new paperback editions of Céline's final three books. Recognizing that many people will believe that he himself shares many of Céline's "authentically vile opinions" (266), Vonnegut nevertheless finds much to admire about the author, claiming that "Céline gave us in his novels the finest history we have of the total collapse of Western civilization in two world wars, as witnessed by hideously vulnerable common women and men" (267).

Channing, William Ellery William Ellery Channing was a prominent Unitarian theologian and preacher in the early part of the 19th century. In January 1980, at a celebration for the 200th anniversary of Channing's birth, Vonnegut delivered a speech at the First Parish Unitarian Church in Cambridge, Massachusetts, in which he credits Channing's accomplishments to the fact that the minister was born into a social group much like the primitive folk societies that Vonnegut talks about repeatedly in his work. This speech is reprinted in the collection *Palm Sunday*.

Chermayeff, Ivan Ivan Chermayeff is a graphic artist and industrial designer whom Vonnegut collaborated with on the children's book *Sun Moon Star*, published by Harper & Row in 1980.

Children's Crusade, The The first subtitle Vonnegut gives his novel *Slaughterhouse-Five* is *The Children's Crusade*. The subtitle comes from a promise Vonnegut tells readers he made to Mary O'Hare, the wife of his old war buddy BERNARD V. O'HARE. Worried that Vonnegut's book about DRESDEN will glamorize war, Mary insists that wars are fought by babies, like her own children upstairs. Upon learning of her concerns, Vonnegut solemnly pledges to Mary that his book will not contain a part for Frank Sinatra or John Wayne. He chooses the subtitle *The Children's Crusade* after he and Bernard O'Hare read about the historical children's crusade. The two men discover that in 1213 thousands of French and German children had been duped into joining an army that was supposed to fight infidels in the holy lands, but the children were actually sold into slavery in North Africa.

Chomsky, Noam   In the novel *Timequake*, Vonnegut, in order to subvert Kilgore Trout's claim that Native Americans were "dumb" (101), quotes M.I.T. linguist and political philosopher Noam Chomsky, who writes about the devastation caused to indigenous people in the Americas by Columbus's voyages. Vonnegut does defend Trout at the end of this passage, saying that Trout is actually trying to raise the question, "perhaps too subtly" (102) of whether great discoveries, such as the visiting of the Americas by Europeans, "really make people any happier than they were before" (102).

Christianity   While not a conventional Christian by any means, Vonnegut, over and over again in his work, expresses admiration for Jesus Christ of the Christian New Testament, and especially for the words Christ is said to have spoken in his Sermon on the Mount. In the novel *Jailbird*, Vonnegut recounts a story in which a judge asks labor organizer POWERS HAPGOOD why a HARVARD-educated man from a privileged background would choose to live and work among coal miners and socialists (*see* SOCIALISM). Hapgood replies, "Because of the Sermon on the Mount, sir" (12), a simple phrase that will echo throughout the novel. Vonnegut even goes so far as to refer to himself as a "Christ-worshipping agnostic" in a sermon he delivered at St. Clement's Episcopal Church in New York on Palm Sunday, 1980 (*Palm Sunday* 298), and in *A Man Without a Country*, he calls Christ the "greatest and most humane of human beings" (95). This admiration, however, does not prevent Vonnegut from critiquing what he considers to be hypocritical forms of Christianity or from rewriting Gospel stories that he believes deliver an incorrect message. In the Palm Sunday sermon, he reimagines Christ as making a "divine black joke"

(300) when he tells Judas Iscariot that "the poor you always have with you, but you do not always have me." Vonnegut also has his fictional alter ego Kilgore Trout, in *Slaughterhouse-Five*, rewrite the story of Christ's crucifixion so that God adopts Christ as his son only after he has been killed, thus delivering the message that it is important to be merciful to all, not only to those who are "well-connected" (109).

City College of New York   For a brief period in 1973 and 1974, Vonnegut was Distinguished Professor of English Prose at the City College of New York, where he taught creative writing courses.

Coffin, Tris and Margaret   Tris and Margaret Coffin, friends of Vonnegut, are publishers of a four-page weekly called *The Washington Spectator*. In the collection *Fates Worse Than Death*, Vonnegut says that the Coffins are among his pantheon of secular saints (191), human beings that he believes make life worth living.

Coleridge, Samuel Taylor   British romantic poet Samuel Taylor Coleridge appears in the novel *Timequake* when Vonnegut quotes his famous line about poetry requiring a "willing suspension of disbelief" (101). While Vonnegut believes that "this acceptance of balderdash is essential to the enjoyment of poems, and of novels and short stories, and of dramas, too," he nevertheless claims that "some assertions by writers . . . are simply too preposterous to be believed" (101). He then goes on to castigate his own fictional creation, Kilgore Trout, for claiming, in his memoir *My Ten Years on Automatic Pilot*, that Native Americans were "dumb" at the time Columbus arrived.

***Cornell Daily Sun*, The**   The *Cornell Daily Sun* is the student-run newspaper of CORNELL UNIVERSITY in Ithaca, New York. Vonnegut worked as a staff writer and managing editor for the paper when he was a Cornell student during the early 1940s. In the collection *Palm Sunday*, Vonnegut reprints a speech he made to the staff of The *Cornell Daily Sun* at the paper's annual banquet in 1980. In the speech, Vonnegut reminisces especially about how he found a family while working for the newspaper and that his happiest memories of his time at Cornell are of walking up a hill very late at night after having "helped to put the *Sun* to bed" (60).

Cornell University   Vonnegut enrolled at Cornell University in 1940 as a biochemistry major. As he discusses in several essays, his father pushed him toward a career in science, hoping Kurt would emulate his older brother, Bernard. Yet, Vonnegut did poorly in his coursework at the university, dedicating himself more fully to his work as editor for THE CORNELL DAILY SUN than to his science classes. Following a bout with pneumonia, and with failing grades, Vonnegut left Cornell in 1943 and later enlisted in the U.S. Army.

Costa, Tony   Tony Costa, a notorious mass murderer on CAPE COD who was convicted in 1970 of dismembering and burying several young woman, and who later hanged himself in prison, was also a friend of Vonnegut's daughter Edith. In the essay collection *Wampeters, Foma, and Granfalloons*, Vonnegut includes an essay on Costa in which he muses about the killer, telling readers of his daughter's surprised reaction to Costa's arrest: "If Tony is a murderer, then *anybody* could be a murderer" (69).

Cox, Riah Fagan   Riah Fagan Cox was the mother of Vonnegut's first wife, JANE COX VONNEGUT YARMOLINSKY. An intelligent and resourceful woman who put herself through college and graduate school, and who later worked as a writer as well as a teacher of Latin and Greek, Riah Cox was "a good friend" to Vonnegut, who writes in the collection *Palm Sunday* that he "liked her a lot" (202). Nevertheless, Vonnegut also points out that Riah Cox disapproved of Vonnegut's use of "certain impolite words" in his work, imagining that he used these words "to cause a sensation" and to make his books more popular (202). Vonnegut uses this example as a stepping-off point for an essay on obscenity, in which he argues that writers must be impolite, that too much politeness makes people blind to problems as they really exist in society.

Crane, Stephen   In *Slaughterhouse-Five*, Edgar Derby, the doomed high school teacher who is a fellow prisoner of war in DRESDEN with Billy Pilgrim, reads a copy of Stephen Crane's famous Civil War novel, *The Red Badge of Courage*, while watching over Billy in the prisoner's infirmary after Billy has been given morphine. Crane's novel, very much about courage and fear during war, is a logical choice for Derby, the only potentially heroic character among the prisoners. Vonnegut undermines the very notion of courage in *Slaughterhouse-Five*, however, as the climax of the book shows poor old Edgar Derby being shot by a German firing squad for supposedly pilfering a teapot.

Crone, Joe   Joe Crone was a fellow prisoner of war with Vonnegut in DRESDEN. In the collection *Fates Worse Than Death*, Vonnegut says that Crone is the model for the character Billy Pilgrim in *Slaughterhouse-Five* (106). Unlike Billy Pilgrim, however, who returns from the war to become a

Dedication to Joe Crone from a manuscript version of *Slaughterhouse-Five (courtesy of The Lilly Library, Indiana University, Bloomington, Indiana)*

wealthy optometrist in ILIUM, New York, Crone died in the Dresden prisoner camp. He insisted on giving away to other prisoners all the food he received to eat. If his fellow prisoners would not accept his food, Crone reportedly threw it away. Consequently, he ended up starving to death. Vonnegut remembers that Crone was buried in Dresden in a white paper suit.

D

Darrow, Clarence Famous defense attorney Clarence Darrow, perhaps best known for his work in the Scopes Monkey Trial of 1925, is one of the dead people whom Vonnegut interviews in *God Bless You, Dr. Kevorkian*. Darrow, from the afterlife, tells Vonnegut his opinion on cameras in courtrooms: "The presence of those cameras finally acknowledges . . . that justice systems anywhere, anytime, have never cared whether justice was achieved or not. Like Roman games, justice systems are ways for unjust governments—and there is not any other sort of government—to be enormously entertaining with real lives at stake" (36).

D'Arthanay, Barbara Barbara D'Arthanay is the wife of Vonnegut's oldest adopted son, JAMES ADAMS, whose biological parents were Vonnegut's sister Alice and her husband, JAMES CARMALT ADAMS. In *Palm Sunday*, Vonnegut describes Barbara as a "former New England schoolteacher who lived and worked with [her husband] for several years on his goat farm on a mountaintop in Jamaica" (225). Vonnegut goes on to claim that the couple "are as uninterested in social rank and property as was Henry David Thoreau" (225).

Darwin, Charles Nineteenth-century naturalist Charles Darwin, author of *On the Origin of Species by Natural Selection* and the father of modern evolutionary theory, figures prominently in several of Vonnegut's works. In *Slaughterhouse-Five*, Billy Pil-

grim claims that the Tralfamadorians are not much interested in Jesus Christ: "The Earthling figure who is most engaging to the Tralfamadorian mind . . . is Charles Darwin—who taught that those who die are meant to die, that corpses are improvements. So it goes" (210). Vonnegut himself expresses a similar view of Darwin when he says, in an interview given to *Playboy* magazine and reprinted in *Wampeters, Foma, and Granfalloons*, that he is "not very grateful for Darwin," because Darwin's ideas "make people crueler" (237). Vonnegut especially laments a form of social Darwinism that teaches that human beings get what they deserve; sick people deserve to be sick, and "any man who's on top is there because he's a superior animal" (238). In *Timequake*, Vonnegut remembers asking his older, scientist brother BERNARD VONNEGUT whether he believes in Darwin's theory. Bernard replies that he does, "Because it's the only game in town" (188). The Vonnegut work that most directly addresses Darwin's theories of evolution and natural selection, though, is the novel *Galápagos*, in which Vonnegut depicts the human species devolving into small-brained, furry sea creatures, a change that the novel's narrator, Leon Trout, sees as a positive one. While Vonnegut recognizes that many popular interpretations of Darwin's theories are inaccurate, he nevertheless argues that *On the Origin of Species* "did more to stabilize people's volatile opinions of how to identify success or failure than any other tome" (*Galápagos* 14).

Davis, Alvin In *Timequake*, Vonnegut tells about his late friend, the journalist Alvin Davis, who was an alcoholic and gambler. According to Davis, the "biggest kick" (31) he ever got from playing games of chance occurred once when he had lost all his money in an all-night poker game. After leaving the table for a few hours to beg and borrow money from friends, he returned and requested that the other players deal him in.

Death of a Salesman In *Timequake*, Vonnegut cites Arthur Miller's play *Death of a Salesman*, along with other modern plays, as moving him tremendously and helping build his moral outlook on life. He speculates that the communal experience of theatergoing is partly responsible for these plays' powerful effects on him.

Debs, Eugene Eugene Debs was a labor organizer and five-time Socialist Party (*see* SOCIALISM) candidate for U.S. president in the early 20th century. An Indiana native like Vonnegut, Debs is one of the writer's personal heroes. Vonnegut dedicates the novel *Hocus Pocus* to him, names his main character Eugene Debs Hartke after him, and includes Debs's most famous quote as the novel's epigraph: "While there is a lower class I am in it. While there is a criminal element I am of it. While there is a soul in prison I am not free." In *Timequake*, Vonnegut tells readers that he still cites this passage from Debs in every speech he gives, but that now he finds it prudent to inform audience members that the quote "is to be taken *seriously*" (142). Vonnegut imagines telling Debs himself that people have begun to ridicule his views in the collection *God Bless You, Dr. Kevorkian*, in which the labor organizer serves as one of the 21 dead people Vonnegut interviews about the afterlife. At the end of this vignette, Vonnegut imagines Debs as an angel, spreading his wings and soaring away. Finally, in the collection *A Man Without a Country*, Vonnegut refers to Debs as one of his "favorite humans" (96) and compares Debs's famous quote to Christ's Sermon on the Mount.

Dees, Morris Morris Dees, founder of the Southern Poverty Law Center, is one of the people whom

Eugene Debs, 1912 *(courtesy of the Library of Congress)*

Vonnegut describes as a "saint" in the collection *Fates Worse Than Death* (191)

determinism In philosophy, determinism is the belief that everything that happens in the universe is the cause of preexisting circumstances and unalterable laws of nature and therefore cannot be changed by human will. Critics have often debated whether Vonnegut's fiction supports a deterministic view of the universe. Often his characters' actions seem doomed to failure no matter what they do. In *Sirens of Titan*, for instance, Winston Niles Rumfoord tells his wife, Beatrice, that she will have to "take the roller coaster ride of the future" that he has foreseen, no matter what he himself does to try to prevent this (54). Similarly, the Bokononist religion in *Cat's Cradle* and the Tralfamadorian worldview in *Slaughterhouse-Five* offer deterministic philosophies of life. Bokononism teaches that God has elaborate plans for each individual human being and the events that occur in a human life serve as nudges toward that final fate.

The Tralfamadorians completely negate the notion of FREE WILL, explaining to Billy Pilgrim that they can see all time at once, the future as well as the past, and that there is no way to change a future that is already in existence. Despite these examples, Vonnegut still admires human beings who refuse to accept a determinist philosophy, who try to change the universe, although he fully realizes that such attempts might ultimately prove futile.

Dillinger, John   John Dillinger, a famed 1930s era bank robber born in INDIANAPOLIS, is mentioned in several Vonnegut works. In his prologue to *Jailbird*, Vonnegut writes that Dillinger was "the Robin Hood" of his early youth (1), informing readers as well that the notorious gangster is buried in Crown Hill Cemetery in Indianapolis, near Vonnegut's parents and his sister Alice, who admired Dillinger even more than her younger brother did. In *Timequake*, Vonnegut again refers to the admiration both he and his sister felt for Dillinger, whom he believes was killed "because he had for too long made G-men . . . look . . . like nincompoops" (41).

Dostoevsky, Feodor   In *Slaughterhouse-Five*, Eliot Rosewater tells Billy Pilgrim, while both men are confined to a mental hospital after serving in World War II, that "everything there was to know about life was in *The Brothers Karamazov*" (101), the 1880 novel considered the culminating work of Russian writer Feodor Dostoevsky. But, adds Rosewater, "that isn't *enough* any more" (101). Because of their traumatic war experiences, Vonnegut explains, Billy and Rosewater try to reinvent themselves and their universe. Older literature, no matter how valuable it was in the past, does not seem to apply to the contemporary world, so the two men turn to SCIENCE FICTION.

Dresden   Vonnegut's experiences as a prisoner of war in Dresden, Germany, in early 1945 serve as the inspiration for his critically acclaimed novel *Slaughterhouse-Five*. An infantry scout captured during the BATTLE OF THE BULGE in December 1944, Vonnegut was transported to Dresden in January 1945, where he worked, with other prisoners, as a slave laborer in a German factory that made vitamin supplements for pregnant women. In Dresden, he was housed in a concrete compound originally built for slaughtering animals and storing meats—the "Slaughterhouse-Five" of the novel's title. On the night of February 13, 1945, Allied forces began a bombing raid on the historic city, causing firestorms that burned thousands upon thousands of people to death and destroyed the city. Relying on the work of British historian DAVID IRVING, Vonnegut claims in *Slaughterhouse-Five* that up to 250,000 people were killed in the firebombings, but best estimates today put the number between 25,000 and 35,000. Following the massacre, the Germans put Vonnegut and his fellow prisoners to work digging out corpses and cleaning up the rubble from the bombings.

dystopic literature   Dystopic literature presents future worlds that are the opposite of utopias, or ideal civilizations. In these books, some crisis has often sparked the institution of an authoritarian form of government that represses individuality. While the best-known pieces of dystopic fiction include George Orwell's *1984* and Aldous Huxley's *Brave New World*, many of Vonnegut's works can also be classified this way, particularly his early novels *Player Piano* and *Cat's Cradle* as well as several of his short stories, including "Harrison Bergeron," "Welcome to the Monkey House," and "Tomorrow and Tomorrow and Tomorrow," among others.

E

Eaker, Ira C. When Billy Pilgrim is hospitalized with a head injury after a plane crash in *Slaughterhouse-Five*, his hospital roommate, Colonel Bertram Copeland Rumfoord, reads a book called *The Destruction of Dresden* actually written by British historian DAVID IRVING. One of the forewords to the book is by Ira C. Eaker, a retired U.S. Air Force lieutenant general. In his foreword, Eaker defends the necessity of the DRESDEN bombing.

echolalia Echolalia is a condition marked by the repetition of verbal utterances made by another person. It is common in those suffering from autism, Tourette syndrome, and schizophrenia. Vonnegut takes a particular interest in this condition, having several characters suffer from it. In *Slaughterhouse-Five*, when Billy Pilgrim is taken to the hospital after the plane crash on Sugarbush Mountain, he shares a room with HARVARD UNIVERSITY history professor Bertram Copeland Rumfoord, who refuses to believe that Billy was actually in the fire-bombing of DRESDEN, and who insists to the doctors and nurses that Billy has echolalia. Also, in *Breakfast of Champions*, Dwayne Hoover, who is slowly going insane, is said at one point to have "incipient echolalia" (135) when he begins echoing the last word of sentences he hears on the radio.

Eden Express, The *The Eden Express: A Memoir of Insanity*, published in 1975, is an autobiographical acccount written by Vonnegut's oldest son,

MARK VONNEGUT, about his mental breakdown in early 1971, his confinement in a mental institution, and his subsequent recovery.

Edison, Thomas Prolific American inventor Thomas Alva Edison figures into several of Vonnegut's works. In *Player Piano*, Dr. Paul Proteus likes to visit Building 58 at the ILIUM Works, which had originally been a machine shop set up by Edison in 1886. Edison in this novel suggests the can-do, engineering spirit that Vonnegut admires in Americans, but that also causes many of the problems in the book as characters invent machines that outperform humans and eventually put large numbers of people out of work. In *Slapstick*, Thomas Edison appears briefly as a guest at a dinner party where Professor Elihu Roosevelt Swain, ancestor of Eliza and Wilbur Swain, and builder of the old mansion in Vermont where the twins are raised, dies of obesity. But the Vonnegut work in which Edison figures most prominently is a short story called "Tom Edison's Shaggy Dog" that appeared in the 1968 collection, *Welcome to the Monkey House*. In this story, an unnamed old man sitting on a park bench in Florida, annoyed by a talkative stranger, tells a tall tale about Edison inventing an intelligence analyzing machine, which he uses to discover that his dog Sparky is brilliant. Sparky gives Edison the tip to use a carbonized cotton thread as a filament in his electric light bulb and thus is the true genius behind Edison's most famous invention.

Einstein, Albert In *A Man Without a Country,* Vonnegut compares his own late-life pessimism to that experienced by Albert Einstein and MARK TWAIN, both of whom, according to Vonnegut, "gave up on the human race at the end of their lives" (88). In this essay, Vonnegut announces that he too, like his "distinct betters Einstein and Twain" gives up on people. Einstein is also a character in the short story "Asleep at the Switch" by Dr. Robert Fender (writing under the pen name "Kilgore Trout), which is described in *Jailbird.*

Eliot, T. S. In *Timequake,* Vonnegut writes that it is "piquant" to him that T. S. Eliot, a writer from St. Louis, Missouri, would deny his origins in the American Middle West. Vonnegut himself writes frequently and thoughtfully about his own INDIA-NAPOLIS roots.

Endell, Mary In chapter 1 of *Slaughterhouse-Five,* Vonnegut goes to visit his old war buddy BER-NARD V. O'HARE, in the hopes that O'Hare can ignite some of his war memories. While a guest at the O'Hare house, Vonnegut sleeps in one of the children's bedrooms, where O'Hare had placed a book—*Dresden, History, Stage and Gallery* by Mary Endell—on the bedside table for Vonnegut to read. The book is a real-life historical account of DRES-DEN published in 1908. In it, Endell describes the 1760 destruction of Dresden by the Prussians, adding to the theme of futility and repeated atrocity Vonnegut develops in the novel.

Epstein, Harold In *God Bless You, Dr. Kevorkian,* Vonnegut imagines having a continental breakfast with the spirit of Harold Epstein, an ordinary man whom Vonnegut admires for his twin devotions, while alive, to his garden and to his wife, Esta.

When asked for a sound bite, Mr. Epstein says, "My only regret is that everybody couldn't be as happy as we were" (40).

existentialism Existentialism is a philosophical belief system most associated with French intellectuals, including Albert Camus and Jean-Paul Sartre, during and immediately after the World War II years. Marked by a belief in the absurdity of the universe, yet the necessity that human beings exert their will and act in good faith with full knowledge of that absurdity, existentialists emphasized the ability of humans to define themselves by the choices they make. It can be argued that Vonnegut shares many ideas with the existentialist thinkers, including a view of the universe as absurd and a recognition that human beings' attempts to bring about meaningful change may be futile. Vonnegut, like Camus in *The Myth of Sisyphus,* frequently depicts characters who exert FREE WILL despite the potential futility of their actions. In *Slaughterhouse-Five,* for instance, Vonnegut himself, as narrator, tells readers that wars are like glaciers—inevitable forces of nature that cannot be stopped—yet he still writes an anti-war novel and warns his sons not to work for weapon manufacturers. With full knowledge that his efforts may do no good at all and an explicit admission to readers of this fact, he nevertheless acts in good faith, as if change is possible. Many of Vonengut's characters, such as the Reverend James J. Lasher in *Player Piano,* display similar attributes. Despite his knowledge that the Ghost Shirt Revolution is doomed to failure, Lasher acts to bring it about anyway, telling Paul Proteus at the end of the novel, "It doesn't matter if we win or lose, Doctor. The important thing is that we tried. For the record, we tried!" (315).

F

Farrell, James T. In *Palm Sunday,* Vonnegut includes the speech he gave at the funeral for his friend, the 20th-century fiction writer, journalist, and socialist (*see* SOCIALISM) James T. Farrell, who chronicled the life of the working-class Irish on the South Side of Chicago. Vonnegut, in his funeral oration, thanked Farrell for showing "through his books that it was perfectly all right, perhaps even useful and beautiful, to say what life really looked like" (130).

Faust In the fictitious "Editor's Note" that precedes *Mother Night,* Vonnegut tells readers that the novel's title was chosen by Howard W. Campbell, Jr. It comes from a speech by Mephistopheles that appears in the early 19th-century play *Faust* written by the German poet, novelist, and scientist Johann Wolfgang Goethe.

> I am a part of the part that at first was all, part of the darkness that gave birth to light, that supercilious light which now disputes with Mother Night her ancient rank and space, and yet cannot succeed; no matter how it struggles, it sticks to matter and can't get free. Light flows from substance, makes it beautiful; solids can check its path, so I hope it won't be long till light and the world's stuff are destroyed together. (xii)

firemen Vonnegut has something of an obsession with volunteer firemen, writing about them in many of his works, although most explicitly in *God Bless You, Mr. Rosewater.* Eliot Rosewater in this novel is said to have shot a 14-year-old volunteer fireman he mistook for an enemy soldier during World War II. As a result, Eliot becomes a fierce supporter of firemen and the work they do. Near the end of the novel, SCIENCE FICTION writer Kilgore Trout explains that Eliot's devotion to volunteer fire departments is evidence of Eliot's underlying sanity and compassion, explaining that firemen present "almost the only example of enthusiastic unselfishness to be seen in this land" (266). Volunteer firemen, like nurses and pediatricians in Vonnegut's work, seem to play the role of secular saints. These saints are compassionate, unselfish human beings who help others and who, as he explains in *Timequake,* make "being alive almost worthwhile" for Vonnegut (239). Vonnegut himself served as a volunteer fireman in the New York state village of Alplaus, during the time he worked for the GENERAL ELECTRIC Company.

Frank, Anne In *Galápagos,* narrator Leon Trout, son of the recurring Vonnegut character SCIENCE FICTION writer Kilgore Trout, tells readers that his mother's favorite quote is from *The Diary of Anne Frank:* "In spite of everything, I still believe people are really good at heart." While readers recognize the chilling irony in this statement from a young girl doomed to die at the Bergen-Belsen concentration camp, it can also be read as a courageous declaration of human optimism in the face of horrific circumstances.

Frankenstein   *Frankenstein*, MARY SHELLEY's 1818 iconic horror novel, plays a role in several Vonnegut works. The play *Fortitude* is about an overly ambitious scientist, much like Shelley's protagonist and sharing his name, who keeps an aged woman alive by replacing her body parts with machines. In *Timequake*, Vonnegut compares Kilgore Trout's awakening of security guard Dudley Prince, who is suffering from Post-Timequake Apathy, to Dr. Frankenstein's waking of his creature in Mary Shelley's novel. In addition, Shelley is one of the departed souls whom Vonnegut imagines interviewing in the whimsical collection *God Bless You, Dr. Kevorkian.*

free will   In philosophical thought, free will is the notion that human beings have control over their own destinies, through the actions they take. Free will is often contrasted to the philosophical stance of DETERMINISM, in which forces outside of human beings control and shape a person's destiny. The pull between free will and determinism is one of the main themes of many Vonnegut novels. Winston Niles Rumfoord, in *The Sirens of Titan*, for instance, believes that he plans the Martian invasion himself, but learns at the end of the novel that he has been manipulated by Tralfamadorian machines without his knowledge. What he believed was free will was merely an illusion. In *Slaughterhouse-Five*, Billy Pilgrim's Tralfamadorian kidnappers tell him that human beings are the only species in the universe that believe in free will. Billy himself can be read as a character who surrenders his free will for a deterministic worldview because free will is so frightening to him. In other works, such as *Breakfast of Champions*, Vonnegut raises the possibility that human beings are merely sacks of chemical reactions; bad human behavior may be caused simply by these chemical misfiring, as happens with Dwayne Hoover. Despite his repeated suggestions that human free will may be an illusion, Vonnegut still seems to advocate that humans behave as if they do indeed control their own destinies, as if their actions matter in the universe. To do otherwise is to give up on life itself.

G

Galápagos Islands The Galápagos Islands play an important role in Vonnegut's novel *Galápagos*. The luxury liner *Bahia de Darwin* is originally scheduled to take tourists on nature cruises of the islands. After war and economic turmoil shake up the country of Ecuador, however, the Galápagos Islands become the destination to which a small band of tourists and native Indian girls escape. This group lands on the northernmost island, Santa Rosalia, where they eventually repopulate the human race.

General Electric Vonnegut worked in the General News Bureau of the General Electric Company in Schenectady, New York, from 1947 to 1951. He frequently credits his experiences at General Electric with providing the inspiration for his first novel, *Player Piano*.

Gettysburg Address In Vonnegut's novel *Mother Night*, Howard W. Campbell, Jr., an American playwright who produces Nazi propaganda during World War II, writes a pageant honoring German soldiers who died fighting. The pageant's working title is "Last Full Measure." Campbell explains to his boss, Joseph Goebbels, that the title comes from Lincoln's Gettysburg Address, and he prepares a translation of the entire address for Goebbels to read. Goebbels, declaring the speech to be "a very fine piece of propaganda" (19), sends a copy to HITLER himself, who is moved to tears by it. Vonnegut also discusses the Gettysburg Address in his collection *A Man Without a Country*, referring to it as one of "the most intelligent and decent prayers ever uttered by a famous American" (72). Vonnegut notes that Lincoln's poetic address was delivered at a time when "it was still possible to make horror and grief in wartime seem almost beautiful" (73), an accomplishment he himself, in novels such as *Slaughterhouse-Five* and *Mother Night*, clearly does not want to mimic.

Goldberg, Rube In *Timequake*, Kilgore Trout writes that "America is the interplay of three hundred million Rube Goldberg contraptions invented only yesterday" (199). Vonnegut then explains to readers that Rube Goldberg was a 20th-century American newspaper cartoonist who drew pictures of "absurdly complex and undependable machines" (200) that accomplished simple tasks in extremely convoluted ways.

Grand Hotel Oloffson The Grand Hotel Oloffson is an actual hotel in Port-au-Prince, Haiti, where Vonnegut stayed with his second wife, JILL KREMENTZ. The hotel also figures in his fiction, when Vonnegut has Rudy Waltz and his older brother, Felix, become the new owners of the Grand Hotel Oloffson in the novel *Deadeye Dick*. The Waltz brothers escape dying in the neutron bomb explosion that kills all the residents of MIDLAND CITY, Ohio, because they are in Haiti at the time.

H

Hallinan, Vivian In *God Bless You, Dr. Kevork-ian*, Vonnegut imagines falling in love with a dead woman, one of the spirits he interviews in the after-life, socialist Vivian Hallinan (*see* SOCIALISM). Von-negut is intrigued when Hallinan is described in her obituary as being from a "colorful West Coast family" (41). When he asks her how she feels about being called "colorful," Hallinan replies that she "would rather have been called what Franklin D. Roosevelt was called by his enemies: 'A traitor to her class'" (43).

Hamlet SHAKESPEARE's most famous dramatic character, Hamlet, is evoked in Vonnegut's *God Bless You, Mr. Rosewater* when Eliot Rosewater compares himself to the famous Danish prince. Eliot resembles Hamlet in that both men have a troubled and complex relationship with a father that sets the plot into motion; each has a sweet-heart who goes insane; and finally, both men have a desire to do right followed by periods of paralysis that prevent them from acting.

Hapgood, Powers Powers Hapgood was a HAR-VARD-educated union organizer and socialist (*see* SOCIALISM) agitator from INDIANAPOLIS in the first half of the 20th century, who was acquainted with the Vonnegut family and who was much admired by Kurt Vonnegut. In the prologue to *Jailbird*, Von-negut says that his character Kenneth Whistler is based largely on Powers Hapgood. Vonnegut also

discusses Hapgood in the collection *A Man Without a Country*, praising him as "a typical Hoosier ideal-ist . . . who thought there could be more economic justice in this country" (13).

Hapgoods, Three Earnest Brothers, The Von-negut refers to the book *The Hapgoods, Three Earnest Brothers*, actually written by Michael D. Marcaccio, in the prologue to *Jailbird*. The book details the lives of William Hapgood, an experi-menter in industrial democracy prior to the Great Depression, as well as William's brothers Norman and Hutchins, both "socialistically inclined jour-nalists and editors and book writers" (10). William Hapgood is also the father of POWERS HAPGOOD, on whom Vonnegut bases the character of Ken-neth Whistler in the novel.

Harding, Warren G. A cast-iron historical marker on the beach at the writer's retreat Xanadu in the novel *Timequake* proclaims that U.S. president War-ren G. Harding declared fictional character Julius King Bowen, a white performer who imitated black Americans in the 1920s and '30s, and who endowed the Xanadu retreat, to be "Laughter Laureate of the United States, Master of Darky Dialects, and heir to the Crown of King of Humor Once Worn by Mark Twain" (89). Later, Kilgore Trout tells Vonnegut that "Warren G. Harding sired an illegitimate daugh-ter by ejaculating in the birth canal of a stenographer in a broom closet at the White House" (89).

Harvard University Harvard University, where Vonnegut briefly taught creative writing in 1970, is the alma mater of several Vonnegut family members, including his paternal uncle, ALEX VONNEGUT, and his son Mark, who received his medical degree there. Harvard University also plays an important role in the novel *Jailbird*. In the prologue to *Jailbird*, Vonnegut writes, "Harvard is all through this book, although I myself never went there" (3). Numerous characters in the novel are Harvard alumni, most notably the novel's narrator, Walter F. Starbuck, a poor boy who is able to attend Harvard because of a wealthy benefactor.

Heliogabalus Kilgore Trout, in *Breakfast of Champions*, tells his parakeet Bill about a Roman emperor named Heliogabalus who purportedly roasted human beings alive inside a hollowed-out bronze bull for the amusement of his dinner guests. Trout's low opinion of human beings leads him to tell Bill that "We're all Heliogabalus" (18). An actual Roman emperor who lived in the early third century, Heliogabalus was known for breaking religious and sexual taboos, though contemporary critics believe that tales of his decadence have been exaggerated.

Heller, Joseph In *Timequake*, Vonnegut claims that the only contemporary American writer he can think of who has given Americans a new word is Joseph Heller, author of the well-known satirical World War II novel *Catch-22*. Vonnegut explains that the title of this novel now appears as an entry in *Webster's Collegiate Dictionary*. Vonnegut discusses Heller more fully in the collection *Palm Sunday*, in which he includes a thoughtful review of Heller's second novel, *Something Happened*. He concludes that, while "*Catch-22* is now the dominant myth about Americans in the war against fascism," *Something Happened* might well become "the dominant myth about the middle-class veterans who came home from that war to become heads of nuclear families" (121).

Hemingway, Ernest Vonnegut opens *Timequake* by discussing the great modern American writer Ernest Hemingway and his well-known novella *The Old Man and the Sea*. Referencing the view that the sharks who eat the old man's fish in the story might be a symbol for the critics who did not appreciate Hemingway's first novel after a 10-year break, Vonnegut compares his own situation to that of Hemingway. Vonnegut claims to have been working on a novel, which he refers to as *Timequake One*, for nearly a decade. Unlike the old man in the Hemingway story, who leaves his fish tied outside the boat for the sharks, Vonnegut decides to "fillet the fish" (xiv), to carve out the best chunks of his novel and throw the rest overboard. Vonnegut's most extensive discussion of Hemingway, however, appears in the collection *Fates Worse Than Death*, in which he includes a speech given to a group of Hemingway scholars in Boise, Idaho. In this speech, Vonnegut praises Hemingway's use of simple, powerful language, while acknowledging that Hemingway's macho subject matter now appears dated.

Hesse, Herman In his collection *Wampeters, Foma, and Granfalloons*, Vonnegut discusses early 20th-century German novelist Herman Hesse, author of *Steppenwolf* and *Siddhartha*, who was extremely popular with young people in the 1960s. Speculating about why Hesse strikes such a chord with that generation, Vonnegut suggests that Hesse offers young people the "hope and romance" that they feel lacking in their lives. In addition, Hesse's politics "coincide with those of the American young . . .: He is against war. He hates armament manufacturers and superpatriots" (113). Finally, in Vonnegut's view, Hesse, who left his native Germany to live in Switzerland, offers the '60s generation an outlet for the homesickness they feel for their own safe, happy childhoods in the face of war, environmental destruction, and political chaos.

Hitler, Adolf German Führer and Nazi party leader Adolf Hitler plays an important role in Vonnegut's third novel, *Mother Night*, when Howard W. Campbell, Jr., an American playwright living in Germany, becomes a key Nazi propagandist working for Hitler and his regime. Although Hitler does not actually appear as a character in the book, unlike several other Nazi officers, he does, at one point, send Campbell a note in which he explains that Lincoln's GETTYSBURG ADDRESS made him weep. Hitler is also one of the dead people whom Vonnegut imagines interviewing in the collection *God Bless You, Dr. Kevorkian*. Vonnegut depicts Hitler in heaven as remorseful for his sins. The brutal engineer of more than 35 million deaths in World War II would like to see a modest monument erected to himself at the United Nations headquarters in New York City, with the words "Excuse Me" carved into its base.

Hoffman, Abbie   Abbie Hoffman was a political activist in the 1960s and '70s, who cofounded the Youth International Party (better knows as the "Yippies"), and who was one of the famous "Chicago Seven," a group of activists tried for interrupting the 1968 Democratic National Convention. Vonnegut admired Hoffman, who died in 1989. In the collection *Fates Worse Than Death*, he describes Hoffman as a "clowning genius" who is high on Vonnegut's "list of saints, of exceptionally courageous, unarmed, unsponsored, unpaid souls who have tried to slow down even a little bit state crimes against those Jesus Christ said should inherit the Earth someday" (189).

Hoyle, Fred   Vonnegut paraphrases 20th-century British astronomer Fred Hoyle in *Timequake*, who said that "believing in Darwin's theoretical mechanisms of evolution was like believing that a hurricane could blow through a junkyard and build a Boeing 747" (188–189).

Hubbard, Kin   Kin Hubbard was an early 20th-century INDIANAPOLIS humorist and cartoonist to whom Vonnegut felt a kinship. In *Timequake*, Vonnegut quotes Hubbard's famous quip that Prohibition is "better than no liquor at all" (174), as he explains to readers that his Lieber ancestors' brewery was put out of business by Prohibition.

Huie, William Bradford   William Bradford Huie is the real-life author of *The Execution of Private Slovik*, about an American G.I. executed by firing

squad in 1945, the only American soldier to be shot for cowardice since the Civil War. In *Slaughterhouse-Five*, Billy Pilgrim finds a copy of this book under the cushion of a chair in the waiting room of his mother's nursing home and opens it to read the opinion of a staff judge advocate who supported PRIVATE EDDIE SLOVIK's death sentence.

humanism   Humanism is a philosophical belief that asserts truth and morality can be found by focusing on human beings and their needs rather than on faith, supernatural entities, or divine revelation. Although there are many sources for contemporary humanism, including ancient Greece and Renaissance Italy, and while the philosophy exists in both secular and religious forms (the religious forms are often associated with Unitarian Universalism), adherents of humanism tend to share a skepticism about received dogma, a belief in science and the scientific method, and a commitment to human rights, civil liberties, and racial and sexual equality. Kurt Vonnegut's interest in humanism is evidenced in his fiction and also in his service as honorary president of the AMERICAN HUMANIST ASSOCIATION since the death of former President Isaac Asimov in 1992 until his own death in 2007. In *Timequake*, Vonnegut defines humanists as people who "try to behave decently and honorably without any expectation of rewards or punishments in an afterlife" (82). He continues, "The creator of the Universe has been to us unknowable so far. We serve as well as we can the highest abstraction of which we have some understanding, which is our community" (82).

Hyannis Port   Hyannis Port, Massachusetts, on CAPE COD, is the famed location of the Kennedy clan's summer home. It is also the main setting for Vonnegut's "The Hyannis Port Story," which depicts an ardent Republican millionaire and staunch Goldwater supporter who lives across the street from the Democratic Kennedys and is fed up with all the tourism and hoopla the Kennedy compound attracts.

I

Iliad, The   Homer's epic poem *The Iliad*, about the Trojan War, serves as part of the background material for Vonnegut's first novel, *Player Piano*, which is set in ILIUM, New York. Ilium is an alternative name for the city of Troy, which is under siege by the Greeks in Homer's poem. Vonnegut's allusions to the *The Iliad* are ironic; in *Player Piano* he depicts a decidedly unheroic age in which human beings are reduced from the epic warriors Achilles and Hector to modern bureaucrats and engineers, men who have become enslaved by the very machines they themselves have created.

Ilium, New York   Ilium, New York, is the setting for Vonnegut's first novel, *Player Piano*. In that book, Ilium has been divided into three areas, one for the managers and engineers and civil servants who run the city, one for the machines that do almost all of the work, and a third area called Homestead, where the masses of unemployed ordinary people live. Ilium, New York, is also the hometown of the Hoenikker family in *Cat's Cradle* as well as of high school biology teacher Mary Hepburn in the novel *Galápagos*. The town appears more incidentally in several other Vonnegut works as well. In classical myth, Ilium is an alternative name for the city of Troy, the city referred to in the title of Homer's epic poem THE ILIAD. Vonnegut uses the name ironically. Despite echoes of a heroic past, in his work, Ilium is a decidedly unheroic place in an unheroic age.

Indianapolis   Indianapolis, Indiana, is Vonnegut's hometown. As he reports in the family history included in *Palm Sunday*, all eight of Vonnegut's great-grandparents settled in Indianapolis in the mid-19th century, so that there was a large extended network of Vonneguts and Liebers and other relatives living in the Indianapolis of his early youth. In many of his works, Vonnegut expresses nostalgia for this time of his life, often lamenting the fact that the Vonnegut clan has largely dispersed from Indianapolis since his childhood and is now spread out all over the country. He frequently praises the excellent education he received at SHORTRIDGE HIGH SCHOOL in Indianapolis, where he served as editor of the daily newspaper and a clarinet player in the band.

Irving, David   In *Slaughterhouse-Five*, Vonnegut relies on facts about the bombing of DRESDEN and the number of civilians killed there that were initially printed in a book by British historian David Irving, *The Destruction of Dresden*. Since that time, Irving has been exposed as a Holocaust denier, accused of racism and anti-Semitism, and charged with wildly overestimating the number of civilians killed in the bombings. While the first edition of Irving's book claimed that between 100,000 and 250,000 civilians were killed in Dresden—the numbers Vonnegut himself cites in *Slaughterhouse-Five*—in later editions, Irving revised the numbers downward to between 50,000 and 100,000 killed.

Best estimates today put the number closer to 25,000 civilians killed. Vonnegut cannot really be blamed for the misinformation in *Slaughterhouse-Five* since Irving's estimates were widely accepted by historians at the time. In 2006, David Irving was sentenced to three years imprisonment upon returning to Austria after being banned from the country because of his Holocaust denials.

J

Jonah *Cat's Cradle* opens with the line "Call me Jonah" (1). The novel's narrator, whose actual name is John, compares himself to the biblical Jonah, who is ordered by God to preach at Nineveh and swallowed by a whale after he shirks his duty. Like Jonah in the Bible, John in the novel is initially reluctant to accept his fate, but ends up warning of the great destruction that will be visited upon Earth as a result of wickedness, in this case, the refusal of scientists to consider the moral outcomes of their relentless pursuit of new technologies.

Jones, James Critically acclaimed author of such World War II novels as *The Thin Red Line* and *From Here to Eternity*, James Jones figures in several Vonnegut works. In the collection *Palm Sunday*, Vonnegut mourns the recent death of Jones, an author he claims as a member of his own generation of novelists, adding that Jones's death "accounts for the autumnal mood" (2) of the essay collection. Jones is also mentioned in the preface to *Deadeye Dick*, where Vonnegut tells readers that he and his wife, JILL KREMENTZ, have stayed in the "James Jones Cottage" at the GRAND HOTEL OLOFFSON in Port au Prince, Haiti.

Jones, Tom Tom Jones was a fellow prisoner of war of Vonnegut's when the author was imprisoned in DRESDEN. When the soldiers were ordered to pair off, Jones's partner was JOE CRONE, whom Vonnegut claims is the model for Billy Pilgrim in *Slaughterhouse-Five*. In the collection *Fates Worse Than Death*, Vonnegut describes receiving a letter from Jones reminiscing about Crone's death in the prisoner camp (106–107). He also includes, in the appendix to this book, a photograph Jones sent to him, which includes Vonnegut and BERNARD V. O'HARE and several other ex-prisoners in front of a German horse-drawn cart shortly after the war ended.

Joyce, John Wesley John Wesley Joyce, owner of the Lion's Head bar in Greenwich Village from 1966 until 1996, the "most famous hangout for heavy-drinking, non-stop-talking writers in America" (47) is one of the departed souls Vonnegut imagines interviewing in *God Bless You, Dr. Kevorkian*.

Joyce, William William Joyce is the real name of a notorious Nazi propagandist nicknamed "Lord Haw-Haw," who broadcast anti-Semitic and pro-German rants over the radio to Britain citizens during World War II. Born in the United States to Irish parents, when Joyce was three he moved back to Ireland, where his Catholic family remained loyal to Britain and staunchly anti-Republican. When his family moved to Britain after the establishment of the Irish Free State in 1922, Joyce became deeply involved in fascist politics. At the outbreak of war, he moved to Berlin, where he soon obtained a job working for German radio's

English service. During the war years, he also worked to help recruit British prisoners of war into a unit called the British Free Corps. Captured at the end of the war, Joyce was executed for treason in England in January 1946. Vonnegut has said in interviews that he modeled the character Howard W. Campbell, Jr., from his novel *Mother Night,* on Joyce, and that the book was an attempt to imagine what an American Lord Haw-Haw would have been like.

K

Keane, Frances In *God Bless You, Dr. Kevorkian,* Frances Keane, a deceased children's book author and expert on romance languages, is one of the dead people Vonnegut imagines meeting in the afterlife. Vonnegut becomes interested in Keane because he believes that her "generally laudatory obit in the *New York Times* cut her off at the knees at the very end with this stark sentence: 'Her three marriages ended in divorce'" (49).

Kennedy, John Fitzgerald John F. Kennedy, 35th president of the United States, appears as a character in Vonnegut's short piece "The Hyannis Port Story," which depicts a storm window salesman and installer who goes to Hyannis Port, CAPE COD, location of the Kennedy's family summer home, to replace the windows on the home of an old Republican and fierce Barry Goldwater supporter named Commodore Rumfoord, who lives across the street from the Kennedy compound. The president actually makes an appearance at the end of the story when he and Rumfoord reach a neighborly détente after Rumfoord's son begins dating a young Kennedy cousin.

Kennedy, Robert In the concluding chapter of *Slaughterhouse-Five,* Vonnegut tells readers that Robert Kennedy, brother of President JOHN F. KENNEDY, and Democratic party presidential contender, was shot two nights previous to Vonnegut's writing this chapter. In this way, Vonnegut moves readers from the past, his account of the bombing

of DRESDEN, into the present time, when he is writing the book in 1968. Wars and atrocities continue in a futile cycle of death and destruction.

Kevorkian, Dr. Jack Dr. Jack Kevorkian, a real-life physician imprisoned in Michigan in 1999 for assisting numerous terminally ill patients to commit suicide, is also the title character of Vonnegut's book *God Bless You, Dr. Kevorkian.* In this odd little collection, Vonnegut imagines himself strapped to a gurney in the Huntsville State Prison in Texas, where he and Dr. Kevorkian perform repeated experiments together in which the doctor injects Vonnegut with just enough drugs that he has near-death experiences and is able to interview people in the afterlife. Vonnegut tells readers that the experiments stop when Dr. Kevorkian is convicted of first-degree murder.

King, Martin Luther, Jr. Vonnegut tells readers in the concluding chapter of *Slaughterhouse-Five* that civil rights leader Martin Luther King, Jr., was shot a month before Vonnegut began writing this final chapter. His point in mentioning King's death, along with that of ROBERT KENNEDY, seems to be to impress upon readers that American atrocities did not end with the bombing of DRESDEN.

Krassner, Paul Paul Krassner was a satirist, comic, magazine journalist and well-known member of the counterculture during the 1960s. Vonnegut praises one of his comic pranks in *Timequake*—the printing of red-white-and-blue bumper stickers during the VIETNAM WAR era that read "Fuck Communism!" Vonnegut sees this slogan, which includes two of the words most loathed and feared by mid-century Americans, as a "particularly elegant commentary on the patriotism and nice-nellyism during the deliberately insane Vietnam War" (191).

Krementz, Jill   The journalist, photographer, and writer Jill Krementz was Vonnegut's second wife. According to an essay he wrote on the occasion of Jill's 50th birthday, included in the collection *Fates Worse Than Death*, Vonnegut first met Jill in 1970 during the production of his play *Happy Birthday, Wanda June* at the Theatre de Lys in Greenwich Village. In this essay, Vonnegut praises his wife's success in her career, her ability to behave as if gender did not matter in a world of professional photography that was still a largely male realm. Although Vonnegut began to live with Jill in New York City in 1971, when he separated from his first wife, JANE COX VONNEGUT YARMOLINSKY, the pair did not actually marry until November 24, 1979. In 1982, they adopted a three-day-old infant, LILY VONNEGUT.

L

Labor's Untold Story   *Labor's Untold Story* is the title of an actual book by Richard O. Boyer and Herbert M. Morais. In *Jailbird,* Vonnegut includes a quote from Webster Thayer, the judge in the SACCO AND VANZETTI case, that he takes from the book by Boyer and Morais. Speaking about Bartolomeo Vanzetti, Judge Thayer said, "This man, although he may not have actually committed the crime attributed to him, is nevertheless morally culpable, because he is the enemy of our existing institutions" (*Jailbird* 235).

Lane, Ora D.   Ora D. Lane was the second wife of Vonnegut's maternal grandfather, ALBERT LIEBER. Lieber married her after the death of his first wife, ALICE BARUS LIEBER. Ora Lane thus became stepmother to the three young children of Albert and Alice, the oldest of whom was six-year-old EDITH LIEBER (VONNEGUT), Kurt Vonnegut's mother. In *Palm Sunday,* family historian JOHN RAUCH reports that Ora Lane treated her stepchildren cruelly, abusing them so completely that each of the children "suffered a distinctive psychic trauma from which they never fully recovered" (35). Albert eventually divorced Lane, but was forced to settle a large alimony on her, which greatly depleted his resources.

Langmuir, Dr. Irving   Dr. Irving Langmuir was an American chemist and physicist who made his greatest scientific contributions while working at the GENERAL ELECTRIC Research Laboratory from 1909 to 1950. Winner of the 1932 Nobel Prize in chemistry, Langmuir's work also contributed to the development of atomic theory in the early part of the century. In a *Paris Review* interview, republished in *Palm Sunday,* Vonnegut says that Dr. Felix Hoenikker in the novel *Cat's Cradle* is a "caricature" (91) of Dr. Langmuir.

Langtry, Meda   Meda Langtry was the third wife of Vonnegut's maternal grandfather, ALBERT LIEBER. Lieber married her after divorcing his abusive second wife, ORA D. LANE. In *Palm Sunday,* Meda Langtry is described as a "nondescript widow" from Canada (36). When she married Albert Lieber, she had a daughter, whom Albert adopted and renamed Alberta. Much younger than her husband, Meda was about the same age as Lieber's daughter, EDITH LIEBER VONNEGUT, Kurt Vonnegut's mother.

Laurel and Hardy   Stan Laurel and Oliver Hardy were a comedy duo who made numerous movies together in the 1920s and '30s. Vonnegut discusses his love of Laurel and Hardy in several of his essays, but the work which the pair figures into most prominently is the novel *Slapstick,* whose title derives from the type of broad, exaggerated physical comedy performed by the two men. Vonnegut tells readers in the prologue to *Slapstick* that he sees his novel as "grotesque, situational poetry" (1), much like the slapstick film comedies of Laurel and Hardy. The reason Vonnegut has such affection for this comedy duo, he explains, is that they are constantly being tested, and they do their best with every test. He adds, "They never failed to bargain in good faith with their destinies, and were screamingly adorable and funny on that account" (1).

Lawrence, Seymour   Seymour Lawrence was Vonnegut's longtime editor and publisher at Delacorte Press. In the opening chapter of *Slaughterhouse-Five*, Vonnegut addresses Lawrence specifically, explaining that his book is a failure, that it is so short and jumbled, because there is nothing to say about a massacre. Seymour Lawrence also appears in *Timequake* when Vonnegut says that the bakemaster at the giant clam bake that ends the novel resembles his late publisher who, Vonnegut adds, rescued him from certain oblivion by publishing *Slaughterhouse-Five* and then bringing all his previous books back into print.

Lewis, Sinclair   In *Timequake*, one of the four guest suites at the Xanadu writer's retreat is named after early 20th-century American writer Sinclair Lewis. Upon his arrival at Xanadu, Kilgore Trout notices that all the suites are named after "certifiable alcoholics" (31).

Lieber, Albert   Albert Lieber was Vonnegut's maternal grandfather. In *Palm Sunday*, Vonnegut calls his grandfather Albert a "rascal," whose "emotional faithlessness to his children" contributed significantly to the later suicide of Vonnegut's mother, EDITH LIEBER VONNEGUT (33). Born in 1863, Albert spent his adult life running the family brewery, P. Lieber & Co., which had been sold to a British syndicate in 1893. Unlike his conservative and retiring father, PETER LIEBER, Albert was, according to family historian JOHN RAUCH, "extroverted, flamboyant, sociable, and a big spender" (*Palm Sunday* 33). He married the musician ALICE BARUS LEIBER in 1885 and had three children with her, including Vonnegut's mother, Edith. After Alice Barus Lieber's death, when Edith was only six years old, Albert married ORA D. LANE, who was an accomplished violinist but an extremely abusive stepmother. Albert eventually divorced her and was married a third time, to a widow named MEDA LANGTRY.

Lieber, Alice Barus   Vonnegut's maternal grandmother, Alice Barus Lieber, daughter of ALICE MÖLLMAN BARUS and KARL BARUS, is said to have been "the most beautiful and accomplished young lady in Indianapolis" by JOHN RAUCH, in his history of the Vonnegut family that is reprinted in *Palm Sunday*. Alice Barus Lieber was a piano player, singer, and composer who married Indianapolis brewer ALBERT LIEBER, but who died when her children were still young. In *Palm Sunday*, Vonnegut reports that his grandmother died of pneumonia; however, in *Timequake* he says that she died while giving birth to her third child, Vonnegut's uncle Rudy.

Lieber, Peter   Peter Lieber was one of Vonnegut's maternal great-grandfathers. Born in Düsseldorf, Germany, in 1832, he migrated to the United States as a young man and served in the U.S. Civil War. Following the war, he moved to INDIANAPOLIS to take up an appointment as secretary to Oliver P. Morton, governor of Indiana. In 1865, Peter Lieber bought a brewery, which he renamed P. Lieber & Co. Although he sold the brewery to a British syndicate in 1893, the business was run by his son, ALBERT LIEBER, until Prohibition. Vonnegut's fullest discussion of this ancestor appears in the chapter titled "Roots" in the collection *Palm Sunday*.

Lieber, Sophia St. André   Sophia St. André Lieber was one of Vonnegut's maternal great-grandmothers. She was the wife of PETER LIEBER, the German immigrant who started the P. Lieber & Co. Brewery in INDIANAPOLIS.

Lincoln, Abraham   Vonnegut greatly admired American president Abraham Lincoln, and he discusses him in several of his works. The play that moves Kilgore Trout to a loud sob at the end of the novel *Timequake* is about Lincoln as a young man, and Vonnegut often refers to the beauty of Lincoln's GETTYSBURG ADDRESS. In *A Man Without a Country*, Vonnegut, recognizing the danger of quoting Lincoln, who "always steals the show," nevertheless does so, citing a comment the future president said about then-president James Polk concerning the imperialist U.S. war in Mexico:

"Trusting to escape scrutiny, by fixing the public gaze upon the exceeding brightness of military glory . . . he plunged into war" (76). Vonnegut clearly cites this remark in light of the Bush administration's war in Iraq, which he deplores.

Lindener, Irma Vonnegut   Irma Vonnegut Lindener was the younger sister of KURT VONNEGUT, SR. In *Palm Sunday*, family historian JOHN RAUCH explains that, after EDITH LIEBER VONNEGUT's suicide in 1944, Irma often came from Germany, where she was living, to stay for extended periods with her brother. The brother and sister "were very congenial and deeply attached to each other," according to Rauch (51).

Lord Haw-Haw   *See* JOYCE, WILLIAM

Lost Horizon   *Lost Horizon* is the name of a 1933 James Hilton novel about a hidden Eden named "Shangri-La" located in the Himalaya Mountains. The book makes an appearance in *Deadeye Dick*, when it is said to have inspired dairy farmer John Fortune to travel to the Himalayas after the death of his wife, a trip that will be the basis for Rudy Waltz's later play, *Katmandu*.

Lot's wife   Lot's wife is a figure who appears in the Book of Genesis in the Christian Bible, where she is said to have been turned into a pillar of salt for looking back at the destruction of the cities of Sodom and Gomorrah. In the opening chapter of *Slaughterhouse-Five*, Vonnegut tells readers that he loves Lot's wife for looking back, "because it was so human" (22). He compares himself to Lot's wife as well, saying the novel is a failure because it was written by a pillar of salt. Vonnegut looks back on the destruction of DRESDEN much as Lot's wife looked back at the biblical cities of Sodom and Gomorrah.

Louis, Joe   Vonnegut's short story "D.P." is about a six-year-old, half African-American, half-German orphan boy living in a German orphanage shortly after the end of World War II. The boy is nicknamed "Joe" by the townspeople after the famous African-American boxer Joe Louis, popularly known as the "Brown Bomber," who defeated German Max Schmeling for the World Heavyweight Championship of 1938.

Ludd, Ned   Ned Ludd is a possibly fictitious workman who supposedly smashed up mechanical knitting machines in the late 18th century, and from whom the group the Luddites took their name. The Luddites were an English social movement in the early 19th century that protested changes brought by the Industrial Revolution, often by smashing machines. The Ghost Shirt Society in *Player Piano* may be partially inspired by the Luddite movement, and Vonnegut refers to himself as a Luddite in *Timequake* when he explains that he still pecks away at a manual typewriter. Kilgore Trout, who writes with pens on yellow legal pads, is said to be even more of a Luddite.

M

Mackay, Charles Charles Mackay, LL.D., is the author of *Extraordinary Popular Delusions and the Madness of Crowds*, published in 1841. In the opening chapter of *Slaughterhouse-Five*, Vonnegut tells readers that he and his war buddy BERNARD V. O'HARE looked up THE CHILDREN'S CRUSADE in this book, which O'Hare had a copy of at his home.

Mahesh Yogi, Maharishi Maharishi Mahesh Yogi, born Mahesh Prasad Varma in India in 1917, was the founder of Transcendental Meditation, a spiritual practice especially popular with the counterculture movement in the 1960s and '70s. Vonnegut writes extensively about the yogi in an essay titled "Yes, We Have No Nirvanas," which is reprinted in *Wampeters, Foma, and Granfalloons*. While believing the yogi himself to be a sincere and well-meaning man, Vonnegut is nevertheless critical of his message that by changing one's self, one can change the world at large and correct social injustices. Suspecting that the yogi's appeal is due largely to the fact that he demands no sacrifices of his followers while promising enormous changes, Vonnegut suggests that the yogi's message, finally, is not that different from what is preached by the American free enterprise system: that any "oppressed person could rise" (38) simply by grasping his own bootstraps and pulling himself up. Eliminating oppression, in Vonnegut's view, is more complicated than that. It depends largely on changing the social and political institutions that oppress people rather than being simply a matter of individual human beings changing themselves.

Markson, David David Markson is a POSTMODERN writer and former student of Vonnegut's old friend, the poet Edward Muir. In *Timequake*, Markson figures briefly when Vonnegut writes Muir a letter complaining of an extended case of writer's block and praising the novel *Reader's Block* by Markson. Muir replies by sending Vonnegut his own letter back in the form of a poem.

Marx, Karl In *A Man Without a Country*, Vonnegut defends 19th-century political philosopher and coauthor of *The Communist Manifesto*, Karl Marx, claiming that Marx should not be held responsible for the later excesses of Soviet leader Joseph Stalin. Although Stalin's suppression of religion in the Soviet Union is often attributed to Marx's famous statement that "religion is the opium of the people," Vonnegut explains his view that, in 1844, when Marx made that comment, opiums were the only effective painkillers available. Marx, Vonnegut argues, had himself taken opiates and was grateful for the temporary pain relief they provided. Thus, according to Vonnegut, Marx, in his famous statement, "was simply noticing, and surely not condemning, the fact that religion could also be comforting to those in economic or social distress" (12).

Maslansky, Dr. Robert   Dr. Robert Maslansky is a physician friend of Vonnegut's who treats addicts at Bellevue Hospital in New York City. In the collection *Fates Worse Than Death*, Vonnegut describes Maslansky as one of the "saints" whom he believes makes human life worth living (191).

Massachusetts Institute of Technology   In the collection *Fates Worse Than Death*, Vonnegut tells readers that the Massachusetts Institute of Technology (MIT) "has played an important part in the history of [his] branch of the Vonnegut family" (117). Both his father, KURT VONNEGUT, SR., and his grandfather, BERNARD VONNEGUT, SR., took degrees in architecture from MIT, while his older brother, Bernard, earned his doctor's degree in chemistry from the school. Vonnegut includes a speech in the collection that he made to the graduating class of MIT in 1985, in which he warns students against practicing immoral science.

Mata Hari   Howard W. Campbell, Jr., the character whose written confessions make up the main text of Vonnegut's novel *Mother Night*, dedicates his work to Mata Hari, a Dutch courtesan and exotic dancer executed as a German spy during World War I. In a chapter that Campbell supposedly later excluded from his confessions, he gives the following explanation for his dedication: "Before seeing what sort of a book I was going to have here, I wrote the dedication—'To Mata Hari.' She whored in the interest of espionage, and so did I" (xii).

Mencken, H. L.   Henry Louis Mencken was an American journalist, satirical writer, and literary critic in the first half of the 20th century, famed for his cynicism and wit. Vonnegut refers to Mencken in *Timequake*, telling readers that the great critic confessed that he did not enjoy the novels of Willa Cather because he was not particularly interested in the Czech immigrants in Nebraska about whom she wrote. Vonnegut says that Mencken's comment explains why he never wrote a novel about his German-American grandfather Albert Lieber. German Americans of INDIANAPOLIS, according to Vonnegut, would not attract universal interest. In the collection *Palm Sunday*, Vonnegut cites Mencken

as well, pointing out that Vonnegut's agnostic ancestors would all have agreed with Mencken's belief that religious people are comical.

metafiction   Metafiction is best understood as fiction that comments on or draws attention to its own status as fiction, in order to explore the relationship between fiction and reality. Vonnegut is considered to be a key practitioner of this technique, which is often used by POSTMODERN authors. In *Slaughterhouse-Five*, Vonnegut devotes the opening chapter to a discussion of the difficulties he had in writing the book. He comments on the form that the novel will take, giving away to readers the beginning, climax, and end of the novel that is to come. In *Breakfast of Champions*, Vonnegut goes even further, appearing as a character in the book, who ends up not only meeting one of his own fictional creations, Kilgore Trout, but also revealing to Trout his status as a character. By the time Vonnegut gets to his final novel, *Timequake*, the line between reality and fiction has become so blurred that he presents Kilgore Trout as a close friend of his, whom he speaks with often. The clambake party that ends the novel includes a mish-mash of people from Vonnegut's real life and the fictional characters he has created over the years. Readers might wonder why Vonnegut relies so heavily on metafiction in his work. The answer has to do with what he sees as the permeable boundary between fiction and reality. Like other postmodern authors, Vonnegut believes strongly in the power of storytelling and language to shape the world we live in. In *Slaughterhouse-Five* for instance, Vonnegut has Kilgore Trout complain that "slipshod storytelling in the New Testament" (108) is responsible for much of the cruelty in the world. The stories people tell about the world and about themselves have a very real effect on how people live their lives. Thus, Vonnegut, through his use of metafiction, suggests that stories and real life are not as distinct and separate as traditionally thought; people actually create reality through the stories they tell.

Midland City   Midland City, Ohio, is a fictional midwestern city that appears as a setting in many Vonnegut works, most prominently in *Breakfast of*

Champions. Perhaps partly modeled after INDIANAPO-LIS, where Vonnegut grew up, Midland City is home to Pontiac dealer Dwayne Hoover and hosts the arts festival that Kilgore Trout is invited to attend. In *Deadeye Dick*, the population of Midland City, hometown of narrator and protagonist Rudy Waltz, is decimated by a neutron bomb, which has killed all the citizens of the city, but left all the buildings intact. Midland City is also said to be the hometown of Eugene Debs Hartke, protagonist of *Hocus Pocus*.

Moby-Dick   In the opening line of *Cat's Cradle*— "Call me Jonah"—Vonnegut echoes the famous opening line of Herman Melville's classic seafaring novel *Moby-Dick*—"Call me Ishmael." Like Ishmael in Melville's novel, John in *Cat's Cradle* is an outsider, a wanderer who witnesses great destruction and survives to tell the tale. *Moby-Dick* might also be referenced in the name given to the protagonist of Vonnegut's novel *Jailbird*—Walter F. Starbuck. The first mate aboard the the *Pequod* in Melville's novel is named Starbuck as well. Both Starbucks are fundamentally moral men who are finally too weak or ineffectual to change the destructive sequence of events they witness.

Moore, Paul, Jr.   Paul Moore, Jr. was an Episcopal bishop in New York City who invited Vonnegut to speak at the Cathedral of St. John the Divine as part of a series against nuclear weaponry in 1982. This is where Vonnegut delivered the speech about "fates worse than death" that would later become the title piece of his third essay collection. In this collection, Vonnegut describes Moore as "a very good man, always on the side of the powerless when they are abused or scorned or cheated by the powerful" (152). He adds that Moore is one of the "saints" who make living, for him, "almost worthwhile" (152).

Mozart, Wolfgang Amadeus   In *Timequake*, Vonnegut uses the composer Wolfgang Amadeus Mozart to illustrate his point that in large societies it is difficult for people to simply do something well and enjoy it, such as playing a musical instrument or a sport, or studying a demanding science at a university, because they are sure to meet someone who is much better at the activity than they are, which will be discouraging. In speeches, he tells listeners: "If you go to a big city, and a university is a big city, you are bound to run into Wolfgang Amadeus Mozart. Stay home, stay home" (149). Vonnegut's views here are linked to his notion that human beings are happier in smaller, more primitive, familylike settings than they are in the huge, crowded modern world.

N

Nathan, George Jean George Jean Nathan was an American drama critic and journalist who worked in the early part of the 20th century. He is mentioned in *Slaughterhouse-Five* when the narrator tells readers that the hotel room where Billy Pilgrim stays on his trip to New York City was once Nathan's home.

Neff, David P. David P. Neff is the leader of the relief organization CARE in Mozambique, whom Vonnegut met when he visited the country in 1989 as part of an effort to publicize the suffering of its war-ravaged citizens. Vonnegut wrote about his trip to Mozambique in an article appearing in *Parade* magazine in 1990. The piece is reprinted in the collection *Fates Worse Than Death*.

New Journalism New Journalism, according to contemporary American writer Tom Wolfe, is a style of reporting that arose in the early 1960s among magazine and Sunday supplement writers such as Jimmy Breslin, Gay Talese, and others. The genre reached its fullest expression in the late 1960s with the publication of Truman Capote's *In Cold Blood* and Norman Mailer's *The Armies of the Night*. New Journalists relied on techniques borrowed from realistic fiction—including dialogue, scene-by-scene construction of a story, a shifting narrative point of view, and symbolic details that delineate a person's class and social status—in order to write journalism that was more lively,

immediate, and in-depth than conventional reporting. In his collection of essays *Wampeters, Foma, and Granfalloons*, Vonnegut expresses his admiration for New Journalists in general and for HUNTER S. THOMPSON in particular. He tells readers that his own essays on the end of the Biafran War and the 1972 Republican National Convention, which are "loose and personal," most likely count as part of the genre of New Journalism. Yet, Vonnegut also informs readers that he does not expect to write many more pieces in this mode since he believes that fiction is an even "more truthful way of telling the truth than New Journalism is" (xviii).

Newton, Sir Isaac Vonnegut expresses admiration for the genius of scientist and mathematician Sir Isaac Newton in *Timequake* when he marvels that "this one naked ape" (120) was able to invent differential calculus and the reflecting telescope, and to discern the laws governing motion, gravity, and optics. He tells readers that his young grandson Max wrote a school report on Newton that contained a fact Vonnegut did not know about the great scientist: that his supervisors advised him to take time out from science to brush up on theology. Vonnegut writes, "I like to think they did this not because they were foolish, but to remind him of how comforting and encouraging the make-believe of religion can be for common folk" (121). Isaac Newton also appears as one of the people Vonnegut interviews in the afterlife in *God Bless You, Dr. Kev-*

orkian. Vonnegut imagines Newton not in heaven, but in the blue tunnel of the afterlife, exploring what the tunnel consists of and how it works. The Newton Vonnegut imagines cannot forgive himself for not coming up with the theories of CHARLES DARWIN, Louis Pasteur, or ALBERT EINSTEIN during his 85 years of life.

Nice, Peter In the collection *Palm Sunday*, Vonnegut tells readers that Peter Nice is the fourth Adams brother, the youngest son of his sister, ALICE VONNEGUT, and her husband, JAMES CARMALT ADAMS. Peter was adopted by a first cousin of his father in Birmingham, Alabama. Despite being raised so far apart, Peter Nice is close to his older brothers, and Vonnegut also claims that "his attitudes toward life," as well as his jokes, are identical to Alice Vonnegut's (228).

Nietzsche, Friedrich Wilhelm In *Timequake*, when discussing the ethical philosophy of HUMANISM, Vonnegut refers to the 19th-century German philosopher Friedrich Wilhelm Nietzsche, who argued that only a person of deep faith could afford the luxury of religious skepticism. Vonnegut agrees with this argument, pointing out that humanists are "by and large educated, comfortably middle-class persons with rewarding lives" who "find rapture enough in secular knowledge and hope" (84). Yet, he also acknowledges that most people cannot do this. Thus, he recommends to a young man about to be released from prison that he join a church so that he will have something like a family to lean on and support him.

Nixon, Richard M. Richard Nixon, 37th president of the United States, appears briefly as a character in *Jailbird* when Walter F. Starbuck serves as his Special Adviser on Youth Affairs. Vonnegut also mentions Nixon in the preface to his collection, *Wampeters, Foma, and Granfalloons*. In this piece, Vonnegut writes that Nixon "is the first President to hate the American people and all they stand for" (xxi).

Odyssey, The Homer's epic poem *The Odyssey* provides inspiration for Vonnegut's 1970 drama, *Happy Birthday, Wanda June*. In both works, a husband who has wandered the world for many years returns home to a wife named Penelope, who has been courted by other suitors during her husband's absence. Vonnegut's play, however, unlike Homer's classic, spoofs traditional masculinity. In a letter to Robert Weide, the producer and director of a 2001 Hollywood staging of *Wanda June*, Vonnegut writes that he "found the behavior of Odysseus after arriving home unexpectedly from the Trojan War hilariously pig-headed and somehow Hemingway-esque." He mocks this behavior with the overly macho character of Harold Ryan in the play.

Oedipus complex Sigmund Freud used the term *Oedipus complex* to describe his theory that very young male children feel a repressed sexual desire for their mothers and an intense jealousy toward their fathers. Freud believed that an unresolved Oedipus complex could lead to neuroses in later life. Dr. Paul Proteus in Vonnegut's *Player Piano* is accused by a prosecutor, at his trial near the end of the book, of harboring an Oedipus complex. The prosecutor argues that Paul's activities in the Ghost Shirt Society are motivated by a hatred of his father rather than a desire to help the oppressed Homesteaders. Paul does not deny the charges, acknowledging instead "that all people are motivated by something pretty sordid" (299) and arguing that frailty is what defines human beings.

O'Hare, Bernard V. Bernard V. O'Hare is the War World II buddy whom Vonnegut describes going to visit in chapter 1 of *Slaughterhouse-Five*. He hopes that O'Hare will help prompt his own wartime memories as he works on his DRESDEN book. O'Hare's wife, Mary, however, perhaps helps Vonnegut with the book more than her husband does. Vonnegut promises Mary that the book he writes will have no roles that could be played by John Wayne or Frank Sinatra and that he will subtitle the book THE CHILDREN'S CRUSADE. Bernard V. O'Hare also figures prominently in the collection *Fates Worse Than Death*, where Vonnegut mourns the recent loss of his longtime friend. Readers find out that O'Hare was a "chain-smoking District Attorney for the first half of his career, and then a chain-smoking defense attorney until his death from cancer a little past midnight, June 9, 1990" (79). The two men had met as new soldiers at Camp Atterbury, just south of INDIANAPOLIS, in 1943. The first time Vonnegut saw O'Hare, he was reading a biography of famous defense attorney CLARENCE DARROW. The men remained friends their whole lives, and Vonnegut includes at the end of this collection a brief speech that O'Hare delivered about his friendship with Vonnegut on the occasion of the writer's 60th birthday. A character with a similar name but different middle initial, Bernard B. O'Hare, appears in *Mother Night*.

O'Keeffe, Georgia In *Timequake*, a painting of a cow's skull in the desert by Georgia O'Keeffe hangs over the desk of Monica Pepper, the secretary for the AMERICAN ACADEMY OF ARTS AND LETTERS. The corresponding artwork hanging over Trout's cot next door at the homeless shelter is "a poster telling him never to stick his ding-dong into anything without first putting on a condom" (55).

Olcott, Colonel Henry S. Colonel Henry S. Olcott, a 19th-century American lawyer and Civil War veteran who immersed himself in Eastern religious teachings and converted to Buddhism, helped found the THEOSOPHICAL SOCIETY in 1875 along with MADAME HELENA BLAVATSKY. Vonnegut writes about Olcott in his essay "The Mysterious Madame Blavatsky," later reprinted in the collection *Wampeters, Foma, and Granfalloons,* painting a picture of an intellectually daring but eccentric man who was devoted to his friend Blavatsky.

O'Neill, Eugene Eugene O'Neill, early 20th-century American playwright, is one of the four writers that the Xanadu writer's retreat in *Timequake* has named its guest suites after. All four are "certifiable alcoholics" according to Kilgore Trout (31).

Origami Express Origami Express is the name of the silk screen printing business founded by Vonnegut and Kentucky artist JOE PETRO III. Vonnegut sent Petro original paintings and drawings that Petro made silk screen prints from. The silk

screens are available for sale on the web through Vonnegut's official site.

O'Shea, Pat Pat O'Shea, Vonnegut tells readers in the collection *Palm Sunday,* is the wife of his son MARK VONNEGUT, and the mother of his grandson Zachary.

Ostrovsky, Erika Erika Ostrovsky is the author of a book about French writer LOUIS-FERDINAND CÉLINE, *Céline and His Vision.* In the opening chapter of *Slaughterhouse-Five,* Vonnegut tells readers that he read portions of Ostrovsky's book while waiting in Boston to catch a plane to Frankfurt, on which he was supposed to meet his buddy BERNARD V. O'HARE for the first leg of their return trip to DRESDEN.

Our Town *Our Town,* a play by Thornton Wilder set in small-town Grover's Corners, New Hampshire, which premiered in 1938, figures into Vonnegut's novel *Timequake* when he tells readers that his 13-year-old daughter, Lily, recently appeared in a school production of it. Vonnegut says the play moved him tremendously, as it has done every time he has watched it, because it reminds him of the INDIANAPOLIS of his youth before the years of the Great Depression. He adds that scenes from *Our Town* and certain other plays served as "emotional and ethical landmarks" (25) for him in his early manhood and that they still do so in 1996, when he is writing the novel.

P

Palermo, Lindsay In the collection *Palm Sunday*, Vonnegut tells readers that Lindsay Palermo, who is an "excellent artist" (228), is the wife of his youngest adopted son, KURT ADAMS.

Pandora In *Timequake*, Vonnegut states that his big brother Bernard had never been a FRANKENSTEIN-like scientist, or a Pandora either. He explains that in Greek mythology Pandora was the first woman made by the gods. Angry at PROMETHEUS for stealing fire, the gods give Pandora a box, which Prometheus begs her not to open. But she does open the box, and all worldly evil flies out of it. The last item to fly out of the box, however, is hope. In telling this story, Vonnegut seems bemused that the gods' act of vengeance is the creation of a woman.

Pellegrino, Peter Peter Pellegrino, an avid hot-air balloonist and a founder of the Balloon Federation of America, is one of the people whom Vonnegut imagines interviewing in the afterlife in *God Bless You, Dr. Kevorkian*.

Petro, Joe, III Joe Petro III was Vonnegut's partner in an artistic business venture called ORIGAMI EXPRESS, a business still in operation after Vonnegut's death. A silk screen artist based in Kentucky, Petro took Vonnegut's original drawings and paintings and made silk screen prints of them, which were then offered for sale. Vonnegut describes the partnership most fully in the author's

Silkscreen, *Absolut Vonnegut* (© 2007 Origami Express LLC, Kurt Vonnegut, and Joe Petro III. www.vonnegut.com)

note that ends the collection *A Man Without a Country*.

Pilgrim's Progress, The Vonnegut's *Slaughterhouse-Five* is seen by many critics as a parody of John Bunyan's 1678 allegory, *The Pilgrim's Progress*, which depicts the journey of an everyman figure named Christian from a "City of Destruction" to a "Celestial City" on Mt. Zion. In Vonnegut's novel, his protagonist, Billy Pilgrim, moves from the fire-bombed city of DRESDEN to a new Eden on the planet Tralfamadore.

Pollock, Jackson   Jackson Pollock was the best known and perhaps the most influential of the ABSTRACT EXPRESSIONIST painters working in New York in the period immediately following the end of World War II. Famous for his "drip" method of covering a canvas, Pollock appears as a colleague and friend of Rabo Karabekian in the novel *Bluebeard*. In the collection *Fates Worse Than Death*, Vonnegut includes an essay he wrote for *Esquire* magazine about Jackson Pollock, in which he compares abstract expressionist painting to jazz music. Both great jazz musicians and great abstract painters, according to Vonnegut, are "champion[s] and connoisseur[s] of the appealing accidents which more formal artists worked hard to exclude from their performances" (42). Pollock is also mentioned in *Timequake*, when Vonnegut's older brother, Bernard, sends him pictures consisting of squiggles of paint that have been squashed between two sheets of glass and asks Kurt: "Is this art or not?" (166). Vonnegut believes that his brother could not have asked such a "jeering" question 50 years before, before the work of "Jack the Dripper," who also "couldn't draw for sour apples" (166), changed the world's view of art.

postmodernism   In literary studies, postmodernism refers to a body of works published during the second half of the 20th century, especially in the 1960s and early 1970s, by authors such as Thomas Pynchon, John Barth, Donald Barthelme, John Fowles, Italo Calvino, Kurt Vonnegut, and many others. Postmodern literature is marked by a fragmented, often nonlinear style, sometimes referred to as "collage" or "pastiche." It tends to be ironic in tone and to draw attention to itself as fiction, often including authorial commentary on the story as part of the story itself. Characters in postmodern fiction, rather than being "well-rounded" or fully fleshed out, often tend to be flat—character types rather than three-dimensional people. (Vonnegut comments famously in *Slaughterhouse-Five* that "There are almost no characters in this story, and almost no dramatic confrontations, because most of the people in it are so sick and so much the listless playthings of enormous forces. One of the main effects of war, after all, is that people are discouraged from being characters" [164]). The flattening out of character in postmodern works results from a skepticism among postmodern thinkers about individuality itself. Postmodernists often view human beings as socially or biologically constructed entities rather than free agents acting independently on the world around them. In addition, postmodern fiction often presents the world as completely commodified: Mass media images not only shape reality but often come to replace the reality they represent. Often, this literature has an apocalyptic feel to it, as postmodern authors are acutely aware that contemporary human beings live under the threat of nuclear destruction, environmental degradation, overpopulation, and depletion of natural resources. It is a literature that tends to be aware of and to explore culturally marginalized and historically oppressed groups, that sees human society as fragmented and various. Above all, postmodern writers are highly suspicious of Enlightenment ideas about human rationality and progress. Vonnegut is one of the writers most frequently mentioned as a postmodernist by critics and literary historians.

Prometheus   In *Timequake*, Vonnegut briefly discusses the Greek mythological figure Prometheus. According to Vonnegut, Promoetheus "steals fire from Heaven and gives it to [humans] so they can be warm and cook, and not, one would hope, so we could incinerate all the little yellow bastards in Hiroshima and Nagasaki, which are in Japan" (195).

quietism Quietism was a form of Christian mysticism popular in 17th-century Europe that advocated stillness and passivity as the best ways for human beings to achieve perfection. Since that time, quietism as a philosophy has garnered more secular connotations, especially through the work of thinkers such as German philosopher Arthur Schopenhauer, who advocated, in a way similar to Buddhism, that humans free themselves from troubling desires. This philosophy is relevant to Vonnegut's fiction in that several critics have accused the writer of advocating in his works a kind of quietism, or, in the words of critic Charles Harris, a "resigned acceptance" to fate. The debate over Vonnegut as a quietist has largely centered on *Slaughterhouse-Five*, with critics such as Harris and Tony Tanner arguing that Vonnegut promotes quietism, while others, chief among them Robert Merrill and Peter Scholl, assert that Vonnegut ultimately rejects quietist principles.

R

Rait, Rita Rita Rait was Vonnegut's Russian translator, whom he greatly admired. She also translated the works of William Faulkner, J. D. Salinger, JOHN UPDIKE, Franz Kafka, ANNE FRANK and others into Russian. In the collection *Fates Worse Than Death*, Vonnegut writes that he has "become fonder of . . . Rita Rait" than he is of anybody else outside his own family (180), and he includes an essay called "Invite Rita Rait to America!" in the collection *Wampeters, Foma, and Granfalloons*.

Rauch, Gertrude Schnull Gertrude Schnull Rauch was a first cousin of Vonnegut's father, KURT VONNEGUT, SR. In *Palm Sunday*, Vonnegut explains that Gertrude's husband, JOHN RAUCH, made a gift to the younger Vonnegut of a manuscript entitled "An Account of the Ancestry of Kurt Vonnegut, Jr., by an Ancient Friend of His Family." Vonnegut quotes extensively from this account in *Palm Sunday*, claiming that it was better written than much of Vonnegut's "own stuff" (18).

Rauch, John John Rauch, whom Vonnegut refers to as his "Uncle John," was actually the husband of a first cousin of KURT VONNEGUT, SR.—GERTRUDE SCHNULL RAUCH. A HARVARD-trained INDIANAPOLIS lawyer, Rauch figures prominently in the autobiographical collage *Palm Sunday*, where Vonnegut quotes extensively from a painstakingly researched account of the Vonnegut family history prepared by his Uncle John.

Ray, James Earl MARTIN LUTHER KING, JR., assassin James Earl Ray is one of the people Vonnegut imagines interviewing in the afterlife in *God Bless You, Dr. Kevorkian*. Unrepentant in Heaven, James Earl Ray says the only reason he regrets shooting King is because his bullet turned the civil rights leader into "some kind of American hero" (58).

Redfield, Dr. Robert Dr. Robert Redfield was the head of the Anthropology Department at the UNIVERSITY OF CHICAGO when Vonnegut was a graduate student there in 1945–46. Vonnegut greatly admired Dr. Redfield's theories about "folk societies"—primitive, close-knit groups of people often related to one another by family ties, in which there was very little division of labor, and in which individuals were valued for themselves rather than for their utility to the group. Vonnegut argues in numerous essays, including his "Address to the National Institute of Arts and Letters, 1971," reprinted in *Wampeters, Foma, and Granfalloons*, that modern humans are chemically engineered to desire to live in such societies and feel alienated and lonely because they no longer do. Dr. Redfield's ideas also inform many of Vonnegut's fictional works, including novels such as *Slapstick*, in which Dr. Wilbur Swain tries to create artificial extended families that will mimic the folk societies of more primitive cultures.

RENAMO RENAMO is the shorthand name for a group called the National Resistance of Mozambique. Vonnegut became acquainted with this group when he traveled to Mozambique as a guest of the Christian charity group CARE in 1989, an experience he describes in the essay collection *Fates Worse Than Death*. According to Vonnegut, RENAMO should be thought of as an "incurable disease" (169). The group has caused enormous suffering in the country through repeated acts of rape, murder, and pillage.

Riley, James Whitcomb   James Whitcomb Riley, known as the "Hoosier Poet," was a native of INDI-ANAPOLIS who wrote humorous and sentimental verse in the late 19th and early 20th centuries. Vonnegut refers to Riley in several of his works as a fellow writer and Indianapolis native. In *Jailbird* and *Timequake*, Vonnegut tells readers that Riley's grave lies on the top of Crown Hill, in the same cemetery where Vonnegut's own family members are buried.

Rivera, Geraldo   Geraldo Rivera, the sensational-ist television journalist, was married to Vonnegut's daughter Edith from 1971 to 1975. Vonnegut men-tions his former son-in-law in the collection *Fates Worse Than Death*, where he describes the marriage as "unfortunate" (27).

Robert's Rules of Order   Wilbur Swain, narra-tor of *Slapstick*, tells readers the story of how West Point graduate Henry Martyn Robert invented a set of rules to govern how meetings are conducted. These rules were published as *Robert's Rules of Order*, a book that Swain believes is "one of the four greatest inventions by Americans" (246). The other three are the Bill of Rights, ALCOHOLICS ANONYMOUS, and the artificial extended families imagined by him and his twin sister, Eliza.

Roethke, Theodore   In the opening chapter of *Slaughterhouse-Five*, Vonnegut tells readers that,

while stranded in the Boston fog waiting for his plane to Germany to take off, he reads part of a book of poems by 20th century American poet Theodore Roethke, *Words for the Wind*. The lines Vonnegut reads, and which he quotes in the novel, are from Roethke's poem "The Waking":

> I wake to sleep, and take my waking slow.
> I feel my fate in what I cannot fear.
> I learn by going where I have to go.

Rushdie, Salman   In the collection *Fates Worse Than Death*, Vonnegut writes about having the British-Indian novelist Salman Rushdie over to his house for lunch in 1981. Rushdie expressed an interest in meeting the American realist writer NELSON ALGREN, with whom Vonnegut was acquainted. When Vonnegut called Algren's home to arrange a meeting, however, he discovered that the writer had died of a heart attack that very morning. Later in the book, Vonnegut tells about writing Rushdie a letter after the author had gone into hiding subsequent to a fatwa, or death con-tract, being placed on him for supposedly insulting Islam in his novel *The Satanic Verses*. Although he never answered Vonnegut's letter, Rushdie did publish a review of the novel *Hocus Pocus*, which argued that Vonnegut "was a burned out case and so on" (*Fates* 131). Vonnegut tells readers he was so upset he considered putting out a contract on Rushdie himself.

Russell, Bertrand   In *Timequake*, Vonnegut men-tions that the British philosopher Bertrand Russell claimed to have lost friends to one of three addic-tions: "alcohol or religion or chess" (32). Vonnegut adds that he himself, like writer Kilgore Trout, is hooked on "making idiosyncratic arrangements in horizontal lines, with ink on bleached and flattened wood pulp, of twenty-six phonetic symbols, ten numbers, and about eight punctuation marks" (32).

S

Sacco and Vanzetti Nicola Sacco and Bartolomeo Vanzetti were Italian immigrant anarchists who were executed in 1927 for robbery and murder in Boston, Massachusetts, in a politically charged case most historians feel was a gross miscarriage of justice. The Sacco and Vanzetti case plays an important role in *Jailbird*. The novel's narrator, Walter F. Starbuck, protested the executions of Sacco and Vanzetti as a young man, fully expecting their martyrdom to be "retold as often and as movingly, to be as irresistible, as the story of Jesus Christ some day" (228). Yet, years later, when Starbuck asks a young hotel night clerk what he knows about the Sacco and Vanzetti case, the young man confuses the two men with 1920s thrill-killers Leopold and Loeb.

Sage, Anna Anna Sage, the notorious "Lady in Red" who betrayed 1930s-era bank robber JOHN DILLINGER to the FBI, appears briefly in *Timequake*. Vonnegut reminisces about how he and his sister Alice, 11 and 16 when Dillinger was killed, both reviled Anna Sage at the time for causing the death of one of their heroes.

Sakharov, Andrei In *Timequake*, Vonnegut points out the irony in the fact that Soviet physicist Andrei Sakharov won a Nobel Peace Prize in 1975 for demanding a halt to the testing of the very nuclear weapons he himself had helped to build. Vonnegut also tells readers about the time in 1987 when he was asked to accept an honorary degree from Staten Island College in New York City on behalf of Sakharov, whose government would not let him attend the ceremony. Although he finds it a "cockamamie exhortation," Vonnegut delivers Sakharov's message to the crowd—"Don't give up on nuclear energy" (6)—one year after the nuclear disaster at Chernobyl, in Ukraine.

Sandburg, Carl In *A Man Without a Country*, Vonnegut praises the early 20th-century American poet Carl Sandburg as a "self-taught workman" who was also a "splendid" writer and speaker. Vonnegut points out that Sandburg, like Vonnegut himself, was a "freshwater person" from the American Great Lakes region.

Saroyan, William In *Timequake*, Vonnegut, noting how many writers seem to have uncontrollable addictions, muses that gambling ruined the American writer William Saroyan.

satire Satire is a literary technique in which an author uses ridicule, wit, and humor to critique social or political ills. Probably the best known satirical piece ever written is JONATHAN SWIFT's 1729 essay "A Modest Proposal," in which he recommends the Irish eat their own children as a solution to the poverty and hunger they face. Vonnegut is frequently classified as a satirical writer. Like other satirists, he uses exaggeration and humor in his works, but also offers serious critiques of society, in the hopes of drawing attention to and possibly remedying what he perceives as societal foolishness and injustice.

Saundby, Sir Robert Sir Robert Saundby was a British air marshal who wrote one of the forewords to David Irving's book *The Destruction of Dresden*, which Colonel Bertram Copeland Rumfoord reads in the hospital room he shares with Billy Pilgrim in *Slaughterhouse-Five*. Saundby's foreword questions whether the Dresden bombings were a military necessity, a view shared by Vonnegut himself.

Schnull, Henry Henry Schnull was one of Kurt Vonnegut's great-grandfathers. Like most of Vonnegut's ancestors, Schnull emigrated from Germany to Indianapolis a few years before the beginning of the Civil War. Henry, along with his brother, August, first made a living by selling farm produce throughout central Indiana. He eventually expanded his operations to become one of the leading merchants in Indianapolis, founding Eagle Machine Works, which later became the Atlas Engine Company, as well as the American Woolen Company, the first textile mill in the United States He died in 1905 an extremely wealthy and well-respected man.

Schnull, Matilda Schramm Matilda Schramm Schnull was one of Vonnegut's paternal great-grandmothers, wife of German immigrant and merchant Henry Schnull. In the account of the Vonnegut family ancestry written by John Rauch

Henry Schnull family photograph, circa 1895 *(courtesy of The Lilly Library, Indiana University, Bloomington, Indiana)*

and reproduced in the collection *Palm Sunday*, she is described as a "stern and tough" woman who also had "a warm, lovable disposition" and who served as "the real matriarch of the family" (30).

science and technology Vonnegut, who refers to himself as a Luddite in *Timequake* and elsewhere—someone who fears and avoids technological change—is often critical in both his fiction and nonfiction of new advances in science and technology. In his first novel, *Player Piano*, for instance, the Ghost Shirt Society sparks a revolution that is intended to destroy the machinery that has put so many people out of work. While the revolution ultimately fails, Vonnegut sympathizes with its intent, showing in the novel the problems that arise when humans have no meaningful work to do, when technological advances take their jobs away. Vonnegut is especially critical of a science and technology that is divorced from moral considerations. Dr. Felix Hoenikker, one of the main contributers to the development of the ATOMIC BOMB and the inventor of *ice-nine* in *Cat's Cradle*, comes off as something of an amoral monster, with no meaningful ties to his fellow human beings. He cannot recognize the sinful nature of his own scientific discoveries. Similarly, in plays such as *Fortitude* and short stories such as "Welcome to the Monkey House," "2BRO2B," and "Tomorrow and Tomorrow and Tomorrow," scientific discoveries that at first promise to be humankind's salvation and discoveries that eradicate disease, stop aging, or extend human life artificially are presented as double-edged swords, creating whole new problems such as overpopulation, depletion of natural resources, and reduced quality of life. Thus, in his numerous essays and speeches, Vonnegut often advocates a new kind of science, one that will be keenly aware of moral issues. This was a science that he believed was beginning to develop amid the youth culture of the 1960s. In a 1969 address to the American Physical Society, Vonnegut argued that "any young scientist . . . when asked by the military to create a terror weapon on the order of napalm, is bound to suspect that he may be committing modern sin," adding, "God bless him for that" (*Wampeters* 104). Vonnegut's optimism

about changing attitudes toward science and technology, however, had largely faded by 2005, when he published the collection *A Man Without a Country*, in which he argues that human beings "have now all but destroyed this once salubrious planet as a life-support system in fewer than two hundred years" (43). The war in Iraq, along with the world's ever-increasing dependency on fossil fuels, pushed Vonnegut to the conclusion that science and technology are not making the world a better place at all, but leading human beings on a path to destruction.

science fiction Vonnegut's early works, in particular *Player Piano* and *The Sirens of Titan* and short stories such as "Welcome to the Monkey House" and "Harrison Bergeron," have often been labeled by critics as science fiction, a genre characterized, in the words of writer Robert A. Heinlein, by realistic speculation about possible future events, based on a thorough knowledge of the physical world and the scientific method. Science fiction elements most often enter Vonnegut's later works through the stories and novels of recurring character and Vonnegut alter ego Kilgore Trout. Several critics have argued that these science fiction elements allow Vonnegut to explore alternative worlds and ways of life when humans themselves seem so bent on destroying their planet and themselves. In the first essay reprinted in *Wampeters, Foma, and Granfalloons*, Vonnegut discusses the genre of science fiction, arguing that serious critics of literature tend to mistake the "file drawer labeled 'science fiction'" for "a urinal" (1). He tells readers that he did not know he was a science fiction writer until he read reviews of *Player Piano*, which he speculates was characterized as science fiction simply because he noticed and wrote about technology in it. While recognizing that there is much bad science fiction writing in the world, Vonnegut nevertheless deplores the notion that "no one can simultaneously be a respectable writer and understand how a refrigerator works" (1) and advises young writers that they could do worse than to throw a little physics or chemistry into their stories. In his essay "Excelsior! We're Going to the Moon! Excelsior!," also reprinted in *Wampeters, Foma, and Granfal-*

loons, Vonnegut argues that good science fiction writers, like all good writers, focus on what it means to be human while also paying attention to the changing world that surrounds human beings. Because significant world changes come largely from SCIENCE AND TECHNOLOGY, these areas constitute one of his concerns throughout his writing.

Semmelweis, Ignaz   In the collection *A Man Without a Country*, Vonnegut describes Dr. Ignaz Semmelweis as "a truly modern hero" (89). Semmelweis, who was born in Budapest in 1818, was an obstetrician working in a maternity hospital for the poor in Vienna, Austria, at a time when one woman out of 10 died of fever following childbirth. After close observation, Semmelweis insisted that physicians begin washing their hands before treating expectant mothers, and the death rate dropped dramatically. Yet, Semmelweis was later forced out of the hospital because of the perception that his insistence on hand washing was an insult to his social superiors. He ended up killing himself in a provincial hospital in Hungary.

serenity prayer   The organization ALCOHOLICS ANONYMOUS has for more than 50 years used a version of what has come to be called the serenity prayer to inspire its members to change their lives and to accept what cannot be changed. The origin of the prayer is uncertain, with some scholars tracing it back to the ancient Greeks and other early sources, and others arguing it was written by American theologian Reinhold Niebuhr in 1943. The best known version of the prayer reads:

> God grant us the serenity to accept the things
> we cannot change,
> courage to change the things we can,
> and wisdom to know the difference.

Vonnegut cites the serenity prayer two times in *Slaughterhouse-Five*. Readers first see the prayer written on a plaque that hangs in Billy Pilgrim's optometry office. Ironically, Vonnegut quotes the words of the prayer, then follows up with this line: "Among the things Billy Pilgrim could not change were the past, the present, and the future" (60), suggesting to some critics a deterministic view of

Illustration of serenity prayer on Montana Wildhack"s locket from *Slaughterhouse-Five (used by permission of Dell Publishing, a division of Random House, Inc.)*

the universe. The serenity prayer is also quoted at the end of Billy Pilgrim's story. Montana Wildhack, Billy's mate in the Tralfamadorian zoo, has the words engraved on a locket that she wears between her breasts. A picture of Montana's locket serves as the book's final illustration.

Shakespeare, William   William Shakespeare is one of the people whom Vonnegut interviews in the afterlife in *God Bless You, Dr. Kevorkian*. Vonnegut tells readers that he and the famous playwright "did not hit it off" (59). He imagines Shakespeare calling Vonnegut's midwestern American dialect "the ugliest English he had ever heard" (59). Nevertheless, Vonnegut is a great admirer of Shakespeare's works, and references to his plays and poems are scattered throughout Vonnegut's own fiction, ranging from comparisons between HAMLET and Eliot Rosewater in *God Bless You, Mr. Rosewater,* to Eliza Swain's broadcasting of Shakespeare's sonnet 39 from a helicopter to her beloved twin brother, Wilbur, in *Slapstick,* to a pun on the famous "To Be or Not To Be" soliloquy in the title of the short story "2BRO2B."

Shaw, George Bernard   George Bernard Shaw, winner of the 1925 Nobel Prize in literature, was an Irish playwright who lived and wrote in England in the late 19th and early 20th centuries. In *Time-quake,* Vonnegut describes Shaw as his "hero"—as a "socialist" as well as a "shrewd and funny play-wright" (141). He tells readers that Shaw, when he was in his 80s, said that if he were considered smart, "he sure pitied people who were considered

George Bernard Shaw, 1934 *(courtesy of the Library of Congress)*

dumb" (141). Vonnegut claims that this is how he feels as well. Vonnegut also writes of his admiration for Shaw's play *Back to Methuselah,* in which Adam and Eve eventually work up the courage to tell God they would like life better if they knew it was going to end sometime.

Shaw, Irwin   Vonnegut delivered a speech prais-ing Irwin Shaw at a banquet in the writer's honor in New York in 1979. In this speech, reprinted in *Palm Sunday,* Vonnegut claims that Shaw "wrote the best American novel about World War Two, which was *The Young Lions*" (125). Although Von-negut apologizes for making the preceding remark while JOSEPH HELLER is present in the audience, he nevertheless praises Shaw for being the only American who was willing to write about the war "from both sides of the line" (125).

Shelley, Mary   Included in the collection *Fates Worse Than Death* is a speech Vonnegut made to the graduating class of the MASSACHUSETTS INSTITUTE OF TECHNOLOGY in 1985, in which he describes Mary Shelley, the author of FRANKEN-STEIN, as "the most effective doubter of the ben-efits of unbridled technological advancement so far" (119). Mary Shelley also appears in *God Bless You, Dr. Kevorkian,* as one of the spirits of the dead whom Vonnegut interviews in the afterlife. In this book, Vonnegut refers to Shelley as author of "the most prescient and influential science fiction novel of all times" (64). When Vonnegut explains to Shelley that many ignorant people in his day believe that "Frankenstein" is the name of the monster rather than the scientist who created him, Shelley gently replies, "That's not so ignorant after all. There are two monsters in my story, not one. And one of them, the scientist, is indeed named Frankenstein" (65).

Shortridge Echo, The   During his high school years, Vonnegut served as editor of his high school's daily newspaper, *The Shortridge Echo,* one of only two high school dailies in the country at the time. In an interview in *Playboy* magazine, reprinted in the collection *Wampeter, Foma, and Granfalloons,* Vonnegut explains that his experience working for

Shortridge High School *(Courtesy of Bass Photo Co. Collection, Indiana Historical Society)*

The Shortridge Echo taught him to write quickly and for a large audience of real readers who were unafraid to give him feedback.

Shortridge High School Shortridge High School is the name of the public high school that Vonnegut attended in INDIANAPOLIS, Indiana. Although his older brother and sister had been given private educations, the Vonnegut family's financial difficulties during the years of the Great Depression made private schools unaffordable for the family's youngest son. Vonnegut writes often of the excellent education he received at Shortridge High.

Slovik, Private Eddie Private Eddie Slovik was shot by firing squad in 1945 for cowardice, the first U.S. soldier to be executed for desertion since the Civil War. Slovik's story inspired the libretto Vonnegut wrote for *L'histoire du Soldat,* a modernist theatrical work updated for the contemporary stage in 1993. Slovik also appears in the novel *Slaughterhouse-Five,* when Billy Pilgrim reads a real-life book called *The Execution of Private Slovik* while sitting in the lobby of his mother's nursing home. Slovik's ignoble death most likely inspired the decidedly unheroic death of Edgar Derby, the American soldier and former high school teacher in that novel who is shot in Germany for pilfering a teapot.

Smith College Vonnegut served as writer-in-residence and distinguished senior lecturer in English at Smith College in Northampton, Massachusetts, during the academic year 2000–01.

socialism Vonnegut, in much of his fiction and in numerous speeches and essays, reveals his sympathy toward socialist forms of government, those which attempt to distribute wealth more evenly among citizens than capitalist systems do. In *Breakfast of Champions,* for instance, Vonnegut describes communism as "a theory that what was left of the planet should be shared more or less equally among all the people" (12), as contrasted to capitalism, which he describes as a system in which "everybody . . . was supposed to grab whatever he could and hold on to it" (13). In his address to the Bennington College graduating class of 1970, reprinted in the collection *Wampeters, Foma, and Granfalloons,* he urges the Bennington students to "work for a socialist form of government" (170). He sees socialism as the political option kindest to "the old and the sick and the shy and the poor and the stupid, and . . . people nobody likes" (170). He echoes these ideas in his final collection, *A Man Without a Country,* in which he argues that "'Socialism' is no more an evil word than 'Christianity'" (11). In fact, Christianity and socialism have much in common, according to Vonnegut, in that each "prescribes a society dedicated to the proposition that all men, women, and children are created equal and shall not starve" (11). Vonnegut admires many socialist activists as well, particularly Indiana native and frequent presidential candidate EUGENE DEBS, whom he quotes frequently in his work.

Solomon, Syd Syd Solomon is a painter friend of Vonnegut's and fellow World War II veteran, whom the writer mentions in several of his essays. In the collection *Palm Sunday,* Vonnegut relates a story about writing an essay for the beginning of a catalogue for one of Solomon's painting exhibits. When Vonnegut asks the abstract painter to describe "what he thought he was doing with paint," Solomon is unable to answer (145). Vonnegut tells readers this inability does not make Solomon's paintings any less "honorable" or "beautiful" (145). For Vonnegut, ABSTRACT EXPRESSIONIST art is connected to "the deeper, quieter, more mysterious parts" of the mind (146). Making art, for a painter like Solomon, is akin to meditation. In *Fates Worse Than Death*, Vonnegut quotes Syd Solomon's advice on how to distinguish good painting from bad painting: "look at a million paintings first" (45), a tidbit that will later be repeated in *Bluebeard* as well as in *A Man Without a Country*.

Steinbeck, John American novelist John Steinbeck is one of the four alcoholic writers that the Xanadu writer's retreat names its guest suites for in *Timequake*. The others are ERNEST HEMINGWAY, EUGENE O'NEILL, and SINCLAIR LEWIS.

Steinberg, Saul Graphic artist and *New Yorker* cartoonist Saul Steinberg was a friend of Vonnegut's, whom the writer describes in *A Man Without a Country* as "the wisest person" he ever met in his life (134). Among many other nuggets of wisdom that he quotes from Steinberg in this book is the artist's statement that what one responds to in any work of art "is the artist's struggle against his or her limitations" (135).

Strange Case of Dr. Jekyll and Mr. Hyde, The A novella published by Robert Louis Stevenson in 1886, *The Strange Case of Dr. Jekyll and Mr. Hyde* is updated by Vonnegut in his play "The Chemistry Professor," which appears as a chapter in the collection *Palm Sunday: An Autobiographical Collage*.

Strax, Dr. Philip One of the dead souls that Vonnegut imagines interviewing in *God Bless You, Dr. Kevorkian*, Dr. Philip Strax was a poet and radiologist who invented mammogram technology after the death of his beloved wife, Gertrude, from breast cancer that was detected too late.

Streetcar Named Desire, A The TENNESSEE WILLIAMS play *A Streetcar Named Desire* is the theatrical piece that is being produced in Vonnegut's short story "Who Am I This Time?" Vonnegut briefly discusses the play as well in *Timequake*, where he states that speeches from this play, and others of its era, serve as "emotional and ethical landmarks" in his life (25).

Stringer, Lee Author of *Grand Central Winter* and *Sleepaway School*, books detailing his three-year stint at a juvenile detention center as a young teenager and the decade he spent homeless and crack-addicted on the streets of New York City, Lee Stringer is an African-American writer greatly admired by Vonnegut. Like *Shaking Hands with God: A Conversation About Writing*, a short book published in 1999, is a transcription of a public conversation held between Vonnegut and Stringer at a Union Square bookstore in Manhattan on the evening of October 1, 1998.

Sturgeon, Theodore Theodore Sturgeon was a prolific American SCIENCE FICTION writer who lived from 1918 to 1985, and who reached the height of his popularity in the 1950s, when he was the most anthologized author alive. Vonnegut has stated that the character of science fiction writer Kilgore Trout is based on Sturgeon, and Vonnegut wrote the foreword to *A Saucer of Loneliness*, the seventh volume of the complete stories of Theodore Sturgeon.

Susann, Jacqueline Jacqueline Susann was the mid-20th-century author of popular, mass market novels, including the 1966 *Valley of the Dolls*, a soap-opera style tale of three women who become rich and famous, which was a smash success and made into a Hollywood movie the following year. Susann's work makes an appearance in Vonnegut's *Slaughterhouse-Five*, when *Valley of the Dolls* is the only book in English the Tralfamadorians have to give Billy Pilgrim, who requests something to read after his kidnapping by the aliens. Billy thinks the book is "pretty good in spots" and notes that "the people in it certainly had their ups and downs" (87). Susann's novel is contrasted to the short, nonlinear Tralfamadorian novels, which Billy also reads on the spaceship.

Swift, Jonathan In the collection *Palm Sunday*, Vonnegut includes a brief preface that he wrote for a new edition of *Gulliver's Travels* by 18th-century satirist Jonathan Swift, which he tells readers was rejected by the book's publisher for being too sentimental. In it, Vonnegut argues that Swift's Gulliver learns from his travels that human beings are "disgusting in the extreme," a view that "is not Swift's own opinion of us" (237). Instead, Vonnegut concludes that Gulliver's disgust with human beings "is meant to be ridiculous" and that "Swift is teaching us a lesson . . . that our readiness to feel disgust for ourselves and others is not, perhaps, the guardian of civilization so many of us imagine it to be. Disgust, in fact, may be the chief damager of our reason, of our common sense" (237).

T

Theosophical Society The Theosophical Society, an organization dedicated to exploring Eastern spiritual practices and to a vision of worldwide brotherhood, was founded in New York City in 1875 by Russian immigrant and mystic MADAME HELENA BLAVATSKY, along with American lawyer and Civil War veteran COLONEL HENRY OLCOTT. Vonnegut briefly describes the group in his essay "The Mysterious Madame Blavatsky," reprinted in *Wampeters, Foma, and Granfalloons.* In this essay, he calls the Theosophical Society a "sane and altruistic" group that "brought America wisdom from the East, which it very much needed" (138–139).

Thompson, Hunter S. Hunter S. Thompson was a journalist and fiction writer famous for inventing "gonzo journalism," a style that abandoned objective reporting in favor of an unconventional and highly subjective style. Among his most well known works are *Hell's Angels: A Strange and Terrible Saga* and *Fear and Loathing in Las Vegas: A Savage Journey to the Heart of the American Dream.* In the collection *Wampeters, Foma, and Granfalloons,* Vonnegut writes of his admiration for Thompson and includes a reprint of a book review of *Fear and Loathing on the Campaign Trail '72,* in which he describes Thompson as "the most creatively crazy and vulnerable of the New Journalists" (231).

Thoreau, Henry David In *Timequake,* Vonnegut quotes the 19th-century transcendentalist writer Henry David Thoreau—"The mass of men lead lives of quiet desperation" (2)—in support of his point that the most "highly evolved Earthling creatures find being alive embarrassing or much worse" (1). In the collection *Palm Sunday,* Vonnegut muses that Thoreau's statement, "I have traveled extensively in Concord" (53), is an expression of the childlike view that "there is surely more than enough to marvel at for a lifetime" in one's hometown (53). Vonnegut is sympathetic to this view as he reminisces about the INDIANAPOLIS of his youth.

Tiglath-pileser the Third The actual ancient Assyrian king Tiglath-pileser the Third figures into Vonnegut's novel *Mother Night* when one of Howard W. Campbell Jr.'s Israeli prison guards, an 18-year-old boy named Arnold Marx, who knows nothing about the World War II, tells Campbell about the burning of the Canaanite city of Hazor by an Israelite army about 1,400 years before Christ. According to Arnold, King Solomon rebuilt the city, but it was burned down again in 732 B.C. by Tiglath-pileser the Third. Vonnegut includes this piece of information not only to emphasize the point that young people, even Jews, are often ignorant of recent history, but also to show a continuing, futile cycle of destruction in the world.

Tocqueville, Alexis de In the collection *A Man Without a Country,* Vonnegut praises the work of French historian and political philosopher Alexis de Tocqueville, who traveled to America in the 1830s to observe and write about the young country. Vonnegut tells readers that he considers "anybody a twerp who hasn't read *Democracy in Action* by Alexis de Tocqueville," adding that "there can never be a better book than that one on the strengths and vulnerabilities inherent in our form of government" (8).

Toynbee, Arnold   In *Timequake*, Vonnegut tells about reading *A Study of History* by the great English historian Arnold Toynbee in a class he took while a graduate student at the UNIVERSITY OF CHICAGO. Toynbee, Vonnegut explains, wrote about how various civilizations responded to challenges. He then goes on to describe how Kilgore Trout responded calmly and rationally to the death and devastation caused by the reinstitution of FREE WILL when the 10-year timequake described in the novel comes to an end.

Tucker, Karla Faye   Karla Faye Tucker (whose name Vonnegut misspells as "Carla Faye Tucker") was a convicted murderer who became a born-again Christian while in prison in Texas. In 1998, Tucker became the first woman executed by the state of Texas since the Civil War. Tucker's death seems to be one of the events prompting Vonnegut's writing of the short, odd little book *God Bless You, Dr. Kevorkian*, in which he imagines being strapped to a gurney in the Huntsville State Prison in Texas—the facility where Tucker herself was executed—and being administered just enough drugs by DR. JACK KEVORKIAN to have near-death experiences during which he is able to interview dead people in heaven. In his interview of Karla Faye Tucker, Vonnegut imagines the executed woman telling him that the governor of Texas is a murderer just as much as she is.

Twain, Mark   Nineteenth-century writer and humorist Mark Twain, best known for his novel *Adventures of Huckleberry Finn*, is cited by numerous critics as Vonnegut's most important literary ancestor. Twain's finely honed sense of humor and increasing pessimism about human beings toward the end of his life make Twain seem quite similar to Vonnegut to many readers. In several of his works, Vonnegut mentions his own appreciation of Twain. In the prologue to *Slapstick*, he explains that he and his older brother, BERNARD VONNEGUT, enjoy the same kind of jokes—"Mark Twain stuff, Laurel and Hardy stuff" (4). In *Timequake*, Vonnegut calls Twain "the funniest American of his time," but he also recognizes the despair that Twain felt in his later life. Vonnegut argues, in fact, that "the most highly evolved Earthling creatures"—such as Twain—"find being alive embarrassing or much worse" (1). In addition, Vonnegut includes in his collection *Palm Sunday* a speech he gave at the 100th anniversary of the completion of Mark Twain's house in Hartford, Connecticut, in which he states his belief that Twain expressed a message similar to that expressed by Christ in the Beatitudes. He also addresses the bitterness that Twain slipped into in later life as well as Twain's distrust of technology. Vonnegut concludes the speech by telling the audience that he named his first born son, MARK VONNEGUT, after Twain. Finally, in the collection, *A Man Without a Country*, Vonnegut mentions Twain frequently, telling readers about the "most humiliated and heartbroken" (75) essay Twain ever wrote, which detailed the slaughter of 600 Moro men, women and children by U.S. soldiers after the Spanish-American War. Vonnegut notes as well that he, like Twain, is giving up on people at the end of his life. Twain's view, expressed in *The Mysterious Stranger*, that Satan, not God, created the planet Earth and "the damned human race" (112) seems to Vonnegut increasingly plausible as Vonnegut himself decries in the book the politics of the Bush administration and the sad state of affairs he believes the country has slipped into.

U

Unitarian Universalism Unitarian Universalism is a liberal faith that respects religious pluralism and individual freedom of choice in matters of belief. It was formed in 1961 by the merging of the Unitarian and Universalist denominations. While Vonnegut actually considers himself to be a humanist (*see* HUMANISM) and a freethinker, in the collection *Fates Worse Than Death*, he tells readers that, "in order not to seem a spiritual quadriplegic to strangers trying to get a fix" on him, he sometimes says that he is a Unitarian Universalist (157). Thus, that denomination, Vonnegut adds, claims him "as one of its own" (157).

University of Chicago In December 1945, after his return from World War II, Vonnegut enrolled as a graduate student in anthropology at the University of Chicago. He also worked as a reporter for the Chicago City News Bureau during this time. Although his master's thesis, "On the Fluctuation Between Good and Evil in Simple Tales," was unanimously rejected, he was awarded his master of arts degree from the University of Chicago in 1971, when the faculty decided that his novel *Cat's Cradle* made a significant contribution to the field of cultural anthropology.

University of Iowa Vonnegut taught creative writing at the prestigious University of Iowa Writer's Workshop from 1965 to 1967.

Updike, John In the collection *Fates Worse Than Death*, Vonnegut tells readers that the well-known 20th-century American writer John Updike was scheduled to lecture in INDIANAPOLIS shortly after the 50th birthday party Vonnegut held for his wife, JILL KREMENTZ. Before going, Updike asked Vonnegut what he should know about the city of Vonnegut's birth. Vonnegut explained to Updike that the city's location was determined by "a pen and straightedge," placed as precisely as possible in the middle of the state and laid out like "an infinitely expandable chessboard of identical squares, each block one-tenth of a mile long, with all streets running exactly east and west or north and south, and with a circle in the middle" (93).

van Gogh, Vincent In *Timequake*, SCIENCE FIC-TION writer Kilgore Trout tells people that his name is Vincent van Gogh because he feels he has much in common with the famous painter: "'The main thing about van Gogh and me,' said Trout, 'is that he painted pictures that astonished *him* with their importance, even though nobody else thought they were worth a damn, and I write stories that astonish *me*, even though nobody else thinks they're worth a damn. How lucky can you get?'" (105).

Vietnam War The U.S. war in Vietnam, raging from the mid 1960s through the early 1970s, figures in several Vonnegut works. In the final chapter of *Slaughterhouse-Five*, Vonnegut mentions the body counts associated with the Vietnam War, as he brings readers from the events of 1945 up to the present time, 1968, when he is writing the book. His reference to the Vietnam War reinforces the notion he explores in the novel's opening chapter—that wars are like glaciers, inevitable and unpreventable. In numerous speeches and essays written during the '60s and '70s, Vonnegut refers to the war as well, critiquing American involvement in Southeast Asia. In his essay "Torture and Blub-ber," for instance, reprinted in *Wampeters, Foma, and Granfalloons*, he clearly deplores U.S. govern-ment policies in Vietnam: "Simply: We are tortur-ers, and we once hoped to win in Indochina and anywhere because we had the most expensive tor-ture instruments yet devised" (171). The work that most specifically addresses the fallout of the Viet-

nam War, however, is the novel *Galápagos*, whose narrator, Leon Trout, is a Vietnam veteran deeply disturbed by his killing of an old woman during the war. At least one critic reads Trout as inventing the deevolution that takes place in the novel as a way of coping with the trauma he experienced in the war, much like Billy Pilgrim's imagined Tralfama-dorian experiences serve as a coping mechanism in *Slaughterhouse-Five*. Eugene Debs Hartke in *Hocus Pocus* is a Vietnam veteran as well.

Voltaire Vonnegut describes the 18th-century French philosopher and writer Voltaire as the "Humanists' Abraham" in *Timequake*, suggesting that he sees Voltaire as the founding father of mod-ern HUMANISM.

Vonnegut, Alex Alex Vonnegut was Kurt Von-negut's paternal uncle, the younger brother of Kurt, Sr. A HARVARD-educated insurance sales-man, who brought the organization ALCOHOLICS ANONYMOUS to INDIANAPOLIS, Alex was much beloved by his nephew. In the prologue to *Slap-stick*, Vonnegut describes how he and his brother, BERNARD VONNEGUT, flew to Uncle Alex's funeral. Alex also appears in the prologue to *Jailbird*, where Vonnegut describes a lunch that he, his father, and his uncle had with labor organizer POWERS HAP-GOOD. In *Timequake*, as well as in several essays, including the introduction to *God Bless You, Dr. Kevorkian*, Vonnegut describes Alex as objecting to the fact that humans so seldom take time to notice the good moments in life. Vonnegut remembers Uncle Alex often interrupting conversations with the question, "If this isn't nice, what is?"

Vonnegut, Alice Alice Vonnegut was Kurt Vonnegut's older sister, who died of cancer in 1958 at the age of 41. Tragically, Alice's husband, JAMES CARMALT ADAMS, had died two days earlier in a commuter train crash. Thus, the Adams' four sons were left as orphans. Vonnegut and his wife at the time, JANE COX VONNEGUT YARMOLINSKY, ended up adopting the three older Adams boys, James, Kurt, and Steven, who ranged in age from eight to 14, and raising them as their own. *Slapstick* is largely a tribute to his sister, Alice. In the prologue to the novel, Vonnegut explains to readers that Alice was the person he had always secretly written for. He also says that the novel depicts him and his "beautiful sister" as monsters (20). The Neanderthaloid twins Wilbur and Eliza Swain, so much more lively and intelligent when together than when separated, represent Vonnegut's love for his sister and his sorrow over her death.

Vonnegut, Bernard Bernard Vonnegut was Kurt Vonnegut's older brother. An atmospheric scientist who spent most of his career working at the State University of New York at Albany, Bernard figures in several of his brother's works. In the prologue to *Slapstick*, Vonnegut describes the airplane trip he and Bernard take to their uncle, ALEX VONNEGUT's, funeral. The brothers leave an empty seat between them for their missing sister, Alice, who had died of cancer many years earlier. *Timequake* depicts an aged Bernard, the scientist who had previously scorned art, experimenting with abstract paintings. A letter he writes to his brother, Kurt, asking whether the "squiggly miniatures" (166) he produces are art or not, prompts Vonnegut to write back a letter in which he explains that "any work of art is half of a conversation between two human beings" (168). He advises Bernard that he must display his squiggles in public and find out whether people like to look at them before he will really know whether they constitute art or not. The epilogue to *Timequake* discusses Bernard's death from cancer in April 1997.

Vonnegut, Bernard, Sr. Vonnegut's older brother, BERNARD VONNEGUT, is named for his paternal grandfather, who was a talented artist from an early age. The first Bernard Vonnegut went on to become an architect in INDIANAPOLIS, although he would have preferred to live in New York City. He died of intestinal cancer in 1908, at the age of 53.

Vonnegut, Carl Hiroaki Carl Hiroaki Vonnegut is Vonnegut's great-nephew, the son of PETER VONNEGUT (himself the son of Vonnegut's older brother Bernard) and MICHI MINATOYA VONNEGUT.

Vonnegut, Clemens, Sr. Clemens Vonnegut, Sr., was one of Kurt Vonnegut's paternal great-grandfathers. Born in Münster, Germany, in 1824, Clemens migrated to the United States in 1848, settling in INDIANAPOLIS in 1850. A well-educated free thinker, Clemens Vonnegut, Sr. eventually founded the Vonnegut Hardware Company, an enterprise still in operation during Kurt Vonnegut's

Vonnegut Hardware Store, 1908 *(courtesy of Bass Photo Co. Collection, Indiana Historical Society)*

boyhood. Vonnegut discusses this relative most fully in the collection *Palm Sunday*, writing that, of all his ancestors, it is Clemens Vonnegut who "most beguiles" him, because he was "a cultivated eccentric," something that Kurt Vonnegut himself tells readers he aspires to be (28). In *Palm Sunday*, Vonnegut quotes the funeral oration that his great-grandfather wrote for himself, in which Clemens denies the existence of a supernatural "Thinking Being" who created Earth and man (176).

Vonnegut, Edith   Edith Vonnegut, born in 1949, is Vonnegut's second child and his oldest daughter. In the collection *Palm Sunday*, Vonnegut describes Edith as a "gifted artist" (232). She is the author of a book of paintings called *Domestic Goddesses*, which uses the style of classical painters to humorously depict women at work in the home. Edith Vonnegut was married to television journalist GERALDO RIVERA for a brief period in the early 1970s.

Vonnegut, Edith Lieber   Kurt Vonnegut's mother, Edith Lieber Vonnegut, daughter of ALBERT LIEBER and ALICE BARUS LIEBER, had a difficult childhood. Her mother died when she was six years old, and she was subsequently raised by an eccentric and abusive stepmother, ORA D. LANE, whom Vonnegut believes inflicted so much psychological damage on the young girl that it contributed to her suicide many years later. In *Palm Sunday*, family historian JOHN RAUCH describes Vonnegut's mother as "a very beautiful woman, tall and statuesque," who had "a lively sense of humor" and who "laughed easily" (43). He also claims that Kurt, Sr., and Edith were a "devoted couple until the day of Edith's death" (43). Vonnegut writes frequently about his mother, speculating that the family's loss of their fortune during the Depression years was more than she could bear. Edith killed herself by taking an overdose of sleeping pills the night before Mother's Day, 1944, when Kurt, Jr., was home on leave from his stint in the army. *Breakfast of Champions* and *Deadeye Dick* can both be read as attempts by Vonnegut to come to terms with his mother's suicide. In *Breakfast of Champions*, Vonnegut compares his own mother to the depressed and drug-addled Celia Hildreth Hoover, who com-

mits suicide by swallowing Drano. In *Deadeye Dick*, Mother's Day 1944 is marked by a tragic accidental death that changes protagonist Rudy Waltz's life forever.

Vonnegut, Emiko Alice   Emiko Alice Vonnegut is the granddaughter of Vonnegut's older brother Bernard and thus Vonnegut's great-niece. She is the daughter of PETER VONNEGUT and MICHI MINATOYA VONNEGUT, a family mentioned briefly in the collection *Palm Sunday* (219).

Vonnegut, Jane Cox   See JANE COX VONNEGUT YARMOLINSKY.

Vonnegut, Katarina Blank   Katarina Blank was one of Vonnegut's paternal great-grandmothers, the wife of CLEMENS VONNEGUT, SR., whom she met when she was working as a waitress in a small German restaurant across the street from the Vonnegut Hardware Company in the 1850s. Like her husband, Katarina was a German immigrant.

Vonnegut, Kurt, Sr.   Kurt Vonnegut's father, Kurt Vonnegut, Sr., was born in INDIANAPOLIS, Indiana in 1884, the oldest son of BERNARD VONNEGUT, SR., and NANETTE SCHNULL VONNEGUT. An architect trained at the MASSACHUSETTS INSTITUTE OF TECHNOLOGY, Vonnegut, Sr. married EDITH LIEBER VONNEGUT in 1913. The couple had three children, Bernard, Alice, and Kurt, Jr. During Kurt, Jr.'s, earliest childhood, the family was affluent and happy, but Kurt, Sr., had trouble finding work during the Depression years, and the family's fortunes diminished greatly. After Edith Lieber Vonnegut's suicide in 1944, family historian JOHN RAUCH reports that Kurt, Sr., "lived almost as a recluse, for some ten years" (*Palm Sunday* 50), eventually buying a small country cottage about 25 miles south of Indianapolis, where he lived until his death from lung cancer in 1957. Vonnegut writes about his father quite often, and *Breakfast of Champions* can be read as his account of coming to terms with his father's death.

Vonnegut, Lily   Lily Vonnegut is Vonnegut's youngest daughter, adopted by the writer and his

Kurt Vonnegut, Sr., 1908 M.I.T. yearbook *(courtesy of The Lilly Library, Indiana University, Bloomington, Indiana)*

ing pediatrician. Mark Vonnegut's book, *THE EDEN EXPRESS*, is an account of his mental collapse and recovery.

Vonnegut, Michi Minatoya Michi Minatoya is the wife of Vonnegut's nephew PETER VONNEGUT. She is mentioned briefly in the collection *Palm Sunday*, as Vonnegut discusses how his family has dispersed from INDIANAPOLIS (219).

Vonnegut, Nanette Nanette Vonnegut, born in 1954, is Vonnegut's second daughter. In *Palm Sunday*, Vonnegut describes Nanette as a "gifted artist" who decides to become a nurse and "make pictures for fun" (232). Nanette also appears in *Slaughterhouse-Five*, when Vonnegut describes taking her and her young friend Allison Mitchell to visit his friend BERNARD V. O'HARE in 1964 and stopping at the New York World's Fair along the way.

Vonnegut, Nanette Schnull Nanette Schnull Vonnegut was the mother of KURT VONNEGUT, SR., thus Vonnegut's paternal grandmother. Daughter of MATILDA SCHRAMM SCHNULL and HENRY SCHNULL, she is described in the collection *Palm Sunday* as "a very beautiful woman" with a "lovely speaking and singing voice," who "laughed readily, enjoyed people, and was greatly admired by a host of friends" (32).

second wife, JILL KREMENTZ, in 1982, when she was a three-day-old infant.

Vonnegut, Mark Mark Vonnegut, named after writer MARK TWAIN, is Kurt Vonnegut's oldest son, born in 1947. Mark suffered a mental breakdown and was hospitalized as a schizophrenic in 1971. He eventually recovered, studied medicine at HARVARD Medical School, and became a practic-

Vonnegut, Peter Peter Vonnegut is the son of Vonnegut's older brother, Bernard. Peter is mentioned briefly in the collection *Palm Sunday* where Vonnegut tells readers that his nephew Peter is a librarian who works in Albany, New York (219).

Vonnegut, Zachary Zachary Vonnegut is Vonnegut's oldest grandchild, the son of MARK VONNEGUT and his wife, schoolteacher PAT O'SHEA.

W

Wakefield, Dan In his collection *Wampeters, Foma, and Granfalloons,* Vonnegut includes a review of a novel called *Going All the Way,* written by his old childhood friend from INDIANAPOLIS, Dan Wakefield. Praising the book highly, Vonnegut says that it is about "what hell it is to be oversexed in Indianapolis" (119). Yet, Vonnegut concludes that this "wildly sexy novel" isn't actually a sex novel. Rather, it is about "a society so drab that sex seems to the young to be the only adventure with any magic in it" (121).

Waller, Fats In *Timequake,* Vonnegut quotes African-American jazz pianist Fats Waller, who used to shout "Somebody shoot me while I'm happy" (3) whenever he played especially well.

Williams, Tennessee Tennessee Williams was a 20th-century American playwright much admired by Vonnegut; his play A STREETCAR NAMED DESIRE figures prominently in Vonnegut's short story "Who Am I This Time?" In *Timequake,* Vonnegut writes that Williams's plays served as as "emotional and ethical landmarks" in his life (25), but he also finds it curious and interesting that Williams, like poet T. S. ELIOT, denied his midwestern roots.

Wilson, Charles Thomson Rees In *Timequake,* Vonnegut explains that his maternal great-uncle Carl Barus was a scientist who concluded that ionization was relatively unimportant in condensation. Almost immediately, a Scottish physicist named Charles Thomson Rees Wilson performed similar experiments using a glass chamber rather than a wooden one and proved Vonnegut's uncle wrong. Vonnegut's conclusion to this anecdote is that Carl Barus "must have felt like something the cat drug in!" (213), a favorite Vonnegut phrase.

Yale, John   John Yale is a worker for an American evangelical Christian charity called World Vision whom Vonnegut met when he made a trip to Mozambique in 1989 to observe the suffering of refugees in the war-torn African country. Vonnegut wrote about John Yale and about his trip to Mozambique in a 1990 article for *Parade* magazine that is reprinted in the collection *Fates Worse Than Death.*

Yarmolinsky,   Adam   Adam   Yarmolinsky, a HARVARD-educated lawyer who held high-ranking positions in the Kennedy, Johnson, and Carter presidential administrations, was the second husband of Vonnegut's first wife, JANE COX VONNEGUT YARMOLINSKY. He later became a professor and provost at University of Maryland at Baltimore before dying of leukemia in January of 2000.

Yarmolinsky, Jane Cox Vonnegut   Jane Cox Vonnegut Yarmolinsky was Kurt Vonnegut's first wife, whom he married in 1945 and divorced in 1979, though they had separated many years before. The pair had met in kindergarten, were high school classmates, and raised six children together: Mark, Nanette, and Edith, their biological children, as well as their adopted sons JAMES, KURT, and STEVEN ADAMS, the children of Vonnegut's late sister Alice. ANGELS WITHOUT WINGS:

A Courageous Family's Triumph over Tragedy, is Jane Yarmolinsky's memoir of these experiences, written as she herself was dying of terminal cancer, and published posthumously in 1987. In his collection *Palm Sunday,* Vonnegut ascribes the breakup of his marriage to Jane as being at least partly the result of her becoming a born-again Christian. In the epigraph to the book, he quotes from one of his ancestors, CLEMENS VONNEGUT, who writes, "Whoever entertains liberal views and chooses a consort that is captured by superstition risks his liberty and his happiness." Nevertheless, the pair remained friendly until Jane's death, and Vonnegut writes quite tenderly of his first wife in many of his books, particularly in *Timequake,* where he says he was happy that Jane was able to believe "in the Trinity and Heaven and Hell and all the rest of it" because he "loved her" (136).

Young, Ida   Ida Young was the Vonnegut family's cook when Kurt Vonnegut was a child growing up in INDIANAPOLIS. In the preface to his collection *Wampeters, Foma, and Granfalloons,* Vonnegut writes that he probably spent more time with her than he spent with anyone else until he got married. Ida Young is possibly the model for the character Mary Hoobler in *Deadeye Dick,* the black family cook who offers Rudy Waltz more warmth and nurturing than his own mother does.

PART IV

Appendixes

Bibliography of Vonnegut's Works (in chronological order)

Novels

Player Piano. New York: Scribner's, 1952. Republished as *Utopia-14,* Bantam Books, 1954.

The Sirens of Titan. New York: Dell, 1959.

Mother Night. Greenwich, Conn.: Fawcett, 1962.

Cat's Cradle. New York: Holt, Rinehart, and Winston, 1963.

God Bless You, Mr. Rosewater. New York: Holt, Rinehart, and Winston, 1965.

Slaughterhouse-Five. New York: Delacorte Press, 1969.

Breakfast of Champions. New York: Delacorte Press, 1973.

Slapstick. New York: Delacorte Press, 1976.

Jailbird. New York: Delacorte Press, 1979.

Deadeye Dick. New York: Delacorte Press, 1982.

Galápagos. New York: Delacorte Press, 1985.

Bluebeard. New York: Delacorte Press, 1987.

Hocus Pocus. New York: Putnam, 1990.

Timequake. New York: Putnam, 1997.

Collected Essays and Stories

Canary in a Cat House. Greenwich, Conn.: Fawcett, 1961.

Welcome to the Monkey House. New York: Delacorte Press, 1968.

Wampeters, Foma, and Granfalloons. New York: Delacorte Press, 1974.

Palm Sunday: An Autobiographical Collage. New York: Delacorte Press, 1981

Nothing Is Lost Save Honor: Two Essays. Jackson, Miss.: Nouveau Press, 1984.

Fates Worse than Death. New York: Putnam, 1991.

Bagombo Snuff Box. New York: Putnam, 1999.

God Bless You, Dr. Kevorkian. New York: Seven Stories Press, 1999.

Like Shaking Hands with God: A Conversation About Writing. New York: Seven Stories Press, 1999.

A Man Without a Country. New York: Seven Stories Press, 2005.

Short Fiction

"Report on the Barnhouse Effect." *Collier's* February 11, 1950, 18–19, 63–65.

"Thanasphere." *Collier's,* September 2, 1950, 18–19, 60, 62.

"EPICAC." *Collier's,* November 25, 1950, 36–37.

"All the King's Horses." *Collier's,* February 10, 1951, 14–15, 46–48, 50.

"Mnemonics." *Collier's,* April 28, 1951, 38.

"The Euphio Question." *Collier's,* May 12, 1951, 22–23, 52–54, 56.

"The Foster Portfolio." *Collier's,* September 8, 1951, 18–19, 72–73.

"More Stately Mansions." *Collier's,* December 22, 1951, 24–25, 62–63.

"Any Reasonable Offer." *Collier's,* January 19, 1952, 32, 46–47.

"The Package." *Collier's,* July 26, 1952, 48–53.

"The No-Talent Kid." *Saturday Evening Post,* October 25, 1952, 28, 109–110, 112, 114.

"Poor Little Rich Town." *Collier's,* October 25, 1952, 90–95.

"Souvenir." *Argosy,* December 1952, 28–29, 76–79.

"Tom Edison's Shaggy Dog." *Collier's,* March 14, 1953, 46, 48–49.

"Unready to Wear." *Galaxy Science Fiction*, April 1953, 7–14.

"The Cruise of the Jolly Roger." *Cape Cod Compass*, April 1953, 7–14.

"D.P." *Ladies' Home Journal*, August 1953, 42–43, 80–81, 84.

"Tomorrow and Tomorrow and Tomorrow." *Galaxy Science Fiction*, January 1954, 100–110. (Originally titled "The Big Trip Up Yonder.")

"Custom-Made Bride." *Saturday Evening Post*, March 27, 1954, 30, 81–82, 86–87.

"Adam." *Cosmopolitan*, April 1954, 34–39.

"Ambitious Sophomore." *Saturday Evening Post*, May 1, 1954, 31, 88, 92, 94.

"Bagombo Snuff Box." *Cosmopolitan*, October 1954, 34–39.

"The Powder Blue Dragon." *Cosmopolitan*, November 1954, 46–48, 50–53.

"A Present for Big Nick." *Argosy*, December 1954, 42–45, 72–73.

"Unpaid Consultant." *Cosmopolitan*, March 1955, 52–57.

"Deer in the Works." *Esquire*, April 1955, 78–79, 112, 114, 116, 118.

"Next Door." *Cosmopolitan*, April 1955, 80–85.

"The Kid Nobody Could Handle." *Saturday Evening Post*, September 24, 1955, 37, 136–137.

"Der Arme Dolmetscher." *The Atlantic Monthly*, July 1955, 86–88. (Originally titled "Das Ganz Arm Dolmetscher.")

"The Boy Who Hated Girls." *Saturday Evening Post*, March 31, 1956, 28–29, 58, 60, 62.

"Miss Temptation." *Saturday Evening Post*, April 21, 1956, 30, 57, 60, 62, 64.

"This Son of Mine." *Saturday Evening Post*, August 18, 1956, 24, 74, 76–78.

"Hal Irwin's Magic Lamp." *Cosmopolitan*, June 1957, 92–95.

"A Night for Love." *Saturday Evening Post*, November 23, 1957, 40–41, 73, 76–77, 80,–81, 84.

"The Manned Missiles." *Cosmopolitan*, July 1958, 83–88.

"Long Walk to Forever." *Ladies' Home Journal*, August 1960, 42–43, 108.

"Find Me a Dream." *Cosmopolitan*, February 1961, 108–111.

"Runaways." *Saturday Evening Post*, April 15, 1961, 26–27, 52, 54, 56.

"Harrison Bergeron." *Magazine of Fantasy and Science Fiction*, October 1961, 5–10. Reprinted in *National Review*, November 16, 1965, 1,020–1,021, 1,041.

"Who Am I This Time?" *Saturday Evening Post*, December 16, 1961, 20–21, 62, 64, 66–67. (Originally titled "My Name Is Everyone.")

"2BRO2B." *Worlds of If*, January 1962, 59–65.

"The Lie." *Saturday Evening Post*, February 24, 1962, 46–47, 51, 56.

"Go Back to Your Precious Wife and Son." *Ladies' Home Journal*, July 1962, 54–55, 108, 110.

"Lovers Anonymous." *Redbook*, October 1963, 70–71, 146–148.

"Where I Live." *Venture—Traveler's World*, October 1964, 145–149. (Originally titled "You've Never Been to Barnstable?")

"New Dictionary." *New York Times* October 30, 1966. (Originally titled "The Random House Dictionary of the English Language," this piece is more a reflective essay than a short story. It is included here because it appears in the volume *Welcome to the Monkey House*.)

"Welcome to the Monkey House." *Playboy*, January 1968, 95, 156, 196, 198, 200–201.

"The Hyannis Port Story." In *Welcome to the Monkey House*. New York: Delacorte Press, 1968, 147–160.

"The Big Space Fuck." *Again, Dangerous Visions: Forty-six Original Stories Edited by Harlan Ellison*. Garden City, N.Y.: Doubleday, 1972, 246–250.

Published Plays, Television Shows, Musical Pieces, Children's Books

Happy Birthday, Wanda June. New York: Samuel French, Inc., 1970.

Between Time and Timbuktu. New York: Dell, 1972.

Fortitude. In *Wampeters, Foma, and Granfalloons*. New York: Delacorte Press, 1974. (Originally published in *Playboy*, September 1968.)

Sun Moon Star. New York: Harper & Row, 1980. (With Ivan Chermayeff.)

The Chemistry Professor. In *Palm Sunday: An Autobiographical Collage*. New York: Delacorte Press, 1981: 239–264.

L'Histoire du Soldat. *The Paris Review* 40, no. 148 (Fall 1998): 188–204.

Requiem. In *Fates Worse Than Death*. New York: Putnam, 1991: 227–230.

Selected Adaptations, Productions of Vonnegut's Work

"Auf Wiedersehen." Adaptation of short story "D.P." Episode of CBS television anthology series *General Electric Theater*. Dir. John Brahm. October 5, 1958.

"The Runaways." Adaptation of short story of the same title. Episode of ABC television anthology series *Bus Stop*. Dir. Arthur Hiller. December 24, 1961.

Happy Birthday, Wanda June. Play premieres off-Broadway at the Theater de Lys. October 7, 1970. Runs through March, 1971.

Happy Birthday, Wanda June. Feature film. Dir. Mark Robson. Columbia Pictures, December 9, 1971.

Between Time and Timbuktu. Teleplay based on Vonnegut material. Dir. Fred Barzyk. National Educational Television, March 13, 1972.

Slaughterhouse-Five. Feature film. Dir. George Roy Hill. Universal Pictures, March 15, 1972.

"EPICAC." Adaptation of short story of the same title. Pilot for proposed NBC television anthology *Rex Harrison Presents Stories of Love*. Dir. John Badham. May 1, 1974.

Next Door. Short (24-minute) independent film. Dir. Andrew Silver, 1975.

Sirens of Titan. Adapted as a two-act play. Dir. Stuart Gordon. Organic Theater Company. Chicago, April 6, 1977.

God Bless You, Mr. Rosewater. Musical adaptation of the novel premieres off-off-Broadway at the W.P.A. Theater. May 1979. Opens off-Broadway at the Entermedia Theater. October 14, 1979.

"Who Am I This Time?" Television adaptation of the short story. Dir. Jonathan Demme. PBS *American Playhouse*, February 2, 1982.

Slapstick (Of Another Kind). Independent film. Dir. Steven Paul, March 1984 (U.S. release).

Displaced Person. Television adaptation of short story "D.P." Dir. Alan Bridges. PBS *American Playhouse*, 1985.

"Long Walk to Forever." Television adaptation of the short story. Dir. John A. Gallagher. A&E Network, October 10, 1987.

"Requiem Mass." Performed at the Unitarian Universalist Church of Buffalo. Buffalo, New York, March 13, 1988.

"Kurt Vonnegut's Monkey House." Television adaptation of short stories "Next Door," "The Euphio Question," and "All the King's Horses." Showtime Series, May 12, 1991.

Make Up Your Mind. Play premieres at the New Group Theater. New York, April 20, 1993.

L'histoire du Soldat. Theatrical piece with music; libretto by Vonnegut. Premieres at Alice Tully Hall. New York, May 6, 1993.

Harrison Bergeron. Television adaptation of the short story. Dir. Bruce Pittman. Showtime, August 13, 1995.

Slaughterhouse-Five. Adapted for stage. Dir. Eric Simonson. Steppenwolf Theater. Chicago, September 18, 1996–November 1, 1996.

Mother Night. Feature film. Dir. Keith Gordon. Fine Line Features, November 1, 1996.

Breakfast of Champions. Feature film. Dir. Alan Rudolph. Hollywood Pictures, February 18, 1999.

BIBLIOGRAPHY OF SECONDARY SOURCES

Books on Vonnegut

Allen, William Rodney, ed. *Conversations with Kurt Vonnegut*. Jackson: University of Mississippi Press, 1988.

———. *Understanding Kurt Vonnegut*. Columbia: University of South Carolina Press, 1991.

Bloom, Harold, ed. *Kurt Vonnegut*. Philadelphia: Chelsea House, 2000.

Bly, William. *Kurt Vonnegut's Slaughterhouse-Five*. Woodbury, N.Y.: Barron's Educational Series, 1985.

Boon, Kevin A., ed. *At Millennium's End: New Essays on the Work of Kurt Vonnegut*. Albany: State University of New York Press, 2001.

———. *Chaos Theory and the Interpretation of Literary Texts: The Case of Kurt Vonnegut*. Lewiston, N.Y.: Edwin Mellen Press, 1997.

Broer, Lawrence R. *Sanity Plea: Schizophrenia in the Novels of Kurt Vonnegut*. 2nd ed. Tuscaloosa: University of Alabama Press, 1994.

Chernuchin, Michael, ed. *Vonnegut Talks!* Forest Hills, N.Y.: Pylon Press, 1977.

Davis, Todd F. *Kurt Vonnegut's Crusade*. Albany: State University of New York Press, 2006.

Giannone, Richard. *Vonnegut: A Preface to His Novels*. Port Washington, N.Y.: Kennikat Press, 1977.

Goldsmith, David H. *Kurt Vonnegut: Fantasist of Fire and Ice*. Bowling Green, Ohio: Bowling Green University Popular Press, 1972.

Hudgens, Betty L. *Kurt Vonnegut, Jr.: A Checklist*. Detroit: Gale, 1972.

Klinkowitz, Jerome. *Kurt Vonnegut*. London: Methuen, 1982.

———. *Slaughterhouse-Five: Reforming the Novel and the World*. Boston: Twayne, 1990.

———. *The Vonnegut Effect*. Columbia: University of South Carolina Press, 2004.

———. *Vonnegut in Fact: The Public Spokesmanship of Personal Fiction*. Columbia: University of South Carolina Press, 1998.

Klinkowitz, Jerome, and Donald L. Lawler, eds. *Vonnegut in America*. New York: Delacort Press/Seymour Lawrence, 1977.

Klinkowitz, Jerome, and John Somer, eds. *The Vonnegut Statement: Original Essays on the Life and Work of Kurt Vonnegut*. New York: Delacort Press/Seymour Lawrence, 1973.

Leeds, Marc. *The Vonnegut Encyclopedia: An Authorized Compendium*. Westport, Conn.: Greenwood, 1995.

Leeds, Marc, and Peter J. Reed. *Kurt Vonnegut: Images and Representations*. Westport, Conn.: Greenwood, 2000.

———, eds. *Vonnegut Chronicles: Interviews and Essays*. Westport, Conn.: Greenwood, 1996.

Lundquist, James. *Kurt Vonnegut*. New York: Ungar, 1977.

Marvin, Thomas F. *Kurt Vonnegut: A Critical Companion*. Westport, Conn.: Greenwood, 2002.

Mayo, Clark. *Kurt Vonnegut: The Gospel from Outer Space*. San Bernardino, Calif.: Borgo Press, 1977.

Merrill, Robert, ed. *Critical Essays on Kurt Vonnegut*. Boston: G. K. Hall, 1990.

Morse, Donald E. *Kurt Vonnegut*. San Bernardino, Calif.: Borgo Press, 1992.

———. *Novels of Kurt Vonnegut: Imagining Being an American*. Westport, Conn.: Praeger, 2003.

Mustazza, Leonard, ed. *Critical Response to Kurt Vonnegut*. Westport, Conn.: Greemwood, 1994.

Mustazza, Leonard. *Forever Pursuing Genesis: The Myth of Eden in the Novels of Kurt Vonnegut*. Lewisburg, Pa.: Bucknell University Press, 1990.

Pettersson, Bo. *The World According to Kurt Vonnegut: Moral Paradox and Narrative Form*. Ebo, Finland: Åbo Akademi University Press; 1994.

Pieratt, Asa B. *Kurt Vonnegut, Jr.: A Descriptive Bibliography and Annotated Secondary Checklist*. Hamden, Conn.: Archon, 1974.

Pieratt, Asa B., Julie Huffman-Klinkowitz, and Jerome Klinkowitz. *Kurt Vonnegut: A Comprehensive Bibliography*. North Haven, Conn.: Archon, 1987.

Rackstraw, Loree, ed. *Draftings in Vonnegut: The Paradox of Hope*. Cedar Falls: University of Northern Iowa Press, 1988.

Reed, Peter J. *Kurt Vonnegut, Jr.* New York: Warner Paperback Library, 1972.

———. *Short Fiction of Kurt Vonnegut*. Westport, Conn.: Greemwood, 1997.

Schatt, Stanley. *Kurt Vonnegut, Jr.* Boston: Twayne, 1976.

Short, Robert. *Something to Believe In: Is Kurt Vonnegut the Exorcist of Jesus Christ Superstar?* New York: Harper & Row, 1978.

Thomas, P. L. *Reading, Learning, Teaching Kurt Vonnegut*. New York: Peter Lang, 2006.

Yarmolinsky, Jane Vonnegut. *Angels Without Wings: A Courageous Family's Triumph Over Tragedy*. Boston: Houghton Mifflin, 1987.

Books with Significant Portions on Vonnegut

Aldiss, Brian W. *Billion Year Spree: The True History of Science Fiction*. Garden City, N.Y.: Doubleday, 1973. 258, 278–279, 313–316.

Amis, Martin. *The Moronic Inferno and Other Visits to America*. New York: Penguin Books, 1987. 132–137, 187, 199.

Berger, Harold L. *Science Fiction and the New Dark Age*. Bowling Green, Ohio: Bowling Green University Popular Press, 1976. ix, 9, 17–19, 20, 22, 25, 37, 65, 69, 77, 123–134, 215n.

Blair, John G. *The Confidence Man in Modern Fiction*. New York: Barnes & Noble Books, 1979. 14–15, 24, 98–111, 113, 132–136, 139.

Bryant, Jerry H. *The Open Decision: The Contemporary American Novel and Its Intellectual Background*. New York: Free Press, 1970. 303–324.

Dickstein, Morris. *Gates of Eden: American Culture in the Sixties*. New York: Basic Books, 1977.

Harris, Charles, B. *Contemporary American Novelists of the Absurd*. New Haven, Conn.: College and University Press, 1971. 51–75.

Hassan, Ihab Habib. *Contemporary American Literature, 1945–1972*. New York: Ungar, 1973. 45–47, 65, 86.

Hauck, Richard Boyd. *A Cheerful Nihilism: Confidence and "The Absurd" in American Humorous Fiction*. Bloomington: Indiana University Press, 1971. 237–245.

Hendin, Josephine. *Vulnerable People: A View of American Fiction Since 1945*. New York: Oxford University Press, 1978.

Hipkiss, Robert A. *The American Absurd: Pynchon, Vonnegut, and Barth*. Port Washington, N.Y.: Associated Faculty Press, 1984. 43–73.

Hume, Kathryn. *Fantasy and Mimesis: Responses to Reality in Western Literature*. New York: Methuen, 1984.

Jones, Peter G. *War and the Novelist: Appraising the American War Novel*. Columbia: University of Missouri Press, 1976. 2, 203–229, 234–235.

Karl, Frederick Robert. *American Fictions: 1940–1980*. New York: Harper & Row, 1983.

Kazin, Alfred. *Bright Book of Life: American Novelists and Storytellers from Hemingway to Mailer*. Boston: Little, Brown, 1973. 82–83, 86–90.

Kennard, Jean. *Number and Nightmare: Forms of Fantasy in Contemporary Literature*. Hamden, Conn.: Archon, 1975. 101–128, 131–133, 203–204.

Ketterer, David. *New Worlds for Old: The Apocalyptic Imagination, Science Fiction and American Literature*. Garden City, N.Y.: Anchor Press, 1974.

Klinkowitz, Jerome. *The American 1960's: Imaginative Acts in a Decade of Change*. Ames: Iowa State University Press, 1980.

———. *Literary Subversions: New American Fiction and the Practice of Criticism*. Carbondale: Southern Illinois Press, 1985.

———. *The Practice of Fiction in America: Writers from Hawthorne to the Present.* Ames: Iowa State University Press, 1980.

———. *The Self-Apparent Word: Fiction as Language/Language as Fiction.* Carbondale: Southern Illinois Press, 1985.

———. *Structuring the Void: The Struggle for Subjects in Contemporary American Fiction.* Durham, N.C.: Duke University Press, 1992.

May, John R. *Toward a New Earth: Apocalypse in the American Novel.* Notre Dame: University of Notre Dame Press, 1972. 172–200.

Olderman, Raymond. *Beyond the Waste Land: A Study of the American Novel in the Nineteen-Sixties.* New Haven, Conn.: Yale University Press, 1972. 189–219.

Scholes, Robert E. *The Fabulators.* New York: Oxford University Press, 1967.

Schultz, Max F. *Black Humor Fiction in the Sixties: A Pluralistic Definition of Man and His World.* Athens: Ohio University Press, 1973. 32–65.

Singh, Sukhbir. *The Survivor in Contemporary American Fiction: Saul Bellow, Bernard Malamud, John Updike, Kurt Vonnegut, Jr.* Delhi: B.R. Publication Corporation, 1991.

Walsh, Chad. *From Utopia to Nightmare.* New York: Harper & Row, 1962. 85–88.

Warrick, Patricia S. *The Cybernetic Imagination in Science Fiction.* Cambridge, Mass.: MIT Press, 1980. 89, 125, 134–139.

Articles in Books

Abádi-Nagy, Zoltán. "An Original Look at 'Origins': Bokononism." In *The Origins and Originality of American Culture,* edited by Tibor Frank, 601–608. Budapest: Akadémiai Kiadó, 1984.

Au, Bobbye G. "Contemporary Novels: A Reflection of Contemporary Culture." In *Modern American Cultural Criticism,* edited by Mark Johnson, 99–104. Warrensburg: Central Missouri State University, 1983.

Benito Sánchez, Jesús. "Pilgrimaging through Time: Puritan Pilgrims and Vonnegut's *Slaughterhouse-Five.*" In *Spanish Association for American Studies (SAAS): Century Ends, Crises and New Beginnings,* edited by María José Alvarez Maurín, Manuel

Broncano Rodrígues, Camino Fernández Rabadán, and Cristina Garrigós González, 33–38. León, Spain: Universidad de León, 1999.

Breinig, Helmbrecht. "Kurt Vonnegut, Jr., 'Tomorrow and Tomorrow and Tomorrow' (1954)." In *Die amerikanische Short Story der Gegenwart: Interpretationen,* edited by Peter Freese, 151–159. Berlin: Schmidt, 1976.

Broer, Lawrence R. "Images of the Shaman in the Works of Kurt Vonnegut." In *Dionysus in Literature: Essays on Literary Madness,* edited by Branimir M. Rieger, 197–208. Bowling Green, Ohio: Popular, 1994.

———. "Kurt Vonnegut vs. Deadeye Dick: The Resolution of Vonnegut's Creative Schizophrenia." In *Spectrum of the Fantastic,* edited by Donald Palumbo, 95–102. Westport, Conn.: Greenwood, 1988.

———. "Pilgrim's Progress: Is Kurt Vonnegut, Jr., Winning His War with Machines?" In *Clockwork Worlds: Mechanized Environments in Science Fiction,* edited by Richard D. Erlich and Thomas P. Dunn, 137–161. Westport, Conn.: Greenwood, 1983.

Collado Rodríguez, Francisco. "On Dreams and Nightmares: Reflections on American Dystopia in the Cyberspace Era." In *Spanish Association for American Studies (SAAS): Century Ends, Crises and New Beginnings,* edited by María José Alvarez Maurín, Manuel Broncano Rodrígues, Camino Fernández Rabadán, and Cristina Garrigós González, 73–80. León, Spain: Universidad de León, 1999.

Cooley, John. "Kurt Vonnegut, Jr." In *Savages and Naturals: Black Portraits by White Writers,* 161–173. Newark: University of Delaware Press, 1982.

Crichton, Michael. "Slaughterhouse-Five." In *The Critic as Artist: Essays on Books, 1920–1970,* edited by Gilbert A. Harrison, 100–107. New York: Liveright, 1972.

Davis, Todd F. "Crusading for the Family: Kurt Vonnegut's Ethics of Familial Community." In *Reading the Family Dance: Family Systems Therapy and Literary Study,* edited by John V. Knapp and Kenneth Womack, 221–235. Newark: University of Delaware Press, 2003.

Davis, Todd F. "Kurt Vonnegut." In *Postmodernism: The Key Figures,* edited by Hans Bertens and Joseph Natoli, 315–320. Malden, Mass.: Blackwell, 2002.

Dimeo, Stephen. "Novel into Film: So It Goes." In *The Modern American Novel and the Movies,* edited by Gerald Peary and Roger Shatzkin, 282–292. New York: Ungar, 1978.

Elkins, Charles L. "Kurt Vonnegut, 1922–." In *Science Fiction Writers: Critical Studies of the Major Authors from the Early Nineteenth Century to the Present Day,* edited by Everett Franklin Bleiler, 551–561. New York: Scribner's, 1982.

Farmer, Philip Jose. "The Obscure Life and Hard Times of Kilgore Trout." In *The Book of Philip Jose Farmer,* 218–231. New York: Daw Books, 1973.

Fischer, Lucy. "Slapstick: From Laurel and Hardy to Vonnegut." In *Purdue University Fifth Annual Conference on Film,* edited by Maud Walther, 111–116. West Lafayette, Ind.: Dept. of Foreign Languages & Literatures, Purdue University, 1980.

Foran, Donna. "Kurt Vonnegut's Search for Soul." In *Issues in Travel Writing: Empire, Spectacle, and Displacement,* edited by Kristi Siegel, 179–196. New York: Peter Lang, 2002.

Frank, Armin P. "Kurt Vonnegut." In *Amerikanische Literatur der Gegenwart,* edited by Martin Christadler, 408–424. Stuttgart, Germany: Alfred Kroner, 1973.

Freese, Peter. "Kurt Vonnegut: Cat's Cradle (1963)." In *Die Utopie in der angloamerikanischen Literatur: Interpretationen,* edited by Hartmut Heuermann and Bernd-Peter Lange, 283–309. Düsseldorf: Bagel, 1984.

———. "Kurt Vonnegut, Jr., The Sirens of Titan (1959)." In *Der Science-Fiction-Roman in der Angloamerikanischen Literatur: Interpretationen,* edited by Hartmut Heuermann, 196–219. Düsseldorf: Bagel, 1986.

———. "Kurt Vonnegut, Jr., Slaughterhouse-Five (1969)." In *Der Roman im Englischunterricht der Sekundarstufe, II: Theorie und Praxis,* edited by Peter Freese and Liesel Hermes, 294–316. Paderborn, Germany: Shoningh, 1977.

———. "Kurt Vonnegut's *Slaughterhouse-Five*: Or, How to Storify an Atrocity." In *Historiographic Metafiction in Modern American and Canadian Literature,* edited by Bernd Engler and Kurt Müller, 209–222. Paderborn, Germany: Ferdinand Schöningh, 1994.

———. "Laurel and Hardy versus the Self-Reflexive Artefact: Vonnegut's Novels between High Culture and Popular Culture." In *High and Low in American Culture,* edited by Charlotte Kretzoi, 19–38. Budapest: Department of English, Loránd Eötvös University, 1986.

Gros-Louis, Doloros K. "The Ironic Christ Figure in *Slaughterhouse-Five.*" In *Biblical Images in Literature,* edited by Roland Bartel, James S. Ackerman and Thayer S. Warshaw, 161–175. New York: Abingdon, 1975.

Group, Robert. "Kurt Vonnegut, Jr." In *Twentieth-Century American Science Fiction Writers Part II: M–Z,* edited by Cowart David and Thomas L. Wymer, 184–190. Detroit, Mich.: Gale; 1981.

Hearron, Tom. "The Theme of Guilt in Vonnegut's Cataclysmic Novels." In *The Nightmare Considered: Critical Essays on Nuclear War Literature,* edited by Nancy Anisfield, 186–192. Bowling Green, Ohio: Popular, 1991.

Hoffman, Thomas P. "The Theme of Mechanization in *Player Piano.*" In *Clockwork Worlds: Mechanized Environments in Science Fiction,* edited by Richard D. Erlich and Thomas P. Dunn, 125–135. Westport, Conn.: Greenwood, 1983.

Hughes, David Y. "The Ghost in the Machine: The Theme of *Player Piano.*" In *America as Utopia,* edited by Kenneth M. Roemer, 108–114. New York: Burt Franklin, 1981.

Humm, Peter. "Reading the Lines: Television and New Fiction." In *Re-Reading English,* edited by Peter Widdowson, 193–206. New York: Methuen, 1982.

Hutcheon, Linda. "Historiographic Metafiction: Parody and the Intertextuality of History." In *Intertextuality and Contemporary American Fiction,* edited by Patrick O'Donnell and Robert Davis, 3–32. Baltimore: Johns Hopkins University Press, 1989.

Jones, Fiona K. "The Twentieth-Century Writer and the Image of the Computer." In *Computers and Human Communication: Problems and Prospects,* edited by David L. Crowner and Laurence A. Marschall, 167–180. Washington, D.C.: University Press of America, 1974.

Klinkowitz, Jerome. "Kurt Vonnegut, Jr." In *Literary Disruptions: The Making of Post-Contemporary American Fiction*, 2nd ed., 33–61, 232–305. Urbana: University of Illinois Press, 1980.

———. "Kurt Vonnegut's Ultimate." In *The Nightmare Considered: Critical Essays on Nuclear War Literature*, edited by Nancy Anisfield, 193–198. Bowling Green, Ohio: Popular, 1991.

———. "*Slaughterhouse-Five*: Fiction into Film." In *Take Two: Adapting the Contemporary American Novel to Film*, edited by Barbara Lupack, 51–59. Bowling Green, Ohio: Popular, 1994.

———. "Toward a New American Mainstream: John Updike and Kurt Vonnegut." In *Traditions, Voices, and Dreams: The American Novel Since the 1960s*, edited by Melvin J. Friedman and Ben Siegel, 150–167. Newark: University of Delaware Press, 1995.

Knorr, John Walter. "Technology, Angst, and Edenic Happiness in Kurt Vonnegut's *Player Piano* and *Slaughterhouse-Five*." In *The Image of Technology in Literature, the Media, and Society*, edited by Will Wright and Steve Kaplan, 99–104. Pueblo: Society for the Interdisciplinary Study of Social Imagery, University of Southern Colorado, 1994.

McConnell, Frank. "Stalking Papa's Ghost: Hemingway's Presence in Contemporary American Writing." In *Ernest Hemingway: New Critical Essays*, edited by A. Robert Lee, 193–211. Totowa, N.J.: Barnes & Noble, 1983.

McGrath, Michael J. Gargas. "Kesey and Vonnegut: The Critique of Liberal Democracy in Contemporary Literature." In *The Artist and the Political Vision*, edited by Benjamin R. Barber and Michael J. Gargas McGrath, 363–383. New Brunswick, N.J.: Transaction, 1982.

McNelly, Willis E. "Science Fiction the Modern Mythology." In *SF: The Other Side of Realism*, edited by Thomas D. Clareson, 193–198. Bowling Green, Ohio: Bowling Green University Popular Press, 1971.

Merrill, Robert. "Kurt Vonnegut as a German-American." In *Germany and German Thought in American Literature and Cultural Criticism*, edited by Peter Freese, 230–243. Essen: Blaue Eule, 1990.

Nelson, Gerald B. "Eliot Rosewater." In *Ten Versions of America*, 61–76. New York: Knopf, 1972.

Pinkster, Sanford. "Fire and Ice: The Radical Cuteness of Kurt Vonnegut, Jr." In *Between Two Worlds: The American Novel in the 1960's*, 1–19. Troy, N.Y.: Whiston, 1980.

Purdy, S. "The American Novel into Film? Nabokov and Vonnegut." In *Purdue University Fifth Annual Conference on Film*, edited by Maud Walther, 130–138. West Lafayette, Ind.: Dept. of Foreign Languages & Literatures, Purdue University, 1980.

Reed, Peter J. "Kurt Vonnegut." In *American Novelists since World War II: Fourth Series*, edited by James R. Giles and Wanda H. Giles, 248–272. Detroit, Mich.: Thomson Gale, 1995.

———. "Kurt Vonnegut, Jr." In *American Novelists since World War II*, edited by Jeffrey Helterman and Richard Layman, 493–508. Detroit, Mich.: Thomson Gale, 1978.

Rhodes, Carolyn. "Tyranny by Computer: Automated Data Processing and Oppressive Government in Science Fiction." In *Many Futures, Many Worlds: Theme and Form in Science Fiction*, edited by Thomas D. Clareson, 66–93. Kent, Ohio: Kent State University Press, 1977.

Scholes, Robert. "Fabulation and Satire—Black Humor: *Cat's Cradle* and *Mother Night*." In *The Fabulators*, 35–55. New York: Oxford University Press, 1967.

———. "'Mithridates, he died old': Black Humor and Kurt Vonnegut, Jr." In *The Sounder Few: Essays from the Hollins Critic*, edited by R. H. W. Dillard, George Garrett and John R. Moore, 173–193. Athens: University of Georgia Press, 1971.

———. "Vonnegut's *Cat's Cradle* and *Mother Night*." In *Fabulation and Metafiction*, 156–162. Urbana: University of Illinois Press, 1979.

Seed, David. "Mankind vs. Machines: The Technological Dystopia in Kurt Vonnegut's *Player Piano*." In *Impossibility Fiction: Alternativity, Extrapolation, Speculation*, edited by Derek Littlewood and Peter Stockwell, 11–23. Amsterdam, Netherlands: Rodopi, 1996.

Segal, Howard P. "Vonnegut's *Player Piano*: An Ambiguous Technological Dystopia." In *No Place Else: Explorations in Utopian and Dystopian Fiction*, edited by Eric S. Rabkin, Martin H. Greenberg, and Joseph D. Olander, 162–181. Carbondale: Southern Illinois University Press, 1983.

St. Germain, Amos. "Breakfast of Champions: Kurt Vonnegut, Jr. Is Still on the Case." In *Proceedings of the Fifth National Convention of the Popular Culture Association, St. Louis, Missouri, March 20–22, 1975*, edited by Michael T. Marsden, 233–243. Bowling Green, Ohio: Bowling Green State University Popular Press, 1975.

Stableford, Brian M. "Locked in the Slaughterhouse: The Novels of Kurt Vonnegut." In *Essays on Six Science Fiction Authors*, 15–23. San Bernardino, Calif.: Borgo Press, 1981.

Szarycz, Ireneusz. "Sinyavsky and Vonnegut: The Themes of Displacement and Alienation." In *Twentieth-Century Russian Literature*, edited by Karen L. Ryan and Barry P. Scherr, 164–179. New York: St. Martin's Press, 2000.

Thorson, James L. "Kurt Vonnegut's Cold War: The Short Stories of the Fifties." In *Tangenten: Literatur & Geschichte*, edited by Martin Meyer, Gabriele Spengemann, and Wolf Kindermann, 102–115. Münster, Germany: Lit, 1996.

Tunnell, James R. "Kesey and Vonnegut: Preachers of Redemption." In *A Casebook on Ken Kesey's One Flew Over the Cuckoo's Nest*, edited by George J. Searles, 127–133. Albuquerque: University of New Mexico Press, 1992.

Vanderbilt, Kermit. "Kurt Vonnegut's American Nightmares and Utopias." In *The Utopian Vision: Seven Essays on the Quincentennial of Sir Thomas More*, edited by E. D. S. Sullivan, 137–173. San Diego, Calif.: San Diego State University Press, 1983.

Visconsi, Elliot. "Technological Signifiers and the Satire on Science in Swift's *Gulliver's Travels* and Vonnegut's *Cat's Cradle*." In *The Image of Technology in Literature, the Media, and Society*, edited by Will Wright and Steve Kaplan, 114–116. Pueblo: Society for the Interdisciplinary Study of Social Imagery, University of Southern Colorado, 1994.

Whitlark, James S. "Vonnegut's Anthropology Thesis." In *Literature and Anthropology*, edited by Philip Dennis and Wendell Aycock, 77–86. Lubbock: Texas Tech University Press, 1989.

Wiedemann, Barbara. "American War Novels: Strategies for Survival." In *War and Peace: Perspectives in the Nuclear Age*, edited by Ulrich Goebel and Otto Nelson, 137–144. Lubbock: Texas Tech University Press, 1988.

Woods, Tim. "Spectres of History: Ethics and Postmodern Fictions of Temporality." In *Critical Ethics: Text, Theory and Responsibility*, edited by Dominic Rainsford and Tim Woods, 105–121. New York: St. Martin's, 1999.

Wright, Moorhead. "The Existential Adventurer and War: Three Case Studies from American Fiction." In *American Thinking about Peace and War*, edited by Ken Booth and Moorhead Wright, 101–110. New York: Barnes and Noble, 1978.

Wymer, Thomas L. "Machines and Meaning of Human in the Novels of Kurt Vonnegut, Jr." In *Mechanical God: Machines in Science Fiction*, edited by Thomas P. Dunn and Richard D. Erlich, 41–52. Westport, Conn.: Greenwood, 1982.

———. "The Swiftian Satire of Kurt Vonnegut, Jr." In *Voices for the Future: Essays on Major Science Fiction Writers*, edited by Thomas D. Clareson, 238–262. Bowling Green, Ohio: Bowling Green University Popular Press, 1976.

Journal Articles (By Decade)

2000 +

Baird, James. "Jeffers, Vonnegut, and Pynchon: Their Philosophies and Fates." *Jeffers Studies* 4, no. 1 (2000): 17–28.

Cacicedo, Alberto. "'You Must Remember This': Trauma and Memory in *Catch-22* and *Slaughterhouse-Five*." *Critique* 46, no. 4 (2005): 357–368.

Cordle, Daniel. "Changing of the Old Guard: Time Travel and Literary Technique in the Work of Kurt Vonnegut." *Yearbook of English Studies* 30 (2000): 166–176.

Doloff, Steven. "Vonnegut's *Cat's Cradle*." *Explicator* 63, no. 1 (2004): 56–57.

Fairfield, James C. "*Slaughterhouse-Five*: A Selected Guide to Scholarship and Resources, 1987–1999." *Bulletin of Bibliography* 58, no. 1 (2001): 49–57.

Freese, Peter. "Kurt Vonnegut's *Player Piano*; or, 'Would You Ask EPICAC What People Are For?'" *Arbeiten aus Anglistik und Amerikanistik* 27, no. 2 (2002): 123–159.

Fumika, Nagano. "Surviving the Perpetual Winter: The Role of the Little Boy in Vonnegut's *Cat's Cradle.*" *Journal of the American Literature Society of Japan* 2 (2003): 73–90.

Giarelli, James M. "On the Metaphysics of Presence." *Philosophy of Education* 34, no. 1 (2000): 11–14.

Guyer, Ruth Levy. "Mind's Eye: Evolving Stories." *Potomac Review* 8, no. 2 [30] (2001): 108–110.

Jarvis, Christina. "The Vietnamization of World War II in *Slaughterhouse-Five* and *Gravity's Rainbow.*" *War, Literature, and the Arts* 15, nos. 1–2 (2003): 95–117.

Magome, Kiyoko. "The Player Piano and Musico-Cybernetic Science Fiction between the 1950s and the 1980s: Kurt Vonnegut and Philip K. Dick." *Extrapolation* 45, no. 4 (2004): 370–387.

Marvin, Tom. "'Who Am I This Time?': Kurt Vonnegut and the Film *Mother Night.*" *Literature Film Quarterly* 31, no. 3 (2003): 231–236.

McHenry, Robert. "If Vonnegut Is Literature, What Is Jacqueline Susann?" *Chronicle of Higher Education* 48, no. 30 (April 5, 2002): B5.

McInnis, Gilbert. "Evolutionary Mythology in the Writings of Kurt Vonnegut, Jr." *Critique* 46, no. 4 (2005): 383–396.

Miller, Gavin. "Literary Narrative as Soteriology in the Work of Kurt Vonnegut and Alasdair Gray." *Journal of Narrative Theory* 31, no. 3 (2001): 299–323.

Morse, Donald E. "The 'Black Frost' Reception of Kurt Vonnegut's Fantastic Novel *Breakfast of Champions.*" *Journal of the Fantastic in the Arts* 11, no. 2 [42] (2000): 143–153.

———. "Sensational Implications: Kurt Vonnegut's *Player Piano* (1952)." *AnaChronist* 6 (2000): 303–314.

Pascual, Mónica Calvo. "Kurt Vonnegut's *The Sirens of Titan:* Human Will in a Newtonian Narrative Gone Chaotic." *Miscelánea* 24 (2001): 53–63.

Ren, Xiaojin. "*Timequake:* A Unity of Incredulity to Metanarratives and Historiographic Metafiction." *Foreign Literature Studies/Wai Guo Wen Xue Yan Jiu* 6, no. 116 (2005): 48–55, 171–172.

Simpson, Josh. "'This Promising of Great Secrets': Literature, Ideas, and the (Re)Invention of Reality in Kurt Vonnegut's *God Bless You, Mr. Rosewater, Slaughterhouse-Five,* and *Breakfast of Champions* Or 'Fantasies of an Impossibly Hospitable World': Science Fiction and Madness in Vonnegut's Troutean Trilogy." *Critique* 45, no. 3 (2004): 261–271.

Tamás, Bényei. "Leakings: Reappropriating Science Fiction–The Case of Kurt Vonnegut." *Journal of the Fantastic in the Arts* 11, no. 4 [44] (2001): 432–453.

Vandersee, Charles. "Naming in Novelizing the Nation: Intertextualities of Ellison, Vonnegut, and Kingston." *Onoma* 38 (2003): 305–324.

Vees-Gulani, Susanne. "Diagnosing Billy Pilgrim: A Psychiatric Approach to Kurt Vonnegut's *Slaughterhouse-Five.*" *Critique* 44, no. 2 (2003): 175–184.

Zindziuviene, Ingrida. "The Author-Reader Educational Dialogue: Kurt Vonnegut's *Timequake* (1997) from the 21st Century Reader's Perspective." *British and American Studies* 10 (2004): 175–185.

1990–1999

Beidler, Phil. "Bad Business: Vietnam and Recent Mass-Market Fiction." *College English* 54, no. 1 (1992): 64–75.

Bergenholtz, Rita. "Food for Thought in *Slaughterhouse-Five.*" *Thalia* 18, nos. 1–2 (1998): 84–93.

Bland, Michael. "A Game of Black Humor in Vonnegut's *Cat's Cradle.*" *Notes on Contemporary Literature* 24, no. 4 (1994): 8–9.

Boon, Kevin A. "The Problem with Pilgrim in Kurt Vonnegut's *Slaughterhouse Five.*" *Notes on Contemporary Literature* 26, no. 2 (1996): 8–10.

Byun, Jong-min. "Some Aspects of Confucianism in Vonnegut's *Cat's Cradle.*" *Journal of English Language and Literature* 37, no. 4 (1991): 973–981.

Coover, Robert. "Pre-Texts to Barthelme." *Review of Contemporary Fiction* 11, no. 2 (1991): 17–33.

Ferguson, Oliver W. "History and Story: Leon Trout's Double Narrative in *Galápagos.*" *Critique* 40, no. 3 (1999): 230–238.

Freese, Peter. "Kurt Vonnegut's *Jailbird:* Recent American History and the Failure of the American Dream." *Amerikastudien/American Studies* 44, no. 1 (1999): 137–165.

———. "Natural Selection with a Vengeance: Kurt Vonnegut's *Galápagos.*" *Amerikastudien/American Studies* 36, no. 3 (1991): 337–360.

———. "Surviving the End: Apocalypse, Evolution, and Entropy in Bernard Malamud, Kurt Vonnegut, and Thomas Pynchon." *Critique* 36, no. 3 (1995): 163–176.

Han, Chun-koong. "Kurt Vonnegut's Humanistic Pessimism." *Journal of English Language and Literature* 41, no. 2 (1995): 477–494.

Han, Eungoo. "Kurt Vonnegut's *Mother Night*: Fiction and Life." *Journal of English Language and Literature* 41, no. 3 (1995): 741–760.

Hattenhauer, Darryl. "The Politics of Kurt Vonnegut's 'Harrison Bergeron'." *Studies in Short Fiction* 35, no. 4 (1998): 387–392.

Hearell, W. Dale. "Formative Pretense in Vonnegut's *Mother Night*." *Publications of the Arkansas Philological Association* 25, no. 1 (1999): 31–38.

———. "Vonnegut's Changing Women." *Publications of the Arkansas Philological Association* 22, no. 2 (1996): 27–35.

Hickenlooper, John. "*Timequake*, Princess Di and the Great Apocalypse." *Bloomsbury Review* 18, no. 1 (1998): 3.

Hou, Weirui. "From the Ladder to the Cobweb: Changes in the Structure of the Novel." *Wai guo yu/Journal of Foreign Languages* 2, no. 84 (1993): 15–21.

Hughes, Joseph J. "Echoes of Gilgamesh in Vonnegut's *Breakfast of Champions*." *Publications of the Missouri Philological Association* 16 (1991): 93–97.

Hume, Kathryn. "Vonnegut's Melancholy." *Philological Quarterly* 77, no. 2 (1998): 221–238.

Kopper, Edward A., Jr. "Abstract Expressionism in Vonnegut's *Bluebeard*." *Journal of Modern Literature* 17, no. 4 (1991): 583–584.

Lazar, Mary. "Sam Johnson on Grub Street, Early Science Fiction Pulps, and Vonnegut." *Extrapolation* 32, no. 3 (1991): 235–255.

Lee, Cremilda Toledo. "Fantasy and Reality in Kurt Vonnegut's *Slaughterhouse-Five*." *Journal of English Language and Literature* 37, no. 4 (1991): 983–991.

Lerate de Castro, Jesús. "The Narrative Function of Kilgore Trout and His Fictional Works in *Slaughterhouse-Five*." *Revista Alicantina de Estudios Ingleses* 7 (1994): 115–122.

Lupack, Barbara T. "Pilgrim's Regress: Cinematic Narrative in *Slaughterhouse-Five*." *Connecticut Review* 12, no. 1 (1990): 15–27.

Morse, Donald E. "Abjuring Rough Magic: Kurt Vonnegut's *Timequake*." *New York Review of Science Fiction* 10, no. 10 [118] (1998): 1, 8–11.

———. "Bringing Chaos to Order: Vonnegut Criticism at Century's End." *Journal of the Fantastic in the Arts* 10, no. 4 [40] (1999): 395–408.

———. "Kurt Vonnegut: The Antonio Gaudi of Fantastic Fiction." *Centennial Review* 42, no. 1 (1998): 173–183.

———. "Kurt Vonnegut's *Jailbird* and *Deadeye Dick*: Two Studies of Defeat." *Hungarian Studies in English* 22 (1991): 109–119.

———. "Thinking Intelligently about Science and Art: Kurt Vonnegut's *Galápagos* and *Bluebeard*." *Extrapolation* 38, no. 4 (1997): 292–303.

———. "'Why Not You?': Kurt Vonnegut's Debt to the Book of Job." *Eger Journal of American Studies* 1 (1993): 75–88.

Noguchi, Kenji. "Vonnegut's Desperado Humor in *Slaughterhouse-Five*." *Studies in English Language and Literature* 45 (1995): 1–15.

Rampton, David. "Into the Secret Chamber: Art and the Artist in Kurt Vonnegut's *Bluebeard*." *Critique* 35, no. 1 (1993): 16–26.

Reed, Peter J. "Kurt Vonnegut: A Selected Bibliography, 1985–1992." *Bulletin of Bibliography* 50, no. 2 (1993): 123–128.

———. "Kurt Vonnegut's Fantastic Faces." *Journal of the Fantastic in the Arts* 10, no. 1 [37] (1998): 77–87.

Shaw, Patrick W. "Too Many Pilgrimages: Travel and Point of View in Kurt Vonnegut's *Slaughterhouse Five*." *Conference of College Teachers of English Studies* 58 (1993): 14–19.

Singh, Sukbir. "Bellow's *Seize the Day* and Vonnegut's *Mother Night*: An Intertextual Approach." *Indian Journal of American Studies* 23, no. 1 (1993): 100–106.

Stralen, Hans van. "*Slaughterhouse-Five*, Existentialist Themes Elaborated in a Postmodernist Way." *Neophilologus* 79, no. 1 (1995): 3–12.

Watts, Philip. "Rewriting History: Céline and Kurt Vonnegut." *South Atlantic Quarterly* 93, no. 2 (1994): 265–278.

1980–1989

Alsen, Eberhard. "Vonnegut's Comedy of Errors." *Transition* 82, no. 3 (1983): 28–36.

Ancone, Frank. "Kurt Vonnegut and the Great Twain Robbery." *Notes on Contemporary Literature* 13, no. 4 (1983): 6–7.

Berryman, Charles. "After the Fall: Kurt Vonnegut." *Critique* 26 (1985): 96–102.

Blackford, Russell. "The Definition of Love: Kurt Vonnegut's *Slapstick*." *Science Fiction* 2, no. 3 (1980): 208–228.

———. "Physics and Fantasy: Scientific Mysticism, Kurt Vonnegut, and *Gravity's Rainbow*." *Journal of Popular Culture* 19 (1985): 35–44.

Brophy, Elizabeth. "Vonnegut's Bird Language in *Slaughterhouse-Five*." *Notes on Modern American Literature* 4 (1980): Item 15.

Burlui, Irina. "Reality and Fiction in the Novels of Kurt Vonnegut, Jr." *Analele Stiintifice ale Universitatii 'Al. I. Cuza' din Iasi (Serie noua), e. Lingvistica* 29 (1983): 77–82.

Chabot, C. Barry. "*Slaughterhouse-Five* and the Comforts of Indifference." *Essays in Literature* 8, no. 1 (1981): 45–51.

Cook, Kenneth. "What's So Damn Funny?: Grim Humor in *The Mysterious Stranger* and *Cat's Cradle*." *Publications of the Missouri Philological Association* 7 (1982): 48–55.

Cooley, John. "The Garden in the Machine: Three Postmodern Pastorals." *Michigan Academician* 13, no. 4 (1981): 405–420.

Cowan, S. A. "Track of the Hound: Ancestors of Kazak in *The Sirens of Titan*." *Extrapolation* 24, no. 3 (1983): 280–287.

Cunningham, Valentine. "The Dilemmas of a Liberal Humanist." *(London) Times Literary Supplement* 4081 (June 19, 1981): 692.

Faris, Wendy B. "Magic and Violence in Macondo and San Lorenzo." *Latin American Literary Review* 13, no. 25 (1985): 44–54.

Fiene, Donald M. "Elements of Dostoevsky in the Novels of Kurt Vonnegut." *Dostoevsky Studies* 2 (1981): 129–142.

———. "Kurt Vonnegut in the USSR: A Bibliography." *Bulletin of Bibliography* 45, no. 4 (1988): 223–232.

Giannone, Richard. "Violence in the Novels of Kurt Vonnegut." *Thought* 56 (1981): 58–76.

Gill, R. B. "Bargaining in Good Faith: The Laughter of Vonnegut, Grass, and Kundera." *Critique* 25 (1984): 77–91.

Greer, Creed. "Kurt Vonnegut and the Character of Words." *Journal of Narrative Technique* 19, no. 3 (1989): 312–330.

Hume, Kathyrn. "The Heraclitan Cosmos of Kurt Vonnegut." *Papers on Language and Literature* 18, no. 2 (1982): 208–224.

———. "Kurt Vonnegut and the Myths and Symbols of Meaning." *Texas Studies in Literature and Language* 24, no. 4 (1982): 429–447.

———. "Vonnegut's Self-Projections: Symbolic Characters and Symbolic Fictions." *Journal of Narrative Technique* 12, no. 3 (1982): 177–190.

Jamosky, Edward and Jerome Klinkowitz. "Kurt Vonnegut's Three *Mother Nights*." *Modern Fiction Studies* 34, no. 2 (1988): 216–219.

Klinkowitz, Jerome. "New American Fiction and Values." *Anglo-American Studies* 2, no. 2 (1982): 241–247.

Martin, Robert A. "*Catch-22* and *Slaughterhouse-Five*." *Notes on Contemporary Literature* 15, no. 4 (1985): 8–10.

———. "*Slaughterhouse-Five*: Vonnegut's Domed Universe." *Notes on Contemporary Literature* 17, no. 2 (1987): 5–8.

Matheson, T. J. "This Lousy Little Book: The Genesis and Development of *Slaughterhouse-Five* as Revealed in Chapter One." *Studies in the Novel* 16, no. 2 (1984): 228–240.

Mathieson, Kenneth. "The Influence of Science Fiction in the Contemporary American Novel." *Science-Fiction Studies* 12, no. 1 [35] (1985): 22–32.

Mayer, Peter C. "Film, Ontology and the Structure of a Novel." *Literature/Film Quarterly* 8 (1980): 204–208.

Merrill, Robert. "John Gardner's *Grendel* and the Interpretation of Modern Fables." *American Literature* 56, no. 2 (1984): 162–180.

Meyer, William H. E. "Kurt Vonnegut: The Man with Nothing to Say." *Critique* 29 (1988): 95–101.

Mills, John. "Return of the Dazed Steer." *Queen's Quarterly* 88, no. 1 (1981): 145–154.

Misra, Kalidas. "The American War Novel from World War II to Vietnam." *Indian Journal of American Studies* 14, no. 2 (1984): 73–80.

Mustazza, Leonard. "A Darwinian Eden: Science and Myth in Kurt Vonnegut's *Galapagos*." *Journal of the Fantastic in the Arts* 3 (1991): 55–65.

———. "The Machine Within: Mechanization, Human Discontent, and the Genre of Vonnegut's *Player Piano*." *Papers on Language and Literature* 25, no. 1 (1989): 99–113.

————. "Vonnegut's Tralfamadore and Milton's Eden." *Essays in Literature* 13 (1986): 299–312.

Nadeau, Robert. "Physics and Metaphysics in the Novels of Kurt Vonnegut, Jr." *Mosaic* 13, no. 2 (1980): 37–47.

Nuwer, Hank. "A Skull Session with Kurt Vonnegut." *South Carolina Review* 19, no. 2 (1987): 2–23.

Orendain, Margarita R. "Confronting the Gods of Science: Kurt Vonnegut, Jr. in 'Welcome to the Monkey House'." *Saint Louis University Research Journal of the Graduate School of Arts and Sciences* 18, no. 1 (1987): 150–167.

Parshall, Peter F. "Meditations on the Philosophy of Tralfamadore: Kurt Vonnegut and George Roy Hill." *Literature Film Quarterly* 15, no. 1 (1987): 49–59.

Rackstraw, Loree. "Vonnegut Cosmos." *North American Review* 267 (1982): 63–67.

Rapf, Joanna E. "'In the Beginning Was the Work': Steve Geller on *Slaughterhouse-Five*." *Post Script* 4, no. 2 (1985): 19–31.

Reddy, K. Satyanaryana. "Structure of Consciousness in the Major Fiction of Kurt Vonnegut, Jr." *Literary Endeavour* 9, nos. 1–4 (1987–88): 91–96.

Reid, Susan. "Kurt Vonnegut and American Culture: Mechanization and Loneliness in *Player Piano*." *Journal of the American Studies Association of Texas* 15 (1984): 46–51.

Saltzman, Arthur M. "The Aesthetic of Doubt in Recent Fiction." *Denver Quarterly* 20, no. 1 (1985): 89–106.

Sandbank, Shimon. "Parable and Theme: Kafka and American Fiction." *Comparative Literature* 37, no. 3 (1985): 252–268.

Schöpp, Joseph C. "*Slaughterhouse-Five*: The Struggle with a Form That Fails." *Amerikastudien/American Studies* 28, no. 3 (1983): 335–345.

Sheppeard, Sallye J. "Signposts in a Chaotic World: Naming Devices in Kurt Vonnegut's Dresden Books." *McNeese Review* 31 (1984–86): 14–22.

Sigman, Joseph. "Science and Parody in Kurt Vonnegut's *The Sirens of Titan*." *Mosaic* 19, no. 1 (1986): 15–32.

Singh, Jaidev. "Self-Reflexivity in Contemporary Fiction: A Note on Ideology." *Creative Forum* 1, no. 4 (1988): 1–11.

Singh, Sukhbir. "The Politics of Madness in Kurt Vonnegut's *God Bless You, Mr. Rosewater*." *Panjab University Research Bulletin (Arts)* 17, no. 1 (1986): 19–27.

Townsend, Roy. "Eliot and Vonnegut: Modernism and Postmodernism?" *Journal of English* 16 (1988): 90–104.

Woodward, Robert H. "Dramatic License in Vonnegut's 'Who Am I This Time?'." *Notes on Contemporary Literature* 12, no. 1 (1982): 8–9.

Ziegfield, Richard E. "Kurt Vonnegut on Censorship and Moral Values." *Modern Fiction Studies* 26 (1980): 631–635.

Zins, Daniel L. "Rescuing Science from Technocracy: *Cat's Cradle* and the Play of Apocalypse." *Science-Fiction Studies* 13 (1986): 170–181.

1970–1979

Abadi-Nagy, Zoltan. "Ironic Messianism in Recent American Fiction." *Studies in English and American* 4 (1978): 63–83.

————. "'The Skilful Seducer': Of Vonnegut's Brand of Comedy." *Hungarian Studies in English* 8 (1974): 45–56.

Auwera, Fernand. "Lucky Punch." *Dietsche Warande en Belfort: Tijdschrift voor Letterkunde, Kunst en Geestesleven* 122 (1977): 783–785.

Bodtke, Richard. "Great Sorrows, Small Joys: The World of Kurt Vonnegut, Jr." *Crosscurrents* 20 (1970): 120–125.

Bosworth, David. "The Literature of Awe." *Antioch Review* 37, no. 1 (1979): 4–26.

Bourjaily, Vance. "What Vonnegut Is and Isn't." *New York Times Book Review* 13 August 1972: 3, 10.

Brier, Peter A. "Caliban Reigns: Romantic Theory and Some Contemporary Fantasists." *Denver Quarterly* 13, no. 1 (1978): 38–51.

Buck, Lynn. "Vonnegut's World of Comic Futility." *Studies in American Fiction* 3 (1975): 181–198.

Burhans, Clinton. "Hemingway and Vonnegut: Diminishing Vision in a Dying Age." *Modern Fiction Studies* 21 (1975): 173–191.

Clancy, L. J. "If the Accident Will: The Novels of Kurt Vonnegut." *Meanjin Quarterly* 30 (1971): 37–45.

Cohn, Alan M. "A Vonnegut Rarissima: A Supplement to Hudgens and to Pieratt and Klinkowitz." *Papers of the Bibliographical Society of America* 73 (1979): 365–366.

Crump, G. B. "D. H. Lawrence and the Immediate Present: Kurt Vonnegut, Jr., Ken Kesey, and Wright Morris." *D. H. Lawrence Review* 10 (1977): 103–141.

Dahiya, Bhim. "Structural Patterns in the Novels of Barth, Vonnegut, and Pynchon." *Indian Journal of American Studies* 5, nos. 1–2 (1976): 53–68.

DeMott, Benjamin. "Vonnegut's Otherworldly Laughter." *Saturday Review* 1 May 1971: 29–32, 38.

Doxey, William S. "Vonnegut's *Cat's Cradle*." *The Explicator* 37, no. 4 (1979): 6.

Edelstein, Arnold. "*Slaughterhouse-Five*: Time Out of Joint." *College Literature* 1 (1974): 128–139.

Engel, David. "On the Question of Foma: A Study of the Novels of Kurt Vonnegut, Jr." *Riverside Quarterly* 5 (1972): 119–128.

Engel, Wilson F., III. "Pilgrim as Prisoner: Cummings and Vonnegut." *Notes on Contemporary Literature* 7, no. 1 (1977): 13–14.

Fiedler, Leslie A. "The Divine Stupidity of Kurt Vonnegut." *Esquire* September 1970: 195–197, 199–200, 202–204.

Fiene, Donald M. "Vonnegut's Quotations from Dostoevsky." *Notes on Modern American Literature* 1 (1977): Item 29.

———. "Vonnegut's *Sirens of Titan*." *Explicator* 34, no. 4 (1975): Item 27.

Flora, Joseph M. "Cabell as Precursor: Reflections on Cabell and Vonnegut." *Kalki* 6 (1975): 118–137.

Friedman, Melvin J. "Dislocations of Setting and Word: Notes on American Fiction Since 1950." *Studies in American Fiction* 5 (1977): 79–98.

Godshalk, William L. "The Recurring Characters of Kurt Vonnegut, Jr." *Notes on Contemporary Literature* 3, no. 1 (1973): 2–3.

———. "Vonnegut and Shakespeare: Rosewater in Elsinore." *Critique* 15, no. 2 (1973): 37–48.

Greiner, Donald J. "Vonnegut's *Slaughterhouse-Five* and the Fiction of Atrocity." *Critique* 14, no. 3 (1973): 38–51.

Gros-Louis, Dolores K. "*Slaughterhouse-Five*: Pacifism vs. Passiveness." *Ball State University Forum* 18, no. 2 (1977): 3–8.

Grossman, Edward. "Vonnegut and His Audience." *Commentary* 58, no. 1 (1974): 40–46.

Hansen, Arlen J. "The Celebration of Solipsism: A New Trend in American Fiction." *Modern Fiction Studies* 19 (1973): 5–15.

Harris, Charles B. "Time, Uncertainty, and Kurt Vonnegut, Jr.: A Reading of *Slaughterhouse-Five*." *Centennial Review* 20, no. 3 (1976): 228–243.

Hartshorne, Thomas L. "From *Catch-22* to *Slaughterhouse V*: The Decline of the Political Mode." *South Atlantic Quarterly* 78, no. 1 (1979): 17–33.

Haskell, John D., Jr. "Addendum to Pieratt and Klinkowitz: Kurt Vonnegut, Jr." *Papers of the Bibliographical Society of America* 70 (1976): 122.

Hayman, David. "The Jolly Mix: Notes on Techniques, Style, and Decorum in *Slaughterhouse-Five*." *Summary* 1, no. 2 (1977): 44–50.

Hendin, Josephine. "Writer as Culture Hero." *Harpers* July 1974: 82–87.

Irving, John. "Kurt Vonnegut and His Critics." *New Republic* September 22, 1979: 41–49.

Isaacs, Neil D. "Unstuck in Time: *Clockwork Orange* and *Slaughterhouse-Five*." *Literature/Film Quarterly* 1, no. 2 (1973): 122–131.

Kael, Pauline. "Current Cinema." *New Yorker* January 23, 1971: 76–78.

Kazin, Alfred. "The War Novel from Mailer to Vonnegut." *Saturday Review* February 6, 1971: 13–15, 36.

Kennedy, R. C. "Kurt Vonnegut, Jr." *Art International* 15 (1971): 20–25.

Klinkowitz, Jerome. "The Dramatization of Kurt Vonnegut, Jr." *Players* 50 (1975): 62–64.

———. "Kurt Vonnegut, Jr. and the Crime of His Times." *Critique* 12, no. 3 (1971): 38–53.

———. "The Literary Career of Kurt Vonnegut, Jr." *Modern Fiction Studies* 19 (1973): 57–67.

Kopper, Edward A., Jr. "Color Symbolism in Vonnegut's *Slaughterhouse-Five*." *Notes on Modern American Literature* 1 (1977): Item 17.

———. "Operation Gomorrah in *Slaughterhouse-Five*." *Notes on Contemporary Literature* 8, no. 4 (1978): 6.

Lawing, John V., Jr. "Kurt Vonnegut: Charming Nihilisit." *Christianity Today* February 14, 1979: 17–20, 22.

LeClair, Thomas. "Death and Black Humor." *Critique* 17, no. 1 (1975): 5–40.

Leff, Leonard. "Science and Destruction in Vonnegut's *Cat's Cradle*." *Rectangle* 46 (1971): 28–32.

———. "Utopia Reconstructed: Alienation in Vonnegut's *God Bless You, Mr. Rosewater*." *Critique* 12, no. 3 (1971): 29–37.

Lessing, Doris. "Vonnegut's Responsibility." *New York Times Book Review* February 4, 1973: 35.

Leverence, W. John. "*Cat's Cradle* and Traditional American Humor." *Journal of Popular Culture* 5, no. 4 (1972): 955–963.

Mangum, Bryant. "*Cat's Cradle*'s Jonah-John and the Garden of Ice-Nine." *Notes on Contemporary Literature* 9, no. 3 (1979): 9–11.

May, John R. "Vonnegut's Humor and the Limits of Hope." *Twentieth Century Literature* 18, no. 1 (1972): 25–36.

McGinnis, Wayne. "The Arbitrary Cycle of *Slaughterhouse-Five*: A Relation of Form to Theme." *Critique* 17, no. 1 (1975): 55–68.

———. "The Source and Implications of *Ice-Nine* in Vonnegut's *Cat's Cradle*." *American Notes and Queries* 13, no. 3 (1974): 40–41.

———. "Vonnegut's *Breakfast of Champions*: A Reductive Success." *Notes on Contemporary Literature* 5, no. 3 (1975): 6–9.

McGinnis, Wayne D. "The Ambiguities of Bokononism." *Iowa English Bulletin: Yearbook* 26, no. 7 (1977): 21–23.

———. "Names in Vonnegut's Fiction." *Notes on Contemporary Literature* 3, no. 2 [4] (1973): 7–9.

McInerney, John M. "Children for Vonnegut." *Notes on Modern American Literature* 3 (1978): Item 4.

Mendelson, Maurice. "Reading Kurt Vonnegut." *Soviet Literature* 8 (1975): 156–159.

Merrill, Robert. "Vonnegut's *Breakfast of Champions*: The Conversion of Heliogabalus." *Critique* 18, no. 3 (1977): 99–108.

Merrill, Robert, and Peter A. Scholl. "Vonnegut's *Slaughterhouse-Five*: The Requirements of Chaos." *Studies in American Fiction* 6, no. 1 (1978): 65–76.

Messent, Peter B. "*Breakfast of Champions*: The Direction of Kurt Vonnegut's Fiction." *Journal of American Studies* 8, no. 1 (1974): 101–114.

Morrow, Patrick D. "The Womb Image in Vonnegut's *Cat's Cradle*." *Notes on Contemporary Literature* 6, no. 5 (1976): 11–13.

Myers, David. "Kurt Vonnegut, Jr.: Morality-Myth in the Antinovel." *International Fiction Review* 3 (1976): 52–56.

Nelson, Joyce. "*Slaughterhouse-Five*: Novel and Film." *Literature/Film Quarterly* 1, no. 2 (1973): 149–153.

———. "Vonnegut and Bugs in Amber." *Journal of Popular Culture* 7 (1973): 551–558.

Nicol, Charles. "The Ideas of an Anti-Intellectual." *National Review* September 28, 1973: 1,064–1,065.

Noguchi, Kenji. "*Slaughterhouse-Five* and Vonnegut's 'Genial Desperado Philosophy'." *Kyushu American Literature* 16 (1975): 17–20.

O'Connor, Gerard W. "The Function of Time Travel in Vonnegut's *Slaughterhouse-Five*." *Riverside Quarterly* 5 (1972): 206–207.

O'Sullivan, Maurice J., Jr. "*Slaughterhouse-Five*: Kurt Vonnegut's Anti-memoirs." *Essays in Literature* 3 (1976): 44–50.

Pauly, Rebecca M. "The Moral Stance of Kurt Vonnegut." *Extrapolation* 15 (1973): 66–71.

Prioli, Carmine A. "Kurt Vonnegut's Duty-Dance." *Essays in Literature* 1, no. 3 (1973): 44–50.

Pütz, Manfred. "Imagination and Self-Definition." *Partisan Review* 44, no. 2 (1977): 235–244.

Rackstraw, Loree. "Paradise Re-Lost." *North American Review* 261 (1976): 63–64.

———. "Vonnegut the Diviner and Other Auguries." *North American Review* 264 (1979): 74–76.

Ranley, Ernest W. "What Are People For? Man, Fate and Kurt Vonnegut." *Commonweal* 7 (May 1971): 207–211.

Rice, Susan. "*Slaughterhouse-Five*: A Viewer's Guide." *Media and Methods* (1972): 27–33.

Rose, Ellen Cronan. "It's All a Joke: Science Fiction in Kurt Vonnegut's *The Sirens of Titan*." *Literature and Psychology* 29, no. 4 (1979): 160–168.

Rovit, Earl. "Some Shapes in Recent American Fiction." *Contemporary Literature* (1974): 550–565.

Rubens, Philip M. "Names in Vonnegut's *Cat's Cradle*." *Notes on Contemporary Literature* 8, no. 1 (1978): 7.

———. "Nothing's Ever Final: Vonnegut's Concept of Time." *College Literature* 6 (1979): 64–72.

Sadler, Frank. "Par-A-Dise and Science." *West Georgia College Review* 11 (1979): 38–43.

Samuels, Charles Thomas. "Age of Vonnegut." *New Republic* June 12, 1971: 30–32.

Schatt, Stanley. "A Kurt Vonnegut Checklist." *Critique* 12, no. 3 (1971): 70–76.

———. "The Whale and the Cross: Vonnegut's Jonah and Christ Figures." *Southwest Review* 56 (1971): 29–42.

———. "The World of Kurt Vonnegut, Jr." *Critique* 12, no. 3 (1971): 54–69.

Scholl, Peter A. "Vonnegut's Attack upon Christiandom." *Christianity and Literature* 22, no. 1 (1972): 5–11.

Schriber, Mary Sue. "Bringing Chaos to Order: The Novel Tradition and Kurt Vonnegut, Jr." *Genre* 10 (1977): 283–297.

———. "You've Come a Long Way, Babbitt! From Zenith to Ilium." *Twentieth Century Literature* 17, no. 2 (1971): 101–106.

Schultz, Max F. "The Unconfirmed Thesis: Kurt Vonnegut, Black Humor, and Contemporary Art." *Critique* 12, no. 3 (1971): 5–28.

Seelye, John. "What the Kids Are Reading." *New Republic* October, 17, 1970: 23–26.

Shaw, Patrick W. "The Excrement Festival: Vonnegut's *Slaughterhouse-Five*." *Scholia Satyrica* 2, no. 3 (1976): 3–11.

Todd, Richard. "*Breakfast of Champions*: This Novel Contains More than Twice Your Daily Requirement of Irony." *Atlantic* May 1973: 105–109.

Trachtenberg, Stanley. "Vonnegut's Cradle: The Erosion of Comedy." *Michigan Quarterly Review* 12 (1973): 66–71.

Uphaus, Robert W. "Expected Meaning in Vonnegut's Dead-End Fiction." *Novel* 8, no. 2 (1975): 164–174.

Vanderwerken, David L. "Pilgrim's Dilemma: *Slaughterhouse-Five*." *Research Studies* 42 (1974): 147–152.

Vinograde, Ann C. "A Soviet Translation of *Slaughterhouse-Five*." *Russian Language Journal* 93 (1972): 14–18.

"Vonnegut's Gospel." *Time* June 29, 1970: 8.

Williams, Melvin G. "Designer's Choice in *Cat's Cradle*." *Papers of the Bibliographical Society of America* 73 (1979): 366.

Wolfe, G. K. "Vonnegut and the Metaphor of Science Fiction: *The Sirens of Titan*." *Journal of Popular Culture* 5, no. 4 (1972): 964–999.

Wood, Michael. "Dancing in the Dark." *New York Review of Books* May 31, 1973: 23–25.

1960–1969

Bryan, C. D. B. "Kurt Vonnegut on Target." *New Republic* October 8, 1966: 21–22, 24–26.

Ciardi, John. "Manner of Speaking." *Saturday Review* September 30, 1967: 16, 18.

Coffey, W. "Gentleness and a Stylish Sense of the Ridiculous." *Commonweal* June 6, 1969: 347–348.

Crichton, J. M. "Sci-Fi and Vonnegut." *New Republic* April 26, 1969: 33–35.

Hicks, Granville. "Literary Horizons." *Saturday Review* March 29, 1969: 25.

Palmer, Raymond C. "Vonnegut's Major Concerns." *Iowa English Bulletin: Yearbook* 14 (1969): 3–10.

Scholes, Robert. "Mithridates, He Died Old: Black Humor and Kurt Vonnegut, Jr." *Hollins Critic* October 16, 1966: 1–12.

Tanner, Tony. "The Uncertain Messenger: A Study of the Novels of Kurt Vonnegut, Jr." *Critical Quarterly* 11 (1969): 297–315.

Weales, Gerald. "Whatever Happened to Tugboat Annie?" *Reporter* December 1, 1966: 50, 52–56.

Interviews

Abádi-Nagy, Zoltán. "'Serenity,' 'Courage,' 'Wisdom': A Talk with Kurt Vonnegut." *Hungarian Studies in English* 22 (1991): 23–37.

Abramson, Marcia. "Vonnegut: Humor with Suffering." *Michigan Daily* (January 22, 1969): 2.

Banks, Ann. "Symposium Sidelights." *Novel: A Forum on Fiction* 3, no. 3 (1970): 208–211.

Bellamy, Joe David, and John Casey. "Kurt Vonnegut, Jr." *The New Fiction: Interviews with Innovative American Writers*, Urbana: University of Illinois Press, (1988). 194–207. Allen 156–167.

Blazejewski, Christopher R. "Vonnegut Unbound." *Harvard Crimson* 12 (May 2000). http://www.thecrimson.com.

Bleifuss, Joel. "Kurt Vonnegut vs. the !&#*!@." *In These Times*. (January 27, 2003). http://www.inthesetimes.com/comments.php?id=38_0_4_0_M.

Bosworth, Patricia. "To Vonnegut, the Hero Is the Man Who Refuses to Kill." *New York Times* (October 25, 1970): D5.

Brinkley, Douglas. "Vonnegut's Apocalypse." *Rolling Stone* (August 24, 2006): 77–110.

Bryan, C. D. B. "Kurt Vonnegut: Head Bokononist." *New York Times Book Review* (April 6, 1969): 2, 25. Allen 3–6.

Cargas, Harry James. "Are There Things a Novelist Shouldn't Joke About?" *Christian Century* (November 24, 1974): 1,048–1,050.

Casey, John. "Kurt Vonnegut, Jr.: A Subterranean Conversation." *Confluence* 2 (1969): 3–5.

Clancy, L. J. "If Accident Will: The Novels of Kurt Vonnegut." *Meanjin Quarterly* (1971): 37–45.

"The Conscience of a Writer." *Publishers Weekly* (March 22, 1971): 26–27. Allen 42–45.

Cook, Bruce. "When Kurt Vonnegut Talks—and He Does—the Young All Tune." *National Observer* (October 12, 1970): 2.

Diskey, Jay A. "Vonnegut Cradles His Fiction in Imagination and Experience." *Indiana Student Daily* (October 5, 1983): 1, 6.

Dunlop, Frank. "God and Kurt Vonnegut, Jr. at Iowa City." *Chicago Tribune Magazine* (May 7, 1976): 48, 84, 86, 88.

Eckholt, Larry. "Vonnegut Vows to Survive Critics." *Des Moines Register* (April 2, 1977): 1B.

Feldman, Michael. "Michael Interviews Kurt Vonnegut." *Whad'Ya Know?* October 2, 1999). http://www.notmuch.com/Features/Interview/1999/10.02.html.

Freedman, David, and Sara Schafer. "Vonnegut and Clancy on Technology." *Inc.* (December 1995): 4.

Friedman, Roger. "God Bless You, Mr. Vonnegut: The Writer on His Eightieth Birthday." *Fox News* (November 11, 2002). http://www.vonnegutweb.com/vonnegutia/interviews/int_fox.html.

Friedenreich, Kenneth. "Kurt Vonnegut: The PR Man Turned Novelist." *Newsday* (August 11, 1975): 12.

Gross, Terry. "Interview: Kurt Vonnegut, Jr." *Applause* (March 1987): 18–21.

Gussow, Mel. "Vonnegut Is Having Fun Doing a Play." *New York Times* (October 6, 1970): 56. Allen 23–25.

Hayman, David, David Michaelis, and George Plimpton. "The Art of Fiction LXIV: Kurt Vonnegut." *Paris Review* 69 (1977): 55–103. Allen 168–195.

Heffernan, Harold. "Vonnegut Likes a Change of Scenery." *Star-Ledger* (June 8, 1971): 26.

Henkle, Roger. "Wrestling (American Style) with Proteus." *Novel: A Forum on Fiction* 3, no. 3 (1970): 197–207.

Hickey, Neil. "Between Time and Timbuktu." *TV Guide* (March 11, 1972): 24–26.

Horwitz, Carey. "An Interview with Kurt Vonnegut, Jr." *Library Journal* (April 15, 1973): 1311.

Houston, Frank. "Salon Interview: Kurt Vonnegut." Salon.com. (October 8, 1999). http://www.salon.com/books/int/1999/10/08/vonnegut_interview/.

Imamura, Tateo. "Vonnegut in Tokyo: An Interview with Kurt Vonnegut." *Eigo Seinen* 130 (1984): 262–266.

Kakutani, Michiko. "Publishing." *New York Times* (January 16, 1981): C4.

Klinkowitz, Jerome. "Lonesome No More: Interview with Kurt Vonnegut." *Washington Post World* (September 2, 1979): 7.

Kornbluth, Jesse, and Robert Weide. "Vonnegut on AOL." AOL.com. (November 22, 1996). http://www.finelinefeatures.com/mnight/aol_qa.htm.

Kramer, Carol. "Kurt's College Cult Adopts Him as Literary Guru at 48." *Chicago Tribune* (November 15, 1970): 5.1. Allen 26–29.

Mahoney, Lawrence. "Poison Their Minds with Humanity." *Tropic: The Miami Herald Sunday Magazine* (January 24, 1971): 8–10, 13, 44.

Mallorey, Carole. "The Joe and Kurt Show." *Playboy* (May 1992): 86–88, 130–135.

McCabe, Loretta. "An Exclusive Interview with Kurt Vonnegut, Jr." *Writers Yearbook—1970* (1970): 92–95, 100–101, 103–105.

McLaughlin, Frank. "An Interview with Kurt Vonnegut, Jr." *Media and Methods* (May 1973): 38–41, 45–46. Allen 66–75.

Merryman, Kathleen. "Vonnegut Blasts America's Lack of Idealism." *Tacoma News Tribune* (April 26, 1985): C10.

Mitchell, Greg. "Meeting My Maker: A Visit with Kurt Vonnegut, Jr., by Kilgore Trout." *Crawdaddy* (April 1, 1974): 42–51. Allen 133–155.

Musil, Robert K. "There Must Be More to Love Than Death: A Conversation with Kurt Vonnegut." *Nation* (August 2, 1980): 128–132. Allen 230–239.

Noble, William, T. "Unstuck in Time . . . A Real Kurt Vonnegut: The Reluctant Guru of Searching Youth." *Detroit Sunday News Magazine* (June 18, 1972): 14–15, 18, 20, 22–24. Allen 57–65.

Nuwer, Hank. "A Skull Session with Kurt Vonnegut." *South Carolina Review* 19, no. 2 (1987): 2–23. Allen 240–264.

Okrent, Daniel. "The Short, Sad Stay of Kurt Vonnegut, Jr." *The Michigan Daily* (January 25, 1969): 2.

———. "A Very New Kind of WIR." *The Michigan Daily* (January 21, 1969): 1–2.

Reasoner, Harry. *60 Minutes.* "CBS News Transcript" (September 15, 1970): 14–17. Allen 15–19.

Reilly, Charles. "An Interview with Kurt Vonnegut, Jr." *Delaware Literary Review* (University of Delaware) (1976): 20–27.

Reilly, Charlie. "Two Conversations with Kurt Vonnegut." *College Literature* 7 (1980): 1–29. Allen 196–229.

Rentilly, J. "The Best Jokes Are Dangerous: An Interview with Kurt Vonnegut, Part One." *McSweeney's Internet Tendency: McSweeney's Quarterly.* (September 16, 2002). http://www.mcsweeneys.net/2002/09/16vonnegut1.html.

Romine, Dannye. "Listening to Kurt Vonnegut, Higgledy-Piggledy." *Charlotte Observer-Sun* (February 18, 1979): 1F, 8F.

Saal, Rollene W. "Pick of the Paperbacks." *Saturday Review* (March 28, 1970): 34.

Schenker, Israel. "Kurt Vonnegut, Jr., Lights Comic Path of Despair." *New York Times* (March 21, 1969): 1, 41. Allen 20–22.

Scholes, Robert. "A Talk with Kurt Vonnegut, Jr." In *The Vonnegut Statement: Original Essays on the Life and Work of Kurt Vonnegut,* 90–118, Allen, 111–132. Delacorte Press, 1973.

Schumacher, Michael. "Vonnegut on Writing." *Writer's Digest* (November 1985): 22, 27.

Sheed, Wilfrid. "The Now Generation Knew Him When." *Life* (September 12, 1969): 64–66, 69. Allen 11–14.

Short, Robert. "Robert Short Interviews Kurt Vonnegut, Chicago—June 8, 1976." In *Something to Believe In: Is Kurt Vonnegut the Exorcist of Jesus Christ Superstar?* 283–308. New York: Harper & Row, 1978.

Stage, Wm. "Mississippi Mud: God Help You Mr. Rosewater." *Riverfront Times.* (March 5, 1997). http://www.riverfronttimes.com.

Standish, David. "Playboy Interview." *Playboy* (July 1973): 57–60, 62, 68, 70, 72, 214, 216. Allen 76–110.

Swaim, Don. "Audio Interview with Kurt Vonnegut, Jr." *Wired for Books.* Athens: Ohio University Telecommunications Center, 1981. http://www.wiredforbooks.org/kurtvonnegut/.

Taylor, Robert. "Kurt Vonnegut." *Boston Globe Sunday Magazine* (July 20, 1969): 10–12, 14–15. Allen 7–10.

Thomas, Phil. "Growing Sales Puzzle Writer." *Ann Arbor News* (December 12, 1971): 41.

Todd, Richard. "The Masks of Kurt Vonnegut, Jr." *New York Times Magazine* (January 24, 1971): 16–17, 19, 22, 24, 26, 30.

Troy, Carol. "Carol Troy Interviews Kurt Vonnegut." *Rags* (March 1971): 24–26.

Unger, Art. "Kurt Vonnegut, Jr.: Class of 71." *Ingenue* (December 1971): 14–18.

Uricchio, Marylynn. "Breakfast with Kurt Vonnegut." *Pittsburgh Post-Gazette* (November 9, 1998). http://www.post-gazette.com.

"Vonnegut's Gospel." *Time* (June 29, 1970): 8.

"We Talk to . . . Kurt Vonnegut." *Mademoiselle* (August 1970): 296.

Wolf, William. "Kurt Vonnegut: Still Dreaming of Imaginary Worlds." *Insight: Sunday Journal of the Milwaukee Journal* (February 28, 1972): 12–18.

Workman, Michael. "Interview with Kurt Vonnegut." *Bridge Magazine.* (November 2000). http://www.bridgemagazine.org/9_02special/vonnegut.html.

Zuckerman, Alicia. "Life During Wartime: Kurt Vonnegut Talks About his 'Desecration' of Stravinsky's Romanticized *The Soldier's Tale.*" *New York* (April 3, 2006): 83.

THE WORKS OF KILGORE TROUT

Kilgore Trout is the fictional science fiction writer who appears in many Vonnegut novels, most notably *God Bless You, Mr. Rosewater, Slaughterhouse-Five, Breakfast of Champions,* and *Timequake.* He is often regarded as Vonnegut's alter ego.

Bibliography of Works by Kilgore Trout

Novels

2BRO2B (God Bless You, Mr. Rosewater)

The Barring-Gaffner of Bagnialto (Breakfast of Champions)

The Big Board (Slaughterhouse-Five)

Delmore Skag [untitled] *(Breakfast of Champions)*

Don [untitled] *(Breakfast of Champions)*

The Era of Hopeful Monsters (Galápagos)

The First District Court of Thankyou (God Bless You, Mr. Rosewater)

The Gospel from Outer Space (Slaughterhouse-Five)

The Gutless Wonder (Slaughterhouse-Five)

How You Doin'? (Breakfast of Champions)

Jesus and the time travelers [untitled] *(Slaughterhouse-Five)*

Language and Music [untitled] *(Breakfast of Champions)*

Maniacs in the Fourth Dimension (Slaughterhouse-Five)

The Money Tree (Slaughterhouse-Five)

Now It Can Be Told (Breakfast of Champions)

Oh Say Can You Smell (God Bless You, Mr. Rosewater)

The Pan-Galactic Memory Bank (Breakfast of Champions)

Pan-Galactic Three-Day Pass (God Bless You, Mr. Rosewater)

Plague on Wheels (Breakfast of Champions)

The Smart Bunny (Breakfast of Champions)

The Son of Jimmy Valentine (Breakfast of Champions)

Venus on the Half Shell (God Bless You, Mr. Rosewater)

Short Stories

"Albert Hardy" *(Timequake)*

"An American Family Marooned on the Planet Pluto" *(Timequake)*

"Asleep at the Switch [actually written by Dr. Robert Fender, published under the pen name "Kilgore Trout"] *(Jailbird)*

"Bunker Bingo Party" *(Timequake)*

"The Dancing Fool" *(Breakfast of Champions)*

"Dog's Breakfast" *(Timequake)*

"Dr. Schadenfreude" *(Timequake)*

"Empire State" *(Timequake)*

"Gilgongo" *(Breakfast of Champions)*

"Golden Wedding" *(Timequake)*

"Hail to the Chief" *(Breakfast of Champions)*

"Kiss Me Again" *(Timequake)*

"Mouth Crazy" [Also called "Pan-Galactic Straw-boss"] *(Breakfast of Champions)*

"No Laughing Matter" *(Timequake)*

"Pan-Galactic Straw-boss" [Also called "Mouth Crazy] *(Breakfast of Champions)*

"The Planet Gobblers" (Speech to graduating class of Hobart and William Smith College, May 26, 1974)

Revised version of the Book of Genesis [untitled] *(Timequake)*

"The Sisters B-36" *(Timequake)*

Skid Row [untitled] *(Breakfast of Champions)*

"This Means You" *(Breakfast of Champions)*

Yeast Particles [untitled] *(Breakfast of Champions)*

Memoir
My Ten Years on Automatic Pilot (Timequake)

Play
The Wrinkled Old Family Retainer (Timequake)

Entries on Works

2BRO2B

2BRO2B, a Kilgore Trout novel described in *God Bless You, Mr. Rosewater*, posits an America in which machines do almost all of the work, disease has been eradicated, and a serious overpopulation problem exists. Thus, the government has set up Ethical Suicide Parlors, where people are encouraged to voluntarily end their lives. The novel's title refers to Hamlet's famous question, "To be or not to be," a question that all citizens of this futuristic America are forced to ask. Interestingly, "2BRO2B" is also the title of one of Vonnegut's own stories, appearing in the collection *Bagombo Snuff Box*, and depicting a similar situation to the one in the Trout novel.

"Albert Hardy"

"Albert Hardy," a Kilgore Trout short story appearing in the novel *Timequake*, is about a working-class Londoner at the very end of the 19th century, who is born with his head between his legs and his genitalia at the top of his neck. Trout is in the middle of writing the story when the timequake occurs, and he is unable to finish it for 10 years, when free will kicks in again. When he finally completes the story, readers discover that the title character, Albert Hardy, is blown to bits in World War I. When he is buried, his body parts are reassembled in the usual order, with his head on top of his neck. His genitalia are never found.

"American Family Marooned on the Planet Pluto, An"

In the novel *Timequake*, Kilgore Trout is said to have written a story called "An American Family Marooned on the Planet Pluto." All readers find out about this story is a one-sentence quote: "Nothing wrecks any kind of love more effectively than the discovery that your previously acceptable behavior has become ridiculous" (33). Vonnegut supplies readers this information in the context of talking about his mother's failure to adjust to the family's loss of its fortune during the Great Depression.

"Asleep at the Switch"

"Asleep at the Switch" is a story published under the pen name "Kilgore Trout," but said to be actually written by Dr. Robert Fender, a character in the Vonnegut novel *Jailbird*. The story is about a reception center outside Heaven, staffed by accountants and business people who require all potential entrants through the Pearly Gates to give a full review of how well they had handled the business opportunities God had sent them while on Earth. These auditors force Albert Einstein to admit he had been "asleep at the switch" to earthly business opportunities before they admit him to Heaven.

Barring-Gaffner of Bagnialto, The

When Kilgore Trout is hitchhiking across country to Midland City in *Breakfast of Champions*, a truck driver who gives him a ride tells him about an experience in which he was jailed for a night in a town called Libertyville, which has so many books that they are used as toilet paper. Imprisoned all night, the driver had nothing to do but read his toilet paper, and he tells Trout about one of the stories he remembers. Trout soon realizes that the driver is referring to one of Trout's own books, *The Barring-Gaffner of Bagnialto*, about a planet that values artworks based on the spin of a roulette wheel.

Big Board, The

When Billy Pilgrim travels to New York City to appear on a radio talk show in *Slaughterhouse-Five*, he enters a pornographic bookstore after noticing some Kilgore Trout novels in the window. He ends up thumbing through a book called *The Big Board*, about an Earthling man and woman who are kidnapped by extraterrestrials and displayed in a zoo on the aliens' planet. As he skims the book, Billy realizes that he had actually read it much earlier, while in the veteran's hospital with Eliot Rosewater years before. This incident is important in *Slaughterhouse-Five* because it suggests that Billy's time travel to the planet Tralfamadore may be a fantasy concocted out of Kilgore Trout novels.

"Bunker Bingo Party"

"Bunker Bingo Party" is a Kilgore Trout story set in Adolf Hitler's bomb-proof bunker in Berlin at the end of World War II. Described in the novel Timequake, the story depicts elite Nazi officers holed up in the underground shelter, absorbed in playing a game of bingo captured from American troops during the Battle of the Bulge and brought to the bunker by the children of Joseph Goebbels.

"Dancing Fool, The"

A Kilgore Trout short story that depicts "a tragic failure to communicate" (58), "The Dancing Fool" is described in Breakfast of Champions. The story is about a flying saucer creature named Zog, who comes to Earth to tell how wars can be prevented and how cancer can be cured. However, on the planet Margo, where Zog hails from, communication is accomplished by means of farts and tap dancing. When Zog lands on Earth, he sees a house on fire and rushes in, farting and tap dancing to warn the people inside. The home's owner, however, brains him with a golf club.

Delmore Skag [untitled]

In Breakfast of Champions, Kilgore Trout is said to have written a novel about a scientist named Delmore Skag, who learns how to reproduce himself in chicken soup. Like Trout's other works, this novel is used by his publisher to sell pornographic images. The text is illustrated with "murky photographs of several white women giving blow jobs to the same black man, who, for some reason, wore a Mexican sombrero" (22).

"Dog's Breakfast"

After the timequake zaps Kilgore Trout backward 10 years in the novel Timequake, he, like everyone else, is forced to relive his life exactly as he had lived it the first time. The first story Trout is forced to rewrite is called "Dog's Breakfast," a tale of a mad scientist named Fleon Sunoco, who does not believe that the human brain, "which is nothing more than a dog's breakfast, three and a half pounds of human sponge" (107), could be capable of composing great artistic works such as Beethoven's Ninth Symphony. Thus, he stays up late at night in his laboratory, dissecting the brains of really smart people, which he believes must have radio receivers transplanted in them. When he eventually finds what he believes is evidence of the devices, Sunoco jumps to his death, realizing that he could not have made such a tremendous discovery unless he himself is controlled by a radio receiver as well.

Don [untitled]

While Kilgore Trout watches a pornographic movie in Breakfast of Champions, he dreams up a new novel, to which he never gives a title. The novel is about an Earthling astronaut named Don, who travels to a planet where all life, except for humanoid beings, has been killed by pollution. The humanoids eat food made out of petroleum and coal. When Don goes to watch a dirty movie with his hosts, the film depicts graphic, close-up shots of people eating real food.

"Dr. Schadenfreude"

In the novel Timequake, Kilgore Trout writes a story called "Dr. Schadenfreude" while he is living at the homeless shelter next door to the American Academy of Arts and Letters in Manhattan. The story concerns a psychiatrist who does not allow his patients to talk about themselves in their sessions. If patients ever uses the words I or me, Dr. Schadenfreude becomes livid, tells them no one cares about them, and orders the patient out of his office immediately.

"Empire State"

In the novel Timequake, Vonnegut quotes from the Kilgore Trout story "Empire State," which is about a meteor the size of a Manhattan skyscraper that is hurtling toward Earth. "Science never cheered up anyone," Trout writes, "The truth about the human situation is just too awful" (121).

Era of Hopeful Monsters, The

The Era of Hopeful Monsters is a Kilgore Trout novel described by his son, Leon Trout, in the novel Galápagos. The book depicts a planet ravaged by pollution and industrial waste. The humanoid creatures who live there begin to give birth to children with all kinds of strange deformities, which Trout describes as Nature's way of experimenting with new creatures who might be better planetary citizens than their parents.

First District Court of Thankyou, The
One of Eliot Rosewater's favorite Kilgore Trout books in Vonnegut's novel *God Bless You, Mr. Rosewater* is said to be *The First District Court of Thankyou*. The novel is about a court that hears cases concerning ingratitude. If a defendant is convicted of being ungrateful, he is given the option of either publicly thanking the plaintiff or being locked in solitary confinement for a month. According to Trout, 80 percent of convicted defendants choose prison.

"Gilgongo"
In *Breakfast of Champions*, Kilgore Trout invents a story called "Gilgongo" while being given a ride out of New York by a truck driver who is a hunter and fisherman as well as a conservationist. "Gilgongo" is about a planet that has too much creation going on, so the inhabitants celebrate whenever a species is wiped out. The word *gilgongo* means "extinct" in their language.

"Golden Wedding"
"Golden Wedding" is a Kilgore Trout story that Dudley Prince, in the novel *Timequake*, rescues from the trash can. It is about a florist who tries to make more money by convincing husband/wife pairs who work together that they are entitled to celebrate several wedding anniversaries per year.

Gospel from Outer Space, The
The Gospel from Outer Space is a Kilgore Trout novel that Eliot Rosewater tells Billy Pilgrim about while the two men are in a mental hospital together in *Slaughterhouse-Five*. In the novel, a visitor from outer space comes to Earth and concludes that Christians find it easy to be cruel to one another because of "slipshod storytelling in the New Testament" (108). The space visitor believes the New Testament, as written, teaches Christians that there are right and wrong people to lynch. Thus, he makes a gift to Earthlings of a new gospel, in which

Jesus is not the son of God, but a penniless nobody. When Jesus is crucified, God adopts him, sending Christians the message that it is not acceptable to torment anyone, even the lowliest and most humble of human beings.

Gutless Wonder, The
The title of a novel by Kilgore Trout that is described in *Slaughterhouse-Five*, *The Gutless Wonder* is about a robot designed to drop burning jellied gasoline on human beings from airplanes. Nobody minds that he does this, but people do object to the robot's bad breath. When his halitosis is cleared up, he is welcomed to the human race with open arms.

"Hail to the Chief"
"Hail to the Chief" is a Kilgore Trout story that is described in *Breakfast of Champions*. It is about "an optimistic chimpanzee who became President of the United States" (90).

How You Doin'?
The Kilgore Trout novel *How You Doin'?*, described in *Breakfast of Champions*, is about "national averages for this and that" (173). An advertising agency on another planet uses these averages to market their products, inviting customers to compare themselves to national averages. Earthlings, wanting to invade the planet, tamper with the statistics in the ads so that the aliens begin to feel inferior. As a result of this demoralizing, the aliens offer only token resistance when the Earthling war ships arrive.

Jesus and the time travelers [untitled]
When Billy Pilgrim goes into the pornographic bookstore in New York City in *Slaughterhouse-Five*, he sees a Kilgore Trout novel in the window that is about a man who built a time machine so that he could go back and see Jesus. In the book, whose title is never given, the time-traveler watches a 12-year old Jesus help his father build a wooden cross to execute a rabble-rouser.

"Kiss Me Again"
"Kiss Me Again," a Kilgore Trout story appearing in the novel *Timequake*, is said to be the only love

story Trout ever attempted to write. In the story, Trout claims that no beautiful woman can "live up to what she looks like for an appreciable length of time" (22). In true, cynical Kilgore Trout fashion, the moral at the end of this love story is: "Men are jerks. Women are psychotic" (22).

Language and music [untitled]
While hitching a ride in the truck that has the word *Pyramid* painted on its side in the novel *Breakfast of Champions*, Kilgore Trout dreams up a story about a planet in which language keeps turning into pure music because the inhabitants who live there are so enchanted by the sounds of words. Government leaders then have to invent new, ugly words that resist being turned into music so that the creatures can continue to communicate. Readers are never given a title for this story.

Maniacs in the Fourth Dimension
Maniacs in the Fourth Dimension is a Kilgore Trout novel that Eliot Rosewater reads in the mental hospital in Vonnegut's novel *Slaughterhouse-Five*. The book is about people with mental diseases that cannot be treated because the causes of these diseases are in the fourth dimension and thus invisible to Earthlings.

Money Tree, The
Readers are told about a Kilgore Trout novel called *The Money Tree* in *Slaughterhouse-Five*. The book is about a tree that has $20 bills for leaves, government bonds for flowers, and diamonds as its fruit. The tree attracts human beings who fight over it and eventually kill one another around its roots, making good fertilizer.

"Mouth Crazy"
When Kilgore Trout's story "Pan-Galactic Straw-boss" is published in a pornographic magazine in *Breakfast of Champions*, it is renamed "Mouth Crazy."

My Ten Years on Automatic Pilot
My Ten Years on Automatic Pilot is the title of the never-finished memoir that Kilgore Trout writes about his experiences during the 10 years he is

forced to relive in the novel *Timequake*. In the memoir, Trout explains that the timequake, which he describes as the Universe suffering "a crisis in self-confidence" (63), zaps Trout and everybody else back from February 13, 2001 to February 17, 1991.

"No Laughing Matter"
Kilgore Trout's story "No Laughing Matter," which appears in the novel *Timequake*, is about a pilot assigned to drop a third atomic bomb on Japan during World War II. When he and his crew refuse to do so, the judge at the court-martial tries to control the courtroom at one point by saying that the trial "is no laughing matter" (12).

Now It Can Be Told
Now It Can Be Told is the Kilgore Trout novel that drives Dwayne Hoover crazy in *Breakfast of Champions*. Written "in the form of a long letter from the Creator of the Universe to the only creature in the Universe who had free will" (57), the novel leads Dwayne to believe that all other people in the world except him are machines. This belief is what instigates Dwayne's violent rampage at the end of the novel. Like most of Trout's publications, *Now It Can Be Told* is illustrated with pornographic images that have nothing at all to do with the story. The front cover of the book depicts a college professor being undressed by a group of naked sorority girls.

Oh Say Can You Smell
In *God Bless You, Mr. Rosewater*, Eliot Rosewater tells his father, the senator, about a novel by Kilgore Trout called *Oh Say Can You Smell*, about a whole country "devoted to fighting odors" (222). The hero of the book, who is also the country's dictator, ultimately solves the odor problem by eliminating noses.

Pan-Galactic Memory Bank, The
The Pan-Galactic Memory Bank is a novel by Kilgore Trout described in *Breakfast of Champions*. The novel's hero is on a space ship that is 200 miles long and 62 miles in diameter. He checks a realistic novel out of a library in his neighborhood, but only reads about 60 pages of it before taking it back,

explaining to the librarian that he already knows about human beings. Vonnegut uses the example of this novel to explain that he agrees with Trout that realistic novels are flawed by their "accumulation of nit-picking details" (286).

"Pan-Galactic Straw-boss"

"Pan Galactic Straw-boss" is a Kilgore Trout story mentioned briefly in *Breakfast of Champions*. When the story is published in a pornographic magazine, it is renamed "Mouth Crazy."

Pan-Galactic Three-Day Pass

Pan-Galactic Three-Day Pass is the title of a Kilgore Trout novel that Eliot Rosewater reads on the bus on the way to Indianapolis near the end of *God Bless You, Mr. Rosewater*. The book is about an Earthling English teacher named Sergeant Raymond Boyle, who is ordered on a space expedition to teach mentally telepathic aliens how to use language. While in space, Boyle is called in to the office of the expedition's chaplain, who gives him an emergency three-day pass since there had "been a death back home" (250). When Boyle asks who died, he is told that the entire Milky Way Galaxy has passed away.

Plague on Wheels

Kilgore Trout's novel *Plague on Wheels*, which appears in *Breakfast of Champions*, is about a planet named Lingo-Three, whose inhabitants resemble American automobiles. The planet dies when the creatures use up all its fossil fuels and destroy the atmosphere. Tiny, one-inch-tall space travelers, however, tell Earthlings about the creatures. Humans then proceed to build automobiles in their image, thus destroying the planet Earth. *Plague on Wheels* is said to be Trout's most widely distributed book, not for the story, but because his publisher has splashed a lurid banner across the front cover, promising "wide-open beavers inside" (22).

"Planet Gobblers, The"

"The Planet Gobblers" is a Kilgore Trout story that Vonnegut refers to in a speech he made to the graduating class of Hobart and William Smith Colleges in Geneva, New York, on May 26, 1974. The story presents Earthlings as "planet gobblers" who "arrive on a planet, gobble it up, and die" (190). Before completely dying, however, Earthlings send spaceships to new planets to repeat the process all over again. In the speech, Vonnegut tells students that poorer nations on Earth think of America as a Planet Gobbler.

Revised version of the Book of Genesis [untitled]

In *Timequake*, Kilgore Trout writes a revised version of the biblical story of Genesis, in which Satan is a woman who sees that God's creatures, Adam and Eve, are going to be either bored stiff or scared silly for their entire lives. So, she makes an apple filled with all sorts of ideas for them to entertain themselves—recipes for beer and whiskey, instructions for gambling and lovemaking, and the like. Trout, in describing the story, says that all Satan wanted to do to was help, and while her ideas had catastrophic side effects for a small minority of people, overall "her record for promoting nostrums with occasionally dreadful side effects is no worse than that of the most reputable pharmaceutical houses of the present day" (30).

"Sisters B-36, The"

"The Sisters B-36," a Kilgore Trout story appearing in the novel *Timequake*, is about three sisters from the planet Booboo in the Crab Nebula, whose last name is B-36. Two of the sisters are artists, while the third is a scientist. The scientist sister, jealous of her creative and talented sisters, invents television and other devices that limit the imagination. When new generations of Booboolings grow up without imaginations, the race becomes "among the most merciless creatures in the local family of galaxies" (21).

Skid Row [untitled]

Bunny Hoover, Dwayne Hoover's homosexual son in *Breakfast of Champions*, lives in a neighborhood nicknamed Skid Row. When the novel's narrator tells readers this information, he also describes a Kilgore Trout story about a town that actually puts up a street sign with the words *Skid Row* on it, so that derelicts can know where they are. The Trout story about Skid Row is never given a title.

Smart Bunny, The

When Kilgore Trout arrives at the Holiday Inn in *Breakfast of Champions*, the hotel desk clerk, Milo Maritimo, tells him that he has borrowed Eliot Rosewater's collection of Trout's work and read every item in it. The only work he has not finished is a novel called *The Smart Bunny*, about a female rabbit as intelligent as Albert Einstein. The rabbit, deciding her brain is a sort of tumor, hops toward the city to have it removed when she is shot by a hunter named Dudley Farrow. Readers are told that this is the only Kilgore Trout novel or story with a female lead character.

Son of Jimmy Valentine, The

At the suggestion of his second wife, Darlene, Kilgore Trout writes a short novel about a man who is such an accomplished lover that he can seduce any woman he wants. Called *The Son of Jimmy Valentine*, the hero, Ralston Valentine, is the son of famous safe cracker Jimmy Valentine. While his father sandpapers his fingers to crack safes, Ralston sandpapers his fingers to better please women. He ends up being elected president of the United States because so many women vote for him. This book is described in Vonnegut's novel *Breakfast of Champions*.

"This Means You"

"This Means You" is a Kilgore Trout short story that appears in *Breakfast of Champions*. Set in the Hawaiian Islands, it is about a group of people who own all the real estate available there. These people put up so many no trespassing signs that ordinary residents have nowhere to stand. Eventually, the government gives all ordinary people who do not own property helium balloons fitted out with harnesses so that they can go on living in Hawaii without trespassing on other peoples' property.

Venus on the Half Shell

In *God Bless You, Mr. Rosewater*, Eliot Rosewater's distant Rhode Island relative Fred Rosewater, while thumbing through racy novels at the local news and coffee shop, comes across a copy of a novel by Kilgore Trout called *Venus on the Half Shell*. The back cover of the novel describes a sexy scene inside, in which Queen Margaret of the planet Shaltoon offers herself to a man identified only as a Space Wanderer. In real life, a novel titled *Venus on the Half Shell* was published in 1975 as a Dell paperback. Although actually written by prolific science fiction author Philip José Farmer, the novel listed Kilgore Trout as the author, leading many early critics and readers to believe that the book was actually written by Vonnegut. Farmer later explained that he wrote the book under Trout's name for two reasons: to make "fantasy become reality," at least for a little while, and as a tribute to Vonnegut, whose works he admired.

Wrinkled Old Family Retainer, The

The Wrinkled Old Family Retainer is a cynical Kilgore Trout play about a wedding described in the novel *Timequake*. While the groom is a heartless womanizer and guests make sarcastic remarks about the proceedings, an aged but loyal family servant weeps sentimentally in a corner behind a potted palm.

Yeast Particles [untitled]

In *Breakfast of Champions*, Kilgore Trout is said to have once written a story about two pieces of yeast that discuss the purpose of life as they eat sugar and "suffocate in their own excrement" (214). They never come close to guessing that they are making champagne. Readers are never told a title for this story.

KURT VONNEGUT CHRONOLOGY

1884
November 24, Birth of father, Kurt Vonnegut, Sr. in Indianapolis, Indiana.

1888
Birth of mother, Alice Lieber Vonnegut, in Indianapolis, Indiana.

1913
November 22, marriage of Kurt Vonnegut and Alice Lieber.

1914
August 29, birth of brother, Bernard.

1917
Birth of sister, Alice.

1922
November 11, Kurt Vonnegut, Jr. born.

1936–1940
Attends Shortridge High School. Works on daily newspaper, *The Shortridge Echo.*

1940
Enrolls at Cornell University. While at Cornell, will serve as managing editor of *The Cornell Daily Sun.*

1942
November 5, Enlists in the U.S. Army.

1943
Drops out of Cornell University after bout of pneumonia.

Attends Army Basic Training, later sent to Carnegie Technical Institute and the University of Tennessee as part of the Army Specialized Training Program (ASTP).

1944
Stationed at Camp Atterbury, just south of Indianapolis, meets Bernard V. O'Hare.

May 14, Edith Lieber Vonnegut commits suicide.

August, Vonnegut sent overseas with the 106th Infantry Division.

December 19, captured during the Battle of the Bulge. Sent to Dresden.

1945
February 13, survives Allied bombing of Dresden in concrete slaughterhouse. Works digging out corpses afterward.

May 22, returns to United States.

September 1, marries Jane Cox.

December, moves to Chicago to study anthropology as a graduate student at the University of Chicago.

1946–1947
Continues graduate studies while working as a reporter for the Chicago City News Bureau.

M.A. thesis turned down by anthropology faculty at Chicago.

1947
May 11, son Mark born in Chicago.

Moves to Schenectady, New York to take job in publicity department of General Electric.

1949
Daughter Edith born in Schenectady.

1950
February 11, publishes first short story, "Report on the Barnhouse Effect," in *Collier's* magazine.
Stories "Thanasphere" and "EPICAC" also published in *Collier's*.

1951
Publishes five additional stories in *Collier's*: "All the King's Horses," "Mnemonics," "The Euphio Question," "The Foster Portfolio," and "More Stately Mansions."
Quits General Electric, moves to Cape Cod, Massachusetts, to write full time.

1952
First novel, *Player Piano*, published by Scribner's. Novel is reviewed by Granville Hicks in the *New York Times*.
"Report on the Barnhouse Effect" included in science fiction anthology edited by Robert A. Heinlein.
Publishes five additional stories, in *Collier's, Saturday Evening Post*, and *Argosy*: "Any Reasonable Offer," "The Package," "The No-Talent Kid," "Poor Little Rich Town," and "Souvenir."

1953
Player Piano rereleased as part of the Doubleday Science Fiction Book Club.
Publishes four magazine short stories: "Tom Edison's Shaggy Dog," "Unready to Wear," "The Cruise of the Jolly Roger," and "D.P."

1954
Player Piano reprinted as *Utopia 14*.
Seven magazine stories published: "The Big Trip Up Yonder" (later titled "Tomorrow and Tomorrow and Tomorrow"), "Custom-Made Bride," "Adam," "Ambitious Sophomore," "Bagombo Snuff Box," "The Powder Blue Dragon," and "A Present for Big Nick."
Daughter Nanette born.

1955
Publishes four magazine short stories: "Unpaid Consultant," "Deer in the Works," "Next Door," and "The Kid Nobody Could Handle."

1956
Publishes three magazine short stories: "The Boy Who Hated Girls," "Miss Temptation," and "This Son of Mine."

1957
October 1, Kurt Vonnegut, Sr. dies.
Publishes two magazine short stories, "Hal Irwin's Magic Lamp," and "A Night for Love."

1958
July, publishes short story, "The Manned Missiles," in *Cosmopolitan*.
September 15, Vonnegut's brother-in-law, James Carmalt Adams, dies in a commuter train crash in New Jersey.
September 16, sister, Alice, dies of cancer.
Kurt and Jane Vonnegut adopt three oldest Adams boys.
October 5, adaptation of short story "D.P" premieres as "Auf Wiedersehen," an episode of the CBS television anthology series *General Electric Theater*.

1959
The Sirens of Titan published as a Dell paperback original.

1960
August, Publishes short story "Long Walk to Forever" in *Ladies' Home Journal*.

1961
Publishes *Canary in a Cat House*, a collection of 12 magazine stories from the 1950s.
Publishes four magazine short stories: "Find Me a Dream," "Runaways," "Harrison Bergeron," and "My Name is Everyone" (later retitled "Who Am I This Time").
December 24, short story "The Runaways" premieres as an episode of television anthology series *Bus Stop* on ABC. The episode is directed by Arthur Hiller with teleplay by Sally Benson.

1962
Mother Night published as a Fawcett paperback.

Publishes four magazine short stories: "HOLE BEAUTIFUL: Prospectus for a Magazine of Shelteredness," "2BRO2B," "The Lie," and "Go Back to Your Precious Wife and Son."

1963

Cat's Cradle published in hardback by Holt, Rinehart & Winston. Graham Greene praises the book as one of the three best novels of the year. Terry Southern writes a positive review in the *New York Times*.

Short story "Lovers Anonymous" published in *Redbook*.

1965

Publishes *God Bless You Mr. Rosewater* with Holt, Rinehart & Winston.

Moves to Iowa after accepting a temporary position teaching at the Iowa Writer's Workshop.

November 16, short story "Harrison Bergeron" reprinted in *National Review*.

1967

Travels to Dresden on a Guggenheim Fellowship with Bernard O'Hare to conduct research for his "famous Dresden novel."

1968

January, short story "Welcome to the Monkey House" published in *Playboy* magazine.

Short story collection, *Welcome to the Monkey House*, 25 pieces previously published in magazines during the 1950s and 1960s, is published by Seymour Lawrence/Delacorte Press.

1969

March, publishes *Slaughterhouse-Five*. Novel goes to number one on *New York Times* best-seller list, brings Vonnegut celebrity status.

1970

Travels to Biafra to report on the collapse of the struggling country.

Accepts a visiting appointment to teach creative writing at Harvard University.

October 7, Happy Birthday, Wanda June premieres off-Broadway in New York at the Theater de Lys. The play runs through March 1971.

Receives grant from the National Institute of Arts and Letters.

1971

Receives M.A. degree from the University of Chicago for *Cat's Cradle*, which is said to make a significant contribution to the field of cultural anthropology.

Son Mark suffers a nervous breakdown, is hospitalized in Vancouver, Canada, and diagnosed as a schizophrenic.

Separates from his wife, Jane Cox Vonnegut, and moves to New York City.

Begins living with photographer Jill Krementz.

December 9, Happy Birthday Wanda June released as a feature film by Columbia Pictures, directed by Mark Robson.

1972

March 13, National Educational Television production of *Between Time and Timbuktu*, an amalgam of various Vonnegut works, premieres. Directed by Fred Barzyk. The teleplay is published in book form with photographs by Jill Krementz later this year.

March 15, Film version of *Slaughterhouse-Five*, directed by George Roy Hill with screenplay by Stephen Geller, is released.

Short story "The Big Space Fuck" published in *Again, Dangerous Visions: Forty-six Original Stories*, edited by Harlan Ellison.

Elected vice president of P.E.N. American Center

1973

Publishes *Breakfast of Champions* with Seymour Lawrence/Delacorte Press as his "fiftieth birthday present to himself."

Teaches creative writing at the City University of New York as Distinguished Professor of English Prose.

Receives honorary doctorate from Indiana University.

1974

Resigns position at CUNY.

Publishes first collection of essays, speeches, and anecdotes, *Wampeters, Foma, and Granfalloons*.

May 1, Pilot for proposed television anthology called *Rex Harrison Presents Stories of Love* premieres on NBC. One of the episodes in the pilot is adapted from Vonnegut's short story "EPICAC," directed by John Badham.

Awarded an honorary doctorate from Hobart and William Smith Colleges.

1975

Mark Vonnegut publishes *The Eden Express: A Memoir of Insanity.*

Release of short (24-minute) independent film, *Next Door*, based on the Vonnegut short story, directed by Andrew Silver.

Elected vice president of the National Institute of Arts and Letters.

1976

Slapstick published by Delacorte/Seymour Lawrence, receives negative reviews, much to Vonnegut's disappointment.

1977

April 6, *Sirens of Titan* adapted as a two-act play by the Organic Theater Company, premieres in Chicago.

1979

Publishes *Jailbird* with Delacorte/Seymour Lawrence.

God Bless You, Mr. Rosewater adapted as a stage musical by Howard Ashman, with music by Alan Menken, premieres in New York City.

November 24, marries Jill Krementz.

1980

Publishes children's book *Sun Moon Stars*, with illustrations by graphic artist Ivan Chermayeff.

1981

Publishes *Palm Sunday: An Autobiographical Collage*, a collection of essays, reviews, and speeches from the previous decade, interspersed with family history and new commentary from the author.

Receives a Literary Lion award from the New York Public Library.

Recipient of Eugene V. Debs Award for public service, from the Eugene V. Debs Foundation.

1982

February 2, American Playhouse television adaptation of short story "Who Am I This Time" premieres on PBS, directed by Jonathan Demme.

Deadeye Dick published.

December, adopts infant daughter Lily.

1984

March, Feature film *Slapstick (of Another Kind)*, directed by Steven Paul, is released in America. The film had previously been released in France in 1982.

Limited edition of two essays, "Nothing is Lost Save Honor," and "The Worst Addiction of Them All" published by Nouveau Press as part of a fund-raiser for the Mississippi Civil Liberties Union.

1985

Publishes *Galápagos*. The novel is praised in a *New York Times* review.

Adaptation of Vonnegut's short story "D.P." premieres as a television movie on PBS called *Displaced Person*, directed by Alan Bridges. Receives an Emmy Award for outstanding children's program.

1986

Vonnegut plays himself in a cameo role in the feature film *Back to School* starring Rodney Dangerfield.

1987

Bluebeard published.

Jane Vonnegut Yarmolinsky publishes *Angels Without Wings: A Courageous Family's Triumph over Tragedy.*

October 10, A&E television premiere of "Long Walk to Forever," an adaptation of the Vonnegut short story, directed by John A. Gallagher.

1988

March 13, premiere of Vonnegut's requiem mass in Buffalo, New York.

1990

Publishes *Hocus Pocus.*

Angels Without Wings premieres as a television movie called *A Promise to Keep.*

1991

Publishes *Fates Worse Than Death: An Autobiographical Collage.*

May 12, Kurt Vonnegut's Monkey House, a television adaptation of several short stories from "Welcome to the Monkey House" premieres in installments on Showtime.

1993

April 20, Vonnegut play, *Make Up Your Mind,* premieres in New York at the New Group Theater. Runs through May 2.

May 6, premiere of *L'histoire du Soldat,* with libretto by Vonnegut, at Alice Tully Hall in New York City.

1995

August 13, short story "Harrison Bergeron" premieres as a television movie on Showtime, directed by Bruce Pittman, screenplay by Arthur Crimm.

1996

September 18, Stage version of *Slaughterhouse-Five* premieres at Chicago's Steppenwolf Theater.

November 1, Mother Night released as a feature film, screenplay by Robert B. Weide, directed by Keith Gordon. Vonnegut has a cameo as a sad man on the street.

1997

What Vonnegut refers to as his "final novel," *Timequake,* is published by Putnam.

Appears in a television commercial for Discover credit cards.

1998

Vonnegut's libretto to *L'histoire du Soldat* published in *The Paris Review.*

1999

February 18, Breakfast of Champions released as a feature film, directed by Alan Rudolph, who also wrote the screenplay. Vonnegut plays a bit role as a commercial director.

Publishes *Bagombo Snuff Box,* a collection of magazine short stories that had previously remained uncollected.

Like Shaking Hands with God, a discussion about writing between Vonnegut and Lee Stringer, published by Seven Stories Press.

Delivers a series of 90-second radio spots for National Public Radio station WNYC in downtown Manhattan as part of a station fundraiser. The spots are transcribed and published by Seven Stories Press as *God Bless You, Dr. Kevorkian.*

2000

Is hospitalized in critical condition with smoke inhalation after his New York brownstone catches fire.

Accepts an appointment to teach creative writing at Smith College as writer-in-residence.

2001

Named a New York State Author by the New York State Writer's Institute.

2002

Appears in television commercial for Nissan Murano minivan.

2004

Exhibition of Vonnegut family artwork at the Indianapolis Art Center organized by Joe Petro III.

2005

Publishes *A Man Without a Country,* a collection of essays, observations and anecdotes. As part of publicity tour, appears on *The Daily Show with Jon Stewart, Now with Bill Moyers,* and *Real Time with Bill Maher.*

2007

The city of Indianapolis declares *The Year of Kurt Vonnegut.*

April 11, Kurt Vonnegut dies after sustaining brain injuries in a fall at his Manhattan home.

INDEX

film versions 11, 178–179, 247, 393

Finch, Dr. Katharine (character) 286–287, 292–293

"Find Me a Dream" **136–137**

Finkelstein, Isadore (Izzy) (character) 44, 51, 112

Finletter Federal Minimum Security Adult Correctional Facility 208, 212, 213, 215, 216, 220, 222

Finnerty, Dr. Edward (character) 283–287, 289–296, 298

firemen 161, 162, 167, 168, 176, 301, 302, 381, **440**

"First Amendment, The" 275

First Book of Bokonon, The 87

First District Court of Thankyou, The (Trout) 508

First Industrial Revolution 286

Flammer, Lou (character) 120, 121

Flemming, Willard (character) 149, 150

folk societies 7, 130, 412, 465

foma 403, 404, 412
  art as 84–85, 92, 405
  Bokonon on 81, 84–85, 88, 90, 92, 211
  religion as 92

Ford, Rose Aldrich (character) 338, 342

"Fortitude" **137–139,** 407, 441, 469

Fortune, John (character) 107, 110, 111, 112, 113, 116, 119, 454

Foster, Alma (character) 140, 141

Foster, Herbert (character) 140, 141

"Foster Portfolio, The" 9, **140–141**

Fourteenth Book of Bokonon, The 86

Francis, Dick 384

Frank, Anne 146, **440–441**

Frankenstein (Shelley) 27, 85, 137, 138, 139, **441,** 471

Frankenstein, Dr. Norbert (character) 137–139, 407

Frascati, Marion (character) 293, 294

Fredonia College 275

Free American Corps 256, 350, 356

Freeman, Charley (character) 177, 271–272, 273–274

Freeman, Sally (character) 111, 112

free will **441**
  in "All the King's Horses" 20
  in *Breakfast of Champions* 57, 60, 61, 65, 71, 76, 380, 441

in *Cat's Cradle* 86
  in existentialism 439
  in *Hocus Pocus* 190
  in *Jailbird* 211
  in *The Sirens of Titan* 312, 317, 441
  in *Slaughterhouse-Five* 61, 211, 350, 355, 361, 437, 441
  in *Timequake* 376, 377, 380, 381, 389, 476

French, Mary Alice (character) 194, 202

Freud, Sigmund 460

Friedan, Betty 104, 236

Friedmann, Tuvia (character) 248, 257

Fuller, Alvan T. 212, 216, 219, 223

Fuller, Corporal Norman (character) 243, 244

Fuller, Mrs. (character) 243, 244

Fu Manchu (character) 331, 338, 346

"Funnier on Paper Than Most People" 282

G

Galápagos **142–156,** 435
  characters in 148–156
  commentary on 144–148
  critics on 12, 146–147
  entropy in 190
  motherless character in 37
  synopsis of 12, 142–144

Galápagos Islands 427, **442**

Galaxy Science Fiction (magazine) 80

Galen, Vermont 330–331, 339

Garth, Fred (character) 289, 293

GEFFCo 50, 55, 145, 149, 150, 152

Gelhorne, Dr. Francis Eldrin (character) 293–294, 295, 297

gender disparity 37, 38, 42, 57, 64

gender roles 103, 104, 105, 180, 235, 236–237

General Electric 8, 9, 248, 256, 344, 367, 411, **442,** 452

General Forge and Foundry Company 81, 90, 92, 94, 95, 97, 98, 374

German Americans 130, 279, 456

German Irregulars (characters) 357, 360, 367

Germany 123–124, 248. *See also* Dresden

Gettysburg Address 63, 258, **442, 445,** 453–454

Get With Child a Mandrake Root (Ulm) 170, 176

Ghost Shirt Society x, 27, 29, 285, 287, 289–294, 296–300, 454, 460, 469

"Gilgongo" (Trout) 508

Gingiva-Tru 257, 258

Glampers, Diana Moon (character) 29–31, 167, 169–171, 183–185

Gloria (character) 138, 139

Gluck, Werner (character) 357, 363

"Go Back to Your Precious Wife and Son" **157–158**

Goblet, The (Campbell) 255, 258

God Bless You, Dr. Kevorkian 13, **158–160,** 450
  afterlife interviews in 158–160, 424, 426, 428, 429, 435, 439, 441, 443, 445, 448, 450, 458–459, 465, 470–471, 473, 476

God Bless You, Mr. Rosewater **160–177**
  Breakfast of Champions compared to 60, 62, 64
  characters in 168–177
  commentary on 163–168
  critics on 10
  Jailbird compared to 211
  "The Kid Nobody Could Handle" compared to 229
  motherless character in 37
  synopsis of 10, 160–163
  utopian schemes in 60, 160, 163–164, 166, 172

Goebbels, Dr. Paul Joseph 258, 384, 442, 507

Goethe, Johann Wolfgang 252, 439

Going All the Way (Wakefield) 482

Goldberg, Rube **442**

"Golden Wedding" (Trout) 391, 508

Goldwater, Barry 204, 205, 206

"Good-bye Blue Monday" 70, 75

"Good Missiles, Good Manners, Good Night" 408

Gorky, Arshile 44

Gospel from Outer Space, The (Trout) 353, 355, 508

Goulding, Ray 282, 428–429

Graham, Jack (character) 208, 216, 220, 227

Graham, James (character) 170, 171

Graham, Mrs. Jack (character) 208–209, 216, 218, 219, 220, 223. *See also* O'Looney, Mary Kathleen (character)

Grand Central Winter (Stringer) 233, 473

Grand Hotel Oloffson 106, 107, 114, 116, **442,** 448

granfalloon 92, 403–404

Grant, Robert 216

Grass, Günther 384

Grasso, Elmer Glenville (character) 339, 344

Gray Shirt Society 29

Great American Experiment 130

Greathouse, Virgil (character) 208, 216, 218, 224

Green Death 332, 334, 335, 339, 341

Greene, Graham 10

Gregory, Dan (character) 35–45, 48, 53–54

GRIOT™ (computer game) 190

Groszinger, Dr. Bernard (character) 371, 372, 373

Guber, Lee 99

Guderian, Heinz 369, 370

Guggenheim Museum (New York) 40–41, 45, 51

Gulliver's Travels (Swift) 28, 278, 473–474

Gummer, Harriet (character) 188, 193, 194

gun culture 108–109, 131–132, 180

Gunther, August (character) 106, 107, 109, 112–113, 115

Gutless Wonder, The (Trout) 508

Gutman, Andor (character) 251–252, 258

H

Hacketts, Elmo C., Jr. (character) 289, 292, 294

Hagstrohm, Edgar R. B. (character) 292, 293, 294, 429–430

"Hail to the Chief" (Trout) 508

Haldeman, H. R. 216

Hale, Nathan 259

Haley, Stewart (character) 21, 22, 56

Halifa Institute for the Documentation of War Criminals 248

"Hal Irwin's Magic Lamp" 24, 81, **177–178**

Hall, Pamela Ford (character) 194–195, 203

Hallinan, Vivian **443**

Halyard, Dr. Ewing J. (character) 284, 288, 289, 294–295, 299, 300

Hamlet 166, 198, 317, **443,** 471

"Protocols of the Elders of
Tralfamadore, The" 189,
193, 196, 198–199
Protocols of the Elders of Zion
(Akbahr) 191, 199
psychoanalysis, and writing
234
Pullman, Mr. and Mrs.
(characters) 305, 306
Pulsifier, M. (character) 325,
329
Puritan character 243, 244

Q

Quezeda, Domingo (character)
151, 153
quietism 87, **464**
Quinn, Bert (character) 228,
229

R

racism/racial prejudice 57, 62,
64, 71, 130, 133, 218, 232,
249, 259, 260, 263
Rackstraw, Loree 388
radio spots 159–160
Rait, Rita **465**
Ramba of Macedon (Rosewater)
173
RAMJAC Corporation 111,
208–210, 213, 215, 216, 218,
220–223
Rampton, David 42
Ramuz, C. F. 229, 230
Random House dictionary
264–265
Rauch, Gertrude Schnull 274,
465
Rauch, John 3, 4, 274, 278,
388, 453, **465**, 468, 480
Ray, James Earl 159, **465**
reading
Fates Worse Than Death on
134–135
*Like Shaking Hands with
God* on 234
Palm Sunday on 134,
274–275, 277
Timequake on 234
*Wampeters, Foma &
Granfalloons* on 134
realistic art 36, 38–39, 41–44,
135, 379, 399, 400, 423
Rebel Without a Cause (film)
184, 228
Red Badge of Courage, The
(Crane) 433
Redfield, Dr. Robert 7, 130,
412, **465**
Red Scare 207, 208, 210
Redwine, the Reverend Homer
C. (character) 316, 325

Reed, Peter 24, 388
Reinbeck, Charlie (character)
268, 269
Reinbeck, Louis C. (character)
268, 269
Reinbeck, Natalie (character)
268, 269
religion. *See also* Bokonism;
Christianity
in *Between Time and
Timbuktu* 27, 28, 29, 30
in *Cat's Cradle* 81, 167
in *Fates Worse Than Death*
130, 133–134, 477
as *foma* 92
in *Jailbird* 212
Marx (Karl) on 455
in *Palm Sunday* 280–282,
432
in *The Sirens of Titan* 314,
316–317, 335
in *Slapstick* 134, 335, 337,
345, 347
in *Timequake* 380–381,
390–391, 459
and war 134
Remarque, Erich Maria 369
Remenzel, Dr. (character)
232, 233
Remenzel, Eli (character)
232–233
Remenzel, Sylvia (character)
232, 233
RENAMO **465–466**
"Report on the Barnhouse
Effect" 8, 9, **307–310**, 398,
429
representational art. *See*
realistic art
Requiem Mass 134
Rettig, John 115–116
Reyes, Guillermo (character)
148, 153
Rice, Ella (character) 177, 178
Rice, Major Allen (character)
371–372, 373
Rice, Margaret (character)
371, 372, 373
Riley, James Whitcomb **466**
Rivera, Geraldo **466,** 480
Rivera, Jerry Cha-Cha
(character) 221, 222
Rivers, Jerry (character) 100,
101, 377, 388
Robert, Henry Martyn 466
Robert's Rules of Order 339,
466
Robo-Magic Corporation 67,
68, 70, 75
Rockefeller, Nelson 75
Rockmell, Dr. Eli W. 338, 342
Roethke, Theodore **466**
Romeo and Juliet (Shakespeare)
198, 205, 310, 418, 419

Roosevelt, Eleanor (character)
116, 117
"Roots" 278
Roseberry, Dr. Harold
(character) 295, 298–299,
301
Rosenau, Dr. Maurice
(character) 325–326
Rosewater, Caroline (character)
162, 167–169, 172–174, 176
Rosewater, Eliot (character)
ix, 7
in *Breakfast of Champions*
58, 70, 74, 75, 76, 511
in *God Bless You, Mr.
Rosewater* 160–177,
211, 360, 428, 440, 443,
471, 508, 509, 510
Helmholtz, George M.
(character) compared
to 229
as motherless character 37
in *Slaughterhouse-Five*
146–147, 348, 353, 355,
360, 361–362, 437, 506,
508, 509
Rosewater, Fred (character)
161–163, 167, 171–173, 511
Rosewater, George (character)
169, 173, 174, 175
Rosewater, Senator Lister Ames
(character) 161–167, 171,
173–176, 428, 431
Rosewater, Noah (character)
163, 171, 172, 174, 175
Rosewater, Sylvia DuVrais
Zetterling (character) 161,
162, 164, 166, 167, 169, 173,
175, 176
Rosewater Law 165, 174–175
Rostand, Edmond 126
Rothko, Mark 49, 202, 423
Rowley, Mrs. Theodore 262
Royalton Coffee Shop 209,
223, 226
Rumfoord, Beatrice (character)
312–329, 436
Rumfoord, Professor Bertram
Copeland (character) 352,
360, 365, 438, 468
Rumfoord, Robert Taft
(character) 204–205, 206,
207
Rumfoord, Commodore
William (character) 204–
207, 450
Rumfoord, Winston Niles
(character) 72, 312–329,
436, 441
"Runaways" **310–311**
Rushdie, Salman 425, **466**
Russell, Bertrand **466**
Ryan, Harold (character)
179–182, 460

Ryan, Paul (character) 179,
180, 181
Ryan, Penelope (character)
179–182

S

Sacco, Dante 209, 221
Sacco, Inez 221
Sacco, Mrs. 221
Sacco, Nicola 209, *210*, 221,
227, 467
Sacco and Vanzetti **467**
committee on case of 216,
219, 223
in *Jailbird* 12, 207, 209,
212, 213, 467
judge in case of 223, 452
protests about 217
testimony in 219
Sacred Miracle Cave 59, 63,
71, 75
Sage, Anna **467**
St. Clement's Episcopal Church
281–282, 432
St. Elmo's Remedy 116, 119
saints 212–213
in *Fates Worse Than Death*
134, 432, 436, 445,
456, 457
firemen as 381, 440
in *God Bless You, Mr.
Rosewater* 161, 173
in *Jailbird* 213
in *A Man Without a
Country* 242
in *Timequake* 242, 381, 440
Sakharov, Andrei 429, **467**
Salinger, Pierre 205
Salo (character) 315, 319–320,
322, 326–327, 328
Salsedo, Andrea 221
samaritrophia 161, 164, 169,
175
Sandburg, Carl **467**
Sandra (character) 81, 97, 98
San Lorenzo 27, 28, 30, 32,
82–84, 86, 87, 89, 90, 91,
94–98, 429
*San Lorenzo: The Land, the
History, the People* (Castle)
82, 91, 96
San Mateo (freighter) 148,
154–155
Santa Rosalia 143, 145, 153,
155, 442
Santayana, George 335
saroon 97
Saroyan, William **467**
Sartre, Jean-Paul 439
Satanic Verses, The (Rushdie)
466
Sateen Dura-Luxe (paint)
40–41, 45, 49, 51, 55